CONTEMPORARY EUROPE:

A Geographic Analysis

CONTEMPORARY EUROPE:

A Geographic Analysis

Seventh Edition

Formerly Entitled: *Europe in the 1990s:
A Geographic Analysis*

Edited by

WILLIAM H. BERENTSEN

The University of Connecticut

Contributing Authors

William H. Berentsen, *University of Connecticut*
Darrick Danta, *California State University Northridge*
Aubrey Diem, *University of Waterloo, emeritus*
George Hoffman, *University of Texas and George Washington University*
Vincent Malmström, *Dartmouth College, emeritus*
Thomas M. Poulsen, *Portland State University, emeritus*
Derek Spooner, *University of Hull*
Craig ZumBrunnen, *University of Washington*

JOHN WILEY & SONS, INC.

New York   Chichester   Weinheim   Brisbane   Toronto   Singapore

Cover Photos: (from top left, clockwise): Randy Wells/Tony Stone Images; Michael Busselle/Tony Stone Images; European Community Delegation, New York; German Information Center; Duomo; Stefano Micozzi/Gamma Liaison; Christopher Morris/ Time/Black Star; Oliver Benn/Tony Stone Images; NRSC Ltd./Science Photo Library/Photo Researchers.

Acquistions Editor   Nanette Kauffman
Marketing Manager   Catherine Faduska
Production Editor   Sandra Russell
Cover Designer   Madelyn Lesure
Manufacturing Manager   Dorothy Sinclair
Photo Editors   Lisa Passmore/Elaine Paoloni
Illustration Editor   Edward Starr

This book was set in 10/12 Palatino by HRS Electronic Text Management and printed and bound by R.R. Donnelly & Sons Company/Crawfordsville. The cover was printed by The Lehigh Press, Inc. The film preparation was done by Jay's Publishers Service. Recognizing the importance of preserving what has been written, it is a policy of John Wiley & Sons, Inc. to have books of enduring value published in the United States printed on acid-free paper, and we exert our best efforts to that end.

The paper on this book was manufactured by a mill whose forest management programs include sustained yield harvesting of its timberlands. Sustained yield harvesting principles ensure that the number of trees cut each year does not exceed the amount of new growth.

Library of Congress Cataloging in Publication Data:
   Berentsen, William, H.
   Contempory Europe: a geographic analysis/edited by William H. Berentsen; contributing authors, William H. Berentsen...(et al.). — 7th ed.
        p.   cm.
   Rev. ed. of: Europe in the 1990s: a geographic analysis/edited by George W. Hoffman. 6th ed. ©1990.
   Includes bibliographical references and index.
   ISBN 0-471-58336-7 (cloth: alk. paper)
   1. Europe–Geography.   I. Berentsen, William H.   II. Europe in the 1990s.
D900.E97   1997
914—dc21   96-37342
                                                                          CIP

Printed in the United States of America
10 9 8 7 6 5 4 3 2 1

This book is dedicated to the memory of George and Viola Hoffman,
whose efforts over a 40-year period produced
the first six editions of this geography of Europe.

PREFACE

Fascination with Europe is common among students young and old. The diversity of the region's landforms and peoples as well as its rich history provides endless opportunity for learning and debating. Europe's diversity and complexity also present a tremendous challenge to authors attempting to provide a reasonably comprehensive survey of the continent from a geographical perspective. For this reason, this text has in all seven editions been completed by a team of authors with complementary knowledge of and experiences in the region.

Contemporary Europe: A Geographic Analysis provides students and instructors with a broad background on contemporary Europe in order to support and complement classroom lecture and discussion activities, which can thereby focus on the strengths of the instructor and the interests of students. No book can bring Europe to life as well as an animated instructor, who can stimulate learning by emphasizing salient features of the region and by providing personal insights and experiences. This book was written as comprehensively as possible in order to free instructors to concentrate on topics of their choice without sacrificing breadth. This edition of the text explicitly focuses on contemporary Europe in the belief that the largest number of students in introductory geography courses on the region want first and foremost to understand and enjoy it as it exists today. The approach is not intended to undervalue the important and intriguing lessons to be learned from a study of the region's historical geography. We have simply chosen to emphasize present-day Europe, and we do so by frequently describing the historical roots of contemporary conditions.

A multi-authored, edited text such as this one poses inevitable challenges for authors, editor, and publisher. The disadvantages of differing approaches and writing styles from chapter to chapter are, however, outweighed by the advantages of tapping the expertise of a number of experienced geographers. In order to allow authors to emphasize in their chapters what they believe to be most important for the topic or region, the editor did not impose a common chapter structure on contributors. Although this approach has some drawbacks, it allows the knowledgeable author to make the best use of available space. We see no benefits, for example, in covering tiny Luxembourg in the same way or with the same array of subtopics as we use to present Russia, the world's largest country. Another difficult choice that had to be made was to present the text in American English. As a result, the text features a more consistent prose, but the reader is also deprived of, for example, the exceptionally well-presented, original text of Derek Spooner which was written in the "Queen's English."

This text has also traditionally presented both topically and regionally focused chapters. This approach inevitably leads to some duplication of material, owing to the use of important regionally based examples in the introductory topical chapters, examples that in some cases are discussed again within the regional chapters. The authors believe that, within bounds, such repetition can reinforce material for students and that in any event the second reading of repetitive material may occur some weeks after the first reading.

There is also, inevitably, room for debate about how regions should be defined for the regional chapters, an issue that is addressed briefly in Chapter 1. It is likely that the regional organization used in the text will be somewhat altered in future editions as the post-socialist experience in the former "East Bloc" unfolds. Russia and the European republics of the former Soviet Union are covered in order to provide text for those instructors who include this region in their course on Europe. Obviously, this chapter can be left unassigned in courses that exclude it, although inquisitive students would benefit greatly from reading on their own Craig ZumBrunnen's masterful presentation of Russia and the newly independent states (NIS).

The limitations inherent in a text like this one preclude publication of color illustrations and the wealth of maps that the topic deserves. For this reason we encourage readers to use this book in conjunction with an atlas, and we particularly recommend Rand McNally's *Goode's World Atlas*. To help readers better visualize the location of less well-known places, the text frequently includes brief locational descriptions. It is hoped that these will help those readers with less well-developed knowledge of place name geography and will not be obtrusive for those with a larger "mental gazetteer." For the sake of consistency, place names in the text are presented as they are in this particular atlas. This means that *Contemporary Europe: A Geographic Analysis* has by default adopted Rand McNally's choice of transliteration schemes that are used for languages with letters other than those used in English (notably the Russian language). However, *Goode's World Atlas* also frequently uses anglicized versions of place names, especially where these names are in common use, such as Kiev instead of Kyyiv. The spelling Kyyiv would be consistent with the atlas's transliteration scheme for the Ukrainian language. The reader should also be aware of both an ongoing transition in the way that foreign-language place names are presented in the Roman alphabet and an ongoing reappraisal by East Europeans of names inherited from a now largely discredited socialist past. Thus, Leningrad has been renamed St. Petersburg, and Karl-Marx-Stadt has been renamed Chemnitz. Other such name changes could easily occur during the life span of this edition, so that instructors and students will need to attempt to keep abreast of changes as gleaned from such sources as newspapers and news magazines.

The reader will note that the late Professor George Hoffman is a co-author of several chapters in the book. Professor Hoffman was one of American geography's most broadly educated experts on Europe and was particularly esteemed by geographers in his home region of Central Europe. To make use of his abundant knowledge, where appropriate, portions of the sixth edition which he authored have been incorporated into this edition. However, it should be noted that the seventh edition is substantially changed from the sixth edition.

Finally, the editor and authors welcome feedback on the book, which would be useful in preparing future editions. The editor, in particular, apologizes in advance for any factual and editorial errors that appear and would be grateful to readers for alerting us to them. We have aspired to eliminate all such problems, but, realistically, some likely remain. Readers' knowledge and editorial acumen would help us improve the book. The authors' primary concern in working on this book has been to produce a text that serves the discipline; readers' comments will help us better achieve this in the future.

William H. Berentsen, editor
Department of Geography U-148
University of Connecticut
Storrs, CT 06269-2148
wberents@uconnvm.uconn.edu

ACKNOWLEDGMENTS

The editor particularly thanks the authors for their help and dedication in bringing this project to fruition. A number of people at John Wiley & Sons, Inc. have also provided a great deal of assistance, especially Nanette Kauffman, Lisa Passmore, Sandra Russell, Madelyn Lesure, Dorothy Sinclair, and Edward Starr, who worked on the final stages of publication.

All of the authors owe debts of gratitude to large numbers of former instructors, to colleagues in North America and Europe, and to discerning students in helping us to make progress in better understanding Europe. In my own case, literally scores of individuals have helped me in innumerable ways over several decades. During the period that the text was being prepared, for example, important assistance and support were provided by many people in the Institutes of Geography at the Humboldt University (Berlin); the Institute of Geography at the Tartu University (Estonia); and the Institute of Geography, Jagiellonian University (Cracow). Support for ongoing fieldwork came from the Fulbright Commission of the Federal Republic of Germany, the U.S. Information Agency, the National Research Council, and the Research Foundation of the University of Connecticut. I am especially appreciative of field trips provided by friends and colleagues which helped me prepare the book. In recent years such help has been given by a number of European geographers: Prof. Dr. Frankdieter Grimm (Leipzig), Dr. Jürgen Peters (Berlin), Prof. Dr. Eike Schamp and Dr. Heike Bertram (Frankfurt), Prof. Dr. Marlies Schulz (Berlin), Prof. Dr. Hans-Wilhelm Windhorst (Vechta); Dr. Györgyi Barta and Prof. Dr. György Enyedi (Budapest); Dr. Jüri Roosare (Tartu); Dr. Bolesław Domanski (Cracow), and Dr. Tadeusz Stryjakiewicz (Poznan). Karl and Lina Baum (Breitnau, Schwarzwald) and my grandfather's extended family in Bavaria have for years taught me about life in southern Germany.

The Department of Geography, the Research Foundation, and the Homer Babbidge Library at the University of Connecticut provided work space and other forms of support during the project. Mr. Tom Kolbe and Mrs. Jeannie Pogmore at the University provided direct administrative assistance on the project. My own interest in wanting to learn about Europe was particularly supported beginning many years ago by fellow geographers, including Professors George Demko, Bob Huke, Dave Lindgren, S. Earl Brown, and the late George Hoffman.

Many long hours, nights, and weekends are consumed by work on a project such as this one. I am grateful for the persevering patience of Sabrina, Rebecca, and Jacob while I was engaged in work on this book.

William H. Berentsen, editor

THE AUTHORS

Craig ZumBrunnen, Ph.D., University of California Berkeley, is Professor at the University of Washington and taught previously at the Ohio State University. He has traveled many times to Eastern Europe and the FSU, including as a member of U.S. Environmental Protection Agency teams under the auspices of the USA-USSR Environmental Accord on river basin modeling for pollution control. He has also worked as a consultant with U.S.A.I.D., the U.S. Department of Energy, Scientific Associates International, and other organizations dealing with Soviet/Russian environmental and natural resource problems. Professor ZumBrunnen is co-author of *The Soviet Iron and Steel Industry* and editor of *Urban Geography in the Soviet Union and the United States*. His published research has focused on Soviet and post-Soviet natural resource management problems, including environmental quality problems, water pollution, mineral resource development, regional economic development, energy resource R&D, and urban geography. His most recent publications have dealt with the role of NGOs in social change within Russia and the NIS, and with topics associated with post-Soviet social and economic transformation processes.

Derek Spooner, Ph.D., University of Cambridge, is Dean of the School of Geography and Earth Resources at the University of Hull in the United Kingdom. He has been a Visiting Professor at the Universities of Maryland and West Virginia. For six years he was the Editor of *Geography*, the journal of the British Geographical Association. His published work includes *Mining and Regional Development* and numerous articles on mining and energy geography as well as on regional economic development problems, especially with reference to the UK. He has first-hand knowledge of much of Europe, with particular interest in Italy.

Thomas M. Poulsen, Ph.D., University of Wisconsin, is Professor Emeritus at Portland State University. He was long Head of Portland State's Geography Department and was Ford Foundation fellow at the Russian Research Center of Harvard University and a Fulbright scholar in Yugoslavia. Professor Poulsen's research has been directed toward the political geography of Europe and Russia, and he is the author of the recently published *Nations and States: A Geographic Background to World Affairs*.

Vincent H. Malmström, Ph.D., University of Michigan, is Professor of Geography Emeritus at Dartmouth College and also taught at Middlebury College, the University of Minnesota at Duluth, and Bucknell University. He has been a Fulbright scholar in Norway and a contributor to all seven editions of this text. Professor Malmström is the author of *Geography of Europe: A Regional Analysis*, *Norden: Crossroads of Destiny*, and *A Regional Geography of Iceland*, as well as numerous articles on the Scandinavian region. His wide-ranging research interests have resulted in publications in climatology, computer mapping, and Mesoamerican calendrics.

The late **George W. Hoffman**, Ph.D., University of Michigan, was Professor of Geography at the University of Texas, Research Professor at George Washington University, and editor of the first sixth editions of this book. He was a Visiting Professor at numerous European universities, Fulbright Lecturer at the Universities of Munich and Heidelberg, and undertook research at the U.N. Economic Commission for Europe and the European Commission in Brussels. He served as a member of the Academic Advisory Committee of the Kennan Institute for Advanced Russian Studies and as Secretary of the Eastern European Program at the Woodrow Wilson International Center for Scholars. He was Project Director for *Problems of Balkan Security: Southeastern Europe in the 1990s,* author of *Regional Development Strategy in Southeast Europe and the Balkans in Transition,* and coauthor of *Yugoslavia and the New Communism* and *The Common Market.* In addition, he published over 150 other scholarly contributions, focused largely on Europe. Professor Hoffman served the Geography and European Studies' disciplines in numerous ways and was recognized for this service by honorary awards from the Association of American Geographers and several European governments.

Aubrey Diem, Ph.D., University of Michigan, is Adjunct Professor at the University of Waterloo. He has traveled and done research in Europe since 1954. Among his publications are *Western Europe: A Geographic Analysis; Switzerland: Land, People, Economy; The New Germany; The Mont Blanc-Pennine Region;* and *First Rains of Autumn,* a novel of love and war in the Alps that includes the memoirs of a partisan hero entitled *Enrico's War.* He has also contributed articles on Europe for *Encyclopaedia Britannica.* His latest project is a photo CD-ROM with 100 slides of Prague that illustrate the changes that occurred in that city from 1962 to 1996.

Darrick Danta, Ph.D., Ohio State University, is Professor at the California State University, Northridge. He has traveled widely throughout Europe, although his research has focused on East Central Europe, particularly Hungary and, more recently, the Balkans. His latest publication is *Reconstructing the Balkans: A Geography of the New Southeast Europe,* co-edited with Derek Hall.

William H. Berentsen, Ph.D., Ohio State University, is Professor of Geography and former Director of the Center for European Studies at the University of Connecticut. He has traveled widely in Europe and researched and taught on several occasions in Germany and Austria, including as a Fulbright Lecturer and Researcher at the Humboldt University in Berlin. His research has included work on patterns and processes of regional development in the United States and Central Europe, with particular emphasis over the past 20 years on eastern Germany. He has co-edited books on *Beiträge zur räumlichen Prozessforschung in den USA (Contributions to Research on Spatial Processes in the USA* with Hans-Wilhelm Windhorst) and *Regional Development Processes and Policies* (with Darrick Danta and Eta Daroczi), as well as numerous publications on Central European topics in American and European journals.

CONTENTS

FIGURES

INSETS

TABLES

INTRODUCTION

What is Europe? Where are its boundaries? Who are Europeans? The answers to these questions are much more complex and controversial than many people would expect. For example, there is no generally accepted agreement on whether Russia is part of Europe or whether Hungarians are "European." Like some other regional designations in the world, Europe is a readily accepted entity without a precise definition of what it comprises. The name "Europe" has an unclear historic origin, although its contemporary usage is quite similar to that which has been operative since the time of ancient Greece. The United States' leading cultural geographer of Europe (Professor Terry Jordan, University of Texas) has maintained that the idea of Europe as a continent is an age-old misconception. Indeed, there is good reason to argue that Europe is simply a western peninsula of Eurasia—a huge combined landmass of Europe and Asia. This book accepts Europe as a physical and cultural construct, albeit one with a rather arbitrary definition and boundary.

Europe comprises dozens of sovereign states (or "countries"), some of which approach the ideal of the nation-state, a country inhabited by a nation of people (Fig. 1-1). Europe also has scores of peoples with varying cultures, many of which could be called "nations." Some of these national groups are minorities in the state where they live, and some nationalities live outside the boundaries of a state that more or less embodies their nation (Fig. 1-2 *a, b*). Lack of political independence or of national unity has enraged some members of ethnic groups to the point that they have created some of Europe's most serious political problems, such as the violent independence movements in Corsica and the Basque lands of Spain; the difficulties between Hungary, Slovakia, and Romania, whose international boundaries have failed to unite large numbers of Hungarians within the Hungarian nation-state; and the terrible wars in the former Yugoslavia. In the last-named case, the overlapping settlement areas of many ethnic and religious groups, especially Croats, Serbs, and Bosnian Mus-

FIGURE 1-1 Europe's countries and adjacent water bodies.

lims, are proving to be unworkable. Conversely, Europe showcases innumerable examples of ethnic and religious tolerance and many regions in which people of different ethnicities and religions live in relative harmony (Fig. 1-3).

Europe also encompasses regions with distinctive "natural" and cultural (i.e., human-created) landscapes, as well as a growing pan-continental awareness of people as "European." In response to the growing identification with "Europe" (comple-

(a)

(b)

FIGURE 1-2 Two inhabitants of the same east Austrian village, (a) one a stereotypical "Austrian," the other a Slav (b). (W. Berentsen)

menting existing identification with countries, ethnicity, and religions), international institutions are being developed in Europe to govern and guide development in the region. The most notable of these organizations is the European Union (EU), but a number of others also exist, several of which are described later in this chapter.

EUROPE DEFINED: BOUNDARIES AND MAJOR REGIONS

In physical geographic terms, Europe's boundaries are defined by the Ural Mountains, Ural River, and Caspian Sea in the east; the northern ridge of the Caucasus Mountains and Black and Mediterranean seas in the south; the Atlantic Ocean in the

west; and the Arctic Ocean in the north. This physical definition is convenient but quite arbitrary, and opens a host of intriguing questions. Europe splits Russia in two, leaving portions in Asia and Europe. So, is Russia "European," "Asian," or neither? Points of view raised in attempts to answer this question may, in fact, be more interesting and important than the answer itself. The same could be said for other countries that are split between continents by the above definition, such as Kazakhstan and Turkey, neither of which is regarded as "European." Places whose designation is left ambiguous by the definition include Iceland, which by convention is considered to be part of Europe, and Denmark's autonomous province of Greenland, which is viewed as part of North America. Further complications are presented by integral parts of France (e.g., French Guiana and

FIGURE 1-3 In many parts of Europe local signs indicate residence of populations speaking different languages, such as here in Brittany, France. (W. Berentsen)

French Polynesia) and Spain (Melilla and Cueta in North Africa) that lie overseas. The accepted view is that these are parts of "European" countries but not themselves "European." More controversial is whether countries close to the defined continent and with cultural affinities to what is perceived as European should also be considered "European," notably Georgia, Armenia, and Israel. Generally, these countries are viewed as overseas "cousins" of Europe and not part of it, much as the United States, Canada, Australia, and New Zealand are viewed as non-European, although they are (or at least were originally) largely political and cultural offsprings of "Europe."

As should be clear from this discussion, cultural considerations are quite important in determin-

ing what is and who are European. Thus, Hungarians and Finns, whose ancestors migrated to Europe from Asia about a thousand years ago, are considered European peoples, although their related, contemporary languages are still not categorized as Indo-European. Conversely, many millions of recent Asian and African immigrants to Europe (and their children born in Europe) are not accepted as "European" and are often not given serious consideration for citizenship status. These people are politely referred to as "guest workers," although many have been "guests" for decades, and their children, though usually brought up within their parents' native, non-European culture, have never lived outside of Europe. The relatively small proportion of immigrants who become naturalized citizens may never feel or be fully accepted. Other peoples in Europe, such as ethnic Turks in Bulgaria, Muslims in Southeastern Europe, and Jews and Gypsies in many places (Romania has especially large numbers of Gypsies), face similar problems, even though their ancestors may have lived in Europe for centuries (Fig. 1-4). An example of the confusing definition of who is "European" and who can become a citizen of a European country is provided by German law. Germany allows uncontested citizenship for descendants of settlers who went to the Russian Empire centuries ago, many of whom now live in Central Asia, but would deny it to descendants of German emigrants to the Americas (including some of this book's authors).

Europe is thus comprised of a kaleidoscope of peoples—and places. Although the strongest perceptions of European landscapes may include verdant hills, towering mountains, quaint villages, and historic cities, the continent also includes the arid plains of Spain, the volcanic "wastelands" of Iceland, sprawling suburbs, and urban skyscrapers. A "European" might conjure up notions of light-skinned northerners, olive-skinned southerners, and villagers in local dress, but the increasingly diverse, mobile European population clad in garb marketed by international corporations un-

FIGURE 1-4 Gypsies in Romania. Gypsies represent a complex ethnic-cultural group, comprised both of people with traditional lifestyles that purposely distance them from non-Gypsies, and of people who are assimilated into non-Gypsy culture. Large families, aggressive panhandling, and unkempt living compounds characteristic of some traditional Gypsy groups often lead to negative responses to Gypsies from other European peoples. Though problematic, this generates a distance between Gypsy and non-Gypsy societies that some Gypsies strongly prefer. (J. Groch-Sygma)

dermines such simplifications, which in any event are of questionable importance in understanding the region.

The diversity of human-derived cultural landscapes and of humans themselves reflects a long, rich, complex history of human settlement in Europe. Humans have lived in this corner of the world for hundreds of thousands of years, adapting to and surviving through the tectonic movements of the land itself (including associated earthquakes and vulcanism), ice ages, ravages of often violent seas, and onslaughts of invaders. The region as it exists today is a colorful and fascinating palette, the result of millennia of changes in the physical environment, the human inhabitants, and interactions between the two.

This book presents an overview of the countries that have been formed and the peoples that live within the physical definition of Europe provided earlier. The "European" republics of the former Soviet Union, including especially Russia, are covered, but note that the term *Europe* as used by this book's authors does not always include the parts of "Europe" within the former USSR. Thus, for example, readers should not be thoroughly confused when someone asserts that Germany is "Europe's" most populous country or that Poland is "Europe's" leading coal producer. Russia's population and coal output would make it the European leader in each case, but parts of each are also contributed from "Asia." In such comparisons, Russia is often treated as a territorial entity separate from both Europe and Asia. In fact, of course, Russia spans much of Eurasia—it is of continental proportions. The potential confusions caused by such usage should be no greater than the somewhat controversial use of the term *Americans* for citizens of the United States.

In addition to the somewhat confusing status of Russia within Europe, other designations can also cause problems. A number of these are associated with the unofficial subregions of Europe, whose definitions and delimitations are even "fuzzier" than the definition for Europe itself. A brief discussion of the conventions used in this book and related ambiguities in defining the regions will undoubtedly help the reader better understand both Europe and this book's coverage of it.

Confusion, for example, abounds over the exact nature of the British Isles, the United Kingdom, Great Britain, and England. The British Isles, a major European subregion, include two large islands (Great Britain and Ireland) and two countries (Ireland, and the United Kingdom of Great Britain and Northern Ireland or "UK"). The UK spans both islands and consists of four major political subdivisions, Northern Ireland, Scotland, Wales, and England. Thus, despite widespread interchangeable usage of England, Britain, Great Britain, and the UK within the public media to refer to the United Kingdom, this book will use only the term *UK* to refer to it. When England is used, it will refer to the UK's specific regional subdivision; Great Britain will indicate an island, not a country. On the other hand, readers need to be alert to clues in the text to infer which "Ireland" is being discussed—the island or the country that covers all but its northeastern portion.

An intriguing aspect of the confusion over the names of places in Europe is that, to the surprise of many travelers, people in the UK often refer to "Europe" as if they were not part of it. Therefore, the continent to which the UK belongs is left unclear. What is clear, perhaps, is that people in the UK may not view themselves as central to Europe as Americans would, or they may believe that the UK, once the center of a far-flung international empire, deserves special consideration and a special designation.

"Western Europe" is another recognized subregion of Europe with quite confusing and ill-defined boundaries. In the past it was often used synonymously with non-Soviet-dominated Europe, so that Greece (far to the east of much of the rest of Europe) was considered to be in the "West" and Soviet "satellites" to the west of Greece were considered part of the "East." This book's chapter on Western Europe uses a very restricted definition of it, including France and the so-called Low Countries—Belgium, Luxembourg, and the Netherlands ("Holland" is the Netherlands' western region). The countries in the region designated "Southern Europe" here (Portugal, Spain, Italy, Greece, Malta, and Cyprus) are uncontested components of the region. Turkey could be defended as part of this group (and is covered briefly within the Southern

Europe chapter), as could the former Yugoslavia, which more traditionally has been considered part of "Eastern" or "Southeastern Europe."

"Eastern Europe" is an especially confusing term. In the United States the term has been used to refer to areas under Soviet domination or influence during the Cold War. However, in Europe itself "Eastern Europe" more often is used to refer to what is now Belarus, Ukraine, Moldova, and European Russia. People in Poland, Hungary, the Czech and Slovak Republics, Slovenia, and Croatia are adamant that they live in "Central" or "East Central Europe." Further confusing the situation is use of the term "Balkans," which is generally synonymous with Southeastern Europe, in this case sometimes including Greece. The end of the Cold War, increased ties between the region and the western part of Europe, and Moscow's greatly diminished influence, reinforces the argument that Central Europe is reemerging as a distinctive European region. However, because of the differential impacts of economic and political developments during the post–World War II era in the western and eastern parts of Europe, it is still difficult to easily include East Central Europe within a description of the other more developed parts of Central Europe—Switzerland, Germany, and Austria. Thus, this book has a chapter on West Central Europe and another on East Central and Southeastern Europe. Our use of "Eastern Europe" will conform to popular usage in the United States—the region that for decades was under Soviet influence, as well as Yugoslavia and Albania. Pending the success of political and economic transition in East Central Europe, distinctions between West and East Central Europe might fade enough to allow the areas to be covered together in a single Central European chapter in future editions of this text.

Even if Central Europe could be defined, it would be difficult to draw the line between it and Southeastern Europe. In this book the countries emanating from the former Yugoslavia are generally treated as part of Southeastern Europe, though Slovenians and Croatians would argue they should be included within Central Europe. The closely allied former Yugoslav republics of Serbia and Montenegro are designated as "Yugoslavia"; the media sometimes call them "rump Yugoslavia." Greece is covered within the Southern rather than Southeastern Europe chapter, although its physical location and a number of geopolitical issues (particularly vis-à-vis Macedonia and Albania) tie it to Southeastern Europe.

"Northern Europe" is as difficult to define as the other regions. The area includes more than "Scandinavia," but how much of the Baltic region should be included is debatable. Estonia, in particular, has shifted its economic and political orientation away from Russia toward Finland and Sweden; Latvia and Lithuania remain more closely tied to Russia but less so than in the past. Reflecting the border status of these small countries, they are formally included here under the European North but are discussed to a certain extent within the context of the regions of the former USSR as well.

The ill-defined boundaries of Europe and its subregions should not consternate readers. First, this is simply the state of affairs in an ever-changing European geopolitical landscape. Second, discussion and introspection about how Europe should or could be defined and subdivided provides a very good reason for learning about it in more detail and offers the basis for virtually unending discussions with other knowledgeable "students of Europe" (see also Inset 1-1).

EUROPE AND THE WORLD ECONOMY

In order to understand the economic conditions and problems in Europe in the mid-1990s, as well as related social and political problems and trends, we must be aware of the economic restructuring that is taking place in the ever more integrated global economy. People's jobs and the goods and services they buy are particularly impacted by increasing levels of international trade and multinational ownership and operations of large businesses. Products from computers and stereos to clothing and automobiles are being manufactured around the world, often by multinational corporations with operations in many different places. Although the number of potential new consumers

INSET 1-1

CONFUSING DETAIL FROM THE
MAP OF EUROPE

The numerous languages of Europe, English-lan-
guage transliterations of local European place
names, as well as outright errors in designating
European places, are two major causes of confusion
for students of Europe. In addition, attention to
detail is needed to correctly interpret the map of
Europe. Some common confusions are noted in the
text, such as the case of "UK," "Great Britain," and
"England." Others should also be noted. "Holland"
actually comprises only the western region of the
Netherlands. "Benelux" refers to the adjacent, small
countries of Belgium, Netherlands, and Luxembourg. "Czechoslovakia" no longer exists; its successors are Slovakia and the Czech Republic.
"Czechia" is not a term that has been widely accepted—at least not yet. The former Ukrainian republic
of the USSR is referred to simply as Ukraine (not
"the Ukraine"). The official name of united Germany is the Federal Republic of Germany (FRG), the
same name as the former "West Germany"; "East
Germany" was formally called the German Democratic Republic (GDR).

The former Yugoslav republics of Serbia and
Montenegro continue to refer to themselves as
"Yugoslavia." Another republic, Bosnia-Herzegovina, is often referred to simply as Bosnia; the "Federation" is used to refer to the cooperative efforts of
Muslims and Croats within it. In Greece "Macedonia" is unacceptable as a name for a country from
the perspective of Greeks and is not uniformly used;
some refer to it as the Former Yugoslav Republic of
Macedonia (FYROM).

Other details of Europe's political geography can
also be confusing. In the far north of Europe, Norway shares a short border with Russia (as well as
development rights on Arctic islands); and the far
northern panhandle of Norway prevents Finland
from having an Arctic coast. A small piece of territory on the Baltic Sea between Poland and Lithuania
(Kaliningrad Oblast) is a detached part of Russia—
in effect, a bit of "war booty" seized directly from
Germany after 1945 (until then part of its province
of East Prussia) and attached administratively to
Russia after World War II. Poland also gained terri-

tory from Germany after World War II, including a
tiny bit of land west of the Oder at its mouth on the
Baltic Sea.

The short, once bitterly contested German-Dan-
ish border is easy to miss on a large map. Germany
includes a small amount of territory west of the
Rhine near Frankfurt am Main in a region which it
and France fought over for centuries. The border
between Ireland and Northern Ireland also requires
attention to detail; this boundary between the UK
and Ireland leaves a sliver of Ireland in the northwesternmost part of the island. Serbia/Montenegro
(the self-proclaimed "Yugoslavia") holds an important territory north of the Danube River, bordering
Romania and Hungary. Ukraine controls a narrow
coastal strip of land between Moldova and the Black
Sea. Immediately to the south, Romania rules a
small but important territory on the Black Sea coast
as well. Greece controls a narrow coastal panhandle
on the northern coast of the Aegean Sea, as well as
most of the Aegean islands—the latter bitterly contested by Turkey. Turkey retains a small chunk of
Europe bordering on Greece and Bulgaria, a tiny
vestige of a once vast European, Asian, and North
African empire. A speck of the once vast British
Empire, Gibraltar, remains in the midst of Spanish
territory. Spain itself includes tiny territories across
the Straits of Gibraltar in North Africa. Most of the
islands in the Mediterranean and all of those in the
Baltic belong to neighboring states. Finally, there are
a number of tiny countries that intrigue and con-
found people carefully studying Europe's complex
geopolitical map (see Inset 1-2).

Many beginning students of Europe also over-
look important details of its physical geography. For
example, note that the Rhine River begins in eastern
Switzerland and flows through the Lake of Constance; the river empties into the North Sea via a
confusing set of distributaries close to the Maas (or
Meuse) River mouth. Though close together at one
point, there exists as yet no natural or human-created link between the Rhine and Rhone rivers, the
Rhone flowing south into the Mediterranean, and
the Rhine north into the North Sea. The Danube's

source is in extreme southwestern Germany, and its mouth is on the Romanian-Ukrainian border. The Volga flows into the Caspian, although a canal links it to the Don, which empties into the Sea of Azov, itself linked to the Black Sea.

There are some confusing names for European mountains. For example, the Pennine Chain is in England; the Apennines in Italy. In addition to the west-east-trending Alps, there are also the north-west-southeast-trending Dinaric Alps in the former Yugoslavia. The Carpathians are hook-shaped and trend east and then south from the Czech-Slovak border through Poland, Ukraine, and Romania.

Many of Europe's major cities are strategically located on the banks or near the mouths of important rivers. For example, London is on the Thames; Rotterdam on the Rhine; Hamburg on the Elbe;

Paris on the Seine; Lyon on the Rhone; Warsaw on the Vistula; and Vienna, Budapest, and Belgrade on the Danube. On the other hand, several other important cities are near but not on the banks of nearby notable streams, such as Berlin (on the Havel and Spree, but near the Oder), Marseille near the Rhone, Milan near the Po, Bucharest just north of the Danube, and Moscow just south of the Volga. Many cities are on or very near the sea, and they or satellite cities serve as major ports—such as St. Petersburg, Stockholm, Copenhagen, Lisbon, Barcelona, Naples, Venice, and Athens. A final surprise—Istanbul, Turkey's major metropolis—is in Europe on the strategic Bosporus, which links the Black Sea to the Sea of Marmara and, ultimately, the Mediterranean.

---

in Western countries has stagnated because of a combination of such variables as falling birth rates and lower economic growth rates, competition among firms to maintain their market shares has intensified. For example, Mercedes and BMW no longer have the world luxury car market to themselves; Infiniti, Lexus, and Acura as well as Cadillac, Lincoln, Jaguar, Saab, and Volvo are all fighting for a piece of this limited market. As the battle intensifies, prices have dropped and profit margins have become narrower. Simultaneously, companies are trying to become more productive on a per worker basis, which means that everywhere the workforce is being sharply reduced as the result of technology and as some jobs are lost to distant competitors. In Germany, companies such as Daimler-Benz, Volkswagen, and BASF have announced that their European labor forces will be cut by the tens of thousands, at the same time that Daimler-Benz, for example, is creating jobs in the United States.

Net job losses are cutting purchasing power, and growth in new, full-time employment opportunities is not keeping pace with growth in labor forces. Although 9 million jobs were created in the EU between 1985 and 1991, unemployment fell by only 3 million. The privatization of former state industries is also expected to further reduce employment by about 500,000 to 1 million persons.

In Spain unemployment of those under 25 years of age is nearly 40 percent, close to 30 percent in Italy, and 25 percent in France. In Eastern Europe, the transition from a centrally planned to a market economy has also resulted in steeply rising unemployment, a situation that could worsen when additional reforms are carried out to make these countries competitive in world markets. Estimates place the number of poor people who live within the relatively wealthy countries of the European Union at between 50 and 70 million; millions more suffer from or are threatened by poverty in Eastern Europe.

Much must be done to make Europe more competitive economically and to help keep it that way. Even people in Europe's strongest economies (e.g., Germany) fear that Europe is losing competitiveness, not only to Japan and the United States, which are widely viewed as successful and threatening economic superpowers, but also to rapidly developing economies such as those on the Pacific Rim. Europeans are also concerned about maintaining the high levels of social services that have become common in most parts of Northern, Western, and West Central Europe in recent decades, although the direct costs of these and related high taxes are frequently viewed as competitive disadvantages in attracting new and maintaining existing employment. Growing numbers of the poor and unemployed, including large numbers of young people, are expressing political frustrations (such as support for demagogues and extremists) that threaten political stability in Western and Eastern Europe.

Thus, the international economic challenges facing Europe are closely related to broader social and political conditions and to problems within individual countries and regions. Some pan-European efforts are being made to face common, pressing problems—and have resulted in both successes and failures in resolving them. These issues are addressed in more depth later in this chapter as well as in succeeding chapters.

PAN-EUROPEAN ORGANIZATIONS

Europe provides the headquarters for a great number of international institutions with global membership, as well as for a host of organizations that have exclusively or primarily European members. Geneva has perhaps the largest number of important international institutions, although Brussels is a close competitor. London, Paris, Vienna, The Hague, and Rome are also notable centers for international institutions (see Table 1-1).

Clearly, as noted earlier, most people and places in Europe today are profoundly impacted both by the integration of the world economy and by ongoing economic integration within Europe, especially within the EU (European Union). There are also some people, particularly within the EU, who would like to see a pan-European government that would have great influence on social and political as well as on economic affairs. Thus, efforts are being made within the EU to extend economic integration by, for example, creating a common currency and a central bank; related efforts have been initiated to develop common social and foreign policies. Thirty years of progress in economic integration and more hesitant steps toward harmonization of environmental, social, and political policies suggests that Europe, or more likely some parts of it, might someday become a federated or united state. This expansion of a pan-European role in political, economic, and social affairs within the EU is referred to as "deep-

ening." At the same time, the EU and other pan-European organizations (e.g., NATO) have been urged through both internal efforts and external pressures to expand their membership, especially by including formerly socialist countries from Central and Eastern Europe, as well as possibly some parts of the former Soviet Union (FSU).

Many citizens as well as some member governments, most notably the UK, oppose the "deepening" of EU integration. Even those who support it often have quite different conceptions of how a united Europe might function. Some prefer a federation of sovereign states, or a "United States" of Europe, with at least some powers granted to a pan-European central government. Somewhat less strongly felt objections have been made to the widening of participation by more countries within European organizations owing to concerns for the economic costs. It would be expensive to include poorer East Central European countries within the EU, and including former Warsaw Pact countries within NATO involves potential political liabilities. In addition, other trends in Europe suggest problems and possible limitations to closer pan-European cooperation, such as ethnic and religious conflict, and strongly felt nationalism.

The "Euro-optimist" can point to the diminished importance of international boundaries in Europe since 1945 and progress in integrating the peoples of Europe economically, socially, culturally, and politically. An unmistakable movement toward European unity has been evidenced in the postwar era. In 1996 even once feared Russia has been incorporated into Europe's broadest international organization—the Council of Europe. "Euro-skeptics," however, emphasize the EC/EU's regular failure to meet its (often purposely ambitious) goals for integration. They point out evidence of persistent divisive tendencies on the continent, suggested by the conflicts in and dissolution of Yugoslavia, Czechoslovakia, and the USSR.

On balance, it is hard to deny the reality of ongoing integration in Europe. People, goods, and investments flow far more easily across borders within the EU, and indeed within Europe, than probably at any time in its history. Though not all efforts toward further integration have been successful or have been achieved very quickly, a

TABLE 1-1

SELECTED INTERNATIONAL ORGANIZATIONS WITH HEADQUARTERS IN EUROPE

Geneva	European Free Trade Association (EFTA), European Organization for Nuclear Research, International Organization for Migration.
	U.N. institutions: Conference on Trade and Development (UNCTAD), Economic Commission for Europe, General Agreement on Tariffs and Trade (GATT) and World Trade Organization (WTO), Institute for Training and Research, International Labor Organization (ILO), International Telecommunications Union, Office of the High Commissioner for Refugees, Research Institute for Social Development, World Council of Churches, World Health Organization (WHO), World Intellectual Property Organization, World Meteorological Organization
Brussels	Benelux, Customs Cooperation Council, European Organization for the Safety of Air Navigation, European Trade Union Confederation, European Union, International Confederation of Free Trade Unions, North Atlantic Treaty Organization (NATO), West European Union (WEU), World Confederation of Labor
London	The [British] Commonwealth, European Bank for Reconstruction and Development (EBRD), International Maritime Satellite Organization, U.N. International Maritime Organization
Paris	European Space Agency; International Energy Agency; Organization for Economic Cooperation and Development (OECD); U.N. Educational, Scientific, and Cultural Organization (UNESCO)
Vienna	Organization of Petroleum Exporting Countries (OPEC), U.N. Industrial Development Organization (UNIDO), U.N. International Atomic Energy Agency, U.N. Relief and Works Agency for Palestinian Refugees in the Near East (UNRA)
Rome	International Fund for Agricultural Development, U.N. Food and Agriculture Organization (FAO)
The Hague	International Court of Justice ("World Court"), Permanent Court of Arbitration
Basel	Bank for International Settlements
Bern	U.N. Universal Postal Union
Helsinki	Nordic Investment Bank
Lyon	International Criminal Police Organization (Interpol)
Prague	Organization for Security and Cooperation in Europe (OSCE)
Stockholm	Nordic Council
Strasbourg	Council of Europe

decades' old trend toward integration seems undeniable. However, ongoing threats of reversals also exist (e.g., owing to conflicts over subsidies for and trade in agricultural products), and there are vocal critics of any further efforts toward pan-European unity. Indeed, some people interpret the UK's initial failure to join the European Community (EC, the previous name of the EU) and its subsequent entry not as a belated commitment to European integration, but at least partly as a tactical move to join the EC/EU so that progress toward integration could be stalled from within.

Although the broad parameters of European integration affect the lives of Europeans, their everyday lives often seem far removed from those of people speaking a different language across a nearby border. Thus, for example, one can usually take a bus in Spain to another nearby Spanish town, but getting to Portugal is dramatically more difficult. The English routinely vacation by jetting to North America and the Mediterranean, but one frequently meets people who have never crossed the few miles to Ireland. Similarly, the Germans, in terms of money spent abroad, are the world's champion travelers, but relatively few seem to venture to neighboring Poland.

In short, Europe is now experiencing an ongoing process of integration, but it remains unclear how far, how complete, and how quickly the process will proceed—or if the process is irreversible. Next is an overview of the European integration process since 1945, focusing on the EC/EU, but also including coverage of other important and well-known pan-European organizations.

Uniting the European Economies and Societies

In order to achieve greater economic prosperity and to promote international understanding and mutual reliance in the interest of lessening the potential for another pan-European war, a post–World War II effort to unite Europe gained support and momentum. Many Europeans have long believed, for example, that only a larger economic union, a common market, can address Europe's underlying economic problems and allow it to compete with the world's economic superpowers, Japan and the United States. The Belgian leader Paul-Henri Spaak once observed that no manufacturing firm in any individual European country was big enough to compete successfully with strong American firms. This is an exaggeration, but it is indicative of the Europeans' insecurity in the face of competition from much larger economic unions.

For decades, some Europeans in business and politics sought to establish an economic unit on a transnational scale, encompassing, for example, a common approach to transport, energy, capital investment, labor, and trade. These people believed that Europe needed a supranational economic development effort, with a complete abolition of tariffs and facilitation of free trade. After World War II, a growing number of people believed that only an economically united Europe would be viable in the mid-twentieth century. Unfortunately, despite factors conducive to Euro-

pean unification in the immediate postwar era, the goal could still not be achieved. Most countries of East Central and Southeastern Europe were instead rapidly incorporated into the new Soviet Empire. Sweden and Switzerland persisted in their traditional neutrality. Austria was militarily occupied for the first 10 postwar years by France, the United Kingdom, the United States, and the USSR, and was then forced to declare neutrality in order to rid itself of Soviet occupation forces. Fascist Spain was shunned by numerous West European governments until a new democratic government was established in the late 1970s. Among Western European countries, traditional disagreements about the future role of an integrated continent made economic integration a slow and difficult process.

The vision of a political union among European countries was presented through Winston Churchill's dramatic appeal in Zurich in 1946, when he urged Franco-German conciliation "to create the European family" and proposed a kind of United States of Europe. Frenchman Jean Monnet proposed a new organization of European countries, and the ultimate development of the European Community during the 1950s ensued.

The emergence of this and several other Western European institutions has markedly changed the character of global political and economic relationships. By its own, often ambitious, schedule for integration, the evolution of the EU might be considered slow, but by more realistic standards the Union has already developed to the point that the continent is far more cosmopolitan in the broadest sense than the Europe of the 1950s and 1960s, which was comprised of many small countries with jealously protected markets and borders.

East Central and Southeastern Europe also embarked on an important, but ill-fated, experiment in regional unification after World War II. There the Soviet Union, using its military might and political influence, tried to override national differences, traditions, and beliefs to form region-wide political-military and economic organizations (the Warsaw Pact and Council for Mutual Economic Assistance [CMEA]). Subsequently, Marxist ideology and the Stalinist model of economic development greatly impacted both bilateral and multilateral relations among the countries of Eastern Europe—quite negatively by most people's evaluation. Yugoslavia, however, charted its own road to socialism during most of the postwar period, tied formally neither to Eastern nor Western economic and political organizations. Albania originally followed a Soviet, then a Chinese, and finally an independent "socialist" path, until, as elsewhere, autocratic socialist rule was lifted a few short years ago.

Evolution of West European Economic Organizations

At the end of World War II, Western Europe had an existing, functioning model and inspiration for multinational economic cooperation—Benelux, the economic union of the Low Countries. In 1921 the small landlocked state of Luxembourg formed a customs union with its neighbor Belgium. The Netherlands, which borders Belgium, became a partner in 1948. Benelux developed by stages, facing and overcoming difficulties. It established a common tariff with the outside world and reduced tariffs among the three countries, thereby increasing trade.

Following World War II, conditions existed to form a similar, larger union of West European states. The U.S.-sponsored Marshall Plan enabled the rebuilding of economies and the rapid recovery of production in Western Europe, although the Soviets prevented participation by East European states. Early cooperative international organizations were launched in the West—such as the Organization for European Economic Cooperation (OEEC) in 1947. The OEEC worked well and has survived, expanding to become the current internationally based Organization for Economic Cooperation and Development (OECD).Through the OECD, "Western" industrialized countries undertake discussion, negotiation, and planning for more productive and harmonious economic relations. Its membership now includes many non-European members, such as the United States, Canada, Australia, New Zealand, and Japan. In addition, the General Agreement on Tariffs and Trade (GATT), concluded in 1948 by many countries inside and outside Europe, did much to facilitate trade, although it also called attention to obstacles to the full economic integration of Western Europe. GATT was instrumental in lowering tariff walls and in preventing tariff wars, but it was not concerned with creating a supranational authority that would lessen economic sovereignty and promote European economic integration and union.

European Coal and Steel Community (ECSC)

Under the leadership and inspiration of Belgian Prime Minister Spaak, a "Little Europe," with a small number of cooperating countries, emerged and achieved marked success when the Schuman Plan for the European Coal and Steel Community was launched on January 1, 1952 (see Table 1-1). Incipient economic interdependence was achieved within the coal, iron, and steel industries of member states, as economic rather than political considerations came to prevail and impediments to the trade of these products were dismantled. The ECSC organized the pooling of the fuel, ore, and scrap resources of "Little Europe" and established a common market in coal, iron ore, and steel. The initial success of ECSC owed much to its timely inception when markets were expanding, but since then it has also successfully weathered many difficulties. These have included recessions and the need to adjust the coal industries of member countries to the changing pattern of demand and to the problem of uneconomic mines in some areas. The ECSC has achieved much politically. Above all, it has brought closer cooperation between France and Germany, which had long been enemies in part based on rivalry over the complementary iron ore (Lorraine) and coal (Saarland) resources along their mutual border.

European Community (EC or Common Market)

The success in launching the European Coal and Steel Community encouraged the six members of the ECSC to consider a broader customs union. After meetings at Messina (Italy) in 1955 and at

Venice in 1956, they agreed to form a common market, declaring their goals in the Treaty of Rome in March 1957:

> The [European Economic] Community's mission shall be, by establishing a common market and gradually removing difficulties between the economic policies of member states, to promote throughout the Community by the harmonious development of economic activities, continuous and balanced expansion, increased stability, a more rapid improvement in the standard of living and closer relations between its member states.

The Common Market was formally launched on January 1, 1958. The six original countries, with an aggregate population of over 160 million, became the world's largest importer, the second largest producer of coal and automobiles, and the third largest producer of steel. The 15 members of today's European Union (EU) have 7 percent of the world's population (370 million people) and nearly a quarter of global economic output. The countries have from 50 to 75 percent of their total trade within the Union; other European countries, especially those still in EFTA (European Free Trade Association) are similarly highly integrated with the EU states (see Table 5-7).

Though known primarily as an economic institution, the EU also includes the European Atomic Energy Community (EURATOM). The Union has achieved a relatively high level of economic integration, and there are ongoing efforts to achieve more. Within the EU, people, goods, and capital are by law allowed unhindered access to all other member countries. In reality, obstacles remain to be overcome in implementing completely unfettered access. The EU is considering political union, as well as establishment of a common currency and a central bank, though these are controversial efforts that have failed in the past. It does appear that a common currency and central bank will be functioning within the EU by around the turn of the century.

The EU has a large budget, a large bureaucracy based in Brussels, and a confusing administrative structure, which includes de facto leadership by the European Council made up of leaders of member states. It also has a Council of Ministers, a Commission with an influential president, and a Parliament. The costs of this administrative structure, the frequent secrecy of EU actions (especially within the Commission), and the arcane political bickering within it, undermine support for the administrative apparatus, despite widespread support within the EU's populace for the Union itself and for European unification. (Support for unification has historically been weaker in the UK and Denmark than elsewhere.) Despite this general commitment to EU unity and the success of EC/EU economic integration in fostering economic well-being and political stability in Europe, the importance of sovereign states as the basic geopolitical entity in Europe has not diminished much, and individuals generally still consider themselves (and actually are) citizens of their respective states rather than citizens of the EU. Still, the possibility of closer political union and evolution of identification with Europe or the EU rather than individual states remains a possibility for the future.

Evolution of the EC/EU The evolution of the European Community from its founding in 1958 is a fascinating example of pan-European politics. The original six members were able to unite based largely on the ability of new and old enemies to discard, or at least set aside, their animosities. Most importantly, France and West Germany ended 300 years of destructive competition and strife in order to lay the basis for a foundation of a more peaceful and unified Europe than has probably ever existed over such a large part of the region. Despite its age-old goal of European and world political leadership, the political realities of post–World War II Europe somehow finally convinced France's leadership that future security and greatness lay not in an adversarial, but in a cooperative, relationship with Germany. Thus, France strove to reduce trade impediments in iron, steel, and the basic natural resources used to produce them, in order to benefit from the economic strength of Germany's heavy industrial sectors, which in the 1950s were concentrated in the Ruhr region. The coal and iron ore fields on and near the French-West German border were tied together physically by way of improved rail and water connections and economically through trade agreements. In 1957 France also begrudgingly allowed the coal-rich Saar region, which it had occupied following the war, to join West Germany as the new state of Saarland. Previously, the Saarland and the iron ore-rich Lorraine had for centuries been a source of conflict between France and Germany.

West Germans sought a variety of goals in joining the EC, including the clear economic advantages of a larger European market, the symbolic political reacceptance of a peaceful Germany within European affairs represented by EC membership, and the peace of mind that potential political extremism in their country could be blunted by its integration into a larger political entity. In fact, these forces continue to be important factors in the ongoing leadership of France and Germany within the EU. The commitment of the two countries' leaders to a close and peaceful relationship is symbolized by regular monthly consultations between the president of France and the chancellor of Germany.

The Netherlands, like France, also saw its political and economic future in a more unified Europe. Twice overrun in this century by German troops and harshly occupied by Germans in World War II (Rotterdam was virtually leveled by air attacks in reprisal for Dutch resistance to the occupation), the Dutch still harbor some anti-German sentiment. This, however, did not and has not stopped the country from developing good relations with Germany. Similarly, the smaller states and economies of Belgium and Luxembourg and the originally weaker economy of Italy benefited from development of the original six-member EC.

The United Kingdom, still considered a world political and economic power in the 1950s, purposely shunned the development of the EC on the European mainland. Instead, it chose to exercise continued, complete sovereignty and to maintain economic trade agreements with the far-flung British Commonwealth, which then still included many overseas colonies. Loss of Empire, the tremendous success of the EC, economic problems on the British Isles, and related decline of the UK's stature in world affairs ultimately led it to seek EC membership during the 1960s. France, led by de Gaulle, twice vetoed UK participation, apparently

because France wanted to maintain its own and reduce the UK's influence in European affairs. After de Gaulle no longer ruled in France, the UK was accepted into EC membership in 1973. At the same time, two countries whose trade was heavily oriented to the UK, Ireland and Denmark, also joined, bringing the EC to nine members.

Despite the prospects of a heavy burden of financial assistance to other, poorer European countries, the EC chose to support fledgling democratic and market-oriented movements elsewhere in Europe by incorporating first Greece (1981) and then Spain and Portugal (1986) within it. As described briefly in a later section, the EC became the EU in 1993 and subsequently greeted Austria, Finland, and Sweden as members on January 1, 1995. The addition of these countries reflects an effort by the wealthier West European EU members to form a broader European market that can more effectively compete with the large, globally oriented American and Japanese economies. However, EC/EU expansion has also been an indication of agreement on the need to promote democracy in previously autocratically ruled countries (Greece, Portugal, and Spain) in order to provide a better basis for European peace and cooperation.

The European Community (EC) became the European Union (EU) on January 1, 1993, following successful implementation of the Single European Act. This so-called Europe 1992 effort was begun in the mid-1980s in order to complete the formation of a true economic union by final elimination of a large number of remaining impediments to intra-European movement of goods, services, capital, and people. Many of the impediments were nontariff trade barriers that existed as law and tradition within the member states, such as strict limitations on beer ingredients in Germany and use of yellow auto headlights in France. The EU membership and their national parliaments made a major effort to pass hundreds of legislative acts in order to finally harmonize the EC/EU market, eliminating local conditions such as those just noted and promoting greater levels of international trade. During this ambitious, successful process, a yet more ambitious, controversial effort to integrate the EC/EU into much more than an economic union was also begun by way of the Maastricht Treaty. This treaty aims to create not only a closer economic union but also a more meaningful political union with, for example, more common political, social, and economic policies.

Based on the implied tenets of EU policy (the promotion of democracy in once autocratically ruled countries and related establishment of a better basis for European peace and cooperation), a number of relatively poor countries have sought incorporation into today's EU. Turkey has had a long-standing interest in joining the EU, although the cost of supporting this large and, by West European standards, poor country has been deemed too difficult. Turkey's age-old frictions with Greece (including current disputes over control of the Aegean Sea, which may have oil under it), as well as the potential specter of the massive migration of poorer, Muslim Anatolian Turks to Western Europe, have thus far precluded more than an associate membership status for the country.

In 1995, however, Greek opposition to Turkish involvement in the EU was muted by an agreement to consider Cyprus for membership in the near future. This move led to a tentative agreement between the EU and Turkey whereby the two parties would drop trade barriers between one another, that is, form a customs union. The European Parliament's acceptance of this agreement was jeopardized by a massive Turkish military incursion into northern Iraq against Kurdish rebels. This operation unleashed strong criticism from European governments, with as yet unknown effects on the tentative customs union agreement.

The issue is complicated by the fact that about 2.5 million Turks live in Germany, where about half a million Shi'ite Kurds are often at odds with the other 2 million non-Kurdish Turks. The Kurdish uprising within Turkey has led to arson and the bombings of Turkish businesses and institutions within Germany, presumably by extremist Kurds.

Besides the problems caused by the Turkish invasion of Iraq, the integration of Turkey into the EU depends on a number of related issues. Cyprus, which is partitioned into Turkish- and Greek-dominated areas, has also applied for EU membership and must have its status clarified. Current EU members must also agree on extending what would likely be massive economic aid to Turkey, which is a much poorer country than any current or prospective member. In fact, full EU membership for Turkey would also allow unlimited access for Turks to live and work in Europe. These conditions do not seem to be politically plausible either now or anytime in the near future.

Since the dissolution of the Soviet Union, many countries in Central and Eastern Europe have also begun clamoring for the perceived economic and political security that EU membership would bring. The hopes of these countries, however, have been put on hold because a number of other, intervening issues have come before the EU, as well as because the West believes that their inclusion would bring potential economic and political perils. Among these dangers are concerns about funding economic development, creating political stability in the relatively poor countries of the region, and placating the political right wing in Russia. Russia's political right fears that extension of the EU, which some Russians see as the economic arm of NATO, would give it influence in areas considered to have great strategic importance to Russia. Those in the West opposed to EU membership for Eastern countries for economic or other political reasons can also use this issue to block EU expansion to the east. In addition, these countries will not easily meet the EU's formal requirements for admission in the near future. The EU requires countries to have stable, pluralistic democracies; guarantees for human and minority rights; market-oriented economies with limited government ownership and limited subsidization of economic activities; low inflation rates and budget deficits; and legal systems in conformity with EU guidelines. The last-named requirement is itself an expensive endeavor.

Nonetheless, at least some East Central European countries will likely join the EU before too long. The Czech Republic, Hungary, and Slovenia are likely candidates, given their political and economic stability and their relatively small sizes. Poland and Slovakia, though politically and economically more complicated cases than the others, are also frequently listed with these three countries as among the most likely earliest entrants. As a first step toward hoped-for admission, several East European states have association agreements with the EU (Bulgaria, the Czech Republic, Hungary, Poland, Romania, and Slovakia), and several others, including the Baltic states and Slovenia, are expected soon to have a similar status. However, before East European states join the EU, Cyprus might be admitted, possibly before the turn of the century (Fig. 1-5).

The EU's Internal Structure The EU has adopted a wide range of actions to promote political, economic, and cultural cooperation within the Union. Restrictions on trade and on the movement of capital and labor have been removed, and common policies on agriculture, transportation, fisheries, and non-EU trade have been formulated. By the early 1990s, the Union had also dismantled a large number of administrative impediments to movements of goods, people, and capital by harmonizing many aspects of members' national policies toward, for example, border formalities, transport and environmental laws, tax rates, and mutual recognition of educational degrees and professional licenses. A controversial abolition of immigration controls at state borders was partially achieved in 1995 between seven so-called "Schengen States," based on an agreement reached in Schengen, Luxembourg. A number of states remain outside the agreement, largely out of concern for loss of sovereignty in controlling illegal immigration, including the potentially easier movement of terrorists to and within Europe.

The Community's administrative, legislative, judicial, and financial machinery consists of four functional units. (1) The Council of Ministers meets primarily in Brussels, though sometimes also in Luxembourg. The Council wields the power of the purse, but since 1975 has shared this power with the European Parliament. Each country acts as president of the Council for a six-month period on a rotational basis. The Council usually acts by a modified majority vote based on ten votes for France, Germany, the United Kingdom, and Italy; eight for Spain; five for the Netherlands, Greece, Portugal, and Belgium; four for Austria

and Sweden; three for Ireland, Portugal, Denmark, and Finland; and two for Luxembourg. Unanimous voting is occasionally required.

(2) The Commission of the EU, located in Brussels, shares executive power with the Council of Ministers and is responsible to the Union as a whole; its 17 members, who reach decisions by majority vote, are nominated by member states. The Commission president plays a vital role within the EU. Energetic Jacques Delors of France (president, 1985–1994) was an outspoken and tireless worker for ever greater integration within the Union. His successor, Jacques Santer of Luxembourg, was a compromise candidate, and has had to grapple with strong resistance to further centralization of power in the EU. The UK, for example, successfully led opposition in 1994 to the election of a more avowedly centralist Commission presidential candidate. The Commission is guardian of treaties and is often the initiator of policy. It commands a large bureaucracy, sometimes disparaged as "Eurocrats". Not all EU citizens are pleased to have their lives impacted by both domestic bureaucrats and these (usually foreign) "Eurocrats."

(3) The European Parliament building is located in Strasbourg, France, but other important parliamentary functions are also carried out in Brussels and Luxembourg. France and Luxembourg have staunchly opposed efforts to move all Parliament offices and meetings to Brussels. Parliament's members, who are directly elected every five years, represent various political orientations that are linked to political parties in member countries with similar political philosophies. Following the 1994 election, social democrats held a plurality in the Parliament; conservatives formed the second largest grouping; and several other coalitions (e.g., Liberals, Greens, Coalition of the Left, and European Rightists) also held seats. Parliament has budgetary powers that give it a vote on all major decisions involving expenditures of the EU budget. It is also charged with reviewing the Commission's activities and must be consulted before proposals go before the Council, though its own powers are limited.

(4) The Court of Justice rules on issues associated with the interpretation and implementation of EU treaties and regulations. It consists of 13 judges

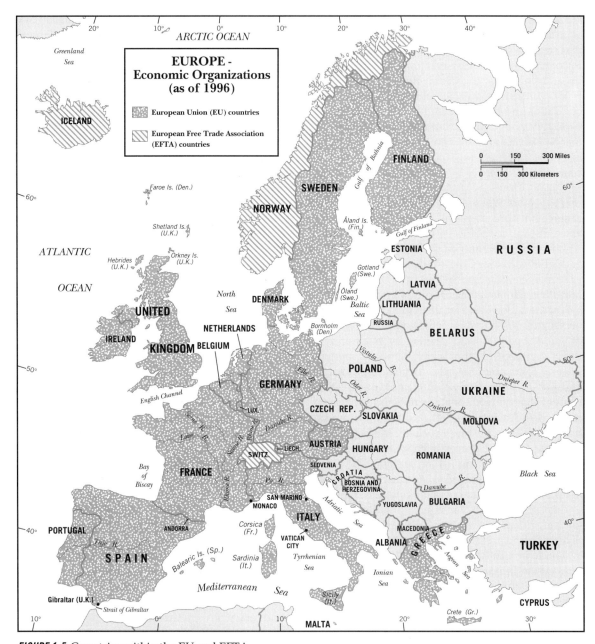

FIGURE 1-5 Countries within the EU and EFTA.

(assisted by six advocates), who are generally appointed for six years. The Court's judgements must be unanimous and are binding on all courts in the member states.

The EU's 1993 income (about $80 billion) was derived from several sources. Value-added sales taxes provide most funding (VAT, 54%); members' dues (22%), custom duties (20%), and duties on imported agricultural products and on EU-pro-duced sugar (4%) provide the rest. In 1993 the largest expenditures were for agricultural policy (51%), regional assistance (31%), and assistance for economic structural change (18%). Aid for agriculture, in fact, accounts for more than two-thirds of the EU budget, since regional aid also goes to support it and is probably the EU's most controversial issue. There are also ongoing controversies about members' dues, which in a few cases are higher than direct financial benefits from the EU. Germany is a very large net contributor. Because of a political choice to support European unity and Germany's many indirect economic benefits from the EU, it has been willing, in effect, to balance the Union's budgets. Other countries (notably the UK and the Netherlands in recent years) have been far less accepting of net contributor status.

A European monetary system was officially introduced in March 1979 with the hope of creating a zone of fiscal stability through the ECU (European Currency Unit), whose value is determined by weighting the currencies of member states. In mid-1995 the ECU was equal to about $1.40 (US). Efforts to inaugurate a single currency have been fraught with a variety of problems. Notable among these are: (1) resistance from countries opposed to greater centralization of power in the hands of the EU; and (2) concerns about the ability of several countries to adhere to strict financial discipline. The maintenance of reasonably balanced national budgets, moderate levels of debt, and stable currency values vis-à-vis other EU denominations are the primary concerns. Strong voices have been heard both supporting and questioning the establishment of a unified currency. The EU and most governments seem to be supporters, but if adopted, a common currency is not likely before the year 2000. Agreement has been reached on changing the currency's name from "ECU" to "euro." When established, the monetary union may, as in the case of the Schengen Treaty, also include only some countries. The related, controversial establishment of a central EU bank is moving forward, with a somewhat predictable choice of Frankfurt, seat of the highly respected German Federal Bank, as winner of a competition to capture the economically important and prestigious institution.

The widely ranging functions of the European Community are supported by the work of a number of committees and other advisory bodies created for specific purposes. For example, the European Social Fund seeks to improve employment possibilities and to assist labor mobility. The European Agricultural Guidance and Guarantee Fund administers levies on agricultural imports into member states, assists European farmers with subsidies, and stimulates improvements in agricultural production and distribution. The Regional Development Fund attempts to reduce unequal economic and social levels within the Community. The Union also has established links with overseas countries such as by way of the Lome Convention of 1975, which developed special relationships between the EU and scores of countries that were once colonial dependencies of France, Belgium, Italy, the United Kingdom, and the Netherlands. The EU gives financial support through the European Development Fund (EDF), a multilateral fund financed by all EU member states, to various development projects. Individual members of the EU also grant bilateral aid; the wealthier EU countries are generally among the world's most generous donors based on aid provided per citizen.

Regional Development Policies Owing to rather large regional disparities between countries and regions in the EU, its second most important budget item, after support of agriculture, has long been a regional development program. The EU and many of its members believe that regional variations are disadvantageous to long-term economic growth and sociopolitical stability, and are inherently unfair. The EU and individual countries like Germany have legally mandated directives to work toward eliminating regional disparities.

At the international level, the EU has allocated for 1994–1999 about $20 billion specifically for transportation and environmental development projects in its four poorest states—Portugal, Spain, Ireland, and Greece. This "Cohesion Fund" was adopted to lessen the financial constraints and feared disadvantages that will face poorly located and developed states as the result of greater EU economic and monetary integration. Although public expenditure will be limited by countries' needs to meet monetary union standards, lower income and more poorly located countries are in need of better infrastructure to compete within the evolving EU. The Cohesion Fund was implemented to help such states develop a better infrastructure, while making it more feasible for them to simultaneously meet the monetary union requirements. A similar fund, the Financial Mechanism, has been established as a result of closer economic ties between EFTA and the EU by way of the EEA (European Economic Area). This fund is described briefly in a later section of this chapter.

The EU's major mechanism for reducing regional disparities within all of its member states is by way of dispersements of money from its Regional Development Fund to members in order for them to support development activities in specifically designated regions. For the period 1994–1999, the EU has budgeted about $25 billion per year for programs with six specific goals. Goal 1, which receives about 70 percent of all funding, is to promote economic development in lagging regions. Eligible areas include Ireland, Northern Ireland, northern and western Scotland, a small area on the French-Belgian border, eastern Germany, easternmost Austria (Burgenland), southern Italy, Greece, Portugal, and most of Spain (excluding Madrid and Catalonia). Goal 2 (10% of budget) is for the economic conversion of declining industrial regions, such as Wales, many parts of northern England, northeastern France, the Ruhr, Barcelona, and Genoa. Goals 3 and 4 (10% of budget) are broadly defined for combatting unemployment. Goal 5 (5% of budget) targets a large number of lagging rural areas within several countries, and Goal 6 (5% of budget) is designed to support development projects in thinly populated regions in Sweden and Finland.

The EU's regional programs have had at best modest success and frequently face severe criticism. Though large in absolute value, the relatively small funding for the programs ($75 per EU citizen per annum) and the politically motivated, wide geographic dispersal of the money, means that they can only exert a limited impact on regions. Given that much support under the EU's agricultural program (CAP) goes to wealthy farmers in prosperous regions, there is persistent criticism that EU programs work at cross purposes.

The precedent of regionally based aid also poses a serious problem for the EU, should it consider including poorer East European or other Mediterranean area members. The relative poverty in much of Poland and Turkey, for example, would put a tremendous burden on the Regional Development Fund's resources and raise objections from countries like Spain that might stand to lose funding. Finally, despite the large absolute financial flows to lagging regions, regional inequalities within the EU hardly changed during the 1980s. For example, in 1991 the EU's 10 wealthiest regions had an average income level 52 percent above the EU average; the 10 poorest regions averaged 42 percent of the EU average. This represented a slight worsening of the situation from 1981, although one can always argue that without the regional development effort conditions would have been worse still.

During the 1957 to 1974 period, regional inequalities in the EC declined sharply, owing to a happier convergence of EU support for poorer regions and then current economic forces, such as a trend toward decentralization of manufacturing jobs away from traditional industrialized centers. In recent years, EU support to poorer regions has not been significant enough to counteract forces detrimental to less developed areas, such as the closure of branch plants. In addition, in recent years the EU has put increased emphasis on making European firms more competitive in the global marketplace. EU aid for research and development projects, usually based in metropolitan growth regions, may be helping to achieve this goal, but also probably work against other EU efforts to reduce gaps in economic opportunity and well-being between prosperous and lagging regions. Thus, EU policies have probably contributed to other forces, such as deregulation of markets and liberalized international trade laws, which have resulted in somewhat increased regional income inequalities within the EU since 1974.

Most individual EU members also have national regional development programs that complement the EU effort. The nature of these programs has varied greatly through time and space, but in general the programs often have goals that are quite similar to EU program goals. Funding frequently is oriented toward agriculturally and locationally disadvantaged regions (earlier including German and Austrian eastern borders regions abutting the CMEA counties), as well as troubled industrial and mining regions. Particularly noteworthy regional development programs exist in the UK and France, where at one time their measures included discouraging further economic growth in their capital cities. Italy had a long-term, controversial *Cassa per il Mezzogiorno* program for developing the south. Germany's regional development program includes both centrally administered efforts and a cooperative state-federal regional development program. In the late 1990s, however, no European regional development effort can really compare with Germany's monumental effort both to support higher living standards and to improve infrastructure in its newly incorporated eastern provinces. This project now consumes about $100 billion annually, more than triple the combined value of all EU regional development programs.

Major Issues Before the Union The EU has clearly moved successfully toward economic integration; political integration remains a distant goal. For example, the establishment of a United States of Europe, an ultimate objective of internationalists, is not imminent. Despite the various complex difficulties involved in harmonizing the activities of so many independent states, trade barriers have been eliminated and common external tariffs are applied to imports from nonmember countries. Numerous difficulties still face the Commission at Brussels in attempts to harmonize the economic, social, and cultural conditions of the member countries; to forge and apply effective policies agreeable to and for the general betterment of all members; and to establish common policies regarding nonmember countries.

One major difficulty lies in achieving a Common Agricultural Policy that serves both producers and consumers, is politically palatable and economically sound, and conforms with economic necessities and political realities of the global economy. There are also the never-ending arguments over the size of member contributions to the Union's budget, as well as development of a monetary policy that can deal with both strong and weak currencies. The monetary policy issue falls within a greater philosophical debate over how much power the EU should have and what level of sovereignty should remain with individual states. Important, too, is the need to help regions within member states that suffer from unemployment and related socioeconomic problems and that require initiatives to restructure local economies. Finally, solutions to serious local and international environmental problems are needed.

The controversial Common Agricultural Policy (CAP) has helped create free trade within the Community. Although agriculture now employs a relatively small proportion of the labor force, agricultural interests are a potent political force within both the EU and its constituent countries. Tens of billions of dollars are spent annually to subsidize producers; the subsidies comprise a majority of the entire EU budget. The original Treaty of Rome that set up the Community ostensibly prohibited national subsidies, but despite the prohibition subsidies still exist, for they are important to individual countries for domestic political reasons. Markets for milk, cereals, sugar, beef, table wines, and some fruits and vegetables are especially affected by government intervention, although price controls and subsidies have been reduced in recent years owing to pressures exerted by selected EU member states and by the United States. Thanks to protection of producers, huge surpluses of butter, wine, skimmed milk powder, and beef accumulate—at a considerable cost to the EU. A system of guaranteed market prices and export subsidies applied under the CAP permitted Europe to emerge as a major agricultural exporter by the mid-1980s.

An EU issue of particular interest to geographers focuses on the efforts of subnational EU governments (such as individual city governments and regions like the German *Länder*) to gain more influence and autonomy. In a trend that began during the 1980s, scores of EU regional governments have established information offices in Brussels, the EU capital, and they have become active in socioeconomic planning and in EU politics. A modest success in the latter regard was achieved by establishing an EU INTERREG program in 1990. The program originally provided funds for cross-border planning efforts between EU members, but the 1994–1999 program, which has funding in excess of $3 billion, includes money for cross-border planning with East Central European states as well.

These formal EU efforts build on a longer tradition of direct interaction among EU regions that includes a variety of earlier links between Baden-Württemberg (Germany) and neighboring and distant regions both within the EU and in Switzerland. Similarly, groups of EU cities have formed associations in a movement dubbed the "Eurocities" movement. Professor Alec Murphy (University of Oregon) has argued (1993) that these efforts and the actions of transnational corporations are indications of the growing importance of nonstate and substate actors within the European political arena. If one includes the actions of international organizations such as the EU itself, one could possibly imagine a time in the future when the central states' roles in European affairs might be more modest than they are today. Though an interesting trend and hypothesis, the role of national governments for now remains a powerful force, both within Europe as a whole and within the EU more specifically.

Whether the EU should be "deepened" by closer integration of existing members before it is further "broadened" by including new members—or if, in fact, neither should occur—is a key current issue within the EU. The issue of membership of several Nordic countries and Austria illustrates a variety of specific factors within countries themselves that affect EU membership decisions as well as more generic issues that currently face the Union.

In 1994 Norway opted, for a second time, not to become an EU member. Although the country's political leadership and urban dwellers generally supported membership, a majority of rural dwellers and those working in protected or heavily subsidized primary sector activities (e.g., agriculture and fishing) opposed it. Norway's farmers are among Europe's most heavily supported, with subsidies as a percentage of producer income

more than 50 percent higher than the EU average and more than double the U. S. average. EU membership for Norway would mean a decline in agricultural subsidies and almost certainly would mean many fewer farmers. Some people in Norway also apparently feared too much EU control over its oil and fishery resources and saw too few tangible benefits from membership, especially given that Norway already has a successful economic relationship with the EU by way of EFTA and EEA. In addition, it is conjectured that nationalism is still particularly strong in Norway, because it has been politically independent for less than a century, following centuries of foreign rule. On the other hand, Norwegian proponents of EU membership emphasize that Norway must look beyond its present oil-dominated economy to a time when oil revenue will decline and new economic bases for continued prosperity must be found. For now, Norway joins two other prosperous, tenaciously independent West European states (Iceland and Switzerland) as outsiders within an ever more EU-dominated Europe.

Sweden, Finland, and Austria only recently became serious candidates for EU membership, but were incorporated rather quickly into the Union beginning in 1995. Sweden's virtually devout neutrality in the Cold War precluded serious consideration of membership until it ended. This coincided with a period of serious economic problems in Sweden and led it to seriously reconsider its future—reflected in the reelection of the pro-EU socialists to power in the country in 1994 and a subsequent decision to join the EU on January 1, 1995.

Finland opted for membership in the EU beginning in 1995 for many of the same reasons as Sweden. Finland fought twice with the Soviet Union during World War II, ultimately losing territory and suffering partial occupation until the 1950s, and was bound by treaty to maintain close economic and political ties to the USSR. The dissolution of the Soviet Union, the disarray of the post-Soviet republics' economies, and a related severe recession in Finland, left the country looking for economic solutions and long-term political security in the form of EU membership.

Austria twice unsuccessfully sought EU membership, based on its Western political, cultural, and economic orientation—especially its very close trade ties to western Germany. However, like Finland, Austria only escaped Soviet occupation after 1955 by proclaiming neutrality, and Soviet objections to Austrian EC membership provided at least a rationale for French vetoes of earlier membership attempts.

The "broadening" versus "deepening" debate within the EU poses a formidable impediment to the inclusion of more countries within the EU. The benefits of "broadening" include the formation of a larger internal market and potentially greater political-military stability across the continent; the costs include increased subsidies and greater difficulty in adopting new EU-wide regulations. "Deepening," closer economic and political cooperation among members, might ultimately result in a United States of Europe. Such a union could, for example, create a common currency, central bank, and common monetary policy, and allow for a joint military force and foreign policy. Some countries are wary of "broadening"; among these are the poorer countries already in the EU, which would encounter more competition for development funds. Others oppose "deepening." For example, the UK leads the opposition to "deepening"; its recent governments have opposed relinquishing more national sovereignty—a concern that, in fact, exists among at least segments of the population in all EU countries.

How this complex debate will evolve within the EU is still unclear. Therefore, it is difficult to predict if or when expansion will occur, and especially when the countries of Central and Eastern Europe might enter an expanded Union. As noted earlier, relatively small and western-oriented Cyprus may join next. Speculation is that, based on their location and economic and political conditions, Poland, Hungary, and the Czech and Slovak Republics, will be the earliest formerly socialist countries to be seriously considered—probably sometime in the early twenty-first century. Given its quite small size, ethnic homogeneity, and political and economic progress, Slovenia could also be considered early, if the Western countries want to show at least some movement toward including the former socialist countries. Estonia, Latvia,

Lithuania, Bulgaria, and Romania are among the Central and East European countries that are holding serious discussions with the EU regarding possible future membership. The sheer size and magnitude of problems in Ukraine and Russia and problems in the former Yugoslav republics of Bosnia-Herzegovina and Serbia-Montenegro will likely defer any consideration of them for membership for many years.

Switzerland, Norway, and Iceland's persistent rejection of EU membership indirectly illustrates the dominance of economic factors in the decision-making processes of most countries seeking EU membership and more directly indicates the potency of the sovereignty issue in such deliberations. These countries are among the wealthiest in Europe, and their electorates see too little benefit from closer association with the EU. Many benefits already accrue to them by their sheer propinquity to the EU as well as by way of the special trade conditions EFTA countries have negotiated with it. Poorer countries, like those in Eastern Europe, cannot afford the luxury of such reasoning. Only a minority of people in Norway, Switzerland, and Iceland, including many leaders, believe that their countries' future security will be best met by EU membership. This is keenly felt by progressive-minded Swiss, who are embarrassed by the ultraconservative views held by other Swiss on issues associated with women's rights and the status of foreign residents. However, the somewhat more understandable concerns for gaining sovereignty over fishing grounds in Iceland and concern for maintaining greater control over rapid growth in international rail, truck, and car traffic and associated environmental degradation in the Alps in Switzerland, play important roles in the voters' rejection of EU membership. Similar concerns, such as fear of potential foreign ownership of land by prosperous Germans in Austria and Denmark, play a role in other countries in their citizenries' reluctance to support open-ended "deepening" of the Union. The potential loss of control over key fishing grounds has also led the autonomously governed territories of Greenland and the Faroe Islands (Denmark) and the Canary Islands (Spain) to reject participation in the EU.

European Free Trade Association (EFTA) and European Economic Area (EEA)

EFTA was formed in 1960 by seven West European countries interested in reducing trade impediments in Europe without agreeing to the level of economic integration sought by the EC. Unfortunately for EFTA, five of its original members as well as a later entry have since joined the EU—most recently, Austria, Finland, and Sweden in 1995. With the defection of one-time members to its more successful rival, EFTA has shrunk to just four countries—Iceland, Liechtenstein, Norway, and Switzerland, with a combined population of 11.5 million people.

Although EFTA states are among Europe's most prosperous, the size of their economies pales in comparison to the EU, which is also a far more important trade destination for EFTA members than the EFTA market itself. EFTA has entered into trade agreements with Central and East European, Southwest Asian, and North African countries, some of which could conceivably one day join the organization. For now membership is not imminent, since some of these countries would prefer to join the EU without the transitional stage of EFTA membership experienced by several current EU members.

The historical evolution of EFTA itself is helpful in understanding the process of European integration. In the 1950s the United Kingdom feared that membership in the European Community would result in losses of its benefits within the British Commonwealth, especially for foodstuffs and industrial raw materials, and would lead to loss of sovereignty. Thus, the UK and its original seven partners in EFTA (Austria, Denmark, Ireland, Norway, Portugal, Sweden, and Switzerland) agreed to form a free trade area. Central to the proposal of a free trade area was the removal of tariffs, quotas, and similar restrictions within the area, although individually determined external tariffs vis-à-vis nonmembers remained in place. Furthermore, EFTA recognized that member countries were unwilling to renounce agricultural subsidies and that it should not allow free movement of labor or infringement of state sovereignty.

EFTA is a loose organization of independent states, which originally had two distinct purposes—first, to create by 1970 a free trade area by removing all trade barriers; second, to establish a good position from which to bargain with the EC. Unlike some EC countries, EFTA states had no interest in ultimate federal union. Three original members were neutral countries—Switzerland, Sweden, and Austria. The United Kingdom had bonds with the Commonwealth, and Portugal had strong ties with its overseas dependencies until they declared independence after the 1974 overthrow of that country's dictatorship. These circumstances at least partially explain the EFTA countries' unwillingness to relinquish sovereignty to the extent required by the EC/EU.

The interests of the members of both EFTA and the EC/EU were and are closely interlocked, and so attempts have been made to bridge the gap between EFTA and the EC/EU. In fact, EFTA has generally functioned as an outer circle of the EC/EU. EFTA countries have had more trade with the EC/EU than with other EFTA members; through time several EFTA countries have shifted allegiances to the EC/EU; and most recently, EFTA and the EU finalized formation of a joint customs union, the European Economic Area (EEA), dropping most impediments to trade in goods and services and movements of capital between them.

The EEA is a joint effort by the EU and EFTA to create a "European economic space" that reduces impediments to the movements of goods between members of the two organizations. Shortly after the implementation of accords to achieve this end, several EFTA members switched membership to the EU and Switzerland opted against joining the EEA, so that the importance of the agreement has been diminished. Nonetheless, it allows much freer trade in services and movement of capital between the EU and EFTA, opening large markets for EFTA countries, but also exposing their *niche* and capital markets to competition from EU firms. An intriguing aspect of the EEA is an associated agreement, the Financial Mechanism, that is to provide nearly $2 billion in subsidized loans and nearly three-quarters of a billion dollars in grants for regional development projects during the late 1990s for the entire island of Ireland, and for Greece, Portugal, and parts of Spain. Besides these benefits to many former EFTA areas now within the EU, net significant economic benefits are expected from the EEA for EFTA countries. The ultimate significance of the accord could also be enhanced if EFTA were to be reinvigorated by new members.

Organization for Economic Cooperation and Development (OECD)

Originally derived from the membership of states receiving aid from the United States during the postwar era, this organization has developed into a more internationally based institution discussing and responding to shared concerns about international economic development. Although most members are from Western Europe, the United States, Canada, Japan, Australia, and New Zealand are also current members. The tradition of holding world economic summits (so-called G-7 meetings) evolved from the OECD's efforts. Non-members have accused it of being a club of rich countries that seek to control rather than guide the world economy.

Council for Mutual Economic Assistance (CMEA or COMECON)

This now defunct organization was introduced in 1949 by Josef Stalin, the Soviet leader from 1928 until 1953, as an effort to encourage East European economic integration and development. It included all of the East European states under Soviet influence following World War II, and later Cuba, Mongolia, and Vietnam as well. Albania, however, ultimately withdrew, and Yugoslavia's role within the CMEA was also curtailed following Marshal Tito's deviations from Moscow's prescribed policies. Although some progress was made toward international economic cooperation within it, for a variety of reasons the CMEA achieved little in comparison to the EC/EU. Some people also argue that it was initially only a propaganda ploy in response to American-supported pan-European development efforts in Western Europe and that later many of its projects were designed to benefit

the USSR, which dominated it and whose demise resulted in its dissolution.

Council of Europe (CE)

Once a dominantly West European institution, the Council of Europe now includes as full or associate members most European states, with the pointed exception of Yugoslavia. It was originally hoped that the Council, established in 1949 to foster European political unity and observance of human rights, would play an important role in European integration, a goal not achieved in either the post-World War II era or at the end of the Cold War. However, the Council has served as a place for East-West dialogue since the end of the Cold War and has worked closely with the Conference on Security and Cooperation (now OSCE) in Europe to assure human rights for Europeans.

Organization for Security and Cooperation in Europe (OSCE)

The OSCE, renamed from its predecessor, the Conference on Security and Cooperation in Europe (CSCE), has had as its primary goals the enhancement of security, economic cooperation, and human rights in Europe. The OSCE today includes virtually all European states as well as all the republics of the FSU, Canada, and the United States. The CSCE's original purposes focused on providing a forum of discussion between Europe's Cold War camps, a role that it played, for example, during the tense period when the United States and USSR were planning deployment of Pershing and SS-20 nuclear armed missiles aimed at European targets in the early 1980s. The CSCE negotiated the Helsinki Accord of 1975 which declared Europe's postwar boundaries inviable and provided stated guarantees for human rights. The failure of East European states to live up to the Accord led to the foundation of a number of dissident cells within those countries to press for greater human and civil rights. In the 1990s the CSCE/OSCE has been working to promote peaceful resolution of conflicts within and between its member states, sending, for example, missions to Yugoslavia (1991), Macedonia and Serbia (1992), Moldova (1993), and the Caucasus republics of the FSU (1992–1993). Although there have been disappointments with the OSCE's abilities to cope with and resolve conflicts in Europe, there remains hope that it can evolve into a premier pan-European political institution.

Western European Union (WEU)

France's rejection of a European Defense Community (which would have been within the EC) led in the mid-1950s to reviving the Western European Union (WEU), a defense initiative that had been largely dormant after the establishment of NATO in 1949. The WEU's membership has closely paralleled (though not been identical to) EC/EU membership, and it has been used to coordinate the European states' activities within NATO. For example, the controversial effort by France and Germany to establish a pan-European army, the "Eurocorps," falls within the jurisdiction of the WEU as well as NATO. Concern at the end of the Cold War that the United States might reduce its military commitment to Europe has spurred interest and membership in the WEU, which has also been expanded to include as associate members many former Baltic and Central and East European states. Thus, although the WEU now functions largely within the shadow of NATO, it provides a ready forum for purely European military coordination should U.S. military commitments to Europe weaken or European governments see a greater need for military consultations or actions independent of NATO and its dominant member, the United States.

North Atlantic Treaty Organization (NATO)

Rising postwar tensions exemplified by the Soviet blockade of West Berlin and the staged *coup d'état* in Czechoslovakia spurred the United States, Canada, and several West European states to conclude a mutual defense treaty in 1949. Primarily a grand alliance for defense among 16 countries, it combines the resources of 15 of these countries for

military purposes, while France participates in political discussions and sometimes joins NATO exercises. NATO generally displayed internal unity when confronting Soviet military power in Europe, but the divergent foreign policies of its members have also led to disagreements on security policies both inside and outside Europe, most recently in the case of the wars in the former Yugoslavia.

NATO has suffered a number of political problems and setbacks. France withdrew from the integrated military command structure in 1965, and the headquarters were removed from Paris to Brussels. France remains a member of the Atlantic Alliance, NATO's political wing, and announced in 1995 that it would rejoin the command structure.

NATO has also had problems in the Mediterranean owing to age-old disputes between members Greece and Turkey and owing to disagreements about policy in the Balkans. On the other hand, some argue that NATO won the Cold War—the so-called Iron Curtain has fallen, the Soviet/Russian military threat to Western Europe has nearly evaporated, and many former Soviet allies are clamoring for NATO membership. The post–Cold War role for NATO (and the United States) in Europe remains somewhat unclear, but it could become a pan-European organization stressing cross-border cooperation and confidence building and a forum for developing common political and military policies and actions, such as it did successfully during the Persian Gulf War.

Warsaw Treaty Organization (WTO)

In response to the organization of NATO, the USSR reorganized a regional defense system, the Warsaw Pact, in 1955, which included Poland, East Germany, Czechoslovakia, Hungary, Romania, and Bulgaria. Yugoslavia and Albania's objections to Moscow's political policies caused their withdrawal from the organization. Although the organization's purported goal was defense from perceived threats posed by the United States, West Germany, and, more generally, NATO, in fact its only military actions in Europe were against its own members during civil uprisings against Soviet-backed rulers (Hungary in 1956 and Czechoslovakia in 1968) and threatened use of force against countries (Romania and Poland), that deviated from Soviet policies. The Warsaw Pact dissolved when the Soviet Union disintegrated and the Cold War ended in the early 1990s.

EUROPE'S GEOPOLITICAL STRUCTURE

Despite the importance of these international organizations, Europe, as most of the world, remains politically dominated by so-called nation-states. The "state," a largely nineteenth- and twentieth-century form of geopolitical organization, theoretically governs "nations"—groups of people identifying with one another as a distinctive cultural-political entity, often based on, (arguably, simply perceived) common ethnicity, and settlement within a common, usually contiguous, territory. In reality many nation-states include peoples of several self-identifying "nations." Notable examples include multiethnic Romania and Belgium. Some countries, such as Switzerland, the United Kingdom, and the former USSR, have more explicitly recognized their multiethnic nature.

Europe's sovereign or "nation-states" have a variety of forms of governments. On the one hand, for example, Switzerland is a decentralized confederation with a virtually invisible national leader, while, on the other hand, the United Kingdom and the Netherlands are centralized constitutional monarchies with visible queens and prime ministers. Europe also has a large number of parliamentary republics, both centralized versions (e.g., France and Poland) and decentralized federal versions (e.g., Germany). A number of European states have experienced or are now ruled by forms of dictatorship, a single political party, or a military (as opposed to civil) government. Notable examples of countries that until recently were so governed include many in East Central and Southeastern Europe, as well as Greece, Portugal, and Spain. Yugoslavia is still ruled by a government that many also view as largely undemocratic.

All countries have official subnational administrative regional units that vary from relative unimportance in centralized states (e.g., the departments of France and voivodships of Poland) to considerable importance in decentralized federations (e.g., states in Germany and Austria, and cantons in Switzerland) (Fig. 1-6 *a*, *b*). There are also a variety of other territorial administrative units, usually reaching down to the level of individual settlements, including villages or groups of neighboring villages. Sometimes ethnic or religious diversity within a country's territory is explicitly recognized by specially constructed, occasionally politically autonomous, territorial subunits. In some cases, such recognition is denied "nations" in order to attempt to quash regional nationalistic movements. Spain experienced the latter under the dictator Franco, but has moved toward attempts to undercut support for separatist extremists and to mollify more moderate autonomy-seeking populations in, for example, the Basque lands and Catalonia by allowing regional autonomy. In other cases, officially designated "national" territories are more illusory than real, as they were in the case of a number of nationality based administrative units within the former, multiethnic Soviet Union, a country that some people feel was the last of Europe's empires. Most of the continent's other imperial, multiethnic states collapsed after World War I (e.g., the Austro-Hungarian and Ottoman Empires).

Finally, Europe includes a number of intriguing, very small sovereign states. Brief overviews of each of these states are provided in Inset 1-2.

EUROPE'S LANDSCAPES

Previous sections have provided an introduction to the political organization of European territory. Here we briefly introduce Europe's "natural" regions and landscapes, including the major characteristics of their human and physical geography.

The "face" of Europe, its varied landscape, displays much more obvious signs of human impact than the sometimes virtually invisible international borders. Europe's varied, and often beautiful, landscapes are the result of historical interactions between the natural environment and human culture. Humans have greatly modified "nature" vir-

FIGURE 1-6 A The subnational territorial organization of France (departments).

tually everywhere in Europe (especially biotic conditions), and current landscapes are a fascinating collage of contemporary and historic architectural and land use elements. The occupance of the same territory over millennia, often by different ethnic/cultural groups (i.e., "sequent occupance"), and rapidly changing technology and tastes mean that a single landscape may include a great variety of elements. Before its ongoing destruction, for example, Sarajevo displayed the

FIGURE 1-6 B The subnational territorial organization of Germany (*Länder*).

cultural features of a number of religions in its Christian churches and mosques, cultural expressions of its multiethnic population (e.g., a "Turkish" bazaar), evidence of "modernity" (e.g., high-rise buildings and automobiles), and artifacts of a simpler life and economy.

Landscapes can be defined and recognized by the combination of a wide range of characteristics. Major factors affecting landscapes include the physical environment, economic processes, cultural preferences and traditions, the expression of political forces on the landscape, and combina-

EUROPE'S MICROSTATES

Although Europe's economy and politics are dominated by large countries, the continent includes seven very small states that are both important and interesting (Table 1-2). The total population of the countries is small (about 1 million people), but several of them play disproportionately important roles in European affairs, albeit modest ones in absolute terms. Three broad generalizations can be made about the existence of these states. First, they are vestiges of medieval, feudal Europe, which was comprised of hundreds of territories with limited autonomy. The great majority of the tiny states (once over 300 in Germany alone) were ultimately incorporated into larger countries and now appear only on historical rather than contemporary maps. The few states described here somehow survived. Second, the small states have complex historical and political ties to other, larger, neighboring states on whose economies they are usually quite dependent. And, third, several of these small states survived as independent entities owing in part to their relative geographic isolation or to their location along the boundaries of states that ultimately agreed to recognize their independence rather than endure problems required to overcome objections to their absorption.

Usually, the economic sustenance of Europe's small states has resulted from their ability to find an economic *niche* by devising laws and institutions that allow them to satisfy demands that cannot or at one time could not be met in neighboring entities, such as gambling (Monaco), tax-advantaged investments (Luxembourg and Malta), business-friendly headquarter locations (Liechtenstein), and untaxed import services, that is, smuggling (Andorra).

TABLE 1-2

EUROPE'S MICROSTATES, CA. 1992

Microstate	Area in sq. miles (sq. km.)	Population (000s)
Andorra	175 (453)	59
Liechtenstein	62 (161)	28
Luxembourg	998 (2586)	390
Malta	122 (316)	357
Monaco	0.6 (1.6)	29
San Marino	24 (61)	23
Vatican City	0.17 (0.44)	1

Andorra is perhaps a classic example of a tiny state that has endured through time as a result of all of the reasons noted here. It is ruled by co-princes from neighboring France and Spain based on an agreement struck in 1278. The agreement has endured dramatic political change on either side of its borders, at least in part owing to the area's relative isolation. Once renowned as a haven for smugglers, Andorra today thrives on retail sales to French and Spanish customers drawn by low taxes, on tourism including skiing, and on low-taxed manufacturing.

The political origins of Liechtenstein (see Chapter 11) date to 1342, though it added small territories up until the eighteenth century. It was part of the Holy Roman Empire until 1806 and is now a constitutional monarchy. The country borders the upper Rhine along the Swiss-Austrian alpine frontier. An agriculturally dominated country until the postwar era, Liechtenstein has developed a prosperous, diversified economy, which also is now based on high value-added manufacturing, tourism, and finance. Like some other small states, it profits by selling stamps collected by people who do not actually use postal services. The worldwide market for stamps brings in more absolute income to large countries like the United States, but the activity is enormously more important as a proportion of total state revenues for microstates like Liechtenstein. Liechtenstein has had very close political and economic ties with Switzerland (e.g., using Swiss currency) since the 1920s, but it has taken a small step away from this relationship by joining the EEA, to which Switzerland has chosen not to belong.

Luxembourg (see Chapter 8), though a very small country, is a relative giant among the countries discussed here. Most people who have flown across the Atlantic on the discount airline (Icelandair) linking the United States, Iceland, and Luxembourg are surprised by both the beauty and charm of the city of Luxembourg, as well as the hour-long drive north through its rural areas toward Liège or the nearly hour-long trip by rail down the meandering, beautiful Moselle River toward Koblenz in Germany. For centuries a strategically located fortress on the frontiers of powerful, often aggressive neighbors, the city of Luxembourg has been a frequent battleground, most recently in the closing stages of World War II, and has frequently changed hands.

Independence was established for Luxembourg at

the Congress of Vienna in 1815. After its declared neutrality failed to save it from German occupation in both world wars, it became a NATO member in 1949. Luxembourg has for decades had close economic ties to neighboring Belgium and the Netherlands via the Benelux union and with all of Western Europe via the EC/EU, in which it was a founding member. Its currency, the franc, is tied to the value of the Belgian franc. The country's economy, like Liechtenstein's, is rather diversified, though its location amidst iron and coal mines resulted in the dominance of iron and steel production within its manufacturing sector, in which a number of other heavy industrial activities are also represented. Luxembourg has important tourism and finance sectors; its financial success is tied to efforts by, for example, highly prosperous Germans trying to use it as a tax haven. Many European firms also have offices or headquarters in the Grand Duchy.

Unlike the three small states just noted, three others are located entirely within the boundaries of other countries rather than at international frontiers—Monaco, San Marino, and the Vatican City State. In each case, the countries' economies and politics are very dependent on and closely tied to single, larger neighbors—France or Italy. Otherwise, these countries share a number of characteristics with the countries already discussed, including rather specialized and unique economic bases. Monaco (see Chapter 10) is a constitutional monarchy on a stunning Mediterranean site, ruled by Prince Rainier, who in 1956 married an American movie actress, the late Grace Kelly. Monaco's dominant tourist industry and posh residential offerings attract other notable and wealthy personalities, but the economy also depends on a tax-sheltered finance sector and a small manufacturing sector.

San Marino and Vatican City trace their independent roots to both the importance of religion in public affairs on the Italian peninsula and to struggles between Church and civil authorities for political power in Italy, a country with which both these tiny states are inextricably entwined. San Marino is the world's smallest republic and possibly Europe's oldest political entity. By tradition, San Marino was founded in the fourth century by a Christian refugee from Dalmatia who was seeking religious freedom. San Marino certainly is the sole surviving state from among many that existed on the Italian peninsula before the unification of Italy in the nineteenth century. San Marino's population, however, is virtually indistinguishable from the Italian-speaking, Roman Catholic inhabitants all around it. The country's economy is joined to Italy's via a customs union, and the country uses Italian currency. San Marino is

heavily dependent on millions of tourists who visit annually, and about 10 percent of its government revenue derive from the sale of stamps. Attempts to diversify the economy have succeeded to some extent, so that now about one-third of the country's workforce is employed in a variety of manufacturing activities.

The Vatican City, or Holy See, is a tiny vestige of the once large Papal States of central Italy. The Pope, the head of the Roman Catholic Church, is supreme ruler of Vatican City's 1000 inhabitants, but more importantly he is the religious and administrative leader of a vast religious and corporate enterprise with hundreds of millions of followers worldwide. In effect, it can be argued that the state exists to allow the international Roman Catholic Church greater political autonomy within Italy and to permit secular rule in Italy.

Malta (see Chapter 10) holds a highly strategic island location in the Mediterranean Sea and has been occupied by a great variety of states and peoples for millennia. Though small in area, the country has, like Luxembourg, a large population in comparison to the other small states discussed here. Malta has been such an important military stronghold and trading outpost that foreign powers controlled the island group until independence was achieved in 1964. Like many other small states, tourism and offshore banking are key sectors, though manufacturing has also been increasingly important.

Finally, a number of small places in Europe with rather unique political statuses share locational and economic characteristics with the ministates reviewed above. For example, Gibraltar (UK), the Channel Islands (UK), and Spanish territories (Melilla and Cueta) on the Moroccan coast are places of historically strategic importance that have generated ongoing political problems between the occupying power and the country near or within which the territory is located. Specialized economic activities such as tourism (Gibraltar and the Channel Islands) and tax-evading financial activities (Channel Islands) result from the places' particular geographic sites and their peculiar political conditions.

More peculiar yet, perhaps, are the ostensibly integral parts of European states that lie well beyond the boundaries of the European continent (e.g., France's Suriname and Denmark's Greenland), not to mention the former colonies and vestigial territories still controlled by European powers around the globe (e.g., the Falkland Islands, UK controlled but claimed by Argentina; French Polynesia; and Netherlands Antilles). These latter, extra-European territories are not considered in this text.

tions of and interactions between all of these. Clearly, the physical environment plays an important role in shaping landscapes, including those heavily influenced by humans. Tectonic movements and the forces of erosion, for example, are especially important in determining relief, and climatic conditions have great influence over distributions of flora and fauna. However, "natural" landscapes have themselves been affected by human economic activities, with increasing impacts following the development of agriculture about 10,000 years ago, the advent of the Industrial Revolution about 200 years ago, and the related explosion of human population. Today about 700 million people live in "Europe," including the European parts of the FSU. Economic activities have had profound influences on shaping European landscapes by radically altering forests; creating huge expanses of farmed and pastured lands; and constructing buildings, transport arteries, and dams. The wastes of economic activities have further altered landscapes by damaging water bodies, flora, and fauna and by scarring the earth's surface with mines and dumps. In densely settled Europe, the impacts of economic activities rival "natural" conditions in determining what the "face" of Europe looks like.

Also important in shaping landscapes are cultural and political systems. Cultural traditions greatly affect, for example, the nature of settlements and the architecture of buildings. Apparently for a variety of reasons, including cultural preferences and traditions, settlements are clustered in some areas, whereas scattered or sprawling settlements are common in others. Cultural innovation combines with local economic needs, available building materials, and prevailing technology to affect architectural styles. Preference and tradition influence the types of regionally prevailing religions and recreational pursuits, for example, thereby affecting the nature of structures and land use. Europe's long Christian tradition and the centuries-long political and economic ascendancy of the Roman and Orthodox Catholic churches have left a stunning legacy of religious art and architecture. Remnant influences of once more prominent Muslim and Jewish religions add diversity to Europe's landscapes as well.

Political systems can also have especially profound effects on economic activities and often result in the construction of distinctive buildings and monuments. Many leaders erect monuments to glorify people and events that support their political agendas. Louis XIV, king of France (1638–1715) and founder of the royal residence at Versailles, began a now widely adopted practice of building imposing structures to provide visible expression of government's power and prestige. Somewhat ironically, East European socialist, "peoples'" republics were especially avid devotees of the use of visual expression of the power of government. Statues of socialist/communist "heroes" were erected widely in Eastern Europe after World War II, and major architectural complexes were constructed to glorify socialism and its leaders (e.g., in East Berlin and Bucharest).

Europe, with a large and culturally diverse population that has occupied the continent for thousands of years, displays a stunning variety of different landscapes. These provide one of the elements that prove attractive to tourists, who can savor a panoply of sights, sounds, and smells within relatively short distances. An overview of these landscapes and their physical, cultural, and economic bases provides a good introduction to a thematic and regional study of Europe.

Europe can be separated into four large physiographic regions, generally associated with the four periods of major mountain building that helped shape the present landscape: (1) the *Northwest Highlands*, comprising the greater part of Scandinavia and the British Isles; (2) the *North European Plain* (and other major lowlands), also known as the Northern Lowlands Region, stretching from the foot of the Pyrenees in southern France, across the Paris and London basins, through Belgium, the Netherlands, northern Germany, Poland, Denmark, and southern Sweden into the FSU; (3) the *Central Uplands and Plateaus*, ranging across Europe from the Spanish Meseta in the west, through central France and Germany to Bohemia in Central Europe; and (4) the *Southern Mountain Region* (or Alpine System) including the French, Swiss, Italian, German, Austrian and Slovenian Alps, the Pyrenees of France and Spain, the Apennines of Italy, the Carpathian Mountains of Central and Southeastern Europe, and a variety of mountain chains in the Balkans. Each of these broad regions has a number of subregions, but each also has some broadly generalizable landscape features in common.

Northwest Highlands

The Highlands consist of two distinct areas, the Fenno-Scandian or Baltic Shield of Sweden, Finland, and southeastern Norway; and the raised remnants of the ancient Caledonian mountain system of the rest of Norway, extreme western Sweden, northern England, Wales, Ireland, and Scotland, as well as the northern portions of the ancient Amorican Mountains in Cornwall-Devon (UK) and Brittany (Bretagne, France).

The Fenno-Scandian Shield consists of rocks up to 2 billion years old in some areas and is related to and in many ways resembles the Canadian Shield of central and eastern Canada (see Fig. 2-15). Local relief is not extreme in most areas; hundreds of millions of years of erosion have softened the contours of the shield's landscape. The Caledonian Mountains are much younger, originating about 420 million years ago. The original mountain system was eroded away long ago, but in recent geologic history sections of the mountains have been uplifted and tilted on their western slopes, creating peaks such as Ben Nevis (4406 feet, 1343 meters), the highest mountain in the British Isles, and 6800-foot high peaks in southern Norway (see Fig. 7-3 and 9-11). Faulting is common, a prime example being the linear lowland partially occupied by Loch Ness in the highlands of Scotland. The ancient Amorican Mountains occupied what is now Cornwall in southwestern England and much of central and western France. The hill country of Cornwall is, for classification's sake only, included within the Northwest Highlands Region. The French hill country in Brittany, Normandy, and the Massif Central with historical geologic roots in the Amorican Mountains is classified with the adjacent Central European Uplands.

Pleistocene glaciation has greatly modified the surface of the Northwest Highlands. Deep U-shaped, elongated valleys, some of which have filled with water to form narrow lakes, roaring waterfalls, moraines hundreds of feet high, winding eskers many miles in length, tens of thousands

of ice-scoured lakes, and deeply indented fiord coastlines extending inland from the open sea in places for nearly a hundred miles, are tributes to the strength of the deep ice masses that covered most of this area as recently as 9000 years ago. The remains of this continental ice sheet may be seen in southern Norway where the Jostedalsbre, Europe's largest glacier, still exists.

The natural landscape and beauty of the Northwest Highlands is the setting for a variety of recreational pursuits. Outdoor recreation, popular among the population of the Nordic countries, has also attracted increasingly larger numbers of travel-minded and affluent Europeans. Because of crowded living conditions and a landscape that is almost completely human-made, Europeans are turning to the remote areas of Northern Europe for their holidays. Here they can camp by secluded mountain lakes, hike in vast forests, swim in the green waters of the fiords, sail among the thousands of low-lying coastal islands, fish the white-water rivers, and ski in a mountain landscape where the few human works blend harmoniously with the natural environment. The midnight sun, glaciers, immense fiords, pristine national parks, and the indigenous Saami culture provide added pleasure for visitors.

The Highlands' southwesternmost areas in Cornwall and Devon have the mildest climates and are highly favored for their beautiful, rugged coastlines and scenic villages with stone cottages. Celtic and Viking heritages offer mysterious human-built artifacts (notably at Stonehenge) and museums illustrating the vibrancy of the Viking raider-colonizer culture such as at York, UK, and Oslo, Norway.

Farming is quite diversified, and evidence of orientation toward the sea can be found almost everywhere. Hundreds of fishing villages with their storage tanks for fish oil and drying racks for cod, as well as the small wooden trawlers sailing along the thousands of miles of mountainous coast are representative Norwegian scenes. Fish farms for the raising of salmon have been established along coasts in Scotland and in Norway. The seascape is also impacted by the development of North Sea oil and gas deposits and associated transport and manufacturing activities.

Central Scotland, the faulted lowland between

Glasgow on the west coast and Edinburgh on the east coast, is a major focal point for industrial development in the region. Over half of the 4 million inhabitants of the area work in occupations that are typical of a modern industrial society, and about three-quarters live and work in cities and towns. Since the end of World War II, there has been a dramatic shift from coal mining and heavy industry into computer-related industries, jet engines, and technology associated with off-shore oil.

Although the Northwest Highlands have urban and industrial landscapes, they also contain Europe's most extensive areas of landscape greatly affected by natural conditions. Even where there are human-impacted landscapes such as in the pasturelands of Scotland and Ireland and in Scandinavia's farmed valleys, human economic activity, as well as human structures (such as the traditional Irish stone cottage and colorful Scandinavian farmsteads), often enhance the variety and beauty of the landscape. Human impact is evident in the Northwest Highlands, but unlike many other parts of more densely settled Europe, it is less obvious and obtrusive.

North European Plain and Other Lowlands

These regions are among the most densely populated and intensively farmed areas of the continent. The North European Plain wraps in an arc from the Pyrenees in southern France across North Central Europe to join the vast areas of relatively low elevation and relief in the western parts of the FSU. Other notable lowlands in Europe include the Rhone (Rhône) Valley; the Swiss Plateau (or Mittelland) and Pannonian Basin, both enclosed between the Central Uplands and Southern Mountain Ranges; and the Po Valley and Wallachian (or Valachian) Plain, both more or less enclosed within the Southern Mountain Region.

Though relatively flat, the North European Plain is not a uniform area. Distinctive physical regions have emerged such as the island of Rügen in Germany, the lakes of Mecklenburg in northern Germany and Mazuria of northern Poland, and the old glacial spillways known to the Germans as *Urstromtäler*.

The geographic factors of low relief and generally moderate climatic conditions have combined with easily worked soils, industrial development, and excellent communication and transportation facilities (airports, highways, canals, and railways) to provide the basis for a large population concentration in the lowland regions of Europe. Many regions of the lowlands were settled over 80,000 years ago. A wide variety of crops are harvested.

Thriving industrial and service activities in lowland Europe help to support the large number of people living in urban areas. Industry evolved on the major lowland regions of northern France, Belgium, and the Netherlands, the area around Hannover and Braunschweig, the Rhine Rift Valley, the Swiss Plateau, the Po Valley, and central and southwest Poland. Service activities including transportation, tourism, and finance have their centers in major cities of lowland Europe such as Paris, London, Frankfurt, Zürich, Hamburg, Berlin, and Warsaw (Fig. 1-7).

The interaction of large population concentrations, abundant food supplies, a dense transportation network, and industrial enterprises have concentrated population in favored lowland locations to the economic disadvantage of other regions, creating urban areas that have become the industrial, commercial, political, and cultural foci of their respective countries. The London basin alone accounts for over 20 percent of the population of the United Kingdom; the Paris region comprises nearly 19 percent of France's inhabitants (see "The Centrality of Paris and the Paris Basin", inset 8-1 in Chapter 8); areas of the Netherlands (the Randstad) average over 400 persons per square kilometer; and the lowland regions of Belgium, northern France, and the Ruhr are also densely populated. The Swiss Plateau, from Lake Geneva to Lake of Constance, is the major urban, industrial, and agricultural region of the country; the Po Valley is the industrial, commercial, and agricultural heartland of Italy; and the Wallachian Plain is the historic core and economic focal point of Romania. In fact, in lowland Europe there is an arc of economic concentration that surrounds London and extends across parts of Belgium, the Netherlands, France, Germany, and Switzerland and ultimately sweeps through the Po Valley in northern Italy.

FIGURE 1-7 Berlin, looking eastward from the Memorial Church (center foreground) in the heart of western Berlin. Berlin developed in the Middle Ages at an important crossing over the river Spree on the broad expanse of the eastern portion of the North European Plain. The site and region have few natural resources, but as seat of political power and ultimately as a crossroads for transport and communication facilities, Berlin developed into a major European urban center. [Courtesy of the German Information Center]

The result of this concentration of humans and their institutions is congestion that is unparalleled in the world over such a large area. Lowland Europe has become a maze of traffic-choked roads and superhighways, canals, railroads, steel mills, derelict industries, coal mines, oil refineries, pipelines, housing estates, and electric power lines. This has created a megalopolis linking London and Paris to the cities of the Netherlands and Belgium and the ports of Bremen and Hamburg, along with separate megalopoli located in the Swiss Plateau and valleys of the Rhine and Po rivers.

Central Uplands and Plateaus

The Central Uplands and Plateaus are a discontinuous combination of hill regions from western Spain into Central Europe. The region has moderate relief, but also includes terrain as diverse as thinly populated low mountains and densely populated valleys and basins (Fig. 1-8). The Uplands of the western parts of Europe were originally formed during the mountain-building era known as the Hercynian period, after the Latin name for the Harz Mountains in central Germany. The original mountains were eroded and many areas then overlain with deep sedimentary deposits. During the Alpine mountain-building period, renewed uplift again created more relief, heightened by ensuing erosion. The great stress and strain on the European continent during the Alpine mountain-building period caused segments of the Hercynian Mountains to fracture and collapse, creating rift valleys such as the Rhine Valley between the Vosges and Black Forest (Schwarzwald). Lava poured from fissures in the earth's surface and covered large areas of the Massif Central and Rhenish Slate

FIGURE 1-8 Central European hill country in northwestern Germany. The meandering Mosel has created a now densely settled, intensively farmed corridor between the thinly populated Eifel (foreground and right) and Hunsrück (left), low mountain ranges within the Central European Uplands. (A. Diem)

Mountains (*rheinisches Schiefergebirge*), and hundreds of volcanoes, some reaching over 12,000 feet (4000 meters), erupted during this tumultuous period. Volcanic activity also created the Kaiserstuhl on the Rhine Plain west of Freiburg, circular lakes in the Eifel Forest, extinct volcanoes in northern Bohemia, and scores of eroded volcanic cones in the Massif Central. Many small basins and valleys are also embedded within the Uplands, notably the valley of the Rhone in France, the Rhine Valley on the French-German border, the Swiss and Bavarian Plateaus, and the valley of the Danube in Austria, as well as the Pannonian and Wallachian Plains.

The Central (or Hercynian) Uplands, like the Northwest Highlands, are popular recreational areas. Because the Uplands are located nearer to the major population centers of Europe, they are frequented by many more people, but they are not nearly as rugged and wild as the Northwest Highlands. Nevertheless, the multitudes of people who travel in Uplands areas throughout the year enjoy a wide variety of recreational pursuits. During the summer months, the jagged and beautiful coasts of northern Spain and extreme southwestern France, with their many cliffs, promontories, and smooth bay head beaches, attract millions of vacationers for swimming and sailing (Fig. 1-9). Hiking trails cut through the Black Forest, Vosges, Rhenish Mountains, Erzgebirge, and the eroded sandstones

of Saxony's "Switzerland" near Dresden. Camping sites are filled with scores of yellow, blue, and green tents, caravans, and camping truck rigs in areas such as the Massif Central, Bohemian Forest (Böhmerwald), and Ardennes. The natural lakes and reservoirs of the Uplands are used for boating and swimming, and diverse scenery, ranging from ancient castles and eroded volcanoes to the rugged Massif Central, attract persons seeking a change from the urban milieu.

Health resorts and spas are located near the many hot and cold springs in the Hercynian Uplands, such as Baden-Baden on the edge of the Black Forest, Wiesbaden at the edge of the Taunus in Germany, and the northern Bohemian resorts of Karlsbad and Marienbad—all of which have offered their patrons relaxing and healthful vacations since Roman times.

The now threatened natural resource base of the Central Uplands has attracted and supported humans for millennia. Sections of "Hercynia," in the Cordillera Cantàbrica of northern Spain and in the wide limestone valleys of the western Massif Central, were settled well over 40,000 years ago. In the vicinity of the present French village of Les Eyzies, along the banks of the Vézère River, cave-dwelling Paleolithic people hunted the abundant game of the region, leaving artifacts such as the stunning works of art discovered by four boys in September 1940 on the walls of the Lascaux cave

FIGURE 1-9 Tourists enjoying sun and sea at Biarritz, France. (W. Berentsen)

physiography, agricultural practices and products vary considerably across the Uplands. Sheltered sunny valleys support grapes for some of the world's greatest wine production regions in France and Germany, and a wide variety of other fruits and specialty crops grow throughout the region, especially in the Rhine Valley. Crops are common both on valley floors and on low elevation plateaus, while areas with harsher climates such as north-facing slopes and higher elevations are in pasture and forest. In the Central Uplands proper, the landscape is typically a mixed pattern of field, pasture, and forest—a landscape mix that hikers and walkers find particularly attractive.

The Central Uplands also offer both rustic and beautifully crafted small towns and villages. The towns of central Germany are especially well preserved, and several, such as Dinkelsbühl and Nordlingen, have thriving tourist industries. The towns' charm and beauty result from narrow, haphazardly routed cobblestone streets; half-timbered architecture; church spires; small shops and cafes; and window flower boxes. Many towns have preserved walls and castles or castle ruins towering over them.

Less appealing landscapes, but economically vital activities, are represented by a number of coalfields on the margins of and within the Uplands. One such major field extends from southern Wales eastward beneath the London Basin and Channel to Flanders, and across the German border to the Ruhr. Other important fields include Upper Silesia in Poland and a small area in the adjacent Czech Republic, as well as the lignite fields of Saxony and northern Bohemia. These industrialized landscapes include large areas covered by cities, towns, and small villages linked together by a web of railroads, highways, canals, and electric power lines. Within lies a mixture of abandoned mine shafts, conical piles of tailings, deteriorating or abandoned factories, planned satellite towns for workers, as well as intensively used farmland, and reservoirs on rivers and in worked-out coal pits. Factories frequently emit clouds of white, black, or red smoke, problems that are now much more typical of the Czech and Polish coal regions than of those in the west.

The Central Uplands and Plateau Region, thus, has landscapes more impacted by human activity

near Montignac. Here, a record of the game of the region—horses, bison, and deer—has been preserved in the limestone walls in vivid hues of black, brown, ocher, and yellow. In 1995 another amazing find of Paleolithic paintings was announced, from the cave of Chauvet in France's Ardèche Valley.

Despite this long history of human habitation, interior sections of the Hercynian Uplands, such as in the central Carpathians in Slovakia, have never supported a high population density. The concentration of inhabitants in the Uplands is greatest along their flanks or where they meet the Atlantic. Some regions in southern Belgium and the Ruhr region are among the most densely populated parts of Europe and in the world, with approximately 2600 inhabitants per square mile (1000 per square kilometer), owing in particular to coal deposits and related urban-industrial development that began during the Industrial Revolution.

Because of differences in climate, soils, and

than the Northwest Highlands but less so than those on the Northern European Lowlands. The ethnic and cultural variety of this region, as well as the geopolitical divide between its eastern and western parts, mean that cultural and political influences on the landscape are quite diverse. The region's landscapes are arguably more diverse than those of the Northwest Highlands and Northern European Lowlands, though probably no more so than Europe's fourth large landscape region—the Southern Mountain Region.

The Southern Mountain Region

The Southern Mountain Region is dominated by three major landscape types—thinly populated mountainous and dryland terrains, more intensively farmed and settled coastal plains, and irrigated valleys. The most spectacular landscapes in

this region are the mountains themselves, whose forms were most recently shaped by alpine glaciation, including ice tongues reaching depths of over 5000 feet (1500 meters) that filled in valleys and overflowed onto plains. Amphitheater-like cirques, arête ridges, and majestic horns, such as the Matterhorn, were shaped from mountain tops; valleys were widened and deepened into U-shapes; and powerful waterfalls began to pour forth from hanging valleys many hundreds of feet above main valley floors (Fig. 1-10). Elongated lakes of great depth such as Lake Geneva and Lago Maggiore filled in many of the ice-scoured valleys both north and south of the main Alpine chain. These dramatic landscapes are most prominent within the Alps in places like central Switzerland and Austria's Tirol and Salzkammergut regions, but also occur elsewhere as in the Julian Alps in Slovenia.

Settlement in the Alpine Mountains began

FIGURE 1-10 The Matterhorn group (Switzerland) displays the ability of ice to shape the landscape. (A. Diem)

many thousands of years ago. An impressive Neanderthal site, dating back at least 90,000 years ago, is presently being excavated in the Alpine foothills of France. Cities such as Aosta at the junction of the Grand and Petit St. Bernard routes, and Chur in the upper Rhine Valley, the focal point for communication over the passes of Graubünden, respectively, date their origin to over 2000 and 5000 years ago. Celtic groups, which mined salt, thrived in the Austrian Alps at Hallstatt during the Bronze Age. Although population densities in the mountains are among the lowest in the western parts of Europe, averaging 15 to 25 people per square mile (5 to 10 per square kilometer), densely populated settlements do exist. Grenoble and Innsbruck have approximately 400,000 and 200,000 inhabitants, respectively, and Granada, situated in a basin south of the Sierra Nevada, also has over 200,000.

The mountains also have economic importance. In high valleys of the Alps grazing is significant, whereas palm, almond, and fig trees grow in Switzerland's Ticino region along Lago Maggiore and Lago Lugano. On the south-facing slopes of northwest Italy, a semitropical vegetation of vineyards, fruit, fig, and nut trees thrive, while the north-facing slopes grow dense stands of larch and spruce. Where supplementary water supplies are available for irrigation, as along the slopes of mountains or in intermontane basins, intensive agriculture is widespread, concentrating on fruit and vegetable cultivation. The forest cover of these southerly mountains has been drastically altered by the grazing of animals, particularly sheep and goats, by fire, and by continuous cutting over the centuries. In many areas of the Mediterranean, erosion is a serious problem, affecting both uplands and coastal plains.

The Southern Mountain Region is not blessed with abundant natural resources to support manufacturing, but mining is and has historically been important in selected areas. For example, iron ore is found at the famous Erzberg (Ore Mountain) in eastern Austria, where mining, begun here in the Middle Ages by means of small quarries, later expanded underground. Presently, the complete mountain is slowly being leveled to the valley floor. More recently, hydroelectric facilities have been developed to utilize falling water for power;

some of these facilities, such as Kaprun (Austria) and Grande Dixence (France), have even become tourist attractions.

Owing to relatively small local markets, lack of resources, problems with transportation, limited space, and efforts at environmental preservation, manufacturing activities are generally limited in size and importance within the Southern Mountains themselves. Development of manufacturing in the region's coastal areas and intermontane basins has also been constrained by political and economic problems at the national and international levels. The region's most important manufacturing centers are generally located at coastal ports (e.g., Barcelona, Genoa, Athens/Piraeus, and Thessalonica). The most economically developed areas of Southern Europe are those with a combination of agricultural resources, larger local markets, and better access to prosperous northwestern Europe, namely, the lower Rhone Valley and northern Italy focused on the Po Valley and Milan. These regions are not, strictly speaking, part of the Southern Mountain Region but could be considered part of Europe's Plains and Lowlands Region.

The Southern Mountain Region is, however, Europe's most important tourist area, with attractions for skiers, hikers, and beachgoers. In both absolute and relative terms, tourism is a very important component of the economies of Southern European countries, with the exception until recently of once isolationist Albania. Combining dramatic beauty with mild weather, favorable snow conditions, challenging peaks, and sheltered valleys and lakes, the Alps offer a wide variety of opportunities for year-round holidays. Furthermore, other mountains formed during the Alpine mountain-building period, such as the Sierra Nevada in Spain, the Pyrenees, the Jura, and the Transylvanian Alps of Romania are also significant tourist regions. In addition, Southern Europe boasts beautiful beaches, cities, and villages. The Mediterranean coasts of Spain, France, Italy, and until recently Croatia and Bulgaria, have been especially sought-after destinations, as are the islands of Greece. Of course, Florence, Rome, and Athens attract tourists owing to their cultural and historical attractions.

Still, economic development, including tourism, has degraded Southern Europe and lessened its natural appeal. There is little recreational land left in a natural state. The Southern Mountain Region's natural and cultural treasures are threatened by centuries of neglectful use. As pressure for industrial and tourist development increases, the time may come when an alpine landscape free from human-made objects will be a rarity and when the region's enticing blue sky and water are too tainted to support the still hugely successful tourist industry.

CONCLUSION

As growing economic demands are made on Europe's limited area and resources by an ever larger, more diverse and affluent population, political and environmental problems are apt to multiply. The quality of life of European countries will depend on several major factors. The first concerns how well people contain and ameliorate environmental problems in all European regions and especially in the former socialist countries. A second factor centers on how all of the European countries adjust to global economic restructuring and world-wide economic competition while maintaining levels of social services that are now generally the highest on the planet. Success in the economic realm also depends on a third factor—the ability of Europe to develop harmonious continent- and worldwide relations between nations and states. The EU provides a successful example of international cooperation, but the Yugoslav wars also indicate the destructiveness of nationalism and extreme intolerance.

Europe is a fascinating and complex region, with countries and subregions exemplifying both successful and unsuccessful political, social, and economic development. Students of the region require both a grounding in broad systematic topics related to it and information on specific regions. Thus, this text continues with topical chapters on physical, population, political, economic, and urban geography, followed by chapters focusing on Europe's major regions. Rather than use a strictly topical or a strictly regional approach for the study of Europe, we believe that a blend of the two is preferable for dealing with this multifaceted region and society.

BIBLIOGRAPHY

Altmann, Franz Lothar. (1995). "European Union Enlargement: Issues for Eastern Europe." The Woodrow Wilson Center, East European Studies Meeting Report (November-December; summarized by P. B. Smith).

Bank, A. S., ed. (1995). *Political Handbook of the World 1994–1995*. Binghamton, N.Y.: CSA Publications.

Clout, Hugh, et al. (1994). *Western Europe: Geographical Perspectives*. 3rd ed. Essex, UK: Longman Scientific & Technical.

Cole, John, and Francis Cole. (1993). *The Geography of the European Community* London and New York: Routledge.

Dinan, Desmond. (1994). *Ever Closer Union? An Introduction to the European Community*. Houndsmills, UK: Lynne Rienner Publishers, Inc. and Macmillan Press Ltd.

Europa Publications Limited. (1995). *The Europa World Year Book 1995*. London: Europa Publications Limited.

European Commission. (1994). *Competitiveness and Cohesion: Trends in the Regions*. Brussels: European Commission.

European Commission. *Eurobarometer: Public Opinion in the European Community*. Brussels: EU Commission, various dates.

European Free Trade Association. (1995). *EFTA Annual Report 1994* . Geneva: EFTA.

European Union. *Europe Magazine*. Brussels: EU, various dates.

Gale Research Inc. (1995). *Countries of the World*. New York: Gale Research Inc.

Gruber, G., et al., eds. (1995). *Neue grenzüberschreitende Regionen im östlichen Mitteleuropa*. Frankfurt/Main: Institut f. Wirtschafts-und Sozialgeographie, Uni. Frankfurt/Main.

Hogan, M. J. (1987). *The Marshall Plan: America, Britain and the Reconstruction of Western Europe, 1947–1952*. New York: Columbia University Press.

Jordan, Terry G. (1996). *The European Culture Area: A Systematic Geography*. 3rd ed. New York: HarperCollins.

Lewis, Jim. (1995). "Regional Assistance in the Enlarged Union: Time for Another Reform." *European Urban and Regional Studies* 2: 1–2.

Murphy, Alexander B. (1993). "Emerging Regional Linkages Within the European Community: Challenging the Dominance of the State." *Tijdschrift voor Economische en Sociale Geografie*: 103–118.

Nystrom, J. W., and G. W. Hoffman. (1976). *The Common Market*. 2nd ed. New York: Van Nostrand.

PHYSICAL GEOGRAPHY

Europe's diverse landforms and climates fascinate student and traveler alike. From rugged, fog-bound coasts in the northwest, across the flat and fertile northern plain, through the forested Central Uplands and the majestic Alps, to the dry and sunny Mediterranean Basin, Europe's landforms and climates offer a splendid panorama. Human activities are affected by the natural environment; sadly, human actions also often degrade the natural heritage. This chapter provides an overview of major characteristics of Europe's physical geography and interrelationships between human societies and the physical environment.

One of Europe's salient characteristics is its intimate relationship with the sea. The Arctic Ocean, the Mediterranean, and the embayments of the Atlantic, along with its many islands, give Europe a coastline longer than that of any other continent. Excepting the former Soviet Union (FSU), only the central Carpathian Mountains region is as far as 300 miles (483 km) from the shore, and approximately 80 percent of Europe's population lives within 100 miles (161 km) of the coast. From prehistoric times, this characteristic has favored the development of trade, not only between one part of Europe and another, but also between Europe and the rest of the world.

Europe is in essence but a long peninsula of the Eurasian landmass from which sprout a number of lesser peninsulas and islands. Its parts fall into half a dozen major assemblages: the British Isles; the Iberian, Italian, and Balkan peninsulas; the Scandinavian lands; and the broad mass of Western and Central Europe merging into the Russian Plain. These units are separated by narrow seas and mountain ranges that have been effectively linked in human history by easily traversed rivers, straits, and mountain passes. Although the Atlantic coast is Europe's unquestioned margin on the west, no clear-cut physical feature marks its eastern extremities. Variously, since classical times, the Don River, the Volga River, and the Ural Mountains have been used as the easternmost limits of Europe; even the Urals form but a minor interruption of a plains region that extends to the Yenisei River in the heart of Siberia.

Europe should be viewed more as a cultural concept than as a unit of terrain. It is far less a physical entity than is peninsular India, which stands cut off from the rest of Eurasia by searing deserts and the lofty Himalayan Ranges. Because the Soviet Union developed a degree of cultural homogeneity and coherence during its seven decades of existence, geographers have generally considered the European and Asiatic parts of the former USSR as a region different from Europe proper, drawing its eastern boundary at the former Soviet western frontier. We use this convention in this text, where the term *Europe* generally is applied to the territory west of the former USSR. Still, the continuities and linkages of Europe proper with the newly independent states to the east are discussed wherever appropriate, and a separate chapter is devoted to the FSU.

PATTERNS OF TERRAIN

In total area, Europe west of the former Soviet border contains about 2 million square miles (over 5 million square km). This is less than two-thirds the size of the continental United States and only one-quarter the size of the former USSR. Roughly half of Europe's total land area is in the main peninsula that sweeps from the Atlantic coast of France to eastern Poland. Even the outermost extremities are not far from each other. It is only about 2500 miles (4025 km) from Gibraltar to North Cape in Scandinavia or from Iceland to Istanbul. Europe's position is in the higher midlatitudes. Its southernmost islands lie north of Atlanta, Georgia, or Memphis, Tennessee, and its east-west midline is about the same location as the U.S-Canadian boundary.

Five billion years of upheavals in the earth's crust have fashioned in Europe a complex of plains, tablelands, hills, and mountains. During the periods of mountain building and the intervals of quiescence, the erosive and depositional forces of running water, moving ice, wind, and gravity were constantly at work to break up and wear away the upland areas and to cover lowlands with great accumulations of the resulting debris.

Although most regions of Europe west of former Soviet territory are characterized by striking variations of relief within small areas, the topography can be grouped into the four terrain belts depicted in Figure 2-1. Three distinctive mountain zones extend from west to east: the Northwestern Highlands, the Central Uplands and Plateaus, and the Southern Mountain Ranges. They are paralleled by the North European Lowlands that fan eastward from western France and southern England to spread eventually into European Russia. Within the mountain belts lie a number of valleys and basins, and along the shores of the Mediterranean and the northern seas are several notable stretches of coastal plain.

Origins of the Mountains

Europe's mountains have been created largely by the heaving and buckling of its surface rather than by the outpouring of volcanic material. Only a few scattered pockets of vulcanism can be identified, mostly in Iceland, the hills of Central Europe, and along the western coast of the Apennine Peninsula. Recently active volcanoes include Vesuvius, Etna, and Stromboli in Italy and the volcanic island of Surtsey off the southern Icelandic coast.

The wrinkling of Europe's surface occurred during three distinctive periods. These upheavals were responses to lateral pressures on the continental landmass from a widening of the Atlantic Basin and a northward movement of Africa. The movements are part of a general floating of brittle and lighter plates of granitic rock on denser basalt. This continental drift has been accompanied by a plunging of earth material below the earth's surface in the Mediterranean Basin and a westward growth of the European landmass. Key to understanding this process is the existence of a shield of very ancient crystalline rock that forms the surface of much of Finland and Sweden and lies at increasing depths under younger rock in Poland and the European FSU. This shield's resistance to movement has been the basis for upheavals along its widening margins.

The earliest uplift of contemporary significance occurred about 450 million years ago. Termed the Caledonian orogeny (mountain-building period), it primarily affected the northwestern fringes of the shield, although some mountain building

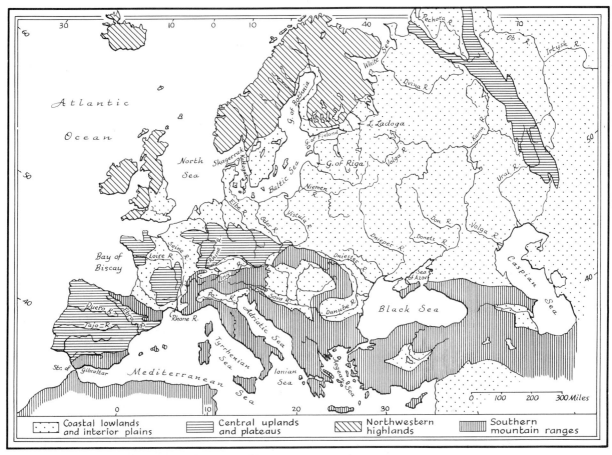

FIGURE 2-1 Major Physiographic divisions of Europe.

occurred as far away as Iberia and the Balkans. Later, erosion reduced the high mountains to plains not unlike the contemporary low-lying surface of the shield in Scandinavia.

A second period of mountain formation began 200 million years ago and resulted in new ranges across Central Europe from France to Slovakia. The mountains of this Hercynian orogeny also were worn down nearly to sea level during a long subsequent period with little tectonic activity.

The most recent mountain formation process started about 50 million years ago and continues today. This Alpine orogeny not only has raised the lofty peaks of Switzerland, Austria, and southern peninsular Europe, but has also rejuvenated the earlier mountain systems. In contrast to the violent overturnings of rock associated with the building of new mountain ranges, uplift in the older mountain regions has resulted in rather uniformly broken, uplifted blocks that retain their horizontal positions and prior erosion surfaces.

Major Mountain Ranges

The Northwestern Highlands are the oldest and most subdued of Europe's three principal groups of mountain ranges. They include the uplands of Ireland, Wales, Scotland, Iceland, and the larger part of Scandinavia. For the most part these are low plateaus of very ancient rock, though in parts of southern Norway, they attain an altitude of 8000 feet (2440 meters) (Fig. 2-2).

The Central Uplands and Plateaus stretch from the Iberian Peninsula to Slovakia, with an outlying region in the Ural Mountains of Russia. They range in elevation from 500 to 2000 feet (150 to 600 meters), with a few parts at 4000 feet (1200 meters) or more. Their major components include the Brittany Peninsula, France's Central Massif, the Ardennes, the Black Forest, the Harz Mountains, and the Bohemian Uplands.

The Southern Mountain Ranges are the most rugged of Europe's highland areas (Fig. 2-3). The recent alpine period of mountain building has lifted them much more than the more northerly belts, and they are in the earliest stages of erosion by running water and moving ice. The sharp jolts by which they have been raised continue to occur, at times with disastrous consequences. Dubrovnik was shattered in 1667, Lisbon was destroyed in 1775, and the Macedonian center of Skopje has had to be rebuilt on at least four occasions, most recently following a catastrophic earthquake in 1963. A series of earthquakes leveled numerous villages in northeastern Italy in 1976, and a sharp tremor in Romania in 1977 caused extensive damage in Bucharest with a loss of more than 1500 lives.

The highest peaks of the Southern Mountain Ranges are in the Alps—Mont Blanc reaches an elevation of almost 16,000 feet (4880 meters). Other ranges include the Pyrenees and Sierra Nevada of Spain, the Apennines of Italy, the Dinaric Alps of the western Balkan Peninsula, the Carpathians

FIGURE 2-2 A characteristic landscape of Europe's Northwestern Highlands near Tromsö Norway. These ancient mountains have been smoothed by the erosive action of the Scandinavian ice sheet. A stream-eroded valley has been deepened and widened by the ice into a fjord through which the sea now penetrates far inland. (Department of Geography, University of Zürich.)

FIGURE 2-3 Alpine topography sharpened by valley glaciers in the Aare massif near the Grimsel Pass of Switzerland. The Alps are the most spectacular of the young southern mountains of Europe. The lakes in the picture are reservoirs, part of the impressive hydroelectric development of the Aare River headwaters (Swissair.)

in Southeastern Europe, and the complex of mountains in the southern Balkan Peninsula. The heights of the more prominent peaks (see Table 2-1) of these ranges are generally from 5000 to 8000 feet (1525 to 2440 meters).

The Lowland Regions

Between the rejuvenated blocks of the Northwest Highlands and the Central Uplands lie the North European Lowlands. Here, in a quietly subsiding zone repeatedly covered by ancient seas, eroded debris from adjacent uplands has accumulated. The continental plate has been deeply overlaid with sediments that under pressure and through the action of natural cements have formed nearly horizontal layers of new rock. In addition to the

shales and sandstones formed, respectively, from silt and sand brought down by streams, other types of sedimentary rock were created. Particularly significant are thick beds of limestone precipitated on the sea floor by minute organisms whose shells consisted of calcium carbonate. When the organisms died, they accumulated on the ocean floor and, under pressure from overlying sediments, eventually formed limestone.

Under certain conditions, another type of sediment accumulated. Plant remains sometimes achieved great thickness in relatively shallow bodies of water. Under the pressure of later sedimentary deposits, they would be converted to organic rock—coal. Coal represents concentrated solar energy locked up in the process of photosynthesis. It is estimated that formation of a seam of coal 1-foot thick (30 cm) requires about 300 years of

TABLE 2-1

EUROPE'S PRINCIPAL MOUNTAINS AND PEAKS

Name	Country	Elevation	
		In Feet	In Meters
Mont Blanc	France & Italy	15,777	4,810
Etna	Italy	10,703	3,263
Finsteraarhorn	Switzerland	14,250	4,343
Gran Paradiso	Italy	13,536	4,126
Jungfrau	Switzerland	13,668	4,167
Matterhorn	Switzerland & Italy	14,698	4,481
Mont Rosa	Switzerland & Italy	15,213	4,638
Weisshorn	Switzerland	14,776	4,505

Source: Kratkaya Geograficheskaya Entsiklopediya, vols. 1–5 (Moscow: 1960–1966).

steady deposition of vegetable matter in a swamp. The harnessing of this energy was the basis for Europe's Industrial Revolution, supported by, for example, extensive coal deposits on lowlands in the English Midlands, in northern France and adjacent southern Belgium, and in Germany's Ruhr region. Although alternative sources of power have developed, many European industrial centers are still in coal regions.

Petroleum is another organic material associated with the sediments of the Northern Lowlands. It appears to be the result of decomposition of plant matter in the absence of oxygen. Its liquid character permits it to flow somewhat like water in the pore spaces of sedimentary rock. Although most eventually reaches the surface and is dissipated, impervious rocks may serve to trap substantial accumulations. The surface rocks of the plain have shown little evidence of such oil pools, but their offshore extensions in the North Sea have been successfully tapped to provide Europe with substantial amounts of this vital commodity. However, these deposits will be exhausted during the twenty-first century, and Europe will resume its

petroleum dependency on the Middle East and other parts of the world.

The Northern Lowlands are not completely flat (Fig. 2-4); forces of erosion have sculpted a network of streams and rivers and have left a fairly rolling surface. Moreover, the geological events that lifted and re-lifted Europe's mountains did not leave this zone of accumulation completely undisturbed. Undulations have been created in formerly horizontal rockbeds as some spots have sunk and others have gently risen. As erosion has attacked the tilted layers, it has removed the less resistant sedimentary rock on the surface first. The result is a pattern of alternating scarps and valleys. Most notable are concentric rings of such features around London and Paris, particularly noticeable to the east of the French capital.

Although the Northern Lowlands and their extension eastward into Russia dominate the map of European lowlands, substantial plains exist elsewhere. These include fringes of coastline, as along either side of the Appenine chain in Italy, and several basins formed within upland and mountainous areas, such as the basins of central Germany and valleys of northern Switzerland and western Austria. Though generally small in territorial extent, they contain the principal areas of population concentration of their respective countries.

Plains in the interior are generally in areas where the earth's crust has sunk. Their surfaces are the result of deposition of sediments from the surrounding mountains. Among the most notable are the Po Valley of northern Italy, the Pannonian Basin shared by Hungary and its neighbors, and the Wallachian Plain of southern Romania. One of the most striking plains is the Rhine Graben in the Central Upland zone between the Vosges of France and the Black Forest of Germany. The Rhine River follows this 20-mile-wide (32 km) gash in the Central Uplands for 175 miles (282 km) along the French-German border before plunging through its own eroded, narrow gorge in the Uplands for another 60 miles (97 km) from Mainz to Bonn, from which it emerges onto the Northern Lowlands.

The coastal plains for the most part are raised segments of extensive past undersea sedimentary accumulations. At the height of the glacial periods when the formation of ice caps lowered sea level

FIGURE 2-4 A characteristically undulating landscape of the North European Lowlands near Amiens in northeastern France. The land is mantled with loess deposited by winds in the period of glaciation. Exceptionally fertile soils have evolved. (Standard Oil.)

by hundreds of feet, these sediments were part of Europe's land surface, and seaward extensions of rivers can be traced across them. These continental shelves may extend 200 miles (325 km) or more off Europe's Atlantic coast, breaking off abruptly to the ocean floor when they have sloped to a depth of approximately 500 feet (150 meters) below present sea level. Their shallow waters have long provided Europe with most of its fish.

Ice Age Legacies

In more recent geologic times, the processes of uplift, erosion, and deposition have been augmented by the sculpturing activity of moving ice.

Between 1.5 and 2 million years ago, snows began to pile up on the northern fringes of Europe and in the higher mountain areas to the south. The mechanism by which more snow began to accumulate than could be melted off each year is the subject of several theories, no one of which adequately accounts for all the observable facts. It is known that on four occasions—and possibly six—the snow reached thicknesses of 2 miles (3.2 km) and more. The great pressure on the lower layers crystallized them into ice, which moved horizontally for hundreds of miles.

The most recent glaciation began 35,000 years ago and reached its maximum extent 10,000 to 15,000 years later. The rate of melting then began to exceed the pace of outward ice flow. The face of the ice thus retreated, averaging perhaps 15 feet (4.5 meters) per year. There were periods of re-advance, stagnation, and accelerated retreat until it disappeared altogether about 9000 years ago.

This most recent stage of glaciation had its principal center of snow accumulation over the Gulf of Bothnia. Its outer edges reached the west coast of Denmark, northern Germany, central Poland, and into the FSU as far as Kiev in Ukraine and to the northern Urals (Fig. 2-5). Lesser ice masses formed over the northern British Isles and in the Southern Mountain Ranges.

In areas near the centers of snow accumulation, the dominant effect of the moving ice was to remove any loose materials and to smooth and groove the bedrock. Because the laminar flow of the ice actually permitted it to flow upward over rocks, it had the ability to excavate zones of rock weakness, creating enclosed basins. After the disappearance of the ice, these filled with water to become rock-bound lakes. Much of Finland and adjacent Russian Karelia is characterized by such a lake-strewn landscape.

Materials taken up by the moving ice were eventually deposited as it melted, to leave a morainic veneer of mixed silt, boulders, sand, and pebbles. Particularly great accumulations occurred at the outermost edge of the ice and at places where the ice face temporarily stabilized during the course of retreat. These deposits remain as ridges that can be traced for hundreds of miles, particularly in northeastern Germany and Poland. Over most of the region covered by the glacier, the slow retreat of the face of the ice left a morainic cover of up to 100 feet (30 meters) of rock fragments, which in certain areas was built up to heights of 1500 feet (450 meters) and more.

At the melting margins of the ice, vast quantities of water accumulated, and as it flowed toward the sea across material earlier deposited by the glacier, it pushed and carried materials along with it. Finer sand and silt particles were moved over considerable distances. Thus, beyond the outer margin of direct deposition of materials by the ice, there are, typically, a succession of gravel beds and sand accumulations formed by materials car-

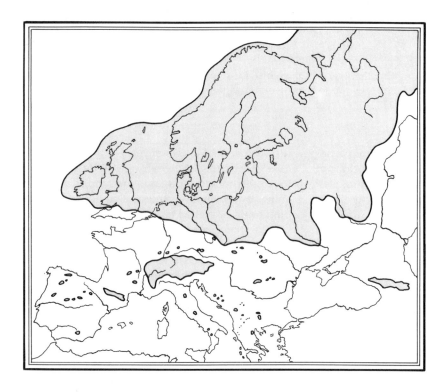

FIGURE 2-5 The maximum extent of glaciation in Europe.

ried outward from the continental glaciers by their meltwaters.

Drainage Disruption Where the face of the ice blocked the preglacial exits to the sea, as in the Vistula River Valley of central Poland, new routes were carved parallel to the ice margins by floodwaters rushing across the low drainage basin divides of the Northern Lowlands. Some streams later resumed flowing within their former channels, but others, including the Vistula, continued to follow the right-angle kinks of their new courses. Several of the abandoned meltwater diversions were used for easily dug canals linking north-flowing rivers during the nineteenth century. The most prominent of these is the Midland Canal (Mittelland Kanal) system across Germany.

The most general characteristic of Europe's glaciated territories is their poor drainage. The indiscriminate dumping of materials by the ice blocked the earlier articulated networks of streams and rivers. Denied former free exits to the sea, waters became impounded in lakes or vegetation-choked bogs. The very unevenness of the glacial deposition gave rise to new water bodies, particularly where material collapsed into hollows formed by the melting of buried ice blocks. More than 50 percent of Europe's lakes are to be found in its zones of continental glaciation.

The great weight of the ice had its own significant effect on the landscape. The region of greatest snow accumulation was depressed several hundred feet into the earth's crust by the weight of the more than 2 miles of ice above. The land is still rebounding at a rate of 30 inches (75 cm) or more per century. Because the depressed rock was flooded by an arm of the sea after its ice cover melted, it was covered by beds of material washed out of adjacent areas and spread evenly by currents and turbulence in the Baltic. Where these sediments have risen to the surface during the process of upward rebounding, they have formed an arable soil that markedly contrasts with the glacially polished bedrock that dominates the region. Already the bed of the Gulf of Bothnia has rebounded more than 800 feet (240 meters) and substantially extended the coastal plains of Sweden and Finland.

Loess Deposits Extensive deposits of windblown sediment—loess—are also an important legacy of the most recent glacial period. Strong wind currents were generated by the great temperature contrasts between exposed land and ice sheet. Winds picked up vast amounts of dust from the material deposited by the glacier and its meltwaters, as the tundra vegetation that followed the retreat offered little protection from the wind. The dust was redeposited, often in thick accumulations, where the force of the winds declined, particularly on the northern margins of the Central Uplands and Plateaus and in the Pannonian Basin.

Although the loess was easily eroded, it served as an excellent medium for soil formation. Its porous, well-drained character was not conducive to the development of thick stands of forest. Loess areas were easily crossed and cleared for farming by humans as they ventured into Northern Europe again, and became the principal regions of prehistoric settlement north of the Alps. An additional advantage for early humans may well have been the ease of constructing habitations by tunneling laterally into loess cliffs exposed by stream erosion.

Mountain Glaciation Glaciers in mountain zones had many effects in common with the great continental ice sheets. Across a broad belt of southern Germany are poorly drained accumulations of rock debris left behind by the retreating face of a piedmont glacier that was formed by the merger of a number of tongues of ice flowing out of the valleys of the Alps. In contrast to the moraines and meltwater deposits characterizing this Alpine foreland, the upper courses of Alpine streams are dominated by the effects of glacial erosion. The glaciers moving downslope tended to steepen valley walls and to undercut them. The characteristic V cross-sectional profile of stream-eroded valleys was transformed into a U-shape. The floors of the valleys were eroded into a series of irregular steps over which streams in their descent form rapids, waterfalls, and natural reservoirs. Glacial debris from the upward-retreating ice face also clogs valley floors.

The most spectacular scenery of the Alps is usually attributable to headward erosion by their glaciers. Particularly striking are serrated ridgelines created by glacial erosion from opposite sides. The famed Matterhorn (Fig. 1-10) derives its unusual form from the headward erosion of several glaciers on its upper flanks.

The Physical Landscape and Human Development

Especially in the past, but also to an extent even today, some people view the evolution of the present European cultural and economic scene as a direct consequence of its environment. Thus, because the plains and mountains have been among the few constant elements during the course of Europe's history, it is often assumed that they hold the key to an understanding of the patterns of human events that have taken place and a guide to the future.

Such a deterministic view is difficult to sustain in a review of the constantly changing panoply of European demography, economics, and politics. To Europeans the significance of terrain features has varied infinitely from group to group, from place to place, and from era to era. It is perhaps most realistic to view Europe's surface features as providing opportunities and limitations for activities that have changed with changing skills and technologies and with changing perceptions of what the opportunities and limitations might be.

Mountains, for example, are frequently seen as barriers to movement. On many occasions population groups have staked their security on the protective character of the terrain, only to find ruefully that their assumptions were incorrect. In Roman times Hannibal crossed the Alps with 30,000 men, and the "impenetrable" Ardennes has three times been the route of a massive invasion during the past century.

Mountains have always been traversable when there was a desire to get to the other side. Even the highest of ranges have had rather easily negotiable crossings, such as the Peartree Pass across the Dinaric Mountains or the Brenner Pass across the Alps. Indeed, several mountain gaps are at water level, including the famed Iron Gate through the Carpathians and the passage of the Elbe through the Ore Mountains (Erzgebirge).

Development in Mountainous Areas The progressive improvement of technology, particularly in transportation, has steadily reduced any limiting effects of mountains on patterns of circulation. Tunnels, cog railways, and improved highway construction techniques have permitted ready passage through the most formidable of features. It is nearly as easy to cross the Alps in Switzerland as to traverse the North European Lowlands in Poland.

Remaining frictions to movement are primarily a function of economic and political conditions rather than inherent properties of the terrain. The building of adequate routeways has followed the development of new types of transport systems based, for example, on railroads, cars and trucks, and pipelines. A steady reduction of handicaps can be traced to circulation of goods and people in Europe from Northwestern Europe to its southern and eastern extremities that is coincident with the pathways of the economic modernization process.

Only recently have the mountainous regions of Southeastern Europe been as easily traversable as the highlands to the west and north. The industrialization of Serbia, Bosnia-Herzegovina, Romania, and other Balkan states has led to the construction of modern railroads and highways that speed up the flow of goods and people and otherwise lessen the isolation long associated with a jumbled terrain.

Progressively changing human capabilities have not only reduced the limitations of topography, but have also multiplied the opportunities for its development. Ski resorts have blossomed on mountain slopes, and luxury hotels have emerged on rocky shores. Improved accessibility and increased demand have unlocked the resource potential of scenery as they have increased the value of mineral and fuel beds.

Despite the greater utilization of Europe's higher and rougher terrain, the bulk of its population is still concentrated in the lowlands. Even Switzerland, habitually viewed as a land of mountaineers, has most of its people concentrated on a relatively low plateau extending from Lake Geneva to the Lake of Constance. Still, exceptions exist—the dissected terrain of the Zagorje region of Croatia retains a much higher rural population density than adjacent plains, reflecting its past role as a refuge from Turkish incursions.

Landforms and Cultural Patterns Mountains have played a role in the evolution of Europe's cultures because of the difficulty they posed in traversing them in the past and their generally sparse settlement patterns. Interaction among people in day-to-day contact that gave rise to broad areas of homogeneity in language and custom tended to be limited by rough terrain, leaving mountain peoples at the margins of evolving cultures on the lowlands. In some instances, this was due to the insulation effect of intervening rugged, unpopulated territory; in others, it was due to the greater ability of groups to resist encroachment of invaders by command of strategic passes. Limited economic or marketing opportunities in mountainous areas also provided fewer inducements for their conquest. Such factors could have played roles in explaining the otherwise very puzzling development in the Pyrenees of the Basque language, which has no known links to any language spoken anywhere. Such an explanation is far from complete, however, because more isolated areas elsewhere in Europe failed to spawn cultures as distinctive as that of the Basques.

Cultural discontinuities are to be found on the flanks of mountains, not at their crests. Except in the very highest areas, access from one slope to another has generally been easier than descent through the valleys to the plains. This is reflected by the locations athwart mountain ranges of the Basques and the Romansch-speaking peoples in the Alps. Where people from the lowlands have invaded mountainous terrain, they have usually progressed to the far side. Thus, the Ukrainians overlap the Carpathians and the South Tirol Germans live on the Italian side of the Alps.

The Linking Function of Rivers Although rivers since classical times have been selected to mark the limits of political jurisdiction, they have barred movement across them even less than mountains have. Indeed, the freedom of movement on water makes any section of shore of equal attainability, whereas opportunities along ridgecrests vary widely between cliff faces and pass routes.

Until the land transportation developments of the nineteenth century, it was far easier to move on rivers and seas than overland. Even now the waterways of Europe (see Table 2-2) play a sub-

	TABLE 2-2	

EUROPE'S PRINCIPAL RIVERS

	Length	
Name	**In Miles**	**In Kilometers**
Danube	1771	2850
Ebro	577	928
Elbe	724	1165
Garonne	404	650
Guadalquivir	423	680
Loire	628	1010
Meuse	518	935
Oder	564	907
Po	405	652
Rhine	824	1326
Rhone	505	812
Sava	584	940
Seine	485	780
Tagus	628	1010
Vardar	600	966
Vistula	679	1092
Weser	470	756

stantial role as arteries of commerce. A person viewing the Rhine practically never loses sight of barges and ships, and much the same can be said on the Danube and the Elbe.

Where overland routes emerged in classical and medieval Europe, they generally paralleled river routes to take advantage of their gentle, stream-carved gradients. Thus, the traditional passage between Central Europe and the Bosporus has followed the corridor of the Vardar and Morava rivers through the Balkan Peninsula and thence along the Danube (Fig. 2-6). The Rhine and the Elbe have played a similar part in the evolution of land communications between Central Europe and the North European Lowlands.

Although modern technology has freed contemporary route builders from excessive concerns with grade, major highways still tend to go along

FIGURE 2-6 Timeworn road follows the Vardar River in the former Yugoslavia. Since ancient times, the Vardar and connecting Morava valleys have served as the principal overland communications route between the southern Balkan Peninsula and Central Europe. (T. M. Poulsen.)

traditional riverine routes to connect the gateway towns and regional service centers that emerged along riverbanks in earlier times.

The use of rivers as commercial arteries is not without its problems. Streams have irregular courses, with rocky rapids in some regions and shallow sandbar reaches in others. The Rhine and Vistula enter the sea through deltas whose channels have shifted repeatedly from one shallow distributary to another. The narrow passages of the Iron Gate and Rhine Gorge have presented problems of swift water and dangerous shoals, as well as the easy opportunity in the past for small groups on their shores to command the river traffic and exact tolls. Additional problems are the inadequacy of water in summer in many areas, especially in Southern Europe, and the freezing of the Central and East European rivers in the winter.

Industrial growth in the eighteenth and nineteenth centuries saw a steady improvement of riverine communications. Channels were stabilized and made self-dredging. Shoals were blasted and streambeds deepened. A railroad was built along the shore of the Iron Gate to tow vessels upstream against the swift waters. In plains areas intricate networks of canals were constructed, linking major stream systems across the continent.

Improvement works have continued to the present. A dam on the lower Danube has changed the torrent through the Iron Gate into a placid reservoir, accessible by large locks to seagoing vessels. A primitive canal system linking the upper Rhine and the Danube has been replaced by a modern system that permits the huge fleet of river barges in Northwestern Europe access to its central and southeastern areas.

The Role of the Seas Europe's seas, like its rivers and mountains, have never been barriers to movement. Despite the dangers of treacherous currents and devastating storms, the seas of Europe since ancient times have bound diverse areas together. The classical empires in the Mediterranean were forged by the ease of travel over water by armies and commerce. The Norse built and maintained a sea-girt state from Russia to Greenland.

Whereas it has been relatively easy to extend political authority across Europe's narrow seas, it has been more difficult to create a homogeneous culture. The seas, like the highlands, have been empty zones interrupting the day-to-day interchange of ideas and the evolution of common cultural characteristics. Although the English Channel has never of itself been an insurmountable barrier to invasions from either side, it has served as an effective discontinuity of the forces that shaped the French and English languages; and despite a common parentage, Icelandic, Faeroese, Norwegian, Danish, and Swedish have emerged as separate languages around the northern seas.

Free movement on the seas has been limited to some extent where small groups have been able to command traffic through the narrows. Turkish control of the Bosporus and Dardanelles Straits has been a constant threat to Russian access to the Mediterranean Sea. The Danes regulated traffic into and out of the Baltic by control of the Oresund. Gibraltar has long been a major prize for control of the outlet of the Mediterranean. Even in wider stretches, such as the Adriatic Sea or the Strait of Tunis, pirate bands based in protective harbors or on offshore islands were successful in frustrating easy passage.

THE CLIMATES OF THE CONTINENT

Europe is endowed with a higher proportion of climates favorable for agriculture and human settlement than any other continent. Its midlatitude position and its intimate relationships with the sea favor moderate temperatures and adequate precipitation. Only its higher latitudes and upper elevations offer marginal opportunities for development. Basic to an understanding of Europe's climatic patterns is its northerly position.

The sun's rays are far less effective in warming the continent than they are in tropical regions, because they reach the surface of this part of the globe at relatively low angles above the horizon. The long (oblique) path of solar rays through the atmosphere causes a higher proportion of their energy to be absorbed by the atmospheric blanket of air than where the sun's rays strike more nearly perpendicular at the earth's surface. Also, low sun angle spreads solar energy over a greater total area than if it came from directly overhead. Actually, more energy is lost to outer space from terrestrial radiation than comes in from the sun in all of Europe poleward of the latitude of Rome. In regions in proximity to the sea, however, this net loss of energy is compensated for by the import of heat from tropical areas, including tropical energy carried to Northern Europe within the North Atlantic Drift, an extension of the Gulf Stream.

Although there is a difference of nearly 40° of latitude between Northern and Southern Europe, the summer months exhibit similar average temperatures throughout the continent—between 60° and 75°F (Fig. 2-7). The lessening intensity of solar radiation as one moves northward is counteracted by a longer period of daylight. The circle of illumination, which divides the earth's spherical surface into lighted and unlighted hemispheres, encompasses an area over the North Pole during the summer. In European latitudes in the summer, a given place travels far more hours on the lighted side of the circle of illumination than on the side away from the sun. London and Copenhagen have 16 1/2 hours of daylight in midsummer, and Rome has more than 15 hours. Indeed, at the June 21 solstice, when the earth's axis is most tipped toward the sun, the solar rays pass as far beyond the North Pole as the Arctic Circle (66 1/2° N). North of this line, the sun is on view around the clock for an increasing number of days, culminating in six months of continuous insolation at the pole itself.

Latitudinal differences in solar radiation are far greater in winter, because the position of the circle of illumination now accentuates rather than counteracts the lessening intensity of radiation poleward. As one goes northward during the December solstice, the period of daylight decreases from a minimum of nine hours at the latitude of Madrid to no insolation at all beyond the Arctic Circle. Average temperatures for the coldest

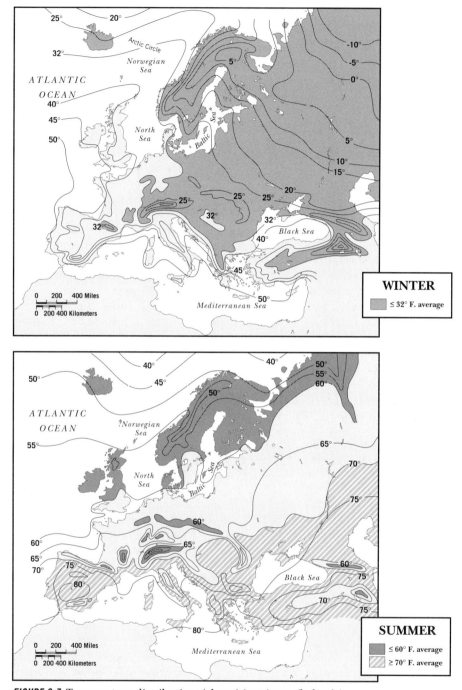

FIGURE 2-7 Temperature distribution: (above) in winter, (below) in summer.

month reflect this difference, ranging from 50°F (10°C) in southern Spain and Greece to below 0°F (-18°C) in northern Sweden (Fig. 2-7).

Maritime Influences

Regional and seasonal contrasts in insolation in Europe are modified over much of the continent, however, by the presence of air warmed by a prior passage over oceans and seas. In contrast to land, which transforms insolation immediately by radiating heat to overlying air and thereby warming it, bodies of water absorb and hold a high proportion of the solar energy that reaches them. Between half and two-thirds of this energy is used to evaporate surface water, and the rest is radiated slowly and evenly to the air. Europe's position in the path of winds blowing across the Atlantic (and its relatively warm North Atlantic Drift), as well as its deep embayments of water in the Baltic and Mediterranean areas, give most regions cooler summers and warmer winters than their latitudes would warrant.

Although the general pattern of circulation of the atmosphere is quite complex, one may visualize a flow of warmed tropical air aloft and away from the equatorial zones toward the energy-deficient polar regions. The rotation of the earth and other atmospheric and surface conditions lead much of this air to spiral downward in the midlatitudes in the form of gigantic outward blowing swirls. These tend to be centered over the eastern sides of the major oceans. Off Europe this persistent counterclockwise-turning subtropical high-pressure cell is termed the Azores anticyclone, although its center shifts seasonally to the north and south of the islands from which it gets its name. In the heart of the Azores anticyclone and for a considerable distance to the east of it, the air moves gently, if at all. Steady winds blow out of its southern margins toward the equator. These are the famous northeastern trade winds, which carried sailing ships to the New World. Other winds, the westerlies, bend around the western and northern fringes of the cell and then drift eastward across Europe and Asia.

Although their moderating effect is felt well into European Russia, the westerlies gradually lose their oceanic temperature characteristics as they pass over the land. In summer they accumulate increasing amounts of energy from the sun-warmed surfaces below them; in winter they transmit heat to the cold landscape underneath. The more direct control of temperatures by incoming insolation alone (without the influence of water bodies) is seen in the greater temperature ranges between warm and cold months in Eastern Europe, furthest from the influence of the Atlantic. Coastal areas generally have ranges of only 20°F (11°C) or less, whereas Polish Galicia and the Balkans experience differences of more than 40°F (22°C).

Local sea breeze circulation is also important in modifying temperatures on the land, particularly in the Mediterranean region. Low pressures over rapidly warming land on sunny summer days draw cooler, heavier air up to 50 miles inland from the adjacent seas. Inland areas of Spain and Macedonia may see land surface temperatures rise to 125°F (52°C), whereas coastal zones reach only 75°F (24°C) or less.

The Clash of Air Masses

Not all maritime air flowing across Europe originates in the tropics. Scandinavia is usually dominated by cooler air masses from the North Atlantic. The zone of contact between this polar maritime air and its tropical counterpart is readily observable in abrupt differences in temperatures and wind direction; the resulting polar front usually has a sinuous pattern across the continent and fluctuates greatly. Its path appears to be guided in part by a 300-mile-per-hour (480 km/hr) river of air in the upper atmosphere called the jet stream.

Shifts in the position of the polar front create variable weather from day to day across Europe in both summer and winter. Such variations become most frequent and acute when cellular perturbations develop on the front and travel along its distance from west to east. The cause of these cyclonic storms is still a matter of controversy. In essence, they arise as spots of low pressure on the front that draw the contrasting air masses from opposite sides into counterclockwise convergent spirals averaging 600 miles (nearly 1000 km) in diameter. The section of the polar front to the west of the low-pressure center sweeps southeastward as an advancing cold front; to the east a warm front swings northward at a somewhat slower pace.

The Arctic front is a similar zone of contact between air masses of different characteristics. Here, the polar maritime air meets even colder air from the frozen Arctic Ocean. On occasion the Arctic front will dip southward to Scandinavia and beyond, with very cold air able to slip as far southeastward as Central Europe. The continent is also occasionally invaded in winter by intensely cold masses of air from Siberia and Central Asia.

Terrain Influences

Because Europe's mountains lie mainly in east-west belts, they do not present barriers to the free passage of air masses and perturbations eastward from the Atlantic as the Cascade Sierra, and Rocky Mountains do in North America. The Alps, however, do tend to keep cold northern air masses out of the Mediterranean Basin through much of the winter, though spillovers occur. The local inhabitants have given names to these cold air invasions. Such a wind blowing down the Rhone Valley is known as the *mistral*; to the east the cold air funneling into the Adriatic is the *bora*.

Several times each winter the polar front crosses the Alps, making the Mediterranean Basin a zone of changing weather as cyclonic storms pass through. This occurs when the Azores anticyclone and its poleward belt of westerly winds move closer to the equator. Also, local temperature contrasts between land and sea, particularly in the Gulf of Genoa, give rise to fronts and the development of cyclonic storms. Storms are generally absent from the Mediterranean in summer, however. The subsiding air of the anticyclone dominates far inland, and only local wind systems prevail. Temperatures remain much the same day after day.

At times Mediterranean air may spill northward across the Alpine passes and create on the north slopes of the mountains a warm, dry wind, the *föhn*, which in the spring can trigger avalanch-

es of snow and in summer can create searing conditions conducive to crop loss and fire. The force of such winds is often sufficient to divert polar front cyclonic storms substantially northward.

Ocean Current Effects

It is commonly assumed that Europe is from 5° to 10°F (3° to 5.5°C) warmer than it should be for its latitude, because warm subtropical waters are imported as far north as Murmansk by the Gulf Stream off the southeastern United States and its continuation northeastward, the North Atlantic Drift. There is, indeed, a significant local effect of this long oceanic river system as winds blow across it off the coasts of Ireland, Scotland, and Norway. By far the most important share of imported warmth, however, comes from the joint effects of surface air of the tropics drawn around the northern edge of the Azores anticyclone into the westerlies and of air descending from aloft within the anticyclone itself, warming as it is more and more compressed in the lower layers of the atmosphere.

The North Atlantic Drift actually splits as it reaches Europe. The portion that moves south is the Canaries Current. Its moving waters become progressively cooler than the surrounding oceanic surface. The cooling effect on winds blowing across the Canaries Current is intensified off Gibraltar, where a surface current moving seaward pulls nearshore surface waters along with it, causing an upwelling of colder waters from the ocean depths.

Patterns of Precipitation

The interplay of atmospheric elements that leads to temperature variations over the face of Europe also creates distinctive patterns of precipitation (Fig. 2-8). The fall of rain or snow occurs when a body of air containing water vapor is forced to ascend. As the air rises it cools; as it cools, its capacity to hold moisture is reduced. As it continues to rise, it cools to the point where its moisture capacity is the same as the amount of water vapor it contains. With further ascent and cooling, mois-

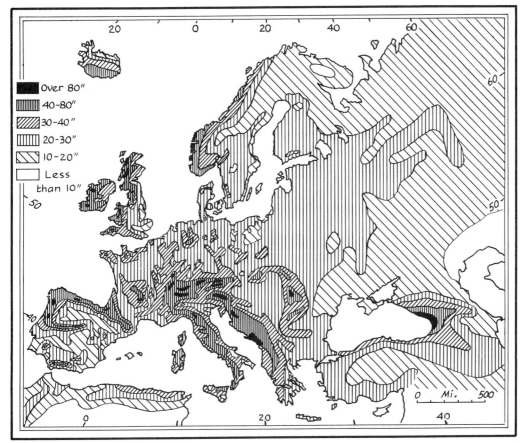

FIGURE 2-8 Annual precipitation.

ture will condense from the gaseous state to a liquid (or solid) state and fall back to earth as some sort of precipitation.

The rising of air and resulting precipitation occur over Europe most often through the convergence of unlike air masses, creating a succession of a hundred or more cyclonic storms each year. Precipitation may also result when a body of air rises as it overruns a topographical barrier or when intensive warming of near-saturated air causes a convectional updraft leading to the rapid cooling and heavy precipitation of a thunderstorm.

The proximity of the Atlantic would seem to guarantee sufficient moisture in the air to provide abundant precipitation throughout Europe. This is, in fact, the situation in the northern half of the continent. Southern Europe, however, has a distinctively dry summer. At this time of year, it is generally dominated by air that has spiraled down through the Azores anticyclone. Almost all previous moisture was precipitated in its original ascent in the tropics, and because it passed over water bodies only briefly, if at all, before reaching the land, the air is generally dry. Seldom is such air able to absorb more than 20 or 30 percent of the water vapor it is capable of holding at its temperature.

In winter the subtropical high-pressure cell shifts southward, and Mediterranean Europe is in the path of the westerlies saturated with moisture from the air's long passage across the Atlantic. Moreover, the Mediterranean region is an area of air mass convergence in winter owing to cyclonic storms that move along the polar front at speeds of 30 to 40 miles (50 to 65 km) an hour. The Mediterranean region receives much of its annual precipitation from these storms, including the impact of orographic enhancement from the area's many mountain chains.

Whereas most of the Mediterranean Basin consequently has its maximum precipitation in winter, the rest of Europe tends to get the larger share of its rainfall in the summer when the warmer air coming off the Atlantic is able to hold greater amounts of water vapor than the colder winter air. Thus, the more intensive summer insolation triggers off convectional activity and large numbers of local thunderstorms whose pelting precipitation augments the region's rainfall from the passing warm fronts and cold fronts that occur during all parts of the year.

Figure 2-8 shows that most of Europe annually receives between 20 and 40 inches (51 to 103 cm) of precipitation, which is sufficient for most agricultural crops. The western coastlines and the windward slopes of mountains receive greater amounts, and interior basins and leeward slopes get substantially less. Differences in precipitation

can be great within short distances. Lovcen, a mountain on the Adriatic coast of Montenegro, receives up to 200 inches (513 cm) annually, whereas the lands immediately behind it seldom receive as much as 30 inches (77 cm).

The mechanisms of the atmosphere leading to precipitation are illustrated by Figures 2-9 and 2-10, which are simplified weather maps of typical days in January and July, respectively. In Figure 2-9 three traveling low-pressure centers are evident—one situated just west of Iceland, a second in the western Mediterranean, and a third in the Aegean Sea. The center of the Azores high-pressure cell is shown extending over the Iberian Peninsula, spinning out currents of maritime tropical air across Europe, some of which is caught up in the low-pressure systems over Iceland and Sardinia. The remainder is streaming north of the Alps, where it mixes with continental polar air coming out of Siberia and Arctic air from an air mass over northern Scandinavia.

A much simpler pattern characterizes the summer situation in Figure 2-10. The Azores high-pressure cell is now to the north of Iberia. The bulk of its maritime tropical air wafts eastward and southward across the continent. Only in the North

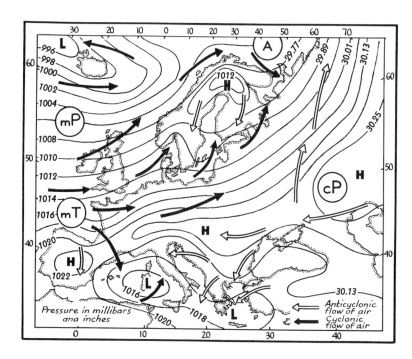

FIGURE 2-9 Pressures, wind flows, and air masses on a typical winter day (January). Bodies of air are classified by their origins: mP, polar maritime; mT, tropical maritime; A, arctic; and cP, continental polar.

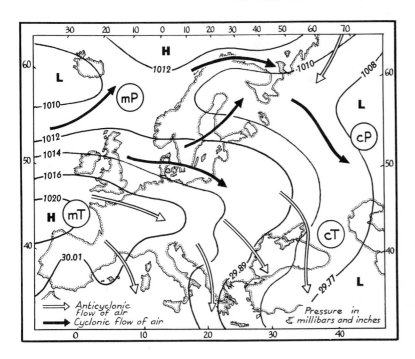

FIGURE 2-10 Pressures, wind flows, and air masses on a typical summer day (June). (See Fig. 2-9 for a legend.)

Sea and Scandinavian areas does its flow converge with maritime polar and continental polar air masses by way of cyclonic storms.

Climatic Regions

The seasonally changing characteristics of precipitation and temperature combine to create a wide variety of opportunities and limitations for the development of vegetation, animal life, and human activity in Europe. Although substantial differences may occur within limited areas, particularly in mountainous regions, broad regional trends may be observed, from the summer drought-resistant trees and shrubs of the Mediterranean zone to the coniferous forests and tundra fringes of Scandinavia.

To gain an appreciation of these climatic variations across Europe, it is useful to divide the continent into a few major type-regions, keeping in mind that such a regional division ultimately must be seen as an arbitrary, albeit useful, breakdown of what is a continuous whole. In this respect, regionalization should be viewed as a technique of analysis similar to the rock classifications of geologists or the periodizations of historians. Just as one

often finds a continuum from basaltic rocks into the granites with no inherent breaks, so combinations of climatic elements often grade almost imperceptibly from place to place without sharp discontinuities, though these do exist on either side of some mountain ranges (e.g., in many places between the relatively humid northern and relatively dry southern sides of the Pyrenees).

An infinite number of possibilities exist for the division of such gradations into types. The utility of any given categorization depends on the task for which it is to be used. Geographers have proposed a number of schemes for climatic regionalization. The most widely used and perhaps most suitable for gaining an appreciation of climatic characteristics on a continental scale is one advanced by Wladimir Köppen in 1900 (see Table 2-3). It is based on aspects of temperature and precipitation that appear to have limiting effects on the expansion of plant communities. Figure 2-11 identifies the major Köppen climatic regions of Europe, and Table 2-3 summarizes their characteristics.

As applied to the continent, the classification system identifies nine distinctive climatic realms as well as a zone of undifferentiated highland climates in areas exhibiting a geographically complex combination of climates owing to great

TABLE 2-3

THE KÖPPEN CLIMATIC CLASSIFICATION

A—Tropical climates. No winter season—all months have average temperatures higher than 64° F (18° C). Precipitation is greater than potential evaporation. (Not found in Europe.)

B—Dry climates. Potential evaporation exceeds precipitation.

C—Humid Mesothermal climates. Mild winter climates—no months have average temperatures below 27°F (-3° C); but at least one month is below 64° F (18° C), and at least one month is above 50° F (10° C). Precipitation is greater than potential evaporation.

D—Humid Microthermal climates. Harsh winter climates—at least one month is below 27° F (-3° C) and at least one month is above 50° F (10° C). Precipitation is greater than potential evaporation.

E—Polar climates. No summer season—all months have average temperatures below 50° F (10° C).

Undifferentiated highland climates. Great variety of climate types within a small area owing to differences in elevation.

Subdivisions Based on Seasonality of Precipitation (Calculated on basis of formulas)

f—Moist. Precipitation adequate throughout the year.

w—Dry winter. Precipitation inadequate in winter months.

s—Dry summer. Precipitation inadequate in summer months.

Subdivisions Based on Characteristics of Temperatures

a—Warm summer. Average temperature of warmest month over 72° F (22° C).

b—Cool summer. Average temperature of warmest month below 72° F (22° C), but at least four months have an average temperature higher than 50° F (10° C).

Subdivisions of the Dry (B) Climates

S—Steppe. Precipitation at least half of the potential evaporation.

W—Desert. Precipitation less than half of the potential evaporation.

h—Warm. Average annual temperature above 64° F (18° C).

k—Cool. Average annual temperature below 64° F (18° C).

Subdivisions of the Polar (E) Climates

T—Tundra. Average temperature of warmest month between 50° F (10° C) and 32° F (0° C).

F—Ice cap. Average temperature of warmest month below 32° F (0° C).

Köppen Climatic Types Present in Europe

Caf—Humid subtropical. Moderate forest climate with warm summers and mild winters.

Cbf—Marine west coast. Moderate forest climate with cool summers and mild winters.

Csa—Mediterranean. Dry summer climate with warm summers and mild winters.

Csb—Mediterranean. Dry summer climate with cool summers and mild winters.

Daf—Humid continental warm summer. Interior forest climate with warm summers and cold winters.

Dbf—Humid continental cool summer. Interior forest climate with cool summers and cold winters.

Dcf—Humid continental short summer. Interior forest climate with short, cool summers and cold winters.

Bsk—Midlatitude steppe. Cool grassland climate.

ET—Tundra. Arctic scrub climate.

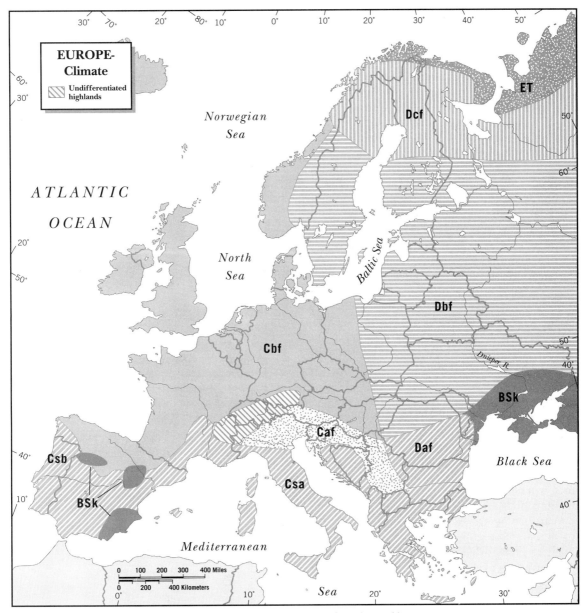

FIGURE 2-11 Köppen climatic regions of Europe. (See Table 2-3 for a legend.)

differences in elevation within small areas. In Europe the principal climatic differentiation is between climates having harsh winters (D—humid microthermal) and those with mild winters (C—humid mesothermal) in which the average temperature of the coldest month is above the freezing level. Climates are further subdivided

between warm summer (July average above 72°F (22°C)) and cool summer (below 72°F) varieties. The humid microthermal category also has a special boreal climate (Dc) that has less than four months of the year with average temperatures above 50°F (10°C). The mild winter climates (humid mesothermal) are also divided between warm summer (humid subtropical—Ca) and cool summer (marine west coast—Cb) variants, as well as a Mediterranean climate (Cs) having dry summers, with warm- and cool-summer varieties. Seasonal patterns of precipitation are indicated by even distribution (f) and summer (s) or winter (w) drought. Thus, for example, Northwestern Europe has a Cbf climate—mild winter, cool summer, with a seasonally distributed pattern of precipitation.

In addition to these climatic types that permit the growth of trees, there are two treeless climates. Several parts of the Iberian Peninsula qualify as subhumid steppe climatic regions (B) where potential evaporation and transpiration exceed the amount of precipitation. In northern Scandinavia summers are too cool for tree growth and reproduction, and this area is distinguished as a tundra region (ET).

An inspection of Figure 2-11 shows that the boundary zone between the mild winter and harsh winter climates runs from central Scandinavia to the Black Sea coast of Bulgaria. The Alps divide the mild winter regions between the marine west coast climate of the north and the Mediterranean climate to the south. Also, there is a humid subtropical zone that extends from the Po Valley of northern Italy to Macedonia. In this area patterns of local winds and the topographical barrier of the Alps minimize any cooling effect in summer by air masses off the Atlantic, yet the southward shift of the polar front in winter permits maritime air to dominate the region and maintain higher temperatures.

Warm summers are also characteristic of the lower Danube region of Bulgaria and Romania, but here greater distance from the Atlantic and Mediterranean places the area in the harsh winter category. The remainder of East Central Europe and southern Scandinavia are harsh winter regions with cool summers. The boreal climate found in northern Sweden and Finland is the western extremity of the broad taiga zone that extends across European Russia and Siberia.

Vegetation

The opportunities and limitations for vegetative growth in Europe's various climates have led to the evolution of distinctive plant associations (Fig. 2-12). The patterns of European vegetation, how-

LEGEND

Forest tracts

Arable land

Lakes and swamps

Arctic and alpine tundra

Moorland

Semidesert

Desert

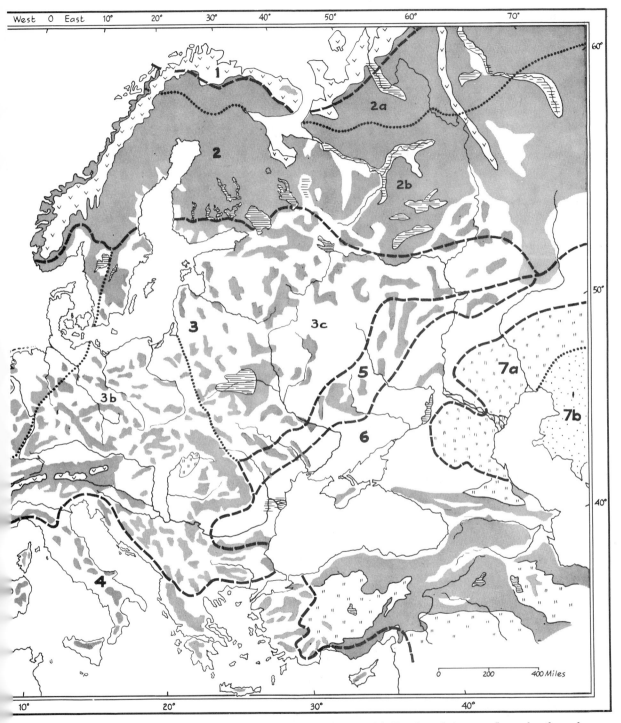

FIGURE 2-12 Vegetation zones and actual distribution of forests. (1) Tundra, alpine meadows, heath, and moorlands. (2) Boreal forest; a, open; b, closed. (3) Mixed forest: a, Atlantic association; b, central association; c, eastern association. (4) Mediterranean hardleaf forest, including large areas of secondary maquis associations. (5) Forest steppe. (6) Steppe. (7) Desert; a, semidesert; b, desert.

ever, are by no means fixed elements of the landscape. Not only have humans substantially altered the physical scene, but also climate has changed significantly over Europe throughout geologic time. In some respects plant life is still recovering from the most recent glaciation. Scientists have been able to reconstruct substantial variations in climatic characteristics by analysis of differences of types of pollen in the year-by-year layering of lake bottoms and scrutiny of differences of annular tree ring growth in preserved wood. Climate has been and is a major controlling factor in the geographic distribution of vegetation on the continent.

The largest share of the continent is characterized by a forest of mixed broadleaf deciduous and needleleaf evergreen trees that stretches from the Atlantic coastline to beyond the Urals in Russia. To the south the summer dryness has led to distinc-tive drought-tolerant evergreen species; poleward the decreasing warmth has caused most broadleaf species to disappear. On the margins of the forests are the dry grasslands of the steppe and the low shrubs of the tundra.

Within the broad mixed-forest zone, the most common species are oaks, maples, and elms in lowland areas; pines, firs, and beeches grow on the uplands (Fig. 2-13). Pines are also characteristic of sandy areas where soil moisture is scant. Most broadleaf trees drop their leaves in the fall to retard the loss of moisture in the dormant period. However, some evergreen species, including the holly, are found in the milder winter areas near the Atlantic coast.

The European mixed-forest region has a significantly smaller variety of trees than the comparable climatic regions of North America. This is quite

FIGURE 2-13 A tree plantation near Doksy, Czech Republic. Much of the original mixed forest of Central Europe has been cleared for cultivation. In upland areas where trees remain, selective forestry practice has promoted pure stands of pine and other fast growing conifers. More recent plantings (foreground) have included rows of oak and other broadleaf species, to more closely replicate the original vegetation pattern and provide a fertilizing leaf mold that will maximize timber yields. (T. M. Poulsen.)

likely due to the elimination of many species during glacial periods. The highland character of Southern Europe and its relatively northern location prevented the preservation of many tree varieties in more equatorial "refuge" areas as occurred in the Western Hemisphere.

An assemblage of low evergreen scrub oaks and shrubs, *maquis*, occurs generally throughout the Mediterranean region (Fig. 2-14). It is much like the chaparral of central and southern California. To resist the hot, dry conditions of summer the plants have narrow, waxy leaves, thick insulating

bark, and root systems that often penetrate 50 feet (15 meters) below ground. Larger evergreens, oaks, cypresses, cedars, and pines are also to be found, but human depredations have caused their former continuous stands to be replaced by maquis in most areas.

The boreal forest of Scandinavia and Finland is the western tip of the needleleaf taiga zone that extends 5000 miles (over 8000 km) across Eurasia. Spruce and pine dominate this European section, although some hardy broadleaf deciduous species are present (see Fig. 9-5). Birch and aspen are par-

FIGURE 2-14 Maquis vegetation on the west coast of Corsica. The remains of a Genoese watchtower stand guard above the cove of the Gulf of Porto. (Miramount, Bastia.)

ticularly well suited to endure the harsh winters and cool summers and tend to be the first trees to regrow in areas cleared by fire or timber cutting.

Low shrubs, mosses, lichens, and grasslike sedges characterize the tundra (Fig. 2-15). Tree growth is discouraged by the extremely cool summers—no month having an average temperature as high as 50°F (10°C)—and by the tendency for local winds to be very strong. A similar assemblage of vegetation is found above the tree line in the Alps and on the upper slopes of the mountains of Scandinavia.

Although areas qualifying as steppe by Köppen's climatic criteria are limited principally to sections of central and eastern Spain, extensive grasslands once characterized both the Pannonian Basin and the Wallachian Plain before these regions were converted to cropland. Because trees will survive when planted in most parts of the latter two areas, the grasslands are likely the result of tree removal similar to the destruction of the Mediterranean forests.

Soils and Their Origins

Soils, like vegetation, are responses to combinations of climatic elements, but they also reflect the nature of the parent rock material on which they have developed and the type of plant life that grows on them. While the soil map of Europe thus becomes complex, some generalizations can be

FIGURE 2-15 At the boundary between tundra and boreal forest in Swedish Lappland. The tundra with its moss, lichen, and sedge carpet is seen in the foreground; the coniferous forest occupies the lower levels in the center; and the Scandinavian mountains, with permanent ice fields, form the backdrop. (Department of Geography, University of Zürich.)

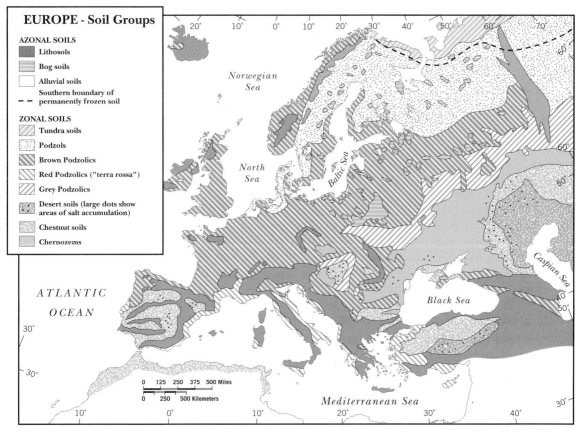

EUROPE - Soil Groups

AZONAL SOILS
- Lithosols
- Bog soils
- Alluvial soils
- - - Southern boundary of permanently frozen soil

ZONAL SOILS
- Tundra soils
- Podzols
- Brown Podzolics
- Red Podzolics ("terra rossa")
- Grey Podzolics
- Desert soils (large dots show areas of salt accumulation)
- Chestnut soils
- Chernozems

FIGURE 2-16 Soil groups.

made (Fig. 2-16), including associations between climate (Fig. 2-11) and soil formation. In the boreal and cool summer humid continental climates, the characteristic soils are podzols—a Russian term meaning "underlying ash," which refers to their light-colored upper layers. For the most part, podzols have developed on poorly drained glacial deposits. Waterlogged and poorly aerated, these soils generally have been leached of their more soluble minerals by acids developed by the slow decay of pine needles on the forest floor. Only grayish insoluble quartz particles tend to remain near the surface, yielding the ash color. Organic humus from the decomposition of vegetation is also scant, leaving these soils poor media for growing crops.

Forest soils outside the glaciated regions are brownish (termed "Brown podzolics" in Fig. 2-16), owing to greater amounts of organic materials and less leaching of minerals. Where they have long been farmed, they show a greater richness than is found in remaining forested areas, because Europe's long tradition of mixed farming has incorporated fixed nitrogen and other nutrients from fodder crops and animal manures. In grassland areas, chernozem (black earth) soils have usually developed. These are rich in organic materials from the decaying root systems of countless generations of plants. Because rainfall is sporadic and tends to come in heavy showers with a consequent rapid runoff, soluble minerals also are retained in the upper layers of chernozem soil.

Substantial portions of the Mediterranean zone are devoid of soils, owing to accelerated erosion following the removal of forests (see Fig. 5-17). Those that do remain are generally light colored, reflecting the lack of a continuous vegetation cover comparable to that in the grasslands. Where the parent rock is limestone, soils develop a bright red color and are known as *terra rossa*.

Seasonal Rhythms

The variations of landscape from region to region in Europe should be seen in another dimension— the changes that occur from season to season. Although seasonal rhythms are moderate in comparison with the great contrasts between summer and winter in the interiors of North America and Asia, they are present and do have a noteworthy impact on human activities in Europe as well.

Seasonal differences are least pronounced in the marine west coast climate areas. The moderating effect of the Atlantic reduces temperature contrasts, and the passage of cyclonic storms across the area throughout the year results in a rather even distribution of precipitation. The principal distinction is in the changing length of daylight. At the summer solstice on June 21, Paris has 16 hours of solar insolation, and at the winter solstice on December 21 it has only 8 hours. Hence, demands for electric power for illumination are notably greater in winter, as they are in all of Europe. This is not to say that the coolness of winters is of no major consequence in Northwestern Europe. Cold air masses drawn from the Arctic or Eastern Europe can bring very chilly weather and a snow cover of 10 days or more duration. Moreover, as temperatures drop below the mid-40s (°F or about 7°C), vegetation lapses into dormancy. This, coupled with a dependable period of almost 250 days between killing frosts, leads to a concentration of crop farming in the warm half of the year. However, the long-standing practice of raising livestock as well as field crops makes agriculture more of a year-round occupation than in more severe winter climate areas.

Seasonal contrasts are greater in Northeastern Europe. Temperatures drop well below freezing in the winter months. Most rivers freeze over, as do the northern and eastern extremities of the Baltic Sea. Snow cover ranges from about 50 days in Central Europe to 150 or more on the margins of the Russian Plain and in northern Scandinavia. Any advantages of having warmer summers than in the west are modified by the greater threat of late spring or early autumn frosts, which limit growing seasons to less than 180 days in much of the area. The interior of Scandinavia and the highlands of Central Europe enjoy less than three frost-free months. Changes between seasons tend to be abrupt. In contrast to Northwestern Europe's rather long transitional periods of spring and fall, the east has notably sharp changeovers from summer to winter. The freeze-thaw activity during these relatively short periods often renders dirt roads unusable, and at the end of winter sudden stream flooding is common. Transportation in Northeastern Europe is also a greater problem in winter. Much more maintenance is required for highways and railroads to remove accumulated snow and to repair frost-heaved roadbeds. Inland navigation ceases, though icebreakers do manage to keep some Baltic ports open that would otherwise be closed by the formation of ice.

The harsher continental climate also affects and limits agricultural activities. Hardier crops must be used, including potatoes and grains such as rye and barley. Relatively few animals are kept over the winter. The snow cover precludes pasturage, so that far more hay must be produced and stored for each animal than is the case in the west. Generally, there is far less to do in the rural areas of Northeastern Europe in the winter, though tasks are often more arduous.

Urban activities also have a pronounced seasonality. The cold weather is inimical to a number of occupations, particularly in the construction industry. Such problems as the curing of concrete are resolved in a variety of ways. The development of prefabrication techniques has become particularly significant in Northeastern Europe. Concrete floors, walls, and even entire apartment modules are cast inside large buildings throughout the year and then fitted into place at construction sites. Although winter cannot be said to place absolute limits on human activities, the economic costs of adapting to cold conditions may be conservatively estimated at 20 percent or more over the costs of performance in the warm period of the year. To this must be added the burden of maintaining workers in agriculture and other fields who can find employment only during the summer months.

In the Mediterranean zone, precipitation rather than temperature is the seasonal differentiating element. Winters share the storminess of Northwestern Europe, whereas summers have much in common with the desert fringes of North Africa. The native vegetation begins growing with the onset of winter rains and goes through its blossoming and fruiting stages generally early in the spring. Grain crops are planted in the fall to take advantage of cool season soil moisture, and they are harvested in the early summer after dry, warm weather matures the crops.

Rural transportation may become bogged down by the winter's succession of cyclonic storms, though the overall impact of seasons is less onerous than in Northeastern Europe. A distinctive problem of the dry Mediterranean summers is the pervasive threat of forest and brushland fires.

Despite the problems that have been cited, it should be stressed that Europe enjoys more favorable climates for agricultural production and other activities than any other continent. Only in the northern areas of Scandinavia and the higher elevations of the southern mountains are growing seasons too short and summer temperatures too cool for the raising of crops. Although a substantial amount of land in Europe is not in agricultural production, this is due more to considerations of economic competitiveness than to absolute limitations imposed by the environment.

Climatic Hazards

Unusual weather conditions that may have devastating effects can also occur in any of Europe's agriculturally favorable climatic regions. In Northwestern and Mediterranean Europe, for instance, bursts of cold air may come from Central Asia or the Arctic that will kill off winter crops and even orchards dependent on prevailing mild winter conditions. Although in most places in Europe precipitation is very much the same year after year, droughts can occur; where the average rainfall is barely adequate for raising crops, they can be serious.

The possibility of drought is a particular problem on the eastern margins of the continent, especially in the more continental regions of Ukraine and Russia. Eastern Europe can also suffer severe crop losses when winter snows fail to occur or are prematurely melted. In such cases, the insulation normally provided for fall-sown crops is lost, making them vulnerable to the bitter cold of air mass invasions from Siberia.

A somewhat similar problem confronts agriculture in the Mediterranean Basin, which characteristically depends on irrigation from streams fed by melting snows of adjacent uplands. Normally, winter precipitation is in the form of snow at altitudes in the mountains above 4500 feet (about 1400 meters). Should it come in the form of rain, there will be no natural reservoir to release water gradually during the growing period. Another hazard, in the normally dry summers, is rain or hail that can flatten ripening crops of wheat and barley.

MODIFICATION OF ENVIRONMENT

Europe's environment is far from being solely the product of the interplay of elemental forces. Since prehistoric times humankind has had a profound effect on its surroundings, modifying and shaping them or otherwise setting into motion processes that have had dramatic, if unanticipated, consequences.

Alteration of Vegetation

The most pronounced environmental effect of human activities has been on vegetation. Before humans became a major force for change, more than 80 percent of Europe was forested. Twothirds of this tree cover has been eliminated over the past 3500 years. Moreover, today's forest lands reflect centuries of selective forestry practices. Some species have been eliminated or reduced, new ones have been introduced from other continents, and for a substantial period in the modern era, the raising of trees has been approached as a long-term variant of cropping.

The forests around the Mediterranean began to

disappear long before the rise of Greece and Rome. Wood was in constant demand for heating, building, and ship construction. The picturesque stone dwellings in Southern Europe are comparatively recent adaptations to the gradual eradication of the woodlands. Trees were also made into charcoal for domestic uses and metallurgy. Many forests were deliberately destroyed to promote pasturage. The removal of forests in the Mediterranean region was usually permanent. The light soils on the steep slopes predominating in the area were subject to sheetwash and gullying when the protective forest cover was removed. The process was so complete that it is difficult for the traveler to Dalmatia or Greece to believe that the craggy hills and mountains now so characteristic of these regions were once green with trees.

The permanence of forest destruction is also traceable to the long-standing practice of the grazing of goats throughout the region. Kept because they could survive on the leaves and branches of the maquis that were indigestible to sheep and other domestic animals, the goats also consumed tree sprouts, effectively blocking forest regeneration. In postwar Dalmatia and other Mediterranean areas where strictly enforced laws require goats to be tethered for grazing and not allowed to roam freely, one can observe the growth of trees again in scrublands where pockets of soil remain (Fig. 5-17).

Deforestation began in Northern Europe at a much later period and had fewer irreversible effects than in the Mediterranean region. Tribal groups moving into the forests north of the Alps confined their clearings principally to the open beech forests associated with deposits of windblown loess, where the soils were more fertile for agriculture and the ease of hunting and gathering edible seeds provided greater direct sustenance than in other parts of the mixed forest. It was only after the fall of the Roman Empire that an increase in population led to a more extensive clearing of forests on old residual soil and glacial moraines.

Over the course of a thousand years, the larger share of the forests of Central and Northwestern Europe was removed. As in the Mediterranean lands, much of the cutting was for the production of charcoal; it was not until the nineteenth century that bituminous coal came into general use for smelting and home heating. Spiraling demands for housing and shipbuilding also took their toll on forests.

Forest removal north of the Alps did not usually lead to the severe erosion that occurred in the Mediterranean lands. In areas that were marginal for farming, the forests that were cut for timber and charcoal quickly regrew, to be cut again and again by subsequent generations. Exceptions occurred where cleared lands were subjected to grazing. Although the goat was not a significant factor north of the Alps, the raising of sheep and cattle was accompanied by frequent burnings to encourage the growth of plant shoots. In Britain in particular, a moorland vegetation of heather, grasses, and sedges became established in former oak forest areas. While the British Isles were once almost completely cloaked in woodlands, owing to the impact of grazing and clearing for cropland, barely one-twentieth now survives.

Although most clearing for agriculture has tended to perpetuate itself to the present, forests have reclaimed some former farming areas, particularly on hill slopes. This began in the earliest periods of clearing when erosion of bared fields forced abandonment. More recently, the commercialization of agriculture has seen marginal hill farms return to a natural forested state. Several governments have encouraged the process by purchasing land for tree farming and recreational use.

The removal of the forests affected other aspects of Europe's environment. Particularly important was the siltation of the Mediterranean Sea following the accelerated erosion of the nearby slopes. Communities that were seaports in classical times are consequently several miles inland in southern France and in the Po Delta.

Human agricultural practices have continued to denude the land. The Agricultural Revolution upset precarious ecological balances in many areas. The consolidation of tiny plots into large fields and the replacement of a variety of subsistence crops by commercial monoculture have usually encouraged greater sheetwash and gully erosion; the depletion of soil nutrients and the mechanization of farming have further speeded up the erosive processes.

Draining the Wetlands

Another significant environmental modification in Europe has been the draining of wetlands. The most spectacular of these efforts is in the Netherlands, where 850 square miles (2200 square km) of farmland have been reclaimed from rivers and seas over the past 1000 years. Two-thirds of this total is the result of the twentieth-century recovery of land from the Zuider Zee, now an inland lake renamed IJsselmeer. In the course of reclamation, more than 3000 enclosed polders have been established by diking and drainage (see Figs. 8-11, 8-12, and 8-15).

Similar poldering has created more than 150 square miles (390 sq km) of farmland in the swamplike fens of eastern England. Other noteworthy areas of land drainage include parts of the North Sea coast of Germany, the Po Valley in Italy, the lower Danubian floodplain of Romania, coastal Albania, and the Landes area of southwestern France. The famous Pontine Marshes southwest of Rome were finally transformed into rich farmland in the 1930s after centuries of futile attempts to drain them from Roman times onward.

Wildlife has been particularly affected by reduction of the wetlands. This includes not only indigenous flora and fauna, but also migratory birds and even some marine life periodically dependent on these areas for shelter and reproduction. Substantial areas of wetlands have now been preserved as natural reserves, including portions of the deltas of the Guadalquivir, Rhone, and Danube rivers.

Industrialization and Its Environmental Consequences

The Industrial Revolution, which began in Britain in the eighteenth century and is now running its course through Southern and Eastern Europe, has had profound consequences for Europe's air, water, biota, and terrain. The ever-increasing combustion of fossil fuels, the continuous growth of metropolitan conurbations, and the intricate networks of canals, railroads, and highways have substantially changed the face of Europe over the past 200 years.

It is, of course, possible to exaggerate the impact of industrialization as well as the doomsday tone of some current concerns about environmental pollution, both of which are sometimes based on limited data and conjecture. Although the evidence of many aspects of human-induced changes in the environment is yet to be documented and understood, it often appears that their impact is less than that of processes set in motion by nature itself. Nevertheless, some consequences of industrialization have been clearly negative and call for redress; a good deal has already been done to clean up rivers and air, and ambitious programs are planned for the future.

Europe's atmosphere in particular has felt the impress of industrialization. Temperatures, for instance, have risen noticeably over Europe's cities, with frost-free periods up to a month longer in duration and the amount of snowfall significantly less. An increased effectiveness of radiation is the principal cause of these urban heat islands. In many ways cities are artificial deserts. Rooftops, sidewalks, and paved streets quickly drain off a high proportion of the precipitation that falls on urban areas; hence, far less incoming solar energy is absorbed by evaporation, which adds to surface heating. Moreover, Europe's increasing numbers of high-rise buildings provide greater total surfaces within a given area for receiving and reradiating solar energy. They also reduce air movement, which allows heat to build up. The burning of fossil fuels for space heating, industrial processes, and transportation adds further energy to the local heat balance.

Air Pollution The development of higher temperatures in Europe's cities is also related to the retardation of outgoing night radiation by a blanket of fine particles in the air, although it should be noted that the smoke and haze of urban atmospheres also limit incoming daytime radiation. It has been estimated that the air over Europe now has perhaps ten times as many particles as before industrialization.

A number of public health problems are associated with the increase in particulate matter. Two centuries ago, the reduction of ultraviolet light by concentration of smoke led to the appearance of the bone-deforming disease, rickets. Although modern vitamin-enriched diets have minimized the threat of this particular disorder, the increasing pollution of the air continues to cause problems, especially for human respiratory systems.

The suspension of fine particles in the air has also significantly reduced visibility in nearly all parts of Europe. Some scientists think that the increased amount of atmospheric dust that settles on Alpine glaciers, and a consequent absorption of insolation, has been a major cause of their accelerated melting and upslope retreat during the past century.

The finest particles add to the number of condensation nuclei that are essential for the precipitation process. This is reflected in a greater number of cloudy days over cities and even a measurable increase in the amount of precipitation. In 1952 a particularly dense combination of fog, smoke, and gaseous pollutants in London was reported to be responsible in a single four-day period for as many as 4000 premature deaths. Thundershowers over London are estimated to result in 30 percent more precipitation than in surrounding areas. The increased amount of chemicals in the air also has had deleterious effects. Venice and Athens, in particular, have begun to experience severe damage to their architectural monuments from a higher air-content of industrial pollutants (see Fig. 11-16).

Acid Rain The growing amounts of chemicals in Europe's air have thus had increasingly deleterious effects on environment and health. Of particular concern in recent years has been the phenomenon of acid rain, which has been blamed for substantial losses in vegetation and aquatic life. Marked increases of sulfur dioxide and particulates in the atmosphere in recent decades have been paralleled by severe damage to forests, particularly in Central Europe, and by the disappearance of fish species from many lakes and streams, especially in Northern Europe.

Relationships are not completely understood, but photochemical reactions in the polluted atmosphere appear to lead to formation of aerosols of solid or liquid matter that may have more deleteri-

ous effects than their parent materials. For example, sulfur dioxide, sulfate, and water combine in the atmosphere, causing precipitation to have acidic characteristics. In the case of forest loss, the acid rain appears to weaken trees and make them more vulnerable to such environmental stresses as heavy snows, gales, and insect pests. Conifers have been particularly susceptible. The "export" of air-borne industrial wastes across Europe's borders also means that forests fairly distant from major industrial areas suffer from pollutants originating far away, such as problems in Scandinavia caused by pollutants from Britain and Germany, in particular.

Although virtually all of Europe's industrialized areas exhibit negative effects from chemical pollution, one of the hardest hit has been the industrial triangle in East Central Europe from Leipzig to Cracow to Budapest. More than two-thirds of the forests of the Ore Mountains (Erzgebirge), which form the border between Germany and the Czech Republic, have been seriously damaged (see Fig. 2-17). The forest damage appears particularly related to a notable increase in the use in the region of local lignites as a fuel, especially for the generation of electric power. The burning of soft coal grew, especially in the early 1980s, when the Soviet Union placed limits on exports of increased amounts of petroleum to its East European allies. Another factor was the increase in the number of personal automobiles in East Central Europe beginning in the 1970s, some of which, like the two-cylinder, plastic-bodied East German Trabant, were notorious for their exhaust emissions.

The harmful effects of air pollution in industrialized Northern Europe are mitigated by the steady succession of cyclonic storms that disperse the waste products of combustion and industrial processing. Severe problems arise primarily when the air remains stationary for several days in a row, particularly when the upper atmosphere is warmer than normal. Under such circumstances smoke and fumes cannot rise, and they achieve adversely dense concentrations close to the surface.

Most pollutants drift back to ground level within a few days. Only the very fine dust particles and carbon dioxide gas remain and accumulate in the

FIGURE 2-17 Increase of sulfur dioxide and other industrial pollutants in Europe's atmosphere has had significant deleterious effects upon its biosphere. These dead and dying trees in the Ore Mountains (Erzgebirge) near Altenberg in eastern Germany stand as mute testimony to the environmental costs of industrialization. (T. M. Poulsen.)

air for extensive periods. The total amount of such materials fed into Europe's atmosphere at any one time, however, has never reached the magnitude of dust and gases that come into the air from the periodic eruptions of such volcanoes as Etna and Vesuvius in southern Italy. Even the explosion of Krakatoa in far-off Indonesia provided sufficient dust particles over Europe to give it spectacular sunsets for several years afterward. However, while controlling naturally occurring volcanic emissions seems impossible (if even desirable), control of human created emissions is both feasible and necessary.

Several European states have taken strong measures to reduce air pollution. The banning of soft coal as a domestic fuel in London in the period following World War II has led to a remarkable clearing of its atmosphere. Winter sunshine has increased by 70 percent and visibility by 300 percent. The number of foggy days has significantly declined, and it has been possible to clean the facades of buildings and brighten the appearance of the city in what formerly would have been an exercise in futility. Now even the skies over the Ruhr and Saxony are often blue rather than gray from perpetual smog.

Europe's terrain has also felt the effects of industrialization. Particularly evident are huge accumulations of waste materials piled up at coal-mining sites and slag heaps of smelting operations (Fig. 2-18). Some 150,000 acres (about 61,000 hectares) of Britain are now such derelict land. These are not only unsightly, but they can also be a serious threat to adjacent settlements. At Aberfan in Wales, for example, rain-saturated coal-mining wastes descended on a school and part of the town in 1966, taking the lives of 144 persons. Destruction of biotic resources, accelerated erosion from hiking trails, and similar depredations have also resulted from an extension of settlements into

FIGURE 2-18 Coal slag heaps near Arras in northeastern France. These hills are the result of decades of accumulation of rocks brought to the surface in the mining of rich beds of underground coal. (T. M. Poulsen.)

Europe's farthest reaches by the ubiquitous erection of weekend houses.

Water Pollution The modernization of Europe has introduced profound changes in its water bodies. Urban and industrial wastes have long been introduced into streams without treatment. Although the wastes of more than 80 percent of the inhabitants of the Netherlands and Germany are now treated, less than 10 percent of the population of Belgium and Portugal are served by sewage-treatment facilities.

The commercialization of farming has also contributed to the decline of water quality. The increasing dedication to a single crop tilled by machines in large fields has led to greater erosion, which culminates in increased stream siltation. The replacement of animal manures by chemical fertilizers has added new contaminants to water bodies, particularly phosphorus and nitrogen. These have stimulated the growth of algae and other forms of plant life that have robbed streams of their oxygen, causing a condition known as eutrophication, so that higher plants and fish life can no longer exist in these waters.

Europe's rivers and seas have been beset by a number of hazardous waste spills that have immediately destroyed wildlife and may well have long-term negative effects. An accidental discharge of chemicals into the Rhine in Switzerland in the early 1980s caused substantial damage down to the river's mouth. In 1967 more than 117,000 tons (106,000 metric tons) of crude oil were discharged into the English Channel when the ship *Torrey Canyon* went aground. A decade later the sinking of the *Amoco Cadiz* off France led to a spill almost twice as great.

Political Factors in Pollution Control

The fragmentation of Europe among more than two dozen rather small states poses significant problems for pollution control. As a general rule, the sources of pollution affecting an area are just as likely to be in a neighboring country as in its home state. European boundaries cut across river basins and prevailing wind patterns.

It has been a challenge for the Europeans to develop a coordinated assault on environmental degradation. Governments in Western Europe have traditionally been concerned about maintaining full employment. They have been reluctant to interfere with the economic process by adding costs and regulatory handicaps for producers. A dependence on the production of goods for export abroad increases the problem. Unilateral decisions that require expensive antipollution equipment, for instance, would place industries at a competitive disadvantage with those of neighboring states, especially when it is likely that the neighbors would benefit most from such measures.

Nevertheless, substantial strides have been made in reducing environmental damage. This progress can be attributed to the citizenry's concern about the quality of life, particularly as Europeans became more affluent in the postwar decades. By the mid-1970s more than 20,000 environmentalist groups had been formed in Western Europe. Some of these, like the Green party in Germany, have developed significant political power bases. These groups have pressured their governments to tackle sources of pollution at home and to develop international agreements. One reflection of this pressure is the establishment of more than 30 international commissions in Western Europe to deal with transboundary environmental problems.

A general environmental protection policy has emerged for the area of the European Union (EU). With the increasing socioeconomic integration of this bloc, member states are required to agree on a common policy in order to avoid unfair competitive advantages that would arise from national variations in environmental regulations.

Private industry itself is finding that sound managerial personnel and skilled workers are more important factors in profitable operation than proximity to raw materials or access to markets. To attract such people requires the availability of environmental amenities, in addition to good housing and educational opportunities. This new approach has encouraged the location of new industrial sites in hitherto unspoiled rural areas, and has slowed the concentration of population and pollution. It has also led to a concern for cleaning up the environment in older regions, notably Germany's Ruhr area.

Special Problems of the Former Socialist Countries

The East European states under communist regimes found it much more difficult to respond to the environmental threat created by their industrialization. These countries apparently had advantages over their market-economy counterparts with regard to environmental protection, because their governments owned title to virtually all lands and industrial facilities. However, their emphasis on rapid industrialization often put them on a collision course with environmental needs. Enterprise managers were all too aware that they would be judged primarily by meeting production quotas. Antipollution devices depend on scarce capital and usually retard productivity. As a result, after World War II these countries suffered from far worse environmental problems than did their Western neighbors.

The highly centralized government management of Eastern economies created special difficulties. A recurring theme in discussions of their situation was the overlapping authority of administrative agencies and their consequent lack of responsibility for meeting problems of air and water pollution and regulating land use. Another factor was the lack of organized public pressure on generators of pollution, although the involvement of a growing number of people in environmental movements increased in the last years before the demise of the communist systems in 1990.

Transborder problems of atmospheric and water pollution also beset the socialist countries. However, the former Council for Mutual Economic Assistance (CMEA) developed no overall environmental policy comparable to that established in the EC/EU. Unlike Western Europe, mutual trade was not between competitive enterprises, but between governmental import/export monopolies based on negotiated quotas. No trade advantages accrued as a result of differences in regulatory laws, as occurred in the West. When these countries did tackle environmental problems, it was by bilateral agreements between states.

Whereas many environmental problems remain throughout Europe, there is increasing recognition of the dangers they pose and substantial amelioration has occurred, especially in Western Europe. A cleanup of the UK's rivers has resulted, for example, in the reappearance of salmon in the Thames after an absence of more than a century. Throughout the Mediterranean region, forests have been planted in areas of ancient land destruction and more recently abandoned farms. Most countries have set aside some of their remaining wildlands as permanent nature preserves. Open-pit mining has been accompanied by the construction of new recreation areas in the exploited lands through leveling and tree planting. Even old areas with disturbed landscapes, such as the coal-mining valleys of Wales, have been rehabilitated and rejuvenated. Europe is becoming "green" again.

BIBLIOGRAPHY

Ager, D. V. (1980). *The Geology of Europe.* London: McGraw-Hill.

Brady, G. L., and J. C. Selle. (1985). "Acid Rain: The International Response." *International Journal of Environmental Studies* 24 (3/4): 217–230.

Brückner, H. (1986). "Man's Impact on the Evolution of the Physical Environment in the Mediterranean Region in Historical Times." *GeoJournal* 13: 7–17.

Chandler, T. J. (1965). *The Climate of London.* London: Hutchinson.

Goudie, A. (1982). *The Human Impact (Man's Role in Environmental Change).* Cambridge, Mass.: MIT Press.

Goudie, A. (1990). *The Landforms of England and Wales.* Cambridge, Mass.: Blackwell.

Hardisty, J. (1990). *The British Seas: An Introduction to the Oceanography and Resources of the North-West European Continental Shelf.* London: Routledge.

Izac, A.M.N. (1985). "Conflicts of Interest in International Environmental Policies: The Case of Transfrontier Pollution in Europe." *International Journal of Environmental Studies* 26 (1/2): 33–42.

Jones, E. L. (1981). *The European Miracle: Environments, Economies, and Geopolitics in the History of Europe and East Asia.* Cambridge: Cambridge University Press.

Wagret, P. (1972). *Polderlands.* New York: Barnes & Noble.

3

POPULATION

Europe's population is far more diverse than popularly conceived. Scores of languages are spoken, some of which are thriving and others, such as Sorbish, which appear to be disappearing. Some languages have ancient Asiatic roots (Hungarian and Finnish), and one, Basque, has entirely unknown origins. Though largely Christian, millions of Europeans profess other religions, including Islam, or belong to a variety of Christian sects, from Lutheran in the north to Orthodox in the southeast. Cultural and socioeconomic conditions also result in widely varying demographic characteristics among Europeans. In short, a "European" is not necessarily a Caucasian Christian; she may be a Jew with Mediterranean roots or a Hungarian with ancient ties to Asia—or he could be an African immigrant.

This chapter introduces the population of Europe in terms of its origins and distribution, density, age structure, demographics, growth, and culture, including language, religion, and leisure activities. It not only provides the basic facts, but also goes beyond the numbers to explain and interpret distributions of people, their changes

through time, and the cultural traits that both unite and divide them. In addition, it shows the relationship of aspects of population to factors such as Europe's physical environment, government policies, and regional conflicts.

POPULATION DISTRIBUTION

Historical Overview of European Peoples

Europe's population has always been characterized by divisions and contrasts resulting from the ebb and flow of groups that gain supremacy in a place, then expand into new territories, only eventually to fade from view. This drama was first performed some 1.5 million years ago as ancestral humanoids, *Homo erectus*, made their entrance onto the European stage. These early humanoids lived a very primitive existence, although they did make crude stone tools, use fire (from 400,000 B.C.), and live in semipermanent structures (from 150,000 B.C.). They held sway until they were replaced by another group, *Homo sapiens*, also known as Neanderthal, around 75,000 B.C. These "almost humans" advanced toolmaking but were in turn overrun by true humans, *Homo sapiens sapiens*, at this stage called Cro-Magnon, about 35,000 B.C. This time frame encompasses most of the Pleistocene, a geologic period dominated in Europe by glaciers that covered its northern and Alpine regions during at least four major advances. Because of the harsh environmental conditions, settlement during this time was restricted to the warmer, more southerly portions of Europe.

About 9000 B.C., the glaciers began their final retreat as the climate in Europe warmed. Human habitation expanded in kind; soon (about 5000 B.C.) humans were farming rich loess soils and keeping animals. They also began fashioning tools, weapons, and other items out of metals. First was

copper, used from about 4000 B.C.; then bronze, an alloy of copper and tin, from 2500 B.C.; and finally iron from 1000 B.C.

These metal ages overlap with the rise of classical European civilizations, whose original roots derived from civilizations in the eastern Mediterranean. From their beginnings in and around the Aegean from 3200 B.C., Minoan, Mycenaean, and the several Greek civilizations spread their influence around the Mediterranean and Black seas and beyond. Early civilizations also developed on the Italian peninsula. First came the Etruscans (530 B.C.), followed by the Romans, who, from their initial expansions in the fourth century B.C., built an empire that, by the third century A.D., encompassed all of Europe south of the Rhine and Danube rivers and included what is now most of England (Fig. 3-1), as well as territory in Africa and Asia. However, the demise of the western portion

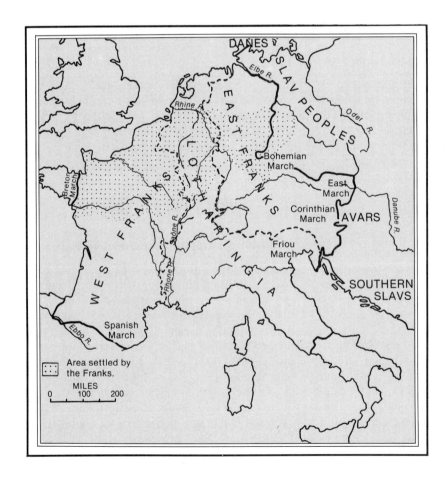

FIGURE 3-1 The division of the Roman Empire in A.D. 395. Imperial capitals are named.

of the Roman Empire in the fifth century led to a shift of power east to Constantinople and the Byzantine Empire at the end of the classical period.

Even at their greatest extent, however, these civilizations controlled only a fraction of the entire European continent. Territory beyond the spheres of classical Europe was inhabited by what Romans and Greeks called "barbarian" tribes and their kingdoms. "Barbarians" were foreigners, people beyond the pale of what was considered civilization by the Greeks and Romans, though, in fact, these peoples had themselves often developed relatively complex and successful cultures that were not well understood in the classical world. The Celts were the most important of these tribes; their origins are generally placed sometime in the second millennium B.C. in West Central Europe. They soon spread across much of Central and Western

Europe into the British Isles, bringing with them their metal-working abilities, burial rites, farming technique, and hill fort construction. Other, often Asian, tribes, such as Huns, Ostrogoths, Vandals, and Visigoths, captured much of Central, Western, and Southern Europe during the third to fifth centuries A.D. The fifth to eleventh centuries saw the movement of such peoples as Avars, originally from Mongolia, into Central Europe; Slavs pushed further westward and into Southeastern Europe; Lombards into the Italian peninsula; Angles and Saxons into the British Isles; Magyars (Hungarians) into Central Europe; Balts across much of Northeastern Europe; and Nordic peoples, collectively called Vikings, into coastal areas of Western Europe, the British Isles, and on to Iceland and Greenland (Fig. 3-2). Although significant movements of people continue to this day, the major

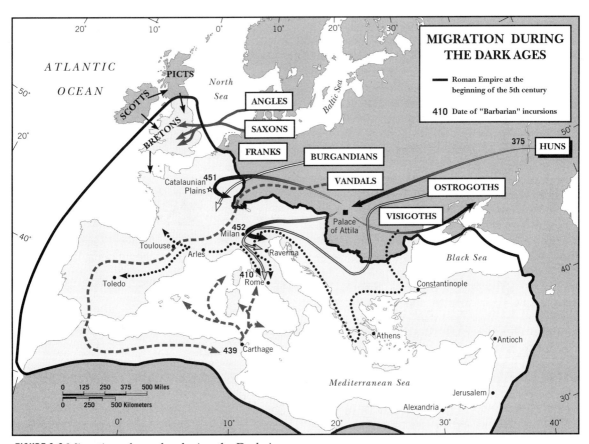

FIGURE 3-2 Migration of peoples during the Dark Ages.

ethnic composition of Europe as we know it was largely in place by about A.D. 1000.

European Population Totals and Distribution

Establishing accurate population figures is always problematic, especially for early time periods. Although figures cannot be determined with any accuracy, the population of Europe for the first million or so years of habitation no doubt fluctuated widely, but probably remained less than 100,000. By the dawn of the historic period around 4000 B.C., the figure jumped to 6.2 million, which would have constituted just over 20 percent of the earth's total at the time. Europe's population experienced periods of growth and decline—both relative and absolute—over the next 6000 years. By A.D. 1, Europe's estimated population of 33 million would have represented about 16 percent of the world's total. The population then generally declined with the fading Roman Empire, so that by A.D. 600 Europe contained only about 18 million, or 6 percent of the planet's total inhabitants. Another period of population growth pushed the totals to 70 million (16%) by 1340, but the Black Death, which arrived in Europe in 1348, together with various wars devastated the population. The numbers then recovered, reaching 100 million (18%) by 1650, 270 million (23%) by 1850, and 392 million (25%) by 1900.

For the twentieth century, the definition of the territorial boundaries of Europe becomes critical to population estimates. The issue concerns whether to include in the population counts the former USSR, and if so, just how much of it. Traditionally, Europe has been defined as the territory west of the Ural Mountains, which would thereby include the most populous portion of Russia, plus Ukraine, Belarus, Moldova, and the Baltic states. However, the Transcaucasus and Central Asian republics of the former USSR would be excluded. Another problem concerns Turkey. Traditionally, only the European portion of Turkey, defined as Istanbul and the rest of the territory lying west of the Bosphorus (eastern Thrace), is included. Finally, the definition of Europe also usually includes Malta and Iceland. Of course, a more restrictive

definition of Europe would not include any portion of the former USSR or, perhaps, any part of Turkey, Iceland, or Malta. Using the most inclusive definition, we can say that Europe in 1930 held 500 million people, 25 percent of the world population; 550 million (21%) by 1950; and 620 million (16%) by 1970. In the mid-1990s the population of Europe stood at well over 700 million (13%), including the European part of the former USSR; the total is 509 million (9.5%) excluding all portions of the former Soviet Union.

The internal distribution of European population (Table 3-1) still reflects the carrying capacity of the land, determined by physical environmental factors and existing technology, despite the fact that the great majority of Europe's population no longer lives on farms. As in other parts of the world, the geographic distribution of societies' infrastructure and economic activities has evolved in close association with agriculture. Our "post-agricultural" society is still very much shaped by the earlier impacts of the distribution of agricultural production, as well as the residential preferences of people for many of the same regions where agriculture is possible.

Two thousand years ago, Southern Europe was relatively more important in terms of European population than today, and ECSEE (East Central and Southeastern Europe) was relatively less important. Changes during the two millennia

TABLE 3-1

EUROPEAN REGIONS' PERCENTAGE OF EUROPEAN POPULATION

Region	A.D.1	1992
Southern Europe	50	16
Western Europe	20	12
East Central and Southeastern Europe	18	49
West Central Europe	10	11
British Isles	1	9
Northern Europe	1	3

reflect a reduction in geographical differences in the availability of technology and, probably, a greater reflection of underlying physical-environmental factors in determining the spatial distribution of population at the macro-scale. Of course, at the micro-scale, Europe's population is now far more concentrated than earlier within cities, most of which, however, also developed in association with support from surrounding agricultural regions.

Determining the most populous country of Europe is also complicated by the definition adopted for its territorial boundaries. At 147.5 million people, the Russian Federation is one of the most populous countries in the world; even the population of its European territory makes it by far Europe's most populous country. The top 10 European countries by population contain about 75 percent of the region's population and include countries from virtually all parts of it (Table 3-2).

TABLE 3-2

EUROPEAN POPULATION, BY COUNTRY, 1995

	Total (millions)	Percent of European Total
EUROPE	729	100
Russia	148	20 (about 3/4 west of Urals)
Germany	82	11
United Kingdom	59	8
France	58	8
Italy	58	8
Ukraine	52	7
Spain	39	5
Poland	39	5
Romania	23	3
Netherlands	16	2
Subtotal	544	75

Source: Population Reference Bureau.

Population Densities

Historically, as noted earlier, population or settlement density has been closely related to various physical geographic factors. Terrain has an obvious influence: flat plains allow much higher densities than mountains, both because of the purely physical constraints of building on steep ground, but also because of the difficulty of growing or transporting food in rugged country. Soil quality also has been an important factor. Areas with well-drained, nutrient-rich soils, typically found in valley floors, have long provided more desirable settlement locations. Finally, climate plays a part in population density. The climatic extremes of hot, cold, or dry have been avoided in preference of more moderate climes. Even the amount of sunlight can play a part in where people live: in the Alps, there is a distinct preference for the sunny, south-facing sides of valleys as opposed to the dark, north-facing sides.

In more modern times, population distribution (Fig. 3-3) has been more closely tied to the availability of industrial resources and jobs, although, as noted earlier, the location of major industrial concentrations has itself been influenced by population concentrations and infrastructure developed when societies were largely dominated by agriculture. The most densely populated portions of Europe are therefore found in a belt extending from the Donets Basin of Ukraine to the Netherlands, with the Rhine, Po, Rhone, and Thames valleys also containing high concentrations of people. These areas have a combination of agricultural and industrial resources, as well as good market accessibility. Local population concentrations are particularly influenced by access to coal (e.g., Silesia), a combination of rich soils and access to market (e.g., Holland in the western Netherlands), or both (e.g., the Cologne and Ruhr basins of northwestern Germany).

Disregarding the so-called microstates (e.g., Monaco), the five most densely populated countries of Europe are (in persons per square kilometer; European average, 105): Netherlands (446), Belgium (330), United Kingdom (236), Germany (220), and Italy (193). The roles of temperate climate and the self-reinforcing benefits of access to

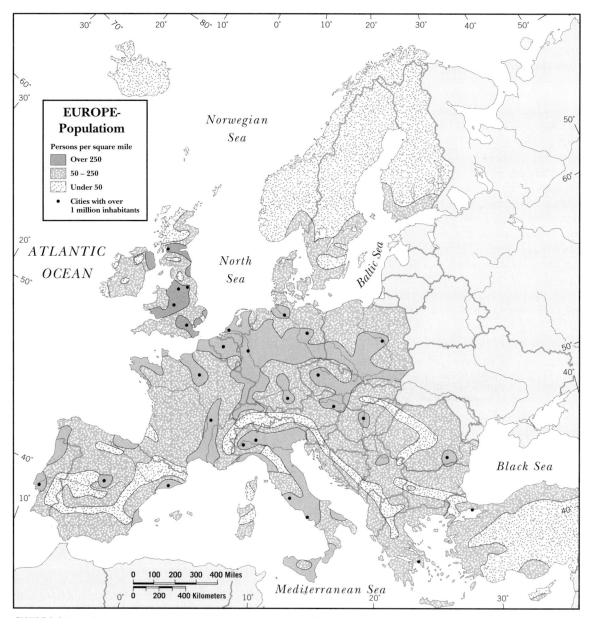

FIGURE 3-3 Population densities in Europe excluding the FSU.

the populous, prosperous Northwest European market are important factors in explaining high population densities in the region. The five least densely populated countries of Europe are all more poorly located in the north and have less temperate climates: Iceland (2.5 people per square kilometer), Norway (13), Finland (15), Sweden (20), and Estonia (35).

EUROPEAN DEMOGRAPHICS

Demographics deals with rates of population change. People are born, they die, and in between they often move. Birth, death, and migration rates, usually expressed per 1000 population, provide valuable insight into the growth and decline of populations. Similarly, demographic rates are closely connected to overall changes in economic development, urbanization, and government policy.

The Demographic Transition Model

One convenient way of analyzing demographic conditions is through the demographic transition model. This model relates birth and death rates through time to illustrate how populations grow by way of natural increase, the difference between the two. Impacts of net migration on **total** population change (natural population growth plus net migration) will also be discussed here. The model has five stages as generalized in Figure 3-4. (Note that in actuality birth and death rates always vary somewhat from the smooth lines depicted on the diagram.) In the first stage, both birth and death rates are relatively high, reflecting a predominantly rural, agricultural population and low levels of medical technology. During this stage, characteristic of primitive societies, the difference between the birth and death rates is slight, so there is little natural increase. The second stage is characterized by falling death rates, produced by improvements in sanitation, medical care, better food, and increased life expectancy. During this stage, birth rates remain at their previously high level, the result being greater natural increase and, most probably, total population growth. Many countries in the developing world are currently in this stage.

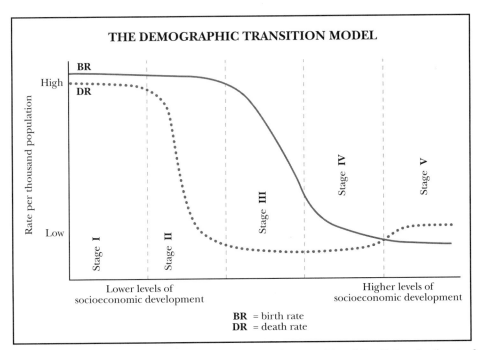

FIGURE 3-4 Diagram of the hypothesized "demographic transition." Declining death rates lead to soaring natural population growth rates in stage II, but growth drops to low or even negative levels after birth rates fall beginning in stage III.

Because of factors such as increased levels of education and urbanization, higher female labor participation rates, establishment of formal retirement programs, greater availability of contraception, and later marriages, birth rates also begin to drop during the third stage. This trend leads to a lowering of the rate of natural increase. Birth, death, and natural increase rates eventually achieve a steady state at low levels in stage four. Most developed countries are in this stage of the demographic transition model. In some countries, death rates can begin to rise, even surpassing birth rates and, thus, herald a fifth stage characterized by population decrease. Rising death rates can come about because of an aging population, increased young adult deaths owing to industrial and auto accidents, and increased incidence of terminal diseases related to health-threatening lifestyles (e.g., smoking, heavy drinking, and consuming foods with high levels of fat).

Of course, reality rarely duplicates the predictions of models such as demographic transition, and so the actual demographic histories of European countries only approximate this kind of neat pattern. Figure 3-5 presents graphs of the birth and death rates for Sweden, France, and Hungary over the past 100 to 200 years. Several interesting aspects emerge from them.

The graph for Sweden shows a fairly typical—albeit more complicated—pattern of stages 2–4 of the demographic transition model. From 1810 to 1820, death rates drop substantially, while birth rates continue at their high level. Birth rates, after a spike in 1860 related to improved maternal health, then drop quickly to 1870 and drop again from 1920 to 1930. Both rates level off during the 1960s but then rise slightly afterward. This rise is especially evident in birth rates, owing, no doubt, to the direct and indirect pronatalist policies adopted by the Scandinavian governments over the past two decades.

The pattern for France illustrates the impact of war on demographic rates. Overall, both birth and death rates drop in tandem over the time frame. However, there are important peaks in the death rate around 1870 and 1940, corresponding to the Franco-Prussian War and World War II. Similarly, birth rates tend to rise sharply after wars, as is the

case in France with the peaks in the 1920s and 1950s "baby booms."

The experience of Hungary illustrates the meteoric declines of both birth and death rates following the 1867 compromise with Austria, which led to political autonomy for Hungary, and were contemporaneous with improved health care, industrialization, and fairly rapid urban development focused on Budapest. The birth rate stabilized at a fairly low level after 1960. However, because of many factors, chief among them increased industrial accidents, disease, alcoholism, and suicide, death rates surpassed birth rates in the early 1980s, and so Hungary is now registering a natural decrease of population. An aged population and a disinclination for children have also helped generate negative population growth rates at times in Germany. Apparently the result of both poor health habits, such as excessive smoking and drinking, poor environmental and working conditions, and increased stress from unsettled political and economic conditions, death rates have been rising in Russia.

Demographic rates can also reveal other aspects of a country, such as the impact of government policy. For example, shortly after taking power, Nicolae Ceausescu banned abortion and all forms of contraception in Romania. Consequently, the birth rate in the country rose from 14.3 births per thousand in 1966 to 27.4 in 1967. Similarly, pronatalist incentives in the German Democractic Republic in the mid-1970s led to an immediate and substantial increase in the birth rate, which, despite a slow and steady decline, remained above West German rates until a 65-percent drop in the birth rate was precipitated in the east by reunification in 1990. The decline can be traced to a severe economic recession and many people's sense of insecurity and disorientation. Birth rates have also fallen about 50 percent in Russia, the apparent result of highly unfavorable economic conditions and related political uncertainty.

Since birth and death rates are commonly quite low for developed countries, rates of natural increase in European countries are some of the lowest in the world. At 19.0 per thousand or 1.9 percent, Albania has by far the highest rate of natural increase in Europe, but Iceland (1.06%), Ire-

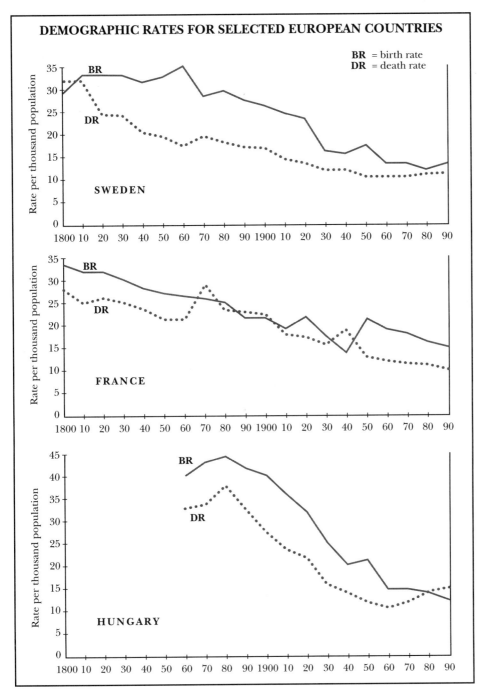

FIGURE 3-5 Demographic transition in sample countries. Clearly, demographic histories vary from country to country. Sweden best illustrates the generalized pattern of "demographic transition."

land (0.60%), Belarus (0.49%), France (0.41%), and Lithuania (0.41%) also have high rates by European standards. Germany and Austria, owing both to low fertility rates (the propensity of child-bearing age women to have children) and to related aged populations, have frequently had negative rates of natural increase in recent years. In Germany this has been enhanced by the extreme drop in the birth rate in the east noted earlier. Similar drops in birth rates have occurred in other parts of ECSEE in the 1990s. Several other countries, including Spain, Portugal, Italy, Greece, Bulgaria, and Denmark, have birth rates that barely exceed death rates. This reflects an especially dramatic demographic transition in Southern and Southeastern Europe, where into the early postwar era rates of natural increase were relatively high by European standards. Several of these countries have very large Roman Catholic populations, which in the past were far more influenced by the de facto pronatalist position of the Church than is currently the case. Different cultural traditions in Europe do remain quite influential in other regards—for example, in Greece only about 2 percent of births occure outside of wedlock, compared to 45 percent in Denmark.

Migration

Migration refers to the movement of people—temporary or permanent. Four distinct types of migration can be discussed: *emigration*, in this case movement out of Europe; *intracontinental migration*, movement from one country to another within Europe; *internal migration*, movement within a country; and *immigration*, movement into Europe from outside the continent. Migration is driven by two sets of factors: "push" factors and "pull" factors. Push factors include relative overpopulation (population exceeding the local carrying capacity of the land), political instability, famine, lack of job opportunities, and political repression. Availability of fertile land, political and religious freedom, and economic opportunity have long acted as pull factors. Improvements in transportation and communication have also been important in facilitating the movement of people.

Emigration Migration of people out of Europe traditionally has been dominated by movement to North America and Australia. For example, the Irish potato famine of the 1840s led to more than 1 million individuals leaving for North America, while another 800,000 died; after 150 years of growth, the population of Ireland (including Northern Ireland) is still only 62 percent of its 1841 population of 8.1 million, in part because emigration of young people from Ireland remains a notable trend. Over the period 1865–1900, some 1.4 million Scandinavians left for the United States, while the period 1850–1920 saw 15.9 million British and Irish, 8.6 million Italians, 4.3 million Germans, 2.3 million people from the Austro-Hungarian Empire, and 1.4 million Portuguese leave Europe. In part, these massive movements resulted from population pressures in the source regions caused by large differences between birth and death rates during stages 2 and 3 of their demographic transitions. Following World War II, large numbers of Britons, Germans, Italians, Spaniards, and Portuguese left Europe; Jewish emigration to Israel also was significant. By about 1970, however, large-scale European emigration had come to a close.

Intracontinental Migration During this century, wars, border changes, and treaty agreements have resulted in the movement of some 33 million people within the European continent. For example, in the 1920s the Treaty of Trianon broke up the Austro-Hungarian (Habsburg) Empire following World War I, thereby creating Czechoslovakia and Yugoslavia, and drastically reducing the size of Hungary. This treaty led to many thousands of people moving across the new borders. Similarly, many Turks and Greeks traded places across the new borders of Turkey, Greece, and Bulgaria, as they were redrawn following the Balkan Wars of 1912 and 1913.

The greatest intracontinental movements, however, are associated with World War II. First, Hitler "called home" some 600,000 ethnic Germans who had previously settled in the territory of Poland, Czechoslovakia, Hungary, Romania, the

Baltic States, and Italy. Then, millions of people—mainly Jews, but also Gypsies and various religious, political, and minority groups—were forced into concentration camps during the war, where millions of them perished (see Inset 3-1). Following the war, 9 million Germans were forced out of Poland along with another 3 million from Czechoslovakia. Finns also had to move following border changes with the USSR.

In the 1960s and 1970s millions of young men, often later followed by their families, moved from Southern to Central and Western Europe. These foreign, or "guest," workers and their families frequently returned to their native countries, but millions have not, resulting in large "foreign" populations within Central and West European countries. In 1995 over 2 million such workers and a total of about 7 million such people lived in Germany, about half of them from Turkey and the former Yugoslavia. Many of these people are second-generation, some even third-generation, German residents and face difficulties integrating into either German or their "native" societies, in part because of stark cultural differences (e.g., between Islam on the one hand, and European Christian and secular traditions on the other) and related xenophobic discrimination. There are also large "foreign" populations in other European states, particularly when one calculates them as a percentage of the native born. Thus, for example, Switzerland and Luxembourg have particularly large "guest worker" components within their resident populations—foreign residents represent over 26 percent of Luxembourg's population. Foreign residents make up large components of other countries' populations as well (notably, 9% in Belgium, 8% in Germany, 7% in France, 4% in the Netherlands, and 3% in the UK).

The evolving EU is also allowing, often encouraging, larger numbers of citizens of member states to live, work, and study in a country other than their native one. For example, it appears that large numbers of Irish citizens are taking advantage of their right to work on the numerous construction projects scattered across eastern Germany. And estimates indicate that by the late 1980s there were already about 250,000 nonnatives who were living in retirement in Spain. Increasing numbers of students are visiting or studying full-time outside their home countries. All of these flows of people seem to be increasing and will likely also result in more young people finding work, spouses, and residences outside their land of birth.

The early 1990s has also been another period of significant population movement within the borders of Europe brought on by the political changes taking place in the countries of the former Soviet Union and ECSEE. For example, between 1990 and 1995 an estimated 1.5 million people sought asylum in Germany alone, most of them from Eastern Europe. In addition, another 1.65 million people "resettled" to Germany. These people are descendants of German emigrants who have a constitutional right to German residence, financial support, and citizenship. Inflows of migrants in both categories are now declining as a result of stricter rules regarding the right to enter Germany in order to seek asylum, as a result of declining numbers of "expatriate" Germans eligible to resettle, and as a result of German aid to countries like Russia to help remaining "expatriates" there and reduce the migrant flows to Germany itself. There have been much smaller but still notable flows of asylum seekers in recent years to France, Switzerland, Sweden, and Austria. In the latter three cases, applicants per thousand population have sometimes exceeded German rates, particularly in Switzerland. Flows in absolute and relative terms have been lowest to Spain and Portugal. Large variations among countries in rates of arrival of asylum seekers clearly indicate the difficulty countries have in distinguishing between people primarily seeking asylum and those more concerned about economic opportunity. Governments and "native" residents have some level of concern and sympathy for people in both categories, although migrants seeking economic opportunity pose a potential and perceived threat to, for example, the unemployed and generate serious financial and political issues in the countries where they try to settle.

About 700,000 people have fled the former Yugoslavia alone, with more than one-half settling in Germany and about 50,000 each in Italy, Austria, and Sweden. The potential for vast movements of people westward from the former Soviet

"ETHNIC TERROR" AND THE HOLOCAUST

The ethnically based hatred and atrocities that have become so evident in the complex wars of the 1990s in the former Yugoslavia echo even more horrifying, similar events in recent European history. Owing largely or exclusively to their ethnic identification, in recent decades people have in several instances been targeted for death by states. During World War I an estimated 600,000 Armenians perished as the direct or indirect result of the policies of the Turkish-dominated Ottoman Empire. During 1932–1933 an estimated 8 million Ukrainians died in a famine that many people believe was purposely engineered by the Soviet government under Josef Stalin to break the political resistance of Ukrainians, who often supported Ukrainian nationalism and resisted collectivization of agriculture.

It will probably be years before even rough, reliable estimates can be made of the number of people who have died owing to ethnic hatred and atrocity in the former Yugoslavia. The number likely reaches the tens of thousands and may be even larger. Deaths alone also do not indicate the extent of physical and emotional suffering endured by millions of people directly affected by the most recent inferno in the Balkans. This human tragedy is itself an echo of a greater calamity that befell the population of Yugoslavia during World War II, when hundreds of thousands of people perished—largely ethnic Serbs who died at the hands of a Croatian-led regime in alliance with the occupying Nazis. To the extent that Serbs have been responsible for "ethnic terror" in the former Yugoslavia, the role of revenge is an important factor in understanding, though certainly not justifying, what has happened.

As catastrophic as the politically and ethnically based human tragedies mentioned here have been, some people believe that Nazi Germany's ruthless attempt to annihilate European Jewry is "unique" in the annals of human atrocity. Indeed, 6 million Jewish men, women, and children were murdered by the Nazis within dozens of death camps spread across its large and brutal empire and as the result of countless other acts of inhumanity. In addition, hundreds of thousands of other members of different population groups—including homosexuals, Gypsies, and the mentally handicapped—were also murdered. Millions more died from deprivation in forced labor camps and in occupied or besieged territories (such as Leningrad/St. Petersburg), not to mention the millions who died as combatants during World War II. In 1941, in one single action alone, an estimated 10,000 Jews were shot and buried in mass graves near the Ukrainian settlement of Babi Yar outside Kiev. In other cases, hundreds of civilians in Nazi-occupied territories were randomly gathered up and shot in retribution for resistance to German aggression. Most "Holocaust" victims, however, perished in carefully planned camps where the preselected, usually Jewish, inmates often suffered greatly before their death.

The Nazis invented a new, arguably "unique" way to mete out its terror. "The Holocaust was not a throwback to medieval torture or archaic barbarism but a thoroughly modern expression of bureaucratic organization, industrial management, scientific achievement, and technological sophistication. The entire apparatus of the German bureaucracy was marshalled in the service of the extermination process" (President's Commission, 1979). Physicians and scientists, investors and business owners/managers, soldiers, and lowly state employees were enticed, coerced, and led to carry out the mass murder. The process was so cold-blooded that great effort was expended to reduce costs per murder, and those who carried out their chosen or assigned tasks in retrospect seldom accept any personal responsibility for the deaths of the millions of noncombatants. The sole officially penitent party has been the central government of the Federal Republic of Germany. The German Democratic Republic, "East" Germany, abjured any blame or responsibility. Heated politically and emotionally charged debates continue over the extent of blame that might be placed on other governments and institutions, such as the Western Allies, *Vichy* France, and the Roman Catholic Church, either for failing to aid the victims or even for collaborating with the Nazis in what many view as humankind's most savage act.

Words cannot describe the enormity of the suffering associated with the madness of Nazi Germany's "ethnic terror." The act decimated

Europe's Jewish population and probably forever changed the relationship between Jews and non-Jews and interrelationships among the ethnically and religiously diverse peoples of the "Near East," to which many Holocaust survivors fled and where they helped to found the state of Israel.

Relatively few people have been called before the law to account for their role in the Holocaust, and some of the guilty show no remorse for their actions. Despite the enormity and inhumanity of the Holocaust, the ethnically motivated and rationalized murders in the former Yugoslavia lead one to wonder if and when all of Europe and the world will discover and cherish life and the very meaning of humanity.

Union to Germany has been one of the primary motivating factors for Germany to take the leading role in providing and seeking economic assistance for the struggling post-Soviet economies. Another factor is Germany's sense of duty to help them, deriving from Nazi Germany's devastation of East Central Europe and the former Soviet Union from 1939 to 1945.

Internal migration The main flow of internal migration in Europe during the past two centuries has been from rural to urban areas. This flow is associated with a change in the labor force from agricultural to manufacturing employment. This process has been especially pronounced in the post–World War II era in ECSEE and the former USSR, where rapid expansion of urban industrial jobs in the period attracted thousands of workers to cities. The temporal process of urbanization in Bulgaria provides an instructive example (Fig. 3-6). During the early era of postwar industrial expansion, there was a high rate of net urban inmigration. Since

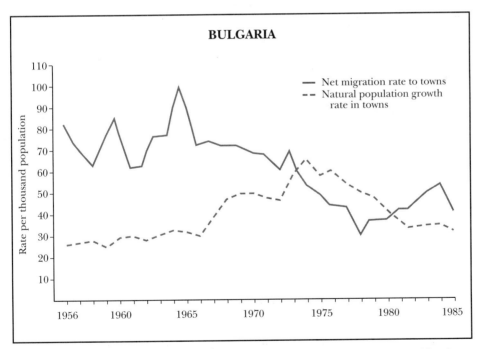

FIGURE 3-6 Population change in Bulgarian settlements, 1956–1985. As indicated by this case, in migration first fuels a wave of urban population growth, followed by a second era characterized by the increasing importance of natural growth, as young immigrants start families. (After material provided by the Institute of Geography, Bulgarian Academy of Sciences, et al.)

migrants almost everywhere tend to be young adults, this generated subsequent, relatively high rates of natural increase in cities (especially 1970–1980) as the young people formed families. As net migration rates subsided, so did both natural and total population growth rates. These stages of urban growth (an era of strong net inmigration; a later, less dramatic era dominated by local natural population increase; and, eventually, a period with a reduced rate of population growth) form a common pattern for cities in Europe, the United States, and elsewhere. How large a city ultimately becomes generally depends on the length (or number of) the net inmigration period(s). From 1861 to 1901, for example, net migration to Paris was so great that, not only did it become a large city, but also 96 percent of all French population growth during those four decades took place within it.

In much of Western Europe, rural-urban migration streams have all but subsided; now, urban-urban, urban-suburban, and even urban-rural movements sometimes predominate. During the 1970s, in particular, many highly economically developed countries and regions experienced patterns of deconcentration—net movement of people away from densely populated metropolitan regions toward less densely settled regions. It is likely that forces favoring concentration of population in metropolitan regions may interact in years to come with forces favoring deconcentration to generate alternating patterns of population concentration and deconcentration. On the one hand, people move to or stay in cities, for example, because of job opportunities created by the advantages of spatially concentrated economic activities (agglomeration economies) and the allure of urban social-cultural amenities. On the other hand, the attractiveness of more pristine and pleasant physical environments in the countryside, in the mountains, and on the seashore draw people away from cities. The nonurban residential preferences are options for large numbers of retirees and locationally unconstrained workers such as artists and consultants.

Subnational trends in total population growth in Europe have shifted and will shift through time.

During the 1980s, regions with relatively favorable economic or environmental conditions grew most rapidly (e.g., southern England, the south coasts of Spain and France, and portions of the Alps), while population losses were recorded in economically depressed (as well as sometimes environmentally damaged) industrialized and rural areas (e.g., the southern German Democratic Republic, northern areas in western Germany, parts of southern Scotland and northern England, northern Norway and Sweden, western Portugal and Bulgaria, and rural Greece). In the 1990s such losses may continue in large areas of the war-ravaged Yugoslavia.

Despite the apparent emphasis in this discussion on the geographic mobility of European peoples, available data on the residential mobility of West Europeans indicate that, in fact, they are only about one-half as likely to move in a given year as people in the United States, Canada, Australia, or New Zealand. From the American prespective, Europeans often exhibit a striking preference to live near family and the places where they were born and raised. Europeans are struck by Americans' apparent indifference to such ties. The differences reflect variations in both cultural and economic characteristics of American and European societies.

Immigration The post–World War II economic boom in many West European countries led to labor shortages, especially for jobs requiring lower qualifications. Initially, workers from Italy and Spain ventured to France and Germany. By the later 1960s and into the 1970s, however, increasing numbers of Turks were going to Germany; people from Algeria, Morocco, and Tunisia moved to France; Pakistanis and West Indians migrated to Britain; and Indonesians went to the Netherlands. Workers from Vietnam, Africa, and Cuba migrated to ECSEE countries to work and learn trades. As an example, by the 1970s, "guest workers" accounted for 10 percent of the total labor force and 30 percent of the manual labor force in Switzerland, whose experience is typical of other Central and West European countries.

France, and to a lesser extent the Netherlands, have particularly large non-European populations, in France's case because of its long and continuing involvement in African political and economic affairs. However, the general economic downturn of the early 1990s, with its attendant unemployment, has been met by calls from some quarters for the expulsion of these workers and strict restrictions on new immigrants. Xenophobic sentiment has been particularly expressed in France and Germany in recent years, sometimes in cruel and crude terms unseen since the time of fascist rule during the 1940s. Chilling episodes of racist violence, however, have also occurred in many other countries, including Austria, Belgium, and Slovakia.

Total Population Growth Rates

The last demographic topic concerns the range of total population growth rates exhibited by the various European countries. These rates are calculated from the estimated populations of the countries for 1991 and 1992, and are expressed in annual percentage growth rates. The fastest growing country in Europe is Albania (2.4%), followed by Iceland (1.3%), Luxembourg (1.3%), Austria (1.3%), and Portugal (1.1%). The slowest growth countries are Hungary (−2.4%), Ireland (−0.3%), Bulgaria (−0.2%), and Spain (0.1%). These figures reflect primarily natural population growth, but include the impact of migration, which are most dramatically evident for Austria, Hungary, and Ireland. In the case of Ireland, the demographic impact of a relatively high rate of natural population growth rate is blunted by net outmigration. As a result, total population growth is only about one-half the rate of natural increase. In Germany net immigration more than cancels out small losses from a negative natural population growth rate. In the Netherlands and Portugal immigration also accounts for about one-third of their relatively low rates of total population increase. The total growth rates of most European countries fall in a narrow range of 0.1 to 0.5 percent.

Age Structure and Life Expectancy

The populations of European countries differ widely with respect to their age distributions, which are a function of birth, death, and net migration rates. Some countries have relatively young populations, others relatively older, while still others exhibit distinct gaps in their age distributions owing to such factors as wars or periods of rapid outmigration. Age distributions are typically portrayed as percentages of the population in five- or ten-year groups (or cohorts) as in Figure 3-7, which shows the age distributions for a sample of European countries. The graph for Albania shows the extremely youthful character of its population, which is both cause and effect of its high birth rate. The structures for Austria, Denmark, and Sweden show progressively older age distributions that are closely related to a long era of low birth rates. France's distribution, though not the oldest, is the most even. The graph for Hungary shows a gap in the percentage of 20–29 year olds, indicating a drop in the birth rate during the 1960s. The graph for Monaco shows an age breakdown dominated by individuals in the 30–70 age categories. (This definitely is not the place to open a toy shop!) Finally, besides age-structure variations between countries, it is important to appreciate that these structures can vary widely between regions and social groups within a society. A classic example is provided by the age structures of the former Czechoslovakia and its large, relatively poor and less-well-educated Gypsy population (largely in Slovakia) (Fig. 3-8).

The last general feature of population to be discussed here concerns life expectancy. How long people live on average is a function of many variables, such as level of medical care, availability of food, occupation, education, and environmental stress. Women generally live six to eight years longer than men in Europe. Life expectancy for women is highest in France, Netherlands, Iceland, Sweden, and Switzerland (all just over 81 years). Men in Iceland, Sweden, and Switzerland can expect to live to an age of 75. At the other end of the spectrum, women in Croatia, Estonia, Romania, and Russia can only expect to live 74 years on

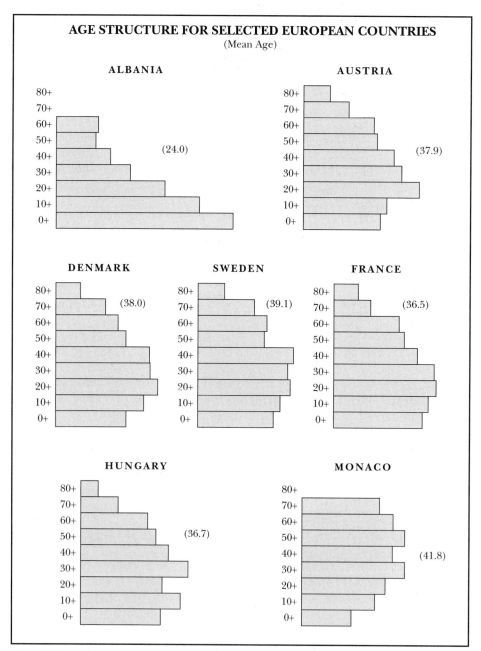

FIGURE 3-7 Age structures of selected European countries. Higher birth rates in less developed countries such as Albania contrast with rates in more developed countries like Sweden, which have fewer young people and generally older populations.

average, while life expectancy for men in Russia is only 63 years (and falling rapidly), 64 in Moldova, and 65 in Estonia, Latvia, and Ukraine. The great-est differences between male and female life expectancies (generally 9 to 10 years) are in East Central Europe and the former USSR. These are

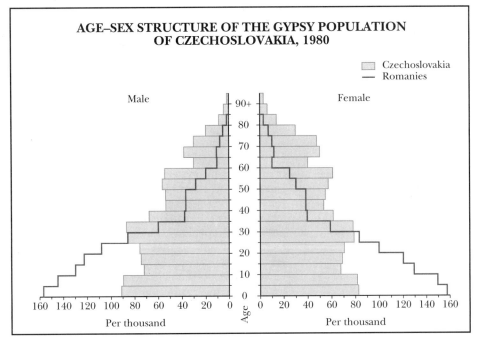

FIGURE 3-8 Population pyramids for Czechoslovakia and Gypsies within it, 1980. A distinctive culture and generally lower socioeconomic levels among some population groups such as this Gypsy population can lead to strikingly different demographic characteristics (Source: Kalibova et al., 1993).

attributed to both occupational and lifestyle differences, heavy smoking, and drinking, especially among the Russians.

CULTURAL ASPECTS OF THE POPULATION

Total numbers of people and their rates of change tell only part of the story of European population. The other part deals with culture: the set of knowledge, practices, preferences, institutions, and skills shared by a group of people. Culture is what defines a people, giving them their identity; it also sets the pattern for interaction with the physical environment, and adds the flavor and texture to the built environment, producing what is called the *cultural landscape*. Fundamental components of culture include language, religion, and a wide range of aspects referred to here as leisure activities (see Inset 3-2). Understanding these aspects of European culture in historical context is necessary

for an accurate picture of the contemporary European scene, especially its diversity and "hot spots" of political/social conflict.

Language

Europe is composed of a kaleidoscope of tongues—some ancient, others relatively new; some dying out, others expanding; some with relatively benign political implications, others creating political flashpoints. Language, besides being a fascinating topic in its own right, is also an important gauge of political and cultural strength, since expansion or contraction of a language goes hand-in-glove with the relative dominance of those who speak it. Similarly, nationally dominant or officially proclaimed languages are usually the form of the language spoken in the capital region of the country. For example, standard French, Spanish, and Russian were originally the dialect spoken in Paris, Madrid, and Moscow. Other existing

LEISURE AND LIFESTYLE "OVER THERE"

North Americans traveling to Europe for the first time will, of course, notice many similarities in the leisure-time activities of people there. However, several surprises are also in store.

People in Europe, on average, spend less time at home than people in North America. Most European cities seem to have more museums, theaters, opera houses, parks, and public squares than U.S. cities, and these always seem to be rather well frequented, and not just by tourists. Most educated Europeans expect a city to have, for example, symphony, opera, and theatrical companies. The theaters of Vienna and London are especially renowned and are an important part of the basis for their thriving tourism. Europeans frequently express astonishment that the arts are often so poorly developed in U.S. cities.

Pubs in Ireland and England; cafes in France and Albania; bars in Germany, Spain, and Italy; and discos, even in Bulgaria, never seem to lack customers. Europeans revel in joining with fellow citizens to socialize, often in these public settings. People linger and chat over coffee or wine, or they savor beer or ale while competing at skat or darts. Little wonder that many Europeans find life in America too hectic and too impersonal.

Daily rhythms vary considerably across Europe. The average American would probably feel most at home in England. Unlike Anglo-Americans, most Central and Southern Europeans typically have their main meal of the day around noon; these are often elaborate affairs lasting two hours, though in recent years the pace of business has altered this pattern somewhat. Still, little wonder that an afternoon nap is also more common in these places than elsewhere. Nowhere is the daily routine as extreme as in Spain, especially Madrid and Barcelona. Here, people of all ages typically have lunch between 2 and 4 in the afternoon, dinner between 10 and midnight, and then stay out dancing and visiting until 2 or 3 A.M.! Just about the opposite occurs in parts of Central and Northern Europe, where grocery stores close in the early evening and restaurants often close at 7 or 8 P.M., and streets become deserted soon afterward. In Vienna many people are out

grocery shopping before work between 6 and 7 A.M., because convenient, small shops have limited hours, especially in the afternoon when they usually only open between 4 and 6 P.M. Shopping hours on the weekend in much of Europe have also traditionally been limited to Saturday mornings, although extended hours are becoming more common, especially on designated "shopping Saturdays." The latter innovation is being reinforced by the greater participation of women in the labor force and the desire of large stores to better utilize their capital investments and to capitalize on their size advantages over small stores by pressing for longer hours.

Vacations are another important aspect of leisure activities. Europeans generally get five to eight weeks of paid vacation per year, which they usually take in the summer. For example, many businesses in France close for a month in July or August while everyone is away. Many Northern Europeans take part of their vacations during winter to escape the cold and lack of sunlight. The crush of travelers can be so great during peak vacation periods that massive traffic jams develop, for example, at passes in the Alps and on the German *Autobahn*. To lessen the impact of such problems, agreements between states in Germany have been developed to stagger the beginning of their (relatively short) summer school vacations.

Singing and folk dancing are typical pastimes for many Europeans. Be it an English stadium, a Bavarian beer hall, or a Hungarian csarda, singing, dancing, and other folk pursuits are still much in evidence. Music is particularly important in Estonia, where composers are national heroes and the annual songfests attract a majority of the country's population. In general, the fine arts play a more central role in European societies than in the United States. Yet, as in the United States, there also coexists a popular media culture, which reflects the dynamism and vibrancy of modern cultures, aspects of which also provoke controversy about taste and propriety.

Sport—participant and spectator—is an important part of life in Europe. Football, called soccer in

America, is by far the most important sport and is widely and well organized around amateur and professional teams. Large professional leagues exist at the national and international levels. Competition is closely followed, especially, of course, the World Cup. European teams have dominated the World Cup, and not surprisingly, three of the four semifinalists in the 1994 Cup were European. Cycling (e.g., Tour de France), track and field, basketball, cricket, skiing events, and auto racing (sometimes it seems, on- and off-track) are also enjoyed. In Eastern Europe, especially Russia, chess is widely played and watched, from formal world championship competitions to widespread informal competition in parks. *Bocche* in the park, dealing cards in a coffeehouse or local bar, and golfing (especially in Scotland, where it originated) are other favorite pastimes. Even if someone is not involved in a competitive sport, weekends especially find Europeans going on hikes in the countryside or walking in city parks and inner-city pedestrian zones, swimming, sailing, going cross-country skiing, or undertaking one of innumerable other locally important activities.

Finally, a major part of Americans' attraction to Europe is its palette of personal dress, food, and beverages. Peoples' dress (or undress on some beaches) in Europe ranges from fashionable and flamboyant to the conservative and somber, as in Slavic Europe. Unfortunately, mass marketing of Europe as a tourist destination and associated clichés (e.g., Dutch wooden shoes and German *Lederhosen*) are poor indicators of the astounding array and meaning of garments across Europe, which are still frequently worn, especially during traditional celebrations.

The preparation and presentation of food is considered a virtual art form in France, and the coffee traditions of Vienna and the Balkans are taken nearly as seriously. The variety and quality of cuisine in France, Italy, and other parts of the Mediterranean region is perhaps most esteemed. However, virtually every European country and region offers popular dishes that are enjoyed elsewhere in Europe and in the world. From pasta to paella, sauerbraten to smorgasbord, bagette to blintzes, and Stroganoff to souvlaki, there are choices galore from the European kitchen. Regional specialties and the emphasis on basic ingredients vary widely. Meat is an especially key food in Western Europe (less so in northern Scandinavia); cost and availability reduce its relative importance in Southeastern Europe. Pork is a favorite in Denmark and Central Europe, whereas fish is especially common in Denmark and Europe's westernmost countries. Cereals provide staples in Southeastern Europe and Italy; potatoes serve the same role in Ireland and Poland. Fruit is heavily consumed in Southern Europe (except Portugal); Greeks eat nearly double the average dose of vegetables of other Europeans, and the Irish nearly as much. France is well known for its diversity and quality of cheeses, Germany especially for its breads, and Denmark for its colorful, delectable open-faced sandwiches. Mere prose cannot adequately describe Belgian chocolates or Austrian pastries. Fortunately for the traveler, Western and Central European countries now offer a pleasing array of European and international foods on their menus.

And, of course, Europeans produce outstanding wine, beer, and spirits (all of which are also the basis for important industries). American wine producers have done well in developing at least some wines comparable to those of France and Italy. In only France, Italy, and Greece do people drink more wine than beer. Virtually every country has a specialty in "hard liquor"—Scotch whiskey is probably the most widely revered in the United States. Few consumers agree that American brews have achieved the quality of English and Irish ales and Central European beers. The Germans are Europe's "champion" beer consumers and have 5000 labels to choose from. (In Bavaria, which has nearly a thousand breweries, the *Steins* seem the size of small buckets.) The Czechs and Irish are close at the rail—all consuming more than double the European annual average (over 60 liters per capita). Unfortunately, the many ways in Europe to toast to health do not often contribute to it. The harmful effects of alcohol are extensive, especially in Central Europe and the former USSR, although strict codes make drinking and driving less commonplace and far less tolerated in Europe than in the United States. In Europe public transport generally provides the "designated driver"—*Cheers! Prosst! Skol! Ege'szse'ge're!*

dialects generally succumb with time to pressure from the center of power. When dominant languages are not spoken by the majority of population in part of a country, it often reflects ongoing conflict between a central government and subnational groups, as reflected by the use of Basque and Catalan in Spain and Celtic languages in the British Isles. ·

Tracing the origin and development of something as fluid as language over the past 5000 years is virtually impossible, so a complete story of languages will never be known. However, clues derived from detailed linguistic evidence suggest that a common root language, called Proto-Indo-European, existed in Europe in about 3000 B.C. The language then began to split and diversify, first into two groups along the so-called Centum-Satem line. This line, named for the word for "100" in Latin and Slavic languages, corresponds quite closely to the present division between Eastern and Western Europe. East of the line, Slavic languages predominate, while in the west, the ancient language (Frankish) itself split into the Romance and Germanic subgroups.[1] Through time, various language branches emerged, most with several modern representatives and dialects as described later in this chapter.

Before proceeding to a discussion of individual languages, however, a few important issues need to be pointed out. First, throughout history there have been both official and common languages in the many regions and countries of Europe. For example, Latin was the language of the nobility, science, law, and religion for much of the Middle Ages and Renaissance eras across most of Europe. But this is not to say that Latin was the language spoken by a majority of the population; indeed, apart from Vatican City and Roman Catholic services, the language has all but disappeared in its spoken form. Similarly, although French was a common language of royal courts (e.g., at times in Russia), it played virtually no role in daily life for masses of citizens except the regions in or near France.

Second, most European languages did not have

a written alphabet until relatively recently. For example, speakers of Slavic languages did not have a written form until the ninth century, at which time the Greek missionaries Cyril and Methodius developed a writing system for them. The alphabet they developed adhered closely to the Greek alphabet—hence the similarities between it and the Cyrillic alphabet. The importance of an alphabet cannot be overstressed: without one, languages become extinct far more quickly than with one; and languages also change much faster when they are passed from generation to generation through spoken forms only. Furthermore, the written form of a language is often an important indicator of its origin and certain other aspects. For example, Serbian and Croatian are essentially the same language, but the Serbs use the Cyrillic alphabet and the Croats use the Latin alphabet, reflecting adherence to Eastern Orthodox and Roman Catholic churches, respectively. These churches, of course, played pivotal early roles in the development of public literacy as the result of the publication of church-related literature.

Third, throughout history and up to the present, many Europeans have spoken more than one language. Americans often marvel at the ability of individuals to speak two, three, or four languages besides their native tongue. (Europeans, on the other hand, are perplexed by Americans' relative linguistic insularity.) Europeans' linguistic flexibility is nothing new, for during medieval times Jewish traders were said to speak Arabic, Persian, Greek, Latin, Frankish, Spanish, and Slavonic! Similarly, many of the words in European languages are borrowed from others, especially for introduced products. For example, the English word "orange" (the fruit) comes from the Arabic "naranj," and the word is "naranja" in Spanish and "narancs" in Hungarian. However, when traveling in Europe, you should keep in mind that place names generally differ from one language to the next. For example, what we call Vienna is "Wien" in German and "Becs" in Hungarian. In Italian "Rome" is Roma, but "Florence" is Firenze. When speaking with Europeans, even those who know English quite well, one must be aware of this problem and always have a map at the ready if travel itineraries are discussed.

Fourth, through the years geographic isolation

---

[1]Languages are classified according to family (e.g., Indo-European), subgroup (Germanic), branch (Western), major language (English), and minor language (Frisian).

related to topographic features has helped maintain language identity. Certain obscure languages, such as Romansch and Vlach, can be heard today only in mountain regions of the Alps and Carpathians respectively. Pressure from people speaking first Saxon and later English isolated Gaelic speakers in Ireland, Wales, and Scotland in the British Isles' far north and west, where they now form the majority in only restricted areas (known as the Gaeltacht in Ireland). A similar process led to concentration of the Breton language in northwesternmost France. Basque may, in part, provide a classic example of the impacts of geographic and, probably, cultural isolation and insularity. As already noted, the Basque language has no known linguistic root; its origin remains one of Europe's greatest, most intriguing mysteries.

Fifth, all languages show regional variation in pronunciation (accent) and vocabulary. When variations are large enough, the different forms of languages are referred to as dialects; in some cases, these dialects are almost mutually incomprehensible. For example, Norwegian exists in two distinct forms (Bokmål and Nynorsk), and Albanian has Tosk and Gheg speakers. Dialects and accents also abound, for example, in Germany, where some are hardly recognizable to "high German" speakers (especially nonnative speakers). These regional variations, often related to the relative isolation of population groups in valleys or on islands, add greatly to cultural richness and regional pride, but provide a humbling reminder of a language's complexity to someone who may think they have achieved linguistic fluency.

Finally, in many countries language is the basis for a heated political issue. Conflict can assume a range of forms, as the following three examples demonstrate:

1. Most place-name signs and other highway markers in the Republic of Ireland are given in both Irish (Gaelic) and English. However, as a form of protest, many of the English names are routinely painted over. Similar actions occur in minority regions across Europe.

2. Tensions between Flemish and French speakers at the Belgian university at Leuven became so caustic during the late 1960s that the university was literally divided along linguistic boundaries. Subsequently, a new university town was built at Louvain-la-Neuve to house the French-speaking faculty and students as well as half the library holdings.

3. Many people in western Romania speak Hungarian as their first language. Since the mid-1960s, Hungarian speakers have endured various degrees of repression, including prohibitions on speaking the language in public. In the early 1990s the mayor of Cluj, an important Transylvanian city, went so far as to make all signs in the Hungarian language illegal, punishable by a substantial fine.

Each of these examples points to the volatile and highly politicized nature of language in the modern European context. In all cases, language becomes a strong indicator of cultural identity and hence of political position with regard to power sharing. The Irish are concerned with gaining political power after centuries of rule from London; the Flemish and French speakers of Belgium have long been at odds with one another; and the Romanians are ever fearful of the Hungarian minority's attempts to gain too much power, lest they should press for a return to the pre–World War I borders, when Transylvania was part of Hungary. Several other examples of these kinds of problems are discussed in Chapter 4 .

Classification of European Languages (Refer to Fig. 3-9 for distributions of each language)

A. *Indo-European*

The Indo-European family of languages is the world's largest, with representatives spoken throughout Europe, the Americas, and South Asia. Eight subgroups of languages are represented in contemporary Europe; most of these are themselves made up of branches, which in turn can be further divided into individual major and minor languages. Each subgroup is discussed in turn in this outline.

1. *Germanic* (also called Teutonic). This subgroup evolved from east Frankish beginnings around the first century B.C. Extinct forms include Gothic, which was spoken in Central Europe, and Norse, which predominated in Scandinavia.

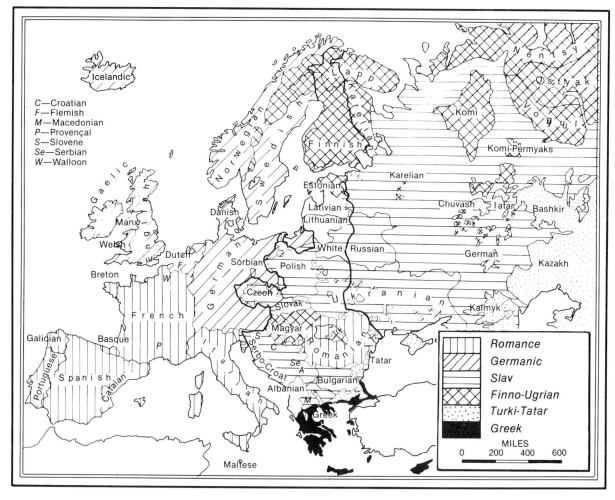

FIGURE 3-9 Europe's major linguistic patterns before World War II. (After Meillet (1928))

Major languages of the western branch are German, spoken in Germany, Austria, and much of Switzerland; Dutch, used in the Netherlands; Flemish, a variant of Dutch spoken in northern Belgium; and English, the main language of the British Isles and rapidly emerging as the *lingua franca* of Europe. English speakers, of course, will note little similarity of English to modern German and can, therefore, legitimately ask where the connection is. The fact that modern German and English

are so different from one another reflects the rapid changes that English has undergone over the past few hundred years. After all, Chaucer, who wrote in Middle English (1150–1500), and even Shakespeare, whose work dates from the late 1500s and early 1600s, are becoming increasingly unintelligible to readers of modern English. To illustrate how pronunciation has changed over the years, Oscar Wilde once proposed the following: take the "gh" sound from rough, the "o" from women, and the "ti" from station. The result is "ghoti," clearly a very different way to spell what would be pronounced as "fish"!

Major languages of the northern branch of the Germanic languages include Swedish, Danish, Norwegian, and Icelandic. The first three are more or less mutually understandable and use essentially the same alphabet. Icelandic, however, has retained much of Old Norse, the language of the Vikings.

Minor Germanic languages include Frisian, Luxembourgian, and Faeroese. Yiddish, a dialect of German mixed with Hebrew and written in Hebrew characters (from right to left), until recent decades was spoken by a majority of world Jewry. Anecdotal information suggests that it has also been experiencing a renewal in recent years.

2. *Romance or Italic*. These are languages descended from Latin; they are spoken in Southern Europe and thus reflect the impact of the Roman Empire on the regions it conquered.

Major representative languages are Italian, French, Spanish, Portuguese, and Romanian. Each of these languages shares a common grammar, vocabulary, and alphabet, though pronunciation can vary widely. For example, the word for the number five in French, Spanish, and Italian, though spelled similarly, has the following approximate English pronunciations: sangk, **theen**ko, and **cheen**gkooay. Romanian may seem out of place in this list, but it is in fact a language descended from the Roman legions that were stationed in the Dacian Province (today's Romania) during A.D. 106–271.

Minor representatives of the Romance languages include Walloon, a version of French spoken in southern Belgium; Galician, a variant of Spanish spoken in northwest Spain; Provençal, spoken in southern France; Catalan, a cross between Spanish and French spoken in eastern, and especially northeastern, Spain in the Barcelona region; Romansch, a language descended from Latin and one of the official languages of Switzerland, though only spoken in the mountains in the south; and Ladino, which is a form of Spanish spoken by Sephardic Jews who, following expulsion from Spain after 1492, settled in various parts of the Balkans.

3. *Slavic*. The term *Slavic* probably comes from the Latin word for race, which came to mean "slave." Slavic languages can be grouped according to geographic location. Major representatives of the eastern branch include Russian, Ukrainian, and Belarussian. The western branch contains Polish, Czech, and Slovakian, with a minor language known as Sorbian or Lusatian. The southern branch is represented by Bulgarian, Serbian, Macedonian, Croatian, and Slovenian. Of these, Russian, Ukrainian, Belarussian, Bulgarian, Serbian, and Macedonian use the Cyrillic alphabet; the rest use Latin script.

4. *Hellenic*. Although there are important dialects, the only representative of this subgroup is Greek. Ancient Greek, the Greek of Homer and the great playwrights of the Classic period, is quite a different language from the modern language. The Greek alphabet, as anyone belonging to a sorority or fraternity knows, is also quite different from Latin script.

5. *Celtic*. This language subgroup was spoken among the Celts, a collection of tribes that probably evolved in what is now southern Germany centuries before the birth of Christ. At one time, Celt was spoken across much of Central, Eastern, and Western Europe.

Major representatives are Irish and Scottish (otherwise known as Gaelic or sometimes Erse), Welsh, and Breton, which is spoken in northwestern France by Celtic speakers who fled Wales and Cornwall during the sixth century. These languages have long been in decline and are now confined to the Atlantic hill country in their respective countries. However, efforts in Ireland and Wales are currently underway to revive the Celtic languages. In areas of Ireland, Scotland, and Wales where the language is still spoken by significant numbers of people, signs are printed in both Gaelic and English (Fig. 3-10).

6. *Thraco-Illyrian*. This language subgroup formerly extended across a broad belt of the central Balkan Peninsula. Today, however, the only remaining representative of the language is Albanian, spoken in that country and by ethnic Albanians in neighboring countries.

7. *Baltic*. Baltic languages formerly extended over a much greater range but were ultimately confined to their current location in the south Baltic coastal areas during the tenth century by advancing Slavs. The Baltic subgroup is the most conservative of the Indo-European languages, having retained archaic features lost elsewhere. The only two remaining representatives are Lithuanian and Latvian (or Lettish).

8. *Indo-Iranian*. Speakers of Indo-European languages, after their emergence in about 3000 B.C., began spreading across Europe in 2500 B.C., through Southwest Asia, all the way to what is now India. The Indo-Iranian branch thus includes many major representatives, such as Sanskrit, Hindi, and Sinhalese. One minor representative is of concern here: namely, Romany, the language spoken by Gypsies. By, in a sense, "returning" their language to Europe, Gypsies have closed the circle of Indo-European language migration. An estimated 9 million Gypsies live in Europe, concentrated dominantly in Southeastern Europe and notably in Romania where about 3.5 million reside.

B. *Non-Indo-European*

Not all languages spoken in Europe by "natives" belong to the Indo-European family. Four language families fall into this group.

1. *Uralic*. This name refers to a family of languages that evolved around the Ural Mountains in present-day Russia. One subgroup is Finno-Ugric, which is divided into the Finnic languages of Finnish, Estonian, and Saami, while the Ugric branch is represented in Europe by Hungarian. These languages have extremely complex grammar systems and many difficult to pronounce letters.

2. *Altaic*. This family includes languages spoken across Central and Southwest Asia. The only representative in Europe is Turkish, which is part of the southwestern branch of the Turkic subgroup. Turkish, of course, is spoken in Turkey and in many parts of the Balkan Peninsula, which was formerly part of the Ottoman or Turkish Empire. The language can also be heard in the many Turkish immigrant communities found throughout Europe.

3. *Hamito-Semitic*. This family includes languages from across North Africa and Southwest Asia. Only two minor representatives are present in Europe: Maltese, which is part of the north Arabic branch of the Semitic subgroup; and Hebrew, which is in the Canaanitic branch. The long reign

FIGURE 3-10 English and Gaelic sign for a settlement in Scotland. (W.H. Berentsen)

of the Arabic Moors in Spain also left Arabic roots in many Spanish and Portuguese place names.

4. *Basque.* Basque is the mystery language of Europe since no connection has yet been established between it and any other. Some believe that the Basque people came from the Caucasus Mountain region; others argue that Basque represents a pre-Indo-European language. In any event, Basque is an ancient tongue, totally unrelated to other European languages. During Franco's reign (1936–1975), speaking Basque in pub-

lic was prohibited in an attempt to homogenize Spanish culture. Since 1976, however, the Basques of northwest Spain have made great strides in reasserting their identity.

Comparative Language Analysis Table 3-3 lists five basic words in 22 languages described in the preceding outline. Several significant points emerge. First, the unmistakable similarity of the Indo-European languages can be seen in the words for mother, three, night, and new; on the other hand, these words are completely different in the non-Indo-European languages. The word for bread, howev-

TABLE 3-3

SELECTED WORDS IN REPRESENTATIVE EUROPEAN LANGUAGES

	mother	bread	three	night	new
English	mother	bread	three	night	new
German	Mutter	Brot	drei	Nacht	neu
Dutch	moeder	brood	drie	nacht	nieuw
Swedish	moder	bröd	tre	natt	ny
Icelandic	móðir	brauð	þrír	nótt	nýr
Latin	mater	panis	tres	nox	novus
French	mèra	pain	trois	nuit	nouveau
Spanish	madre	pan	tres	noche	nuevo
Portuguese	mãe	pão	três	noite	novo
Italian	madre	pane	tre	notte	nuovo
Romanian	mamă	pîine	trei	noapte	nou
Russian	мать (mat')	хлеб (hleb)	три (tri)	ночь (noch')	нóвый (novy)
Polish	matka	chleb	trzy	noc	nowy
Slovene	máti	hléb	tři	nóč	nòv
Greek	μητέρ (meter)	ψωμί (pomi)	τρία (trea)	νὺκτα (nykta)	νέος (neos)
Gaelic	máthair	arán	trí	oíche	nua
Albanian	nënë	búkë	tre,tri	natë	i ri
Lithuanian	motina	duona	trys	naktis	naujas
Finnish	äiti	leipä	kolme	yö	uusi
Hungarian	anya	kenyer	három	éjszaka	új
Turkish	anne	ekmek	üç	gece	yeni
Basque	ama	ogi	hirur	gai	berri

er, shows the difference between the three main European subgroups (Germanic, Romance, and Slavic). Finally, the table shows examples of the Cyrillic and Greek alphabets, along with some of the distinctive characters used in other languages, such as Turkish, Slovene, and Icelandic, which still uses Runic letters.

Among the Indo-European subgroups, Slavic is spoken by the greatest numbers of Europeans, some 309 million in all, followed by Romance at 210 million and Germanic with 204 million speakers. The numbers of speakers for individual languages are shown in Table 3-4.

English, though not the most important official language in Europe, is understood by far greater numbers and is rapidly becoming the first language of business and pop culture. Indeed, English is used routinely in many parts of Western Europe and southern Scandinavia; English speakers are a scarce commodity only in the more remote parts of Southern, Eastern, and Northern Europe.

Religion

Religion is another major cultural influence on developments in Europe. Religion, dominated by Christianity, has been both a unifying and progressive force and, in other ways and at other times, a destructive force. Some of the conflicts we see in Europe today have a religious element. This section first presents an overview of early religion in Europe before treating the three great belief systems of Christianity, Judaism, and Islam (Fig. 3-11).

The first Europeans practiced religions based on animism, totemism, and the worship of elements of the natural environment thought to have supernatural powers, such as trees, rock outcrops, or caves. However, far from being unsophisticated, Europeans by the Stone Age were practicing fairly elaborate rituals that exhibited a high level of development; Stonehenge, Carnac, and other monoliths stand as vivid reminders of prehistoric accomplishments. A basic difference, however, existed between Northern and Southern Europe. In the north, mainly Scandinavia, religion was predominantly patriarchal and associated with the

TABLE 3-4

NUMBERS OF NATIVE SPEAKERS OF EUROPEAN LANGUAGES (IN MILLIONS)

Russian	127
German	103
French	70
Italian	63
English	61
Ukrainian	46
Polish	43
Spanish	25
Romanian	25
Dutch-Flemish	21
Serbo-Croatian	20
Turkish	15
Hungarian	14
Greek	12
Czech	12
Portuguese	10
Belarussian	10
Bulgarian	9
Catalan	9
Swedish	9
Finnish	6
Albanian	5
Danish	5
Norwegian	5
Slovak	5
Provençal	4
Lithuanian	3
Galician	3
Latvian	2
Estonian	2
Slovene	2
Macedonian	1
Romany	1
Celtic (total)	0.6
Basque	0.6

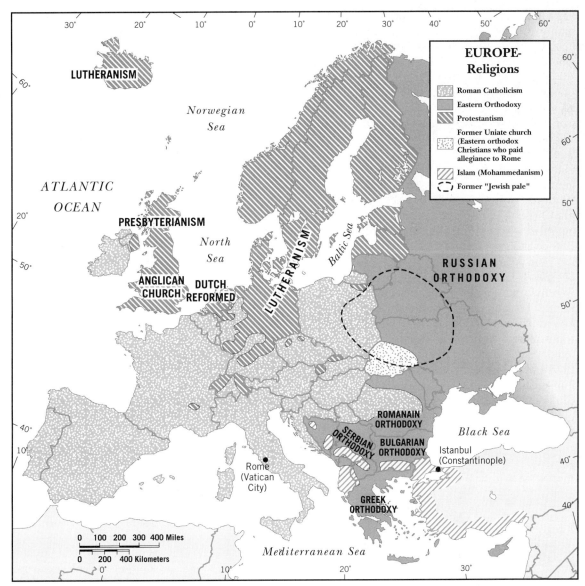

FIGURE 3-11 The major regional patterns of religion in Europe. (After Jordan)

sky and forest; in the south, matriarchal religious practices associated with the earth and fertility were the norm.

Polytheism—the worship of many greater and lesser gods and goddesses—evolved in the classical civilizations of the Aegean and Mediterranean. Most closely associated with the Greeks and Romans, these religions were associated with elaborate rituals, impressive temples, and a well-established hierarchy of priests and priestesses. Polytheism, however, generally did not survive into the Christian era.

Not all elements of the other pagan religions were so easily supplanted. In fact, many of the earlier rituals were readily incorporated into Christianity. The burning of the Yuletide log at Christmas is a holdover from the forest worship days, whereas the practice of Easter in general, and dancing around the May Pole in particular, are examples of ancient resurrection and fertility rituals. All Saints Day (Halloween) is a direct holdover from pagan times, as are many of the superstitions and other practices of modern people. Significantly, even though Christianity has spread over nearly the entire European continent, certain pockets hold to the earlier practices, such as the Saami of far northern Scandinavia. In like manner, other pre-Christian practices, among them magic, astrology, and witchcraft, still have their adherents in Europe and elsewhere (Fig. 3-12).

Christianity Christianity arose in Southwest Asia, which at the time of Christ was controlled from Rome. The religion spread slowly within the Roman Empire, largely because Christians were sometimes persecuted quite vigorously. However, religious tolerance was finally granted in the early fourth century A.D. by the Emperor Constantine, himself a nominal Christian. Under his influence, Christianity eventually became the state religion of

Rome. Afterward, the diffusion of Christianity occurred more rapidly, as converts now came from the ranks of the nobility eager to reinforce and consolidate their powers, as well as from commoners who heeded the call of the many missionaries spreading the word of the Messiah to every corner of Europe.

Beginning in the late fourth century, division in the Roman Empire between the West, ruled from Rome, and the East, ruled from Constantinople (later Istanbul), was echoed in the Church by the emergence of the Roman Catholic and Eastern Orthodox branches. Officially, the First Schism occurred in 484, and complete division was final in 1054. Members of each branch busied themselves with spreading their religion to new territories. Thus, by about the year 300 Roman Catholicism was practiced in limited areas of what is today Italy, France, Spain, and Germany. Missionaries—such as St. Patrick, who arrived in Ireland in 432—actively spread the religion throughout Western Europe and the British Isles during the period 400–600, moved into Central Europe during the period 600–1000, and thence onward to Scandinavia and the Baltic lands by the latter 1300s.

Greek Christians of the Byzantine Empire, representing Eastern Orthodoxy, were not as active in missionary work as their western counterparts. The Serbs and Bulgarians generally were converted by the late 800s; the Russians, Ukrainians, and Romanians followed suit by around the year 1000. Significantly, Eastern Orthodoxy was spread in much more of a hierarchical fashion than was the case for Roman Catholicism. That is, efforts were first made to convert rulers, who in turn would then impose the religion on the lesser nobility and on down the line to commoners. The pattern of authoritarian rule thus set by Orthodoxy, and reinforced by feudalism, may still be evident in the ECSEE citizens' seemingly ready acceptance of strongly centralized political power structures.

As mentioned earlier, religion and alphabet are closely tied. Slavic countries that use the Cyrillic alphabet are Orthodox; those that use Latin script are Roman Catholic. Romanians, Orthodox by religion but with a Latin-based language, used Cyrillic script until 1860, at which time they switched to the Latin system.

FIGURE 3-12 Covering all bases: Christian and pagan symbols atop a European granary. (D. Danta)

Throughout its history Christianity has been threatened from both external and internal forces. Initially, external pressure came from the many unconverted tribes of Central and Eastern Europe. More serious threats came in the form of various Asiatic tribes who attacked Eastern Europe periodically during the Middle Ages. Particularly significant was the advance of the Mongols under the leadership of Genghis Khan. In 1241–1242, the Mongols annihilated the armies of Kiev, Poland, and Hungary, effectively bringing European Christendom to its knees. However, the death of the Khan, and other disputes among the Mongols, led to their withdrawal. Had they pushed further west, European history, no doubt, would have been substantially different.

European Christianity was also threatened by the followers of Islam. The first incursions were made by the Moors, who moved into Iberia in the early 700s, reaching southern France by 732. Civilization in Moorish Iberia flourished. Other religions were tolerated; architectural advances were made; and great centers of learning were established. But the Spanish kings, intent on ridding the peninsula of nonbelievers, set forth on the "Reconquest," which finally pushed the last of the Moors from Iberia in 1492. Soon afterward, Jews were expelled or forcibly converted, and the infamous Spanish Inquisition, begun in 1481, was intensified in an effort to "cleanse" the peninsula of any vestige of heresy.

Islam also made its appearance in the Balkan Peninsula under the auspices of the Ottoman Turks. Their push into the Balkans began in the middle 1300s; by 1529 Suleiman the Magnificent had advanced to the gates of Vienna. Combined forces of Central European armies, joined at times by Russia, began pushing the Turks toward Asia Minor following a second siege of Vienna in 1683. However, the present borders of Turkey were not established until after World War I. The Ottomans thus held parts of the Balkans for some 500 years, during which time many mosques and other structures were built in the region. Many individuals also converted to Islam during the Turkish occupation; Muslims still form majorities of the population in Albania and many parts of Bosnia.

For their part, European Christians engaged in military excursions to recapture the Holy Land from Islamic Arabs. The Crusades, five in all lasting from 1095 to 1291, contributed greatly to the unification of European Christendom and to the forging of alliances. They also helped introduce many new products to Europe, such as spices, silk, and other luxuries, which in turn stimulated interest in exploration and trade. There also developed a deep-seated cultural-political rift between European and Islamic societies. Military victories and losses against Islamic armies are, for example, particularly important in the national histories and lore of Spain, Austria, Hungary, Bulgaria, and Yugoslavia (Serbia/Montenegro).

The 1500s saw increased internal challenges to the Catholic Church within Europe. The Reformation, begun by Martin Luther in 1517, resulted from discontent within the Church and led to the creation of several new churches—Lutheran, which now exists over much of Scandinavia, Germany, and Switzerland; Anglican, also called the Church of England; Anabaptist, which exists in several pockets in Central and Eastern Europe and in the United States as Amish and Mennonite; and Calvinist, or Reformed, which exists in Scotland as Presbyterian, in France as Huguenot, and in England as Puritan.

Other Religions in Europe Of course, Christianity is not the only major religion to be practiced in Europe. Judaism also deserves careful attention. After their expulsion from Palestine, many Jews moved into Europe, forming two initial concentrations. The first was in the Iberian Peninsula, where they gained the name Sephardic Jews, even though most worked as diplomats, physicians, merchants, translators, or in other professional occupations rather than shepherds. On the Balearic Islands Jews, for example, played an important role as cartographers during the Renaissance. As indicated above, Jews were tolerated under the Moors, but were persecuted by Christians after the Reconquest. After their expulsion in 1492, many simply stayed in Spain and practiced their religion secretly; others, however, left for France, Holland, and the Balkan Peninsula, where they established important communities. The other early concentration of Jews was in southern and western Germany. This group also faced persecution, particularly during the late Middle Ages when Jews were forced into the so called Jewish Pale, an area located in East Central Europe (see Fig. 3-11).

Throughout much of history, Jews were persecuted in many ways in Europe. They were long forbidden from owning land, holding public office, or voting. Furthermore, they were segregated into distinct parts of cities, which often were walled off. These districts, which date to Roman times, provided the origin for the term *ghetto*. Despite these handicaps, many of the early developments in trade, banking, and industry, not to mention achievements in the sciences and arts, are attributable to people of Jewish faith.

Prior to World War II, Jews formed at least significant minorities in nearly every city of East Central Europe. During the war, some two-thirds of the Jewish population of Europe (along with other religious and ethnic groups) were killed, and many synagogues and ghettos destroyed. After the war, Jews left Europe for the United States or Israel, so that today Jews are not nearly as numerically important in Europe as was the case prior to 1939. Many former Jewish communities are just now starting to rebuild; even young Jews in Europe fear that the horrors of the Nazis could someday be repeated.

Ironically, religious persecution in one part of Europe has often resulted in the migration of highly skilled and motivated people to other parts of the continent and the world. Dramatic examples include the flight of Jews in the fifteenth century from Spain to Central and Eastern Europe as well as the more recent migration to the United States, and movement of minority Protestants from France to Berlin (the Huguenots), from Western Europe to North America (Puritans), and from Austria to the Georgia colony ("Salzburgers").

The other major non-Christian religion in Europe, Islam, is practiced by many individuals in the former Turkish-held lands of the Balkans (Albania, the former Yugoslavia, Bulgaria, and Greece). It is also practiced among the Turkish and North African guest workers in Central and West European countries. Mosques—many of which

have been destroyed in the Balkans—are becoming more prominent in many cities elsewhere in Europe. Cultural and political differeces between Christians and Muslims frequently lead to misunderstanding, animosity, prejudice, and, sometimes, conflict—despite the fact that most European societies have become increasingly secularized. There are a variety of bases for problems between Muslims and non-Muslims in Europe, including concern for lack of women's rights in traditional Muslim societies and homes, anger over violence and terrorism that spills over into Europe from primarily internal conflicts in Turkey (the struggle between Kurdish separatists and the Turkish state) and North Africa (conflict between Islamic fundamentalists and central governments, as in Algeria), as well as outright xenophobia on all sides. Conflicts are most common in countries where there are large Muslim minorities—notably in France to which Muslims come largely by way of immigration from North Africa, in Germany where the Muslim population derives from immigration of Turkish "guest workers", and, of course, in the former Yugoslavia where Muslims have resided in Bosnia, in particular, for centuries. Although prejudice toward Muslims in Europe is real and occasional violence in some way associated with the religious group is fairly common, by far the greatest number of interactions between Muslims and non-Muslims is peaceable and matter-of-fact. Women in traditional, modest Islamic dress are common sights on European streets, Muslim and non-Muslim workers go about their tasks side-by-side, and people from a variety of ethnic and religious backgrounds frequent eating places run by Muslim immigrants—all without apparent conflict or incident.

The Church in Modern Europe Religion has a strong influence in Europe, both on people and on the built landscape. The most important landscape feature associated with religion is the architecture as seen in cathedrals, churches, synagogues, and mosques. Indeed, many of the most impressive structures in Europe are cathedrals. They were usually the tallest buildings in a town and have retained their role as a focal point in cities. Furthermore, these structures led to many engineering and architectural advances. Apart from churches, many small shrines, crosses, and other markers are a common sight throughout Europe, especially in regions dominated by Catholicism and Orthodoxy.

Religion has also been associated with pilgrimage sites. For example, soon after what were thought to be the remains of Saint James were discovered in the early 800s in a field in northwest Spain, the site became an important destination for Christians from across Europe. After a cathedral was constructed (1078–1211), Santiago de Compostella became Christianity's greatest place of pilgrimage after Rome and Jerusalem; the first tourist books were written during the Middle Ages to assist travelers in their journey to this site. Modern pilgrimage sites include Lourdes in southern France, whose waters have long been attributed with curative powers (Fig. 3-13). Important religious pilgrimage sites from the earliest times (e.g., Stonehenge and Delphi) persist and new ones, often associated with alleged or perceived miracles, continue to emerge.

Religious practice is generally on the wane in Europe, although Italy, Ireland, Poland, and Spain remain strongly Roman Catholic, and Serbs and Bulgars hold fast to Orthodoxy. In general, religion tends to be stronger in rural areas and in the less developed countries of Europe. Furthermore, religion is at least a contributing factor in political conflict (e.g., Northern Ireland) and can be a rallying point for protest against oppression. For example, when the Polish government frowned on church attendance during the communist period, attending mass on Sundays became a way for some to show passive resistance. Many in Poland feel that the ascension of their own John Paul to

FIGURE 3-13 Pilgrims at Lourdes, one of the world's most visited religious pilgrim sites. (D. Danta)

Pope was a more significant factor in the overthrow of the communist regimes than even Gorbachev's reform efforts. The Protestant church was also a key rallying point for East Germans against the autocratic rule of the Socialist Unity party.

Figures for religious affiliation, as of 1990, are as follows. At 83 percent, the continent is overwhelmingly Christian. Among Christians, 63 percent are Roman Catholic, 26 percent Protestant, 9 percent Orthodox, and 2 percent other. The next highest group, at 10 percent, is nonreligious, followed by Muslims with 3 percent and other religions with 4 percent. The Jews of Europe currently constitute only 0.3 percent of the total population, or about 1.5 million practicing individuals.

BIBLIOGRAPHY

Besemeres, John F. (1980). *Socialist Population Politics: The Political Implications of Demographic Trends in the USSR and Eastern Europe.* White Plains, N.Y.: M. E. Sharpe Inc.

Cameron, Rondo. (1989). *A Concise Economic History of the World: From Paleolithic Times to the Present.* New York and Oxford: Oxford University Press.

Campbell, James, and Barry Cunliffe, eds. T*he Peoples of Europe.* Oxford, UK and Cambridge, USA: Basil Blackwell. This series includes books on the European tribes and peoples from their origins to the present, including *The Mongols* by David Morgan; *The Basques* by Roger Collins; *The Franks* by Edward James; and several more.

Chadwick, Nora. (1971). *The Celts.* Harmondsworth, Eng.: Penguin Books.

Coleman, David A. (1993). "Contrasting Age Structures of Western Europe and of Eastern Europe and the Former Soviet Union: Demographic Curiosity or Labor Resource?" *Population and Development Review* 19 (3) : 523–555.

Coleman, David A. (1992) "Does Europe Need Immigrants? Population and Work Force Projections." *International Migration Review* 26 (2) : 413–461.

Dawson, Christopher. (1994). *The Making of Europe: An Introduction to the History of European Unity.* New York: Barnes & Noble.

Euromonitor. (1994). *European Marketing Data and Statistics 1994.* London: Euromonitor.

Fassmann, Heinz, and Rainer Münz. (1992). "Patterns and Trends of International Migration in Western Europe," *Population and Development Review* 18 (3): 457–480.

Hall, Ray, and Paul White, (1995). *Europe's Population: Towards the Next Century.* Bristol, Penn.: UCL Press.

Hatton, Timothy J., and Jeffery G. Williamson, (1994). "What Drove the Mass Migrations from Europe in the Late Nineteenth Century?", *Population and Development Review* 20 (3): 533–559.

Kalibova, Kveta, Tomas Haisman, and Jitka Gyuricova (1993), "Gypsies in Czechoslovakia: Demographic Development and Policy Perspectives". In: J. O'Loughlin and H. van der Wusten (eds.), *The New Political Geography of Eastern Europe.* London and New York: Belhaven Press.

Kulczycki, Andrzej. (1995), "Abortion Policy in Postcommunist Europe: The Conflict in Poland." *Population and Development Review* 21 (3): 471–505.

Institute of Geography, Bulgarian Academy of Sciences and Department of Geography, Sofia University (1987). Unpublished materials on Bulgarian migration and urban growth.

Jordan, Terry C. (1988). *The European Culture Area.* 2nd ed. New York: Harper & Row.

Mallory, J. P. (1989). *In Search of the Indo-Europeans: Language, Archaeology and Myth.* London: Thames & Hudson.

Meillet, A. (1928). *Les langues dans l'Europe nouvelle.* 2nd ed. Paris: Payot.

Mellor, P. A. (1992). "Archaeology and the Population-Dispersal Hypothesis of Modern Human Origins in Europe." *Philosophical Transactions. Series B Biological Sciences* 337 (1280): 225–234.

Noin, Daniel and Robert Woods, eds. (1993). *The Changing Population of Europe.* Oxford, UK and Cambridge, USA: Basil Blackwell.

Population Reference Bureau. (1995). *1995 World Population Data Sheet.* Washington, D.C.: Population Reference Bureau.

Pounds, N.J.G. (1990). *An Historical Geography of Europe.* Cambridge, New York and elsewhere: Cambridge University Press.

President's Commission on the Holocaust. (1979). *Report to the President*.

Renfrew, Colin. (1989). "The Origins of Indo-European Languages." *Scientific American* 261 (4): 106–114.

The Times Atlas of European History. (1994). New York: HarperCollins.

Todd, Malcolm. (1972). *Everyday Life of the Barbarians: Goths, Franks and Vandals*. New York: Dorset Press.

van de Kaa, Dirk J. (1987). "Europe's Second Demographic Transition." *Population Bulletin* 42 (1): 1–59.

van der Knaap, Bert and Arend Odé. (1994). "Population Dynamics and Interregional Migration in Western Europe." In P. Hooimeijer et al., *Population Dynamics in Europe*. Utrecht: Royal Netherlands Geographical Society and Department of Geography, University of Utrecht. Netherlands Geographical Studies No. 173, pp. 37–51.

Watkins, Susan C. (1990). "From Local to National Communities: The Transformation of Demographic Regimes in Western Europe, 1870–1960," *Population and Development Review* 16 (2): 241–272.

White, Paul. (1994). "Migration Research." In P. Hooimeijer et al., *Population Dynamics in Europe*. Utrecht: Royal Netherlands Geographical Society and Department of Geography, University of Utrecht. Netherlands Geographical Studies No. 173, pp. 53–67.

World Facts & Maps. (1994). Rand McNally & Co.: Skokie, Ill.

4

EUROPE'S UNROLLING POLITICAL MAP

Although Europe west of the former borders of the Soviet Union is relatively small, it is culturally diverse, as the preceding chapter on population has demonstrated. Europe also is politically diverse. Within a territory barely two-thirds the size of the United States, a total of 36 states currently function. To these should be added six states that recently emerged from the ashes of the former USSR, whose inhabitants properly consider themselves to be Europeans.

The number of European states will likely continue to grow, for several contain minorities with aspirations for separate statehood. These include the Catalans and Basques of Spain, the Flemings and Walloons of Belgium, and the Corsicans of France. Five similar groups—the Slovaks, Slovenes, Croats, Bosnian Muslims, and Macedonians—only gained their independence in the early 1990s, after decades of minority status within the larger states of Czechoslovakia and Yugoslavia. Paradoxically, as will be demonstrated later

in this chapter, the establishment of the European Union as an economic common market appears to be encouraging rather than discouraging separatist threats to the territorial integrity of existing states.

Europe's international boundaries are no longer the focus of tension between states as they were before World War II. However, some borders are under pressure for revision to reflect geographic patterns of national groups. Thus, after 1990 Serbs fought to incorporate Serbian settlements in Croatia and Bosnia-Herzegovina into a "Greater Serbia", and Hungary has voiced concerns about the status of Magyar minorities within Slovakia, Romania, and "rump" Yugoslavia (Serbia-Montenegro).

The likelihood of future alterations in the map of Europe represents a continuation of a process of constant change that has characterized the continent's political configuration since Roman times. When successive political maps of Europe over the past 2000 years are viewed in sequence, they form an animated motion picture.[1]

THE HISTORICAL EVOLUTION OF EUROPE'S POLITICAL MAP

Since the age of Classical Greece, many theories have been advanced to explain Europe's changing political patterns, but none can account for all the specific changes or successfully predict the course of future alteration. One of the most widely known of such theories is the doctrine of Geopolitics, which emerged in Germany in the 1920s (see Glossary). It provided a rationalization, if not motivation, for the expansionism that characterized Germany before and during World War II. Although no current theory in political geography provides a thoroughly satisfactory basis for comprehending the process of political geographic change in Europe, an historical review of Europe's geopolitical evolution from stateless tribes to the formation of contemporary nation-states offers insights into recurring regularities in Europe's changing political divisions.

Tribes

The initial migrations into Europe in the post-glacial era were of tribal groups that moved more or less constantly out of Anatolia, the hearth of Indo-European civilization. In contrast to later homeland-based political forms, individuals within tribes were linked together through kinship rather than through sharing common territory, a situation that perhaps parallels the present political situation of Europe's Gypsies. Even now, tribal groups do not tend to be bound to particular lands, but instead wander into new areas as opportunities present themselves and adversities appear. Although by the beginning of the Christ-

---

[1] A particularly innovative and useful computer program involving Europe's changing political maps permits such viewing. It has been developed by Clockwork Software in Chicago under the name "Millennium".

ian era the Roman Empire constituted a land-based political organization covering more than half of Europe, tribal associations continued to characterize the rest of the continent. When the Roman Empire collapsed, tribal groups formerly kept at bay on its periphery were able to invade and ravage nearly all its former territory.

Tribal identities persisted into medieval and even modern Europe. Thus, we need to consider tribal antecedents when contemplating the basis for regional distinctions among Bavarians, Saxons, and Prussians in modern Germany, and Ghegs and Tosks in Albania. Indeed, tribal distinctions continue at an even more local level based on the tribal occupancy of individual mountain ridges and valleys throughout Albania, and throughout the adjacent territory of Montenegro.

City-States

Another early form of European political organization persisting into the twentieth century is the city-state. Vatican City and Monaco maintain diplomatic offices, coinage, and other modern trappings of sovereignty despite the fact that their territories are measured in acres rather than square miles. Earlier this century, Danzig (Gdansk), Trieste, and Fiume (Rijeka) enjoyed similar independent city status, and to these West Berlin might be added. Until Germany's unification in 1871, many German towns functioned as nearly sovereign entities, including the former Hanseatic ports of Hamburg, Oldenburg, and Lübeck.

Europe's earliest significant city-states were founded by the Greeks who established a number of self-governing entities along the shores of the Aegean, Ionian, Adriatic, and Black seas. These trading communities served as marketing and distribution centers for surrounding areas whose rural villages were often characterized by languages and cultures quite different from Greek civilization. The Greek city-states formed broader political alliances with each other when threatened by foreign powers, most particularly by the Persians.

Under the leadership of Alexander the Great, the Greek city-states forged a broad empire that incorporated lands in Egypt, India, and Central

Asia. Like similar personal empires created before and after, the empire of Alexander scarcely lasted beyond the lifetime of its creator. Still, Greek city-states and Alexander's empire left a legacy of Greek language and customs in Southeastern Europe and adjacent parts of Asia and Africa that, after Roman conquest, resisted the Latinization that took place, for example, in Etruscan and Celtic lands conquered by Romans farther west (see Fig. 3.1).

The Roman Empire

The founding of the city of Rome in the eighth century B.C. marked the beginning of a process of territorial aggrandizement that over the following millennium brought together under one political organization all the Mediterranean lands, most of Northwestern Europe, and substantial parts of the Middle East. Romans expanded outward from a tribal home in the Tiber Valley, their legions conquering virtually all of the Appenine (Italian) Peninsula by the fourth century B.C.[2] The empire reached its zenith in the second century A.D. Its western section collapsed in the fifth century after Rome itself was sacked by a Germanic tribe. Its eastern portion, which came to be known as the Byzantine Empire, continued well into the Middle Ages, until the last small remnant around Constantinople was liquidated by the Ottoman Turks in 1453.

The many centuries of Roman authority left a permanent imprint on the face of Europe. It provided a lingering sense of association of being "European" that has eluded such comparable territories as Southeast Asia, which was never politically unified, or South Asia, which was united for the first time only at the beginning of the nineteenth century through British negotiation and

conquest. The Roman Empire, by establishing a uniform set of laws and institutions throughout its provinces and by making Latin the language of commerce and government—at least in Western Europe—homogenized the disparate linguistic and cultural diversity that had evolved during the process of migration and settlement following the melting away of the glaciers. A profound influence was Rome's official adoption of the Christian religion in the fourth century A.D., which implanted Christianity firmly on the continent, where it remains today, though riven by schisms and heresies.

The Roman Empire also established an economic coherence throughout its lands that reinforced political and cultural homogenization. Under Rome a system of law and order prevailed that fostered regional specialization in production based on the comparative economic advantages of different places. Goods were exchanged over broad areas. In addition, Roman military engineers built a transportation infrastructure of more than 50,000 miles of paved roads. Although routes were constructed primarily to permit rapid overland movement of military legions to threatened areas, they also linked inland areas to navigable rivers and seas. These remained Europe's principal commercial arteries for moving materials and goods well into the railroad era of the nineteenth century.

The Dark Ages

The fall of the Roman Empire was accompanied by an outpouring of tribal groups throughout most areas of Roman civilization. Germanic tribes moved as far west as the Iberian Peninsula, the Vandals giving their name in corrupted form to the later Spanish province of Andalucía. Slavic-speaking tribes, moving southward from East Central Europe, overwhelmed and assimilated most of the native Thraco-Illyrian peoples of the Balkan Peninsula. This period of wandering peoples witnessed a return of extreme political fragmentation to Europe, with power devolving to individual towns and river valleys. A substantial Roman legacy remained, however, including broad areas of linguistic homogeneity. The tribal

---

[2] It should be noted that Rome remained essentially a city-state throughout its centuries of imperial dominance. The northern part of the Appenine Peninsula was treated as a segment of the Celtic world identified as Cisalpine Gaul ("Gaul on the Roman side of the Alps") and the southern part of the peninsula and the island of Sicily were considered part of Magna Graecia ("Greater Greece").

Franks conquering northern Gaul soon found themselves, in turn, conquered culturally by their new subjects, yielding their Germanic speech to the Latin-based local language. However, the Franks did immortalize themselves in their western conquests, giving their name to the large-scale political unit that subsequently arose in their captured territory—France.

Conquering Germanic and Slavic tribes also witnessed a loss of their polytheistic traditional religions to Roman Christianity. However, the division of the later Roman Empire into eastern and western sections resulted in fundamental differences in the subsequent organization and teachings of that faith. The arbitrary border between the two segments extending north from the Libyan Gulf of Sidra became a major European cultural discontinuity whose legacy is seen in the continuing rivalry and conflict between Serbs and Croats, Magyars and Romanians, and Poles and Russians. Slavic and other tribal groups advancing southward into the Balkan Peninsula in the sixth and seventh centuries were converted to Christianity by competing missionaries from Rome and Constantinople. These two urban centers remained dominant religious seats despite loss of their former political significance.

Charlemagne's Empire

Although the Roman Empire disappeared, the memory of its achievements did not perish. Christian monasteries kept Rome's renown alive during the Dark Ages, and its restoration remained an ideal. The Dark Ages gave way in the eighth century to a period known as the Middle Ages during which strong individuals organized local areas into large land-based kingdoms. Chief among these individuals was Charlemagne (Charles the Great), king of the Franks, who, in alliance with Roman Catholic popes, welded together an empire that extended from the Pyrenees and North Sea to the Czech lands and central Italy. In the year 800 the Pope crowned Charlemagne emperor of the western realm of the Roman Empire. The coronation of an emperor again did not signal a resurrection of the old empire's laws and institutions,

however. Rather, it marked the beginning of the feudal system in Europe, during which lands personally inherited or otherwise acquired by a ruler were apportioned among vassals, who controlled smaller holdings on the basis of personal bonds to those in positions of higher authority.

Charlemagne brought together and maintained a vast domain through personal skills and good fortune (Fig. 4-1). His accomplishment did not last more than a generation after his death in 814, however. Unlike the Roman Empire, Charlemagne's state lacked such bolstering institutions as an organized bureaucracy, a money economy, a well-maintained infrastructure, and a standing military force. Internecine struggles by Charlemagne's heirs led in 843 to the Treaty of Verdun, which formally divided the empire into three parts: Francia Occidentalis (Kingdom of the West Franks), Francia Media (Kingdom of Lotharingia, after Charlemagne's grandson Lothair), and Francia Orientalis (Kingdom of the East Franks). Francia Occidentalis evolved into the modern state of France; Francia Orientalis became the medieval Holy Roman Empire; and Francia Media soon disintegrated, its parts largely joining Francia Orientalis.

Outside Charlemagne's empire large territorial units also grew. For example a half-dozen kingdoms emerged among the Saxon conquests in Great Britain. Danes, Swedes, and Norwegians became organized into dynastic states, although many Norwegians, disgruntled at the forced political consolidation of their traditional tribal units, emigrated to uninhabited Iceland in 874, where they formed Europe's first parliamentary democracy. Farther east, ambitious rulers forged large-scale territorial units among Lithuanians, Poles, and Russians. Magyar tribesmen out of Central Asia invaded the Danubian plains of Central Europe at the end of the ninth century, creating a large Kingdom of Hungary. Slavic tribes to the south also were welded into larger states, challenging the authority of weakening Byzantine emperors, whose domain steadily shrank. Finally, during the Middle Ages much of the Iberian Peninsula was controlled by Muslim Moors from Africa, although several Christian states maintained a precarious independence along the peninsula's northern seaboard.

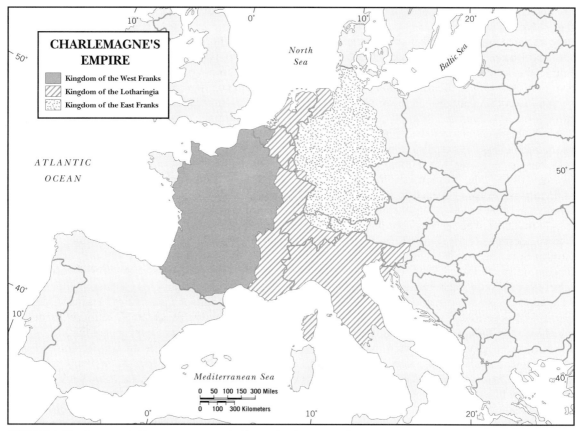

CHARLEMAGNE'S EMPIRE

- Kingdom of the West Franks
- Kingdom of the Lotharingia
- Kingdom of the East Franks

FIGURE 4-1 Charlemagne's Empire in A.D. 843. (From Poulsen, 1995.)

The Prussian Kingdom and Habsburg Empire

Charlemagne, in his efforts to defend his empire, followed the general practice of Frankish tribal states of creating special military frontier zones. Rulers of these *Marken* (usually termed "marches" or "marchlands" in the English language) received special privileges in return for accepting responsibility to defend the empire's other components from foreign invasion. As Francia Orientalis developed into the Holy Roman Empire, the rulers of several marches on its eastern frontiers not only served their functions of protecting the empire, but also expanded territories under their direct control well into the tribal lands of Slavs, Avars, and other groups. Chief among these border entities were the Mark Brandenburg (or Brandenburg March) centered on Berlin and the Ostmark (Eastern March), which came to be run from Vienna.

Rulers of the Brandenburg March conquered the Baltic-speaking Prussian people, who earlier had created a kingdom of their own recognized by their neighbors and the papacy. The Germanic Brandenburgers then appropriated the name—and particularly the independent royal status—of the old Prussians, who subsequently became assimilated or otherwise disappeared from European history. To the south, beginning in the ninth century, the Ostmark similarly expanded to acquire Slavic territories, including the Kingdom of Bohemia. The Habsburg family became Ostmark rulers in 1281 and eventually extended the family domain not only to the east to embrace the adjacent, broad Pannonian Plain and peripheral areas of Central Europe, but also in the north by incorporating the Low Countries and in the west by including Spain and parts of Italy.

The Habsburgs ruled a territory comparable in size and population to France, but it lacked France's high degree of cultural homogeneity (Fig. 4-2). Although much of the Habsburg Empire had been within the Roman Empire, the bulk of its population consisted of descendants of more recent tribal invaders of Roman territories—Germans, Slavs, and Hungarians. A major bonding force of the Habsburg lands was Roman Catholicism, which received strong support from the imperial dynasty. The Habsburgs also impressed their native German tongue as a *lingua franca* throughout their empire, particularly within the towns. Although Habsburg territory lay mainly north and east of the Alps and was essentially landlocked, the empire benefited from easy access by waterway throughout its principal regions by way of the Danube River and its tributaries. The empire built roads and improved streams to foster commerce and industry.

The Ottoman Empire

Europe's last great external invasion occurred during the fourteenth century, when Turkish tribes originally from Central Asia swept into the Balkan Peninsula from a base established a century earlier in Asia Minor. They soon conquered most of the Byzantine Empire, save the city of Constantinople itself, which did not finally fall until 1453. Moving northward through the Balkan Peninsula, the Ottoman Turks destroyed the fledgling Serbian state of Raska at the Battle of Kosovo in 1389. (In the 1990s the Serbs cited this event as justification for their policy of "ethnic cleansing" of Muslim

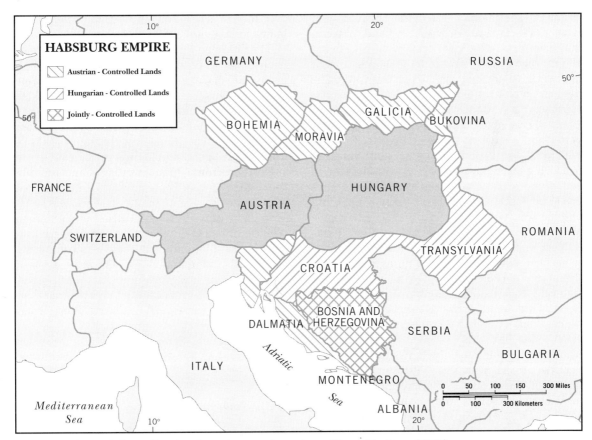

FIGURE 4-2 The Habsburg Empire, late nineteenth century. (From Poulsen, 1995.)

Slavs in Bosnia-Herzegovina.) Ottoman forces defeated the Hungarians in 1526 and in 1529 and 1683 unsuccessfully laid siege to Vienna, seat of Habsburg power.

The Turkish advance northward into the Balkan Peninsula led many Christians to flee to Habsburg lands for haven. Except in Bulgaria, few ethnic Turks settled in their abandoned villages. The Turkish presence in the Balkans was confined mainly to garrisons of soldiers at fortified strong points. However, Illyrian-speaking Albanians, who had accepted the Islamic religion of their conquerors, expanded their areas of settlement eastward into the deserted Serbian hearthland of Kosovo.

A few other Balkan Christian groups also converted to Islam. One was the Bogomils, a heretical Christian sect in Bosnia. They earlier had suffered persecution for their distinctive faith at the hands of both Roman Catholic and Eastern Orthodox churches. Their nobles saw in the philosophy of Islam parallels to their own views, and they certainly appreciated the personal benefits of being able to retain ownership of their estates, a right denied Christians by their Turkish overlords. The descendants of the Bogomils in today's Bosnia-Herzegovina retain the Serbocroatian speech and Islamic heritage of their ancestors. A similar converted South Slavic-speaking group is the Pomaks, who inhabited sections of southwestern Bulgaria.

During the eighteenth century, the Habsburgs settled many Slavic refugees from the Ottoman-occupied Balkans in a special defense zone facing Ottoman forces across the Sava and Danube rivers. Most of these refugees who organized into paramilitary units along this Croatian Military Frontier were Orthodox in religion, although nearly all the population of historic Croatia were Roman Catholic. This regional religious difference is reflected at the end of the twentieth century; the descendants of military frontiersmen form the secessionist Orthodox Serbian minority in the Knin area of predominantly Roman Catholic independent Croatia. In a quirk of history, the Ottoman Empire also recruited its own frontiersmen from local Orthodox Christians to counter any move southward by Habsburg forces. In effect, each empire was defended by Serbian mercenaries. Descendants of the Ottoman border defenders now form a major component of Serbian separatists in independent Bosnia-Herzegovina.

In addition to lacking the religious homogeneity of the Habsburg Empire, the Ottoman Empire also lacked its counterpart's economic coherence. The ancient amber road through the valleys of the Vardar and Morava rivers provided the Turks with a water level route that was passable by wagons from the Aegean Sea to the Danube. However, the two streams were not navigable for most of their distances and could not be compared to the Danubian backbone of the Habsburg Empire. Unlike the Habsburgs, the Turks did little to improve the commercial infrastructure of their territories, although they did build a number of bridges—notably across the Neretva at Mostar (Fig. 12-5), which was destroyed in recent fighting, and across the Drina at Višegrad, the latter a focal point in Ivo Andric's award-winning historical novel *Bridge on the Drina*. For the most part, however, the Turks relied on the roads the Romans had built a millennium earlier.

The Ottoman Empire also lacked the effective civil service of its Habsburg counterpart. A high proportion of Ottoman officials and officers came from Rumelia (a term derived from the Turkish designation of Rome and applied to the empire's European holdings). Although many were from Bogomil families, others rose through the ranks from groups of 13 year-old boys periodically taken as taxation from Christian villages and forcibly converted to Islam. These boys were the principal recruitment source of the feared military Janissaries, who often involved themselves in Ottoman politics. Christian Greeks and Armenians controlled a substantial part of the empire's commerce. Greeks also dominated the empire's Eastern Orthodox church organization. They often generated opprobrium from other groups by their dogmatism and sometime venality. These roles essentially represented continuations of characteristics associated with the Byzantine Empire, which may be said to have conquered its conquerors.

The Emergence of Europe's Nation-States

Although Europe in the Middle Ages had become a complex map of empires, kingdoms, dukedoms, bishoprics, free cities, and similar feudal units, only a tiny fraction of its population shared any sense of identification with such political areas. Most people lived on the land and saw government primarily as a remote agency that demanded taxes from them and took their sons off to war. Identities were local, tied to villages or towns. Any broader commonalities were based on religion and were activated principally when challenges came from groups of a different faith. Conflicts were between "papists" and "heretics" rather than between "Irishmen" and "Englishmen." This state of affairs is understandable when we consider that the Church was virtually the only educational, social, and economic institution that ministered to ordinary people.

Near the end of the eighteenth century, this circumstance changed rather abruptly throughout Europe. Individuals, particularly in the burgeoning cities, began to see themselves less in terms of religious confessions and more as members of distinctive nations, groups of people based on traditions, languages, and territories shared in common. This new attitude is enshrined in the phrase "We the People" that begins the Preamble to the Constitution of the United States of America, which some historians regard as the first of the world's nation-states—states largely comprised of or at least controlled by a self-identifying nation of people. Europe's political map came under severe pressures for change, specifically from nationalism as emerging national identities challenged inherited patterns of political organization.

Northwestern Europe underwent economic and political ferment during the 1700s as the commercialization of agriculture, the harnessing of inanimate energy, and the launching of the Industrial Revolution led to unaccustomed stresses on the population. People uprooted from traditional rural, subsistence ways of life and faced with uncertain futures in urban slums had difficulty finding solace from established religions, which themselves had been split because of the religious wars. New belief and value systems began to emerge which called for change in the social and political structure. Some focused on growing class distinctions within society and promoted a universal perspective culminating in the proclamations of Marx and Engels. Others focused on rejection of the religious-sanctioned divine rights of rulers, who habitually treated their lands as personal estates. Dissenters adhering to these new belief systems called for governments that functioned on the basis of a social contract that met the desires of their citizens. Such views led to the revolt against established authority in the English colonies in North America in 1776. A rebellion against the French monarchy began in 1789.

The rapid development of national identity in Europe had different impacts in different parts of the continent (Fig. 4-3). Europe in about 1800 can be viewed as consisting of three rather widely differing political-geographic regions: western, middle, and eastern.

Europe's western fringes, including the British Isles and Scandinavian countries, were organized into relatively large dynastic states. France remained the largest, preserving and expanding its patrimony of Francia Occidentalis. On the Iberian Peninsula, the Castillians had defeated the Moors and consolidated the territories of the Galicians, Basques, Catalans, and Andalucíans into the state of Spain, although Portugal, which had expelled the Moors from western Iberia nearly two centuries earlier, remained a separate state. Similarly, the English had united the peoples of the islands of Great Britain and Ireland into a single political unit. The Danes maintained a broad state that embraced Iceland, Greenland, Norway, and the Faroes Islands. Sweden included its modern territory, plus Finland. Sovereign states of the Dutch and Swiss also had emerged. All but Holland and Switzerland were ruled by royal dynasties.

The *middle belt of Europe*—essentially modern Germany and Italy—remained a collection of tiny territorial units. Germans were loosely grouped within the lingering Holy Roman Empire, but power was divided among more than 300 separate political entities. Northern Italians also were fragmented into tiny states, whereas those in the center of the peninsula were controlled by the Pope in Rome in the so-called Papal States. Italians in the south were organized into the Kingdom of the Two Sicilies dominated by Spain.

A very simple political organization characterized the peoples of *Eastern Europe*. Essentially all these notably diverse religious and linguistic groups were apportioned among just four em-

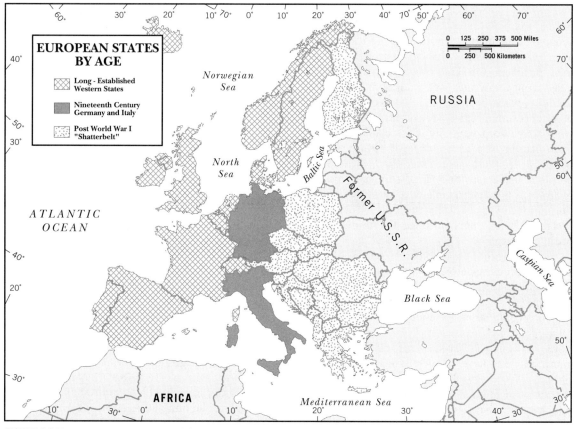

FIGURE 4-3 European states grouped by relative age. (From Poulsen, 1995.)

pires. The formerly large dynastic states of Lithuania and Poland were divided in the eighteenth century among Russia, Prussia, and the Habsburg Empire. The Habsburg Empire also had expanded eastward to absorb the Kingdom of Hungary, with its component parts of Slovakia, Transylvania, and Croatia. Other territories in the Balkans remained parts of the Ottoman Empire.

The overthrow of the French monarchy in 1789 signaled a profound turning point in European history. An ardent revolutionary group, the Jacobins, attacked vestiges of the old order in France and propagated the notion throughout that country that its citizens were "Frenchmen". Their ardent anticlericalism found popular resonance in the economically developing northeast of France but met forceful resistance in the outer regions of the French state, where strong support for the

Roman Catholic Church as an institution remains to this day.

France soon became embroiled in struggles with other European states, whose rulers feared the consequences to themselves of the disorder that was manifesting itself in France. However, France's revolutionary government, under the brilliant military leadership of Napoleon Bonaparte, was able to defeat its foreign adversaries and eventually to dominate much of the European continent, although the British Isles, Scandinavia, and the Ottoman Empire remained outside its control.

The triumphant French legions had a profound political impact on their conquered lands. Their slogan of "Liberty, Equality, and Fraternity" struck a responsive chord among peoples who also had grown dissatisfied with their own traditionalist regimes. However, those inspired by contact with the French soldiers did not thereupon become Frenchmen. Although the traditional elite groups of Europe's dynastic states had habitually used French as a medium of international communication within the continent, these ruling classes had become increasingly discredited, and ordinary people spoke languages quite different from French. Growing up under different cultural heritages, they could not identify with the perceived glories of French civilization as celebrated by members of the French armies. Moreover, increasing numbers chafed under France's continuing occupation and financial demands.

By the time of Napoleon's final defeat in 1815, a majority of Europe's inhabitants had made the switch from religious- to a national-based self-identity. Language proved a principal differentiating factor, but other factors also played important separating roles. Religious heritage remained a significant part of a person's identity, since values, institutions, and standard operating procedures in communities derived largely from religious tradition. Common to all the newly forming nation-states was a sense of linkage to a specific homeland. Those national groups that found themselves minorities in states and empires were united in their quest for a sovereign status of their own. In many ways, the establishment of national identities represented the foundation of secular religions, each with its own sacred texts, martyrs, and icons.

Geographers group the collected cultural attributes that distinguish one nation from another under the concept of national iconography. This concept is best described as a collective national consciousness in which individuals share values, symbols, and historic recollections of the past glories and adversities that have occurred on the specific lands where they live. Thus, a majority of Frenchmen share negative notions of the Roman Catholic clergy, however much they may observe the church's propagated values and take part in its sacraments of marriage, baptism, and final rites. They have an emotional response to France's tri-color flag, its anthem *la Marseillaise*, and its egalitarian values and slogans. They also share images of the glories of Joan of Arc and the perfidiousness of the English. The iconography of many groups also includes popular cultural traditions, including the distinctive games of cricket among the English and Jai Alai among the Basques, and the love of group singing among the Estonians and the Welsh.

Lack of Coincidence of Nations with States As Europeans changed from broader religious to narrower national-based identities during the nineteenth century, serious political problems ensued. The inherited pattern of states only partially corresponded to the territorial patterns of national groups. The discordance was most severe in Eastern Europe, where the four empires found themselves trying to maintain control of multiple and increasingly assertive minority nationalities. In the Habsburg Empire the common Roman Catholicism that had bound Austrians, Hungarians, Czechs, Slovaks, Poles, Croatians and others together became less and less a uniting force. By 1863 the dominant Austrians found it necessary to concede political equality to the Magyars, dividing the state into two parts and renaming it the Austro-Hungarian Empire. In their half of the empire, the Magyars themselves then had to contend with national separatist pressures from their minorities—Slovaks, Romanians, Croatians, and Serbs. Napoleon's short-lived creation of the so-called Illyrian Provinces within the Habsburg lands as an ethnic territory for Slovenes and Croatians had set a precedent for nation-building among the empire's South Slavic peoples.

Similar manifestations of minority national identities appeared in the Ottoman Empire. In the 1830s the Greeks gained independence for the Peloponnesus Peninsula and a narrow strip of land north of Athens and the Gulf of Corinth, although expansion northward to the present boundaries of Greece occurred only after the beginning of the twentieth century (Fig. 4-4). The Serbs began their struggle against the Turks for a country of their own in the first decade of the nineteenth century. By midcentury the Ottoman sultan had recognized the Serbs' right to self-rule, although full sovereignty came only in 1878 as a consequence of a successful Russian campaign against the Turks in the Balkan Peninsula. Romanians and Bulgarians also achieved separate statehood at that time as a result of the Russian victory.

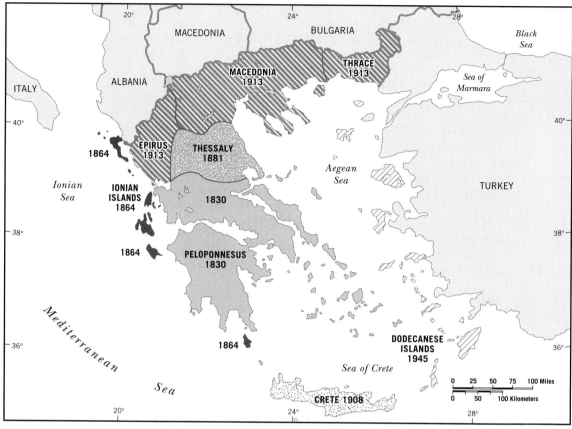

FIGURE 4-4 The territorial growth of Greece. (From Poulsen, 1995.)

To the north, Prussians, Russians, and Austrians faced increasing difficulties during the nineteenth century as a result of Polish national aspirations to reestablish a state of Poland. The Treaty of Vienna in 1815 created a so-called Congress Poland as an autonomous subdivision of the Russian Empire. However, the Russians abrogated this status in 1863 following a Polish rebellion.

The long-established dynastic states of Western Europe faced less intensive pressures from minority nations within their borders than did the broad empires in Eastern Europe. Over the several centuries that most had been functioning, a high degree of cultural homogeneity and economic interlinkage had emerged. A standard written language, introduced and reinforced by products that were off the then relatively new printing press, and a common religion had developed in each.

Thus, after the religious wars that followed the Protestant Reformation, nearly all states had adopted a policy requiring the populace to accept the religion of their rulers. The construction of post roads in England and France facilitated a sense of association among individuals living great distances apart. As a consequence of this homogeneity and coherence, the bulk of the populations of Western European states in the early decades of the nineteenth century generally made an easy transition from religious-based distinctions to common national identities based on the states in which they were born.

Minority national feelings among groups that had preserved distinctive group characteristics, especially languages, were to be found within most states of Western Europe. The Spanish monarchy faced growing threats to the unity of its realm from dissident Basques and Catalans, whose languages and traditions differed markedly from those of the dominant Castillians. France faced regional opposition from its Celtic Breton population of the northwestern Brittany Peninsula, which opposed the anticlericalism of the new republican regime. The dominantly Protestant United Kingdom faced continuing difficulties with its Roman Catholic Irish. Even Denmark had to deal with national separatist sentiments from its populations in Iceland and Norway, and Finns had grown restive in Sweden before their transfer to the Russian Empire during the Napoleonic wars.

In contrast to national pressures for fragmentation besetting the states of Eastern and Western Europe, rulers of the tiny political units of the Germans and Italians witnessed a reverse trend that involved growing popular demands for nationally consolidated states. These ultimately were achieved during the second half of the nineteenth century (Fig. 4-5). Napoleon had initiated the process in Germany during his occupation by abolishing the Holy Roman Empire and simplifying its complex political map into about 30 agglomerated units. His troops encouraged a sense of German identity, if only by establishing

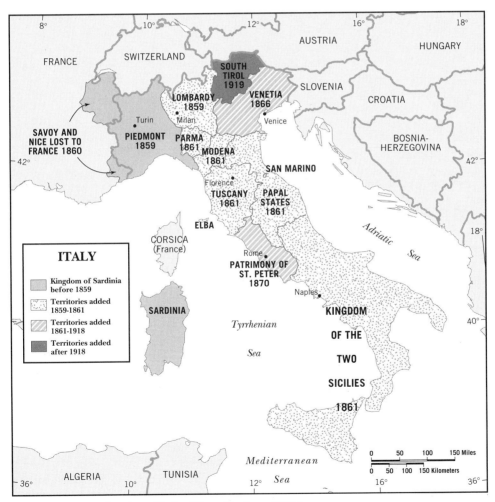

FIGURE 4-5 The unification of Italy. (From Poulsen, 1995.)

strong German resentments toward the French occupying troops. On the Appenine Peninsula, Napoleon also set a precedent for future national unification by creating a Kingdom of Italy. Before other Europeans developed a national identity, virtually no one had advanced the idea of a single state for inhabitants of the Italian peninsula.

The problems of lack of coincidence between Europe's newly forming nations and long-standing states raised substantial questions of boundary location. In the past, boundaries generally had been honored more on maps than on the ground. Before the nineteenth century, European states met at frontier zones whose inhabitants, though officially divided, in fact had closer economic and social connections with each other than with the cores of their nominal state. Even during wartime, battles were fought by opposing armies, but civilian populations continued to trade with each other and otherwise preserve customary economic and social linkages.

This situation changed when state regimes came to represent national groups rather than ruling dynasties. Boundaries became firmly rooted objects on the landscape, as governments sought to encourage local manufacturers and commercial agriculture by setting tariffs on goods produced in other states. Nation-states also tended to seek boundary revision that would incorporate all members of their linguistic-based national groups within state borders. This policy was particularly adopted by the Kingdom of Italy after unification in the 1860s. Italian-speaking minorities in France and the Habsburg Empire were officially termed *irredenta* ("unredeemed"), and Italy continuously sought their incorporation within its borders. The designation became a generic one, with national groups situated in states outside the state of their nominal nation generally designated as "irredentist minorities."

States responded to such internal pressures by seeking to denationalize or expel minorities. In the early years of the French Republic, it was decreed that all citizens unable to speak the French language were to be shot. The decree was directed particularly against the German-speaking Alsatians, who had been incorporated into France a century and a half earlier in 1648. The decree happily was not carried out. Later, during his struggle for mastery of Europe, Napoleon announced, "Let them [the Alsatians] speak German as long as they use their swords in French!"

World War I

Throughout the nineteenth century, national-based tensions continued to develop within Europe, particularly within the multinational empires of Eastern Europe. Actual warfare began in the Balkan Peninsula in 1912 among the forces of Serbia, Bulgaria, Greece, and the Ottoman Empire. At this time, the Albanian and Slavic Macedonian peoples of the Ottoman Empire had not yet formed their own national unities with accompanying quests for separate sovereignty. Bulgarian and Serbian pretensions to Albanian territory during the Balkan wars succeeded in galvanizing Albanians into demands for a nation-state of their own, which the Ottoman Turks conceded in 1913. Development of Macedonian nationalism can be dated only to the trauma of World War II.

The Balkan Wars were a prelude to World War I, which began in 1914 over a terrorist incident by Serbs in Bosnia-Herzegovina who were seeking to incorporate that territory into a greater Serbia. Austria-Hungary had seized the province from the Ottoman Empire in 1878 and had formally annexed it in 1910. The Serbian plurality feared a rumored plan to join Bosnia-Herzegovina to Croatia and to make the Habsburg Empire a tripartite Austro-Hungarian-Croatian state. Because of a network of alliances, all the major European powers were soon drawn into war.

Each of the four empires dominating Eastern Europe emerged a loser in World War I and saw large territories stripped away to form separate new nation-states. Finland, Estonia, Latvia, and Lithuania became independent of Russia, as did Russian Poland, which was joined with former German (Prussian) and Habsburg Polish areas to create a reconstituted Polish state. Austria was separated from Hungary, and Austrian-controlled Bohemia and Moravia were joined with Hungarian-ruled Slovakia and Ruthenia to form the Czechoslovak Republic. The South Slavic-speaking peoples of Austria-Hungary were joined together with independent Serbia and Montenegro, as well as a Macedonian segment of the Ottoman Empire, to establish the multinational state of Yugoslavia.

European borders significantly changed following World War I. To give Poland access to the Baltic Sea, the victorious powers granted it a "corridor" along the Vistula River across traditional Prussian territory. Poland also gained the predominantly German-speaking territories of former Austrian and Prussian Silesia, as well as a sizable strip of long-held Russian territory inhabited primarily by Belarussians, Ukrainians, and Jews. Romania grew by its acquisition of Hungarian Transylvania, Austrian Bukovina, and Russian Bessarabia. Italy gained former Austrian territory south of the Alps and on the Istrian Peninsula. Defeated Germans, on the other hand, in addition to the territories that went to Poland, lost Memel (Klaipeda) to newly independent Lithuania, the Hanseatic town of Danzig (Gdansk) to an independent "free city" status, northern Schleswig to Denmark, and the Saarland to France. Peace treaties also transferred to France the German-speaking territory of Alsace-Lorraine, which Germany had annexed from France in 1871.

World War II

Despite Europe's redrawn map, national tensions remained in many of its parts. The slicing off from Germany of territories that were clearly inhabited by members of the German nation planted the seeds for World War II, which erupted a generation later. The young republican regime in Spain that came to power in 1931 during the world economic crisis sought to appease national agitation by its Catalan and Basque minorities by granting them a degree of internal autonomy. This and other liberal policies generated opposition to the government from Spain's dominant and more politically conservative Castillians. These regional and ideological antagonisms culminated in 1936 in a Spanish civil war that after four years resulted in termination of autonomy for the minorities and suppression of any public use of their distinctive languages. Germany and Italy supported the antirepublican revolt in Spain, which gave them the opportunity to test military technology that would

soon be used to redress territorial grievances against their neighbors.

A strongly nationalistic party, the National Socialists (Nazis), came to power in Germany in the early 1930s. Among its announced goals was revision of the punitive World War I treaties that had taken away territory with German-speaking peoples from the German state. The Nazi's won an early victory in the 1935 referendum in the French-occupied Saarland in which 90 percent of the population favored its return to Germany, which then occurred. The Nazi regime reversed the Prussian policy of 1871 of keeping the rival German-speaking Austrians out of the unified German state. In 1938 the Nazis achieved an *Anschluss* ("unification") of Austria with Germany.

The militant German regime also zeroed in on the supposed persecutions of German minorities in Czechoslovakia and Poland. Following a conference in Munich in 1938, Germany gained French and British assent to annex German-inhabited territories of the Czech borderlands. In the following year, German troops occupied the remainder of western Czechoslovakia, designating the territory officially as "the Protectorate of Bohemia and Moravia." Germany granted nominal independence to the Slovaks of eastern Czechoslovakia, who increasingly had perceived the Czechs as domineering. At the same time, Hungary seized Czechoslovakia's extreme eastern Carpatho-Ukraine region (Ruthenia). With Nazi assent, Hungary also took northern Transylvania from Romania.

In September 1939, Germany, which styled itself the Third Reich,[3] invaded Poland on the pretext of alleviating suffering among German minorities living in the Polish corridor and Upper Silesia. Shortly before the invasion, it had reached a secret accord with the USSR to divide Poland into spheres of control between Germany and the Soviet Union. The Molotov–Ribbentrop pact (named after the Soviet and German foreign ministers respectively) also gave the Soviet Union a free hand in dealing with the formerly Russian-controlled Baltic states of Estonia, Latvia, and

---

[3] By Nazi reckoning, the Holy Roman Empire constituted the First Reich and the German Empire of 1871 the Second Reich.

Lithuania. Germany quickly incorporated the Free State of Danzig and seized Memel from Lithuania, although it then transferred the formerly Polish-held Vilnius area to the Lithuanians. Lithuania's gain was short-lived, for in the following summer the Soviet Union annexed Lithuania and the other two Baltic states. The USSR also seized substantial territories from Romania and Finland, conquering Finland after several weeks of heroic resistance by the Finns.

The United Kingdom and France reacted to the Germans' invasion of Poland by declaring war. During the ensuing Second World War, Germany soon occupied Denmark, Norway, the Netherlands, Belgium, and Luxembourg, and defeated the forces of France. It then formed alliances with Hungary, Romania, and Bulgaria. When such a similar alliance with the Yugoslav regime was rejected in 1941 by a popular uprising, Germany quickly occupied Yugoslavia and territorially divided the state along ethnic lines. Croatia became independent, and Germany, Italy,

Hungary, Albania, and Bulgaria annexed other former Yugoslav regions. Italy earlier had made Albania a protectorate, and from it had launched an attack on Greece. When that invasion faltered, Germany came to the aid of its struggling Italian ally and occupied Greece. In midyear Germany invaded the Soviet Union.

The war ended in 1945 with the complete defeat of Germany and its allies. The continent did not return to prewar political borders, especially within its eastern tier of states. The USSR retained prewar territorial gains from Romania, Poland, the Baltic states, and Finland, and it also secured the western allies' acquiescence to annex the former Czechoslovak Carpatho-Ukraine and the northern part of Germany's East Prussian province, which became the Russian Republic's Kaliningrad Oblast. Poland was "compensated" for loss of its eastern regions to the USSR by being granted German territories in Pomerania, Silesia, and southern East Prussia (Fig. 4-6). Up to 10 million Germans living in those areas were expelled westward.

FIGURE 4-6 Poland's territorial changes, 1939–1945. (From Poulsen, 1995.)

Czechoslovakia regained its Sudetenland, forcing all German-speaking inhabitants to leave. Slovakia lost its wartime independence and again became part of Czechoslovakia. Italy yielded Istrian Peninsula territory south and east of the city of Trieste to Yugoslavia.

Germany itself was divided into zones of occupation by troops from the USSR, the United States, the United Kingdom, and France. These areas eventually hardened into the two sovereign states of the Federal Republic of Germany in the west and the German Democratic Republic in the east. Austria was formally detached from Germany and remained under separate four-power occupation until an international agreement allowed it to become unified and independent again in 1955.

Collapse of the Communist States

National tensions in Europe were generally held in check for 45 years following the end of World War II. The Soviet Union maintained control of its occupied areas of Eastern Europe by putting into power loyal communist regimes in Poland, Czechoslovakia, Hungary, Romania, Bulgaria, and Albania. Yugoslavia, under the communist dictatorship of Josip Broz Tito, defied increasing Soviet economic and political penetration in 1948, and received material support for its independent stance from the United States and other Western countries. Communist Albania broke away from Soviet control in 1961 and received substantial aid from the People's Republic of China. Pursuing avowed internationalist goals, the Soviet and East European communist regimes effectively suppressed minority national movements within their borders, although they permitted minorities an illusion of sovereignty through creation of "socialist republics" and other "autonomous" areas.

In Western Europe, minority groups generally remained quiescent. Spain's fascist dictatorship under General Francisco Franco continued to suppress the national ambitions of its Basques, Catalans, and Galicians until his death in 1975. Would-be nationalist leaders of relatively small minorities, such as the Bretons of France, South Tiroleans of Italy, or Flemings of Belgium, had difficulty rallying support against the states in which

they were found because of the popularly perceived view that small territorial units were unable to support themselves economically.

Substantial political changes in Eastern Europe followed the collapse of the USSR in 1991. Each of the 15 constituent republics of the USSR became a new independent state. Estonia, Latvia, and Lithuania reappeared as sovereign entities. Belarus and Ukraine declared formal independence, with the western portions of their territories continuing to include substantial lands of interwar Poland. Ukraine also retained the former Czechoslovak Carpatho-Ukraine and Romanian Bukovina. Farther south, the Romanian-speaking, former Moldavian Soviet Socialist Republic also assumed independence, although it soon was embroiled in struggles with its Russian and Turkic Gagauz regional minorities.

The USSR's political, and ultimately military withdrawal from Central and Southeastern Europe had particularly profound effects on Germany. The German Democratic Republic, unable to withstand popular pressures for reunification with the Federal Republic of Germany, disappeared in 1990. Its fall was symbolized by the destruction of the massive concrete wall the East Germans had constructed in 1961 around West Berlin. That city technically had remained a zone of occupation by the Western Allies, although it functioned as part of the Federal Republic and received substantial subsidies from that government. Today eastern neighbors of reunited Germany are nervous about the possible designs a German regime might have on lost traditionally German lands in western Poland and the Czech Republic, although no popular mood has yet emerged in Germany seeking their recovery. Moreover, united Germany has officially recognized the German-Polish border established after World War II.

East European countries released from Soviet tutelage also found themselves with activated dissident minority movements. Slovaks agitated for separation from the dominant Czechs of Czechoslovakia and finally regained sovereignty in 1993. Romania found itself pressed to maintain control over its large Transylvanian Hungarian minority, which the previous communist regime had sought to denationalize through a series of repressive measures. Post-communist Bulgaria responded to majority sentiments by continuing to suppress that country's Turkish minority, whose population was growing at a more rapid pace than the Bulgarian majority.

The overthrow of the Soviet-dominated communist regimes of Eastern Europe paved the way for the downfall of the independent communist regimes of Albania and Yugoslavia. In Albania, Gheg tribal groups of the north agitated against Tosk tribes of the south, whom they viewed as favored by the communists. Albania also contended with its Greek minority's increasing assertiveness in Northern Epirus.

In Yugoslavia, the discredited communist government faced overt separatist pressures from Slovenes and Croatians in 1991. Both ultimately declared their independence and were later joined by the former internal Yugoslav republics of Bosnia-Herzegovina and Macedonia. The remaining rump of Yugoslavia—Serbia and Montenegro—responded militarily to these secessionist actions. The Belgrade regime was particularly motivated to ensure that Serbs living in Croatia and Bosnia-Herzegovina did not become subjects of new "nation-states" led by minority groups formerly dominated by the Serb plurality in interwar and communist Yugoslavia. The Serbian-Montenegrin state also devoted substantial resources to suppress its large Albanian minority concentrated in the so-called autonomous province of Kosovo. Newly independent Macedonia also had to contend with an increasingly irredentist Albanian minority.

Minority separation and general restiveness in Central and Southeastern Europe are matched by increasing activism among minorities to the west. Post-Franco republican Spain found it necessary to restore a degree of autonomy at once to its dissident national minorities. In 1978 it conceded the right to establish "autonomous communities" with official status for local languages and the right to fly traditional flags. Catalans, Basques, Galicians, Andalucíans, and others immediately took advantage of the opportunity, and by 1983 17 such self-governing areas had been created. Similarly, a new constitution in Belgium has bestowed some administrative authority to newly comprised,

regionally based legislatures in Flanders, Wallonia, and (bilingual) Brussels.

EUROPE'S INCREASING ETHNIC PARTICULARISM

The last decades of the twentieth century have witnessed increasing political agitation by ethnic minorities in Europe. Corsicans and Bretons in France and Ulster Catholics in the United Kingdom engaged in bombings and other terrorist acts to press separatist demands. Minority groups in other areas made political aspirations manifest in a less overt manner. Walloons and Flemings created segregated ethnic provinces within Belgium. Welsh and Scottish activists in the United Kingdom successfully pressed for referendums on separation from England, although both votes failed. In Italy, a Northern League political party won substantial adherents in its quest for autonomy of that country's prosperous northern part. Even the tiny island of Cyprus, with an area of only 3500 square miles and a population barely reaching 700,000, split into two de facto states owing to tensions between its Turkish and Greek inhabitants.

Contributing to minority disaffection are notable regional inequalities in economic development within several states. Generally speaking, the Industrial Revolution may be viewed as having slowly diffused from its origins in England southward and eastward over a distance approximating 750 miles. The line between primarily urbanized, industrialized, and commercialized Northwestern Europe and predominantly rural, agricultural, and subsistent Southern and Eastern Europe roughly passes across northeastern Spain, southern France, and central Italy. To the east it separates Croatia from Serbia and Bosnia-Herzegovina, Hungary from Romania, the Czech Republic from Slovakia, and western Poland from eastern Poland.

Exceptions to this generalization abound, of course. The Republic of Ireland is best grouped with the nonindustrialized states, even though it lies just across the Irish Sea from the relatively prosperous United Kingdom. Pockets of poverty exist in most industrialized European states, and zones of modern development surround capital cities and centers of resource complexes within the predominantly nonindustrial states of Southern and Eastern Europe.

Minority problems are exacerbated in areas where the boundary line between development and underdevelopment passes between a minority group and the dominant nation of a state. The Corsicans' disaffection lies in their slower economic growth in comparison with that of the mainland French. Nationalistic emotions are not always based on perceived deprivation, however. Basque and Catalan national feelings in northeastern Spain in part reflect anger that group income has been siphoned off to meet welfare needs in the less developed lands of the politically dominant Castillians. Earlier Slovenian and Croatian separatist activities in communist Yugoslavia reflected similar frustrations over the transfer of resources from them to poorer parts of the state.

EUROPEAN MOVEMENT TOWARD POLITICAL UNIFICATION

Chapter 1 of this book details the progressive establishment of a common market on the continent since the end of World War II. Associated with measures to end tariff barriers among European states and to harmonize agricultural subsidies have been the announced goals for eventual political unification. Since 1958, a European Parliament headquartered in Strasbourg, France has functioned in conjunction with the European Union. At a 1991 meeting of political leaders in Maastricht, the Netherlands, EU member states agreed to establish closer political ties and eventually to create a common currency.

However successful Europe's common market has been, a future politically united Europe seems unlikely. There is little evidence that parochial national feelings will wither away in favor of a continent-wide common identity. If the decisions of a European federal government negatively affect the inhabitants of one of its components, a strong movement for secession surely will follow. An instructive example here is the experience of the former USSR, where coercive bonding elements of pervasive secret police and monolithic party control failed. The clearly demonstrated economic benefits of continued unity could not temper enthusiasm for separate national sovereignties. The fact remains that although socialists in Europe have confidently predicted the demise of national identities ever since at least the middle of the nineteenth century, such national feelings have, if anything, intensified, particularly since World War II.

Indeed, the European Union's very success may well encourage the political fragmentation of its existing member states. If a tiny country like Luxembourg, with only 999 square miles, can provide high living standards for its inhabitants within a broad common market, why not an independent Flanders or Brittany? The successful separation of economic sovereignty from national sovereignty in the European Union has demonstrated that a people may "have their [political] cake, and eat it too [economically]." Although a national group must agree to give up the right to create measures favoring local production and commerce within the EU, it may, succeed in establishing and maintaining separate political self-government.

EUROPE'S NATIONS WITHOUT STATES

The successful recent secession of national minority groups from the states of Yugoslavia, Czechoslovakia, and the Soviet Union may portend similar future fragmentation of other European states. The following discussion summarizes the principal dissident European nations that lack states of their own. (In nearly all cases, the map of European linguistic groups in the previous chapter approximates regional patterns of national identities.) Interestingly there are relatively fewer minority national groups in East European states today than there were earlier in the century. As a result of the post-World War I breakup of the old empires, as well as the post–World War II forced resettlement of Germans and the postcommunist fragmentation of Yugoslavia and Czechoslovakia, some East European states are now purer nation-states than most of their counterparts in the West.

Although it is impossible to predict which, if any, of the following stateless nations will secede to form new nation-states, it is clear that governments of the respective states within which they are located will continuously be required to take their special interests into account. As parliamentary democracies in multinational states have learned, politics virtually always becomes ethnic. The result may be a variety of political adjustments, ranging from ethnic quotas in hiring to regional autonomy. Preservation and enhancement of a minority group's distinctive language are almost always associated with ethnic particularism.

France

Although France is often cited as an archetype of the nation-state, it faces increasing challenges from at least four major national groups: Corsicans, Bretons, Alsatians, and Occitanians. Corsicans (representing less than 1% of France's total population) have long chafed at control from Paris; their island has been part of France for far less time than other regions of the country. More devout sentiments toward the Roman Catholic Church prevail in Corsica than in the Paris Basin. Moreover, the Corsican language is closer to Italian than to French, and Corsicans live outside the area of France where processes of modernization have raised the standard of living.

Bretons (3%) in the northwestern Brittany Peninsula have a Celtic-based language and cultural heritage, although most have become bilingual, using both their Celtic and French. Their ancestors resisted incorporation by France until the sixteenth century and remained self-governing until the French Revolution. Attitudes toward the Roman Catholic Church, as among the Corsicans, have remained devout in contrast to the secularism of the Paris Basin. Through the middle of the twentieth century, French governments sought to eradicate their cultural distinctiveness, particularly in language, and Bretons have not participated in the growing affluence of the rest of northern France.

The Alsatians (2%) of northeastern France speak a Germanic language that French governments have periodically suppressed. Alsace did not become part of France until the mid-seventeenth century, and Alsatians maintain strong cultural and economic ties with adjacent Rhineland sections of Germany. They have prospered on a par with inhabitants of the Paris region, but remain more devout to the Roman Catholic Church than citizens in the rest of developed France.

Occitanians (3%), who populate the southern French area known as Provence, are a relatively new addition to the map of European national groups. Their vernaculars is less Germanized than Parisian French, and they are generally grouped together as the Langue d'Oc (thus their name, "language of those who say 'yes' with the word *oc*"). In recent years, their local intelligentsia has reinvigorated collective memories of Parisian suppression in the Middle Ages of their formerly rich culture and distinctive Albigensian Christian religion. Their region remains comparatively less developed economically than northern French territories.

Spain

The dominant Castillians of Spain face regional challenges from four distinctive groups that have evolved into separate nations: Basques, Catalans, Galicians, and Andalucians (Fig. 4-7). The Basques in northeastern Spain (making up 2% of Spain's population) speak Eskerra, a distinctive language unrelated to the Romance languages of the rest of Spain. They still mourn the loss of their historic *fueros* (group rights) following military defeat by Castillian forces in 1876. The present generation retains bitter memories of brutal suppression under the Franco regime from 1936 to 1975. Sometimes known as the "Yankees of Spain," they resent the drain of profits from their successful regional economy to less developed Spanish regions.

Catalans (16%) in the eastern region speak a Romance language that is closer to the Langue d'Oc of southern France than it is to standard Castillian Spanish. Like the Basques, the present generation of Catalans well remembers Franco's suppression, including their loss of rights to use their language in public. They resent the substantial modern influx of Castillians and other Spanish groups into their historic region. Catalans tend to be more secular than the traditionalist Castillians, and they also are unhappy about the outflow of profits accruing from their more highly developed commerce and industry to the rest of Spain.

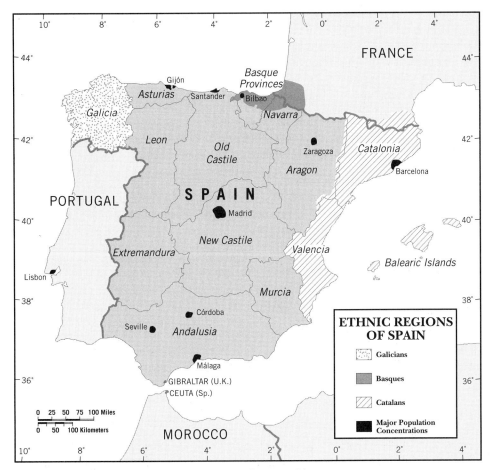

FIGURE 4-7 Ethnic regions in Spain. (From Poulsen, 1995.)

Galicians (8%), who live in the northwest corner of Spain, speak the Galego language, whose pronunciation and vocabulary are closer to Portuguese than to Castillian. Most Galicians believe that they are descendants of Celtic tribes, although scant reflections of Celtic heritage are to be found in their language and popular culture. They inhabit a poverty-stricken region from which a surplus population traditionally has found itself forced to emigrate to other parts of Spain or to Latin America.

Andalucíans (12%) dominate the former Moorish territories of the western Mediterranean coast of Spain. Their dialect is distinctive, but not as different from Castillian Spanish as the Galego and Catalan languages. Through history, the Andalucíans have felt themselves to be the victims of discrimination by Castillians for their past existence under Muslim Moorish control, despite sharing a common language and religion with the Castillians. Their region has not developed economically, in part because a large proportion of the rural population became landless when the Spanish kings gave grants of large estates to favored military officers.

The Netherlands

The Netherlands is justifiably renowned for its warm welcome and characteristic tolerance of foreign immigrants, notably Jewish refugees during periods of European repression, yet it does contain one distinctive minority group that resists assimilation. West Frisians (3% of the Netherlands' total population) occupy a compact area of 1300 square miles (nearly 3400 square km) northeast of the IJsselmeer (Zuider Zee). Their language, though related to Dutch, remains closer to the Low German Frisian spoken along the North Sea coasts of Germany and Denmark. Teachers and intellectuals have kept alive group resentments of forcible incorporation into the Netherlands during the Middle Ages, though few Frisians currently espouse separatist views.

Belgium

The Belgian state has long sustained animosities between its Dutch and French speakers. A common Roman Catholicism has not been enough to allow Belgium to overcome linguistic-based differences. Flemings (52% of Belgium's population), live in the north, speak a Dutch vernacular, and use standard Dutch as a writing medium. They share a strong sense of identity with the historic land of Flanders that they occupy. As traditionalist Catholics, however, they have few irredentist feelings toward the predominantly liberal and Protestant Netherlands. After becoming a constituent part of Belgium in the 1830s, Flemings felt themselves to be at an economic and political disadvantage to the dominant French-speaking Walloons, although Flemings have enjoyed cultural parity with Walloons since the 1890s and their regional economy has overtaken that of Wallonia.

Walloons (42%), who live in southern Belgium, speak and write the French language. Although they identify with French culture, most consider themselves to be part of a separate Walloon nation. They resent the demographic and political ascendancy of Flemings, whom they dominated well into the twentieth century.

The United Kingdom

Through a long-term policy of accommodation, compromise, and political devolution, the dominant English have forged a united British state throughout most of the UK. Still, strong regionalist sentiments short of nationhood prevail among Scots, Shetland Islanders, Welsh, Manx, Channel Islanders, Cornish, Protestant Ulster Irish, and others. The homelands of these groups are characterized by less vigorous economic development than that in affluent southeastern England. Among the regionalists, Scots appear most likely to evolve into a separatist nation. Scots hearken back to a Scottish kingdom that was integrated with England only in the eighteenth century, and many resent English control of petroleum wealth derived from the wells off Scotland in the North Sea.

In addition to these regionalist groups, one clear national group antagonistic to the British state also has evolved in the United Kingdom. Catholic Ulster Irish (less than 1% of the UK's population) have been waging guerrilla warfare against the UK government for more than 25 years in the six Northern Ireland counties that were retained as part of the United Kingdom after a referendum resulted in creation of an Irish Free State in 1920. An unwise British decision to use ancient county lines to separate the Irish Free State from the United Kingdom left a pro-separatist Catholic minority of 30 percent in Ulster. A boundary based on election precincts still would have left many Catholics against their will in loyalist Ulster, but probably would have resulted in a group insufficiently large to be able to support guerrilla activities. The Catholic Irish faith, though not itself a motivating factor for hostilities, serves as a badge to separate them from loyalist Protestants of Ulster, who have a sorry record of job denial and other forms of discrimination against Catholics dating back to the nineteenth century. Although their major goal is to unite Ulster with the Irish Republic, Irish Catholics receive little popular support from south of the border.

Germany

Like the United Kingdom, Germany is characterized by pronounced regionalisms, but none has yet developed to the point of separate nationhood. Inhabitants of the former German Democratic Republic remained part of the German nation during 45 years of enforced separation from the Federal Republic. Since unification of the two states in 1990, however, the east Germans have lost many romantic national illusions and have come to resent the wealth and arrogance perceived in the more developed western provinces. Ancient tribal identities still separate Saxons from Prussians in eastern Germany, and Bavarians from Hessians and other regional groups in the west. Such divisions are reinforced by contrasts between Catholic predominance in the south and west and Protestant majorities in the north and east, although the divisions seem unlikely to be nearly strong enough to ignite separatist movements.

Italy

Regionalisms also are to be found in Italy, mainly between the more affluent north, once part of the medieval Holy Roman Empire, and the poorer south, once part of the Papal States and the Kingdom of the Two Sicilies. A relatively new political party, the Northern League, has galvanized regional sentiments against the perceived endemic corruption and lawlessness emanating from the southern peninsula and islands, although political differences have not yet reached the level of national division. Italy does have one pronounced national minority, however. South Tiroleans (under 1% of Italy's population) occupy about 3000 square miles (7770 square km) of the southern slopes of the Alps adjacent to western Austria. These German-speaking people were forcibly joined to Italy in 1918 under a mistaken Italian belief that the action would result in greater security of its Alpine borders. South Tiroleans have created problems for Italian regimes ever since; past attempts to denationalize them and dilute their numbers with immigrants from the south were unsuccessful. Although they share a common culture with Tiroleans of western Austria, their political goals have not identified them with Austria, whose capital Vienna appears to them as distant and nearly as foreign as Rome.

The Czech Republic

In contrast to the former Czechoslovakia, this successor state comprised of the Czech lands is remarkably homogeneous. Its troublesome 30 percent German Sudetenland minority was expelled at the end of World War II. Still, the Czech nation does experience some regional divisions. Bohemians of the Elbe (Labe) River Basin face increasingly strong localist feelings by Moravians to the east, although frictions have not escalated to the point of becoming national sentiments.

Slovakia

Having achieved their own national self-determination through separation from the Czechs in 1993, Slovaks appear unwilling to allow similar sentiments among their own national minorities. Indeed, they have abrogated some minority privileges granted by the former Czechoslovak government. In this action, they have seemingly followed the lead of their own former national oppressors: after the Kingdom of Hungary gained separate and equal status with Austria in the former Habsburg Empire in the 1860s, it sought to Magyarize the Slovak, Romanian, and Croatian minorities within its territory. Slovakia is treading on dangerous ground because its two principal minorities are potentially irredentist.

Magyars (making up 10% of Slovakia's total population) had their lands added to the Slovak portions of Czechoslovakia after World War I, because regional centers for the predominantly mountain-dwelling Slovaks were situated on adjacent plains in settlements dominated by Magyars, who differ from Slovaks mainly in their Finno-Ugrian language. Hungary gained these lands temporarily during World War II before being forced to relinquish them at the end of the war. Magyars in Slovakia had a brief opportunity to express unhappiness with Slovak domination of their lives during the short-lived, liberal "Prague Spring" in Czechoslovakia in 1968. An increasingly self-confident postcommunist Hungary may well take up their cause.

Ruthenians or Rusyns (7%), themselves including several self-identifying ethnic subgroups, represent but a remnant of the formerly large number of Ukrainians in prewar Czechoslovakia. Most of the Ruthenians lived in the Carpatho-Ukraine province seized by Hungary in 1940, annexed in 1944 by the USSR, and now within independent Ukraine. They have contacts with the strongly nationalistic western part of Ukraine. Like Slovakia's Magyars, the Ruthenians remain angry over former linguistic and cultural privileges that were canceled by the new Slovak regime, though their cultural status has in the meantime improved.

Croatia

Since achieving independence from Yugoslavia in 1991, Croatians have been confronted by hostilities of a militant national minority within its historic borders. Serbs, who constituted 11 percent of Croatia's pre-independence population, declared their own "Krajina Republic" in the former Habsburg Croatian Military Frontier zone. Their cause was originally aided by Serbian forces of the rump Yugoslavia as well as by Serbs inhabiting newly independent Bosnia-Herzegovina, although during 1995 most of the territory was occupied by Croatian forces. Though sharing a common Serbocroatian language with Croatians, the Serbian Orthodox faith and a Byzantine heritage distinguish them from the Roman Catholic Croats, who were formerly part of the Habsburg Empire. The largest part of Croatia's Serbs lived outside the Krajina region in cities like Zagreb and Osijek, and most fled to Serbia and Serbian-controlled territories or were interned in concentration camps after fighting began within the former Yugoslavia.

Bosnia-Herzegovina

Muslims in pre-independence Bosnia-Herzegovina functioned as a secular nation comparable to Catholics of Northern Ireland and were so recognized by Yugoslavia's communist regime. They constituted a plurality of 40 percent in Bosnia-Herzegovina and shared the republic with two militant minorities. Serbs (32%) rebelled against Bosnia-Herzegovina's declaration of independence in 1992 and subsequently engaged in open warfare with the republic's Muslims and Croats. Serbs share the Serbocroatian language with the Muslims and Roman Catholic Croats, but are dis-

tinguished from both, as noted earlier. Their political goal is to become part of a "Greater Serbia" that includes rump Yugoslavia. Croats (18%) are concentrated particularly in the western Herzegovina part of the republic. They identify with the Croat state of Croatia and have alternatively struggled with and found common cause with Bosnia-Herzegovina's Muslims during warfare in the republic.

"Yugoslavia"

After the secession of Slovenia, Croatia, Bosnia-Herzegovina, and Macedonia, only the former socialist republics of Serbia and Montenegro remain to the rump Yugoslavia. It supported Serbs in the secessionist republics, including engaging its army in severe fighting during the early 1990s. The rump Yugoslavia faces potential troubles from three principal minorities. Montenegrins (5% of "Yugoslavia's" population) share Orthodox Christianity and the Serbocroatian language with the Serbs, and in fact are viewed by the Serbian nation merely as "mountain-dwelling Serbs." Relatively few Montenegrins have this view, however, and most take particular pride in the fact that, unlike the Serbs, their ancestors never were conquered by Ottoman forces. Nearly all Montenegrins live in the southwest corner of Yugoslavia adjacent to the Adriatic Sea.

Albanians (14%) are particularly concentrated in the southern, so-called autonomous province of Kosovo. Although not irredentist during the communist era, they have increasingly found common cause with Albanians of Albania as Serbian pressures on them have mounted. They differ from the Orthodox Slavic-speaking Serbs by their predominantly Muslim religion and distinctive Illyrian-based language. Serbs particularly resent their presence in Kosovo, since most Serbs believe that Kosovo was their cultural hearth until Ottoman forces drove them out after 1389 and allowed Albanians to settle in their former villages.

Magyars (4%) live adjacent to Hungary in Serbia's northern Vojvodina region. They differ from Serbs by their Finno-Ugrian language and Roman Catholic religion. Serbian curtailment of customary rights enjoyed under the past Yugoslav communist regime has generated some irredentist feelings, as has recent settlement in their traditional lands by Serbian refugees from Croatia and Bosnia-Herzegovina.

Macedonia

Macedonian feelings of nationhood emerged mainly during World War II, distinguishing them from their neighboring, fellow Slavic-speaking nations of Bulgarians and Serbs. Since independence in 1992, they have struggled for international recognition of their nation and state in the face of opposition by the government of Greece. Macedonia has one major national minority problem. Albanians (20%) dominate its western valleys and constitute a significant component of the population of eastern cities. Their Muslim religion and Illyrian language set them apart from the Slavic-speaking, Orthodox Macedonians.

Romania

The Romanian state grew at the end of World War I when it received the province of Transylvania and the Banat of Temesvar from the Kingdom of Hungary, Southern Dobrogea from Bulgaria, the Bukovina from the Habsburg Empire, and Bessarabia from Russia. It subsequently lost all but multinational Transylvania, whose large German minority has mostly emigrated to Germany in recent decades. One principal national minority remains: Hungarians (11% of the total population of Romania), concentrated in eastern and northern Transylvania. Their Finno-Ugrian speech differs markedly from the Latin-based Romanian language, and the Roman Catholic and Protestant religions of the Transylvanian Magyars contrast with the Orthodox Christianity of the Romanians. Hungarians resent the many decades during which precommunist, communist, and postcommunist Romanian regimes sought to denationalize them. Although separated from Hungary by a zone of Romanian settlement, Hungarians in Romania generally harbor irredentist views.

Bulgaria

The Bulgarian state has long held expansionist views towards adjacent territories, including Grecian eastern Thrace and all of Macedonia. It briefly achieved its aims three times—in the 1878 Treaty of San Stefano, the Balkan War of 1912, and World War II—although in each instance it soon lost all its acquisitions. Bulgars have unsuccessfully sought to assimilate three internal national minority groups: Turks, Pomaks and Macedonains.

Turks (9% of Bulgaria's population), live mainly in northeastern Bulgaria, speak an Altaic language, and have a Muslim heritage, in contrast to the Slavic-speaking, Orthodox Bulgarian majority. Many of these Turks emigrated to Turkey after World War II and again during a period of denationalization pressures by the Bulgarian regime during the 1980s, when the communists, among other measures, sought to force them to adopt Christian Bulgarian names. Bulgarians fear their Turkish minority because of its notably high rate of natural increase.

Pomaks (less than 1%) speak the Bulgarian language but have retained the Muslim religion of Slavic ancestors converted from Christianity. They live mainly along Bulgaria's southern border and have faced the same discrimination as Bulgaria's ethnic Turks.

Macedonians (3%) in Bulgaria's western Pirin region, like their counterparts in independent Macedonia, essentially speak a Bulgarian dialect and share the Orthodox religion of the Bulgarians. They remained part of Turkey until the end of the Balkan wars in 1912 and consider themselves to be distinctive from their eastern neighbors. Bulgarian regimes have sought to denationalize the Pirin Macedonians since communist Yugoslavia's establishment of an internal Macedonian Socialist Republic in 1945. Thus, Bulgaria has refused to recognize the existence of a Macedonian ethnic group in census returns, and an irredentist potential exists.

Greece

Although Greece appears to many observers to be a homogeneous nation-state, its many islands and patchy mainland ecumene result in numerous pronounced regionalisms. Greece lost virtually all its Turkish minority in population exchanges with Turkey in 1920, but it has had to contend with two significant minority groups: Macedonians and Albanians.

Macedonians (up to 20% of Greece's population), termed Slavophones by the Greek government, live in northern Greece adjacent to Macedonia and Bulgaria. Public use of their Slavic language has long been forbidden, but they have retained a sense of distinctiveness over four generations since Greece acquired their territory in 1913 after the Balkan wars. Fearing future nationalist agitation among Slavophones, Greece has sought to delay European Union recognition of independent Macedonia on the grounds that it is an "artificial" entity using a name that is inherently Greek.

Albanians (less than 1%) live in the Epirus region of northwestern Greece adjacent to Albania. Although many share the Greeks' Eastern Orthodox religion, they differ by way of the Illyrian language and tribal traditions.

The Consequences of Fragmentation

The separation of any or all of these enumerated minority nations from states in which they are now located should not be deplored on principle, any more than the political independence from European overlordship by former colonies in Africa and Asia during the 1950s and 1960s. Indeed, in many instances, relationships between a minority nation and the majority nation dominating its state tend to closely parallel past European colonial relationships with overseas peoples. Although a minority's quest for sovereignty may appear to be clearly unwise in terms of its own economic or other interests, that would seem to be the province of the group itself to determine (Fig. 4-8). Efforts by outside parties to thwart separatism on grounds such as preservation of international stability may prove counterproductive to intended aims. The United States government erred at the end of the Cold War when it enunciated foreign policies favoring preservation of the territorial integrity of the postcommunist USSR and Yugoslavia. Through monolithic one-party and secret police controls, both multinational states had operated in effect as colonial empires of their dominant nations, Russians and Serbs, and their regimes were, if anything, less benevolent than past Dutch or British colonial regimes. While it might have been more convenient for the U.S. State Department to deal with a single united former Soviet state rather than 15 separated fragments, nothing the United States ultimately could do would be able to stem the process of national self-determination after the collapse of the USSR.

The terrible internecine war within the former Yugoslavia was likely exacerbated, if not provoked, by American policy. Revulsion had developed among Yugoslavia's Slovenes, Croats, Albanians, and Muslims against the Serbian-dominated regime's heavy-handed suppression of minority national sentiments and clumsy interference with local economies. If the U.S. and European governments had perceived that national separation was inevitable following collapse of the Yugoslav communist system, they might well have played a positive role in assuring a peaceful transition to separate nation-states. The Serbs interpreted U.S. policy favoring continuation of a unified Yugoslavia as support for continuing Serbian hegemony over the other nations. A strong American statement denouncing any use of force by the Yugoslav regime to counter moves toward separate sovereignties could have held Serbian nationalists in check and led to a separation in which the newly independent states might continue to trade and otherwise complement each other. After hostilities began, national antagonisms and sentiments of revenge fed upon themselves, and any policies and demands by external states became virtually irrelevant.

A prevailing misconception is that political sovereignty must be based on a large enough economy to guarantee autarkic economic development and well being. The experience of the twentieth century yields a quite different perspective. Europeans have demonstrated that the small size of sovereign units need not be a deterrent to economic efficiency gained through regional specialization and exchange that is based on inherent territorial comparative advantages in production.

An ever-growing proportion of European states have joined together into a common market that

FIGURE 4-8 Selected regions with serious ethnically based political problems in the 1990s. (From Berentsen, 1993.)

permits scale and other efficiencies found in large territorial units such as the United States. European states have always found ways to cooperate economically to overcome individual limited land spaces. For example, although the five Norden states (Iceland, Denmark, Norway, Sweden, Finland) have long jealously maintained their individual national political sovereignties, they have cooperated for decades in order to tackle economic and social problems. Thus, Norwegians have no apparent desire to join politically with either Sweden or Denmark again, but they have no problems in harmonizing laws and regulations with their former mother countries on matters such as pensions, or in permitting free movement of individuals and capital funds throughout the Norden region as opportunities present themselves.

Before the advent of a united Germany in 1871, the tiny independent German states successfully achieved mutual economic benefits under the nineteenth-century *Zollverein*, or customs union. Luxembourg is an example of a small state that has succeeded in developing itself through linkages with other states in economic matters. Originally a member of the *Zollverein*, Luxembourg found itself detached from the German economy after World War I. Rebuffed in its efforts to tie itself to France, it then formed a customs union with Belgium. After World War II, it became part of the Benelux union with Belgium and the Netherlands that later merged with other European states to form what became the European Union.

Similar international organizations are in the process of forming in European territories that remain outside the current boundaries of the EU, including an association of states astride the Danube that were formerly part of the Habsburg Empire and an Alps-Adria consultative body composed of Austria, Slovenia, and parts of Italy. Russia, Belarus, Ukraine, and other former republics of the Soviet Union cooperate in production and trade through the so-called Commonwealth of Independent States. The group emotion of national identity is a powerful one that can be satisfied through achievement of political sovereignty. And political sovereignty need not be incompatible with broader regional cooperation with other states in economic and other spheres of life.

BIBLIOGRAPHY

Anderson, J. (1988). "Nationalist Ideology and Territory." In *Nationalism, Self-Determination and Political Geography*, eds. R.J. Johnston, D. Knight, and E. Kofman. London: Croom Helm, pp.18–39.

Anderson, James. (1990). "Separatism and Devolution: The Basques in Spain." In *Shared Space: Divided Space: Essays on Conflict and Territorial Organization*, eds. Michael Chisholm and David M. Smith. London: Unwin Hyman, pp.135–156.

Berentsen, William H. (1993). "A Geopolitical Overview of Europe," *Social Education* 57 (4): 170–176.

Boal, F. W., and J. N. H. Douglas, eds. (1982). *Integration and Division: Geographical Perspectives on the Northern Ireland Problem*. London: Academic Press.

Darby, J., ed. (1983). *Northern Ireland: The Background to the Conflict*. Belfast: Appletree Press.

Demko, George, and William B. Wood, eds. (1994). *Reordering the World: Geopolitical Perspectives on the Twenty-First Century*. Boulder, Colo.: Westview Press.

East, W. G. (1966). *An Historical Geography of Europe*, 5th ed. New York: E. P. Dutton.

Foster, Charles R. (1980). *Nations Without a State: Ethnic Minorities in Western Europe*. New York: Praeger.

Glassner, Martin, and Harm de Blij. (1989). *Systematic Political Geography*, 4th ed. New York: John Wiley & Sons.

Hooson, David, ed. (1994). *Geography and National Identity*. Cambridge, Mass.: Blackwell.

Jordan, T. C. (1988). *The European Culture Area*, 2nd ed. New York: Harper & Row.

Knight, David B. (1982). "Identity and Territory: Geographical Perspectives on Nationalism and Regionalism," *Annals of the Association of American Geographers* 72 (4): 514–531.

MacLaughlin, J. G. (1986). "The Political Geography of 'Nation-Building' and Nationalism in Social Sciences: Structural *vs.* Dialectical Accounts," *Political Geography Quarterly* 5 (4): 299–399.

Medhurst, J. (1982). "Basques and Basque Nationalism." In *National Separatism*, ed. C. H. Williams. Cardiff: University of Wales Press.

Mohan, J., ed. (1989). *The Political Geography of Contemporary Britain*. London: Macmillan.

Murphy, Alexander B. (1988). "Evolving Regionalism in Linguistically Divided Belgium." In *Nationalism, Self-Determination and Political Geography*, eds. R.J. Johnston, David B. Knight, and Eleonore Kofman. London: Croom Helm, pp.135-150.

Pacione, Michael, ed. (1985). *Progress in Political Geography*. London: Croom Helm.

Poulsen, Thomas M. (1995). *Nations and States: A Geographic Background to World Affairs*. Englewood Cliffs, NJ: Prentice-Hall.

Pounds, N.J.G., and S. S. Ball. (1964). "Core Areas and the Development of the European States System," *Annals of the Association of American Geographers* 54: 24–40.

Pringle, Dennis. (1985). *One Island, Two Nations? A Political Geographical Analysis of the National Conflict in Ireland*. Letchworth: Research Studies Press.

Pringle, Dennis. (1990). "Separation and Integration: The Case of Ireland." In *Shared Space: Divided Space: Essays on Conflict and Territorial Organization*, eds. Michael Chisholm and David M. Smith. London: Unwin Hyman, pp.157–177.

Reynolds, D., and D. Knight. (1989). "Political Geography." In *Geography in America*, eds. G. Gaile and C. Willmott. Columbus, Ohio: Merrill.

Stephens, Meic. (1976). *Linguistic Minorities in Western Europe*. Llandysul, Wales: Gomer Press.

Williams, C. H. (1991). *Linguistic Minorities, Society, and Territory*, Multilingual Matters No. 78. Clevedon: Multilingual Matters Ltd.

5

ECONOMIC GEOGRAPHY

Despite Western Europe's continued concern about economic problems and its seeming inability to achieve its grandest designs to unite economically and politically into a United States of Europe, economically it is in fact, one of the world's most successful regions. Many of the world's most affluent countries and, unquestionably, the world's most successful international trading community, the European Union, are located within it. Although Eastern Europe and the FSU are poor compared to the West, economic growth and development in at least parts of the latter region, especially East Central Europe, provide hopeful signs that it is beginning a process that will lead to higher levels of development.

In 1994 Europe was the headquarters for 31 of the world's 100 largest business enterprises by revenues—including 12 in Germany and 11 in France. The largest are Royal Dutch Shell (10th largest in the world), Daimler-Benz (20th), Siemens (30th), British Petroleum (31st), and Volkswagen (34th), with revenues ranging from $95 billion to $49 billion in that year. In addition, despite the small size of most European countries and the general shortage of natural resources (except in Russia and

Ukraine), a number of countries rank high in the production of raw materials and manufactured products—most notably Germany and France (Table 5-1). Russia has perhaps the world's most abundant natural resource base and is a major producer of a wide array of products (Table 5-2).

Many parts of the world economy are closely tied by trade and investment to Europe, including it's major economic rivals, the United States and Japan. In the mid-1990s the United States' total trade with Europe (excluding the FSU) was about $250 billion annually, around 80 percent of which was between the USA and EU. An estimated 2 million jobs in the United States are tied to exports to Europe; EU-owned companies employ 2.8 million American workers. In addition, American firms and individuals have invested about $200 billion in properties within Europe. For example, about one-half of U.S. foreign manufacturing investments are in Western Europe. The United States' economic presence in East Central and Southeastern Europe and the FSU is also expanding. Similarly, Europe's ties to the USA are extremely important. In recent years Europe's exports to the USA have exceeded its imports, greatly helping

TABLE 5-1

EUROPEAN COUNTRIES' WORLD RANK AND PERCENTAGE OF WORLD PRODUCTION
IN SELECTED PRODUCTS, EARLY 1990S (EXCLUDING THE FSU)[a]

Country	Product	World Rank	Percent of World Production
Natural Resources			
Netherlands	Natural gas	5	4
Poland	Coal	6	6
UK	Oil	9	4
Albania	Chromite	10	1
Poland	Copper	8	4
Spain	Mercury	3	16
Norway	Magnesium	3	10
Germany	Potash	2	15
Sweden	Roundwood	7	2
Germany	Salt	3	7
Poland	Silver	8	6
Poland	Sulfur	5	4
Portugal	Tin	9	3
Agricultural Products			
Germany	Apples	2	6
Germany	Barley	3	7
Germany	Oats	4	5
Spain	Olive oil	1	28
Spain	Oranges	4	7
Germany	Rape seed	4	10
Poland	Rye	2	24
France	Sugar	7	4
France	Sunflower seed oil	3	11
Italy	Tobacco	9	2
France	Wheat	5	6
UK	Wool	7	3
France	Cheese	2	15
France	Eggs	6	2
Norway	Frozen fish	6	3
Germany	Hogs	4	3
Manufactured Products			
Norway	Aluminum	7	4
Germany	Autos	3	11
UK	Book titles	2	NA

(continued)

	TABLE 5-1		

Country	Product	World Rank	Percent of World Production
Manufactured Products – (continued)			
Italy	Cement	6	3
Germany	Merchant ship tons	4	11
Sweden	Newsprint	4	6
Netherlands	Nitrogenous fertilizer	6	3
Germany	Pharmaceuticals	3	7
Germany	Steam turbines	4	11
Germany	Steel	5	6
Germany	Synthetic rubber	4	5
France	Tires	3	7
Belgium	Tractors	4	4
France	Trucks	5	4
Italy	Woven woolens	2	16
Germany	Zinc	3	5

[a] Based on production by quantity. Most data are for 1993 or 1994, but 1991 or 1992 in some cases. Ranks and production vary somewhat annually. NA= not available

Source: Knight-Ridder (1995); U.N. (1994); U.S. Department of Agriculture (1993).

many countries' balance of payments; European investments in the USA have also grown rapidly. From 1984 to 1993 the United States attracted 58 percent of all EU foreign investment. The UK has been far and away the leading investor in the USA, accounting for nearly a quarter of foreign capital invested in the country. UK corporations, for example, now control numerous widely renowned "American" businesses, such as Hilton, Holiday Inn, Burger King, and Pillsbury. In short, though hampered somewhat by continued political fragmentation and relatively high costs of production, the European economy is a key component of and quite competitive within the global economy.

This chapter provides an introduction to Europe's economic geography, including, in particular, the locational pattern of economic activities and why this pattern exists. Prior to discussion of the location of primary, secondary, and service activities, introductory sections of this chapter

briefly survey the historical evolution of economic activity in Europe, and cover selected aspects of the contemporary European economy, such as levels of national economic development and characteristics of countries' sectoral structures and labor forces. Following a review of the location of sectoral activities, the chapter concludes with sections on trade, the relationship between economic development and the environment, and problems of regional development.

HISTORICAL ECONOMIC GEOGRAPHY: A BRIEF INTRODUCTION

Despite the importance to Europe of what is commonly called the Industrial Revolution of the nineteenth century, the historic roots of the region's economic geography can easily be traced back from one to two thousand years. Over these mil-

TABLE 5-2

PRODUCTION OF SELECTED PRODUCTS IN RUSSIA[a]

	Product	World Rank	Percent of World Production
Natural Resources	Coal	5	2
	Diamonds	4	14
	Gold	5(t)	7
	Magnesium	2	11
	Natural gas	1	28
	Nickel	1	25
	Oil	3	10
	Roundwood	3	NA
Agricultural Products	Hogs	3	3
	Rye	1	27
	Wheat	4	7
	Wool	4	6
Manufactured Products	Cement	3	7
	Cotton fabric	3	9
	Footwear	2	8
	Electricity	2	8
	Gasoline	2	5
	Harvesters	2	31
	Linen fabric	1	52
	Newsprint	5	5
	Nitrogenous fertilizer	3	9
	Steam turbines	2	30
	Steel	3	11
	Tractors	2	7
	Trucks	4	5
	Woolen fabric	3	12

[a] Most data are for 1992 or 1993. Ranks and production vary somewhat annually. Based on production by quantity. (t) = tie   NA = Not Available

Source: Knight-Ridder (1995); U.N. (1994); U.S. Department of Agriculture (1993).

lennia, countless important technological changes and innovations have been made, which, when combined with the regional and temporal differentiation of resources, markets, and public policies result in a highly complex history of one of the world's greatest economic regions. Although there certainly are and have been regional variations in access to resources and markets, an historical economic geography must inevitably underscore the role of political decisions in economic development and their expression in countries' (or empires') regional economic development. This is emphasized by, for example, scrutiny of the economic decline of the once powerful Spanish Empire as the result of poor policy choices (especially in the sixteenth and seventeenth centuries) and the economic decline and abrupt demise of the Soviet Empire in the twentieth century. In contrast, the rise of the Prussian/German and British economies during the seventeenth to nineteenth centuries can be partly explained by wiser policy choices (Cameron, 1993).

Nearly 2000 years ago, much of Europe was united within what was a relatively well-organized political and economic empire centered on Rome. Although many individuals within the empire were slaves and many others, no doubt, were poor, the empire also allowed the development of a

small, wealthy class and provided a modicum of economic and political protection for large numbers of people. Infrastructure, notably roads and water systems, were constructed that survive to the present, and, indeed, in some cases are still in use (Fig. 5-1). Political stability, protection for merchants, and a rudimentary monetary and financial system permitted interregional trade within the empire and between it and other territories. However, population growth, deteriorating discipline among bureaucrats and the military, and lack of technological progress made the western portion of the empire too weak to survive invasion, and it collapsed. The eastern portion of the empire, Byzantium, survived in Southeastern Europe for 12 more centuries. Collapse in the western empire was probably also closely related to lack of personal incentives for the great majority of workers, who

FIGURE 5-1 Roman viaduct at Segovia, Spain. Monuments to engineering skills within the Roman Empire, impressive public works such as this one still stand in many places all around the Mediterranean region. (W. H. Berentsen)

were virtually or actually enslaved and had little to gain personally by innovating. In addition, workers may have surmised that time and effort not placed into what was viewed as constructive work would prove a disadvantage for them in the short term, with no prospects for any long-term benefits from innovative behavior. (This problem was echoed 1600 years later in the economic conditions and policies of the Soviet Empire.) The fall of Rome resulted in a long period of economic stagnation and political instability known as the Dark Ages.

The Dark Ages were characterized by generally poorer standards of living. Political and economic stability were ultimately regained following the development of a feudal economic and political system through which individuals traded their freedom for high levels of economic and political subservience to an hierarchically organized noble class which, in theory, offered the masses protection from external threat. By the tenth century, many parts of Europe also began on the long, halting political and economic path that ultimately led to the Industrial Revolution and to today's highly specialized and regionally interconnected global and European economies.

The first step in this process—improvement in agricultural yields—seems modest in retrospect. Yields rose owing to the adoption of a heavier, horse-drawn plow and use of a new crop rotation system, the three-course system in place of the earlier two-course system. Each of these innovations helped boost output and levels of productivity. Largely urban-based artisans also produced hand-manufactured products that entered into the expanding trade organized within far-flung empires ruled from Venice and Genoa and within the Baltic-based trade federation known as the Hansa or Hanseatic League. Improved financial institutions (especially banks and insurance companies) and more reliable currencies supported increased interregional trade.

In then prosperous Northwestern Europe, Brugge (in modern Belgium) initially emerged as the major early port and trading center for the region, but with the growth of ship sizes and the silting of the small river that served as its outlet to the sea other major ports emerged through time—first Amsterdam, later Antwerp, and in the last century or so, Rotterdam. Brugge had access to the sea and a good location within relatively densely settled Northwestern Europe. It also had an initial advantage owing to the role of Flanders, other parts of Belgium, and northern France as centers for the earliest concentrations of European manufacturing—with an emphasis on textile production. (Northern Italy was another such early center.)

Small-scale metal production, especially iron production, was also an early European industry. At first, production was widely scattered, based on small local iron ore deposits and use of charcoal as another major raw material input. Later, when more advanced smelting technology was developed and higher levels of output were demanded, wood resources became scarcer and iron and steel production developed rapidly on and near coalfields.

On average, development levels continued to improve in Northwestern Europe, especially during the medieval period. However, the temporal pattern of economic development was by no means unilinear. Severe setbacks, for example, occurred during the fourteenth century, owing largely to worsened climatic conditions and rampant plague, and again in the seventeenth century, owing to the destruction and political instability wrought by international warfare (notably the devastating Thirty Years War, which drastically reduced the population of Central Europe).

By the late seventeenth century, patterns of European economic development that were to hold firm well into the twentieth century began to emerge. For example, although inanimate power had yet to be widely harnessed for manufacturing, England established itself as a leading exporter of manufactured products, especially woolen cloth. International trade was expanding rapidly, not only within Europe, but also between it and emerging empires in Asia and the Americas. The American trade was also somewhat complex—simple manufactured products were sent to Africa, where slaves were purchased, who were delivered to American plantations, from which agriculturally derived products came back to Europe, notably sugar and rum, in the so-called triangular trade system. In the sixteenth and seventeenth centuries, Dutch shipping dominated the seas, although England was emerging as the second most important merchant shipper.

During the eighteenth and early nineteenth centuries, one of the world's most important economic eras came to fruition—the "Industrial Revolution" (Fig. 5-2). Many economic historians are unhappy with this popularly accepted term, because it suggests a sudden explosion of innovation and investment in manufacturing without due regard to the slow creation of necessary foundations for this economic blossoming during several preceding centuries. Nonetheless, the early Industrial Revolution (extending from about 1770 to 1850) was certainly a time of more rapid change and expansion in manufacturing than had ever occurred previously in human history. Earlier economic achievements, such as increased agricultural productivity and improved conditions for interregional transportation, greatly facilitated the inventions and innovations of the Industrial Revolution era, such as those in cotton ginning and

mechanized spinning and weaving, in the harnessing of steam and then electric power for machines, and in the production of metals. According to Walter Rostow, Europe reached a "takeoff" stage in its economic development, which resulted in successive, "rapid and sustained" growth in a number of key sectors, such as shipping, railroads, and metallurgy. This provided a stimulus for collateral development in other economic sectors and a basis for ongoing structural economic change and growth (Rostow, 1969).

Although various authors (see Pounds and Cameron) provide very good, thorough overviews of the Industrial Revolution, their descriptions of what really occurred differ somewhat. They generally acknowledge the following components: development of commercialized agriculture and availability of an agricultural surplus that helped feed urban-industrial workers; im-

FIGURE 5-2 Hanley, England: a pottery town created by the Industrial Revolution (School of Architecture Library, University of Texas, Austin.)

proved transportation and an interlocking transport system comprised of canals, roads, railroads, ports, and seagoing shipping; harnessing of inanimate energy to run newly developed, labor-saving machinery within fixed factories; application of science to advance economic production and related development of human-made products (e.g., specialized chemicals); and changes in the organization and management of firms (e.g., incorporation) to allow concentration of capital required for activities that benefited from economies of scale. Scale economies especially influenced the development of railroads, mining, steel, and later, auto production as well.

Europe also benefited from related innovations that emerged from a developing American economy, which was both dependent on and interlinked with the European economy. Notable innovations that came "back" to Europe from the United States included the use of mass-produced, interchangeable parts for facilitating faster, cheaper assembly of final products, and the adoption of assembly-line production techniques. Important political developments, such as the German *Zollverein* (Customs Union) in 1833, the later complete consolidation of the German Empire (1871), and, for a time, the relaxation of impediments to international trade among Northwestern European states (during 1860–1930), further enhanced the positive impacts of all these developments.

Europe's early industrial growth was sustained by the availability of key resources and infrastructure: cheap labor; coal, iron ore, and waterpower; widely scattered metal and mineral ore deposits; access to many advantageous transportation routes; and adequate investment funds. Before charcoal was replaced by coke as a smelting agent, the forests of Europe provided ample charcoal for the industry. The emergence of coal as the major energy source, however, coincided with the rapid development of Europe's earliest large industrial concentrations.

The United Kingdom became the world's first industrialized country during the early nineteenth century, followed fairly quickly by Belgium, France, and Germany. Thereafter, countries originally disadvantaged by the lack of coal also "industrialized"—Austro-Hungary, Denmark, the Netherlands, Sweden, and Switzerland. Italy and Spain lagged somewhat further behind, while many parts of Southern and Southeastern Europe were the last areas to become more industrialized. Many parts of Southeastern Europe are still not fully "industrialized," such as the agrarian Alentejo region of southeastern Portugal.

Early during the era of industrialization, the main area of manufacturing industries in Europe was in proximity to Europe's main coalfields in a belt from the British Midlands through Belgium and northern France to the Saar-Lorraine and Ruhr regions. All of these areas remain industrialized, although several now have problems owing to inadequate structural change over the ensuing one and one-half centuries of economic and technological transformation.

In the late ninteenth century and the beginning of the twentieth century, Europe's core industrial area expanded into numerous small areas located in central and southern Sweden, northern Italy, the Swiss Plateau, and the Barcelona region of Spain. In addition, numerous small manufacturing centers and individual manufacturing enterprises were dispersed into Austria (Styria); parts of Bohemia (the Sudeten region); northern Slovenia; a number of areas in Germany, including ports (Hamburg, Bremen, Lübeck); and the Rhone-Saone valleys of France. Industrial centers originally established during the period of the Austro-Hungarian monarchy in Austrian Silesia, Bohemia, Slovenia, and western Transylvania were expanded during the 1920s and 1930s.

Many European industrial areas expanded greatly during the early years of World War II and then were badly damaged during the latter phases of the war. Areas in Western Europe were hit by Allied bombing, whereas those in the East were damaged by both fierce ground combat and later, in eastern Germany and in other places where Nazis had owned businesses, by the heavy-handed dismantling of manufacturing plants for displacement to the USSR. Ultimately, Western Europe's economic renewal was sparked by the Marshall Plan, an enlightened, multifaceted effort implemented by the United States to rebuild Western Europe's economy and to prevent the rise of another demagogue like Hitler, who had exploited Germans' hatred of the harsh World War I peace settlement policies.

Contrary to the view of some Americans, the United States did not singlehandedly fund the rebuilding of Western Europe after World War II. A reasonable analogy would be to argue that substantial Marshall Plan assistance over several years provided the seeds that Europeans worked very hard to nurture, in the meantime suffering many years of relative deprivation. The development effort was greatly assisted by important collateral efforts, such as currency reform and the evolution of the ECSC, EC, and EU, discussed previously in Chapter 1. Eastern Europe was forced to forego these advantageous conditions. Because the USSR was suspicious of the United States' motives for funding the Marshall Plan and supporting the EC, its leaders feared U.S. influence within its empire and often chose to sponsor economic development that best served the interests of the Soviet Union.

State intervention in the economy and protection of markets by imposing restrictions on trade and direct investment were common everywhere in Europe before World War II. Although impediments to international trade and cooperation began to be dismantled in Western Europe after World War II, Soviet occupation of most of Eastern Europe resulted in a continuation there of isolationist policies, including efforts to achieve economic independence and adherence to so-called socialist principles of locational decision making. Initially, Yugoslavia was included in Soviet planning directives, but, after its break with the USSR in 1948–1949, it introduced policies specific to Yugoslav conditions. Among other things, Yugoslavia attempted to spread industrial investment throughout the country, both to respond to regional problems and to placate nationalistic political pressures from the country's diverse ethnic and religious communities.

Traditional Soviet planning tenets emphasized heavy industry, particularly iron, steel, machinery, and petrochemical plants; hydro-, fossil fuel, and nuclear power plants; and some light manufacturing. Policies favoring spatial concentration of industrial centers sometimes prevailed; at other times and places, plants were widely dispersed, often located near raw materials and at ports and medium-sized cities. Emphasis was often given to the expansion of existing industrial regions, although new industrial activities were also developed in areas that were previously unindustrialized, not infrequently by building industrially dominated "socialist cities" (see Chapter 12). Western regional scientists have often criticized the locations chosen for these new, usually heavy industrial areas as economically irrational. For example, steel production facilities at Dunaujvaros (Hungary) and Eisenhüttenstadt (Eastern Germany) are not located near iron ore or coal resources and are not at a port where these can be easily assembled. Few, if any, similarly located, large steel complexes have been built in Western Europe during at least the last 50 years. Not surprisingly, after German unification in 1990 the iron and steel plant at Eisenhüttenstadt suffered severe job cuts and threats to its ultimate survival.

The Soviet Union planned highly specialized industrial centers in the East European CMEA countries, and CMEA policies favored the more industrially advanced countries of the bloc—East Germany and Czechoslovakia. However, Romania in particular balked at Soviet-led efforts for an industrial emphasis in East Central Europe and an agricultural emphasis in Southeastern Europe. In a long-running political feud with the USSR, Romania adopted a fairly independent political-economic agenda that included creating a better balance between agriculture and manufacturing. When Romania showed signs of political and economic independence from the USSR, the United States gave Romania "most favored nation status." As indicated elsewhere in the book, economic development in the CMEA countries suffered from a number of deficiencies, including virtually ignoring the environmental costs of economic development, the legacies of which will haunt these countries for decades.

Eastern Europe experienced relatively rapid growth in the 1950s and 1960s, but growth waned thereafter through the late 1980s, by which time many CMEA countries had relatively poor living and environmental conditions, uncompetitive economic structures, and mountains of debt. In the meantime, Northwestern Europe had surged ahead, partly through the help of millions of guest workers from Southern Europe, Turkey, and North Africa. Western Europe faces several economic problems, but Eastern Europe has even more serious problems, as discussed later in this chapter.

DEVELOPMENT LEVELS OF EUROPE'S COUNTRIES AND REGIONS

The countries of Northwestern Europe (Norden and countries northwest of Austria, Switzerland, and France) are, excepting Ireland, among the wealthiest in the world. Switzerland and Luxembourg, in particular, rank near the top of world incomes (Fig. 5-3). On average, Italy also falls within the group of the most developed European states, although the northern part of the country is far more prosperous than the southern region. Measures of social well-being, such as infant mortality (death rate of children from birth to age one), life expectancy, and levels of education, also indicate Northwestern Europe's high quality of life by international standards. In fact, contrary to the assumptions of many of its citizens, the United States does not compare favorably to leading Northwest European countries on all measures of social well-being, apparently because of its less-well-developed national social welfare programs and the relatively poor socioeconomic status of many minority Americans.

Southern, East Central, and especially Southeastern Europe, though still within the broadly defined "developed world," generally have much lower levels of socioeconomic well-being than Northwestern Europe. The southern parts of Europe evince particularly great differences in well-being between regions within individual countries, and especially between more developed urban areas and rural areas. Regional differences in well-being, discussed in more detail later in the chapter, are particularly great, for example, between northern and southern Italy and within Spain and Portugal. Such differences, though generally less severe, also exist in Northwestern Europe, most notably within the UK.

Unlike other countries in Northwestern Europe, Ireland has standards of living that are more similar to those of Spain than to other countries in Northern and Western Europe. These two states probably lie somewhere between more prosperous Northwestern Europe and poorer Southern and Eastern Europe in terms of overall levels of well-being.

A third group of European countries in terms of levels of development would probably include Portugal, Greece, and the states of East Central Europe (including Slovenia and Croatia). Among the remaining states in Eastern Europe, Estonia, Latvia, and Bulgaria may be somewhat more developed than the others, and, Macedonia and Albania are among the least developed of Europe's countries.

Despite the fact that Western Europe is relatively prosperous, many of its regions lag far behind the most developed regions on many indicators of well-being (Fig. 5-4). Northern and western Scotland and Northern Ireland lag particularly far behind both southeastern England and the EU average. Southern Italy and eastern Germany are also relatively poor regions in comparison to the respective countries as a whole, despite many years of north-to-south income transfers within Italy. Similar transfers from west-to-east in Germany are more likely to lessen disparities in that country, where human resources and infrastructure are and will be far superior to those in the Italian south or *Mezzogiorno*.

Western Europe also has several wealthy growth regions in which residents generally have high levels of socioeconomic well-being and where economic conditions have continued to improve for many years. Notable among these regions are southern England, Holland (the western Netherlands), the Paris and Brussels regions, Luxembourg, the Alsace region, southern Germany, western Austria, and much of north central and northeastern Italy.

At least a couple of cautionary notes on evaluating European income data should be heeded. First, average income levels for countries and other areal units often camouflage large internal regional and social variations. As noted earlier, regional variations are especially large within Italy. Variations between social group are more difficult to ascertain but are, for example, usually relatively large between native-born Europeans and "guest workers." Second, comparing income data across countries is greatly affected by levels of and temporal changes in currency exchange rates. Thus, for example, the actual local purchasing power of incomes in East European states, where currencies are now weak, are probably understated. Finally, official income statistics do not include

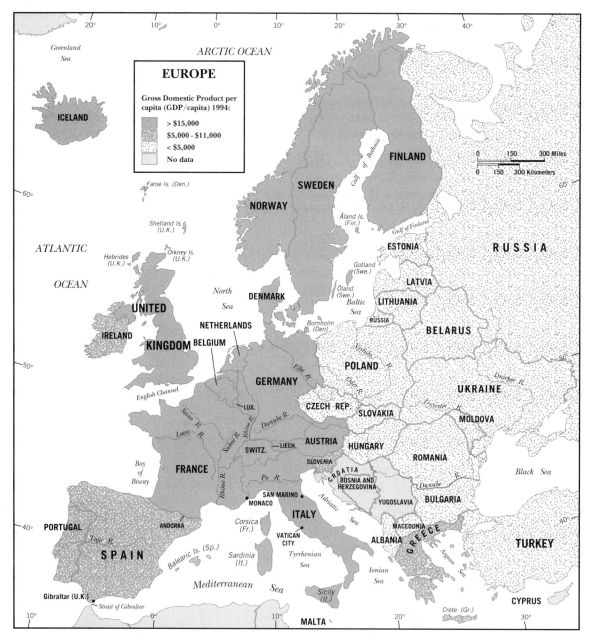

FIGURE 5-3 European income by country. With the exception of Ireland, European income levels by country tend to decline from northwest to southeast. (Data from the Population Reference Bureau)

the value of goods and services provided by people for themselves, thereby underestimating the true economic well-being of, for example, many rural Southern and Eastern Europeans. In addi-

tion, official statistics fail to capture the full value of many "black market" activities, which are estimated to be about 10 percent of domestic output (GDP) in most EU states but much higher in

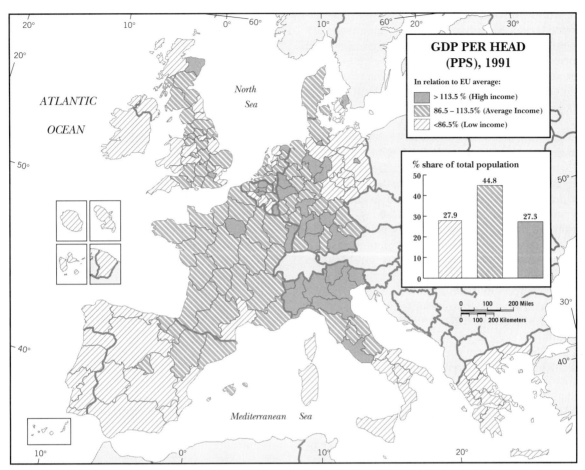

FIGURE 5-4 Income in EU regions in comparison to the all-Union average, 1991. Large income differentials often exist within EU countries, most notably between northern and southern Italy. (After the European Commission (1994)).

Greece (29%), Italy (17%), and Portugal (16%) (Williams and Windebank, 1995). This means that economic conditions in these three countries are on average better than officially reported, although our broad income generalizations likely remain valid.

We can point to other, more fundamental causes for national and regional variations in general levels of socioeconomic well-being, including factors related to natural resources, accessibility to markets, and, especially, historic patterns of public policies. Many of these factors and their importance are discussed in the preceding historical section and within chapters on Europe's regions later

in the book. A number of efforts are also being made at the international, national, and local levels in Europe to combat "backwardness" in some regions and to maintain high standards of living in others. These public policy initiatives are discussed briefly in later sections on the EU and within later chapters on specific regions.

SECTORAL STRUCTURE AND EMPLOYMENT

The sectoral structures of Europe's national economies both reflect and affect patterns of economic well-being and development. The more developed economies have a combination of more efficient agriculture and alternative employment opportunities in the manufacturing and service sectors. Thus, although most Northwest European countries have less than 6 percent of total employment in their primary sectors, such employment is very high in countries and regions in the Southeast (e.g., Romania, 32%) and rather high in East Central Europe (especially Poland, 27%), Southern Europe (e.g., Greece, 23%), and Ireland (14%). Even these levels, however, indicate progress toward more modern sectoral structures and related occupational specialization in these regions' economies. In the years immediately prior to World War II, the percentage of employment in agriculture was about 75 to 80 percent in Southeastern Europe, 40 to 60 percent in East Central Europe, and 50 percent in Ireland.

Unemployment rates prior to the recessions of the 1970s in Western Europe and before the fall of communism in Eastern Europe were quite low, partly resulting from underemployment in the agricultural sector (large numbers of people working at jobs with low incomes) and from labor shortages related to imbalanced gender ratios. The gender imbalance was due to catastrophic reductions in the number of young and middle-aged males during the carnage of the world wars. Unemployment levels rose rapidly during the 1970s, however, and reached especially high levels in countries with too poorly developed and competitive manufacturing and service sectors in the early 1990s (e.g., Albania, 32%; Macedonia, 30%; Spain, 21%; Ireland, 18%; Poland, 16%). In war-torn Bosnia unemployment rates exceeded 60 percent in the mid-1990s. Prosperous European countries also suffer high unemployment rates owing to slow job-creation rates. In 1993 the high EU-wide unemployment rate (10.5%) was far worse for workers under age 25 (over 20% unemployed). Finland (18% overall average unemployment level, 33% for workers under 25), Italy (11%, 31%), France (11%, 23%), and the UK (10%, 17%) offered prime examples of this situation, which also exists in poorer Spain (21%, 37%). Among the prosperous EEA countries, only Germany and Luxembourg had youth unemployment rates under 11 percent.

Relatively high rates of unemployment and, on average, relatively slow rates of economic growth have plagued the EU as a whole since the early 1980s. Until the 1970s, EU economic growth rates were relatively high and unemployment rates low. This changed during the 1970s, and since then "Eurosclerosis," the corrosion of Western Europe's economic strength, has been a recurrent concern during tough economic times—such as the early 1990s.

Pessimists envision a gloomy future: "Europe lacks the hardware, the software, the financial policies and the methods of social organization to participate fully in any of the major technological revolutions under way in the industrial world.... Europe continues to excel only at selling overpriced goods and services to itself (via the European Union's single market) and is losing its global market share while so doing" (Roche, 1994, p. 109). As indications of changing conditions that promise a better economic future for Western Europe, optimists would cite falling real unit wage costs in the EU, down about 10 percent in the 1980s from earlier levels; Europe's large market and established infrastructure; generally high levels of education among citizens; and shifts in economic policies in many countries as they attempt to slow public spending, increase incentives for workers and businesses, and privatize publicly held enterprises. Two of the poorest current EU members, Portugal and Spain, experienced well above average EC/EU economic growth rates in the 1960s, 1970s, and 1980s (also Greece during the 1960–1980 period). In addition, the EU's poorest states— Portugal, Spain, Greece, and Ireland—experienced among the highest percentages of net foreign direct investment during the late 1980s and early 1990s (along with the UK). Similarly, there is hope for the restructuring economies in East Central Europe, which following severe economic downturns around 1990, showed indications of recovery and economic resurrection by 1994 (Figs. 11-22 and 12-17). Unfortunately, the economic situation in easternmost Europe and parts of the war-torn former Yugoslavia indicates less recovery and reform (see Chapter 12).

Clearly, basic economic challenges for the economies of European countries include creating more jobs, maintaining preeminence and competitiveness in sectors and regions that are now successful, and winning new markets in emergent manufacturing and service activities. This must be accomplished during a time of increasing international competition for European economies from rapidly developing countries such as those on the Pacific Rim; at a time when there is increased pressure on the EU to reduce its import barriers and include new, much poorer members; and at a time when there is little room for publicly financed initiatives. European tax and government expenditure levels as a proportion of GDP are already quite high by international standards. The task for the poorer countries of Southern and Eastern Europe is aided by lower labor costs, but made more difficult by relatively poor infrastructural and capital bases, EU trade restrictions, and a disgruntled citizenry in Eastern Europe that expected the end of Soviet/communist domination to lead to rapid improvements in living standards. Similarly, ethnic and economically based regional political problems, notably in Italy and the former Yugoslavia, complicate the task of economic development.

Foreign Workers

Another simmering political and social problem that has potential economic consequences for many countries is the foreign or guest worker issue (see Chapter 3). The issue is not a new one. For example, the Huguenots were invited to Berlin after they fled from France in 1685 following revocation of the Edict of Nantes, which stripped Protestants of protection from persecution. Jews were also invited to Cracow in the Middle Ages in hopes of spurring that city's economic development. Economic advantages subsequently did accrue to both cities, although, ultimately, catastrophe befell Cracow's Jews during World War II. In the contemporary era, millions of workers have been drawn to Western Europe from Southern and Southeastern Europe, as well as from North Africa, to satisfy labor needs. These migrations helped spur economic growth in Western Europe, but they have also resulted in a number of contentious social and political issues revolving around migrants' rights and the influ-

ences of migrants' countries origin and destination on one another.

Problems of lack of social integration and pressure on social infrastructure ultimately led host countries to become concerned about constantly increasing the number of foreign workers, and the countries of origin also no longer considered the emigrant citizens a universal blessing. Earlier, these workers had helped their home coutries in acquiring foreign currencies, training unskilled labor, and reducing unemployment rates. However, the departure of migrants often contributed to family hardships at home, including issues of welfare and education of children with one and often both parents gone—not to speak of the loss of taxes to the home community. An added problem involved the future of foreign workers' children educated in host countries. Could they expect employment in host countries, or would they return to their native country, where many were no longer able to speak the native language? In short, the combination of these problems led to an end of an era of importation of workers into Northwestern Europe by the mid-1970s, but many of the problems persist, since millions of earlier migrants remain as "guest" workers.

As early as 1973, the ghettolike existence and generally poor housing conditions of the politically disenfranchised foreign workers (those from non-EC countries) had become a serious problem for host countries. A series of conventions and agreements approved by the United Nations and the Council of Europe (e.g., on human rights and social security, as well as the Convention on Social Medical Assistance and the EC Social Charter) were designed to ensure that signatory states applied their social legislation equally to foreign nationals and countries' own citizens. In addition, the EC agreed in July 1968 to grant migrants from EC countries equal rights with nationals in seeking employment and to adhere to a series of other measures, including the right to have foreign workers' families accompany them. Moreover, EC migrants received equal representation rights on local worker bodies, became subject to the same local tax and social welfare systems, and usually enjoyed equal access rights to housing and property ownership. Within the EC the Italian workers were the greatest beneficiaries. Foreign workers from non-Community countries could receive these rights only by intercountry agreement.

In view of the problems associated with migrant workers, it is not surprising that some countries with especially large numbers of foreign workers have been concerned about reducing dependence on them altogether. Switzerland was the first country to institute countermeasures (after a national referendum) by instituting regional ceilings, cutbacks on work permits for new applicants, and a drastic reduction of the total permissible number of foreign workers. Still, by the mid-1980s, over 17 percent of the working population in Switzerland was foreign. Currently, the Swiss seem to worry most about large numbers of refugees and asylum seekers, emanating largely from Eastern Europe.

France also instituted measures for control of illegal immigration after 1971, and the number of its foreign workers decreased by 20 percent between 1973 and the mid-1980s. The UK's foreign workers, mainly from former colonies, created a serious political issue, which in 1971 resulted in an Immigration Act terminating any further large-scale permanent immigration into the country. In early 1973 West Germany instituted mild control measures; later, because of the energy crisis, all non-EC labor recruitment efforts were stopped. During the 1980s West Germany and other Western countries initiated special inducements—for example, a year's pay—to encourage the departure of their foreign workers. Italy, too, although sending large numbers of its population job hunting into other EU countries, has a serious problem with illegal immigrants arriving from Africa and Asia at a rate of tens of thousands yearly. Hundreds of thousands of illegal immigrants and many legally registered non-EU immigrants—from Albania, Libya, Tunisia, Morocco, and Ethiopia—now reside in Italy.

NATURAL RESOURCES

Increases in population, increased industrialization, and rapid improvements in the standard of living in Western Europe have resulted in ever greater demand for a variety of natural resources, especially energy resources. On the other hand, Europe's modest raw material base has been depleted by centuries of exploitation. Not surprisingly, then, most European countries are quite dependent on importation of a wide range of industrial raw materials.

Europe's indigenous industrial raw materials, including energy fuels, are limited, though the fuel picture has improved somewhat for the Western European countries owing to the oil and gas discoveries in the North Sea, as well as various conservation measures implemented since the early 1970s. Historically, streams provided waterpower; solid fuels (hard coal and lignite) were the basis of energy during the Industrial Revolution and for many decades afterward. However, Europe has become increasingly dependent on energy imports.

Europe's major fossil fuel producer is the UK—the only country with notable production levels of all major fuel types (oil, natural gas, and coal). It produces in total about as much fossil fuel energy as it consumes. Norway, Europe's leading oil producer, third leading gas producer (after the Netherlands and UK), and leading net energy exporter, exports only enough to provide about two-thirds of Germany's imports alone. Most European energy imports thus originate outside Europe. Germany's and Poland's (European leading) coal production is highly subsidized and covers only part of these countries' total domestic energy needs (about 10% in Germany). Coal producers face increasing competition from lower cost producers of a range of energy products.

Poland, the UK, and poorly developed Albania are the only energy self-sufficient countries; the Netherlands is about 15 percent import dependent. All other European countries are quite dependent on energy imports. In descending order of import dependence, Cyprus, Malta, Portugal, Luxembourg, Italy, Belgium, Finland, Switzerland, Austria, France, and Slovenia all import 70 percent or more of their energy needs.

Although well supplied as a whole with coal and hydropower, Europe (apart from the Netherlands, Norway, and the United Kingdom) lacks adequate petroleum and natural gas production and reserves. Other energy sources are often quite important (e.g., coal in Germany and the UK; natural gas in the Netherlands, Italy, Norway, and

UK), but oil was the most important primary energy source for all West European countries in 1993, except in France where nuclear power was slightly more important. In 1993 oil accounted for 40 percent of energy consumed in Europe, coal for 26 percent, and natural gas for 18 percent. Figure 5-5 shows the extent of the oil and natural gas resources in the North Sea.

Starting with the discoveries of the onshore gasfields in Groningen in the northeastern part of the Netherlands in 1959, commercial production in the North Sea region began in 1965. The British discoveries in the southern part of the North Sea in the late 1960s; the Ekofisk complex in the southern part of the Norwegian-British sector boundary; and a series of other important oilfields and gasfields dis-

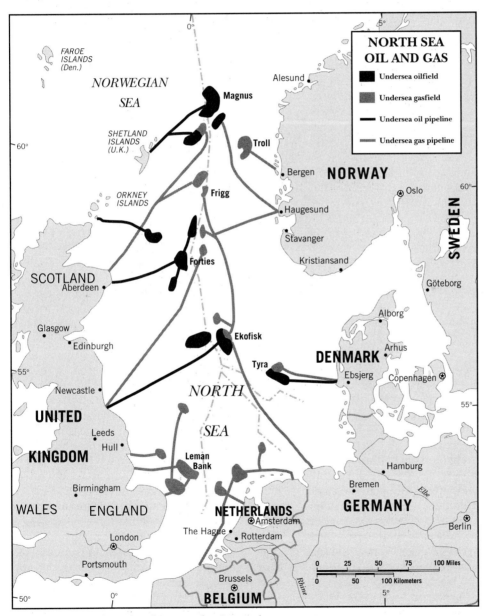

FIGURE 5-5 North Sea oil and gas production regions.

covered (with sites north of the Firth of Forth, around Shetland Islands, and off the Norwegian coast) have resulted in an ever-increasing supply of fuel reserves. These have changed Western Europe's energy supply situation. The newest oil-fields, Troll near Bergen and Heidrun near Trond-heim, began producing off the Norwegian coast during 1995. These fields and improved technology in existing oilfields make it likely that anticipated declines in Norwegian production will be forestalled for at least several more years. The development of the giant Norwegian offshore gas-field at Troll 65 miles (105 km) northwest of Bergen, Norway, and the Sleipner gasfield 190 miles (306 km) southwest of Troll will supply gas to Western Europe, via Emden in Germany and Zeebrugge in Belgium, for at least 25 years, and will help offset possible future declines in Norwegian oil production. Norway's oil production has probably now peaked, but natural gas output is expected to grow for about the next 10 years. Thus, Norway will likely be the world's second largest hydrocarbon exporter (behind Saudi Arabia) in the late 1990s; it was the world's second largest oil exporter (also behind Saudi Arabia) in 1995.

Europe's relatively precarious position with regard to access to oil at stable prices became evident in the aftermath of the Arab oil boycott of October 1973 and again after the sizable oil price increases in 1979. Europe has also become increasingly aware of its dependence on overseas supplies for many of its industrial minerals. Individual European countries have supplies in varying degrees of only a few selected raw materials. Industry in most European countries is wholly dependent on non-European raw material suppliers, because production of them in Europe is simply insufficient to meet demands.

Although the production of coal has declined since the 1950s, sizable reserves of coal and lignite are Europe's most important raw materials, and have prevented periodic energy crises from being even more serious. Figure 5-6 shows the location of Europe's most important coalfields, which stretch from Britain to the Donets Basin of Ukraine and Russia. The declining share of coal in the overall energy balance of Western Europe since 1962 was not even halted by the oil crisis in the 1970s.

Although bituminous coal became competitive with imported oil between 1974 and the early 1980s, the relative demand for coal and solid fuels has hardly changed owing to shifts toward other energy sources, notably natural gas.

Poland has been Europe's leading coal producer in recent years, based on production in Upper Silesia. By 1993 sharp declines in coal production that began in the late 1980s put it in a virtual first place tie with Germany in terms of total energy derived from domestically mined coal. German production has also been declining, however, both in underground hard coal mines in the Ruhr and in open-pit lignite mines in the southern parts of eastern Germany. Coal output also fell by about 25 percent in the UK during the 1980s, by 50 percent in France, and by 90 percent in Belgium. Associated job losses have played a role in increased unemployment rates in all of these countries.

Western Europe's massive replacement of coal by oil over recent decades has drastically increased Europe's dependence on non-European supplies, as indicated earlier, and has thus made most European countries (exclusive of the FSU, the UK, and Norway) vulnerable in the supply of this vital resource. A shift toward oil in Western Europe was brought about by environmental advantages of oil in comparison to coal, by decreasing productivity in coal mines with the exhaustion of easily worked seams, by increased demand for gasoline from ever larger numbers of private cars, and by the obvious cost advantages of relatively low-priced, imported liquid fuels. Even very high taxes on liquid fuel have not led to gains for coal. In addition, the basic structural change in the use of energy resources has contributed to serious social and regional problems that necessitated considerable adaptation (such as the closing of coal mines), a process that will certainly continue for some time. Most Western European coal-producing countries have been forced to support the industry with subsidies. The EC/EU has assisted its members financially in closing uneconomic mines and has contributed to costs of resettlement and retraining of workers.

Until about 1990, East European countries did not experience such a radical energy-source transformation as Western Europe, because the iron and steel industry and electric producers were

FIGURE 5-6 Major European coal production areas. The early development of manufacturing in Northwestern Europe was greatly aided by local coal supplies, and the resource still remains important in selected areas. There are many fewer important production areas than in earlier decades, and most are in western parts of Europe. Production in Eastern Europe is often accounted for by relatively low quality lignite. The coal areas indicated on the map accounted for about 98 percent of coal produced in Europe (excluding the FSU) during the early 1990s. Poland, Germany, and the UK—where the most important mining areas are located—accounted for about 75 percent of Eurpean coal output in the early 1990s.

major energy consumers and depended especially heavily on coal. Thus, in the mid-1990s, coal was the primary energy source of most East European states (excepting, for example, Hungary where oil and natural gas are most important). For a number of reasons, Eastern Europe experienced an increased resource dependence on the USSR in the 1970s. The Soviet Union's willingness to supply its Eastern European allies with needed fuels and a variety of raw materials, sometimes at subsidized low rates, cushioned the East from the impact of the 1970s oil price increases. In the 1990s, however, these countries are facing increased demand for oil (now only available at world price levels), and, in many cases, declining coal output (especially in Poland). Difficult choices—most notably in the Czech Republic—have to be made between continued dependence on highly polluting coal-fired facilities, expensive and dangerous nuclear power, or expensive energy imports.

Nuclear energy is important in Europe for the generation of electricity; about 170 nuclear power stations have been constructed there. Electricity produced from oil is three to four times more expensive than nuclear power, but safety issues, capital costs, and the length of time necessary to construct nuclear plants will likely limit their future role. Still, in 1993 a total of 16 European nuclear power stations were under construction (all but one in Eastern Europe and France), and nuclear energy supplies 12 percent of Europe's overall energy. It is of special importance in France and Sweden, where it represented 40 percent of total energy consumption in 1993. Many countries derive 25 to 45 percent of their electric power from nuclear plants—France (78%) and Belgium (59%) much more. Several countries derive about 10 percent of their total energy from nuclear power, including Germany, the UK, and Spain. Spain has halted construction on several reactors and, instead, has a new pipeline to bring natural gas from North Africa to help meet future energy needs.

In this century especially, the waterpower of Europe has been harnessed for hydroelectricity, principally in Northern Europe and the Alps. In Norway (46%), Sweden (16%), Austria (13%), and Switzerland (10%), hydroelectricity is an important component of total energy use, particularly in comparison to Europe as a whole (2%). Alterna-

tive energy sources that await technical breakthroughs before being put to wider commercial use are solid waste, solar energy, oil shale, tidal and windpower, and geothermal energy. Geothermal energy has seen some commercial use in Tuscany (Italy) since before World War II, and examples of experimental production exist for the other alternative sources as well. Germany is the world's second largest user of windpower, which now provides about 4 percent of all electric production.

Earlier discussion indicates the historically important role of a variety of European mineral and metal resources in establishing industrial activities. Today, however, Europe is not a very important producer of most such resources and, instead, is usually a large importer. Iron ores once mined together with coal in some areas have now been worked out. Several other iron ore deposits are available, most notably the high-grade hematite ores of both Arctic Sweden and Kryvyy Rih in Ukraine. These important European sources are supplemented by less important deposits in France, Spain, and Norway. Although once well known for the production of iron ore, Sweden, France, and Spain (Europe's leaders, in order) now produce only a fraction of world output. Even the current reduced demand for iron ore by the European steel makers has far outgrown European supplies, and much iron ore is imported from Canada, North Africa, Venezuela, Brazil, India, and elsewhere.

Europe's naturally occurring biotic resources are limited owing to centuries of intensive human impact on its land and seas. Europe's once expansive and rich primeval forest on the North European Plain and Central Uplands is now entirely gone, replaced largely by fields. Still, small patches of less valuable, though still quite useful, forests remain. Sweden and Finland are particularly important in pulp and paper production. In recent decades, forests have been damaged by air pollution and related acid rain. In the most badly affected areas, as in the Ore Mountains on the Czech-German border, forests have been destroyed over large areas. More commonly, the damage has been less severe, but it still affects large proportions of Europe's forests, including its largest contiguous stands in central and northern Sweden and Finland. Careful management of many European forests helps to provide an important raw material basis for significant wood products industries in many Northern and Central European countries.

Overfishing and pollution have also greatly diminished Europe's fisheries habitats, especially in the Mediterranean Sea. The eastern North Atlantic and North Sea remain important for fishing, but pressure on Europe's shrinking fishery resources by its large fishing industry was clearly illustrated during 1995, when a rather un-unified EU was forced to negotiate a new settlement for fishing rights between itself and Canada. The Canadian government had taken rather drastic actions to deter what it viewed as rapacious harvesting of fish off its coast by Spanish boats, a charge echoed by fisheries interests in the UK and Ireland but denied by other international observers. Similar disputes in the past on the seas around Iceland, numerous large sealife kills caused by oil spills and other environmental calamities, and declining catches of many of the most valuable fish species, also indicate an apparently ever-degrading natural resource base and ongoing political struggles to balance national economic interests and environmental concerns. Little real progress appears to have been made to curtail fishing enough so that stocks can rebuild. The first steps have finally been taken to reduce pollution of European seas as well as to protect important shallow coastal breeding grounds for all types of sealife.

AGRICULTURE

Agriculture is an important employment sector as well as a supplier of food and raw materials for the European economy. France and the Netherlands are also two of the world's largest exporters of agricultural products. However, agricultural productivity levels vary widely between regions and countries, reflecting a variety of factors affecting agriculture that go beyond differences in natural environments. Agricultural problems cause serious political and economic problems for individual countries and for the EU in their relations with non-EU states. Ironically, these problems have worsened owing to the very success of early EC/EU agricultural policies and to increased levels of productivity by European farmers.

The basic character of European agriculture can be generalized by:

- Private ownership of small farms, except in Eastern Europe where such ownership is being reestablished.
- Increasing output per unit of labor and land, owing to technological change, greater capital inputs, and organizational restructuring, such as development of specialized agro-industrial complexes.
- A high degree of political involvement in agricultural markets.
- A kaleidoscopic spatial pattern of production of a wide range of products across the continent.

Each of these characteristics is discussed in turn in the following section.

The Structure of Agricultural Holdings

Structural problems in European agriculture are closely related to farm size and land ownership patterns. Historically, many parts of Europe had inheritance laws whereby family farms were repeatedly subdivided among heirs over a number of generations, creating independent farms run by "peasants" who lived in thousands of scattered, small villages. Some parts of Europe, especially northern and eastern Germany and Eastern Europe, were dominated by large, wealthy landowners, who had great political and economic power. In Prussia and Mecklenburg, for example, just prior to World War I *Junker* estates over 250 acres (over 100 ha) accounted for more than 40 percent of all farmland, while such large farms comprised only about 8 percent of the land elsewhere in Germany. Very large holdings continue to dominate agriculture in southwestern Spain and adjacent Portugal (Alentejo). Generally speaking, the domination of agriculture by large landholders has historically resulted in an impoverished and disenfranchised "peasant" population, whose status sometimes differed little from serfdom. Such conditions persisted in many areas well into the twentieth century, and standards of living in the Alentejo, for example, are on average still among the lowest in the EU. The pressures of a growing rural population related to declining death rates and soaring rates of natural increase and mass poverty were relieved only by rapid industrialization, by rural to urban migration, and by emigration abroad (especially to the Americas), where millions of poor Europeans hoped to, and often did, find better opportunities. The appeal of advertised factory jobs and free land under the Homestead Act brought millions of European immigrants to the United States in the nineteenth and early twentieth centuries.

Twentieth-century reforms of landholdings by way of "land consolidation" (voluntary or legally required amalgamation of tiny, fragmented fields into more geographically compact private farms), as well as land seizures and forced collectivization of farms in Soviet-dominated Europe, brought some order out of the chaos of the many small and increasingly uneconomic holdings in Eastern Europe. In Western Europe the emphasis has been on creating more viable private farms, which have been further supported by heavy agricultural subsidies. Still, the generally quite small West European farm (an average 36.3 acres (14.7 ha) in the EU) has proven over the long run to be both relatively unattractive as an employment option and exceedingly costly for national and EU budgets to support. Increased technological input requirements, greatly increased capital investment needs, related specialization of production by the introduction of industrial methods (e.g., production of broilers, eggs, pork, and veal in massive, enclosed, highly spatially and economically integrated agroindustrial complexes), and changed farm management and organization have been revolutionizing West European agriculture. In Western, and increasingly in Eastern Europe, farming has become highly mechanized. Thus, despite only average farm size by EU standards, intensively cultivated holdings in Belgium and the Netherlands produce among the EU's highest average farm incomes.

Where labor is abundant and holdings are very small, notably in the Mediterranean countries, there has been less mechanization and the economic performance has been poor. For example, the EU's smallest average farm sizes are in Greece (10 acres, 4.0 ha), Italy (14 acres, 5.6 ha), and Portugal (16.5 acres, 6.7 ha), where farm income is low. Often, areas with the highest density of agricultural population can have the lowest agricultural yields, especially if capital is lacking and labor, albeit plentiful, is inefficiently employed. As a result, such areas suffer underemployment that could be considered "concealed" unemployment.

Land Reform in Western Europe Especially as the result of the market forces noted above, but also influenced by governments' agricultural policies, the number of farms and farmers in Western Europe has been falling steadily for decades. At the same time, the sizes of farms have slowly increased, though they remain quite small in comparison, for example, to those in the United States—and too small to be competitive internationally without continued subsidies. From 1975 to 1985, 25 million farmers left the land, and about 2 million farms have been given up since 1970. The majority of farmers in Western Europe now work only part-time on their farms; a relatively small number of large and efficient farms are becoming increasingly important in terms of total agricultural output. Structural reform in West European agriculture, which is of considerable importance to the modernization and rationalization of agriculture because of the rapidly declining agricultural labor force, is not a problem that can or likely will be solved quickly. The expense involved is formidable, and the job so large that it will require years to complete. For example, France, Germany, the Netherlands, and Belgium have spent billions of dollars in the past two decades on farm rationalization (e.g., encouraging larger farms and consolidated fields), structural improvements, and pensions to farmers. These allocations continue, and billions more will be spent before structural reform and farm rationalization result in a successful adaptation to international economic conditions. The cost will be great and the time frame long.

Despite pressure from the continuing, huge costs of subsidies and despite the political outcries from major international trade partners (including especially the United States and Canada), enormous political clout supports the European farm lobby, which includes not only farmers but also a great number of businesses and people who depend indirectly on the farm economy, such as food processors and producers of farm inputs. Other pro-farm lobbies include environmental and landscape protectionists and tourism interests. Rules governing political representation within countries and the EU give agricultural and rural interests disproportionate political power. Lingering, arguably romantic, notions about protecting the increasingly mythical family farm provide further support for agriculture. Support for "rural traditions," the rural landscape, and the family farm are particularly strong in France, which often leads resistance within the EU to reduced support for agriculture. Other important agricultural countries in the EU such as Germany can also use strong French resistance as an excuse for slower reduction in their own farm subsidies, which lessens domestic political problems with the farm lobby.

Land Reform in Eastern Europe Land reform in Eastern Europe during the interwar period affected large semifeudal estates, but only the reforms after 1945 forced drastic changes. First, numerous small, private holdings were created, but shortly afterward, and following the Soviet pattern, collective and state farms were formed and became dominant. The exceptions were Yugoslavia and Poland, where private farming occupied about 80 percent of arable land, with other land held mostly by a variety of cooperative, collective, and state farms. In the other East European states, over 90 percent of agricultural land was in state-owned farms or in state-dominated collective farms. Under socialism, output and productivity were constrained by shortages of capital and inputs, poor incentives, and inefficiently bureaucratic management—and by small-sized farms in Poland and Yugoslavia (Fig. 5-7). During the last couple of decades under

FIGURE 5-7 Indications of small-scale, labor-intensive farming in Zakopane, Poland in 1995. Farm size remains small, and percentage of employment in agriculture relatively high in many less developed regions of Europe. (W. H. Berentsen)

socialism, the number of farm units in Eastern Europe was further reduced, and farm size increased with the establishment of large agro-industrial complexes. Since about 1990, farmland has been reverting to private ownership, but the great time demands and capital requirements of private farming are leading in most places to a speedier decline than ever in the number of farmers, especially in eastern Germany. Those still in farming are remaining, for at least the time being, in cooperative agricultural enterprises that offer advantages in marketing, access to capital, and division of labor. It will only be a matter of time, however, until even more dramatic structural changes affect East European agriculture as the result of market and, possibly, political pressures.

Government Support and Trends in Agricultural Output

Total agricultural output grew 15 to 30 percent in most West European countries between the early 1980s and early 1990s, except in Norden, where some countries experienced declines in output. Political and economic problems have arisen in Western Europe from surplus production of a number of commodities caused by sizable price supports, at the expense of taxpayers and the urban consumer. Growth in output was mixed in Eastern Europe during the 1980s, and all countries experienced steep rescissions in output beginning around 1989. Under socialism agriculture in Eastern Europe was subsidized, though poor management, low capital inputs, and few incentives for individual farmers resulted in lower levels of output than in Western Europe. Basic food needs were usually met during socialist times, but crop choice, lack of incentives to assure quality, and import restrictions meant, for example, that fresh fruit and quality meat products were often in short supply or unavailable. Exceptions were relatively high-priced, domestically produced fruit sold on the small private markets during the growing season.

Although food prices have fallen in relative or absolute terms on world markets, subsidies to farmers in the EU countries have increased to more than $100 billion a year. Farmers receive a guaranteed price for their dairy products, cereals, and sugar. When market prices fall below a floor price, intervention agencies buy the surpluses. In addition, import levies and export subsidies are set. EU farm support largely aids the largest and richest farmers, who are disproportionately concentrated in wealthier northern regions, while fewer benefits go to smaller, poorer southern farmers.

Regional Patterns of Land Use and Production

In general terms, market demand and climatic conditions result in an emphasis on animal products in Northern Europe and plant production in Southern Europe. The far north and west of Europe is dominated by forestry, grazing, and production of hardy crops. Many areas near ports in Northwestern Europe (especially in the Netherlands and Germany) specialize in animal production based on huge, wealthy urban markets and readily available, inexpensive imported grain. Production of crops also supports animal husbandry on the better soils of Central Europe. Southern Europe is dominated by grain and specialty crops like wine, olive, fruit, and vegetable production.

Croplands occupy especially large proportions of total area on the North European Plain, the Po Valley, and the Pannonian and Wallachian basins. Lands in the north, on southern drylands, and in highlands everywhere are much more commonly in pasture, including much of Norden, the British Isles, the Alps, Dinaric Alps, Iberia, and Greece. The greatest part of Norden as well as large parts of the Alps and Carpathians, the German hill country, and Iberia are forested. The 12 pre-expansion EU countries have 40 to 65 percent of all land in agriculture. In Denmark and Hungary more than half of the land can be sown to crops, whereas Finland and Sweden are heavily forested.

Irrigation of cropland is greatest in absolute and relative terms in Spain (22% of cropland); Romania, Italy, and Bulgaria (33–35%); and Greece (42%). In other words, areas most affected by drought and higher evapotranspiration rates during the growing season have the most irrigation. Iceland (77%) and Norway (70%) have by far the largest amount of unforested and unfarmed land (much of it being bare rock or under ice). However, excepting Iceland, all the European states have at least modest-sized regions with comparatively good soils and environmental conditions for at least some major crops.

Only a few selected regions in Europe, however, benefit from all of the major factors that positively affect agricultural output—adequate and reliable precipitation (or source of irrigation water); a long and warm growing season; good soil; relatively level ground; and good access to capital, technology, and large markets. Except for access to capital, technology, and markets, parts of the Mediterranean lands (e.g., the Mediterranean coast of Spain) and portions of Romania and Bulgaria are fairly well endowed. Parts of Belgium, the Netherlands, and the Pannonian Basin have still better conditions. The Po Valley, parts of France including the Paris Basin, and selected loess-covered lowlands in Germany are perhaps the best endowed regions.

Of course, a number of regions have environmental conditions that are also particularly favorable for specialized crops, such as citrus growing along Mediterranean coasts; olive production in Spain (the world's leading producer) and Italy; tomato cultivation in Italy and Spain; and grapes for making wine in France, Germany, and Southern Europe (Fig. 5-8). Seasonal movement of sheep over great distances has long been common in Spain to best utilize pastures. Though generally cool, the humid conditions and mild winters in the British Isles, Denmark, and other parts of Northwestern Europe are ideal for dairying. Regions in North Central and Northeastern Europe with harsh winters and, frequently, poor soils can focus crop production on hardy crops like barley, rye, and potatoes. Poland, for example, leads Europe in the production of rye and potatoes. (Ireland is now a relatively minor potato producer; dairy and animal rearing are far more important there.) In the far north and in mountain regions where agriculture is difficult, specialized animal husbandry, fishing, or wood production dominate. In many mountainous areas, herders have long moved animals into upland pastures in early summer and down again in the fall, in order to utilize the short mountain growing season for pasturing and to conserve lowland areas for summer fodder production to support animals in winter. Norway, Denmark, and Iceland lead in fish landings. Areas near large markets, such as in Holland (eastern Netherlands), the Po Valley, the Paris Basin, and near Hamburg, Cologne, and the Rhine-Main conurbation (Stuttgart-Frankfurt), often specialize in the production of high-value perishable fruits

FIGURE 5-8 Grape harvesting for wine production on the shores of the Lake of Constance in southen Germany. Labor-intensive, high value added sectors of agriculture are important pillars of many regions' economies. (German Information Center)

and vegetables. The historical evolution of high-value-added and technologically demanding activities by farmers facing environmental constraints for crop production has resulted in specialized production regions for flowers (Holland), poultry (southern England, the Netherlands, and northwestern Germany), and pork and veal (the Netherlands and northwestern Germany). In northern Scandinavia reindeer herds are fed on sparse vegetation.

In most agricultural categories and for many important crops, Germany and France are Europe's leading producers (Table 5-1). They are, for example, the two leading producers of wheat, barley, beef and veal, milk, cheese, butter, eggs, and sugar beets; and one of the two is also near the top for a number of other products. Note that the FSU outproduces other European states for most agricultural products.

Important trends in European agriculture include not only the increasing importance of capital, technology, corporate-style management, and the spatially integrated agroindustrial complexes noted here, but also long-term trends in farmers' shifts of crop choices. Owing to higher incomes and changing tastes, Europeans are eating more refined and less coarse bread than in the past (wheat in place of rye bread, for example) and are consuming more meat and less starch. Wheat production has increased, as has the output of corn, barley, and sugar beets (all feed crops), whereas rye and potato production has been falling. If the example of eastern Germany is instructive, changed ownership patterns and increased incomes in, for example, Poland could quickly lead to similar shifts in crop choice.

TRANSPORTATION AND COMMUNICATION

Natural resource-based products require delivery to processing sites and to market. Obviously, the development of transportation systems is basic to this effort, to the ongoing trends of occupational and regional specialization, and to interregional trade, all of which generally lead to lower production costs and increased efficiency in production. Communication systems develop to facilitate the

movements of goods, to move information in the burgeoning service sectors, and to improve the ability of ever more mobile people to communicate personally with one another.

The transportation of goods was an expensive and time-consuming proposition until the development of the steam engine and its adoption in shipping and railroading in the nineteenth century. Earlier, shipments of bulk goods were generally limited to fairly short distances between points linked by water routes, and much trade focused on the exchange of relatively high-value products. The development of a dense rail network in Northwestern Europe, with fewer lines penetrating into its southern and eastern peripheries, helped to begin to allow the economically efficient movement of goods over longer distances. This furthered the ongoing process of regional and occupational specialization, lowered production costs, and raised both actual and potential total economic output. What might be called a transportation revolution that began in the nineteenth century and continues through our own time was furthered by several factors.

- The development of the internal combustion engine allows motor vehicles to access a high proportion of Europe's territory and permits rapid travel when limited-access highways are in place, as they now are in Northwestern Europe and Italy.
- The development of containerized transport lowers costs and promotes multimodal shipping.
- Electrified rail allows for speedier (and less locally polluting) travel/transport.
- Air travel, especially jet travel, moves people and valuable freight over long distances in a fraction of the time required just a few decades ago.

This transport "revolution" continues in Europe, with the rapid growth in air traffic and with the expansion of high-speed passenger rail links.

Similarly, communications on the continent, originally improved by the invention and application of telegraph, radio, and telephone technology, has improved further with microwave and satellite transmission and ongoing development of ever more rapid ways to send and retrieve digitally encoded messages. An ever lower proportion of information arrives to individuals in the relatively costly, printed format. (Look for future editions of this and other textbooks, for example, to be in digital formats.)

Railways

Until the late 1950s, Europe was still basically in the "railway age." Railroads helped launch its rapid economic development and ascent to leadership in the world economy. Inland waterways (rivers and canals) had a distinctly secondary role in the transportation of goods. During the last 100 years, rail transportation made good use of successive technologies—steam, the diesel engine, and electricity. It benefited from several advantages such as relatively low, often subsidized, fares; fast and dependable service, generally unimpeded by local weather; the capability to transport large numbers of people and large amounts of freight over long distances directly to urban destinations; and generally smaller investments in terminal facilities than required, for example, by waterborne shipping.

After World War II, rapid rebuilding of destroyed railways in many parts of Europe and the USSR was the top priority for getting goods and passengers moving again. At the same time, the first steps toward cooperation and the possible integration of the many national railway systems were taken by way of regionwide cooperation in all modes of transport, such as in the creation in 1947 of the Inland Transport Committee (ITC) of the Economic Commission for Europe (a United Nations entity). The prewar European transport system, initiated by separate, highly nationalistic governments, created autarkic, relatively isolated national transport systems with bottlenecks and barriers to interaction at frontiers. As an outgrowth of Allied cooperation during World War II and as a result of the ITC, intergovernmental cooperation in transport received priority in the postwar era. Today Europe, especially Northwestern Europe, is far better served by interlinked transport services than ever before.

Cooperation between national governments has been successful in dealing with technical problems affecting future rail service. For example, development of a common-users system for the railcar fleet has reduced empty return journeys.

Many countries belong to TEE (TransEurope Express), organized in 1957, which runs first-class air-conditioned trains as well as special freight trains, now linking well over 100 cities.

The European rail system has had strong governmental support at the national level (Fig. 5-9). The rail network was built with government subsidies; and governments largely determined routes, just as has been the case more recently for highways. This special relationship continues and, owing to the lack of competition and to other market-based influences, has probably also contributed to low profits or even to deficits. Most railways in European countries have been publicly owned since their foundation. In 1948 the United Kingdom became the last country to nationalize its railroads, which are now being reprivatized. European governments have always subsidized public rail transportation and have given much attention to modernizing its service. Considerable research to improve tracks, engines, speed, safety, and freight-loading techniques, as well as standardization of equipment and computerization of freight tracking and passenger ticketing, bring continuous improvements to Europe's rail services.

Continued financial support from governments for railroads is based on a variety of concerns and interests, including slowing the growth in demand for fuel for motor vehicles and associated dependence on imported oil, for which availability and price proved dangerously unstable in the 1970s. There is also concern for reducing the air pollution, noise, and traffic congestion associated with road traffic, and for placating voters and satisfying regional interests that seek continued accessibility to the rail network. In fact, the relatively flat terrain and the dense population of Northwestern Europe, in particular, make it one of the best places on the globe to invest in the expensive capital requirements of modern rail systems.

Until the 1950s, railways still carried between 50 and 90 percent of the countries' cargo traffic. Today rail's share in Western Europe is generally only 10 to 25 percent, but it is higher in Eastern Europe. Rail ton miles (movement of 1 ton of freight over 1 mile) fell about 25 percent in Western Europe between 1977 and 1992, while road ton miles grew 60 percent. In Eastern Europe during the same period, rail ton miles fell about 50 percent, especially rapidly after 1989, and road ton

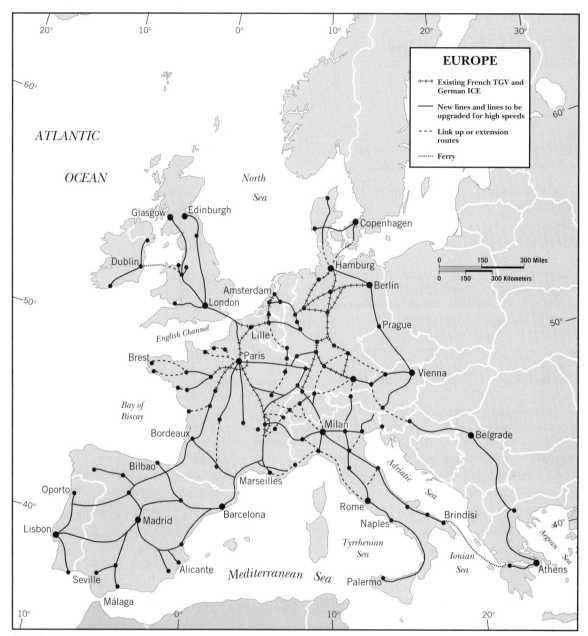

FIGURE 5-9 Europe's future high speed rail net? Based on proposals by the EU Commission, plans by national railroads, and existing service, this map indicates where high speed rail service could be offered by the early part of the 21st century. High speed rail is a reality on many lines in France and Germany in particular, as well as on portions of most other West European rail nets. Hopes for a network as extensive as the one shown are probably not very realistic in the short run. For example, for now the planned Italian high speed rail net (to be completed by about 2002) only includes lines from the French border to Venice and from Milan to Rome; only a short distance is now operational north from Rome toward Milan. The pattern also indicates the vast head start that Western Europe will have over Eastern Europe in this particular transport mode, an advantage that has existed historically for most other transport and communication modes as well. (Based in part on a map from Cole (1993)).

miles grew by 30 percent. In France and Germany, for example, rail carries about one-third the level of trucks, but in the UK only one-tenth. In Eastern Europe, despite declining traffic in absolute and relative terms, rail still dominates. This will change, as more limited-access highways are constructed and the East begins to tie into Western Europe's existing transport network.

Although the relative importance of passenger traffic has declined over the years, railroads continue to be important. Thus, for example, in Germany about 10 percent of long-distance passenger travel is by rail, making it the second most important carrier after private vehicles (which carries 77%). Railroads are also important employers and large revenue earners. The French national railway, SNCF, is the world's second largest transport firm, with over $17 billion in revenues in 1992; Germany and Italy's rail systems also each collected in excess of $10 billion.

Europe's railroads, although no longer the preeminent travel or transport mode (having been surpassed by cars and trucks), are by no means dead. With the congestion of highways and ports, the tremendous increase in urban agglomerations, and pollution caused particularly by motor traffic, Europe has again begun putting more emphasis on railroads. The technological innovations of the last 25 years have contributed to the modernization and specialization of railway services and the building of additional, selected rail lines.

The most ambitious, recently completed transport project is the Channel rail tunnel (Chunnel) between England and France. It was constructed over a seven-year period by a joint Anglo-French company, opening a few months late and many billions of dollars over budget in 1994. Plans for such a tunnel were first drawn up nearly 200 years ago, and the first of several tunneling efforts was aborted over 100 years ago. The 31-mile-long (50 km) crossing consists of two railway tunnels and a service tunnel. In connection with the Chunnel, a high-speed rail network linking the biggest cities of Northwestern Europe is also under construction. British Rail will eventually construct a high-speed railway link between the Channel tunnel and London and beyond, but due to much domestic opposition in southern England (Kent),

this vital link will not become available for some years to come. On the other hand, high-speed links to the Chunnel are already in place from Paris, and as a result, northern France may especially benefit from the project, at least during the next few years.

Another important new project is the so-called Betuwe Line—a planned 130-mile (209 km) container freight line from the German border through the Netherlands' rural Betuwe region to Rotterdam. This $5 billion, 7 year long construction project to commence in 1997 is designed to assure Rotterdam area ports the best possible accessibility in the coming century and to reduce problems associated with heavy truck traffic between them and Germany. Protests related to landscape/land-use disruptions have been overridden, but noise abatement measures costing $500 million are planned.

The rail service of the future is the international high-speed train, modeled after the Japanese Shinkansen system inaugurated in 1964. In Europe comparable service was initiated in 1958 with the *Mistral*, which ran at 90 mph (140 kph) between Paris and Lyon. The TGV (*train a grande vitesse*), inaugurated in 1981, now averages 134 mph (215 kph) between these cities, and TGV services have been extended to Tours and on toward Bordeaux. Germany, too, is building fast trains and new modern rail routes. The newest proposal is to build an exceptionally fast train (310 mph or 500 kph), the *Transrapid*, between Hamburg and Berlin during the coming decade. An ambitious effort among all of the countries of Western Europe is underway to cooperatively build a 155-185 mile per hour (250–300 kph) rail system, the basic components of which should link up by around the year 2000. This would allow rapid transit among a network of large cities, including London, Paris, Lille, Brussels, Antwerp, Rotterdam, Amsterdam, Cologne, and Aachen (Fig. 5-9). The most astonishing proposed project (*Swissmetro*) is a 500-mile-long (800 km) network of underground tunnels that is to link major Swiss cities by speedy trains. A feasibility study of the projected 25-year-long, $20 billion undertaking is in progress.

The ongoing development of high-speed rail in Europe faces several major hurdles, including funding new routeways through densely populated areas; overcoming environmental impacts, such as noise from fast trains; and dealing with the incompatibility of system components such as signals. The current French and German high-speed systems are still incompatible, and the electric current requirements of other, existing lines that will be partially used by the high-speed trains differ considerably across the continent. Other problems for the eventual integration of European rail systems include gauge differences between Spain, Portugal, Finland, and the FSU and the rest of Europe, and the great competition faced by ever-growing passenger travel over (generally) short distances by car and over long distances by air. The railroads' traffic share, much of it squeezed into the middle distances, must constantly battle to maintain ridership on all fronts.

Waterways

Canals and rivers are among Europe's oldest means of transport. Their role rapidly declined, however, with the development of the railroad network in the nineteenth century. Locks were simply too small to permit passage of large barges or boats that could have better competed with railways. It was only with the increased postwar demand for transportation of goods in bulk that inland waterways again emerged as a viable alternative.

Freedom of river navigation across international borders became an important issue centuries ago. The modern affirmation of the right of safe and unobstructed passage for inland shipping was established at the Congress of Vienna in 1815, which served as a model for later conventions on Europe's great rivers—the Danube in 1856 and the Rhine in 1831. With some modification, these treaties are still the basic transportation guidelines for European river transport, permitting free transportation for all European countries.

Emphasis on specialization in the handling of goods, together with the introduction of other new technologies, have resulted in a revival of inland shipping in recent decades (Fig. 5-10). The introduction of 24-hour navigation on the Rhine and other important West European waterways by installation of radar and inauguration of barge pusher techniques has made inland shipping competitive. These barges, concentrating on shipment of ore, phosphates, and building material, have given inland shipping an important place among Europe's transport modes. In 1950, for example, there was talk of a permanent crisis of Rhine shipping, but the Rhine now carries hundreds of millions of tons on its 522 miles (835 km) of navigable waterways. Total goods carried on German and Austrian sections of the Danube approximate 100 million tons. Increased use of inland waterborne shipping contributed to the decision to build the long-planned Rhine-Main-Danube Canal

FIGURE 5-10 The Rhine, here at St. Goarshausen within its dramatic gorge through the Central Uplands, is Europe's busiest inland waterway. (Ulrike Welsch/Photo Researchers)

between Bamberg and Regensburg, Germany, which should result in traffic increases on all the rivers. However, other than passenger cruise trips, there are no expectations of Black Sea to North Sea through traffic, and total freight traffic on the upper Danube remains quite modest.

Based on low traffic and expected ecological disruptions, growing opposition has arisen in Bavaria to damming and canalizing the last free-flowing portion of the Danube east of Munich. Discussions also continue about building a long-desired and controversial Rhone–Rhine Canal that would link Rotterdam and Marseille by way of an inland waterway.

For now, however, and likely in the future as well, by far the greatest amount of tonnage moved on European waterways travels back and forth between Germany and the Netherlands, largely between the Ruhr and Rotterdam. Smaller amounts move within and through Belgium, mostly in low-land Flanders; and much smaller amounts move on French waterways, primarily to and from Paris and within the Normandy region.

In general, European waterways, as well as other inland transport modes, focus on Europe's ports, which are among the world's busiest. Rotterdam, strategically located amidst Europe's wealthiest and most densely populated region at the mouth of the heavily traveled Rhine, is Europe's greatest port. It and other great ports like Antwerp (the world's eighth busiest port), Hamburg (the world's sixth busiest container port), and Marseille (Table 5-3) provide Europe with its vital links to the rest of the world, from which it receives vast quantities of imports (especially raw materials) and through which it exports smaller quantities of higher value products, particularly manufactured goods. Rotterdam has especially important ties to Germany, trade which accounts for over a third of the port's total traffic. Most goods going through Rotterdam area ports use connecting inland waterways. About one-third of shipments out from Rotterdam go over pipelines (reflecting the port's very important trade in oil); about a third of the much lower volume of incoming traffic arrives by truck.

Ships now use intermodal containers that can be transshipped by truck, barge, and railcar. The development of intercontinental containers for

TABLE 5-3	
EUROPE'S MAJOR PORTS, 1993 (CARGO IN MILLIONS OF TONS)	
Rotterdam	282
Antwerp	102
Marseille	87
Hamburg	66
Le Havre	55
Amsterdam	49
London	46
Genoa	41
Dunkerque	41
Zeebrugge	33
Wilhelmshaven	31
Bremen	28
Ghent	22

Source: Rotterdam Municipal Port (1994).

maritime transport has further contributed to the transformation of European transport. Containerization of long-distance hauls is now popular in transoceanic barge-carrying ships, which can be unloaded outside established port installations for subsequent transport by inland waterway pushers. For example, although Rotterdam is especially important for movement of bulk commodities (77% of total tonnage), container shipments (16%) have grown over the last 20 years and should grow further after completion of the Betuwe Line described earlier. Oil movements have dropped off considerably. Hamburg, as already noted, is also the world's sixth most important container port, with over 40 percent of that traffic being with Southeast Asia.

Goods moving by sea to and from Europe are increasingly carried on non-European-built and -registered ships. Both shipbuilding and ship registry have declined dramatically in Europe in recent years. Greek registry, Europe's largest, has held steady, but Norway saw registered tons fall by nearly one-quarter between 1977 and 1993. There were similarly sharp drops over the same period in many other countries with previously

TABLE 5-4	
CHANGES IN REGISTERED FREIGHTER TONNAGE, SELECTED COUNTRIES, 1977–1993	
Malta	+9987%
Cyprus	+719%
UK	-82%
Spain	-76%
Sweden	-67%
France	-63%
Germany	-48%
Netherlands	-42%
Italy	-37%
Poland	-23%
Norway	-23%
Greece	-17%

Source: Euromonitor (1995)

large merchant fleets (Table 5-4). Taxes, wages, and regulations have resulted in the re-flagging of vessels to other places, including Malta and Cyprus. Malta now has Europe's fourth largest fleet, which developed almost entirely after about 1980. Cyprus, whose fleet was Europe's second largest in 1993, also grew spectacularly during the 1980s.

Road Vehicle Transport

By far the most important passenger and freight transport modes in Europe now are cars and trucks, respectively. The first European superhighway, built in 1924 between Milan and Venice, was envisioned as the beginning of a new international highway system ultimately connecting much of Europe, a system that has yet to be completed. The limited-access highway heralded an end to the absolute supremacy of railways and contributed greatly to other postwar changes in Europe, including a key role in increased intra-European tourism and suburbanization.

Highway freight grew much faster than railway haulage after 1950, with road haulage carrying about two-thirds of the increase in inland goods traffic in Western Europe. Rail freight movement stagnated and, more recently, declined rather precipitously. On the other hand, in Eastern Europe over 90 percent of increases in freight movement was hauled by rail as late as the 1950s; by the 1980s this too had changed dramatically, with rail movements in decline and road traffic increasing as well.

The number of private cars in Europe has also increased dramatically since the 1960s. In the mid-1950s Europe had about 10 million registered cars; there were more than 150 million in 1990 (about the same number as in the United States). Between 1950 and the early 1990s, the number of private cars per 1000 inhabitants in Italy increased from 7 to 391, in France from 20 to 392, and in West Germany, where auto ownership is most widespread, from 18 to 460. In 1992 in Germany, over 80 percent of all miles traveled by passengers were in private cars; conditions are probably similar in other Northwest European countries.

The problem of increased traffic and insufficient highways was of great concern for the 1950 Geneva Declaration, which called for new roads and improvements in existing ones. Ultimately, about 46,500 miles (75,000 km) of high-speed international highway across Europe will be numbered (E1 to E30) as will linking roads (E31 to E125). Another planned development is to build missing links across waterways and between countries in the form of bridges, rail connections, or tunnels. For example, bridges are planned between Denmark and southern Sweden, Copenhagen and the mainland of Europe, and Spain and Morocco. More tunnels will be built through the western, central, and eastern Alps, and a bridge is planned across the Straits of Messina, linking Italy and Sicily. A second bridge over the Bosporus at Istanbul has already been completed.

Pipelines

The increased tonnage of maritime shipping and greatly increased demand for oil and petrochemicals has led to the building of a large network of inland pipelines for distribution of oil and natural gas. By the early 1980s, hardly a region in Europe was not served by pipelines (Fig. 5-11); pipelines

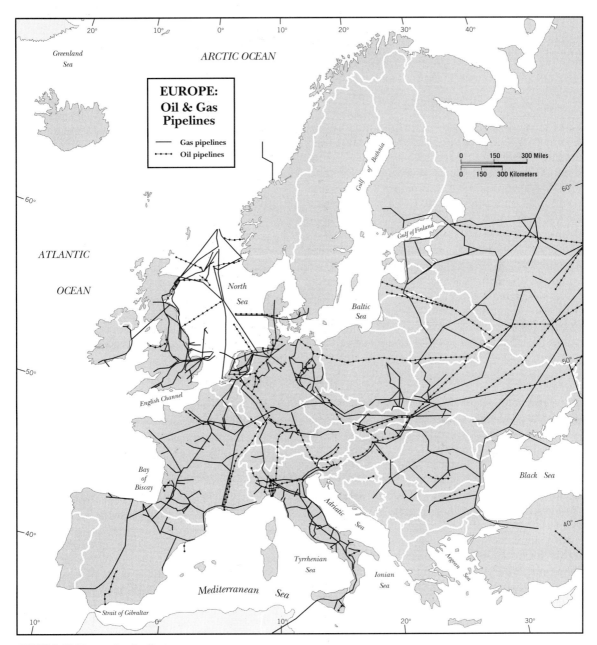

FIGURE 5-11 Europe's pipelines.

and trucking have been the fastest growing freight haulers in Europe. The FSU built the Friendship (Drushba) pipeline to bring oil and natural gas from its fields on the western slopes of the central Urals through Poland to eastern Germany, with a later branch south, which now also continues into western Germany. The Orenburg pipeline in the FSU is carrying Russian natural gas to both Eastern and Western Europe. Pipelines in Western Europe carry crude oil from ports on the Mediterranean and the North Seas to inland refineries. Natural gas and oil in the North Sea are distributed by pipeline to the UK, Norway, and many EU countries.

Air Transport

Until the mid-1960s, air transport played a minor role in the movement of goods and people. Since then, the number of passengers as well as the volume of freight has grown faster than any other form of transport, though comparatively speaking it still plays only a minor role. Three of the world's largest airlines by revenue in 1992 were European—Air France (#3), Lufthansa (Germany, #4), and British Airways (#7). London, Paris, and Frankfurt (in that order) are Europe's busiest airports.

European airlines are generally either partly or wholly state owned, have long been protected from external competition, set high fares within Europe (by American standards), frequently require subsidies, and in many cases now face financial difficulties. Privatization (such as recently by Germany's Lufthansa) may increase in the future; deregulation is underway, and mergers and links between European and U.S. carriers are probably needed to keep smaller lines in business. Already Swissair has bought a nearly 50 percent share of Sabena (Belgium) for $230 million, giving Swissair better access to the EU market and Sabena needed capital. Scandinavian Airlines System (SAS) has decided to coordinate routes, cargo, and sales with Lufthansa in order to improve its position and chances for survival after deregulation. The European airlines' competitive problems are suggested by declining numbers of transatlantic flights by the Concorde, and governments' intentions to give huge subsidies to Air France and Iberia (Spain) to help keep them competitive. The subsidies have drawn outcries and legal action from numerous other carriers.

MANUFACTURING

The location of modern manufacturing is affected by more factors, and also more important factors, than simply the location of raw materials. Though of continuing importance, the effect of resources on manufacturing is being eroded throughout the economically developed world by many factors. (1) Improved technology has resulted in an ever-declining need for raw material inputs. For example, a ton of iron once required many tons of coal for production; now less than a ton of coal will suffice. Technological advancements, of course, have also led to the development of products that embody more skilled labor and capital costs in proportion to final output. (2) Improvement of and relative cost reduction for transport services make it easier to move resources to production sites, now often closer to markets, rather than the reverse. This is particularly true in Europe, where many raw materials were never plentiful and those that were have, in any event, been greatly depleted. (3) The sizes of markets have grown enormously over the years, so that individual metropolitan areas and megalopolitan areas (e.g., the Cologne-Ruhr conurbation) now contain tens of millions of quite prosperous consumers as well as thousands of firms. The ability to reliably move massive amounts of food and energy, for both industrial and consumer use, to these geographic concentrations and the ability to construct high-performance commuter passenger services and high-rise offices and apartment buildings, have made these large, concentrated urban concentrations possible. The draw of these huge markets has proven attractive for many producers.

The major population and economic centers on the western part of the North European Plain have Europe's best location for market-oriented economic activities, including manufacturing. They possess centrality within Europe's densest, wealthiest market region, access to skilled labor, and excellent telecommunication and transport ties to Europe and the world. Measures of accessibility to the EU market indicate that Paris, London, Amsterdam, the Ruhr, and Frankfurt have perhaps the best locations (Keeble, 1986). The advantages of these cities will increase by 1998, when all but Frankfurt will be linked within a planned international high-speed rail network. Taking all of the European market into account except the FSU, Karlsruhe (based on European income) and Ulm, Germany (based on European population), have the best locations. Including the FSU's income and population the best market locations shift eastward to Dresden and Warsaw (Cole and Cole, 1993). The benefits of centrality within the European space economy accrue in particular to Germany, but also substantially to Switzerland, northern France, southern England, and the Low Countries.

Changing patterns of industrial organization have also favored the concentration of many higher-value-added activities like research and development in cities in general, particularly in areas that develop new and better ways to organize production (e.g., highly interconnected, flexible, and responsive small-firm networks in northern Italy). Such sites often become centers for the development and production of new products like those from the aerospace and computer industries in and near Munich. In contrast, areas in which things are done more or less as in decades past, have suffered devastating economic losses, such as many of Europe's textile, steel and shipbuilding regions. Although the inertia of existing capital investment, infrastructure, and local markets can help maintain a region's economy for some time in the face of ever mounting extraregional competition, inevitably a downward spiral of economic misfortune can begin in regions where sectoral and organizational structures and labor skills no longer match contemporary needs. Such areas are desperately in need of what is generally called "restructuring."

Planners and others who study regions ("regional scientists," including economic geographers) agree that governments can play key roles in restructuring, but the precise nature of this effort remains rather contested. Some people favor greater free market orientation and deregulation (as conservatives did in the UK in the 1980s). Others simply advocate new styles of government economic involvement—a position typical now among "reformed" socialists in parts of East Central and Southeastern Europe.

One generally successful governmental action has been the development of regional trading areas in Europe. Most notably, the ever-expanding EC/EU began nearly 40 years ago with 6 members and now numbers 15, with many other countries clamoring for the right of entry. The EU especially, but also EFTA and its trade alliance with the EU

(the EEA), have brought liberalization of and increases in trade, resulting in considerable impetus for European economic growth. The EU is also causing adjustments in the production and marketing of nearly all manufactured goods, and has influenced the locational pattern of newly established industrial investments from member and nonmember countries. For example, many U.S. firms that do business within the EU are particularly interested in having investment and production footholds within it in order to assure optimal market access.

Some economic changes and decisions affecting Europe's economies are largely beyond the control of their governments. Technologic and organizational change appear to be greater among Europe's international competitors in Japan and other parts of the Pacific Rim, including the United States, than among EU firms, leading to concern for "Eurosclerosis." Still, geographic concentrations of skilled labor, technology, and innovative behavior have resulted in a number of successful high-technology production regions in Europe. These and various other generalized types of industrial regions in Europe and their locational determinants are described briefly in the following sections.

Manufacturing Output

Germany, the UK, France, Italy, and Spain (in that order) are by far Europe's leading manufacturers by value added, producing well in excess of a trillion dollars annually in output. The value of Germany's production is nearly double that of the next three producers; it alone accounts for about a quarter of EU manufactures. Germany leads the continent (excepting Russia, which in turn leads Germany) in production of a wide range of goods, including iron, steel, cars, cloth, synthetic fibers, plastics, and electricity. However, Europe's relative position among the world's industrial regions has been falling, and it lags particularly far behind in such fields as computer and aerospace production, where the United States and Japan dominate. For example, none of the world's top 10 computer chip firms is in Europe; 9 out of 10 are American and Japanese; and about 75 percent of personal computers sold in Europe are made elsewhere. The four top-selling PC companies in Europe are American based; Olivetti of Italy is fifth. Although the giant Phillips electronics firm (based at Eindhoven, the Netherlands) was an early developer of CDs and VCRs, it has been in serious difficulty and cut companywide employment during the first half of the 1990s from 297,000 to 238,000. In an effort to gain a portion of the world's civilian aircraft market, a consortium of French, German, UK, and Spanish producers organized Airbus; it has now become competitive, holding about one-third of the world's share of sales. As in other fields, however, U.S. and European aerospace firms complain about one another's heavy government subsidies. Europe's world share in production of "older" industrial products has also declined, notably in steel production, although European production of steel still comprised about 24 percent of total world production in the early 1990s.

Traditional Resource-Based Centers for Heavy Industry

Europe's unquestioned world leadership in manufacturing was clearest at the height of the early Industrial Revolution when many manufacturing sectors were drawn toward large coalfields. In fact, earlier centers of manufacturing had also already developed around raw material sites, such as the relatively small ore deposits both in the Ore Mountains (Erzgebirge) in southeastern Germany and in Bohemia. The concentrations of manufacturing in large coalfields during the latter part of the nineteenth century reached unprecedented proportions. During this heyday of capitalism, old industries like mining and metal-smelting and –working expanded greatly, and new industries, like the complex of production associated with railroads (e.g., locomotives, railcars, and rails), developed rapidly. Renowned industrial regions emerged which became their respective countries' economic heartlands. The names of these regions are still virtually synonymous with heavy industry —the Ruhr, the English Midlands, Upper Silesia, and, in Ukraine and Russia, the Donets Basin. Other important nineteenth-century coal-based heavy industrial regions included southern Wales; the flanks of the Pennines and Northumberland in

England; central Scotland; Bilbao in northern Spain; an area around Lyon; a series of regions from northern France through southern Belgium to Aachen in Germany; the Saarland on the oft-disputed French-German border; southern Saxony from Zwickau east to Dresden; the Miskolc region in northern Hungary; and in what was then Austria, areas in upper Styria, western and northern Bohemia, and parts of the Silesian region in Moravia. In addition, heavy industry based on local iron ore and nearby coalfields thrived in Lorraine and adjacent Luxembourg. There were no important resource-based heavy industrial regions in Southern or Southeastern Europe, which are short on coal resources and also developed industry rather late.

By the outbreak of World War I, Germany, the UK, and France dominated Europe's production of heavy industrial output, with about 80 percent of total output of products such as steel, machinery, and chemicals. The three countries' share of coal production exceeded 90 percent at that time. Austria and Belgium (as well as Russia) were distant competitors.

Industrial concentrations attracted inmigration and investment in a broad range of infrastructure, most notably in transport facilities (Fig. 5-12). Thus, industrial areas developed large local consumer and producer markets as well as an infrastructural base, all of which helped maintain their industrial importance until at least the early post–World War II era, when a variety of problems began to become apparent. By the 1950s, shifts in relative energy prices to the detriment of coal, depletion of local resources and better access to imports at coastal sites, new technology favoring larger and more integrated plants, and international competition began to erode the advantages of the traditional, resource-based, heavy industrial regions. Many people would argue that the decline of these regions was exacerbated by inflexible, large firms and unions that began to understand too late the variety of economic and related locational disadvantages facing them. Crumbling and unsightly buildings, polluted skies and water, an aging and stagnating population, and dearth of recreational and cultural amenities emerged as cause and effect of a downward spiral of job losses and falling relative incomes in many traditional

FIGURE 5-12 Duisburg in the Ruhr region. The Ruhr region is served well by many transportation modes; inland shipping moves a variety of bulk goods, including raw materials for the region's iron and steel plants. (W. H. Berentsen)

coal-based industrial regions. These conditions began to be clear in Western Europe by the 1960s and generally worsened thereafter. The EU, for example, experienced declining coal output, and 500,000 workers lost jobs in the steel industry in the 1970s and 1980s. In the 1990s, efforts are continuing to further reduce excess output, with more jobs certain to be lost when it becomes politically palatable.

The effects have been compressed in time in East Central Europe, where coal-based heavy industrial regions have been hit especially hard during the current era of industrial restructuring. Exposed to international competition first, eastern Germany's coal and metal-producing sectors and regions are reeling from job cuts. In Silesia, owing to continued short-term government protection, conditions are almost certain to get much worse before too long.

Still, there remains a great deal of production of a number of major products like coal, chemicals, metals, machinery, and transport equipment in Europe's traditional resource-based manufacturing regions. For example, chemicals production is frequently located within complex associations with other heavy industries, which both deliver to and buy from chemical firms like those concentrated in the Ruhr and the Halle-Leipzig agglomerations. More isolated large complexes also occur, as in Ludwigshaven and Basel. By far the three largest European chemical firms (Hoechst, BASF, and Bayer) are all German owned.

Some traditional heavy industrial regions (e.g., central Scotland, the West Midlands of England, and the Ruhr) are showing some indications of revival or, at least, stabilization. For example, the West Midlands, which lost about 500,000 jobs from the mid-1960s to the mid-1980s and had an unemployment rate of 14 percent in 1982, had reduced its unemployment rate below the EU average to about 6 percent by the early 1990s. The Ruhr has also lost hundreds of thousands of jobs. For example, in the 1980s Germany's leading steel cities, Dortmund and Duisburg, lost a staggering 36 percent and 47 percent of their manufacturing jobs, respectively. In 1988 the Ruhr had a peak unemployment rate of 15 percent. By 1990 that stood at 11 percent, and the region was making efforts on a variety of fronts to attract new jobs—investing in infrastructure, education, and environmental restoration and protection, as well as launching a public relations campaign to attempt to change the region's image.

Once gloomy Glasgow and depressed Edinburgh have perhaps made the greatest headway, now attracting investments and jobs in a variety of microelectronics fields, and successfully creating the image of a "Silicon Glen." It remains to be seen whether the Ruhr, the West Midlands, and other heavy industrial regions that have yet to achieve Silicon Glen's level of transformation can again prosper in the next century, or whether they will become permanent problem regions.

Labor-Intensive Manufacturing Regions

Other early, and often now problematic, manufacturing regions, are those specializing in the labor-intensive production of textiles, leather goods, and toys. Textile production regions were among Europe's earliest specialized manufacturing areas, although the scale and organization of production were far different than at present. Textile production is now carried out in large, far more capital-intensive and technologically advanced factories than in decades past. The earliest textile production areas, dating to the Middle Ages (e.g., Flanders and northern Italy), involved small groups of people spinning and weaving in small shops, or individuals working at home. Woolen and linen production was more important than cotton cloth production, which flourished after invention of the cotton gin (1793). After increased international trade in the nineteenth century, the cotton gin led to greatly expanded importation of cotton, little of which has ever been grown in Europe itself.

In the nineteenth and early twentieth centuries, textile production (cotton, woolen, and linen) was rather widespread in Europe, including fairly important production regions in Catalonia; Lyon (silk) and northern France; Flanders; Manchester, the flanks of the Pennine chain, and Northern Ireland in the UK; the Rhineland and Ruhr regions, southern Bavaria, and an area focused around Chemnitz in Germany; parts of Switzerland; parts of Bohemia; and Silesia and especially Łódz in Poland. In several of these cases, producers employed female workers who offered an inexpensive potential labor reservoir in heavy industrial regions that otherwise offered work primarily for men.

Although there have been different temporal phases in the growth and decline of European textiles depending on region and product specialization, in general only relatively low-labor-cost producers can now compete for the broadest spectrum of the world market, while high-quality, specialized products have faced less severe competition. In the 1980s more than 400,000 textile workers lost their jobs in the EU alone, the majority of them women, owing to mechanization and international competition. By quantity, woolen production peaked in most places between about 1910 and 1940, linen production during the inter-war period, and cotton cloth manufacturing in about 1960 (a few years earlier in the UK). Synthetic fibers production appears to have peaked in Northwestern Europe in the 1970s and 1980s, although definitive indications of the relative decline of this industry across Europe are not yet apparent. Italy is now the EU's leader in textile and apparel production; the UK, Germany, and France are also quite important. The relative position of Portugal (with production regionally concentrated around Porto in the north) has improved. During the 1980s and 1990s, however, employment in this sector declined by from 25 to 40 percent in all of these countries. Clearly, Western Europe is increasingly at a disadvantage internationally in competing with lower cost producers. One such European competitor, Romania, has become a much more important producer in recent years.

In general, a clearly negative trend is evident in the European textile industry. Beginning in the 1980s, in part owing to changes in international trade agreements, growth in demand for cloth made in Europe was less rapid than demand for imports. Most of Europe's textile regions now face rather severe problems owing especially to international competition. An indicator of this difficulty was the plummeting textile employment in the Chemnitz region of Germany after its large industry was exposed to international competition. Between 1991 and 1993, Saxony lost 45,000 jobs in the textile sector (a 75% decline), and thousands more positions in other labor-intensive sectors—19,000 jobs in clothing production (-76%) and 8000 in leather working (-84%). Low-cost, labor-intensive industries, though still rather important overall for employment in both Western and Eastern Europe, do not offer regions long-term development opportunities. In order for Europe to maintain competitiveness in the manufacturing sector, production of other higher cost and quality industrial goods must be and are being emphasized.

Seaport and Coastal Manufacturing Centers

European ports have long been important manufacturing sites, building ships and processing and using imported raw materials to produce finished and intermediate products such as food, steel, and chemicals. Notable examples include Liverpool, Newcastle, and other north English ports, Glasgow, Rotterdam/Europoort, Bremen, Hamburg, Barcelona, Marseille, and Genoa (Fig. 5-13). By the 1960s manufacturers using bulky, imported raw materials turned increasingly to coastal locations to benefit from economies of sea transport. Examples of new coastal industrial sites include the iron and steel industry at Dunkirk; Fos in southern France; Bremen; Ijmuiden on the coast of northwest Holland; Cornigliano and Bagnoli on the west coast of Italy and Taranto on the east coast; Port Talbot, Newport, and Danwem in south Wales; and Lackenby and Appleby on the east coast of England. Development of oil refining and petrochemicals are found in coastal areas, especially along the lower parts of estuaries—for example, on the Humber and Tees in Britain, and at Europoort (downstream from Rotterdam) in the Netherlands.

Although some of these industrial regions continue to do well or are recovering, in part because of economic and employment gains in transport and other service sectors, many port-based industrial regions have been especially hard hit by job losses in shipbuilding. These places have experienced ongoing economic problems in recent years—for example, Liverpool, Bremen, Nantes (France), Genoa, and Gdansk (formerly Danzig). Bremen is currently threatened by the collapse of Germany's leading shipbuilding firm, Vulkan Verbund AG, which employed over 22,000 workers in 1996. Other ports, such as Antwerp, Lübeck, and Trieste have also suffered, at one time or another, from lost trade hinterlands as the result of changing geopolitical conditions. Apparently, port cities that are part of more economically diversified regions, such as London and Hamburg, or regions that are diversifying, such as Glasgow and Barcelona, have the brightest futures.

High-Value-Added, Engineering-Oriented Production Regions

Once specialized in the manufacture of relatively "old," metals-based products, some industrial regions have continued to thrive, or at least to compete reasonably well, by producing ever more sophisticated machinery. The best example of such a region, one of Europe's most prosperous, is the Neckar Valley region in Germany. Focused around Stuttgart, the region is home to a variety of

FIGURE 5-13 The port of Rotterdam in 1987. Rotterdam, at the mouth of the heavily trafficked Rhine River and amidst wealthy and populous Northwestern Europe, has long been among the world's busiest harbors. (Sam C. Pierson, Jr./Photo Researchers)

industries, most notably the complex of firms associated with Daimler-Benz, makers of Mercedes-Benz cars, which many people consider the best engineered in the world. Another good example of this kind of region is offered by the Aachen-Cologne area, also in Germany.

Historically, Germany had other leading regional engineering complexes, one stretching from Magdeburg to Dresden in Saxony and another in what is now in Polish Silesia. In East Central Europe, western Bohemia was historically a relatively prosperous industrial region based in part on engineering manufactures. During the socialist era, these three regions were prosperous only by CMEA standards; disadvantages associated with the economic conditions within that bloc have left them unproductive and poor by Western standards. These East Central European regions are expected to become reestablished as competitive areas for such products as machinery and transportation equipment. The engineering sector is also an important component of a number of broadly based industrial regions, described earlier as traditional, resource-based, heavy industrial areas (notably the Ruhr) and later in this chapter under the title of "metropolitan market-regions" (such as Paris).

High-Technology Regions

Perhaps the late-twentieth-century analogue to engineering-oriented regions, which often had a high level of preeminence from the latter part of the nineteenth century to about 1975, is what today we call "high-technology" regions. These areas generally have concentrations of research-intensive activities and rapidly evolving subsectors of the electronics, aerospace, optics and instruments, telecommunications, chemical, and biomedical industries. Regions with this type of industrial structure tend to be among the world's most prosperous, rapidly growing, and changing economic areas. They usually attract and encourage the local development of leading industrial sectors by way of an assortment of locational advantages. Such regions may, for example, be characterized as having access to skilled labor and technology (in university and business research

laboratories); to excellent, rapid means of transportation and communication; and to a local "quality of life" attractive to both entrepreneurs and workers. Specialized "high-tech" regions now exist to one extent or another around Cambridge and Glasgow–Edinburgh ("Silicon Glen") in the UK; and Lyons, Grenoble, Montpelier, and the Cote d'Azur region in France.

The Cote d'Azur region is attempting to benefit from its climatic and scenic allure by attracting high-technology and headquarters facilities. A research and development, or "science," park with over 1000 international firms and 16,000 workers has developed near Cannes at Sophia Antipolis. The park was begun in 1969 when many people were skeptical of its success, but today it represents the second most important economic activity after tourism on the French Riviera. Other, similarly structured technology parks are now being planned in the region, notably one on 2500 acres between Nice and Monaco called Plateau Tercier.

High-tech activities are also important components of industrial structures of the Munich, northeastern Italy (especially Milan), Paris, Manchester-West Midlands-London, and southern Wales regions. For example, once largely a university town and regional market center, Cambridge now employs about 20,000 workers in high-technology activities. Munich, Germany's third largest industrial concentration (fourteenth largest in 1950), has more than 2000 large and small high-tech firms and has become Germany's leading center for aerospace and software development.

Fast-paced technological change and rapidly developing competition for the manufacture of new products require that such regions have firms that are constantly improving on older products or developing new ones to replace the production of items that either become obsolete or whose production can be moved to lower cost regions. In addition, the regions must combat some of the disadvantageous outcomes of their own success, such as higher levels of local commercial land development, higher housing and labor costs, congestion, and pollution. Ironically, the absence of these problems was often the original stimulus for the development in today's leading high-tech regions. Regional planners and local politicians usually want their region to achieve the status of a "high-tech" concentration, but the competition is too fierce for most areas ever to succeed. Developing a high-tech component within a local industrial structure is both more likely and more often realized.

Metropolitan Market Centers

As noted earlier, decreasing transport costs, reduced relative importance of raw materials in total production costs, and greatly expanded market sizes in cities have all enhanced the role of market orientation in European manufacturing. Thus, industrial regions have developed in and around all the major metropolitan areas of Europe, which also benefit from concentrations of skilled labor and access to transport and telecommunication services. Manufacturing activities are often particularly well developed in capital cities, where the concentration of government employment, decision making, and, usually, cultural amenities enhances urban concentrations of the countries' populations and economic activities. Despite avowed public policy goals to decentralize manufacturing and other economic activities from these concentrations, market forces and government policies working at cross purposes have generally checked such efforts. Besides Europe's capitals, other major urban manufacturing centers that are important metropolitan market centers include Amsterdam, Frankfurt, Düsseldorf, Hannover, Munich, Berlin, Zürich, Geneva, Milan, and Barcelona. In some cases, a "market center" may also be classifiable within another of the manufacturing region categories noted earlier, such as Munich and Milan which can also be called high-technology regions.

Generally, the sectoral employment structures of metropolitan regions are much better balanced than regions described earlier, and their inhabitants enjoy relatively good socioeconomic conditions. Metropolitan-based industrial regions are likely to be forever a part of Europe's manufacturing landscape and will probably continue to experience fewer boom-and-bust economic cycles than, for example, resource, port, and low-cost labor-based regions.

Manufacturing in the "Periphery"

Although most of Europe's manufacturing output occurs in more advanced countries and developed regions, manufacturing has also often grown rapidly in selected poorer regions. The less prosperous regions may offer some benefits from local resources (notably in Southeastern Europe), lower cost labor, or lower cost access to the EU market for nonmembers, as in the cases of Portugal and Spain. National development efforts as well as EU and other international development funds (e.g., the World Bank and the European Bank for Recovery and Development [EBRD]) further support manufacturing investment. Spain and Portugal have had higher than EU average growth rates in manufacturing for over three decades; Greece and Ireland had similar patterns in the 1960s and 1970s. Although the formerly socialist countries of Eastern Europe experienced plummeting industrial output for several years beginning in about 1989, several are now showing good signs of recovery, especially Poland, Hungary, and Slovenia. These countries, the Czech Republic, and possibly Slovakia and Estonia will probably do better than other East European countries before the year 2000. Recovery everywhere in the East, however, is tied to: level of Western financial help and investment (by far the greatest in relative terms in Hungary, Table 5-5); reduction of EU import barrier; and domestic political will and stability. The resolution of threatening political problems in Northern Ireland and the Baltic states, as well as lasting peace in Bosnia-Herzegovina and settlement of related disputes in Croatia, Serbia-Montenegro, and Macedonia, are needed for these areas to attract international investment and to prosper. Another problem that likely has negative impacts on investment in manufacturing is the high level of strike activity in Spain and Italy, especially in comparison to Austria, Germany, and Switzerland, where such problems are few by international standards.

Industrial "Restructuring"

In the parts of Europe that are already highly industrialized, as elsewhere in the highly developed

TABLE 5-5

PER CAPITA FINANCIAL COMMITMENTS BY
(A) DEVELOPMENT INSTITUTIONS 1990–1993 AND
(B) THE WORLD BANK GROUP 1990–1995 TO
EUROPEAN TRANSITIONAL ECONOMIES
(IN DOLLARS)

	A	B
Hungary	280.0	166.3
Romania	185.0	62.0
Poland	132.0	99.8
Slovenia	113.0	40.0
Bulgaria	92.0	85.5
Slovakia	73.0	25.0
Czech Republic	66.0	31.3
Albania	44.0	55.4
Belarus	21.0	16.5
Moldova	19.0	40.0
Russia	12.7	31.8
Estonia	7.0	73.3
Latvia	4.0	49.2
Lithuania	3.0	31.9
Ukraine	0.7	13.0
Croatia	NA	55.1
Macedonia	NA	92.3

Source: World Bank, 1994, 1995.

world, rapidly changing technology and intense international competition have created tremendous pressure for manufacturers to cut production costs. Germany, in particular, has had a national debate in recent years assessing its locational attractiveness for industry, especially given the country's high wages and benefits, as well as increasingly stringent environmental standards. German business leaders rank their country poorly in terms of its attractiveness for investment, although in other countries it still maintains a quite high ranking as a place to do business.

Similar scrutiny of competitiveness within Europe as a whole has been one of the motivating factors to develop an ever larger, more efficient economic union within the EU. Huge job losses within some of Europe's biggest firms during the early 1990s has created some urgency, resulting both from the longer term restructuring process and a recent, sharp recession. These jobs, often relatively well paid, will be difficult to replace in the service sector, which has recently experienced losses among large employers such as the German and Italian national railways (94,000 jobs lost), and the British and German national telecommunications systems (60,000 lost jobs) (Table 5-6).

The automobile industry provides a good example of industrial restructuring in European manufacturing. Although at one time it was characterized by a large number of primarily (often small) European-based firms, pressure from U.S. and Japanese competitors has led to many changes in the organizational and territorial structure of production. At least 20 formerly independent European firms have been absorbed by other larger European firms and by American companies over the last three decades. Smaller, weaker firms have been unable to remain independent in the face of competition from the large firms. Acquisitions have helped the large firms utilize economies of scale in production and management, while also expanding marketing opportunities by adding recognized names to their product lines. Notable examples include acquisition of Alfa Romeo and Ferrari by Fiat; Lotus, Saab, and Lamborghini by Chrysler; Aston Martin and Jaguar by Ford; and Rover by BMW. A hoped-for merger of Renault and Volvo has been derailed primarily by nationalist tendencies, whereby countries are reluctant to see trade-

TABLE 5-6

JOB LOSSES IN FIRMS IN THE EARLY 1990S
(IN THOUSANDS)

Philips (Netherlands, electronics)	75
Daimler-Benz (Germany, cars)	63
Volkswagen (Germany, cars)	63
British Coal	31
ICI (UK, chemicals)	21
Fiat (Italy, cars)	20
Michelin (France, tires/rubber)	20

mark auto (or airline) firms come under foreign control. This factor and others have resulted in a slow movement of European auto firms toward globalization of production, a strategy that U.S. and Japanese firms have followed for many years. Ultimately, economic pressure will probably lead to greater integration of European auto producers and an expanded presence of overseas firms—or bankruptcy for relatively small European firms based in small domestic markets. German firms have taken the most aggressive steps by European firms to produce off the continent by opening assembly plants in the Americas—for example, Volkswagen in Mexico and Brazil, and Mercedes and BMW in the United States. Volkswagen made an earlier attempt in the United States, but failed.

European auto firms have also pursued cost-cutting measures by forming alliances with other firms, by streamlining the number of firms from which they draw parts, and by shifting production to lower labor cost areas. While still independent, Rover joined in alliances; Renault has also been involved in several. Renault illustrates the efforts by many auto firms to reduce production costs by concentrating their sources of supply. Its suppliers shrank from nearly 1000 in the late 1980s to 630 in 1992. Many firms have cut labor costs by seeking lower cost production sites in Southern and Eastern Europe and in the United States; Spain and Portugal are particularly favored. And West European firms have sought to tap larger markets through their East European and American production sites.

Strategies such as these in the auto sector should help Europe maintain production in other traditional manufacturing sectors. In addition, as in the United States, there must also be (and indeed is) planning and support for development of dynamic new employment sectors, some of which must rely on smaller firms in high-technology manufacturing. These jobs would help generate increased employment in related manufacturing and service sectors. European governments support the development of these new, future-oriented sectors by way of funding for advanced education and public-private technology park projects, as well as by way of research programs co-funded by the EU in emerging technologies. Despite serious concerns about national competitiveness within the global economy, especially in Germany, surveys indicate that business leaders from other countries continue to view West European states, especially Germany and the UK, as attractive, competitive locations for economic activities.

SERVICES

Despite a relatively high level of industrialization and unusually high employment levels in manufacturing in, for example, Germany, Europe's major employment sector is comprised of a wide range of service activities. In general, service-sector employment is highest in the more developed European countries and lowest in poorer, agriculturally dominated ones. Similarly, service employment tends to be lower in agricultural regions and higher in urban and tourist areas. Employment levels in services are 70 percent or higher in many urban regions, but as low as 30 to 40 percent in agricultural areas.

Europe's thousands of villages and small towns provide relatively common service functions such as primary education, basic health care, local government administration, retailing, and entertainment. In recent years, however, owing to the population's improved ability to move through space in private vehicles and owing to the generally lower costs of providing services at larger service centers, these places at the lower end of the urban settlement hierarchy have lost jobs to larger urban places. In addition, higher incomes and a more complex international economy have led to the development of large numbers of jobs in specialized service functions in transportation/communication, finance, marketing, media, entertainment, and consulting activities, which have generally concentrated in large cities. Though sometimes located in the central city, some jobs also often end up in the suburbs. Retail services have been especially pulled to the edges of Europe's cities by growing populations, in contrast to stagnating or declining central city populations. Service-sector jobs have also concentrated in newly developed office centers outside of cramped city centers, such as in Le Defense in Paris and Canary Warf in London. Other than Leipzig, an interesting but special case, European cities have yet to experience the level of suburbanization of population and jobs common in the United States.

Services are especially important within the economies of towns and cities, which themselves evolved and grew largely proportionate to their role as market-oriented service centers for surrounding territories. As interregional commerce and communication have improved, some large cities have also increasingly become exporters of services to more distant regions. For example, London serves Europe and the world as a major center for specialized financial services; Geneva, Zürich, Paris, and Frankfurt are somewhat less important, but nonetheless also serve large market regions. London has by far Europe's largest stock market; stock sales in Frankfurt, the second most important center, were about one-half the level of London in 1994. Large sales volumes in absolute terms also take place in Paris, Milan, and Amsterdam, although they are relatively small in comparison to London. London is also the leading European city for production of advertising, for hosting conferences, and probably also for provision of consultants' services and book publishing. (The UK and Germany are the top European providers of consultants' services and the world's second and third largest producers, respectively, of new book titles.)

Important concentrations of firms in the finance sector have grown up in places with particularly favorable tax regulations, such as Luxembourg, the Isle of Man, and the British Channel Islands. Other small, politically autonomous territories have also specialized in attracting customers from larger neighbors by offering low costs—for example, retailing in Andorra and headquarters' locations in Liechtenstein (often simply post boxes). Paris has traditionally been an important fashion center for Europe and the world, Milan somewhat less so, and Düsseldorf primarily for Germany's domestic fashion market. A recent survey of international investors indicates that Frankfurt is a preferred site for corporation headquarters, though an expensive one. Somewhat less preferred but viewed as a better economic value for headquarters sites are the regions in and near Paris, London, Brussels, and Randstad Holland (including Rotterdam, The Hague, Amsterdam, and Utrecht). The importance of market location, and Northwestern Europe's advantage in this regard, are rather evident from

this list. However, new telecommunications technology also allows poorly located regions with other locational advantages to offer specialized services to the international market. Thus, owing to a high-quality telecommunications network, educated and yet relatively low-paid workers, Ireland is attracting large numbers of pan-European telephone call centers from which firms can service existing customers and reach out to new ones.

Besides a concern for loss of competitiveness in manufacturing, the EU and many individual European countries are also concerned about the weak development of certain European service sectors. For example, Hollywood producers provide Europe with about 80 percent of its feature-length films, up from about 60 percent in the early 1980s; the United States also produces most of the movies shown on European television. Furthermore, U.S. firms hold about 60 percent of the European market for computer software sales. Of the top 30 software firms selling in Europe, about two-thirds are American; most of the rest are French and German. These trends reflect in part the scale advantages of producers within the huge U.S. domestic market, whose lower marginal costs make it easier to compete in foreign markets. Most countries offer much smaller bases for domestic producers. For example, the United States has more than five times as many PCs as Germany, Europe's largest PC market. American service firms are also aggressive franchisers and marketers in Europe. Obviously, McDonald's is a classic example of an aggressive franchiser. The U.S. film industry is a good example of an industry emphasizing marketing, spending as much as one-half of production costs on it, well above European levels. Finally, it is also likely that public ownership of many service providers in Europe (typical in the transportation, telecommunication, health, and education sectors) has stifled innovativeness and limited international marketing efforts by providing too much protection for domestic firms. European service-sector firms often are now struggling to become competitive internationally (e.g., national airlines). They are preparing belatedly for international competition, sometimes assisted by denationalization and deregulation, such as in the telecommunication industry. Thus, many firms are only now emerging as private commercial enterprises without state ownership and domination, as in broadcasting and higher education, or they are only surviving financially by way of subsidies, as in the cases of air and passenger rail services.

The telecommunication sector, in particular, faces radical change as a result of technological advances, privatization, and related increased competition. The EU expects that its telecommunication sector will finally be open to worldwide competitors by 1998. The more than one-half million workers in the world's third through sixth largest telephone companies (Deutsche Telekom, British Telecom, France Telecom, and SIP [Italy]) will be impacted by privatization and layoffs. However, consumers should see better service and, in many cases, lower prices. In response to privatization, as well as anticipated enlarged markets and greater international competition in telecommunications, Deutsche Telekom, France Telecom, and Sprint (USA) are planning joint operations as are the USA's MCI and British Telecom. Changes are also coming to the long-protected, relatively high-cost European airline services. American airline firms and the U.S. government are pressing the EU to open its market, which is limited by treaty to 262 transatlantic flights per week by U.S. airlines through 1997. To the chagrin of the EU, the United States has been successfully establishing bilateral "open sky" agreements with individual countries, including EU members. Despite the pressure, the EU wants to restrict U.S. firms' access to its market, fearing the ability of these large carriers to outcompete Europe's smaller, still nationally based carriers. It seems likely, however, that before too long both economic and political pressure will require the EU and its members to open its air passenger market and for European airlines to restructure, creating larger, probably multinational firms out of today's single-country-based companies. This process is already underway, with initial joint business operations among several American and European airlines—Swissair with TWA (USA) and Sabena (Belgium) Airlines; and Lufthansa Airlines (Germany) with Lauda Air (Austria), Luxair (Luxembourg), and Scandinavian Airline Systems (SAS—Denmark, Norway, and Sweden).

Of course, there are exceptions to the generalizations about the problems of European service-sector companies. Bertelsmann (Germany), one of the world's two largest media companies behind Time-Warner of the United States, as well as Holiday Inn (UK, hotels), Benneton (Italy, retailing), British Airways, and Greek and Cypriot shippers, provide examples of quite successful, internationally competitive service providers.

Tourism, a sector particularly impacted by geographic conditions, also has great international importance. In 1993 tourists spent nearly $150 billion in Europe, and nearly 300 million tourists crossed international frontiers. Tourism receipts nearly doubled within EU countries between 1986 and 1993, and international arrivals more than doubled. In short, tourism is a big business that is growing more rapidly than most other sectors within the European economy.

Tourism is officially defined as traveling for pleasure; it consists of at least two types of travel—brief leisure trips and longer vacation travel. With the increased mobility of Europeans (and non-European visitors), the pervasive urbanization of the world's population, and a corresponding deterioration of its environment, more and more people are traveling for recreational purposes. In Europe as a whole, over half of the population annually goes on holiday away from home, made possible by the virtually universal availability of paid holidays of up to six weeks each year and salary arrangements that provide extra income during peak travel periods (Christmas time and in the summer).

The French and Germans are particularly avid travelers. Nearly 90 percent of the French take their vacations in July and August, a peculiarity of French life that creates problems for the French economy as the result of temporal peaks in demand for transportation and hotels. Germans disperse to the far ends of the planet, especially during vacation periods, and in financial terms they are the world's champion globetrotters. No country has a wider gap between tourist receipts at home and expenditures abroad than Germany—a gap of $33 billion in 1994. No European country's citizens even approach the Germans' expenditures abroad; citizens of the UK, Italy, and France are distant competitors.

Domestically generated tourism receipts are quite a different matter. In 1993 France, Italy, and Spain were clear leaders; all accumulated about

$20 billion in income, as they had done throughout the early 1990s. Austria, UK, and Germany were the only serious rivals ($10–15 billion generated each throughout the 1990s). Tourist receipts are particularly important within the economies of smaller (e.g., Austria) and poorer (e.g., Portugal, Greece, and Spain) countries, but there are also especially large net positive receipts in France and Italy (and at one time in the former Yugoslavia).

In 1995 seven of the ten world's most popular tourist destinations were European. There were over 60 million international arrivals in France, over 45 million in Spain, and 18 to 29 million in Italy, the UK, Hungary, Poland, and Austria.

The large majority of tourists from Northern Europe, Germany, the Netherlands, and Austria travel south to the Mediterranean coasts for sun (Fig. 5-14). Greece and its islands, the Italian cities and the north Italian-Swiss lakes, the Italian-French Riviera, the Mediterranean resorts of Spain, the Alps, and German spas are among the most popular vacation areas. Many tourists also enjoy beaches on the south coast of England (Torquay, Brighton), and those on the continent near Ostende and Sylt in Germany. The Norwegian fjords are popular during a short vacation period.

There are special tourist resorts with modern condominiums and elaborately planned recreation—for example, the Costa Brava, Costa del Sol, Costa Bianca, and the Balearic and Canary Islands of Spain. More modest resorts can be found on the Bulgarian Black Sea coast, which are oriented toward package tours and mass tourism. Large numbers of Europeans visit theme parks, from permanent carnival-like operations scattered across the continent to larger parks like Legoland (Denmark), EuroDisney in Paris (9 million visitors in 1994), and the newly opened Port Aventura (Spain), a park built on a site rejected by Disney and one that hopes to avoid EuroDisney's financial problems by learning from its apparent errors.

For vacationers seeking the quiet enjoyment of rustic scenes, there are beautiful, historic villages throughout Europe, especially in the German hill country and in the Alps. Some regions are particularly renowned for specific tourist features, such as the Loire Valley and Rhine Gorge for wines and castles and the Salzkammergut region (Austria) and Lake Balaton (Hungary) for lake watersports. Europeans and non-Europeans (notably Americans and Japanese) are drawn to historic buildings, museums, and other cultural attractions of scores of cities, including large places like Paris, Vienna, Rome, London, and Prague, as well as many smaller ones such as Florence, Venice, York, Edinburgh, Brugge, and Salzburg.

Prague, undamaged by World War II and relatively unchanged within its historic core during the socialist era, has been rapidly redecorating its facades and expanding tourist services. It has

FIGURE 5-14 Monaco is one of the focal points of tourism along the French Riviera. (A. Diem)

FIGURE 5-15 Following dramatic political and economic change in Eastern Europe since 1989, tourism to East Central Europe in particular has boomed. Prague, especially its Charles Bridge and majestic castle on Hradcany hill in the background, is a mecca for tourists, *especially Americans*. (Paul S. Conklin/Monkmeyer Press Photo)

become a favored tourist destination in East Central Europe, apparently now earning close to two billion dollars annually in tourist receipts (Fig. 5-15). Elsewhere in Eastern Europe important tourist industries developed during the socialist era in Bulgaria and Romania near the coastal cities of Varna and Mamaia, respectively; in Hungary on Lake Balaton; and in Poland and Slovakia in the mountainous areas of the High Tatra Range of the Carpathians.

The former Yugoslavia once had the largest number of foreign tourists (2.8 million in 1990) and derived considerable foreign currency income ($8 billion in 1990) from tourists on its scenic Adriatic coast, in its historic towns, and in northern Alpine regions of Slovenia. After the war erupted there, tourism virtually collapsed in many parts of the country. Foreign visitorship on the Croatian coast, the core region of the former Yugoslavia's tourist industry, plunged by more than 90 percent between 1988 and 1991, and by 1993 had rebounded to only somewhat less than 20 percent of the foreign visitor levels of the late 1980s. It appears that only Slovenia and possibly the northern areas of the Croatian coast are in a position to revive their once vibrant business in the short run. A viable peace accord in Bosnia would probably greatly assist Croatia in rebuilding the infrastructure and visitorship of much of its Dalmatian coast tourism business.

Bulgaria has also lost a great deal of business

(suffering 90% revenue decline from 1989 to 1991 alone) owing both to diversion of many former East European customers to West European destinations and to economic disruptions within the Bulgarian economy. On the other hand, tourism receipts grew twentyfold (to $4 billion) in Poland between 1989 and 1992; receipts in Hungary and the Czech Republic have also grown quickly in the post-Soviet era.

Higher incomes, more leisure time, and increased personal mobility across space by Europeans have begun to result in some convergence of European and American tastes for free-time activities. Thus, for example, many vacation carnival and theme parks have developed in Europe, including the multibillion dollar EuroDisney park near Paris, patterned after Florida's DisneyWorld. Over a dozen new golf courses, many with associated homes and entertainment services, have sprung up around Berlin since the fall of the wall now that it is possible for relatively prosperous West Berliners to spend some of their considerable free time in the surrounding state of Brandenburg.

Not too surprisingly, given what has been noted earlier about German travel patterns, they are the most ubiquitous international tourists in many European countries, and are among at least the top three origins of visitors in all 18 EU and EFTA member states. The French (leading tourists in Spain and among the top three origins of visitors in three other countries), the UK (leaders to Ireland

and Greece, and among the top three in four others), and the Dutch (leaders to Belgium and among the top three in three others) are distant competitors. Visitors from the United States are relatively most important in Northwestern Europe, notably in Germany and the UK, where they outnumber arrivals from other countries. Large numbers of Americans also visit Ireland and Switzerland, where they are the second most important national tourist group, as well as the Netherlands (third most numerous).

Tourism has economic, environmental, and sociological effects on resort areas. The economic impact is well known and documented. Tourist expenditures, with effects on local tax bases, employment opportunities, and agriculture, bring needed income to regions that are often depressed areas. Tourism is of special importance in regions if there are two or more peak travel seasons and benefits can be distributed over the whole or most of the year, as in the case of winter and summer seasons in the Alps. National governments derive valuable benefits from tourist receipts, which often are an important factor in balancing trade. However, with rapid growth it has become clear that some forethought and improved recreational planning are necessary if the European countryside is to be protected from haphazard exploitation (see the discussion of the Alpine region in Chapter 8).

INTERNATIONAL TRADE

The development of economic interrelationships among European countries and between Europe and other parts of the world has led to rapidly increasing levels of international trade for a variety of reasons.

- European countries are small in area but have large populations and economies.
- The economies of many European countries require imports of raw materials.
- In turn, most countries specialize in the production of goods and services that require large-scale production (based on economies of scale), and exports are essential, both for firms to operate successfully and for national economies to balance payments.

- Europe, especially Northwestern Europe, has a well-developed, geographically integrated, multimodal transport network.
- Europeans have high incomes and are fully aware of consumer options available in other parts of the world, creating demand for imported products and a highly attractive market for exporters.
- And the economies of European states are bound within an enlarging and intertwining set of international organizations and regulations that encourage trade.

These conditions lead to high levels of international trade within Europe and between Europe and the rest of the world. In 1993 European countries engaged in total trade of about $3.5 trillion, more than half of which was among the countries now in the EU. Germany, by far Europe's largest economy, usually holds second or third place among the world's leading exporters each year, in close competition with the United States and Japan.

Several broad generalizations can be made about the geography of European trade (see Table 5-6). First, trade in Europe is dominated by flows within the EU and between the EU and other European countries. EU countries have from 60 to 80 percent of their trade with EU partners. EFTA countries have also historically had only slightly less trade with EU partners. In the early 1990s, EFTA countries had only about 10 to 20 percent of total trade with EFTA partners. By the early 1990s, several former CMEA countries also had about 50 percent of their trade with EU countries, only about 20 percent among themselves, and 10 to 15 percent with the FSU.

The dramatic reduction of trade between Eastern Europe and the FSU underscores a second major generalization that can be made about European trade–Germany's great, and increasing, importance as a trade partner. Germany's location, size, and outward-looking economic and political policies have made it Europe's single most important center for international trade (Figure 5-16). This status is reflected by a variety of indicators, such as value of trade flows, movement of goods through ports serving it (notably Rotterdam and Hamburg), and choice of Frankfurt as center for the EU's emerging central bank. Germany is also

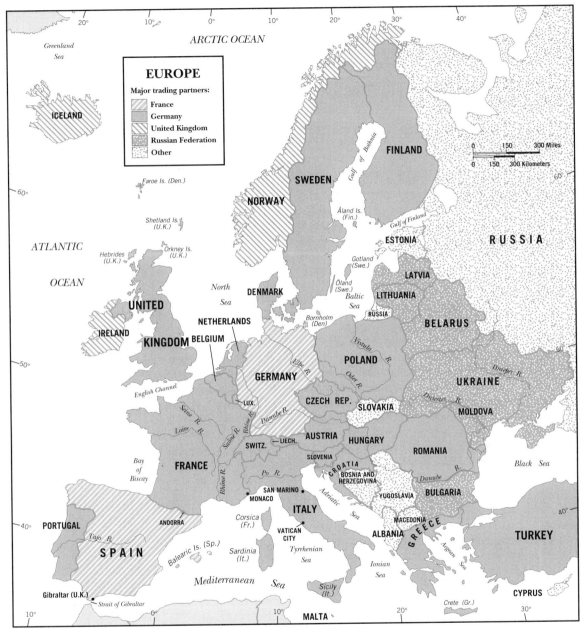

FIGURE 5-16 European countries' major trade partner. Since 1989, Germany has become increasingly important as a dominant partner for more countries in Europe. (Data from International Monetary Fund, 1995, and U.N., 1995)

important for East European trade. Between 1989 and 1992, its proportion of total trade with several countries rose dramatically, most notably Poland (from 20 to 28%), the Czech/Slovak Republics (15 to 27%), Hungary (20 to 26%), the former Yugoslavia (17 to 23%), and Bulgaria (8 to 17%). Bulgaria's trade patterns are changing the most rapidly; it experienced a huge relative decline in total trade with the FSU—going from 56% in 1989 to 23% in 1993.

A third important generalization that can be made about European trade is the importance of bilateral trade links among neighboring countries (Table 5-7). This rather unsurprising pattern is closely related to the ease of communications and lower transport costs associated with common borders. For example, trade ties among the Nordic countries have always flourished despite the fact that the countries have for decades been split among EC/EU and EFTA membership. More recently, Estonia has also been drawn into the Nordic trade circle, with especially close ties to Finland and Sweden. The much reduced political importance of the East-West Europe divide has led, as noted earlier, to Germany's dramatically increased role as a trade partner in East Central Europe. The historic importance of Eastern European trade for Austria and Greece has also been enhanced.

Fourth, historically evolved political and economic ties, rather than geographic propinquity, are also frequently important. For example, Cyprus and Malta have closer ties with the UK than might be expected, based on British influence on those islands when commercial and military fleets dominated the world's oceans and seas. Based on other colonial ties, the UK has nearly 15 percent of its trade with Asian countries, and France and Portugal about 5 percent of their trade with Africa—at levels far higher than typically low African-European interaction. Although most EU countries have about 5 percent of their trade with the USA, closer ties between the USA and the UK, Ireland, Iceland, and Sweden have nearly doubled that level. Switzerland also has about 10 percent of its total trade with the United States. European trade with Japan has grown to be comparable with, though generally still lower than, U.S.-European trade.

Finally, some broad generalizations can be made about the sectoral composition of European trade. As indicated earlier in this chapter, European countries generally import more raw materials than they export, though many countries have important raw material and primary product exports. The UK and Norway are especially important fossil fuel exporters, while several other

countries export a variety of raw materials, such as the Netherlands, natural gas; Poland, coal; and Sweden, iron ore. Other important bulk and primary commodity exporters include Sweden and Finland (wood), and Iceland and Norway (fish). The proportionate value of agricultural product exports varies greatly in Europe, from less than 2 percent in Sweden to nearly 25 percent in Denmark. More than 20 percent of exports also come from agriculture in Ireland, Greece, and Hungary, and 10 to 18 percent in the Netherlands, Cyprus, Bulgaria, Spain, France, Poland, and Belgium. West European countries are world leaders in marketing relatively high-value-added food and agricultural products, such as Denmark (furs, meat, butter, and cheese), France (wine and cheese), the Netherlands (flowers, cheese, and meat products), and Belgium and Switzerland (confectionery products).

Still, by far the most important products traded by European countries are manufactured products, which are especially important exports. Germany is, for example, a particularly important exporter of machinery (50% of exports). Most EU countries have about 25 to 40 percent of their exports in this category, with the notable exception of Greece (only 5%).

Domestic, EU, and international political issues play an important role in European trade. For example, the United States and other non-EU agricultural exporters such as Argentina, Australia, and Canada frequently object to EU policies that protect its agricultural markets and promote subsidized agricultural exports to the non-EU countries' customers. The USA and EU have also differed sharply on guidelines for procurement of goods and services by governments, and on how to compute the levels and sizes of subsidies given to aircraft producers. Though increasingly achieving access to the EU market, East European countries argue that their economic restructuring is impeded by the EU's protective measures in, for example, steel and agricultural production.

The United States has had, and continues to have, a number of serious disagreements with the EU over the access of U.S. companies to the EU telecommunication and media markets. The EU has placed restrictions on the proportion of non-EU-produced television programs that can be

TABLE 5-7

Country	Leading Total Trade[a] Partner	Year	Pct. of total Accounted for	Source
Albania	(probably Italy)			
Austria	Germany	1993	40.4	ITSY
Belarus	Russian Fed.	1994	69.1	DOTSY
Belgium-Luxembourg	Germany	1992	23.4	ITSY
Bosnia-Herzegovina	Croatia	1994	29.4	DOTSY
Bulgaria	Russian Fed.	1993	23.0	ITSY
Croatia	Germany	1993	22.0	ITSY
Czech Republic	Germany	1994	34.9	DOTSY
Denmark	Germany	1992	22.6	ITSY
Estonia	Finland	1994	25.4	DOTSY
Finland	Germany	1993	14.3	ITSY
France	Germany	1993	17.5	ITSY
Germany	France	1993	11.5	ITSY
Greece	Germany	1992	21.4	ITSY
Hungary	Germany	1993	23.7	ITSY
Iceland	United Kingdom	1993	15.4	ITSY
Ireland	United Kingdom	1993	31.8	ITSY
Italy	Germany	1993	19.6	ITSY
Latvia	Russian Fed.	1994	25.5	DOTSY
Lithuania	Russian Fed.	1992	43.0	ITSY
Macedonia	Italy	1994	20.9	DOTSY
Moldova	Russian Fed.	1994	64.9	DOTSY
Netherlands	Germany	1993	24.2	ITSY
Norway	United Kingdom	1993	18.0	ITSY
Poland	Germany	1992	27.3	ITSY
Portugal	Germany	1992	16.4	ITSY
Romania	Germany	1993	15.2	ITSY
Russia	Ukraine	1994	11.0	DOTSY
Slovakia	Czech Republic	1994	41.1	DOTSY
Slovenia	Germany	1993	27.2	ITSY
Spain	France	1993	18.0	ITSY
Sweden	Germany	1993	15.9	ITSY
Switzerland-Liechten.	Germany	1993	27.7	ITSY
Turkey	Germany	1993	18.3	ITSY
Ukraine	Russian Fed.	1994	54.2	DOTSY
United Kingdom	Germany	1993	13.3	ITSY

[a]Total trade is defined as the sum of all imports and exports.

Sources: ITSY-International Trade Statistics Yearbook; DOTSY-Direction of Trade Statistics Yearbook (International Monetary Fund, 1995 and U.N., 1995).

broadcast within the Community. Italy has taken measures beyond those of the EU to protect its film industry. France has stiffer restrictions on media content than the EU in several areas, mandating minimum levels of EU- and French-produced television programs and radio music transmissions. The French restrictions reflect more than simply protection of business interests; the French have also made many efforts to prevent incursions of non-French language terms into local usage. Many French people view these "language laws" as quite reasonable measures to "protect" the country's venerated language and culture, but its critics argue that such laws are ultimately ineffective and perhaps harmful for France's economic competitiveness and international relations.

Despite these kinds of restrictions, other economic indicators suggest the European economy's high level of integration into the world economy. Several countries experience huge capital movements into and out of their economies by way of foreign direct investment (FDI) and stock, security, and currency sales. The UK, the Netherlands, Belgium, Sweden, and Switzerland have especially high levels of bidirectional FDI in proportion to GNP. Ten of the world's top 20 nonfinancial multinational corporations ranked by foreign assets are European based, including the world leader—Royal Dutch Shell (UK and Netherlands based; $69 billion in foreign assets in 1990). Companies in several countries (especially in the UK, but also in the Netherlands and Germany) have very large holdings in the United States. More than half of all manufacturing assets in Ireland are controlled from abroad, including much non-European ownership.

ECONOMIC DEVELOPMENT AND THE ENVIRONMENT

Human impact has perhaps been greater in Europe than in any other part of the world. Europe has been inhabited by humans for at least tens of thousands of years and in recent centuries has had a relatively high level of inhabitants per square mile or kilometer. In addition, it has experienced the world's longest period of industrialization,

and its relatively high levels of economic development have meant particularly great human impacts on the environment by way of energy use and creation of waste materials. Thus, there are virtually no regions and biospheres in Europe that have not been greatly impacted by humans, and many of its originally indigenous plants and animals no longer live in the wild.

Although the impact of humans on the environment has undoubtedly been greatest in recent centuries and decades, the effects of early human habitation on the continent were sometimes dramatic. For example, the barren and dry Dalmatian coast of the former Yugoslavia (now largely in Croatia) once boasted forests stretching from the slopes of the Dinaric Alps to the Adriatic Sea. Systematic logging over centuries and introduction of sheep and goats dramatically reduced the forest, hindered revegetation, resulted in soil erosion, and heightened periods of drought throughout the region (Fig. 5-17). The starkly unvegetated, dry landscape now common on the Adriatic coast is almost certainly a human-created landscape. Similarly, centuries of forest clearing to secure wood and open up farmlands radically transformed many other parts of Europe, notably the now unforested highlands of the British Isles and Balkans, as well as large areas of the North European Plain. Even the unique landscapes of the Lune–burger Heath (Germany) and Norfolk Broads lake country (UK) appear to have been created in centuries past by human activities.

Today, virtually all of Europe's landscapes and natural environments show clear marks of human impact, and usually these are negative. The most disturbing scenes include the smog-filled skies and dead forests in the "dirty triangle" between Germany, Poland, and the Czech Republic; dead seals and fish washing up on Baltic shores; and the now empty villages and escalating cancer rates in the wake of the Chernobyl disaster in Ukraine and Belarus. An avalanche of mud from a coal slag heap in Wales once engulfed a school, killing scores of people, primarily children; other "coal tips" mar the landscape across the continent. Spectacular chemical spills and even fires have ravaged European rivers, many of which have at least stretches that are considered virtually biologically dead.

FIGURE 5-17 Vegetation disruption associated with grazing animals on the Dalmatian coast, Yugoslavia (1975). Centuries of unwise forestry and agricultural practices have harmed many areas in the seasonally dry Mediterranean region, where plants are reestablished slowly after disturbances and bare soils can be easily eroded by winter rains that follow the summer dry period. Here regrowth of forest is promoted by fencing out foraging goats. (W. H. Berentsen)

Air pollution, particularly in industrial regions and metropolitan areas, provides one striking example of negative human impacts on the European environment. Although it is increasingly feasible to reduce emissions by way of "scrubbers" on smokestacks, catalytic converters in motorized vehicles, and cleaner mixtures of liquid fuels, progress toward adopting such ameliorative measures has been slow in some places, virtually nonexistent in others. In Germany, where people treasure forests and leadership has been taken in reducing solid wastes and increasing recycling, a national love affair with automobiles (rivaling that of the United States) has stalled progress toward adopting speed limits that would reduce emissions (and accidents). Unleaded gasoline, which reduces the harm from emissions, has also been only slowly accepted in Europe.

Air pollution has taken a great toll on life and property in Europe. Periodic, severe smog caused by inversions has sometimes resulted in an increased death toll; it once killed hundreds over a period of several days in London. Long-term exposure to the hazards of air pollution has undoubtedly shortened the lives of untold numbers of Europeans. Though less dramatic than the human costs, high property costs are another concomitant of air pollution which damages buildings, monuments, forests, and crops (Fig. 11-16). For example, most European trees suffer high levels of defoliation owing to airborne pollution. More than 40 percent of trees in Poland, the Czech Republic, and the UK are at least partially defoliated as the result of pollution (World Resources Institute, 1994). Large contiguous areas of forest on the Czech-German border are dead as the result of emissions from lignite-burning power plants and factories. Receding glaciers and landslides triggered by the thawing of underlying permafrost in the Alps may also be a response to rising global temperatures, partly caused by large gaseous emissions from Europe itself.

Europe's most populous countries and largest economies are responsible for the majority of carbon dioxide, carbon monoxide, and nitrogen oxide emissions. The biggest offenders are Germany, the UK, Italy, France, and Spain, more or less in descending order of total emissions. However, countries dependent on coal, especially lignite, for energy produce relatively more sulfur oxide emissions. Thus, eastern Germany, the UK, Poland, and the Czech Republic put the greatest amounts of sulfur dioxides into the air. None of these emissions respects international boundaries, and large movements of air pollutants take place back and forth across boundaries, particularly in Central Europe's "dirty triangle." There are generally net imports by countries from western neighbors owing to common westerly winds. Thus, Scandinavia is the recipient of many airborne pollutants from the UK, with quite negative impacts on forests and freshwater bodies.

Water pollution is an equally sad story in Europe. Great concern has been expressed about the increasing levels of all sorts of pollutants in the Baltic, North, Black, and Mediterranean seas, coupled with indications of disappearing or sickening sea life. Overfishing and destruction of wetland breeding habitats compound the problems. Europe has few pristine water courses and has many rivers and lakes that are badly polluted. For example, the Rhine and Elbe rivers are polluted from sewage, industrial chemical pollutants, and wastes from mining of industrial salts. Despite notable improvements, in the case of the Rhine in particular, many rivers remain relatively unclean.

Water pollution derives largely from the heavy use of river water in Europe for industrial cleaning and cooling and as transport routes. Waterways are also heavily used to produce hydroelectric power. All of these uses greatly impact the rivers' ecology. Many, if not most, parts of rivers used as major transport routes, like the Rhine and Danube, have largely human-engineered beds, following construction of dams, locks, and dredged and channelized beds. Massive undertakings at the "Iron Gates" on the Danube and on the Main-Danube Canal are only two recent examples of a long tradition of human engineering of European watercourses. Although no huge interbasin water-transfer schemes such as those actually initiated and originally planned in Russia have been contemplated in Europe, a number of more modest transfers have been considered or implemented.

Perhaps the most dramatic and controversial of these transfers is the recently completed Gabcikovo-Nagymaros project in Slovakia. During the 1970s Austria, Hungary, and Czechoslovakia agreed to dam and divert a portion of the Danube along the countries' common borders. The project was designed to provide energy that would otherwise have had to come from expensive oil imports or from environmentally damaging and threatening nuclear and coal-fired thermal power plants. However, after construction began, growth in energy consumption rates slowed, oil prices moderated, and the project's environmental impacts—most notably habitat destruction and changes in water table levels along the Danube—became better understood by larger numbers of Central Europeans. Protests led by "environmentalists" in Austria and Hungary, as well as the huge capital costs required by the project, led these countries to back out of it, despite their already huge investments. Newly independent Slovakia, arguably faced with more severe energy constraints than the other original participants, decided to complete a modified project on its own. A portion of the Danube along the Hungarian-Slovak border now flows through a newly dug channel and has resulted in the previously feared, drastic fall in water tables along the old riverbed (now carrying about 15% of its former flow) and dramatic changes in riverside wetland habitats. Power from the project will provide 20 percent of Slovak electric needs and greatly reduce its dependence on electricity from coal-fired thermal plants (now) in the Czech Republic.

Concerns for groundwater disruption along the central Danube are but one instance of negative human impacts on that important, invisible resource. Besides local depression of groundwater levels from pumping (usually for irrigation purposes), groundwater resources in Europe are also threatened by pollution from agriculture. Heavy use of fertilizers and pesticides has damaged groundwater, particularly in Eastern Europe. Areas where intensive animal rearing is common, notably in the Netherlands and northwestern Germany, also suffer nitrate contamination of groundwater as the result of heavy dumping of liquid manure on to fields. Initiating the growing of corn to capture the nitrogen for economically useful purposes is only a partial measure to address the problem.

Wetlands and tidal areas in Europe have also been greatly impacted by human action. Centuries of effort to drain wetlands and impound tidal areas within or behind dikes, in order to expand agricultural areas, prevent flooding, and control disease have dramatically altered large areas. The most dramatic actions have been taken in Holland during the past 850 years to secure land from flooding caused by both North Sea storms and the Rhine, Maas, and Scheldt. Other large areas have also been drained and diked—for example, the fens of southeastern England, the lower courses of rivers in France such as along the Garonne River near Bordeaux, areas in the Po Valley and in coastal wetlands of Italy, former wetlands along the coast of Albania, and areas along the Rhine and in the estuaries of German rivers. Sharp declines in wetlands are believed to have worsened downstream flooding of rivers and sharply reduced the marine and bird life of European seas by destroying critical breeding and feeding areas.

Pollution in the open sea is becoming an increasingly important and contentious issue in Europe. Many North Sea production facilities are nearing the end of their useful life, and it remains unclear what will become of them and their stored wastes. In order to prevent a precedent-setting deep-sea disposal of the wreckage and wastes of a large oil platform, the international environmental organization, Greenpeace, organized a consumer boycott and undertook dramatic actions at sea against Shell Oil during June 1995, preventing the firm from completing the disposal. Now, oil firms, governments, and environmental organizations are reconsidering the comparative economic and ecological costs of land- versus sea-based disposal of such waste.

In recent years, the solid waste disposal generated by hundreds of millions of consumers with ever-rising levels of material consumption has become a controversial issue. Numerous scandals have erupted with knowledge that hazardous materials have been shipped from Western Europe to the developing world or Eastern Europe in exchange for cash payment. Within Eastern Europe dumping of all sorts of wastes, including hazardous chemicals and radioactive materials, went unchecked under the former socialist regimes, which pushed rapid industrialization without comprehensive waste disposal plans. In Estonia a virtual lake of radioactive waste threatens to spill into the Baltic Sea, with potentially horrific consequences. In eastern Germany, where such problems are being systematically addressed, hundreds of dangerous disposal sites have been found and are being treated, at the cost of many billions of dollars.

Somewhat ironically, owing to both need for raw materials and avowed environmentally friendly policies, the former GDR developed one of Europe's first and most comprehensive recycling programs for domestic waste. The concentration of large populations within huge housing estates helped make it practicable to set out bins collecting paper, glass, metal, and organic matter (the organic matter sometimes being used for animal feed). A similar tradition has evolved within united Germany, which requires retailers to recycle packing material. Over the objections of companies like McDonald's, it has been proposed that disposable eating plates and utensils be taxed. Solid waste disposal is much less well organized in poorer parts of Europe and in Mediterranean areas, where litter on landscapes and streets is more common than in Northwestern Europe. The Dutch, the Germans, and in particular the Swiss, have a reputation for tidiness that is visible on the landscape. It is not unknown there for pedestrians to return litter to people who have "inadvertently" dropped something.

The European landscape clearly displays the problems of centuries of more or less unregulated waste disposal. The clearest signs of this neglect are evident in the huge, generally unvegetated slag heaps in Europe's mining areas, which take on the proportions of hills in many places. Often the heaps emit dangerous runoff into streams, toxic dust during dry periods, and even radioactive emissions, as in the case of uranium mine wastes in Saxony. Similarly, wastelands have been created by huge open-pit coalfields, especially in northern Bohemia, Saxony, and southern Brandenburg (eastern Germany). In eastern Germany whole forests were killed or damaged by falling groundwater levels due to pumping within the nearby pits, entire rivers were diverted (and towns and villages razed) to allow exploitation of underlying coal, and large areas remain unreclaimed. Similar problems have plagued lignite-mining areas in western Germany. In this case, however, earlier requirements to recultivate land and stricter enforcement of environmental regulations have led to less wide spread ecological damage.

The European landscape has been changed by a variety of other economic activities. As noted earlier, deforestation plagues many areas. Visual disruption of the landscape has resulted from the construction of tourist facilities on Mediterranean coastlines and in the Alps where second homes are scattered along the sides of valleys. Other problems include construction of controlled-access highways, and along the German coast and in British highlands erection of "wind farms." Propeller-like machines turn wind into about 4 percent of Germany's electricity demands. This example, however, illustrates the often ironic conflict between competing uses of European resources. The use of windpower, or waterpower in tidal estuaries or from rivers, reduces the need for burning fossil fuels or using nuclear materials in power plants, but they have their own environmental consequences. Governments and individuals are faced with difficult choices and tradeoffs in making decisions about the exploitation and consumption of European (or imported) resources.

Despite this litany of environmental problems, Western Europe has also been in the forefront of efforts to ameliorate environmental problems and adopt policies and lifestyles more amenable to environmental protection. The EU and individual countries have strengthened environmental legislation, reflecting both greater cognizance of the need for it as well as the growth of "green" political movements. "Green" coalitions, for example, work to reduce dependence on nuclear power and private, motorized transportation. Frequent protests have been made against cutbacks in support for railways and against further construction of highways (often, also airports), and pressure has been mounted to adopt use of lead-free gasoline, speed limits, and limits on trucking.

In Germany, the Netherlands, Austria, and Switzerland, "green" movements have helped create Europe's highest levels of recycling. The UK has particularly lagged in this area; for example, its level of recycling of paper and glass was far below that of the European leaders in the early 1990s (Euromonitor, 1994). An environmentally friendly, or "green," lifestyle is advocated by individuals and organizations. Specifically, fellow citizens are urged to consume fewer packaged goods, eat "organically" grown produce (which forsakes chemical fertilizers, herbicides, and pesticides), and travel by way of public transport. These positions overlap the long-held beliefs and practices of the population in Northern and Northwestern Europe, which have traditionally supported strict land-use planning and protection of forests and wildlife. These traditions appear to have emanated in part from the practices of large landholders (e.g., to support hunting for sport) and in part from the bitter historic experience of negative human impacts that have left Europe virtually devoid of a once immense primeval forest and stock of wild mammals.

In an attempt to protect the natural heritage that remains, most European states are establishing large numbers of protected areas, including "national parks" modeled on the U.S. pattern. Similarly, enhanced efforts are being made to protect culturally valuable urban landscapes by, for example, rehabilitating historic buildings or in some cases entire settlements. UNESCO has designated Quedlinburg, Germany; Csesky Krumlov, Czech Republic; and several other European towns as "world heritage sites"—places worthy of international recognition and protection. In an experiment to protect the architectural heritage and decrease auto exhaust in the EU's most polluted city, the Greek government has experimented with closing central Athens to most motor vehicle traffic.

Protection of Europe's environment in the future will become a more difficult task. Although populations are not growing very rapidly, standards of living are, and so increasingly difficult decisions have to be reached regarding the relative value of economic growth, job security in polluting economic activities, personal freedoms such as private auto travel, and environmental protection. European leadership in the global environmental protection movement is also problematic, because some people in the "Third World" view European environmental attitudes as hypocritical, given the harmful worldwide activities of European-based corporations, Europe's own environmental degradation, and Europeans' relatively high standards of living, in part derived from environmentally damaging behavior.

BIBLIOGRAPHY

Cameron, Rondo. (1993). *A Concise Economic History of the World*. 2nd ed. New York: Oxford University Press.

Clout, Hugh, ed. (1994). *Europe's Cities in the Late Twentieth Century*. Utrecht/Amsterdam: Royal Dutch Geographical Society and Department of Human Geography, University of Amsterdam.

Clout, Hugh, et al. (1994). *Western Europe: Geographical Perspectives*. 3rd ed. Essex, UK: Longman Scientific & Technical.

Cole, John, and Francis Cole. (1993). *The Geography of the European Community*. London and New York: Routledge.

Commodity Research Bureau, (1993). *1993 CRB Commodity Year Book*. New York: Knight-Ridder.

Euromonitor. (1996). *European Marketing Data and Statistics 1996*. London: Euromonitor. Issues in 1994 and 1995 also used.

European Commission. (1994). *Competitiveness and Cohesion: Trends in the Regions*. Brussels: European Commission.

European Commission. *Eurobarometer: Public Opinion in the European Community*. Brussels: EU Commission, various dates.

European Union. *Europe Magazine*. Brussels: EU, various dates.

Fortune. (1995). "The Global 500," August 7.

German Information Center. *The Week in Germany*. (New York), various dates.

Harenberg, Bodo, ed. (1994). *Harenberg Lexicon der Gegenwart, 1995*. Dortmund: Harenberg Lexicon-Verlag.

Ilbery, Brian W. 1986. *Western Europe: A Systematic Human Geography*. 2nd ed. Oxford, UK: Oxford University Press.

International Herald Tribune. 1995. Various dates.

International Monetary Fund. (1995). *Direction of Trade Statistics Yearbook*. Washington, D.C.: IMF.

Jordan, Peter. (1995). The Impact of the Wars in Croatia and Bosnia-Herzegovina on the Tourism of the Croatian Coast. Unpublished paper, Austrian East and Southeast Europe Institute, Vienna.

Keeble, David. (1989). "Core-Periphery Disparities, Recession and New Regional Dynamisms in the European Community." *Geography* 72: 322, Part I: 1–11.

Klohn, Werner. (1995). "Landwirtschaft in Europa." *Praxis Geographie* 25 (5): 4–10.

Knight-Ridder Financial/Commodity Research Bureau. (1995). *1995 CRB Commodity Yearbook*. New York: John Wiley & Sons.

Miosga, Manfred. (1995). "Räumliche Dispäritäten in Europa und Perspektiven zukünftiger Entwicklung." *Geographische Rundschau* 47: 144–149.

Newsweek. (1994). "Road Kill on the Infobahn—Computers: Why American and Japanese Firms Are Leaving the Europeans in the Dust." October 10, pp. 42–43.

Oelke, Eckhard. (1995). "Rotterdam—grösster Seehafen der Erde." *Erdkundeunterricht* 1: 17–25.

Office of the U.S. Trade Representative. (1994). *Foreign Trade Barriers*. Washington, D.C.: Office of the U.S. Trade Representative.

Pinder, David, ed. (1990). *Western Europe: Challenge and Change*. London: Belhaven.

Pinder, David. (1983). *Regional Economic Development and Policy: Theory and Practice in the European Community*. London: Allen & Unwin.

Population Reference Bureau. (1995). *1995 World Population Data Sheet*. Washington, D.C.

Pounds, Norman J. G. (1969). *Eastern Europe*. London: Longman.

_____. (1985). *An Historical Geography of Europe: 1800–1914*. Cambridge, UK: Cambridge University Press.

_____. (1990). *An Historical Geography of Europe*. Cambridge, UK: Cambridge University Press.

Robert, Jean. (1994). "Paris and the Ile-de-France: National Capital, World City." In Clout, Hugh, ed. *Europe's Cities in the Late Twentieth Century*. Utrecht/Amsterdam: Royal Dutch Geographical Society and Department of Human Geography, University of Amsterdam, pp. 13–28.

Roche, David. (1994). "You Ain't Seen Nothing Yet." *Euromoney*, June: 109–114.

Rostow, Walt W. (1960). *The Stages of Economic Growth.* Cambridge: Cambridge University Press.

Rotterdam Municipal Port. (1994). *Rotterdam Port Statistics 1994.* Rotterdam: Rotterdam Municipal Port.

Savary, Julien. (1995). "The Rise of International Cooperation in the European Automobile Industry: The Renault Case." *European Urban and Regional Studies* 2: 3–20.

Schätzl, Ludwig, ed. (1993). *Wirtschaftsgeographie der Europäischen Gemeinschaft.* Paderborn: Schöningh.

Senat für Wirtschaft und Technologie des Landes Berlin. (1994). *Die Wirtschaft der Neuen Bundesländer.* Wiesbaden: Gabler.

U.N. (1994). *1992 Industrial Commodity Statistics Yearbook.* New York: U.N.

U.N. (1995). *1993 International Trade Statistics Yearbook.* New York: U.N.

U.S. Department of Agriculture. (1993). *Agricultural Statistics 1993.* Washington, D.C.: U.S. Government Printing Office.

Williams, Colin C., and Jan Windebank. (1995). "Black Market Work in the European Community: Peripheral Work for Peripheral Localities?" *International Journal of Urban and Regional Research*, 19: 23–39.

Windhorst, Hans-Wilhelm, ed. (1993). *Räumliche Verbundsysteme in der Agrarwirtschaft.* Band 11, Vechtaer Studien zur Angewandten Geographie und Regionalwissenschaft. Institut für Strukturforschung und Planning in agrarischen Intensivgebieten (ISPA). Vechta, FRG.

World Bank. (1994). "Development Institutions' Assistance in Numbers." *Transition* 5: 6, 7–8.

World Resources Institute. (1994). *World Resources 1994–95.* New York: Oxford University Press.

Zahn, Ulf, ed. (1988). *Diercke Weltatlas.* 3rd ed. Braunschweig: Westermann Schulbuchverlag.

6

URBAN GEOGRAPHY

The importance of cities to Europe, both today and in the past, is immense. Indeed, although there is much more to Europe than its urban places, the great cities—London, Paris, Rome, Berlin—are often what first come to mind when we conjure images of the region. Cities historically have been the sites of innovation, political and military control, and centers of business, finance, commerce, religion, and the arts. If there is such a thing as a European culture, it is largely an urban one: our word "civilization" comes from the Latin *civitas*, which is also the root for "city." Conversely, the word "pagan" has its origins in "peasant," or rural dweller. Besides their importance to European life and the interest they generate, cities closely mirror the prevailing economic, political, and social conditions in their respective countries. They are, therefore, important items of study for a fuller understanding of the geography of Europe.

Although for statistical purposes governments have set out official definitions of what is considered "urban," usually based on population size and density, identifying what is truly urban and what is truly a city is ultimately based on more qualitative than quantitative criteria. When the qualitative criteria are fulfilled, a settlement will generally have a population size and density great enough to fulfill quantitatively defined norms, usually at least 2000 people, and will have a concentration of economic, political, social, and economic institutions. Mumford (1961) argues that a city is a nucleated settlement that "is not so much a mass of structures as a complex of inter-related and constantly interacting functions…[a] polarization of culture" (p. 85). The city is a focal point of a culture's major activities—government, commerce, the arts, and social interaction. Rousseau argues: "Houses make a town, but citizens make a city" (Mumford, 1961, p. 93). The variety of cultures in Europe, its relatively high level of economic development over many centuries, and more than 2000 years of urban heritage have combined to create a large number and fascinating diversity of great cities.

This chapter reviews the history of European urbanization, in particular with regard to the close connection between cities and economic conditions, and outlines aspects of the European urban system—the collection of cities, their relative sizes, and patterns of interaction. Also discussed is urban structure—the spatial arrangement of land uses within individual cities. Particular emphasis is placed on the difference between structures that developed under market economies and those that have been influenced by socialist planning. The final portion of the chapter highlights urban problems in contemporary European cities and policies to address them.

FIGURE 6-1 The Acropolis of Athens, Greece. Inhabited for at least 5000 years, a fortress site for 3400 years, and a religious shrine since the time of ancient Greece, the Acropolis dominates modern Athens as a surviving symbol of the roots of Western civilization. (D. Danta)

HISTORY OF URBAN DEVELOPMENT IN EUROPE

This historical review of urbanization in Europe is necessarily brief, somewhat selective in approach, and broken into rather arbitrary periods for presentation. Much fuller treatment of the subject is provided in the references cited in the bibliography at the end of the chapter.

The Classical Period (800 B.C. to A.D. 450)

Although permanent settlement in Europe extends back to the Iron Age, true cities, places that satisfy the "urban" conditions discussed earlier, did not appear until around 800 B.C. in the lands in and around the Aegean Sea. The first European cities were built by the Minoans on what is now Crete; however, city-building technology soon spread among the Aegean islands and to the Greek mainland.

Given the continual threat from pirates, the typical city was built on high, easily defended ground, and so was called the *acropolis*, or high town (Fig. 6-1). Each city contained temples, government buildings, and an *agora*, or marketplace, where important issues of the day were discussed. This tradition of grass–roots democracy continues to the present in Greece—the many squares of Athens frequently become jammed with people engaged in heated political debates well into the night. In addition, early Greek cities were open in the sense that they included the agricultural population living in the surrounding territory, or hinterland; facilities were available to all citizens equally; and city patrons (originally called "tyrants") helped enhance the urban environment by funding works of public art and other beneficial projects.

As cities grew, groups of people emigrated to found new towns elsewhere. In this way, Greek cities spread beyond the Aegean to the Black Sea (e.g., Constanta), the Italian peninsula (Bari and Naples), southern France (Marseille), and into Iberia (Gerona). These cities were laid out in strict grid patterns aligned on a north-south axis, generally without regard for local terrain. Cities remained quite small by today's standards. Although ancient Athens in its prime probably reached a population of around 150,000, most large places were in the range of 10,000 to 15,000, whereas the vast majority of cities at this time held no more than a few thousand inhabitants.

Greek influence in Southern Europe gradually gave way during the second and first centuries B.C. to the expanding Roman Empire. Cities founded under Rome's direction were similar in some respects to their Greek predecessors: they were based on the grid system; they contained central squares or marketplaces; and they were consciously spread to new territories. However, whereas Greek cities functioned as independent city-states and were designed along egalitarian lines, Roman cities functioned within a well-organized empire and were designed along hierarchical lines, reflecting the rigid class structure of the Roman society. For example, Rome, which remained the Empire's capital until 330, contained distinct areas for use by senators and generals, whereas lower classes were clustered in the world's first tenements.

By the second century A.D., the Romans had expanded control over an area extending across the southern half of Europe below Hadrian's wall in Britain and the Rhine-Danube rivers in West Central Europe (Fig. 6-2). Virtually every contemporary city in this part of Europe can trace its origin to the Roman period; traces of the original inhabitants are still plainly visible in many of them (Fig. 6-3). Conversely, the area of Europe lying outside of Roman influence—Northern and most of Central Europe—did not participate in Roman urbanization. This part of Europe benefited neither from the direct siting of cities, nor from the accompanying infrastructure (such as roads, aqueducts, and sewerage

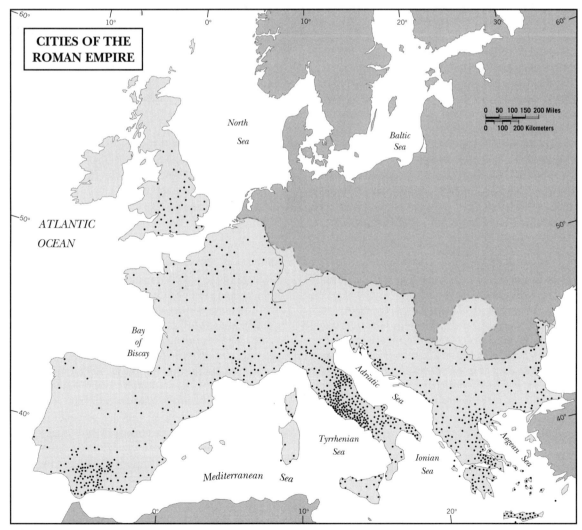

FIGURE 6-2 Distribution of Roman cities. (From Pounds 1990, p. 56)

FIGURE 6-3 A Roman theater in Lyon, France. Lyon, renowned in modern times for its vibrant economy and distinctive cuisine, also has many architectural treasures, including still-functioning twin Roman theaters on a spectacular site above the city. (W. H. Berentsen)

systems) that played such a large part in the subsequent development of Southern Europe. City building was thus delayed by several hundred years.

The majority of Roman cities, however, were small. Still, Rome reached a population of over 1 million by A.D. 100—a feat not repeated until London reached this mark in 1800. The next most populous places were between 15,000 and 30,000 people, whereas most urban places held no more than 2,000 to 5,000 citizens.

The Dark Ages and Medieval Periods (450–1300)

The period of European history lasting from the collapse of the Roman Empire to the Renaissance, especially during the so-called Dark Ages from 476 to 1000, did not augur well for the process of ur-

banization. The withdrawal of Roman legions and the breakdown of civil order left most cities without good administration or protection. In addition, the hostile activities of various Germanic tribes greatly disrupted urban patterns. Although in some cases invading tribes used existing cities as the capitals of their new empires (e.g., Valencia under the Visigoths from A.D. 413), many cities became depopulated and fell to ruin. For example, Aquinicum (Budapest), Serdica (Sofia), and even Rome itself experienced varying periods of abandonment following destruction by "barbarian" tribes. During these periods structures generally collapsed, often providing materials for the construction of other buildings at later times. Furthermore, waves of attacks by various Asiatic tribes, such as the Scythians and Huns (4th-5th centuries), and Mongols (13th century), as well as the Vikings (9th–11th centuries), caused considerable damage to European cities, particularly in the east (e.g., Kiev) and in northern coastal regions.

Economic developments were more important in the evolution of European cities during the medieval period. Feudalism, arising from the ashes of the hierarchical social structure of the Roman Empire and the chiefdoms of medieval tribes, was a highly structured, rural/agrarian-based, introverted economic system that was not at all conducive to city maintenance or formation. The self-contained country manor became the basic building block of settlement. Frequent warfare associated with this period further inhibited urban growth and led to the building of massive fortifications and castles in cities. Existing Roman structures, such as the arenas in Nimes and Arles, were fortified and became tiny, densely packed urban sanctuaries. The ever more crowded and densely built cities became more susceptible to terrible plagues that at times decimated urban populations.

Cities, of course, survived during this period and several interrelated forces—including the influence of the Roman Catholic Church, the settlement of Germans in East Central Europe, and increased interregional trade—provided important bases for the evolution of European urban development. The Church was particularly important in maintaining cities during medieval times. It was a largely urban-based institution, so the location of a cathedral, which marked the seat of a bishop, defined a city and vice versa. In many cities, bishops more or less assumed the role of mayor, exercising power in both the secular and spiritual realms. Furthermore, the Catholic Church was the largest landholder in Europe and in many cities was a major employer and significant determinant of land use. For example, the siting of cathedrals, cloisters, monasteries, and cemeteries took first precedent within cities; a long-standing rule was that a cathedral tower had to be the tallest structure in each town, reflecting the preeminent position of the Church vis-a-vis secular institutions (Fig. 6-4). In addition, some towns, especially Santiago de Compostela (Spain) and Lourdes (France), became important pilgrimage sites and thus prospered from Europe's first form of tourism.

The Church, as well as local rulers' interest in promoting economic development, also played an important role in the expansion of Germanic settlement and "German law" cities throughout much of the western parts of Central Europe—areas in today's central and eastern Germany; in Austria, Hungary, the Czech Republic; and in western and southern Poland. Germans were attracted as settlers to these areas, where "German law" (or rule) meant tacit political agreements and

FIGURE 6-4 Cathedral at Bern, Switzerland. The pointed spires of high Gothic architecture emphasize movement to Heaven. (W. H. Berentsen)

enticements that included offers of special privileges, most notably considerable economic freedom and municipal political autonomy. Based on models that evolved early in, for example, Lübeck and Magdeburg, "German law" was ultimately adopted in scores of cities across the region. From about the year 1143 (Lübeck) into the sixteenth century (Vitebsk, 1547) and from Frankfurt am Main in the west to Kiev in the east, a vast area was influenced by the development of German law cities. These cities became focal points for the development of early handicraft-based manufacturing and specialized urban services. Thus they also became centers of innovation, skilled labor, and development of civil liberties for individual citizens. They set early precedents in urban planning and popularized particular urban features (e.g., the planned central marketplace). It can be argued that the pattern of settlement and political-economic change in Central Europe associated with German law cities represent some of the earliest foundations of modern forms of urban morphology, democratic rule, and market-based economic development in the region. German law cities also spread further eastward during the fourteenth to sixteenth centuries.

In addition to and associated with the roles of the Church and the spread of "German law," medieval towns grew as a consequence of increasing trade with a local market area (hinterland) and as a result of being located along the important trade routes that criss-crossed Europe. Chief among these were the main north-south routes that linked Dordrecht (in the Netherlands) to Mainz (Germany), Pavia (Italy), and Venice; and the east-west route from Mainz to Prague, Cracow, and Kiev. Other towns prospered as sites of annual or more frequent fairs. These fairs often specialized in particular goods, and so the town became synonymous with the product (e.g., Toledo for weapons, Bordeaux for wine, Leipzig for metals, and Skane, in southern Sweden, for fish). Still others, the medieval *bastides* (walled towns), were new towns built in previously underserved regions to act as collection points for agricultural products (Fig. 6-5).

In contrast to Greek cities, a major characteristic of medieval European towns was their closed nature. The cities were physically enclosed by one

FIGURE 6-5 The walls of Carcassone in southern France show the need for defense of medieval *bastide* cities. (D. Danta)

high wall or even multiple sets of them with limited numbers of gates that were kept closed at night. In like manner, they did not automatically welcome people living in the area surrounding the town. To become a city resident, a person needed to gain permission, typically by becoming an apprentice in one of the many craft guilds that practiced in the cities. The custom of closed towns, as well as the generally stagnant nature of feudalism, greatly impaired both social and geographic mobility during the medieval period. It particularly inhibited a thorough blossoming of the potential for trade between cities and their rural hinterlands, which during medieval times remained locked within the stifling confines of feudalism.

Not surprisingly, urbanization in Europe during

the medieval period did not occur evenly. Much of the discussion thus far applies only to that portion of Western and Southern Europe that was under the control of the Roman Empire. Urban development did not occur even to these limited levels in the areas of Southeastern Europe under the control of the Byzantine Empire, and much of East Central and especially Northern Europe remained largely in a pre-urban state throughout the Middle Ages. On the other hand, the Moors, who began pushing into the Iberian Peninsula in the early 700s, founded and restored many cities and generally elevated urban culture in Iberia.

Cities remained small during the medieval period. At the end of the period, there were just over 3000 recognized cities in Europe containing approximately 4.2 million people, or 15 to 20 percent of the total population. Of these, over 90 percent had fewer than 2000 inhabitants, while only a handful of cities—Milan, Venice, Genoa, Florence, Paris, Cordoba, and Constantinople—were in excess of 50,000 people. Other large cities at the time were concentrated in northern Italy and West Central Europe (again reflecting the importance of trade), and in Moorish Spain (Fig. 6-6). Apart from Prague, East Central, Southeastern and Northern

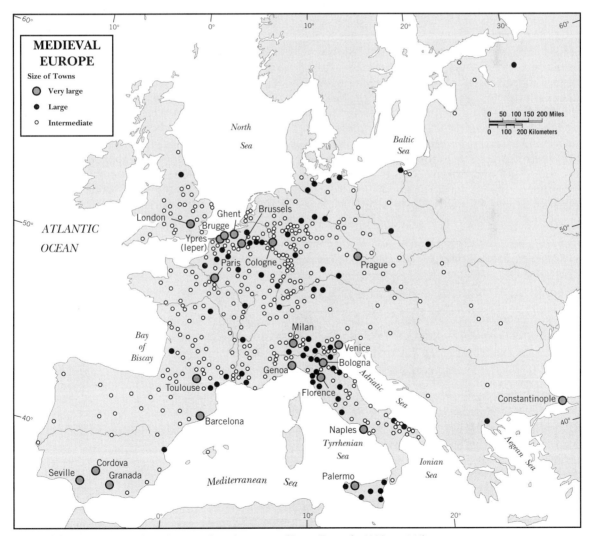

FIGURE 6-6 Distribution of cities in medieval Europe. (From Pounds 1990, p. 164)

Europe were almost wholly lacking in significant urban places at the close of the Middle Ages.

The Renaissance and Early Modern Periods (1300–1760)

The process of urbanization during the Renaissance period was driven by mercantilism and associated long-distance trade. This form of economic organization, which gradually replaced feudalism in Western Europe, had its greatest impact on the many port cities ringing the European landmass (Fig. 6-7). Beginning in the thirteenth century, the merchants of Venice and Genoa became fabulously wealthy, supplying goods, such as spices, silks, and other luxuries, to the aristocracy of Europe, whose appetite for such products had been whetted by contact with the east during the Crusades (1095–1291). Somewhat later, cities on the North Sea (Brugge [Bruges] and Antwerp) became involved in the cloth trade and were in turn quickly joined by other cities forming the Hanseatic League—the trade association that by the fourteenth and fifteenth centuries stretched from London to Riga and included such coastal cities as Bremen, Hamburg, Rostock, and Bergen, as well as many inland towns that also participated in trade.

Besides the growth and alignment of towns in Europe, important changes also occurred in the "look" of cities during this period. The Renaissance is known for new forms of art and architecture. In particular, greater emphasis was placed on the control of visual perspective and on the rediscovery of Classical models. As such, many cities, in particular capitals, were redesigned by straightening some of the tortuous medieval street patterns into wide boulevards that provided vistas of important buildings in the cities. For example, in Paris the Avenue des Champs-Élysées was built to provide a fitting promenade for the kings and queens of France as they traveled between their palaces at the Louvre and Versailles. This new concept of urban design was extended to formal gardens, and the grandeur of Versailles' buildings and grounds was subsequently imitated during the Renaissance era across Western and Central Europe. The status and power of imperial authority exemplified at Versailles echo across Europe and beyond in the form of imposing architectural ensembles in national and provincial capitals, including dazzling examples in Vienna (Schönbrunn Palace), Berlin-Potsdam (Sanssouci and Charlot-

FIGURE 6-7 The wealth of empires is reflected in these buildings along a Venetian canal. Merchants grew rich during the long era that Venice dominated trade in the eastern Mediterranean. (W. H. Berentsen)

FIGURE 6-8 Schönbrunn Palace, a lavish imperial residence in Vienna, Austria. (W. H. Berentsen)

tenburg Palaces), and St. Petersburg (Winter Palace) (Fig. 6-8).

Another form of art and architecture to make its appearance at this time (especially during 1550–1750) was Baroque. Gaudily ornate and emphasizing curves and color rather than straight lines and subdued hues, this style had its greatest impact on buildings and churches in Central Europe.

The growth of European cities that occurred during the Renaissance period, however, generally was confined to the western half of Europe. First, as mentioned earlier, the impact of Classical urbanization, which in many ways provided a template to subsequent development, had little impact on much of East Central, Southeastern and Northern Europe. Second, the Church, which, again, was so important in city maintenance in Western Europe, did not have an impact in the east and far north until around the period 1000–1300. Third, feudalism, which had been all but eliminated in the west by the end of the medieval period, survived in the east and was even strengthened in

the fifteenth and sixteenth centuries through the so-called second serfdom. Fourth, the long-distance trade experienced by Western European cities during the Age of Mercantilism, particularly after 1492 and the rise of trade with overseas colonies, bypassed Eastern Europe, and the re-alignment of trade routes further isolated this region. Finally, the invasions by Mongols and other Asiatic tribes in the 1200s, and the domination by the Ottoman Turks from the early 1300s, greatly retarded urban development in East Central and Southeastern Europe.

Still, urban development in East Central Europe was positively influenced by the establishment and modest growth of urban places that were allowed to become German law cities. In this way, an incipient process of modern urbanization began during the fourteenth and fifteenth centuries in much of what is today central and eastern Poland, the Baltic states, Slovakia, Transylvania, Belarus, and western Ukraine. However, the impediments noted here restricted the potential benefits of this early development, and more rapid urban growth in the region did not occur until much later during the Industrial Revolution.

In terms of population totals, the Renaissance period represented only a quantitative change in the size of urban places, since during that era essentially the same distribution of towns prevailed that had existed at the end of the medieval period. Cities simply got bigger. By the sixteenth century, 16 cities in northern Italy, West Central Europe, and Iberia had grown to over 50,000 people, while several others had reached the 25,000 to 50,000 range. Cities in Northern, East Central, and Southeastern Europe, such as Cracow, Prague, and Thessaloniki, had grown to over 25,000, while others reached the 5000 or 10,000 mark.

The Industrial Period (1760–1945)

Several innovations–chief among them being the invention of the steam engine, the development of blast furnaces, and the construction of mechanical looms—heralded the Industrial Revolution in Europe. Large-scale manufacturing, which began in the English Midlands in the middle 1700s and then spread to Belgium, France, Germany, and reached eastward to Hungary by the 1870s, was part of a massive urban, economic, political, and social restructuring of society. The many new mines and textile and iron mills acted like magnets pulling former agricultural workers from rural to urban locations. Similarly, developing rail lines, which used iron from 1830 and then steel after 1870, created an enormous demand for these products while providing a cheap and an efficient means of transporting both raw materials and finished products to and from points of production. Thus, before too long large concentrations of population were possible both in resource-based industrial regions (e.g., the English Midlands, the Ruhr region, and Silesia) and in cities that also served as major ports or capitals (e.g., London, Paris, and Berlin).

Most of the great industrial cities of Europe developed during this period. Chief among them are Manchester, Leeds, and Newcastle in England; Brugge and Ghent in Belgium; the German, Swiss, and French cities along the Rhine and Ruhr rivers, such as Dortmund, Essen, Strasbourg, and Basel; Plzen and Brno in the Czech Republic; and, later, Milan and Turin in Italy, and Poznan, Łodz, and Wrocław in Poland. Furthermore, not all parts of Europe participated in industrialization during this period. Expansion of the industrial sectors in the countries of Southeastern Europe did not occur until the early or middle part of this century.

Of course, the early industrial cities, especially in England, were incredibly polluted, cramped, and generally unhappy places in which to live, as was well documented by authors such as Dickens, Balzac, and Zola (Inset 6-1). These cities provided ample backdrop for the *Communist Manifesto*, Marx and Engles' 1848 call to arms that influenced a wave of revolutions that spread across Europe.

A map of the urban geography of Europe in 1815 (Fig. 6-9) demonstrates the impact of early industrialization on city growth on the island of Great Britain. Rapid growth had pushed the population of London past the million mark, while several of the industrial towns in the English Midlands and Scotland reached over 100,000 and the portion of the population living in cities greater than 10,000 had grown to 30 percent. Table 6-1, which shows population figures for selected European cities for the period 1750–1990, indicates the impact of industrial technologies as they diffused across the face of Europe.

Finally, we must note the impact of the two world wars on European cities. Although nearly all parts of Europe suffered either directly or indirectly during the wars, East Central Europe bore the lion's share of damage. Besides the many boundary changes, destroyed economies and governments, crumbled lines of transportation and communication, and the death or debilitating injury of several millions of people, most cities received substantial physical damage. Indeed, 85 percent of Warsaw was destroyed during World War II; Sofia received almost as much damage; and central Budapest and Berlin were left in rubble. Dresden was callously firebombed at the war's conclusion, killing nearly all the inhabitants of the former "Paris on the Elbe." Of the 6 million Jews killed during World War II, most came from East Central Europe; a rich, urban-focused cultural her-

ENGLISH INDUSTRIAL CITIES

The following passage captures some of the flavor of industrial cities in Victorian England (1837–1901):

It was on a cold, damp, foggy morning in December that I took my leave of Manchester. I rose earlier than usual, it was just at the hour when, from all quarters of the busy town, the manufacturing labourers crowded the streets as they hurried to their work. I opened the window and looked out. The numberless lamps burning in the streets, sent a dull, sickly, melancholy light through the thick yellow mist. At a distance I saw huge factories, which, at first wrapt in total darkness, were brilliantly illuminated from top to bottom in a few minutes, when the hour of work began. As neither cart nor van yet traversed the streets, and there was little other noise abroad, the clapping of wooden shoes upon the crowded pavement, resounded strangely in the empty streets. In long rows on every side, and in every direction, hurried forward thousands of men, women and children. They spoke not a word, but huddling up their frozen hands in their cotton clothes, they hastened on, clap, clap, along the pavement, to their dreary and monotonous occupation. Gradually the crowd grew thinner and thinner, and clapping died away. When hundreds of clocks struck out the hour of six, the streets were again silent and deserted, and the giant factories had swallowed the busy population. All at once, almost in a moment, arose on every side a low, rushing, and surging sound, like the sighing of wind among trees. It was the chorus raised by hundreds of thousands of wheels and shuttles, large and small, and by the panting and rushing from hundreds of thousands of steam-engines.

Source: J. G. Kohl, *Ireland, Scotland and England*, Book III (London, 1844), p. 146; cited in Richard Dennis, *English Industrial Cities of the Nineteenth Century: A Social Geography* (Cambridge: Cambridge University Press, 1984), p. 78.

---

itage associated with them ended with their annihilation. On the other hand, a few cities, Prague being the most prominent, came through World War II virtually unscathed.

The Contemporary Period (1945–Present)

For most of the post–World War II period, Europe has existed in two essentially separate spheres: a western half characterized by market economies that have mirrored trends in other advanced countries; and an eastern half, characterized by command economies that have had very different approaches to industrial, urban, and social planning. Given these differences, some of the following discussion of urban patterns in the contemporary period will treat the two spheres separately.

Similarities in urban trends do exist between east and west. The obvious, first task in post–World War II Europe was to repair the physical damage to buildings, reestablish communication and transportation infrastructures, reconstruct industrial capacity, and stabilize political and economic systems. Of course, West European countries were aided in these tasks by financial support from the United States in the form of the Marshall Plan. Because East Europe did not benefit from such outside help, its recovery took much longer (Fig. 6-10).

During the 1950s and 1960s, large-scale industrialization resumed in Western Europe and either was renewed or commenced in Eastern Europe. This process again put in motion the pattern of rural-urban migration characteristic of industrialization and was concomitant with both a rapid growth of cities and an increase in the overall percentage of urban population living in places. Rapid industrialization was particularly pronounced in Eastern Europe, where expansion of heavy industry in existing and newly created cities took place at a greatly accelerated pace. In a process known as underurbanization, the number of urban industrial jobs in socialist countries expanded at a faster rate than available housing

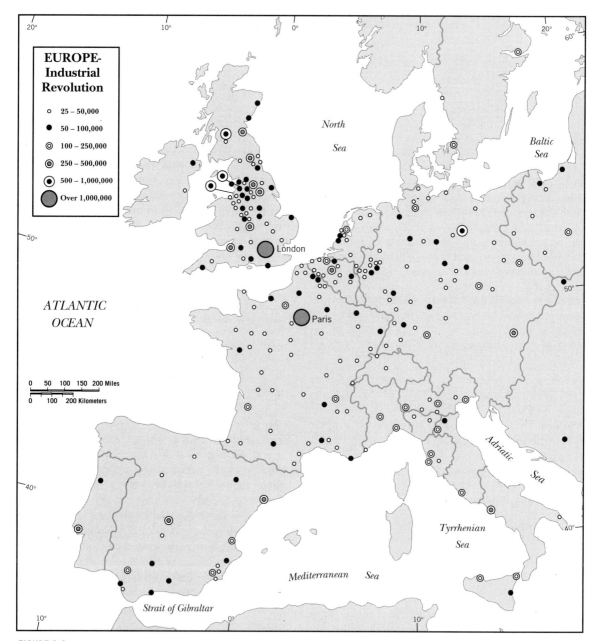

FIGURE 6-9 Distribution of European cities in 1815. (From Pounds 1990, p. 325)

units, and so workers had to commute, sometimes over long distances, for up to a week at a time.

Industrialization in Europe was also accompanied by an influx of foreign-born "guest workers."

These workers—who came mainly from Turkey, Yugoslavia, North Africa, Pakistan, and Jamaica to Western Europe and from Cuba, Vietnam, and Mongolia to Eastern Europe—formed distinct

TABLE 6-1

POPULATION TOTALS FOR SELECTED EUROPEAN CITIES, 1750 TO 1990 (IN THOUSANDS)

City	1750	1800	1850	1870	1900	1930	1960	1990
Amsterdam	210	201	224	264	511	752	865	1038
Athens	10	12	31	45	111	453	628	3027
Belgrade	—	25	15	26	69	267	585	1470
Berlin	90	172	419	826	1889	4243	3261	3301
Birmingham	24	74	233	344	523	1003	1107	1400
Brussels	60	66	251	314	599	840	1020	970
Bucharest	—	32	120	142	276	631	1226	2014
Copenhagen	93	101	129	181	401	771	1262	1339
Cracow	20	24	50	50	91	221	497	744
Essen	—	4	9	52	119	654	730	623
Lisbon	148	180	240	—	356	594	817	1612
London	675	1117	2685	3890	6586	8216	8172	6378
Madrid	109	160	281	332	540	834	2260	3101
Marseille	68	111	194	313	491	610	778	1080
Milan	124	135	242	262	493	992	1583	1464
Paris	576	547	1053	1852	2714	2891	2790	8510
Prague	59	75	118	157	202	849	1005	1209
Stockholm	60	76	93	136	301	502	809	1471
Vienna	175	247	444	834	1675	1874	1628	2044
Warsaw	23	100	160	252	638	1179	1136	1674

Sources: For the years 1750–1960: B. R. Mitchell (1992), *International Historical Statistics: Europe 1750–1980,* 3rd ed. (Stockton Press), Table A4, pp. 72–75; for 1990: Graham Bateman and Victoria Egan, eds. (1993), *The Encyclopedia of World Geography*. (New York: Barnes and Noble Books).

neighborhoods and communities in their destination cities (see section on "Foreign Workers" in Chapter 5).

Since the 1970s, the type of industrial expansion that characterized Europe after the Industrial Revolution has given way to more dispersed development, including smaller scale production in formerly peripheral locations. Variously referred to as deindustrialization, transition to a postindustrial economy, or development of flexible production, this change was accompanied by a general decline in the growth of large cities, a leveling of the urban hierarchy by diminished importance of leading cities, counter-urbanization (growth of nonurban places), and an increase in the process of suburbanization across Western Europe.

In Eastern Europe, the process of socialist-led intensive industrialization resulted in urban growth. Suburbanization has not been as typical in these countries as in the west. The events of 1989, however, have thrown the region into a state of flux. Many cities are currently losing population as workers emigrate to the west, whereas others (e.g., Bucharest) are growing rapidly as former restric-

FIGURE 6-10 The World War II destruction is only now disappearing in Dresden, Germany. On February 13/14, 1945, Dresden was razed, and tens of thousands of people died in a firestorm that erupted from a vengeful, controversial bombing raid on the city, whose population was swollen by hundreds of thousands of refugees fleeing the oncoming Red Army. (D. Danta)

tions on migration are lifted. In eastern Germany, in particular, suburbanization of commercial and residential urban functions has proceeded at a surprising pace.

THE EUROPEAN URBAN SYSTEM

An urban system represents a network of interconnected cities in a given territory. Discussions of urban systems typically include treatment of levels of urbanization in countries, relative city sizes and trends in city growth rates, urban hierarchies, interurban linkages, aspects of government policy, and city functions (Inset 6-2).

Urban Size and Growth

In 1990 Europe (excluding the territory of the former Soviet Union) contained approximately 363 million urban dwellers, or 73 percent of the total population. (The United States, by comparison, was 76% urban.) However, levels of urbanization

vary considerably among European countries. Belgium, Iceland, and the UK are 90 to 95 percent urban, whereas Albania and Bosnia are 34 percent urban (Table 6-2). These values illustrate the general relationship between level of urbanization and overall level of development: Northwest European countries are, with the exception of Ireland, economically advanced, whereas East Central and Southeastern Europe remain more poorly developed and have more rural-based economies. However, physical conditions, for example, Austria's Alps and Finland's vast tracks of sparsely populated land, also play a role in determining levels.

Although Europe is the most urbanized of all world regions, relatively few of the world's largest cities are found here. Indeed, according to *The World Almanac*, Europe contains only 17 of the world's largest 92 cities. London, the largest city in Europe, ranks only sixteenth on this list. Other cities in the top 92 include Paris (18th), the Ruhr conurbation (22nd, with Essen its largest individual city), Istanbul (27th), Milan (36th), Madrid (40th), Barcelona (44th), Manchester (45th), Athens (55th), and Berlin (63rd). The main reason for these relatively low world rankings is the current rela-

CITY DEFINITIONS

The analysis of urban systems is complicated by problems of definition. Everyone, of course, knows exactly what a city is—that is, until they are asked to define one. About the only thing that governments and academics can agree on is that cities are places containing a concentration of people. But just how many people constitute a city? In the United States, a city is any place with a population greater than 2500, which was a significant size in 1790 when this value was selected, but which is now hardly a metropolis. In Europe, minimum size requirements for classification as a city vary from a low of 200 in Norway and Sweden to a high of 20,000 in Greece and Spain. On the other hand, on the Great Hungarian Plain there are so-called giant villages: places containing 20,000 population, but functioning only as agricultural centers. Obviously, trying to make valid comparisons over such a great range is almost impossible.

The task is even more complicated because of problems connected with defining a city's boundaries—that is, exactly where the city ends. As cities grow and expand outward, they begin to incorporate villages and small towns that previously were independent entities. Governments usually lag behind such growth in their annexation process,

and so the city stays "underbounded," with the result that population counts remain low. Some cities, however, anticipate growth and extend their municipal boundaries well beyond the current built-up area; this practice results in "overbounding" and consequent high population counts.

In any given year, the problem of boundary definition greatly complicates attempts at analysis. However, definitional problems become acute whenever long time spans are under investigation. In these cases, boundaries are usually set at the most recent, largest definition, and totals for previous periods are calculated to these boundaries. This practice, of course, inflates early counts, but this is the only way to minimize data bias. Also, because of the difficulty of determining urban boundaries and great differences in the way city sizes are calculated (e.g., metropolitan population *versus* population of a political entity like the "City of London"), reported populations of cities can vary widely. This is especially true for London, for which metropolitan population figures alone range from about 7 to about 9 million people for 1990. Given problems such as these, statistical data in general, and city population totals in particular, should always be viewed critically and, perhaps, with a degree of skepticism.

tively slow pace of both population and urban growth in most countries of Europe. Over the period 1980–1990, the average annual growth rate for the urban population of Europe was 2.6 percent. This is the lowest rate for any large region and is far below the rate of 12.0 percent for East Asia and the Pacific, or 5.9 percent for Sub-Saharan Africa. Similarly, many of the individual countries of Europe experienced average annual growth rates over this period below 1.0 percent.

Urban Hierarchies, Interlinkages, and Functions

The European urban hierarchy is in at least one respect far different from the American urban hierarchy. The existence of dozens of sovereign states

in Europe, the development of national capitals as administrative centers, and their adoption of economic policies based on perceived national self-interest, mean that boundaries between European countries are much more significant than those between American states. As a result, no European city has achieved the relative significance of New York City within the United States, although Moscow, London, and Paris have somewhat comparable pan-European roles. Though smaller than New York, these cities are large and have approximately equivalent metropolitan population sizes—about 9 to 10 million people based on a uniform standard for delimiting metropolitan boundaries. A number of other European metropolitan areas are also clustered around the 4 to 5 million population level—Milan, St. Petersburg, Madrid, Barcelona, and Manchester.

TABLE 6-2

THE URBAN POPULATION IN EUROPE 1990 (PERCENTAGE)

Country	Urban Percentage
Monaco	100
Vatican City	100
Belgium	97
United Kingdom	92
Iceland	91
Netherlands	89
Luxembourg	86
Denmark	85
Germany	85
Malta	85
Sweden	83
Czech. Rep.	75
France	74
Norway	73
Russia	73
Estonia	71
Latvia	69
Belarus	68
Cyprus	68
Italy	68
Lithuania	68
Switzerland	68
Ukraine	68
Bulgaria	67
Turkey	67
Finland	64
Spain	64
Greece	63
Hungary	63
Poland	62
Macedonia	58
Ireland	57
Slovakia	57
Romania	55
Austria	54
Croatia	54
Slovenia	50
Moldova	47
Serbia/Montenegro	47
Albania	37
Bosnia-Herzegovina	34
Portugal	34

Source: H.J. de Blij and P.O. Muller, Geography: Realms, Regions, and Concepts, 8th ed. (New York: John Wiley & Sons, Inc., 1997).

Several European cities play important international roles. London is not only the largest city in Europe (excepting Moscow), but is also considered, along with New York and Tokyo, a "world city" owing to its preeminent position within the global economy, and particularly in money markets, stock exchanges, insurance, and advertising. Similarly, the Vatican City remains the center of the Roman Catholic Church. Paris and Milan have long been centers of culture, especially in the worlds of high fashion and opera. Furthermore, many cities are known internationally for particular products or services, such as Amsterdam for diamonds or Bologna for meat products. Brussels and Strasbourg (France) contain the headquarters of the European Union and the Council of Europe, whereas various cities run regional stock exchanges. In addition to these specialized roles, over the years Western European cities have become closely interconnected through trade and other types of economic, political, and cultural exchanges.

The bunching of Europe's largest cities at quite similar size levels is closely associated with the importance of these cities within their own countries: Of course, these and other large cities serve European-wide functions in addition to their strictly national roles. The relative importance of cities' nationally based service roles in Europe largely explains the roughly similar size of many large European cities—in contrast to the differing population sizes of American metropolitan centers.

Cities play an especially important role both within their own country and within the region they dominate economically. Capital cities are seats of government and almost always the centers of business, industry, and culture in their states. Bern, the capital of Switzerland, is one exception. Capitals are also usually the most connected places in their country in terms of transportation networks. For example, the rail network of Hungary focuses on Budapest; getting from one provincial town to another usually involves going to the capital, even though such a trip may add considerably to the distance and to the time of travel. The situation in much larger France is not too dissimilar. Even small urban places, however, also provide goods and services to their surrounding territories, or hinterlands, thereby acting as central places.

Cities, of course, are places where people live, work, shop, and enjoy recreational and cultural facilities. Cities provide these facilities not only for residents, but also for people living in smaller towns and villages in their hinterlands. Furthermore, larger cities provide specialized goods and services—such as advanced medical facilities, expensive or hard to find merchandise, and professional sports—to smaller places down the urban hierarchy. For example, a person living in Le Puy in central France no doubt would buy bread in a local bakery, but may patronize a hairdresser in St. Etienne, have a medical test performed in Lyon, shop for clothes in Paris, and may even travel to Milan, Vienna, or London for an opera or rock concert.

Although each European city serves a rather standard function as servant for its immediate hinterland, most places perform more specialized functions and some are particularly specialized. For example, Bonn, the capital of the Federal Re-public of Germany, from 1949 until German Unification, is a rather unremarkable place apart from its administrative functions. Other towns are much more narrowly defined as mining and industrial towns. Still others are known as religious, spa, or university cities (Inset 6-3; Fig. 6-11).

It will be fascinating to see how the ongoing economic integration of Europe and possible steps toward political integration might affect the relative economic importance and population size of European cities in the future. The potentially profound impact of political-economic integration on European cities was reflected in competition between, for example, London and Frankfurt am Main to serve as home for the future EU central bank. Frankfurt acquired this function, owing to the respect for and influence of Germany's central bank (Bundesbank), located in the city.

One commonly used technique for analyzing urban systems is to arrange a region's cities into a

---

INSET 6-3

TOWN AND GOWN

The earliest models for universities in North America, exemplified by Harvard, were originally located in the country, far from the distractions of the city. The original universities, however, were urban based. Of the three main medieval institutions—Church, empire, and university—only the last was a creation of the period itself. Universities are important not only in their own right, but also because a study of their diffusion across Europe and of the relations between universities and their towns paints a picture of the intellectual history of the region from the first stirrings of the Renaissance and the rise of humanism.

The modern university differs from its precursors—*lyceums* of ancient Greece and the monastic schools—in that they were chartered, the curriculum and the right to teach was controlled by a group of masters, and successful scholars were awarded credentials. The first universities in Europe were located in Bologna (founded 1088), Salerno (the first medical school founded in the eleventh century), and Paris (chartered in 1200 but dating from much earlier). Universities soon spread to other parts of Europe: Oxford (dating from 1167) and Cambridge (founded 1284) in England; Florence (1321) and several others in northern Italy; and Charles University in Prague, the first in East Central Europe (founded in 1348).

Universities were important institutions in their cities, providing prestige, employment, and revenue. However, they were not without problems. Then as now, students often caused conflict with local youths and shopkeepers; reports of fights and general rowdiness were frequent. By and large, however, universities have added greatly to the texture of their urban environments. The left bank of the Seine in Paris—long dominated by the Sorbonne and still called the Latin Quarter because of the former use of this language in instruction—is a landscape of bookshops, cafes, and other *avant-garde* "hangouts" just like most campus communities in the United States. That universities have made substantial impacts on their towns is illustrated by a saying concerning the "other" great English university: "Cambridge the town is the university is the town."

FIGURE 6-11 The classic neo-Gothic architecture of Cambridge University, UK. (D. Danta)

rank order according to population size and then assess the urban hierarchy. A rule of thumb is that the population size of a city should be approximately that city's rank divided into the population of the largest city. For example, the second largest city in a country should be about half the size of the largest, the third ranking city should be one-third the size of the largest, and so forth. When this condition holds, the urban system is said to exhibit a rank-size distribution. On the other hand, many urban distributions exhibit what is called a primate distribution—a situation in which the largest city is much larger than the next sized city (usually taken to be five to ten times greater). In primate urban systems the largest city, typically the capital, dominates the rest of the urban system and the country's economy, culture, and politics.

Owing to the division of Europe into many relatively small states, its overall urban hierarchy is much "flatter" than is the case, for example, in a politically unified territory like the United States. Thus, Europe has no dominating urban center, but a number of competitors for this role. At the national level, both rank-size and primate city urban hierarchies can be found in Europe. Belgium, Germany, Italy, Norway, Poland, and Switzerland all have well-balanced, rank-size urban systems. However, the following countries exhibit primate distributions (the first number in parentheses indi-

cates the factor by which the largest city is more populous than the second largest city; the second number indicates the city's percentage of its country's total population): Hungary (10.0; 20%), Iceland (9.1; 37%), Austria (8.0; 27%), UK (6.8; 13%), Denmark (5.8; 27%), and Romania (5.5; 9%). In each of these states, the capital city also dominates life in a variety of ways. For example, in Hungary people speak of living in Budapest or in "the country"; London is simply known as "The Smoke." The dominance of capitals in countries not included in the preceding statistics has also been an issue of some national concern, notably in France, Greece, and Ireland.

On the other hand, in some European states the largest city is less than twice the size of the second largest, usually indicating a condition of dual primacy. Representatives in this category are the Netherlands (1.2), Portugal (1.3), Sweden (1.5), and Spain (1.7). The rest of the countries of Europe exhibit city-size distributions intermediate between rank-size and primate.

During the communist period cities in Eastern Europe, unlike their western counterparts, generally did not establish close linkages with other cities. First, border and trade restrictions stifled the flow of goods and people between Eastern and Western Europe, and even between Eastern Europe and the Soviet Union. In particular, close connections that had existed between Berlin and cities in Poland, and the special relationships that Vienna had with Prague and Budapest, were all but severed after World War II. In like manner, suspicious, sometimes outright hostile, relations among the Balkan countries greatly reduced interaction among Tirane, Belgrade, Sofia, Athens, Thessaloniki, and Istanbul. Second, even though close cooperation and trade relations as part of an international division of labor were explicit goals of the Council for Mutual Economic Assistance (CMEA), the nature of centrally planned economies prevented hoped-for levels of interaction. In particular, because currencies were nonconvertible, trade arrangements had to be negotiated in barter fashion—a practice that obviously undermined efficiency and reduced trade. Third, the low level of technology and transportation infrastructure in the region further inhibited close international ties. Finally, and related to all these factors, the countries of Eastern Europe spent most of the communist period following varying degrees of autarkic (economic self-sufficient) policies.

Since the breakdown of the communist governments of Eastern Europe in 1989, the situation has been changing. As the number of joint ventures with the west increases and as more Western goods appear in shops, the countries of Eastern Europe will become less isolated, and so interconnections will be forged. More important, however, is the reemergence of former regional centers, notably Berlin and Vienna. After 50 years of relative obscurity, these centers are quickly assuming important roles in the development of post–Cold War East Central Europe. Unfortunately, continuing strife in Southeastern Europe has thus far prevented the reemergence of similar regional centers in this region, such as Athens and Istanbul.

In the future, greater levels of economic and political connectivity, no doubt, will characterize all the cities of Europe. Indeed, greater interaction within the European Union, as well as the changing nature of industrial production, can only lead to closer levels of interurban cooperation. However, a few cities that owed their development to special circumstances that existed during the communist period could be relative losers in post-socialist Eastern Europe (e.g., planned industrial cities like Eisenhüttenstadt in eastern Germany and Leninváros in Hungary).

Contemporary European cities have a broader range of functions now than in the past. Although some remain dominated by industry (e.g., Katowice, Poland) or port activities (e.g., Rotterdam), many larger European cities incorporate a broad array of economic activities within them (e.g., London, Paris, and Berlin). A few have become specialized service centers for provision of services at the global or European scale—London and Frankfurt/Main in financial services, for example. Many smaller cities and towns that escaped major wartime damage and whose city centers at least were not major participants in the massive urban growth and change associated with the Industrial Revolution now prosper as magnets for tourists—for example, Brugge (Belgium) and Regensburg (Germany). Ironically, many small towns bypassed by the Industrial Revolution and economically stagnant for decades have now refurbished their architectural heritage and have emerged as major tourist centers or much-valued residential cities owing to their clean air, architectural beauty, and, often, tradition as centers of culture. There are a few large examples of such places (e.g., Salzburg and Cambridge) and many smaller examples (e.g., Rothenburg ob der Tauber [Germany], Ribe [Denmark], Colmar [France], Český Krumlov [Czech Rep.]).

Urban Systems Policies

Government policy, whether direct or indirect, intended or inadvertent, plays a critical role in the growth of cities and hence in the development of urban systems. All governments adopt policies or pursue development strategies that impact cities. For example, governments' efforts to encourage industrialization led to the growth of larger cities; the siting of military bases can have a great impact on the development of one region versus another; the design of transportation networks and provision of other types of infrastructure can affect how cities in a country grow; and social policies on immigration and internal migration can affect population redistribution within countries. Of course, governments also become involved in planning the internal structure of cities, as discussed later in this chapter.

Selected West European states have adopted the most explicit urban policies. Chief among these is the growth-pole strategy used first by the French beginning in the late 1950s and by the British in their New Towns scheme. Growth-pole strategies, which many other countries, including the United States, have also adopted, typically have two related goals: (1) to stimulate economic growth and development in lagging regions (usually located in peripheral parts of a country); and (2) to direct growth away from overdeveloped regions or primate cities. In the French example, planners sought to divert growth away from Paris to other, less developed parts of France. The policy instruments adopted included restrictions on the siting of new facilities or expansion of existing ones in and around Paris; reduced shares of national investment in housing, education, and infrastructure in the Paris region; and provision of various incentives, such as tax breaks, to firms in designated "equilibrium metropolises" located around the country (specifically Lille, Nancy, Strasbourg, Lyon, Marseille, Toulouse, Bordeaux, and Nantes). Given the more balanced state of the French space economy and urban system today, the growth-pole strategy can be viewed as a success. Several other European governments have also used elements of a growth-pole strategy in their regional development programs.

During the post–World War II period, the countries of Eastern Europe exercised far greater control over aspects of urban planning than did their Western counterparts. Planners were guided by several important concerns derived from Marxist-Leninist philosophy, such as eliminating excessive concentration in big cities, which they viewed as negative consequences of capitalist development; balancing the urban system; removing the "contradiction" between urban and rural lifestyles; and providing infrastructure equally to all parts of the country. To achieve these goals, planners placed restrictions on industrial expansion and inmigration to capital cities, while adopting aggressive forms of the growth-pole strategy by locating new plants in peripheral locations. Furthermore, all of the countries of Eastern Europe built new industrial towns to increase industrial output, decentralize production, balance the urban hierarchy, and provide urban functions to underserved areas. In addition, at least one author has suggested that urban policies in some of the Eastern European countries sought to develop cities along borders to improve their overall defensive posture. On the other hand, governments were wary of placing important industries and sensitive military establishments too close to borders, lest they should end up in another state following one of the many border changes that have plagued this part of Europe for so many years.

An extreme form of settlement planning was pursued in Romania under its former dictator, Nicolae Ceausescu. His plan, called "systematization," was to reorganize Romania's entire settlement system, mainly by transforming villages to towns and creating architectural uniformity across the country (Fig. 6-12). In all, some 300 to 400 villages were transformed, thereby eliminating any signs of traditional life, while other villages were simply destroyed. Similar efforts to concentrate population in larger urban centers and reduce the number of small villages were also pursued in other socialist countries (e.g., the GDR) in order to achieve both economic and political goals.

FIGURE 6-12 The Romanian village of Navodari was "systematized" to create conformity in all settlements. (D. Danta)

THE MORPHOLOGY OF EUROPEAN CITIES

European cities are palimpsests: "texts" of wood, brick, mortar, concrete, steel, and glass written on the parchment of the physical site. As "texts," cities can be read to reveal the historic processes and events, the practical considerations and limitations, and the interplay of competing interests that have shaped them through the ages. This section deals with the internal arrangement of European cities, a topic referred to as urban structure or morphology. Topics include site conditions of cities, location of land use categories and determinants of their location, aspects of urban planning, and the social geography of cities. As was the case with urban systems, the structure of cities in Western Europe is very different from that which developed under socialism in Eastern Europe, and so treatment will be separate for the two regions.

Nearly all European cities have certain locational characteristics in common. Cities are either located along the coast at ports (e.g., Lisbon, Barcelona, Amsterdam, Dublin, Belfast, Hamburg, Copenhagen, Reykjavik, Oslo, Stockholm, Helsinki, Gdansk, Genoa, Athens, Constanta), along a river (e.g., Cordoba and Seville on the Guadalquivir; London—Thames; Paris—Seine; Lyon—Rhone; Brussels—Senne; Cologne—Rhine; Bern—Aare; Milan—Po; Rome—Tiber; Vienna, Bratislava, Budapest, and Belgrade—Danube; Cracow and Warsaw—Vistula; and Prague—Vltava), on prominent hills offering protection (e.g., Salzburg), or at sites of natural resources (e.g., Kiruna, Wrocław, Ploiesti). Only a handful of large European cities—Madrid, Bucharest, and Tirane are three—do not fit into these categories, indicating that political rather than locational factors played a greater role in the original establishment and subsequent growth of these places.

The initial characteristics of a city's location, referred to as its site conditions, reflect the logic prevailing when the city was founded. For example, Classical and medieval cities needed sources of water as well as protection from pirates and warlords, and industrial cities needed rivers to attain power and to access inexpensive transportation. Of course, not all cities were consciously located with such geographic factors in mind. However, the list in the previous paragraph is so extensive for the simple fact that cities illogically situated either usually failed to develop into major places or ceased to exist.

Whereas locational characteristics (sometimes referred to popularly as "geography") matter with regard to where cities develop, history has been important in shaping their internal structure. The vast majority of cities in Southern and Western Europe have existed for some 2000 years, in Central Europe for nearly a 1000 years, and in Eastern and Northern Europe for around 500 years. "New" cities that have been in existence for only a matter of a 100 years or less are the exception, though several evolved on coalfields during the Industrial Revolution (e.g., Bochum, Germany) or as planned industrial cities in socialist Eastern Europe (discussed in Chapter 12 on East Central and Southeastern Europe). Given their longevity and general inertia of land use, cities in Europe usually exhibit many historical elements. First, cities retain their original square or plaza, which today is usually restricted to pedestrian traffic. This square generally features the cathedral, old town hall, craft and guild halls, and what were originally apartments of the wealthiest citizens, but now are more likely small, rather rundown rooms rented by students and artists. These squares and the connecting pedestrian streets, or *ramblas* as they are known in Barcelona, are important gathering points. They are usually packed with people who come to meet friends, feed the pigeons, or just sit and watch the world go by. Many people play musical instruments or put on comedy routines to make money from passersby; some evenings, the streets become crowded with these "baskers." The streets and lanes in these city centers are usually narrow and winding, reflecting their origin in pre-industrial and pre-automotive eras.

Often interspersed with the people-oriented gathering places in European cities are a vast number of small shops and vendors selling anything from simple goods such as newspapers and ice cream to much more expensive, specialized products. European cities almost always also have major commercial zones that provide clusters of

FIGURE 6-13 The old castle of Bratislava, Slovakia overlooks the newer suburbs below and socialist housing in the background. (D. Danta)

large and small shops, concentrations of banks and other specialized business services, and, often, entertainment districts with theaters and restaurants. Museums, churches, government ministries, and some residences also crowd into the central parts of European cities. All of these areas may be incorporated to a greater or lesser degree within a walking-oriented part of the city that serves as a magnet for strolling residents and tourists alike.

Ringing the original cities are often either walls, remnants of walls, or spaces where walls used to be. For example, the two large curving boulevards of Budapest are built along the former courses of walls that defined the boundaries of the city at different times in the past. Vienna's *Ringstrasse*, with grandiose architectural gems along it, was built on the land that once held the city's fortifications. Germany's smaller city of Münster is ringed by a park, which was also once the site of the city walls and defenses. In other cities, a castle still perches on high ground overlooking more recent settlements that grew below the original city or "urb," namely, the "sub-urbs" (Fig. 6-13). Many cities in Southeastern Europe retain traces of their character from Turkish times in the form of mosques, bazaars (markets), and specially designed bridges.

European cities tend to be compact and have high population densities. This pattern results from a variety of interrelated factors, including especially the nature of European cities' housing, transport, and planning systems as well as great appreciation for urban life and amenities within European cultures.

Apartment living is common in Europe and represents the primary form of residential land use in its cities. Europeans have lived in apartments for centuries, but construction of apartment buildings and row housing proceeded at an especially fast pace in cities during the Industrial Revolution in order to shelter workers who flocked to them from the countryside. This working-class housing still dominates large districts in many industrial cities throughout Europe. Similarly, during the twentieth century many European governments have built large tracts of public housing. Single-family detached houses in suburban locations are more costly in Europe than a comparable unit would be in the United States. Therefore not as many are built, with the result that suburbanization is generally not taking place there at the same rate as in North America, although it exists now to some extent around most European cities. Apart from public, working-class, and other types of tenement housing, however, apartments are often quite elaborate affairs, encompassing whole floors or multiple levels of the same building. In addition, wealthier individuals in European cities tend to live closer to the city center than do their American counterparts. As a final point, Europeans do not tend to move as frequently as North Americans. Indeed, although many Europeans rent, leases are often for 10 years or even longer, and tenants are generally required to supply appliances and some plumbing fixtures in the apartments. Permanency of residence leads to much greater neighborhood stability than is the case in other parts of the world. As mentioned previously, many urban neighborhoods are composed of migrant groups from various parts of the world.

European cities usually also have excellent systems of public transportation. Systems of buses, trams, streetcars, and subways permit quick and efficient travel to all parts of town, but they particularly benefit the city center on which they generally focus. This aspect of European cities is both cause and consequence of their compact shape. European cities are also well provided with parks, which are usually public but can also be for the exclusive use of nearby residents. Many of these parks were created at the close of World War II on the sites of bombed buildings or derive from the nineteenth century when outmoded fortifications were torn down and partially transformed into public green space. Another form of semipublic space are cemeteries, such as the *Zentralfriedhof* in Vienna; these are important, though often overlooked, aspects of urban land use (Fig. 6-14).

A major difference between European and other cities is the lack of relatively tall buildings marking the downtown. Because land is so expensive in the centers of North American cities, developers

FIGURE 6-15 La Défense on the outskirts of Paris contains the tall buildings and corporate headquarters that would mark the downtown of a North American city. Strict planning within the historic center of Paris helped generate a repressed demand for office space that was partially met by this complex. (D. Danta)

build upward to garner the greatest profit. Cost of land explains the appearance of skyscrapers and other tall buildings in the downtowns of American cities. However, building restrictions in the centers of most European cities prevent this type of high-rise development, and so their skyline remains much flatter. Modern high-rise construction still often takes place, but at the edges of cities rather than at their centers. This situation especially holds for Paris, which has exercised height controls for well over 100 years. Although the Île de la Cité, the elongated island in the Seine that marks the Roman nucleus and contained much of the city until the 1800s, is still considered the center of Paris, a new development just outside the municipal boundaries of the city—La Défense—contains the tall buildings, corporate headquarters, and other amenities characteristic of modern urban centers (Fig. 6-15). This reflects the irrepressible demand for space in the modern city, including historic European cities. The repressed supply of quarters in cities like Paris leads to even greater inner-city population density and often to pressures for suburban development.

Many structures in European cities exhibit historical building materials and architectural styles,

FIGURE 6-14 Land became so scarce in Prague's Jewish cemetery that graves were stacked 15 deep. (D. Danta)

and the populace and governments usually put great emphasis on their preservation. Although the Industrial Revolution and the post–World War II commercial boom in European cities have caused much more cumulative loss of the historic fabric of the region's cities, there has been an ongoing and growing concern about maintaining the historic character of cities, especially the city centers, as much as possible. These centers are the source of great civic pride and of enjoyment for both residents and tourists. Regional variations in architectural styles also allow many cities to develop and cultivate a "cityscape" that is quite distinctive. For example, most historic buildings in northern Germany and around the Baltic are made of red brick, whereas half-timbered buildings from the medieval period are still evident in many cities of England, central and southern Germany, and France (Fig. 6-16). Bremen (Germany), Chester (England), Heidelberg, and Colmar (France) provide attractive examples of these styles. In like manner, roof materials vary across Europe—slate in parts of Wales and Northern Europe, thatch across a broad belt from Ireland to Hungary, sod in northern climes, and red ceramic tile in Southern Europe.

A number of European cities display a similarity in the location of preferred, higher income resi-

FIGURE 6-16 These black and white half-timbered buildings in Chester, England, have remained unchanged for hundreds of years. (D. Danta)

dential communities—namely, development in close-in western suburbs. In some cases, this is at least partly related to landscape features, such as the Buda Hills and Vienna Woods (*Wienerwald*) in Budapest and Vienna, respectively, or to political conditions, as in the case of Berlin (with American influence in the west and Soviet influence in the east from 1945 to 1989). In other cases, a socioeconomic gradient of residential neighborhoods that displays tendencies of a decline from west to east may more closely reflect the preference of the well-to-do and the well connected to live upwind from noxious urban manufacturing emissions, given that European cities are generally influenced by relatively frequent westerly winds. Besides the cities noted here, other examples of cities with west-to-east-trending socioeconomic gradients include London, Paris, Prague, and Moscow.

Finally, in general, European cities illustrate much more clearly than American cities the impact of urban planning and its general acceptance. The cultural preferences of the population and the socioeconomic policy preferences of governments join to favor central city preservation and development as opposed to a more common pattern of suburban preferences in the United States. Restrictions on the growth of distant suburbs; guidelines for and restrictions on types of allowable central city development; high energy taxes on private transportation, impediments to the movements of cars and trucks in the central city, development of pedestrian zones, and subsidized public transport; policies favoring small, family owned as opposed to large shops (e.g., restrictions on the number of hours shops may be open weekly); and subsidized cultural programs in the form of performing arts theaters and museums—all play a role in maintaining stronger central city cores in Europe than in the United States. To a large degree, this is possible because Europeans continue to support a high level of taxation and a great deal of government control in shaping the structure, and especially the land use, of European cities. The net result is that European city centers generally have more residents, consumer-oriented services, and round-the-clock activity than cities in the United States. Moreover, their residential suburbs are usually less dispersed and more oriented toward trade with city center businesses rather than the typical decentralized pattern of malls and shopping centers in the United States.

The Socialist, East European Variant

Cities in Eastern Europe during 1947–1989 developed under quite different economic and political conditions than did those in Western Europe. Private ownership of land, most forms of private development, and hence urban land and real estate markets simply did not exist. Similarly, greater control by planners and urban planning principles derived from the socialist philosophy had consequences for the structure of these cities (Inset 6-4).

First, because there were no land markets or profit motive, no rationale existed for constructing very tall buildings. Where they do exist, tall buildings are intended for public use as meeting halls, cultural centers, and other civic activities (Fig. 6-17). Like those in the west, the centers of cities in the east ideally are open squares. However, the reason for this arrangement is symbolic—to represent the socialist heart of the city and to provide room for political rallies.

Cities that developed under socialism tend to be less spatially segregated than those under capitalism. Some parts of these cities, of course, continued to attract and concentrate prosperous and politically well-connected residents. But the overall level of residential heterogeneity—except perhaps at the intra-building level—was and is lower than that in most American cities. In attempts to erase vestiges of their bourgeois past, governments in socialist countries converted former mansions to political uses, such as providing accommodations for ministries, branches of the Academy of Science, or foreign delegations.

Under socialism, housing was viewed as a right, not as a commodity. Technically, each family was entitled to its own apartment and each family member to a separate room. In order to achieve this ideal, governments undertook massive building programs during the 1950s–1970s based on construction of so-called housing estates with multistory, prefabricated, multifamily apartment

FIGURE 6-17 The House of the Republic in Bucharest shows the type of "wedding cake" architecture typical of the socialist period. Ironically, the ostentatious style was, in part, designed to illustrate the power and glory of the Ceausescu regime which fashioned it—a regime subsequently driven from power by a popular revolt. (D. Danta)

blocks. Apartments in these blocks are small (generally from about 500 to 700 sq ft, or about 50 to 70 sq m), poorly constructed, and lack amenities. Residents generally dislike them as much as those living, for example, in British Council flats (also public housing). Typically, housing estates were built in large clusters, usually near the edges of cities on available land, sometimes forming massive concrete curtains on the landscape. As a result, population densities in Eastern European cities may increase near the city boundary, contrary to normal expectations.

Housing estates were constructed in groups to form what is called a neighborhood unit (also known by the Russian name *mikrorayon*). A neighborhood unit usually consists of three to four apartment blocks arranged into a quadrangle surrounding shops, green space, and play areas for children. The rationale for these units, according to the socialist planning philosophy, was to promote greater social interaction. Unfortunately, in practice most housing estates in socialist Eastern Europe had a shortage of commercial and social services within them. Though often planned, shortages of funds prevented their completion. Owing both to low rents and general economic

PLANNING A NEW INDUSTRIAL TOWN: LENINVÁROS

Leninváros (Lenintown) is typical of the new indus-trial towns that were built in the socialist countries of Eastern Europe during the 1950s through 1970s. These new towns are important, for they offer the clearest view of socialist planning philosophy in operation.

Leninváros was intended to increase industrial output, specifically of chemical products, offer employment in this part of Hungary, and supply urban services to its hinterland. Situated on the Tisza River in the Great Hungarian Plain, the town was built on the site of a former village that con-tained only 1700 people in 1945. Construction of the power station and massive chemical works, which is the reason for Leninváros' existence, began in 1953–1954; its construction commenced in 1955. Originally planned to house 10,000 inhabitants, in 1964 the target population was increased to 40,000. The town was given official recognition in 1966 (using its village name, Tiszaszederkény), but the name was changed in 1970 to commemorate the centenary of Lenin's birth.

As seen in its map (Fig. 6-18A), Leninváros was planned in four sections, each to contain a popula-tion of 10,000 arranged into neighborhood units. At the center is the town council, shopping district, and park land surrounding an artificial lake. Leninváros is slightly better provided with schools, infrastruc-ture, and recreational facilities than most compara-bly sized Hungarian towns. In particular, the town has an outdoor skating rink and Olympic-sized swimming pool located adjacent to the plant. It is separated from the chemical works by a 600-meter-wide forest belt.

Leninváros's population growth has been rapid, increasing from 3377 in 1960 to 11,033 in 1970; 18,677 in 1980; and 18,696 in 1990. This total falls far short of the anticipated 40,000 because of the gener-al restructuring of Hungarian industry during the 1970s and 1980s. Another reason perhaps is the town's failure to attract the hoped-for numbers of people. Even 20 years after its construction, it still has a very sterile, inhospitable feel to it. In spite of every good intention, the place never got past its small "company-town" stage. Similar problems exist in other planned, new socialist cities, notably Halle Neustadt in eastern Germany and Katowice in Poland, as well as, to some extent, in planned towns (Fig. 6-18B) in the west such as Zwolle and other towns on Netherlands' polders.

FIGURE 6-18A Leninváros, a planned city south of Budapest. (D. Danta)

FIGURE 6-18B Eisenhüttenstadt, a planned city in the GDR. (W. H. Berentsen)

inefficiencies, there were always too few funds to meet the demand for both more and improved housing. Long waiting lists for better housing were a general characteristic of life in socialist East Europe. Since the fall of socialism, a profusion of small shops have begun to spring up in many parts of the region's towns and cities (Fig. 12-16).

The construction of neighborhood units and related aspects of socialist urban planning were particularly developed in the new industrial towns (Inset 6-4). The kind of social engineering attempted by planners through the neighborhood unit concept quickly fell from grace, however, and so countries in Eastern Europe abandoned this practice, along with housing block construction, by the mid-1980s.

A major problem facing city councils across the region these days is just what to do with these blocks. The obvious answer is to sell or "privatize" them. However, assuming for the moment that demand exists for them, a major problem concerns valuation, that is, establishing a selling price. Under socialism, the prices of goods, services, and rents were determined in an arbitrary way. Determining the "worth" of an apartment block, therefore, is nearly impossible. Some governments have decided to auction off individual apartments for 50 percent of their maintenance cost. Many individuals have taken advantage of this low price to buy apartments and then resell them at a handsome

profit. On the other hand, governments continue to provide services and charge the same rents until all the units in a building are sold. Thus, there is an incentive to ensure that at least one tenant in a building holds out.

Public transportation is even more important in the cities of Eastern Europe than in Western European cities. Generally, governments in the region have made a strong commitment to provide reasonably convenient, inexpensive, and extensive public transport systems—and have made it difficult to own a private vehicle, although such ownership was increasing steadily in the 1970s and 1980s. Still, a greater proportion of the cities' residents use public transport systems than their counterparts in the west, because private ownership of autos has been so low. Private cars were even banned in Albania until the early 1990s. Major transport hubs, in particular where different modes of transport meet, are now emerging as important retail and commercial centers in these cities. Eastern Germany is leading the way in the construction of numerous western-style, auto-oriented shopping complexes.

Department, fashion, cosmetic, fast food, and even video rental stores are cropping up across the downtowns of Eastern European cities just as in the west. However, the retail structure of most towns in the region, in particular the arrangement and specialization of particular shops in a given block of a city, is usually more haphazard than that in a comparable block in Western Europe or North America, reflecting an early stage in the evolution of market-oriented retail land use in eastern cities.

A final point concerns public art in the cities of Eastern Europe. All European cities contain various monuments, statues, and other forms of art that add to the distinctive character of these places. Until very recently, the countries of Eastern Europe also prominently displayed expressions of socialism. For example, nearly all government buildings had large red stars attached to them; statues of Marx, Lenin, and other communist heroes were displayed in many cities along with other statues in socialist realism style; political banners and murals were often conspicuously displayed; and larger cities had monuments to the Red Army's role in ending the Nazi occupation.

FIGURE 6-19A Glorifying the accomplishments of socialism in Albania. (D. Danta)

FIGURE 6-19B Karl Marx in Chemnitz, Germany (formerly Karl-Marx-Stadt), an example of the immense "socialist realism" statues formerly found throughout the cities of East Central and Southeast Europe. (W. H. Berentsen)

have been changed back to pre-World War II designations, canceling out socialist-era efforts to honor socialist "heroes" by naming streets after them. Similarly, cities have reverted to using presocialist names, so that Karl-Marx-Stadt is again Chemnitz and the former Leningrad is St. Petersburg.

URBAN PROBLEMS AND POLICIES

Despite the many attractions of European cities, they, like cities everywhere, face a number of problems and challenges, including adapting to a more globalized and service-oriented economy, improving urban infrastructure while preserving historic urban structures, balancing preferences to maintain strong city centers while responding to increasing pressures for suburban expansion, and addressing ever-evolving patterns of socioeconomic and ethnic segregation and associated ethnic-based conflicts. An in-depth study of the socioeconomic condition of West European cities by Cheshire and Hay (1989) up to the mid-1980s indicates the wide variety of urban problems in West European cities, as well as the variation in level of problems among cities within the same region and country. Though difficult to generalize, their study did indicate that a number of cities faced problems especially rooted in their overreliance on heavy industrial activities (e.g., steel production and shipbuilding, notably in Northwest European cities and particularly those on coalfields) or those with rather poor infrastructure (especially cities in Southern Europe). Cities in regions with diversified economies and a good infrastructural endowment (e.g., southern Germany and much of northern Italy) had lower levels of social and economic problems. Although the authors were not able to gather comparable data for East Central and Southeast European cities, it is probably reasonable to conjecture that many cities in the region suffer the infrastructural shortcomings of Southern European cities, and, in some cases, problems of poor economic structure as well (e.g., Katowice, Poland and Košice, Slovakia).

In response to the challenges of a highly competitive international economy and in the face of relatively expensive land and labor, the economic

(Fig. 6-19a,b). Since 1989, however, red stars have been removed from buildings, and statues of communists have been taken down. In Budapest, a special "statue cemetery" has been erected in a field just outside the city boundary. Street names

structures of European cities have been evolving toward much more specialized service employment (e.g., financial services) and away from manufacturing. A number of cities have been particularly successful in this transformation (e.g., Luxembourg, Dublin, London, and Paris), often as the result of aggressive public sector involvement in attracting new kinds of jobs. Thus, for example, public involvement in resolving a serious office space shortage in Paris led to the development of a huge La Défense office complex outside of, but near, the center of the historic city. La Défense complex now employs about 110,000 workers; the development has allowed the city to preserve its cherished (and, for tourism, economically valuable) historical center, while establishing new space within the city for the extremely important service sector. A somewhat similar project involving more private initiatives in the previously derelict Docklands of East London (see Chapter 7) has also led to provision of space for about 53,000 service sector jobs. Other cities that were previously overly dependent on manufacturing and suffering from rapid loss in jobs (e.g., Manchester and Turin) are also trying to diversify their employment structures. Among formerly industrial cities, Glasgow may perhaps provide the best example of success in moving toward achieving this rather difficult task. Other, previously nonindustrialized, often modestly sized cities with "livability" appeal for highly skilled and educated workers have also succeeded in developing policies to attract new high-technology firms, notably Cambridge (UK), Montpellier (France), and Munich.

Cities across Europe have been working to strengthen the economic basis of city centers. As noted earlier, they have a number of advantages in this regard in comparison to cities in the United States, but pressures for suburbanization persist. In addition and in harmony with the inherent advantages associated with the relative affordability and convenience of public transportation as well as cultural preferences and political support favoring maintaining a strong city center, city governments have frequently developed inner-city pedestrian zones to enhance the social, recreational, and shopping experiences of visitors to the city center. Suburbanization has also proceeded, responding to a variety of residential preferences

and economic factors at work in Europe as in the United States. Thus, for example, expanding demand for city center space for services has raised prices and reduced housing alternatives for residents. Expanded public transport has often made it easier for commuters to reach these jobs from bucolic, relatively low-cost residential areas in the suburbs. Suburbs have also often developed in and around planned new towns (especially in the UK) that originally were conceived as independent satellites of nearby large cities (notably London), in order to reduce their dominance and congestion within them. In fact, these satellites often have evolved as somewhat spatially detached "bedroom communities" from which workers commute into the major city. Some such new towns have grown to rather phenomenally large sizes— for example, Milton Keynes outside of London (approximately 220,000 people).

Beginning as early as the 1920s, regional planning over large metropolitan areas was begun in order to coordinate development of transportation, water supply, and land use. Pioneers in these activities included the many, densely packed industrial towns in Germany's Ruhr River Valley, the Randstad region in western Netherlands (encompassing especially the cities of Rotterdam, The Hague, Amsterdam, and Utrecht), as well as the London region. Ongoing cooperation in the Randstad and London regions continues, though cooperative government efforts have been set back by conservative UK government efforts to dissolve cooperative government in and around London previously undertaken by the Greater London Council (GLC). Planning in the Randstad region, on the other hand, has been a long, continuing effort to preserve the urban region's intensively farmed "green heart" from further encroachment by urban activities. Preservation of green space is seen as a way of improving regional air quality, providing recreational space, and maintaining a portion of the region's historic land use patterns (Fig. 6-20).

Despite the power and efforts of planners in Europe, urban sprawl and poorly planned settlement developments are also not uncommon. The edges of Madrid, areas on Spain's southern coast and Bulgaria's Black Sea coast, as well as the fringes of many eastern German cities, all illustrate

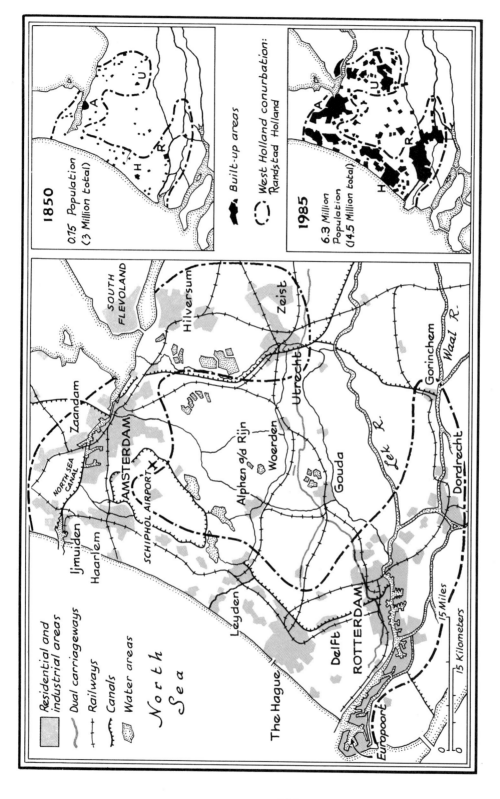

FIGURE 6-20 Randstad, Holland, where a regional and urban planning effort is being made to preserve the "green heart" within highly urbanized western Holland.

the negative impacts of unplanned or poorly planned urban and commercial development. In eastern Germany the expanding role of privately owned cars, the allure of economic gain by poorly developed regions, as well as weak (in some cases, probably, corrupt) planning authorities, have been among the more important factors behind urban sprawl. The building of commercial strips, shopping malls, and brightly lit gas stations on the outskirts of eastern German cities is particularly jarring, given Germany's long tradition of strict land use planning, the German culture's sensitivity to aesthetic appearance in almost all other aspects of the environment (e.g., local planning authorities often have control of the pitch and color of private home roofs), and the drab nature and lack of commercialism during the East German socialist era.

Finally, European cities often need to struggle with problems of social and ethnic segregation. West European cities are particularly prone to the development of low-income residential regions owing to a partially market-oriented housing and land price system. Land use planning provisions, a relatively high level of income security, rent controls, and provision of public housing, however, produce less ghastly conditions in low-income urban areas in Europe than in the United States, including far less dereliction, street crime, and drug trade—although these problems are of increasing concern in many places in Europe.

Despite socialist rhetoric, poor districts inherited from earlier capitalist eras were not always subsequently well-developed in Eastern Europe (e.g., Prenzlauerberg [East Berlin] and Sonnenberg [Dresden]), and residential areas were provided for the privileged elite (e.g., Wandlitz north of east Berlin and the dacha district northwest of Moscow). In addition, there is concern that poor ghettos may now evolve in the east during a chaotic era of incipient capitalist development, possibly focusing on the poorly built, poorly served, and generally unpopular large housing estates that were constructed during the socialist era or in inner-city areas where very old housing has been neglected. Fear of the development of more poor regions in East European cities reflects a more general concern for the possibility of greater socioeco-

nomic stratification within the former socialist countries in the near future. Given socialism's level of public discussion about this particular "evil" of capitalism as well as increased social and economic insecurity in the east, the specter of ghettos and an economic underclass generates great anxiety and discussion in the region.

Western European cities often display considerable ethnic residential segregation. During the 1960s and 1970s literally millions of guest workers poured into Northwestern Europe from Southeastern Europe, northern Africa, and other former colonies to take advantage of job opportunities in labor-short Europe. Most migrants came with little capital and education, and generally took low-paid jobs that native residents found undesirable. The inmigration included large numbers of Muslims, whose presence quickly began to create cultural misunderstandings and clashes. This problem intensified after severe recessions and the development of persistently high levels of unemployment in many European countries beginning in the 1970s, and especially after many guest workers began to bring their families from abroad and to raise families in Europe. In Germany guest workers and their families ultimately numbered over 5 million people, most from the poorest parts of Italy, Turkey, and the former Yugoslavia. Many children of these immigrants have been born or raised in Germany, so that they are not really at home either within their native or the German society; under current conditions, they have few future economic opportunities and rather slim chances of acquiring German citizenship. In Germany and elsewhere, these immigrants have tended to live spatially and socially separated from the native population. The trend has been accelerated by a tendency over the last one to two decades for many European cities to experience net outmigration of natives but ongoing net inmigration of nonnatives, including many non-Europeans.

Apparently racially motivated strife has broken out in numerous European cities over the past couple of decades (e.g., in Germany, UK, and France), and sometimes in places that are otherwise rather well respected for tolerance (e.g., the Netherlands and Sweden). Some of the most recent and highly publicized outbreaks of violent xenophobia have occurred in places with relatively few minority populations, but where social and economic anxiety has made immigrants the local population's targets of frustrations, notably in eastern Germany. Equally disturbing have been apparently increased numbers of anti-Semitic acts or political rhetoric in countries with poor or suspect records of tolerance toward this (now rather tiny) ethnic-religious minority—notably in Germany, Austria, France, Russia, and Poland. Fewer Europeans will now argue, as many did, for example, in the late 1960s, that racism is a largely American problem. Indeed, Germany's greatest future urban problem may not be reconstructing and integrating its eastern cities into the national economy and urban system, but rather addressing a potential time bomb in the neglected resolution of the political rights of guest workers and their social relations with other "Germans."

In short, Europe has beautiful cities that in many ways reflect broader "European" cultural traits, overlain in individual cities by historical and national elements. However, the region's cities also suffer the problems of urban centers of all developed countries in the contemporary era—from combating ethnic discrimination and crime to simply providing basic infrastructural needs ranging from adequate housing to contemporary modes of telecommunication. As intriguing as the European cities' historic heritage is to Americans, they continue to evolve and change, though generally accompanied by historic preservation efforts. Like cities in all parts of the globe, Europe's cities are the focal points of economic growth and change as well as architectural innovation.

BIBLIOGRAPHY

Bairoch, Paul. (1988). *Cities and Economic Development: From the Dawn of History to the Present*. Chicago: The University of Chicago Press.

Balfour, Alan. (1990). *Berlin: The Politics of Order*. New York: Rizzoli.

Bender, Thomas, ed. (1988). *The University and the City: From Medieval Origins to the Present*. New York and Oxford: Oxford University Press.

Benevolo, Leonardo. (1993). *The European City*. Oxford, UK and Cambridge, Mass.: Basil Blackwell.

Berentsen, W. H. (1992). "The Socialist Face of the GDR: Eastern Germany's Landscape—Past, Present, and Future", *Landscape and Urban Planning*, 22, 137–151.

Braunfels, Wolfgang. (1988). *Urban Design in Western Europe: Regime and Architecture, 900–1900*. Chicago and London: The University of Chicago Press.

Burtenshaw, David, Michael Bateman, and Greg J. Ashworth. (1994). *The European City: A Western Perspective*. New York: Halsted Press.

Cheshire, Paul C., and Dennis Hay. (1989). *Urban Problems in Western Europe*. London: Unwin Hyman.

Clout, Hugh, ed. (1994). *Europe's Cities in the Late Twentieth Century*. Netherlands Geographical Studies 176. Utrecht/Amsterdam: Royal Dutch Geographical Society & Department of Human Geography, University of Amsterdam.

Danta, Darrick. (1993). "Ceausescu's Bucharest." *The Geographical Review* 83, (2): 170–182.

Dawson, Andrew H., ed. (1987). *Planning in Eastern Europe*. New York: St. Martin's Press.

French, R. A. and F. E. Ian Hamilton. (1979). *The Socialist City: Spatial Structure and Urban Policy*. New York: John Wiley & Sons.

Dennis, Richard. (1984). *English Industrial Cities of the Nineteenth Century: A Social Geography*. Cambridge: Cambridge University Press.

Girouard, Mark. (1985). *Cities and People: A Social and Architectural History*. New Haven and London: Yale University Press.

Gutkind, E.A., ed. (1972). *International History of City Development*, Vols I–VIII. New York: Free Press.

Hernández, Xavier, and Pilar Comes. (1990). *Barmi: A Mediterranean City Through the Ages*. Boston: Houghton Mifflin Company.

Hernández, Xavier, and Jordi Ballonga. (1991). *Lebek: A City of Northern Europe Through the Ages*. Boston: Houghton Mifflin Company.

Knox, Paul, and Darrick Danta. (1993). "Cities of Europe." In: *Cities of the World*, 2nd ed. Stanley D. Brunn and Jack F. Williams, editors. New York, HarperCollins College Publishers. pp. 85–149.

Kostof, Spiro. (1992). *The City Assembled: The Elements of Urban Form Through History*. Boston, Toronto, London: Little, Brown and Company.

Kostof, Spiro. (1991). *The City Shaped: Urban Patterns and Meanings Through History*. Boston, Toronto, London: Little, Brown and Company.

Magocsi, Paul Robert. (1993). *Historical Atlas of East Central Europe*. Toronto: University of Toronto Press.

Mumford, Lewis. (1961). *The City in History: Its Origins, Its Transformations, and Its Prospects*. New York: Harcourt, Brace & World.

Pirenne, Henri. (1925). *Medieval Cities: Their Origins and the Revival of Trade*. Garden City, N.Y.: Doubleday & Company, Inc.

Pounds, N.J.G. (1990). *An Historical Geography of Europe*. Cambridge, UK: Cambridge University Press.

Pounds, N.J.G. (1969). "The Urbanization of the Classical World." *Annals of the Association of American Geographers* 59, (1): 135–157.

Rugg, Dean S. (1985). *Eastern Europe*. London: Longman.

Strong, Ann Louise. (1971). *Planned Urban Environments: Sweden, Finland, Israel, The Netherlands, France*. Baltimore and London: The Johns Hopkins Press.

Turner, Bengt, József Hegedüs, and Iván Tosics, eds. (1992). *The Reform of Housing in Eastern Europe and the Soviet Union*. London and New York: Routledge.

7

THE BRITISH ISLES

To the north and west of mainland Europe, and separated from it by the North Sea and the English Channel (only 21 miles or 34 km wide at the Straits of Dover), lies a group of numerous islands—the British Isles. Their total area is about 94,475 square miles (excluding inland water), or 244,755 sq km—roughly the size of Oregon. This includes the small Channel Islands—part of the United Kingdom, but south of the Channel and close to the French coast. Two large islands—Britain and Ireland—dominate the group, with Britain almost three times the size of Ireland (Fig. 7-1). With a total population of over 60 million, the group is densely populated, but there are marked variations, especially between the scantily populated uplands of the northern and western periphery in Scotland, Ireland, and Wales, and the crowded lowlands of southeast England.

The British Isles is a term that is rarely used today outside weather forecasts, for they no longer form a single, unified state. In 1921 most of the island of Ireland broke away to form the Irish Free State. This became the Republic of Ireland in 1949. Part of Ireland—six northern counties in the his-

toric province of Ulster—remained part of the United Kingdom of Great Britain and Northern Ireland. For 50 years Northern Ireland had its own separate Parliament and administration, but increasingly violent conflict between Protestants and Catholics led to the imposition of direct rule from London in 1972.

The other three countries of the United Kingdom—England, Scotland, and Wales—have been joined under one monarch since 1603. With the government and its associated institutions based in the capital city of London, England has dominated the Union—politically, economically, and culturally. However, loyalties to Scottish and Welsh culture remain strong—circa 500,000 of the 2.9 million population of Wales speak Welsh; in Scotland 80,000 still speak Gaelic (Figs. 7-2 and 3-10). Many Welsh, Scots, and Irish people retain a powerful sense of their different ethnic origins. In the 1960s and 1970s there was a strong revival of Scottish and Welsh nationalism, leading the London government to make some concessions, but genuine devolution (decentralization of political authority) has not occurred. The Welsh Language

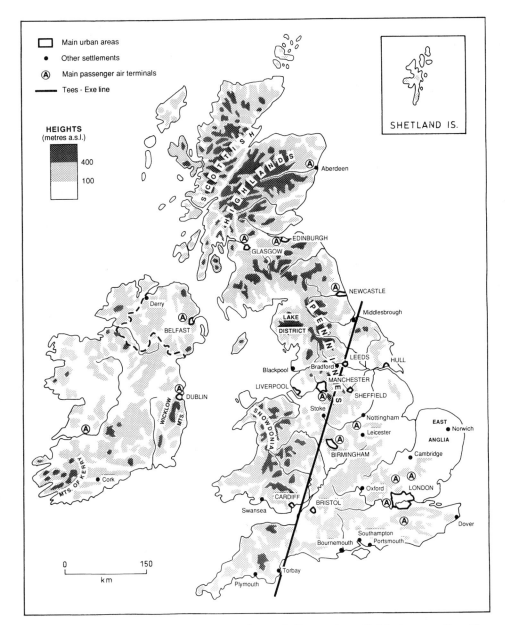

FIGURE 7-1 Orientation map of the British Isles, including major relief features, national boundaries, selected towns and cities, and main passenger airports.

Act of 1967 gave equal validity to Welsh in public administration in Wales.

The economic dominance of England, and in particular the London-centered southeast region has been reinforced by London's dominance of the national media. Radio, television, and newspapers tend to promulgate British national values, which are often strongly rooted in southern middle-class England (the notion, for example, of what is "standard English" in broadcasting terms), although

FIGURE 7-2 Anglicized and Gaelic names for a settlement in western Scotland. (W. H. Berentsen)

since the 1970s Wales has had a Welsh-language channel. Within England regional identities are often not clear-cut, and no genuine regional tier of government exists. Regional and local variations in social and economic conditions are often complex and suggest a kaleidoscope of local fortunes.

Loyalties are often strongest to localities—to cities like Newcastle-upon-Tyne (with its fanatical "Toon Army" supporting the local soccer team), to ancient counties like Cornwall (on England's southwestern peninsula), or even to tiny Rutland (officially abolished in local government reform in 1973 but still fighting a rearguard action). In some cases, the counties of England reflect administrative and sociocultural divisions that go back a thousand years.

NORTH VERSUS SOUTH

One broad regional difference in England that *has* been discernible for much of the twentieth century is that between a struggling north and a prosperous south, and the notion of a "north-south divide" in Britain achieved considerable media prominence in the 1980s. The precise location of the divide was often unclear, oscillating somewhere in midland (central) England, but sometimes defined by a southwest- to northeast-trending line from the Severn estuary (mouth of the Severn River at the boundary of southeastern

Wales and England) to the Wash (the large bay on the North Sea about 80 miles [130 km] north of London).

The north-south divide, in fact, referred to the UK as a whole, and in this sense the terms *center* and *periphery* would be more appropriate, for Scotland, Northern Ireland, and Wales are classified as part of the north (as would be the Republic of Ireland, but for its political separation). However, the opposition (and complementarity) of northern and southern England is a longer established notion, with its roots in the nineteenth-century industrialization that gave birth to the mining and manufacturing regions of the north, and produced a set of images reinforced by writers as diverse as Charles Dickens, Elizabeth Gaskell, and George Orwell and by the paintings of Turner and Lowry.

According to this stereotyping, the north became the homeland of a traditional working class and the culture associated with it—miners and mill-girls, cloth caps and fish and chips, allotments (garden plots) and pigeon-racing, beer drinking, rugby league football—and with its landscape dominated by "the dark satanic mills" of William Blake's *Jerusalem*. Elizabeth Gaskell called Lancashire "Darkshire" in one novel, and George Orwell in his celebrated exploration of "the road to Wigan Pier" (Wigan is an inland coal-mining town in Lancashire) was conscious of entering "a strange country" across some line "a little north of Birmingham." Orwell painted a striking verbal picture of his journey north in the 1930s;

> The train bore me away, through the monstrous scenery of slagheaps, chimneys, piled scrap-iron, foul canals, path of cindery mud criss-crossed by the print of clogs.... As we moved slowly through the outskirt of the town we passed row after row of little grey slum houses at right angles to the embankment. (Orwell, 1937)

The distinctive paintings of L. S. Lowry of industrial Manchester, with their "matchstalk men" and "matchstalk cats and dogs" (in the words of a recent popular song) reinforced these images of a second-class England, dominated by grimy work and industrial production. This "legendary north," peopled by the warm-hearted working class inhabiting an industrial wasteland, was set against the effete but civilized south—where the wealth was consumed, and the traditional conservative values of rural England were retained. This has become an increasingly romanticized and mythologized picture, and may bear little relation to reality, but, as we shall see, it remains true that the south retains the reins of economic and political power. Indeed, there are continuing crucial differences between the economic structures and performance of the southeastern core and the northern and western periphery of Britain.

PART OF EUROPE?

In the 1990s, the British Isles, and the UK in particular, stand at a critical juncture in their history, as they anxiously contemplate closer union with "continental" Europe. Debates about the relationship with Europe have dominated British politics in the early 1990s. The UK's dilemma can only be understood by reference to the location of the British Isles. Their geographical position has been crucial to the trajectory of past development.

Centuries ago, when the known world was centered around the Mediterranean Sea, the British Isles lay on the margins. The ancient name of Albion suggested by the white chalk cliffs of Dover on the English Channel, reminds us that they were approached, explored, subdued, and settled from mainland Europe. This marginal, even terminal, position on Europe's periphery ceased to be a disadvantage in the "long sixteenth century," when with the discovery of the Americas, Britain's Atlantic position became an opportunity to gain a dominant position in the developing world economy. Britain's development became closely tied to a worldwide Empire and dominance of global trade. Although drawn into numerous European wars (concerned with rivalry for power within the world economy), Britain remained in many respects aloof from "continental" Europe, and the countries of "the Continent" were more foreign to

the people of Britain than the more distant inhabitants of the United States or the countries of the British Commonwealth, like Australia.

When the European Community was formed in 1958, it is therefore not surprising that the UK stayed outside it. However, the loss of its hegemonic position as a Great Power by midcentury produced a gradual reassessment of its place in the world, and the UK finally joined the European Community in 1973. Ireland too threw in its lot with Europe.

In the two decades since, the UK has remained in many respects a reluctant participant in European integration. The drive toward closer European union has brought many disputes with its European partners and produced significant cleavages within British society.

The British in the 1990s find themselves drawn in two directions, and this ambivalence is exemplified in their material culture and social behavior. Thus, while more British still go to Spain for their holidays than to any other country, Florida is now the third most popular holiday destination. Many British people have second homes in France, while timeshare owners—of whom there are more than 150,000—particularly favor Spain. British high streets ("main streets") and highways are densely populated with American fast food outlets like McDonald's, Burger King, and Pizza Hut, but the British are also major consumers of European wine, yoghurt, pizza, and pasta. British cinemas and TV are still dominated by American films, but the British drive European and Asian cars. On Sunday afternoon they may tune in to watch live Italian soccer on their TVs, but increasing numbers have become avid followers of televised American football and events like the Superbowl. And while supersonic flights on Concorde aircraft in the 1970s seemed to shrink the Atlantic, bringing New York within three hours of London (and vice versa), the opening in 1994 of the Channel Tunnel, linking Britain and France by train, symbolized for many the end of separation from Europe.

This chapter introduces the geography of the British Isles, with a particular emphasis on patterns of regional development, and the diversity of fortunes of different places—regions, cities, localities. The themes of contrast and complementarity between core and periphery, north and south, run through the chapter, which begins with an introduction to the physical environment and the resource base.

THE PHYSICAL ENVIRONMENT AND RESOURCE BASE

Climate and Weather

In latitude the British Isles lie a long way north; their position is comparable to that of Labrador or northern British Columbia. They enjoy a climate, however, that is more favorable than that in any other land so far from the Equator, principally because of the influence of the North Atlantic Drift—the movement of warm water and of correspondingly warm air northeast from the Gulf Stream toward the open channel between Iceland and Norway. The existence of a continental shelf with shallow seas around Britain enhances the ameliorating effect, spreading warm water over a wide area and enabling it to exert a strong influence on the temperature of overlying air.

While the climate is *temperate*, with maritime influences keeping winter sea-level temperatures abnormally mild for the latitude, the weather exhibits great daily and year-by-year variability, albeit within a narrow band of extremes. This unpredictability (which makes the weather an obsessive topic of conversation) relates to the competing influence of tropical warm and polar cold air masses. While for most of the year the island lies wholly within the belt of westerly winds (with southwesterly winds *dominant*), the sequence of weather is determined by the passage of cyclonic storms (or depressions) formed by whirls and eddies in the atmosphere as air masses from north and south clash at the Polar Front.

In winter, a great mass of heavy, cold air lies over Eastern Europe, and British weather may be affected by cold outblowing winds; eastern Britain tends on average to be colder and drier than western parts of the island. Moisture-laden winds from the Atlantic give heavy winter precipitation on the uplands of the west. The warmest parts of the

British Isles in winter lie in southwest England, including the Scilly Isles off the southwesterly coast, with an average January temperature of 45°F, as well as in southwest Ireland. The popularity of the southern and southwestern coast of England as a destination for retirement migration —notably resorts like Bournemouth and Torbay —reflects these places' moderate temperatures. In summer, southern Britain comes under increasing influence from the high-pressure atmospheric system reigning over the Mediterranean and the Azores, and may experience long spells of fine weather. This however, is not guaranteed, and there may be summers when southern Britain lies in the track of eastward-moving storm systems, giving cool, wet weather.

In general, we can make a distinction between the drier east and wetter west, with the areas of heaviest annual rainfall (more than 60 in. [1500 mm]) on the uplands of Scotland, the Lake District of northwestern England, Wales, the Pennines in northern England, and western Ireland. Small areas in these regions may experience 200 in. (5100 mm) of precipitation annually. By contrast, lowland areas of eastern and midland England have less than 30 in. (760 mm), with only 20 in. (500 mm) in the neighborhood of the Thames estuary near London. In all parts of the British Isles, rainfall is adequate for agricultural purposes, although irrigation systems may be employed in the lowlands. However, the increase of water consumption in the densely populated south and east of England in recent years has led to concerns about the long-term sustainability of water supply and to increasing anticipation of water shortages. Such concerns were intensified by the occurrence of a severe drought sequence from 1988 to 1992, when parts of southeast England received less than 80 percent of the long-term average rainfall in a period with above-average evaporation losses. Debates about possible climatic changes related to an enhanced greenhouse effect also suggest that southeast England may become hotter and drier in summer, worsening the problem. Since the 1970s a variety of engineering schemes have been proposed, which would transfer water on an intraregional basis—for example, from upland Wales to the Thames, or from the massive Kielder reservoir in Northumberland (northern England) into Yorkshire to the south, but so far most water transfers have been more local than this.

In the far north and west, the problem for farming may be an excess of rainfall, making agriculture difficult or impossible, with waterlogging of soils and cool summer temperatures leading to crop failure. However, where relief conditions permit, the climate is conducive to the growth of grass and the support of a pastoral economy.

By global standards, the British Isles are relatively free of extreme weather events, which present hazards to life and property, but such events are not unknown. For example, in 1879 two waterspouts (tornadoes over water) destroyed the Tay railway bridge in Scotland with the loss of 79 lives, as a train plunged into the river. The great storm of October 16, 1987, which took weather forecasters by surprise, uprooted millions of trees, killed 19 people, and wreaked £1.5 billion ($2.25 billion) worth of damage.

In the 1990s the windiness of the British Isles is increasingly being viewed as an asset in the quest for new renewable energy resources. The UK has the largest potential wind-energy resource of any country in the European Union, and while it has been relatively slow (compared, say, to Denmark or the Netherlands) in pursuing this technology, the last five years have seen the development of windfarms in Cornwall, Wales, and the Pennines in particular. In some cases, the inevitable preference for highly visible upland sites has brought conflict with those anxious to preserve the quality of the upland landscape, presenting a considerable dilemma for environmentalists keen to promote renewable energy in preference to fossil-fuel-based or nuclear electricity generation. By 1994 around 20 windfarms had been constructed, but as yet wind power is making only a tiny contribution to electricity-generating capacity in the UK.

The Land

The land of Britain itself presents within a small area an amazingly rich variety of landscapes, which reflects both the diversity of the underlying geology and the strong influence of different processes in operation during the, geologically speaking, recent era of glaciation (Quaternary period). In

particular, ice sheets and glaciers have left a set of superficial deposits of rock and sand known as drift, which obscure the underlying solid rocks in large areas of lowland Britain. In the uplands ice scouring (scraping and gouging) has left sometimes bare, rocky terrain that is comparatively useless for agriculture.

The "natural landscapes" of the British Isles have played a major role in the historical pattern of human settlement—for example, influencing the position of routeways, providing defensible urban sites, and supporting the development of rich farmlands. However, in recent centuries, this relationship has often been reversed, with the natural landscape substantially modified by human impact. The draining of the great fenlands (a type of wetland) of eastern England since the sixteenth century is an obvious example, converting most of it into featureless but productive arable farmland, but no parts of the landscape remain untrammeled by the human hand, even the so-called wildernesses of the Scottish Highlands.

The preservation of the wildscapes of upland Britain has become an important theme in countryside planning and nature conservation since the 1940s, but the landscapes preserved, for example, in the 11 national parks of England and Wales are cultural rather than natural. Indeed, the most recently (1989) created such park, the lakeland of the Norfolk Broads northeast of London, which is very popular with the boating fraternity, has been shown to be a waterscape created by large-scale peat-digging in the early medieval period, and subsequent inundation. The area of open water has also declined significantly through silting (deposition of water-borne sediments) over the last century.

Within a very detailed pattern of local variation, a broad distinction can be drawn between highland and lowland zones in Great Britain. Traditionally, these zones are divided by an irregular line joining the Tees estuary on the North Sea in the northeast with that of the Exe on the English Channel in the southwest. This line approximately separates the outcrop of older (Palaeozoic era) rocks to the north and west from the younger (Mesozoic and Tertiary) rocks to the south and east. The ancient mountains of the northwest have been worn down over immense periods of geological time and now reach only modest elevations. The highest, Ben Nevis, is only somewhat more than 4500 feet high (1341 m), and they generally present rounded outlines (Fig. 7-3). The most extensive upland area, the Highlands of Scotland, forms an irregularly surfaced plateau, predominantly between about 1950 and 2925 feet (600 and 900 m). Glaciation has produced scoured and deep U-shaped valleys here and in Snowdonia (northern Wales) and the Lake District in northwestern England.

Ireland physiographically forms part of the upland zone of the British Isles, and its geological structure and divisions express continuity with those of Great Britain. A broad description that is sometimes made is of a central plain with an interrupted rim of mountains and hills. Much of the lowland center is more strictly speaking a low limestone plateau, but this is plastered with glacial deposits that have produced impeded and irregular drainage, which, combined with the moist climate, have produced huge bogs and pastures.

Distinctive in the northeastern part of the island is the basaltic lava spread of the Antrim Plateau (most famously exhibited in the Giant's Causeway); prominent uplands include the granite mass of the Wicklow Mountains in the southeast, and the sandstone ridges of Kerry and Cork (in the west) and the Mountains of Mourne (northwest).

Whereas igneous and metamorphic rocks are heavily represented in the upland zone of the British Isles, the lowlands are dominated by gently disturbed (tilted and folded) sedimentary rocks. To the south and east of the Tees–Exe line lie first the broad plains (mainly Triassic age) rocks of the English Midlands, occasionally interrupted by small remnants of older mountains (e.g., like Charnwood Forest in south central England). Much of southern England is made up of alternating low ridges and shallow valleys, though southernmost England has a bit rougher terrain, such as the Weald of Kent, Surrey, and Sussex—classic fieldwork country for the disciples of the geomorphologist William Morris Davis. The ridge country

FIGURE 7-3 Ben Nevis, the highest point in the British Isles. (W. H. Berentsen)

(scarplands) in southeast England tends to be formed of (Jurassic) limestones or the (Cretaceous) chalk. East Anglia, the stubby peninsula northeast of London, consists of a low plateau, where superficial glacial deposits for the most part obscure the underlying geology.

Eastern England's fragile coastline provides a reminder of the dynamic and transitory character of the physical environment, and recent predictions of sea-level change enhanced by global warming have intensified debates about interference with, and management of, the coast. The sea reached its present level approximately 6000 years ago, and in recent centuries, land reclamation, port construction, and the building of sea defenses have created an engineered coast that is now vulnerable to sea-level rise. Parts of the coast are also experiencing very high rates of erosion, most notably Holderness, north of East Anglia and the Humber River, where the soft boulder clay cliffs are retreating at an average rate of 9 feet (2.75 m) per annum, threatening farms, villages, and holiday resorts.

Mineral Resources

The varied geological base of the land of the British Isles—and increasingly of the seas that fringe them—has been of immense importance to economic development. In particular, the abundant coal derived from fields in northern and midland Britain provided the energy base for nineteenth-century industrialization. Since the 1960s, natural gas and oil from the North Sea have provided an immense bonus to the UK's national exchequer (Treasury), transforming the regional economy of Scotland and giving the UK—uniquely in the EU—a favorable trading balance in energy.

Coal is the UK's most abundant energy resource, and known reserves could sustain recent levels of production for perhaps 300 years, although such calculations have been rendered irrelevant as the political and economic climate has turned sharply against coal mining in the last decade. Coal reserves are located mainly in the regions of northern and western Britain—the biggest fields lie in central Scotland, northeast England,

central England (Lancashire, Yorkshire, and the East Midlands), and south Wales—but there are a scatter of smaller fields in the West Midlands and elsewhere (Fig. 7-4). Mining conditions vary considerably between fields. Historically, there has been a shift of mining in some fields, for example, Yorkshire, from shallow seams (which could be worked from the surface) toward deeper "concealed" fields, although in the recent past surface mining has again expanded and now accounts for almost one-quarter of total production.

Initially, the most successful fields were coastal, exploiting their potential for export and coastal shipment of "seacoal" to major urban markets, especially London. In the twentieth century, however, the inland fields of Yorkshire and the Midlands became increasingly dominant, based on more favorable geological conditions for automated deep mining and the development of large-scale electricity generation, which by the 1960s had become the dominant market.

In 1947 the coal industry was taken into public ownership, a symbolic moment for the British labor movement, but the problems of labor relations in the industry remained. Coal began to lose ground to oil in energy markets, and although the oil crises of the 1970s brought some respite, the decline gathered pace in the 1980s, especially after the year-long strike of 1984–1985, which failed in its attempt to preserve miners' jobs. In the 1970s the National Coal Board invested heavily in new equipment, and "greenfield" mines (those in quite new regions) were sunk in central England (at Selby, Yorkshire, and Asfordby, Leicestershire). These mines survive as the core of a shrunken industry that returned to the private sector in 1995. Coal's problems in retaining a place in the market have been compounded by the rise of natural gas in electricity generation since 1990, and the growth of coal imports from countries like the United States and Colombia, but an increasingly significant underlying problem has been the growing pressure from Europe to reduce sulphurous emissions from burning coal. The UK's largest coal-fired power station (Drax in Yorkshire, 4000 MW) has been fitted with desulphurization equipment, but most other plants rely on less effective technology.

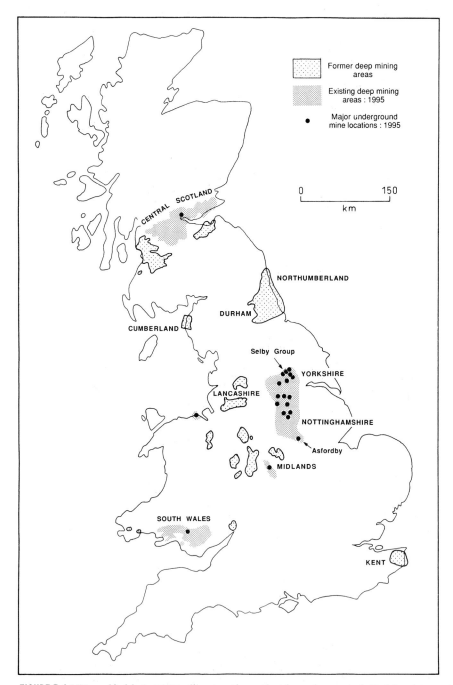

FIGURE 7-4 UK coalfields in 1995, showing those that have been exploited by deep mining in the recent past. Note that surface mining continues in several areas.

In 1994 coal production totaled only 75 million tons (68 million metric tons). The workforce of less than 20,000 in 1994 compared, incredibly, with 1 million in 1913, when 322 million tons were produced. Many coalfields are no longer worked, and some preserve underground mines only as part of the heritage industry.

Until the 1960s the UK's oil supplies came mostly from large-scale imports (the basis for a set of major coastal refineries), and gas supply was based on the manufacture of gas from coal, or on imports of liquid methane from Algeria. This position has been drastically altered with the development of hydrocarbon supplies from sedimentary rock in the North Sea (Fig. 5-5). Interest in the potential of these (Permian age) geologic structures followed the exploitation of natural gas in the Netherlands after 1959. The first North Sea gasfield to be discovered was West Sole in 1965; oil was discovered in 1970 and first landed from the Forties field in 1975. It was particularly fortunate for the UK that in 1964 it had ratified the 1958 Law of the Sea, which divided offshore areas along median lines (demarcating equal distances to the nearest landfalls), giving the UK an important share of the productive fields associated with the central region of the North Sea (in grabens, or rift structures).

The North Sea is a relatively high-cost area for hydrocarbon production by global standards, but the hikes in the oil price on world markets in the 1970s, related to geopolitical pressures from OPEC, ensured its viability. Initially, development was concentrated in the gasfields off the east central English coast (Norfolk and Humberside) in the southern North Sea, in the comparatively shallow waters of Great Britain's continental shelf. The focus of development then shifted northward to the deeper waters off eastern Scotland and the Shetland Islands. Here oilfield development was linked especially to the growth of Aberdeen as an oil supply base, but terminals for pipelines and tankers were also constructed at Peterhead and on the offshore islands of Orkney and Shetland, at Flotta and Sullom Voe. Although in the 1970s the UK government established the British National Oil Corporation, this experiment proved short-

lived, and the development of the North Sea oil province has been undertaken mainly by the private sector.

In the 1980s a new phase of development began in the southern North Sea with the discovery of additional gasfields, but attention has also shifted to the waters west of Shetland. Since 1993 important new discoveries have been announced by British Petroleum (BP) in this area, which presents particularly hostile conditions (deeper water and stormy weather) for offshore production. BP plans to use technologies tested in the deep-water fields of the Gulf of Mexico. Other parts of Britain's fringing seas have also attracted attention, with some gasfield development in the Irish Sea. There are also some onshore developments, of which Wytch Farm Oilfield in Dorset in southwestern England is the only one comparable in size to the larger North Sea fields.

The scale of the oil and gas resources of the North Sea province has been the subject of considerable debate and of a wide range of estimates. In the early days official forecasts suggested that oil production might peak by 1982 and then decline quickly, but this has proven pessimistic. Although the industry has suffered occasional setbacks (e.g., the Piper Alpha oil platform disaster in 1988 in which explosion and fire led to the loss of 166 lives), producing temporary reduction in output, oil production reached a new peak in 1994 of 140 million tons (127 million metric tons), and the predicted decline is likely to be slower than originally anticipated. Total remaining reserves of oil are 2288 million tons, and of gas over 20 trillion cubic feet (1.91 trillion cubic meters). In total, 93 oilfields (73 offshore) and 56 gasfields (53 offshore) have been developed, and some of the early fields are now in decline. Seasonal demand for gas (which is used especially in the domestic market) is managed in part by storing gas pumped from more northerly fields into a depleted field off eastern England. Gas production has grown by over 50 percent since 1989, reaching nearly 750 cubic billion cubic feet (70 billion cubic meters) in 1994.

The geology of the British Isles and their fringing seas has given the UK the most balanced energy resource base in Europe outside the former

USSR. The UK still has abundant reserves of coal, which now seem unlikely to be exploited; the oil and natural gas resources available in the North Sea are rivaled only by those of Norway. As the world moves towards an era of new energy technologies, it is also well placed for the exploitation of renewable energy resources. Hydroelectric power has been successfully exploited in the past, particularly in Scotland and in Ireland on the River Shannon, but there is relatively little potential for further large-scale development. However, geographical conditions are particularly suitable for the development of tidal power. The large tidal range and the availability of numerous river mouth (estuarine) sites give considerable potential, and a number of schemes have been put forward, of which the most dramatic would be a Severn barrage (dam) linking England and Wales across the Bristol Channel on the countries' southern border. This has the potential generating capacity of five conventional thermal power stations. The impediments to development here and elsewhere are considerable, however, and reflect the significance of the estuaries for nature conservation. Bodies like the Royal Society for the Protection of Birds (with nearly one million members) are strongly opposed to estuary development. Wave power is another possibility in the longer term, either offshore or at coastal sites (there is a small prototype station on Islay off the west coast of Scotland), while the potential of wind power has already been noted.

The enormous contribution of the energy minerals should not obscure the fact that the geological variety of the British Isles has provided the base for many other mineral industries that have played (and still do play) an important part in economic development. In tonnage, the largest volume of mineral production in the modern UK comes from those industries that supply the copious amounts of construction materials required by the modern economy (for buildings and roads especially), although these industries—sand and gravel, limestone, igneous rock—have never remotely approached the employment generated by the coal industry. In the postwar period, the volume of output of construction materials has grown rapidly. The relatively low value of many of these materials means that production is often close to major urban centers in order to reduce transport costs, and this sometimes produces conflicts of interest with agriculture, housing, recreation, and other urban fringe developments. This is true, for example, of the extensive workings of gravel pits along the Thames in the London Basin. Upland areas of great landscape quality have often become the target for mineral developers, leading to conflict with conservation groups. Some of the minerals, like limestone, are also raw materials for a wide range of industries besides construction. For example, the high-quality limestone of the Peak District (in central England) and Yorkshire Dales National Parks (east central England) is exploited on a scale that many would see as inappropriate in areas set aside "for the preservation and enhancement of natural beauty", and "for encouraging the provision...of facilities for the enjoyment thereof."[1] A substantial new source of demand for limestone emerged in the 1990s with the installation of scrubbers at some power stations.

By contrast, the production of metallic minerals has declined significantly. In the nineteenth century the older rocks of upland Britain were exploited on a large scale for copper, tin, lead, and zinc. Cornwall at one time supplied 50 percent of world copper production. These industries declined swiftly with competition from low-cost overseas areas. Cornish copper production disappeared completely, but tin lingered on a small scale and actually experienced a revival of interest in the 1970s when uncertainties on world markets and political instability led some international companies to re-focus their interest on locations in the "safe havens" of developed countries. However, the collapse of world tin prices in the 1980s squashed the revival; by 1995 only a single mine survived.

Another industry now much in decline is iron ore, where the low quality of domestic ores increasingly offsets its transport cost advantage. Imports overtook domestic output in the 1960s. It should not be overlooked, however, that domestic ores played a key role in the historical development of the iron and steel industry and its loca-

---

[1] as prescribed by the 1949 National Parks and Access to the Countryside Act.

tional shifts. Initially, the presence of ores played a considerable part in coalfield industrialization, while from the 1840s the discovery of (Jurassic age) deposits in a variety of locations in central England from Yorkshire to Oxfordshire underpinned the development of the iron and steel industry in many areas, including new towns (at Middlesborough, Scunthorpe, and Corby). Scunthorpe's development from the 1850s in east central England was due to the presence of what one geographer described as "the worst iron ore field in the world" (with an iron content of only 20 to 22%) (Pocock, 1963); despite contraction in the 1980s, it remains one of the four great centers of British steel production. The major source of ore for this area (as in the steel industry generally) is now imports.

Mineral production has had considerable impact on Britain's landscape. Surface mines for common minerals have been widely scattered so that the landscape from the air often appears pockmarked. Locally concentrated areas of dereliction have been left. Large-scale working of china clay in southwestern England in Cornwall (and to a lesser extent Devon), has produced an extraordinary landscape of conical white sand heaps and deep blue-green pools, sometimes described as the Cornish Alps. In north Wales the vast slate quarries and even vaster waste heaps have considerably altered the natural landscape of Snowdonia. The concentration of brickworks in the Oxford region (around Peterborough, Bedford, and Bletchley) has also presented a formidable challenge for restoration and landuse planning. Thus, while the exploitation of minerals has in the past often transformed regional and local growth patterns, in the postwar period it has presented an increasing challenge in reconciling the demands of a growing industrial economy with the desire to protect open space and preserve landscape quality. Arguments about the expansion of mineral exploitation in the UK's national parks since the 1960s—potash in North Yorkshire, limestone and fluorspar in the Peak District, china clay on Dartmoor (southwestern England), gold in Snowdonia (north Wales)— were the front-line of a much broader struggle between developers and environmentalists, which continually resurfaces. Because many of these upland areas in peripheral Britain have very limit-

ed economic opportunities, the argument is sometimes presented as jobs *versus* scenery, with some local people resenting what they see as interference by middle-class conservationists based elsewhere. In 1994, for example, proposals for a massive stone quarry on the Hebridean island of Harris bitterly divided the local population, while the pressure for surface coal sites (despite the decline of deep mining) continues to arouse strong emotions in affected communities in Yorkshire, the Midlands, and northeast England.

INFRASTRUCTURE

Transport and Communications

Transport infrastructure is a vital element in a country's economic development, while in the informational society traditional forms of communication like mail service have been complemented (and to some extent are supplanted) by computer-based networks. Britain has a digital telephone network (completed in 1988) and a national system of data highways.

Over a long period, transportation investments and improvements have reduced journey times, and increased time-space convergence (i.e., reduced the amount of time required to traverse distance). This process has continued to the present day through developments such as rail electrification on selected routes like the east coast mainline from London to Edinburgh. The impact of such processes has tended to reinforce the advantages of the major cities, drawn closer together by high-speed rail and road routes. London is the hub of the national network, as well as the fulcrum for international travel through the UK's major airports. London's airports, dominated by Heathrow and Gatwick, carry approximately 65 percent of UK air traffic. In the 1960s the pruning of the rail network increased the comparative disadvantage of many peripheral rural areas, which lost their railway connections, while the construction of the motorway network (now about 1850 miles or nearly 3000 km) also tended to be to the advantage of the country's core areas. The M25 (Motorway (or Highway) number 25), completed in the 1980s, encircling London, is the most heavily used road in the UK. It carries 14 percent of all highway traffic and has already exceeded its design capacity.

Although its potential influence on regional development patterns is still debated, the opening of the Channel Tunnel in 1993, linking England and France by rail, would appear to reinforce the advantages of southeast England (Fig. 7-5). This huge engineering project—at a cost of about $11.5 billion (£7.5 billion), the largest ever undertaken in Europe—is producing significant time-space convergence between some of Europe's major capital cities. Although Britain has been slow to develop high-speed links between the Tunnel and London, with serious disputes over route alignment, journey times from London to Paris are down to three hours. The Tunnel, which was financed by the private sector, carries through services as well as shuttle trains onto which cars are loaded for the short international transfer. This development is probably the most momentous single infrastructure project undertaken in the UK in the postwar period and carries enormous significance in the UK's reorientation toward Europe.

Recent years have been characterized by the increasing domination of the British transport scene by motor vehicles and by the decline of public transport. In the last decade the government's em-

FIGURE 7-5 The Channel Tunnel road-rail interchange. The town of Folkstone, Kent, is visible. (Photo by permission of Q. A. Photos Ltd.)

phasis on privatization and deregulation has obviously been influential, but its neglect of public transport services is of much longer standing, especially that of the railways, where apart from the intercity high-speed services the quality and competitiveness of the system have declined. Transfer to the private sector looms. Transport of freight is now dominated by heavy-goods road vehicles. Together with the rise of car ownership and use, this shift is now coming home to roost in terms of traffic congestion, environmental problems, and conflict over road-building programs.

In the 1980s the number of cars in the UK grew by over one-third (there are now over 21 million) and traffic volume by over 60 percent. Use of the private car remains a powerful expression of consumer preference and status, and the pro-car lobbies wield huge political influence. Controversy over new road construction came to a head with the spirited but ultimately unsuccessful attempts by environmentalists to prevent the carving of a huge swathe for the M3 highway across the beautiful chalklands of Twyford Down, near Winchester west of London. The protestors may have lost this particular battle, but the war between motor vehicle and environmental interests is not yet over.

The environmental problems associated with the growth of car and truck use are most acute in the cities, where air pollution has become a serious issue, and pollutant levels often exceed the thresholds identified as harmful to health. A few cities have begun to invest in light-rail schemes to combat congestion and pollution, notably Manchester, with its Metrolink network, Sheffield, with its "Supertram," and Newcastle. But in London comparatively little headway has been made outside Docklands, and the absence of a proper citywide government makes integrated new initiatives difficult. Car movement dominates in London, accounting for over 50 percent of journeys, while the railways and underground network are severely overcrowded on many lines into the central area. London is still the major European city for financial services, but because of the problems of traffic congestion and pollution, there is a risk that it will become increasingly less attractive for investment compared to its European rivals.

Congestion has been an increasing problem at London's major airports, especially at Heathrow to the west, and recent years have seen more rapid growth of traffic at its subsidiary airports, particularly Stansted to the north. In the provinces, Manchester has emerged as the third major international gateway in the UK (behind London's Heathrow and Gatwick), and Birmingham has also made major strides, in conjunction with its growing role as an international conference and exhibition center.

Changes are also evident in the port system. Many of the older docklands have declined as traffic has moved to deeper water terminals or shifted to new routes, and new elements have been added in the form of container terminals and North Sea oil jetties. The major regional shift has been toward the "south east angle" and the short sea routes to Europe (e.g., at Felixstowe in Suffolk northeast of London), while ports in the west like Liverpool have tended to decline, particularly where much of their trade had been based on the colonial links of the past.

Energy

Another vital support to the UK economy has been the development of its commercial energy system. As we have already seen, the UK possesses a particularly rich and varied resource base, with its abundant reserves providing the historic basis for industrialization and the gas and oil wealth of the continental shelf producing a completely new dimension to the country's economic geography from the mid-1960s onward. These fossil-fuel sources, especially coal, have provided the foundation for the UK's electricity supply system (Fig. 7-6). The demand for electricity has grown at an average rate of 2.7 percent per annum since 1960.

Until 1989 the electricity industry was in public ownership, and the Central Electricity Generating Board (in England and Wales) planned a strongly integrated system for electricity production, transmission, and distribution to consumers. In the 1960s major investments were begun in large coal- and oil-fired plants, the former principally in coal-field locations in Yorkshire and the East Midlands. The last and largest of these, Drax (4000 MW), was not completed until the 1980s, by which time coal accounted for over 70 percent of electricity genera-

tion. However, a major rival for coal was developing in the form of nuclear power.

The nuclear industry in its initial phase of development linked the civilian use of "atoms for peace," with its promise of cheap, clean, unlimited electricity, and the military need for plutonium for nuclear weaponry. In the 1950s a set of eight "Magnox" nuclear power stations were constructed, which in the 1990s have begun to be phased out of production and decommissioned. A second round of six Advanced Gas-cooled Reactors (AGRs) followed in the late 1960s; these were larger but suffered from major construction problems and cost overruns. Most of the nuclear stations are in coastal locations, and many are in the coal-deficient south of England. In 1979 the new Conservative government of Margaret Thatcher announced a major expansion of nuclear power. It was motivated both by faith in the technology and by the desire to reduce the power of the National Union of Mineworkers, whose strikes in the early 1970s had helped bring down an earlier Conservative administration. The expansion was to be based on the Pressurized Water Reactor (PWR), with 10 new stations to be constructed over the next decade. The reality, however, proved very different. Lengthy planning inquiries and delays in obtaining permits, added to the bad publicity the industry received from Chernobyl, but above all to the growing doubts about the financial basis of the industry, have meant that only one new station has been built. Sizewell B in Suffolk finally opened in 1995, 14 years after it had been first proposed. Thus, although nuclear power's share of electricity production in the UK has now risen to 26 percent, this proportion is almost certain to decline as older stations close.

In the 1980s the problems of waste disposal and reprocessing spent fuel became the industry's Achilles' heel. Although in 1978 a major expansion of reprocessing facilities was begun in northwest England at Sellafield, the difficulties of finding sites for waste dumps mounted. Contamination of local beaches at Sellafield and fears about potential health hazards (including possible links to local child cancer clusters) did little to help the nuclear industry's cause with the general public. In 1993 the thermal oxide reprocessing plant (THORP) at Sellafield was finally completed, leading to fresh

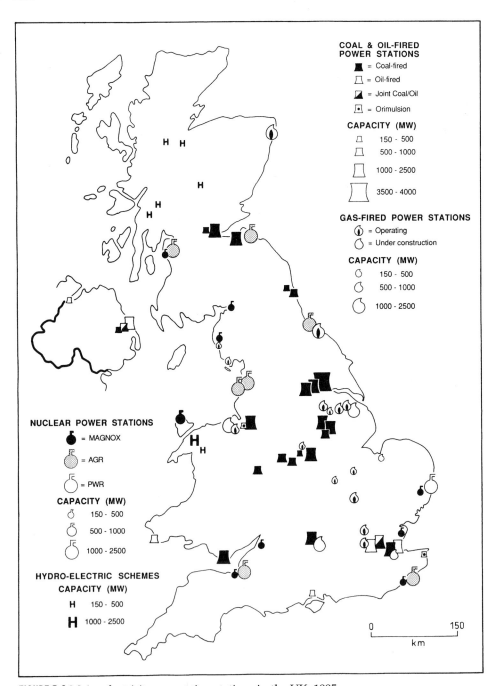

FIGURE 7-6 Major electricity-generating stations in the UK, 1995.

disputes over whether it should be allowed to operate. This facility has global significance, for it handles Japanese and German, as well as British, waste.

The problems of nuclear power in the UK crystallized in 1989 when the decision was made to withdraw the industry from electricity privatization because of the financial risks involved. Nuclear power has remained in public ownership and has continued to benefit from subsidies, although privatization was again proposed in 1995.

The privatization of electrical production in 1989 has had another significant impact on the geography of electricity generation, with the new private companies "dashing for gas." Since 1990, 20 combined-cycle natural gas-fired plants have been constructed (most are already complete), and by 1994 gas had taken 12 percent of the electricity market. Gas-fired stations are seen to offer advantages in lower outputs of greenhouse gases and help the new companies to attain targets for emission reductions; they are also cheaper and quicker to build. The rise of gas in electricity generation is *the* major new feature of the energy map of the 1990s and is accelerating the shift away from coal. Some government forecasts suggest that gas may eventually take at least 50 percent of the electricity market.

THE PEOPLE

The British Isles is among the most densely populated and urbanized parts of the world, but geographical patterns are highly variable. There is an obvious contrast between the UK, the third most densely populated country in the EU, and the Republic of Ireland, one of the least densely populated. But *within* the UK there are also great variations, which bear some broad relation to the underlying pattern of highland, upland, and lowland, though considerably adapted and distorted by the history of industrial development. Some highland areas in Scotland are relatively empty of people, whereas at the other extreme areas like London are highly congested. Despite dense population, 80 percent of the land is still devoted to agriculture, and an efficient farming industry produces over 60 percent of the nation's food requirements.

Since the mid-nineteenth century, the UK has been classified as an urban country, and by the 1990s 90 percent of its population were living in urban areas. Precise definition of urban populations is difficult because administrative boundaries used for statistical purposes often bear little relation to the functional realities of urban life.

However, any method of definition indicates that London is far and away the largest city. The metropolitan area defined as Greater London has a population of 6.9 million, about 14 percent of the population of England. Three other metropolitan areas—the West Midlands (focused on Birmingham), Greater Manchester, and West Yorkshire (focused on Leeds-Bradford)—each have populations of over 2 million. If we define cities in local labor market terms, we find that there are four cities in the UK with populations in excess of 1 million—London, Birmingham, Glasgow, and Manchester.

During recent decades, the population of the UK has grown slowly, but this conceals significant geographical and compositional changes. Geographers Tony Champion and Alan Townsend have identified three particularly important geographical trends in the second half of the twentieth century: the change in balance between north and south, the urban to rural shift, and suburbanization and metropolitan decentralization.

First, the "drift to the south" is a phrase that has often been used to describe geographical changes in twentieth-century Britain and is sometimes challenged as imprecise or even misleading. Nevertheless, it is true that the dominant movement of population and employment for at least half a century has been from north to south, reversing the trends established during nineteenth-century industrialization. The dominance of the national capital, London, and the rich agricultural lowlands of the south and east, a dominance which existed before 1750, has been reasserted. The movement of people into the Midlands and south slackened in the 1960s and 1970s, but reemerged in the 1980s—reopening the north-south divide. It is also evident that the renewed strong growth of the southeast in particular has been based in part on selective migration of younger and better qualified people from the less dynamic north.

The second phenomenon, the urban-rural shift, has been occurring widely in the Western world—the tendency for small cities, towns, and rural areas to grow at the expense of large cities. In the UK the large cities have generally experienced large population losses over the last 40 years. This "counter-urbanization" has led to population growth in the more remote and rural regions, and has been the most dramatic change in the UK's population distribution in the last 30 years, al-though it waned somewhat in the 1980s. It was stimulated in part by the development of New Town and overspill policies for the large cities, while the baby boom of postwar Britain worked its way through into greater demands for family-sized housing with lawn and garden space, which were often satisfied in ex-urban locations with attractive residential environments. Much of the basis for the shift, however, was a locational change in the availability of jobs, as we shall see.

The third phenomenon—the flight from the inner urban core to the suburbs and the city fringe —is a longer-standing trend, and has been stimu-lated in postwar Britain by slum clearance and re-housing policies, the decline of inner-city industry and jobs, and the desire to escape an unattractive physical and social environment. Tight planning controls and the protection of Green Belts around many cities have often pushed suburbanization into counter-urbanization.

Since the 1980s, both suburbanization and counter-urbanization have appeared to slacken as policies have been introduced to support inner-city development, as the New Towns Program was wound up, and as young professional populations have begun to colonize a few favored and newly fashionable inner-city districts. Thus, paradoxical-ly, back to the countryside and back to the city movements have been occurring simultaneously.

Nevertheless, the most striking feature of change in the population distribution in Britain in the 1980s was the high growth rate in the rural south, espe-cially in "Roseland" (the rest of southeast England outside London) (Fig. 7-7). Counties in an arc from Norfolk in the northeast to Dorset in the southwest grew most rapidly in population, with Cambridge-shire north of London leading the group between 1981 and 1992, adding 15 percent. This area com-bined the gains from both north-south and urban-rural shifts. In the north, rural areas have not grown as rapidly as their southern counterparts, although they have been more dynamic than the urban areas.

Alongside these geographical changes have been interconnected changes in the composition of the population. There has been a substantial growth, for example, of the elderly and retired component. In some coastal communities in south-ern England, over 30 percent of the population is

of pensionable age. The most momentous change, however, has been the growth of the "nonwhite" ethnic minorities, and the decline of the "white" population of the UK (reflecting in part a decline in the birth rate). In 1951 only about 200,000 inhabi-tants of the UK belonged to ethnic minorities; by 1991 there were 3 million (5.5% of the population).

The main period of immigration of these groups was the 1950s and early 1960s, when it was encouraged by labor shortages in some areas, es-pecially in poorly paid manual work in traditional industries like textiles and in many urban services. The major sources of immigrants were former colonial territories in the New Commonwealth countries, a potent reminder of Britain's imperial past. Although the 1962 changes in the UK's immi-gration policy reduced the flow, the relatively high birth rates among the ethnic minority groups have enabled them to increase their share of the nation-al population. There were also important infusions of refugees from East Africa in the late 1960s and early 1970s.

The largest concentration of ethnic groups is of South Asian origin, with 49 percent in 1991 from India, Pakistan, and Bangladesh, and another 17 percent from the West Indies. The ethnic minori-ties are highly concentrated spatially, with over two-thirds living in England's four largest metro-politan areas; particularly heavy clusters are found in the central English urban centers of Birming-ham, Bradford, and Leicester (where one in five household heads are from an ethnic minority) and in parts of inner London. By contrast, in most rur-al areas ethnic minorities form less than 1 percent of the population. These patterns reflect the origi-nal availability of work and of low-cost housing, but they have been reinforced by direct or indirect racial discrimination. All low-income groups in cities face considerable obstacles to dispersion into suburban environments, but these obstacles are undoubtedly greater for ethnic minorities.

"Blacks" are often disadvantaged and discrimi-nated against in the housing and labor markets, and have become clustered in urban ghettos where unemployment, crime, and drug abuse fes-ter. From the Notting Hill riots of 1958 in London to the widespread urban disturbances of the early 1980s, the failures of integration are depressingly evident. The pattern of geographical segregation

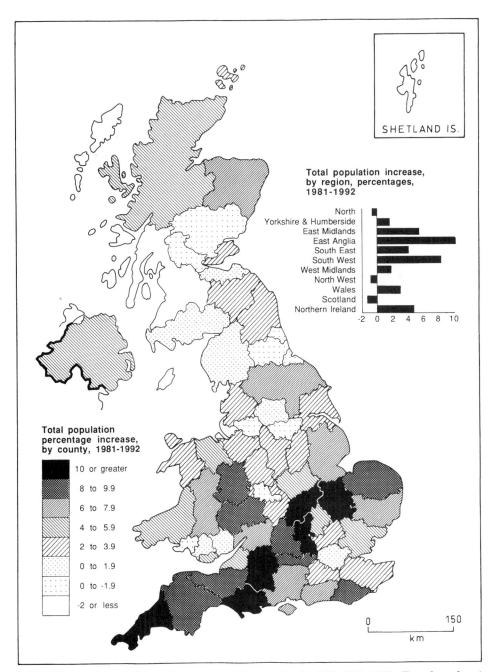

FIGURE 7-7 Population change by county and region in the UK, 1981–1992. (Based on data in Ordnance Survey's *Statlas UK*)

that has developed undoubtedly has restricted the labor market opportunities and life chances of people from ethnic minorities, especially given the

changes in location of economic activities that have been taking place. Yet the development of substantial "nonwhite" populations has added

FIGURE 7-8 The Notting Hill Carnival, South London, a graphic reminder of the multi-racial nature of many British cities. (Photo by permission of M. Knobil)

greatly to the diversity and vitality of British culture, as events such as the annual Notting Hill Carnival show, while "blacks" make a major contribution to many aspects of public life such as professional sport and entertainment (Fig. 7-8). And on the streets of British towns, numerous Asian restaurants and take-out food outlets are an ever-present and pervasive reminder both of the imperial past and the multicultural present.

MODERN BRITAIN: THE EMERGENCE OF A CENTER-PERIPHERY PATTERN AND REGIONAL INTERVENTION

In the twentieth century Britain's decline from Great Power status has been accompanied by significant changes in the relationship of its economy to that of the wider world; these changes have pro-

duced significant shifts in its internal geography. The center-periphery pattern that began to emerge in the interwar period, and that became most evident by the 1950s and 1960s, was linked to changes in the international division of labor and to shifts in national sectoral employment patterns.

The origins of the regional problem that was first starkly manifest in the interwar depression lay in the decline of Britain's imperial power and the loss of its ability to dominate world markets. The First World War acted as a catalyst to these changes. It left major industries such as shipbuilding with gross overcapacity; the capacity of the world's merchant shipyards had doubled during the war. In 1920 the UK's expanded shipyards built over 2 million gross tons, but by 1923 only 660,000 tons. Coal, iron and steel, machinery, ships and textiles accounted for two-thirds of exports in 1913. Coal and steel exporters faced new competition. The industries of the old order were in disarray.

In the nineteenth century, industrial development had been associated with considerable regional and local specialization; regions and towns were often dominated by a narrow range of industries. Such regions were over-committed to particular economic activities now in decline, leading to intense problems of unemployment. Particularly important in the former scheme of things had been the coastal coalfields—especially Northumberland and Durham in northern England, south Wales, and central Scotland—looking outward to export markets. These coalfields now became the focus of depression and unemployment. In some regions unemployment exceeded 20 percent of the workforce, but locally rates were much higher. In small towns like Jarrow, a shipyard town on northern England's River Tyne, or Merthyr Tydfil in the south Wales coalfield, unemployment at its worst was well over 50 percent. Unemployment was, in fact, a serious problem in *all* regions in this period, but in relative terms it was much less acute in the southeast.

The new industries—engineering, vehicles, and consumer-goods manufacturing—were developing in this period according to a different locational logic. These industries were initially based on the internal market rather than exports; the distribution of the national population, dominated by the metropolitan area of London, gave particular advantage to southern and especially midland locations. A factory 70 miles (113 km) northwest of London might be within 80 miles (129 km) of half the national market. The new industries were also based on electric power—the establishment of a national power grid in 1926 meant that there was little difference in costs between locations. Moreover, many of the new industries grew out of the more varied and flexible industrial base of the Midlands and southeast, where small-scale engineering and metal-working firms had developed a richer entrepreneurial tradition than in the peripheral coalfields dominated by a few large companies. Sometimes there was an element of chance in the origins of new industry; it was fortuitous that William Morris's original bicycle shop was located in Oxford in the South Midlands. Oxford, however, proved to be a particularly appropriate central location for the development of Morris' car manufacturing. Auto manufacturing was particularly important as it began to develop as an assembly industry along Fordist lines (i.e., in big assembly-line plants). Car manufacturing generated a large multiplier effect on other industries (i.e., it generated still more jobs) and led to the development of the external economies of agglomeration (benefits of spatial concentration), both of which promoted further economic growth in the Midlands.

London already dominated the national economic space. By 1800 it had become the largest city in Europe (with 900,000 people). Before the First World War, it had the largest concentration of market-oriented industries producing for final consumer demand, such as clothing and furniture, often tightly packed in specialized quarters or districts close to the City of London. It was already the greatest service and retail center; the presence of the court, government institutions, and the like ensured that it would have the greatest concentration of wealth and consumption. It is sometimes suggested that the emergence of depressed areas in the 1930s in peripheral Britain represented a *reversal* of the geography of inequality. This is a fallacious theory. Even in the heyday of the coalfields, their relationship to London and the southeast was a subordinate one. During the depression of the 1930s, London's historically pre-eminent position increased.

Foreign investment, especially American, also played an important role as a catalyst to industrial growth in the London area in the interwar period. U.S. companies seeking a place in the British market often established themselves in the southeast. Especially popular were districts in the suburban zone between 5 and 15 miles (8 to 24 km) from central London along major highways (places like Chiswick and Wembley).

J. B. Priestley's *English Journey* in 1934 took him down the Great West Road outside London, and he provides a wonderful description of the appearance of this new industrial landscape to someone brought up in Bradford in the industrial north:

> After the familiar muddle of West London, the Great West Road looked very odd. Being new, it did not look English. We might have suddenly rolled into California. Or, for that matter into one of the main avenues of the old exhibitions, like the Franco-British Exhibition of my boyhood. It was the line of new factories on each side that suggested the Exhibition, for years of the West Riding have fixed forever my idea of what a proper factory looks like; a grim blackened rectangle with a tall chimney at the corner. These decorative little buildings, all glass and concrete and chromium plate, seem to my barbaric mind to be merely playing at being factories.... Actually I know, they are tangible evidence, most cunningly arranged to take the eye, to prove that the new industries have moved south. They also prove that there *are* new enterprises to move south. You notice them decorating the western borders of London. At night they look as exciting as Blackpool [a major British vacation destination].

Many of these firms had not in fact "moved south," but were from overseas—Gillette, Firestone, and other U.S. companies. They increased the innovative base of the southeast and reinforced the upward spiral of growth. One significant shift southward, however, was the American Ford Motor Company, which moved from Trafford Park in Manchester to open a major new plant at Dagenham, east of London on the Thames estuary.

The interwar period saw the formation of the effective area or axial belt of twentieth-century

Britain (sometimes described as coffin-shaped)—the core of the British economy, dominated by Greater London. The outer limits of this heartland were perhaps reached in a line linking the Wash, Manchester, Bristol, Southampton, and lower Thames. This zone had the highest economic potential now that the distribution of consumer income had replaced mineral resources as the key location factor. Later, some geographers thought this area suggested the development of a British megalopolis, a set of overlapping metropolitan areas on the model of the northeast seaboard of the United States, with the highways built from the 1950s onward acting as its main streets.

Beyond the core lay the disadvantaged periphery, including the islands of industrial depression in the coalfields and specialized manufacturing zones, but also extensive upland areas, facing declining labor requirements for agriculture and a lack of alternative employment opportunities. Many of these areas had already suffered a severe hemorrhage of outmigration in the nineteenth century. Ireland formed an integral part of this periphery. These areas faced an even greater comparative disadvantage in the twentieth century. The size of local communities made it difficult to support a range of services, and distance from the center of the national market militated against the development of new industries. Paradoxically, as transport links began to improve, the protection afforded by distance from larger scale, more efficient competitors was eroded, leading to the decline or extinction of local, small-scale, traditional industries. Within the peripheral areas, seasonal inactivity was also a problem in coastal holiday resorts—a problem that affected towns in southern and eastern England too.

These problems of uneven development and acute depression in the interwar period led to government attempts to intervene to ameliorate the situation. The new Labour party drew much of its growing support from the working-class communities of northern England, Wales, and Scotland. The Conservatives, the party in power for most of the period, became concerned by the potential emergence of "Two Nations" that weakened their power base and might even threaten national stability. The march in 1936 of unemployed shipyard workers from Jarrow to London (almost 300 miles [485 km]) to publicize their plight, attracted considerable attention and alerted the government to the acuteness of the situation.

As early as 1928, a scheme had been established to help the unemployed migrate to new opportunities. The weakness of this approach was that even the more successful regions like the southeast had substantial reserves of unemployed labor. From 1934 on, the emphasis shifted to moving work to the workers; this principle has underlain most regional policies ever since. Four areas were identified as Special Areas, where financial assistance was available to support new industries. Predictably, they were the coastal coalfields, including the small Cumberland coalfield in northwest England. Industrial parks were established with government money, the most famous at Team Valley in northeast England. Although some new industries were established, the impact on unemployment was only modest, especially because many of the jobs in new light industries were for newly employed women rather than unemployed male miners or shipyard workers. However, the approach of world war and the need for rearmament led to a revival in the economies of the depressed areas, which also received a substantial boost during the war itself from the strategic dispersal of industry away from southeast England to avoid German bombing.

Shortly before the war, the government had set up a Royal Commission to investigate the problems of the growth of London and its dominance of the distribution of population. The Barlow Report that resulted in 1940 laid out the directions for much postwar regional and urban policy; the report favored restraint of London's physical expansion, decentralization of population and industry, and a quest for greater regional balance. In 1945 a reforming Labour government was elected and set about zealously to build a better, fairer Britain, committed to full employment and greater social equity. This was a time of dramatic innovation in many fields. Industries like coal were taken into public ownership, New Towns were established to decant population from London, the basis of the postwar town and country planning system was established, and the principle of free medical attention for all was enshrined in a new National Health Service. A strong commitment to regional policy was evident, and the dispersal of industry to the less successful regions, now renamed Development Areas, was aided by the drive to reestablish a peacetime economy. Measures were taken for the first time to control industrial expansion in the southeast by issuing Industrial Development Certificates. This action, combined with the use of financial incentives, produced a high level of industrial mobility.

Although the postwar energy for reform was soon dissipated and the enthusiasm for regional policy slackened, the problems of regional inequality did not seem particularly serious in the boom years of the 1950s, when as Conservative Prime Minister Harold Macmillan reminded the voters, the British had "never had it so good." The high level of demand for coal masked the problems of the coalfield regions. Changes were taking place, however, in the structure of the national economy, which had serious potential implications, in particular the growing relative importance of the service sector. The southeast continued to benefit from this growth in the 1950s and 1960s,—notably in professional and financial services, government institutions, and business headquarters—while investments in infrastructure, especially transport, were continuing to reinforce the advantages of the axial belt over the periphery. The development of air services, particularly international flights, was heavily concentrated at London's Heathrow airport. The construction of the highway network brought particular benefits to the central sites on the southeast-northwest trending London-Midlands-Lancashire axis, while the rationalization of the railways in the 1960s axed many lines in peripheral rural areas and focused services on an intercity network. The comparative disadvantage of the periphery intensified.

Beginning in the late 1950s, the problems of the peripheral regions again became apparent, and regional policy was reactivated. Britain's failure to modernize its industrial base was leading to renewed problems of international competitiveness, and the coal industry was beginning to decline in the face of competition from cheap imported oil. The industrial structures of the peripheral regions were still skewed toward declining industries.

Many small areas were added to the map of assisted areas; alongside the industrial problem towns of northern England, Wales, and Scotland, for the first time numerous rural districts in the southwest, Wales, and Scotland were included, as well as a scatter of peripheral localities in the east and south—principally fading coastal resorts like Skegness, Great Yarmouth, and the Isles of Wight and Thanet.

Policy was considerably strengthened after 1964 and the return of a Labour government whose narrow majority was precariously dependent on support in the problem areas. The strategy of assistance was redrawn; instead of a scatter of small districts, now large areas of the country were designated, within which it was hoped that growth might gravitate to the areas of greatest potential. Regional planning strategies were drawn up, if rarely implemented. By the early 1970s assisted areas covered well over half the national territory, and aid was graded according to the severity of problems between Intermediate, Development, and Special Development Areas. The last, predictably, were mainly coalfields. Belatedly, the problems of concentration of office-based employment in London were addressed by the introduction of a permit system for new office development in 1965. A drive to remove the problem of derelict land was also begun, as it became increasingly evident that the ugly image of the north was hampering attempts to attract footloose industry.

Regional policy was so vigorous in this period that by the mid-1970s there was some optimism that the core-periphery problem was waning. Regional unemployment rates were converging. Many parts of the periphery were showing marked improvement in their economic performance and had attracted substantial numbers of manufacturing plants. Pressed by the government, parts of the auto industry had been decentralized to Merseyside (the Liverpool area) and central Scotland. A significant development of electronics factories, many of them owned by international companies, was taking shape in Scotland's Silicon Glen. However, many of the factories established in the peripheral regions tended to be branch plants, sometimes with relatively low levels of skill required in the work, and with higher order functions (management, research and development) remaining in the southeast. The quantity of new development was not matched by its quality. Where firms relocated completely from London, they were more likely to establish in the outer part of southeast England, with its easy access to the capital and a high-quality social environment, attractive to management and skilled staff, than in Northern Ireland, Merseyside, or northeast England.

With regard to the dispersal of offices from London, success was much more limited anyway. Private firms that moved out of London (encouraged by government policy) tended to remain within 100 miles (161 km) of the capital, while many preferred to go only as far as suburban centers like Croydon and Richmond. Long-distance moves were rare and were largely confined to sporadic attempts by the government itself to relocate parts of government departments (the Vehicle Licensing Centre to south Wales and Social Security to Newcastle, for example). These attempts to shift the civil service out of London became increasingly halfhearted as the problems of cities like London became ever more apparent. The "paper metropolis" remained relatively concentrated. Thus, while it briefly appeared that a turning point in the development of the center-periphery relationship had been reached, serious weaknesses in the position of many peripheral regions were still evident.

By the 1970s the effects of deindustrialization were beginning to be visible. The national level of manufacturing employment began to decline in 1966; output turned downward in 1974 and reached a nadir in 1981. These trends reflected in part the increasing turbulence in the international economy, and arguably the ending of the long boom, for which the 1973–1974 oil crisis was a catalyst. The slowdown in growth of demand for established consumer goods, the outflow of British capital, and growing competition from Japan and the Newly Industrializing Countries (NICs) were all factors.

The late 1970s and early 1980s thus witnessed the devastating impact of deindustrialization in the UK. Decline spread to most manufacturing sectors (though there were important exceptions such as high-tech industry), and the divide between the regions became strongly pronounced. The pattern of imbalance became identified as the north-south

divide, reviving memories of, and eliciting comparisons with, the interwar period. By 1985 regional unemployment differentials were greater than at any time since the 1930s. Four southern regions—the southeast, East Anglia (northeast of London), the southwest and the East Midlands—were opening a distinct gap with the rest of the UK in their economic performance.

Deindustrialization hit the manufacturing regions hard, and this included the West Midlands, centered on Birmingham, Coventry, and "the Black Country," (primarily in Staffordshire, with other portions in Warwickshire and Worcestershire; the name derives from black smoke from factories) which lost one-third of its manufacturing jobs between 1974 and 1982 and seemed thereby to have joined the depressed north. The wave of factory closures across the country included many that had been established in the success years of postwar regional policy. In many regions (and not just in the north) crisis localities appeared— towns where the dominant employer closed down or severely contracted operations. Steel plant (e.g., in Corby, Consett, and Scunthorpe) and dockyard closures (e.g., the Medway towns of Kent southeast of London) were obvious examples.

There was, of course, another side to deindustrialization. It was coupled with the growth of the services economy. In particular, private producer services (financial and business), key sources and mediators of change, and those where the southeast in particular had a high proportion of national employment, played an important role. From 1983 until 1990 a boom in service activity was concentrated in the south.

A clear inverse relationship obtained between deindustrialization and service sector growth in the regions. The south also led in high-tech industry and research and development, especially in the towns of the M4 corridor west of London, and in Cambridge north of London, with its university-linked science park. According to Manuel Castells and Peter Hall (1994), the Cambridge phenomenon has become a worldwide symbol of the innovative milieu, based on genuinely entrepreneurial new-firm-based growth in computing, scientific instruments, electronics, and biotechnology, spun off from university research on the Silicon Valley model. Here, if anywhere, lies an English technopole.

A further dimension of the emerging new economic geography was a nationwide shift by manufacturing industry from urban to rural localities —or at least away from the inner urban and older suburban districts of major cities and conurbations (including London) to smaller towns and rural districts. This was an important ingredient in the success of outer southeast England and East Anglia, which was becoming the fastest growing area in the UK. This shift was rooted in many factors, and was linked to skilled, "flexible" labor and the attraction of prestige areas with attractive natural and cultural environments. It was popular with highly qualified staff involved in research and other specialist activities.

Some of the boom towns of the 1980s have been in the more attractive rural districts of the north, for example, in Cheshire, North Yorkshire, or the fringes of the Lake District. But these so-called "Northern Lights" have nevertheless been outperformed by those south of the north-south divide. In 1990 a study of 280 localities by Tony Champion and Anne Green (1991) picked out west of London a crescent zone in which were located the 35 most prosperous places (Fig. 7-9). A decade earlier Peter Hall (1981) had noted that "if you want to find the really booming places of Britain you should travel diagonally," from (southwest to northeast) Exeter to Swindon, Oxford, Cambridge and finally Nor-

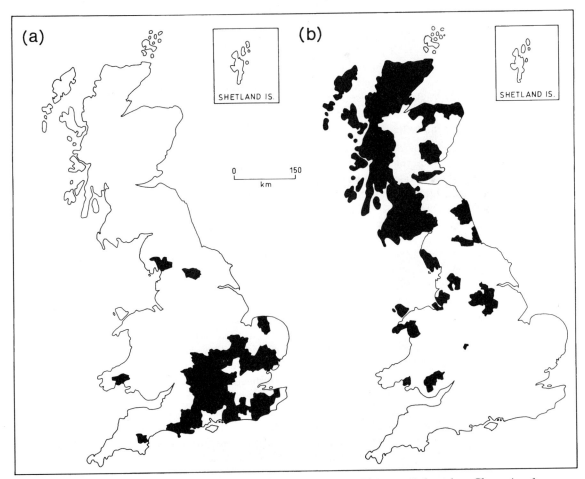

FIGURE 7-9 The north-south divide and the mosaic of local fortunes. This map is based on Champion & Green's (1991) analysis of the performance of 280 local labor market areas according to a range of socioeconomic indicators (including employment and unemployment) in the late 1980s. The two maps show (*a*) the best performing 20 percent and (b) the worst performing 20 percent of these areas.

wich. That analysis has proven perceptive. Here lie the UK's new industrial spaces.

This conclusion is reinforced by analyses of 1991 census data. Forrest and Gordon, (1995, p. 7) describing the pattern of poverty and wealth in England as one of social polarization with strong spatial characteristics, noted the following:

- There was an evident persistence of a north-south divide.

- The southeast, excluding the inner and some outer boroughs of London, emerged in strong contrast to the rest of the country, as the number one region for service and informational employment and the region in which the highly educated and multiple earning households were concentrated.

- Although there were pockets of prosperity further afield, there was a broad *crescent* of wealth, of relative affluence, curving around London, taking in parts of East Anglia and the southwest and stretching up through the Cotswolds and into parts of the East Midlands.

- By contrast unemployment, poverty, and ill health were concentrated in the major cities; the depressed industrial north, especially in a belt from Merseyside through Manchester to South Yorkshire (central England) and in the northeast; and in the "forgotten corners" of England.

Deindustrialization, growth in services, and the urban-rural shift combined in the 1980s to provide a complex mosaic of local fortunes in all regions, with crisis localities and boom towns sometimes not far apart. It is only 50 miles (80 km) from Corby, a depressed former steel town, to prosperous Cambridge, for example. This local pattern of spatial inequality overlays the broader regional division of the north-south divide.

In the second half of the 1980s government policies, including financial deregulation and tax reductions, encouraged a boom in the British economy, and that boom was led by the service-industry. Nationally, unemployment was almost halved, and regional differentials narrowed, suggesting that, as the government argued, growth was trickling-down to the peripheral regions.

Stranger things were to follow. With the collapse of this boom in the early 1990s, unemployment again rose nationally, but regional differences continued to *decrease*. This recession hit the services sector and the housing construction industry hard, as well as manufacturing, leading to a steep rise in unemployment in the southeast. The south now led the way into recession. Specific local problems also began to be felt in some towns in the south from the reduction of government expenditure on defense (a result of the end of the Cold War). Many towns in the south and southwest like Bristol had been major beneficiaries of government defense contracts. Others like Weymouth had depended on the presence of military bases and defense installations. The problems of coastal holiday resorts in the face of competition from abroad continued.

In the 1990s, therefore, there has been some debate about the continuing validity of a north-south divide. In 1993 the unemployment rate was lower in Scotland than in southeast England. However, the problems of the service sector which have so badly affected the southeast may be largely cyclical and the result of boom-bust policies. By 1995 there were signs of recovery in the southeastern economy. On the other hand, the quest for productivity gains in the service sector to meet competitive international pressures may continue to produce job losses in service industries. It is also true that there are increasing indications of divergent performance within the periphery. In Scotland the variable impact through time of the North Sea oil phenomenon has produced an aberration from broader regional trends. The Welsh economy (especially in south Wales) has seen some remarkable transformations and has performed strongly in the recent past.

In the long-run perspective, however, the southeast seems likely to retain its dominant position. Economic and political power is still strongly based there. Within the UK regional prospects are still shaped by a spatial division of labor that sees corporate headquarters, high-tech industry, producer services, and research and development strongly represented in a greater southeast. The peripheral regions are still heavily dependent on manufacturing, with a strong presence of branch plants and declining public services. Closer ties with Europe also tend to be to the advantage of the southeast corner, while arguably the center of gravity in Europe's own axial belt is shifting southward.

Regional Policy under Margaret Thatcher

How has regional policy changed in the last 20 years, and what influence has government policy had on the changing fortunes of the regions? In the mid-1970s the worsening position of the national economy and the pressure for public expenditure cuts forced regional policy on to the defensive. Labor subsidies to manufacturing employers in Development Areas, for example, were curtailed in 1976. However, the most significant changes followed the election of Margaret Thatcher, a radical right-wing Conservative, to prime minister in 1979.

Margaret Thatcher's long period in power (1979-1990) was characterized by a quite different approach to economic management and social issues to that of her predecessors (whether Labour or Conservative). The political agenda of Thatcherism was characterized by a redefinition of the role of the state and an abandonment of the Keynesian approach to economic management with which regional policy was traditionally associated. The Welfare State was to be cut back; free market conservatism and the promotion of "the enterprise culture" were to be the solutions to the country's economic problems—and to the difficulties of those places struggling to adapt to economic change. The defeat of inflation became an overriding objective; the goal of full employment was abandoned. The all-party political consensus on the need for regional policy was broken. This new approach likely contributed to the intensity of problems the regions faced during the recession of the early 1980s.

The Thatcher years were characterized by a decline in the significance of national government regional policy. The *geographical* scale of aid was reduced—the new assisted areas map in place by 1984 was much more fragmented—there was a return to the locality as the basis for regional poli-

cy. The scale of *financial* assistance was cut back; standardized grants were abolished in 1988, and the system of locational controls (the IDC or Industrial Development Certificate—required for locating factories in selected areas) was abandoned. Regional agencies established in the 1970s were given a greater enterprise orientation. *Ad hoc* initiatives, often designed to promote a new economic localism, became important. Some initiatives like the Enterprise Zone (see Inset 7-1) indicated a blurring of the divide between urban and regional policy. Regional aid still played an important part in encouraging inward investment from overseas. Famous examples include Nissan, the Japanese car manufacturer, which established a major factory in the north in the 1980s, and more recently Samsung, the Korean electronics company, which in 1994 announced its decision to build a complex of factories in the same region. Much more emphasis in government aid was placed on the promotion of indigenous entrepreneurship, innovation, and small firms. The government appeared to see traditional regional policy as social welfare policy, and was happy that major responsibility for regional policy was being shifted to the European Community. The main target for government spatial policy became the cities rather than the regions, and these began to appropriate the lion's share of expenditure, as we will see.

The Thatcher map of assisted areas lasted from 1984 until 1993, when a further review was undertaken. Under a new prime minister (John Major), the Conservative government responded to the changing regional and local fortunes—and perhaps to the decline in its electoral fortunes in the southeast (though this is difficult to prove). The new map covered 34 percent of the UK's working population ("the worst third") and again was heavily based on the unemployment criteria (Fig. 7-10). The map is notable for a shift in policy focus toward the south. Over half of the new assisted areas were in East Anglia, the southeast and southwest—including, again, coastal localities like Great Yarmouth and the Isle of Wight, echoing policies introduced briefly more than 30 years previously, but also new localities along the Channel coast (e.g., Dover, Hastings, and Weymouth). Most striking of all, however, is the inclusion for the first time

ENTERPRISE ZONES

Peter Hall's concept of an essay on "nonplan" within Britain's ailing cities, as a last attempt to resuscitate their economies, was taken up by the Conservative government in 1980. In this way, perhaps the government could remove "the dead hand of the state" and the "blitzing" effect of planning, thereby enabling enterprise to flourish, and create jobs and wealth. Enterprise Zones (EZs) were an experiment to test whether greater freedom from government interference could lead to faster growth, and they were the forerunner of other policies designed to lift the burden of government interferences. As initially conceived, they were declared to target economic decline and environmental decay. In practice, however, they have been above all an economic initiative, offering, in Prime Minister Thatcher's words, "a real prospect of stimulating investment and job creation."

The 1980 legislation led to the designation of small areas as Enterprise Zones for 10 years, with benefits in the form of freedom from normal planning permission and exemption from local taxes on industrial and commercial property, as well as tax allowances on capital expenditure. Research has shown that firms have been attracted mainly by the financial incentives, especially where Enterprise Zones lay in Development Areas and, thereby, also provided the opportunity for capital investment grants.

Twenty-five EZs were created between 1980 and 1984 (Fig. 7-13), varying considerably in size (and sometimes split between more than one site), ranging from about 1100 acres (454 ha) in Gateshead (Tyneside) to about 130 acres (53 ha) at Flixborough on the lower Trent. Most lay in the assisted areas, but some were in problem locations in southeast England, notably the Isle of Dogs in London Docklands. Not all were in the inner city, or even in cities at all. The towns of Corby and Scunthorpe were affected by steel mill closures; Wakefield's EZ was in declining mining villages in the Yorkshire coalfield. EZs have quite frequently been used as a response to a local economic crisis resulting from industrial collapse. In 1988 the government announced that there would be no general extension of the EZ idea—with an admission that the experiment had been expensive—but six more EZs have, nevertheless, resulted from "exceptional circumstances."

EZs have met varying success in attracting investment. The Isle of Dogs EZ helped to finance a bonanza of speculative office development in Docklands, while both Corby and Scunthorpe proved particularly attractive to inward manufacturing investment. Many EZs, however, have tended to encourage boundary-hopping by local companies seeking to cash in on the tax benefits, with little genuine net addition of jobs, whereas others have become magnets for retail development (sometimes to the chagrin of city-center stores). Two of the four new super-regional shopping centers built in the UK in the late 1980s, Metrocentre at Gateshead and Merry Hill at Dudley, have located in Enterprise Zones, while Swansea and Scunthorpe also have much smaller but locally significant retail complexes. Metrocentre is probably the largest enclosed shopping center in Europe with 1,630,000 sq ft (154,300 sq m) of floor space, and Merry Hill also tops 1,250,00 sq ft (11,899 sq m).

Critics of Enterprise Zones argue that they were too small, too local, and too few in number to make a significant impact on the inner-city problem. The main beneficiaries, they maintain, have been capital interests and property developers, and not enough real impact has been seen in encouraging small enterprises. The major effect of EZs was perhaps at least as much ideological as anything else, in shifting the balance between industrial and community interests. Nevertheless, they have helped some localities to illustrate that "something was happening," and they have been coveted by local authorities as strengthening the enticement of externally derived investment.

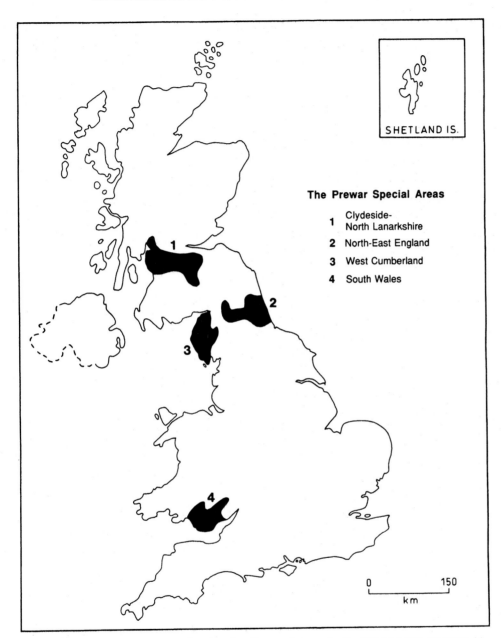

FIGURE 7-10 The changing map of regional policy assistance in the UK (*a*) 1934, (*b*) 1979, (*c*) 1984 and 1993. The maps illustrate the ebb and flow of regional fortunes as well as changing government attitudes.

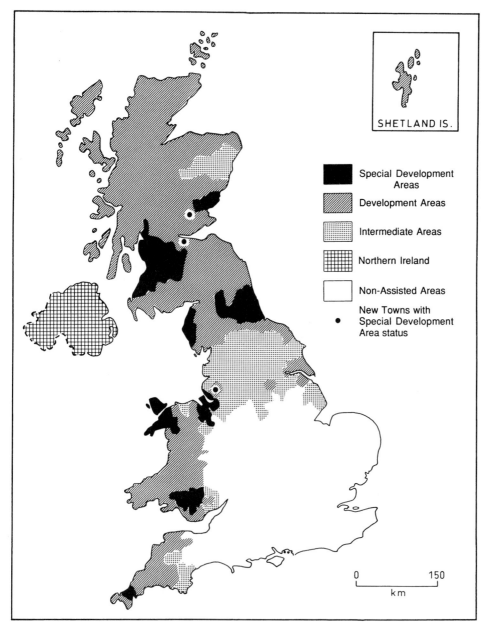

FIGURE 7-10 B Regional policy assistance areas in 1979.

of localities in London itself, including some of those districts, like Park Royal, which were so successful in an earlier phase of manufacturing growth. In the north, some towns lost their assisted status (including some that appeared to have successfully converted after steel closures, like Scunthorpe), but the dismantling of the coal industry in the 1990s produced new "blackspots" in Yorkshire

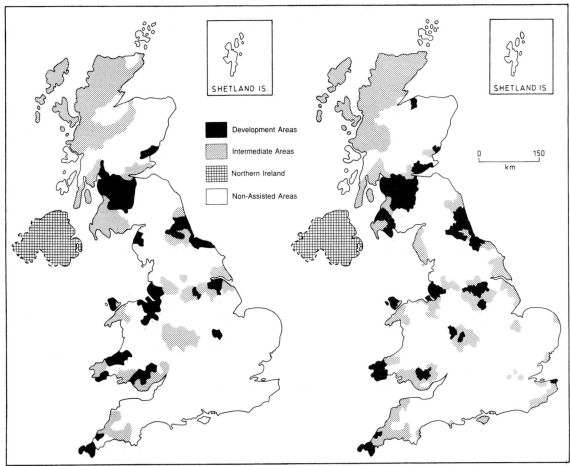

FIGURE 7-10 C Regional policy assistance areas in 1984 (left) and 1993 (right).

and the East Midlands. Regional policy in the 1990s thus represents a response to a mixture of influences—long-term structural shifts as well as shorter term cyclical changes and political expediency.

URBAN CHANGE: SPRAWL, DECAY, AND REVITALIZATION

Britain's society is essentially urban. Industrialization in the nineteenth century laid the basis for

rapid and often chaotic urban growth, characterized by unsanitary and squalid housing for the working classes and poor public health. Cities like Manchester were in many ways shocking places, as Friedrich Engels, so vividly portrayed. The need for public intervention to protect people from the excesses of urbanization was becoming rapidly apparent. A few enlightened factory owners built ordered, quality settlements for their workers (e.g., Titus Salt at Saltaire, near Bradford, George Cadbury at Bourneville outside Birmingham, William Lever at Port Sunlight on the Mersey), but such philanthropy remained the exception rather than the rule (Fig. 7-11). Legislation to impose minimum standards was badly needed and began to make an impact beginning in the 1880s.

In the early twentieth century, powerful ideas about planning and the urban environment were propagated by Ebenezer Howard and Patrick Geddes, in particular, which led to new initiatives to combat sprawl and regulate urban development. Howard's solution to the problems of overcrowding and sprawl was proposed in *Garden Cities of Tomorrow* (1902)—the development of self-contained, balanced communities based on the decentralization of industry and people from the city. The first garden city (really a small town), Letchworth, was built according to these ideals in Hertfordshire, northwest of London, in 1903, and was followed in the interwar period by nearby Welwyn Garden City. These settlements in many respects formed the prototypes for the New Towns of post–World War II Britain.

In the interwar period, local authorities in Britain became increasingly involved in urban renewal and expansion. Low-income, or Council housing as it was popularly known, became important, accounting for around 50 percent of all new housing built in the period. Some of this housing was of relatively high quality—certainly compared with what was to follow. The cities had become in many ways public cities, with facilities and services as well as housing provided by the municipal authorities. At the same time, speculative private housing led to ribbon development of residential areas, culminating in a government response in the form of town planning acts, which served to regulate and zone the development of land.

The control of metropolitan sprawl, and especially the growth of London, was a matter of in-

FIGURE 7-11 Saltaire, Bradford. Titus Salt's great textile mill is now home to a complex of cultural, commercial, and residential uses, including the Hockney Art Gallery. In the background are the chapel and model village built by Salt for his workers. (Courtesy of Bradford EID Marketing)

creasing concern. It was addressed by the Barlow Report of 1940, which advocated controlling the growth of London. The Barlow Report was to provide the basic guiding principles for the development of urban and regional planning in postwar Britain. The control of London's growth was taken up by the great planner, Patrick Abercrombie, through the concept of a green belt girdling the suburbs, with beyond it the planned expansion of existing towns, and the construction of New Towns, to house "overspill" populations. The town and country planning system assembled in the early postwar years gave the government the vital weapon of development control on the use of land, while housing construction (in part to remedy massive bomb damage) by the public sector was a key priority of a reforming and energetic Labour government.

The New Towns Act of 1946 established the basis for the designation of New Towns—ultimately 28 in number—and undoubtedly was one of the major British achievements of the postwar period. The mechanism was the establishment of development corporations for each New Town, financed by central government, which controlled construction and growth. The New Towns were designed on the basis of self-containment and social balance; they were not to be simply dormitories for the cities. In general, the early New Towns achieved this and their other goals; they provided good housing and a decent environment.

Fourteen New Towns were designated by 1950, eight of them in the so-called London Ring (e.g., Welwyn Garden City), between 20 and 40 miles (32–64 km) from the center of the national capital, and with target populations (after later revision) generally between 40,000 and 100,000. The rest had a more varied set of circumstances and locations. Corby in the East Midlands was a blueprint for an industrial settlement based on a new iron- and steel-making complex, Peterlee in the northeast and Glenrothes in Scotland provided new foci in coal-mining areas. Others served the overspill needs of provincial conurbations—East Kilbride for Glasgow, for example (Fig. 7-12).

A second major phase of New Town designations came in the 1960s but in a different mode. Several of these New Towns were based on quite substantial preexisting settlements; Warrington, near Manchester, and Northampton, in the East Midlands, for example, each already housed more than 120,000 people. The aim of several New Towns in this phase was to provide larger countermagnets to the growth of metropolitan areas. Those for London lay further from the capital than the earlier ring and were linked to regional planning strategies for the whole of southeast England. Several of the major proposals for expansion during this period—like the South Hampshire city—never came to fruition, and those New Towns that have been built have tended to have smaller populations than originally intended. The most famous of the second wave has been Milton Keynes outside London, which has capitalized on its central location in attracting strong inward investment, including several foreign companies, as well as providing a home for one of the most successful educational innovations of the postwar period, the Open University. The Open University was a radical experiment in the education of adults introduced by the Labour government of Harold Wilson in the 1960s, though it actually opened in 1971. Its aim is to extend educational opportunities to all, and its method of teaching is centred on correspondence courses, backed by TV programs and a nation-wide network of tutors. Students thus are basically being educated 'at a distance'.

The New Towns in general have proved particularly attractive to manufacturing companies, both decentralizing from London and investing from overseas. Indeed, the presence of New Towns like Stevenage and Crawley (close to Gatwick airport) near London provided a significant loophole, weakening attempts to divert manufacturing growth away from London to the assisted areas of peripheral Britain. On the other hand, *within* the peripheral areas New Towns like Washington and Glenrothes have proved to be key locations in restructuring problem regions and were very much part of the growth center strategies pursued in these regions after the 1960s (if now unfashionable). In the 1980s Washington New Town in northeast England became the new home of the Japanese car giant, Nissan, seeking a location inside the EU for car manufacture—one of the most significant new developments in post-war industrial UK and one that has been followed by many other Japanese investments in the same

TARGET POPULATION

●   Over 200,000

●   100,001–200,000

•   50,001–100,000

·   50,000 or less

'47   Date of designation

     Major urban areas

Glenrothes '48
Cumbernauld '55
East Kilbride '47   Livingston '62
Irvine '66
Londonderry '69
Ballymena '67
Antrim '66
Craigavon '65
Washington '64
Peterlee '48
Newton Aycliffe '47
Central Lancashire '70
Skelmersdale '61
Workington '68
Runcorn '64
Newtown '67   Telford '63   Peterborough '67
Corby '50
Redditch '64   Northampton '68
Milton Keynes '67   Stevenage '46
Welwyn Garden City '48   Harlow '47
Cwmbran '49   Hemel Hempstead '47   Basildon '49
Hatfield '48
Bracknell '49
Crawley '47

0   50

Miles

FIGURE 7-12 The New Towns of the UK.

region. Most New Towns, even those in the southeast, were much less successful in attracting service activities, and the lack of controls on office development in London until 1965 undoubtedly contributed to this failure.

As a planning concept, New Towns are no longer fashionable, and their Development Corporations have been terminated. Beginning in the 1960s, the problems of population loss, social deprivation, and economic decline were becoming increasingly evident in the major cities of Britain, especially in their inner areas. Many cities, particularly London, were becoming increasingly unwilling centrifuges, and the political clamor grew over the discriminatory policy practices against the cities.

The Inner Cities

As we have already noted, housing development was a major priority in Britain in the aftermath of the Second World War. Bomb damage in London, and in a few devastated provincial targets for the Luftwaffe—Coventry, Hull, Plymouth—presented urgent demands. In some cases deterioration could be stemmed only by providing "prefabs" (single-story, prefabricated homes with corrugated iron roofs), but the problem, in fact, went much deeper. Removal of slum housing was desperately needed, and this endeavor was carried out by establishing Comprehensive Redevelopment Areas from 1947 onward and by building extensive new housing complexes, often including high-rise apartment blocks, sometimes on greenfield outer-city sites. Much of this housing has proven to be of low quality and itself needed refurbishing or demolition in the 1980s and 1990s. The outer estates have often become desolate sumps of deprivation, unemployment, crime, and vandalism—in many people's views, the critical urban problem places of the 1990s. However, this is to jump ahead of the story: in the 1960s and 1970s the inner city remained the focus of concern, as comprehensive redevelopment failed to keep pace with urban decay. In some cities, notably Birmingham, London, and Bradford, large-scale immigration of Commonwealth Asians and West Indians was leading to the development of large ethnic communities and a potential for racial problems. Such problems were an especially powerful concern for Labour governments (1964–1970 and 1974–1979), which derived much of their political support from working-class populations concentrated in the inner cities.

New policy initiatives began to appear in the 1960s, with a growing fashion for rehabilitation rather than clearance, the development of area-based renewal for districts with special social needs, and positive discrimination for areas of multiple deprivation under the 1968 Urban Program. Schemes included the General Improvement Areas (1969) and Housing Action Areas (1974), while between 1969 and 1977 a small number of experimental Community Development Projects were established on a neighborhood basis, aimed at finding new ways of meeting the needs of people living in areas of serious social deprivation. The approach was shifting towards economic solutions, treating the inner city as a problem region arising from the decline of its employment in industry. This was confirmed in the government's White Paper of 1977, which was followed by the Inner Urban Areas Act of 1978. This act set up 15 Urban Program Areas and provided financial support for property improvement in Industrial Improvement Areas within cities.

The change in approach was enormously accelerated by the election of a Conservative government in 1979, which increasingly identified the causes of inner urban problems as the incompetence and bureaucracy of (Labour) local authorities rather than disinvestment by the private sector. Urban policy was shifted unequivocally to the support of wealth creation through the enterprise culture, and away from the distribution of welfare. Whereas in the past the public sector had been seen as the natural mechanism to promote urban reconstruction, it was now considered a major contribution to the problem. Local authorities were to be reduced in power or bypassed. As one government minister, Michael Heseltine, explained—"we took their [local authorities] powers away from them because they were making such a mess of it. They are the people who have got it all wrong." The urban riots of 1980 and 1981 in inner districts of London, Liverpool, Birmingham, Manchester, and Bristol were a further galvanizing influence on policy change.

The new emphasis on the enterprise culture as the urban salvation was nowhere better exemplified than in the establishment of Enterprise Zones from 1980 (see Inset 7-1 and Fig. 7-13). The idea is attributed to the geographer Peter Hall, who advocated a last-ditch, freeport experiment based on free enterprise (akin to the Hong Kong model), although Hall claimed that the model that ultimately emerged was a watered-down version of the concept, bearing a suspicious resemblance to conventional regional policy. The prime purpose of Enterprise Zones was to encourage and stimulate the creation of enterprise through a mixture of tax breaks and deregulation. The locations favored, in fact, were not by any means restricted to inner-city situations, with several in depressed

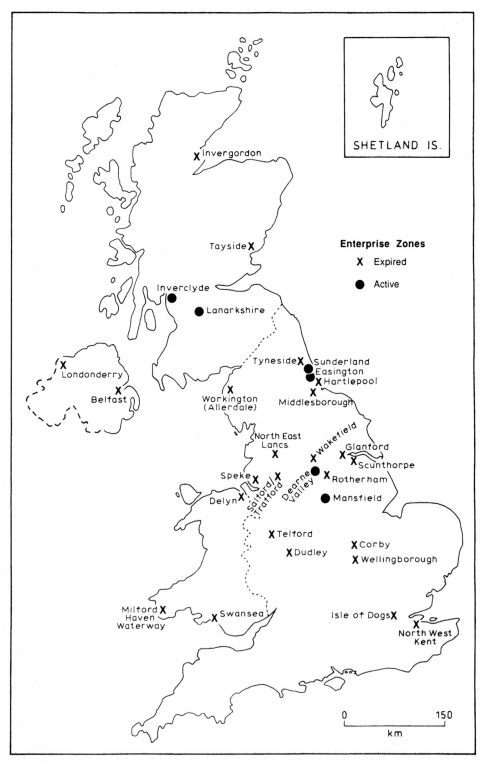

FIGURE 7-13 The location of Enterprise Zones in the UK, 1995.

area locations. This is particularly true of the later additions—Sunderland in the northeast (shipyard closures), Ravenscraig (steel mill closure) and the three coalfield Enterprise Zones announced in 1994. A confusion of regional and urban policy instruments is indeed apparent.

If the Enterprise Zone could be claimed as a British invention, subsequently copied in other countries, the second major instrument developed by the Conservative government owed much more to experience elsewhere. American models of urban revitalization and concepts of privatism and leverage were particularly influential. *Privatism* refers to confidence in the private sector's capacity to create the conditions for personal and community prosperity, and *leverage* to the use of relatively small quantities of public funds to lever large quantities of private investment. These concepts underpinned the new Urban Development Corporations (UDCs) introduced in 1980. Sometimes described as the in-town New Towns, these bodies were financed and appointed by the central government and given full planning powers within designated areas, taking them out of local government control. But whereas the New Towns resonated with an ethos of careful planning and design, the UDCs are concerned with marketing and place promotion. As one UDC chief executive put it, "the era of the grand plan was dead." Charged with the economic, social, and physical generation of their areas, UDCs had the power to acquire and develop land, carry out building and other operations, and provide infrastructure. They have been seen as a deliberate bypassing of Labour local governments—a centralization of power. UDCs emphasize property development and the recycling of old structures to new uses. There is a strong emphasis on "flagship projects" and changing the image of an area.

Britain's first two UDCs were established in 1980, both for zones centered around the redundant spaces created by changes in port locations—London Docklands and Merseyside (see Inset 7-2 and Fig. 7-14). Others followed in major provincial cities from 1987, with a wide range of sizes. Most contained some waterfront areas. Urban Development Corporations attracted a mounting share of the urban policy cake, while urban policy funding overtook the financing of regional policy. The channeling of government money into UDCs was, however, accompanied by reductions in funding of local government, forcing many authorities to cut back on services and encouraging them to increase the selling off of public housing (introduced by the Conservatives in 1979). Nationally, over 1 million Council houses have been sold off under the right to buy policy. In the major cities like London and Manchester, metropolis-wide government was abolished in 1986, making strategic planning increasingly elusive.

The record of UDCs has been controversial, and their undemocratic nature has attracted much criticism. The spectacular redevelopment of London Docklands dwarfs developments elsewhere and took on particular significance as the flagship project for Mrs. Thatcher's Britain (Fig. 7-15). As one critic put it, however, in the early 1980s the flagship appeared to be "on the rocks." In Liverpool, the other early UDC, large expenditure of public money produced relatively little private industrial development, and in the mid-1980s the strategy was shifted toward leisure and tourist-based development. In this respect, Liverpool's Albert Dock redevelopment has been more successful, and developments like the Tate Gallery and quayside shopping and housing have helped provide a new image for a city once described as a museum to the depression and demoralized by local political crises.

Since the mid-1980s other new initiatives for Britain's beleaguered cities have followed. City Challenge—a competition between cities for limited funds—was introduced in 1991. Some derided it as devaluing urban policy to a regeneration game, but others applauded it, because bids had to be based on partnerships between business, communities, and local governments. The whole urban program was restructured into a Single Urban Regeneration Budget in 1993.

Cities in the UK are now locked into a fiercely competitive game in which national boundaries are transcended and in which promotion and city marketing play a vital role. Many cities have attempted to shed their industrial images, emphasizing their postindustrial qualities as centers for consumption and leisure. The revitalization of city centers and waterfront areas is closely linked to these marketing efforts. One of the most success-

INSET 7-2

LONDON DOCKLANDS

The redevelopment of London Docklands since 1980 has changed the skyline of central London in a dramatic way, with the 800-ft (244 m), 50-story tower of 1 Canada Square at Canary Wharf—the highest building in Europe—seen by many as a potent symbol of Britain's new enterprise culture.

Docklands lies in the heart of London, less than 3 miles (5 km) from the great financial center of the city. The opportunity for physical redevelopment in this zone was provided by the closure by 1981 of the docks of the Port of London Authority, as shipping activity moved downstream to Tilbury, leaving 55 miles (88km) of abandoned waterfront. Manufacturing decline also affected the area, whose 40,000 residents lived predominantly in poor-quality public (Council) housing. In 1985 one-third of the workforce was unemployed. The constituent districts of Tower Hamlets, Newham and Hackney, are among the poorest in the UK and house some of the highest concentrations of immigrants, especially Bengalis.

The Urban Development Corporation established in 1980 replaced the needs-led schemes of the local authorities with property-led development. The property boom on the Isle of Dogs in the late 1980s was fueled by available capital subsidies because this area had an Enterprise Zone. Speculative office development took place on a massive scale, led by the Canadian developers of Canary Wharf, Olympia, and York, who perceived the potential of Docklands as a global business location. Canary Wharf was conceived as a 12-million-sq ft (1.1 million sq m) development in five stages, of which only two have so far been completed. Several newspapers relocated their operations from Fleet Street to Wapping, despite acrimonious disputes with the unions. Up-market private housing schemes proliferated, and the Docklands Light Railway was constructed to provide access to the area. There is a small airport.

The vision of "Wall Street on the Water" proved elusive in the 1990s. The City of London resisted the potential competition by opening up more office space, while the recession of 1990 led to gross problems of oversupply. London lost 50,000 jobs in the financial services sector, and house prices slumped, leaving many residents trapped with debts larger than the value of their property. The problems of Docklands culminated in the bankruptcy of Olympia and York, whose 4.2 million sq ft (390,000 sq m) of completed office space was only 50 percent occupied.

This dramatic development reinforced the dissatisfaction of Docklands' critics, who had deplored the lack of benefits to local people from the property boom. Most of the jobs in the new office developments were taken by commuters. Two Docklands were said to exist, with luxurious enclaves for wealthy incomers side by side with underfunded housing projects, parks, and community facilities serving the original residents. Here was a Porsche-hamburger economy: the juxtaposition of terrific growth and people excluded from it. Planning was criticized as inadequate and transport systems as congested. Although the Urban Development Corporation claimed high leverage rates, others argued that there were substantial hidden subsidies through the EZ tax allowances and huge expenditures by the Ministry of Transport.

Yet, it would be premature to write off Docklands as a failure. The physical renewal is undeniably spectacular. The government is financing extension of the London Underground Jubilee Line to link Canary Wharf with the West End. Canary Wharf, now owned by a consortium of banks, is over 75 percent occupied, and property values have revived. In late 1995 the Canary Wharf project appeared to have moved full circle, with its projected purchase by a consortium led by its original developer, Paul Reichmann of Olympia and York, for about $1.25 billion (£800M). The developers avowed intention was to realize the original vision of a development more than double the present size. In the long term, Docklands could well still provide a vital impetus to the sustained redevelopment of the East Thames corridor—a neglected sector of the national capital.

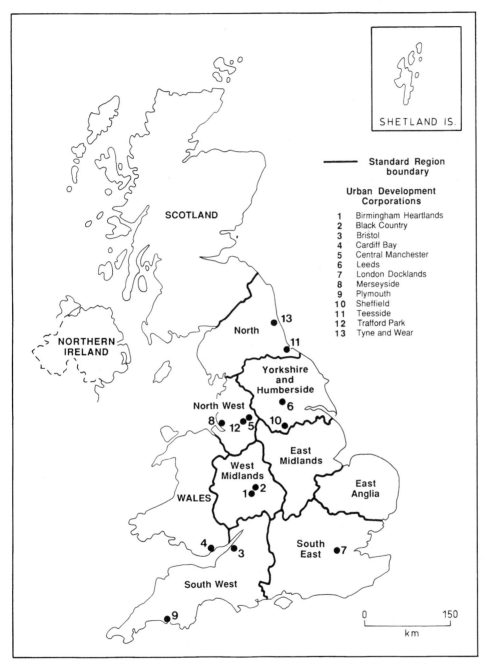

FIGURE 7-14 The location of Urban Development Corporations in the UK, 1995. The map also shows the standard regions of the UK.

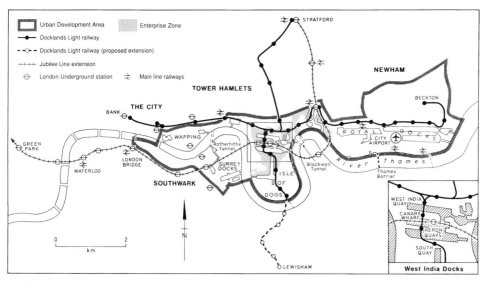

FIGURE 7-15 London Docklands in 1996: the UDC area.

ful re-imaging campaigns was conducted by Glasgow, Scotland's largest city. Having raised its profile and its people's morale with the slogan "Glasgow's Miles Better," it successfully transformed its image from that of declining industrial city to that of cultural center, using its designation as European City of Culture in 1990 to stage a series of festive events. Another city that has shaken off its image as a place of "dark, satanic mills" is the wool textile town of Bradford in West Yorkshire. Bradford's new image was constructed around leisure and tourism, combining the ingredients of ethnic culture ("the flavors of Asia"), literary landscape (the Bronte country of *Wuthering Heights*), industrial heritage (Salt's mill now exhibits David Hockney paintings), and the capture of the National Museum of Film, Photography and Television. By 1990 Bradford was attracting 6 million visitors a year. Cities are also in competition to stage sporting events, with Manchester's unsuccessful bid to host the Olympic Games nevertheless providing the basis for considerable investment in sports facilities, and a focus for urban renewal. Manchester will host the Commonwealth Games in 2002.

As with the renaissance in the downtowns of America, however, the spectacle and conspicuous consumption of redeveloped city centers are viewed by some observers, such as the socially critical

geographer David Harvey, as a carnival mask, leaving the social problems of the inner cities (or the outer estates) largely unchanged. Issues of equity and deprivation remain. A recent review of urban policy in the UK concluded that, while public resources had achieved a turnaround of fortunes in specific areas, in the most deprived areas inroads had not been made. Indeed, the biggest and most deprived of the urban areas had generally experienced a continuing deterioration, with inner-city conditions spreading. As the city promoters conceded, the Glasgow's Miles Better campaign looks like "a sick joke for people living in damp houses in Easterhouse", a notoriously deprived suburb (*Financial Times* 25 June, 1992). Today the areas of most concentrated poverty in the UK are still in urban areas, and these include cities on both sides of the north-south divide.

THE REGIONS OF THE UK

As we have seen, the geography of the contemporary UK still exhibits the macro-patterns of core-periphery and north-south, although the precise extent of these regional divisions is difficult to define, and they overlie a complex mosaic of local fortunes. The final sections of this chapter review the regions of the British Isles that are at an intermediary scale of analysis—the 11 standard regions of the UK, as well as the Republic of Ireland, a separate state. In England there are eight such regions (Fig. 7-14), which can be grouped into three sets—the southeast, southwest, and East Anglia, which constitute a broader south in economic and cultural terms; the Midlands, divided into east and west, which lie on the hinge of the north-south divide; and the three unequivocally northern regions—the northwest, Yorkshire and Humberside (east central England), and the north. To these are added the national regions of the periphery—Wales, Scotland, and Northern Ireland. (For socioeconomic data on the UK's regions, see Table 7-1.) These countries stand in different formal relationships to the United Kingdom as a whole, and each retains its own nationalist aspirations. These aspirations are manifest in different ways, however. While many in Scotland and Wales hanker after greater political autonomy and independence from Westminster, the loyalist majority in Northern Ireland remains anxious to retain their membership in the Union.

Southern England

Southern England is dominated by the largest English region, *the southeast*, which leads the UK in both economic and political terms. It is the wealthiest region and the one with the highest proportion of its employment in the service industry. In turn the southeast is dominated by London, lying in a central position within it. In the last half century, the growth of its service economy, and in particular of government functions, corporate headquarters, and financial and other producer services, has reinforced its hegemony within the British regional system (Fig. 7-16). London is also the UK's major tourist attraction and is unrivaled in the UK in the concentration of entertainment, leisure, and cultural facilities. The southeast region also has major representation of high-tech industry—including the M4 corridor west from London itself, and the growth poles of Heathrow and Gatwick airports. The sphere of London's influence continues to move outward, with decentral-

ization of population and employment especially benefiting growing centers to the north and west, and placing strong development pressures on London's Green Belt and on rural areas beyond it. By contrast, the heart of the metropolitan area has lost population and economic activities and contains many problem districts.

After the growth-dominated 1980s, the early 1990s were a rude shock for this region, as the recession in the service sector led to big increases in unemployment. However, the southeast remains the strongest region in long-run perspective, and there are few signs that its political hegemony is likely to be overturned. As we have seen, the Channel Tunnel presents an opportunity to strengthen its position compared to other regions, and to reaffirm its claim to be part of the geographical core of the European Union.

East Anglia is a small lowland region, but nevertheless it is the UK's fastest growing region in terms of population and economic activity. This new vitality in part reflects the spread of growth impulses outward from the southeast into adjacent areas. Historically, this region has been characterized by sparse rural populations and small or medium-sized towns, and a dependence on agriculturally based activity (especially arable farming). Agriculture in much of this area exemplifies many of the trends characteristic of efficient lowland farming—larger capital-intensive farms with bigger fields and fewer hedgerows; a growing influence of modern technology and factory-farming methods for rearing pigs and poultry; and a growing influence of agribusinesses (companies that produce, process, and market farm products).

Recent growth is based in part on manufacturing. This is the UK's leading growth area for high-tech industry, especially around Cambridge. Cambridge houses the UK's leading scientific university, which plays a key role in technology transfer. Even more important than manufacturing growth has been the expansion of business and professional services, while tourism is important in Cambridge and along the coast. The growth of small firms plays a particularly important role in the economic success of East Anglia.

The region has benefited especially from its perception as an attractive residential environment offering a high quality of life to an affluent and

TABLE 7-1

REGIONAL DIMENSIONS AND INDICATORS

	Area	Population		Employment, 1991[a] (pct.)			Unemployment Rate	Income	Car Ownership	GDP
	000 sq mi (km)	1992 Million	Annual Growth Rate, 1981–1992	Agriculture	Industry	Services	1993	Average Gross Weekly per Household 1992 £	Private Cars per 1000 pop. 1990	Index p.c. 1991
Southeast	10.5 (27.2)	17.70	0.4	1.2	25.4	72.5	10.2	407.3	388	117.3
East Anglia	4.9 (12.6)	2.09	0.9	4.0	29.2	66.3	8.1	350.2	409	100.4
Southwest	9.2 23.8	4.75	0.7	4.6	29.0	65.6	9.5	346.5	401	94.3
East Midlands	6.0 (15.6)	4.06	0.5	2.7	38.0	58.5	9.5	344.4	341	97.1
West Midlands	5.0 (13.0)	5.28	0.2	2.1	39.1	57.7	10.9	304.2	377	92.4
Northwest	2.8 (7.3)	6.40	-0.1	1.5	33.3	64.4	10.7	317.1	325	90.4
Yorkshire and Humberside	5.9 (15.4)	5.00	0.2	2.5	34.8	61.7	10.3	303.2	313	91.7
North	5.9 (15.4)	3.10	-0.1	1.7	34.9	62.0	11.9	285.1	284	90.5
Wales	8.0 (20.8)	2.90	0.3	3.1	32.7	62.9	10.3	294.6	328	85.1
Scotland	30.4 (78.8)	5.11	-0.1	3.0	30.2	65.9	9.7	313.7	280	95.8
Northern Ireland	5.4 (14.1)	1.61	0.4	4.5	28.0	66.4	13.9	281.3	281	81.1
UK	94.2 (244.1)	58.0	0.3	2.3	30.9	65.9	10.3	342.9	352	100

Source: Central Statistical Office (1994) *Regional Trends*, 29, London.

[a]Figures derived from annual European Community sample survey on labor forces; definitions may differ from those used in UK statistical series.

(a)

(b)

FIGURE 7-16 The West India Docks on the Isle of Dogs, London Docklands in (a) 1982 (shortly after their closure) and (b) in 1993. Both pictures provide a view toward the west and the City of London. The elevated Docklands Light Railway is visible in the 1993 photograph, which is dominated by the office complex at Canary Wharf. (Photos by permission of Chorley and Handford Ltd.)

mobile population, and from the urban to rural shift in manufacturing and service location.

The southwest is a large and elongated region containing significant internal contrasts. Its northern and eastern parts contain the major urban centers, notably Bristol, and have also benefited from proximity to the southeast and decentralization of activity from that region, along the M4 corridor. They house important sunrise industries such as aerospace and electronics. The high quality of the region's environment, with fabulous coastal scenery and two national parks, has made the southwest the UK's major region for inward migration, including large numbers of retired people to resorts like Bournemouth and Torbay. Much of the region has a pastoral farming economy, with particular emphasis on milk production.

The *far* southwest, however, has many of the hallmarks of a rural depressed area, and its remoteness has made the attraction of new investment difficult. Cornwall's traditional economy has suffered many setbacks: the once-great tin-mining industry is all but extinguished, fishing has been negatively affected by European Union policies, its holiday resorts face competition from the overseas package holiday market, and some of its farming is marginal.

In many parts of the region, the recent cutback in defense industries has had a serious impact, particularly in Plymouth, the major city in the peninsula, where employment in the large naval dockyards has been drastically reduced. Elsewhere the closure of military bases and the reduction in aircraft contracts have had serious effects.

Midlands England

The increasing mobility of people and capital and the reduction of journey times have tended to blur the identity of the English Midlands. The *West Midlands*, focused on England's second largest city, Birmingham, and the Black Country conurbation, remains the industrial heartland of Britain and is in many respects the pivot or hinge between north and south. The region has traditionally been dominated by auto and engineering manufacture, especially in cities like Coventry, while another important specialization has been ceramics in "the Potteries" of North Staffordshire. The region has suffered considerably from deindustrialization, but has been successful in attracting a large amount of inward investment from overseas. The regional economy is becoming more diverse with the success of Birmingham and Coventry in attracting office relocations from London, especially in the banking sector. Birmingham's image has improved, too, with the development of its airport and exhibition and leisure facilities. In times of recession the West Midlands tends to align with the north, but in other periods it appears to be part of the enlarged southeast.

The *East Midlands* is a more diverse region lacking a single focus, and it has performed well in recent years economically. Rapid growth in those parts of the region adjacent to the southeast contrasts with the decline of the coal-mining towns and villages of Derbyshire and Nottinghamshire. Much of the East Midlands appears to have been able to capitalize on its central location within the UK national market, on its excellent highway connections, and on its greater freedom from congestion than the metropolitan areas of the West Midlands. Most analyses of its economic performance set it in the southern group of regions.

The region is especially important for clothing and footwear manufacture. Nottingham in particular has made a successful transition from large-volume, low-cost goods to high-quality, design-based production as a city of fashion. A notable coup in the attraction of inward investment was the establishment of Japanese automobile maker Toyota's major UK plant in Derbyshire. This development is already leading to important spin-offs in many parts of Midlands England.

Northern England

Northern England subdivides into three major regions, each of which has a strongly industrial, urbanized core, but it also contains outstanding scenery in the uplands of the Pennines and the Lake District. There are four national parks within this greater north—a reminder that the traditional images of industrial depression convey stereotypes that do little justice to the northern reality. Much of northern England is rural, but rurality carries its own problems, as primary sector employment continues to decline and the characteristic pastoral hill-farming of many areas struggles to survive, remaining precariously dependent on subsidies. Tourist income is vital to the rural economy.

The *northwest* is the smallest standard region in mainland Britain, but it has a population second in size only to the southeast. This intensely urbanized area could fairly claim to be the cradle of the Industrial Revolution; the development of industry worldwide began in the cotton textiles villages and towns of Lancashire. Most of its towns are industrial, but the region also contains some of the first mass holiday resorts for the British working class, notably Blackpool. The Pleasure Beach at Blackpool is still the top individual tourist attraction in the UK. However, other smaller resorts in this region and elsewhere now struggle in the face of international package tourism for the masses.

In recent years, the northwest has been in both absolute and relative decline. Its two major metropolitan areas, focused on Liverpool and Manchester, have faced particularly serious problems of adapting to the impact of global competition and of converting from dependence on traditional industries. Liverpool's problems have been compounded by local political wrangles and its reputation for militancy. Merseyside has the dubious distinction of being the only area in England which qualifies as an Objective 1 region for aid from the European Union. However, urban revitalization has begun to make an impact in some parts of the northwest too, including the redevelopment of the old docks at the head of the famous Manchester Ship Canal, Salford Quays. Manchester is the largest city in the north, and its critical mass is helping it to assume the role of the north's unofficial capital. The northwestern economy is increasingly oriented to the service sector, including tourism and leisure, and the region has also played a key role in the development of English popular culture. Liverpool was the home of the Beatles and the "Mersey sound," while Manchester is the base for "Coronation Street," television's longest running and best-loved soap opera.

Within the north, there is increasing evidence of a growing west-east Transpennine axis, linking the ports of the Mersey and the Humber, and the conurbations of Lancashire and West Yorkshire. The *Yorkshire and Humberside* region shares with the northwest many common elements of industrial history, although in West Yorkshire the traditional specialization was woollen rather than cotton textiles. West and South Yorkshire are heavily urbanized and contain major provincial cities in Leeds, Bradford, and Sheffield. Paradoxically, the southernmost parts of this region have struggled most, in economic terms, in the last two decades, as the contractions of metal manufacture (especially steel) and coal mining have taken their toll. West and South Yorkshire had become the heartland of the British coal industry, but the region's strength as an energy producer is tilting eastward to the gas terminals and power stations, the oil ports, and refineries of Humberside. Leeds is the major regional center, and like Manchester has experienced rapid recent growth in the financial services sector. This growth is based in part on an influx of banking activities (especially data processing) from elsewhere, and in part on West Yorkshire's traditional strength as the center of the UK's building society movement. Leeds also benefits from improved journey times from the southeast. It is now only two hours by intercity train from London, as

is historic York, a small city but a major tourist attraction.

If the northwest and Yorkshire and Humberside have often been viewed as "intermediate" in fortune and regional aid benefits, the third northern region, known confusingly as *the North*, has been the archetypal depressed area of twentieth-century Britain. This region has been focused on the coalfield of the northeast and the industrial potential of the lower Tyne, Wear, and Tees rivers, but it also contains a broad tract of rural uplands stretching west across to the tourist mecca of the Lake District National Park, beyond which lies a further narrow fringe of isolated decaying industrial towns—truly one of the forgotten corners of England, though home now to the Sellafield nuclear complex.

Until the eighteenth century, the Lake District was seen as the "embodiment of inhospitality," but its lakes and mountains became popular with writers and artists in the late eighteenth century, culminating in its association with the Lake poets, Wordsworth and Coleridge. This laid the basis for its making as a cherished English landscape, to the extent that it now attracts 17 million visitors a year and has begun to suffer from visitor pressure.

Despite much hype about "the New North" and "the Great North," the industrialized core of the region continues to suffer from the contractions of its staple industries, especially coal (with the closure of its last deep mines) and shipbuilding. The shipbuilding industry was formerly dominant on the Tyne and Wear, but is now hanging on precariously: all of Sunderland's shipyards have closed, and the last major yard on the Tyne, Swan Hunter, was recently reprieved from its creditors. Hope for the future is provided by such major new investments as the Metro Centre and the Nissan factory, with its 4000 strong workforce and substantial stimulation of component suppliers. Newcastle-upon-Tyne, the major regional city, has recently fostered a more dynamic image.

In the northeast, the distinctive "Geordie" accent has helped to give a strong sense of identity, but it also carries negative associations with a working-class, male-oriented culture. Many of the improvements seen in the region have been heavily underwritten by large amounts of public money from London or Brussels (EU), both in infrastructure investment and incentives for foreign companies like Nissan or Samsung—leading to references to the north as "a global outpost" or "Whitehall colony." The region continues to score very poorly by many indicators of social well-being, such as educational attainment, crime levels, and mortality rates.

Wales

Whereas the English regions described have little or no political status and imprecise identities, the situation is quite different in Wales and Scotland, both of which in the distant past had separate existences. Wales contains persistent elements of Celtic culture and tradition, largely extinguished in England by the Anglo-Saxons many centuries ago. The Welsh language survives, especially in rural west and north Wales, where for many it is still the first language (though relatively few speak *only* Welsh). Welsh nationalism revived in the 1960s, and a small number of members of Parliament have been elected for "Plaid Cymru," a Welsh nationalist party. Regional devolution, the redistribution of authority in the UK and the restructuring of its political framework, remains an important issue. Concessions to Welsh nationalism were made after 1960 by the appointment of a secretary of state for Wales and the establishment of the Welsh Office as a government department, based in Cardiff, which deals with the administration of government business in Wales on an integrated basis. A further recognition of Wales, special circumstances and needs came in 1975 with the setting up of the Welsh Development Agency (WDA) to play a lead role in Welsh regional development. There are no equivalent development agencies for individual English regions.

Nevertheless, Welsh nationalists and other critics argue that Wales has been the victim of "internal colonialism," with its economic dependency reinforced by political domination and exploitation from London. The English conquered Wales in the thirteenth century, and the principality of Wales was integrated into the kingdom of England in 1536. Wales' economic dependency developed in the nineteenth century as it was drawn into the world of industrial capitalism. This process fo-

cused on the south Wales coalfield, which drew population from rural Wales as well as from England. This area developed an anglicized and cosmopolitan economy dominated by external capital (and after World War II by state industry). In the twentieth century, its working-class population became a major stronghold of trade unions and the Labour party. Coal and steel were the mainstays of a south Wales economy based on exports; the valleys—Rhondda, Taff, Rhymney, Ebbw—became home to strings of settlements devoted largely to the production of the single commodity, coal. A much more spatially restricted coalfield-based development took place in northeast Wales.

As in other peripheral coalfields of the UK, south Wales suffered decades of decline and contraction of its key industries during the twentieth century. Steel became increasingly concentrated at a few major coastal sites like Port Talbot and Llanwern (built in the 1950s). These traumas have, however, begun to recede in the 1990s. Coal mining has been reduced to a tiny shadow of its former self, but a slimmer steel industry has emerged with claims to be the most efficient in Europe. Aided by regional policies and the rapid access to southeast England provided by the Severn Road Bridge (opened in 1966) and associated highways, traffic over which is now relieved by a second, longer span, the south Wales economy has begun to benefit from a major wave of inward investment from the rest of the UK and overseas.

In the 1990s Wales has received about 20 percent of all overseas investment in Britain, and its 40 Japanese companies form one of the largest concentrations of Japanese investments in Europe, led, for example, by Sony, Hitachi, and Aiwa. Wales has an increasing share of the British manufacturing workforce. Although it remains in the lower reaches of the rank of UK regions according to many indicators, there is substantial evidence of successful restructuring of its economy, and it is experiencing population growth (partly from retirement inmigration). A special WDA Program for the Valleys was introduced in 1988, and there have been many other central government-financed initiatives. The coalfield has in part become a dormitory area for people commuting to the industrial sites and service industries of the lowlands along the Swansea-Cardiff axis. (These are the two major urban centers.) Completion of the second Severn Bridge in 1996 has strengthened access eastward.

Rural Wales has experienced mixed fortunes in recent years. Pressures from the EU's Common Agricultural Policy have caused substantial reductions in the number of small sheep and dairy farms, and have led to population losses in the uplands. The population of rural Wales has become more urban, focused on the small market towns supported by government initiatives (like Newtown), or on coastal resorts and retirement centers.

Scotland

The kingdom of Scotland was joined with England voluntarily in 1603, and the two kingdoms unified with a single Parliament in 1707. It retains many of the trappings of a separate state, however, with its own bank notes and its own legal and education system. But it shares with Wales a history of resentment against English (and London) domination of the "United Kingdom." This resentment has found strong expression in the clamor for devolution, the rise of the Scottish Nationalist party, and the demise of the Conservative party (as the party of national government since 1979). This sentiment has been illustrated in both parliamentary and local government elections. Overall, the Labour party dominates the political scene in Scotland, with particularly strong support in the industrial and urban districts of its central area, but the Scottish Nationalists have easily overtaken the Conservatives. In the 1995 local elections, for example, Labour won 613 seats, the Scottish nationalists 181, and the Conservatives a mere 82. As in Wales, central government has made concessions to Scotland's particular status and aspirations, but much earlier, with the establishment of the Scottish Office in 1886. Since 1975 there has also been a Scottish Development Agency (SDA, now renamed Scottish Enterprise).

There are parallels too in the integration of west central Scotland—especially Clydeside (areas near the mouth of the River Clyde) and the city of Glasgow—into the British space-economy during nineteenth-century industrialization. Here development was on a larger scale and more diverse than in south Wales, with particular emphasis on coal, iron and steel, engineering, and shipbuilding, and strength was drawn from local coal and iron reserves and the Clyde's harbor. However, the regional economy was still prone to the dangerous consequences of specialization. Indeed, the economic historian Sydney Checkland believed that many of Glasgow's subsequent economic problems were due to an "Upas tree" effect: he compared the monolithic industries of the region to the fabled Javanese tree that poisoned other life in its shade. During the intense deindustrialization of the British economy in the early 1980s, the area lost many of its major industrial plants.

In the 1980s, the continuing decline of the traditional heavy industrial base in west central Scotland had a severe impact on the Scottish economy. During the decline of the British steel industry, the Ravenscraig complex in Lanarkshire became one of the UK's five major integrated works, although far from ideally located for the import of ore. However, its loss of major markets with the retrenchment of shipbuilding on the Clyde, and the failure of Scottish car plants established in the 1960s (Chrysler closed at Linwood in 1981), led to its closing in 1992, with profoundly negative consequences.

Thus, despite the bravura associated with Glasgow's campaigns to project a new image, the urban-industrial environment of west central Scotland remains depressed. By the late 1980s manufacturing employment on Clydeside had fallen by two-thirds since the early 1950s. Some of the deprived districts of Glasgow still have unemployment rates of over 40 percent, and the concentration of socioeconomic disadvantage in outer suburbs like Castlemilk, Pollok, and Easterhouse presents an enormous challenge to regional and urban policymakers.

This depressed economic outlook holds, despite the success story of the growth in electronics in the central belt of Scotland, leading to the nickname Silicon Glen. Major international companies are distributed from Greenock in the west on the Clyde (IBM) to Edinburgh in the east (Ferranti). Electronics now accounts for 21 percent of Scottish manufacturing output and employs 45,000 people. The Scottish electronics industry accounts for 10 percent of world PC production. Foreign companies (especially American) dominate, attracted by generous regional incentives, the engineering tradition, and the advantages of agglomeration. However, technology transfer to local companies has been limited, with comparatively little research and development in Scotland. This has produced fears that Silicon Glen may become vulnerable to global shifts as lower cost production opportunities arise, perhaps in Eastern Europe.

The problems of Clydeside can be compared with more buoyant economic conditions elsewhere in Scotland, and a west-east contrast is particularly apparent. Edinburgh, Scotland's historic capital, is still the financial, educational, and cultural heart of Scotland, and in 1988 it received the accolade of being identified as the most desirable city in the UK in which to live—decided by a team of researchers from Glasgow! However, the west-east contrast has received its most significant input from the development of North Sea oil and gas, for which Aberdeen has become the major center in the UK, with only limited spillover effects benefiting other subregions. The oil industry employs 97,500 people, or 5 percent of Scotland's workforce, and the effect of oil exploitation has been to decouple Scotland's economic performance from that of the UK as a whole. This effect was illustrated when the oil price fell steeply in 1986, leading to a major increase in unemployment in Scotland, while it was falling in many English regions.

Aberdeen on Scotland's eastern, North Sea coast has developed as the major base for the offshore fields of the northern North Sea, and as a terminal for oil and gas landfall, with the development of Dyce airport and a substructure of firms supplying equipment to the offshore operations. As a result, in much of the Grampian area in which Aberdeen is located unemployment rates have often been below the national average, and so this area has been omitted from the list of assisted areas since 1984. The same has been true of the Orkney and Shetland Islands off the northern tip of the mainland, where major oil terminals have been established. Concern about the disruptive impact of the oil economy with its massive influx of short-term construction activity (including an immigrant, largely male workforce) led the Shetlands to negotiate special arrangements to establish a dis-

turbance fund, for extracting revenue from the oil companies in order to safeguard the post–oil future.

North Sea oil has made a massive contribution to the British economy over the last 20 years, and in particular to government coffers through taxation measures extracting revenue from the oil operations. This has led to Scottish demands for a specific share of these revenues, but such pressure has generally been resisted.

In the remote and sparsely populated Highlands and islands, the disruptive social impact of oil-related activity on traditional communities has caused considerable concern. Thus, Shetland's population fell by 14 percent between 1981 and 1992, mainly reflecting the loss of temporary oil construction residents. In the same way, the construction of major industrial sites on the remote west coast of Scotland, to build platforms for the offshore industry, was contested as environmentally damaging in one of the last great wildernesses of Western Europe. The damage appeared all the more culpable in that some of the yards, once built, did little business. Fears have similarly been expressed over the risk of oilspills to marine and coastal life, but despite a few scares, these fears have so far proven to be largely unfounded.

While oil has benefited Aberdeen and Shetland and a few other scattered localities, the major part of the Highlands and islands to the north of the Highland line struggles to adapt to the changing circumstances of late twentieth-century Britain and to overcome the comparative disadvantage of location at Europe's periphery. This area is a traditional source of emigration, and its inaccessibility and low population density make the attraction of new sources of employment difficult. With agriculture and fishing in decline, provision of jobs for males is particularly problematical. It is a major challenge to the Highlands and Islands Development Board (HIDB), now renamed the Highland and Island Enterprise, which since 1965 has been attempting to diversify the area's economy. There have been some successes—with tourism (the major growth sector), with small-scale manufacturing, and with fish-farming (for salmon) in the sea-lochs.

Tourism tends to provide mostly female part-time employment and is highly seasonal, except in a few limited areas of winter sports development, as in the Cairngorms. There the development of ski lifts and access roads now threatens environmental impacts opposed by nature-lovers and conservationists. The problems of Highland development remain intractable.

Northern Ireland

The six counties of Northern Ireland, part of the historic province of Ulster, is the UK's smallest region by population, the poorest economically, and the most problematical politically. Long-term unemployment is substantial, and incomes are more than 30 percent below the national average. The political instability and violence (with over 3000 deaths from terrorism) over the last 25 years have had a major debilitating effect on its economy, but we should not forget that this effect has been compounded by a comparative disadvantage arising from peripherality, spatial separation from the mainland market (leading to higher costs in supplying it), small scale of the internal market in Northern Ireland, and weaknesses of its economic structure. Taking its political and economic problems together, it is not surprising that Northern Ireland qualifies as an Objective 1 region within the EU. There are, moreover, internal differences within Northern Ireland. The most disadvantaged areas lie in the west (around Derry) and in the south, close to the border with the Republic of Ireland, but there are also localities within Belfast, the province's leading city, where unemployment exceeds 50 percent of the workforce.

As early as the 1980s, there were signs that the Northern Ireland economy was becoming detached from the performance of the rest of the UK; it failed, for example, to participate in the boom of the 1980s. Nevertheless, in the 1990s there have been some signs of hope: the long-standing tradition of net outmigration has been reversed, and most importantly, the warring paramilitary loyalist and republican groups announced a cessation of violence in 1994. The peace process that was put in place was apparently consolidated by President Clinton's visit to Ireland in 1995, but, sadly, the Irish Republican Army (IRA) resumed its bombing

campaign in early 1996, targeting the streets of London, including the Docklands.

The roots of the political troubles in Northern Ireland and the sectarian conflict between Protestants and Catholics can be traced back to the English conquest of Ireland in the seventeenth century, expropriation of good agricultural land, and establishment of mainly Protestant English and Scottish settlers in Ulster in particular. The closeness of Scotland to Northern Ireland is worth emphasizing—it is only 12 miles (19 km) as the crow flies at the narrowest point, and close Scottish association with Ulster predates the seventeenth-century settlement. Northeast Protestant Ireland became increasingly integrated into the British economy during the nineteenth-century industrialization, whereas the Catholic remainder of Ireland was effectively deindustrialized and became dependent on agricultural exports. The Irish linen industry concentrated in the Belfast area, where industrialization was further boosted by textile-oriented engineering activities and, from the 1850s, by shipbuilding.

Protestant settlement was most marked in East Ulster, and here the settlers were too numerous and well-organized to be easily assimilated. As the industrial north and the agricultural south of Ireland diverged economically, Catholic migration took place to the north, especially during the disastrous Famine of the 1840s. By 1861, 34 percent of Belfast's population was Catholic, and competition between Catholics and Protestants for jobs frequently led to riots and discrimination against Catholics (Fig. 7-17).

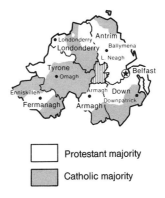

☐ Protestant majority

▨ Catholic majority

FIGURE 7-17 Religious affiliation in Northern Ireland.

Northern Ireland was established in 1921 when the solution of Britain's "Irish problem" was decreed to be partition: establishing a political unit tied to the UK and sending MPs (members of Parliament) to Westminster, but with a separate Northern Ireland Parliament too at Stormont.

Discrimination against Catholics by employers continued in the new state. In the postwar period, the two Irish economies converged leading to the Anglo-Irish Free Trade Agreement in 1965 and joint application to join the European Community. The consequent need for, but lack of progress toward, greater economic and political cooperation between north and south, and in particular for a reduction in anti-Catholic discrimination in the north, led to renewed violence. The quest of Catholics for civil rights and social justice led to a Protestant backlash to preserve their jobs in a context of deteriorating economic conditions in the UK. The deepening civil disturbance and increasing terrorist activity by the Provisional Irish Republican Army (IRA) in 1968 led to the suspension of the Stormont Parliament, the imposition of direct rule from London in 1972, and the introduction of 15,000 British troops.

Northern Ireland thus became deeply divided, with terrorist atrocities multiplying on both sides. The problem appears to be deeply intractable, with reunification of Ireland difficult to attain with a 2:1 UK-oriented, Protestant majority in the north. Parts of Belfast have developed into a Catholic ghetto, characterized by high levels of social deprivation, whereas Derry City has a Catholic majority. Nevertheless, in the 1990s signs of a breakthrough have at last been sighted, as both sides have become exhausted by the violent stalemate and appear prepared to negotiate. The permanent cessation of hostilities could produce either a peace deficit or a peace dividend in economic terms. Pessimists point out that over 20,000 people are employed in the security forces and related occupations; optimists argue that such potential job losses will be outweighed by increased inward investment, tourism, and other commercial development.

Northern Ireland offers a particularly favorable regional policy investment incentive package, with grants of up to 40 percent of capital expenditure available—much higher than on the British mainland. Only one week after the IRA ceasefire began, Hilton International announced that it would build a luxury hotel as the centerpiece of the new Laganside waterfront development in Belfast. This was an encouraging sign, while even before the ceasefire American disc drive manufacturer Seagate chose Derry for a $65 million (£45m) high-tech factory.

For the present, the Northern Ireland economy retains serious flaws. A quarter of its employment is based on public expenditure, the shipyards of Harland and Woolf have a doubtful future, and the low-wage levels could be interpreted as either a strength or a weakness. For the people of Northern Ireland, however, the 1995 peace dividend in personal freedom was incalculable, and the return of the bombing in 1996 brought mass protest onto the streets of Belfast.

THE REPUBLIC OF IRELAND

The partition of Ireland in 1921 and the establishment of the Irish Free State—later to become the Republic of Ireland (1949)—brought to an apparent end domination by the English and the sense of colonial occupation by an alien power. However, it would be a mistake to believe that the ties to Britain were severed. Western Europe's newest independent state, in fact, retained strong economic, social, and demographic connections with mainland Britain, and proximity to Great Britain has remained the single most important factor in Ireland's human geography. The UK has been, for example, the principal destination of Irish migration and is the Republic's most important trading partner. It has been observed that when the UK economy is thriving, the rate of population decline in Ireland tends to lessen.

The nineteenth century was a traumatic period for Ireland, when it functioned as a periphery to the British core. Catholic Ireland was largely rural and agricultural; it supplied large quantities of food and cheap labor to the expanding industrial economy of England. In contrast to what was happening in Protestant Ulster, it also suffered deindustrialization. One million Irish died in the Great Famine of 1845–1848, when the potato crop failed, and nearly twice that number emigrated (Fig. 7-18). Between 1841 and 1911 the population of what is now the Republic fell from 6.5 million to 3.2 million people. In this period urban growth was extremely limited, rural areas were depopulated by emigration, and fertility was reduced.

The Irish economy suffered from grave locational handicaps compared with England, while the Irish market was too small to provide a strong basis for industrial development. After independence, tariffs were used to protect the home market, but the impact was modest, and despite high birth rates, the size of the Irish population remained static. In the western parts of Ireland, population decline continued, especially in the receding *Gaeltacht*, the territorial pockets of native Gaelic culture on the Atlantic margins. Here lived the remaining Gaelic speakers (of whom there were still 58,000 in 1981).

In the early postwar period, the problems of Irish development became very apparent. The policy of protectionism had largely failed. Irish workers had free entry to Great Britain. Between 1951 and 1961 the population of the Republic again declined, and emigration reached its highest levels since the turn of the century. Ireland was still a stagnant periphery to England's dynamic core.

In the 1960s and 1970s the situation improved markedly, as deliberate policies were introduced to attract foreign capital and to encourage industrial development in the west in the "Underdeveloped Areas" (from 1952)—later renamed the "Designated Areas." The *Gaeltarra Eireann*, a Development Board to sustain the Irish-speaking

FIGURE 7-18 House in a village in western Ireland deserted by its inhabitants during the potato famine. (W. H. Berentsen)

areas, was established in 1957 (Fig. 7-19). A major showpiece was the establishment near Limerick of the Shannon Free Airport Industrial Estate as a free trade area in 1959. This successfully attracted numerous international manufacturing companies and laid the foundation for development of a growth-centered approach to rural industrializa-

tion. Shannon, tended to exist as an enclave, however, with comparatively little influence beyond the Limerick labor market.

A major boost came from EC membership in 1973, with financial benefits to many areas under the Common Agricultural Policy and with foreign industrial investment taking off, especially from

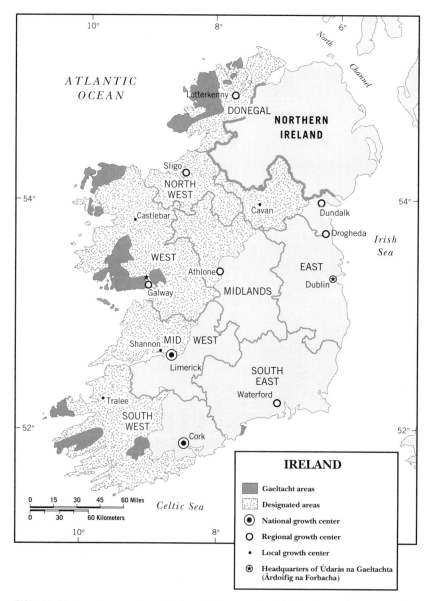

FIGURE 7-19 Planning regions, designated areas, the Gaeltacht, and proposed growth areas in the Republic of Ireland in the mid-1980s. (after Brunt, 1988)

the United States, the UK, and West Germany, attracted by the low-cost environment and the lowest wage rates in the EC (until Spain, Portugal, and Greece joined). The Irish population grew by 15 percent between 1971 and 1981, and all regions experienced immigration (a trend doubtless aided by the weakness of the UK economy). However, problems reemerged in the 1980s. Growing competition in the global economy led export-based industrialization to falter and inflation and unemployment rose. The Republic had also become a major debtor country, and austerity measures had to be introduced. Although between 1979 and 1986 Ireland had the highest population growth rate in the EC, after 1986 total population decline returned—the result of both renewed net emigration and lower natural increase. The lower birth rate indicated the effect of social changes—the reduction in family size and wider adoption of birth control, and the feminization of the workforce as the result of rural industrial development.

Both the economy and geography of the Republic are still in a stage of transition, but it is clear that the core-periphery pattern within the British Isles is replicated within the Republic itself. The east-west contrasts in development noted in Northern Ireland are mirrored south of the border, and just as Belfast dominates Northern Ireland, so Dublin dominates the Republic. Dublin is a primate city and has received a major boost from the restoration of its functions as national capital; its position as a control center has been enhanced since 1973 by its role as an EU capital (Fig. 7-20). It is the most attractive location in the Republic for most types of development, including financial and business services. Sprawling greater Dublin houses 30 percent of the Republic's population, though growth has also brought a less attractive side. Some of its large

FIGURE 7-20 Ireland is increasingly being used as a back-office location for U.S. companies. (By permission of Chris Duggin, Daily Telegraph)

housing estates have the highest unemployment and worst poverty levels in the country.

Ireland has made the shift to an urbanized society. More people now live in towns than in the countryside, but outside Dublin there are no large cities; this is a handicap in any attempt to create more even patterns of regional development. Cork, the second largest city, had a population of only 127,000 in 1991, despite considerable growth since independence.

Industrial growth has tended to create a branch plant economy, with foreign-owned plants purchasing a low proportion of inputs in Ireland. In the 1980s some of these plants were closed. The indigenous industrial sector has remained retarded, and self-sustaining industrial growth has not been achieved. Foreign firms currently provide 60 percent of export earnings. Despite some success in industrial dispersal in the 1970s, the fundamental core-periphery pattern of development within the Republic remains, with the Dublin-centered east the favored core region.

Western Ireland, particularly the Atlantic fringe, continues to be quintessentially a place on the margin. Although the landscape is beautiful and the environment unpolluted, prospects are limited and the comparative disadvantage for many forms of economic activity is great. Tourism is one exception (it now provides 6% of employment in the Republic as a whole), but the Gaeltacht hardly offers opportunities for mass marketing. The environment is relatively harsh for farming. The need for structural reform in agriculture has not been fully met, and the benefits of EU membership are now much reduced for the Irish farmer. In the Republic as a whole, 15 percent of the workforce is still in agriculture (compared to 2.4% in the UK).

The Republic of Ireland's economic performance shows few signs of convergence with the EU average. Incomes are still more than 25 percent below that average, qualifying the entire country for Objective 1 status under EU regional policy. The population density is one of the lowest in the EU, and with a population of only 3.5 million in 1991 only Luxembourg has fewer people. The optimistic view is that growth will trickle down in Europe, and that information technology will offer

escape from the disadvantages of peripheral location and the lack of critical mass. There are some positive signs of this effect in Ireland's growing role as a back-office for firms headquartered in Europe's core or in the leading U.S. cities. Thus, a leading U.S. data processing firm employs more than 600 people in the Shannon area who are on line each day to its mainframe computer in Colorado via a satellite link leased from AT&T, with 20,000 items of electronic mail sent daily. A New York life insurance company takes advantage of the five hour time difference with Shannon to process claims that are flown in overnight, with the decisions relayed back by satellite on the same working day. However, it will be more difficult to attract higher order, decision-making functions. Pessimists fear that marginality may increase. While the Channel Tunnel may draw England closer to Europe's core, there is no equivalent in prospect for the Irish Sea.

There are, however, signs of convergence within divided Ireland between Northern Ireland and the Irish Republic, with increasing similarities in various aspects of their human geography. Both have problems of peripherality, and both are characterized by the growth of a dominant city, uneven rural depopulation, and severe long-term unemployment. Economic growth in both parts of Ireland has been based on investment from outside, and both, therefore, face the dilemmas of the branch plant economy—namely, that employment will be cut in the Irish branches whenever a recession occurs. Demographic behavior has become more similar across the border. Convergence has been complemented by growing economic and political cooperation (although the currencies remain different), and the arrival of the peace process in 1994 (though still incomplete) offers hope that this cooperation may be enhanced in the future. However, the prospect of a united Ireland remains remote.

CONCLUSION

In the last 100 years, Britain has lost its position of political and economic hegemony within the world system. It is no longer the workshop of the world, and it has lost its worldwide Empire; however, it has entered into new political relationships in Europe. It is not possible to unravel the complex identity of the UK today without appreciating the impact of the world role that the country played in the past. Similarly, the changes that have taken place in the country's internal geography and in the fortunes of different localities are comprehensible only in terms of relationships to the international economy. Thus, the continuing dominance of the South in Britain is linked to the legacy of the past by the position of London as a world city. London, with New York and Tokyo, remains one of the great financial nodes of the global economy, and its continuation in that role appeared to be secured in the 1980s by a relaxation of trading regulations (the so-called Big Bang policy changes in 1986). The financial activities of the city of London predate modern industrialization and have survived Britain's manufacturing decline. Their continuing success appears crucial to both national and regional performance.

During the two decades since the UK entered the European Union, despite the success of the financial services industry and the substantial benefits of North Sea oil development, the country has continued to slide toward the position of an average European country. Among the major world economies it has fallen behind Germany, France, and perhaps even Italy, and by 1995 it had slipped to eighteenth position in world rank of total domestic output (GDP) per capita—even behind its former colonies Hong Kong and Singapore. Within Europe, the British Isles occupy a peripheral location, and there is a real danger that this position will be converted into second-tier status in the EU for the United Kingdom as well as the Republic of Ireland. Alternatively, changes in spatial relations and accessibility to "continental" Europe may accentuate the existing patterns of core and periphery *within* Britain.

Certainly, the consequences of economic and social change in the last 20 years have been the intensification of uneven development at a variety of scales. Arguably, however, inequalities have been heightened by the policies adopted by Conservative governments since their return to power in 1979, with the Thatcherite emphasis on the benefits of competition, the virtues of the enterprise culture, and the roll back of state intervention and support. The 1980s saw increasing divergence between the haves and have-nots in British society, with the reemergence of a deprived underclass (and visible poverty in the beggars and the homeless on the streets of London), the shrinking of the core full-time workforce, and the expansion of peripheral part-time and temporary employment. Identifying the haves and have-nots on a geographical basis has become complicated, but despite some faltering in the recession of the early 1990s, the winners appear to lie especially in outer southeast England and adjacent districts. There employment growth has taken place in the attractive residential milieu of small and medium-sized towns and cities like Cambridge, Bracknell, Newbury, Milton Keynes, and Bournemouth.

The UK's economy has evolved over a long period into one where service industries dominate the employment structure. The shift to a postindustrial society has gone furthest in southeast England. The key components of growth have become the producer services of finance and business and, despite encouraging growth in other centers like Birmingham, Leeds, and Edinburgh, these are most strongly represented in southeast England. The southeast also contains a disproportionate share of the more dynamic sectors of manufacturing, especially high-tech industry, particularly in Silicon Vale west of London and centers like Cambridge. Another growing service industry is tourism and leisure. The number of overseas visitors to the UK more than doubled in the 1980s (although still considerably exceeded by the number of UK residents visiting overseas). Despite the problems of foreign competition facing their traditional holiday resorts, southeast and southwest England together still account for over 40 percent of tourist-related employment in the UK.

Although much of affluent southern England has moved firmly into the postindustrial era—and increasingly suffers the problems of competition for land and overloaded infrastructure—there are other districts where the negative aspects of deindustrialization remain more evident than the positive aspects of postindustrialism. The principal losers in late-twentieth-century Britain include many of the traditional industrial towns and cities of the north and west. Despite considerable efforts at revitalization and image reconstruction, cities like Liverpool, Belfast, Sunderland, and Glasgow consistently feature among the worst performing cities in the EU based on a wide range of economic and social indicators. The inner areas of cities throughout the UK also continue to face major problems of decay and poverty, although increasingly these problems have spread to include the desolate outer city public housing estates built in the 1950s and 1960s.

The political map of the British Isles in the twentieth century has seen momentous changes, with the partition of Ireland and the establishment of a new nation-state. Devolution and nationalism have emerged as critical issues in Wales and Scotland, while sectarian conflict in Northern Ireland has been a running sore in the life of the UK since the 1960s, with bombing and murder spreading intermittently to the streets of English cities and threatening the security of government itself. These remain major problems, although there were more hopeful signs for resolution of the Northern Ireland problem in 1995 than for many years. But then came renewed IRA bombing during 1996. While antagonism to Westminster in Scotland in particular remains strong, it may be that opportunities for development of a federal structure within the broader context of the European Union may help to preserve the stability of the United Kingdom of Great Britain and Northern Ireland.

BIBLIOGRAPHY

Balchin, P. N. (1990). *Regional Policy in Britain: The North-South Divide.* London: Chapman.

Brownill, S. (1990). *Developing London's Docklands: Another Great Planning Disaster?* London: Chapman.

Brunt, B. (1988). *The Republic Of Ireland.* London: Chapman.

Castells, M., and P. Hall, (1994). *Technopoles of the World.* New York: Routledge.

Champion, A. G., and A. E. Green. (1991). "Britain's Economic Recovery and the North-South Divide." *Geography,* 76 (3): 249–254.

Champion, A. G., and A. R. Townsend. (1986). *Contemporary Britain: A Geographical Perspective.* London: Arnold.

Daniels, P. W. (1995). "Services in a Shrinking World." *Geography* 80 (2): 97–110.

Department of Trade and Industry. (1995). *The Energy Report.* London: HMSO.

Forrest, R., and D. Gordon. (1993). *People and Places—A 1991 Census Atlas of England.* Bristol: SAUS.

Gold, J. R., and S.V. Ward, eds. (1994). *Place Promotion: The Use of Publicity and Marketing to Sell Towns and Regions.* New York: John Wiley.

Gordon, D. and R. Forrest. (1995). *People and Places 2: Social and Economic Dimensions in England.* School of Advanced Urban Studies: Bristol.

Hall, P. (1981). "Issues for the Eighties," *The Planner,* 67, pp. 4–5.

Hall, P. (1988). *Cities of Tomorrow.* Cambridge: Blackwell.

Hall, P. (1992). *Urban and Regional Planning.* 3rd ed. New York: Routledge.

Harrison, R.T., and M., Hart eds. (1993). *Spatial Policy in a Divided Nation.* London: Kingsley.

Hechter, M. (1975). *Internal Colonialism: The Celtic Fringe in British National Development, 1536–1966.* Berkeley: University of California Press.

House, J. W., ed. (1979). *UK Space.* London: Weidenfeld & Nicolson.

Hudson, R., and A. Williams. (1986). *The United Kingdom.* London: Chapman.

Imrie, R., and H. Thomas, eds. (1993). *British Urban Policy and Urban Development Corporations.* London: Chapman.

Johnson, J. H. (1994). *The Human Geography of Ireland.* New York: John Wiley & Sons.

Kearns, G., and C. Philo. (1993). *Selling Places.* New York: Pergamon.

Keeble, D. E. (1976). *Industrial Location and Planning in the United Kingdom.* New York: Methuen.

Law, C.M. (1980). *British Regional Development since World War 1.* New York: Methuen.

Massey, D. (1984). *Spatial Divisions of Labour: Social Structures and the Geography of Production.* New York: Methuen.

Mohan, J., ed. (1989). *The Political Geography of Contemporary Britain.* Basingstoke: Macmillan.

Ordnance Survey. (1995). *Statlas UK: A Statistical Analysis of the United Kingdom.* Southampton: HMSO.

Pocock, D.C.D. (1963). "Iron and Steel at Scunthorpe." *East Midland Geographer* (3):124–138.

Robson, B. (1988). *Those Inner Cities*. Oxford: Clarendon.

Smith, J., ed. (1992). "British Passenger Transport: Into the 1990s," *Geography* 77 (1): 63–93.

Spooner, D. J., ed. (1995). "Regional Development in the UK. Part 1." *Geography* 80 (1): 72–89.

Spooner, D. J., ed. (1995). "Regional Development in the UK: Part 2." *Geography* 80 (2): 163–191.

Stamp, L. D., and S.H. Beaver. (1971). *The British Isles: A Geographic and Economic Survey*. 6th ed. London: Longman.

Townroe, P., and R. Martin, eds. (1992). *Regional Development in the 1990s: The British Isles in Transition*. London: Kingsley.

Urry, J. (1995). *Consuming Places*. New York: Routledge.

Wild, M.T., and P. Jones. (1991). *De-industrialization and New Industrialisation in Britain and Germany*. London: Anglo-German Foundation.

Literary References

Howard, E. (1902). *Garden Cities of Tomorrow*. London: Swan Sonnenschein.

Orwell, G. (1937). *The Road to Wigan Pie*r. London: V. Gollancz, Ltd.

Priestley, J. B. (1934). *English Journey*. London: Heinemann.

8

WESTERN EUROPE

Western Europe comprises a variety of regions, including those countries that during the Cold War were outside the realm of Soviet influence, as well as a more narrowly defined region made up of the mainland states of Northwestern Europe. The latter definition is used here for a region comprised of the Netherlands, Belgium, Luxembourg, and France. These countries account for 84.7 million inhabitants living on 238,929 sq miles of territory (618,826 sq km), an area about the size of the province of Alberta in Canada. Population densities by country vary considerably, with France having 277 people per sq mile (107 per sq km) compared to 862 per sq mile (333 per sq km) for Belgium and 980 per sq mile (378 per sq km) for the Netherlands, a country with one of the world's highest population densities. Numerous significant cities are found in this region, such as Amsterdam, Brussels, and Paris. With over 9 million inhabitants, Paris is the largest urban agglomeration in Europe (see Inset 8-1). All of the Western European states were original members of the European Community, now called the European Union, which by 1995 had grown to include 15 countries.

Three of Europe's four major physiographic regions are found in Western Europe (Fig. 8-1). The North European Lowland (and other major lowlands, including some captured from the seabed), embraces most of the Netherlands, western Belgium, the Paris and Aquitaine basins (Aquitaine in southwestern France), and the Rhine Valley of France. The Central Uplands and Plateaus physiographic region is found in the southern extension of the Netherlands, eastern Belgium, Luxembourg, and throughout France, and includes the Ardennes, Armorican Massif of Brittany, the Vosges near the French-German border, and Massif Central in south central France. The Alpine system is represented by the Alps, the Jura (on the Swiss-French border), and the Pyrenees on the border between France and Spain.

Western Europe, with the exception of Luxembourg, is decidedly maritime in orientation, its western edge fronting on water bodies such as the Gulf of Biscay, the Channel, and the North Sea—all part of the Atlantic Ocean. France also borders on the Mediterranean. Navigable rivers that ultimately flow into the sea, such as the Rhine in the Netherlands, the Scheldt in Belgium, the Mosel in

THE CENTRALITY OF PARIS AND THE
PARIS BASIN

The Paris Basin, the geographical heartland of France, is an area of low-lying sedimentary rocks, and covers almost one-quarter of its total surface. The Seine and its tributaries form the main river system for the Basin. However, sections of the Loire, Meuse, and Moselle have also played major roles in shaping the region's geography.

At one time the Paris Basin was inundated by a succession of seas into which were deposited sedimentary beds over 2000 m thick. These beds were flexed and raised by violent earth movements associated with the Alpine orogeny (mountain building era), and then subsequently eroded. The present landscape is the result of renewed river erosion caused by a more recent phase of general uplift, accompanied by additional deposition of materials.

Structurally, the Basin can be compared to a nest of broad, shallow bowls with jagged edges, each bowl and edge representing a different rock layer and escarpment (ridge), respectively. The escarpments and their outliers can best be understood by examining a geological map of Europe and detailed topographical sections of specific areas within the Basin.

The combination of a variety of rock types, variations in erosion, and location of superficial deposits have given rise to a number of natural regions. Within these regions, differences in physical geography have encouraged differences in cultural geography, such as settlement patterns and agricultural practices. Beauce, for example, where the soil is rich loam, is an area of extensive wheat cultivation, whereas the Brie region southeast of Paris has a topsoil of clay and is noted for dairying. Moreover, the communication net linking the natural regions has been influenced in many places by structure and erosion, as road and rail lines often follow river valleys and breaks in the escarpments. Climactic conditions within the Basin generally vary in relation to distance from the coast and elevation. Both summer and winter temperatures are more extreme farther inland, and although precipitation decreases from the coast, the higher eastern areas of the Paris Basin are wetter then the center.

The focal point of the Paris Basin is the country's capital, Paris. Occupying 2.2 percent of France's territory, in 1992 the Paris region, the six Departments of the Ile-de-France, held 18.8 percent of the country's population. A quarter of the workforce was engaged in the secondary sector and three-quarters in services. Per capita income was nearly three times the figure for the rest of France. Whereas the population of the city increased from 1.9 million in 1876 to a peak of 2.9 million in 1921, the population of the entire Paris region grew during the same period from 2.8 million to nearly 6 million. From 1946 to 1962, the city grew from 2.6 to 2.7 million, whereas the region increased from 6.4 to 8.4 million. Although the city's population declined in recent years from 2.9 million in 1962 to 2.1 million in 1990, the region has grown to 10.9 million (1993).

The growth of Paris has all but wiped away the original landscapes of the city's site. A Celtic tribe, the Parissi, built the walled settlement of Lutetia on the Ile-de-la-Cité, the highest of a number of islands in the meandering Seine. Crossing the Ile was the main north-south land route that intersected with east-west river traffic. Coming down from the Butte St. Geneviève on the south bank, this overland road headed through the gap between Montmarte and Belleville, the route taken today by roads, rail lines, and a canal.

Although early Roman expansion took place on the southern bank of the slopes of the Butte St. Geneviève, later development spread onto the low-lying northern bank that was part of the ancient river plain of the Seine. Following the downfall of the Romans, a period of stagnation ensued, lasting through the ninth-century Norman attacks. Finally, under the Capetian dynasty, Paris, which was still chiefly confined to the Ile-de-la-Cité and two bridge-heads north and south of the river, revived. The steady growth of the monarchy attracted commercial and industrial enterprises that combined with administrative functions to give the city its essential character. Centered on the Ile-de-la-Cité was the royal and ecclesiastical administration, the north bank became the predominant commercial quarter with port facilities and market areas, whereas the educational complex was located on the south or left bank.

Between 1180 and 1210, the first wall was built around the city, the forerunner of four other walls. The last one, constructed in the 1840s, formed the present limit of Paris, except for the Bois de Boulogne and Bois de Vincennes. Population, which remained about half a million during the eighteenth century, increased in 1841 to almost 1 million. By 1861 the incorporation of additional communes into the city raised the total to 1.7 million. During the latter half of the nineteenth century, Paris was transformed by Baron Haussmann, whose work resulted in the basic layout of the present city. Streets were widened, new roads were built, the railway stations were placed in a circle outside the old city, cultural activities were enhanced, and parks such as the Bois de Boulogne were laid out.

Continuing industrialization and improving communications gave impetus to and facilitated the city's expansion. By the early years of the twentieth century, the built-up areas filled in the city limits and spilled out unchecked into the suburbs, swallowing up rural villages. After World War I, development pushed even farther out into the countryside, spreading in a linear fashion along the main lines of communication.

Today, Paris can best be portrayed as a congested inner city, corresponding to the limits of the 1840 wall, in which the commercial, cultural, educational, and administrative functions are carried out, and a sprawling, expanding suburban area, the Parisian agglomeration, in which the larger industries are located and the newer residential areas are concentrated. Because of a lack of amenities in the suburbs, residents commute to Paris, adding to the crowded living and working conditions in the inner city.

The French government has attempted to solve some of the problems caused by the growth of Paris. Beginning in 1928 and continuing through the war years, various schemes were drawn up, but little was accomplished. Finally, in 1960, the Plan for Development and General Organization for Paris (PADOG) was approved. PADOG attempted to limit the growth of Paris, while at the same time it planned to rebuild the transport network, create new commercial development centers in the suburbs, and renew the inner city.

To implement PADOG, the District of the Region of Paris was established in 1961 in an area covering the Departments of Seine-et-Marne and Seine-et-Oise, and the Department of Seine, which has since been reorganized. Covering an area 10 times larger than the Paris agglomeration, the District is a unique administrative unit with a total of 1315 communes, more than 1000 of which are rural. The agency's main functions are to study the problems of the Paris region, to finance proposed solutions, and to continue a comprehensive planning policy in an ever changing environment.

In 1965 the District published a new master plan for the Paris region, the *Schéma Directeur d'Aménagement et d'Urbanism de la Région de Paris*, which set out guidelines until the year 2000. The PADOG scheme to halt the physical growth of Paris was replaced by a plan forecasting at least 14 million people in the Paris region. A number of significant planning proposals have been brought forth in the *Schéma* to provide more favorable living conditions for the forecasted population increase. Taking into consideration the region's physical, economic, and human geography, the planners have laid out two development axes extending on both sides of the Seine westward toward Rouen, Le Havre, and Caen, and eastward to Meaux and Melun. To maintain the region's natural landscape, existing green spaces and wooded areas are being preserved, recreation areas have been established, and the urban zones have been set back several miles from the river, thereby protecting the banks from speculative building. Five new cities have been created in both underdeveloped areas or from renovated or extended suburbs. Similarly, six urban centers in the inner suburbs have been renovated. A nationwide food distributing center, which replaced the congested Les Halles in the heart of Paris, is located at Rungis. Furthermore, Europe's largest warehousing complex, Eurostore, has been established near Le Bourget airport, whereas Charles de Gaulle airport near Rossy-en-France handles most international flights.

The most ambitious scheme outside the city is La Défense, a massive office and residential development across the Seine to the north of the Bois de Boulogne (see Fig. 6-15).Which consists of apartments, flats, shopping centers, *la Grande Arche*, and skyscrapers. Numerous national and international companies, such as Esso, Fiat, Roussel Hoechst, and Rank Xerox, have their headquarters there. A fast, regional metro connects La Défense to the inner city.

Within central Paris a number of projects have been completed, including a shopping center and transportation node at the site of the old Les Halles, new museums, such as the Orsay and Pompidou Center, the renovation of the Louvre, a new opera at the Bastille, and the station complex on the site of the old Gare Montparnasse. Towering nearly 200 m above the city, this skyscraper block is completely out of scale with the rest of the city's low skyline but provides a superb view of the Eiffel Tower and inner city from its observation floor. All of the areas earmarked for urban expansion have been or will be connected by new transit facilities. A 155-mile (250-km) regional express metro network crossing through the center of Paris has been built to serve the outer suburbs. The lines, sections of which were linked together in 1978 in a station under les Halles, have eliminated much commuter congestion. In addition, an expanding network of highways and *autoroutes* is trying to keep pace with the traffic congestion of the urban agglomeration.

The centrality of Paris may be understood by examining the multifaceted functions of the city and the Ile-de-France. Administrative roles include the city, region, and the country; thus, all of the political parties have their main offices in Paris. Economic power is reflected in the head offices of 50 percent of French companies, including 96 percent of French banks. The city is a major financial, publishing, media, and educational center. For example, nearly 42 percent of all foreign students in France study in Paris, and 80 percent of all French books are published there. The city is the dominant cultural center in Europe and is a tourist magnet for the whole world. Industries in the region include electronics, automobiles, aerospace, pharmaceuticals, food processing, and textiles and clothing. Paris is the second largest European city for air traffic, and its port accounted for nearly 21 million tons of barge traffic in 1993. Thus, the Ile-de-France region, including Paris, despite official attempts to decentralize the Paris region, benefits from the centripetal nature of the situation, generates its own economic momentum, and continues to expand.

Luxembourg, and the Rhine, Seine, Loire, Garonne, and Rhône in France allowed access to the hinterlands and resulted in the development of ports such as Rotterdam, the world's largest, at the Rhine's mouth, Antwerp on the Sheldt estuary, Le Havre where the Seine flows into the Channel, St. Nazaire on the estuary of the Loire, Bordeaux where the Garonne meets the Gironde estuary, and Marseille-Fos to the east of the Rhône delta.

Another result of the proximity of the sea is the maritime climate that prevails over much of Western Europe. The mean January isotherm of 32°F (0°C) trends north-south from the Jutland Peninsula so that in nearly all regions of Western Europe January temperatures are above freezing. July isotherms register less than 64°F (18°C) in the north of France and most of Belgium and the Netherlands, to over 72°F (22°) in the south of France and along the Mediterranean littoral (coastal area).

The physical landscape has also affected the historical evolution and economic development of Western Europe. For example, all of the countries, except Luxembourg, played a role in the voyages of discovery and at one time or another maintained large colonies in Africa, Asia, and North America. France's proximity to German lands resulted in wars that ravaged Europe from the time of the breakup of Charlemagne's empire until the end of World War II. The Central Uplands and Plateaus were vital in the establishment of iron and steel industries based on both iron and coal situated within or on the fringe of these areas. The coal mines and steel mills of northern France and the Massif Central, southern Belgium, and southern Netherlands, many of which are now closed, bear witness to these developments. Several of these areas are undergoing industrial restructuring that includes the introduction of high-tech industries (see section on Flanders and Wallonia). Furthermore, good soils along with a maritime climate led to the development of intensive agricultural practices such as dairying, market gardening, and greenhouse cultivation, as well as the growing of grain.

The rural landscape of Western Europe is characterized by distinct regions ranging from the intensely cultivated flat lands of northern France, western Belgium, and most of the Netherlands to the bocage or hedgerows of the Armorican uplands

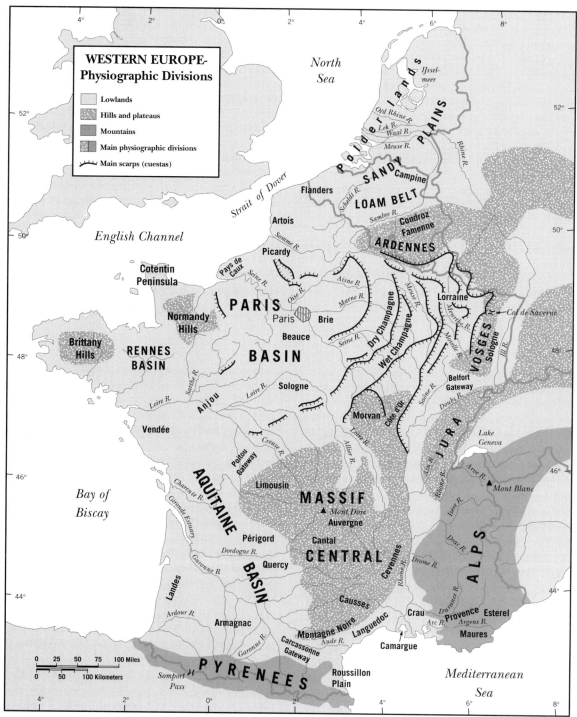

FIGURE 8-1 Physiographic divisions of Western Europe.

of western France and the pasturelands of the Massif Central, Pyrenees, Jura, and Alps (Fig. 8-2).

Urbanization, especially in France, dates to Celtic times; the Romans built on the Celtic foundations. Cities such as Paris in the north, Lyon at the confluence of the Saône and Rhône, and Arles, Orange, and Nîmes in the south, prospered, their Roman ruins being important tourist attractions today. Both rural and urban landscapes are linked by rail, including the high-speed TGV (Trains à Grande Vitesse), national highways, four to six lane divided, toll *autoroutes*, frequent air service, and canals (found mainly in the north). The Channel Tunnel and ferry service connecting England with France, Belgium, and the Netherlands completes this admirable network that represents one of the densest transportation systems in the world.

FRANCE

France, the largest of the Western European countries (roughly the same size as the states of California and New York) and encompassing many distinct physical and cultural realms, extends from the North Sea to the Mediterranean and from the western tip of the Armorican Massif to the Rhine Valley. As mentioned, three of the four physiographic regions of Western Europe are found in France. The ancient rocks of Hercynian Europe, the Central Uplands and Plateaus, are represented by the low hills of the Armorican Massif of Brittany and Normandy, the dissected block of the Ardennes, and the mountains of the Vosges and Massif Central; the younger Alpine system

FIGURE 8-2 The bocage landscape of Brittany. Rolling countryside with fields and pastures enclosed by hedgerows. Some of the farmsteads are isolated; others are clustered in hamlets and villages (French Embassy, Press and Information Division).

includes the folded mountains of the French Jura, and the peaks of the Alps and Pyrenees; whereas the low-lying sedimentary deposits of the Paris and Aquitaine basins and the Rhine Valley are part of the North European Lowlands.

This variety of physical landscapes, subjected to contrasting climatic conditions, permits a mixture of agriculture ranging from dairying, wheat, and flax cultivation in the north to the growing of rice, olives, and citrus fruits along the Mediterranean coast and in Corsica. In addition, industrial development based on local supplies of raw materials initially occurred in key regions of the country, but especially in the north (coal) and east (iron ore).

The diversity of both the agricultural and industrial sectors complemented by a population that has grown to 58 million has provided France with a powerful economic base that expanded strongly during the post–Second World War period. Per capita income was $21,706 ($18,709 purchasing power parities—PPPs) in 1993. Growth in recent years has been hindered by conflicting government policies. For example, the Socialists nationalized many sectors of industry and commerce in 1981, whereas the conservative governments of 1986–1988 and from 1993 on began a process of returning them to private ownership. Thus, observers have questioned the long-term competitiveness of French industry. Although there are exceptions, investment abroad has not kept pace with that of its other European competitors. Too many firms have not achieved economies of scale by enlarging output; far too few companies have strategies that go beyond the domestic market. In addition, the debt of French companies is higher than that of their British or German counterparts.

The positive aspects for the future may be summarized as follows. Certain French companies have strengthened their balance sheets because of profits and the raising of capital on the stock market; mergers and acquisitions have provided a European or worldwide dimension for many French firms; and the country finally realizes that a European vision, rather than a limited nationalistic French one, will pay more dividends in industry, economic policy, and defense. Nevertheless, in 1994 there were only 5 French companies among the top 50 European firms by market assets, com-

pared to 21 from the UK (of which 2 were Anglo-Dutch) and 8 from Germany.

As the last decade before the twenty-first century winds down, inflation has been cut to under 3 percent, unemployment is a record high 12 percent, and the latest conservative government not only must boost economic growth and find meaningful jobs for its citizens (for example, in 1993 unemployment was 23.2% among the under 25-year-old labor force), but must also find ways to neutralize the largest extreme right-wing party in Europe, the National Front. Characterized by ultra-xenophobia, the right exploits the country's racial problems and focuses on rising levels of crime and terrorism.

Historical Perspective

The borders that separate France from the neighboring states of Belgium, Luxembourg, Germany, Switzerland, Italy, and Spain are relatively old and stable. In the past 200 years, except for minor alterations, the general hexagonal shape of the country has been maintained. Parts of the French frontier correspond approximately to "natural" divisions: the massive Pyrenees to the south; and the glaciated Alps, undulating Jura, and Rhine depression to the east. The northern boundary, largely the result of historical circumstances, reflects neither physical geography, economic interests, nor cultural traditions and often divides peoples and activities between countries. For example, iron ore (France) is separated from coal (Germany) deposits, Germanic-speaking Alsatians live in France, and French-speaking people reside in Belgium.

Since prehistoric times, France has been a geographic stage on which a multitude of invaders have played diverse roles, either as settlers, destructors, or conquerors. The Phoenicians settled the site where later the Greeks founded Massalia (Marseille) just east of the Rhône Delta in about 600 B.C. Between the eighth and tenth centuries, raiding parties of Britons and Normans sailed many miles inland up the drowned river valleys of the Seine and Loire, pillaging and laying waste to the countryside. France's land barriers have also been easily breached. The Pyrenees were crossed with relative facility along the Atlantic and

Mediterranean coasts. Today, the Basque and Catalan peoples live on both sides of these mountains. Between the Pyrenees and Massif Central, the Carcassonne Gap provided a low-level routeway. From the Mediterranean shores to Burgundy (east central France) and beyond, the valleys of the Rhône between the Massif Central and the Alps, and the Saône, dividing the Paris Basin from the Jura, have allowed access for intruding armies from pre-Roman times until World War II. Movement around the Vosges has been facilitated in the south by the Belfort Gap between the Vosges and the Jura and in the north by the Saverne Gap west of Strasbourg. The North European Plain curves southwest between the North Sea and Ardennes in northern France, providing an easy route into the Paris Basin. This was the direction the German armies took during the Franco-Prussian War, the First World War, and again in World War II after the Nazi panzer units had broken through the Ardennes near Sedan on the Belgian border.

The distinct historical evolution of the French population has resulted in strong regional identities that have resisted the French government's traditional efforts at centralization. Economic and political autonomy, initiated by the Socialists in the early 1980s, for peoples such as the Bretons, Basques, Catalans, Alsatians, and Corsicans will continue to be necessary to defuse political unrest. In the Corsican case, even these measures have failed to halt the spate of bombings, murders, and assassinations, perpetuated by small separatist groups and criminal elements, that have racked this beautiful, mountainous island.

For nearly 1400 years, Paris has been the center of gravity in France. Focal point of the Paris Basin, the city became dominant because of historical and physical circumstances. The French kings expanded their domains outward from the nucleus of the Ile-de-la-Cité in the Seine and the surrounding area, the Ile-de-France (Fig. 8-3). Then, Paris was an important crossing point for land and water routes; today, the city serves a similar function. The major lines of communication and transportation from all over France converge on the capital. The centrality of Paris is further emphasized by demographics: nearly 20 percent of the French population lives in the region of Ile-de-France (10.8 million) and over 25 percent of the country's GDP originates from this area. Comprising just 2.2 percent of the country's land area, the Ile-de-France (the historic city of Paris with about 2 million population, as well as seven surrounding departments) accounts for over 22 percent of the economically active population, 25 percent of the major industrial establishments, 38 percent of office workers, and 50 percent of head offices (see Inset 8-1).

Population and Economy

France had a population of 58.5 million in 1996, inhabiting a geographically diverse landscape of 211,200 sq miles (547,000 sq km). Following World War II, the country's birth rate began to rise, reversing the trend that had existed since the early nineteenth century. Although population had increased by only 12.5 million between 1800 and 1945, it rose by the same amount between 1945 and 1975. Thus, the birth rate, which was one of the lowest in the world before World War II, 14.6 per 1000 in 1939, rose to more than 20 per 1000 immediately after the war. It has since declined to about 14 per 1000, reflecting the downward trend among the industrialized countries of Western Europe. The age structure, in common with most countries of Western Europe, reveals nearly 70 percent of the population between 15 and 64 years of age and only 21 percent under age 14. There are about 3.75 million foreigners, mainly Portuguese, Algerians, and Moroccans, who comprise about 5 percent of the labor force and as much as 20 percent of the country's unskilled workers. As elsewhere in Western Europe, they do the dirty, noisy, dangerous, and heavy work unacceptable to the native citizens. Ethnic tension relating to the large number of foreigners, especially "Blacks" and North Africans, has given the right-wing National Front (a political party) its raison d'être. Population is shifting from the industrial rust-belt of the north (Nord-Pas-de-Calais) and eastern France to the more economically promising and milder climatic regions of the west, southwest, and Mediterranean. The movement may be explained both by young people searching for work and by pensioners retiring in these areas. In addition, many North African immigrants with birth rates up to five times as high as the French are settling along the

FIGURE 8-3 Aerial view of the Île-de-la-Cité St. Louis in the heart of Paris, in the middle of the Seine River. Notre Dame Cathedral is at center (French Tourist Office).

Mediterranean. In 1995, capitalizing on the fears of locals, the National Front elected mayors in Nice, Toulon, and Orange—all in the south.

Following the trend of other Western European countries, the percentage of the labor force engaged in the primary sector has dropped, as has the percentage engaged in the secondary sector. There has been a profound shift to the service sectors. For example, between 1977 and 1986, nearly 500,000 jobs disappeared in farming and 1.4 million in industry. Services expanded to absorb most of the losses. In 1993 the percentages of employment were as follows: primary 5.1; secondary 27.7; and tertiary 67.2. All told, between 1983 and 1993

there was an increase of 6.3 percent of the civilian labor force to 25.2 million. Between 1987 and 1990, roughly 800,000 new jobs were created; however, the number of jobless fell by only 160,000 because of a hidden labor supply and population growth. Unemployment, as mentioned, remained at 12 percent in 1994.

Energy and Electricity

France, highly dependent on foreign energy sources, ranks second after Germany in Western Europe's production of electricity. Output is characterized by a declining use of fossil fuels, a steady level of hydroelectric production, and an increasing reliance on nuclear plants. Production in 1993 was over 474 trillion kwh compared to 346 trillion kwh in 1986; 15 percent was derived from hydro sources and 78 percent from nuclear power plants. France's use of nuclear power is the highest in Western Europe; in fact, it is the world's most nuclear dependent country in the world.

Coal production, mainly from mines in Lorraine, has steadily diminished from a postwar high of 53 million tons in 1963 to only 8.6 million in 1993. The same year 15 million tons were imported, the United States (4.7 million tons) and Australia (2.8 million tons) providing the bulk of imports. Natural gas production declined from 270 million cu ft in 1974 to only 124 million cu ft in 1993, as the deposits in the southwest near Lacq are being depleted. Imports of 1075 million cu ft from Russian, Algeria, Norway, and the Netherlands serve over 5000 municipalities and 25 million consumers. In 1994 a new 20-year contract was signed with Norway that will increase Norway's share of gas from 18 percent to 30 percent. Petroleum output was only 2.8 million tons in 1993 from wells in the Paris and Aquitaine basins. Imports were over 78 million tons from numerous sources in the Middle East (50.3% of the total), Africa (19%), the North Sea (18%), and the former Soviet Union.

France has been a pioneer in the use of hydroelectric energy; however, the best sites have already been exploited, and new plants are less efficient and more expensive than the old facilities. Aside from the Alps, Pyrenees, and Massif Central, the remaining areas of major production are the Rhine and Rhône River dams constructed after World War II. The country also boasts the world's first tidal power-generating station. It was inaugurated in 1966 at a dam across the Rance Estuary near St. Malo on the Brittany coast, and the rise and fall of the tides provide the motive force.

France has a significant oil refining industry, with an annual capacity in 1993 of 84 million tons, fourth in Europe after Italy, Germany, and the UK, and ninth in the world. The major locations are coastal: l'Etang d'Berre, Fos, and Lavera near the Rhone Delta in the south; Marseille; the lower Seine between Rouen and Le Havre in the north; and the Gironde region near Bordeaux. Lyon, on the South European pipeline, which terminates at Karlsruhe, Germany in the Rhine Valley, is also a significant refining center. Because of too many installations in Western Europe, however, refining has been a contracting industry.

In 1992 oil accounted for 40.3 percent of primary energy consumption, natural gas 12.7 percent, coal 8.4 percent, electricity (including nuclear) 38.3 percent, and new energy sources such as solar power, 1.9 percent. Taking into account France's domestic coal and gas output, and the 15 percent of electricity generated by hydroelectric plants, home-based resources accounted for nearly 50 percent of consumption. This is up from 42 percent in 1984 and only 22 percent in 1973, when nuclear power accounted for just 1.8 percent of primary energy. The country's goal is to meet 50 percent of its energy needs through domestic resources.

Raw Materials

Because of its geologic diversity, France possesses a number of raw materials. Nevertheless, it still lacks large quantities of basic materials necessary for modern industry. Iron ore, bauxite, potash, rock salt, and sulfur are the only commodities available in generous amounts. Iron ore production, second in Europe after Sweden, declined from 16.7 million tons in 1974 to just 1.27 million in 1993 as uneconomic mines were closed. Moreover, because of decreasing demand and foreign competition, the European steel industry has been in a contracting state for over a decade. Bauxite, named after the Provençal village of Les Baux, is found in large quantities in Provence and Languedoc in the south. Production, once second in Europe after Greece, has dropped from 2.9 million tons in 1974 to zero. The reasons for the cut in production include cheaper bauxite from overseas, low demand for aluminum, and imports of aluminum from the former Soviet Union—all factors depressing the market.

In 1904 large deposits of high-quality potash were discovered in the Rhine Valley northwest of Mulhouse. The Germans, who then controlled this region, protected production elsewhere in Germany by doing little to develop them. After 1918 the area became part of France and production was expanded. In 1974 a total of 2.3 million tons were mined to be used for fertilizer and for primary material in the chemical industry. Production, second after Germany, was only 1.2 million tons in 1992. One serious problem resulting from the mines is the salinization of the Rhine from mine wastes (tailings). Lastly, France has become one of Europe's major producers of sulfur, a chemical associated with the natural gas deposits discovered after the war at Lacq near the Pyrenees in the southwest.

Industry

The changes that affected French industry during the 1980s and 1990s illustrate the impact of this sector on the overall economic strength of the country. Factors such as location, regional disparities, unemployment, inflation, GDP and economic growth were directly related to how well industry fared. Thus, in order to understand the contemporary geography of France, a detailed analysis of the industrial sector is necessary (Fig. 8-4).

In the decade 1980 to 1990, industry, located mainly in the north and east of France, underwent fundamental restructuring. In fact, it has been buffeted by changes in governmental policy as never before in the country's history. After the Socialist election victory in the early 1980s and the subsequent nationalization of sectors such as steel, aluminum, and electronics, the government had to inject enormous sums into the nationalized sector to compensate for the previous private owners' lack of investment. In addition, state companies, such as the Renault automotive concern, were losing enormous sums. Despite the capital stimulant, losses continued and even became greater as French industry was subjected to the full fury of international competition. Iron and steel, automobile, aluminum, and consumer electronics production and shipbuilding were particularly hard hit. As losses mounted, the government was forced to change from a policy of *dirigisme*, or control, a policy strongly entrenched before the Socialists took over, to one of allowing market forces to establish

direction. As a result, the steel industry contracted, and the two main nationalized companies, Usinor and Sacilor, merged. Because of severe losses, companies such as Renault in the state sector, and Peugeot and Michelin controlled by private interests, were forced to rationalize and develop new strategies for the 1990s.

Other moves were necessary. The diversification that occurred during the 1960s and 1970s was redressed, and companies had to give up acquisitions that did not fit into their overall strategy. Thus, Péchiney, an aluminum firm, Thomson, an electronics concern, and Saint-Gobain, primarily a manufacturer of glass, led the way. Other firms, such as Creusot-Loire, an engineering group, did not survive and were liquidated.

The restructuring can be traced to a number of factors. First, the Socialists' initial policies boosted already high wage and social security costs. Second, high interest rates hurt those firms that had plunged into debt in the 1970s rather than raising fresh equity capital. Third, many companies were slow to adapt to changing world markets, maintaining excessive capacity and failing to move fast enough into new technologies. French research and development spending has been most effective in big, state-run projects like space, nuclear power, and armaments. The benefits for industry as a whole, and particularly for the consumer goods sector, have been limited. Generally, the country's industrial structure has been too rigid. The question is whether investment, privatization, and restructuring alone can revive France's industrial prospects, especially since unemployment has reached record levels.

The conservatives, after replacing the Socialists (1986–1988), made the recovery of French industry's competitiveness their top priority. Rather than state intervention, steps were taken to create a market economy in order to encourage the development and profitability of the industrial sector. Thus, the franc was devalued, taxes were reduced, exchange constraints eased, regulations concerning the firing of workers simplified, price controls lifted, energy and telecommunications deregulated, and privatization of state banks and industries was undertaken. For example, in 1987–1988, the

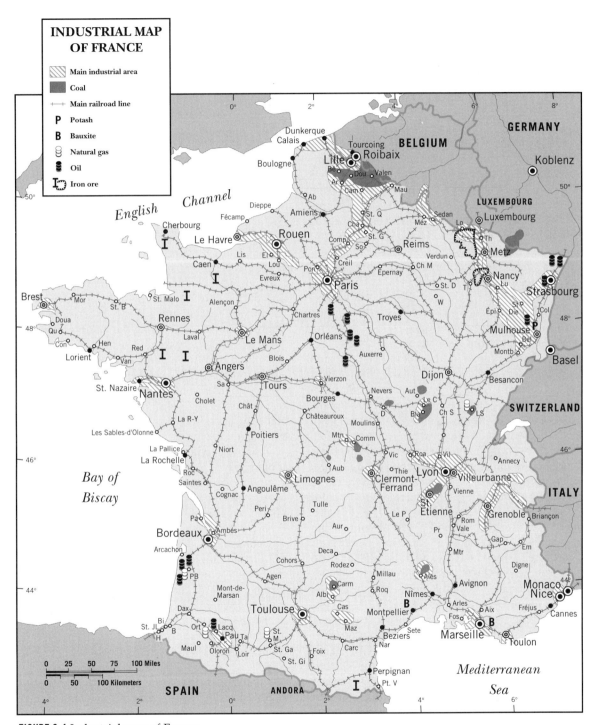

FIGURE 8-4 Industrial map of France.

conservative government sold off 13 state-owned firms, including Saint Gobain, Compagnié Generale d'Electricité, Paribas, Suez, and one of the big three French banks.

Privatization under a new, firmly entrenched conservative government has continued during the 1990s. This time it was not a question of ideology but rather of searching for money so that the national deficit would not increase. Companies scheduled for privatization include both firms heavily in debt such as Renault, the computer firm Bull and the steel concern Usinor-Sacilor, as well as money-making companies such as Rhône-Poulenc (privatized in 1993) in chemicals and Elf-Aquitaine in petroleum products. All told, 21 firms including Air France, banks, and insurance companies are scheduled for privatization. In the meantime, the state continues to inject funds into deficit enterprises such as Bull and Air France, although this practice has come under increasing scrutiny by the European Union.

As is evident from these factors, since the end of World War II French industry had been directed and protected, with decision making often subject to government regulation. In contrast, France's most important European competitor, Germany, has operated in a more dynamic laissez-faire fashion, despite certain state-owned sectors. In fact, France's overall industrial situation was in worse condition than the government had thought. Not only were the traditional sectors such as vehicles, steel, and shipbuilding suffering severely, but also general competitiveness, profitability, and investment were lagging behind those of contending countries. Studies showed that investments in France fell between 1980 and 1984 and by 1986 only reached the level of 1979. On the other hand, investments in Germany, Britain, the United States, and Japan had surged ahead. French investment abroad was also outstripped by other countries. For example, in 1984 French enterprises invested only $3.2 billion compared with higher levels in Germany ($4.7 billion), Japan ($6.1 billion), and the United States ($18.8 billion). Another indicator of the weakness of French industry was the foreign penetration of the home market. It rose steadily from 26.8 percent in 1979 to 33.1 percent in 1985. At the same time, French penetration of export markets declined from 10.4 percent in 1979

to 8.2 percent in 1985. Both of these trends have continued to the present, as reflected in the plunge in the country's industrial goods trade surplus. In 1986 France's trade balance on goods and services was almost in surplus; in 1990 it was about $10 billion in deficit. Among the reasons was a decline in exports of civil engineering projects, aeronautics, and armaments.

Still, overall there have been a number of positive signs. Companies such as Elf-Aquitaine, Alcatel-Alsthorn in telecommunications and transportation, Renault, Rhône-Poulenc, and Péchiney were profitable in 1993. Profits have also grown in Saint-Gobain and CGE, the electronics, telecommunications, and engineering group that purchased control of the European business of ITT. French technology has been a leader in sectors such as nuclear energy, space, military technology, and digital communications. The productivity of the French engineering industry is second only to that of Germany, outpacing the UK. For example, French productivity was 79 percent of Germany's, compared to only 56 percent for the UK. In addition, France is home to one of the largest construction companies in the world, Bouygues, with sales of $1.2 billion in 1994. Both in 1992 and 1993, the trade balance and balance of current accounts were again positive.

A closer look at some examples of French industry will reveal the changes that have occurred in the steel industry and will illustrate the actions specific companies are taking to meet international competition. Beginning in 1960, the French iron and steel industry underwent a period of technical reorganization and economic concentration that ultimately resulted in the emergence of one state-controlled company, Usinor-Sacilor, formed in 1987. Historically, the iron and steel industry was characterized by a series of locational changes caused by replacements in raw materials. Because of scattered iron ore deposits and timber resources, the dominant locational characteristic of the industry, until the middle of the nineteenth century, was dispersion. After 1840, coal was widely substituted for charcoal, and the iron and steel industry migrated to the small coalfields. The major development areas were the coalfields of St. Etienne near Lyon and Le Creusot to the north toward Dijon. A third change occurred with the introduction of the Bessemer and open hearth processes in about 1860, which required imported iron ore and coal. The result was coastal locations that developed in the late nineteenth and early twentieth centuries at Boulogne, Outreau, Isbergues, and Calais in northern France, and at Marseille, Étang de Thau, and Beaucaire in southern France. The invention of the Thomas Gilchrist basic furnace, which could utilize the high phosphorus Lorraine ores, brought about the fourth change in location. The Lorraine ore fields of the northeast became the focus of development, while many of the smaller centers disappeared, leaving only large nuclei such as St. Etienne, Montluçon, and Le Creusot, all in central France.

After World War II, the government encouraged the development of two massive steel complexes, one located in the north at Dunkirk (Fig. 8-5) and the other near the Rhône Delta at Fos. Both utilized green field sites that were located on tidewater in order to expedite the import of inexpensive raw materials.

As the 1970s drew to a close, the steel industry was in serious trouble. Heavily in debt because of new construction and suffering losses because of declining demand, European overcapacity, and foreign competition, obsolete plants were closed and manpower was slashed. The interior locations of the north, Lorraine, and central France north of the Massif Central suffered the most (Fig. 8-6). Steel production plunged from 27 million tons in 1974 to only 17.1 million tons by 1993 (part of the overall EC restructuring that saw over 32 million tons of overcapacity shut down after 1980), and yet the losses continued. For example, the nationalized steel companies accounted for half of the state's capital grants to nationalized firms. In 1984 alone, Usinor and Sacilor received six times as much as the state put into the Bull computer group. These funds could have been better utilized for expanding "sunrise" industries that would provide future employment rather than for propping up "sunset" industries that were destined to fail. Operating losses were in the billions of dollars, and Usinor-Sacilor alone lost nearly $1 billion (Fr5.8 billion) in 1993, before making a small profit in 1994. The saga of iron and steel in France reflected the traditional penchant of French administrators, be they Socialist or conservative, for *dirigisme* and state intervention.

Along with the iron and steel industry, the French automobile sector, which included the government-controlled Renault and the privately owned Peugeot, suffered severely in the early 1980s during the period of Socialist control of the economy. Production dropped to a low of 2.8 million units. A number of factors were responsible, including price controls, a bloated labor force, growing competition, marketing mistakes, and an inferior product. Both firms, unable to compete with the American and Japanese giants, stopped exporting to the world's largest market, the United States and Canada.

Thus, Renault with factories in the Paris region

FIGURE 8-5 The coastal industrial complex near Dunkirk (W. H. Berentsen).

FIGURE 8-6 The depressed industrial center of Montceau-les-Mines is located near a small coal basin in the northeast Massif Central close to the vineyards of Burgundy. This interior location, far from the major population centers of the country, has not remained competitive with the more dynamic industrial regions of France (A. Diem).

and at Le Mans and Rouen, west and north of Paris respectively, lost $600 million in 1981 and nearly $1 billion in 1984. Peugeot with an important plant at Sochaux southwest of Mulhouse lost $200 million in 1981 and $260 million in 1983. In addition, the auto makers' share of both the home and the European market declined. For example, in 1981 Renault was the European market leader with 14.9 percent of sales. By 1993 the figure had dropped to 10.5 percent, and so it lagged behind Fiat, Volkswagen, Ford, GM, and Peugeot. In France Renault's market share tumbled from 40 to about 28 percent. Its debts in 1987 totaled $8.2 billion, a figure that has not been reduced to date. Because of restructuring and a financial breakeven point of 1.2 million cars rather than an earlier 2 million, Renault finally showed a modest profit, which

reached about $1 billion in 1992 before dropping to about $200 million in 1993. After losing heavily, it sold its share of American Motors to Chrysler as part of a new strategy to leave the North American market and consolidate its European position. A merger was planned with Volvo; however, because of the Volvo stockholders, reticence, these plans collapsed in 1993. Owing to impending privatization, the government has changed Renault's legal status from that of a *régie* or government-controlled agency that precludes bankruptcy, to that of a normal nationalized company that will have to compete without special status.

Peugeot's European market share also deteriorated from 14.5 percent in 1980 to 12 percent in 1993; however, in France, it kept about one-third of the market. The firm showed a profit of $558 million for 1994, after a loss the previous year. In addition, fresh capital has been raised on the stock market. Restructuring has resulted in a breakeven point of 1.3 million cars compared to 2.2 million in 1980, and although the labor force has been cut, productivity has been improved. Though shut out of the North American market, Peugeot is in a strong position to benefit from the booming market for automobiles in China as it has a joint venture that will produce 150,000 cars a year there. Aside from foreign competition, Peugeot is concerned that government proposals to aid Renault will distort competition between the two French auto makers. Based on past patterns, this concern is well founded, although ultimately Renault is scheduled for privatization.

France's automobile industry is an archetype example of the forces that affect all major industries in the "world region." Competition from the United States', European, and Japanese manufacturers has forced both Renault and Peugeot to become more efficient in order to survive. Whether they will succeed or collapse has still not been ascertained as the relentless international pressure only increases in intensity.

France is also attempting to compete on a world scale in a number of high-tech areas. A company that fits this mold is Thomson, with plants across France in Nancy, Tours, Grenoble, and Aix-en-Provence. It comprises a group that includes divisions in consumer electronics, engineering, electronic components, and defense and aerospace. The government has already invested more than $380 million, and the company is seeking additional billions in order to become a high-volume chip producer and gain a 3 percent share of the world semiconductor market. The firm has come face to face with intensive Japanese competition, and many analysts question the massive spending of government funds as the chip business continues to be a losing proposition.

In 1987 Thomson merged its manufacturing and research and development activities in silicon chips with those of the state-owned Italian company SGS, forming the firm of ST. The merger resulted in sales of 10.1 percent of the European semiconductor market, second after Philips with 14.8 percent. ST is now the world's tenth largest semiconductor producer, employing 17,000 people

and accounting for about 3 percent of the world market. Productivity has improved dramatically. Whereas at the time of the merger ST was generating $44,000 of sales per employee, it is now close to or above its foreign rivals at $120,000 per employee. Profit was $447 million in 1994.

Thomson has also undergone draconian restructuring in other divisions in order to return to profitability. Moves were taken to buy Germany's Telefunken; Ferguson, Britain's largest television manufacturer; as well as the U.S.A.'s General Electric consumer-electronics arm that included RCA. The last-named takeover was in exchange for an estimated $800 million and Thomson's medical equipment division, thereby consolidating the company's position as Europe's second largest consumer electronics group after Philips of the Netherlands. Deals have also been struck with Oki of Japan, a manufacturer of computer printers and automated machinery, and with IBM in order to improve Thomson's productivity.

If industry in France is to be successful and provide meaningful employment, an example to emulate is the sailboat manufacturing concern, Beneteau. Developing from a local firm to a world-class competitor in but a few years, the company, with its main plant in Saint-Hilaire-de-Riez, Brittany (there are eight other plants in France), produces more than 5000 sail, power, and fishing boats a year and grew by 20 percent annually during the decade 1977 to 1986. Beneteau's boats are well designed, fast, and light, and are produced in efficient, technologically advanced, low-cost assembly plants. Sales of $91 million were registered in 1986, and the company employed 1100 people worldwide, compared to only $250,000 and 17 employees in 1964, when Annette Beneteau Roux took over the company. In 1991–1992 sales reached $115.5 million. The firm became a leader in its field, even as its home market declined. Nearly 60 percent of all sales were outside France, of which Europe accounted for 24 percent and North America 28 percent. Expansion is underway in the Far East. Presently, the company holds about 17 percent of the European market, but only 6 percent of the vast U.S. market. To raise the U.S. figure to 15 or 20 percent, a yacht assembly plant has been opened in Marion, South Carolina.

Beneteau provides a model for successful development in the industrial sphere. The CEO and personnel work together and are strongly motivated. There is little or no government interference in the daily running of the business. The product is innovative, well constructed, well designed, aimed at a particular segment of consumers, and is sold in worldwide markets. Price is not prohibitive. Finally, research and development has priority in order to fend off competition. Unfortunately, government policies directing the postwar industrial development of France rarely took these factors into consideration.

Agriculture

In 1993 agriculture, food products, and forestry and fishing comprised 7.9 percent of the GDP compared to 33.8 percent in industry and 58.3 percent in services. The same year, basic agricultural products accounted for 6.6 percent of total exports, whereas processed agricultural products accounted for a further 10 percent and the country experienced a $9 billion surplus in basic and processed agricultural and food products, compared to one-half that in 1986. Thus, agriculture is a significant element in the French economy.

As we have seen, the percentage of the labor force engaged in the primary sector steadily dropped from 27 percent in 1954 to 5 percent in 1992. Although the 5 percent figure is higher than that in the United Kingdom, Germany, Belgium, and the Netherlands, the decline reflects a continuing change in France's occupational structure to that of an industrialized and service-oriented country. At the same time, agriculture, generously aided by the Common Agricultural Policy of the European Union, has been transformed from a labor-intensive, inefficient, high-cost sector to an efficient, mechanized, relatively low-cost producer. Presently however, supports and subsidies are being reduced because of large surpluses of food products. The country has the largest agricultural output in the EU and is the second largest exporter of agricultural products in the world after the United States, of which wheat exports are particularly significant. In addition, France is self-sufficient in most agricultural and livestock products.

The French Agriculture Ministry estimates that a fifth of the country's farmland, about 15 million acres, will still have to be taken out of production. Because of the large exodus from the countryside, the number of farms with a corresponding increase in farm size has declined. The larger farms of more than 50 ha (123 acres) are generally found in the wheat-producing areas of the Paris Basin. Medium-sized holdings of 20 to 50 ha (50–123 acres) predominate in Franche Comté along the Swiss border, in the west with the exception of Brittany, and in the center of the Aquitaine Basin. Small farms of less than 20 ha are found mainly in regions where agriculture is often a secondary activity, such as in Rhône-Alps and Alsace in the east, and in the south where many smaller holdings specialize in market gardening, vineyards, and flower cultivation. The average size of the French farm in 1975 was 59 acres (24 ha), increasing in 1991 to 74 acres (30 ha), which was larger than that in the other countries of the EU with the exception of the United Kingdom.

Over 80 percent of the area of France was productive in 1993. Of the utilized agricultural land, 58 percent was arable land, 4 percent land under permanent crops, and 37 percent permanent grassland. Vineyards, about 3 percent, accounted for about 2.5 million acres (just over 1 million ha) compared to over 4 million acres for Spain and 2.7 million acres for Italy, France's major European competitors. Wooded areas made up 26 percent of the country's total land.

In 1992 over half of the arable land in France was sown with cereals, and over 50 percent of the cereal land was devoted to wheat. By far the area with the highest yields and the greatest production was found in the north and in the Paris Basin. Here are some of the largest and most modern farms in France. Barley, used for livestock feed and in the production of beer, was grown on 19 percent of the cereal land. Once again the north and Paris Basin stood out as centers of production. Cultivation of corn, used for animal fodder, accounted for 20 percent of the cereal lands, primarily in the Paris and Aquitaine basins. Rice, grown on the lands of the Rhône Delta, utilized only 0.03 percent of the arable land. All told, per acre yields of cereals have increased by nearly 50 percent since 1965. The value of cereal production accounts for approximately 17 percent of the total value of agricultural products.

Fruits and vegetables, while grown on about 1.4 percent of the arable land, account for about 12 percent of the total value of agricultural production. Production is scattered throughout the country, with fruit and vegetable areas often coinciding. Market gardening is evident near large cities, especially Paris; the valleys of the Garonne, Seine, and Loire are particularly important, and so is the Brittany coast. Finally, the Mediterranean coast from Roussillon on the Spanish border, east through the lower Rhône Valley to the Côte d'Azur, is a major region for fruit, vegetable, and flower cultivation.

Vineyards occupied nearly 8 percent of arable land and account for close to 13 percent of total value of agricultural production. A combination of climate, soil condition, and exposure favor six main regions of production, of which the Languedoc-Provence-Côte d'Azur in southern France is the largest producing region, mainly of *vin ordinaire* (table wine). The better wines, *apellation controlée*, grown in the regions of Champagne, Burgundy, and Bordeaux, are produced in areas close to the climactic limit for the vine. Both quantity and quality of the wines depend on such yearly climactic conditions as the lateness of frosts and amounts of precipitation and sunshine.

Viticulture is undergoing restructuring. The period from 1988 through 1990 was marked by market expansion, mainly to the United States and Japan. They were vintage years and prices were high; however, during this time a surplus of wine resulted that has been hard to sell off. Prices have dropped; competition from Spain, Australia, California, Chile, and South Africa became fierce and exposed the weaknesses of the French industry. There are too many producers, and the industry is too fragmented. The majority of French wines are red, whereas the world's wine drinkers now prefer white wine. In addition, there is a general trend against alcoholic drinks in France. All of these factors, as well as the fact that the EU wants to reduce France's wine-growing area by a million and a quarter acres (500,000 ha) by 1997, means that rationalization is occurring. Already major beverage groups from Japan, the UK, and Canada have taken over French firms.

Sugar beets, grown for the manufacture of sugar and industrial alcohol and colza, used for vegetable oil, are among the most important of the industrial crops. Grown mainly in the northern regions where they are rotated with wheat, they account for nearly 7 percent of the total value of agricultural production.

The significance of animal raising is reflected in its contribution of about 49 percent of the total value of agricultural products. Marginal lands formerly used for cereal production have been put to natural pasture, especially in the mountains and in the humid west where mild climactic conditions allow year-round grazing. At the same time, livestock farming has nearly disappeared from the prosperous grain areas of the Paris Basin. France is self-sufficient in dairy products and is a major exporter. In recent years, the number of animals and the output of animal products have remained relatively constant.

Sea fishing in France is underdeveloped compared to that in other Western European countries. With nearly 1860 miles (3000 km) of coast, France is one of the most favored countries of Europe; however, the total catch in 1993 was only 811,000 tons, fifth among the Western European countries. If total catch per inhabitant were used, France would rank even lower. Boulogne on the Channel is by far the most important fishing port, followed by Lorient and La Rochelle, both on the Atlantic. Unrest among fishermen resulted in the destruction of imported fish and serious riots in 1994, when they reacted violently against the import of less expensive fish to France from other countries both within and outside of the EU.

Tourism

In 1993 over 60 million tourists arrived in France, the largest figure in the EU. By comparison, only 36 million were recorded in 1986. With over $23.4 billion in receipts and just $12.8 billion spent abroad by the French, the country had a positive balance of over $10 billion. The largest number of visitors by far were from Germany, followed by the UK, Netherlands, Switzerland, and Belgium. Through massive investments in a number of schemes, tourism has become the fourth largest industry in the country. Development has been concentrated in four major regions: Languedoc-Rousillon in the south, Corsica, Aquitaine in the southwest, and the Alps (Fig. 8-7).

Of particular interest is the Languedoc-Rousillon project, covering 100 miles (161 km) of coast west of the Rhône Delta. Construction began in 1968 and has resulted in the completion of six tourist nuclei, the expansion of existing villages, and the creation of small-craft harbors. Tourist capacity is 2 million persons annually, with harbor space for 12,000 boats. The most futuristic development is La Grande-Motte, southeast of Montpellier, a new city of white concrete pyramids, which contrasts with the more traditionally designed new town of Cap d'Agde farther west along the coast. These two resorts alone accommodate nearly 100,000 tourists nightly. The Côte d'Azur from east of Marseille to Menton on the Italian border is

also a favorite tourist destination, especially during the summer months. (See section on southern France in Chapter 10.)

The development of French ski resorts such as Flaine, Avoiraz, and Val d'Isère has led to an increase in the number of nights spent by tourists in the Alps. A boost was given to winter tourism by the 1992 Olympic games, which were centered in the Alps in Albertville. Massive infrastructure was required, and there were many negative environmental impacts. Paris remains the focal point of tourist action, accounting for about one-quarter of all tourist nights spent in hotels. EuroDisney has located just east of the capital; however, financial projections were far too optimistic, and the facility lost substantial amounts of money before recovering. Environmental problems associated with tourist development will be discussed later in this chapter in the section on environment.

FIGURE 8-7 A marina, apartment buildings, and hotel at La Grande-Motte, southeast of Montpellier on the Lanquedoc coast, southern France (A. Diem).

Trade

From 1980 to 1992, France registered an annual deficit in trade. The sum reached a high of about $16 billion in 1991. In 1992 and 1993 the trade balance was positive. Close to 60 percent of the country's imports and 63 percent of exports were carried out within the EC in 1992, with Germany the most important single country, accounting for 17.6 percent of exports and 18.7 percent of imports. Trade with former French colonies was insignificant. The largest percentage of imports involved investment goods such as machinery and equipment with 24.6 percent of the total; this was followed by nondurable consumer goods, 16.5 percent; chemicals, 14.8 percent; and automobiles and land transport equipment, 10.2 percent. Investment goods at 26.8 percent of the total were the largest sector for exports, followed by nondurable consumer goods, chemicals, and automobiles, all at about 14 to 15 percent. Overall, imports have been rising, boosted in areas like machine tools or consumer electronics where French products have disappeared from the market or are under strong competitive pressure. Exports have been hit by the contracting markets of oil-producing and developing countries that have been strong customers for French plant equipment and for aerospace products and arms. As we have seen, French industries, such as the automotive sector, were ill prepared to take advantage of the strong dollar when the United States was amassing its record trade deficit. Presently, competition among foreign suppliers for a portion of the vast U.S. market is keener than ever. Missing out in the U.S. market is part of a trend that has seen a continuing reduction of France's share of the world market in manufactured goods, a shrinking in the traditional French surplus in industrial goods, and a deepening bilateral trade deficit with its main trading partner, Germany. A greater emphasis from both the private and public sector is being placed on trade and investment in Asia and the Pacific Rim, where the potential for growth is far greater than in the overcrowded European market. Recent successes include the award of a $2.2 billion contract for a TGV railway in South Korea, a joint venture for cement production and Peugeot's investment in

China, and BSN's acquisition of a New Zealand food group.

The country's current account (net flow of foreign currency from all economic activities) recorded a surplus in 1986 for the first time since 1979, and then it plunged into deficit in the late 1980s and early 1990s. In 1992 and 1993 the current account was positive again and reached about $5 billion in 1993. A strong performance by tourism and by services compensated for the deficit in trade and the servicing of foreign debt.

Transportation

France has an excellent network of road, rail, water, and air routes. Of particular interest are the country's rail system and its highways. France is in the vanguard of railway development with its TGV trains. Operating at speeds of 170 miles (270 km) per hour, the TGV connects Paris with Lyon in just two hours and, then, partially using regular tracks connects with the south of France and to the Swiss cities of Geneva, Lausanne, and Bern. Other TGV trains link Paris to Bordeaux and Brittany, and a TGV train connects to London through the Channel Tunnel. Ultimately Brussels, Amsterdam, and Cologne will be part of the TGV network. Since its introduction in 1982, the TGV has steadily accounted for more of the total national passenger miles (number of passengers times average travel distances), reaching about 50 percent in 1994, proving that high-speed trains have an edge over air travel for intercity journeys of up to three hours and more.

Despite the growing TGV network, 1993 was a dismal year, with passenger traffic falling by 7.5 percent to 30 billion passenger miles (48 billion km) and freight volume by 10 percent to 27 billion ton miles (total tons carried times average distance of haul; 43.5 billion ton km). SNCF (the Societé Nationale des Chemins de Fer) lost well over $1 billion, and total indebtedness was over $24 billion (Fr150 billion). The decline can be attributed to a recession, rigid price structuring, and problems with the introduction of a new computer system that turned off many passengers. To boost traffic, SNCF has responded with a better fare structure and a modernization of freight services, especially containers that will use both rail and roads. Furthermore, about 6 million tons of freight will travel through the Channel Tunnel. Fares will be steep for automobiles using the tunnel and could reduce the projected number of travelers, for there will be strong competition from the existing ferry services. Calais and stops to the east such as Lille will get an added economic boost from tunnel traffic.

Continuing rationalization is reducing employment in the SNCF by about 5000 annually; presently, the labor force is under 200,000 (down from a postwar peak of 500,000). As we have seen in the case of French industry, the SNFC has also suffered from the misguided Socialist economic policies of the early 1980s, when employment in the public sector was boosted for no other reason than to provide work. Thus, between 1981 and 1983, the SNCF took on 35,000 more people at a time when freight traffic was falling and other European railroads were reducing employment to increase productivity. The result was reflected in exploding deficits that were compounded by high finance charges for borrowed money to cover losses. A later attempt to retrench by reducing employment and holding down salary increases precipitated costly strikes that further eroded passenger and freight traffic. The challenge for the SNFC is not a technical one; its equipment is among the world's best, though maintenance of the regular trains has declined. Rather, the company must maintain the loyalty of the workforce, be innovative in its attempts at a continued rationalization, and attract more passengers and freight in order to meet the competition from highway and air traffic.

Air traffic climbed to 51.4 million passengers in 1993, and air freight totaled nearly 1 million tons. The largest airports are in the Paris region,— Orly being the most important, followed closely by Roissy-Charles-de-Gaulle. The state airline, Air France, scheduled for privatization, is in deep financial trouble, having lost well over $1 billion in 1993 with total debts at about $6 billion (Fr38 billion). In 1993, an initial restructuring package resulted in a violent and costly strike. However, a referendum on new reforms was supported by more than 80 percent of the company's staff. Five thousand employees from a total of 40,000 will be cut, salaries frozen, and working hours increased, the first step in the difficult process of reform. The

government has promised a capital injection of about $3 billion (Fr20 billion), which has been approved by the EU, to tide the company over through the restructuring period. The airline has lagged behind its competitors in productivity and in order to survive must modernize, increase efficiency, and rise to the challenge of its competitors .

French highways that admirably web the country have been supplemented by a network of toll *autoroutes*. These high-speed, divided, four-lane routes are the funnels for intercity and international traffic. Though aiding in a smooth flow of traffic, they are themselves jammed during peak tourist periods and can be subject to blockades by irate truck drivers. Over 4100 miles (6600 km) of *autoroutes* radiate from Paris, thus efficiently connecting the capital with the many distinct regions of the country. Unfortunately, in 1993 over 9000 persons were killed on French highways, the highest figure in Europe.

Economic Planning and Regional Development

Economic planning has been an important factor in both the sustained growth of the economy and the regional well-being of the country. Since 1946 various plans have affected many segments of French life, including transportation, agriculture, industry, the environment, and regional development. The objectives of the plans were to increase production, foster economic stability, balance foreign trade, guarantee full employment, improve living standards, and decentralize production by promoting growth in the peripheral regions or those affected by economic decline. The results, as one would expect from such lofty goals, have been mixed (see Fig. 8-6). On the positive side, as we have seen, agglomerations, such as Marseille, Bordeaux, Lyon, and Toulouse, have grown, countering the pull of Paris. Toulouse, sited on the Garonne River in the southwestern part of the country, is one of the outstanding examples of decentralization. Because of the policies of Datar, the state organization for regional development, Toulouse has developed high-tech industries in aeronautics and space as well as in electronics, medical equipment, and biotechnology. Aérospatiale, Alcatel, and Matra have factories there, and foreign firms include Siemens, Bosch, and Motorola. Nevertheless, Paris has maintained its momentum because of the synergies resulting from its immense economic strength (see Inset 8-1 and Fig. 8-8).

Technopoles similar to Sophia-Antipolis and Haute-Alsace have been established throughout the country in order to create employment in advanced technological sectors. Rural areas, particularly the Massif Central and Brittany, have been aided in modernizing and restructuring agriculture. Furthermore, tourism in both the mountains and along the coasts has been boosted by the development of marinas and the construction of hotels and condominiums. In addition, regional

FIGURE 8-8 A view of Paris looking from Montparnasse to the Eiffel Tower and beyond the Bois de Boulogne to the commercial and residential development of La Défense (A. Diem).

parks, national parks, and protected shorelines have been established. France's regions no longer look only to Paris for economic largesse. They are now competing among themselves for new industry and are finding that they must compete not only against other French regions, but also against regions in other countries. France is witnessing an historical revolution that some have likened to a decolonization of the regions from Paris. In the long term, such a move can only benefit this regionally diverse country.

Environment

The preservation of France's natural landscape is an important part of environmental planning. Attempts have been made to alleviate water shortages and to address the problem of air pollution. Maintenance of the scenic beauty of the countryside also has high priority, and regional and national parks have been established. Agencies have been organized to study the environmental problems and to propose meaningful solutions. New laws have been enacted to ensure results; however, as in many countries, a great gap exists between the relatively easy step of passing legislation to protect the environment and enforcement of the law.

In a number of cases, France has lagged behind neighboring countries in matters of the environment. For example, the Swiss have strict laws governing air pollution and were leaders in insisting that new automobiles had to be equipped with catalyzers. In contrast, in France a rear-guard action was fought against the use of catalyzers. This situation has now changed as a result of strict EU legislation. Large industrial projects have been undertaken in France with little consideration for the environment. Examples are the complex at Fos, near the nature reserve of the Camargue in the Rhône Delta, and the many refineries that have been sited on estuaries such as the Gironde and Seine. Nuclear plants have been placed in environmentally sensitive areas such as the Rhône Valley, with little consideration for the scenic surroundings. The vital bird and wildlife sanctuary of the Camargue has been seriously threatened by the expansion of tourism. Finally, the Côte d'Azur has been developed for tourism in a laissez-faire manner that has destroyed much of the natural beauty of this unique area. One of the ecological tragedies relating to both the Côte and to Corsica has been the terrible fires that ravage the Mediterranean forests each summer, destroying tens of thousands of acres of pine, mimosa, Mediterranean oak, and olive trees. They are set accidentally by campers or tourists, or deliberately by pyromaniacs and criminals who wait for the high winds of the Mistral before starting a blaze. Hundreds of thousands of acres of forest have been destroyed, and much property damage has resulted.

One of the more positive aspects of environmental planning in France has been the rehabilitation of Lac d'Annecy in the pre-Alps south of Geneva. Through a rigorous cleanup program and strict sewage controls, it has been transformed from a lake used as a dumping ground and suffering from eutrophication and high bacteria counts into a healthy body of water enjoyed by both tourists and the inhabitants of the city of Annecy.

Conclusions

France is a country of strong regional contrasts. Not only are there distinct physical areas such as the limestone canyons of the Massif Central, glacial festooned Alps, and escarpments of the Paris Basin, but there are now clear differences in the composition of the population caused by an influx of migrants. For example, the center of Marseille and the Montmartre in Paris are progressively resembling parts of Africa.

The country must address three basic problems if the future years are to be free from conflict. One is the maintenance of a physical environment that insures a healthy life for the country's inhabitants. As indicated earlier, this can be a formidable task in France, where environmental concerns have never had top priority. The second problem is the integration of recent African migrants into the country's mainstream cultural and economic life. Grievances against these individuals have been exploited by the extreme right wing and have led to violence and bloodshed directed against the Arab and "black" population. The third and most

significant problem is the restructuring of the economy to ensure ongoing competitive strength.

From 1955 to the mid-1980s, the French economy was one of the strongest in Western Europe. Industrial expansion was fueled by large-scale investment in locales such as Dunkirk and Fos. Communications were strikingly improved as reflected in the TGV trains and *autoroutes*. The drain of population from the provinces toward Paris was slowed. And regional development produced fundamental changes, with growth occurring in such cities as Lyon, Grenoble, Bordeaux, Toulouse, Montpellier, Cannes, and Nice. For example, Nice had a population of under 200,000 in 1966; by 1990, however, it had climbed to over 450,000, 27.5 percent of whom were under 25 years of age. In addition, annual revenues generated by new high-tech and scientific activities in the Nice region have overtaken the combined annual turnover of the tourist and convention business. Furthermore, the electronics and data processing sector and bioengineering and marine research, employed nearly 10,000 persons each. Although much growth took place in certain regions,— for example, the population of Provence-Alpes-Côte d'Azur increased to 4.3 million by 1992,— other regions such as Nord-Pas de Calais stagnated, where hopefully the Channel Tunnel will provide a much needed economic boost to this area.

As the year 2000 approaches, the French themselves are questioning whether the country is prepared for the economic wars that have characterized the emergence of "the world region." Disgruntled farmers, truck drivers, Air France employees, students, and fisherman have taken to the streets, battled the police, blocked highways and rail lines, and destroyed property to protest against the economic restructuring that inevitably means lost jobs. In 1993 alone, a year that *Le Monde* described as one of the blackest years since the end of the Second World War, 260,000 jobs disappeared. Industrial investment was stagnant; unemployment reached a record 12 percent and was even more serious among the young; and the trade balance was in a deficit position.

Indicators reveal that in the last decade French industry has become less competitive in world markets. Whether that trend will reverse itself now that many of France's industries are stronger, having restructured, merged, or acquired companies, remains a question mark. Certainly, companies such as Peugeot, Renault, Bull, Thomson, and Saint-Gobain are tougher today than they were a few years ago; however, the same may be said about their competitors. And herein lies the dilemma for all the industrialized countries. There will be no respite to the savage combativeness that characterizes the present world order. Will everyone be able to prosper in this boiling economic crucible? Are the French prepared mentally and physically to join battle with the Japanese, other Asians, Americans, and Germans? Are their industries and institutions, long insulated from economic realities by paternalistic governments, strong enough to compete in the forthcoming years?

In the past, a country such as France could live rather well within its own borders, acquire a few colonies, and protect itself from outsiders by means of a strong army. In contrast, the present order relies on economic strength as a prescription for social harmony and the foundation for national security. Thus, to truly understand France, the complexities of the country's economic structure must be analyzed and carefully monitored.

BELGIUM

Belgium, one of the smallest countries in Western Europe, is one of the most densely populated with over 862 persons per sq mile (333 per sq km) in 1996 and 10.2 million inhabitants. Like Switzerland, Belgium has more than one official language. But unlike tranquil Switzerland, Belgium has been the scene of an intense political struggle between its Flemish- and French-speaking inhabitants. The Flemish segment comprises about 57.8 percent of the population and mainly inhabits the five northern provinces; the French-speaking population account for about 32.5 percent of the total and lives for the most part in the four southern provinces (Fig. 8-9). Brussels, the capital, is officially bilingual, but in reality it is four-fifths French speaking, though surrounded by Flemish territory. To ease linguistic tensions, a process of devolution of political power from the central government to the

regions has occurred, changing Belgium from a highly centralized unitary state into a federation of regions and language communities. Known as the St. Michael accords, they give Flanders, Wallonia, (the small German speaking region in eastern Belgium), and Brussels each an elected assembly. A new constitution was adopted in 1993 and has legalized this process. Thus, the regions are now responsible for such sectors as local economic policy, foreign trade, research, agriculture, environmental protection, public works, and education. Already, Flanders has signed a treaty with the Netherlands on water policy and has invested in the ailing Dutch truck manufacturer DAF (see the section on Flanders and Wallonia).

Belgium, along with the Netherlands and Luxembourg, is a member of Benelux, a forerunner to the establishment of the European Union. Benelux was established in 1948 as a common customs union with the above-mentioned countries. Belgium joined the North Atlantic Treaty Organization (NATO), and the European Coal and Steel Community and was a founding member of the European Economic Community. The headquarters of both the EU and NATO are located in Brussels.

A variety of geology and relief is found within the country's 11,778 sq miles (30,506 sq km). The most prominent feature is the contrast between the southern (Hercynian) uplands, all lying over 650 feet (200 m), that reach their highest elevations in the Ardennes, and the northern plains and low plateaus that open to the North Sea and are composed of younger deposits. The east-west Sambre and Meuse valleys form a rough demarcation between these two physiographic regions. Accordingly, the mean annual temperature in the maritime north is warmer, and there is less precipitation than in the rugged south. Because of the more favorable climate and physiography in the north, agriculture is more developed and population density greater than in the south.

Belgium is a highly industrialized country, though services now employ a greater percentage of the labor force. In 1992, 27.7 percent of the labor force was engaged in industry, compared to 2.6 percent in the primary sector (the lowest figure in Europe after the UK) and 69.7 percent in the service sector. There has been a major shift from

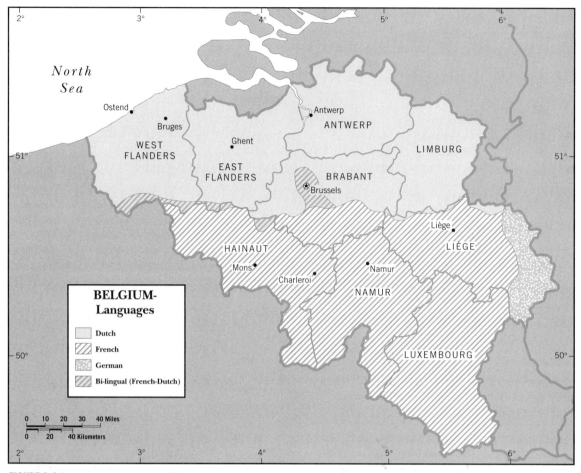

FIGURE 8-9 Language regions in Belgium.

industry, with 39 percent of employment in 1976, to services. In fact, in 1992 services accounted for 69.4 percent of the GDP compared to 29 percent for industry. Old established industries such as iron and steel, nonferrous metals, textiles, and heavy engineering predominated but have been hard hit by restructuring. Oil refining, chemicals, and consumer goods have grown in importance.

Because of the sharp decline in coal mining after the Second World War, government policy tried to revitalize the aged industrial areas in the French-speaking area of the country. Special incentives encouraged foreign investment in this region. Unfortunately, economic development became entangled in the fierce politics of language, espe-

cially because the "rust-belt" was in the French area of Wallonia, whereas the bulk of investment flowed to the Flemish north, particularly around the port facilities of Antwerp (see section on Flanders and Wallonia).

Population

From 1900 to 1996, the population of Belgium increased by about 30 percent. The Brussels district grew by nearly 50 percent, whereas the increase in the Flemish provinces was more than three times that of the Walloon provinces. Of all of the provinces, Antwerp (Antwerpen) registered the greatest growth in both total numbers and share of the country's population, followed by Brabant (see Fig. 8-9). A number of provinces, such as East Flanders and Hainault, while increasing their numbers slightly, have experienced a declining share of the country's population. Whereas in 1900 about 35 percent of the population lived in communes of more than 10,000, today the figure is over 50 percent. By North American standards the country is highly urbanized. Brussels (960,000 in 1991), for example, is within 37 miles (60 km) of Antwerp (468,000), the capital of Flanders, Charleroi (207,000), Ghent (230,000), Mons (92,000), and Namur (104,000) and within about 60 miles (100 km) of Brugge (117,000), and Liège (195,000), the capital of Wallonia.

The country's birth rate, in common with the other EU countries, has gone down to under 10 per 1000 as a result of which the bulk of the population is now between the ages of 14 and 64. The proportion under age 14 is only 8 percent. Foreigners comprise 8.6 percent of the population, one of the highest figures in the EU. They are mainly Italians, Moroccans, French, and Turks.

Economic Factors

In 1993 Belgium produced nearly 71 trillion kwh of electricity compared to about 47 trillion kwh in 1976. Only 1.4 percent was generated by hydro sources; however, just under 60 percent was nuclear from seven power stations, the second highest figure in the EU after France. After the Chernobyl disaster, a proposed eighth nuclear station was instead built as a gas-fired plant. Most of the thermal stations that originally relied on high-grade coal now consume low-grade coal products. Production of electrical energy was one of the few remaining uses for low-grade, high-priced Belgium coal; coal mining that accounted for 8.1 million tons in 1974 has collapsed, producing only 218,000 tons in 1992. The shift in fuel use between 1981 and 1992 was dramatic; although oil remained the most important energy source, both oil and coal experienced drops in use. Nuclear power output increased 230 percent, thereby displacing coal as the second most important energy source,

while natural gas use also climbed so that its relative importance became virtually equal to coal.

The country is dependent on fuel imports for over half its energy consumption, natural gas coming from the Netherlands. Belgium has a refining capacity of 34.5 million tons; five refineries are located in the Antwerp port area, two in Ghent, and one in Feluy in south Belgium. The Petrofina-BP-Esso refineries at Antwerp are connected to the port of Rotterdam by pipeline. Thus, the oil companies can use the Rotterdam-Europoort facilities where tankers of up to 250,000 tons can unload. Ghent is supplied by pipeline from Zeebrugge on the coast, and the Feluy installations receive crude oil by a pipeline from Antwerp.

Belgium has no major deposits of ores or minerals. The country depends on imported ores for both the iron and steel industry and for the refining of lead, zinc, and copper. Rare metals such as cobalt and radium are also imported. The old established industries, such as iron and steel, nonferrous metals, textiles, and heavy engineering accounted for a smaller percentage of GDP than the more modern chemical, electronics, and light engineering (assembly of automobiles and aerospace industries). In 1990 metal manufacturing and engineering registered 25.1 percent of gross value added by industry; food, drink, and tobacco 17.1 percent; chemicals and rubber 10.8 percent; and textiles only 3.9 percent.

The country's iron and steel industry dates from the thirteenth century and is located mainly in Wallonia. However, a newer facility was built at Zelzate north of Ghent in order to facilitate importation of iron ore. Production of iron in 1992 was 8.5 million tons (13 million tons in 1974), and steel output was 10.3 million tons (16.2 million in 1974), still placing Belgium among the top six producers of each in Europe. The decline of both iron and steel production, with sharp reductions in the labor force, is part of the EU's strategy to reduce overcapacity and restructure the industry.

Contrasting with the decline of iron and steel production has been the growth of a diversified chemical sector, located mainly in the Antwerp region. The German companies, Bayer and BASF, and the American company Dow all have plants in Belgium. Solvay, the country's second largest company and the largest chemical concern in Belgium, has expanded in the United States as well as taking over a plant in the former East Germany that had been seized by the Nazis and then run by the communist regime.

Of particular significance is the assembly of over 1 million automobiles in Belgium in 1993, with Ford, GM, Renault, VW, and Volvo all having plants, mainly in Flanders. Although the bulk of each car comes from elsewhere, an increasing number of components are manufactured in Belgium. About 40,000 people work directly in the industry, with another 700,000 indirectly connected to the assembly operations.

Textiles are the oldest industry in Belgium, concentrating in Flanders during the eleventh century and processing local and imported wool for cloth and carpets. Later the linen industry developed, followed by cotton spinning and weaving. Today, artificial and synthetic fibers are significant, whereas linen has declined sharply. One of the largest textiles companies, De Witte, was recently purchased by the major textile group, Gamma Holdings of the Netherlands. De Witte's sales are derived from cotton spinning, 12 percent, and household linen, 44 percent. The rest comes from sales of materials for automobiles, such as for seats and panels and sales of household textiles such as napkins, sheets, and tablecloths. Because of unrelenting competition in textiles, particularly from Asia, the textile companies must restructure if they are to survive.

Brussels is the hub of Belgium's main industrial region. Stretching north along the Wittebroek Canal and south paralleling the Charleroi Canal are textile and clothing factories, leather works, printing establishments, chemical plants, auto assembly lines, firms fabricating scientific instruments, food concerns, and breweries.

Tourism in Belgium can be divided into three main components. The well-developed seaside resorts cater mainly to Belgium nationals. A fair number of foreign tourists visit Brugge, Ghent, and Brussels, primarily for cultural reasons, whereas Brussels, because of NATO headquarters and its role as the institutional capital of the European Union, has become a magnet for international business travelers and politicians. Receipts from tourism (for the Belgium-Luxembourg Economic Union combined) amounted to over $4 billion in 1993 (a 115% increase from 1983), while expenditures by Belgians abroad were $6.4 billion (almost a 170% increase from 1983), thus leaving the country with a deficit in tourism of $2.4 billion. That same year tourism accounted for 1.9 percent of the GDP, compared to 1.6 percent for the Netherlands and 1.9 percent for France.

As noted earlier, only 2.6 percent of Belgium's working population was employed in agriculture in 1992. The same year the primary sector accounted for about 1.8 percent of the GDP, compared to 3.6 percent in the Netherlands and about 1.4 percent in Luxembourg. Except for the Ardennes highland, the climate of Belgium is relatively mild and humid, thus favoring pasture and meadowland. January mean temperatures are generally above freezing, and July mean temperatures are between 61° and 64°F (16° and 18°C). All regions of the country receive at least 29 in. (750 mm) of precipitation; therefore, livestock rearing and production of milk are well developed and play a significant role in the agricultural economy. Climactic conditions also favor the cultivation of root crops such as potatoes and sugar beets.

Agriculture is characterized by a large number of very small part-time holdings; a relatively small average size of full-time holdings; and an excessive fragmentation of holdings. The number of holdings dropped from 106,000 in 1970 to 85,000 in 1990. The largest number of farms, 20,200 or 23.8 percent, was between 2.5 and 12 acres (1 and 5 ha). The average farm size has slowly grown to 40 acres (16 ha), and mechanization is widespread. The total amount of arable land declined from 2.14 million acres (866,000 ha) in 1975 to about 2 million acres (820,000 ha) in 1992. Only 2 percent was planted in permanent crops, the rest being permanent pasture. Wheat was the main crop, followed by sugar beets and potatoes. Crop cultivation is largely on the flat and fertile plain of Flanders, an area ideal for intensive cultivation.

Forests cover about 19 percent of the country, especially in the uplands of the Ardennes, and contribute about 6 percent of output in the primary sector. Over half of the productive forests are deciduous with such species as oak, ash, beech, and poplar; and 44 percent are coniferous with spruce, larch, and various types of pine. Imports of timber amount to about 50 percent of needs.

Although bordering the North Sea, Belgium does not have an important fishing industry. In 1993, 36,600 tons were landed, contributing only 2 percent of the value of the primary sector. Almost all of the fish landed supply the home market.

Trade and Finance

Belgium and Luxembourg form a customs and economic union (BLEU), and so their trade and payments accounts are amalgamated. In 1993 exports amounted to over $122.4 billion, whereas imports were just under $125 billion for a trade balance of -$2.3 billion. In 1992 the EU took 75 percent of all exports; the largest single country was Germany with 23 percent, followed by France, 19.1 percent, and the Netherlands 13.8 percent. The EU accounted for almost 72 percent of imports, and Germany was the largest supplier with 24 percent, followed by the Netherlands, 17.4 percent, and France, 16.3 percent. Principal imports and exports were metal products, chemicals, and minerals; energy products are an additional important import. The current account deficit was over $1 billion in 1990 and $4.7 billion in 1992.

Brussels, Capital of Belgium and the European Union

Brussels, the capital of Belgium, is also home to NATO, Euratom (European Atomic Energy Community), and the European Union. The city is the largest in Belgium with just under 1 million inhabitants living in 19 autonomous communes and over 1.8 million in the agglomeration. However, because of the country's linguistic split, it has never dominated national life as has Paris or London. The original site of Brussels was an island in the Senne River; goods from Antwerp could be transported upstream via the Schelde and Senne to the small settlement from where they were than transshipped. Crossed by the east-west Brugge-Cologne highway, Brussels also became a stopping place for merchants and travelers. Known as a thriving textile center, the city became a residence of the dukes of Brabant in the eleventh century and expanded onto the sandstone uplands to the east. By the middle of the fifteenth century, population was about 45,000 and the famous Hôtel de Ville was soon built. Later, the dukes of Burgundy and the Habsburgs established their court residences in Brussels. After the splitting of the 17 provinces, the city became the capital of the Spanish Netherlands, and in 1830 it became the capital of the kingdom of Belgium. By the middle of the nineteenth century, Brussels began to expand over the alluvial plain on the left bank of the Senne and onto the more distant western uplands. By 1880 the population of Brussels and its communes was over 431,000, growing to 749,000 by 1910 and to over 912,000 on the eve of World War II.

Today, this affluent administrative, commercial, and manufacturing metropolis is developing largely uncontrolled by any town planning legislation. Central Brussels, more than ever before, is merely an administrative district. Population of the Brussels commune, which reached a peak of nearly 219,000 in 1910 has fallen below 150,000. More office blocks have been built to house the burgeoning bureaucratic workforce (Fig. 8-10). The Brussels World Trade Center occupies 125 acres (51 ha) near the Gare du Nord. It is a minicity complete with skyscrapers that house offices, data centers, shopping facilities, exhibition halls, luxury apartments, and a hotel that is linked directly to the transportation system which converges on the capital. The former residents of this and other central areas have moved to the periphery of the city or into the small villages surrounding the capital.

In addition to its administrative and commercial functions, Brussels is the hub of Belgium's main inland industrial region noted above. Interspersed with industrial enterprises are horticultural districts, and crop, poultry, and livestock farms. Of special interest are the greenhouses in the region of Hoeilaart-Overijse that occupy over 1200 acres (486 ha) and produce grapes, fruits, and flowers for home and export markets.

Flanders and Wallonia Within the Single Market of the EU

On January 1, 1993, the customs posts of the EU were dismantled and the internal frontiers of the EU ceased to exist, thus creating a single trading region of over 365 million consumers, the largest such market in the world. Paradoxically, a reemergence of European regions based on geography, history, culture, and economics has occurred with-

FIGURE 8-10 EU Commission headquarters, the Berlaymont, in Brussels. The direct and indirect EU employment impacts on Brussels create thousands of jobs in the city, including many of 16,000 full-time employees of the EU Commission (European Community Delegation, New York).

in this common market. Two of the most distinctive are the major regions of Belgium. In the north of the country lies Flanders, with a population of close to 6 million, mostly Flemish-speaking people, a per capita income of about $20,000, a highly educated workforce, and an admirable infrastructure suited to modern industry. All told, 386,000 firms are found in Flanders (195,000 in Wallonia). Unemployment in the region is about 8 percent (Wallonia 17%). Since the end of the Second World War, Flanders with its five ports of Ostend, Zeebrugge, Brugge, Ghent, and Antwerp, has become an economic powerhouse, the source of 70 percent of all Belgian exports. South of Flanders, bordering on France, is Wallonia, a French speaking region of 3.25 million with a per capita income of about $15,000. Wallonia is trying to recover from the decline of the coal, iron, and steel industries that characterized its former economic strength.

The political and cultural tensions of the post–Second World War years that pitted the Flemish-speaking north against the French-speaking south have resulted in the devolution of powers in Belgium and a new constitution, so that both regions now have authority over institutions that were formerly wielded by the state. For example, today foreign trade is the domain of the regions; thus, Flanders runs 69 trade missions abroad and Wallonia controls over 55. The regions also compete with each other for foreign investment and provide economic incentives where necessary. They also control diverse sectors such as agriculture, energy, water, and the environment.

A brief geographical analysis will illuminate the differences between the two regions, revealing positive or negative factors that affect each area. Since 1945, over 1000 industrial companies and 13,000 trading and service companies have located in Flanders, contributing to the economic expansion that has marked the postwar years. Concerns such as Volvo, BASF, Upjohn, and Bayer have thrived from locations in Flanders, and the trend shows no sign of diminishing. For example, in 1993 Nike, the U.S. footwear manufacturer, opted to base its European distribution center at Meerhout/Laakdal. A number of other companies engaged in distribution, such as the French Gondrand and TNT Express, have also located in Flanders in Bornem.

An important factor is the centrality of the area, close to the four international seaports of Antwerp, Zeebrugge, Ghent, and Ostend, with high productivity and together handling the highest volume of general cargo in the world. In addition, Flanders' excellent infrastructure, with the densest, most modern rail, road, and waterway network in the world, is vital to Flanders' economic ties to Europe, from Portugal to the Baltic countries and Scandinavia.

Antwerp, the second largest port in Europe, with over 102 million tons handled in 1993, is expanding its container terminals to accommodate increasing traffic. The port has the lowest handling costs and the highest output of all major European terminals and has developed as a vital hub for inland waterways, linking to 930 miles (1500 km) of canals in the country as well as the European network. Furthermore, Antwerp has excellent rail connections and is the largest railway port in Europe, handling about 28 million tons of merchandise annually. The nearby motorway stretches are integrated with the European web, and Antwerp has its own airport for air-freight traffic. Thus, it is not surprising that industrial areas surrounding the port have attracted multinationals such as GM, Ford, Exxon, l'Air Liquide, Fina, and Solvay. Two industrial sectors stand out—chemicals, which account for 20 percent of turnover in manufacturing and 75 percent of export turnover, and auto-related industries. Ford, GM, Renault, VW, Honda, and Volvo all have plants in Flanders that either produce parts and manufacture or assemble automobiles.

Other factors contributing to Flanders' success include high educational standards; only Germany and the Netherlands spend more on a per capita basis. Research and development (R&D) invest-

ment continues to grow in such key sectors as microelectronics, new materials, environmental technology, medical technology, and biotechnology. Furthermore, monetary stability, a low inflation rate, and a spectrum of financial incentives, some of which have since been suspended by the Commission of the European Union, attracted companies to Flanders. These incentives, which included subsidies, interest-free loans, and tax concessions, coupled to a multilingual, skilled, motivated, and productive workforce, were vital factors in the economic renaissance of the Flanders region.

Wallonia, an area of manufacturing activity since the Middle Ages and one of the foremost industrial regions of Europe during the nineteenth and early twentieth centuries, witnessed the near collapse of its industrial base because of the restructuring of iron and steel industries after World War II and falling output from its coal mines. As late as 1974, coal output was over 8 million tons, whereas in 1992 it was only 218,000 tons. During the same period, iron production declined from 13 million to 8.5 million tons and steel output from 16.2 to 10.3 million tons.

As high unemployment figures testify, it has been difficult to rejuvenate the economy of Wallonia. Progress, however, is being made. Helped by financial incentives, over 2500 small and medium-sized companies, including Alcatel Alsthom, British Petroleum, Daewoo, Oerlikon Bürle, and Sandoz, have located in the region. In the Liège and Charleroi basins, historic industries such as metals, chemicals, and glass making have become sophisticated high-tech operations involved in space exploration, software, telecommunications, computer graphics, and petrochemicals.

Wallonia also has an excellent educational infrastructure; for example, there are five universities within a 30-mile (50-km) radius of Charleroi. The transportation infrastructure is also admirable and will be further enhanced when the region is finally linked to TGV trains that will connect London to Germany via the Channel Tunnel, Brussels and Liège. The old industrial regions, including the Charleroi-Namur-Liège axis, have been divided up into local development zones that are slowly shedding their obsolete past and emerging into the twenty-first century.

A good example is the transformation that has

taken place around Brussels' South Charleroi airport. Known as Aeropole, the site close to the airport is attracting small to medium-sized companies in such fields as information technology and the environment, management consultancies, finance, and engineering. Both light industries and research and development agencies are being served. The area is eligible for EU grants and assistance, thus keeping costs low—about 10 percent of that for similar land in Brussels itself. The airport, only 28 miles (45 km) from the capital, has evolved mainly as a freight and charter location, rather than for scheduled passenger service. However, ultimate capacity will be 4 million passengers annually. The area in proximity to the Aeropole has become an established center for the Belgian aerospace industry with firms working on the European space rocket Airiane, Airbus, and F16 military aircraft.

Other areas of Wallonia that have undergone significant restructuring include Louvain-la-Neuve, southeast of Brussels, where biomedical and pharmaceutical companies are located, and Nivelles, northwest of Charleroi, where research facilities have been installed. All told, within Wallonia 120 industrial zones have been established where firms are mainly producing for export. In fact, two-thirds of all turnover comes from markets abroad.

Flanders and Wallonia, because of their past history, have reversed their former economic roles. Whereas in the past, French-speaking Wallonia was the economic focus of the country, today it is Flemish-speaking Flanders. After 1945, the resources of Wallonia such as coal, stone, and the forests were no longer the main factors in continued economic growth. Aging iron and steel industries were not competitive within the emerging European and world economies. By contrast, the strategic location of Flanders, focusing on the port of Antwerp and the North Sea coast, was ideal for the expansion of industries, such as chemicals and automobiles, that took place after World War II within the framework of the European Economic Community. Today, Wallonia is fighting to regain its former economic strength and to do this must develop modern industries whose main inputs are high technology, brain power, and marketing resources.

The examples of Flanders and Wallonia developing within the matrix of rapid worldwide economic change and fierce competition both from within and without the European Union clearly portray the way geographic regions must evolve in order to remain dynamic and solvent. No longer are the old criteria of resources and favorable location adequate to ensure prosperity. Of all the new factors necessary for sustained growth, none are more important than education, highly skilled labor, and continuing research and development.

Conclusions

Belgium has been plagued by divisive separatist forces because of language differences. Like Italy, the country has also been living beyond its economic means for a long time. Both problems have been aggravated by worldwide economic restructuring and the deep recession of the early 1990s. The constitution of 1993, which legalized the different ethnic regions of the country, is an historic document. Real power was finally transferred to the linguistic areas, with the federal government only retaining control of foreign policy and defense, justice, taxation, and social security. However, the new constitution did little to placate right-wing Flemish autonomists, the *Vlaams Blok*, located mainly in Antwerp, which has become synonymous with neo-Nazi activity. Their appeal has been heightened by Belgium's weak economic position. Although inflation is under 3 percent and per capita income was a respectable $21,037 ($19,517 PPPs) in 1993, unemployment was over 10 percent; the under 25 years age group was especially hard hit. For example, one in five in this group in Flanders and one in four in Wallonia is out of work. Furthermore, the public debt at 130 percent of GDP is the highest in the EU and is increasing annually at 7 percent.

Worldwide restructuring and the recession have affected all segments of industry; however, the older industries of Wallonia have borne the brunt of the transformation. In 1993 the OECD chided Belgium for failing to address its financial problems, mainly through reduced social spending and greater flexibility on the labor market; otherwise the OECD warned that the Belgium franc could become a target for speculative devaluation. Thus, in late 1993 the Global Plan was adopted, a package designed to rein in budget and social security deficits, boost industrial competitiveness, and freeze wages until the end of 1996. The Plan will raise certain taxes, reduce spending on health care, family allowances and pensions, as well as sharply reduce the costs of hiring labor, especially for people under 26. In addition, a four-year plan to privatize government assets, from banks and insurance to the state telecom company, is expected to add over $2 billion to government coffers.

Ultimately, many Belgians believe that the country should become an example to the European Union as a diverse ethnic state within firm supranational structures provided by growing EU integration. Furthermore, many believe that the country is a test case for tackling the problems presently plaguing the European Union, such as slow economic growth, high production costs, excessive public debt, and disenchantment with political elites as a result of Euro-wide corruption.

NETHERLANDS

The Netherlands, with its predominantly flat terrain, is an amalgam of grazing cows, clusters of greenhouses, high tension towers, an occasional windmill, and a succession of church steeples strung along a thin strip of land set against an enormous expanse of sky and moving clouds. On the IJsselmeer, in the southwestern delta region, or in the northern lake district of Friesland, water and sky reign supreme, punctuated by a scattering of white sails and lines of distant trees that appear to be shimmering on the water's surface. Along the coast, the foam of the breaking surf washes against the yellow beach sands, backed by a low swell of grass-covered dunes. Only in the cities and towns does one experience a closed-in feeling. The perspective changes when the countryside is viewed from a water tower, a tall building, or, best of all, low-flying aircraft. Then the human-made angularity of the Dutch landscape comes sharply into focus. Thousands of greenhouses brilliantly reflect the

sun's rays. Hundreds of odd-size plots are surrounded by drainage canals. New polder areas stand out as a formation of green and grey-brown rectangular fields which might have been painted on the earth's surface by Mondrian. The Afluitsdijk, the longest dike in the country, closing off the IJsselmeer from the North Sea is a fragile ribbon of earth, concrete, and four-lane highway surrounded by oceans of slate grey water (Fig. 8-11). In the distance are the supertankers, refineries, and quays of Europoort-Rotterdam, the world's largest port, and the North Sea Canal, on which river barges skim and ocean freighters slowly glide. The Canal cuts a wide swath through the fertile fields of grain and forage crops that stretch between the busy wharves of Amsterdam and the smoking blast furnaces of Velsen.

Survival for the Dutch has meant constant battle against the sea. From 1200 to 1930, they gained a total of 1.28 million acres (519,140 ha) by reclaiming land from the sea and draining inland lakes (Fig. 8-12). However, during this period, because of powerful sea storms, 1.4 million acres (565,600 ha) were lost for a net deficit of over 100,000 acres (46,460 ha), nearly 180 sq miles. This trend was reversed in 1930 when the Wieringermeer polder, the first in the Zuiderzee scheme, was pumped dry. Then came the Northeast polder, East Flevoland, and South Flevoland. Another mammoth undertaking has been the Delta Plan, which has sealed off the mouth of the Rhine and provides a barrier against sea storms such as the one in 1953 that inundated nearly 500,000 acres (202,000 ha) and killed 1835 persons (see Inset 8-2 and Fig. 8-13).

In 1996 the Netherlands was Europe's most densely populated country with about 980 persons per sq mile (378 per sq km) compared to only 35 per sq mile (14 per sq km) in Norway. In order to prevent chaotic living conditions and misuse of the limited resources, intelligent long-range planning of urban and rural development has been undertaken at municipal, regional, and national levels. Nationwide legislation began with the Housing Act of 1901 and has continued to the present with the *Second Report on Physical Planning in the Netherlands*. Providing a framework for the country's development until the year 2000, the *Second Report* presents in an integrated manner, the

FIGURE 8-11 Afsluitdijk, toward the northeast, with shipping lock and discharge sluices. These sluices control the water levels of Lake IJssel (IJsselmeer). Extreme left, the fishing village of Den Oever on the former island of Wieringen; left, Wadden Zee; right, IJsselmeer. The last gap of the enclosing dike was closed in 1932 (Luchtfoto Bart Hofmeester, Rotterdam/The Netherlands).

philosophical, administrative, economic, and physical outline for future expansion.

One of Europe's most dynamic countries, the Netherlands has witnessed enormous changes since the end of the Second World War. Pushed by a swelling population and the discovery of vast natural gasfields in the northeast of the country, industrialization accelerated, particularly in the chemicals, electronics, and metals sectors. In 1992 industry contributed 28.1 percent to the GDP; services, 68.2 percent; and agriculture, 3.6 percent. Employment in these sectors was, respectively, 24.6 percent, 71.4 percent, and 4 percent. Per capita income in 1993 was $20,211 ($17,593 PPPs). Thousands of foreign firms have opened branches in the Netherlands or have started jointly operated enterprises with Dutch counterparts. Generally, over 30 percent of industrial production is exported.

Possessing efficient and comprehensive rail, road, and canal systems, one of the world's largest natural gasfields near Groningen, and enormous beds of salt, the Netherlands appears to have a solid industrial future. However, a number of structural and economic problems have emerged as increased costs have outpaced productivity and the strong guilder has deterred exports. Therefore, the Dutch must strive to improve their competitive position, for close to 50 percent of the GDP is derived from exports.

Physiographic Divisions

The Netherlands is part of the contact zone between Hercynian and Caledonian Europe. This area, within the North Sea geosyncline, has been slowly subsiding for millennia. At the same time,

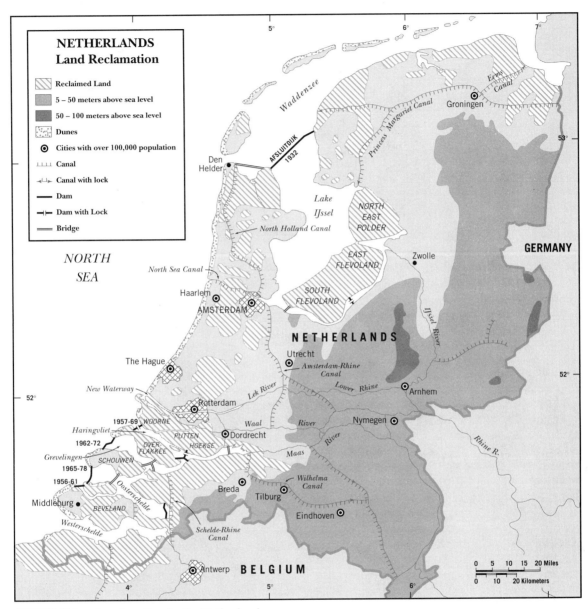

FIGURE 8-12 Land reclamation in the Netherlands.

sedimentary beds of great depth have been accumulating, deposited by the ancient Rhine and Maas rivers as they meandered over a large part of the country. Scandinavian ice sheets of the Riss glaciation covered the northern part of Holland, penetrating just below the present cities of Haar-lem on the west and Nijmegen on the east. Extending over much of the present North Sea bottom, the glacial mass coalesced with another ice sheet which covered most of the British Isles.

The waters of the Rhine, Maas, and other rivers, and the meltwaters from the glacier formed a large

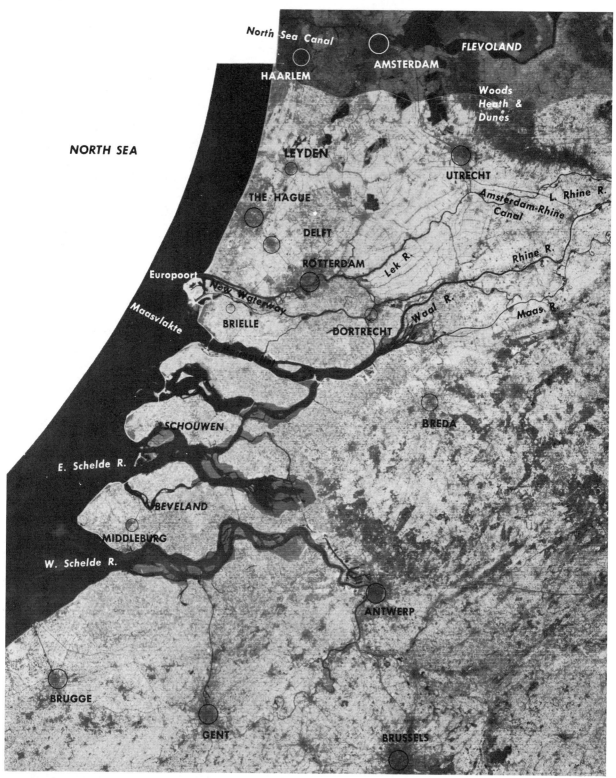

FIGURE 8-13 Landsat (ERTS) multispectral image (channel 6) centered southeast of Utrecht, including Randstad, Holland, and northern Belgium (U.S. Department of the Interior, EROS Data Center).

lake in front of the ice that could only drain in a southerly direction through the present Channel between England and France. The slow and irregular retreat of the glacier left the moraine ramparts of western Gelderland, as well as ground moraine deposits containing boulder clay and large erratic boulders of Scandinavian origin in Drenthe, Friesland, and Groningen. Glacial lakes and drumlins emerged in Friesland, marshes and bogs were formed, and loess deposits accumulated. In addition, vast quantities of sand, originating from the glacier and rivers, were deposited on the floor of the North Sea.

The retreat of the ice, was followed by a marked rise in sea level. Except for the moraine remnant islands of Texel and Wieringen, the rising waters inundated the west coast of Holland and deposited the "old sea clay," some of which remains on the west side of the IJsselmeer. As the sea advanced, the sand masses left by the glacier were reworked by the combined action of waves and currents, and a barrier beach was formed outside the original shoreline. When the sea subsequently retreated, peat deposits accumulated east of the barrier beach. Then from the ninth century A.D. on, the relative rise of sea level caused much flooding, resulting in the destruction of the old barrier beach, the formation of new dunes, the deposition of "young sea clay," and the creation of the Zuiderzee from the freshwater lake known to the Romans as *Flevo Lacus*. At this stage the Dutch had to intensify their struggle against the onslaughts of the sea, a battle that has continued to the present. Today, 40 percent of the country lies below sea level, protected by an intricate system of dikes, canals, pumping stations, and the delta works (see Inset 8-2).

As a result of the work of the ice sheet, fluvial action, and the impact of the sea, the Netherlands may be divided into four main physical regions, all lying within the North European Plain. The largest is the low coastal zone of clays and peats that stretches from the islands of Zeeland in the south to the German border in the northeast (Fig. 8-14). A second region consists of the broad alluvial valleys of the Rhine, Maas, and IJssel. In the east and south are the sandy areas that form another distinct landscape. And in the far south lies Limburg, the only region of the country not affected by the sea, fluvial action, or glaciation. This is the north-ern rim or the Belgian Plateau, below which lies coal in the Limburg field in which mining was closed down in the mid-1970s.

Population

Between 1830 and 1996 the Netherlands' population increased sixfold. The population, only 2.6 million in 1830 and 5.2 million in 1900, passed the 12 million mark in 1960 and was 15.6 million in 1996. About 40 percent of the population is Catholic, 40 percent Protestant, and 18 percent claim no religious affiliation. With a death rate of about 8 per 1000, one of the lowest in the world, and a birth rate of 13 per 1000, natural growth amounts to about 70,000 people annually. Projections, including the impacts of immigration, indicate that by the year 2000, the Dutch population could be over 16 million with a density of over 1000 inhabitants per sq mile (388 per sq km), one of the highest in the world.

Present settlement patterns reflect the unequal distribution of population. On the one hand, the western urban agglomeration known as Randstad Holland ("Ring city," because of its rural center), including Amsterdam, Rotterdam, and The Hague ('s-Gravenhage), has population densities ranging from 385 per sq mile (1000 per sq km) in rural areas and over 10,300 per sq mile (4000 per sq km) in urban regions. On the other hand, population density in the north and east is well below the national average and drops to only 52 per sq mile (135 per sq km) in Drenthe near the German border. Amsterdam and Rotterdam have populations of just over 1 million, whereas Utrecht numbers over 500,000 and Eindhoven nearly 400,000. Immigration from former Dutch colonies and Eastern Europe is over 100,000 annually, putting additional pressures on urban areas. Foreigners accounted for 4.3 percent of the population in 1990, mainly Turks and Moroccans, many of whom are unemployed (see section on Amsterdam and Rotterdam).

Economic Factors

Coinciding with rising industrialization, the gross output of electricity more than quadrupled from the 15.5 billion kwh produced in 1960 to the nearly

HUMAN RESPONSE TO GEOGRAPHICAL HAZARDS: ZUIDERZEE RECLAMATION AND THE DELTA PLAN

The large tracts of land that were once lakes or part of the sea are a unique feature of the Netherlands' geography. Early inhabitants struggled against the elements in the north of the country. Here, Frisian peoples of Scandinavian origin settled in about the fifth century. Living close to the sea, they built artificial refuge mounds above the high-tide level called *terpen*. In the Netherlands alone these mounds numbered about 1500. Dike construction began in Friesland in the ninth century, and the building of *terpen* ceased in the thirteenth century. The early dikes, however, were no match for the powerful thrusts of the sea, and in 1287, as many as 50,000 people perished during a December flood. The south of the country also suffered from the storms that periodically swept the North Sea coast. Initial reclamation schemes were purely defense measures against the sea. However, during the end of the sixteenth and beginning of the seventeenth centuries, inland lakes were drained by windmills to provide new land for cultivation. In the nineteenth century, the Haarlemmermeer, the largest lake in the country, was pumped dry by steam-pumping stations, and a flood threat was removed against Amsterdam.

Still the country was menaced by the shallow Zuiderzee. A freshwater lake during Roman times, it was enlarged by successive storms transforming the lake into an arm of the North Sea. Then in 1916 the dikes that surrounded the Zuiderzee were breached by a devastating storm, and Amsterdam was again at the mercy of the sea. A scheme was proposed that would both dam off the Zuiderzee forming a fresh water lake fed by the IJssel River and create five polders. In 1918 the Zuiderzee act was passed, and by 1932 an earthen dam, 19 miles (30 km) long from Wieringen to the coast of Friesland, had been completed. The more than 185 miles (300 km) of dikes protecting the former Zuiderzee were no longer exposed to tidal action, and the province of Noord Holland was connected directly to Friesland by road. Furthermore, the formation of the IJsselmeer provided a reservoir of fresh water for the increasing needs of agriculture and industry and helped to check the salinization of groundwater. The way had been prepared for creating new polders, and in 1930 the Wieringermeer polder was drained, followed in 1942 by the Northeast polder. After the Second World War, the East Flevoland and South Flevoland polders fell dry, leaving the Mark-

erwaard polder, which was scheduled to be drained by 1980 but will remain as open water because of changing needs. Land use in the IJsselmeer polders has been mainly agricultural. However, because of the dispersal of population from the Randstad, especially from Amsterdam, and the diminishing need for agricultural land, as well as because of food surpluses within the EU, the percentage of land used for residential, industrial, and recreational space has been increased in the South Flevoland polder.

With the completion of the main dike (Afsluitsdijk) across the Zuiderzee, the threat to central Holland had been blunted. However, one region, the delta, subjected to repeated floodings, remained vulnerable. The floods of February 1953, which left 1800 persons dead and drowned thousands of cattle, galvanized the government into action, and so in 1958 the Delta Act was passed. The principal object of the delta project was to shorten and strengthen the total length of coastline and dikes open to the sea by damming off the sea arms of the delta. The 19 miles (30 km) of new dams, some of which are barrier sluices that can be closed, thereby keeping out the sea, have reduced the length of the sea defenses by about 435 miles (700 km). In the unlikely situation that the new dams should be breached, the existing dikes, which lie along arms of the rivers, would become secondary defenses. Water behind the dams and barrier sluices is either salt water that is tidal, salt water that is nontidal, or fresh water. Furthermore, the delta project has ended the isolation of the islands by building connecting bridges and roads and using the new dikes and sluice dams for roadways. Throughout the project, recreation and tourist areas have been constructed.

Both the Zuiderzee reclamation and the Delta Plan have increased the security of the Netherlands from sea flooding. However, one threat remains—that of inland flooding from the Rhine and Maas waterways, a situation that occurred at the end of 1993 and in early 1995. A combination of factors are responsible, including higher than normal rainfall, less absorbing capacity of the watershed because of urban and industrial expansion, canalization of the rivers, and forests that have been weakened by acidification. This problem will remain formidable in the future and must be addressed, not only by the Netherlands but also by Belgium, France, Germany, and Switzerland.

FIGURE 8-14 "Dijk" settlement, Southlands, Zeeland Province (Netherlands Board of Tourism).

78 billion kwh generated in 1993, about 5 percent of which was nuclear. In 1992 crude oil accounted for 4.5 percent of primary energy production, natural gas over 93.2 percent, and nuclear 1.3 percent. Coal production, mainly from mines in Limburg, faced with competition from oil and natural gas, declined from 12.6 million tons in 1960 to only 0.8 million tons in 1974. The last mine closed in 1975. Crude oil output, mainly from wells in the North Sea and north of Enschede, reached a high of 3.9 million tons in 1990 and declined to 3.1 million by 1993. Reserves were estimated to be 189 million barrels in 1988, of which 56 percent were offshore. Imports of oil rose from 19.9 million tons in 1962 to a high of 85.4 million tons in 1973. By 1990 imports had dropped to 44.5 million as the country reduced its reliance on imported petroleum. Refining capacity reached a peak of over 98 million tons in 1976; however, because of worldwide overcapacity, it dropped to 59.2 million tons in 1993. The refineries are concentrated mainly in the port of Rotterdam.

Natural gas is the most important natural resource in the Netherlands, and the Slochteren field near Groningen has developed into one of Europe's most significant energy sources. From 1974 to 1993, production held steady at around 2930 to 2970 billion cu ft annually. Reserves, at present rates of production, are estimated to last at least until the year 2017, and the outlook for exports continues buoyant, because natural gas is the cleanest of the hydrocarbon fuels. Pipelines link the Netherlands with Switzerland, Belgium, Italy, France, Austria, and Germany. Domestically, an aluminum smelter was built at Delfzijl near the gasfield, and a chemical complex was built near Vlissingen in Zeeland in the southwest. Paradoxically, because of gas exports, the Dutch have imported natural gas from Algeria and Norway.

The country's nuclear power plant of 400-mw capacity was built at Borssele near the port of Vlissingen. The power is being used mainly by the French firm, Péchiney, for its nearby aluminum smelting works.

The only significant raw material other than oil and natural gas is salt. Found in the eastern part of the Netherlands in Overijssel Province, thick deposits about 1000 to 1300 feet (300 to 400m) below the surface are sufficient to meet the country's demand for years to come. The salt is used as a raw material for the chemical industry, for the production of industrial salt, and for a soda plant at Delfzijl. Production was 3.7 million tons in 1991.

Formerly, lack of raw materials limited the development of primary industry; since the Second World War, however, growth has occurred in the steel, aluminum, and chemical industries. Historically, the major industrial centers evolved in the west and south of the country where raw materials (coal) were found and where basic geographic factors such as a large population, access to water transportation, and proximity to domestic and foreign markets favored industrial development. Thus, the west, especially the ports, and the south of the country became the core industrial areas. After the Second World War, industry, often aided by government subsidies, or because of the discovery of natural gas, dispersed to other regions of the country.

The only major steelworks in the Netherlands is the Hoogovens integrated plant at IJmuiden, 15 miles (24 km) west of Amsterdam. A complex of coke ovens, sintering plants, blast furnaces, and rolling mills, Hoogovens accounted for almost all of the Dutch steel production of 6 million tons in 1993, an amount that has remained constant since the 1970s. When Hoogovens was founded in 1918, the IJmuiden site was chosen partly for political reasons. Steel experts were against the location, because it was far from coalfields and farther from iron mines. Since then, location factors have changed radically, and the IJmuiden site is unsurpassed. Ocean vessels supply the plant, located outside the entrance to the North Sea canal, with cheap ore and coking coal from abroad. Additional supplies of coking coal come from the Ruhr, and limestone arrives by rail or barge from Germany and Belgium. Because of a limited domestic market, the steel industry has been heavily export oriented. Semifinished and finished products are loaded directly from the plant to ocean vessels or barges. Because of European and worldwide competition, productivity has been continually upgraded and the industry has been restructured and rationalized.

Aluminum smelting was established by the Alusuisse and Hoogovens firms at Delfzijl northeast of Groningen in 1966 and by Péchiney at Vlissingen in Zeeland in 1971. Both sites offer deep-water harbors that allow imported alumina to be unloaded adjacent to the smelters. Natural gas is the main fuel for generating electric power. The aluminum industry has been hard hit by low cost imports from Russia; production, which was 264,000 tons in 1991, dropped to 232,000 tons in 1993.

The chemical industry, producing items such as fertilizers, detergents, pharmaceuticals, and basic chemicals, has grown considerably since 1945. Two basic factors have been responsible: the Netherlands' geographic situation and the creation of the EC/EU. Because the modern chemical industry handles large volumes of raw materials and finished products that amount to millions of tons annually, efficient cheap transportation and adequate port facilities are imperative. Large ships, deep channels, and efficient rapid handling are necessary. With its North Sea location on the deltas of the Rhine, Maas, and Schelde, close to the industrial centers of Belgium, France, and Germany, blessed with the ports of Rotterdam, Amsterdam, and Vlissingen, the country commands a superior geographic position. Prior to the EC, the country was too small to provide an outlet for giant chemical concerns, but once a vast market protected by an external tariff was created, Dutch concerns were able to boost production and international firms could establish subsidiaries in the Netherlands.

The Dutch created new industrial sites, mainly between Rotterdam and the North Sea, and multinational enterprises such as ICI (Imperial Chemical Industries), Du Pont, Esso, and Hoechst have built large complexes. To meet this international competition, the Dutch companies have expanded. Two major Dutch firms are AKU, which produces artificial and synthetic fibers and filaments, and KZO, a manufacturer of heavy chemicals, pharmaceuticals, cosmetic products, paints, detergents, and foodstuffs. AKU and KZO have merged with the German company Glanzstoff to form the AKZO concern. In 1993 AKZO acquired the

Swedish company Nobel, creating the world's largest paint group. AKZO NOBEL is one of the world's leading firms in certain aspects of the chemical business. Employment is over 61,000 in 50 countries worldwide.

Developments in the chemical sector have taken place in the south on both sides of the Westerschelde, in the north near Delfzijl, and in the southeast where a chemical industry emerged after the closing of the coal mines. Related to the expansion of the chemical industry has been the pollution of air, water, and soil, which presents a serious situation in such a densely populated country.

Metal products, machinery, vehicles, shipbuilding, and aerospace are significant components of industry. Because of competition, shipbuilding has declined; however, specialized vessels are being constructed such as tugs, dredges, and ships for the offshore oil and gas industry. In 1993 the Dutch launched 170,000 tons compared to 723,000 in 1974. Fokker aircraft, with a factory at Schiphol airport near Amsterdam, was partially taken over by Daimler-Benz and struggled to stay alive in a fiercely competitive market. After hundreds of millions of dollars in losses, it finally declared bankruptcy and closed its core aircraft assembly operation during 1995 with the loss of 5700 jobs. The state-owned truck concern, DAF, has also suffered financially and filed for bankruptcy in 1993. Somewhat surprisingly, it had profits in 1994 and 1995 ($100 million in 1995) and expected to substantially increase production beginning in 1996.

The electronics sector is another pillar of Dutch industry, but it too has downsized as a result of the recession of the early 1990s and rivalry from Asia. Philips Electronics is a multinational renowned for its inventions such as the compact cassette and CD. Unfortunately, its marketing skills lag behind research and development. Active in products such as stereos, color TVs, electronic microscopes, and X-ray apparatus, the company employed 252,000 in 1994, compared to over 390,000 in 1977. Philips has undergone massive rationalization and restructuring in order to improve its balance sheet. In 1993, on sales of $32.16 billion, the company lost $273.7 million. However, a profit of $878.8 million was recorded in 1994. World headquarters are in Eindhoven in the south central part of the country.

Two multinational Anglo-Dutch firms, Royal Dutch/Shell and Unilever are among the largest companies in Europe by market capital. Royal Dutch, employing 117,000 employees and ranked number one in 1994, had a profit of over $9 billion; Unilever, employing 294,000, was in seventh place and had a profit of over $3 billion.

Overnight stays by tourists expanded by 33 percent in the Netherlands from 1983 to 1991, but declined from 1992 to 1993 by 5.1 percent. The balance between tourist receipts and Dutch tourist expenditures is in the red. In 1993 receipts accounted for $4.6 billion, whereas expenditures were $8.9 billion; leaving a balance of -$4.3 billion. Most visitors to the country are German, followed by the British and Americans. Amsterdam is the country's major tourist attraction, accounting for about 40 percent of all tourists, but the vivid bulb fields south of Haarlem, handsome old villages, Europoort, the delta works, and excellent beaches also draw many visitors. Camping is popular with both Dutch and foreign tourists, and modern facilities have been built at many locations along the coast and in the large cities and small villages of the interior. The country, with thousands of miles of bike paths, is a key destination for the renaissance of ecologically sound biking holidays that has swept many countries of Europe, especially Germany. The unstable summer weather, often cool and rainy, can severely curtail outdoor tourism.

Agriculture, Forestry, and Fishing

In 1994 agricultural land accounted for about half of the country's 16,000 sq miles (41,500 sq km). The agricultural regions relate for the most part to geologic and hydrological conditions. The climate of the country is fairly uniform, temperate, and influenced by the sea. Average annual precipitation varies from 20 in. (500 mm) in the southeast to 35 in. (900 mm) south of the IJsselmeer. January mean temperatures range from just above freezing in the delta to just below freezing in the northeast; July mean temperatures range from 68°F (20°C) near the coast, warming to 73°F (23°C) in the southeast. Thus, coastal areas are warmer in winter and cooler in summer than inland areas.

Agricultural productivity has benefited from reclamation measures. Much of the farmland has been recovered from the sea and lakes, and soil conditions of inland areas formerly unfit for cultivation have been improved (Fig. 8-15). Four broad soil divisions are recognizable: the alluvial soils, mainly clays, of the polders and river valleys; the podzolic sands and gravels south and east of the IJsselmeer and north of the Belgian border; the organic soils between Amsterdam and Rotterdam and in the northeast; and the brown podzolic soils of the southeast, often covered with fertile loess.

Extensive agriculture such as the growing of cereals, potatoes, and sugar beets accounts for about 36 percent of the agricultural land and is found mainly on marine clays in the north and southwest of the country, on old and new polder lands, and on old peat lands in the east. Here the farms are relatively large, about 100 acres (40 ha), in comparison to the rest of the country. Over 50 percent of the agricultural lands are devoted to pastures on poorer soils, which are used mainly for dairying, the products of which are domestically used and exported. The south and east of the

FIGURE 8-15 Farmsteads and planned village of Nagele in the Northeast polder (toward west-northwest) reclaimed from former Zuiderzee. Top right, farms along the road to the village of Tollebeek (Luchtfoto Bart Hofmeester, Rotterdam/The Netherlands).

country have sandy soils and feature many mixed farms that raise or import fodder for the industrial production of pigs and chickens. This industry has expanded rapidly. For example, in 1974 only 6.7 million pigs were raised, a figure that reached 13.7 million in 1993. These figures compare to those of the dairy herd that remained more or less constant, just under 5 million, during the same period. The fallout from this enormous increase in pigs has resulted in severe environmental problems related to the vast amounts of manure, especially in the east and south of the country, that have been spread onto the land. Soil pollution is especially serious, as is the unpleasant smell across wide areas of the countryside.

Horticulture, which takes up about 3.4 percent of the agricultural land, is practiced in many agricultural regions of the country. Behind the dunes on the west coast are the fields of flowers and bulbs. Other areas devoted to horticulture produce vegetables such as peppers, tomatoes, cucumbers, and lettuce in greenhouses, as well as flowers. A major export market is Germany, especially the nearby Ruhr. Products are also exported to other parts of Europe and to North America. The main greenhouse region, Westland, is found between the Hague and Rotterdam. In all, greenhouses occupy nearly 25,000 acres (over 10,000 ha).

In 1993 the number of agricultural holdings was 120,000, a figure that has declined steadily since the Second World War. The average farm size has increased to over 40 acres (16 ha). Although only 4 percent of the labor force is employed in the primary sector, the value of output has increased considerably.

The country began specialization in high-value products that could be exported at the end of the nineteenth century. Today, agricultural products account for between 20 and 25 percent of the total value of exports, most of which go to the EU, and contribute 3.6 percent of the GDP. The Common Agricultural Policy (CAP) of the EU has been beneficial for Dutch farmers. Being better organized than other countries, highly competitive, and concentrating on export-oriented products, they at one time were able to pull ahead of their European rivals. Competition has increased, however, and the CAP, because of surplus production, has reduced quotas. As already mentioned, because of the intense nature of animal production and the resulting increase in urine and manure, problems of air, soil, and groundwater pollution are serious. Because of a Euro-wide surplus of agricultural and livestock products, the trend will be to take land out of production and return it to a natural state.

Compared to agriculture, forestry is of minor importance; the area of woods and forests comprises 8 percent of the total land, one of the smaller figures for Europe. Forestry is rarely part of farm activity, and trees and shrubs are planted to serve as windbreaks or for ornamental purposes. In other areas trees have been planted as part of recreation zones. The largest wooded regions are found in the provinces of Gelderland south of the IJsselmeer and in Noord Brabant and correspond with the sandy soils of these areas. Government policy forbids cutting without a license.

The Dutch fishing fleets, no longer the mainstay of the economy, are based in the southwestern ports of Scheveningen, Vlaardingen, and IJmuiden. Consisting mainly of herring, mackerel, and eel, the catch was 487,200 tons in 1992, up from 326,000 in 1974.

Trade and Finance

In 1993 the EU was the main trading partner of the Netherlands, receiving 74 percent of all exports and accounting for 61 percent of all imports. Germany was the largest single trading partner, taking 29 percent of exports and providing 25 percent of imports, followed by Belgium/Luxembourg. In 1993 a favorable balance of trade in goods of $5.5 billion had been achieved. Manufactured products accounted for 65 percent of the total export commodity trade. Machinery; food, drink, and tobacco; and metal goods comprised the major import and export categories; chemical products represented another significant export. The country's current account has been strongly in the black since 1987, with the transport sector being a major contributor.

The mergers in Dutch banking during the early 1990s have prepared the banking industry for the financial wars that are part of the globalization of the economy. Though strengthened domestically, they must compete on the international scene as well as be able to resist further penetrations by foreign banks that have established themselves in the traditionally open Dutch markets. The Amsterdam Stock Exchange, one of the oldest in the world, is in a struggle with London to remain the principal place for the buying and selling of Dutch securities. Known for their conservative and wise investments, Dutch banks are financially stable and have expanded abroad in London and Chicago from their strong home base. ABN Amro Holding, the largest bank in the Netherlands, is the nineteenth largest bank in the world by assets; its profits in 1994 were over $1 billion.

Transportation

Because of the Netherlands' superb geographical situation between the British Isles and Germany and between Scandinavia and France, as well as its river access to the "continent" via the Rhine and Maas rivers, the transport industry plays a prime role in the economy, contributing large surpluses to the country's balance of payments. In fact, from 1987 to 1991, the figure did not fall below $4 billion annually.

Fronting on the world's busiest sea and being the outlet of Europe's most traveled river have provided the Dutch with natural advantages that they have improved on by means of engineering projects such as the New Waterway, North Sea Canal, and Amsterdam-Rhine Canal. Furthermore, the opening of the Main-Danube Canal has linked the country to the Black Sea by way of inland waterways. Germany, Luxembourg, France, and Switzerland, as well as Eastern European countries, Russia, and the independent states of the former Soviet Union are linked to Dutch ports. In addition, the Maas outlet and the mouth of the Schelde connect with eastern and western Belgium, respectively. The Netherlands has become the "gateway to Western Europe" and will play a more important role with Eastern Europe than in the past (Fig. 8-16).

In 1991 the Dutch inland fleet comprised over 6000 vessels, including tankers, push barges, and container barges. The length of navigable inland waters was over 3100 miles (5000 km), with the Rhine and its outlets at Rotterdam and through the Amsterdam-Rhine Canal being by far the most important waterway. The goods carried by Dutch ships are either brought from overseas to Dutch ports and then transshipped into barges or are brought down the river for transshipment into seagoing vessels at Dutch ports. This transit traffic comprises mostly bulk goods consisting of iron ores, phosphates, coal, and grain that move upstream, and sands, gravels, fertilizers, cement, and timber that move downstream. Besides these bulk goods, appreciable quantities of higher value merchandise such as seeds, sugar, coffee, and tropical products are carried upstream, while metal, machinery, and chemicals are shipped downstream, many of which now arrive in containers. In 1992 a total of 125.6 million tons passed the German-Dutch border at Emmerich (see section on Amsterdam and Rotterdam).

The Netherlands' railway network has a density about half that of Belgium. Traditionally, the railway has been a passenger traffic system; goods traffic moves mainly by inland waterway and road. In 1990, 70 percent of the 1740-mile (2800-km) rail network was electrified, the rest being used by diesel-electric locomotives. Amsterdam, joined in 1981 to the Schiphol airport, is linked to major European cities by fast EuroCity trains. For example, Basel is only 8 hours and 45 minutes away, Paris 5 hours and 26 minutes, and Bonn 3 hours and 10 minutes.

One of the densest networks of roads, highways, and motorways in the world links the various regions of the country and connects with the international highway system. There are over 1240 miles (2000 km) of four-lane divided highways in the Netherlands, and because of projects such as the Delta Works and the IJsselmeer reclamation, highways now connect formerly isolated sections of the country. There were 2.7 inhabitants per car in 1993, a figure that is below that of other countries, such as Belgium and France. However, because of the dense traffic in the Randstad region, traffic from Germany and Belgium, as well as the many tunnels and bridges, there are often traffic jams, especially during the rush hours. Because of their strategic location, Dutch shipping companies, play a vital role in inter-European road transport.

Schiphol, the national airport, only 6 miles (10 km) southwest of Amsterdam, serves the Rand-

FIGURE 8-16 In Rotterdam, part of the prewar ports on the southern riverbank (Waalhaven), looking eastward. In the foreground, a container vessel; in the left background, the river Neuwe Maas, and right, the Maashaven. Upper left (in front of the white tall building), the Euromast (tower) (Luchtfoto Bart Hofmeester, Rotterdam/The Netherlands).

stad conurbation of over 5 million inhabitants. Passenger traffic in 1993 was 21.2 million persons, up 11.1 percent from the previous year. Freight tonnage was also up by 11.6 percent, reaching 770,000 tons. Schiphol is the fourth largest European airport in terms of passengers, after London, Paris, and Frankfurt, and the fourth largest in terms of freight handled. Whereas the airport is far below London in passengers—71 million in 1993— it is not so far behind in London's freight handling of 1.1 million tons. Many industries have established

branches at the airport to utilize the bonded warehouses. Here goods may be unpacked, sorted, repacked, and then distributed throughout Europe, all without special customs permission or the payment of import duties. Thus, the Dutch, as is the case with port facilities, have made the good geographical situation of Schiphol even better by providing greater efficiency for users and by pursuing a continuing policy of modernization.

Traditionally a seafaring country, the Netherlands had a merchant fleet of 4.1 million tons registered in the Netherlands and the Netherlands' Antilles in 1993. Rotterdam, the world's largest port with over 282 million tons of shipments (43% of which was oil), and Amsterdam, with 30.5 million tons in 1993, are the main ports (see section on Rotterdam and Amsterdam).

Physical Planning and Environment

Physical planning in the Netherlands has been instrumental in preventing the chaotic development of the country's urban areas and in preserving agricultural and recreational land. Modern physical planning at the national level dates from the Housing Act of 1901, intended for the improvement of housing. With the addition of various amendments, however, to a considerable extent, it became a law governing physical planning. After World War II, in response to mounting pressures created by population growth, industrial development, and the increase in motor vehicles, the old legislation had to be revised. To ensure a proper balance of land use, new legislation was enacted in 1965 providing for coordinated planning at the national, regional, and municipal levels.

In 1966 the publication of the *Second Report on Physical Planning in the Netherlands* showed the government's great concern about maintaining high environmental standards. It was not an act of legislation but a policy statement that presented guidelines for municipal and regional development within the national framework. According to the *Report*, problems such as the need for recreational space, traffic and parking, purity of water, land for urban expansion, and certain other matters must be addressed, especially in such a small, densely populated, highly urbanized country as the Netherlands. The problems were not necessarily new. However, the stronger the pressure on the available space and the more complicated the social and technical development process, the more the well-being of the population depended on guidance given to physical development. A third report was published between 1975 and 1977, and in 1983, a report relating to urbanization was also released.

Because of high population density, the constant threat of the sea, and the creation of polders,

government practices to control and guide development had existed for a long period. However, because development was taking place on a much larger scale and at a much faster pace than ever before, larger units for physical planning were necessary. Planning at the municipality level was followed by planning at the regional and then at the national level. Furthermore, the Netherlands' relations to the rest of Europe, especially the neighboring countries of Belgium and Germany, were considered. Thus pipelines, motorways, improved rail service, and strategic recreation areas were all vital to physical planning.

The Dutch planners have prevented the deterioration of living standards by controlling growth and over-concentration and by encouraging decentralization. Dispersal areas for additional population were designated in the north, parts of Overijssel Province, the tip of Noord Holland, the southern IJsselmeer polders, and the province of Zeeland. Thus, the Randstad areas, a name given to the major cities of the southwest of the country, were protected from uncontrolled expansion. Amsterdam, Rotterdam, the Hague, and Utrecht have kept their specialized functions without merging with one another, and a central green area of small villages for agriculture and recreation has remained. Nevertheless, because of continuing population pressure, development has not been stopped within the Randstad (Fig. 8-17).

Although there have been problems, planning has enabled the country to evolve from a population of 5.5 million at the turn of the century to over 15 million in 1993. Compared to other countries in Europe, Belgium, France, and Italy, for example, space is intelligently utilized in an efficient manner. There is adequate land for urbanization, industry, recreation, and nature protection in a country with one of the highest population densities in the world.

The Dutch have fought not only against the sea, but also against pollution and environmental degradation. These problems have been accentuated because of high population density, limited land, and a location at the mouth of the Rhine and near major industrial centers in their own country, as well as in Germany, France, and Belgium. Thus, serious difficulties have arisen with water, air, and soil pollution, as well as salinization of fresh

FIGURE 8-17 Brielle. Air photograph of the medieval town and planned residential extension encroaching on fertile farmland (see farmhouses, lower right). Brielle is west of Rotterdam on Vorne-Putten Island, south of Europoort (Information and Documentation Center for the Geography of the Netherlands, Utrecht).

water. Water pollution takes many forms. First, the Rhine is heavily polluted before it reaches the Netherlands. Groundwater has been contaminated by industrial discharges and by application of too much manure on the land because of intensive raising of animals. In addition, the North Sea has suffered serious pollution, caused in part by container ships losing their containers stacked on deck in heavy weather. In 1994 packaged toxic chemicals washed up on the beaches of the country from such a situation. Air pollution results from refineries on the west coast, especially in Europoort; from incinerators, also mainly in the west; from dense vehicular circulation, primarily in the Randstad area; and from nearby industrial

concentrations in other countries. Acid rain, as in most parts of Europe is serious, particularly in the southeast of the Netherlands. Soil pollution has led to too much nitrites and phosphates in the groundwater; this is a serious situation, for two-thirds of the potable water comes from the ground. Furthermore, dredging of the canals and harbors has brought up material that is polluted with chemicals and heavy metals. It must be stored in specially designed reservoirs. Finally, serious noise pollution has resulted from the intense urban development.

The government is attempting to limit environmental degradation through laws, the building of purification systems for waste water, the encouragement of recycling, and more ecological construction. A good example of the ecological construction is Ecolonia near The Hague, where the houses have been built to save water, and fuel, and where materials using toxic chemicals have been eliminated and have been chosen for their recyclability.

Rotterdam and Amsterdam: A Functional Approach to Urbanization Within the Randstad

Randstad Holland is comprised of the three largest cities in the country: Rotterdam with a population in 1992 (agglomeration) of 1.06 million; Amsterdam, 1.08 million; and The Hague, 693,000 (see Fig. 6-20). Respective figures at the end of 1974 were 1.03 million, 991,000, and 679,000. The different functions of these three great cities have created a polycentric urban region with an agricultural core. Government pursuits are centered in The Hague; large-scale port development and commercial activities in Rotterdam; and financial, cultural, service, and smaller commercial activities in Amsterdam. A detailed look at Rotterdam and Amsterdam will compare the unique methods by which they are solving their urban problems, all of which must be considered within the framework of an expanded Randstad by the year 2000.

For over 600 years, the ports of Rotterdam and Amsterdam have modified their original sites and situation by reclaiming land for urban growth, deepening their waterways, and digging new channels and canals to the open sea. Because of differences in location and function, historical evolution, past and present planning laws, and the destruction of World War II, the cities are using different methods to solve the problems created by the growth of their metropolitan areas. These problems, common to all modern cities, become magnified in the densely populated Randstad where the failure to solve them would result in Rotterdam and Amsterdam's inability to function as normal urban areas. They include the shortage of land for port, industrial, and commercial facilities; the need to provide efficient public transportation, adequate housing accommodations, and recreational land for their populations;

severe traffic congestion; and environmental degradation.

The history of Rotterdam has been closely connected with its location in the Rhine Delta. A little over 100 years ago, the port was far behind its international competitors; within the last century, however, Rotterdam has climbed rapidly to become the world's largest port (Fig. 8-16). Total goods traffic in 1993 was 282 million tons, followed by the second largest port, Singapore, with 238 million. The next largest European port was nearby Antwerp registering 102 million tons. Furthermore, the Dutch city has become Europe's leading oil distribution and refining center and largest container port.

Rotterdam's history may be discussed in three phases. First, it originated in the fourteenth century as a small fishing village located on a bend of one of the estuary branches of the Rhine. The second phase began in 1872 with the excavation of the channel known as the New Waterway by which Rotterdam was directly connected with the North Sea. The third stage commenced in the early 1950s with the establishment of the European Community and the development of large new port and industrial facilities at the mouth of the New Waterway, known as Europoort.

The original site of Rotterdam was on the north bank of the Nieuwe Mass, one of the Rhine's distributaries. A study of the map of the delta region will show the Rhine and its many distributary streams flowing through Belgium and the Netherlands. It will not show the many changes along their beds effected by nature and humans in the centuries since the last continental glaciation. These streams, often swollen by flood, meandered aimlessly across the marshy wastes here picking up, there depositing great quantities of sand and gravel laid down by the Riss ice mass. Efforts to control these river movements began with settlement in the region and have continued with increasing skill and ingenuity to the present day. This area was a flat, windswept coastal region with little natural defense against the great smashing storms that swept out of the North Sea.

The old town of Rotterdam grew up in the fourteenth century where the south-flowing Rotte River emptied into the Nieuwe Mass. A dam was built across the Rotte (hence the name Rotterdam) to act as a barrier against the sea floods that often accompanied the severe storms, drowning great tracts of low-lying land. Rotterdam suffered greatly from the feudal wars that laid waste to much of this area of the Netherlands during the fifteenth century, and its development was hampered by the competition of older and more powerful towns, especially Dordrecht. During this period, boats made their way up the 20 miles (32 km) from the North Sea to Rotterdam by sailing up the inlet known as the Brielsche Maas. But by the middle of the eighteenth century, sailing vessels had increased in size, and hundreds of years of continuous silting had added considerable land surface to the island of Rozenburg in the Brielsche Maas, thus choking the channel. This route had to be abandoned, and a new one, requiring many days to sail eastward through Dordrecht and then westward through the distributaries of the Rhine and out to the open sea, was established. In 1829 a canal was dug through the island of Voorne south of Rotterdam as an alternative direct route to the North Sea, but the estuary leading to it became silt laden in 30 to 40 years. Failure greeted all efforts to provide direct access from the North Sea to Rotterdam. By the latter half of the nineteenth century, however a new plan was undertaken, and with the help of powerful steam dredges, work was begun on the New Waterway. By 1872 a channel had been completed through the dunes at the Hoek van Holland connecting the Nieuwe Maas River with the North Sea. At last Rotterdam and one of the world's busiest waterways were connected by a lock-free, bridge-free channel that has been continuously deepened to accommodate ever-larger vessels.

The opening of the New Waterway couldn't have come at a better time. In 1868 the Mannheim Convention assured free navigation and equal rights to shipping traffic of all nationalities on the Rhine and its tributaries from Basel to the North Sea. The Ruhr-Westphalian industrial complex in Germany was rapidly expanding under the full force of the German industrial revolution, and large amounts of Swedish and Norwegian ores were necessary to augment domestic sources. Growing volumes of other bulk goods such as timber and grain, much of which was transferred from ocean freighter to river barge at Rotterdam and carried up the Rhine to the Ruhr-Rhenish

industrial centers, were also imported. The reaction to this steadily growing demand for bulk goods was immediate. The Rotterdam area augmented its port facilities, and the number of its incoming vessels rose sharply from nearly 2000 in 1850 to over 7000 by 1900.

Starting in 1890, a series of harbors were constructed on the north and south banks of the Maas, and development continued downstream without interruption until the construction in 1938 of two petroleum harbors at Pernis. In spite of rather difficult times after World War I and during the Depression, Rotterdam had sufficiently recovered traffic so that by 1930 a record total of over 15,000 oceangoing vessels entered the port and over 42 million tons of seaborne cargo were handled, a figure not surpassed until 1954.

On May 14, 1940, German bombers deliberately destroyed the heart of Rotterdam. Nearly 25,000 dwellings, as well as thousands of shops, many churches, the railway stations, hotels, and schools, were burned beyond use. Astonishingly, four days later, a plan for the reconstruction of the city was authorized, and by December 1941, the first official drawing of the plan was completed. The city, meanwhile, carried out an extensive expropriation program, including the ruins and sites of the bombed buildings, a large number of undamaged buildings and sites on the fringe of the devastated area, and a large tract of land outside the city for future housing and industrial areas. Work on the new plan began during the occupation. Roads and canals were built, bridges constructed, houses and shops completed, and the Maas tunnel, started before the war, was finished. The Germans put a stop to all rebuilding operations in July 1942, and before they left in May 1945, they further destroyed one-third of the wharves and about 40 percent of the harbor equipment.

Restoration of the port had immediate priority after the war. Thus, by the end of December 1949, the destroyed docks were rebuilt and modernized, and Rotterdam was prepared to service the increasing number of incoming ships. Nevertheless, it was still necessary to prepare the port for future growth. Before the war, the dock facilities were designed to handle mainly bulk cargo and oil traffic. Now these docks were redesigned to handle various kinds of general cargo, whereas bulk cargoes such as oil, chemicals, and iron ore were to be discharged in new docks built closer to the sea. Here, the larger vessels of the future could be moored, and new industries such as refineries, chemical works, and steel plants could process the raw materials. In 1947 the Botlek harbor plan transformed the large tract of polderland lying west of Pernis into a harbor and industrial area of nearly 3000 acres (1200 ha). Such firms as Dow Chemical and Esso Nederland soon leased industrial sites, and despite initial skepticism the venture was a success.

Two years after the completion of the Botlek scheme, a decision was made to further expand the port facilities. The agrarian island of Rozenburg, which had forced the cutting of the New Waterway, was transformed into the Europoort. It became the gateway to the EC, handling bulk carriers and tankers up to 350,000 tons that discharged the raw materials for the iron, steel, petrochemical, and oil industries of the Rhine hinterland. A new oil terminal was built at Maasvlakte at the western approach to Europoort that could handle fully laden tankers of up to 500,000 tons. Companies such as Chevron, Texaco, Shell, Esso, and BP located here, and oil flowed by pipeline to their refineries at Europoort, Botlek, and Pernis, and by the Rhine pipeline to the Ruhr-Cologne industrial conurbation. Rotterdam is also connected by pipeline to both Amsterdam and Antwerp. In addition, a container port opened in 1967, which is now the third largest in the world after Hong Kong and Singapore. The number of vessels using Rotterdam's varied and efficient facilities reached a high of 34,252 in 1975 and was 32,255 in 1992. During the same period tonnage grew from 273,000 to 293,000. The decline in the number of vessels was compensated by the increasing size of bulk carriers and container ships.

Presently, plans are underway to handle 400 million tons annually by the year 2010, which will require about 6200 acres (2500 ha) of new facilities. This will mean renovating all installations and building a new dock on the north side of the New Waterway, bordering on the Westland market gardening area, that would be used for the distribution and transportation of horticultural products. There will also be a westward extension of the Maasvlakte. A guiding factor in the port expansion

plans calls for increasing the value of products during the handling of the cargo. For example, such procedures as grading, blending, repacking, and processing of goods all add considerable value to the original materials. A second factor will be an active industrial policy to attract firms, especially those that can utilize some of the raw materials, such as basic chemicals, and transform them into high-quality chemical products. Additional aspects to boost the port's growth will include the strengthening of central distribution facilities for the European market and an addition to the bulk agricultural docks that will include refrigerated and deep freeze works for vegetable, fruit, and fruit juice concentrates.

As in all cities, problems remain, especially air pollution from the refineries, but they are being tackled or solved in a well-thought-out manner. Polluted silt and port sludge coming mainly from the Rhine are being contained in a large 620-acre (250-ha) reservoir situated at the northeast point of the Maasvlakte. It is hoped that a future reduction of pollutants in the rivers will forestall the building of a new reservoir when the present one fills up by 2000. The Maas River remains a barrier to commuters, as almost 300,000 people travel across or under it each day. New tunnels and bridges have been constructed, and a rapid transit system connects both sides of the river between the central station and the Zuidplein.

The CBD (central business district) of Rotterdam, completely rebuilt after World War II, remains a pedestrian zone surrounded by high-rise apartments, and in the Oude Haven, or old port, an imaginative waterfront development has been constructed combining housing, offices, restaurants, and pubs. Satellite towns have been built in the suburbs, and recreation land has been established for urban inhabitants.

The city of Amsterdam was founded in the thirteenth century at about the same time as Rotterdam and only 37 miles (60 km) to the north. It grew rapidly to become the principal commercial city of Europe in the seventeenth century. The location of Amsterdam at the narrows where the IJ flowed into the Zuiderzee was a vital factor in the city's development. By the thirteenth century, floods had transformed the freshwater lake, the *Flevo Lacus*, into a great shallow bay of the North

Sea. The IJ had become a broad tidal arm of this bay, later known as the Zuiderzee, leading into the interior of Noord Holland. Amsterdam was founded where the Amstel River flowed into the IJ. In about 1270, a dam, built across the Amstel a short distance from its mouth, provided a small, sheltered harbor where seagoing boats were suited to navigation on the interior waterways connecting with the IJ.

Amsterdam's early situation brought the city into contact by way of the sheltered Zuiderzee and Waddenzee with the major centers of the Hanseatic League. Beer was imported from Hamburg in 1323, and the demand for ships to transport the brew encouraged the inhabitants to become traders. Local products such as cloth, fish, and agricultural produce were exchanged for English wool; for wine and millstones from the Rhineland; and for spices, oil, salt, and wine from or through France and Flanders. By the fifteenth century, Amsterdam had become powerful enough to challenge German interests in the Baltic. Because of commercial ventures and the need for shipyard space, the town expanded into the surrounding waterlogged expanse of peat and tidal flats. Solving problems such as adequate water supply, sewage disposal, and land reclamation required a cooperative effort because of the cost and difficulty involved. Therefore, the city did not grow continuously but in a series of well-defined and regulated stages beginning in 1382.

Historical events favored Amsterdam's continued growth in the late sixteenth and early seventeenth centuries. Antwerp fell to the Spanish, and the Treaty of Westphalia closed the Schelde to navigation. An influx of highly skilled Flemish, Huguenot, and Jewish refugees swelled the population to approximately 105,000 in 1620. In comparison, Rotterdam was but a small village of 15,000. Commercial contacts developed with the Mediterranean Basin, Africa, the Americas, and the Far East. The East India Company was founded in 1602, and Amsterdam was established as the predominant colonial entrepôt (entry point) for Europe. Its position, protected from the danger of seaward assault, and capable of defense by flooding in case of landward attack, was secure and civic authorities responded to the opportunities at hand and deliberately planned the territorial expansion of the city in a manner unique to contemporary Europe.

From 1610 on, the city was enlarged by adding canals, roads, living quarters, public and commercial buildings, and dock space. The basic idea of the plan was a semicircle of concentric canals with the IJ as their base (Fig. 8-18). This plan, which would eventually result in a fourfold increase in area, gave the central city its present unusual half-moon shape. By the middle of the eighteenth century, population had reached 200,000. Amsterdam did not grow larger for almost a century because the rise of England as a powerful maritime country and the occupation of the Netherlands by Napoleon's armies interrupted the flow of commerce and severed communications with the East Indies. Furthermore, access to the port was becoming increasingly difficult as ships grew larger and the channels through the Zuiderzee silted up.

In the early nineteenth century, a solution to both these problems was attempted. Amsterdam was reestablished as an entrepôt for the East Indian trade, and the North Holland Canal from the IJ to Den Helder was cut. However, the canal twisted north from Amsterdam and was inadequate to cope with modern shipping. The city found itself in the same position as Rotterdam and, like it, sought a solution to the problem of being cut off from the open sea. Amsterdam's answer was almost the same. A direct route from the city through the dune coast to the North Sea was realized with the opening of the North Sea Canal in 1876. This canal, unlike the New Waterway, has two sets of locks, one at the mouth near IJmuiden and the other near Amsterdam connecting with the IJsselmeer. The entrance lock has been enlarged three times and accommodates the longest vessels afloat. The existing entrance to the canal has been rebuilt to suit vessels of up to 100,000 tons with a draft of 43 feet (13 meters).

Although Amsterdam finally had an outlet to the open sea, its communications to the great rivers, which formed the connecting links with the European hinterland, remained poor, to the detriment of the port's economic development. In 1893 the Merwede Canal was opened, giving better access to the Rhine, but it was not until 1952, when the Amsterdam-Rhine Canal was completed, that this problem was overcome. However, because of

FIGURE 8-18 Amsterdam, the largest city in the Netherlands and about 700 years old. The photograph shows the striking location of the canals in the oldest part of the city (KLM Aerocarto, Rotterdam).

congestion and new types of transport such as push barges, widening of the canal has also now become a necessity.

After the opening of the North Sea Canal, a new period of vigorous economic expansion began. Docking and storage facilities were extended to the east and west of the city along the IJ. By 1897 the population approached half a million, more than twice the figure for 1849. In order to house the influx of people, new residential areas were built with little regard to the existing pattern of the city. This expansion was poorly controlled and monotonous; unplanned quarters appeared that quickly deteriorated into slums. Fortunately, the Netherlands' Housing Act of 1901 brought a stop to this unplanned development, and since 1931 all

municipalities in the Netherlands have had to establish a master plan.

Between the two world wars, Amsterdam was the vanguard of scientific town planning. In the early 1920s, two garden cities north of the IJ, Oostzaan and Nieuwendam, were built. Between 1928 and 1934, a comprehensive plan for the city, designed to cover the physical requirements of housing, work, traffic, and recreation to the year 2000, materialized. Delayed during the war years, the plan was realized with the construction of other garden cities north and south of the old city, including a highly developed complex of apartments around the artificial lake of Sloterplas. The lake provides excellent recreation facilities such as sailing, swimming, and fishing in the midst of about 125,000 people who dwell in this area. The satellite towns are connected to the old central city of Amsterdam by express highways whose medians are reserved for high-speed tram lines joining the main tram net of the city.

Construction of a new residential and industrial area southeast of the city began in 1966. Known as Bijlmermeer, the complex houses 110,000 persons in apartments and row houses that are separated from all motor traffic. Cars are parked in garages located within walking distance of the dwellings, and a network of cycle tracks and footpaths lace the area. A subway connects Bijlmermeer to central Amsterdam.

Problems of traffic congestion are most severe. Buses, autos, trams, scooters, and bicycles clog the narrow streets of the central city during morning and evening rush hours. Bypass highways, tunnels under the IJ, and the rapid transit system have relieved the situation somewhat, but the problem remains acute.

The rehabilitation of old Amsterdam is an ongoing part of the master plan. The historical flavor of the seventeenth-century city with its beautiful churches, rich homes, and narrow streets and canals has been preserved when possible and renewed when necessary. Skyscraper construction has been forbidden, not only for aesthetic reasons but also because of the increased traffic and pedestrian congestion that inevitably follows. Instead, new sites for commerce and industry, as well as space for parklands are being carved out of the nineteenth-century slum districts surrounding the central core. The Amsterdam of the future will occupy a far greater area than it did in the early 1950s, even though total population will be less.

Amsterdam is continuing to prosper as a result of the interplay of old and new economic forces. The conurbation, stretching for about 25 miles (40 km) east and west, includes important development areas such as the mouth of the North Sea Canal with its blast furnaces, steel plants, and other industries; the older but important Zaan region to the north; the industrial and commercial area in proximity to Schiphol International Airport; and the reclaimed land of the IJsselmeer, South Flevoland, to the east of Amsterdam, which has become an entirely new hinterland for the city, with sites for new towns and recreational facilities.

The port of Amsterdam has reacted favorably to this increasing activity and accounted for 30.5 million tons in 1993, 29 percent of which was petroleum products. After 1945 it was necessary to restore the capacity and facilities of the port, and by 1960 the area of harbor basins had been doubled. The city has developed from a purely national port into an international transit harbor. Especially since the opening of the Amsterdam-Rhine Canal, many of the favorable conditions that apply to Rotterdam's situation are also applicable to Amsterdam. Facilities for storing and handling bulk goods have been enlarged and modernized, a container center and roll on/roll off facilities established, a refinery has been sited, and a passenger terminal opened. As a result, the tonnage handled has doubled since the early 1970s. Harbor development continues to take place along the North Sea Canal from the Amerikahaven on the west of Amsterdam to Velsen. The city is one of the few European ports with spacious ready-made industrial sites bordering deep water. Significant factors behind expansion are the reserves of natural gas in the north of the country and the continuing prospects for discovery of hydrocarbons elsewhere in the Netherlands and in the North Sea.

Conclusions

Challenge has been the keynote to Dutch survival. The first challenge was to stay alive in the inhospitable low-lying coastal area subjected to repeated storms and flooding. Then came the challenge of draining inland lakes, reclaiming marsh and heathlands, and wresting land from the sea. In the twentieth century, large-scale projects such as the Zuiderzee scheme and Delta Works that would seal the country from potential floods fired the imagination of the Dutch. And finally, a new and perhaps greater challenge arose: how to plan for 15 million people living and working in a complex industrial and agricultural country limited in area and still maintain individual freedom, high living standards, and good environmental conditions.

The challenge is not totally economic; however, industry must remain competitive in worldwide markets or prosperity may be undermined. Instead, it is the myriad of problems, magnified in

FIGURE 8-19 The Rhine-Meuse estuary toward the west. The Hollandsch Diep (foreground) is the principal outlet of the Rhine-Meuse system. Small, mostly irrigated plots on both sides (KLM Aerocarto).

this small, densely populated country, that plague the industrial societies of Europe. Can the Dutch ameliorate air pollution? Will they prevent the further poisoning of the Rhine that raised such a scare in 1986 when toxic chemicals were spilled into the river following a fire at Schweizerhalle in Switzerland? Will the floods that affected the country in 1994 and 1995, because of the high waters of the Rhine, Maas, and Waal, be controlled? Can noise levels from jet aircraft and traffic be reduced? Can urban and industrial expansion continue to utilize rural land without creating a "Nederlands-stad"— a completely urbanized Netherlands? If the government controls and regulates so many aspects of growth and development, can individual freedom be maintained? Finally, will the new immigrants to the country, asylum seekers, and refugees be absorbed into the mainstream of Dutch life with-

out aggravating social tensions, especially in times of restructuring and recession?

Based on previous attainments, the answers to these questions appear to be positive. The old saying, "God made the World, but the Dutch made Holland" should be revised by adding, "and they will likely make sure that it will continue to function efficiently and harmoniously" (Fig. 8-19).

LUXEMBOURG

Surrounded by France, Belgium, and Germany, the 998 sq miles (2585 sq km) of the Grand Duchy of Luxembourg's landlocked territory comprises two distinct natural regions: the Oesling in the north, a continuation of the Ardennes that accounts for 32 percent of the country, and the Bon Pays in the south, part of the Lorraine scarplands, that comprises 68 percent. Unlike the other "pocket" states of Liechtenstein, Monaco, Andorra, San Marino, and the Vatican, Luxembourg has maintained itself as a genuine state with a strong economic base and political influence far greater than size alone would indicate. Traditionally dependent on the steel industry, the country has become a significant international banking center, and has succeeded in diversifying and enlarging its industrial base. Industry's share of the GDP fell from 37.9 percent in 1981 to 33.7 percent in 1991, whereas during the same period, services increased from 59.5 to 64.9 percent. Luxembourg's importance as a political center for the EU is second only to that of Brussels; the Court of Justice, the Statistical Office, and the European Investment Bank are among the EU agencies located in Luxembourg city. With a per capita income in 1993 of $32,477 ($28,368 PPPs), the country's inhabitants enjoy one of Europe's highest living standards.

A favorable location close to major industrial centers in Belgium, Germany, and France, as well as liberal tax legislation toward holding companies registered in the Grand Duchy, have made Luxembourg a base for international firms, particularly those from the United States. The financial sector included 213 banks in 1992, up from 111 in 1980, as well as the European Investment Bank, which provides development funds for poor regions in the EU and loans to Eastern European countries. Another valuable source of income has been Radio-Tele-Luxembourg, which beams programs to the surrounding countries, including by way of cable and satellite. Self-supporting through the sale of advertising, the station is one of the Grand Duchy's most important companies. Thus, Luxembourg has diversified its formerly steel-based economy.

Population

Luxembourg's population increased from 246,000 recorded by the 1905 census to over 395,000 in 1993. Over 30 percent of the population are foreigners, the highest ratio in the EU. Portuguese account for the largest number followed by Italians. Two cantons in Luxembourg beyond the city of the same name, Esch-sur-Alzette and Dudelange, account for about 30 percent of the population. The country's main commercial and industrial activity takes place in Dudelange. In 1993 the primary sector accounted for only 3 percent of the workforce, secondary 28.2 percent, and service sector 68.2 percent, reflecting the ongoing shift toward services. The country's birth rate rose to 13.1 per 1000 inhabitants from a low of 11 per 1000 in 1980. All told, close to 50,000 persons, *frontaliers*, from France, Belgium, and Germany cross the borders daily to work in Luxembourg.

Transportation and Communication

The country's transport infrastructure is excellent, with an efficient network of highways (including over 60 miles [100 km] of motorways), railroads, and the airport at Luxembourg city. The Moselle has been canalized and barge traffic, though down since 1980, still plays a role in the overall economy, with steel products being exported and fuels imported. Fast EuroCity trains connecting Zürich to Brussels and Amsterdam stop at the capital. Air traffic, both passengers and freight, has grown steadily, and the city is connected to major European centers and to North America via Icelandic Airlines.

Because of the EU's directive to permit freer transmission of television, Luxembourg has enhanced its hold on transfrontier broadcasting. Radio Luxembourg goes back many years, but now the country is seeking investment by outside broadcasters. Companie Luxembourgeoise de Télédiffusion (CLT), the largest with 500 employees, Radio-Tele-Luxembourg (RTL), and Société Européenne de Satellites (SES), the top operator of European satellites, are well positioned to further diversify and strengthen Luxembourg's economy as they involve more media companies in European commercial television and radio.

The Economy

Production of electricity, which was over 2000 million kwh in 1974, slumped to 1019 million in 1992, mainly because thermal-generated electricity comes from power stations associated with the iron and steel works that have cut production by half during this time. Some hydroelectric production is generated by stations on the Our River in the Ardennes; however, the country is almost 100 percent dependent on foreign supply for primary energy sources. In 1992 oil consumption was the most significant source accounting for 51.1 percent of the total, followed by coal, 26.5 percent, and natural gas, 12.3 percent. Iron ore was mined in the Grand Duchy; however, in 1992 all ore for the steel industry was imported.

Evolving from crude seventeenth-century ironworks at Dommeldange north of Luxembourg city, the modern phase of the iron and steel industry developed during the late nineteenth century within the framework of the German *Zollverein*. After 1867, concessions were granted in the southern *minette* regions where the Lorraine iron ore deposits extended into Luxembourg, and intensive exploitation began, especially around Esch-sur-Alzette. In 1884 the first modern blast furnaces and the first Thomas steel converters in Luxembourg were installed at Dudelange, transforming this agricultural region into an industrial landscape of mines, steel works, rolling mills, railroads, and accompanying urban agglomerations. By 1900 iron ore production was over 6 million tons annually, pig-iron production nearly 1 million tons, and raw steel production about 250,000 tons. Before World War I, these figures grew to 7 million tons, 2.5 million tons, and 1 million tons, respectively.

In 1975 the iron and steel industry, then the backbone of Luxembourg's economy, employed 27,000 workers. By 1993 that figure had dropped to only 7390, as the EU-wide rationalization had taken effect. Still, this was the largest total of laborers in any one industry. In addition, because of restructuring, iron and steel production have become highly competitive, with productivity levels comparable to Japan. Output dropped from 4.6 million tons of steel in 1980 to only 3 million tons in 1992 before climbing to 3.3 million tons in 1993. The importance of the industry to the Luxembourg economy declined, falling from over 25 percent of GDP in 1974 to under 8 percent by 1992, with value added to industrial production dropping from 44 percent in 1980 to 29 percent by 1990.

One company ARBED, (Aciéres Réunies de Burbach-Eich-Dudelange), dominates production. It was formed in 1911, when existing steel works in Saarbrücken, Esch-sur-Alzette, and Dudelange were merged. In 1967 another company, Hadir, was added to ARBED, and a major modernization program was initiated. The company also has interests in the Belgian Sidmar works north of Ghent and in the Bremen-based Klöckner Stahl. Surprisingly, ARBED is Europe's third largest steel maker after France's Usinor-Sacilor and British Steel.

After the Second World War, Luxembourg's reliance on the iron and steel industry, based on a single export commodity, tied the country's economy to the fluctuating demand for steel. At the end of the 1940s, the government embarked on a program of industrial diversification. By 1950 Goodyear constructed a tire manufacturing plant that employed over 3500 persons north of the capital at Colmar-Berg. Other companies followed including Du Pont and Monsanto. However, in 1979, Monsanto closed its doors. Fortunately, the gap it left has been filled by other firms, including TDK, the Japanese company specializing in audio and video tape and floppy disks, and Villeroy & Boch, a manufacturer of porcelain dishes for household use. Today the industrial sector is characterized by a mixture of companies that produce a variety of products, all of which are capital intensive and use high-technology techniques. The location of Luxembourg near the Netherlands, Belgium, France, and Germany is perfect for their needs. In addition, the country's modern infrastructure and social and political stability are significant factors for the success of these firms.

Tourists come to this diminutive country because of its reasonable prices, medieval buildings, and variety of landscapes, including the scarplands of the south, the rugged Ardennes in the north, and the Moselle Valley vineyards in the east. The number of overnight stays in 1992 was 2.2 million, with the Belgians and Dutch accounting for the largest number of foreigners. The central region, including the capital, hosted the greatest number of visitors staying in hotels and pensions, while the Ardennes was the main region for campers. Infrastructure for international business and political conferences has been improved in the capital region.

The country's financial sectors have grown steadily since the early 1970s and today, helped by a liberal tax policy and banking secrecy laws, have emerged as strong European competitors. The number of banks, which was only 37 in 1970, totaled 213 in 1992 and employed nearly 17,600 persons. The largest number of banks are German with 63 establishments, followed by Belgian and Luxembourgian, 24; French, 21; and Swiss 17. In addition, private banking, which caters to wealthy clients, is increasing. The number of investment funds registered in the Grand Duchy increased from 75 in 1981 to over 600 by 1992. Moreover, because of favorable legislation, the number of holding companies, which constitute an important source of "invisible" earnings, presently exceeds over 5000.

Germans, who want to escape taxes on savings stash their cash in "offshore" banks, especially in Luxembourg. A large slice of the $170 billion that left Germany from 1990 to 1993 was deposited in Luxembourg. Much of these "tax free" deposits then flowed back into the German capital markets, where the banks invested them in German government securities. Although the Germans are exerting some pressures to harmonize tax on interest income within the EU, money held in Luxembourg's banks can still go to Switzerland or other offshore havens. Thus, Luxembourg's status as a favorable center for depositing money appears to be secure.

Agriculture's contribution to GDP in 1991 was 1.4 percent and accounted for only 3.3 percent of the workforce. The total number of holdings dropped steadily from 5173 in 1980 to only 3542 in 1992. During those years, the average size of holdings increased from 73 to 122 acres (29 to 49 ha).

Climactic conditions in Luxembourg are not overly favorable for agriculture. Precipitation in the north of the country ranges from 35 to 39 in. (900 to 1000 mm), diminishing in the southeast to less than 27 in. (700 mm) in the sheltered Moselle Valley. January mean temperatures range from just below freezing in the west to just above freezing in the Moselle Valley, and July mean temperatures are 61°F to 64°F (16° to 18°C). Over 50 percent of Luxembourg's area is agricultural land, of which 46 percent is arable. About 53 percent of the agricultural land is permanent grassland, and 1 percent is in vineyards. In addition, nearly 32 percent of the country is covered by forest.

Conclusions

A combination of factors has contributed to Luxembourg's economic prosperity. The country is socially and politically stable, and it has been open to Europe. For example, foreigners account for more than half of the working population. Three languages, Letzeburgish, French, and German, are spoken. Furthermore, the decline of the steel industry has been more than compensated for by the growth of a variety of other industrial firms; the rise of the service sector, especially banking and finance; the growth of tourism; and the strengthening of the communications industry. In addition, the Grand Duchy is, after Brussels, the second capital of the EU. In order to maintain and secure its high living standard, the country will continue with past policies. Because Luxembourg depends on exports of goods and services, 98 percent of the GDP to maintain prosperity (the highest figure in the EU), it will continue to further its position as a European service capital. Furthermore, the Grand Duchy will continue to champion greater European integration and continuing worldwide cooperation.

CONCLUSIONS

The countries of Western Europe are vying to compete both within the EU and the "world region." They have been restructuring their industries so that there are more competitive, privatizing state-run companies, and expanding sectors such as banking and finance that were not part of their economic matrix at the end of the Second World War. Blessed with a favorable location, an admirable infrastructure, especially in transportation, and a highly educated and skilled workforce, they are well positioned to function efficiently within the EuroArc, a prosperous region that leads from southeast England to the Po Valley. Likened by the French geographer Brunet to a banana because of its general shape, the Arc has many offshoots, and embraces urban agglomerations and industrial concentrations that include London, Paris, the Randstad, Brussels, the Ruhr, the Rhine-Main conurbation, southwest Germany, the Swiss Mittelland, and the Po Valley. This region is the economic nexus of the EU. It is an area of dense population and diverse urban areas that include the magnificent capitals of London and Paris; great productivity; serious social problems such as unemployment and the integration of asylum seekers, refugees, and immigrants; and formidable environmental problems. The EuroArc will receive a strong economic boost from the Channel Tunnel and the extension of Europe's high-speed rail network. The Arc's southern extension intersects with the Mediterranean Arc, a densely populated, highly developed, narrow corridor, backed by highlands and mountains, that extends from Barcelona across southern France to Genoa (see section on southern France in Chapter 10). Within these Arcs natural synergies are emerging that previously were hindered from developing by artificial political boundaries, which because of the European Union no longer exist to hinder economic evolution.

BIBLIOGRAPHY

Beaujeu-Garnier, J., A. Gamblin, and A. Delobez, 1987. *Images économiques du monde.* Paris: Sedes.

Belgium Information and Documentation Institute. (1985). *Atlas of Belgium.* Brussels.

Burtenshaw, D. (1976). *Saar-Lorraine.* Problem Regions of Europe series, ed. D. I. Scargill. London: Oxford University Press.

Clout, H. D. (1975). *The Franco-Belgian Border Region,* Problem Regions of Europe series, ed. D. I. Scargill. London: Oxford University Press.

_____. (1972). *The Geography of Post-War France.* Oxford: Pergamon Press.

_____. (1973). *The Massif Central.* Problem Regions of Europe series, ed. D. I. Scargill. London: Oxford University Press.

_____ ed. (1987). *Regional Development in Western Europe.* 3rd ed. London: David Fulton.

_____ ed. (1977). *Themes in the Historical Geography of France.* London: Academic Press.

Demangeon, A. (1946–1948). *France économique et humaine.* Géographie Universelle, 2 vols., pt. 2. Paris: Librairie Armand Colin.

Diem, A., ed. (1984). *The Mont Blanc-Pennine Region.* Waterloo: Department of Geography Publication Series, Occasional Paper No. 1. Reprinted 1988.

_____.(1979). *Western Europe: A Geographical Analysis.* New York: John Wiley & Sons, Inc. (Reprinted by the author with additions, 1988).

Dutt, A. K., and F .J. Costa, eds. (1985)., *Public Planning in the Netherlands.* New York: Oxford University Press.

Financial Times Survey. "Belgium." *Financial Times,* June 2, 1994, pp. I–IV; July 12, 1993, pp. 7–9; June 16, 1992, pp. I–IV.

_____. "Business Locations in Europe." *Financial Times,* October 11, 1993, pp. I–VI.

_____. "Dutch Banking and Investment." *Financial Times,* September 10, 1993, pp. 9–12.

_____. "European Finance and Investment: France." *Financial Times,* October 13, 1992, pp. 31–34.

_____. "Flanders." *Financial Times,* May 8, 1990, pp. 27–30.

_____. "France." *Financial Times,* September 27, 1995, 1–6; July 12, 1994, I–VI; June 24, 1993, pp. I–VI; June 22, 1992, pp. I–VIII.

_____. "Luxembourg." *Financial Times,* October 19, 1994, pp. I–IV; October 25, 1989, pp. I–VI.

_____. "Rhône-Alpes." *Financial Times,* February 19, 1993, pp. I–IV.

_____. "Southern France." *Financial Times,* March 25, 1991, pp. 11–15.

_____. "Toulouse and the Midi-Pyrenees." *Financial Times,* May 18, 1994, pp. 23-25.

Information and Documentation Centre for the Geography of the Netherlands. (1986). *Randstad Holland,* 2nd ed. Utrecht/The Hague: Henk Meijer.

"La Camargue en danger." (1992). *Le Point,* June 27– July 3, pp. 44–49.

Lawrence, G.R.P. (1973). *Randstad Holland.* Problem Regions of Europe series, ed. D. I. Scargill. London: Oxford University Press.

Le Monde. (1994). "Bilan économique et social 1993: L'EUROPE EN BERNE."

Martonne, E. de. (1942). *France Physique,* Géographie Universelle, vol. 6, pt. 1. Paris: Librairie Armand Colin.

Meijer, H. (1992). *Bulletin de l'idg 1992, les polders de l'IJsselmeer.* Utrecht: Centre d'Information et de Documentation pour la Géographie des Pays-Bas.

_____.(1987). *Petite géographie des Pays-Bas.* Utrecht: Centre d'Information et de Documentation pour la Géographie des Pays-Bas.

_____. (1986). *Randstad Holland*. Utrecht: Centre d'Information et de Documentation pour la Géographie des Pay-Bas.

_____ ed. (1993). *The South-west Netherlands*. IDG Bulletin. Utrecht: Information and Documentation Centre for the Geography of the Netherlands, 1993.

_____. (1987). *Zuidersee-IJsselmeer*. Utrecht: Centre d'Information et de Documentation pour la Géographie des Pays-Bas.

Minghi, J. V. (1981). "The Franco-Italian Borderland: Sovereinty Change and Contemporary Development in the Alpes Maritimes." *Regio Basiliensis* 2 (3): 232–246.

Ministry of Foreign Affairs, Centre for Geography of the Netherlands. (1985), *Pictoral Atlas of the Netherlands*. Compiled and text by H. Meijer, IDG. 2nd ed. The Hague.

Murphy, A. B. (1988). *The Regional Dynamics of Language Differentiation in Belgium: A Study in Cultural-Political Geography*. Chicago: University of Chicago Geography Research Papers 227.

Pinchemal, Philippe, et al. (1987). *France: A Geographical, Social, and Economic Survey*. Cambridge: Cambridge University Press.

Pounds, N.J.G. (1954). "France and 'Les Limites Naturelles,' from the Seventeenth to Twentieth Centuries." *Annals of the Association of American Geographers* 44: 51–62.

——. (1957). "Historical Geography of the Iron and Steel Industry of France." *Annals of the Association of American Geographers* 47: 3–14.

Raun, L. (1989). "Flood Tide of Environmental Concern Engulfs the Dutch." *Financial Times*, February 16.

Thompson, I. B. (1973). *The Paris Basin*, Problem Regions of Europe series, ed. D. I. Scargill. London: Oxford University Press.

Wever, E., and M. de Smidt (1989). *An Industrial Geography of the Netherlands*. Boston: Routledge.

CHAPTER

9

REGION NORD:
THE EUROPEAN NORTH

On Europe's northern periphery, extending from the shores of the Baltic and North seas into the farther reaches of the North Atlantic and Arctic oceans, lies a region that has come to be known as "Norden." Its name means simply "the North" in Scandinavian, a term introduced to the English-speaking public in the first edition of this text some four decades ago. In its strictest sense, the region may be thought of as being composed of the three Scandinavian countries (Denmark, Norway, and Sweden), together with Finland and Iceland—all countries that have shared many common threads in their historical and cultural evolution. Their most striking similarity is that they are all relatively small countries that have been repeatedly caught up in the intrigues and machinations of the great powers that surround them—Germany on the south, Russia on the east, and the Anglo-Saxon powers (i.e., Britain and more recently the United States) on the west.

Sweden, alone among the Nordic countries, has never been a "client-state" of a larger neighbor. In-deed, during the late Middle Ages, in the absence of a strong Germany or Russia, it briefly played the role of a Great Power itself. Although a Scandinavian interest in the Baltic states had begun as early as the Viking Age and had been revived by the imperial expansionism of Denmark in the thirteenth century, it was during the seventeenth century—when the Baltic Sea was a "Swedish Lake" —that both Estonia and Latvia were drawn most strongly into the Scandinavian sphere of influence. (Interestingly, in both of these countries many people still refer to this period as "the good old Swedish days.") During this same hiatus in Great Power strength, Lithuania launched its own political expansion toward the south and east, but the rise of Germany and Russia soon forced it back into the mold of a small buffer state as well. Small wonder, then, that with the collapse of the Soviet Union the Nordic countries should have moved so quickly to reestablish relationships with the three Baltic states whose geopolitical experience so closely mirrors their own. In doing so, however, the realities of a new Europe have impelled them to broaden their definition of "the North" to include both "Norden" and the Baltic countries—an area for which their preferred term is "Region NORD."

The present challenges facing the European North are more economic than geopolitical. Denmark already broke with its Nordic neighbors in 1972 to join the European Community at the same time as the UK, because it wanted to ensure that its agricultural exports would continue to have free access to its principal markets in both the UK and Germany. Finland, once the Soviet Union dissolved and its trade ties to Russia collapsed, became eager to join the European Union and reorient its economy westward. It became an EU member effective January 1, 1995. Although serious economic difficulties also confront Sweden, many of its citizens remained ambivalent about joining the EU until the end of the Cold War and difficult domestic economic problems led it to reconsider membership. In a relatively close referendum vote in late 1994, the Swedish populace recommended to its political leadership that Sweden join the organization, in which it became a member effective January 1, 1995. Norway, driven by the concerns of its farmers and fishermen, is still openly distrustful of

such a move. In another close referendum vote, and despite the normally pace-setting precedent of Sweden, Norwegians for the second time declined EU membership. Iceland and the Faeroes (Færoes), a self-governing territory of Denmark, have also indicated that they are not interested in joining. Greenland, which as a part of Denmark was given membership, has since chosen to withdraw. How soon the Baltic countries will be ready for membership in the EU remains to be seen, although in late 1994 the EU expressed the intent to include them at some time in the future.

To understand these very different reactions to membership in an expanded European Union, it is important to understand how their differing physical geographies have contributed to the distinctive economic, social, and political personality which each of them has today. Aside from their shared location in the subcontinent's higher latitudes and an historically interwoven cultural evolution, the countries of the European North demonstrate a remarkable variety of environmental settings and resource endowments. Some idea of this diversity may be gained by an examination of Table 9-1 and the following discussion of the region's physical geography.

TABLE 9-1

SELECTED STATISTICS FOR THE EUROPEAN NORTH

Country	Population (in millions)	Area (in km2)	Density (per km2)	Percent of Area Arable	Pasture	Forest
Iceland	0.25	103,000	2	0.1	1.2	0.0
Faeroes	0.05	1399	36	2.0	NA	0.0
Norway	4.2	323,878	13	2.9	0.3	21.7
Sweden	8.6	449,964	19	7.2	1.4	55.2
Finland	5.0	338,145	15	8.0	0.4	66.0
Denmark	5.1	43,084	120	62.0	5.4	11.6
NORDEN	**23.2**	**1,259,470**	**18**	**7.6**	**0.1**	**42.8**
Estonia	1.6	45,125	35	22.0	11.0	31.0
Latvia	2.7	64,589	41	27.0	13.0	39.0
Lithuania	3.8	65,200	58	49.1	22.2	16.3
Region NORD	**31.3**	**1,434,385**	**22**	**10.8**	**2.0**	**41.1**

Sources: *Population Data Sheet*, Population Reference Bureau, and *World Factbook*, CIA, 1993.

LOCATION, SIZE, AND CONFIGURATION

The countries of the European North occupy a position in the Old World that is almost directly comparable to that of Alaska in the New World. The Danish-German border, Norden's southernmost boundary, is situated in the same latitude as the southern tip of the Alaskan Panhandle (55ºN), while the southernmost limits of Lithuania reach a degree farther to the south. The North Cape of Norway, the northernmost point of "continental" Europe, is at the same latitude as Point Barrow (71ºN). Longitudinally, the distance from the eastern extremity of Finland to the western extremity of Iceland is as great as that from the Alaskan Panhandle to the outermost islands of the Aleutian chain. When the Norwegian islands of Spitsbergen (Svalbard) are included, however, the plane of reference must be altered, for the only regions in the New World at a corresponding latitude (74º to 81ºN) are the northernmost islands of the Canadian archipelago and the northern quarter of Greenland.

In size, the European North is only slightly smaller than Alaska, for it embraces nearly 554,000 sq miles (1.43 million sq km) compared to Alaska's 591,000 sq miles (1.53 million sq km). With an area that makes up almost a quarter of that of non-Russian Europe (which includes the westernmost republics of the former Soviet Union, that is, the Baltic states, Belarus, Ukraine, and Moldova), its population of 31.3 million is 60 times greater than that of the United States' northernmost state. On the other hand, the fact that this represents little more than 6 percent of Europe's total inhabitants dramatically illustrates how environmentally challenging and sparsely inhabited this region is.

Unlike Alaska, the European North is not a single, relatively unbroken expanse of land (Fig. 9-1). Instead, it is a region composed largely of peninsulas and islands, each separated from the other by varying widths of open sea. By far Norden's largest continuous landmass is what we may call the Fennoscandian Peninsula. Joined to the subcontinent along a front extending from the Gulf of Finland to the Arctic Ocean's White Sea, this neck of land stretches northward from the Gulf of Bothnia (the northernmost portion of the Baltic Sea) to the White Sea, and then mushrooms out into the Scandinavian Peninsula (which extends 1200 miles

[2000 km] to the southwest), and the Kola Peninsula (which extends some 300 miles [480 km] to the east). That this appendage is divided politically between Norway, Sweden, Finland, and Russia in no way detracts from either its physical continuity or the essentially peninsular character of the area as a whole. Norden's only other land contact with the subcontinent is on the Jutland Peninsula where Denmark borders Germany. Owing to its location, this peninsula has been an infinitely more important link between the northern countries and the remainder of Europe than the broader but far less accessible Fennoscandian Peninsula.

Apart from these two peninsulas, Norden lacks contiguity, for its remaining constituents are islands. Among these are Iceland and the Faeroes in the North Atlantic, Spitsbergen and Jan Mayen in the Arctic, the Danish archipelago and the Swedish islands of Gotland and Öland in the Baltic, and the Åland archipelago at the entrance to the Gulf of Bothnia. As a consequence of this peninsular and insular configuration, Norden stands somewhat apart from the rest of Europe. Its relative isolation has played an important role in the historical and cultural development of the region and in large part explains the sense of community among the Nordic nations today.

Unfortunately, lying as they do on the European mainland, the three Baltic states have seldom enjoyed the benefits of such geographic detachment. Located on the edge of the North European Plain, with no natural boundaries of any consequence, they have a history that is virtually the antithesis of that of the Nordic countries. Too poor to be strong, they have also been too vulnerable to remain free for any appreciable length of time.

THE ENVIRONMENTAL CHALLENGES

The environment of the European North has always posed a number of challenges to human occupance of the region. As the last area of Europe to be free of the glaciers, the North was the last major region of the subcontinent to feel the tread of human footsteps. In no other part of Europe were people for so long dependent on hunting, gathering, and fishing rather than agriculture to support

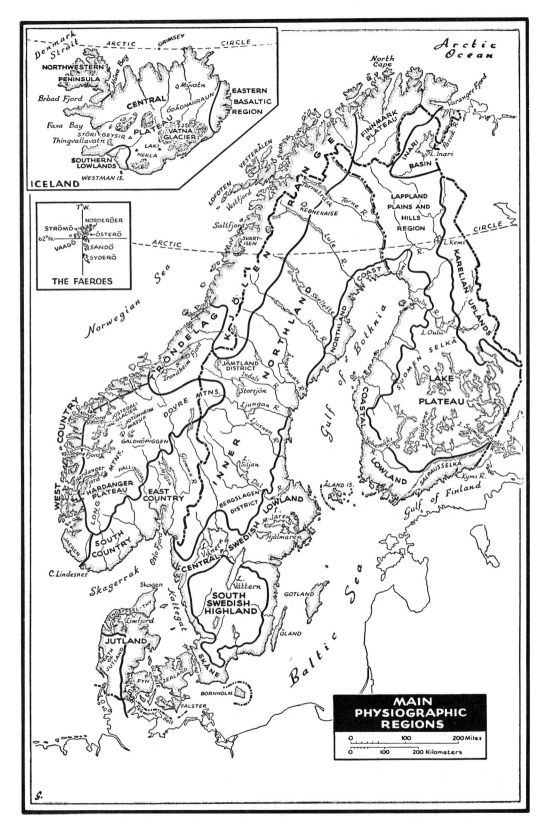

FIGURE 9-1 Main physiographic regions.

themselves. In no other part of Europe did the Neolithic Agricultural Revolution arrive so late or advance so falteringly. And apart from the eastern reaches of the subcontinent, the European North was the last major region to feel the impact of commerce and the urban revolution. That such developments were so tardy in the European North is due, of course, to the region's out-of-the-way location. Although the innovations of the Industrial Revolution did reach the region relatively early, their implementation was largely precluded by the area's meager and uneven resource base.

A direct consequence of the European North's high latitude is its great seasonal variation in insolation. Psychologically, it can be argued that human responses to these extremes can range from midsummer exuberance at the time of the midnight sun to a depression born of darkness at midwinter. Indeed, all life in the North, plant and animal, experiences a strong seasonal regimen attuned to the wide fluctuations in light and warmth. Thanks to a pronounced maritime exposure, however, the European North is spared the types of continental temperature extremes that beset Alaska (Fig. 9-2). In fact, no other region in the world so near the Pole enjoys such radical temperature anomalies. Nevertheless, no part of the European North is immune from frost, and in the higher mountains of Scandinavia and in the interior of Iceland there are extensive areas where the air temperature never rises above freezing. As a result, Norway boasts the largest ice fields on the European mainland, and no less than one-eighth of Iceland is covered by glaciers. Altogether, more than two-fifths of the land surface of the European North has a climate too cold for trees to grow, and throughout most of the area below the tree line the agricultural growing season is less than five months. Within the European North, all of the subcontinent's staple food crops and domesticated animals reach the poleward limits of their distribution.

Low annual temperatures and evaporation rates combine with an almost continuous influx of moist air off the Atlantic to give the more exposed parts of western Norway and southern Iceland a quite humid climate. Even over the more continental areas, in Sweden, Finland, and the Baltic states,

lack of moisture is seldom a problem. On the contrary, drainage of excess water from the fields is a common agricultural practice in these countries. The need for drainage results from low levels of evaporation and transpiration of plants (i.e., evapotranspiration) and from drainage problems related to glaciation.

Because all parts of the European North were subjected to Pleistocene glaciation, most soils are derived from glacial till, glacial deposits of a highly variable nature left on the land as glacial ice sheets recede. Where the underlying bedrock happened to be limestone or chalk, as in Denmark and parts of the Baltic states, the till is quite productive. But elsewhere, where the parent material is crystalline rock, as in most of Norway, Sweden, and Finland, or volcanic as in Iceland, the development and productivity of soil tend to be rather poor. In these latter areas, by far the better developed and most productive are soils derived from clays deposited in postglacial seas that overlapped the lower coastal fringes.

Topography poses the most serious challenge in Norway, where, together with high latitude, it greatly complicates communications and has rendered nearly three-fourths of the country unproductive. It was not until 1909 that Norway's two largest cities were linked by a year-round overland connection, the Bergen Railway, and this was possible only with the burying of 15 percent of its mileage in tunnels and snowsheds. In Iceland, too, rugged terrain has rendered no less than seven-eighths of the country unproductive, and it wasn't until the 1970s that a circum-island road could be completed across the vast areas of sand and gravel deposited from streams ushering from glaciers, called outwash plains, on the south coast. Iceland's intense volcanic and seismic activity also constitutes environmental challenges that on occasion have had serious repercussions. For example, the devastating eruption of Laki in 1783–1784 destroyed nearly three-fourths of the island's livestock, leading to the starvation of one-fifth of its human inhabitants. Most of the recent volcanic activity has been centered just off Iceland's southern coast. There a new volcano, Surtsey, was born in 1963, and much of the town and harbor of Vestmannaeyjar was destroyed by an eruption in 1973.

FIGURE 9-2 Farming along the Ulvik Fjord, a branch of the Hardanger Fjord, east of Bergen, Norway. Although lying far in the north and confined by soaring walls of rock, farmlands along Norway's fjords benefit from the influences of the sea, which moderate temperatures and make agriculture feasible. (Tony Craddock/Tony Stone Images)

Human Responses to the Environment

To argue that people have triumphed over the environment of the European North is scarcely accurate; in much of the region, they have at best reached only a tenuous accommodation with it. As long as their livelihood was derived principally from the soil, whenever the climate tended to deteriorate—growing either cooler or wetter—they had little option but to stand their ground and suffer famine or to retreat. Fortunately, at the very dawn of the Agricultural Revolution, during the Bronze Age (2500 B.C.), so congenial were the prevailing conditions that cultivation spread along the Norwegian coast as far as 68°N, as well

as to the northern extremities of the Gulf of Bothnia. Later, during the colder and wetter Celtic Iron Age (500 B.C.—A.D. 1), virtually all cultivation ceased north of 62° latitude. As the climate improved during the Roman Iron Age (A.D. 1–500), the farmer once again began the readvance of settlement, which culminated in the widespread settlement witnessed in the Viking period (A.D. 800–1100). Beginning in the thirteenth century, however, another turn for the worse saw the total abandonment of the Norse settlements in Greenland and their irregular contraction elsewhere in Norden throughout the Middle Ages. Indeed, famine—whether caused by a wetter than average summer or an earlier than usual frost—remained a frequent occurrence in Norden until the late nineteenth century.

As long as agriculture was the mainstay of the region's economy, the population that could be supported within the European North remained necessarily small. As late as 1750, there were scarcely 4–5 million people in the entire region, or about the same as the present population of Norway or Denmark. Even so, the density per square mile of food-producing land averaged 100 people for the region as a whole. In such marginal areas as Norway and Iceland, the figure was two to three times higher.

The late eighteenth century saw economic expansion in fishing, shipping, mining, and commerce. It also witnessed the introduction of the potato—a staple food crop that revolutionized the carrying capacity of the North's anything but bountiful soils. By 1800 the region's population had grown to nearly 6 million, and by the middle of the nineteenth century it had increased by 50 percent to about 9 million. However, the North's demographic expansion was already beginning to exceed the region's capacity to absorb this increase, and overseas migration, which began as a slow trickle in the 1820s, swelled to a torrent in the 1880s. This wave of emigration began first in Norway and Denmark and then moved eastward to embrace Sweden and, later, Finland. Although greater freedom of movement was permitted in Czarist Russia after the passport reform of 1863, for the Baltic states overseas migration was relatively unimportant until after the political upheaval and reforms in Russia in 1905, and especially after they became independent following World War I. Nevertheless, by the beginning of the twentieth century, the population of the European North had grown to nearly 15 million inhabitants, and by midcentury it totaled something over 20 million. Although the rate of demographic growth had crested by the First World War, without the safety valve of emigration to North America, one can scarcely imagine what the economic, social, and political repercussions would have been within Norden, for in the century between 1850 and 1950 no fewer than 3 million people had been siphoned off—nearly 1.4 million from Sweden, about 860,000 from Norway, some 375,000 from Denmark, about 365,000 from Finland, and nearly 20,000 from Iceland.

During the same period, the Baltic states suffered grievous casualties in both world wars, a massive flight to the West in 1944, and large-scale Soviet deportations of Baltic citizens and their replacement by Russians following the war. By the early 1990s, when the Baltic states had once again regained their independence, the population of the European North totalled just over 31 million—an increase of nearly a third over the last half-century.

Thus, it can be seen that in Norden the transformation from a subsistence agricultural economy to a modern urban industrial society consumed more than two centuries and was accompanied by a population explosion whose impact would have been very different had it been confined to the region rather than projected to the New World where large Nordic communities became established in the United States' upper midwest region. In the Baltic states, where a medieval form of serfdom wasn't abolished until a hundred years ago and where foreign intervention and exploitation continued until very recently, the process of economic modernization still has a way to go.

Today, although Norden has the lowest overall population density of any major region in Europe—a direct reflection of its marginal sub-Arctic environment—it ranks among the wealthiest regions in the world when measured in terms of gross national product (GNP) per capita (Table 9-2). Although the three Baltic states have income levels that range from only one-sixth to one-fourth those of the Nordic countries, they, too, rank among the "wealthiest" of the former Soviet republics. However, raising their living standards to West European levels, much less to Nordic ones, will no doubt be a long and arduous task.

That such a uniformly high level of well-being has been achieved in one of Europe's most unpromising physical settings is an eloquent testimony to the energy, perseverance, and pragmatic good sense of the Nordic peoples. Although the three Scandinavian countries retain monarchical forms of government, in all five Nordic states democracy is an economic and a social reality as well as a political fact of life. Humanitarianism, social concern, cooperation, and planning are the key elements in these welfare states. Guided by the belief that by right every citizen should have access to low-cost health services, higher education, decent housing, productive jobs, and a clean environment, the peoples of Norden have built societies that support what are arguably the highest socioeconomic living standards in the world (e.g., high incomes, long life expectancies, political democracy, and stability; see Tables 9-2 and 9-3). In the subsequent pages, we examine how they

TABLE 9-2

SELECTED STATISTICS FOR THE EUROPEAN NORTH, 1990

| Country | Per Capita GNP ($) | Employment in Percent | | |
		Agriculture	Industry	Services
Denmark	20,510	5.6	19.8	44.1
Finland	23,196	8.6	24.3	28.5
Iceland	21,962	13.2	28.3	25.5
Norway	21,850	6.2	18.0	33.8
Sweden	25,863	3.2	22.6	37.0
Estonia	5,209	20	42	38
Latvia	4,500	16	41	43
Lithuania	3,759	18	42	40

Sources: Yearbook of Nordic Statistics, 1990; CIA, World Fact Book , 1993.

TABLE 9-3

DEMOGRAPHIC DATA FOR THE NORTH EUROPEAN COUNTRIES

| Country | Rates per 1000 | | | Longevity | |
	Births	Deaths	Infant Mortality	Male	Female
Denmark	12.0	11.4	7.1	73	79
Finland	12.6	9.9	5.4	72	80
Iceland	17.0	6.7	4.0	76	81
Norway	13.7	10.5	6.4	74	81
Sweden	13.8	11.0	5.8	75	81
Estonia	14.0	12.1	19.5	65	75
Latvia	14.0	12.7	22.0	64	75
Lithuania	14.9	10.9	16.9	66	76

Source: CIA, World Fact Book, 1993.

accomplished this and some of the problems encountered in the process.

REGIONS OF THE EUROPEAN NORTH

How the people of Northern Europe make their living depends largely on the environmental setting in which they find themselves. Using the geological structure of the European North as a basis, we can distinguish six major subdivisions, each embracing one or more physiographic regions: (1) the Scandinavian mountains, (2) the Fennoscandian Shield, (3) Sweden's Baltic Islands, (4) Denmark and southern Sweden (Skåne), (5) the Baltic mainland, and (6) the Faeroes and Iceland (see Fig. 9-1).

The Scandinavian Mountains

Norway has fallen heir to most of Scandinavia's mountain backbone. Fully 72 percent of its land area is of swamp and unproductive highland rock wastes (see Fig. 9-3). In its various portions, the mountain ridge is known by several local names. The southern part of the ridge is called the Long Mountains (Langfjellene) and separates the country into the East Country (Østlandet) on the east-facing slopes and the West Country (Vestlandet) on the western side. In the Jotunheim Massif, where the highest peaks are located (Galdhø-

piggen, 8019 ft [2468 m]), the ridge turns in a more east-west direction and bears the name of Dovre Mountains (Dovrefiell), separating the East Country in the south from Trøndelag in the north. Here the main ridge is broken by the Trøndelag-Jämtland Gap, but it is resumed once again to the north as the Kjølen Range. Associated with this range is the mountain bulwark that makes up the Lofoten Islands and the coast of Norway's Finnmark region in the far north. In its northern reaches, the main ridge of the Kjølen runs through Swedish territory, reaching its highest point in Kebnekaise, 6965 ft (2123 m). Finland's highest mountain, Haltiatunturi, 4344 ft (1324 m), is also found in this section.

The Scandinavian mountains have a marked weather-divide effect, for they separate the distinctly maritime west coast from the more continental eastern interior. Thanks to the moderating influences of the North Atlantic Drift and the prevailing westerlies, winter temperatures average above freezing along the coast as far north as the Lofotens. Although the maximum precipitation in these coastal districts comes in winter, most of it falls as rain. Over the mountains and to the east, where winter temperatures are considerably lower, moisture at that season contributes to a deep and stable snow cover. Indeed, until recently virtually all transmontane roads linking eastern and western Norway have been blocked by snow from six to seven months, but now several of the main roads are kept open throughout the year. Every-

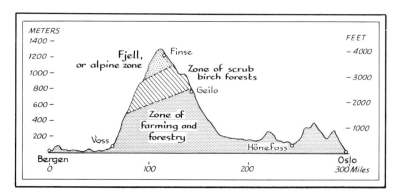

FIGURE 9-3 Profile of the Scandinavian mountains along the Oslo-Bergen Railway. More than 30 miles (48 km) of this railway, which links Norway's two largest cities, are above timberline, and another 30 miles are above the limit of permanent agricultural settlement. Owing primarily to the differences in climate, the limits of the respective zones are lower on the west than they are on the east. (From Rutebok for Norge)

where on the western slopes the average annual precipitation exceeds 40 in. (100 cm), and in the higher parts of the West Country it totals between two and three times that amount. In the area between Sogne Fjord and Nord Fjord, as much as 230 in. (580 cm) of moisture fall each year, helping to nourish the Jostedal Glacier, the largest ice sheet on the European mainland. East of the mountains the average annual precipitation everywhere drops to under 40 in. (100 cm), and in some sheltered valleys and in the far north to less than 20 in. (50 cm). Summers are warmer and sunnier than they are to the west, although this is also the season of maximum precipitation.

In the southern Scandinavian mountains, the coniferous tree line is reached at an elevation of less than 3000 ft (915 m); in Trøndelag the limit falls to 2000 ft (610 m) and in the far north to 1200 ft (365 m). Although scrub birches struggle upward an average of 800 ft (245 m) higher, the greater part of the mountains lie well within the zone of alpine meadows. It is these open highland wastes that best typify the fjeld (*fjell*) of Scandinavia, barren plateaus above the tree line.

Although their height is not impressive when compared to such ranges as the Alps, the Scandinavian mountains have always constituted a distinct barrier to movement. Except near their northern and southern extremities, they are crossed by only one pass at less than 2000 ft (610 m) elevation. This is the strategically located Trøndelag-Jämtland Gap, which breaks across the range near the middle of the Scandinavian Peninsula. With two exceptions (at either end of the Dovre Mountains), all the passes within Norway itself are higher than 3300 ft (1000 m), and hence above the tree line. The Bergen Railway makes its east-west crossing at 4271 ft (1302 m) (Figs. 9-3 and 9-4).

Three similar, but nevertheless distinct, subdivisions make up the western slope of the mountains—from south to north, the Norwegian West Country, Trøndelag, and the Kjølen Range. The most distinctive feature of the Norwegian West Country is its narrow steep-sided valleys, which in

FIGURE 9-4 The Bergen Railway crosses the mountains above timberline near Finse. (Norwegian State Railways)

many instances have been scoured by ice far below the level of the sea, leaving deep fjords. The greatest of these are Sogne Fjord, some 125 miles (200 km) long and near its outer end over 4000 ft (1220 m) deep, and Hardanger Fjord to the south, 105 miles (170 km) long and at its deepest over 2900 ft (885 m). Tributary streams join the main valley far up the fjord sides, and as a consequence waterfalls gushing from these hanging valleys are numerous. Habitation is limited to the more sheltered of the islands lining the coast, to the low strips of land rimming much of the shore, and to small patches of lowland at fjord heads (Fig. 9-2). The Jaeren (Jæren) district south of Stavanger affords a noteworthy exception, for here the coastal lowland is covered with rolling glacial moraine deposits. Jaeren's early spring and longer growing season help make it one of Norway's best agricultural areas. Although the more sheltered parts of the West Country were once covered by mixed forest, this region today possesses only a small fraction of Norway's productive woodland.

North of the Dovre Mountains, centered on Trondheim Fjord, is the region of Trøndelag. Thanks to its easily eroded bedrock, this is Norway's second most extensive lowland area and agricultural district. Although its clayey soils have been cultivated for centuries, the region is still largely clothed in a forest of spruce and pine.

Northward from Trøndelag, Norway is squeezed into the lower western slopes of the Kjølen Range. The varying geological character of the range gives it very broken relief, ranging from the sharp alpine peaks of the Lofotens to the relatively broad interior valleys extending from Trondheim Fjord to Salt Fjord. In the more sheltered valleys, good stands of conifers are found, whereas along the coasts a cover of scrub birch is characteristic.

The Arctic Circle, which bisects the Kjølen Range, is scarcely reflected in the relatively mild climate, although its presence is keenly felt in the marked seasonal variation in solar insolation. As in Lappland, where Norway, Sweden, and Finland meet in the north, this region at midsummer knows no darkness at all. In the far northern latitude of the North Cape, the sun remains above the horizon from mid-May until the end of July, and still further north in Spitsbergen continuous sunlight holds from mid-April until the end of August. In contrast, at the winter solstice, the regions north of the Arctic Circle receive no sunlight whatsoever—at the North Cape, darkness holds from mid-November to the end of January, and in Spitsbergen the sun does not rise from the end of October until mid-February.

The Fennoscandian Shield

East of the Scandinavian mountains lies the vast Fennoscandian Shield. It may be likened somewhat to a broad, shallow saucer, for it rises not only along its western edge, but also in the east where it culminates in the Karelian Uplands of eastern Finland. Its southernmost outliers, in the South Swedish Highland, northeastern Skåne, and the northern part of the Danish island of Bornholm, do not show this same east-west warping, but they do reveal the extensive faulting that has left its print on much of the rest of the region.

The eastern slope of the Scandinavian mountains (the highest and westernmost part of the shield) is shared by both Norway and Sweden, with by far the larger part in Sweden. The long, gradual southeasterly slope drains into Northern Europe's largest rivers, among them the Glomma in Norway and the Dal in Sweden, each well over 300 miles (500 km) long. Many of the valleys are occupied by deep finger lakes, the eastern slope's counterpart of the western fjords; typical are Norway's largest lake, Mjøsa (140 sq mile/363 sq km), and Siljan, Storsjön, and Torneträsk in Sweden (Fig. 9-4).

The valleys of the Norwegian East Country and of the Inner Northland of Sweden (Norrland) are relatively broad and open. Those of the East Country converge in the region of Oslo Fjord, whereas in the South Country, the valleys are narrower and extend more nearly north-south. There is also a convergence of several large valleys in the Swedish Northland, where the mouths of the Ångerman, Indals, and Ljungan rivers are located within a few miles of one another. In both areas, the hilly terrain of the interior comes down to the edge of the sea without a bordering coastal plain.

Most of the Norwegian East Country and Sweden's Inner Northland lie well above the highest postglacial limit of the sea; hence, their soils are almost entirely derived from coarse glacial (morainic) materials. In the lower valleys of the East Country, however, easily eroded bedrock have contributed not only to the region's essentially lowland character, but also to its distinction as the most productive farming area of Norway. Apart from those in the Jämtland district, no similar deposits are found in Inner Northland. This fact coupled with higher latitude and a more severe climate makes this vast region the least productive agricultural area of Sweden (Fig. 9-5).

The irregular terrain of Sweden's Inner Northland merges imperceptibly into that of Norway's Finnmark Plateau and that of the Lappland Plains and Hills of northern Finland. Moraine deposits interspersed with resistant rock outcrops (monadnocks) and swampy plains characterize both

regions. A major difference is in their drainage. In Finnmark, which slopes northward, the edge of the plateau meets the ocean in a series of bold and barren headlands—the North Cape, for example, rising nearly 1000 ft (300 m) out of the water. Most of Finnish Lappland drains by way of the Kemi River system into the Gulf of Bothnia. Finland's only area of Arctic drainage, the Inari Basin, centers on the lake of that name, which is also the country's largest body of water. Its most important outlet is the Pasvik River, which for most of its length serves as the Norwegian-Russian frontier.

South of the Oulu River, the character of the Finnish countryside changes as the pattern of land and water becomes increasingly complex. This part of the Shield constitutes the Lake Plateau, Finland's most distinctive landscape. Delimited on

FIGURE 9-5 An isolated farmstead in Inner Northland. Although agriculture in this vast region is handicapped by poor soils and a short growing season, Inner Northland ranks as Sweden's chief source of timber, minerals, and hydroelectric power. (Swedish Tourist Office)

the south by the Salpausselkä (two great moraines that run roughly parallel to the Gulf of Finland) and on the north by the Suomen moraine (a secondary watershed), the Lake Plateau rises into the Karelian Uplands in the east and is even more poorly defined in the west. Its distinctive character, however, is its great profusion of lakes, interspersed with irregular, low-relief glacial features (eskers and drumlins), and low hills composed of resistant rock. The Plateau's elevation averages between 300 and 500 ft (90 and 150 m) (Fig. 9-6).

The Karelian Uplands form the watershed between the Gulf of Bothnia and the White Sea. Compared to the Scandinavian mountains, they are merely a rise in the landscape, averaging 500 to 700 ft (150 to 215 m) in elevation. In the southern half of the region, individual points top 1200 ft

(365 m), whereas in the north a number of summits range from 1400 to 2100 ft (425 to 640 m). The Finnish-Russian border runs through this region but does not coincide with the summit line at all points.

Portions of the Shield that were sufficiently downwarped to be inundated by the postglacial antecedents of the Baltic Sea differ in several important respects from the remainder of the Shield. They became, first of all, areas of deposition from earlier seas (marine clays), which markedly distinguishes their soils from those above the highest marine limit. They are inherently more productive, and hence have long been preferred for agricultural settlement. Besides contributing to a difference in soil, however, the marine deposits have largely tended to obliterate local variations in relief, pro-

FIGURE 9-6 Tavastehus fortress, built by the Swedes during the conquest of Finland in the thirteenth century, has become the nucleus of the modern city of Hämeenlinna, the birthplace of the country's foremost composer, Jean Sibelius (1865–1957). (V. H. Malmström)

ducing in the process the most extensive unbroken plains within the Shield region. For example, the plains that form the coastal lowland of western and southern Finland average from 20 to 80 miles (30 to 130 km) in width, and their continuation, the Northland coast of Sweden, from 20 to 30 miles (30 to 50 km). Although the Northland Coast is pinched out by the hills of Inner Northland south of Umeå, it is resumed near Sundsvall and broadens into the Central Swedish Lowland. Though not a coastal plain in the strict sense of the term, the Central Swedish Lowland once formed a postglacial strait between the Baltic and the North Sea. It is characterized by relatively extensive flat plains, broken at intervals by low hills associated with faulting and large lakes. In the eastern half of the Lowland, the hills are aligned principally east-west, and off the coast they continue as a chain of stepping-stone rocks and islets through the Stockholm skerry guard (derived from the Swedish "skärgård," a maze of low, rocky islands) to the Åland archipelago and into the southern Finnish mainland. In Sweden's Western Lowland, fault lines trend more north-south. Vänern, the largest of Sweden's lakes, owes its existence partly to faulting and partly to inundation of the low plain. Vättern to the east occupies an ancient fault valley and is Sweden's second largest lake.

South of the Central Swedish Lowland is an upland region, which like most of the higher portions of the Shield, was not covered by the postglacial lakes. This is the South Swedish Highland, whose moraine-strewn erosion-resistant hills culminate at an elevation of 1237 ft (377 m) about 20 miles (30 km) south of Lake Vättern. Traversed by numerous fault lines running roughly north-south, the region has an uneven surface and in the south many small lakes and swamps. On either coast the region slopes down to a narrow coastal lowland. The southernmost outcrops of the Shield are to be found in hills that trend northwest-southeast through the northeastern parts of the province of Skåne, and in the granite cliffs that line the northern coast of the Danish island of Bornholm.

With the exception of the South Swedish Highland, most of the Shield region lies in the lee of the Scandinavian mountains. As a consequence, the greater part of eastern Norway, Sweden, and Fin-

land receives only between 20 and 30 in. (50 and 75 cm) of precipitation a year, with the maximum concentration in the summer. Along the more exposed western edge of the South Swedish Highland, the annual precipitation is nearly twice as great. Cloudiness is less pronounced than west of the mountains, and summers are warmer. Winters are correspondingly more severe than along the Norwegian coast, with temperatures falling off progressively toward the northeast. The snow cover over most of the Shield region is deep and stable—from two to three months in the south to more than seven months in parts of Lappland. Ice normally interrupts navigation in the Baltic for about two months of the year, in the southern reaches of the Gulf of Bothnia for three months, at the inner end of the Gulf of Finland for five months, and in northern Bothnian waters for as long as seven months.

Apart from the areas of good soils where extensive clearings have been made, the Shield region is primarily a land of forest. In southern Sweden and along the southern coasts of Norway and Finland, one finds a mixed forest including both deciduous and coniferous species, but by far their greater part falls into the zone of northern coniferous forests, where spruce and pine are dominant. In Norway the land in forest is almost a quarter of total land area, whereas in Sweden it is more than half and in Finland nearly two-thirds. In no other region of Europe are the per capita ratios of productive woodland as high as in these countries of the north.

Sweden's Baltic Islands

Sweden's two Baltic islands, Gotland and Öland, afford a unique variety of landscape within the Northern European area. Both of them are composed of limestones that dip slightly to the southsoutheast; on southern Gotland, sandstones are found. Owing to their generally level surface, low rainfall, and porous bedrock, there are no true valleys anywhere on the islands. In the southern half of Öland, an area known as the Alvaret, the limestone is clothed by a shortgrass vegetation reminiscent of the steppe. Elsewhere on the islands there are patches of mixed forest in which both drought-tolerant pine and ivy are common.

Denmark and Skåne

Thanks to their common geological background, the landscapes of Sweden's southern province, Skåne, and most of Denmark are similar. Structurally, the lowland of southwestern Skåne, the Danish islands, and eastern parts of the Jutland Peninsula form a gently to moderately rolling plain interrupted only by shallow arms of the sea. This till plain, composed as it is of lime (calcium oxide) rich moraine deposits and clays resting on a bedrock of limestone and chalk, is among the most productive farmland in all of Northern Europe (Fig. 9-7). Only in a few scattered localities is the bedrock exposed at the surface, as, for example, on the eastern end of the island of Møn, where the

chalk cliffs rise more than 400 ft (120 m) out of the Baltic. Running through central and southern Jutland is a chain of hills that marks the terminal moraine of the last glaciation. It is in these hills that Denmark's highest point is located—Yding Skovhøj, a mere 567 ft (173 m). To the west of the moraine, glacial streams built up extensive outwash plains of sand and gravel, an area that today constitutes Denmark's least productive region—the so-called Heath of Jutland. Sweeping sand beaches and shifting dunes characterize Jutland's low western coast.

Owing to their location on the extreme southern margin of Northern Europe, Denmark and Skåne enjoy the mildest climate of any part of the region. Temperatures average near or above freezing dur-

FIGURE 9-7 The rolling, lime-rich morainic soils of eastern Denmark constitute the most productive agricultural area in all of Norden. (Danish Agricultural Council)

ing most winters and up to the mid-60s°F (18°C) during the summer. Precipitation, the bulk of which falls as rain, totals between 20 and 30 in. (50 and 75 cm) a year. The native vegetation supported by this mild, moist climate was originally a dense deciduous forest in which beech trees were particularly common. However, as the land was taken under cultivation, the forests were gradually felled, until today only about 10 percent of Denmark and Skåne remain in woods. Owing to long exploitation, even these remaining groves have a parklike character, and they can in no way be compared with the forests found in most of Northern Europe. Humans have also altered the originally barren Heath of Jutland, where there have been numerous plantations of spruce and pine, and considerable cultivation.

The Baltic Mainland

Like the islands of Gotland and Öland, the northern portions of the Baltic mainland are chiefly underlain by limestones, sandstones, and shales. Only along the north and west coasts of Estonia, however, is the bedrock exposed at the surface; here it appears as an escarpment (low cliff) some 50 to 65 ft (15 to 20 m) in height, known as a glint.

This escarpment separates the ancient rock core of the Fennoscandian Shield from the younger geologic formations to the south and east. Beginning in the White Sea and continuing through Lakes Onega, Ladoga, and the Gulf of Finland, it dives beneath the Baltic to reappear along the western shore of Öland. Everywhere else the countryside of the Baltic states is mantled in thick deposits of glacial and glacially related fluvial (glacio-fluvial) debris. As in Denmark, the highest elevation (1040 ft [317 m], in southeastern Estonia) is found in the terminal moraine pushed up by the last advance of the continental icesheet. This rolling country is a tapestry of fields, forests, and small glacially derived (kettle) lakes. Somewhat lower elevations (the highest being 768 ft [234 m]) are found in the recessional moraines that stretch across the western portions of Latvia and Lithuania. Between these hillier upland areas are more poorly drained pockets of lowland that were once occupied by postglacial seas or lakes (like the Jel-

gava lowland in Latvia), by valleys once filled by large streams from melting glaciers (glacial spillways), such as that between Panevezhis and Kaunas in central Lithuania, or by the valleys of present watercourses. Although broadleaf deciduous forests predominate over most of the region, along the low sandy coasts of Latvia and Lithuania, wind-sheared pines take over.

The Faeroes and Iceland

Having once been part of the same tabular island (Greater Iceland), the Faeroes and large sections of Iceland demonstrate a striking similarity of landscape. Gently dipping layers of basalt (rock from lava) form bold headlands of over 2000 ft (600 m) along the northwestern edges of the Faeroes and in eastern and northwestern Iceland. In the Faeroes the inclination is toward the southeast, so nearly all habitations are on this lower and more accessible side of the islands. In Iceland the layers dip chiefly toward the interior of the island, indicating a zone of subsidence. In the basalt areas mountain glaciation has produced numerous U-shaped valleys, many partially submerged as fjords, and other boldly etched features (e.g., cirques, arêtes, and horn peaks; Fig. 9-8).

In the subsidence zone, which runs diagonally across Iceland from southwest to northeast, volcanism and subsurface forces (diastrophism) continue as active agents in landscape formation. As a result, the features are jumbled and chaotic. Most of interior Iceland is a plateau averaging about 2000 ft (600 m) in elevation, although numerous isolated mountains rise above the general level to heights of 5000 ft (1525 m) and more. Some of these are blocks of rock thrust upward by faulting (horsts), others are volcanic cones, and still others are old volcanic necks (exposed volcano cores) that remain where the volcanoes themselves have been eroded away. Dramatic, abrupt variations in relief (such as fault scarps, like the one at Thingvellir) and extensive lava flows, of which the largest is the Odádhahraun in the northeast, further break up the terrain. In the higher parts of the island, particularly on the highlands that cross the country east-west, lie several plateau glaciers, of which the largest is Vatna Glacier—2200 sq miles (5700 sq

FIGURE 9-8 A small settlement in the Faeroes. Most habitation in this rugged island group is concentrated near the lower, southeastern ends of glacial troughs that dissect the basalt bedrock. The mild, maritime climate is too cool for tree growth, other than in the lee of the houses. (Danish Information Service)

km). Extensive lowlands are found only in the south and southwest, although even there large areas are uninhabitable owing to lava flows and the continuing deposition of outwash from the great glaciers.

Iceland is one of the most intensively volcanic regions in the world. Perhaps the best known of its volcanoes is Hekla, which within historic times has had more than a dozen eruptions, the most recent in 1947–1948. Occasionally, volcanic activity occurs beneath one of the glaciers, resulting in the spectacular and destructive phenomenon known as a glacier burst, the most recent of which

occurred during the fall of 1996. Hot springs, found in virtually every part of the island, total several thousand in all. Many boil over periodically, sending great columns of superheated water and steam into the air, the most famous being the Stóri Geysir in Haukadalur in western Iceland, from which our word *geyser* derives.

Owing to the surrounding water, both the Faeroes and Iceland have decidedly maritime climates. In the Faeroes, winter temperatures rarely dip to the freezing point, and summer temperatures seldom get much above 50°F (10°C). About 60 in. (150 cm) of precipitation are received each year, the maximum in winter, and almost all in the form of rain. There are long periods of overcast skies, and winds of gale force are not infrequent. As might be expected, such a climate has not been conducive to tree growth; hence, most of the Faeroes are covered with grass.

The very size of Iceland contributes several aspects of continentality to its climate. The south and west coasts, bathed by a branch of the North Atlantic Drift, the Irminger Current, have a milder and wetter climate than the northern and eastern coasts, which come under the influence of the cold East Greenland Current. Winter temperatures in the southwest seldom average below freezing, but in the north and east they normally drop around the low 20s°F (-5°C). Snow is thus more common and longer lasting in the latter regions. In summer, temperatures around the low 50s°F (10°C) are common to all the island's coastal districts. Precipitation averages between 30 and 60 in. (75 and 150 cm) a year in the south and west, but over most of the northern half of the island usually amounts to less than 20 in. (50 cm).

The dominant vegetation in Iceland today is grass, although in the lowlands, at the coming of the first settlers, there were rather extensive wooded areas, chiefly of scrub birch. Small birch groves are now found only in isolated or sheltered valleys where they are protected by law. The greater part of the island is covered by a sparse mountain vegetation—mosses and lichens together with grasses, heather, and dwarf birches. In recent years, conifers have been successfully introduced from other subarctic regions, demonstrating that the climate is not hostile to their growth. Forestation and tree panting are being seriously pursued; the country's largest experimental forest is at Hallormstadhur in the northeast.

POPULATION GROWTH AND URBANIZATION

In the last decade and a half, population growth in Norden has slowed markedly, and in the core states of Denmark, Sweden, and Norway it has all but reached a stagnant or negative condition. Indeed, apart from the Faeroes and Iceland, all the Nordic countries are projected to have smaller populations in the first decades of the new millennium than they do at present. Moreover, the structure of the population is changing, with a rapid increase in aging taking place among the Scandinavians themselves and a progressive increase in ethnic diversity occurring as more and more immigrant minority groups are absorbed into the fabric of Nordic society. In view of these circumstances, whether or not projected labor shortages in the 1990s will trigger demands for more foreign workers remains to be seen. One unforeseen circumstance in Nordic population projections has been the arrival in Norden of many refugees from the war-torn former Yugoslavia.

Modest as the population growth of the Nordic countries has been, it has also been geographically uneven. Although the inner-city areas of Copenhagen, Stockholm, Oslo, and Helsinki have tended to lose population, their adjacent suburbs have all experienced substantial increases. By far the most densely populated region in Norden is that flanking the opposing shores of the Öresund, the strait that separates the Danish island of Sjaelland from the Swedish province of Skåne. In this one region live about one-seventh of all the citizens of Norden, or nearly a quarter of the combined populations of Denmark and Sweden. This focal region is the true heart and core of Norden—a strategic crossroads in the maritime linkages between the North and Baltic seas but even more important as the bridgehead for all overland movement between Scandinavia and the rest of the European mainland. In Denmark the largest population growth has taken place to the north and west of Copenhagen, while on the Swedish side there has been corresponding growth in the western coastal corridor between Malmö and Göteborg. The completion of the Öresund bridge and tunnel project between Copenhagen and Malmö will unquestionably spur the growth of this region as Scandinavia's principal core area in the future. Elsewhere in Sweden, the largest increases in population have been around Stockholm, both on the axes leading northward to Uppsala and southwestward into the heart of the country.

In Norway the Oslo Fjord region is becoming steadily more urbanized, especially in the areas both to the northeast and southwest of the capital. In the counties along the south and southwest coasts the population has grown relatively rapidly, reflecting primarily the development of the off-shore oil industry and related inmigration. However, in the interior districts of the East Country, in West Country north of Bergen, and in Trøndelag, a small absolute growth has not forestalled a relative decline in the region's share of national population. In north Norway, a population peak was recorded in about 1980, and since then the region's population has declined both in absolute numbers and in terms of its share of the country's total population.

In Finland the largest increases in population have also been recorded in the south and south-western coastal districts, particularly in the triangle bounded by Helsinki, Tampere, and Turku. In both the Faeroes and in Iceland, urbanization has also continued apace, so that by the 1990s no fewer than one of every three Faeroese lived in or near Tórshavn, the islands' capital, and well over half of all Icelanders lived in the metropolitan area of Reykjavík. In each of the Nordic countries, therefore, the dominance of the historical core areas of the respective states has been further strengthened at the expense of many of the more remote or out-lying parts of their national territories.

Urbanization in Norden has produced two cities of over 1 million inhabitants, Stockholm and Copenhagen, both of whose metropolitan areas contained about 1.5 million people in the early 1990s. Three other metropolitan areas have well past half a million people—Helsinki, the Finnish capital; Göteborg, Sweden's west coast port; and Oslo, the Norwegian capital. Next in size are Malmö in southern Sweden, Århus in Danish Jutland, and Bergen, Norway's west-coast port.

Among smaller sized cities, in the range between 100,000 and 200,000 population, Finland has its interior industrial center of Tampere and historic capital of Turku; two relatively new suburban satellites of Helsinki, Espoo and Vantaa; and Oulu, the regional capital of the north. In the same size-category in Norway are an ancient cathedral center, Trondheim, and, soon to enter this range, the oil-boom town, Stavanger. Sweden has eight small-sized cities stretching across the middle of the country from Uppsala to Hälsingborg. They include Norrköping, Västerås, Örebro, Linköping, Jönköping, and Borås, all of which are industrial hubs that have grown from medieval roots. Metro-

politan Reykjavík with 152,000 inhabitants (central city 90,000) is Iceland's only urban center of any size, and in the Faeroes, the population node in the Tórshavn area numbers 15,000.

In the Baltic states, major demographic shifts have taken place as a result of the population losses that these countries sustained during World War II as well as due to massive flight to the West, large-scale Soviet deportations, changes in their administrative boundaries, and the influx of other Soviet citizens into the area following the war. In Estonia alone, perhaps as many as 200,000 were victims of the war, and deportations may have involved as many as 80,000 others. During the same period immigration probably accounted for up to 180,000 non-Estonians moving into the country, chiefly into centers of Soviet industrial development, notably at Narva in the northeast. Thus, not only did the proportion of Estonians in the total population decline sharply but also the urbanization of the country increased rapidly from hardly a third in 1940 to well over half by the end of the Stalinist era and to 72 percent in 1990. It is much the same story in Latvia, where 77 percent of the people were Latvians at the outbreak of World War II and only one-third of the population lived in cities. Today scarcely 52 percent of the populace is ethnic Latvian, but no fewer than 71 percent of them live in urban areas. In Latvia, and especially Estonia, great political difficulties have been encountered in determining who deserves citizenship, owing in particular to large numbers of immigrant Russians, toward whom there is often considerable antipathy.

In Lithuania, the proportion of ethnic Lithuanians today is virtually the same as it was in the pre-war era (82%), although Jews, who then numbered over 7 percent of the total population, were almost all killed by the Nazis. The German minority, which comprised more than 4 percent of the pre-war population, nearly all fled to the West at the war's end. In their place have come various Soviet nationalities and Poles. Moreover, the cities of Lithuania now house fully 69 percent of the country's population, as opposed to only about one-third in 1940.

The Baltic states boast nine cities with over 100,000 inhabitants each. The three capital cities are the largest, with Riga topping the list at

917,000, and Vilnius (597,000) and Tallinn (498,000) somewhat smaller. Kaunas, which served as independent Lithuania's capital between 1920 and 1940, ranks fourth (434,000). There are a further half-dozen transportation and industrial centers, each of which numbers between 50,000 and 100,000 inhabitants.

ECONOMIC GEOGRAPHY

Agriculture

In all the countries of the European North, the marginal nature of the environment has favored the production of livestock products more than field crops. Indeed, in the most rugged and more maritime areas of Norden—Iceland, the Faeroes, and Norway—emphasis has been placed on sheep and goats rather than dairy cattle, because they are more tolerant of the rough pastures that dominate these areas. In fact, Norway has nearly two-thirds of Norden's sheep and virtually all of its goat population, with the majority of the region's remaining sheep being found on the Atlantic islands. In all three areas the chief field crops are hay, potatoes, and fodder roots; only in the lower, warmer, and drier areas of Norway is any attempt made to grow some cereals. Even here the principal emphasis is on more tolerant grains such as oats and barley.

Both Sweden and Finland are more congenial to agriculture, because they are predominantly lowland countries; elevation does not further exacerbate a climate already made marginal by the region's high-latitude location. Moreover, they have much more extensive areas below the highest marine limit, and consequently they have a higher proportion of more productive soils. They also experience more continental climates, so they are both warmer and drier than Norden's maritime fringes during the growing season. As a result, in both Sweden and Finland the relative balance between livestock production and crop production shifts toward crop production, but even in these countries livestock activities account for some 70 percent of all commercial farm output. With just over 30 percent of Norden's crop area, Sweden produces like proportions of many commodities,

including wheat, rye, potatoes, sugar beets, and milk. Finland, with about 28 percent of Norden's cropland, only exceeds its expected share of agricultural output in oats, but comes close in other hardy crops like rye and potatoes.

Because of a favorable combination of topography, climate, and soils, Denmark, despite its small size, ranks as Norden's preeminent agricultural area. With less than 3.5 percent of Norden's total land area, Denmark has some 28 percent of the region's land under cultivation and accounts for nearly 50 percent of its poultry; more than 50 percent of its wheat, sugar beets, and barley; and about two-thirds of its rye and pork production. Indeed, Danish farmers produce between a fifth and a quarter of their country's total annual exports.

Within Denmark, cereal cultivation tends to be concentrated on the lime-rich morainic soils of the islands and eastern Jutland, and sugar beets are especially important on the southwestern islands of Lolland and Falster. Potatoes, oats, and fodder roots find their heaviest concentrations in the poorer soils and damper areas of western and northern Jutland. In Jutland as a whole, the emphasis on livestock products tends to be greater than in the islands to the east where field crops are more favored both by soil and climate. Of Danish agricultural output, 90 percent of the value is derived from animal products, with meat the most important.

Not too surprisingly, the proportion of the Baltic states which can be cultivated compares more favorably with that of Denmark than it does with the remainder of Norden, and for much the same reason. Within the Soviet economic orbit, the Baltic states played much the same role that Denmark does in Western Europe—that of a purveyor of dairy products, meat (especially bacon, ham, and pork), poultry, and eggs to foreign urban markets, in this instance to St. Petersburg and Moscow. Whereas two-thirds of farm income is derived from livestock products in Estonia, this proportion decreases somewhat as one moves southward into Latvia and Lithuania, where a longer growing season and better soils tend to favor such crops as cereals, potatoes, sugar beets, and flax.

In Sweden the regional contrasts in agriculture are much more pronounced, because the spectrum of latitude, climate, soils, and topography is much greater than it is in Denmark and the Baltic states. The Skåne Lowland, which is similar to the adjacent Danish islands in most of its physical attributes, is far and away Sweden's most prosperous agricultural region. With less than 3 percent of the country's land area, it has more than one-sixth of its area under cultivation and the highest yields of cereals and sugar beets. The Central Swedish Lowland, despite its more northerly latitude, also is a major agricultural region, thanks both to its soils and terrain; with scarcely 15 percent of the country's total land area, it accounts for nearly half of Sweden's cultivated area. Together, Skåne and the Central Lowland grow about two-thirds of Sweden's grain, the bulk of which goes to feed livestock. The higher, cooler, rockier South Swedish Highland has a proportionate share of cultivated area, but much more of its land is dedicated to pasture and forest than to field crops. Norrland, which comprises some 70 percent of Sweden's entire area, is and always has been the country's agricultural frontier, for latitude, topography, climate, and soils all conspire against the farmer in this region. Even after centuries of colonization, it scarcely has more land under the plow than Skåne.

In Finland, the optimal agricultural lands are those located along the south and west coasts, precisely where the postglacial seas provided the most extensive lowlands of marine clays and where the Swedish immigrants moved in during the Middle Ages. These same areas have the mildest climate and the longest growing season in the country, and stand in sharp contrast to the morainic soils and more continental climates of the eastern and northern interior. A transect from southwest to northeast across the country would reveal a decline from over 40 percent under cultivation in the Turku area to less than 5 percent in the northeastern borderlands. Finland's dwindling Swedish-speaking population, now constituting scarcely 6 percent of the total, still occupies many of the best farmlands in Finland.

Norway has less than 3 percent of its area under cultivation, and most of this is found in the lower valleys of the East Country and adjacent to the shores of Oslo Fjord. Here too, latitude, topography, climate, and soils come together in the optimal blend that the country possesses. The farther one moves from this agricultural core, the more marginal the environment becomes, resulting in shifts of emphasis from field crops to pasture and from cattle to sheep and goats. What the Trøndelag lowland offers in the way of topography and soils is partially offset by latitude and climate, but nonetheless it ranks second only to the East Country as a producer of agricultural products. The district of Jaeren, south of Stavanger, capitalizes on its location for the mildest climate and longest growing season in Norway, and as a result it specializes in early vegetables, as well as dairying and egg production. No other region contributes a greater proportion of the country's output of dairy products, poultry, and pork. Hence, no other region enjoys so high a level of agricultural income.

In the Faeroes the physical geography of the land means that the small proportion of their area which is devoted to agriculture is found at lower elevations on the southeastern sides of the islands. The islands are self-sufficient in dairy products and mutton, but most vegetables and fruits must be imported. The local production of beef and eggs is discouraged by cheap imports of these commodities from Denmark. In Iceland, the most extensive lowlands fortunately coincide with the mildest climate the island has to offer; thus, the south and westerly coastal areas are the primary sources of most agricultural produce in the country. The principal emphasis is on sheep raising, and the only local crops of importance are hay, potatoes, and turnips. Geothermally heated greenhouses supply some vegetables and cut flowers to the Reykjavík market.

Beginning at the end of the Second World War, but accelerating during especially the last decade, major changes in the organizational structure of Nordic agriculture have taken place. In all of the countries except Iceland, there has been a marked reduction in the number of active farmers, as well as in the total area in agricultural use. Iceland has experienced a slight increase in both. This rationalization has been accomplished by a consolidation of farm holdings into more viable economic units and by rapid mechanization. Because the respective governments have encouraged the phasing out of farming in more marginal areas and the concentration of production in the more favorably endowed and situated areas, overall output has not only remained high but in many sectors has substantially improved. Indeed, overproduction, principally of dairy products, has become a problem in virtually all the countries.

In the Baltic states perhaps the major challenge facing agriculture today is the privatization of landholdings. Whereas Estonia had 140,000 private farms on the eve of Soviet occupation, these were quickly consolidated by the communists into 300 giant state farms. Since regaining its independence, Estonia has established some 10,000 private holdings, but problems with financial credit, mismanagement by "novice" farmers, and stiff foreign competition within a relatively open economy have caused production to fall sharply. Latvia, too, has created more than 50,000 new private farms, many of them too small to be economically viable, and agricultural output has suffered here as well. In Lithuania, disappointment with the land privatization scheme was so strong that the new liberation government was turned out of office by the electorate in 1992, who gave their vote of confidence instead to the former communists. Unfortunately, a severe drought in that year only made the problems of agriculture worse throughout the entire region. In all the Baltic countries, choosing appropriate levels of agricultural subsidies is a potent political issue.

Forestry

The productive forests of Norden form part of the great boreal forest, or taiga, that stretches across the Eurasian landmass from the Atlantic to the Pacific. Almost half of Norden's total forest area is in Sweden; Finland has about three-eighths and Norway one-eighth. Because of the great north-south extent of these countries as well as their variations in elevation, the character and quality of the forest differs markedly from region to region.

In the Skåne Lowland of southern Sweden, only 13 percent of the area is in forest—a figure slightly above that of Denmark, with which it is most comparable in terms of climate, soils, and vegetation. (Denmark has only 1 percent of Norden's productive forest area.) Skåne has the highest annual regrowth rate in Sweden—averaging upward of 100 cu ft (3 cu m) per acre; but the forest itself is

composed chiefly of such hardwood varieties as beech and oak, which are of limited commercial importance. In the South Swedish Highland, where the forest is more mixed, the proportion of wooded land rises to over 60 percent of the total area. The mixed forest continues through the Central Lowland into the lower valleys and southern coastal region of eastern Norway as well as into the southern coastal districts of Finland. Although all of these areas represent some of the more attractive districts for agricultural settlement in each of the respective countries, in most places the proportion of land in forest averages more than 40 to 50 percent of the total.

The taiga proper, the northlands' vast coniferous forest, begins in the interior valleys of Norway, embraces most of the Norrland region of Sweden, and includes virtually all of Finland apart from its southern and northernmost extremities. Annual regrowth varies from over 50 cu ft (1.5 cu m) per acre on the southern fringes of the zone to less than half that rate near its northern and high-elevation margins. Pine and spruce are dominant everywhere, with birch constituting the most common hardwood species. In Norway more than four-fifths of the volume of the forest and even more of its annual regrowth is concentrated in the East Country, with the region of Trøndelag accounting for most of the remainder. Within Sweden, the region of Norrland accounts for over two-thirds of the annual timber cut, by far the greater volume coming from the more productive forests of the southern half of the region. In Finland no less than seven-tenths of the volume and a greater proportion of the annual regrowth of the forest are concentrated in the southern half of the country. At elevations averaging above 3000 ft (915 m) in southern Norway and something over 1500 ft (460 m) in most of Lappland, the upper limit of productive forest is reached, beyond which clusters of mountain birch grade into the alpine zone of tundra vegetation.

Ownership patterns of the forest differ markedly in the three countries. For example, in Norway over three-fourths of all the productive woodland belong to individual farmers, a small amount to governments, and very little to companies. In Finland about two-thirds is owned by farmers, nearly one-quarter by governments, and smaller amounts by companies. In Sweden only about one-half of forest is farmer owned, one-quarter by companies (principally the more productive areas of south central Norrland), and the smallest share by governments.

The actual number of people totally dependent on forestry as a livelihood is small in Norden. Nevertheless, lumbering has traditionally provided an important source of seasonal income and employment for farmers in all three countries. Norden's forests are principally important as sources of raw materials for the woodworking industries and thus make major contributions to the exports of the region. In total output, Sweden produces three-fifths of Norden's pulpwood and over half of its saw timber; Finland ranks second, producing about one-third of each. All told, Norden's forests produce over 4 billion cu ft (113 million cu m) of wood each year, or about the same as the woodlands of Canada.

In the Baltic states, where the native forest consists of mixed coniferous and broadleaf species of trees, forestry plays an intermediate role in the economy between that of the Nordic north and Denmark on the south. Wood and paper goods are produced in all three countries, but their relative importance declines from about 14 percent of the value of the nation's output in Estonia to lower levels in Latvia (7%) and Lithuania (5%).

Fishing

Each year the countries of Norden account for a total catch of well over 5 million tons of fish, with Norway, Iceland, and Denmark each accounting for about 30 percent of the landings. Throughout the region, the effects of overfishing and pollution may be seen not only in the steady decline in employment but also in the changing composition of the catch. In the last decade alone, the number of fishermen has dropped by about 20 percent, whereas the kinds of species caught have increasingly been of the lower-value industrial varieties. In Norway, for example, the blue whiting, mackerel, and pout are all caught in greater volume than the once more traditional herring and cod. In Iceland, almost half of the annual catch is made up of

capelin, and in Denmark over 40 percent of the tonnage landed consists of sand-eels.

Of the roughly 50,000 persons employed in Nordic fisheries, over half are Norwegians and one-seventh are Icelanders. In Norway, fishing remains essentially a small-scale family operation. Hence, vessels are both numerous and small, and most fishing is done relatively close to home. In Iceland, on the other hand, the emphasis is on larger trawlers that spend extended periods at sea. As a result, the average catch per Norwegian fisherman is less than 60 tons of fish a year, compared to his Icelandic counterpart who lands some 200 tons annually.

Spatially, Norway's fishermen are concentrated along the Atlantic and Arctic coasts, with almost half of the total residing in north Norway and most of the remaining half living in the West Country. Although the age-old Lofoten cod fisheries today attract fewer than one-tenth the participants than they formerly did, cod remains the most valuable species caught in northern waters. Because younger men are being enticed away from fishing by better paid, less onerous jobs on land, the median age of the average Norwegian fisherman has been steadily rising. However, one of the more positive trends in the industry in recent years has been the development of fish farms in the fjords of the West Country, with a consequent increase in the export of high-value species such as salmon and rainbow trout.

Denmark's fishermen derive the bulk of their catch from the North Sea; the ports where most of the fish are landed therefore lie along the west coast of Jutland, notably Esbjerg. Three-quarters of the entire Danish catch goes to industrial uses such as the production of fishmeal and oil, although the remaining one-quarter, consisting principally of cod, flatfish, lobster, and shrimp, accounts for no less than four-fifths of the total value of the catch.

In Iceland, where one-eighth of the workforce earns its livelihood from fishing and three-fourths of the country's exports are derived from it, the dangers of overfishing were realized early. In 1952 the country extended its territorial waters from 3 to 4 nautical miles, in 1958 from 4 to 12, in 1972 from 12 to 50, and in 1975 from 50 to 200 nautical miles. These unilateral efforts to widen and protect its exclusive fisheries zone were met with foreign opposition, especially from the United Kingdom. Moreover, they have not prevented the depletion of the marine resources on which Iceland is so critically dependent. For example, the annual herring catch, which used to provide the very raison d'etre for such north-coast towns as Siglufjördhur and Húsavik, has declined so catastrophically that it now generates less than 2 percent of the country's income from fishing. Geographically, the industry's center of gravity has increasingly shifted to the southwestern coast where the principal ports of landing are Reykjavík and Vestmannaeyjar.

Sweden's access to the North Sea is provided primarily by the county of Bohuslän, north of Göteborg. Well over half of the entire Swedish catch, measured both by volume and value, is landed at ports in this region—cod, herring, and industrial fish being most important.

In the Faeroes, fishing and the production of fish products have contributed more than one-third of the islands' gross product and provided some 95 percent of the islands' exports up to the 1970s. Since that time, however, because many nations have extended their fisheries zones to 200 nautical miles, Faeroese fishermen have increasingly been forced to stay in their home waters. Despite government attempts to maintain production by setting quotas, the nearby fishing areas have been seriously depleted. An industry that once employed about one-fourth of the islands' population is now in grave recession and plagued by bankruptcy. Heavy subsidization from Denmark—totaling some $130 million annually—has resulted in one of the heaviest per capita external debts in the world, amounting to nearly $30,000. The Danish government has threatened to cut off its aid unless drastic measures are taken to balance the islands' budget. Once viewed as a model for such regions as the Shetlands and Orkneys, the Faeroes are now suffering the same exodus of young people as has long characterized the Scottish archipelagoes.

Lacking access to the open ocean, Finland and the Baltic states all have relatively modest fishing industries. In Estonia, which has the longest coastline and the best harbors of the Baltic states, fishing contributes something over 5 percent to the gross domestic product, but in Latvia, Lithuania, and Finland it totals less than 1 percent.

Mining and Quarrying

In the early 1990s mineral industries employed about 35,000 people in Norden, nearly 60 percent of them in Norway. Sweden had about 24 percent of the region's mineral workers, Finland just under 13 percent, and Denmark about 4 percent. When measured by value of production, however, oil and gas wells in the North Sea now account for over 90 percent of Norden's mineral output, with Denmark and especially Norway steadily increasing both the amount they produce and the revenues they receive.

Until the oil and gas boom, the extractive mineral industries in Denmark were largely limited to the quarrying of road-building materials. In Iceland the same was true, but in 1969 the extraction of diatomite (used for making filters) began at Myvatn (lake) and exports since then have averaged about 24,000 tons annually, contributing about 1 percent of the country's exports by value.

In large part, of course, these differences in the relative importance of mineral industries within Norden (Fig. 9-9) can be traced to the diverse geologic structures of the individual countries. Iceland and Denmark are geologically homogeneous—Iceland being composed almost entirely of volcanic materials, and Denmark being underlain almost entirely by sedimentary formations in which limestones and chalks are the most important. In contrast, the other three countries have complex structures dominated by ancient, diverse rock types (including igneous and metamorphic).

Sedimentary formations in Denmark, Skåne, and the Central Lowland and Baltic islands of Sweden, as well as in a few restricted areas of Norway and Finland, account for the localized concentration of cement industries in these places. Because of the total absence of limestone in Iceland, the cement plant at Akranes uses seashells dredged from the floor of Faxa Flói as its raw material. Among the other minerals derived from sedimentary structures are petroleum, uranium, and coal.

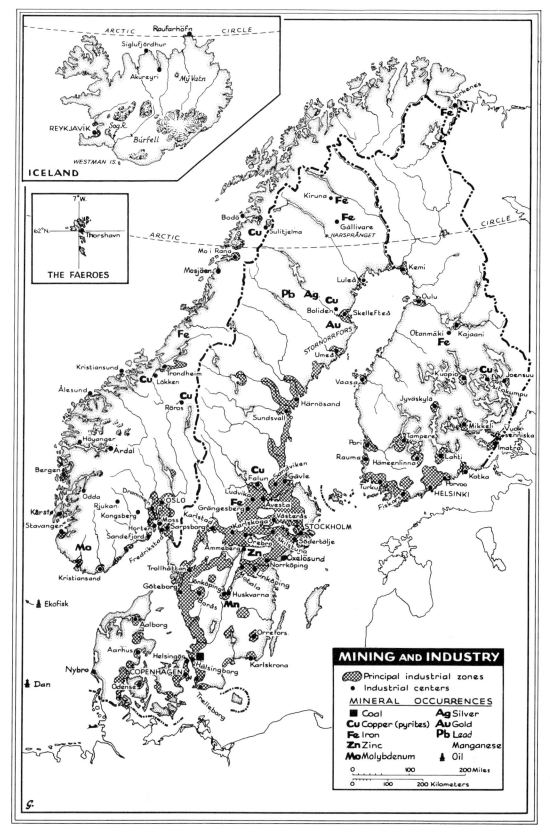

FIGURE 9-9 Mining and industry.

The most significant deposits of these minerals are found in the Norwegian Arctic archipelago of Svalbard, or Spitsbergen, where about half a million tons are mined annually by Norwegian mines and about the same amount by the Russians. Until the early 1970s, the chief regional sources of petroleum and uranium were oil shale deposits in the Central Swedish Lowland. However, discoveries of vast petroleum and natural gas reserves offshore in the North and Norwegian seas have shifted the exploration and exploitation of energy minerals to the adjacent coastal areas of western Norway and Denmark.

Norway's North Sea oilfields lie on the very outer edge of its territorial waters, separated from the Norwegian mainland by a deep submarine trench. Initially, therefore, all oil was piped to the English coast (Teesside), and gas was piped to Emden in Germany, thus going into export without ever touching Norway itself. However, as new fields were discovered farther to the north, these options became less realistic, even though oil from the Heimdal wells is piped ashore near St. Fergus in Scotland, as is the gas from the Odin and Frigg fields. With the development of the huge Statfjord gas deposits northwest of Bergen, the technological challenge of "bridging" the trench with pipelines became a virtual necessity, and now large-diameter pipes converge from both the northern and southern fields on a major processing and distributing facility constructed at Karstø north of Stavanger. Similarly, oil from the Oseberg and Vesle Frikk fields is now piped ashore at Sture, north of Bergen. In coming years it is anticipated that both oil and gas production will shift farther north in Norway, inasmuch as the known reserves south of the 62nd parallel total only 5 billion tons of oil equivalent, whereas those already proven north of that line total 400 billion tons of oil equivalent. By the mid-1990s, Norway was producing well over 100 million tons of oil equivalent annually and about a trillion cu ft (28 billion cu m) of gas. In Denmark, both oil and gas are brought ashore by pipeline near the west-coast port of Esbjerg, and although its output is a fraction of Norway's (e.g., about 7% of Norwegian oil output) it is quite important within the domestic market.

In the ancient crystalline rocks underlying most of Finland and the Scandinavian Peninsula,

a variety of both metallic and nonmetallic minerals are being exploited. For example, on the northern half of the island of Bornholm, the only part of Denmark where rocks of the Fennoscandian Shield outcrop at the surface, granite is quarried for building stone and kaolin is dug to make porcelain. Large granite quarries are also found at accessible locations along the southern and western coasts of Sweden, Norway, and Finland, but in these countries the production of metallic minerals is far more important. In Sweden high-grade iron ores are found both in the Bergslagen district at the southern edge of Norrland and in the Lappland district in the far north. However, competition from low-cost producers such as Australia and Brazil has made it increasingly difficult for Sweden to continue to mine iron ore profitably. As a result, in Lappland production has declined steadily for the last 20 years, and in the Bergslagen the last two mines were closed in 1990. More modest, both in quality and in quantity, are the iron ores found in the far north of Norway and in north central Finland, although each of them contributes significantly to their respective domestic steel industries. Another major mineral district is found along the Skellefte River in northern Sweden, where polymetallic ores have been exploited for lead, zinc, copper, gold, silver, and arsenic. Although they are being rapidly depleted, the Aitik copper deposits may have a viable future. Sulfur is extracted from many of these mineral ores as a byproduct to be used in the pulp and paper industries. Finland's largest mining operation is located in the eastern interior at Outokumpu, whereas Norway obtains copper ores at a variety of locations and produces some titanium, molybdenum, and columbium from mines near the south coast.

Apart from construction materials such as sand, gravel, and clay, the Baltic states are deficient in mineral resources. The only quarrying operations of any significance are the extraction of oil-shale and of phosphorite in northeastern Estonia. Although oil-shale has been used to produce oil, some 70 percent of it is burned to generate electricity, in the past chiefly for export to nearby areas in Russia. Today it is an important domestic energy source. The phosphorite goes primarily into agricultural fertilizers. Both of these industries have been responsible for high levels of hazardous pollution within the surrounding region.

Energy Balance

As a region, Norden produces over 60 percent of the energy it consumes, although wide variations obtain from country to country. By 1980 Norway had become a net exporter of energy, thanks to the growing output of oil and gas from its North Sea reserves and its vast hydroelectric potential. By 1995 it had become Europe's leading energy exporter and the world's second leading oil exporter. Even though Denmark's production of North Sea oil and gas is far more modest, by 1990 it was able to supply some 70 percent of its energy needs from these sources. Iceland, by drawing both on its waterpower and geothermal resources, can cover about two-thirds of its energy needs domestically. Sweden ranks fourth in energy self-sufficiency, producing about 45 percent of the energy it consumes from hydroelectric and nuclear sources. Finland covers a like proportion of its energy needs from a combination of hydroelectric and nuclear installations, wood, sawdust, peat, and several Finnish-owned oil platforms in the North Sea.

More than 60 percent of all the electricity generated in Norden comes from waterpower, with Norway alone contributing over half of the total and Sweden more than one-third. In both Norway and Iceland, electricity is almost solely derived from hydro sources, whereas in Denmark virtually all electricity is generated by burning fuels. Finland and Sweden have a mix of sources, with Finland obtaining about 80 percent of its electricity from nuclear and gas-fired power plants, and Sweden about 50 percent. Plans for a massive expansion of nuclear power generation in Sweden were stalled after the mishap at Three Mile Island in 1979, and in 1980 a national referendum called for the closing of the four existing plants by 2010. The Chernobyl accident in April 1986 further accelerated plans for nuclear shutdowns in Sweden and caused Finland to shelve its own plans to construct a new 1000-mW reactor.

No region in the world has a higher per capita consumption of electricity than Norden. Even energy-poor Denmark's consumption lies above that of the European average, while Finland's is twice as great, Sweden and Iceland consume three times as much, and Norway, with the highest per capita consumption in the world, averages nearly five times that of Europe as a whole. These high levels of consumption, in part, reflect high income levels, relatively inexpensive hydroelectric power, and related energy-intensive manufacturing, notably the production of fertilizer and aluminum in Norway.

Thanks to the configuration of the Scandinavian mountain system, most of Norway's hydroelectric potential is advantageously located in the south, that is, in the East and West Countries. In contrast, over 80 percent of all of Sweden's hydroelectric potential is in Norrland (e.g., from large installations on the Ume and Lule rivers), requiring Sweden to build some of the longest high-tension transmission systems in the world to convey the electricity to its populated areas of the south. In Finland, too, the major sources of hydroelectric power are peripheral to the country's centers of population and industry. It has an installation in the south on the Russian border, but the biggest power stations are in the north along the Oulu and Kemi rivers. Iceland's largest hydroelectric station is at Búrfell in the Southern Lowlands. Augmenting the electricity supply for central and southern Sweden and the coastal districts of southern and western Finland are a number of large thermoelectric-generating stations that depend on imported coal and oil for their fuel. It is in these same areas that all of the region's nuclear power plants are located.

As early as 1912, the Swedes and the Danes linked their electric grids with a cable beneath the Öresund. Since that time, the inter-Nordic exchange of power has continued apace. At the present time there are no fewer than 18 interconnections between the Norden countries, varying from 60,000- to 400,000-volt capacity each, and at least two further links are planned in the future. Norwegian planners are arguing for a submarine transmission line to the United Kingdom which would obviate the need to construct more pollution-causing, coal-fired plants in the UK. Iceland is also considering a plan to export geothermally produced energy by submarine cable to Britain.

Reflecting their historic dependence on imported crude oil, the refineries of the Nordic countries also have been built at coastal sites. Norway's largest refineries are on Oslo Fjord near Tönsberg and near Sola in Jaeren on the west coast, which is also advantageously situated for processing some of the oil from Norway's own North Sea fields. Another major refinery and storage installation has been constructed north of Bergen, in anticipation of the increased offshore oil activity in that region in coming years. In Denmark, all the major refineries have been built at deep-water ports in the eastern part of the country. Sweden's largest refineries are near Göteborg and south of Stockholm on the east coast. Finland's refineries have been built in the southwest (near Naantali) and just to the east of Helsinki. Thanks to its common frontier with Russia, Finland also imports natural gas from its eastern neighbor. In 1987 Sweden also began importing 21 billion cu ft (600 million cu m) of natural gas each year from Denmark as part of a 20-year plan to reduce its dependence on nuclear energy.

By all odds, the most dramatic economic undertaking in Norden during the last two decades has been the discovery and development of the offshore oil and gas resources in the North and Norwegian seas. Even so, these would appear to be only the tip of the iceberg, for similar oil- and gas-bearing formations apparently continue well into the Arctic Ocean and Barents Sea. Nevertheless, compared to the relative ease of developing the Ekofisk field in the North Sea, where water depths were only about 240 ft (74 m), the exploitation of the more northerly fields, such as Troll about 70 miles (113 km) northwest of Bergen, will necessitate working at depths greater than 1000 ft (300 m). In 1986, in anticipation of bringing the Troll gasfield online, Norway signed a 14 trillion cu ft (400 billion cu m) contract with buyers from the European Union, and deliveries were started in 1993. This agreement, which is to continue for more than 20 years, will assure Norway's status as a major gas supplier to Europe in the decades to come. But great as the economic rewards may be, so too, will be the technological and environmental challenges in exploiting these resources along the stormiest edge of the European continental shelf.

Norway, long the "poor cousin" among the three Scandinavian states, suddenly has become the wealthiest. The oil and gas sector already dwarfs all other elements in the Norwegian economy, contributing one-seventh of the country's gross national product, absorbing about one-fifth of its capital investment, and contributing over half of the country's merchandise exports by value. Of the merchandise exports, the majority accrues to the Norwegian government in the form of taxes and royalties, and inasmuch as a minimum of 50 percent ownership of all producing fields is reserved to the national oil company, Statoil, Norway is currently awash in oil- and gas-generated revenues. On the other hand, this windfall has not been an unmixed blessing, for it has created a situation in which wages and prices have skyrocketed, personal debt has more than doubled, and the more traditional sectors of the Norwegian economy, including agriculture, fishing, and manufacturing, have all become less productive and less competitive. Government expenditures for capital improvements and social programs, long restrained by limited funding, now burgeon as if there were no end to the money available. In the last decade, more than four-fifths of all new jobs created have been in the public sector. In short, the oil boom has encouraged the Norwegians to live far beyond their means, although the sharp fall in oil prices in 1986 provided a sobering reminder of the fragility of the country's economic base.

The development of offshore oil and gas resources has also manifested itself in growing regional inequalities in Norway, one of which has already been mentioned—the loss of population in the interior and northern counties versus the rapid growth of the southwest, especially Rogaland County. As exploration and exploitation inevitably shift northward, the more peripheral regions of Scandinavia—North Norway and the adjacent parts of Swedish and Finnish Lappland, a region which the Scandinavians term the "Nordkalott" or the "Northern Cap"—will increasingly feel the impact of industrial development, especially as the infrastructure of pipelines and refineries is put in place. However, even if and when the Askeladden field west of Hammerfest comes into production, there is every reason to expect that the real beneficiaries will continue to be the traditional core areas to the south, where population, agriculture, and industry are already concentrated.

Because of their essentially lowland character, the three Baltic states have only modest hydroelectric potential, the largest generating stations being located near Kaunas in Lithuania and Narva in Estonia. Deposits of oil shale in Estonia and peat in all three of the countries are used to generate power in thermal-electric stations, but oil and gas imports from Russia make up the critical difference in each of their energy budgets. In Estonia, fully half of the country's energy is derived from such imports, whereas in Latvia the degree of dependence on Russian energy amounts to 93 percent. Lithuania also imports crude oil from the Samara region of Russia, and in return for processing it for export through the Latvian port of Ventspils, is allowed to keep one-fifth for its own domestic uses. However, fully 90 percent of Lithuania's electricity comes from a Chernobyl-type nuclear reactor located at Ignalina, which is subject to frequent shutdowns. Because of their key location near the western seaboard of Russia, all three of the Baltic states capitalize on the flow of transit traffic, not the least in petroleum products. Lithuania controls the flow of oil not only between Russia and its Kaliningrad oblast to the southwest but also to Russia's major export terminal at Ventspils, Latvia. In addition, Lithuania is making plans for a major oil terminal of its own at Butinge, just north of Klaipeda, much to the displeasure of its northern neighbor, Latvia, which fears loss of business at Ventspils. Estonia has considered a major oil-export installation at the deep-water harbor of Muuga, just east of Tallinn, but Russia is contemplating the construction of a super-oil depot near St. Petersburg to obviate transit fees to all of its former republics.

Manufacturing

Nearly 2 million persons are employed in manufacturing industries in Norden, with one-third of the total residing in Sweden and about one-quarter in Finland. In terms of the number of people they employ, both Danish and Norwegian enterprises tend to be smaller in size, the Danish accounting for just under one-fifth of the region's value added by manufacture and the Norwegian for about one-seventh.

Although food products account for about one-fourth of Denmark's value added by manufacture, they make up the largest single sector of Danish industry in terms of total value of output and rank second only to the engineering industries in number of persons employed. Denmark produces more than half of Norden's meat, cheese, sugar, and beer, and nearly half of its butter.

It is in the realm of nonfood manufactures that Sweden most clearly demonstrates its industrial strength and diversity—with all of Norden's car, bus, and truck production, over half of its steel and saw timber, nearly half of its pulp, three-eighths of its pig-iron, and 30 percent of its cement. Norway, on the other hand, leads the region in aluminum and nitrogenous fertilizer production, both of which are massive consumers of hydroelectricity. Finland is first in newsprint output and has surpassed Sweden and is narrowing Denmark's lead in shipbuilding. Norway's shipbuilder, Kvaerner, which builds ships in yards in several other European countries, is a surprising success in a sector where most of these countries' output has plunged.

Although manufacturing has been one of the strongest urbanizing forces at work within Norden, it has not given rise to the sprawling industrial complexes typical of the German Ruhr, the English Midlands, or the Pittsburgh-Cleveland corridor in the United States. This is, of course, because Norden lacks the prime coalfields that serve as magnets for such concentrations. Manufacturing in Norden began in earnest only when electricity came into widespread use, whether generated by waterpower—as in Norway, Sweden, Finland, and Iceland—or by imported coal and oil as in Denmark. Raw materials came from the farms, fisheries, forests, and mines, with the major markets for domestic consumption growing up around the respective national capitals. Increasingly, the industries of Norden have turned to foreign markets and sources of supply, some of them becoming multinational corporations of world stature, such as Finland's Nokia, producer of mobile phones.

In Norden, as elsewhere, the geographical distribution of manufacturing reflects locational compromises, chiefly among the factors of power sources, raw materials, and markets. Where perishable foodstuffs, such as dairy products, meat, and fish, are involved, the processing plants are as close to the source of supply as possible. Thus, dairies and slaughterhouses are scattered through the most productive agricultural areas, and fish-canning and fish-freezing installations dot the coasts of Norway, Iceland, and western Sweden. Among the leading centers of the fish processing industry are Stavanger, Bergen, and Hammerfest in Norway; Reykjavík in Iceland; and Göteborg in Sweden.

The wood-processing industries, owing to the bulky nature of the raw materials, also tend to locate near sources of supply. Most sawmills, and pulp and paper factories are situated near the mouths of rivers where they can assemble the timber and ship the finished products most easily. The seasonal flotation of logs down the rivers in spring has all but given way to year-round transport by road and rail.

Several industries have been located near power sources, including some older enterprises that use waterpower directly and some newer ones that are based on hydroelectricity. At older waterpower sites (e.g., Sarpsborg in Norway; Trollhättan, Borås, and Norrköping in Sweden; and Tampere in Finland), a variety of textile mills and wood- and metal-working industries came into being almost at the dawn of the industrial age in Norden. Then, in the period when steam power gained ascendancy (and before electricity was harnessed), a great expansion of manufacturing occurred in the port cities of Norden where the imported coal (from Britain or Germany) was unloaded. Much of the earlier industrialization of Oslo, Bergen, Trondheim, and Stavanger in Norway; Copenhagen, Århus, Odense, and Ålborg in Denmark; Göteborg, Malmö, and Stockholm in Sweden; Turku and Helsinki in Finland; and Reykjavík in Iceland belongs to this period. With the advent of the electric age, most of these industries switched to the new energy source that, except in Denmark, derived chiefly from domestic hydroelectric installations. The development of vast amounts of exceedingly cheap hydroelectricity, especially in Norway and more recently in Iceland, has given rise to a number of electrometallurgical and electrochemical industries. For example, the famed Norsk Hydro firm, which manufactures nitrate fer-

tilizers by extracting nitrogen from the air, began operations near the great waterpower site of Rjukan in the mountainous Telemark region west of Oslo, although most of its production now takes place at its plant on the southern coast near Porsgrunn. Similarly, other metal refineries have shifted locations from exhausted ore sites to coastal locations where it can easily be imported. The greatest expansion in the electrometallurgical industry, however, has been in the smelting of aluminum, Norway's first smelter being built at Høyanger on Sogne Fjord north of Bergen in 1915. Since World War II several large, new plants have been built.

For all but the massive power consumers like the electrochemical and electrometallurgical industries, the dawn of the electric age has liberated most industries from their dependence on local energy sources and permitted them to locate closer to domestic consumer markets or near the coast for easier export to foreign markets. In Norway this has meant a growing concentration of industries in the lower valleys of the East Country, especially in the area of Oslo Fjord. In Sweden there is a heavy concentration of manufacturing in the Stockholm and Göteborg areas and in the central lowland between them. Similarly, the west coast of Sweden between Göteborg and Malmö is an area of industrial concentration that extends into the Copenhagen-Helsingør area of Denmark. Elsewhere in Denmark, the largest manufacturing nodes are found around such port cities as Odense, Århus, and Ålborg. In Finland, Tampere remains the most specialized industrial center, although the southern coastal areas, including Helsinki and Turku, have concentrated on manufacturing as well. In Iceland the major node of industrial activity is centered on Reykjavík in the southwest, but Akureyri, the regional capital of the north, also has a number of small, diversified industries.

The Baltic states ranked among the most industrially advanced regions of the former Soviet Union and enjoyed a good reputation for the quality of their manufactures. The changeover from centrally planned economies to market-oriented economies caused each of them to experience serious dislocations and declines in output during the early 1990s. How many of these industries will remain competitive as they gear themselves to trade with the West is yet to be seen. In Estonia, in addition to the processing of oil-shale for the distillation of fuel and the generation of electricity, the chief emphasis was on the construction of ships, electric motors, and earth-moving machinery; Latvia concentrated on the production of buses and vans, street- and railway-cars, agricultural machinery, and household appliances; and in Lithuania, key industries included machine tools, electronics, television sets, refrigerators, and freezers. Firms from Germany, Sweden, and the United States have already evinced considerable interest in developing joint ventures, but Russia is also continuing to invest in the region. While on the one hand seeking and needing such external investment, on the other hand it brings some related problems for the Baltic states, such as a high concentration of new investments in Estonia in the Tallinn region.

Transportation

Because of their insular and peninsular configuration, the countries of Norden depend more heavily on shipping to conduct their foreign trade than do any other countries in Europe, save the Low Countries. Only the Netherlands and Belgium carry on a larger volume of ocean commerce per capita than the Nordic countries, owing to the specialized entrepôt functions of their cities of Rotterdam and Antwerp. For Norden as a whole, nearly 60 percent of the tonnage handled is outbound, with Norway accounting for over half of the total due to its increasing exports of oil. Indeed, as a result of the oil industry, Norway now generates more than five times as much tonnage for export than it receives in imports. In the other Nordic countries, more goods are unloaded than dispatched, with both Iceland and Denmark having about two-thirds of their trade comprised of imports. Both Finland and Sweden have more equal traffic flows, owing to the large volume of timber and wood products that move into export.

Functionally, the seaports of Norden fall into four principal classes: (1) major population centers that generate large volumes of diversified imports and exports; (2) specialized oil-import ports; (3) specialized raw material export ports; and (4) ferry ports. In the first class are all the Nordic capitals—Copenhagen, Stockholm, Oslo, and Helsinki—as well as Århus, the regional capital of Jutland, and Turku, Finland's most accessible winter port. Most important of all the Nordic ports, however, is Göteborg on the west coast of Sweden. Because it effectively serves as the Atlantic gateway for the entire country, the tonnages it handles each year total nearly one-fourth of Sweden's overseas commerce.

The second class of ports are those that specialize in oil imports. The largest of these, and hence the second-ranking port in all of Norden, is Brofjorden, a deep-water anchorage on the Swedish coast north of Göteborg, which can handle ships up to 300,000 tons. From here, smaller coastwise tankers distribute refined petroleum products to the remainder of Sweden. In Denmark, Norway, and Finland the location of the oil-import ports represents a compromise between harbor depth and market orientation. In Denmark two such ports serve the Copenhagen market from the western side of the large island (Saelland) where it is located, and a third is strategically located between the markets of the other large island, Fyn, and the Jutland Peninsula. In Norway, the country's major eastern market is supplied from Tønsberg at the mouth of Oslofjord, whereas much of western Norway is served from a distribution center at Sola near Stavanger. Both of Finland's specialized oil-import ports are located in close proximity to the urban markets of Helsinki and Turku.

Among the specialized raw material export ports are Narvik in north Norway and Luleå, Sweden, located at the head of the Gulf of Bothnia, both of which still retain a sizable, even if somewhat diminished, export of iron ore. In the same general class of ports are specialized timber export ports in Sweden and in Finland, as well as major cement plants in Denmark. Finally, because of Norden's insular and peninsular configuration, several ports within the region are totally dominated by ferry traffic. For example, each year the Helsingør-Hälsingborg crossing of the Öresund between Denmark and Sweden carries over 16 million passengers as well as 1.75 million cars, trucks, and buses. The major crossing on the Copenhagen-

Jutland route (over the Great Belt) carries 10 million passengers and 2.5 million motor vehicles a year; the Rødby-Puttgarden route from Denmark to northern Germany moves 7.5 million persons and 1.25 million cars; and the Copenhagen-Malmö crossing transports some 5 million passengers and nearly half a million automobiles. Similar large-scale ferry movements cross the Baltic from Stockholm to Finland via Mariehamn in the Åland Islands, and a sizable traffic also exists across the Skagerack and Kattegat from Denmark to Norway and Sweden, and across the southern Baltic from Trelleborg in southern Sweden to Germany and Poland (Fig. 9-10). There is a great deal of traffic between Helsinki and Tallinn, Estonia, amounting to over 3 million passengers during 1995. This reflects strong economic ties between Finland and Estonia, as well as especially heavy traffic reportedly generated by highly taxed Finns seeking lower cost alcoholic beverages in Estonia. Direct ferry connections also link Tallinn and Stockholm, the route on which a tragic accident in 1994 took the lives of hundreds of people, stunning Sweden and small, newly independent Estonia.

In recent years, in the face of a depressed shipping market and growing competition from vessels flying "flags of convenience," the Nordic countries have drastically cut back the size of their merchant fleets. Indeed, by the mid-1990s their combined tonnages were less than half of what they were at the beginning of 1980s. Unable to attract youthful seamen at competitive wages from their own domestic labor pools, Scandinavian shippers had increasingly adopted the practices of their competitors by recruiting cheaper labor from abroad. Moreover, to escape the growing burdens of taxation and regulation imposed by their own authorities, they have "reflagged" their vessels in countries where labor and social legislation is either minimal or nonexistent. Certainly, international shipping is one industry in which Nordic social and political idealism has been forced to capitulate to economic realism in order to survive. Nowhere is this "compromise" better illustrated than in Norway, which still maintains a merchant fleet of over 23 million tons, but lists most of it in a special "Norwegian International Ship Register."

For the domestic movement of goods, the truck has become the principal carrier in all the Nordic countries, except Norway. There, where topography and climate pose severe challenges to overland transportation, nearly two-thirds of all goods continues to move by ship, although trucking now accounts for more than four times as much internal freight movement as do the railways. In Iceland, where railways were never constructed, nine-tenths of all goods move overland by truck as compared to only one-tenth moving by ship along the coasts. In Denmark, about three-fourths of domestic goods traffic moves over the road, and another one-sixth is carried by ships operating between the islands and the Jutland Peninsula. Sweden places a rather heavy reliance on coastwise shipping for domestic traffic, amounting to about three-eighths of its total movement. Finland, which lacks such an option, especially during the winter, depends on over-the-road haulage for more than two-thirds of its freight movement. The railway plays its most important role in Sweden and Finland where it handles about one-fourth of the goods traffic.

With respect to the movement of people within Norden, the automotive revolution has been even more dramatic. In all of the countries, well over three-fourths of all person/miles are generated by private cars. With over 8.8 million automobiles in circulation, Norden has one of the highest per capita ownerships of passenger cars in the world.

FIGURE 9-10 Baltic ferry between Turku, Finland, and Stockholm. Turku and Stockholm are just two among a number of busy ports in Northern Europe, many of which are on the Baltic Sea. This large ferry is part of a fleet of Silja Line boats that ferry passengers and vehicles across the Baltic between Finland, Sweden and Germany. (Hannu Vallas/Woodfin Camp & Associates)

To keep pace with the rapid growth in the number of cars, buses, and trucks, the Nordic countries have accelerated the improvement of their highways so that today nearly all roads in Denmark are hard-surfaced, as are three-fourths of those in Sweden, two-thirds of those in Norway, and more than half of those in Finland. Over 1400 miles (2250 km) of dual-motorways have been constructed, chiefly along the major "E-roads" between the urban centers of Denmark and Sweden, and on the approaches to Oslo and Helsinki. In Iceland a circum-island road was completed in 1974 when a gap across the quick-sands to the south of the Vatna Glacier was closed, but only 60 percent of it has been hard-surfaced to date. Planning began in 1973 for the construction of a combined bridge and tunnel link between Copenhagen and Malmö and a railway tunnel between Helsingør and Hälsingborg. Although some preparatory work has been carried out, both economic and environmental concerns have slowed their progress.

Denmark is also the node of Nordic international air transportation, with Copenhagen's Kastrup airport annually handling over 11 million passengers, only one-fifth of whom arrive or depart on domestic flights. Because of its strategic location, Kastrup was made the principal base of operations of The Scandinavian Airlines System (SAS), a consortium in which Denmark and Norway each hold two-sevenths of the stock and Sweden holds three-sevenths. The traffic shadow cast by Kastrup is so large that the only Danish airports to handle any significant volume of passengers are those serving the more distant peninsula of Jutland and the island of Bornholm.

Owing to Denmark's location, small size, and the excellence of its surface transport, its volume of domestic air passenger traffic is considerably smaller than that of its three Nordic neighbors. Both Oslo and Helsinki handle nearly 7.5 million passengers a year, whereas Stockholm annually serves nearly 13 million passengers—in all cases heavily dominated by movements of the countries' own citizens. Norway, with its rugged terrain, difficult surface communications, but affluent economy, epitomizes a country in which air passenger traffic has really come into its own. As a result, the airports for Bergen, Stavanger, and Trondheim all generate more passenger traffic each year than

Göteborg, Sweden's second city, despite the fact that Göteborg is as large as all three of the Norwegian cities put together. This is a forceful illustration that, for air traffic, location is more critical than population size. Similarly, in Iceland where surface alternatives are relatively poor, heavy reliance is placed on air transport for linking the outlying regions of the country with the capital.

The Baltic countries have a surprisingly dense system of roads and an increasingly high level of auto and truck traffic. The railroads are in relatively poorer condition, and there has been a steep decline in cross-border traffic and cooperation in the region since the countries emerged to freedom from the USSR. The crossing at the strategic Polish-Lithuanian border linking the Baltics by land to Western Europe is particularly associated with the ills of bureaucracy, corruption, and interminable delays. The Baltic countries' air service has quickly reoriented itself westward, so that Copenhagen and its SAS service is prominent, though small nationally based airlines are also emerging.

Trade

The Nordic countries carry on a volume of international trade that ranks among the highest in the world on a per capita basis. In 1990, for example, it averaged half again more than that conducted by the members of the European Union, more than three times that of Japan, and from three to four times that of the United States.

A little over one-fifth of Norden's trade is conducted within the region itself. Both Sweden and Denmark sell more to their Nordic neighbors than they buy, whereas the remaining countries import more from Norden than they export to it. The bulk of Norden's former (European Free Trade Association) trade was also within the Nordic region itself rather than with EFTA's more distant members such as Switzerland and Austria.

Over half of all of Norden's trade has been with the European Union, a pattern that will be strengthened by Sweden's and Finland's membership. Germany is the region's largest trading partner, and the United Kingdom ranks second. Only Norway sells more to the EU than it buys from it, and its surplus is steadily increasing as sales of oil and gas continue to grow.

Trade with the countries of Eastern Europe averages about 4 percent for Norden as a whole. However, as late as 1991 Russia supplied just over 10 percent of Finland's imports and was the destination for just under 6 percent of its exports. When the remaining countries of the subcontinent are included, we find that no less than three-fourths of all Norden's exports are sold within Europe and that the same proportion of its imports are derived from Europe. The region's leading overseas trading partner is the United States, which accounts for just under 7 percent of Norden's total commerce.

The overall composition of Nordic imports varies little from country to country, except in their relative importance to the individual states. In each of the countries, the chief imports include machinery, transport equipment, electrical apparatus, chemicals, and iron and steel. In all but Norway, mineral fuels also loom large, whereas in all but Denmark, foodstuffs constitute a significant import. The list of exports, on the other hand, is far more diversified, with the most important products moving into trade being oil and gas, paper and paper products, automobiles, machinery and equipment, iron and steel, nonferrous metals, woodpulp, meat, and fish. In Iceland, fish and fish products, aluminum, alloy metals for steel production, diatomite, and woolen knitwear dominate the list of exports. In Norway, oil and gas dwarf its other exports, which include nonferrous metals, fish, and chemicals. In Denmark, although machinery and equipment and metal manufactures lead in value, meat, chemicals, and fish are also important. In Finland, machinery and transport equipment, chemicals, and iron and steel all surpass in value its traditional exports of wood products. Sweden, the region's largest exporter, exports in particular automobiles, paper and paper products, iron and steel, machinery, pulp, and saw timber.

Norden's present trading configurations began to evolve in 1973. At the beginning of that year, Denmark joined the European Economic Community, along with the United Kingdom and Ireland. Although Norway declined to enter this expanded trading bloc, it negotiated a separate trade treaty with the EC, as did Sweden, Finland, and Iceland to prevent discriminatory tariffs from being erected against certain of their critical exports. Finland also became the first market-economy country to sign an agreement of economic, scientific, and technical cooperation with the CMEA group. However, the collapse of the Soviet Union in 1989 not only necessitated a major shift in the Finnish economy toward the West, but it also caused both Finland and Sweden to reevaluate their positions of neutrality in the new Europe. Subsequently, the governments of both countries and also of Norway applied for membership in the European Union. In May 1994, after lengthy negotiations, all three of them (along with Austria) were accepted for admission, which was ultimately also accepted by Sweden and Finland based on the results of referenda on the issue. For the second time, Norwegians voted against EC/EU membership, and Norway remains outside the organization and within the now tiny EFTA—although membership within this organization does give it special trade privileges with the EU by way of the EEA agreement.

The Soviet collapse also ushered in an entirely new era in the economic life of the Baltic states. Suddenly, the centrally planned patterns of specialized agricultural and industrial exports to the Soviet market, which had been predicated on the importation of raw materials and energy from other regions of the Soviet Union, were called into question as the three republics regained their political independence. How viable these Moscow-created industries will be in a world where Estonia, Latvia, and Lithuania increasingly seek to reorient their trade to the West is something only the future will reveal. By mid-1993 Estonia had succeeded in substituting Finland for Russia as its major trading partner, selling to it just over one-fifth of its exports and buying from it just over two-fifths of its imports. Although Russia occupied second place, now Sweden and Germany came in third and fourth, respectively. Machinery, oil, chemicals, and foodstuffs constitute Estonia's most important imports. Because Estonia's leading exports are textiles, wood products, metal goods, and dairy products, perhaps the most rational market will continue to be in the east; but politics complicates this greatly. Owing to many Russians' negative perceptions of both Estonia's role in the demise of the USSR and its treatment of a large Russian minority, Russia has imposed double tariff duties on Estonian imports.

In both Latvia and Lithuania, however, Russia has retained its predominant trading position. Russia is the recipient of more than one-fourth of Latvia's exports and the supplier of nearly three-eighths of its imports, while it buys more than two-fifths of Lithuania's exports and provides more than two-thirds of its imports. Both Latvia and Lithuania depend heavily on the import of oil and gas from Russia, as well as on raw materials and intermediate products such as metal goods. In return, Latvia has exported transport equipment, agricultural machinery, and household appliances to Russia, whereas Lithuania has sold it such items as machine tools, electronic products, and refrigerators. Again, only time will tell how many of these kinds of goods from the Baltic states will find a ready market in the West.

Tourism

As a result of high incomes, generous paid vacations, and widespread automobile ownership, the peoples of Norden are among the most avid tourists in Europe. They are sun worshippers of long standing, and so their own preference is for the countries of the Mediterranean, where getting a summer tan is a surer bet than it is in their home latitudes. Though for now poorer, people from the Baltic states, long confined to travel within the Soviet bloc, also frequently head south. Lack of economic and political integration within the Baltics and the appeal of the Mediterranean result in relatively more interest in the Mediterranean than in neighboring countries.

Over 15 million non-Nordic tourists visit Norden each year. More than five-sixths of these were Germans crossing the border into Denmark, usually on short shopping trips. Throughout Norden there is a marked seasonality to the influx of tourists, with nearly half of all hotel overnights and about seven-eighths of all camping overnights concentrated in the three summer months.

Denmark, with its central location and overland connections with the rest of Europe, is by far the most frequently visited. For many Europeans and overseas tourists it is the northern limit of the

"Grand Tour," and it is the only impression many of them ever get of Scandinavia. The tourist's most popular goal in Denmark is Copenhagen, where two-thirds of all foreign visitor overnights are recorded, whereas the Danes themselves prefer to vacation on the beaches of western Jutland. Denmark receives more than one-third of all Nordic receipts from tourism. A considerably smaller number of foreign tourists find their way into Sweden each year, and there, too, the principal goal is the capital city, Stockholm. Norway, on the other hand, attracts a greater number of visitors who come to see its fjords and Midnight Sun in summer, and to ski at its mountain resorts in winter (Fig. 9-11). Tourist travel in both Finland and Iceland tends to suffer somewhat from their out-of-the-way locations. In Finland, most foreign-

FIGURE 9-11 A Norwegian fjord. Norway's spectacular west coast is characterized by numerous U-shaped glacial valleys that were scoured by ice to levels far below sea level. Now filled by the sea, the fjords are favorite destinations of summer cruise ships as well as hikers. (© Matti Kaups)

ers seldom get beyond the south coast and the capital, though improved highways are tempting more of them to make the jaunt northward to the North Cape. Even so, about 30 percent of all hotel overnights are in the Helsinki area. Iceland receives more than 150,000 visitors a year, about one-third of whom are Americans; most of the remainder are Germans, Britons, and Scandinavians. In sum, however, the tourist balance of payments for the Nordic countries is markedly negative; in all of them save Denmark, they earn considerably less from foreign visitors than what they themselves spend traveling to other countries. For now foreign travel to the Baltics is quite dominated by visits from neighboring countries, Germany, Sweden, and Finland.

PROBLEMS AND PROSPECTS

Despite their noteworthy economic and social achievements, all of the Nordic countries face serious challenges to the continuance of their affluent lifestyles. Some of these challenges have grown out of their own evolution as postindustrial welfare states—high wages that make their industries uncompetitive with those in other, less developed countries; social services that require large governmental bureaucracies to administer and high levels of taxation to support; and a populace whose living standard and educational status are so high that it is no longer willing to perform the more menial tasks in society, relegating them instead to foreign immigrant workers. On the other hand, some of the challenges arise from external forces over which they have little or no control—for example, the steep rise in energy costs during the 1970s; increasing unemployment as the globalization of the world economy forces a major restructuring of their manufacturing industries; the pressure to accommodate their economic, social, and political structures to the regulatory mechanisms of the European Union as the price of their admission to an integrated Europe; their adjustment to an entirely new geopolitical climate in the European sub-Arctic following the Soviet Union's fragmentation; and their continued commitment to international humanitarian assistance, especial-

ly as it relates to the problem of refugees from the war-ravaged former Yugoslavia.

With no domestic energy sources of its own prior to the oil crisis, Denmark was especially vulnerable to external economic pressures. Although its first North Sea oil platform began production in 1972 and natural gas came onstream in 1984, these developments were not rapid or timely enough to forestall the doubling of Denmark's foreign debt during the 1980s. By 1990 the country could supply nearly 70 percent of its domestic energy requirements, and it was hoped that this would rise to 90 percent by the end of the century. However, just as the energy crisis was being met and the country's balance of payments registered a surplus for the first time in over a quarter of a century, the economic slowdown that began in 1989 has pushed the budget deficit and social welfare costs higher as unemployment has risen beyond 12 percent. During this same critical period, Denmark experienced five elections and as many changes of government as the various political parties struggled to formulate policies that would win broad popular support. In a June 1992 referendum, the Danish electorate shocked the architects of a united Europe by rejecting the Maastricht Treaty, and not until it was resubmitted in amended form did a second referendum narrowly approve it in May 1993. As minority and coalition governments came and went, political fragmentation went on to such a degree that the election of 1994 was contested by no fewer than eleven parties, compared to only five a decade earlier.

In Finland, where no political party has ever held a majority in Parliament, economic and social policy has always rested on fragile coalitions. The cornerstone of all Finnish policymaking during the Cold War period, however, was the maintenance of cordial relations with the Soviet Union. To this end, their treaty of mutual friendship and cooperation was extended right up until the USSR's disintegration in 1991. Because of its own dependence on imported oil, Finland had increasingly looked to its eastern neighbor as a source of supply. Following the drastic fall in world oil prices in 1986, Finland had managed to build up a huge trade surplus with the Soviet Union, but because Finland's trade with the Eastern bloc was on a barter basis and was not in hard currency, that surplus turned out to be rather illusory. With the Soviet collapse, not only did Finland lose its major market but its principal energy supplier also became quite undependable. On the first score, Finland has scurried to reorient its economy westward, including applying for and gaining membership in the EU; even so, its ailing industries have been forced to lay off large numbers of workers, giving the country an unemployment rate approaching 20 percent. On the second count, the country has revived its plans for both a controversial new nuclear reactor and a large hydroelectric installation, purchased some oil platforms in the North Sea, and formulated plans to scale up its use of peat threefold. With an agricultural sector that has been among the most heavily subsidized in the world and a forest industry whose resources are being used to capacity, it is clear that the Finnish economy is in for some drastic rationalization in the coming years. On the domestic political front, this was signaled by the election in 1991 of Finland's first nonSocialist government in over a quarter of a century.

Although Iceland was spared the downturn in employment that afflicted much of the industrialized world during the 1980s, it has often suffered from almost runaway inflation during the post–World War II era. Within the last 20 years alone, its currency has been devalued more than half a dozen times. Its volatile balance of payments depends primarily on the volume of its fisheries catch and favorable world prices for aluminum, both of which are notoriously unstable. Fortunately for Iceland, although its own catch of cod has been ominously decreasing, the overfishing of both European and North American waters has been even worse, so this has driven up prices. Until 1979, the country's political spectrum was represented by four parties, and in 1980 Iceland inaugurated the world's first popularly elected female head of state. In the election of 1983, two new splinter groups appeared, one of which was the Women's Alliance. But for whatever government has held office, the central issue has been the reconciliation of the electorate's demand for an ever-rising standard of living within the framework of a modern welfare state with the realities imposed by a lopsided dependency on a single and highly erratic resource—fish. Although the

country does not seek membership in the European Union, the Althing (the Icelandic Parliament) voted in early 1993 to ratify the European Economic Area treaty linking it to the EU via EFTA.

The last decade has marked a period of dramatic economic and political change in Norway as well. Because it has never been able to derive a living from its land, Norway has always depended on the sea for its livelihood—in the past by means of fishing, sealing, whaling, and shipping, and at present by extracting the vast deposits of oil and natural gas that the adjacent seafloor contains. The fortuitous discovery of its North Sea wealth, just as the energy crisis gripped the industrialized world, spared Norway many of the dislocations suffered by its Nordic neighbors. At the same time, it posed a number of other problems, some of which have already been mentioned. The boom in the oil and gas industry has tended to obscure the fact that the traditional economic underpinnings of the country are in a state of stagnation or actual decline. Overfishing and pollution are making serious inroads in the annual catch of the coastal fisheries; revenues from shipping, which once paid for one-fourth of the country's imports, now pay for scarcely one-twentieth; and key industries such as chemicals and engineering are finding it difficult to market their products, because Norwegian labor costs are among the highest in the world. Indeed, as Norway has lost markets both at home and abroad, manufacturing's share of the gross domestic product fell from 18 percent in 1980 to 13.5 percent in 1991. As the plight of many private firms has worsened, the state has found itself bailing them out, much as the Swedes had misguidedly done 10 years earlier, while at the same time pouring substantial subsidies into farming and fishing to keep the primary sector afloat as well. Moreover, while expanding its program of social services, Norway has inflated public sector employment to such a degree that two-thirds of all jobs created in the last decade have been in the government.

The 1972 referendum on Norway's entry into the Common Market proved to be a political watershed for the country. The Liberal party, the country's oldest, first split and then collapsed over the issue. A radical faction broke out of the Labor party, which was in favor of joining, to form a new

Socialist Left party, which was hostile to the idea. Similarly, on the right another strongly nationalistic faction, also opposed to joining, formed itself into the Progress party, thereby cutting into the strength of the Conservatives, who favored membership. The remaining two of Norway's traditional political parties, the Center (or Farmer's) and Christian People's parties, also adamantly opposed membership. Nearly two decades later, the bitter divisiveness of the EC membership question again took center stage, when a second referendum was held in December 1994—and, again, Norwegians voted down EU membership. A brief interlude of a Conservative coalition government ended in 1995 when the two-seat Progress party refused to support an increase in the gasoline tax, and a Labor-Socialist Left coalition took over, headed by the country's first woman prime minister. Norway's political leadership will continue to be tested. While the country's dependence on oil continues to grow, employment in all sectors of the Norwegian economy except public and social services continues to contract, and today the overall unemployment rate is over 6 percent.

Sweden also experienced some major economic and political changes following the oil crisis and recession of the early 1970s. After 44 years in office, the Social Democrats were turned out in 1976 and replaced with a nonSocialist coalition. Although the principal issues in the election had been "creeping socialism" and nuclear power, because of growing economic recession in the wake of the energy crisis, the new government resorted to expensive state-financed rescue operations to bail out a number of ailing industries. These operations included nationalization of the steel and shipbuilding industries, as well as heavy subsidization of textile- and shoe-making. By 1978 the nuclear issue had brought down the coalition government, and two years later it was referred to the Swedish electorate in a national referendum. In the meantime, a new nonSocialist coalition took office following the election of 1979, but by 1981 it too fell apart over the question of taxation. As a result, the Social Democrats were returned to power in 1982 but without a majority, making them dependent on communist support to enact legislation. Early in 1986 the party, Sweden, and the world were shocked as the country's dynamic

prime minister, Olof Palme, was shot by an unknown assailant on the streets of Stockholm. The controversial head of the Social Democratic party, Palme was also an outspoken critic of injustice, oppression, and violence throughout the world. That a champion of human rights could be gunned down on a city street in highly prosperous and peaceful Sweden was a traumatic affront to the sensibilities of its citizens and those of Norden. Unfortunately, however, it was just one more illustration that even this, sane and idyllic corner of the world was not immune to the cross currents of international terrorism that swirl around it. The loss of Palme was a further blow to the fortunes of Social Democracy in Sweden, for his successor, Ingvar Carlsson, was perceived by the labor wing of the party as being more interested in the middle classes.

In the 1988 elections, environmental issues figured so prominently that the "Green" party won no fewer than 20 seats, all but one of which was at the expense of the nonSocialist coalition made up of the Conservative, Liberal, and Center parties. By the early 1990s with the economy once more in recession, the public opinion polls gave the Social Democrats the lowest rating they had received since the end of the Second World War. Though still the largest party in the country, after the results of the 1991 elections were in, the Social Democrats were no longer able to form a government, and a four-party bourgeois coalition assumed power in their place. United only by their opposition to the socialists, this Conservative-Liberal-Center-Christian Democrat coalition is so fragile and divided that it must depend on a new, right-wing splinter party called the New Democracy to enact any legislation. Ironically, in the same election the environmental issue was all but displaced by the economic recession, causing the "Green" party to lose all of its seats in the Parliament, but enabling the communists, renamed the "Left" party, to retain their grip on no fewer than 16 of them.

The primary objectives of Sweden's nonsocialist coalition government were to ready the country for membership in the European Union by reducing the tax burden of Swedish citizens toward the EU's average, encouraging a more market-driven economy, and trimming the level of such social services as health, education, and welfare. However, during their three years in office, the public debt doubled and unemployment tripled. Thus in the parliamentary elections of 1994, the Social Democrats were once again returned to office but without a majority, thereby obliging them to govern with the support of the Left party. In the referendum of November 1994, the Swedish electorate approved the country's entry into the EU in January 1995 by a slim majority. However, several issues remain to be settled before Sweden can mesh itself seamlessly into the European alliance. Among them are the very special provision in Swedish law known as *allemansrätt* (literally, "every man's right") guaranteeing rights of access to the fields, forests, and lakes of Sweden to all its citizens; the probable dismantling of the state monopoly on alcohol in the face of EU pressure for open sales of beer, wine, and other alcoholic beverages; and the reduction of inspection standards for food, as Swedish levels of sanitation are brought down to those prevailing within the EU. Lower prices and lower taxes may appeal to many Swedes, but lower food and sanitation standards do not. Indeed, fewer than six months after their country's admission to the EU, more than 60 percent of the Swedish electorate were complaining of their disenchantment with the decision. As a consequence, when it came time to elect Sweden's members to the European Parliament in September 1995, only an apathetic 43 percent of the people turned out to vote—chiefly for adherents of parties opposed to EU entry.

Within their marginal, sub-Arctic environments, all of the countries of Norden have tried to promote equality of opportunity in all of their diverse regions. That they have not been entirely successful in defying their geography is apparent from the fact that the peripheries of their states continue to lose population to the traditional core areas, where economic, social, and cultural opportunities remain greater. Certainly, they cannot be faulted for not having tried, for in the process they have created what many people believe are the most prosperous, equitable, and democratic societies found anywhere on our planet.

At the level of international policymaking, the so-called Norden Society has been actively promoting cooperation on economic, social, and cultural matters among the five Nordic states ever since its founding at the end of the First World War, and in 1952 the quasi-governmental Nordic Council was established to formalize and intensify their cooperative efforts. The fact that these countries already shared such features as a common labor market and customs union, as well as the reciprocity of many social benefits, well before the European Community came into being has somewhat complicated the relationships between them since, especially because first Denmark, and then more recently Finland and Sweden, have opted to join the European Union. One illustration will suffice: the only way in which the Nordic customs union could be reconciled with the Schengen Treaty (see Chapter 1, section on the EU's Internal Structure) on freedom of movement within the European community was either to have the three Nordic members of the EU not covered by it, or to have nonmember Norway enforce the agreement—which it consented to do.

On the other hand, split as they are over membership in the EU, the Nordic countries have continued to work closely together as a regional unit. In fact, once Finland and Sweden had gained admission to the EU, they immediately set about to persuade that body to establish a regional development program for the Baltic, similar to that already in place for the Mediterranean region. One of its principal goals is the early admission of the former Baltic Republics to the European Community. The Nordic countries are leaders in a pan-Baltic planning effort and in development efforts of all types in the Baltic states, which, short of another disastrous occupation by Russian forces (as threatened by radical-right and communist politicians there), will need their political and economic support for some time. The emergent Baltic states are complicating this cause with nationally based, divisive political spats, such as those between Lithuania and Poland over the Polish minority in Lithuania and between Estonia and Latvia over territory in the Baltic Sea that may have oil deposits.

In keeping with an expanded vision of its future, the Nordic Council has also reorganized itself into three commissions. One deals with intra-Nordic affairs; a second with Norden's relations to its surrounding regions, especially the Baltic, Arctic, and Barents seas areas; and a third with Norden's broader European relationships. Similarly, in the wake of the expanded international cooperation that has become possible following the collapse of communism in Eastern Europe, the Baltic Sea Institute has been established in Karlskrona, Sweden, whose mission is to promote research and development in the entire area stretching between the North and White seas.

Apart from the challenges posed by the changing political configurations of a "New Europe," the people of Norden are fully aware that as citizens of a global community, they are subject to forces and influences from beyond their boundaries which can seriously impact their relatively tranquil and pristine corner of the planet. Acid rain blowing in from the industrial districts of the English Midlands and the German Ruhr was already recognized as a serious problem in the early 1960s. During 40 years of communist rule, East European states often dumped hazardous wastes into the Baltic Sea, a shallow body of water that takes as long as 20 years to flush itself out; as a result, the marine life of the region has declined precipitously. The disastrous meltdown of the Chernobyl reactor in April 1986 wafted radioactive clouds over much of northern Sweden, contaminating plant and animal life over large areas and threatening the traditional lifestyle of the nomadic Same (Saami in Finnish). The knowledge that a similar "time-bomb" exists in the Soviet-built Ignalina reactor in Lithuania has prompted Nordic engineers to help improve its construction and safety standards, and hopefully obtain its early decommissioning. Similar concerns about the horrendous pollution emanating from the Russian nickel smelters near the Arctic frontiers of Norway and Finland have obliged the Scandinavians to assist in cleaning up this operation as well. Somewhat farther afield but of rapidly increasing concern is the recognition that the ozone layer over the north polar region is also thinning, with the resultant increase of ultraviolet radiation over the Nordic countries. On the other hand, the concerns of some foreign environmentalists focus on the Nordic states themselves, especially on whaling along the Norwegian coast and sealing along the Bothnian coast of Sweden. In both of these areas, however, the Scandinavians view the carefully monitored harvest of whales and seals as more of a protection for the fishing industry than any threat to the environment.

Of course, the countries of the European North are no more insulated from the economic and political cross currents of the planet than they are from the environmental ones. Already the largest per capita donors of humanitarian aid of any of the United Nations, how much farther can they go in welcoming additional migrants from disadvantaged Third World regions or from the war-torn republics of the former Yugoslavia, especially as their own economies face contraction and restructuring? Can the idealistic welfare states they have created over the last half-century continue to ensure their citizens "the good life" in the face of such momentous changes as those posed by the continuing integration of Europe and the globalization of the world economy? In a world where the "bottom line" is profitability, often based on low-cost labor, it will be for the coming decades to reveal whether the states of the European North can retain their presently privileged position.

BIBLIOGRAPHY

As might be expected, articles dealing with limited aspects of the geography of Norden frequently appear in the geographic journals of the individual countries, and many of them are now published in English. The primary geographic serials emanating from Norden are the *Geografisk Tidsskrift* (Denmark); *Fennia* (Finland); *Norsk Geografisk Tidsskrift* (Norway); and *Geografiska Annaler* and *Lund Studies in Geography* (Sweden).

Ahlmann, Hans W., ed. (1976). *Norden i Text och Kartor*. Stockholm: Generalstabens Litografiska Anstalts Förlag.

Central Bank of Iceland. (1987). *Iceland 1986* . Reykjavík: Central Bank of Iceland.

Danmarks Statistik (annual). *Statistical Yearbook of Denmark*. Copenhagen.

Economist Intelligence Unit. (1994–1995). *Country Report* and *Quarterly Economic Review*. Baltic States (Estonia, Latvia, Lithuania); Denmark and Iceland; Finland; Norway; Sweden.

Færoernes Landstyre (annual). *Rigombudsmanden på Færoerne. Årbog for Færoerne* [Yearbook for the Færoes]. Tórshavn: Færoernes Landstyre.

Hagskyslur Islands (occasional). *Statistical Abstract of Iceland*. Reykjavík.

Iceland Review. Quarterly.

John, Brian S. (1984). *Scandinavia: A New Geography*. New York: Longman.

Malmström, V. H. (1965). *Norden: Crossroads of Destiny*. Searchlight Book No. 22. Princeton, N.J.: Van Nostrand.

_____. (1958). *A Regional Geography of Iceland*. Washington, D.C.: National Academy of Sciences–National Research Council.

Mead, W. R. (1964). *An Economic Geography of the Scandinavian States and Finland*. London: University of London Press._____. (1981). *An Historical Geography of Scandinavia*. London: Academic Press.

_____. (1974). *The Scandinavian Northlands*. In Problem Regions of Europe Series, ed. D. I. Scargill. London: Oxford University Press.

Murphy, A. B. and A. Hunderi-Ely (1996). "The Geography of the 1994 Nordic Vote on European Union Membership", *The Professional Geographer* 48: 284-297.

Nordic Council. *Nordisk Kontakt* and *NK Tema* [Both are excellent sources, but are published only in the Scandinavian languages. Each issue of *NK Tema* explores a single theme in depth. Recent topics have included regional development; self-government in the Faeroes, Greenland, and Åland; equality of the sexes; Nordic relations with Europe; political disaffection of the electorate; and so on.]

Nordic Council (annual). *Yearbook of Nordic States*. Stockholm: Nordic Council.

Norwegian Information Service. *News of Norway*.

Royal Danish Ministry of Foreign Affairs. *Danish Journal; Denmark Review*.

Somme, Axel, ed. (1960). *A Geography of Norden*. Oslo: J. W. Cappelens Forlag.

Statistiska Centralbyrån (annual). *Statistical Yearbook of Sweden*. Stockholm: Statistiska Centralbyrån.

Statistisk Sentralbyrå (annual). *Statistical Yearbook of Norway*. Oslo: Statistisk Sentralbyrå.

Swedish Information Service. *Current Sweden; Human Environment in Sweden; Political Life in Sweden; Social Change in Sweden; Working Life in Sweden*.

Tilastokeskus (annual). *Statistical Yearbook of Finland*. Helsinki: Tilastokeskus.

Varjo, Uuno, and Wolf, Tietze, ed. (1987). *Norden: Man and Environment*. Berlin: Gebrüder Borntraeger.

10

SOUTHERN EUROPE

A TOPICAL OVERVIEW

Southern Europe—influenced by a distinctive climate and a unique Greco-Roman historical tradition—is a region of divergences. The congestion of major urban areas and glitter of new coastal tourist developments contrast starkly to poorer and more isolated rural areas. The emergence of the EU has transformed Southern Europe's economic base, strengthening manufacturing and tourism and intensifying agriculture, which now services international rather than mainly local markets. National and regional economies have been restructured, often with lessened government proprietorship in economic activities and increased emphasis on private ownership and foreign investment. The complex nature of Southern Europe's physical and human geography cannot be easily generalized. However, two vital elements have emerged. Southern Europe has become increasingly integrated and dependent upon the European Union. Simultaneously, regions of Southern Europe are cooperating as never before because of the reduced significance of former national boundaries.

Southern Europe consists mainly of three great peninsulas, the Iberian, Italian, and Grecian, as well as a number of distinctive islands. Some of the islands such as the Balearics, Corsica, Sicily, or Crete belong to an adjacent country; others such as Malta and Cyprus are countries in their own right. Within the matrix of Southern Europe, the following countries are discussed in this chapter: Portugal, Spain, Italy, Greece, Malta, and Cyprus. Furthermore, the littoral areas of Mediterranean France are analyzed, and brief comments are given on Turkey and Gibraltar. All told, over 122 million people live in this area, occupying about 350,000 sq miles (907,000 sq km), an area about the same size as France and western Germany or the states of Texas and Idaho. Turkey, though physically not part of Southern Europe, has in recent years been drawn toward the economic orbit of the European Union (EU); when included with the above figures, an additional 63 million inhabitants living on 301,000 sq miles (780,000 sq km) must be counted.

The physical landscape of Southern Europe is complex and includes low-lying plains such as the Po Valley in northern Italy; elevated tablelands, which are best represented by the Spanish Meseta (the central part of the country); hill country, good examples of which are on the north coast of Crete and interior Sicily; rugged mountain ranges, including the Pyrenees in Spain, the Alps and Apennines in Italy, the Pindus in Greece and the Taurus in Turkey; and distinctive drainage systems represented by the Duro in Iberia, the Po in Italy, the Axios in Greece, and the Menderes in Turkey. In addition, because of tectonic instability there are numerous volcanoes such as the island of Thira in the Cyclades, the Eolean islands of Vulcano and Stromboli, as well as Europe's highest, Mount Etna, 10,095 ft (3340 m), in northeast Sicily. Although the Mediterranean climate with summer drought is prevalent in many areas, because of the varied topography and different locations of the peninsulas, climatic conditions are not uniform.

Throughout history, the interplay of the region's particular climate and distinctive vegetation with the juxtaposition of sea, plains, hills, mountains, and rivers, has been a fundamental element in the evolution of the geography of Southern Europe. At times natural disasters such as earthquakes, floods, forest fires, avalanches, landslides and volcanic eruptions have had harsh consequences for the region's inhabitants. All of the countries have been affected by different physical, historical, political, and cultural factors, and all of their economies have developed in a distinctive fashion. Although it would be easier to stress the similarities among these countries, to understand them one must analyze their unique characteristics, not only in comparison with other states in Southern Europe, but also in relation to the diverse regions found within each country.

The most profound political and economic change to occur in modern times in Southern Europe has been the inclusion of the four main countries, Portugal, Spain, Italy, and Greece, within the political framework of the European Union. Europe's tariff-free trading market, the European Economic Area or EEA (including the EU and EFTA, excluding Switzerland), now encompasses more than 370 million people, the largest such block in the world. Barriers to the unhindered movement of goods, services, and people among 18 countries have been eliminated in principle.

Furthermore, Malta, Cyprus, and Turkey have applied for membership in the EU, although Turkey's application has been turned down for the present.

The geopolitical status of Southern Europe, especially Italy, Greece, and Turkey, was profoundly affected by the Persian Gulf War, the collapse of the Soviet Union, and the civil war in the former Yugoslavia. Italy has been impacted by the Yugoslav conflict and by Albanian refugees; Greece has been affected by both the war in the former Yugoslavia and by the creation of the country of Macedonia; whereas Turkey's role in Central Asia and in the Middle East has changed because of its role in the Gulf War against Iraq, because of the independence of former Soviet lands that border on its northeast regions, and because of the civil war between Kurdish separatists and the Turkish state. Furthermore, Southern Europe has been and will continue to be affected by the rise of fundamentalist Islam in North Africa, Egypt, and the Middle East.

Major Geographic Components: The Major Peninsulas and Islands, Southern France, and Turkey

Southern Europe as defined here is composed of three large peninsulas (Iberia, Italy, and Greece), a number of major islands (including the Balearic Islands; the islands of the states of Malta and Greece, notably Crete; Corsica, Sardinia, and Sicily; and the dynamic southern part of France, which physically links Spain and Italy. A small part of Turkey lies within the area generally defined as "Europe," and Turkey has a number of important ties to Europe, so it is covered briefly as well.

Separated from France by the jagged Pyrenees Mountains, the Iberian Peninsula is surrounded by the waters of the Atlantic Ocean and the Mediterranean. Gibraltar on the south coast of the peninsula has a commanding position, controlling the strategic Straits of Gibraltar between these two water bodies (see Inset 10-1). With over 230,000 sq miles (596,900 sq km), 66 percent of the total territory, and 40 percent of the population of Southern Europe, Iberia has the largest area of Southern

INSET 10-1

GIBRALTAR

Gibraltar, situated at the extreme south of the Iberian Peninsula, is a distinct limestone rock mass, 1394 ft (425 m) at its highest elevation and 2.32 sq miles (6 sq km). The present population is about 30,000. Strategically, the rock controls the narrow straits through which the surface waters of the Mediterranean flow into the Atlantic. Gibraltar's border with Spain was closed in 1969 as a protest against British control since 1704. However, the land frontier was opened again in February 1985, a forerunner of Spain's entry into the EC in January 1986. Presently, there is considerable trade between Spain

and Gibraltar. About 1000 Spaniards are also employed on "the rock," and Spanish construction companies are active in Gibraltar's real estate boom. The rock's tourist trade expanded from only 600,000 visitors in 1984 to over 3 million by 1992, aided in part by its airport. It also has become a growing offshore financial center, with over 3800 tax-exempt registered companies and branches or representative offices for 15 British and foreign banks. Many of the clients are drawn from the 300,000-strong British expatriate community on the Costa del Sol.

Europe's three peninsulas. Jutting into the Atlantic as far as western Ireland, the northwest of Iberia has a wet and mild climate that is influenced by the ocean. Because of its size and rectangular shape, interior locations on the peninsula have their own mini-continental character with a wide range of precipitation and temperatures between the summer and winter seasons. In addition, a complicated geologic structure has resulted in deposits of resources such as iron ore, mercury, potash, and pyrites that are commercially viable.

Unlike the Italian and Grecian peninsulas, the mountain ranges in Iberia trend east-west rather than north-south. Historically, this has separated Iberia into distinct political and cultural regions. Five main ranges and five great river valleys can be differentiated. From north to south these mountain chains or *cordilleras* are the Cantabrian-Pyrenees, the Castillan Mountains, the Iberian chain, the Sierra Morena, and the Sierra Nevada. Only one of the principal rivers, the Ebro, flows into the Mediterranean; the others, the Duro, Tagus, Guadiana, and Guadalquivir, rise in the east and flow into the Atlantic, thus emphasizing the east-west tilt of the peninsula.

Stretching from the glaciated Alps to southern Sicily, the Italian peninsula and the islands of Sardinia and Sicily comprise 115,000 sq miles (301,000 sq km), or only 33 percent of the territory of Southern Europe but 47 percent of the population. The distance from the northern borders of Italy to the southern coast of Sicily, a few score miles from

Africa, is quite great—the same as from the Alps to southern Sweden. This lengthy landmass divides the Mediterranean into two separate basins. The peninsula can be delineated into a number of distinct physical regions, which include the Alpine peaks that form the Italian frontiers with the neighboring countries of France, Switzerland, Austria, and Slovenia (Fig. 10-1); the flat expanse of the Po Valley that has been Italy's traditional industrial and agricultural heartland; the volcanic region of Tuscany; and the elongated Apennines that form the peninsula's backbone.

The peninsula and adjacent islands that belong to Greece are the smallest of the major land areas

FIGURE 10-1 Windsurfers near the village of Limone on Lake Garda. The lake was formed by the scouring action of a glacier that originated in the Alps. (A. Diem)

of Southern Europe with only 51,000 sq miles (132,000 sq km), of 14.6 percent of the land area and 8.5 percent of the population. The country controls maritime movement between the Mediterranean and Black Sea through the Aegean waters. Although the land area is relatively limited, it is spread throughout the eastern Mediterranean over 500 miles (805 km) north-south and over 375 miles (600 km) east-west, with some of the islands, such as Rhodes and Kos, just a few miles from Turkey. There is also a large Greek population on the island of Cyprus.

Most of mainland Greece is composed of mountain ranges interspersed with numerous small intermontane basins. Related to this landscape, the country's early development resulted in independent city-states that occupied the low-lying lands for agricultural purposes. Even today, remote parts of Greece suffer from poor communication with the rest of the country. A number of rivers, including the Axios which flows into the Aegean west of Thessaloniki, the Pinios in Thessaly (east central Greece), and the Kephisos north of Athens, provide much needed waters for irrigation.

There are five main islands or clusters of islands in Southern Europe. Beginning in the west are the Balearics off the east coast of Spain. They include Formentera, Ibiza, Mallorca, and Menorca and are a continuation of the Sierra Nevada mountain range. Together they comprise just over 1930 sq miles (5000 sq km) and have a population of 768,000, a figure that does not include the millions of tourists who visit these islands annually. For example, Ibiza and Formentera alone host over 1 million tourists each year.

Corsica, part of France, and Sardinia, belonging to Italy, are found to the west of the Apennine Peninsula. With over 9200 sq miles (24,000 sq km) and over 1.5 million inhabitants, Sardinia is almost three times as large as Corsica and has a population six and one half times greater. Both islands are structurally part of "Hercynian" Europe, ancient mountain regions formed about 300 to 400 million years ago. Whereas Sardinia is integrated within the Italian state, many people on Corsica, because of separatist elements unappeased by a regional government, have still not completely reconciled themselves to inclusion within France. Thus, Corsica has been rocked by assassinations, murders, bombings, and arson for many years.

Separated from the toe of Italy by the narrow straits of Messina is Sicily, the largest island in the Mediterranean, 9900 sq miles (25,700 sq km), and the most populated (5.2 million inhabitants). Most of Sicily is geologically related to the Apennine Peninsula; however, the eastern tip is Hercynian in origin. The island's economy depends on agricultural exports, such as citrus fruits and wine, some industry, tourism, and especially on an illegal drug trade that is controlled by the Mafia.

Less than 60 miles (100km) south of Sicily is Malta, a set of islands that became a republic in 1974. Only 122 sq miles (315 sq km), by far the smallest of the islands discussed in this section, Malta had a population of 362,000 in 1993. Without natural resources or an agricultural base, the islands depend on industry, trade, and tourism for prosperity.

Crete, southeast of Greece's Peloponnesos Peninsula, and Cyprus in the eastern Mediterranean south of Turkey, are the remaining significant islands. Crete is structurally related to the Dinaric Mountains that sweep south through the Greek mainland and Peloponnesos before trending eastward. With nearly 3500 sq miles (9000 sq km), it is the largest of the islands of Greece, and was only united with the mainland in 1913 (Fig. 10-2). Cyprus 3550 sq miles (9200 sq km), structurally a continuation of the Taurus ranges of Turkey, became an independent republic in 1959, but has been divided into two distinct political units as a result of the Turkish invasion of 1974.

FIGURE 10-2 Snow-covered mountains of the Psiloítis Range in western Crete during the month of June. Meltwaters play an important role in irrigation at lower altitudes. (A. Diem)

Similarities among the three peninsulas and the islands include basic physiographic and climatic conditions as well as vegetation associated with the Mediterranean climate, although the climate has been modified everywhere to different degrees by humans. There are high mountains that are covered with deep snows during the winter months. The population tends to be the densest along the coasts of Iberia and Greece, whereas on the Italian peninsula, interior locations, especially in the Po Valley, are significant for their concentration of inhabitants. Specialized agricultural products, many of which require irrigation, are typical of the Mediterranean region. Reliance on the growing of fruits, vegetables, olives, and grapes for manufacture of wine is evident (Fig. 10-3). For the most part, these crops, the cultivation of which has been aided by EU monies, are in surplus and are often "dumped," that is, sold at low cost, often abroad. Italy has also developed an important animal husbandry and dairy industry.

All areas lack large quantities of basic resources, especially oil, coal, and natural gas (hydrocarbons), although this is changing some-what because of offshore drilling and the discovery of both gas and oil. Furthermore, freshwater shortages are endemic. Portugal, Spain, Italy, and Greece depended on agriculture as the mainstay of their economies for a longer time than did countries in Central and Northern Europe and were late to industrialize. All four had nationalized many industries that later became uncompetitive and were chronic drains on their respective country's economy, losing hundreds of millions or billions of dollars annually. All the countries are now trying to privatize their state holdings, are seeking foreign investment, and are searching for high-tech industries and specialized products to manufacture in order to secure their economic future in both European and world markets. Finally, all of the countries of Southern Europe, because of their Mediterranean climate and classical ruins, have significant tourist industries that on the one hand contribute handsomely to their balance of payments and on the other hand create serious environmental problems.

Though historically not a part of Southern Europe in the strictest sense, Turkey must be

FIGURE 10-3 The hills of Tuscany near the Etruscan city of Volterra south of Florence. Vineyards are evident in the foreground. The olive trees in the background were killed by the severe winter of 1985. (A. Diem)

included in the geography of the area. The territory comprising European Turkey (part of Thrace), which borders on Greece and Bulgaria, and the immense peninsula of Asian Turkey, which borders Syria, Iraq, Iran, and the new republics carved out of the former Soviet Union, are all that is left from the vast holdings of the Ottoman Empire. Before the First World War, that realm extended from the Balkans to Mesopotamia and included sections of present-day Greece and the former Yugoslavia, and most of the countries of the current "Middle East" (also referred to as Southwest Asia). Turkey is somewhat larger in size than the state of Texas and borders on both the Black and Mediterranean seas.

A continuing factor that contributes to Turkey's strategic significance is its control of the Dardanelles, the Sea of Marmara, and the Bosporus, the water bodies that connect the Black and Mediterranean seas. Though by international agreement only warships require permission to pass through the narrow, dangerous passage, Turkey can block their entry in time of war. The Bosporus, one of the world's most crowded waterways, is under increasing pressure, because maritime traffic has expanded sharply following the collapse of the Soviet Union. Traffic will continue to grow because of the opening of the Main-Danube Canal connecting Rotterdam with the Black Sea and because of oil exports from Kazakhstan and Azerbaijan to Europe. Turkish fears of accidents on the narrow Bosporus are well founded; in March 1994, a tanker collision left many dead and serious pollution from an oil spill. Fewer than half of the 40,000 vessels that traverse the Bosporus yearly take a pilot on board, and, thus, the Turkish authorities have tightened regulations covering the passage of large vessels. Another strategic factor is the headwaters of the Euphrates and Tigris rivers, which rise in the mountains of eastern Turkey. Both rivers are vital for agriculture in Syria and Iraq. However, Turkey, because of the construction of giant dams and irrigation projects, controls the ultimate amount of water that reaches its neighbors.

The country may be divided into three general geographic regions. European Turkey consists of the plateau of Thrace, a continuation of the same structure in Greece. Asian Turkey comprises the vast Anatolian Plateau bordered in the north by the Pontic Mountains that plunge into the Black Sea and in the south by the Taurus that rim the Mediterranean coast. The extreme east, characterized by a continental climate, includes the mountains of Armenia in the north and of Kurdistan in the south. The biblical Mount Ararat, a volcano of 16,950 ft (5167 m), forms a section of the frontier with Armenia.

Post–1945 Development Stages

Economic development in Southern Europe after the Second World War can best be understood by examining three distinct stages. The first gathered momentum during the 1960s and gradually ran out of steam in the early 1970s. At this time, all of Western Europe was experiencing an economic renaissance as it recovered from the tremendous damage wrought by World War II. New capital expenditures were evident, often funded by government sources, and private companies were expanding. For Southern Europe, this meant a break with the past, as heavy industry was sited on what was in many instances coastal locations that had never been utilized or were under agricultural cultivation. Thus, refineries, steel mills, and shipyards sprouted in such places as the estuary of the Tagus River near Lisbon, the Mediterranean coast north of Valencia, the mouth of the Rhône River west of Marseille, the heel of Italy adjacent to Taranto, and west of Athens near the island of Salamis.

For the most part, development was capital- rather than labor-intensive; it used large chunks of terrain, and polluted the land, air, and water. Because of the oil crisis of the 1970s, increasing competition from the Far East and Third World countries, and a drop in demand for products such as ships and steel, and commodities such as oil, these industries went into decline during the late 1970s and early 1980s.

A second stage of development was related to tourism, for which Southern Europe is strategically placed because of a unique combination of historical and cultural factors, a Mediterranean climate that guaranteed sun, the azure waters of a great water body, superb scenery, and fascinating ruins that included Minoan, Greek, Etruscan, and Roman examples (Fig. 10-4). Prior to World War II, tourism was concentrated in a number of select resorts such as Cascais on the Atlantic coast near Lisbon, San Sebastian on the northeast coast of Spain, Nice and Menton in France, nearby Monaco, and the Ligurian Riviera west and east of Genoa in Italy. For the most part, tourism was for the wealthy few rather than for the masses, and its economic and physical impact was limited. The pattern changed during the 1960s and 1970s. As Western Europe became more affluent, tourism for the masses developed. A growth industry emerged that required a modern infrastructure of highways, railroads, and airports; water and sewage systems; accommodations; and the "development" of the natural amenities of Southern Europe. Land that had remained relatively undisturbed for centuries was now subjected to the full impact of modern technology. High-rise dwellings and condos replaced fishing villages and forests. In short, the values of urban Europe overwhelmed the values of rural, "sleepy" Southern Europe. Today, there is barely a stretch of natural coast from southern Portugal to Naples. Development for tourism has also affected Greece, Malta, and southern Cyprus and has spread to the west and south coasts of Turkey.

The third stage of development is presently occurring. Realizing that the industrial future of the area will be better served by less-polluting, labor-intensive, high-tech and consumer product industries, rather than traditional heavy industries, the countries of Southern Europe are rationalizing and selling off state-controlled companies and searching for private companies that would like to invest in state-of-the-art enterprises. Domestic and foreign firms have been attracted, including a number from Japan. Competition is keen, and the results so far have been mixed. For every carefully planned science park such as that found at Sophia Antipolis between Cannes and Nice (5000 people employed, with tenants including IBM and Hewlett-Packard), there have been laissez-faire equivalents similar to the small factories sited without environmental consideration within the valleys of the Apennines north of Genoa, between Bologna and Florence (Italy), and in the suburbs of Barcelona in northeastern Spain.

Because of world competition, economic restructuring, and the severe recession of the early and mid-1990s, all the countries of Southern Europe have seen a decline in economic growth. Nevertheless, the infrastructure for tourism continues to be developed, with much irrevocable damage being done to the unique natural landscape and ecosystem. A key question remains unanswered. How will Southern Europe continue to be developed so that employment levels remain high and the very amenities that attracted tourists in the past be preserved for both future tourists and the indigenous population?

Overview of Economic Development, Tourism, and Environmental Degradation

Both economic development, which includes industrialization and increasing numbers of motor vehicles, and the growth of tourism have been responsible for Southern Europe's currently severe environmental and social problems. Three areas have been hardest hit, all of which have fragile ecosystems. They are the Pyrenees Mountains, forming the border between Spain and France; the Alpine regions of Southern France and Italy; and the Mediterranean coast and sea.

The Alps and Pyrenees have been affected by (1) indiscriminate dumping of solid waste and raw

FIGURE 10-4 The tourist attraction of the Pantheon in the Piazza della Rotonda, Rome. The building was built in 27 B.C. by Marcus Agrippa, restored by Hadrian in A.D. 120–125, and converted into the Christian church of Santa Maria Rotonda in 609. (A. Diem)

garbage; (2) air pollution, from older metallurgical industries and from dense vehicular traffic, made worse by temperature inversions (warm, polluted air trapped beneath a blanket of cooler, denser air, especially in mountain valleys); (3) water pollution in Alpine lakes, resulting from lack of adequate sewage facilities and the runoff of pesticides, herbicides, and fertilizers from agricultural enterprises; and (4) the cutting of forests and the erosion of terrain in ski-related developments.

Despite harsh climates at high altitudes, lack of space because of rugged terrain, and limited areas for construction owing to avalanche dangers, tourist expansion in Southern Europe's mountain regions has not been planned and continues unchecked. Future consequences will include increased flooding and landslides similar to that which ravaged parts of the Italian Alps during the exceptionally wet summer of 1987 and again in the autumns of 1993 and 1994.

Presently, there is serious air and water pollution throughout the Mediterranean realm. Cities such as Athens, Nice, Milan, Rome, and Barcelona have been hard hit by ozone and smog formed from industrial and vehicular emissions. Enormous damage has been done to historical monuments and buildings, and the health of humans has been affected. Trees are dead and dying throughout the Alpine arc and especially along the highways that funnel traffic through the mountains. Indiscriminate dumping of noxious substances such as industrial chemicals, garbage, sewage, and solid toxic waste is evident and has fouled much of the coastline and polluted the sea. Forests have been illegally cut in Greece so that construction can occur. Forest fires, often set by pyromaniacs during high wind and drought, have destroyed tens of thousands of acres throughout Spain, southern France, Corsica, and Greece, where because of a unique Mediterranean climate, woodlands are necessary for the survival of the ecosystem. A sunken oil tanker off of the Ligurian coast near Genoa is a time bomb waiting to release its cargo of oil when the vessel rusts through. Finally, the Mediterranean Sea, once famous for its giant tunas, dolphins, sponges, and coral, has become, because of overfishing and pollution, a virtually dead sea.

Traffic problems during the spring and summer holiday seasons resemble those in the great cities of Central and Northern Europe. Especially hard hit have been the Algarve in southern Portugal, the Costa Brava and Costa del Sol in Spain, the Côte d'Azur in France, and the Ligurian Riviera in Italy. In these areas, because of topographic limitations, cars, trucks, and buses are forced to use one or two coastal roads or the toll highway. Chaos ensues!

Many of the Greek Cyclade Islands southeast of Athens and the Balearic Islands of Spain have been transformed into playgrounds for tourists and retirement colonies for Northern Europeans, irrevocably altering the physical, cultural, and economic character of the areas, with little consideration given for the local residents. Land speculation and urban sprawl are everywhere; the Costa Brava, Costa del Sol, and Côte d'Azur bear witness to this phenomenon. Unfortunately, the cost of servicing and maintaining what are mainly unplanned developments falls on local communities. And finally, criminals, often professionals from elsewhere, prey on unsuspecting tourists and pensioners, marring their "carefree" lives.

A type of modern feudalism is developing whereby local populations, though benefiting somewhat economically, must subordinate their lives to the needs and whims of tourist hordes. Discos, water-slides, motorcycle tracks, high-rise apartments, and shopping centers encroach on fishing villages and the rural countryside and on the mountain valleys of the Pyrenees and Alps. Development capital often comes from abroad; thus, the bulk of profits also goes abroad and does not pay for the needed infrastructure. Most tourists, coming from crowded urban areas of Europe, are unconcerned about environmental degradation in holiday resorts. They are unaware of the delicate ecological balance of the Alpine and Mediterranean world that is fast being altered and destroyed. The end result will be the ruination of two of Europe's most unique natural landscapes.

To be sure, some positive attempts have been made to limit degradation in the Mediterranean region under the sponsorship of the Mediterranean Action Plan of the United Nations' Environment Program. For example, cities such as

Naples and Genoa in Italy, and Marseille, Nice, and Toulon in France, finally have or are building sewage treatment plants. Beaches are also being monitored for pollution. Nevertheless, it is still too early to know whether the tide of degradation is being reversed. The question of how the Southern European economies will continue to expand, so that employment remains high and the amenities that attract tourists are preserved, has not been addressed. Two case studies of the clash of economic forces and Southern Europe's fragile environment follow.

Venice: A City Threatened by Environmental Degradation

Where the North Italian Plain meets the Adriatic Sea, a variegated coast of lagoons, offshore bars, spits, and deltas has been formed (Fig. 10-5). The coastal region, or littoral, is constantly being altered by natural forces, such as tidal action, storms, and the deposits of the Po, Adige, Piave, and Tagliamento rivers, as well as by human actions, such as channel dredging, filling in of marshes, deposition of pollutants, and industry's use of underground freshwater supplies.

Venice, the city most affected by these conditions, was founded in the fifth century by mainland refugees fleeing from barbarian invaders. Originally built on a group of islands in the center of the Laguna Veneta, the city is now connected to its mainland industrial suburbs by a rail and road causeway that was built by the Austrians in the nineteenth century. The glorious period of the Venetian Republic, which reached its zenith at the beginning of the fifteenth century when it was the main commercial force in the eastern Mediterranean, provided the wealth to construct this unique island where internal movement is still by foot or boat.

The millions of tourists who visit Venice see the outward trappings of the city's wealthy past: great houses lining the Grand Canal, the Doge's Palace, and Piazza San Marco and its basilica. One might think that tourism, which injects tens of millions of dollars annually into the economy of the city, along with local industry, would be able to sustain the city's functions. Unfortunately, this is not the case. The romantic strains of orchestras playing in Piazza San Marco help shield the outsider from the *verità* that is contemporary Venice. The city is polluted and dying, losing its population, and slowly sinking beneath the waters of the Adriatic. High tides that sometimes cover Piazza San Marco are becoming more frequent as the city continues to subside about an inch (2–3 cm) every 10 years. The stability of buildings is being undermined. The backwash from motorboats that carry out all the urban functions, from hauling garbage to burying the dead, is one of the main causes of the rotting of building foundations, nearly all of which are on wooden pilings sunk into the lagoon bed.

Basic factors in the decline of Venice are the city's critical shortage of housing and its living conditions that would be unacceptable anywhere else in northern Italy. Between 1951 and 1971, about 70,000 Venetians fled to the mainland from decaying, unhealthy, water-soaked, and rat-infested buildings. The islands' population dropped from 176,000 to well under 100,000 by 1990, the lowest figure since the late nineteenth century, whereas the number of people living in the mainland industrial suburbs of Porto Marghera and Mestre increased from 96,000 to over 200,000, many of whom commute daily to work in Venice.

Two opposing forces have been competing to shape future developments. On one side are technocrats who wish to further the industrial expansion that began in the early years of the twentieth century when Porto Marghera was reclaimed from the mainland marshes. Here are concentrated large-scale refining, metallurgical, engineering, and chemical industries that continued to expand in the postwar period, contributing to air and water pollution. In addition, a vast industrial zone of 7900 acres (3110 ha) has been created by filling in marshy sections of the mainland to the south. Ships going to Porto Marghera may cross the Laguna Veneta by a deep-water channel that passes next to Piazza San Marco. However, a new channel has been completed directly to Porto Marghera through the Porto di Malamocco to the south of Venice.

These developments are most disturbing to those groups that envisage Venice as the heart of a much larger economic region that would include the nearby cities of Padova and Treviso. According to the association known as *Italia Nostra*, a group

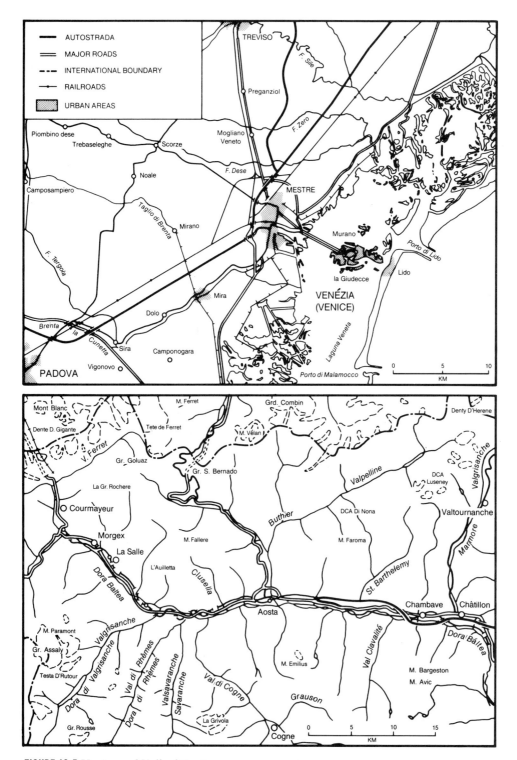

FIGURE 10-5 Venice and Valle d'Aosta.

that has endeavored to defend the country's historical monuments and landscape from disfigurement by ruthless developers and speculators, present industrialization is destroying Venice. *Italia Nostra* points out that air pollution is defacing architectural masterpieces. They also claim that the new deep channels will intensify the flow of high tides into the lagoons and that filling in of coastal marshes will deprive the lagoons of a buffer against which high tides used to spend themselves harmlessly by flooding the marsh islets. Moreover, a third industrial area whose enterprises would require more fresh water from underground wells would hasten the subsidence of the whole lagoon bed, including Venice. New industry, according to *Italia Nostra,* should be built well back from the coast nearer to Padova and Treviso, and these cities should be linked by a high-speed railway that would tunnel under the lagoon to Venice. Another alternative would be to develop an industrial zone near Rovigo at the mouth of the Po.

The strain on the historical center of Venice is further compounded by the enormous growth of tourism that at times has suffocated the city. Over 8 million tourists attack Venice each year, many of whom stay in relatively new hotels that have been constructed on the offshore bar of the Litorale del Cavallino and take the ferry to and from Venice. The garbage problem alone from these hordes has necessitated the banning of picnic lunches in Piazza San Marco; plastic garbage receptacles studded throughout the piazza detract from the harmony of its visual attraction. At peak periods, such as Easter and carnival, the police have had to close the causeway from the mainland in order to prevent a gridlock of humans.

Added to pollution related to tourism is industrial air pollution from the mainland and solid organic and toxic wastes that are discharged or dumped into lagoons and canals. Thus, most of the major ingredients contributing to environmental catastrophe are evident. Not only has the city been threatened by high tides and floods, but also during the summer of 1988 tons of algae formed in the lagoons because of phosphate and nitrogen pollution, killing fish, causing a nauseating smell, and resulting in a proliferation of insects because of the death of marine life.

Fortunately, there is a positive side to this bleak picture. The Italian and Venetian governments, international agencies (e.g., UNESCO), and individual benefactors have restored damaged buildings and art works, reduced pollution, closed off artesian wells, provided water from mainland rivers, and upgraded housing. Folding barriers have been proposed at the three seaward entrances of the Laguna Veneta to help control high tides, although there is a question as to whether they will ever be built. Finally, the EU is partially funding a sophisticated computer program that will be used in Venice to provide a database to catalogue levels of pollution, their sources, and the type of emissions pouring into local waters. This has already been done for the industrial complex of Porto Marghera. The focus has shifted to Venice itself and to nearby Murano, famous for its artisanal glass. Both areas are large polluters. Venice daily accounts for vast amounts of human wastes that are dumped into the lagoon with other residues from thousands of service industries such as hotels and restaurants. Murano adds such pollutants as arsenic and lead which are used in the making of glass. The database will be supplemented by chemical analysis of lagoon water by automatic instruments, thus providing local governments with hard data that can be used to force offenders to alter their ways.

The solutions to Venice's problems must be balanced with other interests in the 214 sq miles (550 sq km) of the Venetian lagoon, which includes Italy's largest petrochemical complex at Mestre, employing 15,000 workers. Fortunately, there has been a shift from a purely engineering approach to one that incorporates environmental factors, such as restoring wetlands and bringing lost sediments back into the lagoon. Furthermore, the scandal and corruption that were evident in past government attempts to solve the problems of Venice have been exposed and are unlikely to be repeated in the near future.

Venice provides a striking example of how a coastal city can be affected environmentally within a matrix of unique historical, cultural, economic, human, and geographical factors. The next example, the Valle d'Aosta, illuminates a similar situation within the geographical realm of the Alps of Southern Europe.

Valle d'Aosta, Italy: Environmental Impact Almost completely enclosed by Western Europe's highest mountains, which include Mont Blanc and the Matterhorn, the Valle d'Aosta in northwestern Italy on the Swiss and French borders has been an important alpine routeway from prehistoric times to the present, because of the nearby Great and Little Saint Bernard passes. The two passes became less important during the first half of the twentieth century when rail lines, such as those on the Gotthard and Simplon routes, first tunneled through the Alps. Another negative factor was that both of the St. Bernard passes were closed during the winter months, usually from November to June, isolating the Aosta Valley from the rest of Europe. Then in 1964, the 3.5 mile (5.6 km) long Great Saint Bernard Tunnel connecting the Aosta Valley with Valais, Switzerland was opened to vehicular traffic; and in 1965, the 7 mile (11.3 km) long Mont Blanc Tunnel between Courmayeur and Chamonix, France, was completed. The impact on the Valle d'Aosta has been enormous. Since the opening of the two tunnels, over 48.2 million vehicles, including millions of heavy diesel trucks and tour buses, have passed through, 76 percent using the Mont Blanc and 24 percent the Grand Saint Bernard routes. No longer isolated, Aosta has been thrust into the mainstream of Europe. Traffic brings pollution, and areas at both ends of the tunnels have suffered. For example, the forests around Chamonix are dying or dead because of acidification and particle fallout.

The Valle d'Aosta, like Venice, depends on tourism for its main economic input (Fig. 10-6). In fact, tourism has become a dominant force in the economy at a time when the valley's traditional industries, such as textiles, mining, and steel, have been contracting. Like Venice, environmental degradation is threatening to erode the very foundations of Aosta's newfound wealth.

The advent of tourism dates back to 1736 when travelers were already writing about the beauties of the valley, such as spectacular mountain scenery and magnificent Roman and medieval remains. By 1830, a thermal spa had been established at Près-Saint Didier near Courmayeur. In 1850 a society of mountain guides was founded at

Courmayeur to take care of an increasing number of English climbers. Later, the royal families of the Kingdom of Savoy and Sardinia hunted ibex in the valleys of the Gran Paradiso. In 1923 a national park was created in this area south of Cogne to protect the unique flora and fauna. At both Courmayeur and Breuil-Cervinia, skiing was already underway before World War II.

Unfortunately, postwar development, spurred by mass tourism, has irrevocably altered the natural environment. A combination of the highways (autostrada), the two tunnels, and expansion of resorts in nearby valleys has, in so many instances, brought forth the undesirable aspects of tourism. Rivers and streams have been polluted; garbage is found everywhere; dumping of solid waste from construction and renovation is uncontrolled; graveling and quarrying is carried out with little regard for scenery and ecology; traffic congestion during the winter and summer tourist seasons is considerable, contributing noise and pollutants that compromise the Alpine ambiance; many of the buildings are more typical of architecture in Milan or Turin than the Alps; and uncontrolled urban sprawl has created a mess in the main valley. Finally, the construction of the last autostrada link west of Aosta to the Mont Blanc Tunnel in the early 1990s has all but destroyed the natural bed of the valley's main river, the Dora Baltea. One positive factor has been the reduction of air and water pollutants that have spewed forth from the steel mill in Aosta since its construction in the 1920s owing to cutbacks in production. Some efforts have also been made to control development in order to preserve the mountain milieu, as witnessed in Courmayeur and in Pila above Aosta. However, in contrast, the expansion of Breuil-Cervinia has desecrated terrain at the base of the Matterhorn.

To be sure, because of the impact of tourism, the Valle d'Aosta has become one of the most prosperous regions in Southern Europe. However, during its transformation from a valley dependent on agriculture and heavy industry to one relying on tourism, the unique physical and cultural characteristics of the Valley have been irreparably degraded.

FIGURE 10-6 Expansion of hotels and apartments at the base of the Matterhorn, Breuil-Cervinia, Valle d'Aosta. (A. Diem)

SOUTHERN EUROPE: A REGIONAL OVERVIEW

Portugal

Portugal, independent since the twelfth century, is one of the oldest countries in Europe. Occupying more than one-sixth of the Iberian Peninsula, the country, along with the islands of the Azores and Madeira, comprises Metropolitan Portugal, an area roughly the same size as Austria, with 9.9 million inhabitants in 1993. Continental Portugal has a variety of distinct landscapes, most of which are part of Hercynian Europe. The country is the only one in Southern Europe that faces the Atlantic and has been described as an oceanic oasis on the western edge of the arid Spanish Meseta. The main rivers of Portugal, the Douro in the north and the Tagus in the center, flow off the Meseta to the Atlantic and are navigable upstream as far as the Spanish frontier. The mountains of east central

Portugal, the central ridge of the Estrela, are almost 6200 ft (2000 m) high. The lower uplands of the Algarve in the south are western continuations of Spanish ranges.

The Tagus divides Portugal into two distinct regions. North of the river the land is mostly mountainous; in the south undulating lowlands predominate. There are other contrasts between north and south in climate, vegetation, land use, and economic activity. The north is wetter, and its annual temperature range is less than in the south, where dry summers necessitate irrigation. In the north corn, rye, and grapes are the main crops, whereas cultivation of wheat, oats, and the cork oak predominate in the south. Furthermore, the greatest population densities are found in the north, as is the largest concentration of industry.

During the sixteenth century, Portugal was a powerful maritime state and a leader during the age of discovery. The country was united as a geographical entity by the attraction of the Atlantic and by the navigable rivers that linked the coast to the interior. By contrast, the frontier with Spain was a rugged, sparsely populated area with limited appeal. Only today, when both countries are members of the EU, is this isolation beginning to break down.

Portugal's golden age of grandeur has long since faded, and the country, once a world power, today plays a quite modest role on the European scene. Portugal's colonial legacy was finally dissolved in the middle 1970s. With a per capita GDP of only $8688 in 1993 ($11,953 at Purchasing Power Parities—PPPs), Portugal was one of the poorest countries in the EU (just above Greece) and one of the least industrialized.

During the late 1960s and early 1970s, Portugal, unlike Spain, did not experience an economic boom. The development of a modern economy has been hindered by the fragmentation of local industry, lack of technological research, small size of the home market, bureaucratic red tape, traditional protection of inefficient enterprises, and curbs on domestic competition. Emigration of workers from the most productive age groups, in excess of 2 million, has also had serious effects on the economy. Furthermore, during the late 1960s and early 1970s there was a massive hemorrhage of resources as

Portugal engaged in an unsuccessful struggle to hold on to its African colonies.

Since 1960, the economy has undergone considerable structural change, particularly in the expansion of industry. In 1953 industry accounted for only 28 percent of GDP. By 1975, this figure had risen to 42.7 percent; but by 1992 it had dropped again to 33.1 percent as services played a more important part in the economy. These figures must be understood within the context of a large "black" economy, especially in construction, which has been estimated to be equivalent to 22 percent of GDP. During the period 1975–1981, industrial employment increased from about 25 percent of the labor force to 37 percent. However, by 1993 it had dropped to 33 percent. Employment in agriculture, forestry, and fishing dropped from 48 percent to about 11 percent, and services climbed from 28 percent to 55 percent in the same year.

In 1993 Portugal had a greater percentage of the working population in the primary sector than any other country in the EU, except for Greece. The diminutive size of farm holdings in the north, and the larger, generally underused *latifundia* (large landholdings) in the south, combined with the ever-increasing flight of rural population to cities and abroad, have precluded a satisfactory development of agriculture. There was general disruption because of a land reform introduced in 1974 that split up large estates in the south and redistributed land to tenants and farm laborers. In part, this has now been reversed. In addition, imposed low food prices helped to keep agricultural investment and production down, resulting in the importation of large quantities of food. This has changed as a result of the Common Agricultural Policy (CAP) of the EU which has raised the price of food. Today, domestic production is facing stiff competition, because Portugal has been flooded with surplus agricultural products from the rest of the Union. Although Portuguese agriculture represents nearly 6 percent of GDP and under 12 percent of employment, yields per acre are less than a third of the European average.

The mining sector has seen an impressive expansion in mineral exploitation, mainly because of the opening of the large Neves Corvo mine in the Alentejo region east of Lisbon near the Spanish border. Here, the output of copper rocketed from 300 tons in 1985 to 152,000 in 1993, the highest figure in Western Europe. Portugal is also a leading producer of tin and tungsten as well as an important source of uranium, zinc, silver, gold, and precious stones.

Indigenous energy resources, with the exception of poor quality coal and waterpower, are limited. Thus, Portugal is dependent on foreign energy sources for about 92 percent of primary consumption, mainly of oil. With EU backing, a natural gas network is being constructed. Textiles and clothing are the largest industries, employing nearly 25 percent of the manufacturing workforce and accounting for 20 percent of the value of manufacturing output. Other significant sectors are chemicals and plastics, vehicles and parts, food processing, pulp and paper, the production of cork, and ship repairs. South of Lisbon in the district of Setubal, a Ford-Volkswagen plant in an industrial park represents the biggest foreign investment in the country. One high-tech company EFACE, a firm based in Oporto, manufactures electric motors, switchgear, and transformers for domestic and export markets. Iberomoldes, founded in 1975 in the Marinha Grande region north of Lisbon, has evolved into a center for plastic factories and excels in precision mould-making, counting among its clients Volvo, Electrolux, and Black & Decker. The government is committed to supporting viable modern companies and to phasing out those firms that cannot compete in the international marketplace.

Tourism, focused on the Lisbon area, the Porto region, the southern coast of the Algarve, and the island of Madeira off the Moroccan coast, has boosted the service sector and accounted for 4.4 percent of GDP in 1992, the second highest figure in Western Europe after Austria (Fig. 10-7). The country hosted over 8.4 million visitors and took in over $4 billion in tourist receipts in 1993, representing a nearly 350-percent increase since 1983. During the same period, expenditures by Portuguese abroad increased by over 350 percent and amounted to over $1.9 billion. Thus, the country posted a positive balance of tourism of $2.1 billion.

Portugal imports more than it exports. However, the current account (balance of all in- and out-

FIGURE 10-7 Tourist development at Albufeira on the Algarve of southern Portugal. (A. Diem)

flowing funds within the economy), after running a deficit for many years, has swung back and forth from positive to negative since 1985. In 1993 the EU received over 75 percent of exports and was the source of 72 percent of imports. Germany was the largest trading partner for exports, receiving 20 percent, whereas Spain provided the largest amount of imports with 18 percent.

A major economic boost for Portugal has been investment in industry, tourism, service, commerce, and the stock market by its EU partners, former EFTA members, and non-European countries, especially the United States and Japan. In 1987 investment was $437 million, over 2.5 times the figure for 1986. Then in 1988 it rose to $1.1 billion and shot up to $7.2 billion in 1991. The Gulf War, the recession in the early 1990s, and the attraction of Eastern Europe have since reduced foreign investment; in 1993 it was only $1.2 billion. The UK, with a strong thrust in the tourist sector, has led foreign investors, followed by Spain. Spain alone has over 300 companies in Portugal engaged in various sectors, including wholesaling, services, manufacturing, and food processing. American companies have been big investors and are represented by firms such as Coca-Cola, Mobil, Ford, and Citibank.

A key factor in the surge of investments has been one of the lowest labor costs in the EU. Now that goods can be shipped throughout the EU without tariffs or taxes, lower labor costs are being sought by firms with headquarters in Portugal's main trading partners (Germany, Spain, and France). A production location in Portugal can often lead to higher profits for companies.

On the surface, the economy appears strong. Billions of ECUs (the EU's currency unit until the "euro" is introduced sometime in the future) have been injected by the EU, and many vital infrastructure projects, such as highways, bridges, and irrigation projects, have been completed, although waste, corruption, and environmental damage have been documented. Between 1986 and 1990, the country received ECU 2.9 billion and is scheduled to gain another 4.45 billion between 1994 and 2000. Most of this investment will be spent on transport infrastructure and will create approximately 100,000 jobs. However, the country's health, education, and social security systems remain weak.

Portugal's economic growth rate was 5 percent in 1987, then the highest in Europe, but declined to 1.1 percent in 1994. Inflation dropped to 5.3 percent the same year from 25 percent in 1985, although it is still too high in comparison to that of the country's major trading partners. Other serious economic weaknesses remain. The country has an accumulated public debt nearing 80 percent of GDP, which requires close to 10 percent of GDP annually for servicing. The annual budget deficit ranges from 8 to 10 percent of GDP, mainly because of accumulated public corporation liabilities. Thus, the apparent strength of the economy must be tempered by the knowledge that Portugal's financial foundation is weak.

To compete successfully in the European Union, Portugal must continue to streamline its government bureaucracy, allow more competition in the financial sector, and modernize and restructure formerly protected industries, especially those in the government sphere. Now that the country is part of a larger market, it must also further develop export possibilities, which is not an easy task. With the opening of the single European market in 1993 and the EEA in 1994, Portugal's industry and its backward agricultural sector have faced competition from far more advanced members of the EU, and cheaper and better quality goods have become plentiful. Finally, because of the collapse of the communist empire, European investment that might have gone to Portugal is occurring in

the Czech Republic, Hungary, and Poland. They can offer even lower wages than Portugal, a strong industrial base, skilled labor, and closer proximity to EU markets.

Spain

Spain, in the sixteenth century the most powerful country in Europe, is today striving to regain its former position as a cultural and geographical crossroads. The complex physical geography of the country, mainly mountains and tablelands, has encouraged the development of isolated and separated regions. The northeastern coastal areas of Catalonia (Cataluña), the Basque provinces on the north coast, and Galicia in the northwest are as different from each other as they are from the central areas of Aragon and Castile (Castilla La Nueva and Castilla La Vieja). Thus, Spain has always been plagued by fear of "Balkanization"—political disintegration into small, bickering states. For example, between 1977 and 1995, separatists in the Basque provinces, Catalonia, and Madrid took over 800 lives in terrorist attacks. The lack of a readily accepted capital such as Paris or London also hindered unity for a long period. The creation of Madrid as the capital in the late sixteenth century was artificial and never welded Spain into a unified country.

The second largest state in Europe after France, Spain is relatively sparsely populated with only 39.2 million inhabitants or 201 inhabitants per sq mile (78 per sq km) in 1996. By comparison, Italy had a population of 58 million or 498 per sq mile (190 per sq km). The most densely populated areas of Spain, over 648 persons per sq mile (250 per sq km), are found along the coast, whereas parts of the interior have densities as low as about 39 per sq mile (under 15 per sq km). Despite a booming economy from the 1960s through the 1980s, Spain is still a relatively poor country by European standards, with great disparities of wealth. Per capita income in 1986 was $5925 ($8050 PPP) and rose to $12,227 ($13,311 PPP) in 1993, the third lowest in Western Europe, after Greece and Portugal. One positive factor has been the growth of a strong middle class since the 1960s.

Data on the production of electricity mirror Spain's great industrial strides since World War II. In 1938 the country produced only 2.7 billion kwh of electricity, 81 percent of which was derived from hydroelectric sources. (The same year Italy produced 15.5 billion kwh.) In 1993 the figure for Spain was 156.2 billion kwh, 16 percent of which was generated by hydro sources and 36 percent by nuclear plants. Of a total primary energy production of 28.8 million tons of petroleum equivalent in 1992, 40 percent was accounted for by coal and lignite, reflecting the deposits in the northwest. Nuclear energy accounted for 47 percent. Oil and natural gas accounted for only .04 percent each; therefore, large quantities of these must be imported.

Ambitious industrial projects increased the percentage of the labor force engaged in industry from 27 percent in 1961 to over 37 in 1970. By 1992 the figure declined to 31 percent; the difference, common to most sophisticated countries, was taken up by services, over 59 percent of all employment in 1992.

Spanish industry is concentrated in three regions: the northeastern coast in the Basque provinces, Madrid, and Barcelona (Fig. 10-8). The disparity in living standards among these zones and the larger remaining parts of the country is considerable. For example, in 1991 the GDP-PPP per capita indicator in Spain in relation to the EU average (100) was 77.3; that of the northeast was 88.9, Catalonia 94.6, and Madrid 96.6; whereas the central region (excluding Madrid) was only 63 and the south 61.8 (Inset 10-2 and Figs. 10-9, 10-10).

A traditional lack of investment resulted in Spanish industry lagging technologically behind more advanced European countries. In recent years, a rapid rise in wage levels has largely deprived the country of its former cost advantage. A recent study on competitiveness put Spain in nineteenth place among OECD countries, with only Turkey, Portugal, and Greece making a poorer showing. The government has taken draconian steps to redress this situation. Industrial restructuring, known as *reconversión industrial*, is attempting to reverse long-standing policies that protected industry and expanded state control, thereby creating gross inefficiencies. This resulted in the loss of tens of thousands of jobs in the industrial sector

and has boosted unemployment from 3.7 percent in 1975 to over 20 percent in 1986. The actual level was somewhat lower because of a rapid expansion of the "black" economy. Nevertheless, about 1 million laborers in the industrial sector lost their jobs during 1976–1986, and the bloodletting has continued. In 1991 unemployment dropped to 16 percent; however, because of the recession among the Western countries in the early 1990s, it rose again to nearly 24 percent in 1994 and was over 39 percent among youth under 25 years of age. Hardest hit have been those industries that have been under pressure throughout the Western world: mining, steel, shipbuilding, and textiles. These have played a far greater role in the Spanish economy than in comparable European countries. For example, tonnage in shipbuilding dropped from 1.4 million launched in 1974 (fourth in the world) to 181,300 in 1986 (fifteenth), before reviving to 766,500 in 1993 (eighth).

The INI (Instituto Nacional de Industria), a state holding company set up after the Spanish Civil War to carry out an autarchic economic policy based on import substitution, is being revamped. It is hoped that this reorganization will stem the massive hemorrhage of tax funds needed to prop up its ailing industries which have cost Spanish taxpayers billions of dollars annually. Attempts are underway to sell off some state companies to the private sector and to restructure others. One result has been the sale of Seat, the state-owned automobile company, to Volkswagen. Nevertheless, much remains to be done before a meaningful transformation of the remaining state industries occurs.

The government has taken a number of steps to soften the *reconversión*, including offering early pensions and severance pay, and establishing a number of zones of priority reindustrialization (ZUR) in which new jobs are being created with the aid of large subsidies. A positive note has been the surge of investments that have been taking place from abroad. Companies such as Alcatel, AT&T, Ford, Fujitsu, Sony, Sanyo, Nissan, SKF, and Renault have invested well over $3 billion since 1985. In addition, Citicorp, Chase Manhattan, and Barclays have opened many branches in what was formerly a protected financial market. A key factor in foreign investment is

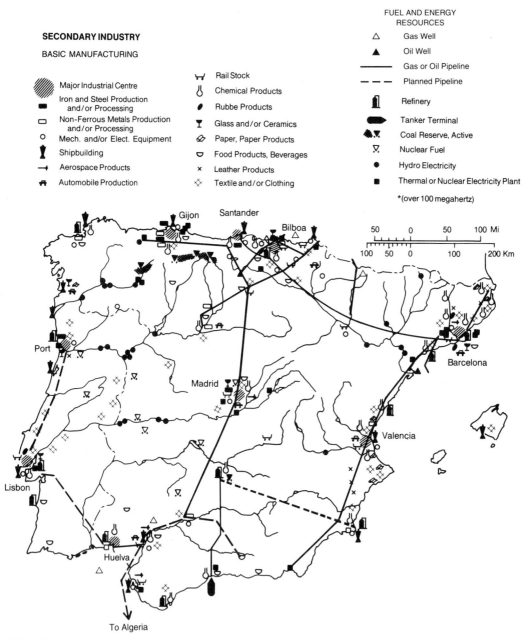

SECONDARY INDUSTRY

BASIC MANUFACTURING

	Major Industrial Centre
■	Iron and Steel Production and/or Processing
▫	Non-Ferrous Metals Production and/or Processing
○	Mech. and/or Elect. Equipment
⚱	Shipbuilding
→	Aerospace Products
⚘	Automobile Production

⊢⊣	Rail Stock
⚗	Chemical Products
⬤	Rubbe Products
⊻	Glass and/or Ceramics
⬨	Paper, Paper Products
▽	Food Products, Beverages
×	Leather Products
⋄	Textile and/or Clothing

FUEL AND ENERGY RESOURCES

△	Gas Well
▲	Oil Well
——	Gas or Oil Pipeline
- - -	Planned Pipeline
⬛	Refinery
⬛▶	Tanker Terminal
▲▼	Coal Reserve, Active
▽	Nuclear Fuel
●	Hydro Electricity
■	Thermal or Nuclear Electricity Plant

*(over 100 megahertz)

FIGURE 10-8 Manufacturing regions and resources in Iberia.

Spain's home market of over 39 million potentially affluent consumers.

Because of the rapid pace of economic change, certain regions such as Asturias in the northwest have suffered severely, whereas others such as Andalusia in the south have benefited. Asturias, because of obsolescence and high production costs, has seen a contraction of its mines, steel

THE BARCELONA REGION: A CASE STUDY OF URBANIZATION IN SOUTHERN EUROPE

An examination of the Barcelona region will provide the reader with an archetype of urban growth that has dramatically changed the face of Southern Europe in the last quarter of a century. By analyzing the city's development characteristics, we may better understand the continuing process of urbanization that has had powerful social and economic impacts on the countries of Southern Europe.

Barcelona, the capital of Catalonia, an autonomous region of Spain, is located on the Mediterranean in northeast Spain. The city region has the country's most diversified economy, accounting for 25 percent of Spain's industrial production and 20 percent of commerce. Within the boundaries of the region are found such dissimilar physical realms as the tourist playground of the Costa Brava, rice fields of the Ebro Delta, and isolated valleys of the Pyrenees.

The city of Barcelona encompasses three distinct physiographic zones: the coastal range, the pre-coastal depression, and the coastal plain. The coastal plain, where some of the most densely populated urban areas are to be found, is composed of recent alluvial debris from the Llobregat and Beos rivers that have formed a delta jutting into the Mediterranean. The coastal range parallels the coast and reaches 1679 ft (511 m). Barcelona's site, on the Mediterranean coast and encompassing two river valleys, has provided, on the one hand, a natural routeway to the trading areas of the world and, on the other hand, a gateway to the interior of Catalonia. Construction of the *autopistas* (toll highways) north to France, west to Zaragoza, and south to Valencia has reinforced the city's strategic situation.

Barcelona was founded by the Phoenicians, occupied by Carthage and Rome, and later became the capital of the Visigoths. By the thirteenth century, it was the largest banking and commercial center in Europe. Because the voyages of discovery diverted much trade to other continents, the city then stagnated. Population was just over 30,000 in the mid-fourteenth century and did not pass 60,000 until the mid-seventeenth century. However, by the end of the eighteenth century, as economic prospects improved, the city became the main destination for emigrants from Catalonia; close to 100,000 inhabitants were packed densely within the city's walls. Spurred by industrialization and the railways, population grew to nearly 190,000 by 1860 and by 1897 was over 300,000.

Thirty years later, Barcelona had grown to over 1 million, which at the time was the largest urban area in Spain. The city expanded into the surrounding countryside and annexed rural villages, in the process attracting immigrants from the coast as far south as Murcia and Almería as well as from the Balearic Islands. During the period 1850–1970, the shift of the central business district may be traced from within the narrow alleyways of the old city, north along the tree-lined Ramblas to the Plaza de Cataluna, and west along the broad diagonal to the modern complex of high apartments and striking office towers near the University, *ciutat universitària*.

The civil war and its aftermath was a dormant period of economic and demographic activity, especially since the city was an economic and political stronghold of the losing Republican side as well as the focus of the Catalan national identify. Spain's autarchic economic policy during the Second World War gradually gave way to more integrated economic relations with the rest of Europe and the city stirred from its lethargy—climbing from 1.3 million citizens in 1950 to 1.7 million in 1970 and reaching 1.8 million in 1990. Between 1960 and 1970, much of the growth was concentrated in the suburbs, with rural communities experiencing a 100 to 200 percent increase in population. This trend continues today as the city's residents try to escape congestion and high taxes. Two factors were originally responsible. First, in 1960 the city acquired a new municipal charter that facilitated the transfer of industry from the city to the outskirts as well as allowing the construction of large blocks of apartments outside the former municipal boundaries. Second, the necessary infrastructure, such as *autopistas*, the extension of the subway, and the enlargement of the airport and port, contributed to the urban growth.

A period of unplanned expansion ensued that was characterized by the establishment of industry and residences side by side, especially along the highways northeast to the Costa Brava. Responding to this growth, the Corporació de Barcelona (CMB) was created in 1974 and was responsible for such sectors as energy, transport, waste removal, and environmental control. The metropolitan area of Barcelona encompassed 185 sq miles (478 sq km) and had a population of 3 million in 1981 and 4 million by 1991. This represented about two-thirds of the population of Catalonia living on just over 10 percent of the region's territory. Characteristic of the CMB is a densely populated core, corresponding to the former boundaries of Barcelona, and a less dense suburban area.

In the mid- to late 1980s, a boom period developed, fueled by Spain's entry into the EC and by the awarding of the 1992 Olympics to the city. Foreign investment was strong, especially from Japan, and 118 firms, 85 percent of Japanese investment in Spain, were attracted to Barcelona. Projects rationalized the city's infrastructure, and the urban area was redeveloped to ensure further coordinated growth. New urban expressways were built, the subway system was extended, and the airport enlarged. A new container port is being built; however, rail connections to France and Madrid are archaic, because of the wide-gauge Spanish system. As a result of the economic success of the high-speed rail line between Madrid and Seville, prospects for Barcelona to link with Europe and Madrid have improved, despite the critical economic situation that the country found itself in during

1994. However, as a result of spending for the Olympics, Barcelona carries the highest debt of any Spanish city, over three times as high per capita as Madrid.

The CMB plays a predominant role in Spain's economy. For example, about 42 percent of the labor force is employed in the secondary sector compared to only 33 percent throughout Spain. The CMB is not an area of heavy industry, but rather its firms manufacture a diverse range of products, including automobiles, chemicals, electronic goods, textiles, and shoes. The industrial sector has experienced many problems. Because of staggering losses in 1993, SEAT was forced to close one of its factories in Barcelona by the parent Volkswagen and Nissan wants to reduce the labor force in its plant near the SEAT factory. Akzo, the Dutch chemicals and fibers group, also closed its Barcelona factory because of losses. The unions refused the Dutch proposal to restructure, thus emphasizing the negative effects of Spain's labor legislation/regulation. It is bureaucratic, job classification is rigid, and employment is fixed, all of which result in higher costs than necessary when the economy is in low gear, thereby making Spain less competitive among the southern EU countries. Like Spain, Barcelona has experienced a recent era of rapid development, but faces a number of challenges to maintain growth into the next century.

mills, and shipyards. The shipyards have prospered because of the International Exposition in Seville and the construction of a science and technology park, as well as the building of necessary infrastructure, such as bridges, highways, and a TGV train that links Madrid and Seville, 293 miles (471 km), in only two hours and forty-five minutes. The new train has been a financial success and carried close to 4 million passengers in 1994.

Progress in agriculture has been slow, but it is beginning to make an impact on living standards, especially in the once backward south. The percentage of the labor force employed in agriculture, forestry, and fishing continues to drop, hitting 10 percent in 1993 compared to 16 percent in 1986. In 1993 the primary sector accounted for about 5 percent of GDP compared to over 7 percent in 1976. There are great regional disparities. For example, in Galicia in the northwest, nearly 40 percent of the

active population works in largely subsistence farming, whereas in Catalonia less than 3 percent still engage primarily in agriculture.

Spurred by entry into the EC, enormous changes have occurred in Spain. Southern provinces such as Malaga, Almeria, and Huelva are being transformed into the "California" of Spain as millions of dollars of new investments have changed once arid regions into efficiently managed, irrigated tracts that are growing crops ranging from sunflowers, strawberries, and asparagus to kiwi fruit, avocados, and oranges (Fig. 10-11). Spain is supplying the EU with increasing quantities of such fruits and vegetables as tomatoes, potatoes, apricots, peaches, apples, melons, artichokes, eggplants, celery, cauliflower, cucumbers, and carrots.

Because of the expansion of irrigated areas, as well as a growing urban population that needs

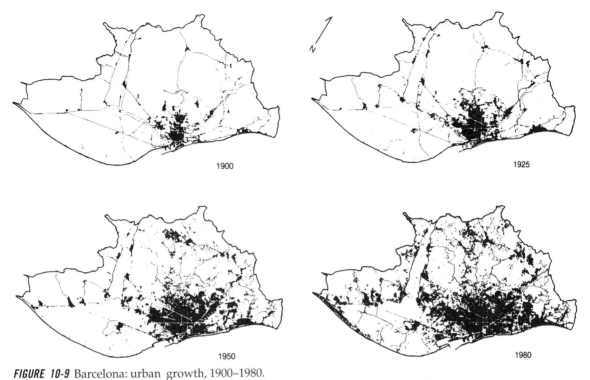

FIGURE 10-9 Barcelona: urban growth, 1900–1980.

FIGURE 10-10 The harbor and city of Barcelona, with the mountains of the Tibidabo in the background. (A. Diem)

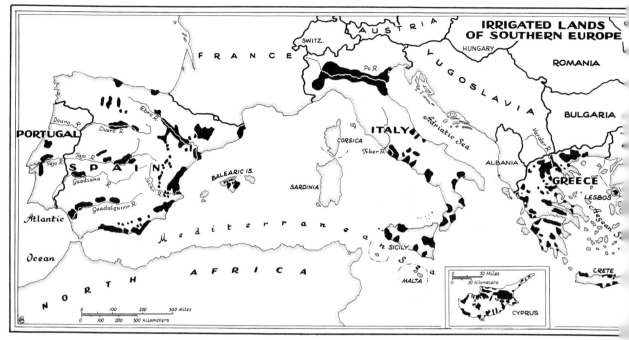

FIGURE 10-11 Irrigated lands of Southern Europe. This map suggests the extensiveness of irrigation in Portugal, Spain, Italy, Greece, and Cyprus. Areas under irrigation have increased and not all in the region may be shown here.

more water, serious shortages have developed. For example, in the dry summer of 1994, the Segura River Basin south of Alicante, one of Spain's most intensive fruit-growing regions, had to receive water by canal from reservoirs on the Tajo River in central Spain 185 miles (300 km) to the northwest. The problem is aggravated by the Mediterranean climate, periods of prolonged drought, loss of much reservoir water by evaporation, reservoirs that are rarely if ever full, and the fact that Spain is producing crops that are in surplus in the EU and are, therefore, often dumped—though the EU has financed many of the irrigation projects.

Numerous irrigation schemes were initiated during the late 1930s and early 1940s when economic priorities were completely different from those of today. Farmers in the north of Spain, as well as Portuguese farmers, have protested against a further siphoning off of northern water. A proposed National Hydrology Plan that will attempt to deal with water resource management remains to be finalized.

The Spanish fishing fleet is, in terms of catch, the second largest in the EU after Denmark; however, the country has been a net importer of fish since 1974. Some conflict has arisen with the French over fishing rights in the Gulf of Gascogne, as well as with the Canadians, Portuguese, and Moroccans in other areas. One of the problems in rationalizing the fleet size is that the approximately 100,000 workers that are employed are concentrated in regions that have high levels of unemployment.

Tourism, concentrated along the coast and on the Balearic Islands, has been a dynamic growth industry, bringing in over $6 billion annually from 1981 to 1984, hitting a then-record $12 billion in 1986 and rising to over $19 billion in 1993. In 1993, 57.3 million foreign visitors arrived, over half of whom stayed in the country for more than 24

hours. Tourist expenditures by Spaniards accounted for only $4.7 billion that year; thus, the country
had a positive balance of nearly $15 billion. The
economic and environmental effects of mass
tourism are discussed later in this chapter.

After Spain entered the EC in 1985, trading patterns began to change. In 1986 imports from within the Community represented 48 percent of the
total compared with 35 percent in 1985; exports to
the EC increased to 61 percent (50% in 1985). In
1994 the EU was taking about 68 percent of exports
and accounted for over 61 percent of imports.
France was the major customer for exports (19%),
and the largest supplier for imports (17%). That
same year imports amounted to $88 billion, where-
as exports were only $72.5 billion. Thus, the trade
deficit was over $15 billion. Because the formerly
protected home market is now open to competition from the EU, Spanish producers are facing
stiff import competition that has affected consumer products, especially in sectors such as auto
and steel production.

Spain's membership in the EU poses both a
challenge and a threat to the country. On the one
hand, the market for Spain's products has
increased enormously and was given another
boost in 1994 with the establishment of the European Economic Area. To benefit fully, exports must
expand at a faster pace than previously. On the
other hand, the lowering of high Spanish tariffs has
resulted in a flood of products from EU countries
that have had the advantage of years of competition to rationalize and modernize their industries.

The question is: can Spain make up for lost
time? To be sure, the foreign exchange levels are
strong, though investment, formerly buoyant, has
tapered off somewhat because of economic uncertainty. On the negative side, inflation is above the
European average, and perhaps more significantly, Spain's former trade surplus with the Union
has turned into a sizable and growing deficit. The
recent recession has taken its toll by way of bankruptcies, closed factories, and layoffs of workers,
driving up unemployment to over 3.3 million.
Reflecting the weak state of the economy, three
devaluations of the peseta totaling 19 percent have
been effected in recent years. The festivities of
1992, the International Exposition in Seville and

the Olympics in Barcelona, only masked the economic problems of the country that must now be
addressed.

Southern France, an Expanding Region within the Mediterranean Arc from Barcelona to Genoa

Southern France, the Mediterranean region linking
Spain and Italy, is a variegated and dynamic area.
It comprises the littoral and hinterlands of the
region of Languedoc-Roussillion from the Pyrenees to the Rhône River, the coastal stretch and
mountains of the region of Provence-Alpes-Côte
d'Azur from the Rhône to the Italian border, plus
the island of Corsica. The coast is divided into two
distinct physical regions by the delta of the Rhône;
a third region, that of the delta itself, overlaps both
regions. To the west of the delta, Languedoc-Roussillion is a low-lying coastal plain of sandy beaches and lagoons that has been transformed into a
tourist region of apartments, hotels, and marinas.
The main urban area of Languedoc is Montpellier.
Delineating the coast to the north is the edge of the
Massif Central. Between the foothills of the Pyrenees and the Massif Central, the Carcassonne
depression links Languedoc-Roussillion to the
Aquitaine Basin to the northwest, whereas to the
south railroads and highways connect with Spanish Catalonia.

To the east of the delta the coast is a rugged
region of capes, peninsulas, and bays that in the
west are backed by the calcareous foothills of the
Alps such as the limestones of the Maritime Alps
that plunge into the sea east of Nice. This coastal
area is the famous French Riviera-Côte d'Azur, a
dilating urban strip-agglomeration that includes
the naval port of Toulon on the west; a string of
tourist cities and villages such as St. Tropez,
Cannes, and Antibes; the major city on this section
of the coast, Nice; and the Principality of Monaco.

The third physical region, the delta of the
Rhône and the stony Crau, which overlaps both
political regions, is a clearly defined expanse of
deposited sediments, silts, and small boulders—
studded with low limestones mountains—that

filled in the sea between the Massif Central and Alpine foothills. The apex of the area is the walled city of Avignon in the north. Roman Nîmes lies at the edge of the Massive Central to the west, whereas strategic Arles is the last bridgehead before the Rhône flows into the Mediterranean through its delta. East of the delta, Marseille, the third city of France and the third largest port in Europe, after Rotterdam and Antwerp, sprawls across a significant undulating site on the coast.

Three main economic engines—tourism, agriculture, and industry—as well as the port functions of Marseille-Fos-Étang de Berre, are behind the growth of southern France since the Second World War. The focus of expansion, for the most part, corresponds to the coast; in contrast is the depopulation characteristic of the mountain and hill country of Provence and the Maritime Alps (Alpes-Maritimes).

As indicated in the chapter on France, the political region of Languedoc-Roussillion, with a population of over 2 million, has emerged as a key summer tourism region since the construction of six projects along the coast that today are capable of hosting 2 million visitors and over 12,000 boats. The area has also become the second French region, after Bordeaux, for the production of quality wines (*appellation d'orique controlée*). In 1992, out of a total production of 555 million gallons (21 million hectoliters), 14 percent were *appellation*. Once known almost exclusively for inexpensive table wines, or wines that were blended with Algerian or Italian varieties, Languedoc-Roussillion upgraded the quality of its vines and now exports high-quality wines, such as Corbieres and Côtes de Roussillon, throughout Europe and in North America. Because of the success of these varieties, Australian and U.S. investors have acquired relatively cheap vineyards and are expanding output. One firm that has benefited from the renaissance of local wines is SABATE, the specialist cork-manufacturing company near Perpignan, which is one of three international firms in this sector. Rising sales, aided by advanced production methods, have boosted the workforce to over 100. The company is represented in California, Spain, and Australia and has

expanded into China and the former Soviet Union.

The dominant city of Languedoc-Roussillion is the capital, Montpellier, 30 miles (50 km) to the west of Nîmes. Center of an urban agglomeration of 250,000, it is known for its university, medical faculty, animated design facilities, and expertise in tropical and Mediterranean agriculture. Industrial firms include IBM, Dell Computer, and GEC-Alsthom, the French-British engineering group. The municipality is attempting to attract other companies by projecting the image of a center of cultural and scientific life and boasts both its *technopole* or science parks and its new opera house. Located just north of the A9 highway, Montpellier will be connected to Paris, and ultimately to Barcelona, by an extension of the TGV line.

The Rhône Delta, which is part of the Department of Bouches-du-Rhône and is mainly within the larger region of Provence-Alpes-Côte d'Azur, is significant for its tourism focusing on the Camargue (Rhône Delta region), Avignon, and Arles. Also important is agriculture, especially rice production in the Camargue, wines (the most famous being Chateauneuf-du-Pape north of Avignon), and early-season fruits and vegetables, reflected in the commercial market at Cavaillon, east of Avignon, the third largest in Europe after those in Rungis (near Paris) and Hamburg, Germany. In addition, the industrial, refining, and port functions that rim the coast from Marseille to the Gulf of Fos are vital to the economy of the region, though because of pollution they conflict with the interests of tourism.

Arles, gateway to the Camargue, is renowned for its Gallo-Roman ruins and edifices as well as the city where Van Gogh painted some of his finest works. Sited on the most direct route between Spain and Italy, the city flourished during Roman times and, because it was closer to the Mediterranean Sea than at present, it was also a major port. Roman ruins, including an arena and a theater, attract tourists from all over the world. The city's attractiveness is also based on its proximity to the natural beauties, especially the abundant bird life, of the Camargue Regional Natural Park located within the delta of the Rhône. Threatened not only by the refining and industry of Fos, but also by tourist expansion on the rim and within the Camargue itself, the Natural Park is slowly being transformed into a commercial area.

Avignon, located just north of the junction of the Durrance and Rhône rivers, owes its fame and architecture to the presence of several generations of Popes who lived there in the fourteenth century. Part of an agglomeration of 181,000, the city, with 87,000 inhabitants in 1990, also has important agricultural, commercial, and administrative functions and in summer is host to the famous Avignon theatrical festival. Because of its situation on rail, road, and water routes that connect the north of France with both the Languedoc coast and the Côte d'Azur, the city is home to over 400 firms that are engaged in the shipment of freight and other goods and has become a vital logistical center at both national and international levels.

The major metropolis of the region is without doubt the city of Marseille, with its sprawling suburbs, industries, and port functions. Founded by the Phoenicians, then occupied by the Greeks and later by the Romans, Marseille had a population of under 900,000 in 1991. As is common to many European cities, however, population in the central area has declined in recent years, because inhabitants are moving to nearby towns which have lower taxes and more pleasant living conditions. The major highway links connecting these towns to Marseille have aided the trend toward dispersion and have resulted in an urban agglomeration that is over 1.2 million. Nevertheless, Marseille has revitalized its center with commercial construction, the building of a World Trade Center, and renovation of the old port into a vibrant marina. To counter centrifugal forces, it has also embarked on a program to attract shoppers to the city center.

Since its founding, Marseille has long been a significant port, establishing trading links with the Catalan coast. It played a major role in the Crusades and was vital to the expansion of French colonial interests in North Africa and the Middle East. After the Suez Canal was built, French colonial interests in the Far East, such as in Indochina, were served from Marseille. The port, which

includes the installations at Fos, continues to function in the same manner today, with over 1 million passengers passing through in 1993, though purely economic interests have taken over from the politically influenced colonial past. Today the port maintains its regional dominance and competes with Pisa and Genoa for business on the Levant coast and in Egypt and North Africa, as well. Over 87 million tons of merchandise were handled in 1993, 73 percent of which were hydrocarbons. Athough there were great hopes for the development of Fos, both as a port and as an industrial area for steel and chemicals, because of recession and reduction of European steel capacity, only 7500 were employed there in 1994, instead of a planned workforce of 50,000. In addition Marseille's airport, Marignane, continues the transport function, handling 5.9 million passengers and 39,288 tons of freight in 1993, each being the third highest in France.

The city's historical connections with the sea have given rise to industries based on all types of offshore activity, such as oceanography and water desalination. In general, however, industry is not the force that it once was during the apogee of French colonial power. Then many mills were processing tropical oils and manufacturing soap, and industries were processing imported and local agricultural products. Today industry employs about 15 percent of the total workforce. Services, especially commerce, are more important, accounting for about 76 percent of employment.

Marseille is the capital of the Bouches-du-Rhône Department and is an important administrative magnet for the Provence-Alpes-Côte d'Azur region. The population of this region increased from 4 million in 1982 to 4.4 million in 1993. The diverse landscape of the Marseille-centered region, as well as the way that it has expanded in an urban and industrial manner, has left Marseille the hub of a semicircle of *laissez-faire* development that requires better integration, organization, and rationalization for efficient growth and, more importantly, for it to remain competitive in the "economic storms" that are swirling across Europe and the world. Manufacturing activity in the metropolitan region of Marseille includes: (1) the industries on the plain of Aubagne to the east, one of which produces Gemplus Card, the memory card that is used in public phones, health care, and commercial television; (2) the Étang de Berre to the north with its refineries, petrochemical plants, and aerospace firms near the Marignane airport and at Istres; and (3) the region stretching to Fos and the Rhône Delta on the west where salt flats, refineries, pipelines, and steel industries are sited.

East of Marseille, past the tourist village of Cassis and the closed shipyards of la Ciotat, the true Côte d'Azur begins at Toulon, a naval port and university town that is home to France's Mediterranean fleet. It has berths for aircraft carriers, the latest being the nuclear-powered *Charles-de-Gaulle*, as well as nuclear-powered submarines, in addition to a vast array of repair docks and facilities. Both during the Gulf War and the civil wars in Yugoslavia, the strategic nature of the port was clearly evident.

Though constantly expanding, the tourist facilities along the coast from le Lavandou to St. Tropez and Ste. Maxime have not as yet totally overwhelmed natural settings on the Maures Massif, an area of low hills composed of rock and a dense Mediterranean forest, mainly of umbrella pines, that rise to over 2400 ft (750 m) back of the coast. Small bayhead beaches stud the coast where the rocks descend into the Mediterranean. Offshore lie the Iles d'Hyères one of which, the Ile de Port-Cros, has been turned into a National Park. From St. Tropez eastward, the impact of tourism intensifies and includes the modern village and marina of Port Grimaud on the Gulf of St. Tropez which has taken some pressure off of the former fishing village of St. Tropez. Further east the coast becomes urbanized with the cities of Cannes, Juan les Pines, and Antibes spreading out along the highway and into the surrounding countryside. The Var lowland to the west of Nice is a small break before the steep Maritime Alps dominate the coast. An urban strip-agglomeration begins, including the Principality of Monaco, which ends in France at Menton, just before the Italian border. However, this coastal agglomeration, rimmed by mountains, then continues eastward past the Italian port of Genoa.

Nice, France's fifth largest city, dominates the eastern edge of the coast as Marseille imposes on the west. Like Marseille it was an early Greek settlement; however, whereas Marseille's destiny was tied up with the growth of the French state, Nice was entwined with the expansion of the House of Savoy and Italy. In 1860, because the French had aided the Italians in their struggle with Austria, the city along with Savoy was ceded to France. Center of a tourist and industrial region of over 500,000 residents, Nice with its university is one of the most dynamic cities in France. The Alpes-Maritimes and Var departments, with their beaches, marinas, mountains, museums and festivals, are among the most intensely developed tourist areas in Europe. In addition, industry, especially high-technology companies, such as Texas Instruments and IBM, plays an ever more vital role in the local economy. A focal point for this type of development is Sophia Antipolis, an International Activities Park located to the west of Nice. Founded in 1972, the park spreads over about 5700 acres (2300 ha) and will be doubled in size. Companies such as Digital, Thompson, Wellcome, and Oréal have attracted skilled employees from all over the world. A total of 700 companies have been installed, and nearly 13,000 persons work in the park and in the department; about 23,000 others are associated with the park's activities.

Modern transportation facilities along the Côte d'Azur, which have contributed to economic expansion and urban growth, contrast greatly to those in the interior hinterland which have hardly been improved at all. Toll autoroutes converge on the coastal region from eastern and northern France and from the Rhine Valley of Germany via the Rhône Valley. The A8 that rims the coast from Cannes past Nice to the Italian border is one of the most amazing highways in Europe. Scores of tunnels pierce the mountains, and great viaducts project over the valleys. South of Avignon, spurs connect with Marseille and Toulon. To the east, three separate autostradas, crossing the Apennines, join the Côte d'Azur with the populous cities of the Po Valley and Switzerland. All of the above routes are heavily traveled by cars, especially during holidays and the summer tourist season, as well as by ponderous trucks connecting Central and Northern Europe with Spain, southern France, and Italy. In comparison to the autoroutes, the normal roads that join the coast to the hilly and mountainous hinterland are twisting narrow highways that move traffic at very slow speeds. They are fine for sightseeing but require patience and much skill on the part of the driver.

EuroCity trains also use the natural gateway of the Rhône Valley to service the coastal regions of southern France, joining the Spanish rail net to the west and the Italian rail net to the east. Frequent commuter trains link the many large and small urban centers along the coast. Considering the rugged nature of the coast between the Rhône Valley and the Italian border, transport infrastructure for vehicles and trains represents a major feat of engineering. In addition, there are airports at Montpellier, Marseille, and Nice.

As good as the present road and rail links are, French planners are preparing for the twenty-first century. An expansion is projected for north-south routes by complementing the main Paris-Lyon-Marseille autoroute with new highways over the highlands to the east and west of the Rhône, a direct Nîmes-Arles-Salon-de-Province link across the Rhône Delta, and a doubling of the Aix-Nice highway with an alternate A8 further inland will alleviate congestion. All are considered necessary to consolidate southern France's position on the Mediterranean axis running from Barcelona to Genoa. The rail planners are extending the TGV trains to Marseille, cutting the Paris-Marseille trip by 90 minutes to 3 hours; a TGV branch east to Fréjus will cut the Paris-Nice journey to 4 hours. Connections would be possible to Italy and west to Montpellier and Barcelona to link with the proposed Spanish TGV trains. However, both rail and road plans have been opposed by environmentalists and residents of the areas that would be transformed. In the case of the autoroutes, noise is a major concern and pollution from vehicle exhausts is serious. Though fast and relatively friendly to the environment, the TGV trains, because of their great speeds, cause intense sound pollution. Furthermore, in both the case of highways and rail lines, new right of ways would cut wide swaths through the countryside.

Southern France is evolving from being the Mediterranean rim of a great country into a section of a dynamic coastal arc that links Barcelona to Genoa. This is but one area that reflects the transformation of Europe from inward-looking national states, rimmed by artificial boundaries, to a Europe that has ended old political divisions and created new "Euroregions" that will function more efficiently and creatively within the European and world matrix.

Monaco

The Principality of Monaco is a ministate on the rim of the Mediterranean coast to the east of Nice and is surrounded by France, with whom it has a customs union (see Fig. 5-14). Monaco's role in the economy of the Côte d'Azur is far out of proportion to its 0.75-sq-mile (1.95-sq-km) territory. With about 30,000 inhabitants, it is fueled by a number of diverse factors. Although tourism, banking, and casinos are important sources of revenue for Monaco, the main generator of funds is industry. It has some 700 small businesses, including 65 companies in chemicals, pharmaceuticals, and cosmetics; 10 in plastics; 60 in electronics and engineering; and 70 in card and paper production. Employment in industry draws about one-third of its workers from nearby France and Italy. Banking employs over 1200 and accounts for nearly 35 percent of financial turnover. There are 38 banks in the Principality that offer their clients freedom from exchange controls, transaction duties, and income or capital gains tax. Customers are mainly citizens of a particular bank's country of origin. Tourism brings in about 250,000 overnight visitors annually and 3 million day trippers; the visitors come to the Grand Prix, a circus festival, sporting functions, and conference and trade fairs. There is a close historical relationship between the Principality's government and the Société des Bains de Mer (SBM). The company, 70 percent controlled by the state, is the largest commercial concern in Monaco, being an employer of 2600 people; it manages Monaco's casinos, most of its hotels, and the main sporting, social, and cultural activities.

Such a small, dynamically active area is bound to have a number of problems. Traffic congestion is very serious, including large diesel trucks that wind their way through Monaco's streets polluting the atmosphere. A tunnel will ultimately connect Monaco directly to the A8 motorway, which is the main traffic funnel for the Mediterranean coast. Space is at a premium because the Maritime Alps rise directly from the sea behind the town. In the last 45 years the size of the Principality has increased by 30 percent. Twenty-two acres (9 ha) in east Monaco were reclaimed from the sea during the 1950s. Then in the late 1960s, 54 acres (22 ha) in the west were created from the sea and are being used as an industrial park, helicopter port, soccer stadium, and low-income housing development. Plans have been discussed to build floating islands in the Mediterranean. However, one wonders how feasible this project would be. In any case, the Principality is certainly close to the saturation point.

Italy

Italy, though lacking major deposits of natural resources, has become one of the industrial dynamos of Western Europe since the end of World War II. The country has been transformed from a predominantly poor, agrarian one into an economically growing, urban, industrial, though nonegalitarian, society. During the late 1980s the country acquired a new, more positive image. No longer was it a place where inflation threatened the economic well-being of the average citizen, strikes crippled industry, terrorism menaced the democratic process, politics were a game of musical chairs, and state industries were burning up tax revenues.

To be sure, many serious problems remained, such as sporadic strikes, a constricting bureaucracy, insufficient funds allocated for education, inadequate air and rail service, poor controls for urban sprawl, a high level of public spending, and the rising ratio of debt to GDP. Nevertheless, between 1984 and 1987, one government lasted almost 36 months, unions were quiet and strikes at their lowest level in many years, and the economy was expanding. Publicly owned companies were being restructured to reduce their huge losses, and the private sector was prospering. Italian entrepre-

neurs, led by the managers of such companies as Fiat, Olivetti, and Benetton, were making their mark throughout the world. Other successful small firms, mainly from the north, were also prosperous. Italy had ceased to be a country in perpetual crisis and was instead challenging the United Kingdom and France for the number four spot among the Western world's leading industrialized countries. By 1993, Italy's per capita income ($17,371 [PPP $17,830]) had passed the UK by about $1000. In many ways Italy had become the model for the other countries of Southern Europe, as they strove to move up the economic ladder.

By 1993, this euphoric situation had collapsed. The political and economic sectors of Italian society had been racked by exposure of corruption on a vast scale that included bribes, contract rigging, kickbacks, fraud, illicit funding for political parties, overpricing, and misuse of funds. Industrial magnates, politicians, and government employees were in jail awaiting trial. A former chairman of ENI, the state energy company, and a leading financial entrepreneur, committed suicide. The major political parties had been discredited in the eyes of the public, and a new separatist political party, the Liga Nord (the Northern League), was establishing itself firmly in Lombardy and the Friuli-Venezia Giulia regions. A national neo-Fascist party was also gaining in strength. At the same time, the humbled Christian Democrats, the most powerful party in the country since the end of World War II, changed its name to the Popular party in an effort to distance itself from years of corrupt rule. Finally, the Mafia openly challenged the democratic process by its spectacular assassinations of two judges in Sicily, and terrorism once again raised its ugly head, as bombs exploded in central Milan and in Florence, killing bystanders and destroying irreplaceable cultural treasures. The public outcry led to new elections, with new electoral laws that have profoundly changed the way the Italian state has operated since the end of the Second World War.

Another profound change within Italian society has been its transition during this century from a demographically high-growth to low-growth society—despite the Roman Catholic Church's official stand in opposition to birth control. The population of Italy, after growing rapidly in the 1960s, increased only slightly between 1983 and 1996 from 56.8 million to 57.7 million. The number of births and the fertility rate are now among the lowest in the world. The growth rate hovers near zero, reflecting the trend that is evident throughout industrialized Europe. Thus, Italy has experienced a shrinking of young age groups and an expansion of the older population.

Population density is about 496 people per sq mile (192 per sq km) and is considerably higher if the mountainous areas of the country are excluded from consideration. The main concentration of people is found in the Po Valley in four agglomerations—Milan, 4 million; Turin, 1.5 million; and Bologna and Venice-Trieste, each with over 500,000. Other regions of high population density include Rome and Naples, with 3 million residents each; Genoa and the Ligurian coast in the northwest, with nearly 1 million; Palermo (Sicily) with over 800,000; and Florence, with over 500,000.

From the end of the Second World War until the beginning of the 1970s, large numbers of migrants moved from the poorer agricultural south to the wealthier industrial north, as well as to other countries such as Switzerland and Germany. During this period, population also shifted from rural areas to the major cities. For the most part these movements have ended. However, the country has been impacted by about 1.4 million immigrants, of whom only 900,000 are legal. Most immigrants come from outside the EU, mainly from the Maghreb (the North African coastal regions), the former Yugoslavia, Egypt, Ethiopia, and the Philippines. Hostility toward the immigrants is evident, and racist attacks have erupted. In an effort to ameliorate this sensitive situation, the government has introduced visa requirements to control illegal immigration. Simultaneously, it offered amnesty to the illegals who had come to the country before 1990.

As indicated by the distribution of population, much of Italy is composed of rugged topography, with over three-quarters of its area being rough hills and rugged mountains. The topography reflects Italy's young geological age, and it has been the setting for catastrophic natural disasters since the time of first settlement. Eruptions of Mount Vesuvius buried the Roman cities of Pompeii and Herculaneum in 79 A.D.; ravaging lava flows regularly radiate from the slopes of Mount Etna; Sicilian and Alpine earthquakes erupt with destructive power; and sudden, devastating floods from rain pouring off of the Alps or Apennines have been accepted as inevitable calamities. In the case of these floods, destruction has been far more severe than necessary because of the lack of forest cover in many mountainous regions and the fact that recent development has resulted in the construction of factories, housing estates, schools, and hospitals in narrow river valleys known for their severe flooding.

Perhaps such natural calamities have been a factor in turning the Italians away from nature. For the most part, Italian urban dwellers have undertaken little activity in the countryside, even though many people once worked in the fields. The Italians, in comparison to societies in Western and Northern Europe, have a deplorable record for the wise utilization of resources and conservation of the rural landscape. As the country became wealthier and more mobile in the 1970s and 1980s, the peace and harmony of landscapes and cities that escaped ravages from earlier civilizations have been violated. Splendid Alpine valleys have been transformed by the *nouveau riche* of Turin and Milan into vast garbage dumps strewn with the fallout from a consumer society. The Po, Italy's longest river, drains the organic and industrial filth from the country's manufacturing and agricultural heartland, with little or no primary sewage treatment, and discharges a toxic brew of bacteria, heavy metals, and chemicals into the Adriatic. South of the Po Delta are bathing resorts such as Rimini and Riccione that have suffered considerable economic damage, because the waters of the Adriatic have become so degraded. Italy's record of pollution control is among the worst in Western Europe. Many of the country's beaches have become cesspools; cities such as Rome, Milan, Turin, and Naples are being suffocated by the exhaust from vehicles; and hundreds of thousands of trees are dead or dying in the Alps and along the shores of the northern lakes from a combination of acid rain and exhaust from dense auto, bus, motorcycle, and truck traffic.

A major factor in this ruination of the landscape, but also a positive factor for the industrialization of Italy, has been the modernization of the transportation network, especially the construction of tollroads (*autostradas*) that extend throughout the north of the country and southward onto Sicily. These four-lane divided highways, constructed through the mountains and along the rugged coasts, have linked Italy as never before in history by connecting the formerly remote south to the central and northern regions of the country and beyond to France, Switzerland, Austria, and Germany. By contrast, Italy's rail network, though extensive, has lagged technologically behind other European countries. Strikes both in the rail and air sectors have consistently played havoc with interregional and international connections.

Italy has relatively few mineral resources but is one of Europe's most heavily dependent countries on oil. In 1992 petroleum accounted for 60 percent of primary energy consumption, down 8 percent from 1982. Natural gas registered 26 percent, coal and lignite about 8 percent, and other sources such as hydro and geothermal together about 7 percent. In a referendum in 1987, Italians rejected the use of nuclear energy. Production of oil, from small fields in the Po Valley, Adriatic, and Sicily, amounted to less than 5 million tons in 1993. Natural gas production, mainly from Po Valley fields, was more substantial at 685 billion cu ft (19.4 billion cu m). Coal, oil, and natural gas must be imported to make up the deficit because of the low production of fuels within the country.

Italy has the largest refining capacity among the countries of Western Europe with 3.3 percent of the world's total in 1993, though in general there is much overcapacity, and the refineries, especially those in the Po Valley, are serious polluters.

The country's planners are emphasizing the continuing need to diversify energy sources by generating more electricity with coal and less from conventional oil-fired stations. However, because the price of coal is relatively high compared to oil and environmental impacts are greater, the use of more coal may be arrested. Benefiting from the success of the French nuclear program, Italy has been able to import surplus power from across the Alps. Consumption of natural gas has continued to increase, thanks to imports from the Netherlands and from the trans-Mediterranean pipeline that links Algerian fields via Sicily to the high use areas of northern Italy.

Two factors will transform the Italian energy sector in the future. On the one hand, ENEL, the country's state-owned electricity-generating utility, signed one of the world's biggest long-term energy contracts with Nigeria that will supply liquefied natural gas worth about $650 million over 20 years beginning in 1997. Further amounts of gas will come from Algeria via an undersea pipeline, and liquefied gas from Algeria will also be imported. Talks are underway with Norway and Qatar about additional supplies of natural gas. On the other hand, Agip, a subsidiary of ENI, the state energy company, has discovered one of the most important offshore petroleum fields in Europe in the Straits of Otranto near the maritime border with Albania. Reserves are estimated to be 70 million of barrels of low sulfur content and also contain natural gas. Future production of oil in Italy should increase by at least one-third over present levels.

National averages indicate that Italy has a relatively well-developed economy, with an accompanying employment structure, although there are great differences between the highly developed north and the severely lagging south (see Inset 10-3). In 1993 the percentage of the national labor force engaged in agriculture, forestry, and fishing was 7.4 (the lowest figure in Southern Europe); 33.3 percent was in industry and 59.3 percent was in services. In recent years, the totals for agriculture and industry have been declining, whereas those for services have been growing.

Agricultural practices in Italy have been conditioned by a variety of physical and cultural geographical factors. The structure and relief of the country, climate, soils, Italy's historical evolution, and government policies have shaped present-day rural economic life. Depending on the region of Italy and the period of history in which it developed, the relative proportion of these ingredients varied. For example, during the Roman era, the south was brilliantly civilized and highly developed agriculturally, whereas the Po Plain, having a good summer climate but only fair soil conditions, was marshy, covered with forest, and almost deserted. From the thirteenth century on, the development of the Po countryside was linked with wealthy townspeople who bought land, cleared and drained it, and introduced better methods of farming.

THE MEZZOGIORNO

Generally corresponding to the former Kingdom of Naples and Sicily, *Mezzogiorno* is the traditional name for the relatively poor part of Italy below Rome, as well as the islands of Sicily and Sardinia. For the purposes of development planning, the *Mezzogiorno* includes the eight regions in this area as well as certain other provinces, communes, and islands. Together this represents about 21.2 million inhabitants, or 36 percent of the Italian total, clustered especially around Naples, the "heel" of Italy in the southeast, Palermo, and the east coast of Sicily. The legacy of the past, responsible to a large degree for the deterioration of the south's physical geography, has retarded economic development in the *Mezzogiorno*. The feudal society that persisted until after World War II was not too concerned with deforestation, waste of water, erosion, primitive agricultural techniques, and exploitation of peasant laborers. Even today, after more than 40 years of directed development, the *Mezzogiorno*, compared to the rest of Italy, is an underdeveloped area with per capita incomes only a little over half of what they are in the northern and central regions of the country. Its lack of economic development has had important economic, demographic, and political impacts on all of Italy for decades.

Still, much has been undertaken to attempt to bridge the gap between north and south. Over $50 billion was spent in the south during the last 35 years, mainly on capital- rather than labor-intensive projects, and many industries were established there. In addition, physical and cultural isolation has been eliminated by the construction of *autostradas*, new airports, and gas pipelines; improvements in ferry service between the mainland and Sicily; electrification; modernization of the railroad; updating of farming techniques; and advances in education, television, and health care. Nevertheless, since 1973, despite some notable regionally focused successes that include the Adriatic coast from Pescara to Bari, the north-south economic gap has been widening rather than closing. According to Bank of Italy data, four-fifths of Italy's

total public deficit is attributable to the south, compared to a surplus in the center and northern regions.

Many factors are responsible. The region is peripheral to the rest of Europe, the physical landscape of much of the region is hilly and mountainous, and the cultural legacy that includes the Camorra organization in the Naples region, the 'ndrangheta in Calabria (the mainland region adjacent to Sicily), and the Mafia in Sicily has retarded attempts to truly modernize the economy. The failure of Sicilian land reform and the fiasco of the proposed Gioia Tauro steel complex in Calabria are but two examples. The steel project was proposed on a site totally unsuited for a steel mill and at a time when the EC was trying to reduce European capacity. Although construction was started, the works will never be finished. Presently, a container port is being established there.

The *Mezzogiorno* is also overpopulated. In the past, surplus labor could seek its fortune in the north of Italy or in countries such as Switzerland and West Germany. The recession of the late 1970s, early 1980s, and especially early 1990s severely constricted emigration. Certainly, the *Mezzogiorno* made far too many investments in heavy industry, such as steel manufacture, chemicals, and refining. These have now become less important and in any case have provided limited employment opportunities. Far too little investment has been made in small and medium-sized companies that could utilize local agricultural products and artisanal skills to provide much needed employment. The south generates less than 8 percent of all Italian exports. Unemployment is running at over 20 percent, compared to 11 percent in central Italy and below 7 percent in the north. The bottomless sink of the *Mezzogiorno*, where millions of dollars have disappeared without a trace, has been a major factor in the success of the Northern League (*Liga Nord*), whose leaders resent the financing of senseless economic projects, "cathedrals in the desert," in the south of the country.

Spurred by nineteenth-century industrialization in the north, the Po Valley has become the richest agricultural region in Italy and one of the most productive in Western Europe, whereas Sicily, which under the Arabs and Normans was one of the best agrarian regions in Europe, declined after the fourteenth century (Fig. 10-12). As forests were felled and soil eroded, coastal marshes developed, malaria became endemic, areas of cultivated land diminished, and the growing of many plants that had required skill and irrigation was abandoned. A long period of agricultural deterioration ensued that was partially halted only after World War II.

Agriculture succeeded in the Po Valley and failed in Sicily not because of the basic physical landscape in either case, but because of human actions. Certainly, relief, climate, and soil conditions had to be contended with, but an unenlightened policy in the Po Valley would have produced the same results there as it had in Sicily. Similarly, wise development policies in Sicily could still raise

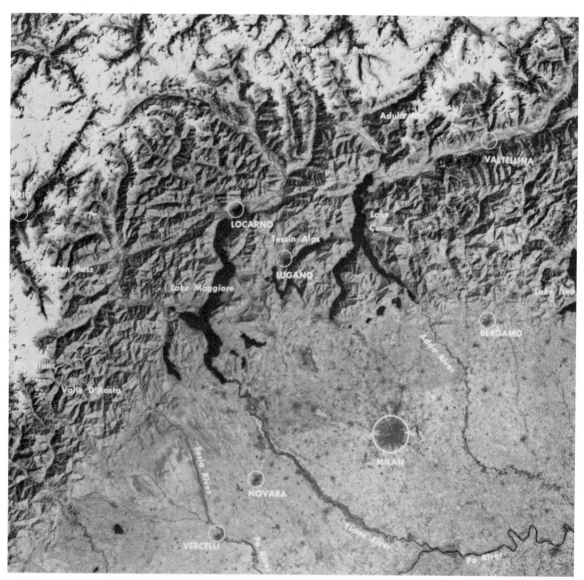

FIGURE 10-12 A Landsat satellite photo of part of northwestern Italy and southern Switzerland showing a rugged, sparsely settled Alpine backdrop to the flat, fertile Po Valley, one of Europe's most densely settled regions. (EROS Data Center)

production efficiency close to the levels of the Po Plain. Physical as well as cultural factors often determine agrarian practices.

Over 75 percent of Italy is classified as hilly or mountainous; yet over 55 percent of the total area of the country is devoted to agriculture, the fourth largest area in Western Europe, after France, Spain, and the United Kingdom. Nevertheless, except for fruit and vegetables, the country runs a deficit on its food trade. Most agricultural sectors are self-sufficient only at the 60 to 65 percent level and livestock at only 50 percent. A number of factors are responsible. Farm units outside the Po Valley tend to be too small, marketing and distribution facilities are in many cases poor, farmers do not speak with a united political voice, and financing is fragmented. In addition, as we have seen, the physical geography in many areas of the country is detrimental to high yields. Furthermore, regional differences are considerable. For example, farmers in the north of the country are closer to their counterparts in Western, Central, and Northern Europe technologically, culturally, economically, and geographically than to farmers in the south of Italy.

New products such as kiwi fruit, soybeans, and the jojoba plant have been introduced; however, the traditional crops, such as citrus fruits, wine grapes, and olive oil are facing serious competition from Spain. The production of wine is 40 percent above consumption within Italy, and olive oil was already a surplus product in the European Community before Spain's entry. A logical step would be to increase output in those sectors that register a trade deficit. However, the CAP (Common Agricultural Policy) imposes quotas on each country, so that Italian production of certain products is blocked. Because Italians voted to do away with the Ministry of Agriculture, administrative responsibility is slowly changing from a centrally to a regionally directed ministry.

Industrial development in Italy has been characterized by an unwieldy, politicized, bureaucratic-ridden, loss-making public sector consisting of large companies and a dynamic, efficient, innovative, market-seeking, profitable private sector made up mainly of small and medium-sized concerns. The former sector includes companies belonging to the three state holding companies

ENI (*Ente Nazionale Idrocarburi*), IRI (*Instituto per la Reconstruzione Industriale*), and EFIM (*Ente Partecipazione e Finanziamento Industrie Manifatturiere*), and it consists of a variety of enterprises, such as banks, the toll autostradas, steel, shipbuilding, and armaments. Alfa Romeo was state owned but has since been purchased by Fiat. The private sector includes companies that are often controlled by family interests, such as Pirelli (tires and industrial rubber products), Fiat (vehicles, railway rolling stock, steel, aerospace, machines tools), Olivetti (computers and telecommunications), Montedison (chemicals and synthetic fibers) which has merged with Ferruzzi (agri-business), Zanussi (domestic appliances), Benetton (clothing and sporting goods), and Bastogi (machine tools).

In 1933 IRI was set up as part of the Fascists' policy of economic self-sufficiency (autarchy). Today, it consists of over 1000 companies and accounts for about 5 percent of Italy's employment and value added, 6 percent of fixed investment, almost 10 percent of GDP, and 30 percent of industry's research and development (R&D). In all, it has shareholdings in about 140 companies that employ approximately 500,000 persons. ENI was founded in 1953 to safeguard Italian interests in the supply of petroleum and natural gas. Both companies have suffered from severe losses that were as high as several billion dollars in 1983 and 1984. Draconian efforts have been required to stop the bloodletting. Thus, tens of thousands of employees have been shed in both companies. In 1991 IRI employed 407,000 and ENI employed 131,000. The cumulated debts of both companies totaled about $55 billion in 1991, and in 1993 IRI lost nearly $7 billion—more than double the 1992 figure. Because of government control and their links with the political process, corruption in the state holding companies has been endemic.

A paradoxical state industry is steel. Surprisingly, Italy is the largest producer of steel in Western Europe after Germany, accounting for nearly 26 million tons in 1993. The steel mills continue to lose money, despite the fact that they, along with Spanish mills, have been the most subsidized in Europe. Because of EU pressure and outrage among the private steel manufacturers in Europe, Italian overcapacity in steel will be cut with the loss of nearly 12,000 jobs, the bulk of which will be from Europe's largest steel plant at Taranto in the south.

Privatization of state companies, such as Agip (oil and gas), Nuovo Pignone (mechanical engineering), Credito Italiano and IMI (banking), and Enel (electricity generation) has been announced by the Italian government. Like their counterparts in Germany and France, who would like the government to sharply reduce its holdings in business, and thus gain monies that could reduce the national debt, Italian politicians are in favor of removing state control of a vast industrial empire. However, in comparison to its EU partners, little has been accomplished because of a combination of political upheaval, vested interests, the early 1990s recession, and the intricacies of the Italian political process. By the end of 1993, Nuovo Pignone had been sold to the United States' General Electric-led consortium, and Credito Italiano, Italy's seventh biggest bank, had been privatized.

Not all has been positive in the private sector during the 1990s. Companies have been stung, both by the recession and by growing international competition. The chairman of Olivetti was jailed and admitted paying kickbacks in order to secure government orders. In addition, Ferruzzi, because of fraudulent practices and enormous debt, was struggling to survive. Nevertheless, most of the larger companies had already restructured before the latest recession. Capacity was reduced and labor needs were sharply lowered, thereby increasing competitiveness.

In recent years small companies, located mainly in northern and central Italy, have made a substantial contribution to the country's economy. The Italian employers' federation, Confindustria, estimates that businesses with turnover of less than about $7 million annually represent 86 percent of all industrial companies in Italy. They employ less than 15 people on average. They are not unionized, and they turn out a wide range of goods, from plastic and plumbing fixtures to ceramics, furniture, clothing, jewelry, and shoes. Many small firms producing the same product cluster in the same city or region. For example, wool textiles are found in Prato (near Florence) and Biella (between Milan and Turin), silk in Como (north of Milan), and shoes in Verona (northern edge of the Po Valley). These firms, all in the north, utilize the latest techniques and equipment and often do piecework for the large manufacturers (e.g., Benetton), which do not wish to tie themselves down to large capital investment.

Substantial weaknesses in Italian industry remain. Few firms are both large and successful: in 1994 only 8 Italian companies were in Europe's top 100 companies by turnover, compared to 32 German, 24 French, and 12 from the UK. (Some of the firms counted are in sectors other than industry.)

Two examples, one in the state sector and the other in the private, reveal some of the problems that Italy faces as it attempts to come to grips with years of corruption and bad management. In both cases enormous sums of money have disappeared. EFIM, the third largest state holding company, controlled 120 firms, including enterprises ranging from armaments and glass to aluminum and helicopters. The proposed liquidation of this chronically loss-making firm will cost Italian taxpayers at least $11 billion. An analysis of the company reveals the worst evils of state ownership. The sheer size and diversity of EFIM precluded efficient operation. Employment totaled 37,000 in six divisions. Sales in 1991 were about $3 billion and losses about $800 million. It was long regarded as a dumping place for loss-making industries that were kept alive to promote political patronage with lavish use of state funds. Five EFIM companies are implicated in kickback investigations. Despite the hemorrhage of public funds, liquidation has been slow, hampered by a crowded government agenda, the recession, and the inexperience of Italians in the liquidation process. As a result, creditors, such as local suppliers and national and international banks, have not been paid. The question that has not been satisfactorily answered is, How did EFIM get into such a mess?

The second company that found itself in trouble was Italy's second biggest private holding company, Feruzzi Finanziaria. In 1992 it had 50,000 employees, and sales were about $13 billion. The net debt of the company is more than $14 billion at current exchange rates. Foreign banks are owed over $4 billion. An intricate restructuring plan, supported by the Bank of Italy, has been approved to rescue the firm. As was the case with EFIM, poor management and corruption were involved.

Among services, tourism makes a significant

contribution to Italy's current account. Nearly 50 million foreign visitors were registered in 1993, down from 53.3 million in 1986, but still injecting $22 billion into the economy. Expenditures abroad by Italians in 1993 were $14 billion, thereby leaving a surplus of $8 billion. The largest numbers of tourists came from Switzerland, followed by Germans. Nearly 60 percent of all visitors arrived between the months of June and September. The main regions affected are Alpine resorts (e.g., Valle d'Aosta and Friuli); northern lakes (e.g., Maggiore, Como, and Garda); the Italian Riviera in the northeast (Riviera di Ponente and Riviera di Levante); the northern Adriatic coast from Trieste to Pescara; and the islands in proximity to Naples. Also, cities such as Venice, Florence, Pisa, Perugia, and Rome and unique archaeological sites such as Pompeii and Herculaneum are favorite tourist destinations (Fig. 10-13).

Since 1986, Italy's trade has been predominantly in deficit, reaching minus $17.7 billion in 1991, before easing somewhat to minus $12.7 billion in 1992. In 1992 devaluation helped exports, whereas a recession reduced imports and by 1994 the trade balance was positive. In the past an invisibles (e.g., transfer of "guest worker" funds from abroad) surplus has alleviated the trade gap. However, the invisibles balance also deteriorated.

The reasons behind a recent rapid increase in exports include the depreciation of the lira by 20 percent since September 1992 and increased trade with non-OECD countries, especially the dynamic, newly industrialized countries of Asia. In China alone, exports between 1992 and 1993 doubled. Among the strongest sectors of this export boom has been industrial machinery and mechanical goods, especially machine tools, an industry that is well established in northern Italy. Italian quality consumer goods have also been in strong demand. In 1993 the EU took about 58 to 59 percent of exports and imports. Germany, by far, was the largest single trading partner, followed by France, the United States, and the UK. In 1991 industrial and agricultural machinery accounted for the largest amount of exports (17%), whereas chemicals were the largest import (13%).

Though not alone, Italy is an archetype example of a country that has lived beyond its means for too long. The economic geography of the country has been deeply affected by such factors as a serious public debt; tax evasion; expensive social programs such as generous pension schemes and free prescriptions; unaccountable public finances; and inflation-indexed wages. All this came together in 1992 when the Italian lira, like the Spanish peseta and Portuguese escudo, was forced outside of the European Monetary System (EMS). The lira's value declined by more than 20 percent, reflecting the true worth of the currency and shattering the illusion that Italy might finally be a country with a strong currency and economy.

A realism not seen in postwar Italy since the economic boom of the late 1960s and early 1970s enveloped the country, and caretaker governments attempted to provide the structural framework to rebuild Italy in a moral, political, and economic manner. Inflation has been kept under control, and serious attempts have been made to tame the runaway government debt, which is one of the highest in Western Europe—10 percent of GDP on an annual basis, and in 1993 an accumulated debt of 120 percent of GDP. Indexed pay has been eliminated, and generous pensions have been

FIGURE 10-13 Piazette San Marco, Venice. (A. Diem)

curtailed. No one has been spared from the government's inquest into corruption.

During 1992–1993 over 200,000 jobs were lost, and a 10.5 percent unemployment rate rose to nearly 12 percent in 1994. In the south unemployment is about twice the national average and endemic among young people between the ages of 14 and 29. Although exports have climbed because of devaluation and are a positive sign of the potential of the country, nevertheless Italy must eliminate practices such as patronage, kickbacks, inefficiency, and overemployment that have insulated the country from the fierce economic competition that is evident within the world region. The infrastructure, especially the ports, airports, and railroads, must continue to be modernized. Finally, the country must reverse its disgraceful record of allowing environmental degradation to damage and destroy the natural amenities of the country, and criminal organizations must be brought to heel. Greater social cooperation is needed in Italy rather than, as in the past, emphasis on individualistically oriented goals. Otherwise, the former excesses and abuses will continue to haunt the country's inhabitants.

Ideologically diverse parties have been unable to reverse a perceived decline in morals and morale that has poisoned so many layers of Italian society. It will take a virtual political, psychological, and social miracle for politicians to succeed. Nevertheless, one must always realize that in Italy, as the saying goes, "anything is possible."

rugged and form a diverse coastline of elongated gulfs and promontories. To the east and south, the islands of Greece are the drowned remnants of the main ranges. Thus, the physiography of the country has contributed to the remoteness of one region from another.

Greece has Western Europe's lowest per capita income—$7071 in 1993 ($8797 PPP); however, these figures do not take into account that the "black" economy is running at levels equivalent to 30 percent of GDP. Thus, the average Greek enjoys a living standard far higher than that measured by official per capita income alone. In 1993 more people were engaged in agriculture, forestry, and fishing in Greece—21 percent of the working population—than anywhere else in Western Europe. Only 24 percent were engaged in industry, one of the lower amounts in Western Europe, and over 54 percent were in services.

When Greece became an independent state in 1830, the population was only 700,000. In 1996 it was 10.5 million. Then, Athens was a poor village of 5000; now it is a bloated capital of over 3 million (Fig. 10-14). By contrast, Thessaloniki (also called Salonika), the second city of Greece, has just under 1 million inhabitants.

Despite periods of political instability since the end of World War II and the lack of most basic raw materials, Greece has made enormous economic

Greece

Greece, bordered in the north by Albania, the new state of Macedonia, and Bulgaria; in the east by Turkey; and surrounded elsewhere by the azure seas of the Mediterranean, lies in relative isolation from other Western European countries. Mountains predominate; plains, found mainly east of the Pindus Range, cover only 30 percent of the country's territory. Nearly 70 percent of Greece is over 650 ft (200 m) in elevation. Although the highest peak, Mount Olympus, 9477 ft (2917 m), is not noteworthy in comparison to the Alps of Italy, its local relief, and that of other mountainous regions, can be significant. The mountains are complex and

FIGURE 10-14 Athens, looking at the hill of the Lycabettus from the Acropolis. The densely built-up nature of the city is evident. (A. Diem)

strides, especially since 1960. Growing exports of manufactured goods, an increase of foreign investment, substantial aid from the EU, modernization of agriculture, the rise of tourism, and remittances from seamen and Greeks working abroad have enabled the country to maintain a viable economy. Nevertheless, Greece, like the other countries of Southern Europe, suffers from an antiquated financial system, excessive inflation (13.7% in 1993, by far the highest in the EU), massive public sector borrowing, and an extensive foreign debt. Recently, exports of manufactured goods have stagnated. In addition, both tourist and worker remittances have fallen, and earnings from shipping have slumped, thereby plunging the current account balance into the red (-$2 billion in 1992). To combat these economic problems, an austerity program was put in effect that resulted in, among other things, a devaluation of the drachma by 15 percent to boost exports and encourage tourism; a two-year freeze in wages and salaries; and a large loan from the European Union to help service the foreign debt. Whether austerity can be maintained now that the Socialists are in power again remains to be seen.

Greece also is the only country viewed as part of Western Europe to be at political odds with its neighbors. Greek-Turkish relations are a source of irritation within the European Union as well as reducing the effectiveness of NATO (the North Atlantic Treaty Organization), of which both are members. The two countries are at odds over sea and airspace rights in the Aegean, militarization of the Greek island of Lemnos, and Turkish occupation of the northern part of Cyprus (Fig. 10-15). In 1988 positive efforts were begun to mitigate these problems. The Turkish premier made a state visit to Athens, and direct talks under UN auspices began between the Turkish and Greek Cypriot leaders. At the time of this writing, however, there have been no concrete results—to the contrary, renewed sabre rattling and naval movements occurred recently over ownership of a barren Aegean island. Furthermore, both countries have been receiving armaments at unprecedented levels, and tension has been high because of the war in Bosnia (Greece has supported Serbia whereas Turkey has supported the Bosnian Muslims) and the Kurdish problem in Turkey, in which case the Turks have accused the Greeks of aiding the Kurdish rebels.

To the consternation of its allies, Greece until recently continued to harass its new neighbor and UN member, Macedonia. Greece objects not only to use of the name Macedonia but also to the new country's flag, a sunburst symbol associated with the ancient dynasty of Alexander the Great. Thus, the port of Thessaloniki, formerly the main outlet for Macedonian exports, was closed for some time to Macedonian trade as the result of a Greek trade embargo on that country. Finally, Greece is quarreling with Albania over the status of ethnic Greeks in that country, freezing Greek investment there and opening the way for Italian companies.

Greece can ill afford these political disputes with neighbors; it is a relatively poor country with limited resources. It has no coal, though lignite deposits, found mainly near Ptolemais in northwest Macedonia and at Megalopolis in the Peloponnesos, are estimated at 6.4 billion tons. Lignite-burning generating stations are significant polluters in these areas. Production of petroleum, near the northern island of Thassos, is limited. Thus, most oil must be imported. The main refineries in Greece are located in the Athens region and near Thessaloniki.

Oil exploration has had both domestic and international repercussions. In the first instance, the North Aegean Petroleum Company (NAPC), an international consortium with strong Canadian investment, has developed offshore oil deposits in the North Aegean. In 1994 the Public Petroleum Corporation (DEP) planned to offer concessions for both onshore and offshore oil exploration in western Greece. Blocks in Epirus and the Ionian Sea were made available to international bidders in areas known to have oil-bearing strata.

In the second instance, an international one, Turkey had warned Greece not to explore for oil beyond its 6.2-mile (10-km) territorial water limits. Otherwise, "the necessary measures to safeguard Turkish rights and interests in the Aegean would be exercised." The Turkish threat appears to have subsided, though it could flare up again.

Greece is a net importer of energy, with over 60 percent of primary consumption being imported in 1992. Official policy aims to reduce dependence on oil, which accounted for over 70 percent of total

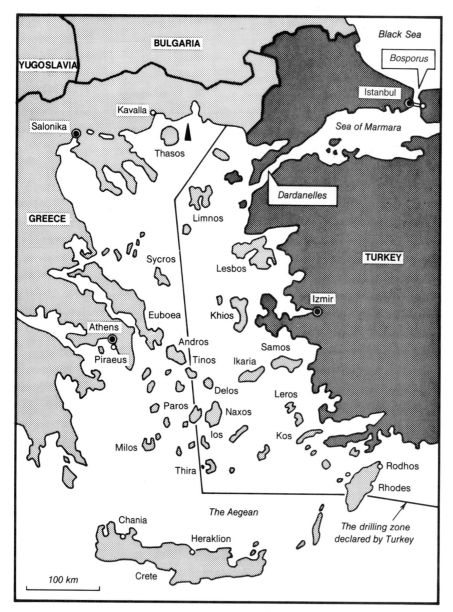

FIGURE 10-15 Areas of conflict between Greece and Turkey. Though Greece controls most Aegean islands, Turkey contests its right to these and associated sea bed resources.

primary energy supply in 1980. By 1992 this had declined to 61 percent, despite an increase in total primary energy demand during this period. One way this is being done is by importing natural gas from the former Soviet Union via a 437-mile (704-km) pipeline from Bulgaria. Eventually, this gas will cover about 13 percent of Greece's annual energy requirements. Algeria will also supply 424 billion cu ft (12 billion cu m) of liquefied natural gas over 21 years. Furthermore, for the first time, the country will import electricity from Turkey by linking the grid systems of the two countries through Thrace.

A large number of minerals and ores are mined in Greece, the most notable of which are asbestos, bauxite (largest production in Europe), nickel, and magnesite. The country also has a major cement industry.

Public Power Corporation, a state-owned enterprise, is the sole producer and distributor of electric energy. Between 1974 and 1993 production of electricity increased over twofold. Presently, most of the country is connected to the national grid. In 1990 nearly 87 percent of the total output of electricity came from the utilization of domestic sources. At the end of 1973, PPC's installed generating capacity was 58 percent lignite and hydro and 42 percent oil. By 1992 the figures had shifted to 88 percent lignite and hydro and only 12 percent oil.

Agriculture illustrates other structural characteristics and changes in the Greek economy. In 1982 agriculture accounted for 16.5 percent of Greece's GDP and about 30 percent of all exports. In 1992 agriculture's contribution to GDP remained relatively high but had fallen to 12.7 percent, while the relative export share was unchanged. Although Greek farmers are more prosperous than ever before, farming is still beset by many problems. This paradoxical situation may be explained on the one hand by favorable EU prices for agricultural products that have boosted income, as well as increased government pensions for farmers and their wives, and on the other hand by low productivity and a reduced annual rate of growth of agricultural output.

Part of the explanation for the lower agricultural growth is the result of structural problems. About 70 percent of the country's land area is used for some sort of agricultural purposes, but only 22 percent is classified as arable. Nearly one-third of the arable land is under irrigation. Just over half of the arable area is level land where productivity is satisfactory, whereas the rest is mountainous or rugged hill land of low productivity. The largest plains are found in the regions of Macedonia and in Thessaly with smaller flat areas scattered throughout the country, often associated with deltas or coastal areas. Another factor that con-

tributes to low productivity is the limited size of farms. Holdings in Greece tend to be noncontiguous and much smaller (13 acres/5.3 ha) than the EU average. About one-third of Greek agricultural output now comes from Epirus, Macedonia, and Thrace in northern Greece, especially from the Macedonian plains. The region accounts for 62 percent of the country's cereals, 50 percent of corn and 80 percent of sugar beets. In addition, about 55 percent of the tobacco crop comes from the north.

Before 1981 the agricultural trade balance with the EC was positive; however, after Greece entered the EC, food imports from other member countries showed a dramatic penetration of the Greek market. For example, today much of the country's famous feta cheese comes from Denmark. Not surprisingly, imports of basic foodstuffs have accounted for over 10 percent of the total import bill in recent years. One of Greece's problems has been the low quality of food processing and lack of imagination in marketing. In addition, Greek products face considerable competition in export markets from Spain, a country that grows many of the same crops as Greece and is closer to Central European markets. Also, the war in the former Yugoslavia cut the main land export route, north through the Vardar Valley, and resulted in a decrease of agricultural exports to the former Yugoslav republics. Exports to Europe now take the longer and more expensive route by ferry to Brindisi in Italy. One result has been the dumping of surplus citrus and tender fruit crops.

A more positive note is the fact that EU payments to Greece for agricultural improvements have increased considerably since 1981, with monies being earmarked both for 22 mountainous and underdeveloped provinces and for modernization in processing, marketing, and production. The result has been a rationalization as well as an internationalization of food processors. Giants such as Philip Morris, PepsiCo, Nestlé, Unilever, and BSN are all firmly established. In fact, food processing is now the largest and most profitable sector of Greek manufacturing.

Fish farming has become a vital new industry, especially since overfishing and pollution have reduced landings from the Mediterranean. The Greeks account for 40 percent of the 423 fish farms that were scattered throughout the Mediterranean region in 1995. Raising mainly sea bream and sea bass for both home and export markets, the industry produces about 12,000 tons annually and output should double by the year 2000.

Traditionally, the main branches of industry have been food processing, textiles, and chemicals. Over 36 percent of industrial establishments in these categories are situated in the Athens region, the next largest industrial center being Thessaloniki with over 12 percent. In 1983, 93 percent of all establishments had under 10 employees. By 1990, however, larger companies had been established. For example, among 4112 manufacturers, 30 percent had over 500 employees.

Government attempts at regional decentralization of industry have been partially successful. For example, many industries have been located along the main highway between Athens and Thessaloniki. In addition, a long-range program has established large industrial complexes and small modern industries throughout the country. Presently, one-third of Greece's manufacturing and over half of its exports originate in the three northern provinces of Epirus, Macedonia, and Thrace.

The industrial concentration west of Thessaloniki is a good example of heavy industry that was located far from the country's capital. The steel plant associated with this complex has helped to boost the production of steel to over 1 million tons annually. Two other industries of note are textiles, which provides the largest share of value added by the manufacturing sector (about 16 percent), and by shipbuilding and refitting, a sector that has fallen on hard times. In 1992 less then 1000 tons were launched compared to over 150,000 tons in 1974. Nevertheless, Greek owners have the world's largest merchant marine with nearly 111 million tons, mainly tankers, 46 percent of which are registered in the country.

Greek manufacturing suffers from a lack of competitiveness. Between 1981 and 1985 more than 40 percent of the country's industrial companies were showing net losses on their annual balance sheets, with losses exceeding profits each year for industry as a whole. Industrial production declined between 1980 and 1985, and investment stagnated. By 1990, the situation had improved, and 77 percent of manufacturing industries report-

ed a profit. The three most profitable were basic metallurgical products, food, and chemicals such as pharmaceuticals, cosmetics, and detergents. It remains to be seen whether the country, because of weak infrastructure, lack of a skilled labor force, and low R&D expenditures, can ever make high value-added products that can sell on an EU-wide basis.

Though on the periphery of Western Europe, potential foreign investors have been reminded of Greece's advantageous geographical location between Europe, the Balkan countries, and the Middle East and its good air connections to the latter regions. In fact, the country has benefited from the relocation of war-ravaged Beirut's financial institutions and companies in Athens. Also, there has been no lack of investment incentives. Overall, however, there has been a dearth of investors compared, for example, to Spain and Portugal. During the 1980s direct investment from overseas in Greek manufacturing and service industries totaled about $2 billion compared to $6.5 billion in Portugal. One reason was the government's ambivalent attitude and constantly changing policies toward private investment. On the one hand, it encouraged private investment in oil exploration, while on the other hand, once NAPC was successful, the government tried to nationalize the operation. Furthermore, during this period Europe's largest cement exporter, Heracles General Cement, was nationalized and then later sold to a company managed by the Italian Ferruzzi firm. Corruption charges have involved kickbacks to Greek officials of the former conservative government. The shifts in government from socialist to conservative and then back to socialist have also dampened investors' enthusiasm. Since returning to power, the Socialists have halted the privatization of the Greek telecommunications company OTE. They have also announced the revival of a large alumina plant near Thisbe with Russian, and hopefully, EU support. A major stake would be held by the Greek government. Because of the world's depressed market for aluminum, the scheme appears to be another money losing, make-work project funded by the Greek and EU taxpayers. Finally, relations with neighboring Albania, Macedonia, and Turkey have been counterproductive for the Greek economy.

Tourism employs directly or indirectly over one-half million persons and is a multibillion dollar industry. In addition, it is a valuable contributor to the country's balance of payments, accounting in 1993 for 4.6 percent of the GDP, the highest figure in Southern Europe. The surge in tourism during the 1960s grew to well over 4 million visitors by the end of the 1970s. In 1986 over 7 million tourists came to Greece, spending more than $1.8 billion; these figures reached 9.4 million and $3.2 billion in 1993. The tourist expenditures of Greeks outside the country in 1993 were only $995 million, leaving the country with a $2.2 billion balance. Present plans call for quality tourism rather than the continued growth of "sun and sea" packages; the extent to which this strategy will be implemented remains to be seen, however. As a start, casinos within luxurious facilities and convention centers are being built throughout the country in order to lure wealthy tourists.

The tourist invasion has precipitated many problems. The building of modern hotels has clashed with the traditional Greek urban and rural landscape. In addition, the atmosphere of seaside villages has been transformed into a tourist ambiance with discos and motorscooter rentals overshadowing local shops, small restaurants, fishing boats, and classical ruins. Tourism has concentrated in favored locations, such as the islands of Crete, Rhodes, Corfu, and Mykonos, leaving other regions untouched. Thus, one island may benefit financially because of tourism, whereas another may remain less disturbed but also at a low economic level. Tourist growth contributes to a general degradation of the environment, including air and water pollution as well as problems associated with the disposal of solid waste and garbage. The seasonality of tourism has meant that expensive facilities go unused for much of the year and employment is only for specific times. Finally, tourism can be severely affected by international terrorism, recession, and inflation. The pros and cons of many of these issues are discussed in the concluding section of this chapter.

In summary, Greece has made enormous economic gains since the end of the Second World War. New industries have been installed, facilities for the production of energy have been developed, new infrastructure has been established, and agri-culture modernized. The EU has contributed significantly to developing the country and will continue to do so in the future, although some of its projects such as the damming of the Acheloos in the southwest corner of the country have been criticized because of the resulting havoc to traditional farming and the destruction of a unique ecological system. Many Greeks have gone abroad in search of employment and have sent back much needed funds. Accompanying these changes has been a massive shift of population from the rural countryside to the urban and industrial centers. To be sure, there is evidence of increased prosperity throughout the country; nevertheless, regional economic disparities, though lessened somewhat, still remain.

The future offers a challenge on many fronts. Politically, the Socialists have returned to power during a recessional period. Will they try to stimulate the economy by more government spending, or will they retain some of the structural changes of the conservatives, such as the ending of price restrictions, privatization, liberalization of labor laws, and strengthening of competition policy? Relations with Turkey remain an enigma, although attempts at reconciliation are being made. Only time will tell whether the established pattern of recurring cycles of tension, followed by a brief period of *détente*, followed by renewed, higher levels of tension will be broken. The collapse of communism has had both positive and negative effects. The war in the former Yugoslavia has shattered normal political and economic links to the north. The country of Macedonia was for a time isolated by Greece, despite previous significant economic ties. Albanians have been pouring over the Greek border searching for work and fueling ethnic tensions. Nevertheless, a new thrust in the Greek economy has involved Bulgaria and to a lesser degree Romania. If the unstable political scene in the Balkans can be secured, then future possibilities for regional economic growth are very positive.

Economically, the country must reduce its escalating public debt and lessen inflation; manufacturing must become more competitive within the EU; and the welfare state must be contracted, public sector employment reduced (the public sector added 30,000 jobs in 1994), tax collection improved, and new wealth distributed over a broader base. Greece must continue its evolution toward a modern industrial country while at the same time preserving those spiritual and material elements from the past that have also become the hallmarks of other parts of the Western world.

Turkey

A short analysis of Turkey, a country of 63 million predominantly Moslem inhabitants in 1993, is necessary in order to understand its geopolitical significance to Europe, the former Soviet Union, the Middle East, and the delicate state of its relations with neighboring Greece. To comprehend the animosity between Greece and Turkey, one must go back centuries to the overthrow of Byzantium by the Ottoman Turks and their subsequent occupation of territories that later became the Greek state. Consideration must also be given to the bloody fighting between the two countries that took place in the chaos following World War I. As we have seen, Turkey controls the Bosporus, the Sea of Marmara, and the Dardanelles, the strategic waterways connecting the Aegean and the Black Sea. As a member of NATO, it anchors the southeastern flank of the organization that the western democracies established after World War II to contain the expansion of the Soviet Union. Paradoxically, Turkish troops, armed with NATO weapons, invaded nearby Cyprus in 1974 to thwart the Greek government's attempt to annex the island. This has led to the division of Cyprus into two countries: one Turkish controlled, with a predominantly Turkish population, and the other the Republic of Cyprus, with a predominantly Greek population. Greece and Turkey's inability to compromise on the Cyprus issue has been a major factor contributing to the state of tension between the two countries.

Turkey was a key partner of the UN forces during the Gulf War with Iraq, providing vital airfields for the United Nations' air strikes. The country has also established close relationships with the independent Islamic lands of the former Soviet Union and is aiding these countries economically. In addition, Turkey's key role in the Middle East cannot be overlooked: it controls the headwaters of both the Tigris and Euphrates rivers, which are vital to the viable agriculture of both Syria and Iraq. Finally, because of its more than 8 million Kurds, living mainly in the east and southeast, Turkey has been drawn into a bloody conflict with separatist and terrorist elements that not only has affected the Kurdish regions of Turkey but has also spread to West European cities, especially those of Germany. Because of large Kurdish minorities in Iran and Iraq, the war has had further international ramifications.

Nearly six times as large as Greece and twice as large as Italy, Turkey is the poorest country in the OECD. As a result of a high birth rate, population has been increasing by more than 1 million people a year. About 35.5 percent of the inhabitants are under 15 years of age. When Ankara, Turkey's political and administrative center, was built in the 1930s, it was designed for 100,000 inhabitants. Today, it boasts over 3.5 million inhabitants in its old and new quarters. The economic focal point of the country, connecting Europe and Asia, is the Bosporus region, home to over 7 million. One serious problem is the contrast between the highly developed, European-style urban areas, such as Ankara, Istanbul, Bursa, Izmir, and Adana which are in the western half of the country and the backward agrarian regions of the Anatolian highlands of the eastern half of Turkey. At least 50 percent of the country's population lives in poorly developed rural areas with inadequate infrastructure and an archaic form of subsistence and barter economy. A major hydroelectric and irrigation project, the Southeast Anatolia Project (GAP) in the upper basins of the Tigris and Euphrates rivers, is a start in overcoming the isolation of the east. However, GAP's success depends on solving the Kurdish conflict.

The gap between the industrial and developing regions of the country is reminiscent of differences between northern and southern Italy after World War II, except that it is more extreme. For example, automobile density in Turkey is only about one-fifth that of Greece; however, almost all the vehicles are concentrated in the urban areas, resulting in chaotic traffic conditions. By comparison, few rural dwellers have cars, although, despite the rough nature of the roads, truck, bus and tourist traffic can be considerable. There are also great differences in income levels. The OECD calculated that per capita income was $2928 (PPP $5410) in 1993; the government states that it should be twice as high, however. Nevertheless, people in the cities appear to have substantially greater purchasing power than statistics would indicate. Their way of life is little different from that of urbanites in Western Europe; however, in the rural areas hardly any cash circulates, and saving traditionally takes the form of gold jewelry.

In the decade 1981–1991, economic growth averaged 5.1 percent annually and was 6 percent in 1992. The production of electricity cannot keep pace with demand. Per capita energy consumption, the lowest in the OECD, is less than half that of Greece. The country's economy has been undergoing a liberalization, with bureaucratic barriers crumbling and foreign products competing alongside domestic products, although in certain sectors, such as automobiles, there is still limited competition. Attempts are being made to reduce government intervention in the economy. Much has been accomplished along these lines, but serious problems continue to face Turkey, among which are a high rate of inflation—66 percent in 1991, reaching 70 percent in 1993, and nearly 150 percent in 1994. Unemployment was also over 8 percent in 1994. Furthermore, the balance of payments deficit was close to $5 billion. Privatization had been blocked by political and legal conflict, and the public sector deficit was close to 16 percent of the GDP. Economic chaos erupted in 1994, forcing the government to devalue the Turkish lira by 38 percent, raise commodity prices to realistic levels, and close loss-making state enterprises in an effort to head off hyperinflation.

Economic underdevelopment is mirrored in employment statistics. In 1993, 45 percent of the working population were employed in the primary sector, which contributed 14.4 percent of GDP. Industry employed only 22 percent but produced nearly 33 percent of GDP, whereas the tertiary sector accounted for 33 percent of the workforce and for 53 percent of GDP. Exports have been strong, with the industrial sector accounting for over 75 percent; however, imports have been growing faster. In 1992 the country had a negative trade balance of over $14 billion. Goods, such as leather, textiles and clothing, semifinished iron and steel products, and machinery—most of which are produced under license—are the main exports, of which nearly 50 percent go to the EU and 25 percent to the Middle East. The balance of trade deficit has been reduced by earnings from tourism and remittances from laborers working abroad. However, tourism suffered during the Gulf War and has been seriously affected by Kurdish terrorist acts aimed against foreign tourists.

Turkey, an associate member of the EU, supplies migrant labor to many countries in the Union, especially Germany, but was turned down for full membership in 1989. Greece has posed strong opposition to Turkey's admission, although the UK and Germany wish to strengthen EU ties with Turkey. A proposed customs union with the EU could be in place during the late 1990s and would bring Turkey a major step closer to European integration. A significant negative factor for full membership is that Turkey is an Islamic state with deep cultural and historical roots in the Middle East and is being affected by the worldwide revival of fundamentalism. By comparison, the EU is a grouping of countries that are predominantly Christian in religion and that share a common Western heritage.

There are certain hypocritical elements in the EU's relationship with Turkey. For example, after selling Turkey machinery to modernize its textile industry, the EU placed quotas on Turkish textiles, a sector that employs about one-fifth of the workforce and accounts for about one-quarter of Turkish export earnings. The EU has also questioned Turkey's record on human rights and is concerned about potential mass migration from Turkey to EU countries.

A number of adverse factors must be overcome for Turkey to become a full member of the EU. First, the disputes between Greece and Turkey must be resolved; second, Turkey's record on human rights must be improved; the Kurdish conflict must be settled; and last, the current EU states must accept the fact that whereas they are all predominantly Christian countries with a common culture, Turkey is a state with roots in Islamic civilization.

Cyprus

Fifty miles south of the Taurus Mountains of Turkey lies a continuation of the mainland ranges, the island of Cyprus. Two chains of mountains (the most southerly of which rises to almost 6396 ft [1950 m]) are separated by a major lowland known as the Mesoria Plain; the three features form the main physiographic regions. Over 248 miles (400 km) to the west is the nearest Greek territory, the island of Rhodes.

Cyprus, after a period of violent resistance led by the Greek Cypriots, obtained independence from British rule in 1960 and became a republic. Nevertheless, fighting between Greek and Turkish Cypriots ensued until a UN peacekeeping force was established in 1964. The Republic of Cyprus became a member of the British Commonwealth and has associated status with the European Union. The involvement of both Greece and Turkey in Cyprus relates to the unconditional support both countries give to their respective ethnic compatriots on the island, especially since the attempted Greek coup and subsequent Turkish invasion of 1974. The present population of Cyprus, about 850,000, is divided between Greek Cypriots, who belong to the Greek Orthodox Church and comprise 80 percent of the total, and Turkish Cypriots, who are Muslims and make up 20 percent of the total.

The contemporary political situation has been complicated by the Turkish invasion. The island was divided along a 68-mile (110-km) frontier into a Turkish-dominated northern and Greek- dominated southern sector that split the capital Nicosia (Lefkosha in Turkish). In 1975 the Turkish Federated Republic of North Cyprus (TFRNC) was established, occupying 38 percent of the island's territory. It was unilaterally declared independent in 1983, and only Turkey, among all the world's countries, recognizes it. Population changes resulting from the invasion have divided the island geographically between Turks and Greeks. Some of the best resorts, agricultural land, factories, and ports, including Famagusta, were taken over by the Turks (Fig. 10-16). Nearly 200,000 Greek Cypriots fled south, and almost 50,000 Turkish Cypriots were forced north. Present estimates indicate that about 170,00 Turkish Cypriots live in the north, including some 40,000 Turkish mainlanders, and at least 27,000 Turkish troops. Only the southern part of the island, the Republic of Cyprus, is a member of the United Nations and is recognized by the international community.

Economically, the north and south of Cyprus are vastly different. Much of the north's budget (estimates range anywhere from 35 to 70%) is financed by Turkey. Per capita income of only $4000 in 1994 was one-third that of the south's, reflecting the north's difficult economic conditions. Agriculture is the mainstay of the north's economy, accounting for about 20 percent of GDP, 40 percent of employment, and 70 percent of export earnings. Because the north has not been recognized as a sovereign state, it suffers economically and cannot exploit its tourist potential. For example, tourists, about 60,000 annually, cannot fly directly to the north because the international airport at Nicosia is still closed. They must come via the Turkish mainland.

The south has a more diversified economy. Agriculture accounts for only about 7 percent of GDP, whereas manufacturing contributes nearly 20 percent. Economic growth has been boosted by the establishment of companies and banks that located in the Republic after the collapse of Lebanon. Today more than 1000 offshore companies, including AT&T, Sony, and Johnson Wax, conduct their regional or worldwide activities from the south of the island. Thus, the southern part of Nicosia has grown by more than 130,000 people since the Turkish invasion, compared to the stagnation of the Turkish sector.

The south also plays a strong commercial role in relations with Lebanon. Less than 124 miles (200 km) from the war-ravaged country, the Republic of Cyprus was a staging area for the movement of goods and people to and from the mainland. A German-Cypriot company, located in Limassol, controls the bulk of container traffic in transit from Cyprus. Principal destinations are Lebanon, Syria, and Egypt. Over 12,000 Lebanese, mainly Maronite Christians, live in Limassol, the main port and second city of the Republic. In addition,

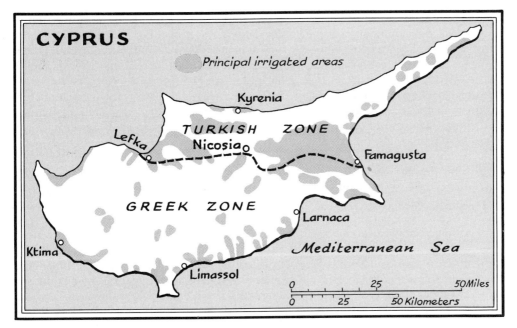

FIGURE 10-16 Divided Cyprus.

Lebanese made up about 7 percent of the more than 2.5 million tourists that visited the republic in 1994. In the summer of 1988 prospects for the unification of Cyprus that would provide iron-clad guarantees for the civil rights of both Greeks and Turks took a positive turn. The Greek and Turkish Cypriot leaders began meeting in Geneva under the auspices of the United Nations; however, by the mid-1990s little had been accomplished, mainly because of Turkish Cypriot fears about territorial concessions and UN plans for a federal solution to end the island's division.

The complex process of European unification has enveloped Cyprus as well as Greece and Turkey. On the one hand, the EU agreed to Turkey's entrance to the customs union. On the other hand, Greece linked the issue to the protection of Greek Cypriot interests and stated that it would not veto Turkey's entry as long as negotiations on Cyprus's membership in the EU would begin by 1998. Once a member, Cyprus would be much less vulnerable to a Turkish military threat. Thus, the Turks are under pressure to unify the island so that the north will not be excluded from Europe's single market.

The division of Cyprus between Turkish and Greek elements is a classic example of tenuous relations between two ethnic and religious groups that have their roots in historical events. At the time of this writing, modern politicians have not been able to overcome this legacy.

Malta

Malta, located less than 60 miles (100 km) from southeast Sicily, is a structural continuation of the limestones of the Italian island. The group of islands, Gozo, Comino, and Malta, that comprise the country of Malta are only 22 sq miles (31.5 sq km) and in 1993 had 366,000 inhabitants. Like Sicily, Malta has been occupied by a series of invaders, ranging from Phoenicians and Greeks to Byzantines and Arabs. The country lacks natural resources and a solid agricultural base and depends on manufacturing, trade, services, and tourism for its economic viability.

For more than 150 years the Maltese economy subsisted largely on earnings and employment provided by the British army. When the last British troops left in 1979, an economic vacuum resulted that was filled with the development of light industry and tourist facilities. Government control of key sectors of the economy was responsible for launching export-oriented industries, such as the fabrication of garments, footwear, plastics, metals, and chemical products that were aimed at West European markets. Investment from Europe followed, and earnings from tourism multiplied. The rapid growth of the economy ended in 1980 as the worldwide recession hit Europe. Malta became uncompetitive as labor costs rose and low-cost products from Asia flooded Malta's overseas markets. Tourism also suffered because of rising prices, the government's political antagonism toward those countries from which the tourist flow originated, and an infrastructure that could not cope with the tourist invasion. To counter the recession the country concluded a series of barter deals with the Soviet Union and Eastern bloc countries and developed trade with North African neighbors, such as Algeria, Tunisia, and Libya. Nonetheless, in 1986 over 60 percent of the island's trade was still with members of the EC. A fresh assault was made on those markets, and by 1993 the percentage had risen to over 77—Italy at 44 percent being the largest single customer for exports.

Government strategy changed in recent years, in part, spurred by the election of the nationalists after 16 years of uninterrupted socialist rule. There was emphasis on upgrading the skills of the hardworking, English-speaking labor force so that high-tech industry will want to invest in Malta. The government's role in directing the economy has been downplayed, although the public sector generated about 40 percent of Malta's GDP and employed 49 percent of the workforce in 1991. Agriculture and fishing contributed only 3.6 percent of the GDP, whereas manufacturing, ship repair, and shipbuilding accounted for 27 percent. Continuing efforts are being made to encourage private investment in key sectors, including banking and finance. Plans called for the creation of between 5000 and 10,000 jobs, mainly in export-oriented and service industries. Favored sectors include high fashion, footwear, small electrical goods, automobile parts, and hospital products. Presently, over 400 firms are engaged in exporting their services or products, including over 200 for-

eign companies. Projects have been initiated to alleviate shortages of electricity and fresh water as well as to improve telecommunications and harbor and airport facilities. For example, new shipbuilding and repair facilities have been constructed, as has a grain terminal. Tourism, which climbed to 728,000 visitors in 1980 and then fell off sharply, climbed to over 1 million in 1993, the vast majority of whom came from the United Kingdom. However, tourism is reaching the saturation level. All told, substantial progress has been made in setting the country back on course to economic stability and prosperity. Annual growth was 5 percent between 1986 and 1993, raising the per capita income above that of Greece and Portugal. Unemployment, as high as 9 percent in 1985, was under 4 percent by the early 1990s. The government has set up the Malta International Business Authority to create a small but reputable offshore financial center and has applied for EU membership—though a socialist government elected in 1996 now opposes entry. It also remains unclear how many of the recent policies supporting economic expansion will be continued by the new government.

CONCLUSIONS

Southern Europe is a complex region characterized by a ruggedly beautiful landscape and fundamental change since 1945. All of the countries and regions it encompasses have made strong economic progress since the Second World War, with Italy and southern France leading the way—though not without environmental costs and damages. The region's countries have been transformed from rural societies into vigorous, industrialized, urban-oriented democratic states that are growing through local and foreign investment in sectors such as manufacturing, tourism, wholesaling, distribution, and food processing.

Southern European countries may be characterized in the following manner: unemployment is relatively high, reaching over 20 percent in Spain and nearly 40 percent in the under age 25 bracket; government deficits are larger than elsewhere because of massive public sector spending on declining industries and social programs, as a result of which inflation rates are higher than in other countries of Europe; all the countries have a "black" or underground economy that contributes as much as 25 percent to the gross domestic product but is not included in official statistics; industrial growth areas that focus on fast-growing cities such as Barcelona, Thessaloniki, Porto, Nice, or Milano are found in every country and a continuous urban strip, the Mediterranean Arc from Barcelona to Genoa, has emerged; environmental pollution has been more severe throughout Southern Europe than elsewhere; and lastly, all the countries were seriously affected by the severe recession of the early 1990s and their currencies have been devalued. Because of the inherent weakness of their economies, the world economic restructuring that characterized this period had a greater impact on Southern Europe than elsewhere.

To further understand Southern Europe, we must consider the region not only within the economic and political framework of the European Union, but also within the physical and geopolitical matrix of the Mediterranean Basin, an area with local characteristics and problems. For example, Southern Europe was drawn into the Lebanese Civil War, the Arab-Israeli conflict, the United States' confrontation with Libya, and the Gulf War. Furthermore, murderous incidents by terrorist groups, both international and local, have left their stain in cities such as Athens, Barcelona, Florence, Milan, Nice, and Rome; on places such as Sicily, Corsica, Cyprus, and northern Spain; and on ships plying the Mediterranean. Bloody conflicts, which have resisted meaningful solutions, are also clearly evident. Basque separatist actions are almost a daily part of contemporary Spain. The Red Brigades, the Mafia, and other extremist groups sporadically surface in Italy. Corsica is racked by separatist bombings and Mafia-type killings. The Greek-Turkish confrontation flares from time to time in the Aegean. And a permanent answer to the division of Cyprus, though possibly closer than in many years, still remains a distant hope. In addition, increasing tension in the nearby Maghreb (Morocco, Tunisia, and Algeria), because of high birth rates, weak economies, and the rise of Islamic fundamentalism, poses a serious threat to the EU and especially the countries of Spain,

France, and Italy, which have borne and will bear the brunt of both illegal and legal immigration to their countries from North Africa. Already, the large African populations in these countries and in southern France have led to racial attacks and are related to social problems such as prostitution, drug-dealing, and petty crime, all of which add fuel to the paranoid political platforms of neo-Nazi or neo-Fascist parties.

Finally, if a meaningful outcome to the problem of pollution in the Mediterranean Sea is to be found, there must be more cooperation among all of the countries, European, African, Middle Eastern, and Asian (the Black Sea states), that comprise the geopolitical mosaic around this historic and strategic body of water.

BIBLIOGRAPHY

Beeley, B. W. (1978). "The Greek-Turkish Boundary: Conflict at the Interface." Transactions of the Institute of British Geographers. 3:351–366.

Collins, R. (1987). The Basques. The People of Europe series. New York: Basil Blackwell.

Diem, A. (1963). "An Evaluation of Land Reform and Reclamation in Sicily." *Canadian Geographer* 4: 182–191.

_____. (1979). *Western Europe: A Geographical Analysis*. New York: Wiley. (Reprinted by the author with additions, 1988.)

_____. (1988). "Pollution on the Roof of Europe." Geographical Magazine (June): 2–8.

Financial Times. Financial Times Survey. (1995). "Turkey," June 12, pp I–VIII.

_____. (1995). "Spain", June 30, pp 21–26; (1994) May 11, pp 27–30; (1993) April 2, pp I-VI.

_____. (1995). "Italy," July 28, pp 7-10; (1994) July 7, pp 27–32; (1993) June 30, pp I–VI; (1992) July 7, pp I–VIII; (1991) June 6, pp I–VIII.

_____. (1995). "Malta," September 22, pp 1–4;(1994) February 18, pp I–IV.

_____. (1995). "Italian Industry and Technology." October 25, pp 27–31; (1993) October 13, pp 25–29.

_____. (1994). "Marmara", July 5, pp 12–14.

_____. (1994). "Greece." July 8, pp 9–12; (1994) November 14, pp I–IV; (1992) July 15, pp 23–26.

_____. (1994). "Monaco." July 19, pp I–IV; (1990) May 14, pp I–VI.

_____. (1994). "Portugal." October 28, pp 11–14; (1993) November 8, pp I–IV.

_____. (1994). "Turkish Finance and Industry." November 3, pp I–IV.

_____. (1994). "Italian Banking and Finance." November 24, pp 25–28.

_____. (1993). "Spain: Banking and Finance." June 23, pp I–VI.

_____. (1993). "The Basque Country." November 24, pp 27–30.

_____. (1992). "Northern Greece." November 4, pp I–VI.

_____. (1991). "Emilia Romagna." May 20, pp 11-13.

_____. (1990). "Italian Industry." October 23, pp I–X.

Financial Times. Financial Times Traveller (1993). "Barcelona." November pp, 1–16.

Friedrich, Michael. (1993). "Wie ein Fluss den Bach runter-geht." Greenpeace, (March–May): 48–54.

Geo. (1993). "Monaco", No. 173. (July): 58–117.

_____. (1989). "Traumstadt im Hoch-Format", (May) 64–86.

Grenon, M., and M. Batisse, eds. (1991). _Futures for the Mediterranean Basin: The Blue Plan_. London: Oxford University Press.

Houston, J. M. (1964). _The Western Mediterranean World_. London: Longmans.

Hudson, R., and J. Lewis. (1985). _Uneven Development in Southern Europe_. London: Methuen.

International Herald Tribune. (1994). A Special Report. "Barcelona." June 15, pp 17–18.

Jouve, A., P. Stragiotti, and M. Fabries-Verfaillie. (1992). _La France des Regions_. Rosny: Bréal.

_____. (1994). _La France des Villes_. Rosny: Bréal.

King, R. (1985). "Italian Migration: The Clotting of the Haemorrhage." _Geography_ (April):171–175.

Lewis, J., and A. Williams. (1985). "Portugal: The Decade of Return." _Geography_ (April): 178–182.

l'Etat de la France 94–95. (1994). Paris: Editions la Découverte.

Malta Information. (1995). Valetta: Department of Information.

Morris, A., and G. Dickinson. (1987), "Tourist Development in Spain: Growth Versus Conservation on the Costa Brava." _Geography_ 72:16–25.

Newbigin, M. I. (1952). _Southern Europe_. London: Methuen.

Organization for Economic Cooperation and Development (1975). _Mediterranean Pilot Study of Environmental Degradation and Pollution from Coastal Development Final Report_. Paris: OECD.

_____ Economic Surveys (Published annually). _Portugal, Spain, Italy, Greece_. Paris: OECD.

_____ (1986). _Tourism Policy and International Tourism in the OECD Member Countries in 1985_. Paris: OECD.

Pastor, X., ed. (1991). _The Greenpeace Book of the Mediterranean_. London: Collins & Brown.

Robinson, H. (1960). _The Mediterranean Lands_. London: University Tutorial Press.

Rodgers, A. (1979). _Economic Development in Retrospect; The Italian Model & Its Significance for Regional Planning in Market-Oriented Economies_. New York: V. H. Winston.

Semple, E. C. (1931). _The Geography of the Mediterranean Region_. New York: Henry Holt.

Siegried, A. (1948). _The Mediterranean_. London: Jonathan Cape.

Stanislawski, D. (1959). _The Individuality of Portugal_. Austin: University of Texas Press.

_____. (1963). _Portugal's Other Kingdom: The Algarve_. Austin: University of Texas Press.

Walker, D. (1960). _The Mediterranean Lands_. New York: Wiley.

Williams, A., ed. (1984). _Southern Europe Transformed: Political and Economic Change in Greece, Italy, Portugal, and Spain_. London: Harper & Row.

Tableaux de l'Economie Française: 1993–1994 (1993). Amiens: INSEE.

11

WEST CENTRAL EUROPE

The politically stable, democratic, and prosperous West Central European countries—Austria, Germany, Liechtenstein, and Switzerland— are four of Europe's success stories. Each, in one way or another, has overcome political problems that severely threatened its social and economic fabric, and each has become a leader in some aspect of international and European integration. The turbulent histories, yet ultimate successes, of these states offer hope for neighboring states in East Central Europe.

Once among the resource-short and poorer of Western European countries, Switzerland invested in its human resources and used its tradition of stability and neutrality as bases for rapid economic growth, which has been particularly strong since the end of the Second World War. Today, though not without social problems and economic difficulties, Switzerland is one of the world's wealthiest countries. Austria's path to economic success has been a more difficult one. Before 1918, the Austro-Hungarian Empire was a vast domain of diverse lands with culturally distinct inhabitants (Fig. 4-2). After the peace treaty, the country was reduced to "rump Austria" and experienced great political and economic difficulty during the tumultuous interwar years. Absorbed into Nazi Germany in 1938, Austria was occupied by the Allied powers, including the Soviet Union, after World War II. Occupation ended in 1955, when Austria emerged as a democratic but neutral country, cut off from neighboring Czechoslovakia and Hungary by the "Iron Curtain." Nevertheless, owing in part to strong trade ties with Germany, the country prospered, and when communism collapsed in the early 1990s, it joined the enlarged EU as one of Europe's most flourishing and stable states.

Germany, first united only about 125 years ago, has suffered through three *Reichs* (empires), two world wars, political and economic instability, physical devastation, and military occupation. Nevertheless, the country experienced two eras of rapid economic growth (1871–1914 and 1949–1974). Today, democratically ruled and politically united for the first time in a half-century, Germany has the largest and strongest economy and one of the most stable currencies in Europe. Furthermore, it has been the leader in the expansion of the European Union and integration of the former socialist countries into the Western sphere.

West Central Europe, formerly a battleground during the Reformation, the Napoleonic wars, the two world wars, and the Cold War, is now central to the European Union and the emerging democracies of Eastern Europe, in both economic and geopolitical terms.

PHYSICAL GEOGRAPHY

The diverse physical landscape of West Central Europe ranges from sedimentary lowlands in northern Germany, covered by thick continental glacial deposits; the eroded, ancient rocks that characterize the Central Uplands regions of Germany and Austria, such as the Black Forest (*Schwarzwald*) and Bavarian Forest (*Bayerischer Wald*); to the glaciated Alps composed of sedimentary, metamorphic, and igneous rocks that trend east-west through all four countries (Fig. 11-1). All of these landform regions are extensions of similar features found in the bordering countries. The climate of West Central Europe is as varied as the landscape, ranging from maritime conditions in northern Germany to more continental conditions in eastern Germany and Austria. The high valleys and peaks of the Alps have great seasonal temperature fluctuations and high levels of precipitation. The southern Alpine flanks of Switzerland and Austria have much more moderate climates; subtropical climatic regions may be found in some of the sheltered valleys.

The North European Plain

This extensive plain extends about 125 miles (200 km) southward from the North and Baltic seacoasts to the Central Uplands. In West Central Europe the Plain is the main physiographic feature of northern Germany, with extensions west into

the Netherlands and east into Poland. Its unconsolidated deposits were laid down by ice sheets that spread southward from Scandinavia and from associated meltwaters associated with glaciation. The terrain is strewn with glacial erratics (boulders brought from the north), clay, gravel, sand, and deposits of windblown loess varying in thickness between 40 and 500 ft (12 and 152 m). Various stages of glacial retreat are marked by moraines that give the region a hilly character. The plain is generally divided into two subregions, one west and one east of the Elbe River. The plain in its western part—between the North Sea coast and the East Frisian Islands—includes extensive tidal flats on the seashore and in the estuaries of the Elbe, Weser, and Ems rivers. The estuaries, like the polders in the Netherlands, were reclaimed by diking and draining; the soil is rich and suitable for grazing and some intensive agriculture, such as the orchards of the Altes Land on the south bank of the Elbe northwest of Hamburg. Beyond the tidal flats, in the adjacent zone of sandy soils, there are usually extensive fens—level, treeless, and covered with grasses. Although the fens still cover a large area, Dutch-inspired methods of draining have made it possible to raise vegetables and cattle, and new agricultural settlements have been established—for example, Papenburg, on the lower Ems. Between the Elbe and the Ems is the Luneburger Heath, a sandy area extending from the Elbe to the Weser-Aller.

The Plain east of the Elbe extends further south into the territory of former East Germany and adjacent Poland. Along the Baltic seacoast is a swath of fairly productive clay soils up to about 30 miles (50 km) inland, and wider still east of Rostock. To the south of this intensively farmed region are sandy soils used for grazing or covered by coniferous forests. This region is criss-crossed by broad river valleys that are ancient glacial spillways now occupied by small streams and canals. In some areas of Mecklenburg and Brandenburg north of Berlin, there are beautifully sculpted glacial moraine landscapes of lakes intermingled with alternating fields and forests (Fig. 11-2). This area and its sandy counterpart west of the Elbe have Germany's lowest population densities.

The climate of the Plain in West Central Europe

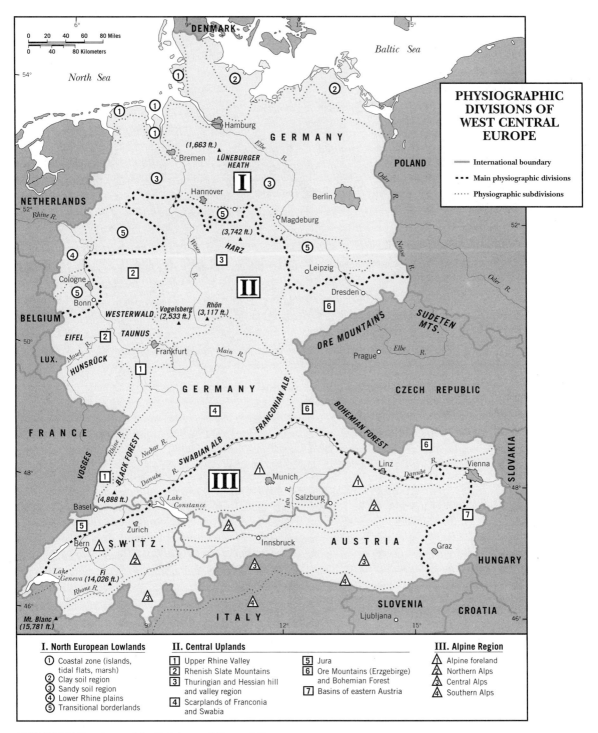

FIGURE 11-1 Physiographic divisions of Central Europe.

FIGURE 11-2 North European Plain in eastern Germany. In most places the Plain is relatively flat, fertile, and intensively farmed. (Daniel Hummel/The Image Bank)

is maritime, with cool summers and mild winters, considerable precipitation, and strong winds. From west to east it is colder and drier in winter because of increasing distance from the moderating influence of the North Atlantic. Thus, for example, although Münster in the west and more easterly Berlin have similar altitudes, Münster has 15 fewer days with frost, is on average 3.5 degrees farenheit warmer in January, and receives several inches more precipitation than the more continental Berlin.

At the southern margins of the Plain there is a transitional borderland, a narrow, noncontinuous belt of land across Germany with highly fertile loess soils. Although the width of this zone varies, it broadens to include several productive lowland embayments important for agriculture—such as the Cologne and Münster Lowlands, the Magdeburger Börde, and the Harz Forelands. The region also possesses great mineral wealth, mainly bituminous coal and lignite deposits in the Rhineland, Ruhr, Magdeburg, Leipzig, and Lusatian regions, and small amounts of petroleum between Han-

nover and Brunswick. The combination of mineral resources and valuable farmland supports a dense rural and urban population. Most of the towns are situated at points where routes from the uplands to the south fan out into the plains, on which there are also important east-west transportation arteries. The Mittelland Canal from the Ems to the Oder—a direct water connection between the Oder, Berlin, the Ruhr, and the Rhine—traverses the Plain (see Fig. 1-7).

The Central Uplands

Between the North German Plain and the Alpine Foreland to the south is a region of great diversity—rolling, forested hills, granite massifs, and old volcanoes—all belonging to the Central Uplands. The hilly and diversified character of this zone is the result of movements in the earth's crust and associated uplifting, faulting, and erosion. There are also volcanic intrusions, especially in the western Uplands. The heights near the center of the

Uplands generally escaped the ice cover, but the peripheral valleys, particularly in the north, were broadened by ice action. Only the highest portions of the Uplands were covered by mountain glaciers, evident, for example, by way of U-shaped glacial valleys in the Black Forest.

The Central Uplands are divided into numerous topographical units. Especially significant is the Rhine Valley, extending from Basel in Switzerland, at the head of Rhine navigation, to Düsseldorf at the edge of the Rhenish Slate Mountains (Rheinisches Schiefergebirge), and then continuing out onto the North European Plain, across the Dutch border to the North Sea. The Upper Rhine Valley, extending from Basel to Frankfurt, is over 180 miles (290 km) long, but only about 25 miles (40 km) wide. The valley is a graben—a feature formed by the collapse of land between two roughly parallel faults, which run along the base of the French Vosges region on the west and the Black Forest on the east. The Rhine, which rises in the Swiss Alps, turns north into the faulted valley at Basel, which is a rich agricultural region.

The ancient Rhine River cut through the Central Uplands as they were being uplifted. North of Mainz in western Germany the Rhine flows through a narrow meandering gorge, about 1450 ft (nearly 450 m) below surrounding heights (Fig. 11-3). Vineyards still cover terraced, sun-facing lower slopes of the steep-sided Rhine Gorge, as well as many tributary valleys, notably along the Moselle. The Rhine is Europe's busiest waterway for barge

FIGURE 11-3 Castle Gutenfels on the Rhine. Ships of many nations must carefully wind their way through this narrow and still dangerous stretch of the Rhine, especially at low water level. (Inter Nationes, Bonn, Federal Republic of Germany)

traffic, a transportation funnel with highways and railways; the Gorge is an important tourist attraction.

The Central Uplands are not a climatic divide within Europe as are the Alps, although higher elevations within the Uplands have a harsher climate than nearby lowlands. Precipitation increases rapidly with increasing altitude, and, of course, temperature declines. Climatic differences within short distances near the Uplands are often greater than the differences caused by continentality between western and eastern locations on the European Plain. For example, the average annual temperature and rainfall differences between London and Moscow, over 1200 miles (1900 km) apart, are 13°F (7°C) and 5.5 in. (60 mm), respectively. Freiburg, Germany (elev. 874 ft/269 m) and the Feldberg, the highest peak in the Black Forest (4771 ft/1468m), are just 12 miles (20 km) apart but have annual temperature differences of 13°F (7°C). The Feldberg is wetter and colder than Moscow and has over 32 in. (830 mm) more precipitation than nearby Freiburg. The more equable climates of lower elevations, especially mild conditions in the Rhine Valley, permit cultivation of wheat, sugar beets, tobacco, hops, fruits, and grapes, with vineyards in foothills of bordering hills.

The Alpine Region

The third major physiographic region in West Central Europe comprises the central part of Europe's Alpine region. The Alps extend into seven countries—Italy, France, Switzerland, Liechtenstein, Germany, Austria, and Slovenia. Of these, Switzerland, Liechtenstein, Austria, and Slovenia are truly Alpine counties. The Alpine region has two primary subregions—the Alpine Foreland or foothills region, and the Alps themselves.

The Alpine Foreland, and related Swiss Plateau, extend from near Geneva eastwards across the northern side of the Alps to Vienna. Its widest north-south extent is in Germany and its narrowest in Austria, but in all three countries this alpine foothill and foreland country is an important area for agriculture and settlement with cities such as Lausanne, Bern, Zürich, Augsburg, Munich, and Linz located on it.

The Swiss section, the Swiss Plateau or Mittland, with elevations varying between 1140 and 2110 ft (350 and 650 m), is by far the most important area for settlement and economic activity in Switzerland. Delineated by the Jura to the northwest, the Lake of Constance (Bodensee) to the northeast, and the Alps to the south, the region's landforms have been greatly influenced by glaciation, resulting in numerous lakes. A wide variety of agricultural activities are supported, including grain cultivation and dairying. The mixture of agricultural activities and interspersed forests, hills, lakes, and settlements—many with preserved and restored historic buildings, and virtually all carefully planned and maintained—offers an appealing landscape (Fig. 11-4).

The similarly attractive German portion of the the Alpine Foreland, the northward-sloping continuation of the Swiss Plateau, has the appearance of a broad plain. It has been covered by deposits from glaciers emanating from the Alps, resulting in moraines, gravels, sands, and erratics. A number of glacial lakes such as the Ammersee and Starnberger See southwest of Munich have been formed. The northern section of the Foreland is relatively flat and well suited for agriculture now that low-lying areas have been drained. The higher southern parts with a harsher climate and less fertile soils, such as the Allgäu, are areas of dairy farming, forestry, and tourism. Rivers crossing the region rise in the Alps and flow north in broad low valleys to the Danube (Donau).

The Austrian extension of the Swiss and German Alpine Foreland is the Danube Valley, an important, narrow transport corridor between the Alps to the south and a portion of the Central Uplands, the Bohemian Massif, to the north. The Valley is a depression 15 to 30 miles (25 to 48 km) wide, through which flows the Danube, navigable from Ulm in Germany to the Black Sea. A canal first considered in Roman times now connects the Danube with the Rhine and Main rivers via the Altmühl Valley in Germany. Thus, river traffic for 1500-ton barges is now possible between the North and Black seas. The attractiveness of the rural landscape of the Danube Valley is enhanced by an amalgam of tidy farms, forested hillsides, quiet villages with characteristic onion-domed Roman Catholic churches, and occasional grand castles

FIGURE 11-4 A typical section of the densely settled, highly industrialized, and intensively farmed Swiss Plateau. Near the center, the Reuss and Limmat rivers join the Aare River, which flows 10 miles farther through the Jura Mountains to reach the Rhine River. (Swissair)

and churches, including the ruins of Königstein, which according to legend served as the first of Richard the Lion Hearted's prisons prior to his ransom, and an imposing abbey above the river at Melk. Eastern portions of the valley have particularly fertile soil, a mild climate, and important fruit- and wine-producing regions (e.g., the Wachau). Though an important transportation artery, the tonnage carried on the Danube does not compare to traffic on the Rhine.

The Alps to the south of the Foreland form an important climatic and cultural divide between Northern and Southern Europe, though numerous low-elevation passes have always allowed trade and population movements. The mountain chain extends in an arc from the French-Italian border on the Mediterranean, then north and eastward across Switzerland, Italy, Germany, Austria, and Slovenia. Waters that rise in the Alps flow into the North Sea by way of the Rhine, into the Black Sea

via the Inn, a tributary of the Danube, and into the Mediterranean via the Rhône and Po.

Tectonic movements resulting in the collision of the European and African landmasses have created three broad, folded bands of upthrusted rock. Massifs of elevated rocks such as the Mont Blanc and Gotthard Massifs are among the highest mountains in the Alps. The northern pre-Alps or Helvetic folds are composed of a variety of different rock types and include the highest mountain in Germany—the Zugspitze. The central East Alpine folds are higher and reflect the impact of erosion from Alpine glaciation. Rising through folded rocks are, for example, the Pennine Alps in Switzerland and the Hohe Tauren in Austria. To the south are the Dinaric folds, which include large areas of Dolomite limestone seen in the Julian Alps of Austria and Slovenia.

A number of distinct geographical characteristics are evident throughout the Alps, in which differences in local relief are immense. The highest mountains, composed of crystalline rocks, are found in the Mont Blanc Massif (15,622 ft/4807 m) and in the huge overthrust fold of the Monte Rosa (15,060 ft/4634 m) that forms the Swiss-Italian boundary (Fig. 11-5). Glaciated river valleys lie far below the surrounding mountains (Fig. 2-3). For example, Sierre in the Rhône Valley of Switzerland (valley floor at 1732 ft/533 m) and Innsbruck in the Inn Valley of western Austria (1865 ft/574 m) lie below peaks of up to 8100 ft (2500 m). Valley climates are far milder than in the surrounding mountains; soils, comprised of glacial moraines and alluvial deposits, are more fertile; and routeways through the Alpine arc are facilitated. For example, Martigny, Switzerland, is situated on

FIGURE 11-5 The Matterhorn in Switzerland, one of Europe's most dramatic peaks. As in many areas of the Alps, hikers and sightseers can approach the mountain by railway. (Courtesy of Swiss National Tourist Office)

passes between Italy (Grand St. Bernard) and France (the Forclaz); and Innsbruck between Italy (Brenner), Germany (Seefelder Sattel), Austria's Vorarlberg Province, and nearby Switzerland (Arlberg Pass) (Fig. 11-6).

People have been living in the Alps since Paleolithic times—50,000 to 90,000 years ago. They hunted game and left artifacts in various sites such as Sion in the Rhône Valley of Switzerland, Lieglhöhle near Taüplitz in Austria, and on the shores of the Hallstätter See in Austria where a distinct Celtic culture thrived. The Romans enlarged old Celtic villages and built many new towns both in the valleys leading up to the Alps and within the Alps themselves, such as Octodurus (Martigny) and Virunum (Zollfield in Austria).

The economic basis of the Alps, which was predominantly agricultural and pastoral in the past, has undergone fundamental change in the last 100 years. In the late nineteenth and early twentieth centuries, with the development of hydroelectricity, heavy metallurgical and chemical industries were attracted to major valleys. One result of this industrialization was depopulation of higher elevation valleys. Today, many industrial enterprises are no longer viable because of foreign competition, the high cost of transporting raw material from coastal ports to interior valley locations, or because indigenous raw materials have been exhausted. Mechanical engineering requiring more specialization has fared better than heavy industry, and so have consumer-related enterprises, but these too have been hard hit by worldwide economic restructuring.

The most significant economic change in the past 30 years in the Alps has been the development of mass tourism. This has been closely linked with the extension of major highways into the mountains with the opening of the Mont Blanc, Grand St. Bernard, Gotthard, San Bernadino, and Felbertauern tunnels. Employment opportunities in the tertiary sector have increased substantially, taking up the slack caused by the decline of agricultural and industrial employment. The arrival of millions of urban dwellers in the mountains has, however, had enormous environmental consequences for the people who inhabit these areas. The financial betterment of their lives must be weighed against the additional costs necessary for tourist services

FIGURE 11-6 Brenner Pass road between Innsbruck and Italy (South Tirol). The Alpine Autobahn crossing Austria is 69 miles long (111 km) and offers the quickest connection between Northern and Southern Europe, crossing the Brenner Pass (Austrian/Italian frontier) at 4404 ft. (1355 m). The Europa Bridge, a few miles south of Innsbruck, was completed in 1963, and is 2674 ft long (823 m) and 623 ft (192 m) above the Wipp Valley. (Austrian Information Service)

such as ski-lifts, improved roads, and water treatment plants. Inexorably, the spread of factories, apartment buildings, and businesses has altered the main valleys of, for example, the Rhône, Rhine, and Inn. These same conditions may be seen on a lesser scale in side valleys as well. Uncontrolled urbanization and water and air pollution have produced unsightly vistas and, in the case of pollution, the health of humans and forests, has been compromised.

The Pannonian Basin

East of Vienna and the last foothills of the Alps (*Wienerwald*, or Vienna Woods) are two small sections of the vast Pannonian Basin that stretch eastward to the Bihor Mountains of Romania. Formerly the bed of an ancient sea, the productive land north of the Danube in eastern Austria comprises the Inner and Outer Vienna Basins, outliers of the Pannonian Basin. Most of the Basin is in Hungary (discussed in Chapter 12). This region has a dry, warm climate, a long growing season that permits some grape cultivation, and sufficient rainfall for high agricultural yields.

Because the western edge of the Vienna Basin, through which flows the Danube, was a natural routeway between the Alps and Carpathians, the area has been of great economic and strategic value since ancient times. Fortifications such as Carnuntum (Petronell) and later Vindobona (Vienna) were Roman legionary strongholds that guarded the converging routes. Throughout history, the Vienna Basin has retained its importance in the political geography of Central Europe. Furthermore, both agriculture and industry make this one of the most important economic regions of Austria.

POPULATION

At the beginning of the Christian era Central Europe was inhabited by various German-speaking peoples, including the Saxons, Frisians, Goths, Vandals, Franks, and Alemanni. The Celts as well as the northernmost Ligurians, Etruscans, and Illyrians lived in the mountainous regions of the south. The Rhine became the western frontier of the Roman Empire after Caesar's conquest of Gaul (57–51 B.C.). An advance farther east to the Danube was strategically desirable for Rome to secure the eastern frontier and command important passes of the Alps. A Roman force advanced through the Aige (Etsch) Valley into Tirol, and in 15 B.C. the province of Rhaetia was created. Shortly thereafter Noricum and Pannonia, both bounded by the Danube River and the crest of the southern Alps, were added (Fig. 3-1). The Romans' attempt to move the frontier east to the Elbe River was checked by Germanic tribes. With Roman fortifications acting as a barrier to their movement westward and southward and limiting their pasturelands, Germanic tribes added agriculture to their primarily pastoral economy. This brought about increased population pressures, which contributed to the unification of various tribes into more powerful units and, ultimately, a breakdown of the Roman defense lines that ran along the Rhine, the Limes (a fortified boundary in southern Germany), and the Danube during the fourth and fifth centuries. The movement of the Germanic peoples toward the west and south also emptied wide stretches of land east of the Elbe, which soon were occupied by Slavic peoples from the east. This event was of major historical importance in the relationship between Central and Eastern Europe.

The Germanic peoples were quick to follow the Roman withdrawal. Alemanni of Swabian stock moved from what is now northeastern Germany (Brandenburg) south- and westwards, occupying the Rhine Valley, the Neckar Lowlands, and the Swiss Plateau. They also settled in parts of mountainous Switzerland and modern Austrian Vorarlberg. Saxons moved from the plains between the Ems and Weser rivers, now in northwestern Germany, into Flanders and northern France; the southeast coast of England; and central and southern Germany. Bavarians occupied the Alpine Forelands of Germany and part of present Austria. Franks advanced from their original homes on the lower Rhine and Westphalia in northwestern Germany across the Rhine into France and the southern part of the Low Countries. Other German tribes migrated beyond Central Europe. The Lombards traversed the Alps into the fertile Po Valley;

the Vandals crossed into North Africa; the Goths settled in Iberia; and Burgundians moved into the valley of the Saone in France. In short, West Central Europe, though now dominated by people speaking the German language, has historically been home to a great variety of ethnic bands, partly explaining the rather late emergence of unified states in the region.

One effect of this resettling of peoples was the establishment of many small political units. These were characteristic of medieval Central Europe and are still evident today in the federated structure of all three large Central European countries. These units are often quite isolated and separated from each other by such barriers as high mountains, deep valleys, and gorges. At various times several of these units were united, and if grouped around a pass controlling important routes, they were known as passlands. The Swiss Confederation around the St. Gotthard and Tirol around the Brenner Pass are typical passlands of the Alps. The Swiss Confederation played an important role in the founding of the Swiss state.

In the contemporary era West Central Europe includes the EU's most populous country, Germany; the other states—Austria, Liechtenstein, and Switzerland—are small by comparison. The populations of Switzerland and West Germany increased steadily between 1950 and about 1970, and Austria's population grew in the 1960s, but thereafter population growth slowed considerably in these countries until large numbers of immigrants arrived in the late 1980s and early 1990s. Inmigration now appears to be declining, owing to factors noted later in this chapter. Another part of West Central Europe, eastern Germany, has been losing population throughout most of the last four decades, as people fled the harsh and autocratic rule of Soviet occupation and East German communist regimes, and more recently flocked to prosperous western Germany. Overall population growth in West Central Europe during the next decade or two will likely be among the lowest of all the world's regions owing to the interrelated low birth rate and relatively old age structure, a situation now common in many other European countries as well.

If estimated future labor demands are to be met and West Central Europe is not to lose a significant proportion of the population, renewed immigration will be necessary. Labor shortages during the mid-1950s to mid-1960s led to massive movements of labor from Southern and Eastern Europe to urban and industrial centers in West Central Europe. Although many of these "guest workers" moved back to their homelands, others stayed and have since been joined by their families or have borne children. During 1993, foreign residents, who accounted for about 7 percent of the German population (9% by 1996), accounted for 13 percent of all births. In 1995 well over 7 million foreigners were living in Germany (from Turkey 1.9 million, the former Yugoslavia 930,000, and Italy 563,000), about 2 million of them recently arrived asylum seekers. Switzerland in 1992 had over a million foreigners (Italy 380,000; Spain and Portugal 219,000; former Yugoslavia 173,000), and Austria well over 200,000 (mostly from the former Yugoslavia and Turkey) (Fig. 11-7).

The economic attractiveness of Germany and, until recently, its favorable asylum conditions have resulted in it receiving an overwhelming share of EU inmigrants seeking political asylum (77% of EU registrants during 1992), although revised laws slowed immigration after 1993. Predictions about the region's total population change in the short term are difficult to make, given impediments for attaining citizenship and the existing negative attitudes of many West Central Europeans toward the long-term residence of guest workers as expressed by occasional street riots, violence against immigrants, and the rhetoric of xenophobic, nationalistic demagogues in the political arena. However, without substantial, additional immigration or a striking increase in the fertility rate, there will be population stagnation in the region, as the percentage of older inhabitants increases and that of younger inhabitants decreases.

In many ways, the West Central European countries are following general European patterns of population change, characterized by slow or stagnant total population growth, a decline in central city populations accompanied by increases in selected metropolitan areas, and declining populations in some rural and remote areas. For example, in Switzerland two-thirds of the population has been concentrated in the geographically advanta-

FIGURE 11-7 Mediterranean people and culture are prominent in parts of many European central cities. Here a Turkish shop in Lübeck. (W. H. Berentsen)

geous Swiss Plateau for well over a century. In this century population growth has been greatest in the metropolitan areas of Geneva and Zürich, although there have been population decreases in central cities and slow growth in the canton of Appenzell (see Inset 11-1).

German is spoken by virtually all the people of Germany and Austria and by 65 percent of the Swiss. A small number of citizens in Germany speak Dutch and Danish as native languages, and in Austria a number speak Hungarian and Slovene. Switzerland's language distribution is unique, with three main national languages, German, French, and Italian. Besides the dominant German language, 18 percent of Swiss speak French and 10 percent Italian as first languages. One percent, living mainly in the southeastern canton of Graubünden, speak Rhaeto-Romansch, the country's fourth official language (Fig. 11-9). In Germany and Switzerland both Protestantism and Roman Catholicism are important faiths; in Austria over 90 percent of the population professed Roman Catholicism until recent scandals in the Church caused defections that, at least for now, have reduced its overwhelming dominance.

Although the role of religion in the political and cultural life of the people has greatly declined in recent decades, it still plays a considerable role in the rural and mountainous parts of West Central Europe.

ECONOMIC DEVELOPMENT

The highly developed economies of the West Central European countries incorporate both agricultural and manufacturing activities that include high-technology and specialized service functions, such as international finance and tourism. In fact, in all of the countries services account for over 60 percent of GDP, whereas agriculture is 3 percent or below; manufacturing employment is between 33 and 37 percent in the three large states. As wealthy, high-skilled/high-wage countries, West Central Europe's manufacturing sectors have increasingly emphasized production of high value-added products in the metals and machinery, transportation equipment, chemicals, and elec-

INSET 11-1

ZÜRICH: SWITZERLAND'S DOMINANT CITY

The city of Zürich is the industrial, commercial, and cultural center of Switzerland. In 1990 it had over twice the population of the next largest city, Basel (Fig. 11-8). The initial site of the city was on well-drained glacial deposits along a narrow strip of land between the Limmat and Sihl rivers, near its entry into Zürich Lake (*Zürichsee*). Most likely, the foundations of modern Zürich were laid along the Limmat by the Helvetii people. Later the Romans fortified the moraine hill, known today as the Lindenhof, which overlooks the river. Turicum (Roman Zürich) was a customs station, *entrepôt* (a commercial center where goods were received for distribution, transshipment, or repackaging), and frontier post between Rhaetia (Roman Switzerland) and Gaul (Roman France), situated on a major trade route between the Rhine Valley and the Po Plain in Italy. During the Middle Ages, the Gotthard and Arlberg Passes were opened, facilitating trade to the south and east, respectively. Boats plying the rivers and lakes enhanced Zürich's situation as a break-of-bulk center (place of transshipment between transport modes) at the head of the Zürichsee. A number of warehouses were built along the Limmat to store a variety of goods. In addition, mills, located on bridges in the river, were used for the grinding of flour, preparation of cloth (notably, silk at one time), tanning, manufacture of paper, and sharpening of

FIGURE 11-8 Zürich, capital of the canton Zürich, is the largest Swiss city and the country's economic center. The city is located on the northern end of Lake Zürich where the River Sihl enters the lake. The main chain of the Alps is in the background. (Verkehrsverein Zürich)

tools and weapons. By the beginning of the nineteenth century, these mills furnished energy to the textile indstry. During the Swiss Reformation, Zürich was transformed from a local center to a European city. Religious and political exiles flocked there, enriching the city's economic and cultural life. From 1550 to 1800, an influx of refugees from Ticino canton, Italy, France, and Holland settled in Zürich, bringing with them manufacturing processes and advanced commercial practices that revived the flagging textile industry and laid the foundation for further industrial development.

The development of Zürich's financial institutions went hand in hand with the steady expansion of industry, especially textiles and engineering works. The first federal industrial census in 1882 showed the canton of Zürich to be the most industrialized in the country. Industry stimulated the growth of even greater savings, and by the end of the nineteenth century, Zürich emerged as Switzerland's most important financial center, strongly linked with leading international centers of finance. In addition, an important insurance business had developed in conjunction with the financial institutions. Another significant factor contributing to Zürich's expansion during this period was the city's growing importance as a railroad junction and manufacturer of rolling stock. For example, the opening of the Gotthard Tunnel under the Gotthard Massif in 1882, the first trans-Alpine rail connection, linked Zürich to Milan.

Spurred both by industrialization and railway building, the rapid physical growth of the city after 1850 resulted in a territorial amalgamation, uniting the old city of Zürich with 11 industrial and residential suburbs. The city's population increased from approximately 28,000 to over 92,000 and its area from 7 to 18 sq miles (17 to 45 sq km). The rapid rise in population continued, reaching 165,000 by 1910. Whereas in 1850 the population of the Zürich region was under 17 percent of the canton's total, by 1910 this figure jumped to over 42 percent. There was a second amalgamation in 1934, almost doubling Zürich's size, while increasing the population nearly 20 percent to over 312,000.

By 1941, 54 percent of the canton's population lived in the city of Zürich. To accommodate the rising numbers, a Master Zone Plan was proposed in 1946, which has been amended a number of times since. It delimits the areas to be used for residences, industry, recreation, and agriculture and forestry. Additional planning has been necessary outside of the present city boundaries to ensure rational land use in the increasingly congested rural-urban fringe. The majority of new factories, distribution centers, warehouses, and shopping centers now locate outside the city in areas of the region, because of the shortage of land for large-scale industrial enterprises within it. Thus, ever more of the employment within the city of Zürich will be in the tertiary sector, a figure that was over 74 percent in 1991.

Within the city, planning problems have included encroachment of business functions and light industry into older residential areas around the periphery of the central business area, a resulting steady decline of population in the city proper, and traffic congestion and related pollution. Only partial resolutions to these problems have been found.

While the population of the city has decreased steadily since 1962 (344,104 in 1992), that of the surrounding suburbs has continued to rise. Six planning areas, representing over 70 percent of the canton's population and composed of the city of Zürich and its surrounding 69 communities, combined in 1958 to formulate a comprehensive plan for the Zürich region (the RZU). Factors such as the use of land for residential, recreational, and industrial purposes; water supply; sewage disposal; and regional transportation systems were included in the plan that will provide for a regional population of 1.5 million by the year 2010.

The growth of Zürich from a Roman settlement to one of the world's most important industrial, commercial, and cultural centers has been accomplished with a minimum of destruction to the city's original site. Today's residents can still stroll through the medieval quarter, promenade along the lake shore, fish and swim in the river and lake, and ride horses and ski in the forests of the Zürichberg and Uetliberg. The preservation of the natural environment is a blessing for the city's inhabitants, having economic as well as aesthetic ramifications. Certainly, it has been a major factor in Zürich's development as one of the largest tourist centers in Switzerland.

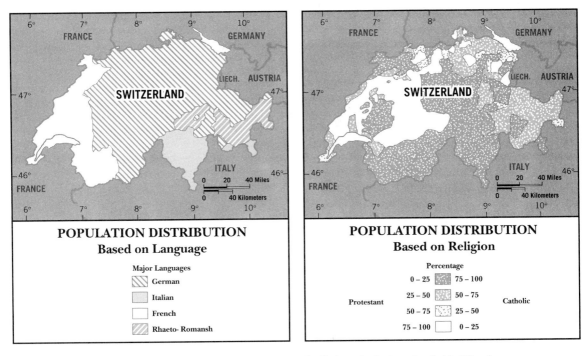

FIGURE 11-9 Regional patterns of dominant languages and religions in Switzerland. (A. Diem)

tronics industries. Similarly, production in other sectors, such as in textile-apparel production, which is especially susceptible to competition from low-wage competitors, has focused on higher value-added, higher quality products for sale in high-income countries. Nevertheless, industry has been moving to lower wage countries within the EU, Asia, and North America. Employment has fallen in many sectors, from textiles and apparel manufacturing to mining, as world economic restructuring takes place.

Employment and production in agriculture have been maintained by government supports in Austria and Switzerland and by the Common Agricultural Policy of the EU in Germany. Special emphasis has been placed on assistance to mountain farmers in order to preserve jobs in relatively remote areas and to maintain cherished traditional landscapes and lifestyles. The highly scenic, well-tended landscapes have led to economic benefits

in the form of well-developed tourism. In the early 1990s Austria had each year nearly 100 million foreign tourist-nights (number of tourists times average number of nights stayed), Switzerland over 37 million, and Germany about 34 million. The tourist industries in Austria and Switzerland are heavily dependent on German visitors, who respectively comprise over 60 percent and 40 percent of all visits. In both countries the regional focus is on the Alps; for example, Tirol (western Austria) alone had about 40 million foreign tourist-nights in the early 1990s and nearly 10 percent of all employment in the hotel and restaurant sector.

The West Central European countries, particularly Germany and Switzerland, are key trade partners and provide vital transport routes for European commerce. Levels of international trade are high, and growth in exports has been especially notable. Germany is the dominant trade partner for its smaller neighbors, accounting for about 40 percent of Austria's total trade and about 30 percent of Switzerland's. Germany, and Austria to a lesser extent, are expected to be able to profit from economic growth in Eastern Europe. Such diverse manufactured products as auto engines, vehicle parts, and textiles are being manufactured for Western firms in Eastern Europe, with their ultimate destination intended for West Central and other Western European countries.

SWITZERLAND

The country that is most representative, and in fact the nexus, of the diverse physical and cultural geography of Western Europe is Switzerland. Switzerland is the crossroads of Western Europe. Main north-south and east-west rail and road arteries converge within Switzerland's boundaries. The three prominent linguistic groups, German, French, and Italian, and the two major religions of continental Western Europe are also represented.

The rivers that flow from its Alpine glaciers empty into four European seas: the Rhine (German *Rhein*—French *Rhin*) drains into the North Sea; the Rhône to the Mediterranean; the Inn to the Danube and on to the Black Sea; and the Ticino to the Po, which empties into the Adriatic. At one point southwest of St. Moritz, the drainage divide among the tributaries of the Rhine, Inn, and Po are but a few miles apart.

The climates of Switzerland include subtropical conditions near the protected Ticino lakes in the south, the perpetual snow and ice of the Alpine massifs, the rain-shadow areas of the Rhône Valley in Valais in the southwest, and the continental-like climate of the Jura valleys in the northwest. Western parts of the Mittelland experience a maritime-influenced climate similar to the rest of Northwestern Europe.

Switzerland's human resource has been effectively educated and efficiently utilized to transform what was a predominantly mountainous, rural, and landlocked country with limited natural resources into one of the most diversified and prominent industrial and commercial countries in

the world. By importing raw materials and converting them into high-quality, high value-added specialized products for export; by pursuing aggressive commercial policies; and by developing a highly efficient transportation system and tourist industry, Switzerland has kept unemployment low, 4.7 percent in 1994, compared to 10.9 percent in the European Community as a whole. In addition, inflation is under control, and Switzerland achieved the highest per capita income among the OECD countries—$33,453 in 1993 (though when taking purchasing power parity into account, the Swiss place third behind Luxembourg and the United States).

Physical Geography and Geopolitics

The physical geography of Switzerland has been a significant factor in the country's history from pre-Roman times until the present. Three major physiographic divisions, discussed earlier, stretch across the country from Geneva on the west to the Bodensee (Lake of Constance) on the east—the Jura Mountains, the Mittelland or Plateau, and the Alps. Much of the country also lies outside of the natural frontiers of the Rhine, the Jura, and the Alps. The site of Schaffhausen is north of the Rhine surrounded for the most part by German territory. Basel, situated on both sides of the Rhine at the southern end of the rift valley, controls important transportation routes through the Jura to the south and east. The canton of Ticino is located south of the main alpine crests looking toward the Po Plain in Italy.

The area that is now Switzerland lay at the intersection of key medieval trade routes. East-west commerce moved from the Danube Basin via southern Germany through Switzerland to the Rhône Valley, southern France, and the Iberian Peninsula. Italy's trade with the textile-producing areas of the Netherlands, as well as goods from Frankfurt and the Baltic and German ports destined for Southern Europe, largely traversed the Rhine Valley and the Swiss Alpine passes. These were in many respects the mainsprings to Swiss history. The severely glaciated mountain valleys led into the heart of the Alps at relatively low altitudes, and the major trans-Alpine routes followed these river valleys until blocked by sheer-sided massifs or Alpine lakes. Boats and barges ferried goods and passengers farther up the lakes to the upper valleys, where narrow roads climbed over the passes. Today, the major Swiss alpine routes, long since improved and modernized, bind the county together and facilitate transportation between Northern and Southern Europe.

Of particular interest is St. Gotthard Pass, which did not come into widespread use until the Devil's Bridge, crossing the Schöllenen Gorge, was constructed over the Reuss River in the early thirteenth century. This route brought the isolated mountain communities of Uri, Schwiez, and Unterwalden into the mainstream of European political life. They were forced into cooperation to defend their independence against the desires of powerful dynasties to control and exploit the Gotthard route. This led directly to the foundation of the Swiss Confederation in 1291.

The history of Switzerland, a complicated series of events, provides the background for an understanding of the country's present-day cultural differences and economic strength. Because of its central location and pass routes through the Alps, Switzerland was coveted by surrounding powers from Roman times through the Second World War. Its location astride the Alps and in the midst of the EU makes it especially important to the EU. Even so, the Swiss populace has thus far steadfastly resisted EU membership and continues to be suspicious of external control and degradation of their Alps.

Swiss history, played out on the battlefields of Alpine Europe, was to a great extent the saga of local peoples trying to prevent foreign aggressors, such as the Habsburgs and French, from taking control of their territory. The early inhabitants, Celtic tribes, were conquered by the Romans, who in turn fell victim to barbaric incursions. By A.D. 400, Roman Switzerland had disintegrated, and the lands of the Romanized Celts were occupied by Germanic tribes such as the Burgundians and Alemannians. The Burgundians, few in number, occupied the lands of western Switzerland. Although they remained political masters, they lost contact with their former homelands and were

assimilated into the Roman Celtic population. Modern French-speaking Switzerland is approximately the territory settled by the Burgundians from the fifth century onward.

The large-scale migrations of Alemannians penetrated south of the Rhine during the sixth and seventh centuries A.D. More numerous than the Burgundians and in direct contact with their kin north of the Rhine, the Alemannians colonized lands that had been only partially under Roman influence, thus facilitating the imposition of their culture and language on the Celts. Germanic hegemony slowly penetrated westward from the Reuss River on the Gotthard route in the sixth century to the Sarine in the thirteenth century. The Alemannians also pushed farther into the upper Rhine Valley, driving the Celts deeper into the Alps. Today, in the valleys of Graubünden, the descendants of these Celts speak the fourth language of Switzerland, Romansch.

During the late fifth and early sixth centuries, Burgundians and Alemannians came under the control of the Franks, and later became part of Charlemagne's Holy Roman Empire. In 843, less than 30 years after Charlemagne's death, the Treaty of Verdun divided the Empire and Switzerland among his grandsons. The Middle Kingdom of Lothair included the Burgundian settlement area west of the Aare, while Alemannia, north and south of the Rhine, formed part of the East Frankish Kingdom of Louis.

The Swiss areas were united again in the eleventh century under a German-dominated Holy Roman Empire. However, the gradual decline of the Empire gave rise to a loose confederation of quasi-independent states, enabling feudal dynasties to emerge as territorial powers by the beginning of the thirteenth century. During the eleventh and twelfth centuries, strategic new cities such as Geneva, Bern, Fribourg, and Winterthur were founded to provide secure stopping places for the increasing numbers of merchants associated with rapidly expanding trade in Western Europe. By the end of the thirteenth century, the Habsburgs had emerged as the dominant family in Switzerland. Their original castle, built in 1020, within a few miles of the confluence of the Aare, Reuss, and Limmat, was strategically situated to control east-west routes across the Mittelland, and north-south passages through the Gotthard Pass and the Wallensee-Zürichsee waterways. The expansion of Habsburg influence and territory, threatening the independence of some of the small communities within central Switzerland, precipitated events leading to the establishment of the independent Swiss Confederation in 1291 (Fig. 11-10).

A succession of wars and conflicts among the cantons and the arrival of the Reformation characterized the events of the ensuing centuries. A major defeat of the Swiss armies on the Po Plain near Milan marked the first step toward neutrality (see Inset 11-2). The Swiss realized that outside their frontiers there was no policy on which their linguistic and religious factions could agree. Either they would continue to involve themselves in the affairs of their neighbors (Austria, France, and Italy), and thereby destroy the Confederation, or they would remain independent. This point of view was reinforced during the sixteenth-century religious wars that ravaged Europe. Thus, the foundations of Swiss neutrality were laid.

Demographic and Economic Development

In 1996 the population of Switzerland was 7.1 million, compared to 2.4 million in 1850, the year of

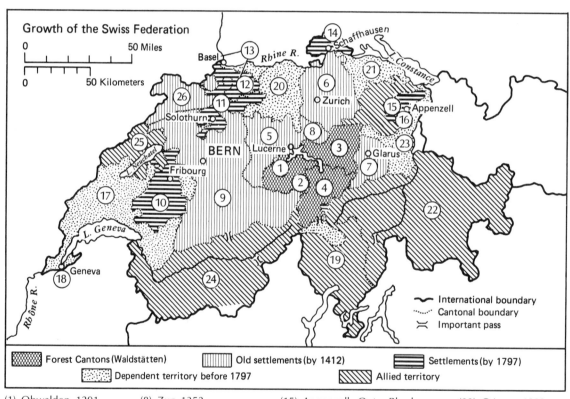

(1) Obwalden, 1291	(8) Zug, 1352	(15) Appenzell–Outer Rhodes	(22) Grisons, 1803
(2) Nidwalden, 1291	(9) Bern, 1352	(16) Inner Rhodes, 1513	(23) Saint Gallen, 1803
(3) Schwyz, 1291	(10) Fribourg, 1481	(17) Vaud, 1803	(24) Valais, 1815
(4) Uri, 1291	(11) Solothurn, 1481	(18) Geneva, 1815	(25) Neuchâtel, 1815
(5) Lucerne, 1332	(12) Basel (rural)	(19) Ticino, 1813	(26) Jura, 1979
(6) Zürich, 1351	(13) Basel (urban), 1501	(20) Aargau, 1805	
(7) Glarus, 1352	(14) Schaffhausen, 1501	(21) Thurgau, 1803	

FIGURE 11-10 Growth of the Swiss Federation.

SWISS NEUTRALITY

Swiss neutrality has been a *leitmotif* of the country's foreign policy since the Congress of Vienna in 1815 and has been a major factor in the country's acquisition of wealth. However, the collapse of communism and the changing geopolitical map of Europe have forced the Swiss to rethink past strategies.

The country remained neutral during the Franco-Prussian War, and neutrality was maintained during the First World War in spite of the country's ethnic split. Because 40 percent of the total food consumed was imported, the country was dependent on the goodwill of surrounding neighbors or the maintenance of supply with foreign food sources. Although many sectors of the economy suffered severely because of the war, others such as machine manufacturing, watchmaking, textiles, food processing, and agriculture flourished.

The peaceful position of Switzerland was reaffirmed after the war by the Treaty of Versailles. It recognized Swiss neutrality as an international obligation for the preservation of peace. Neutrality was further strengthened by the Declaration of London in 1920, when the Council of the League of Nations recognized that its permanent neutrality and a guarantee of Switzerland's territorial integrity, as stated by the treaties of 1815, were justified in the interests of general peace and, therefore, consistent with the League's principles. In May 1930 the Swiss voted for entry into the League of Nations, and the League headquarters, at the insistence of President Woodrow Wilson, was established in Geneva.

The disintegration of the League, weakened by the rising power of Fascism and Nazism during the troubled 1930s, induced the Swiss to give up collective security for their old position of absolute neutrality. Fearing the worst, they prepared themselves psychologically, economically, and militarily for any possible conflict. When World War II broke out in September 1939, the Federal Council issued a declaration of neutrality that was backed by a strong army and air force. Ultimately, 650,000 soldiers were mobilized out of a population of only 4 million.

A fortress in the central Alps, the *Rédouit*, was prepared with arms, ammunition, medical supplies, food, water, hydroelectrical plants, and factories so that the Swiss army could fight against the Nazis even if the cities of the Mittelland were lost. This action spared the country from the destruction and havoc that engulfed Europe by making seizure of Switzerland too costly an undertaking for Germany. Despite being surrounded by Nazi and Fascist enemies, Switzerland survived as the only democratic state in Central Europe. Nevertheless, the country also aided the Nazi war machine long after it was doomed to defeat, and forbade the entry of Jews who were desperately seeking to escape the Nazis' grasp, many of whom later perished in the death camps. Strict neutrality has persisted until the present. Although volunteer units of the Swiss army were being trained for peacekeeping roles with the UN (to which Switzerland does not belong), their use was voted down by a national referendum.

One dilemma that the Swiss now face is how to exist with an economically powerful European Union, while having little or no say as to how the EU formulates policy that affects Switzerland. A second dilemma is how to balance its soldier-citizen tradition with changing social and political circumstances. Although the Swiss army has been an important integrating factor in modern Swiss history, it has operated as if it could do no wrong. In recent years a number of difficulties have arisen, including a series of deaths and injuries to both Swiss citizens and tourists, because live ammunition that did not go off during exercises exploded when found and handled by civilians who were hiking or on outings. In addition, the military's quest for more areas for storage and operations poses difficulties in a country where space is at a premium, and military exercises held in the Alpine valleys during spring and fall are noisy and disruptive.

In accordance with Swiss law, the army serves solely to preserve the independence of the country. Defense is based on a system of universal conscription under which every Swiss male is liable for military duty between the ages of 20 and 40 years and, for officers, to 45 years. The Swiss are the only soldiers in the world who keep their equipment, including arms and ammunition, at home and who perform obligatory gunnery duty each year in civilian clothes—a manifestation of the extraordinary degree of trust between citizen and government. However, many Swiss have questioned the necessity for compulsory service in a nuclear age. A number of conscientious objectors have spent periods in jail, inasmuch there have been no social alternatives to military service. Alternative service is now in the planning stage. In November 1989 a national referendum saw more than one-third of the electorate, mainly those between the ages of 20 and 30, and a majority in the cantons of Jura and Geneva, vote to do away with the Swiss army. This came as a shock to the establishment of army officers, who are also members of Parliament and executives in the country's banks and multinational corporations. Nevertheless, despite the end of the Cold War the country has not noticeably changed its stand on the place of the army in Swiss society. For example, in 1993 the Swiss voted in favor of buying 34 F18 jet fighters from the United States at a cost of about $3 billion, and fallout shelters are still being built. Thus, despite controversy, Switzerland's commitment to neutrality, backed by military readiness, will likely persist well into the next century.

the first official census. Today Switzerland has an aging population with a relatively low birth rate. The number of inhabitants under 15 dropped from 24 percent in 1960 to 17 percent in 1991, whereas those between 15 and 64 increased from 63 percent to 68 percent, and those over 65 went from 10 percent to 15 percent of the total population. Population density in 1996 was 446 inhabitants per sq mile (172 per sq km), but if the uninhabitable mountain areas, about one-fourth of Switzerland, were deducted from the total area of the country, the density figure would rise to about 550 persons per sq mile (212 per sq km). In any case, Swiss population density is comparable to Germany (591 persons per sq mile/228 per sq km) and greater than France (277 persons per sq mile/107 per sq km).

In 1992 foreigners accounted for 18.5 percent of the population and 30 percent of the labor force. The largest number with residence permits were Italian (30% of the total) followed by people from the former Yugoslavia (13%), Spain (9%), and Portugal (8%). Certain employment sectors, especially construction, hotels, and restaurants are almost totally dependent on non-Swiss laborers. Because of the civil war in Yugoslavia, Switzerland has also taken in over 70,000 refugees.

Of the 16,294 sq miles (41,387 sq km) that comprise Switzerland's territory, only 74.5 percent is productive for some kind of agriculture or forestry. The area in settlement and infrastructure is 6 percent. The remaining areas are too rocky, too steep, or in perpetual snow and ice and so are unsuitable for either agriculture or forestry. Forests cover 30 percent of the country, and 38 percent of the land is used for agriculture. Of that total, 60 percent is pasture and arable land, 36 percent is *alpine pasture*, and 4 percent tree culture, fruits, vineyards, and horticulture. Cultivated land is found throughout the country with the largest concentrations on the Mittelland and in the valleys of the Jura and the Alps.

Agricultural workers represented 20 percent of the labor force in 1939 but only 5.6 percent in 1993. The number of farms decreased from 239,000 in 1939 to 108,000 in 1990. The number of small units dropped considerably; however, farms over 50 acres (20 hectares) increased in number. Average farm size is about 25 acres (10 ha). Related to the decline of small farms, agricultural productivity rose by about 75 percent from 1955 to 1967 and has continued to increase because of mechanization, scientific techniques, fertilizers, improved crop varieties, and the consolidation of holdings. Another key factor in increased output of agricultural products, such as cheese and wine, is government subsidy. Thus, market prices for food are among the highest in Europe.

The small size of average farms presents problems of efficiency; still, domestic production of foodstuffs covers about 60 percent of consumption. The bulk of food imports comes from EU countries, which are the main purchasers of such Swiss agricultural exports as cheese, breeding cattle, and potatoes.

Government policy has strongly supported agriculture, ostensibly because Switzerland must be able to feed itself in case of war, but more realistically because a large number of Swiss believe that farms are a good thing and they want to preserve a balance between the rural and urban population. This thinking is changing as the urban population pressures the government to reduce subsidies.

The agricultural regions of Switzerland are relatively easy to define. The Mittelland is the prominent area for cultivation, because of adequate precipitation, moderate temperatures, and large amounts of cultivable land with good soil and moderate slope. Fruit trees abound throughout the Mittelland; cereals, root crops, as well as specialty crops such as flowers and tobacco are cultivated. In the higher elevations of the Jura, the pre-Alps, and the mountain pastures of the high Alps, cattle grazing is most extensive, whereas in the deeply protected Alpine valleys, especially the Rhône between Martigny and Sierre, the valleys of Ticino, and the Rhine north of Chur, fruit, vegetable, and vine cultivation is widespread. Vineyards are also found on the south-facing slopes of lakes Geneva, Biel, Neuchâtel, and Murten. Many of the local wines are outstanding in quality; however, because of subsidies there has not been much incentive to export.

Of the more than 30 percent of Switzerland covered by forest, public corporations own over 67 percent of the total; the rest is held by private and cantonal interests. Federal forests account for less than 1 percent. Yields are insufficient to meet home requirements; therefore, approximately 25 percent of the quantity consumed must be import-

ed. Because of the Federal Forestry Laws of 1902 and 1991, permission must be granted to cut any tree. Nevertheless, trees have been cut illegally, often to build new ski runs. Clear-cutting of the forests in Switzerland is not allowed, as it is in North America, because forests provide protection against floods and avalanches. On the Mittelland, the forests serve as recreation areas for riding, hiking, and cross-country skiing.

Because of widespread air pollution, the Federal Office of Forestry has classified over a third of the country's forests as damaged, sick, or dying. Of these, more of the forests in the mountains are affected compared to the Mittelland (Fig. 11-11). Valleys along the Gotthard highway suffer from especially serious air pollution owing to intense traffic. A special study of the forests around Zürich has confirmed that they too are slowly deteriorating.

Damage to trees by air pollution and acid rain varies because of altitude, bedrock, soil types, and exposure. Thus, forests in the Jura are less susceptible to damage from acid rain, because the bedrock is limestone that tends to buffer the acidity. Areas such as the basin of St. Moritz show the widespread effects of air pollution, caused mainly by the intense traffic, especially during the summer months. Forests in many side valleys, such as the Val d'Anniviers in Valais, exhibit the classic signs of acid rain damage. There are fewer needles on the branches, the crowns are bare, and the trees

FIGURE 11-11 Air pollution in the Rhône Valley. (A. Diem)

are dying. Such conditions are evident throughout the Alps of Europe. (For further information on the effects of acidification on forests, see a pictorial in the German magazine *Stern*, November 2, 1989.) The question being asked among researchers is, "How long will the forests of Switzerland be able to contain avalanches, stop falling rock, and inhibit earth slides?" If national and international measures to control air pollution are not effective, the future appears grim.

Switzerland has few natural resources besides substantial hydroelectric resources along the Rhine and in the Alps. In the postwar era, Switzerland followed the trend in Western Europe that saw the proportion of petroleum used in total energy consumption increase dramatically. In 1950 petroleum products represented only 24 percent of the country's energy requirements; this increased to 51 percent by 1960 and reached a high of 77 percent in 1970. Because of the oil crisis of 1973, an energy policy of diversification reduced the use of oil to only 51 percent in 1992. The percentage of coal used declined sharply from 41 percent in 1950 to about zero today. Gas has increased its contribution to total energy requirements from 3 percent in 1950 to 8 percent by 1992. Much of the balance of energy derives from hydroelectric sources.

Until 1960, all electricity in Switzerland was produced by waterpower. By 1992 hydro sources accounted for only 58 percent of total production and nuclear stations for 42 percent. The bulk of hydroelectricity is produced in the more mountainous southern part of the country.

Electricity exchanges with the French, German, and Italian grids are common. In summer when water from melting glaciers is plentiful, the amount of power exported may be one-half or more of domestic consumption, making Switzerland, along with Norway and France, one of the largest exporters of electrical energy in Western Europe, in both per capita and absolute terms.

After the Second World War nuclear plants were constructed. There are five reactors in operation; however, the plan to build a sixth station at Kaiseraugst near Basel has been canceled because of environmental protests. Though ostensibly "cleaner" than other forms of thermal power generation, nuclear plants are unsightly and pose potential risks of release of radioactive isotopes.

The clouds produced from the cooling towers sharply reduce the amount of surrounding sunshine, and the storage problem for the radioactive waste material from the reactors has not been solved. Finally, the Chernobyl accident in 1986, which doused Europe and Switzerland with radioactivity, aroused widespread public concern about the safety of nuclear energy. In 1990 the Swiss voted for a 10-year moratorium on the construction of nuclear power plants.

One politically acceptable way by which additional energy has been supplied has been through the use of natural gas. From 1974 on, the period that natural gas has been available in the country, consumption has grown considerably, and systems of gas transport and distribution have expanded. Some natural gas is produced, but most is imported. Switzerland is on the main European north-south pipeline from the Netherlands to the Po Plain in Italy.

The federal government has launched an energy conservation program designed to stabilize and rationalize energy consumption by the year 2000. By setting energy standards for buildings, cars, and appliances and by implementing a carbon tax on gasoline and heating oil, wasteful consumption will be discouraged.

Manufacturing

Despite resource scarcity, industrialization in Switzerland was well under way during the nineteenth century. By 1888, approximately 42 percent of the labor force was already engaged in industrial production. In 1993, industry accounted for 33 percent of the labor force; the service sector had grown to over 61 percent.

Diversity of product line and the small number of large firms are characteristics of Swiss industry. However, several Swiss enterprises have worldwide operations: two firms in 1994, Nestlé and Roche Holding, ranked among the top 10 of the largest corporations by market capitalization in Europe. Three others, Sandoz, Ciba-Geigy, and ABB (Asea Brown Boveri, jointly owned by Swiss and Swedish interests), were among the top 50.

The rural nature of many Swiss industrial sites can be attributed partly to the fact that manufacturing began with cottage industries and that, as mechanization progressed, they remained in the areas where skilled labor was available. This is illustrated by two of the leading Swiss industries: textiles in the northeast of the country and watch-making in the Jura in the northwest. Decentralization was also encouraged by the fact that waterpower was initially more readily available away from the towns. An exception to the rural location of manufacturing was the chemical industry, located near salt and potash deposits in the Rhine Valley in the vicinity of Basel. In the late nineteenth century when electricity could not be transmitted very far, branches of both the chemical and aluminum industries settled near sources of hydroelectricity that was generated in the Rhône Valley in the canton of Valais.

The industrialization of Switzerland began with the manufacture of cotton and silk. For a long time the textile industry employed the largest number of workers; however, in the twentieth century, machinery and vehicle manufactures took the lead and are now the largest employers, with 22 percent of the total manufacturing workforce in 1993. Initially, the machinery and metallurgical industries, located mainly in the northeast of Switzerland near the traditional industrial centers of Zürich, Winterthur, St. Gallen, and Baden, manufactured spinning frames, power looms, and water wheels. They are now engaged in a wide variety of sophisticated activities, including production of enormous generators and turbines, textile machinery, complex machine tools, internal combustion engines, and transportation equipment, as well as products such as surveying instruments, photographic apparatus, electronic equipment, and instruments. This highly diversified sector accounted for the largest percentage in value of Swiss exports—32 percent in 1984 and 58 percent in 1993.

Lack of indigenous raw materials such as coal and oil has not prevented the chemical and pharmaceutical industries from becoming the second largest export industry. This sector employed 72,000 workers in 1993, and accounted for 24 percent of all exports. Products included chemicals, dyestuffs, pharmaceuticals, cosmetics, perfume essences, and food flavorings. The export figures, important as they are, do not tell the complete sto-

ry of the chemical industry's contribution to the Swiss balance of payments. Firms such as Ciba-Geigy, Sandoz, and Roche Holding have plants throughout the world that distribute the home product as well as manufacturing chemicals for local markets. In this way protectionist measures of foreign countries are overcome and currency fluctuations are mitigated.

An industrial sector closely related to the machine industry is watchmaking. Concentrated in the valleys of the Jura, especially at La Chaux-de-Fonds, Le Locle, Biel, and Neuchâtel and in Geneva, the industry employed 76,000 persons in 1965, only 31,000 in 1984, and 35,000 in 1993. The industry was a classic example of one that had been overtaken by world competitors. In the early 1970s, serious problems confronted this tradition-bound sector. Wages were high compared with Japanese and Soviet competitors, and foreign electronic watches were reducing the market for traditional Swiss mechanical movements. Furthermore, there was a revival of protectionism in certain Swiss markets, and the increasing value of the Swiss franc was fast eroding Swiss competitiveness. Finally, the marketing of Swiss watches was behind the times, for they were sold mainly in specialty shops. Thus, the Swiss saw their exports of watches and movements (about 95 percent of production) shrink from 34 percent of the world's total in 1970 to only 14 percent in 1985. Nevertheless, watch exports by value represented about 22 percent of the Swiss total exports and 40 percent of the world watch market.

A necessary rationalization and reorganization of the industry was carried out. For example, many of the fragmented suppliers were grouped into two large holding companies that accounted for about one-third of watch output. The companies were later merged to form SMH (La Société Suisse de micro-électrique et d'horlogerie-Swiss Corporation for Microelectronics and Watchmaking Industries) with headquarters at Biel/Bienne. As a result of restructuring, exports of watches again began to climb. Companies that sought a particular segment of the market prospered; others that failed to heed the economic warning signs provide mute testimony to their failure by way of empty factories in the Jura.

The Swiss watchmaking strategy has followed

two distinct paths. One is the manufacture of prestige watches, as exemplified by such firms as Audemars Piguet, Ebel, Patek Philippe, Piaget, and Rolex. These companies manufacture no more than about 10 percent of Swiss production but account for about 40 percent of export income. The other path, the automatic fabrication of inexpensive plastic fashion watches, such as Swatch and Mondaine, has been highly successful. The Swatch, manufactured by new technology on robotized production lines, and strongly marketed as a fashion accessory, was unveiled by SMH in 1982. By 1992 Swatch had sold over 100 million units, making it the biggest selling watch in history. A continuing parade of new models has resulted in ever-increasing sales, exceeding 25 million in 1992.

Chocolate is another of Switzerland's specialized, quality products. One producer, Nestlé, is more than a manufacturer of candy bars; it was the largest Swiss firm in total sales in 1992, and it is one of the three largest food manufacturers in the world. In 1994 the firm ranked fourth in size among all European companies with a turnover of $44.5 billion and a profit of $3.6 billion or over 10 percent of sales.

Another company based in Switzerland with most of its interests abroad is A-L Holdings (Alusuisse-Lonza Ltd.), the world's sixth largest aluminum producer, manufacturer of chemicals and aluminum products, and packaging fabricator. Although its main plants are in the canton of Valais, A-L owns or controls installations throughout the world.

Swiss industry is characterized by a number of significant factors. For the most part, raw materials are imported; the labor force is skilled, motivated, and rarely strikes; wages are high; there is a high value-added component to products that are of a specialized nature; export markets are found worldwide; and subsidiary operations, employing the bulk of each company's workers, are found on every continent. Swiss companies, like their counterparts in Europe, the United States, and Canada, are undergoing structural changes because of the intense worldwide competition that has emerged in all sectors of industrialization. Companies must boost profits and eliminate all unnecessary expenses to survive. The restructuring may be characterized as follows. (1) Employment, whenever possible, is being reduced; (2) production may be shifted to low-wage countries; (3) divisions that chronically lose money or that do not fit into the major strategy of a firm may be sold or closed down; (4) mergers or agreements with other firms may be undertaken to reduce costs in all phases of production; and (5) new markets such as those in former communist countries or in Asia are being opened.

Service Sectors: Tourism, Finance, and Trade

Tourism also provides an important source of revenue for Switzerland, especially in rural and mountainous areas. In 1993 total earnings from tourism amounted to $7 billion, of which nearly 60 percent was accounted for by foreign receipts. From 1986 to 1991, the growth of foreign earnings from tourism was over 30 percent. However, in 1993, because of the strong Swiss franc and uncertainty in the economy, tourism receipts declined. Swiss tourist expenditures abroad in 1993 were $5.8 billion. Thus, the country still had a favorable tourist balance of $1.2 billion, an important factor in the country's balance of payments.

Because expenditures by foreigners in Switzerland have the same effect on the Swiss balance of payments as the export of goods, 14 percent of export earnings can be attributed to tourism, an "invisible" export. In fact, tourism was the third largest export earner after the metal and machine industry, and the chemical industry. Compared to other European countries, Switzerland ranked eighth in tourist arrivals in 1992, accounting for 4.5 percent of the European total. As a share of tourism in the GDP, the Swiss figure in 1993 was 3 percent, the fourth highest in Europe. Furthermore, tourism is an important employer, with about every eleventh laborer, most of whom are foreigners, working directly or indirectly in the industry. The figures are much higher in the mountain regions than in the urban agglomerations.

The country offers a variety of tourist attractions: cosmopolitan cities, stunning scenery, diverse climates, and a culture shaped by German, French, Italian, and Romansch elements. Even more important in a harassed urban society is the tranquillity of rural Switzerland, although this serenity has become increasingly more difficult to find because of expansion of economic activities in the mountains.

Tourism has had a double impact on the Swiss landscape and economy. On the one hand, it has injected much needed funds, not only in traditional tourist areas such as Interlaken, Luzern, and St. Moritz, but also in newer resort areas such as the Val d'Anniviers and Val d'Héremence in Valais. However, the very process of development in the mountain regions has led to serious environmental degradation, such as air pollution and forest damage. Where limited-access highways and tunnels have been built to carry international traffic through the narrow Alpine valleys, such as on the Gotthard and San Bernadino routes, the fallout from vehicle pollution has reached crisis proportions. In addition, erosion in the high mountains because of the development of ski areas, quarrying for rock and gravel, the cutting of new roads and trails, and construction of avalanche barriers is evident in a number of mountain cantons. In many resorts, the natural attributes that have attracted tourists from all over the world are being steadily degraded (Fig. 11-12).

Another service sector, finance, also makes important economic contributions to Switzerland's economy. Swiss banks, though not among the largest in the world, are notable within Europe. Besides labor expertise and a reputation for political stability, Switzerland has benefited from laws that have traditionally given account holders more protection from scrutiny than they have gotten in other places. The big three—Union Bank of Switzerland, Swiss Bank Corporation, and CS Holding (Credit Swiss)—were among the top 50 companies by market capitalization in Europe in 1994. Restructuring has been going on within the Swiss banking sector to improve competitiveness, especially since cartel-like conventions providing protection of various types of banks was abolished. There are over 600 domestic banks and finance companies in the country, as well as 230 foreign banks. Rationalization among the Swiss banks is necessary, and perhaps as many as 100 could disappear in the next decade. The banks, like industry, derive a major share of their net income from foreign markets. For example, in 1991 the figure was 30 percent for Crédit Suisse, and by the first half of 1993 the figure for UBS reached 40 percent. Though slow to adjust to the liberalization of the world banking industry during the 1980s, the big three Swiss banks are now among the most profitable in the world.

FIGURE 11-12 Overdevelopment in the Alps; a parking lot in Täsch. (Zermatt Tourist Office)

The Swiss have traditionally been among the forerunners in liberalizing and facilitating international trade. The geographical distribution of Switzerland's foreign trade shows dependence on Western Europe and especially the EU countries. In 1994 imports from the EU (12 countries) accounted for 73 percent of all imports, whereas shipments to the EU accounted for 56.5 percent of all exports. Switzerland had a total of about 7 percent of imports and 6 percent of its exports with other EFTA countries. The largest single market for Swiss goods was Germany, taking 21 percent of Swiss exports and providing 33 percent of imports.

From 1986 to 1992, the country registered annual trade deficits. However, in 1993 and 1994 surpluses were recorded, with over $2.4 billion in 1994. During the deficit years, with the exception of 1992, the proportion of imports covered by exports was over 85 percent. Thus, if the export of manufactured goods was the only means of paying for imports, the country would have been in financial difficulty when trade did not balance. Fortunately, "invisible" exports ameliorate this situation. Money flows into Switzerland from the many investments abroad. In addition, the activities of banks, insurance companies, international business firms, and transit operations bring in considerable sums, as does tourism. Since 1965, with minor exceptions, the inflow from "invisibles" has been able to offset any adverse balance of trade.

The Swiss, long before the Japanese and Germans, sought out world markets for their products. The proportion of exports in most industries is extremely high: 95 percent in dyestuffs and watches, 90 percent in textile machinery, 80 percent in machine tools, 70 percent in the silk industry, and 45 percent in textiles. The formula for Swiss success in industry may be summarized as follows. (1) Build a specialized product with a high added value; (2) guarantee the delivery date; (3) offer the necessary financing through an efficient banking network; (4) provide effective after-sales service; (5) sell the product all over the world, thus achieving economies of scale; and (6) where necessary, build local factories in order to overcome trade barriers. The end result has been an economy that has weathered the various slowdowns since

the end of the Second World War and has provided the country's inhabitants with the highest per capita incomes in the Western world.

Transport and Communication

Because of its geographical position and the importance of international trade to its economy, Switzerland has become an integral part of various inter-European and worldwide transportation and communication networks. The increasing movement of people and goods throughout Europe and especially through the Alps has resulted in new road and rail projects to help lessen the impact of the problem. Nevertheless, no solution will be perfect. For example, the number of trucks using the Gotthard through the canton of Uri climbed from less than 70 a day in 1980, before the opening of the road tunnel, to over 2400 by 1992, with a projected 4500 by the year 2000. Now that a new rail tunnel is to be constructed on the Gotthard route, the valleys of the Reuss and Leventina will become giant construction sites. No one can foresee the outcome of this massive project that will allow 40-ton trucks to cross the Alps on rail flat cars.

Rhine navigation is vital for the flow of goods into this landlocked country. Swiss policy has succeeded in keeping down the cost of transportation from European seaports to the Swiss frontier in order to minimize the disadvantages of the interior location of industry. The Mannheim Act of 1868 guaranteed the international status of Rhine shipping by forbidding the levying of dues and providing for equality of access to all countries. Since the end of World War II, barges of up to 2000 tons have been able to reach Basel without difficulty (Fig. 5-10). Traffic to ports in the Basel region, which was 1 million tons in 1930, exceeded 8 million in 1991.

Switzerland's rail network plays a significant role among the country's transportation modes. The dense rail network of 800 stations and over 3100 miles (5000 km) of track has been completely electrified. Swiss cities are linked by hourly trains, many of which are designated "InterCity" and stop only at major centers. One can go across the country from St. Gallen to Geneva, a distance of

230 miles (370 km), in just over four hours, stopping for a few minutes at Zürich, Bern, Fribourg, and Lausanne.

The main international rail connections are the Basel-Chiasso line linking France and Germany to Milan via the Gotthard Tunnel; a parallel route via Basel, Bern, the Lötschberg, and Simplon Tunnels; the Simplon route connecting Paris to Milan via Geneva or Vallorbe and the Rhône Valley; and the Geneva-Zürich line linking Switzerland to Germany and Austria. Geneva, Lausanne, and Bern are connected to Paris by French TGV (*Train à grande vitesse*), which on winter ski season weekends continues up the Rhône Valley to Brig. There are also many specialized trains, such as the line that reaches the summit of the Jungfraujoch at 11235 ft (3457 m) of altitude and over 465 miles (750 km) of cable cars.

There are five tunnels through which small vehicles can be carried by rail on flat cars. By far the largest, the Lötschberg, between the cantons of Bern and Valais, accounted for over a million vehicles in 1991, followed by the Furka between Valais and Graubünden with 197,000. New tunnels designed to transport 40-ton trucks on flat cars have been proposed for construction by 2015— under the Gotthard, over 30 miles (49.2 km), Monte Ceneri north of Lugano (7.8 miles/12.6 km), and the Lötschberg (17.5 miles/ 28.1 km). However, because of financial considerations, only one of these will most likely be constructed.

Despite all that has been done to encourage more passenger traffic, the Federal Railway continues to register operating deficits. During 1991–1993 the figure was well over $200 million annually. To reduce expenses, more regional trains will be shifted to buses, and the hourly cadence of some lines will be reduced during periods of infrequent use.

Switzerland, with 3.1 million cars, is a highly motorized country with one automobile for each 2.3 inhabitants in 1993, comparable to conditions in Germany (2.3), the United States (1.8), and Canada (2.1). The wide use of the private passenger car results in traffic and parking congestion, especially in the major cities, and contributes to air pollution, although all Swiss automobiles must be checked biannually for emission levels. Because of the Alpine barrier and the excellent goods transport provided by the Federal Railways, there are fewer heavy trucks than in most West European countries. The network of main highways and motorways is congested, especially during the summer and winter tourist seasons when millions of foreign automobiles pass through the country. In July 1993 the longest traffic jam ever recorded in Switzerland, 15 miles (24 km), kept holiday traffic to a standstill. Major highways connect the main cities of the Mittelland, and additional sections have penetrated the Alps. The most significant project was the 10.1-mile (16.3-km) tunnel under the Gotthard Pass. Another major obstacle was overcome when the 3-mile (5 km) N5 road tunnel under the city of Neuchâtel was completed in 1993.

Because of Switzerland's strategic position in Western Europe, the pressure on the country's highways from foreign motorists has been steadily growing. The total number of nondomestic vehicles of all types entering Switzerland is close to 60 million. The heavy traffic loads on the new highways, bridges, and tunnels have been higher than expected and require greater maintenance than anticipated. Thus, since 1984 an annual fee has been levied on all vehicles, both foreign and domestic, that use the motorways.

During the period 1971–1991, airline traffic by Swiss and foreign lines increased steadily. The number of flights expanded from over 153,000 to over 187,000. The number of passengers carried grew from 7.5 million to nearly 16 million, and freight increased twofold to over 443,000 tons. In 1991 Zürich-Kloten, Switzerland's largest airport, accounted for over 54 percent of all flights and over 62 percent of all passengers, followed by Geneva-Cointrin (29% and 28%) and Basel Euroairport (17% and 10%). The same year Zürich ranked fifth among European airports in flights, tenth in passengers, and fifth in freight.

Swissair, founded in 1931, is the country's main carrier, with over 19,000 employees in 1992, about 18 percent of whom work abroad. The company provides a good example of how Swiss firms aid the economy of their country. Swissair provides services that are exported abroad, thus earning foreign currency that can be used for payments of imports. In fact, some 65 percent of flight operations revenue comes from sales outside Switzerland and, therefore, benefit the country's balance of payments. To help survive the savage air wars that have taken their toll of established airlines, Swissair has made a number of strategic moves to ensure greater operating economies and maintain access to the EU countries. There are agreements with Delta, Singapore, SAS, and Austrian airlines that will consolidate functions, reduce expenditures, and provide easier access to a larger passenger pool. Furthermore, an aircraft maintenance center has been established at Shannon in Ireland with Lufthansa and Guinness Peat Aviation, and Swissair has share holdings in both the Galileo and Covia computer systems for travel agents. Finally, Swissair has purchased a majority share of the Belgian airline, Sabena.

Perspectives on the Swiss Success Story

Switzerland, as portrayed in this chapter, is a progressive, dynamic democracy, with a strong, well-managed economy and an educated, affluent, urban populace. The country has business contacts throughout the world and has considerable investments abroad. The deep recession of the early 1990s affected Switzerland severely, but less so than France and Germany. In 1994 unemployment in Switzerland was a "high" 4.7 percent compared to 12.6 percent in France and 9.5 percent in Germany, while inflation remained low (0.9%).

A number of factors have been responsible for Swiss economic strength. The country, unlike others in Europe, did not have to spend billions of dollars to prop up declining industries in sectors such as steel, coal mining, petrochemicals, and shipbuilding, because these industries were not found in Switzerland. The high value-added Swiss industries, despite some closures, maintained almost full employment levels. However, the severity of the 1990s recession hit Swiss exports and led to greater unemployment than at any time during the past quarter century. Both in the recession of the 1980s and the 1990s, govern-

ment funds were not used to restructure declining industries. A good example is watchmaking, where money came from private investors and the banks. Historically, Swiss investment has come from the private sector; government plays little or no part in directing investment. Consequently, costly schemes that can lose billions of taxpayers' dollars are avoided. Also, because of decentralization, there is no bloated government bureaucracy that must be maintained at taxpayers' expense. Therefore, in terms of economic efficiency, the Swiss are at the top of the league.

Because of unstable international political and economic conditions, people from all over the world have looked to Switzerland as a land of asylum. During the 1960s, many Swiss spoke out against the erosion of traditional values because of the influx of foreigners. At that time the finger was pointed at the Italians. Many, who arrived carrying their meager possessions on their shoulders, have now become financially successful and for the most part have been accepted by the Swiss. Today, the same questions are being asked about asylum seekers among refugees from countries such as Sri Lanka, Turkey, Afghanistan, and the former Yugoslavia. However, many workers from the former Yugoslavia and those of Portuguese and Spanish descent have made vital contributions to the economy. Certain sectors, especially tourism, construction, hotels, and restaurants, would not be able to function if the workers were not allowed to stay.

Finally, the question of continuing neutrality must be faced. No one doubts that the reasons for Swiss neutrality were valid until 1945. As long as Germany, France, and Italy were potential enemies of each other, an alliance with any of them would have resulted in national dismemberment. Today, with the collapse of the communist empire, Switzerland has to seek justification for its neutrality on a larger stage than that of Europe alone. Many Swiss feel that in a world of increasing economic and political interdependence, neutrality on the Swiss pattern is anachronistic and only serves to avoid international responsibility. Switzerland voted against joining the European Economic Area, sending peacekeeping forces to the UN, and allowing foreigners to buy property in Switzerland; the country is still not a member of the United Nations.

Surely, neutrality has its place. A good example is the work of the International Committee of the Red Cross (ICRC), an international organization that is private and composed exclusively of Swiss citizens, though non-Swiss will be allowed in the future. The ICRC has been operative since adoption of the first Geneva Convention in 1864. In honor of the founder, the Swiss Jean Henry Dunant, Switzerland's flag with colors reversed was adopted as the organization's symbol. Today, 164 countries are part of the organization. By being Swiss, the ICRC benefits from neutrality and maintains an impartial position in relation to the countries involved. Without question the work of the ICRC is vital in today's violent world. Nevertheless, it is not enough to justify Swiss neutrality.

The Swiss are living in "the world region." Their companies are located throughout the globe and are active in buying up firms in other countries. Furthermore, without exports the economy would collapse. The concepts of neutrality are flawed when armaments manufactured by Swiss companies find their way to warring states. Can the Swiss avoid world responsibility by claiming that they are neutral? Arguably, the country cannot remain an isolated island in an integrated Europe. Because of the international nature of the Swiss economy, the EU can apply great pressure on the Swiss, as has been the case of European trucks heavier than 28 tons passing through the country. Swiss banking practices are being more closely scrutinized and impacted by international pressures owing to alleged negligence (or worse) of Swiss banks in the handling of accounts of European Jews who perished in the Holocaust and as a result of the possibility that Swiss banking secrecy laws could be used by drug dealers and dictators to hide money illegally collected within their own countries. Whether or not one likes it, the world has changed dramatically and fundamentally since the end of the Cold War; the collapse of the Soviet Empire is proof of that. We have seen how the government's attempts to sell Europe and the United Nations to the Swiss have been rejected in national referendums. Nevertheless for the economic, political, cultural, and environmental welfare

of the country, in addition to moral obligations, the conservative Swiss must eventually become part of the European Union and the United Nations. Although it may take some time, it is an inevitable evolution of Swiss history.

GERMANY

Switzerland's large northern neighbor, the Federal Republic of Germany, long a major economic and political force in the EU, has emerged, after unification and the dissolution of the Soviet Union, as Europe's most powerful economy. The unified country now has over 80 million inhabitants, second only to Russia in Europe, and is the fourth largest European state in area west of the former USSR. The present incarnation of Germany has no historical precedence. It is a "New" Germany—but one that retains deep cultural and historic traditions. Although Germanic peoples occupied much of what is today Germany, the country's geopolitical roots date to 843 when Louis the German came to power in one of the territories of Charlemagne's divided empire. Subsequently, however, what was to become Germany splintered into a great number of small, relatively weak and poorly integrated states, though they were often loosely united in the long-lived Holy Roman Empire (800–1806). German lands were frequently the scene of conflict, especially during the Reformation and the devastating Thirty Years' War. The seeds of modern Germany were germinated by the formation of the Prussian Kingdom in 1701—an unlikely but, ultimately, a highly successful competitor with its primary territorial rivals, France and Austria. By the nineteenth century many of the small German states joined the Prussian-dominated German Confederation, and following stunning military victories over Austria and France, a German Empire was established under Prussian rule.

In 1871 the newly united German Reich covered an area of 212,600 sq miles (540,000 sq km), at that time the third largest among the European powers. Since then, it has undergone five territorial changes. By the Treaty of Versailles, Germany lost over 27,500 sq miles (70,000 sq km) and 6.5 million of its population. It expanded again, between 1938 and 1945, seizing the Sudetenland from Czechoslovakia and incorporating Austria and many other parts of Europe. After defeat in World War II, Germany was divided into four occupied zones. The western zones united in 1949 to become West Germany (Federal Republic of Germany), to which the French-occupied Saarland was annexed in 1957 (the "little reunification"). The eastern zone, occupied by the Soviet Union, became East Germany (German Democratic Republic) in 1949. The full sovereignty of East Germany was recognized by the Soviet Union in 1955 and, following a Western agreement with West Germany, by the United States and most other countries in 1974.

The city of Berlin also was divided into four occupied zones, later reduced to two sectors—East (Soviet) and West (USA, French, and British). East Berlin was absorbed into East Germany and become its capital. West Berlin became de facto one of 11 West German states (*Länder*), but was represented in the West German Parliament by nonvoting observers. Owing to the Four-Power agreement of 1945, West Berlin had a special status and could not officially belong to West Germany.

It remained an enclave within East Germany, with precarious lines of communication with parent West Germany (Fig. 11-13). The former Prussian-German provinces of Pomerania, Brandenburg, and Upper and Lower Silesia became part of Poland; and East Prussia was split between the USSR (Kaliningrad Oblast) and Poland.

Finally, in 1990, following the failure of Soviet and East German political and economic development policies, East and West Germany were united within an enlarged FRG. United Germany has officially recognized its postwar boundaries as final in response to concerns by neighbors, especially Poland and the Czech Republic, that the once again powerful country might seek to reassert claims to territories formerly under German control. Despite rhetoric and exhortations from a small minority of Germans for reestablishment of Germans' "rights" or control in these regions, neither the contemporary German state nor the great majority of its populace gives much indication that any such effort can be expected. To the contrary, official German state policy is one of conciliation with its neighbors, with the republics of the former USSR, and with the remaining German as well as Israeli Jews.

FIGURE 11-13 The Berlin Wall from West Berlin (right) looking toward the east (left). Until autumn of 1989, West Berlin was encircled by walls and other impediments that were intended to isolate the city from East Germany and prevent the escape of East Germans to the West. Similarly fortified barricades stretched along the entire East-West German border. (German Information Center)

Population

Germany has had striking patterns of regional population change during the postwar era. Western Germany had population gains between 1945 and about 1960, with little total change thereafter. Much of the growth in the immediate postwar era was fueled by the infusion of nearly 8 million refugees from territories lost by Germany during the war. Owing to the common cultural heritage (they spoke the same language), the newcomers were quickly integrated into the society. Eastern Germany experienced large population losses after the war owing to emigration prior to construction of "the Wall" in 1961 (nearly 3 million refugees), and relatively little change thereafter until a wave of emigration of nearly a million people beginning in 1989 that tapered off sharply by the early 1990s. Small numbers of East Germans had also fled or were ransomed by the FRG from politically based imprisonment after the East-West border was sealed in 1961. The large numbers of refugees from the east, with a high percentage in the most productive working age group, contributed immensely to the rapid postwar rehabilitation and economic growth of West Germany.

During the 1970s and 1980s in western Germany, the southern provinces (Länder) grew the most rapidly, notably in metropolitan areas—Nuremberg, Würzburg, Freiburg, Regensburg, and especially in the Munich-Augsburg and Stuttgart-Karlsruhe-Mannheim regions. For example, the two southern *Länder* (Bavaria and Baden-Württemberg) accounted for about 30 percent of all population growth in western Germany in the 1950s, nearly 50 percent in the 1960s, and nearly 60 percent in the 1970s and 1980s. The growth reflects both somewhat higher birth rates and inmigration affected by appealing natural environments and employment growth in high-technology engineering and electronics industries. Population growth was also relatively great during the 1970–1990 period near other German cities, such as Cologne, Bonn, Bremen, Hannover, and Hamburg, while central city populations themselves stagnated or fell (including in West Berlin). Relatively high population losses were also recorded in many western rural areas, especially along the border with eastern Germany and in economically depressed coal-and metal-producing areas of the Ruhr region. Eastern Germany experienced widespread population losses in most areas; population gains were largely confined to larger cities and towns and their immediate hinterlands.

More than 90 percent of Germany's resident population is composed of ethnic Germans, including millions of postwar ethnic German immigrants from Eastern Europe. For example, from 1990 to 1995 over 200,000 people were admitted each year into Germany from Romania, Poland, and the former Soviet Union, with a peak of 430,00 in 1992. The remaining approximately 2 million ethnic Germans in Eastern Europe, many of whose ancestors emigrated three centuries ago, are often far removed culturally and socioeconomically from modern German society. Those who have come to Germany face a variety of problems integrating into society, despite support from the central government, local communities, and individual Germans.

Among the minorities now living in Germany are 60,000 Jews. These are largely people who have come to Germany in recent years from the FSU (former Soviet Union) and Eastern Europe. A Jewish community is being reestablished in Berlin, where Jews first settled in the year 1295 and where in 1933 there were 173,000 in the Jewish community. Today's community of 10,000 offers Berlin and Germany an opportunity to establish a new relationship between Germans and Jews—one that could stand in contrast to the horrific annihilation of German Jewry during the Nazi era. Other notable, small population groups in Germany include ethnic Danes (in Schleswig-Holstein) and Sorbs (Slavic people in Brandenburg and Saxony).

Many millions of foreign guest workers and asylum seekers reside in Germany but as yet have little prospect of becoming German citizens. Because of once lenient laws, hundreds of thousands of asylum seekers and refugees came to Germany from places as diverse as Afghanistan, Nigeria, and the former Yugoslavia. In 1992, the last year before entry became more difficult, over 450,000 entered the country. One specific problem involves Vietnamese who came to East Germany as guest workers and presently are stateless. Ultimately, most will return to Vietnam, many probably unwillingly, as the result of an agreement between Vietnam and united Germany. In all there are about 7.2 million foreigners living in Germany, the largest number, 1.8 million, being Turks and Kurds.

Germany's "guest worker" population is almost entirely associated with rapid immigration to Germany during a long period of economic expansion and labor shortages from the 1950s into the mid-1970s. By mid-1955 only about 80,000 foreign workers (*Gastarbeiter*—guest workers) were counted in West Germany. However, in 1961 a dependable stream of people from East Germany was slowed by the erection of the Berlin Wall and similar obstacles along the entire East-West German border (see Fig. 11-14). With a constantly increasing demand for additional labor, the West Germans started systematically recruiting citizens from foreign countries—at first from Italy, then from Spain and Greece, and ultimately from other Mediterranean countries, especially Yugoslavia and Turkey. A widespread official recruitment system was established with the official permission of individual countries, which in the departure of their unemployed, underemployed, and uneducated citizens envisioned a great advantage to their economy.

Thus, the German economy was able to rely on a dependable supply of workers. The trickle of the 1950s (guest workers represented 0.4 percent of the total employed in mid-1955) became a flood by 1973 (10 percent of the labor force in late 1973). During the last 20 years there has been on average a slow decline in the absolute and relative importance of guest workers, who now comprise less than 5 percent of the labor force, but who, with their families, continue to represent a numerically large population group. Birth rates are also relatively high among many guest worker subpopulations, so that combined with segregated residential patterns, many German cities have large minority populations and large numbers of minority school children. In many cities more than 10 percent of the resident population are non-Germans—notably Frankfurt (25%); Stuttgart (19%); Munich (17%); Düsseldorf, Mannheim, Cologne (all 15%); Berlin (14%); and Hamburg (12%). In addition, EU regulations allowing free movement of labor as well as illegally working foreign residents account for an estimated 150,000 workers in Germany's construction industry, a sector that has an estimated 130,000 unemployed German citizens.

Cultural conflicts have arisen between the traditionally Christian German culture and the Islamic culture of many Turks, and there are jealousies related to the existence of high unemployment among Germans and continuing employment of foreign labor, in both menial and skilled positions. There is a significant level of xenophobia among ethnic Germans, though hostility based on race or ethnicity seems no greater there than, for example, in the United States. Xenophobic attitudes, jealousies toward guest workers, and the feeling by many "ethnic Germans" that Germany should not be an "immigration country" have played a role within the politics that make it difficult for immigrants to gain German citizenship. This is in spite of the fact that many guest workers have lived for decades in Germany and their children have been born and raised there. These serious political and social issues are, arguably, greater long-term problems for the country than are the issues surrounding the incorporation of eastern Germany into west German society.

Two world wars, a major depression, and the recent period of prosperity, all within a relatively few years, have left a deep mark on the age structure of Germany's population. The natural population increase (excess of births over deaths), which in 1910 stood at 13 per 1000, diminished steadily until in 1933 it reached a low of 3.5 per 1000. There was a brief postwar "baby boom," but by mid-1989 West Germany recorded a decrease of -0.2 per 1000. In East Germany owing to various pronatalist policies, there were positive rates of natural increase in the 1980s, but beginning in 1989 the rate was again negative (-0.4 per 1000) and fell sharply in the early 1990s owing to emigration of young people and insecure social and economic conditions. In the mid-1990s united Germany's natural population growth rate remained negative. Given Germany's age structure and low birth rate, a natural population decline is predicted well into the future. In order to fill future jobs, especially menial jobs often disdained by Germans, immigration of more foreign labor may be inevitable—despite unemployment among highly educated Germans and tensions between ethnic Germans and nonethnic German residents in Germany.

Economic Geography

Like Japan, Germany only belatedly became one of the world's leading economies. The country first went through the Industrial Revolution after its political unification in 1871. Although other European countries had gained a head start, Germany, with a reservoir of human and material resources, fertile soils capable of feeding a growing industrial population, and centrally located position in Europe, soon overtook its rivals in production and trade. Despite defeat and territorial losses after World War I, Germany rebounded economically in the 1930s, but the Nazi leadership used the country's renewed strength to launch Europe's most devastating war, which resulted in widespread destruction in Germany. At the end of World War II, Germany's economic life was scarred by bombed-out cities, infrastructure, and industrial plants. Dismemberment of the nation into three occupied zones also disrupted traditional economic linkages between the diverse German regions. For example, the hinterland of the port of Hamburg, which formerly included Dresden and Bohemia in Czechoslovakia, was cut by the Iron Curtain a few miles to the southeast of the city.

Following some years of bitter poverty, West Germany rapidly recovered. East Germany also recuperated, though more slowly and incompletely owing in part to heavy Soviet reparations payments, as well as to the GDR's incorporation into the CMEA bloc rather than the EC. Ultimately, these disadvantages—together with the political and economic successes of West Germany; the Socialist Unity party's autocratic, economically ineffective leadership in East Germany, and the decline of Soviet power—led East Germans to choose union with the West in hopes of repeating West Germany's postwar "economic miracle." Thus far, only a portion of their hopes has been met.

An analysis of West Germany's economic strength will help to explain the country's postwar recuperative power. The growth of agriculture and manufacturing in Germany after 1871 was made possible by the presence of domestic resources (such as coal, potash, and iron ore), a skilled labor force, a government committed to economic development, and a culture that valued education, work, and accomplishment.

Thanks to pioneering efforts in applying scientific methods to agriculture, Germany greatly increased its crop yields and attained world leadership in the production of sugar beets, potatoes, and rye. By 1937 Germany produced close to 85 percent of its food needs. After World War II, despite destruction and a reduced area, and because of the Common Agricultural Policy of the EC, the country rapidly became self-sufficient in most foodstuffs.

Industry, Germany's greatest asset, owed its early, rapid growth to the extensive coal deposits of the Ruhr, the Saar, and Upper Silesia (after World War II incorporated into Poland). Plentiful coal, lignite, and some low-grade iron ore provided the basis for the iron and steel industry, which in turn supplied the basic materials for such vital industries as shipbuilding and the manufacture of rails, rolling stock, machines, and armaments. Germany's other raw materials, including large potash and salt deposits for the fertilizer and chemical industry, also contributed to its position among Europe's principal manufacturing countries.

By the end of World War II and during the subsequent postwar era, the importance of these resources waned, owing to the high cost of their development (especially coal), the relatively modest resource base in the first place, and their depletion through long periods of use. In West Germany the burgeoning demands of the rapidly expanding economy were increasingly met by substantial levels of resource importation, especially oil and iron ore, despite the fact that the West inherited prewar Germany's best coal and (modest) iron ore deposits.

Western Germany's economic structure has changed greatly during this century. Although wartime loss of manpower was offset by a great influx of immigrants and the reconstruction of German cities and industrial establishments, territorial losses constituted a serious impediment to the restoration of normal economic life after World

War II. Nevertheless, western Germany has once again become one of the world's major economic centers. West Germany received important financial support from the Marshall Plan (European Recovery Program) funded by the United States, which provided the seeds that ultimately helped sow West German success. Tremendous effort by the population as well as decades of relatively low standards of living and high levels of investment brought West Germany economic success and living standards comparable to U.S. levels by about 1970. West Germany has also benefited from actively participating in many important European organizations (see Chapter 5), foremost being the European Union. Linked with France, it has been a primary advocate of greater European economic and political unity, as well as being by far the largest direct net financial supporter.

On the other hand, after Germany was divided into two states in 1949, East Germany remained more agriculturally oriented (about 10% of all employment in the late 1980s); more dependent on "old" industries like lignite, iron, and steel production; less technologically advanced and oriented; and far less productive than West Germany. Although East Germany did well within the autarchic and relatively backward CMEA economic bloc, it was no match for the world's advanced market economies. Despite Socialist Unity party rhetoric that deceived some persons in the West, visual evidence both before and after the demise of the GDR revealed the shambles that socialism/communism made of the country.

East Germany inherited from Germany's postwar division far fewer resources than West Germany and was especially short of energy resources, although it did have potash deposits used in the chemical industry and extensive low-quality lignite deposits. As a result, the GDR developed open-pit lignite mines at great expense that resulted in serious environmental problems, including disastrous air and water pollution problems (Fig. 11-14). It became dependent on oil and hard coal imports, particularly from the USSR. The GDR also mined a variety of minerals in the eastern Harz and in southernmost Saxony regions that were uneconomic. The mining was undertaken largely as a result of attempts to be self-sufficient, and was based on inadequate data and methods

FIGURE 11-14 Lignite-fired power plant at Lübbenau southeast of Berlin. Huge areas of eastern Germany are scarred by open pit lignite mines, which resulted in a variety of direct and indirect environmental problems, including the severe air pollution evidenced here. (Vivianne Moos/The Image Bank)

for evaluating the cost-benefit ratio of the operations. Moreover, the economic planning was inept, undertaken with a managerial force that was often chosen based on political motives rather than on ability. Uranium, one such mined product, was used for export to the Soviet Union.

Although it was considered the CMEA's most advanced industrial economy and had the highest level of per capita consumption, the GDR's physical plant became technologically dated and its infrastructure was literally crumbling to pieces. The workforce became dispirited, was poorly motivated, and unproductive, and generally unbeknownst to the populace, the country's budget was dependent on indirect aid from the FRG. The East German economy was unprepared to integrate and compete within the German or global economies of the 1990s, and it continues to suffer severe problems more than six years after unification, many of which have deep roots and will not be quickly resolved.

Eastern Germany now benefits from western German capital, labor skills, and technology, as well as the EU market and agricultural, industrial, and infrastructural subsidies. An estimated $700 billion was transferred from west to east within Germany during the early 1990s, dwarfing aid from the EU. However, eastern Germany must also face economic competition inherent both within the EU and a united Germany. In the short run, it has been doing poorly, with drastically reduced industrial output (about a 75% decline in the mid-1990s in comparison to 1989) and high unemployment rates—officially about 15 percent in 1995, but probably much higher.

United Germany's economy functions with much more government intervention than is the case in the United States, though far less than was the situation in the former East Germany. East Germany directly controlled about 95 percent of the country's GDP, whereas U.S. federal budget resources amount to less than 25 percent of GDP (low by developed world standards). West Germany's federal expenditures were running a little below 50 percent of GDP prior to unification (around the European average). United Germany now has a large federal budget deficit, and the budget is about 52 percent of total GDP, of which eastern Germany contributes only about 7 percent.

Unlike the GDR's highly centralized, politically and publicly dominated economy or the United States' relatively capitalist-oriented one, united Germany functions with the mixed "social market" economic system that dominated throughout most of its postwar history and is generally supported by all large German political parties. The government has more economic power and influence than the government in the United States. Germans have much higher taxes; publicly owned industries and utilities (such as railroads, the national airline, television and radio broadcasters, and telecommunication providers) employ about a million workers; and the population has a denser, more secure social safety net, including a national health care system. However, the direct and indirect costs of all these services (e.g., high taxes and reduced individual incentives) have been called into question, and, as in many European countries, the German government has been and will in the future privatize some of its holdings. Lufthansa, the national airline, is now 65 percent privately owned, and the huge government telecommunications monopoly, Deutsche Telekom, will soon be split into three privatized portions. Similarly, united Germany has almost completely privatized the thousands of previously government-owned

enterprises in the east, or has shut them down. Ironically, when this process began, the institution established to accomplish the mammoth privatization process, the *Treuhandanstalt*, was the world's largest employer with literally millions of workers. On January 1, 1995 the "Treuhand" ceased to exist, although its controversial impacts, such as the sale and closing of nearly 14,000 firms that once employed 4 million workers but now only 1.5 million, will reverberate across Germany's economic and political landscape for at least a generation to come.

The reunited German economy experienced a brief, largely publicly financed, boom after unification that benefited employment and production in the west and flooded the east with consumer goods. Thereafter, however, Germany suffered its most severe postwar recession in the early 1990s. Western Germans were subjected to higher tax rates, and eastern Germans lost their jobs by the millions as eastern German producers were, possibly too quickly, subjected to the full brunt of competition from more efficient producers in western Germany, the EU, and the world economy. By the mid-1990s fully one-third of all former East German workers were in an unwanted labor status and official unemployment was at about 15 percent—double the western German average and well above the EU mean (11%).

Employment in particular sectors has been especially hard hit in eastern Germany, including agriculture, mining, metallurgy, and textiles and apparel production. Hoped-for economic leadership by high-technology industries such as the computer industry has yet to materialize, and there has been a net decline rather than an expansion in the automotive industry. Leading economic sectors in the east thus far have been those thriving on investments and massive transfer payments from the federal government, especially in the construction industry and service sectors. Although the German economy emerged from a severe recession in 1994, the painful, expensive, and slow process of economic restructuring and environmental clean-up in eastern Germany will require many years until the rash unification promise by Chancellor Helmut Kohl of a blossoming eastern German landscape can be realized. In the meantime, a number of social and economic problems face eastern Germany, resulting in huge financial drains and political problems for all of Germany (see "The Transition in Berlin and Eastern Germany" in this chapter and the section on "A Post-Socialist, Post-Soviet *ECSEE*" in Chapter 12).

Beyond these problems, Germany has also been increasingly concerned about its ability to remain competitive as a place of manufacturing and business within the world economy. German wage rates and benefits (including the world's longest paid vacations—about 30 days per year) are among the world's most expensive. Investment by German firms abroad has increased, and leading firms like Mercedes-Benz and BMW are locating production in lower cost U.S. production sites. There is some evidence, and probably a wider perception, that Germany is becoming less competitive as a production site and is losing its chance to join new technology industries dominated by the United States and Japan (e.g., in computer hardware and software) and in industries where Germany once held clear dominance (e.g., machine tools). Unemployment has increased, especially among the young, among highly educated subgroups, and in eastern Germany. Tax rates are high; federal budget deficits have burgeoned; inflation and interest rates have gone up; and national indebtedness has increased. There are clear, associated indications of social insecurity. For example, birth rates have plunged in the east; the time needed to complete degrees at universities has lengthened; and attacks have been made against ethnic minorities as well as their homes and places of worship, including synagogues. Political frustration is evident in the declining proportion of votes being cast for the established, major parties. Traditional ruling coalitions, notably the CDU/CSU/FDP national coalition, are receiving less electoral support; and there are increasing tendencies for small parties, including extremist parties, to gain notoriety, such as the right-wing *Republikaner*, the protest *Statt Partei*, and the Greens.

Observers also note that these problems and concerns are exaggerated and that actions to address them, rather than panic or inaction from despondency, are the appropriate response. Though expensive, German wage costs are not exorbitantly high, given the high levels of labor productivity. Investment abroad in order to reduce production costs can improve profits for German firms, more of whom, in any event, will need to develop new high value-added products and services to produce in Germany and market abroad in order for both the firms and the national economy to prosper. National budget deficits were a virtually unavoidable outcome of unification; they should subside in time as the benefits of investment in the east begin to pay dividends and government moves to rein in spending.

For Germans, and outside observers, it is difficult to ascertain whether the more pessimistic or the more optimistic of these scenarios accurately reflects likely future trends in the German economy and society. Given the past political and economic successes of the Federal Republic, however, one must assume that appropriate responses to all these concerns will at least allow reasonable adaptation to changing domestic and international circumstances.

Agriculture

The economic importance of agriculture within Germany and German society is, as in France, greater than one would expect given its very small share in GDP and employment. Agriculture dominates a traditional rural way of life respected by many people, based on factors such as farmers' thrifty and hard-working lifestyle and their role in preserving a traditional landscape of mixed field and forest (Fig. 11-15). Noteworthy features of German agriculture are: (1) European leadership in the production of a number of goods; (2) a relatively high percentage of land under cultivation in selected areas; (3) relatively high yields by European standards, particularly in the west; (4) rapidly falling levels of employment and cultivation in the east; and (5) ongoing structural change in the size of holdings and levels of employment and capitalization. High-level efficiency in production contributes to the country's high degree of agricultural self-sufficiency.

Both owing to its sheer size and to the productivity of its farm sector, Germany is among the top producers in Europe (excepting the former USSR)

FIGURE 11-15 Allgäu landscape in the foothills of the Alps in Germany near the Austrian border. (W. H. Berentsen)

for animal products such as pork, beef, milk, and butter, as well as many crops suitable to its climates, including sugar beets, oats, and rape seed. It is also second only to either France or Poland in the production of wheat, barley, and rye.

The most productive agricultural areas in Germany result from a combination of favorable natural conditions and support from good infrastructure and government policies, the latter with greater positive impact in the west. Three general areas of the country have the highest yielding cropland: (1) the Cologne and Münster lowlands in the west; (2) a series of valleys and basins in the southwest near Stuttgart, Mainz, and Frankfurt; and (3) an arc-shaped area in central Germany that is more or less in a line between the cities of Hannover, Leipzig, and Erfurt. All of these areas benefit from the natural productivity of their underlying loess soils, as well as from relatively mild lowland climatic conditions. Another relatively large and productive agricultural region is in the northern part of the Alpine Foreland (north of Munich), which also contains many loess soil areas and a good climate, though one that is somewhat colder in the winter than the other regions noted. Other agricultural regions, including small, quite productive ones, are scattered throughout Germany. Because of historic settlement patterns as well as current government subsidies, agricultural activities also continue in many hilly and

mountainous regions of the country (see Fig. 11-16). Farming in these regions requires greater effort and expense, with lower returns, so that farmsteads in, for example, the Black Forest are declining in number. Farming in these areas continues, in part because farmers and family members can supplement incomes by other employment, including employment in expanding tourist industries.

The bread grains (oats, barley, rye, and wheat) and potatoes, of which Germany has been one of Europe's chief producers, constitute, along with more recently expanded meat production and con-

FIGURE 11-16 Restoration of statues at the Zwinger Palace, Dresden. (W. H. Berentsen)

sumption, the historic basis of Germany's diet. Rye, the most important cereal crop, is made into dark bread, often mixed with other grains including wheat. Wheat has grown in importance through time, and is displacing rye and potato production on many east German farms. Barley is in special demand for brewing beer and for animal fodder; oats are a typical crop of the moist regions along the Baltic coast and the North Sea. Industrial crops, such as hemp, flax, tobacco, hops, sunflower, and rape seed, have increased in importance, but the area under cultivation is relatively small. Sugar beets, a source of sugar and fodder, are grown for the most part on loess soil in the borderlands between the North European Plain and the Central Uplands, in a distribution similar to that of wheat. Vegetable and fruit production is widespread, though often taking advantage of sheltered river valley locations in proximity to large urban markets, such as along the central Rhine, the lower Elbe near Hamburg, and the Havel in the Potsdam-Berlin region. Intensive agriculture is also practiced in the mild coastal and small island regions of the Lake of Constance, where a variety of fruits and vegetables are grown. Vineyards are located on the slopes of the Rhine Gorge and in the Neckar, Main, Moselle, and Nahe valleys. German wines, notably the Rhine and Mosel wines, are of good quality and are exported globally (Fig. 5-8).

A combination of factors is responsible for the higher agricultural yields in the west compared to the east, but the primary factors have been associated with the better access to capital and advanced technology and the personal incentives offered by the west's free market-oriented economic system. Failed economic policies in the socialist east retarded farmers' access to technology and severely dampened incentives to produce and innovate. Now in eastern Germany, owing to the reorganization of very large state-dominated farms and the failure of high levels of private farming to emerge, levels of agricultural employment and cultivation are plummeting. In fact, employment has declined an astounding 80 percent. Literally hundreds of thousands of eastern farmers have changed careers, are trying to do so, or are unemployed. The steep decline in eastern agriculture is due to the farmers' lack of access to adequate capital,

reluctance to return to the long hours required in private agriculture, keen competition in the EU and Germany, and financial incentives to leave land idle.

A number of economic and related political factors are resulting in an ongoing process of structural change in German agriculture. Notably, in order to meet growing domestic and international competition, western German farms are becoming progressively larger and more specialized, and production everywhere is more capital intensive and technologically advanced. For example, in 1960 in West Germany 74 percent of farms were smaller than 25 acres (10 hectares); by 1991 this figure had fallen to 47 percent, and many of the smaller farms were operated by part-time farmers. Similarly, levels of mechanization have risen and use of inorganic fertilizer has rapidly increased (e.g., a threefold increases in nitrogen- and phosphate-based fertilizers per hectare between 1960 and 1990). In the west, the northern *Länder* have larger farms, and the southern *Länder* have smaller farms, owing largely to historic inheritance laws that favored splitting farms among heirs in much of the south. The south also has climatic conditions that offer more opportunities for intensive use of smaller plots by, for example, vineyards, specialized fruits and vegetables, hops, and tobacco. Furthermore, southern farmers are more likely to have off-farm work than their northern counterparts. Thus, Schleswig-Holstein in the far north has, on average, Germany's largest farms (94 acres/38 ha) and Baden-Württemberg in the southwest its smallest (32 acres/13 ha).

Paradoxically, some of western Germany's most intensive agriculture is also located on its poorest lands. In northwestern Germany, the portion of the country north of the Ruhr and west of Hannover and Hamburg (and especially around the towns of Vechta and Cloppenburg), rural economies once based primarily on grazing have over the last century been transformed by the increased raising of pigs, poultry, and calves. The change has been based on a number of locational advantages and changes in organization of production. Until at least the beginning of this century, farmers in the area were poor and found it difficult to compete against producers in regions with better drained land, better soils, and longer growing seasons. However, based on improved rail connections to North Sea ports, farmers began importing grain, fattening animals and fowl for slaughter, and then shipping them to the large, relatively prosperous industrial cities in the vicinity, particularly the huge market in the Ruhr region. Wastes from the animals were also used as fertilizers to improve productivity on wet pasturelands, on which drainage was improved in order to allow production of silage crops, notably field corn. Progressive improvements in the productivity of breeds of animals and poultry; investment in specialized feedlots and feed storage and delivery systems; careful attention to critical issues of health of animals and quality of product; and development of a complex agroindustrial structure, including both very large firms and small private producers specializing in tasks such as breeding, feeding, slaughtering, and marketing, have transformed the region's landscape and economy. Boggy fields and marshes have been replaced by fields of corn and a landscape dotted with small factories, feedlots, and prosperous private farms. The agroeconomic structure, once dominated by family farms, is now also comprised of vertically integrated agroindustrial corporations and cooperatives as well as smaller, specialized product and service providers. All these actors are bound together in what has been described as a territorially bounded, joint production system—interrelated, specialist producers agglomerated in space. This development—in effect, the "industrialization" of agriculture—is found elsewhere in the most developed agricultural regions of Europe, most notably in the neighboring Netherlands.

On the one hand, the ability of farmers in northwestern Germany to overcome natural disadvantages by ingenuity and to capitalize on locational advantages is an economic success story. On the other hand, controversies related to negative environmental impacts (especially leaching of nitrogen compounds into groundwater and drainage of wetlands) and treatment of captive animals have arisen. Efforts are underway to reduce or eliminate the negative environmental consequences of intensive agriculture in the northwest.

Elsewhere, in both western and eastern Germany, farmers in other disadvantaged agricultural regions have also focused on products for which they have at least a comparative advantage. Thus, for example, there is a concentration of milk production in the hill country of Saxony in eastern Germany and in the Bavarian Forest and Alpine foothills of the southwest. In a particularly beautiful part of the Alpine region, Allgäu milk cooperatives have successfully developed recognition for their cheeses—an excellent way for the producers to gain advantages of selling a more value-added product than perishable milk alone.

Agricultural development in eastern Germany shares some characteristics in common with the west, but in other respects it is quite distinct. Under socialism farmland was at first more equitably distributed among farmers, following seizure of land from church estates and from large landowners (especially in the north), many of whom were alleged Nazis or Nazi collaborators. Later, farmland was almost entirely collectivized under government supervision and control beginning in the early 1950s and culminating in a strong party-led campaign in the early 1960s. Economic, social, and political pressures for private farmers to join collectives were among a number of factors that led to massive emigration from the east, a movement ultimately stemmed by construction of closely guarded fortifications along all east-west German borders. Thereafter, huge, frequently highly specialized farms emerged in eastern Germany. As in the west, these farms became increasingly mechanized, more heavily dependent on chemical fertilizers and pesticides, and more environmentally unfriendly. In the late 1980s East German farms ranged in size from 8 to 12 thousand acres (approx. 3 to 5 thousand hectares) and could have thousands of animals. In contrast, West Germany's private farms averaged 44 acres (18 ha) and had a fraction of the number of animals of the eastern farms.

Since unification, employment and cultivated areas in the east have undergone a drastic decline. Large cooperative farms, controlled primarily by socialist-era managers, still dominate the economic and physical landscape. However, EU agricultural subsidies encouraging reduced areas of production have also resulted in large areas of fallow land. The continued power and growing economic and political clout of socialist-era farm bosses in rural areas has become a national issue.

There is fear that unification has led to the reintroduction of powerful eastern landlords who once supported Nazism and were disowned by the occupying Soviets. Ironically, most of the new capitalist era lords of the land are formerly "red" barons.

An EU-wide move to cut cereal surpluses and farm subsidies has and will result in lower levels still in employment and cultivation across Germany, but as in other advanced industrial countries, the country must also deal politically with a powerful farm lobby and socially with a large rural population and a tradition of "family" farming in the west that rallies support from other segments of society. Agriculture is apt to continue to employ a higher percentage of workers than in, for example, the United States well into the next century, and U.S.-EU controversies associated with subsidies and impediments to trade may never be completely resolved.

Forestry, Fishing, and Mining

With the exception of mining, other primary sectors in Germany are far less economically significant than agriculture. The North Sea and North Atlantic provide most of the fish catch. Fishing grounds in the Baltic Sea are less productive. Competition, overfishing, and the impacts of pollution have sharply reduced the German fish catch (e.g., the 1988 West German catch was less than a quarter of the 1960 catch). Landings increased somewhat in the late 1980s and early 1990s, but the industry's problems remain, and it is a relatively minor sector within the German economy.

German forests (21% of the land) today differ greatly from the forest of ancient times—none of which has survived millennia of human use and abuse. Once predominantly broadleaved, the forests are now composed chiefly of conifers, which have been found to be especially suitable for reforestation. Thanks to strict and effective conservation measures, large tracts are preserved for wood production, as small-animal habitat, and as recreation areas for the German people, who enjoy walking and revere forests. Most tracts of forest lands have been in state or community hands (*Gemeindewälder*) since 1919. Unfortunately, acid rain negatively impacts forests, especially those in the higher elevations of the south, where over 50 percent of the stands have been damaged. Besides pollutants from industry and thermal plants both in Germany and abroad, much forest damage is attributed to vehicular exhaust, especially from diesel motors that use oil with a high sulfur content. Heavy traffic and the German passion for driving at unlimited speeds on the extensive *autobahn* system contribute to the problem.

Because of the country's areal extent and market size, as well as its careful forestry planning and harvesting, Germany is, after Russia, Europe's major wood producer. It leads other important competitors like Finland, France, and Sweden in most production categories, including total roundwood production, sawnwood, and paper output.

Germany's mountain regions in particular have for centuries produced a wide range of minerals and metals. However, this production, as well as oil and natural gas extraction on the country's northern plain, is not significant by either international or domestic standards, although it did at one time play an important role in helping to establish the earliest eras of manufacturing in a number of regions such as the Ore Mountains on the Czech border. Small amounts of crude oil production come from the fields in the Hannover-Emsland, Weser-Ems, and Alpine Foreland areas, but domestic production covers only about 3 percent of consumption. Imports of oil and, to a lesser extent, of natural gas have increased dramatically through time, and expectations of oil discoveries in the German sector of the North Sea thus far have not materialized. Given that nearly 70 percent of the oil imported in 1974 came from the politically unstable Arab world (15% alone from Libya), the potentially serious economic impact of Germany's dependence on oil imports can be easily understood. All together, in 1990 Germany depended on foreign sources for about half of its energy.

Germany is still one of the world's top 10 coal producers and the third largest in Europe, not including the former USSR, after the UK and Poland. It is also the third largest producer of potash. Both industries face difficult production conditions, are cutting back the number of mines and workers, and cause significant environmental problems. Germany's higher grade coal ("hard coal") is produced primarily in the Ruhr region, long one of Europe's major coal-producing and, largely as a result, manufacturing regions. Because coal has been mined for centuries, the best and most accessible coal seams have been largely exhausted, and today relatively thin, deep, and fractured seams are exploited. The major scene of mining, once concentrated in shallower shafts south of the Ruhr River, is in deeper shafts north of the river, as miners are forced to utilize the field's unmined reserves, which remain primarily in north- and downward-trending seams. Coal has been mined in the Ruhr region since the late 1830s, with 1.7 million metric tons in 1850. Rich deposits of coking and other types of coal also occur, most importantly in the Ruhr, but also in lesser quantities in the Saar region.

Also important are Germany's numerous lignite fields, the most important of which are in areas west of Cologne, near Helmstedt on the former East-West German border, around Leipzig, and in Lusatian fields north of Dresden (see Fig. 11-15). Lignite is a low-quality coal that cannot be economically transported very far; it has generally been burned for power or processed into chemicals or fuel briquettes near the mine sites. Lignite occurs in thick deposits close to the surface and is extracted mainly by open-pit methods, requiring the displacement of fields, factories, villages, and even river courses. With the postwar losses of the important Upper Silesian bituminous coal mines to Poland, lignite assumed an even more important position in the West German industrial fuel picture, and especially within the energy budget of the GDR. The GDR, lacking significant supplies of all other hydrocarbons, greatly expanded lignite production, thereby creating Germany's, and one of Europe's, worst air pollution problems, as well as disrupting water tables and landscapes over large areas. Many of the GDR's mines were both uneconomic and quite environmentally harmful. Since unification, many have closed and coal-related employment has plummeted. For example, the Lusatian open-pit lignite mines employed 80,000 workers in 1990 and 12,000 in 1995, and will have only about 7000 by the year 2000. For the first time in decades, at least skies over Saxony are sometimes blue. There remains the huge and expensive task of rebuilding power plants so that they burn cleaner, repairing damage to buildings and monuments from decades of air pollution, and cleaning up the poisonous wastes from chemical plants (Fig. 11-16). Around Bitterfeld, where problems are extreme, experts have recommended evacuating residents owing to soil contamination. Recultivation of the hundreds of square miles of lignite mines is alone expected to cost about $20 billion.

Germany's large supply of coal was once an important reason for its key position in the European economy. The production picture radically changed after 1957, with the greatly increased role of oil as a major source for industrial and household fuels. The rapid increase in use of oil and a constant drop in demand for coal have combined to bring about important changes in the Ruhr. For example, the last pit in the Dortmund area was closed in 1986. Coal production in Germany today can only be preserved by heavy subsidies. Production costs are high, and without ongoing supports, imports from the United States could undercut coal prices in the Ruhr itself, as well as many other parts of Europe. Despite the problems and associated mine and employment cutbacks, Germany remains, and likely will remain, a major coal producer. In 1993, for example, the Ruhr accounted for over one-quarter of all EU "hard" coal production.

Primarily because of its coal output, but also in part owing to domestic nuclear power production (21 nuclear plants produce about 11 percent of all energy), Germany satisfies about one-half of its basic energy needs from domestic sources. At one time it was expected that an increasing amount of nuclear power would be produced, and additional reactors were planned. However, environmental opposition to nuclear power and the impact of the Chernobyl accident in the Soviet Union, which doused radiation on parts of Germany, increased the fear of more installations. Not surprisingly, future increases in nuclear power use are now in doubt. Waterpower plays a small role in Germany's energy budget. Germany remains highly dependent on imports of oil and natural gas, which combined accounted for the one-half of the country's needs not met by domestic production.

The only other internationally important mining activity in Germany besides coal production is the mining of potash, a significant resource in fertilizer production. Germany produces about one-sixth of the world's output. Production is in the heart of Germany, evenly split between a number of mines in the west and east, though many of the eastern mines have closed, primarily for economic reasons but also to reduce what has been serious pollution of the Elbe with salt.

Iron ore was mined beginning in 1850 in the hill country southeast of Cologne and provided an important, original basis for Germany's metallurgy industries. Now, however, the country is quite dependent on imports, as is the case for most industrial raw materials. The impacts of Germany's most important domestically mined industrial raw materials, coal and potash, on the location of manufacturing are discussed later in this chapter.

The Transport Sector

Germany's postwar economic growth depended on an efficient, highly integrated transportation system. Railroads serve well most of the country, with densities highest in the Rhine-Ruhr region. The division of Germany had a negative effect on a number of railway lines, notably in the discontinuation of much of the former dense east-to-west and northeast-to-southwest traffic. These lines and traffic are now being reestablished. A newly developed postwar rail pattern in the FRG was north-to-south, connecting North Rhine-Westphalia and the North Sea ports with the south along the highly strategic Rhine River transport corridor. This orientation remains important even as the traditional east-west flow pattern reemerges.

Rail travel for passengers and for freight movement has been encouraged in order to cut back on vehicle exhausts and reduce highway congestion. The federally operated railway system has received large subsidies to improve freight and passenger services. The railways have seen a steady decline in geographic coverage, but speed and quality of service have improved dramatically. High-speed express trains now run between major destinations every one or two hours during peak travel periods with good on-time records. In

addition, high-speed Intercity Express (ICE) trains are traveling at speeds of up to 175 miles/hour (280 km/h) on several routes. Even faster trains are planned for the Hamburg-Berlin line. In the future many of these lines will become part of the expanding European system of high-speed trains that include France's TGV operations (see Fig. 5-9). Though losing relative importance to highway, pipeline, and air transport, railways still carry a substantial portion of passengers and freight, in the latter case about one-half of trucked freight in 1991.

Eastern Germany's rail system is in need of massive levels of investment to repair, upgrade, and electrify tracks and to introduce more modern locomotives and rolling stock. In order to conserve liquid fuel that was in short supply in the GDR, railroads were relatively more important in the East German economy than in the West's, carrying the great majority of cargo and thereby putting pressure on a system that received far too little investment until unification. As indicated earlier, investment in reestablishing rail connections between eastern and western Germany is also underway.

Germany's waterways are the country's oldest transport arteries (Fig. 11-13). Four large, navigable rivers flow south-to-north across the North German Lowlands: the Rhine, with the Dortmund-Ems Canal extension to Emden; the Weser; the Elbe; and the Oder (now part of the German-Polish border). The three east-west arteries are the Danube and two canals, the Mittelland and Kiel (Fig. 1-7). The Mittelland Canal, completed in 1938, links the Ems with the Elbe and is extended eastward by various canals to the Oder. The Rhine carries more passengers and freight than any other German waterway. Because the mouth of the river is in foreign territory, Germany constructed the Dortmund-Ems Canal as a bypass through German territory to the North Sea. The canal is too shallow and too narrow for modern barges, so most shipping continues to travel down the river into Dutch territory to the world's busiest port, Rotterdam. The canalization of the Mosel River, completed in early 1964, brought a direct connection to the northern French industrial region by making a connection between the drainage basin of the Meuse and the rivers flowing to join the Seine and the Rhine. Inasmuch as the Rhine flows through Europe's greatest industrial concentrations, traffic is heavy with coal, coke, grain, timber, potash, and crushed rocks—raw materials that are well suited to low-cost water transport.

The Elbe provided a natural link between the North Sea and landlocked Czechoslovakia, but owing to the reorientation of Czechoslovakia's foreign trade and division of Germany, river traffic declined, creating some economic problems for the port at Hamburg at the end of World War II. West Germany lost all direct contact with shipment on the Oder River, which after World War II became part of the East German-Polish border. In order to give Hamburg easier access to its hinterland, the Elbe lateral canal, between the Elbe and the Mittelland Canal near Brunswick (Braunschweig), was completed in 1976. The canal cuts the distance by water from Hamburg to the Ruhr by 155 miles. The Danube has always had less importance as an east-west artery, largely because of its isolation from other German waterways, the absence of major industry along its banks, and its eastward direction of flow toward less well-developed parts of Europe.

The idea of linking the Danube, Main and Rhine rivers was considered by the Romans and attempted at various times over the centuries. A nineteenth-century canal cut from near Nuremberg to the Danube above Regensburg was too small for much modern commercial traffic. A modern canal similar in capacity to the Main River was recently completed and furnishes an important link between the Rhine-Main and Danube systems. There are various projections about ultimate traffic levels on the canal. Initially, little or no actual North to Black Sea traffic is expected, but rather more local movements of bulky products for which transport is encouraged by the relatively low line-haul costs offered by river barge.

Germany, especially in the west, also has an excellent road system; indeed, it is the densest in Europe for any relatively large country. Despite Europe's most extensive superhighway network, even these roads are no longer able to adequately carry the steadily growing traffic—50 percent growth in total ton miles carried during the 1980s, for example. Although they originally were built

primarily to facilitate troop movements, the superhighways are now used by a large number of overland truck carriers and are being expanded. Increased use by trucks and autos, especially at peak holiday travel times, leads to massive traffic jams, particularly near cities, at major intersections, and on stretches leading up to mountain passes in Austria and Switzerland. Road surfaces and capacities in eastern Germany are being improved as part of the massive infrastructural investment program paid for largely by western taxes.

Pipelines, such as the one between Rostock and Schwedt and Wilhelmshaven and the Ruhr have become more important. They were especially important in GDR days, bringing that country vital oil and natural gas from the USSR by way of lines extended across the Polish-East German border. An undersea line brings natural gas from the North Sea fields to northern Germany.

The movement of seaborne goods through German ports grew little during the 1980s. German ports loaded and unloaded less tonnage than the ports of several European countries. For example, amounts are less than one-half the total volume of ports in the Netherlands and less than two-thirds that of the UK; these two states are Europe's leading oceangoing traders. Nonetheless, in absolute terms, significant amounts of goods move through German ports, more than twice as much arriving by volume than departing owing to imports of many raw materials. Hamburg with 66 million tons handled in 1993 is Europe's fourth largest port after Rotterdam, Antwerp, and Marseille, and it is one of the world's largest container ports. Wilhelmshaven, the German oil port, is the second most important German port in tonnage (33 million).

Air freight plays only a minor role in the transport of goods in Germany, although ton miles grew by 250 percent in the 1980s and passenger service expanded more rapidly than the air traffic control system could easily accommodate. Lufthansa, 35 percent government owned (compared to Air France (100%) and British Airways (0%), is Europe's fourth largest airline, and the third most important carrier of international travelers. Although air travel is growing in Europe and Germany, it has been restrained somewhat by relatively high prices (despite large subsidies) and competition from high-speed trains. Frankfurt is the country's largest airport and third in Europe after London and Paris with 32.5 million passengers passing through in 1993.

Manufacturing

Germany is Europe's leading industrial producer, with 37 percent of the labor force engaged in that sector, the highest figure among the major industrial countries of the world. Germany's industrial development began relatively late, following the building of the first railroads in the 1830s and 1840s, the decline in customs duties between the numerous German states in the mid-nineteenth century, and, especially, German unification in 1871. As a result of railroad expansion and adoption of steam power, industrial concentrations spread into many parts of the country and thus were not strictly tied to the location of raw materials and waterways. The most rapid era of growth in German manufacturing followed a few years after unification, when Germany emerged as a major producer of, for example, coal, metals, machinery, and chemicals. Following several decades of rapid growth and development, most of Germany's major twentieth-century industrial regions including the Ruhr, Saar, Saxony, Berlin, and Silesia were well developed by the outbreak of World War I. Despite political and economic turmoil resulting from German defeat in the war as well as substantial territorial losses, German industry diversified and grew, and played a key role in Germany's massive military buildup before and during World War II.

West Germany had a number of geographically based advantages for postwar industrial development, especially an excellent market location within populous, prosperous Northwestern Europe and a variety of transport ties to markets including rail, road, pipeline, and inland waterways. Other geographically related advantages included large urban areas that offer concentrations of skilled labor and attractive cultural amenities, excellent infrastructure, and large markets that enable economies of scale. In many ways Germany benefited more than any other country from the ongo-

ing process of European economic integration. This situation is reflected in its political leadership and also in the fact that it is by far the major net contributor to EC/EU activities.

East Germany's industrial sector also recovered and grew after World War II, in part because of the socialist government's emphasis on it. However, because of a number of disadvantages, industry became increasingly uneconomic and outdated. East Germany was cut off from Western markets because of political reasons, as well as because it was less well endowed with most resources, excepting potash deposits. The country was especially hard hit by the artificial dissection of once economically integrated Germany into three parts: East and West Germany, and those eastern lands transferred to Poland and the USSR (in the latter case, the Königsberg area, now Russia's Kaliningrad Oblast). Major German transport lines and freight movements that once moved goods primarily along an east-west axis (from Silesia, Berlin, and Saxony to the Ruhr and the urban-industrial centers in the Rhine-Main-Neckar region) were cut by north-south international boundaries between the Germanies and Poland. In addition, postwar geopolitics and COMECON economic policies undercut these transport and associated trade ties. The relatively small East German state was required to build a new transport network focusing on north-south linkages, tying together major industrial regions in the south, with Berlin, and newly developed ports, especially Rostock, on the northern Baltic coast. Rostock had no real chance to be tied into the east-west trending river and canal systems linking the Elbe and Oder rivers in the central part of the country. Good rail service to northern ports was never completely established, although some progress and improvement of shipping ties between the GDR and other Baltic ports was achieved. Similarly, the relatively poor GDR was unable to maintain the *autobahn* routes that it inherited from the Third Reich, and some deteriorated to the point that traffic instead had to use narrow two-lane routes congested with trucks and buses. The best roads in the East were those constructed with funds from West Germany in order that it could have better access to West Berlin, embedded deep within East German territory.

Most importantly, however, East Germany's

industrial revival was impeded by economic policies adopted as the result of misguided economic development strategies and confrontational political positions vis-à-vis Western Europe and NATO in general and West Germany in particular. Under the avowed pretext of seizing economic power from capitalists, the socialist government gained control of virtually the entire national economy, thereby undercutting the incentives for efficient production and for innovative policies that are common to a private enterprise system.

Under the USSR's influence the GDR and other COMECON countries reoriented trade patterns away from Western Europe toward (1) greater domestic self-sufficiency (a bad decision for countries as small as the GDR) and (2) greater trade with the more backward and much less dynamic Soviet economy. Ignoring economic realities, the GDR sought to become more self-sufficient in sectors of the economy missing from its inherited economic structure (e.g., coal mining, and mining and refining of metals). It invested heavily in uneconomic and highly polluting metals and lignite mining, as well as in iron and steel production. In several cases, entirely new "socialist" industrial cities were founded such as Eisenhüttenstadt, first known as Stalinstadt, which was noted for iron and steel production. Others included Schwedt, engaged in oil refining and paper production, and Hoyerswerda, where lignite mines were developed with adjacent thermal-generating stations. Despite achieving some success, including supporting higher living standards than most other places in the Soviet bloc, GDR policies ultimately proved unsuccessful economically and politically. The eastern German economy, especially manufacturing, will suffer for decades from the failures of socialism.

Historically, the major regional concentrations of German manufacturing were in a discontinuous belt of unequal width, extending from Aachen on the German-Belgian border to the German Czech border at Dresden (Fig. 11-17). Prior to World War II, this industrial region extended into the Silesian regions of what is today Poland. The belt includes a number of regional concentrations, many of which developed their earliest roots on local raw material dependency, especially coal. The most important industrial clusters exist in the vicinities of Aachen and Cologne, the Ruhr Valley, Hannover-Brunswick, Magdeburg, and in the Dresden-Leipzig-Chemnitz (formerly Karl-Marx-Stadt) triangle. Other important, local concentrations also occur in the "belt," such as at Bielefeld-Herford. The Saar represents an old, important heavy industrial region outside of the belt (and depending on the date in history, sometimes also outside of Germany). In addition, important industries are located in the larger urban concentrations scattered throughout the country. Most of these latter regions have been historically less dependent on local natural resources and have been more market oriented.

Two south German states, Bavaria and Baden-Württemberg, have gained a reputation as prosperous, high-tech regions in comparison to the northern "rust-belt" that was once characterized by mining and basic iron and steel industries. If figures for unemployment alone are considered, this statement is correct, but it is an oversimplification of the actual situation. The present regional pattern of economic development and potential is a more complicated one. The northern states have higher unemployment levels owing to the many declining industries and the need for important structural adjustments. This results in slower economic growth than in the southern states, where unemployment is lower. But two small northern urban states, Hamburg and Bremen, still have much higher levels of GDP/capita than the southern states. However, the southern states of Baden-Württemberg, Hesse, and Bavaria all now have lower unemployment rates, higher GDP/capita levels, and higher population and economic growth rates than, for example, Germany's largest and once economically dominating state of North Rhine-Westphalia. Other northern states, Schleswig-Holstein and Lower Saxony, also have rather high unemployment rates and lower GDP/capita values than the leading southern ones. Of course, eastern Germany, discussed separately below, is now by far Germany's poorest and most economically troubled region.

The state of North Rhine-Westphalia, which includes the Ruhr region, was once the German economy's major regional engine and dynamo; it remains Germany's major industrial and population concentration. For example, it accounted for

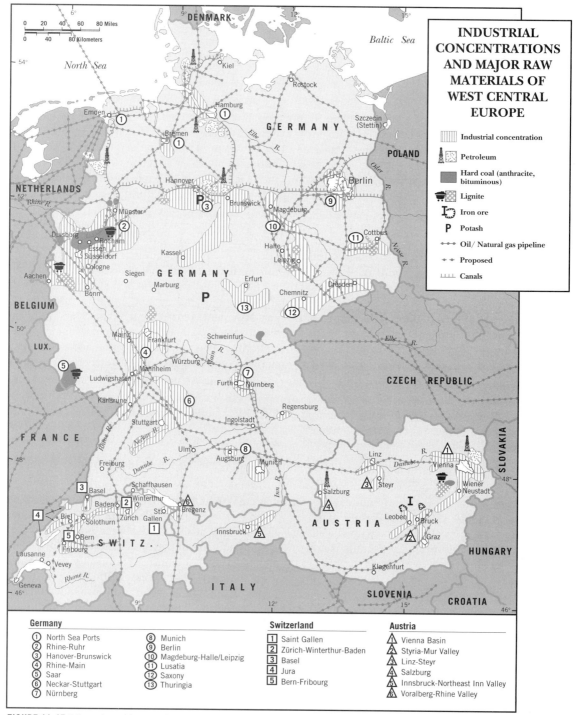

FIGURE 11-17 Manufacturing regions in West Central Europe.

42 percent of western Germany's GNP in 1950 and about 25 percent in 1992. The Ruhr region accounts for one-quarter of all EU coal production and one-sixth of all steel production, the total value of production exceeding the national economies of, for example, Ireland, Portugal, and Denmark. Now, however, North Rhine-Westphalia has a concentration of "old" industries and has suffered in recent years from relatively high unemployment rates (15% in 1988, dropping to 11% in 1994) and a relative loss of importance within the German economy.

As production of the Ruhr's major traditional products has declined, considerable efforts have been made to diversify the regional economy. Thus, employment in chemicals, electrical engineering, and vehicle manufacture has increased. However, many more thousands of additional jobs must be found to make up for the hundreds of thousands that have been eliminated.

The Ruhr has been important historically because of its high-grade deposits of coking coal; its proximity to western Germany's only source of iron ore; and the unrivaled artery of trade provided by the Rhine and its tributaries such as the Ruhr River. A dense network of canals connect the region with most parts of Germany and the wealthy Northwest European market of 60 million people within a 155-mile (250-km) radius (Figs. 11-18 and 5-13).

The core of the Ruhr area extends about 35 miles (56 km) from Duisburg on the Rhine in the west to Dortmund in the east and has a north-south extent of less than 15 miles (25 km). Traditionally, the region has been divided into a northern coal-mining area and a southern steel-producing region, especially as newer mines moved northward as coal seams in the south were gradually exhausted. With over 5 million people in 4432 sq miles (11,257 sq km), the Ruhr is the most populous part of North Rhine-Westphalia, Germany's most heavily populated state. Three urban agglomerations have more than half a million inhabitants, and many of Germany's biggest companies have either their headquarters or main plants in the region.

The Ruhr area is remarkable for its concentra-tions of cities. Its core area encompasses 10 urban centers with populations over 100,000, among which are the Rhine port at Duisburg (839,000), Essen (630,000), and Dortmund (609,000). The Ruhr is dotted with manufacturing plants that until recently were mostly iron- and steelworks, locomotive and chemical plants, and factories producing equipment for mines and steel mills. Owing to this specialization, unemployment rose faster in the region than in any other part of West Germany during the 1980s, especially as world steel demand slackened and international competition increased. Twenty-five years ago, mining and steel accounted for 70 percent of the region's jobs, with mines alone employing over 600,000 people; by 1987 this figure had fallen to 164,000. In Bochum, for example, between 1958 and 1973, all 17 coal mines closed and all 40,000 mining jobs were lost (Fig. 11-19). During the 1980s alone over 150,000 industrial jobs disappeared in the Ruhr region, most of which were in coal, iron, and steel production.

German-mined coal is more expensive than imported coal, and production can only be preserved by considerable federal, state, and community subsidies. With an increased production of nuclear power, a drastic cutback in the demand for coking coal for steel production, and a declining need for coal in power plants, the western German mining industries have only survived by higher subsidies. Increasing political and economic pressures have been exerted to reduce subsidies and further cut production.

Steel makers have diversified their output, moving into new steel products and processes, and are buying firms that produce goods often completely unrelated to steel. Governments in the Ruhr region are actively courting a variety of employers, especially those in high-technology fields and in service sectors. They also support more than a dozen local universities that have ties to business and to publicly sponsored technology centers. Planners would like to have more large investments such as those made by General Motors in the late 1960s, which created 20,000 jobs. GM built for its Opel subsidiary an automobile plant on the site of an old coal mine outside

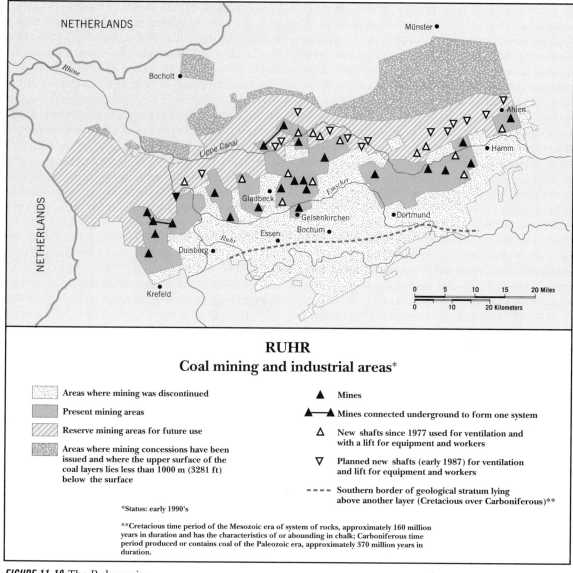

RUHR
Coal mining and industrial areas*

Areas where mining was discontinued

Present mining areas

Reserve mining areas for future use

Areas where mining concessions have been issued and where the upper surface of the coal layers lies less than 1000 m (3281 ft) below the surface

▲   Mines

▲——▲   Mines connected underground to form one system

△   New shafts since 1977 used for ventilation and with a lift for equipment and workers

▽   Planned new shafts (early 1987) for ventilation and lift for equipment and workers

----   Southern border of geological stratum lying above another layer (Cretacious over Carboniferous)**

*Status: early 1990's

**Cretacious time period of the Mesozoic era of system of rocks, approximately 160 million years in duration and has the characteristics of or abounding in chalk; Carboniferous time period produced or contains coal of the Paleozoic era, approximately 370 million years in duration.

FIGURE 11-18 The Ruhr region.

Bochum (Fig. 11-19). However, neither the auto sector nor other heavy industrial activities are likely candidates for large employment increases in the 1990s and in the next century, when jobs are more likely to be generated in smaller numbers by a larger number of individual employers. Employment growth in service sectors has been a partial economic savior for the region, as more than 200,000 such jobs were added during the 1980s.

New industries are being attracted to the Ruhr. Industries specializing in pollution control equipment have flourished, and some success has been achieved in attracting high-technology activities. The chemicals industry has also benefited from nearby oil refineries. An integrated rapid transport system, augmented by a modernized railway and urban highway system, has improved internal accessibility. Environmental programs have also

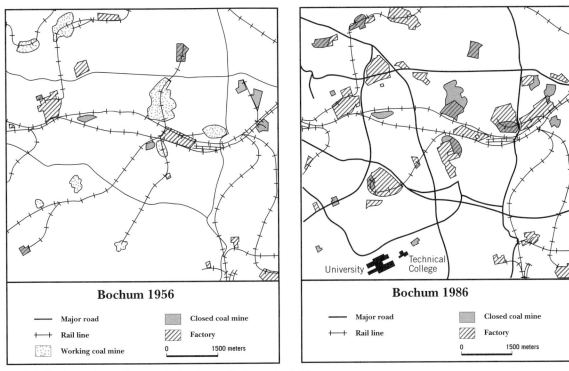

FIGURE 11-19 Land use changes in Bochum (Ruhr region), Germany.

made the Ruhr a more attractive place to live; air pollution is at its lowest levels since records began being kept in the 1960s. Still, the Ruhr must struggle with widespread perceptions that it largely has a polluted environment; unsightly, derelict transport and manufacturing facilities; and a relative lack of historic structures and cultural traditions.

The area surrounding the Ruhr also has a great variety of industries, such as textile and synthetic fiber, chemical, coal, and steel production. Industrialization was closely linked to the coal basin extending from Belgium and the Netherlands into Germany, but especially to the important lignite deposits stretching northwest from Bonn to northwest of Cologne. The region benefits, of course, from the same excellent market access facilitated by a dense multimodal transport system as is enjoyed by the Ruhr. However, some places in the area, especially Cologne and Düsseldorf, have been able to avoid the perceived stigma associated with the Ruhr that undoubtedly have made its conversion from a mining and manufacturing region more difficult.

Cologne is Germany's third largest city and a major cultural, industrial, and service center, noted especially for auto, chemicals, and machinery production; radio, television, and film companies; and banking and insurance. Aachen is the center of a diversified industrial area, producing hardware, textiles, steel, and high-technology products. Düsseldorf has traditionally been a major administrative and financial center for Ruhr area firms as well as being Germany's fashion industry center. During the last couple of decades, the city has compensated for the economic impacts on the neighboring Ruhr both by industrial expansion and by attracting a wider range of business headquarters for multinational corporations. The city currently is home to over 3000 such firms, including more than 300 Japanese firms, making it one of the most important centers for Japanese firms outside of Japan.

The Rhine-Neckar region is one of Germany's newer and more rapidly developing urban-industrial areas and includes several of Germany's larger cities by population, including Frankfurt/Main,

Stuttgart, and Mannheim. It benefits from a good transport and market location, and its nearness to a number of productive agricultural regions. Frankfurt is Germany's, and one of Europe's, most important banking and finance centers, as well as headquarters for many German and multinational firms. The city was transformed by reconstruction following World War II destruction and has emerged as a modern, major business center, which many Germans regard as atypically German in appearance. Because of its many skyscrapers and location on the Main River, Frankfurt is often referred to as "Mainhattan" (Fig. 11-20).

The Rhine-Neckar industrial area, extending roughly from Stuttgart on the Neckar in the southeast to Ludwigshafen on the Rhine in the north-

FIGURE 11-20 Untypically German or European, a number of skyscrapers dominate Frankfurt am Main, Germany's major financial center. (A. Diem)

west, is Germany's premier center for engineering and automotive production, as well as a major production center for a range of other products, notably chemicals. Porsche and Mercedes cars are produced in and around Stuttgart, where Germany's largest firm in sales and third largest employer is headquartered (Daimler-Benz, with sales turnover of $63 billion and employment of 371,000 in 1993). The huge chemical multinational, BASF, Germany's eleventh largest firm by sales with employment over 115,000 workers, is focused on Ludwigshafen. The Rhine-Neckar region is strewn with small and medium-sized firms producing an array of high-quality machinery, supplying local automotive as well as broader German and international markets.

Berlin and Munich, respectively, Germany's largest and third largest cities, have each attracted a wide variety of manufacturing and service activities based on their roles as early seats of government, transport nodes, major cultural centers, and large population centers serving extensive hinterlands. Neither city has near it any especially notable industrial raw materials. Berlin has traditionally been a manufacturing site for machinery, electronics, and pharmaceuticals, as well as a major administrative center for government and business activities and a major center for education and the arts. All but education and the arts suffered in West Berlin during its 28 years of relative isolation within East Germany. Though stagnating demographically, it appeared to prosper economically, in part owing to large subsidies from West Germany, which have now ceased.

East Berlin also prospered, but only by Eastern bloc standards; its relatively large industrial sector is unproductive by Western standards, and parts of the city still suffer from the drab, dilapidated pall resulting from years of coal-fired air pollution and neglected maintenance. Whereas the designation of Berlin as the capital and seat of government of a united Germany will boost the city's status as a center for both German and European business, it has been speculated that this will mostly favor prosperous, fashionable western Berlin. This could leave parts of eastern Berlin—especially parts of decaying old worker residential areas like Prenzlauerberg and poorly designed and constructed housing estates like massive Marzahn—as concentrations of the city's poor with associated social problems (Fig. 11-21).

United Berlin has lost thousands of industrial jobs, as the result of the restructuring of formerly subsidized firms in both the eastern and western sectors of the city. A building boom in the former historical center near Friedrichstrasse signals a clear orientation of Berlin's economy toward business and government employment. Although manufacturing will remain important, its relative significance has declined.

Munich, one of Germany's most dynamic cities, has been growing rapidly and attracting a variety of high-technology firms, especially in the computing and aerospace sectors. The country's largest employer and third largest firm by sales, Siemens (electronics), is headquartered in the city. Production of autos, including high-quality, status-symbol cars such as BMW and Audi, occurs near Munich, which is also a center for production of films. Once viewed by many Germans as a provincial town in a relatively poor and backward state, Munich has become a vibrant, cosmopolitan center in the heart of Germany's second largest state economy, Bavaria—with about 18 percent of total German GDP. The city, located near the Alps and but a few hours' drive from the resorts of Austria and Italy, has achieved the status of a preferred residential site for both workers and students. It appears to have a bright future, if it can preserve its "livability" during this era of rapid expansion.

Following World War II, West Germany's ports suffered because of the loss of their hinterland. However, they have recovered in recent years, largely because of the greatly increased need for imports of key raw materials by both Germany and other European economies, as well as demands emanating from exploration for North Sea oil and natural gas. The major ports, Hamburg and Bremen, also lost much of their major shipbuilding industry to lower cost producers in the Far East. This sector has been partially replaced by relatively diversified manufacturing activities, in addition to the growing importance of service sector activities. Hamburg has traditionally been Germany's wealthiest state and continues to have, by far, its highest levels of GDP/capita. Bremen has also been relatively prosperous and continues to enjoy relatively high levels of GDP/capita, but several more rapidly growing southern states appear poised to overtake it.

Hamburg, on the lower Elbe and Germany's most important port, was hard hit in the postwar period. The city's inaccessibility to supertankers and increased German trade within the EC/EU further accentuated its geographical disadvantage compared with Rotterdam, which is nearer the heart of Europe's growth axis and Germany's main manufacturing concentrations. Nonetheless,

FIGURE 11-21 Housing estates in eastern Berlin. Massive, Soviet-era housing complexes on the edge of town are a common feature of eastern German cities—as well as cities throughout East Central and Southeastern Europe. (W. H. Berentsen)

Hamburg remains Germany's major port, with a specialization in movement of containers. The city has diversified its economic base with a variety of manufacturing activities ranging from aerospace to refining. The service sector is also strong; Hamburg is Germany's major publishing center and a headquarters for trading companies. Linkages with Hamburg's extensive hinterland in eastern Germany have been restored, and are once again contributing to the city's prosperity. In fact, construction is booming as multinational firms have been investing in the city and its surrounding area to profit from its enhanced location.

Bremen, a state comprised of the city itself as well as its outport of Bremerhaven at the mouth of the Weser River on the North Sea, is Germany's second most important port. Its shipbuilding and machinery industries have declined in importance, but the twin ports continue to be especially important for the importation and processing of raw commodities, including oil refining.

Eastern Germany has traditional industrial regions besides Berlin, particularly within the Halle/Leipzig-Chemnitz-Dresden triangle, most of which are in the state of Saxony. There are, however, a number of other industrial nodes in the east, primarily in the regions south of Berlin, in which there has been either a long tradition of manufacturing based on local resources and labor skills or on more recently exploited, massive lignite coal deposits. Beginning in the 1950s, the socialist regime sought to spread industry beyond then existing sites and in a few cases did so by developing so-called socialist cities focused on new, often uneconomically, located industrial plants.

Some of the earliest industrial activities in eastern Germany began centuries ago using small mineral and metal deposits and waterpower in the Ore Mountains (Erzgebirge) on the border with the Czech Republic. Some mining continues in this area today. Especially since the demise of the GDR, however, mines have closed owing to exhausted resources and high production costs. The legacy of mining has included the establishment of a tradition of manufacturing and skilled labor that spans several centuries, and a variety of industrial activities are still scattered throughout the low mountain region. Activities include metal

processing, woodworking, textile and apparel production, and toy manufacturing. Though sharply reduced in importance because of the factors noted earlier and because of the relatively high cost of German labor for such things as textile and toy production, limited output continues in all the aforementioned sectors.

Based in part on the regional heritage of manufacturing, but also on the ability to exploit lignite and potash resources and sell them in expanding, post-World War II German and European markets, industry grew on a much larger scale somewhat later in the cities and towns north of the Ore Mountains. By the end of the GDR era, major industrial concentrations had developed throughout the region, most of which produced various kinds of machinery—the GDR's preeminent industrial product. Cities and regions have also developed other traditional specializations as well, such as in Halle and Bitterfeld (chemicals), Leipzig (chemicals and publishing), Zwickau (cars), Chemnitz (in the GDR era called Karl-Marx-Stadt, textiles), Jena (optics), and Dresden (electronics).

Many of these places and sectors have been decimated by economic restructuring in the post–GDR era. Despite massive subsidies for investments in the east, factories have been closed because of their outdated, inefficient machinery and facilities, as well as because of the frightening level of air and water quality problems that they caused. In addition, even in plants that have managed to stay open, there have been massive layoffs of workers resulting from obsolete technologies and low labor productivity that produced high levels of overemployment. Exposure to Western competition and real budget constraints forced many plants to greatly trim their workforces to survive. Thus, for example, total east German industrial employment, nearly 3 million workers in 1990, fell by about three quarters within the next three years. The decline was particularly steep in selected sectors, especially those in which the GDR had tended to specialize. As a result, east Germany now produces only a small proportion of German manufacturing output, unemployment among former manufacturing workers is high, and related social problems and political disagreements abound.

Some of the most difficult adjustments appear

to be occurring in the most specialized industrial cities of the GDR era, including several that were founded or greatly expanded based on communist doctrine. The "socialist city" of Eisenhüttenstadt (Iron Mill City) has experienced massive employment cuts in its mill, whose future remains problematic (Fig. 6-18). Similar problems face other cities like Hoyerswerda where coal mining and electric generation were keys to the local economy, and Rostock, which was the GDR's major international port, a function now largely taken over by Hamburg. Local governments are attempting to transform Rostock's economy. For example, a large new regional power plant is to replace smaller, less efficient plants scattered throughout northeastern Germany and the closed Soviet-technology nuclear plant near Greifswald. The Rostock plant will require large quantities of imported coal (and building materials during the construction phase) that will provide employment for a port that must now compete with Lübeck for the Baltic Sea business and has lost most of its former shipbuilding industry (largely oriented to the Soviet market). Also, Leipzig, once overly dependent on highly polluting and relatively inefficient chemical industries, is quickly regaining its role as a major business center for the populous region south of Berlin.

The Transition in Berlin and Eastern Germany

The dissolution of the former GDR and unification of Germany have obviously led to dramatic political, social, and economic changes within Berlin and eastern Germany. The totalitarian rule of the Socialist Unity party (SED), its vast secret police system (the "Stasi"), and the Stasi's pervasive informer network have been replaced by the western German political system dominated by multiple political parties and political interest groups. Among the interest groups are powerful business concerns and labor unions, which have a history of relatively successful cooperation. The former SED, now transformed into a more open Western-style political party, the Party of Democratic Socialism (PDS), has a small following focused on areas of East Berlin where former SED leaders reside. The hypocrisies of SED rule leave disgruntled eastern

German voters' support split largely among Germany's main conservative (CDU) and left-of-center (SPD) parties. Both of these parties have erred in their positions relative to the east, especially the CDU, whose leader, Helmut Kohl, rashly promised a flourishing eastern Germany economy without costs to the west. Voters in the east have also subsequently learned that political scandal and hypocrisy plague western parties, and political frustration and cynicism in the former GDR are quite apparent.

The eastern economy is recovering, owing to huge west-to-east financial transfers, but it is not flourishing. Eastern voters' apparent patience with the polemical nature of Kohl's promises, weaknesses in the SPD leadership, and a perception that the SPD lacks commitment to the development of the east, have reduced the SPD's potential strength in the region. Thus, during the first five years after unification, eastern Germany has not developed into a region with a highly distinctive political profile. Yet it has continued to generate a number of German political issues, including how to deal with the abuses of SED and GDR power and how best to lessen tensions between western and eastern Germans.

The successful integration of eastern Germans into German society is hindered by real or perceived social problems within eastern Germany, which are a major issue of concern among residents. Unemployment and undesired employment status (e.g., early retirement or required occupational change owing to job loss) is the major issue, because employment provides the greatest level of future economic security and personal satisfaction as well as social status within German culture. Loss of a job, especially for those closely associated with the discredited SED state, has been particularly traumatic for eastern Germans. Jobs lost in uneconomic enterprises are also sometimes interpreted by eastern Germans as the result of economic colonization policies directed by west German business and their political supporters, especially the CDU.

Although incomes and economic well-being appear to have increased rapidly in absolute terms for many people, relatively rapid increases in rents and food prices worry many easterners. Special concerns have been expressed for the large number of single mothers, relatively far more numerous in the east than the west, whose social and economic position has deteriorated since unification. Contributing to this has been the sharp reduction in state support for child care and the proportionately high level of job loss among young women. Job losses for women have, for example, been great in eastern Germany's labor-intensive public administration and textile sectors.

Street crime has surged, apparently the combined result of weaker central political control and less intrusive police practices, and the existence of large numbers of disgruntled and relatively poor people from both eastern Germany and Eastern Europe. Eastern Germans are also vexed by the perception that they are treated disdainfully by western Germans and that they hold mere second-class citizenship status, as well as by the rapid appearance of beggars, drug pushers, and homeless people within their midst. In addition, people are also confronting the pressures and contradictions of the much more pluralistic society and economy of west Germany, within which they have been plunged. That many eastern Germans feel disoriented and insecure is reflected in an unprecedented, drastic decline in the eastern German birth rate that is expected to rebound slowly, and only partially, during the next few years.

Despite concerns by the majority of eastern Germans, most are still doing much better in material terms under the west German economic system than they did within the SED's Soviet-style economy. Although huge job losses have resulted from the closing, privatizing, and streamlining of the former GDR's large publicly owned manufacturing combines, new jobs are opening in the construction and service sectors, and remaining jobs in manufacturing are more productive and more highly paid.

The east faces many disadvantages for attracting economic activities, as well as countervailing advantages. On the one hand, disadvantages include the backlog in unclarified ownership of property because of property seizures by the Nazis, Soviets, and GDR; the dangerous environmental pollution of many industrial sites; a relatively high cost of labor in comparison to output in many sectors; and lack of high-quality recreational activities and residential properties that would

appeal to most highly skilled managers. The latter problem is enhanced by western Germans' poor image of eastern Germany. On the other hand, advantages include a large market of 16 million people with a pent-up, as yet unsatisfied, demand for many consumer goods and services; a well-educated labor force; and an improving, modern infrastructure. Ongoing, high levels of public investment in basic infrastructure such as rail lines, highways, telecommunications, and water and sewer lines are bringing eastern Germany closer to West European standards. Public financial support and private investment are also improving housing conditions, although the unpainted, falling stucco facades of older housing and uninspiring rows of newer high rises in the east are apt to remain as drab reminders of the socialist era for decades to come.

Thus far, the net result of economic change has been an increasingly regionally and socially differentiated pattern of economic development. Parts of Berlin and Saxony are booming, while serious problems loom in selected monostructural manufacturing and mining regions and in many rural areas, especially in the north. High job losses in the textile/apparel sector around Chemnitz, in mining in many southern regions, in metallurgy in places like Eisenhüttenstadt, and in farming in rural areas have produced high levels of unemployment and concern for future job prospects. Disastrous environmental damage by chemical production near Bitterfeld and uranium mining regions in the Erzgebirge threaten residents as well as their economic future. Some people have coped with these problems by commuting, often over long distances, whereas others, about a million people since 1989, have simply migrated to the west. Luckier people have retained or found new jobs locally.

In Saxony, especially around Leipzig and to a lesser extent Dresden, a huge building boom offers jobs and an apparent indication of likely future economic prosperity (Fig. 11-22). Leipzig's traditional role as a center for international fairs is being supported by the construction of new facilities. Warehouses, business complexes, North American-style shopping centers, and up-scale housing have or are being built on the city's outskirts. Simultaneously, shops and offices are being

FIGURE 11-22 Cranes over Dresden, illustrating ongoing reconstruction in eastern Germany that is also particularly notable in Leipzig and eastern Berlin. (W. H. Berentsen)

strewn former Soviet bases mar the landscape. On the other hand, the region boasts lovely tree-lined roads through rolling forest and field country in Mecklenburg, the dramatic Elbe River gorge south of Dresden, scenic hill country in the Thuringian Forest and Harz Mountains, and existing (e.g., Quedlinburg) or potentially (e.g., Stralsund) architecturally stunning towns and villages.

Thus, both success and disappointment have resulted from the unification of Germany. Although the great majority of former east Germans are, overall, satisfied or pleased with many features of their new circumstances, they are not happy about all aspects of life in united Germany. Unification will be a long social, economic, and psychological process that will leave most people satisfied and others angry or disappointed. Despite Helmut Kohl's promises and many Germans' assumptions in 1989 and 1990, the unification of Germany will take decades, trillions of dollars, and a great deal of patience and understanding among individual Germans across what was once the major Cold War boundary. Germans appear to be prepared for these historic tasks. Failure to complete the social, economic, and political integration of their country could result in costs similar to those the United States paid for over a century following the failed "reconstruction" and reintegration of the South into the Union. Although comparisons between the U.S. and German cases can be made, particularly in the original psychological positions of the United States' North and South versus Germany's west and east, all indications are that Germany's unification will largely succeed, though it will take longer than most people ever expected.

constructed in the central city, including renovation of the central rail station—one of Germany's largest and most impressive. In relative terms, Leipzig has experienced more rapid economic change than any other place in eastern Germany. East Berlin, however, is a close second to Leipzig and in absolute terms has seen and will see even more development based on both the city as national capital and as a more important European and world business center. However, Berlin has lost vast numbers of manufacturing jobs in the short run, owing to closure of decrepit plants in the east and previously subsidized, and likewise uneconomic, plants in the west. In the longer run, Berlin will no doubt prosper economically, possibly to the detriment of many nearby rural areas whose inhabitants will seek greater economic opportunities in the city.

The eastern German landscape is changing rapidly as paint and repairs improve the look of selected buildings. Outdoor advertising colors and clutters views. There are more autos and trucks on the roads and highways. Lax planning has resulted in urban sprawl that is noticeable everywhere, particularly outside Leipzig and Berlin. Many drab villages remain untouched in visual terms by unification. The ghastly hulks of closed manufacturing plants; abandoned and decaying workers' housing, warehouses, and rail yards; and thousands of small, improvised waste disposal sites and litter-

AUSTRIA

For centuries one of Europe's great powers, Austria is now a relatively small country, but one that has adapted astonishingly well to both political and economic conditions that are radically different from those that existed when Vienna was capital of the far-flung, multinational Habsburg Empire. Despite current internal political problems associated with a politically splintered electorate, resurgence of a nationalist right-wing political movement (22.5% of the vote in the 1994 general election), and very belated national recognition of complicity in Nazi horrors when the country was a province within the German Third Reich, Austria also has an enviable record of political stability and international engagement.

Among the many contradictions in modern Austrian political history is the fact that one of its elected presidents, Kurt Waldheim, was UN secretary general but has since been shunned because of his alleged complicity in World War II Nazi atrocities. Although the recent electoral successes of nationalist, xenophobic candidates have made headlines, Austria has for decades also served as the initial Western sanctuary for tens of thousands of Jews fleeing the former Soviet Union. More recently, the country has become a haven for refugees from the civil wars in the former Yugoslavia. Thus, as is the case for most countries, sweeping generalizations about Austria must be tempered with the factual realities of its complex history.

Population

Austria's approximately 8 million citizens are divided unequally among its nine provinces. Nearly 40 percent live in the capital, Vienna, and nearby Lower Austria. Less than 20 percent of the population lives in the three western provinces (Vorarlberg, Tirol, and Salzburg), although these provinces have grown rapidly since about 1970, while the population of the six more easterly provinces has declined slightly. Between 1951 and 1991 the western provinces, which in 1951 had but one-sixth of the total national population, registered nearly half of Austria's population growth. The three easternmost provinces (Burgenland, Vienna, and Lower Austria) with nearly 50 percent of Austria's population in 1951 had no net growth over the next 40 years. High levels of immigration to eastern Austria have not offset negative population growth resulting from interrelated low birth rates and an aged population structure. Population losses related to emigration have been especially notable in rural areas along the eastern borders, across which little trade and movement

occurred for decades owing to severe restrictions imposed by Austria's formerly socialist neighbors. The west of the country has experienced both natural population growth and net immigration, with immigration related to positive patterns of economic development as discussed later in this chapter. As elsewhere in West Central Europe, central city populations have stagnated, while the suburbs and environs of larger cities have grown most rapidly, especially around Innsbruck, Salzburg, and Linz, and to a lesser extent in the environs of Vienna and Graz.

Although Austria's population is largely German-speaking and Catholic, there are still notable ethnic and social variations within the country. Important ethnic minorities live along Austria's once disputed eastern boundaries, notably Hungarians, Slovenes, and Croatians (Fig. 1-2). The cultural and economic integration of these peoples into Austrian society has been so successful that, although their ethnic distinctiveness and identity have been threatened, their officially recognized status has not been questioned. More problematic is a large foreign-worker and foreign-resident population that grew rapidly as the result of immigration in the late 1980s and early 1990s. A xenophobic response by some Austrians has been one of the bases for the increased electoral success of far right political candidates, especially because of rapid increases in the number of immigrants from Asia and Africa. For example, the non-Austrian population of Vienna (dominantly Turkish) grew by over 80,000 between 1981 and 1991 to nearly 200,000 persons; the number of Asians (excepting Turks) and Africans grew from about 6000 in 1971 to 75,000 in 1994. The population growth of foreigners in Austria has resulted especially from immigration from the former Yugoslavia, other parts of Eastern Europe, Turkey, Africa, and Asia. There are now about a half million non-Austrians in the country, with nearly 40 percent in the capital.

Given that Austria is playing a much more important role as a center of development for East Central and Southeastern Europe, foreign immigration may well continue—and it is hardly new. Owing to political problems in Hungary in 1956–1957, in Czechoslovakia in 1968–1969, and in Poland in 1981-1982, approximately 150,000 to

200,000 people from each of these countries fled to or through Austria. Considering the fact that many of these and other migrant peoples, as well as generations of migrants from the Empire to Vienna, have stayed in Austria, the ethnic character of the country is complex. Furthermore, Austria's renown for the arts, especially music, results in part from the country's historical role as a meeting place of East and West. Many of Vienna's most common names, foods, and drinks can be traced to Czech, Hungarian, or Turkish origin.

Landscape, Resources, and Environment

One of Austria's most important natural resources is the country's landscape. It is a source of enjoyment, pride, and tourist-related employment. The country encompasses a major portion of the glacially sculpted, thinly populated Alps, as well

as often scenically cultivated valleys and basins (Figs. 11-6 and 11-23). Well-preserved, architecturally varied buildings from churches to castles enhance the appeal of cities and countryside alike. The well-known beauty of the Alps and cities such as Innsbruck, Salzburg, and Vienna are complemented by many other, less well-known areas in Austria, such as the Wachau in the Danube Valley and Burgenland, the country's easternmost province.

Austria has no major sources of mineral or metallic resources, although between 1500 and 3000 workers are employed in each of several extraction activities, including oil and gas production, and magnesite, iron ore, and lignite mining. Many other minerals and metals are mined in small quantities, but, in general, Austria depends heavily on imported raw materials to support its well-developed manufacturing sector. For example, domestic supplies provide only about 10 percent of the country's oil needs, which are met by

FIGURE 11-23 The Alps in Tirol. The sheds in the foreground are associated with *Alpenwirtschaft,* in which animals are driven into the high country during the summer months to utilize mountain pastures while valley plots produce hay that is stored for winter use. (W. H. Berentsen)

imports through pipelines from the south and east. Natural gas demand is met largely by deliveries from a pipeline running from Russia through Austria to Italy. Nuclear power generation is not allowed by law, though an unused, completed nuclear power plant has been held in reserve, apparently in case of a dire national energy emergency. Austria's logging industry provides important wood exports as well as a basic resource for the domestic wood products and furniture industries. Hydroelectric power derived both from alpine and lowland rivers, including the Danube, provides an important proportion of the country's total energy (one-sixth) and, especially, electric supplies (two-thirds) (Fig. 11-24).

Important relations exist between human environmental impacts and economic development in Austria, given the natural environment's relatively high priority and its relevance as the basis for the vital tourist industry. For example, Austria has long provided relatively high agricultural subsidies to alpine farmers in order to help maintain the traditional cultural alpine landscape, which includes maintenance of a mixture of highland pastures and forests. The pastures and forests serve in part as protection against avalanches. Four of Austria's six existing or planned "national parks" are located in the country's mountain lands. Though offering less protection for forests and wildlife than allowed by international norms, Austria's national parks do provide protection to plant life and landscape resources. For aesthetic, environmental, and economic reasons related to tourism, Austria's mountains are a highly prized and revered resource for a country frequently referred to as the "alpine republic."

Like Switzerland, Austria is also concerned about rapidly increasing trans-Alpine vehicle traffic and associated air and noise pollution. This is especially true in Tirol along the Brenner Pass. Similarly, concerns have been voiced about the proliferation of tourist facilities and second homes in alpine areas, particularly those scattered on the landscape outside of traditionally spatially contained settlements. The direct and indirect impacts of tourism include clearing of land, building of roads and parking lots, proliferation of ski-lifts, canalization of streams, and decline of agriculture. All have led to the increased incidence of

FIGURE 11-24 Kaprun hydroelectric station, with storage lakes Wasserfallboden and Mooserboden (completed in 1957), located in a southern valley of the Upper Salzach Valley (Pinzgau, Salzburg Province, Austria). Two dams enclose the valley, which stores the water during the summer and makes it available during the winter period for energy production. Mountains in the background belong to the Glockner Mountains. Today, a road from the valley leads to the upper lake, and the whole area has been opened for tourists. (Tavernkraftwerk AG, Salzburg, Austria)

such environmental catastrophes as avalanches, landslides, and floods. Efforts are made both by way of local planning and by way of transport agreements within the EU to contain and reduce these problems.

Severe air pollution from sources both within and without the country further threaten the environment. For example, the government estimates that approximately 166,000 tons of sulfur oxides *annually* waft into the country, largely from Germany, the Czech and Slovak Republics, Italy, and Poland, whereas about 17,000 tons are "exported." Austria has adopted stricter air pollution standards than most European states by, for example, requiring catalytic converters on new cars and reducing allowed sulfur emissions from heating oil. As a result, total emissions of sulphur dioxide and dust were sharply reduced during the 1980s, and carbon monoxide and nitrogen oxide emissions were held constant. Nevertheless, air pollution's impact on Austria's forests may be seen, especially along heavily traveled highways such as the Brenner, where thousands of trees are dead or dying.

Finally, Austrians mobilized during the 1980s to block government participation in the controversial Gabcikovo-Nagymaros project on the Danube, which has subsequently been completed by Slovakia without Czech or Austrian participation (see Chapter 5). The construction of a power plant associated with the project on the Danube at Hainburg east of Vienna was eventually stopped, and negotiations are underway to create a national park along the river. However, smaller power plants with less intrusive environmental impact, may yet be constructed along the Austrian stretch of the river.

Economic Development

As in other Western European countries, Switzerland excepted, transport of goods and passengers in Austria is increasingly reliant on automotive carriers. About two-thirds of domestic and one-half of transborder goods movement is by way of truck. Another one-tenth of domestic and one-third of international goods movement is by pipeline. These figures illustrate both the importance of these transport modes within Austria and Austria's role as a transit country for trucks between Italy and Germany, and for natural gas from Eastern to Western Europe. Transborder movement of trucks and buses more than doubled to nearly 700,000 per year between 1989 and 1991, while auto transit traffic leaped from about 8 to 13 million cars. This resulted in part from the opening of Eastern Europe to the West; however, to Austria's relief recent growth has tapered off.

Rail movements now account for about one-

fifth of goods movements, and shipping on the Danube and its tributaries only about 3 percent. The completion of the Rhine-Main Canal in Germany indirectly linking the Danube with the North Sea could increase the importance of transport by water in Austria; however, there are many limiting factors.

Modern Austria has one of the world's highest standards of social and economic well-being, an achievement that seemed highly implausible during the 1919–1955 era. Then Austria was beset by political and economic problems associated with the dissolution of the Habsburg Empire, the rise of Fascism and incorporation into Nazi Germany, and postwar Allied occupation until 1955. Despite inherited problems from the 1945–1955 era, relative lack of mineral and metallic resources, and disadvantageous location relatively distant from the core West European market and abutting the "Iron Curtain," Austria achieved economic success even prior to its recent entry into the EU.

The basis for Austrian economic growth came from a mixture of factors, including a "social partnership" that stressed compromise and conciliation among labor unions, employers, and government; and relatively high levels of training and education. Increases in labor productivity in Austria were among Europe's highest rates of improvements in the 1960s and 1970s. There was a high national savings and investment rate, and emphasis was placed on continual restructuring of the national economy by support for a relatively high-technology manufacturing sector. Also, specialized business service functions evolved, especially in Vienna, as well as tourism, primarily in the western provinces. Finally, and most importantly, close economic ties to Germany's large and growing economy cushioned Austria from economic downturns. For example, in 1990 Germany accounted for over 40 percent of Austria's total trade, and German tourists spent nearly 57 million nights in Austrian tourist facilities. As in other advanced industrial countries, employment in many traditional manufacturing sectors has stagnated or declined in Austria over the past 25 years, especially in mining, metal production, and the leather-working, textile, and apparel sectors. However, as indicated earlier, production and employment in higher value-added sectors have increased, including machinery, transport equipment, electronics, and pharmaceutical production. The service sector, including finance, insurance, real estate, medicine, education, and research and development, has expanded. Unlike most other West European countries, Austria still has a large publicly owned manufacturing sector that is particularly important in iron and steel (e.g., Voest Alpine), energy, and chemical production.

By West European standards, Austrian farms are quite small, being more comparable with Spain than its otherwise economically similar West European EU partners. In addition, farms are highly subsidized, and many will likely face serious difficulties competing, even within the EU's highly subsidized and protected agricultural economy. Still, Austrian farms are following the European-wide trend toward larger size and higher levels of mechanization. For example, during the 1970s and 1980s almost all of the 18 percent decline in farm numbers, about 600,000, occurred among smaller farms with fewer than about 44 acres (20 ha) .

Tourism is relatively more important in Austria than in any other European state. Receipts in 1993 accounted for 7.4 percent of GDP. In 1991 over 170,000 people worked in tourist-oriented jobs. In 1993 Austria recorded Europe's third largest number of tourist-nights and the fourth largest tourist revenue. Only France, Italy, and Spain took in more money from tourism. As a small country, Austria has a much higher per capita income from tourism ($1700 in 1992) than competitors such as Greece ($450), and the UK ($250). The Alpine republic's 1993 trade deficit in commodities was paid for by earnings from services, including tourist income. Although Austrians frequently vacation outside of their own country, their 1993 expenditures abroad, $8.3 billion, when compared to receipts of $13.5 billion, left them with a surplus of $5.2 billion. Germans are the most important tourists. Tirol has by far the country's largest numbers of total and foreign tourist-nights and, in relative terms, the greatest employment dependence on tourism. However, in Vienna large numbers of visitors, who spend on average much larger sums of money while visiting (double the level in Tirol), help support more hotel and restaurant jobs (about 30,000 in 1991) than in other provinces. Vienna draws larger numbers of visitors from East Cen-

tral, Southern, and Southeastern Europe and from outside Europe than the western provinces. However, the western provinces have huge advantages in attracting the larger number of visitors that come to Austria's Alps from Northern and Northwestern Europe. Tourists come to Austria in both summer and winter, though there has been strong growth in winter tourism, whereas the number of summer visitors has not risen since about 1970.

The geographic core of the Austrian economy lies in the eastern provinces of Vienna, Upper and Lower Austria, and Styria, though in terms of per capita production and income, only Vienna has economic conditions comparable to those of the sparsely populated western provinces of Vorarlberg, Tirol, and Salzburg. In recent years eastern provinces faced difficulties related to the decline of traditional industries, such as in the mining and metals sectors, as well as the locational disadvantages of being virtually encircled by poorer, relatively uncooperative socialist states and distant from Western Europe. The problem of declining tradional industries has been slowly but steadily addressed, while since 1990 eastern Austria has begun to benefit more from its location next to the revitalizing Czech Republic, Slovakia, Hungary, and Slovenia. Vienna, for example, is increasingly regaining its role as an international business and political center for Southeastern and East Central Europe. In relative terms, Austria has become an important participant in economic change in Hungary and the Czech and Slovak Republics.

Besides being a national and international center for specialized political and commercial service functions, Vienna is also an important, diversified manufacturing region and eastern Austria's most important tourist destination. The city's stunning architectural and artistic treasures, its broad palette of cultural events, especially in music and theater, its many educational institutions, and the quality of its residential ambiance appeal to tourists as well as to people in business who now need to have closer proximity to Eastern Europe. Thus, the relative importance of Vienna as a commercial gateway to East Central and Southeastern Europe is increasing. It has always been at the heart of the Austrian economy, often to the point that the city is envied and chided by Austrians from other regions, where people frequently feel that too much of the country's economic, cultural, and political life focuses on what was once, but is no more, an imperial capital.

The combined provincial economies of two other eastern provinces, Upper and Lower Austria, are larger than that of Vienna owing to their relatively high proportion of the country's total population (38%) and related service activities; their relatively productive agricultural sectors in comparison to other provinces (incomes per farm are about two-thirds higher than in the Alps); and especially their vital manufacturing sectors—by far Austria's most important with about half of all the country's production in 1993. The manufacturing sector is fairly diverse in both provinces, although there are notable geographic concentrations of metal production and metal-working activities around Linz in Upper Austria, and chemicals and machinery production in the suburbs and satellite towns of Vienna within Lower Austria. Despite Upper and Lower Austria's importance in absolute terms, GDP per capita is below the national average and far below Vienna, especially in Lower Austria.

Austria's other eastern provinces, Styria and Burgenland, have less healthy economies than their neighbors and are the country's poorest in terms of per capita income. Styria has particularly troublesome problems in its declining mining and metals-producing sectors. Austria's easternmost province, Burgenland, has been its most agriculturally oriented, least industrialized, and poorest region ever since the area's controversial annexation to Austria from its historic attachment to western Hungary 75 years ago. However, socioeconomic conditions have changed radically for the better in Burgenland in the postwar era, in part owing to considerable commuting of workers from the province to work in metropolitan Vienna.

Carinthia, Austria's southern province, also has economic problems, as reflected in a relatively high unemployment rate and an income level below the national average. Its economy is overly dominated by primary sector activities and tourism. Although tourism is important, it has not been successful enough to provide the generally high standard of living that prevails in Austria's western provinces.

Western Austria includes the country's wealthiest provinces outside Vienna. The economies and incomes in Salzburg and Tirol, in which mountain farmers were once poor, have grown rapidly over the last 30 years based mainly on a booming tourist industry. Tirol is especially dominated by tourism, chiefly from adjacent Germany. In 1990 there were 43 million tourist-nights spent in Tirol (population about 600,000), about 95 percent of which were accounted for by foreign tourists. Vorarlberg, bordering on Switzerland, has an economy dominated both by tourism (again heavily supported from neighboring Germany) and by textiles and apparels. Although employment growth in the textile/apparel sector has lagged, value of production has grown rapidly with increasing labor productivity and more emphasis on ever higher quality and higher priced products (including ski fashions).

LIECHTENSTEIN

Liechtenstein is a sovereign Central European state—a constitutional monarchy. It receives only brief treatment here because it is hardly larger than a Swiss, Austrian, or German local political subdivision, having an area of 62 sq miles (160 sq km) and a population of about 29,000. Although the state shares many things in common with neighbors that surround it, Liechtenstein is also in some ways distinctive.

The Liechtenstein landscape is virtually identical to that of its neighbors. The country includes largely forested alpine hills and mountains and a section of the largely arable upper Rhine River Valley floor. The majority of the population is ethnically indistinguishable from the majority populations in neighboring regions of Austria and Switzerland and stems originally from Allemannic tribes. A large resident foreign population is mostly, though not entirely, from Austria and Switzerland. Most people in Liechtenstein speak German and, like Austrians and south Germans, are largely Roman Catholic.

The roots of Liechtenstein's independent existence extend back to 1342, but in 1719 it was declared the Principality of Liechtenstein, a territorial subunit of the loosely organized Holy Roman

Empire. Following the demise of the Empire during the Napoleonic era, Liechtenstein was part of the loosely organized Germanic Confederation. The Confederation collapsed with Prussia's military victory over Austria in 1866, and Liechtenstein has since then had a strictly sovereign identity. The country has been able to manage its independence by way of close cooperation with its neighbors and other European states. From 1852 until the end of World War I, Liechtenstein was tied closely to Austria; its rail lines are still owned by the Austrian federal railway system. Since the 1920s Liechtenstein has had especially close political and economic ties to Switzerland, with which it has a postal, customs, and currency union. Switzerland also represents it politically in most foreign capitals. Its relationship with Switzerland, however, is not so close that it functions merely as an appendage. For example, although Switzerland is the largest trade partner, it still only accounts for about 14 percent of total trade, most of the rest of which Liechtenstein conducts with EU and EEA (European Economic Area) countries. Unlike Switzerland, Liechtenstein belongs both to the UN and the EEA, but like Switzerland, it is among the small number of remnant EFTA states.

Again like its neighbors, Liechtenstein has a balanced economy and a very prosperous populace. In 1930, 70 percent of the workforce worked in agriculture (below 2% now); today it has thriving manufacturing and financial sectors. Over 50 factories produce a variety of high value-added products, and over 70,000 firms, including important banks, have their nominal headquarters in the Principality. Firms are lured by stable political conditions, strict banking secrecy guarantees, and low, indirect taxes. About 20 percent of the country's income derives from levies on its firms and another 4 percent from selling stamps, largely to collectors worldwide. Economic activity is so intense that Liechtenstein has a labor shortage; more than half of the labor force is comprised of foreign workers, about two-thirds of whom commute from Austria and Switzerland.

Life in tiny, somewhat isolated Liechtenstein is so peaceful and prosperous that people beyond its immediate vicinity seldom notice it, unless, perhaps, you pass through it on the Vienna-Paris rail line that traverses it, or you collect some of its stamps. The country's stability and prosperity, along with its very small size, shield it from the glare of public attention that often focuses on places with serious problems.

BIBLIOGRAPHY

Berentsen, W. H. (1981). "Regional Change in the German Democratic Republic." *Annals of the Association of American Geographers* 71 (1): 50–66.

———. (1987). "Settlement Structure and Urban Development in the GDR 1950–1985." *Urban Geography* 8 (5) 405–419.

———. (1992). "The Socialist Face of the GDR: Eastern Germany's Landscape—Past, Present, and Future." *Landscape and Urban Planning* 22: 137–151.

———. (1994). "Implications of German Unification for Regional Development in the Former GDR." *Local Governments and Market Decentralization: Experiences in Industrialized, Developing, and Former Eastern Bloc Countries*. R. J. Bennett, ed., UN University Press, pp. 476–504.

Bergmann, Eckhard. (1992). "Räumliche Aspekte des Strukturwandels in der Landwirtschaft." *Geographische Rundschau* 44: 143–147.

Breitfeld, K., et al. (1992). *Das vereinte Deutschland: Eine kleine Geographie:* Leipzig: Institut für Länderkunde Leipzig.

Diem, A. (1984), "The Alps," *The Geographical Magazine* 56: 414-420.

———. (1988), "Pollution on the Roof of Europe: Are the Alps Dying?" *The Geographical Magazine* 60 (6): 2–8.

———. (1993). *The New Germany. 2nd ed.* Waterloo: Media International.

———. (1994). *Switzerland: Land, People, Economy.* 4th ed. Waterloo: Media International.

Eckart, Karl, Hans-Friedrich Wollkopf, et al. (1994). *Landwirtschaft in Deutschland.* Beiträge zur Regionalen Geographie 36. Leipzig: Institut für Länderkunde Leipzig.

Elkins, T. H., and B. Hofmeister. (1988). *Berlin, Spatial Structure of a Divided City.* London: Methuen.

Europa Publications Limited. (1995). *The Europa World Year Book 1995.* London: Europa Publications Limited.

"Federal Republic of Germany." (1988). *Geographische Rundschau.* Special edition. Braunschweig: Westermann Schulbuchverlag.

Gale Research Inc. (1995). *Countries of the World.* New York, Gale Research Inc.

Harenberg, Bodo, ed. (1994). *Harenberg Lexicon der Gegenwert.* Dortmund: Harenberg Lexicon-Verlag.

Hoffman, G. W. (1951). "The Survival of an Independent Austria." *Geographical Review* 41: 606–621.

Jelavich, B. (1987). *Modern Austria. Empire and Republic 1815-1986.* New York: Columbia Press.

Lichtenberger, Elisabeth. (1995). "Schmelztiegel Wien." *Geographische Rundschau* 47: 10–17.

Mellor, Roy E. H. (1978). *The Two Germanies: A Modern Geography.* London: Harper & Row.

Organization for Economic Cooperation and Development. (1991). *OECD Economic Surveys: Austria.* Paris: OECD.

Österreichisches Statistische Zentralamt. *Statistisches Handbuch für die Republik Österreich.* Vienna: Österreichisches Statistische Zentralamt. Various years.

Schmid, Gerhard Friedrich. (1989). *Kleine Deutschlandkunde.* Stuttgart: Ernst Klett.

Seger, Martin. (1995). "Umweltschutz: ausgewählte Probleme und Lösungsansätze." *Geographische Rundschau* 47: 38–45.

Statistisches Bundesamt der Bundesrepublik Deutschland. (1989). *Länderbericht Österreich.* Wiesbaden: Statistisches Bundesamt.

———. *Statistisches Jahrbuch für die Bundesrepublik Deutschland.* Wiesbaden: Statistisches Bundesamt. Various years.

Wild, M. T. (1980). *West Germany: A Geography of Its People.* Totowa, N.J.: Barnes & Noble.

Zimmerman, Friedrich. (1995). "Tourismus in Österreich." *Geographische Rundschau* 47: 30–37.

12

EAST CENTRAL AND SOUTHEASTERN EUROPE

For decades largely cut off from the West and under the shadow of Soviet dominance, countries in East Central and Southeastern Europe (ECSEE) suddenly made headlines in 1989. East Germans occupied Western embassies in Eastern Europe seeking escape from their authoritarian rulers. Reform-minded party members and leaders, emboldened by Mikhail Gorbachev's new and more open policies in the USSR, took power in East Berlin. Unaware of the true depth of the populace's disdain for its rule, the party in East Germany soon lost control of political events— and, thankfully, unlike previous such crises in East Germany and elsewhere, neither the Soviet nor East German military intervened. Before long the Berlin Wall opened, and autocratic, leftist governments dissolved across ECSEE, in part owing to the heretofore unimaginable neutrality of the Soviet military.

Until 1989 relatively few people in the United States knew much about ECSEE, where the region is generally referred to as Eastern Europe. Most West Europeans had also become accustomed to the political division of Europe between East and West, and by the 1980s their lives were usually not directly affected by events there. This situation changed dramatically, with startling developments including the peaceful opening of the Berlin Wall, the brief and violent political revolution in Romania, and the catastrophe of civil and inter-republic war in the former Yugoslavia. Also making news, however, was a wave of democratic reform and economic change based on greater market orientation. Rapid economic restructuring began reshaping the formerly centrally planned economies. Soviet troops withdrew from ECSEE, in part as the result of a dramatic lessening of tensions and a number of agreements between the

United States and the USSR. By the early 1990s, political change struck the Soviet Union itself, as first the Baltic republics and ultimately all Soviet republics emerged as independent states. The reverberations of this "revolution" of 1989–1990 continue to be felt across the region, as new economic structures are being built and new democratic forms of governance in the region's countries are emerging.

Unfortunately, nationalism and long-held ethnic animosities, dampened in some countries by the dictates of Soviet power for more than 40 years, have reemerged in Eastern Europe causing war in the former Yugoslavia and the threat of it elsewhere. From about 1991 to 1993, the economies and living standards of most ECSEE countries also deteriorated sharply. Much of the region experienced dramatically worsened economic conditions for millions of people, owing to the demise of large socialist-era firms without countervailing job creation in the emerging private marketplace. At the same time, a small number of people began to accumulate vast wealth, sometimes via questionable or clearly illegal activities. Economic distress, as well as the social-political outcry associated with increasing social inequalities and crime, resulted in both acrimonious political debates and the return of "reformed" socialist parties to national leadership roles in several countries. By 1994 the economies of most countries began to improve, but the socioeconomic problems persist and probably cannot be resolved in most places before some time in the next century.

Now much more politically and economically engaged in the region, the United States and Western Europe are also seeking to expand the domain of the EU and NATO in order to help spur economic growth and assure peace in countries freed from Soviet domination. This effort is being made without needlessly strengthening the political position of radical Russian nationalists and unreformed communists who demand the reconstitution of the Soviet Union—if necessary by force.

In retrospect, in the early 1990s Eastern Europe began what is now viewed as a long and uncertain path toward political democracy and economic prosperity. Some countries, like the Czech Republic and Hungary, have progressed far along the path, whereas other places like Romania and Albania have much further to go. This chapter provides a basic overview of the ECSEE, a region whose importance to the United States and Western Europe has clearly, then, increased.

The ECSEE encompasses a large area, about the size of combined France, Germany, and the UK, and has a population of about 120 million people. The region is comprised of countries and peoples that share both similarities and dissimilarities. The entire region was recently ruled by centralized communist or socialist governments, most of which were greatly influenced by policies emanating from Moscow. The region has fairly low levels of socioeconomic well-being by European standards, though considerable regional variations exist both within and between the individual states. Multiple ethnic identities within the countries have created serious domestic and international political and social problems (Table 12-1)—excepting, for the most part, Poland. In that country ethnic diversity was largely eliminated by the flight and deportation of Germans after World War II, the exchange of Belarussian and Ukrainian refugees across the Polish-Soviet border in the late 1940s, and the death of millions of Jews during the Holocaust. The relatively low socioeconomic status and great ethnic diversity of the ECSEE countries are also related to a common, relatively negative impact of external, imperial rule over long periods of time, including the critical late-nineteenth-century era of rapid industrialization in Europe.

The ECSEE region has been called the shatterbelt, a term referring to its fragmentation into many political and cultural units. Such names as the Eastern Marchlands, the *Cordon Sanitaire* of the interwar period, the Iron Curtain of the postwar period, or simply satellite or captive countries (Yugoslavia and Albania excluded in the case of the last two expressions) have also been applied. Today the region is compromised of 18 countries west of Russia—six former republics of the USSR; five former Yugoslav republics; the two, now sep-

TABLE 12-1

ETHNIC COMPOSITION OF ECSEE COUNTRIES, CIRCA 1990[a]

Dominance of Titular Ethnic Group

Hungary	Hungarians 99% Other 1% (esp. Germans, Slovaks, Romanians, Gypsies)
Poland	Poles 97% Germans 1% Other 2% (esp. Ukrainians, Belarussians)
Albania	Albanians 97% Greeks 2% Other 1% (esp. Vlachs, Gypsies, Montenegrins)
Czech Republic	Czechs 94% Slovaks 4% Other 2% (esp. Poles, Germans, Hungarians)
Slovenia	Slovenes 90% Croats 3% Serbs 2% "Yugoslavs" 1% Other 3% (esp. Muslims, Hungarians, Montenegrins, Macedonians)

One Major Ethnic Minority

Romania	Romanians 89% Hungarians 7% Gypsies 2% Other 1% (esp. Germans, Ukrainians, Serbs, Croats, Russians, Turks)
Slovak Republic	Slovaks 87% Hungarians 11% Czechs 1% Other 1% (esp. Rusyns, Ukrainians, Poles)
Croatia	Croats 75% Serbs 11% "Yugoslavs" 8% Other 5% (esp. Hungarians, Slovenes, Muslims, Montenegrins, Macedonians, Albanians)
Macedonia	Macedonians 67% Albanians 20% Serbs 2% Muslims 2% Other 9% (esp. "Yugoslavs", Montenegrins, Croats)

Multiethnic

Bulgaria	Bulgarians 73% Turks 15% Gypsies 6% Macedonians 3% Vlachs 2% Other 1% (esp. Armenians, Russians, Albanians)
Former Yugoslavia	Serbs 36% Croats 20% Muslims 9% Slovenes 8% Albanians 8% Macedonians 6% "Yugoslavs" 5% Montenegrins 2% Hungarians 2% Other 4% (esp. Gypsies, Turks, Slovaks, Bulgarians, Romanians, Vlachs, Czechs, Ukrainians, Ruthenians)
Serbia/ Montenegro	Serbs 63% Albanians 14% Montenegrins 6% "Yugoslavs" 5% Hungarians 4% Muslims 3% Croats 2% Other 4%
Bosnia-Herzegovina	Muslims 39% Serbs 32% Croats 18% "Yugoslavs" 8% Others 2% (esp. Montenegrins, Macedonians, Slovenes, Albanians)

[a]All data for the former Yugoslavia and its former republics are from the 1981 census. Figures may not total to 100 percent owing to rounding procedures. Roma/Sinti are usually reported as "Gypsy." Hungarians are, in fact, an interrelated group of peoples, including most notably the Magyars. In the former Czechoslovakia "Ruthenians" were sometimes reported as people claiming Rusyn, Ukrainian, or Russian ethnicity.

arate, portions of the old Czechoslovakia; four other countries once coerced into military, political, and economic union with the USSR; and the region's political renegade, Albania. Once inappropriately homogenized as "Eastern Europe" within the minds of many people in the West, the area is now more accurately viewed as complexly bewildering and fraught with both opportunity and danger for the future of Europe.

In terms of physical geography, ECSEE contains both well-defined, homogeneous areas like the Great Hungarian Plain (*Alföld*) and highly complex regions such as the Dinaric Ranges (Fig. 12-1). Its mountains and other highlands, howev-

FIGURE 12-1 Physiographic map of ECSEE.

er, never seem to have been barriers to the movement of peoples, allowing the settlement of a great variety of European and Asian peoples. Many easily accessible passes, river valleys, and most of all the Danube River have allowed interaction, including conflict, among peoples within and beyond the region. For example, the eastern portion of the North European Lowland has been a traditional invasion route from Russia into Central and Western Europe, and vice versa. The Polish Uplands were an important routeway between Western Europe and northwestern and central Russia. The Morava-Vardar corridor in the southeast assisted the Ottoman Turks in their easy penetration to the gates of Vienna. And control of important passes and basins facilitated Austrian rule over important lands in the Carpathian Mountain region.

Many different peoples have used these routes since the dawn of European history, and it is not surprising that for some the Danube corridor became their permanent home. Major migrant groups include Poles, Czechs, Slovaks, Hungarians (Magyars), Germans, Romanians, Bulgars, Illyrians, and the South Slavic peoples (Slovenes, Croats, Serbs, and Macedonians) of the former Yugoslavia (the latter meaning Land of the South Slavs). As a result of their movements, the area was occupied by people of many different cultures, and this fragmentation has contributed to the region's lack of a stable political-territorial framework.

The ECSEE also has a great variety of climates, including the Mediterranean climate along the Adriatic littoral of the former Yugoslavia (the bordering Karst Mountains preclude inland extensions), the semiarid steppe along the lower Danube in the Dobruja region of Romania, and the relatively harsh continental climate of East Central Europe. This variety in climatic conditions is matched by a great diversity of soils and vegetation.

East Central and Southeastern Europe is not particularly rich in natural resources. The agricultural activities of a large, though rapidly declining, rural population still play an important role, but increased industrialization in every one of the countries has rapidly altered the economic structure of the area. With the exception of Albania and the former Yugoslavia, all East European countries

had close economic ties with the Soviet Union, adopted post–World War II economic policies favoring industrialization, and were members of the Council for Mutual Economic Assistance (CMEA). Now Germany is becoming the dominant trade partner and the origin of foreign investment for most ECSEE countries.

East Central Europe generally has less ethnic diversity than Southeastern Europe, is more economically developed, and is undertaking more rapid political and economic reform. Thus, for example, Hungary, the Czech Republic, Poland, and Slovenia are much more likely candidates for earlier inclusion in the EU than, for example, Romania and Albania.

The unifying characteristics of ECSEE countries, ironically one of them being internal complexity, are used here as the rationale for discussing them within a single group, but differences among them will also be a consistent subtheme within the chapter. It is possible that the strong desire of the people of East Central Europe to be identified with Central and Western Europe rather than Eastern Europe may be achieved in the next century. However, for now, owing to many factors not the least being 45 years of Soviet influence, East Central Europe has commonalties with Southeastern Europe that justify analyzing the region as a single, if diverse, region.

PHYSIOGRAPHIC REGIONS

Despite the complexity of East Central and Southeastern Europe's physiography, five major regions may be identified: (1) the North European Lowlands; (2) the Polish and Bohemian Uplands; (3) the Carpathian Ranges and Moldovan Tablelands; (4) the Pannonian and Walachian Plains; and (5) the Southeast European Highlands and Dinaric Ranges.

The *North European Lowlands* are part of a continentwide European Plain extending from France in the west to Russia in the east (discussed in Chapter 2). Two clear-cut divisions can be distinguished, the Baltic Coastal Zone and the Glacial Valley Zone further south. The Coastal Zone extends into Poland from the west and continues on to the east. It is flat and sandy, and long sand bars created by strong ocean currents enclose low coastal depressions. This shoreline has only a few good ports, for example, Gdansk (formerly Danzig) and Szczecin (formerly the German port city Stettin) on the mouth of the Oder. Lakes are plentiful in the region, especially in Mazuria in northeastern Poland. Mazuria's tangled, glaciated, thinly populated landscape played an important role in Germany's defeat of Russian Empire forces at the very beginning of World War I, documented in Alexander Solzhenitsyn's novel *August, 1914.*

South of the morainic hill country is the Glacial Valley Zone, extending east to west and comprised of lowlands where broad valleys alternate with somewhat higher ground of mainly sandy soils. The valleys are glacial "spillways," created by the meltwater of continental ice sheets. They are broad, flat, generally east- to west-trending depressions. In successive advances the ice sheets, which spread southward from Scandinavia, encountered no obstacles to their advance until they reached the Uplands in the south. Unconsolidated materials were deposited; boulders, clay, gravel, sand, and deposits of windblown loess now vary in thickness between 40 and 159 ft (12 and 52 m).

Between the Lowlands and the Uplands in Poland, as in Germany, lies a belt of glacial soil partially covered by loess. In Poland this includes the plain in Lower Silesia. This transitional loess region, situated between the Uplands and Plains, has been cultivated for thousands of years and was of great importance to the settlement of the whole region.

The *Polish and Bohemian Uplands,* located in Poland, the Czech Republic, and Slovakia, are a continuation of the western portion of the Central European Upland extending into East Central Europe from Germany and Austria. The region is divided into numerous topographical units intermittently covered with fertile loess. Because of their east-west orientation, the Uplands are not a climatic divide, though rainfall increases rapidly with increasing altitude. The various upland regions and enclosed basins and plateaus show great contrasts in economic development. Manufacturing regions are intermixed with agricultural areas based on loess soils (e.g., east of Cracow) and primarily forested regions. The Polish Uplands include the Sudeten Mountains and the plateau lands east of the Oder River, containing one of Europe's largest coalfields (upper Silesia) as well as other minerals. The Uplands also include the Bohemian Massif and surrounding heights, an ancient geologic structure of wooded mountains, and the fertile, loess-covered intermontane Bohemian Basin.

South of the Polish Uplands and east of the Bohemian Massif is a transitional zone, the rolling hills of the Carpathian Foreland and the Moravian Depression. Located between the Danube Basin (Pannonian Plain or Basin) and the low gap of the Moravian Gate, this depression offers one of Europe's most important routes connecting the North European Lowlands with the Danube Valley. The depression is itself an important agricultural region.

The *Carpathian Ranges,* comprised of the Carpathian Mountains and related subregions, constitute a third major physiographical region of ECSEE. The arc of the Carpathian Ranges and their forelands extend a thousand miles from the Vienna Basin to the Iron Gate, where the Danube River squeezes through a narrow gorge in the southern Carpathians and forms the border between Romania and Serbia. The Carpathians stretch across about the same distance as the Alps, but they are lower, reaching an elevation of at most 8700 ft (2600 m) in the High Tatra on the Polish-Slovak border. The Carpathians are widest in the northwest but are penetrated by rivers, which facilitate transportation and settlement. The central Carpathians include the strategically placed territory of Carpatho-Ukraine, which in the interwar years was part of Czechoslovakia (known then as Ruthenia), next became part of the Ukrainian SSR in 1945, and now is part of Ukraine. A militarily important, scenic pass has allowed movement through this region between the Pannonian Basin and central Ukraine since medieval times. The eastern Carpathians are located entirely within Romania and form an arc through which a pass provides the main route between the Pannonian Basin and Bucharest on the Walachian Plain. The southern Carpathians, known as the Transylvanian Alps, also have important routes traversing them at low altitudes, connecting the Basin with the Walachian Plain.

The *Pannonian and Walachian Plains* are lowland basins contained within surrounding, more rugged terrain. The Pannonian Basin, surrounded by the Carpathians, the Alps, and the Dinaric Ranges, is also sometimes referred to as the Alföld or Carpathian Basin. The Danube River flows through the whole length of the region. The Basin, over 110,000 sq miles (286,000 sq km) in area, is not uniform in relief. It is divided into minor basins, hill lands, and mountains. Much of the Basin was covered by an inland sea until rivers from the surrounding mountains filled it with alluvial deposits. The Little Alföld extends from the foothills of the Alps in Austria to the slopes of the Trans-Danubian Hills in western Hungary and north across the Danube to the foothills of the western Carpathians in Slovakia. Neusiedler Lake, at the Austro-Hungarian border, and Lake Balaton in the Trans-Danubian Hills are shallow freshwater lakes remaining from the one-time inland sea and are today popular tourist areas.

The Great Alföld stretches east and north of the Danube across Hungary into Slovakia and south into Romania and the former Yugoslavia. Southeast of Kecskemét, Hungary, lies the treeless grassy *puszta*, covered with windblown sand, and near Debrecen is the Hortobagy, a steppe region covered with highly alkaline soil unsuited to most commercial crops. Most of the Banat region in the south, where the Hungarian, Serb, and Romanian borders converge, is composed of fertile black soil.

The Walachian Plain is a depression that was a gulf of the Black Sea, but like other Central European basins was entirely filled by river deposits from nearby uplands. The steppe plateau of Dobruja on the eastern Romanian-Bulgarian border blocks the straight course of the Danube and forces its flow northward. The Danube, especially during floods, is extremely difficult to navigate in its middle and lower reaches because of the sluggish course of the river and its many braided channels. For this reason, the Danube-Black Sea Canal was

FIGURE 12-2 (a) View of the Dinaric Alps from the Adriatic coast near Zadar. (T. M. Poulsen)

commissioned in 1984 to facilitate traffic. The canal, which connects Cernavoda at the Danube bend with Constanța, is nearly 40 miles long (64.2 km) and shortens the journey to the Black Sea by some 250 miles (400 km). Bordering the floodplains, on both the Romanian and the Bulgarian side, cliffs rise as much as 300 ft (90m) above the marshes.

Four physiographical subregions can be defined within the *Southeastern Highlands*: (1) the Alps; (2) the Dinaric Ranges, including the Adriatic littoral; (3) the Transitional and Basin Lands of the Morava and Vardar rivers; and (4) the Rhodope Massif, Balkan Ranges, and interspersed depressions. The structure and relief of these Highlands is complex and diverse. Volcanic intruded rock indicates that the Highlands are an area of instability; earthquakes are common. Steep mountains, small intermontane basins, and heavy erosion, especially in the Southern Highlands, are typical. A large part of the Highlands is composed of soluble limestone, with characteristic landscape features including

caves and sinkholes. Indeed, the term *karst topography* used by geomorphologists to describe such landscapes was taken from this region.

In the north, the Karawanken and Julian Alps form a scenic and, in many ways, major political divide between Central and Southeastern Europe. The new, small country of Slovenia now spans this largely mountainous region within which its capital, Ljubljana, occupies a fertile central valley. The Dinaric Ranges region itself includes coastal and mountain zones. The Adriatic littoral, also called the Dalmatian coast (famous for its indigenous dog breed), a narrow coastal zone with many islands and inlets of the Adriatic Sea, presents a picturesque landscape that attracted millions of tourists before wars broke out following the collapse of united Yugoslavia (Fig. 12-2). Access from the Adriatic coast to the mountainous interior is blocked by the High Karst (part of the Dinaric Massif), a barren, mainly limestone zone extending from northwest to southeast for 350 miles (563

FIGURE 12-2 (b) The same view with recently built new weekend and summer homes. (T. M. Poulsen)

km) with elevations averaging 8000 ft (2440 m). South of the Dinaric Ranges, a series of parallel mountains extends further southward and merges with the Albanian Epirus Ranges.

The transitional and basin lands of the Morava and Vardar, a region of great diversity, includes the Morava-Vardar depression, which affords a short route about 300 miles (480 km) from the lowlands of the north to the Aegean Sea and its strategic port of Thessaloniki. Eastern Serbia and Bulgaria lie within the fourth broad physiographic region in the Southeastern Highlands, comprised of the rather unproductive Rhodope Massif, the Balkan Ranges, and associated depressions and plateaus. The Rhodope Massif is rugged land in which the most important economic resources are metal ores. The Balkan Ranges are an extension of the Carpathians south of the Danube River. Within Bulgaria the Balkan Ranges separate the hilly farmland of the Danube or Bulgarian Plateau in the northern part of the country from the productive Sofia and Rumelian basins in the south. The southernmost Balkan Range, the Sredna Gora (Old Mountains), presents a scenic and imposing barrier when viewed from the basins.

POPULATION AND URBANIZATION

As noted in Chapter 3, East Central and Southeastern Europe was settled by a number of European and Asiatic peoples through time. The earliest inhabitants of the region are shrouded somewhat in prehistory, but by two thousand years ago Roman historians indicate that Germanic, Celtic, Thracian, Illyrian, Hellenic, and Scythian tribes occupied parts of East Central and Southeastern Europe. Later, a variety of Asian invaders, including the Avars, Huns, Mongols, and Turks, greatly impacted settlement patterns in the region.

Today Slavic peoples dominate. Their origin is somewhat obscure, but they spread over the region and have played a substantial, and usually dominating, role in development of the region

over about the past 1500 years. They cut the ancient forests, farmed, practiced seasonal pasturage, and ultimately played a role in establishing urban places.

After the twelfth century, German settlers drained the swampy valleys and began clearing the extensive forests in what is now western and central Poland. By 1900, millions of German-speaking people lived within what is today Poland, the Baltic and the Czech Republics. Fewer and less spatially contiguous German settlements occurred on some of the fertile land in what is now Hungary, Slovakia, Romania, and Serbia (especially in the Banat and other parts of the northern Vojvodina region). Jews, who migrated to ECSEE from the south and west, often faced impediments to holding land and frequently lived in urban centers working in commerce and crafts. The Ottoman Turk occupation of Southeastern Europe began 500 years ago, and the modern Turkish state still controls territory in eastern Thrace, including the one-time capital of the eastern Roman Empire, Byzantium—today's Istanbul. Ottoman occupation generally did not result in new settlements, but their armies, merchants, and bureaucrats lived in the cities, usually surrounded by rural areas dominated by local peoples. The Islamic faith spread under their rule, and most of Southeastern Europe's Muslim population traces its cultural lineage back to the time of Ottoman rule, especially in Bosnia, Macedonia, and part of eastern Bulgaria. Ottoman political and economic impact on the region has, on the whole, been regarded as negative, and most formerly subject peoples view the long era of occupation in very dark terms (Fig. 12-3).

Ottoman rule, thus, also played a role in the late and slow evolution of the process of urbanization in the region. In the Carpathian Basin, to protect the croplands against constant pillaging, the so-called village towns, or peasant villages, were developed, with outlying houses occupied only during harvest times. Scattered hamlets with stone houses on protective steep slopes are typical for some of the southern Dinaric regions of Montenegro and Albania. Dispersed settlements in mountain areas all over East Central and Southeastern

FIGURE 12-3 Memorial in Bulgaria to soldiers who fell in the 1876 uprising against Ottoman rule. (W. H. Berentsen)

Europe were typical for people in pastoral or lumbering occupations or in regions of poor soil. Closely packed villages with narrow streets are common in the mining communities of Bohemia and the western Carpathians, and in the coastal towns along the Dalmatian littoral. Some of the latter settlements have histories dating to Roman and pre-Roman times, including Split, which has city streets lying in the pattern of an earlier, huge Roman palace (Fig. 12-4). Austrian influences are observable in the market centers of the Bohemian and Polish Uplands; in Transylvania, where there is often a well-laid-out marketplace from which streets radiate to towns' edges; and in the architecture of many churches and other public buildings.

Ottoman Turkish influence on urban morphology is also often important. Turkish settlements are characterized by houses that are closed toward the street and opened toward the interior. Sometimes a high wall with a heavy gate encloses a central courtyard. In the center of the Turkish part of towns is the fascinating oriental bazaar, a place for trade and commerce. Central Sarajevo had a classic example of such a bazaar before the Yugoslav civil war. The Ottoman Turkish settlements usually were divided into quiet living and more

bustling business quarters. The houses of tradespeople and artisans (metal and armament industries, silk and gold embroidery) were usually concentrated in the center of the towns. Mosques and minarets as well as skillfully constructed stone bridges, once rather common urban landscape features, are now increasingly rare (Fig. 12-5).

On the whole, areas long under Ottoman occupation developed fewer and smaller urban concentrations. Many towns in the Carpathian Basin are relatively new, rebuilt after the region was reoccupied following the Ottoman military defeats in the seventeenth and eighteenth centuries. They consist largely of one-story whitewashed stone buildings with tile roofs, with wide tree-lined streets leading to a central square. The only large settlements in the Slavic regions during the era of Ottoman control were Belgrade, at the northern end of the Morava-Vardar depression at the confluence of the Sava and Danube rivers; Skopje, an important transport junction; and Sofia.

Towns within the Hapsburg Empire, the Prussian state, and Poland developed along important trade routes or near strategic sites. Good examples are Cracow on the upper Vistula River, for centuries one of Europe's leading trading cities and

FIGURE 12-4 Split, on the Adriatic coast with the Diocletian palace in the center and the high Karst in the background. The city is an important port and is the administrative, economic, and cultural center of Dalmatia, Croatia's Adriatic coastal region. The city was an Illyian-Greek settlement in ancient times. At the end of the third century, a palace was built for the Roman Emperor Diocletian, who is buried here. (T. M. Poulsen)

FIGURE 12-5 Mostar, Bosnia-Herzegovina. The main span of the centuries-old Mostar bridge recently toppled into the river resulting from damages suffered during fighting here. (W. H. Berentsen)

cultural centers; Warsaw, the capital of Poland after 1596, located on an important east-west route; Prague, roughly in the center of the Bohemian Basin; Buda, on the high, western bank of the Danube River (see Fig. 12-14); and Pest, the commercial town on the Danube's low bank, where the Danube is easy to bridge before its marshy course through the plains to the south. Although Budapest's location is extremely favorable geographically, in trade and strategic location it never was able to rival Vienna, its neighbor to the west and long-time political and cultural center of the Habsburg Empire. Many of these cities have still earlier roots; Budapest and Vienna, for example, were Roman settlements.

The importance and implications of class structure for the people of this region should be briefly noted. Generally speaking, two structures existed in East Central and Southeastern Europe prior to World War I: (1) that of the Hungarians (Magyars) and North Slavs, as well as those South Slavs under control of the Austro-Hungarian Empire; and (2) that of the peoples in areas south of the Danube and Sava rivers formerly controlled by the Ottoman Empire, especially the territory of the Serbs, Albanians, and Bulgarians. People in the first, northern region were ruled by feudal states (e.g., Prussia, Poland, Bohemia, Hungary) where the landed gentry was the leading class and the mass of the peasants were either serfs (in most regions until 1848; in the Russian part of Poland until 1867) or partially free. The landed nobility together with the high clergy had a dominant influence on the central government, which was often weak and unstable. After the Middle Ages, and closely related to the growing importance of trade and commerce, a small but growing middle class living in towns and villages exerted an increasing influence in the northern region.

The situation in the Ottoman-dominated southern areas was quite different. Here a landed nobility and middle class were largely nonexistent. The dominant class was comprised of Ottoman Turk officials, military leaders, and large landowners. Trade was often in the hands of Greeks and Jews. The original Serbian feudal state of the fourteenth century, with its landowners, high and low nobility, clergy, and dependent peasantry, was completely destroyed by the Turkish conquerors. Peasant families in the region lived in groups referred to as *zadrugas* (joint family units), whose origin goes back to the tribal organizations of the early South Slavic peoples. Many who could escape from Ottoman rule fled into the impassable mountains, mainly in Montenegro, where their descendants carried on guerrilla warfare for generations. Among the people living in the mountains, especially the Montenegrins and Albanians, clan rivalry evolved, and the constant struggle for freedom from foreign oppressors became part of daily life. These struggles were led by local leaders and encouraged by the Orthodox Church, which during the Slavic struggle for survival played an important role in preserving the memory and ideal of a Serbian state.

The few intellectuals in the East Central and Southeast European countries came largely from the middle class; they frequently had to fight to uphold their beliefs and often were forced to emigrate. Without the impact of the Industrial Revolution on the masses in the Ottoman-controlled lands, long-established modes of life remained unchanged in the region for a longer time than in nearly any other part of Europe.

During the nineteenth century, railways were built in East Central Europe to link important commercial and strategic centers, and the Danube was made navigable at the Iron Gate. With easier transportation of goods over longer distances, industry and trade began to develop, and thousands of agricultural workers moved into rapidly expanding towns. By the end of the nineteenth century, Bucharest, Prague, Łódź, Breslau (Wrocław), and Warsaw had populations of over 100,000, and Budapest over half a million. Industrialization came later and much more slowly to other parts of Hungary and the countries of Southeastern Europe. The first function of these regions was to supply raw materials to the newly expanding industries of Western and Central Europe, and heavy industry developed slowly. Industrialization was slowest to emerge in the former territory of the Ottoman Empire, where it did not start in earnest until after World War II.

The process of urbanization greatly accelerated during the postwar period, but then slowed following the initial communist/socialist drive for industrialization. Increased urbanization has been the result of rural-urban migration, natural growth, and administrative reclassification. The few urban concentrations where industrialization began early experienced the most dynamic change. As explained in more detail in Chapter 5, rapid industrialization in the countries of ECSEE, especially from the 1950s through the mid-1970s, led to the dramatic growth of many towns and cities. However, expenditures on basic infrastructure, on cultural, medical, and educational facilities, and on housing did not keep pace with industrial expansion. The result was a set of urban places too strongly tied to heavy industry and lacking service functions. In many cases, workers could not find adequate housing and were forced to commute to their jobs from villages, thereby limiting their use of what limited facilities existed in cities for permanent residents. Finally, these mainly industrial cities did not develop strong ties with their surrounding territory and, thus, generally have not grown into central places (centers that serve a surrounding hinterland). On the other hand, rural population in great numbers poured into the cities, and in some cases dramatically impacted urban life.

In the post–World War II period, a number of new cities were created, the so-called socialist cities discussed in Chapter 6. Besides increasing industrial output, they were intended to demonstrate new principles and ideologies of urban construction. Central planning gave special attention to planned urban development in order to prevent the uncontrolled, rapid growth of cities. Several countries had strict laws, especially in the 1950s and 1960s, limiting the influx of migrants into capital cities, though eventually these were widely circumvented. While for political reasons many countries announced the resolution of problematic differences between life in the rural villages and in the cities, urban life actually remained quite different from and generally more advantageous than rural life. Settlement policies were usually urban biased, assuring advantages for cities and their residents.

Ideological motives lay behind the socialists' urban-centered policies. Cities were declared "the stronghold of the working class," although they also represented a spatial concentration of white-collar workers. Governments in the socialist countries of Eastern Europe were initially suspicious of individualistic rural people, who were difficult to control; this concern formed a primary political motive for the collectivization of agriculture.

The general neglect of infrastructure under socialism conserved backward conditions in rural settlements and some small towns. Ironically, "freezing" these places in time may offer them better future prospects for architectural revival and related tourist promotion. On the other hand, numerous cities, especially those industrialized during the socialist era, today feature uniformly drab architecture, an ill-fitting combination of historic and socialist-era buildings, and serious air pollution problems (see Fig. 11-16).

POLITICAL GEOGRAPHY: THE "SHATTERBELT"

East Central and Southeastern Europe, as noted earlier, has often been called a "shatterbelt." Frequent boundary changes and the distribution of many ethnic groups in the region are cause and effect of the political instability inherent in this designation. The most prominent and tragic aspect of the shatterbelt phenomenon is the especially virulent and persistent forms of ethnic hatred that have repeatedly resulted in catastrophic loss of life in the region. Obviously, the existence of ethnic problems in the region is by no means unique; these problems are, sadly, endemic to human society and occur across the globe. However, it can be argued that interethnic conflict has been more frequent and severe in Central and Eastern Europe than in Western Europe, particularly during the nationalist or "postcolonial" eras—that is, after the withdrawal of dominating imperial forces (Austrian, Ottoman, and Soviet) and following the establishment of so-called nation-states.

In fact, of course, the many, generally small countries of Central and Eastern Europe are, with the exception of Poland and Hungary, anything but ethnically homogeneous and are generally states with many nations within them (Fig. 12-6). "Ethnic mixing" resulting from forced and voluntary migrations has occurred over many centuries

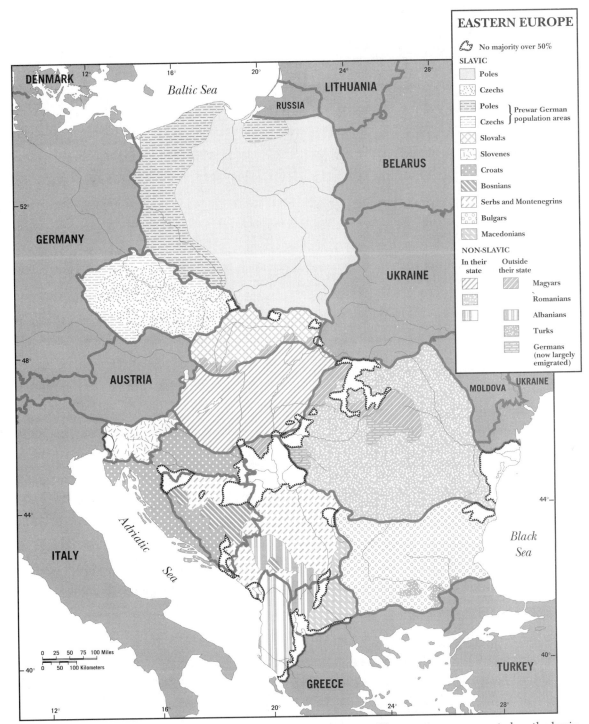

FIGURE 12-6 Ethnographic patterns of Eastern Europe. Majorities over 50 percent are represented on the basis of censuses taken between 1945 and the late 1980s.

throughout the region, in part a legacy of its frequent status as a "borderland." However, many peoples also willingly sought out opportunity by migrating to the region during times of economic growth, political stability, and social open-mindedness. Examples of such movement include the inmigration of Germans and Jews (especially following the pogroms associated with the Spanish Inquisition).

Regrettably, however, ECSEE has frequently employed a political and social tactic called "ethnic cleansing" in response to (often politically manipulated) popular outcry and hysteria against supposedly nonnative ethnic groups. Although the frightful Holocaust, in which Jews and Gypsies were particularly targeted, is the most extreme example, vicious attacks on huge numbers of people occurred during World War II in Yugoslavia (especially against Serbs) and is recurring in the same region. Millions of Germans were also expelled (or earlier fled in fear) from their native areas in ECSEE—especially western Poland, the Sudetenland, the former East Prussia, and Hungary—during and following World War II. Millions more Germans from Central and Eastern Europe had been resettled within the Third Reich by the Nazis themselves shortly before the war. The Soviets moved hundreds of thousands of people from Poland, Ukraine, and Lithuania eastward during World War II as the result of changed borders between the USSR and its western neighbors. Tens of thousands of other ECSEE residents were similarly displaced as the result of other boundary changes in the region during the war. "Exchanges" of about 2 million people took place both between Greece and Turkey in the 1920s and the USSR and Poland in the 1940s. Smaller such exchanges and agreements after World War II occurred between Czechoslovakia and the USSR; Czechoslovakia and Hungary; Hungary and Yugoslavia; and Bulgaria and Greece. Territorial losses by Finland and Italy during World War II resulted in hundreds of thousands of refugees flooding into those countries. Between 1944 and 1948 alone, Magocsi (1993) estimates that over 31 million ECSEE people moved involuntarily. In response to these movements, additional movements of population took place *within* countries, for example, into

Poland's western and northern territories from other parts of the country.

The seemingly never-ending movements of European peoples and boundaries, both historically and during this century, have resulted in a complex spatial mixing of peoples. Perhaps because so much of the population movement has been involuntary and the changes in borders unwanted, apparently little progress has been made toward the concept of the ethnic "melting pot," which in the United States, though somewhat disputed today, has played at least some role in lessening ethnic identities and has blunted politically dangerous expressions of nationalism.

In the early 1990s, many unresolved political problems in ECSEE were linked at least in part to ethnically based disputes within and between countries in the region (Fig. 4-8). The most severe problems are associated with the dissolution of the former Yugoslavia (a topic discussed in some detail later in this chapter). However, many other serious or potentially serious problems occur across ECSEE.

One example of such problems based on ethnic groups concerns ethnic Hungarians living outside the present boundaries of Hungary. In 1918, following World War I, Hungary was reduced in size by two-thirds, while 40 percent of the Hungarian population thereby found itself living in another country (see Fig. 12-6). Other boundary changes, especially in the Carpathian region, further complicate the picture. People in the region joke about this situation by accurately claiming that you could have been born in Hungary, grown up in Czechoslovakia, worked in the Soviet Union, and retired in Ukraine—all without ever leaving your native village. Currently, Hungarians living in Slovakia, Serbia, and Ukraine are pushing for greater representation and other minority rights, such as education in Hungarian and bilingual road signs.

A particularly thorny issue concerns Transylvania, the northwestern portion of Romania, which contains some 2 million Hungarian speakers. The people include both Magyars, who live along the border region of present Hungary, and Szeklers, a closely related people who are found concentrated in the Carpathian hills of eastern Transylvania. The original inhabitants of this region are unknown; however, the Romanian claim that an ancient tribe, the Dacians, was in place at the time of Roman occupation in the second century is credible. After the withdrawal of the Roman legions, whose legacy was a Latin-based language still spoken in the country, the region was overrun by various Germanic and Slavic tribes. Settlement by Szeklers, Vlachs, and German Saxons began in the ninth century, but Transylvania was conquered by Hungary in 1003. The region was made a principality in 1540, was recognized as a separate entity within the Ottoman Empire, and became a grand principality in the Austrian Empire in 1765. After the creation of the Dual Monarchy with Austria in 1867, Transylvania became a more integral part of Hungary but was ceded to Romania by the Treaty of Trianon (the same document that created the so-called successor states of Czechoslovakia and Yugoslavia). A portion of Transylvania was captured briefly by Hungary during World War II, but was returned to Romania at its close.

During the 1950s and early 1960s, a portion of Transylvania containing the highest concentration of Hungarians was designated an autonomous region. However, after gaining power in 1966, the new Romanian leader Ceausescu quickly abolished this zone and began systematic efforts to ethnically dilute the area. Supposedly, his plan to "systematize" villages throughout Romania was a further attempt to eradicate traces of ethnic consciousness, but the effort was also not directed solely at Hungarians.

Tensions between Romanians, Hungarians, and Germans in the region remained more or less in check over the years. However, the conflict escalated after 1989. Ethnic Hungarians were beaten; signs in Hungarian were made illegal by the ultranationalist mayor of Cluj-Napoca; and the democratically elected leaders of the two predominantly Hungarian counties of Transylvania were summarily dismissed in 1992 and replaced by ethnic Romanians.

A complete "solution" to the Transylvania question is highly unlikely, though problems associated with German ethnicity will likely lessen now that a large proportion of Romanians with German ancestry have emigrated to Germany. The Romanian government, along with most Romanians, views Transylvania as an integral, historic part of the country and is always on the alert for irredentist moves by the Hungarians. For their part, many Magyars in Hungary speak of the "Tragedy of Trianon" and call for the "return" of Transylvania. Cooler heads in the government and in academic circles, however, do not echo these sentiments. The residents of the region, who surprisingly are not generally considered in this debate, point out that Transylvania has long been a separate province and perhaps should be considered so, rather than merely as a ping-pong ball at the mercy of Bucharest and Budapest. This sentiment is especially prevalent among the Szeklers, who, though sharing a common language, do not hold particularly close ties with the Magyars of Hungary proper and who generally would not embrace attempts somehow to join with that country. Differences of opinion on this topic are sharp, and discussions inevitably become heated. Neither Hungary nor Romania is apt to be considered for EU membership until saber rattling, propaganda, and veiled threats of force disappear in the face of an official compromise agreement between the countries. In late 1996 steps in this direction were taken in the form of a "friendship" agreement between Hungary and Romania that assures the rights of Hungarians in Romania in exchange for a Hungarian renunciation of territorial claims. A similar agreement had already been reached between Hungary and Slovakia, where there is another large Hungarian minority.

Romania has similar ethnically based political problems in its relationship with Moldova and Ukraine. Moldovians in both Moldova and southwesternmost Ukraine are related ethnically to those people who inhabit northeastern Romania. There has been speculation about various possible new geopolitical alignments in the region, including the apparently unlikely scenario of Moldova becoming part of Romania, with which it was joined from 1918 to 1945. Ethnic and political complications make such a union fraught with danger, not the least because of a sizable Russian population group in eastern Moldova.

Hungary has other, though generally less severe, problems than those with Romania, related to the residence of large numbers of Magyars in Slovakia and the Serbian-controlled Vojvodina. Political problems associated with the large Magyar minority in southern Slovakia compound Slovakia's other ethnically based problems (notably within ethnically complex, easternmost Slovakia). Slovakia also has a complicated economic interrelationship with the Czech Republic, from which it had a political "velvet (i.e., peaceful) divorce" after the collapse of communism and the USSR. Fortunately, the small and dwindling Magyar minority in Austria, who live primarily in its easternmost province of Burgenland, has resulted in few problems and presented no impediment to ever closer relations between the two countries. Burgenland, originally part of the province of West Hungary, was awarded to Austria in a complicated and disputed plebiscite after World War I.

Bulgaria also faces a number of potential ethnoterritorial disputes. Most importantly, Bulgarians generally have an extremely negative view of the long, harsh rule of the Ottoman Turks over its people and territory, and the country has many problems associated with its large Muslim population. At least some Bulgarian Muslims identify themselves as Turks (and are so recognized by the government of Turkey), whereas the old autocratic socialist regime under Todor Zhivkov argued that these people were Slavs who converted to Islam under Ottoman rule and should rightly reacquire Slavic family names. A campaign to enforce this process led to a large migration of Muslim peoples to Turkey and a related return flow when these people found poor economic and political conditions awaiting them there. The as yet unresolved tensions between ethnic Bulgarians and Muslims have caused social, economic, and political problems within Bulgaria and strained its relations with bordering Turkey. In addition, Bulgaria has also historically had ethnoterritorial problems with all of its other neighbors—Macedonia, Romania, and Greece. Like Slovakia, Bulgaria's struggling new government hardly needs these issues to add to the burden of its serious domestic economic and political problems.

Besides serious ethnoterritorial problems with Serbia over Kosovo, discussed in a later section, Albania has also had problems with Greece. The opening up of Albanian society and its borders has led to the emigration of ethnic Greeks to Greece. However, in addition, large numbers of Albanians crossed the frontier seeking economic opportunity. They have found work based largely on their willingness to accept very low wages, but they face animosity within Greece, reportedly based both on ethnic discrimination and competition for employment.

Even the relatively ethnically homogeneous Czech Republic and Poland are not without ethnic-based domestic and international troubles. In the Czech Republic some lingering problems are associated with the rights of Slovaks residing within it as well as indications of rising ethnic/regional consciousness among Moravians (closely related to Czechs) and Silesians (many with Polish ties). The ethnic and regional consciousness of Moravians was demonstrated by a 1991 census in the Czech Republic, in which 1.4 million Moravians identified themselves as Moravian rather than Czech. Fortunately, these issues have thus far created no serious international problems. The Czech Republic's relationship with Germany is complicated by the expulsion of millions of Sudeten Germans from Czechoslovakia after World War II. Rhetoric intensified between the neighboring states in 1996, emanating from political pressure by refugee organizations in Germany which have been seeking apologies and compensation for lost property from the Czechs. An agreement in 1997 between the countries seems to have defused the problem.

In Poland, political change has led to some increased self-identification of citizens with their German ethnic roots, ties that would have probably been ignored or suppressed earlier. Some people believe that millions of Poles may have such ethnic links, though assimilation and outmigration have without doubt substantially reduced the minority group. The extent to which a resurgence of identification with German ethnicity could unsettle German-Polish relations or impact domestic Polish politics, especially in once German-dominated Silesia, is not clear. However, by the mid-1990s the issue was posing no serious threats to official German-Polish relations, which are reasonably good.

Finally, the lessening of authoritarian rule in ECSEE countries in the late 1980s, as well as the Yugoslav conflicts, have resulted in a wave of emigrants from the east toward the west, particularly to Germany. Some of these people claim to be political asylum seekers; most are more likely seeking greater economic opportunity. Some ethnic Germans, especially from Romania, have exercised a constitutional right to acquire residency and German citizenship.

Several other ethnically based international disputes could be elaborated on here—such as those between Estonia and Russia (Russians comprise one-third of the Estonian population) and Lithuania and Poland (based primarily on complaints of a Polish minority in the Vilnius region). There are fewer examples of concrete steps toward resolution of ethnic problems. One such example is Slovakia's official acceptance of codification of the Rusyn language. The Rusyns are comprised of several subgroups, who live predominantly in the Carpathians of eastern Slovakia but also in neighboring areas of Ukraine, Hungary, and Poland (where they have been referred to as "Lemkos"). The Rusyns have historic ties to Ukraine, and some people, including some among the group itself, believe they should be considered Ukrainian. However, it appears that the long-simmering issue of recognition of the population group within Slovakia has been resolved, supported by that country's government, a number of international institutions, and Rusyn cultural organizations in Central Europe.

Despite some positive steps toward ethnic conciliation such as the Rusyn case and agreements between Slovakia and Hungary on the rights of Slovak-Hungarians, the persistence of ethnically based intolerance and international problems in ECSEE, including real and potential boundary disputes, presents serious problems to the world and to Europe. The tragedies in the former Yugoslavia punctuate this reality. Higher levels of ethnically based intolerance in Central and Southeastern Europe in comparison to Western Europe could be based on lower levels of education and intercultural contact in the former region. Intolerance could also be related to one of the basic roots of relatively low levels of education—relatively low levels of economic development. In any event, ethnic and religious diversity and intolerance play an important role in the turbulent political history of East Central and Southeastern Europe and the geopolitical instability that gives the region its appellation as a "shatterbelt." Among other impacts, these conditions threaten the region's ability to improve what today are often poor economic conditions by "developed world" standards.

ECONOMIC GEOGRAPHY

Economic Conditions in the ECSEE Countries in 1918

Most of the countries of East Central and Southeastern Europe were poorly developed economically before World War I. With the exception of some mineral exploitation and the establishment of a few industries—especially in the Czech lands, the Banat in today's Romania, Slovenia, Upper Silesia, and some of the main cities such as Prague and Budapest—the area was predominantly agricultural. The output of minerals was most often shipped to industries located in the Vienna Basin, to other developing manufacturing centers in the Austro-Hungarian Empire, or to foreign countries in exchange for needed manufactured goods. The iron industry, with relatively wide distribution, was closely related to local raw materials and fuels. The availability of the metal encouraged engineering, and the distribution of coalfields, mainly lignite, laid the basis for chemical production. Urban settlements, with few exceptions, were small and separated, and between 70 and 90 percent of the population was rural—except in Bohemia, Upper Silesia, and parts of Hungary. In East Central Europe, agriculture was dominated by large private and church estates, often owned by absentee landlords, and the land-hungry peasantry had little opportunity to obtain property. Large numbers of peasants migrated to the United States between the late nineteenth century and the beginning of World War I, with a smaller number going to Canada, Australia, South Africa, and Brazil. Communications tied regional urban centers with Vienna and to a lesser degree with Budapest, Berlin, and St. Petersburg.

Basic socioeconomic and political changes followed the breakdown of Central and Eastern Europe's empires in 1918, resulting in the incorporation of some of the small independent states of Southeastern Europe into newly organized, larger units as well as the emergence of several new independent states. Agriculture, the basis of the economy for every one of the newly independent countries, increased output between 1919 and 1938, but in spite of land reforms, the land hunger of peasants could not be satisfied. Peasants, on the whole, were highly taxed, paid high interest rates, and were frequently caught in a price squeeze between industrial and agricultural prices. The population was rapidly expanding, roughly three times as fast as in Western Europe, and agriculture was characterized by large surpluses and low labor productivity.

With the exception of Czechoslovakia, the newly created states after World War I lacked a satisfactory basis for the development of industry, even though individual plants, which laid the foundation for later industrialization, did exist in Poland (Upper Silesia), Hungary, and Slovenia. However, local raw materials, which could have been the basis for a prospering industry, were sold abroad, and finished products were purchased at high prices. Foreign capital for fresh investments was scarce, and available funds usually found their way primarily into extractive industries. The exploitation of raw material was largely in the hands of foreign investors. In Yugoslavia, for example, all the capital in the copper mines at Bor (French concession), the lead mines at Trepca (English concession), and the manganese and bauxite mines was foreign. Little attention was given to the possibility of developing consumer goods from local raw materials, such as agricultural products and timber. Industries often produced goods for export only, without thought of developing a domestic market.

It was, therefore, not surprising that the world depression of 1929, the after-effects of which were felt throughout the 1930s, had a devastating impact on the economies of these countries. The few foreign investments for the most part dried up. Political rivalry among the small states encouraged a drive for autocracy, and what little reasoning was originally manifest in economic development in the region was clouded by divergent nationalistic aspirations.

Except in Czechoslovakia, and to a lesser degree in Poland, the pattern of trade consisted of export of agricultural products and other raw materials (e.g., ores and oil) and import of manufactured goods. ECSEE also served as Europe's only grain export region. However, total interwar trade volume was small—less than 7 percent of Europe's imports and less than 10 percent of its exports.

Actually, ECSEE had only about 10 years of peaceful, independent development prior to the socialist era—from 1919 to the outbreak of the world depression in 1929. The depression found the Eastern European countries still in the midst of making adjustments and major decisions related to their newly created independence. Although the height of the depression was passed by 1934, its repercussions were felt until the beginning of World War II. Unfortunately, these problems only compounded a host of other economic problems impeding economic development in ECSEE.

Origins of Regional Development Problems in Eastern Europe

Although some of the reasons for the relatively low level of economic development in Eastern Europe are reasonably well substantiated and accepted, there is still a rather surprising diversity of views and related, unresolved ambiguity about the root causes of the region's lagging performance in comparison to Western Europe. The following provides a short overview of the diverse, yet often interrelated, factors that appear to have held back East European development.

First, agriculture has traditionally been less productive in Central and Southeastern Europe than in the West, owing only partly to adverse environmental conditions (e.g., a somewhat colder, drier, continental climate in Northeastern in comparison to Northwestern Europe and rugged terrain with associated poorer soils in many parts of Southeastern Europe). However, the Pannonian Basin and the Walachian Plain do offer comparatively good conditions for agriculture. Perhaps more important explanations for a lagging agricultural sector are a long era of feudalism, particularly imposition of the so-called second serfdom in the fifteenth century as well as the more recent era of socialized agriculture, both of which were punctuated by national economic policies adverse to agriculture. In neither era was the potential for technological change in the sector ever achieved (Fig. 12-7). The emergence of a more important peasant agricultural sector in the nineteenth century and maintenance of substantial private agricultural holdings under socialism (in Yugoslavia and Poland) were

FIGURE 12-7 A Romanian farmer with relatively primitive wooden tools. (W. H. Berentsen)

not especially mitigating factors, since the farms were generally small, undercapitalized, technologically backward, and too poorly linked to both domestic and international markets.

In Southeastern Europe agriculture was especially disadvantaged by relatively little influence from skilled German settlers, whose productivity positively influenced parts of today's Poland, Czech Republic, Hungary, Slovenia, and Croatia. Bulgaria, in particular, had one of Europe's highest proportions of agriculture on very small farms, with more than 50 percent of holdings by area in farms smaller than 25 acres (10 hectares). The conditions described above were compounded by relatively rapid natural population increases and high population densities in rural areas.

A second complex of factors retarding East European development was, of course, the relatively poor performance of the industrial sector and the relatively poorly developed infrastructure. Again, lagging industrial development can only be partially explained by the natural resource base. ECSEE's resource base includes a diverse set of metals and minerals, but it is characterized by relatively small, scattered deposits and a serious shortage of fossil fuels. Romanian oil and gas resources are by international comparisons of comparatively minor importance. Lack of coal probably played an especially important role in

the slow development of industry in Southeastern Europe during the Industrial Revolution, a period during which Western Europe's levels of development rapidly outdistanced those in the East and opened a gap that has never been closed.

The lack of many navigable rivers and the difficult conditions for railroad construction also disadvantaged Southeastern Europe. The region was comparatively distant from the rapidly developing West European rail network, making it more difficult to integrate rail systems with the West, although areas now in Poland, the Czech Republic, and Hungary were more fortunate in this regard. Construction of reliable hard-surfaced roads has also been slow and late in coming to most regions of East Central and Southeastern Europe.

Policies for the development of infrastructure and manufacturing were especially poor in areas under Ottoman rule; they were not substantially better in areas controlled by the Russian Empire or in the parts of the Austro-Hungarian Empire ruled from Budapest. Dramatic differences in, for example, the density of rail lines in the 1990s remain obvious between areas under the control of more economically progressive governments and those dominated by unresponsive governments during the late nineteenth and early twentieth centuries, a critical developmental epoch in European history. Western Poland (formerly German) has a far higher rail density than eastern Poland (formerly Russian dominated). Slovenia (formerly ruled from Austria) has a better network than Serbia and Macedonia (long dominated by Ottoman rule).

The economic development policies of the newly emerged, independent countries of ECSEE immediately before and after World War I were constrained by the lack of trained, experienced managers; by ongoing ethnic conflicts and rampant "small-state nationalism"; by the disruptions and devastation of the world wars and regional conflicts (e.g., Balkan Wars); and by the depression of the 1930s. Although subsequent socialist regimes partially addressed infrastructural problems, they showed a striking inability to sponsor forward-looking industrial policies. Industrial growth under socialist rule came at a frightful cost in resources, environmental quality, and human health.

The small, geographically splintered ECSEE markets and the region's poor trade and transport-communication linkages between regional and international markets are a third group of factors that have always curtailed economic growth. This situation has been exacerbated by autarchic economic policies engendered by nationalism, Stalinist thought, and the more recent failures of the poorly developed market within the CMEA. The CMEA originally discouraged trade with the West, and later could not provide the financial resources and technology needed to benefit from burgeoning trade within Western Europe. Poor economic development policies and related worsening terms of trade have long resulted in too few trade linkages between the ECSEE and the world economy. Intensifying this negative picture have been the inadequately developed East European financial institutions, which need to encourage savings and support trade and capital investment. Too little trade and investment have reduced productivity in several ways, including shielding producers from competition and reducing the importation of badly needed technology.

Needless to say, poor levels of economic development and the related lack of middle class savings constrained development of a local source of capital and, thereby, reduced investment, a fourth complex of factors that has negatively affected economic development in ECSEE. Urban growth in the East was slowed by lack of occupational specialization in services and manufacturing. This was cause and effect of the slow development of a consumer and mercantile-oriented middle class in the region. A middle class also failed to emerge in ECSEE owing to political conditions (e.g., feudalism and foreign domination/exploitation) and to slow economic growth. The lack of a strong, historic middle class, as well as the policies adopted during the era of socialist rule, also deprived the region of a source of motivated, educated workers and managers; aspiring inventors, investors, and industrialists; and related acquisitive consumers. Individualism, individual achievement, and consumption are less well developed in East Central and Southeastern Europe than in Western Europe. Although the relative and comparative merits and problems of the capitalist versus socialist, and Protestant versus Catholic social milieus continue to be debated in Europe (especially in the rapidly changing East), the development of Western markets and productivity has unquestionably benefited from the political and economic rights of the individual and perhaps also from a "Protestant work ethic"—though this last named factor is disputed.

Investment from external, international sources has been discouraged by many factors—the small local markets; poor infrastructure (especially transport systems); poorly developed local financial systems; political instability; and, most recently, socialist economic policies that encouraged self-sufficiency within the CMEA and limited private ownership and personal incentives. The enervating bureaucratic morass of the socialist societies further disadvantaged their economies. Thus, the possible advantages of using inexpensive labor, access to the enormous West European (and potential Russian) market, and imported technology to entice external capital to help support economic development have not been utilized. The avowed social and economic advantages of socialism never compensated for these foregone, potential sources of growth.

Political instability represents a fifth factor retarding development in ECSEE. Investments and economic development policies have been made more difficult by the virtually ongoing political uncertainty and crises in East Central and

Southeastern Europe over the last century. The weakening and dissolution of the Ottoman Empire in Europe was accompanied by strife among the Austro-Hungarian and Russian empires and several emergent, nationalist-minded new states in the region (e.g., Serbia and Bulgaria). There followed, of course, an era of world war and the complete collapse of the empires, without the emergence of political and economic cooperation among the dominantly Slavic successor states in the interwar period. The depression, World War II, and an era of politically harsh, economically disadvantageous Soviet occupation and domination covered the 1930–1990 period. In the 1990s the region's small states face not only the problems ensuing from a century of neglect, but also heightened economic competition from a host of European and Asian countries and resurgent nationalism within and across ECSEE borders.

Finally, despite avowed concern for reducing regional inequalities and for efficiently using regional human and natural resources, socialist societies implemented few explicit, successful programs to achieve these goals. Regional problems in socialist societies—including backward rural areas, relatively overdeveloped capital cities, and severely polluted mining and industrial regions—were of secondary concern in comparison with attempts to cope with pressing national economic problems and with socialist/communist parties' concerns for maintaining political power. Regional problems and inequalities under socialism appear to have been as great as those in the capitalist world, whereas regional policies in East Central and Southeastern Europe seemed, if anything, less responsive to them than in Western Europe.

In sum, a host of interrelated factors offer a reasonable explanation for the symptoms of lagging socioeconomic development in ECSEE. Shortages of natural resources, capital, technology, skilled workers, and managers; inadequately developed infrastructure and markets; and relatively poor access to large Western markets, all appear to have combined with centuries of poor political and economic management to put the region where it is today. In general, the countries of East Central and Southeastern have relatively poor levels of development in terms of current levels of output and productivity and in terms of an economic struc-

ture. They also have limited immediate prospects for successful adaptation to current international economic conditions.

Economic Change in the Socialist Era

Despite both political rhetoric and actual development efforts, the economic goals of socialist planners were not achieved during the several decades of autocratic socialist rule in ECSEE. Efforts to modernize the economies of East Central and Southeastern Europe were based on adoption of the Soviet model of socioeconomic planning, though approaches varied somewhat both between countries and through time.

After World War II, the ECSEE market economies were replaced with Soviet-type central planning economies under large bureaucracies controlled by the Communist party. Through such forced central control, the communists hoped to achieve rapid industrialization and lay the foundation for modern industrial states. Industry, especially heavy industry, received the highest priority in investment planning and became the prime vector of change in the spatial economic structure. Location decisions for investments in industry became an important aspect of state and party policy. A great effort was made to improve skills and to absorb the large surplus of agricultural labor force existing in all of the East Central and Southeastern European countries. In each country emphasis also was placed on self-sufficiency and reliance on internal sources of capital accumulation. This economic nationalism resulted in increased similarities in the development pattern of the individual countries and in the absence of specialization and regional cooperation, not to speak of integration. In spite of the organization of CMEA in the early 1950s, most countries' development was heavily directed by Moscow, with the exceptions of Romania, Albania, and Yugoslavia, which established considerable economic independence from it.

The USSR exerted its influence through political and economic leadership, including at times threatened or actual military intervention and warnings to withhold petroleum deliveries. Industrialization on the scale attempted was often impossible without key raw material shipments from the Soviet Union. In view of the deficiencies in the natural endowment of the Central and Southeastern European countries, the massive industrialization could only be accomplished with the USSR's economic and political support. The region's dependence on Soviet raw material shipments gave the Soviet Union a key economic and political lever.

Economic and political changes during the 45 years of communist rule in the ECSEE countries led to great structural changes in the economy, marked by an increase in industrial capacity and relative share of manufacturing in total economic output. The share of industry and services in total domestic output (GDP) of the relatively highly developed economy of Czechoslovakia exceeded 85 percent in the late 1980s, and in the other ECSEE countries it ranged between 40 and 80 percent. Certainly, the most dramatic change in the economies of the Eastern European countries was in the agricultural sector. Owing to rapid industrialization, the share of agricultural labor had declined greatly by the early 1990s to 10 to 30 percent of the total employed, with Albania (60%) as well as Bosnia and Romania, having high percentages and the Czech Republic the lowest. Additional decreases in agriculture's contribution to GDP are expected by the end of the century. The growth of industry's contribution to GDP was leveling off in all countries of the region by the 1980s and fell in most countries during the difficult era of economic transition during the early 1990s, while the service sectors have been growing in importance.

Several eras of postwar economic development are identifiable in ECSEE through the mid-1990s, although developments in individual CMEA countries vary somewhat from the following pattern. First, from the end of World War II to the late 1940s, governments emphasized reconstruction and then expansion of already existing industries throughout the region. During this period, the state acquired considerable land through expulsion or withdrawal of foreign landowners, outright nationalization, and restrictions on the size of private holdings.

Second, the period from the late 1940s to the end of the 1950s, the so-called command economy

development phase, emphasized industrialization and centralized methods of planning and management. Some variations among countries, however, occurred after Nikita Khrushchev became Soviet premier in 1953—Yugoslavia diverged from these patterns after 1950 and Albania after 1953. With regard to agriculture, the period on either side of 1950 was characterized by emphasis on collectivization, despite considerable peasant resistance. In Poland after 1956 and in Yugoslavia after 1953, most collectives were disbanded, and both of these countries thereafter had much more private agriculture than other parts of the region. Collectivization was again emphasized elsewhere in ECSEE late in the 1950s and was concluded by the early 1960s. Finally, the party, in cooperation with different government bodies, including central planning authorities, established at each administrative level mandatory five-year and annual plans for enterprises in all of the countries.

Third, only when the negative consequences of these planning methods and forced growth policies became obvious were serious discussions about possible changes initiated. The gradual dismantling of the Stalinist development model by Khrushchev and his increased emphasis on the CMEA as a vehicle of economic integration in the region were suspended as a policy in the early 1960s owing to resistance led by Romania. A trend toward increased trade with the West both reflected and necessitated economic reform efforts beginning in the mid-1960s. The economic reform in Yugoslavia initiated in 1965 went furthest, giving emphasis to decentralization of major economic and political decision making, although the party reemerged as an important force in key policy decisions in the 1970s. In the new system of economic reforms, the countries in the region tried to move cautiously toward decentralization of planning and management functions, but generally without relaxing party control over vital economic decisions. The economic reform movement after 1965 caused considerable political upheaval in ECSEE, as exemplified both in the political turmoil in Poland during the 1970s and in the domestically initiated liberalization within Czechoslovakia in 1968, which led to Soviet intervention and occupation. Opposition by party bureaucracies ultimately was the major reason for the collapse of the reform movement. Always the maverick, however, Albania developed strong ties with the People's Republic of China and adopted its own Maoist development strategy based on emphasis upon the rural sector.

Fourth, by the 1970s the failure of economic reform made the Central and Southeastern European countries more anxious to gain access to Western technology, to become more competitive in Western markets, and to adjust to sharply higher raw material costs. The Soviet Union was interested in such a development in view of the beneficial impact it would exert on its own long-term industrial development. Worldwide price increases of oil and raw materials during the 1970s, including those sold by the USSR, as well as the cost of imported technology, left most ECSEE countries with sizable foreign debts by the early 1980s. The debt became particularly large in Poland and Romania; Romania then took drastic actions to eliminate the debt at great cost and burden for its average citizens. Albania broke its ties with China in 1976, and for a time became completely isolated in political and economic terms.

Fifth, the CMEA countries were under considerable pressure in the 1980s to follow the Soviet example under Gorbachev to initiate economic reforms in order to resolve their economic problems. However, the countries responded in quite different ways depending on ever growing political independence from Moscow. The GDR, Romania, Bulgaria, and Czechoslovakia initiated reforms very slowly. Reform and relatively open discussion of potential options occurred earlier and proceeded faster in Hungary and Poland. Albania remained isolated and unchanged, and internal political problems in Yugoslavia overshadowed efforts toward economic change, although an important part of this dispute was the desire by relatively prosperous Slovenia and Croatia to have greater political and economic autonomy within the Yugoslav federation. The Hungarian reforms of 1968 favoring greater private initiatives, especially in agriculture, and reduction in government controls—so-called "goulash" communism—were particularly cited

by Gorbachev as a model for development in the Soviet Union and the other countries.

Gorbachev's open discussion of the need for political and economic reform, his growing reluctance to use Soviet military force to impose policy from Moscow, an ever worsening economic situation across the region, and the long-held contempt of most citizens for their governments' policies combined to ignite a series of sometimes peaceful, sometimes violent political revolts across Central and Eastern Europe in 1989. One inflexible regime after another fell in the face of internal pressure, and, for the first time in 50 years, the Soviet military did not take action. Among the more dramatic events of this startling era were the opening of the Berlin Wall (for Americans a primary symbol of the Iron Curtain), ascension to power of once imprisoned Lech Walesa in Poland and Vaclav Havel in Czechoslovakia, violent revolution in Romania, and, somewhat later, the opening of Albania to the outside world.

Following this era of revolutionary change, all of Central and Eastern Europe is now experiencing a trying period of structural changes in political and economic organization. In most, but not all, countries, the role of private enterprise, more open markets, civil institutions ("civil society"), and democratic rule has increased dramatically. This is especially true in Poland, Hungary, the Czech Republic, Slovakia, Slovenia, and eastern Germany, and least true in Serbia and Romania. Political and economic evolution in the other states of the region is somewhat mixed.

Removal of central authoritarian power, virtual elimination of the Soviet military threat, and the end of the Cold War also unleashed dramatic domestic political forces in Central and Eastern Europe. The Germanys rapidly united; separate Czech and Slovak states were proclaimed; and war ravaged the disintegrating Yugoslavia. The wars in the former Yugoslavia have threatened to reignite international conflict among the many small, highly nationalistic states of Southeastern Europe, which have dangerously overlapping aspirations for territory and strikingly different interpretations of history. Thus, for example, the weak and small Macedonian state has been threatened on all sides by neighbors (Serbia, Bulgaria,

Albania, and Greece) that dispute the existence of a separate ethnic identity for Macedonia or, in the case of Greece, are suspicious of its potential territorial claims on them. In the mid-1990s the maintenance of a unified, independent state in war-torn Bosnia-Herzegovina remains in doubt, despite a newly instituted peace plan.

The economic transition is also proving to be a painful one, with high levels of unemployment and falling standards of living for many people across the region, some of whom are convinced more than ever that instituting capitalism means greater inequality among classes, greater vulnerability to foreign influence, and increased crime. These problems have resulted in resurgent xenophobia and increased political extremism, including both rejuvenation of the political fortunes of (often altered) socialist political parties and ultraconservative, ultranationalist movements. These conditions will likely lead to at least some level of domestic political instability in most countries of the region well into the twenty-first century.

Regional Patterns of Socioeconomic Well-being

An overview of the cumulative impacts of the socialist regimes' inherited regional strengths and weaknesses as well as the legacy of their policies is provided by studying Figure 12-8, which presents an intriguing survey of the socioeconomic well-being of the regions of East Central and Southeastern Europe in the mid-1980s. Zaniewski (1992) provides an index of social well-being based on variables measuring health care standards (infant mortality and per capita hospital bed availability), housing space per capita, and social infrastructure (telephone and television access per capita). The construction of such broad indices of well-being is fraught with problems and difficult choices for a researcher, but the survey's results in this case, for the most part, confirm widely accepted generalizations.

Relatively high levels of social (and economic) well-being in Hungary, the Czech Republic, and Slovenia conform well with most people's perceptions of the regions, although the relatively favorable position of Bulgaria in the mid-1980s generally comes as a surprise. Bulgaria's position at that time was verified, however, by one of the region's lowest rates of infant death and an income level comparable to Hungary's. Relatively high levels of well-being in urban regions, such as in Warsaw, Poznan, Łódź, Wrocław (all in Poland), Budapest, Bucharest, and Sofia, and low levels of well-being in rural Galicia (southeastern Poland), Walachia and Moldovia (eastern Romania), Bosnia-Herzgovina, Kosovo, and Macedonia (former Yugoslavia), are also not surprising.

Regional inequalities are greatest in the former Yugoslavia; there living standards range from relatively good in Slovenia to very poor, by European standards, in Kosovo and Macedonia. For example, in 1992 infant mortality rates differed from 8.9 in Slovenia to 35.3 in Macedonia. Inequalities in well-being were important underlying factors in the ethnic and political disputes that led to the demise of the Yugoslavia federation, a topic that will be discussed in more detail in a later section of this chapter. Regional inequalities have led to political and ethnic problems in other countries as well, notably in the former Czechoslovakia. But the level of inequalities in these cases is lower than in Yugoslavia and usually results from rural-urban differences, especially between relatively prosperous capital regions and poor rural hinterlands.

Some relatively good news in Zaniewski's study is that, in general, between 1970 and 1987 regional inequalities declined within all of the countries, and standards of social well-being improved more rapidly in the less well-developed regions. This finding is partial verification of socialist claims of policy emphasis on and achievement of reduced social and regional inequalities. However, similar trends during much of the same period in the capitalist world and comparable levels of regional inequality in both capitalist and ECSEE countries in the late 1980s place doubt on the socialist governments' claims that they had greater success in dealing with regional inequalities than governments in Western Europe. Depending on how one defines things, it does seem tenable to argue that social inequalities were

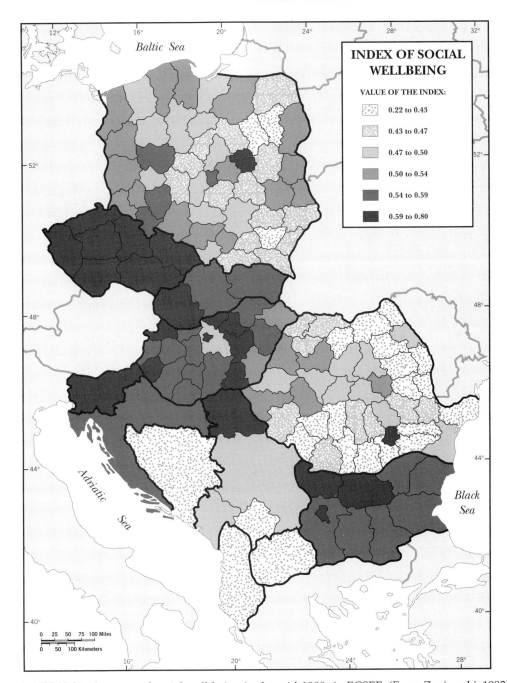

FIGURE 12-8 Indications of social well-being in the mid-1980s in ECSEE. (From Zaniewski, 1992)

smaller in socialist than in capitalist societies, related both to the absence of extremely wealthy capitalists and to relatively low material living standards for common people. Common people generally did have a rudimentary social "safety net" in ECSEE; but well-connected politicians and celebrities (e.g., sports stars) lived better.

Unfortunately, social inequalities in particular, and probably regional inequalities as well, have been widening in ECSEE during the current period of rapid political and economic change. This at least in part reflects uneven abilities among social groups and regions to respond to the problems and opportunities resulting from these changes. Thus, for example, people with better education and political connections, and regions with better infrastructure and favorable sectoral structures, are adapting better than others. Increasing inequalities are causing considerable social unrest and political change, as dramatically indicated by the election victories in the early 1990s in many ECSEE countries (e.g., Poland, Hungary, Slovakia, Bulgaria, Slovenia, and Lithuania) of left-leaning parties, whose socialist-communist predecessors were widely rejected in earlier elections held around 1990.

Natural Resources

As one possible basis for economic development, the countries of Eastern Europe possess a variety of natural resources; unfortunately, these are limited in quality and quantity. During the socialist era, until the early 1960s restrictions on imports from non-Soviet bloc sources and Western restrictions on trade with ECSEE resulted in overdiversification and uneconomic investments in expensive raw materials production. Still, rapid industrial growth during the last 50 years placed great demands on available fuels and minerals. Hence, the region became increasingly dependent on imports, most often from the Soviet Union. The USSR sometimes provided raw materials at relatively low cost, but this advantage was undercut by sporadic supply problems and fluctuating prices.

Soviet-enforced industrialization programs emphasized abundant use of capital and labor, and cheap raw materials, which were largely lack-

ing in East Central and Southeastern Europe. The intensive development of high-cost, energy-intensive industrialization in the region during the early postwar period yielded high economic growth rates, but ultimately at high environmental and health costs, import dependence, and an outmoded and structurally weak manufacturing sector. Industrialization was a basic part of Soviet ideology, however, and added economic strength to Soviet-CMEA political ties. This development was also beneficial to the Soviet Union's own strategic requirements, especially that of obtaining urgently needed goods from the more advanced ECSEE countries. Thus, efforts to create socialist autarchy, especially during this accelerated drive for industrialization, overcommitted the region's available fuels and raw materials.

Coal is generally the foremost fuel and raw material resource of the East Central and Southeast European countries, but (with the exception of bituminous coal in Poland) most of it is lignite (or "brown") coal. With the exception of Romania, all the region's countries relied on coal for their domestic industries during the socialist era, often without regard to cost and invariably at the expense of the environment. Significant changes in the energy mix only began to occur in the 1960s or 1970s and lagged behind developments in the West. Poland, East Germany (the GDR), and Czechoslovakia relied heavily on coal. All countries deficient in high-grade coal resources (particularly the GDR and Bulgaria) imported Soviet coal, with an increasing share originating in the Donets Basin of the eastern Ukraine. Poland, ECSEE's preeminent coal producer and exporter, supplied substantial quantities to the USSR's fuel-deficient western border regions and to other CMEA countries. Lignite was widely mined and used for a variety of industrial and domestic purposes—to the detriment of the environment and human health.

By the early 1990s a number of changes became apparent in the fuel supply situation for East Central and Southeastern Europe. Although coal remains the most important fuel source in most countries, its importance has waned considerably in Hungary (where oil and natural gas are now dominant) and in the Czech and Slovak Republics (where oil and nuclear power now claim a larger share of fuel consumption).

Poland has long been the region's major net exporter of fuels owing to its own sizable bituminous coal deposits, located mainly in the Upper Silesian district. Despite steep declines in production after 1989, Poland remains by far Europe's major coal producer, and coal accounts for about 75 percent of the country's total energy consumption. Natural gas and oil production is minimal. Poland's only other industrial raw material of note is copper, for which it leads Europe in production.

The Czech and Slovak Republics' petroleum and natural gas requirements have traditionally been largely met by imports from the Soviet Union and now come from Russia. Some oil is drilled in southern Moravia, and natural gas is produced near Ostrava (both in the eastern half of the Czech Republic) and near Košice (eastern Slovakia). Oil and gas pipelines between Russia and Western Europe through Eastern Europe allow good access for the Czech and Slovak Republics to fossil fuel supplies, assuming that Russian oil production, which began falling rapidly after 1988, stabilizes and the countries can afford to pay for the imports.

The Czech Republic's reserves of bituminous coal and lignite are at the Ostrava-Karvina Basin in Silesia on the Polish border. Bituminous coal resources are limited; poorer quality lignite is available in ample quantities, although it is highly polluting. Production of both coals began falling in 1987, but the country remains one of Europe's larger producers of both. The Czech Republic also possesses considerable reserves of uranium. Following the end of World War II and up to recent years, the former Soviet Union had priority in exploiting these reserves. Several nuclear power plants were completed, and many more are still under construction, at least one with involvement of capital and technology from the United States. Projections for the future are for higher levels of nuclear power generation. However, the country faces the hazardous choice of a fuel supply mix of either highly polluting coal or increased nuclear power use with fear of nuclear accidents. It appears that the relative importance of nuclear power may gain somewhat in the near future.

With the exception of bauxite, manganese, and uranium, Hungary has a poor mineral supply, and the great majority of its industrial raw materials must be imported. Notable bauxite deposits are found largely along the Bakony Hills. In the past Hungary exported alumina and manganese to the Soviet Union. Fossil fuel production is quite small and began declining still further after the late 1980s.

Romania, with its relatively modest petroleum and natural gas reserves, was once an important exporter of crude oil. In spite of expanding drilling areas, including a thus far unsuccessful search offshore in the Black Sea, and some of the world's deepest wells, increased supplies of indigenous production have not kept up with needs. Romania has therefore been faced with ever-increasing imports, especially to supply its large petrochemical industry. Output for all fossil fuels declined dramatically in the early 1990s, both reflecting and contributing to the country's precarious economic situation. Important oilfields are at Ploesti and along the eastern and southern flanks of the Carpathian Mountains (Oltenia and western Moldovia), and in some parts of the middle and lower Danubian Plain. These developments laid the basis for the growth of important oil-refining and petrochemical industries. Because of possible pollution at coastal sites near developing tourist areas on the Black Sea, imported oil is refined inland.

Natural gas resources make important contributions to Romania's energy consumption. Gas first replaced oil for fuel purposes, but owing to the energy crisis, power stations have utilized more lignite; thus, additional gas can be made available to the chemical industry. Much of Romania's coal production is located near Oltenia south of Bucharest. Some hard coal (anthracite) is located in the Jiu Valley in the southwest. An accelerated development of Romania's considerable hydroelectric potential, including a joint development with the former Yugoslavia of the Iron Gate hydropower dam on the Danube (output of 2 billion kwh) (Fig. 12-9), increased hydropower but has not provided the country with sufficient energy production.

Romania's one-time independence from fuel and raw materials imports was a major contributing factor in its quasi-independent foreign policy. Romania also produced notable amounts of iron ore, manganese, bauxite, chrome, nickel, molybde-

FIGURE 12-9 Joint hydropower station built by Romania and the former Yugoslavia across the Danube River southeast of Turnu-Severin. The hydropower station, the dam, a highway that connects Romania and Serbia, and a lock on both the Romanian and Serbian sides of the river were completed in 1971. The station produces more than 2 billion kwh of electricity. The view is from the Romanian side, with the power station and a lock in the foreground, looking toward Serbia. The hydropower station is located at the eastern end of the 90-mile long (145-km) Iron Gate (Djerdap) gorge of the Danube River. (Romanian Library, New York)

num, and a variety of nonferrous metals such as copper, zinc, lead, and mercury-bearing ores. At the same time, some raw material imports have become a necessity in response to increased industrial needs and the rapid decline in Romania's oil production.

Bulgaria has few fossil fuel resources, although it does produce a modest amount of lignite coal. It has a better supply of a broad range of minerals and metals (especially lead, zinc, and iron ores), which help supply domestic consumption and are located primarily in the Balkan range.

Albania is a small fossil fuel producer, although it has substantially developed its hydroelectric potential. It exports both oil and chrome. Albania is the leading European producer of chrome and cobalt. Exploration for and development of Albanian natural resources are likely to evolve more rapidly now that the economy is becoming far more active in the global economy and it has better access to capital, technology, and markets. However, there do not appear to be prospects for resource discoveries or developments that will materially affect European production patterns.

The former Yugoslavia produced about one-fifth of its petroleum and natural gas needs in the Croatian-Slavonian fields and in the Banat, both in the northeast. Rapid increases in oil consumption during the 1970s and 1980s forced the country to import increasing quantities of oil from the Middle East and Libya, with whom it had good political relations. Not surprisingly, fossil fuel production fell sharply beginning in about 1990. The production of hydropower received considerable attention, and the former Yugoslavia was a large producer. One of the largest hydroelectric installations in Europe is the Djerdap power plant on the Danube, east of the Iron Gate gorge; its capacity is close to Grand Coulee Dam on the Columbia River in the United States (see Fig. 12-9). Territories within the former Yugoslavia, especially Serbia, Macedonia, and Bosnia-Herzegovina, produced a wide array of minerals and metals in relatively small quantities, notably bauxite, in which the former Yugoslavia led Europe in production. Undoubtedly, production of all of these resources has been negatively affected by the disruptions caused by war.

In general, East Central and Southeastern Europe is deficient in industrial resources, and in cases where resources are available, terrible environmental impacts have been associated with their exploitation. These problems are discussed in a later section of this chapter.

Agriculture

Excepting Albania and Bosnia, industry is the most important branch of the national economy in all East Central and Southeast European countries, but agricultural production does play a more important role there than it does in Northwestern Europe, for example. In the past, agriculture in ECSEE was often neglected and had a low priority in investment allocations. Not until new policies were adopted in the mid-1960s were most countries able to achieve better harvests. Mechanization played a slowly increasing role in expanding agricultural output, and introducing higher yielding varieties for cereals and the greatly increased use of fertilizers also raised yields. However, in both levels of mechanization and agricultural yields the region still lags behind Western Europe.

Although there were differing natural and economic conditions for each country, a common ideology and similar economic structures were clearly expressed in the agricultural policies of the CMEA countries under Soviet domination. Six basic factors typified the system of agricultural production and management in them, as well as to a certain extent in Albania and Yugoslavia.

First, agriculture was dominated by large-scale collective and state farms, which had little authority to set their own pricing and production goals and were ideologically committed to large-scale, communal agricultural operations (Fig. 12-10). Collectivization was halted and then reversed in Poland and the former Yugoslavia, although some large farms under public ownership remained. In Poland and the former Yugoslavia, a high percentage of arable land was farmed privately, not always with great success, owing to small farm size and undercapitalization. Second, emphasis on greater efficiency by way of increased investments did not produce the desired results; investment costs consistently increased faster than agricultur-

FIGURE 12-10 Private homestead engulfed by a collective farm in central Hungary. (W. H. Berentsen)

al output. Increased livestock production produced mixed results, in part owing to poor planning and related, sporadic feed shortages. Third, increasing demand for energy as well as environmental constraints became a real problem for most countries, in spite of the increased labor efficiency on large farms. The large farms, including livestock facilities, were often wasteful users of energy. Fourth, air and water pollution and misuse of areas with marginally productive soils were additional problems. Large-scale livestock facilities produced enormous quantities of wastes, which were often poorly stored or simply dumped into rivers, and were in part responsible for the increas-

ing environmental problems of the region. Fifth, technical innovations in agriculture in the Soviet Union and other CMEA countries proceeded slowly, with heavy dependence on imported technology. In part, this was the result of capital and foreign-exchange constraints. Even a long- established practice, such as the mechanized harvesting of grain, was not universal, because domestic production of harvesters had a low priority. Agriculture continued to employ large numbers of people, often at low levels of productivity (Fig. 12-11). Finally, agricultural development in ECSEE was characterized by increasing numbers of agroindustrial complexes. They linked industrial activities to

FIGURE 12-11 Arduously gathering hay in the Bialystok region of northeastern Poland. Small, labor intensive farms pose inherent limits on productivity and income in most cases for Polish farmers. (David Woodfall/Tony Stone Images)

the basic production processes of the farm and coordinated inputs, processing, and marketing under a single management unit, reducing bottlenecks and stabilizing seasonal labor requirements. The rural labor force was also usefully occupied with other economic activities in the off-season, and farms could simply shut down small, collateral industries during harvest season. State farms and agricultural cooperatives became large-scale agricultural industrial combines, selling products to other state enterprises.

Land reform played an early, important role in many of the ECSEE countries, and by 1948 most of the land was actually in the hands of the peasantry. However, land reform in the 1950s brought collectivization, often forcibly introduced, and state control. This, in turn, wrought basic structural changes. By the early 1960s the socialist sector (state and collective farms) controlled 85 to 95 percent of total agricultural land, except in Poland (15 percent) and Yugoslavia (23 percent). The attitude of most governments toward agriculture followed closely that of the Soviet Union. State farms were established mainly for breeding and experimental purposes, with workers paid an hourly rate. Collective farms of various types with land and labor contributed by the farmers were the most common form. They allowed the farmer to retain a small private household plot (1 acre, or 0.4 ha) usually for vegetables and fruit, a cow, a few pigs, and poultry. Farmers were allowed to sell their surplus on the nearby open market or to the collective.

The pattern of irregularly shaped, small strips of farmland, typical of the prewar landscape, was largely replaced by large fields suitable for combines and tractors, except in most parts of Poland and Yugoslavia where agriculture remained largely privatized (see Figs. 5-7 and 12-11). During the socialist era, the rural landscape often underwent a dramatic transition, especially impacting the traditional system of settlements, such as the ethnic German settlements of the Romanian Banat and the Yugoslav Vojvodina. Small, colorful, clustered farm buildings mostly disappeared and were replaced by larger stables, equipment, and repair buildings.

Except in Poland and the former Yugoslavia, where agricultural production has long been dominated by small private farms, the private agricultural sector of East Central and Southern Europe until around 1990 consisted mainly of very small plots, usually half a hectare (1.2 acres) in size, allocated by collective farms to their members. Often, urban dwellers were also allotted a small garden plot outside cities. In Bulgaria, Czechoslovakia, the GDR, Hungary, and Romania, private agriculture accounted for a small share of agricultural production and was intended to complement rather than supplant socialist agriculture. Individual farmers owned a sizable share of the livestock, 30 to 40 percent or more, and held similar shares in the production of meat, milk, eggs, fruits, and vegetables (the latter as much as 50 to 60 %), but government-dominated farms produced the vast majority of other crops, most notably grains for human and animal consumption. Relations between private producers and the socialist sector were formalized in contracts, whereby private farmers committed themselves to deliver a given quantity of output to the state or cooperative farms at government set prices. In return for signing such contracts, the farmers received improved access to inputs such as seed and fertilizer.

During the 1980s and into the early 1990s, while most West European countries were experiencing net gains in both total agricultural output and food production, most countries in East Central and, especially, Southeastern Europe showed little improvement. In many cases, production declined in ECSEE after 1989 or 1990. Hungary and Czechoslovakia were the only states in the region that demonstrated the modest progress more typical of Western European agriculture.

During the last couple of decades of socialist rule, Poland and Romania suffered periodic food shortages and related civil discontent. Complaints about poor quality and inconsistent supply of some food items, as well as the lack of fresh meat and produce, became common across the region. Efforts to develop animal husbandry through the introduction of industrial-type animal-rearing technologies, in which, for example, as many as 4000 dairy cows were managed at East German farms, did not achieve the hopes of central planners.

Several reasons account for the agricultural problems of the region's states. Poor climatic conditions led to annual fluctuations in agricultural output. Bureaucratic inefficiency and lack of personal incentives in collectivized agriculture resulted in the slow growth of productivity. Poor access to modern machinery, farm supplies, and infrastructure, and misdirected pricing policies further hampered production. Artificially low food prices under socialism led to increased demand and expectations by consumers that could not be satisfied. Many governments tried to meet consumer demands, especially for meat and bread, by increased feed grain imports, largely from the West. These imports often resulted in supporting low food prices and related, reduced domestic production. The sometimes serious food situation led the governments to provide incentives for the development of private plots, small areas of land permitting citizens to grow food for their personal needs and for sale in farmers' markets (except in Albania).

The agricultural exporting countries of ECSEE were adversely affected by protectionism, especially from the European Union countries. ECSEE countries lost their historical markets in Western Europe during World War II and the subsequent socialist era. In the current era a painful transition has occurred from a heavily state-dominated agricultural system to one with a mix of private farms and cooperative ventures that have evolved from the preexisting collective farms. The difficulty of easily transforming the old system to a viable new one is exemplified by falling agricultural output in several countries in the early 1990s, greatly expanded amounts of fallow land in eastern Germany, and Bulgaria's change from an important food exporter to a food importer. Privatization of agricultural holdings and establishment of efficient agricultural farms and firms have lagged. In Bulgaria, for example, by 1994 no more than one-half of farmland had been privatized, and most of that was in less productive agricultural regions. Where private farming exists, farm sizes are often too small to allow efficiency or reasonable living standards. In the south and east of Poland, average farm size is little more than 12 acres (5 ha). Romania has 5 million private farms, but most are only 2.5 to 8.5 acres in size (1 to 3.5 ha). Changes also have caused food prices to rise rapidly. In Romania, for example, average family expenditure on food jumped from around 20 percent of total income to nearly 80 percent over the period 1989–1992.

Regional patterns of agricultural production in the ECSEE countries vary according to environmental conditions. Polish farmers, because of often waterlogged soils and a short growing season, have traditionally relied on hardy potatoes and cabbage as the main root crops, rye and barley as the main cereal crops, and pig and some cattle production. New hybrid strains of wheat allow its cultivation in the large, open fields characteristic of the North European Lowlands along with sunflowers, used for making cooking oil. Much of the Czech lands and Slovakia are too hilly for extensive cultivation of cereal crops. However, yields of wheat, rye, barley, oats, and potatoes are comparable to those of other European countries. Hungary's generally good soils and long, hot summers allow for excellent agricultural production. Extensive fields of wheat and other cereal crops, along with sunflowers and rape seed, are grown in the Great Plain and the hilly country of Transdanubia in the west. Hungarians also produce a variety of root crops, fruits, nuts, and vegetables, in particular the famous paprika and tomatoes. (Anyone who has tasted one will understand why the Hungarian word for tomato, *paradicsom*, is the same as the word for paradise.) Various wines are also produced in Hungary, ranging from the rich "Bull's Blood" of Eger to the sweet dessert wines of Tokaj.

The rich agricultural lands of Romania also yield wheat, vegetables, and orchard crops; cattle, pigs, and poultry are produced in quantity. Besides the crops mentioned above, Bulgaria produces wine and brandy, and it is the world's major producer of attar, the essence of rose, used in the manufacture of perfume. This cash crop, which is harvested in the Valley of Roses in central Bulgaria each spring amid colorful ceremonies, is becoming an important source of income. Agriculture in the countries of the former Yugoslavia is limited by the steep terrain of the Dinaric Mountains and poor soils in the extensive limestone areas. However, advantage is taken of the fertile lands lying along the Sava and Danube rivers to grow wheat, corn, and sunflowers. Similarly, fruit and other orchard products, as well as significant amounts of tobacco, sheep, and pigs, are important market and cash crops. Agricultural production in Albania, despite the large workforce, is hampered by the generally steep terrain and by the lack of fertilizer, seeds, and machinery. During the socialist period, however, the Albanian government drained large tracts of land, thereby making them available for agriculture. Besides growing cereal and orchard crops on terraced hills and lowlands, vegetables and tobacco are produced. Timber and related forest products are also important to Albania's economy, as they are in Bulgaria, Romania, Slovakia, and the Czech lands.

Manufacturing

Socialist industrial policies resulted in very high growth rates during the 1950s and 1960s, achieved by high rates of investment and large-scale labor migration from agriculture to industry. However, production of consumer goods, provision of services, and investment in infrastructure were neglected. Accelerated industrialization was the core of economic development in ECSEE until the mid-1970s. While, disadvantaged by resource deficiencies, East European industrialization was supported by the availability of imports of iron ore, petroleum, natural gas, and key minerals from the Soviet Union.

Primary attention was given to heavy manufacturing industries. Chemical production tripled between 1960 and the late 1980s, and generally as in the United States and other Western countries, the emphasis was placed on such products as synthetic fibers, plastics, and fertilizers. Per capita output of certain products, such as fertilizers, equaled or even exceeded the West European output.

Perhaps most important was the expansion of iron and steel production effected by modernizing older plants and establishing many new ones. Those in Nowa Huta (Poland), Košice (eastern Slovakia), Eisenhüttenstadt (GDR), Dunaújváros (Hungary), Victoria (Romania), Kremikovci (near Sofia, Bulgaria), Elbasan (Albania), and Zenica (Yugoslavia) were among the major new developments (Fig. 12-12).

The location of metallurgical and associated chemical industries was confined, on the whole, to the modernized, established industrial centers, but a few new large growth centers, built around one or two heavy industries, were added in every country, as, for example, the above-mentioned Košice, Eisenhüttenstadt, and Dunaújváros. As new industrial activities developed throughout ECSEE, polarization in a few areas often increased, contrary to early socialist planning principles and rhetoric.

During the early 1990s, manufacturing output fell precipitously in all the countries of the former CMEA. Declines in manufacturing output resulted from a number of interrelated factors. Cumulative, basic economic problems hinder all the ECSEE countries, most importantly overreliance on large factories with old technologies and production of relatively poor-quality goods destined largely for the sheltered CMEA market. Export orders have declined rapidly as a result of several factors. Problems of acquiring industrial inputs owing to rapidly changing (often falling) production in other former CMEA countries, such as drops in Russian oil and Polish coal production, as well as rapidly shifting import patterns by former CMEA countries in favor of West European suppliers, are cutting ECSEE exports. Exporting to the West has been made difficult because of problems with product quality, marketing, finance, and EU import constraints. Financial problems associated with inflation, debt, and currency stability have further hampered exports.

Industrial output initially fell by about 40 to 50 percent in all the former CMEA countries (as well as Serbia). Recovery is now underway, beginning first in Poland. Manufacturing output was rising again in many ECSEE and post-Soviet countries by 1995.

A simplified description of regional industrial patterns in the ECSEE countries is as follows. Four major regions exist in Poland: the north Polish port cities (Szczecin, Gdynia, and Gdańsk), specializing in shipbuilding and machinery; the Central Region consisting of several nodes, Warsaw-Łódź, Poznan-Bydgoszcz, producing iron and steel, metallurgy, chemicals, and textiles; Lower Silesia (Wrocław-Wałbrzych), manufacturing textiles, precision instruments, chemicals, glass, and ceramics; and Upper Silesia (Katowice, Cracow, Nowa Huta), with metals, machinery, and chemi-

FIGURE 12-12 Major manufacturing regions in ECSEE. Eastern Germany: (1) Berlin-Brandenburg; (2) Magdeburg-Halle-Leipzig; (3) Thuringia-Saxony. Poland: (4) North Polish Ports; (5) Central region; (6) Lower Silesia; (7) Upper Silesia. Czech Rep.: (8) North Bohemian region; (9) Central region; (10) Moravian region. Slovakia: (11) Northern region. Hungary: (12) Budapest region; (13) Western Transdanubian region; (14) Northeastern region. Romania: (15) Banat; (16) Walachian region; (17) Southern Carpathians region; (18) Eastern region. Bulgaria: (19) Sofia region; (20) Central region. Slovenia: (21) Lubljana-Maribor region. Croatia and Bosnia: (22) Central Sava region; (23) Northwest coastal region. Yugoslavia: (24) Belgrade region; (25) Morava region. Macedonia: (26) Skopje Basin. Important urban-industrial nodes are also indicated by appropriate letters for specific cities.

cal production. The Upper Silesia region benefits from traditional access to production in Silesia of a wide array of raw materials or intermediate goods, including copper, cement, coal, zinc, lead, silver, sulfur, salt, and building materials. Small, private, often specialized, firms are in some cases prospering, such as in furniture production near Poznan and west of Cracow. Many large, still subsidized shipbuilding firms in the north and metallurgy plants in the south likely face problems in the near future owing to low levels of productivity. More than half of Poland's industrial labor force still worked within publicly owned plants in the mid-1990s, while employment in the agriculture and retail/wholesale sectors was well over 90 percent in private firms. In the heavily industrialized Katowice region (Upper Silesia), only about 22 percent of the manufacturing labor force was in private firms in 1994. On the other hand, by then the more prosperous and dynamic Warsaw and Poznan regions had more than 65 percent of manufacturing workers within privately owned firms. Developments in leading centers such as these, the dynamic small and private firms, and significant levels of foreign investment are helping to lead industrial restructuring in Poland and increase its trade and investment ties with the EU (Fig. 12-13). For example, between 1990 and 1995 over $5 billion of foreign investment was made in Poland (e.g., by Coca-Cola at several sites and GM near Katowice), and the number of joint ventures increased very rapidly (over 15,000 by 1993 compared to 1645 in 1990).

Industry in the Czech Republic is also concentrated in four main zones: North Bohemia (Plzeň, Chomutov), focusing on metallurgy, machinery, and chemicals; the Central Region (Prague, Kladno), with a similar production pattern, but also electrical equipment; central Moravia (Brno, Olomouc, Gottwaldov), dominated by metallurgy, textiles, and chemicals; and Czech Silesia (Ostrava), metallurgy, machinery, and chemicals. In the early 1990s, the Czech Republic was attracting far more foreign direct investment (over $2.5 billion) than other ECSEE countries, with the exceptions of Hungary and Poland. Slovakia has a main industrial area at Bratislava, where metallurgy, textile, and precision instruments are the major products,

FIGURE 12-13 Evidence of foreign investment in post-socialist Poland. (W. H. Berentsen)

and less important, smaller manufacturing centers such as at Košice (iron and steel).

Manufacturing regions in Hungary are found in an arc from north of Lake Balaton to the northeastern part of the country. Particular concentrations exist in western Transdanubia (Székesfehérvar, Tatabánya), central Hungary (Budapest), and northeastern Hungary (Salgótarján, Ozd, Miskolc). Each of these specializes in metallurgy, machinery, and textiles. Foreign investment has been higher in Hungary than in any other ECSEE country, totaling over $6 billion by early 1995. Foreign auto assemblers have shown particular interest; Suzuki, GM, and Audi (a unit of Volkswagen) all have made or announced investments.

Industrial production in Romania exists in four main regions spread across Walachia and Moldova: the Banat (Timişoara, Hunedoară), with metallurgy, textiles, and machinery; the Bucharest region (Bucharest-Ploeşti), dominated by chemicals, machinery, and petroleum refining; the southern Romanian region (Craiova-Piteşti), petroleum refining and textiles; and the eastern Romanian region (Galaţi, Bacău, Iaşi), chemicals, metallurgy, and pharmaceuticals. Romanian industry, however, is plagued by illogically located, technologically backward plants that often specialize in the production of goods ill suited for a country with only a modest natural resource base. For example, Romania overbuilt its chemical industry, which depends heavily on imported fossil fuels. Romania has also yet to privatize manufacturing and was attracting relatively little foreign investment until 1994.

Bulgarian industry is concentrated in two areas: the Sofia region (Sofia, Pernik, Kremikovci), dominated by machinery and electrical equipment; and the central Bulgarian region (Plovdiv, Dimitrovgrad, Stara Zagora), with metals, chemicals, and petrochemicals production. A smaller industrial region exists on the Bulgarian Black Sea coast focused on Burgas.

Manufacturing regions in the countries of the former Yugoslavia include the central Slovenian region (Ljubljana, Maribor) specializing in engineering, electrical equipment, and machinery; the central Sava Valley in Croatia (Zagreb, Sisak) engaging in metallurgy, petrochemicals, and machinery production; the Belgrade region (Belgrade-Pančevo) and central Serbia (Niš to Kruševac), both of which have metallurgy, textile, and equipment industries; and, finally, the Skopje region in Macedonia, which has metallurgy and chemical production. War; trade blockades affecting most directly Yugoslavia (Serbia/Montenegro) and Macedonia; and slow government responses to liberalize economies plague several Yugoslav successor states. Reports in the mid-1990s indicate that owing to a variety of problems, 1993 industrial production in Yugoslavia was only 20 percent of 1990 production. Yugoslav industrial output began to increase again in 1995. Slovenia, and to a lesser extent Croatia, are progressing faster and doing far better than their neighbors to the south.

Albania has small industrial zones in Tirana, Shkoder, and Elbasan. Its political situation was one of the last in ECSEE to improve, and its economy is only now partially liberalized. However, given that Albania was once a virtually "closed" country, it is attracting a surprising amount of attention and interest from investors within the various parts of its small economy.

Once heavily industrialized, eastern Germany (covered in Chapter 11) has been devastated by the closing of relatively inefficient and often highly polluting plants, in part owing to sudden exposure to and keen competition from west German firms. Some people in the east argue that they are being "deindustrialized" and "colonized," although

public and private investment, especially in infrastructure that could help resurrect industry, dwarfs total investment from nondomestic sources in all other former Eastern bloc countries combined. From 1990 to 1995 western Germany sent an estimated $700 billion eastward by way of welfare, subsidy, and direct investment programs.

Not surprisingly, the industrial structure of ECSEE countries is changing rapidly. Many plants are outdated, and highly polluting, and require massive subsidies to remain in operation. Furthermore, the energy needed to run these plants is becoming more difficult and costly to acquire. For example, the alumina industry located in western Transdanubia was originally developed to take advantage of the bauxite deposits found there. However, the significant energy needs of this industry were always a problem, and the plants have now closed, unable to compete with the cheap energy sites available in Norway (see the section "The Economic Transition" later in this chapter). The textile industries in eastern Germany and Poland (notably at Łódź), once large employers, have drastically reduced their number of workers. Many steel plants and shipyards have closed or are in deep trouble—including the Gdańsk shipyard where former Solidarity leader and Polish President Lech Walesa worked. Many more large, nonprivatized plants in ECSEE (notably in Polish Silesia) are expected to close or sharply reduce their staffs once largely politically motivated subsidies are withdrawn.

Tourism

A study in the late 1980s referred to ECSEE as one of the world's rapidly developing new tourist areas. The former Yugoslavia was in the forefront of this dynamic development after 1964. Tourist trade greatly increased, and receipts in convertible currencies in 1987 amounted to $3.4 billion, accounting for 8 percent of Yugoslavia's hard currency earnings that year. Although the CMEA countries lagged far behind Yugoslavia and Western countries in tourist income, increased tourism during the late 1980s was of particular significance for their economies. Tourism by citizens of the

CMEA countries themselves was channeled by governments toward other socialist countries, primarily because of currency problems and the reluctance of many countries to approve visits to the West. Eighty percent of the tourists in Hungary and 60 percent of Bulgaria's tourists in the early 1980s came from the other socialist countries, although citizens from the West were coming in increasing numbers to some East European countries.

The growing tourist industry in all ECSEE countries, but especially Yugoslavia, was a hard currency earner and produced an important multiplier effect on regional economies—creating jobs in related activities. Each ECSEE country had specific sites preferred by tourists, with mountain regions, coastal areas, lakes, and sites of cultural/historical significance the preferred destinations.

The dramatic political and economic changes in ECSEE have brought a number of changes in tourism. The first effect was a brief surge in foreign travel by ECSEE citizens around the year 1990, reflecting a long-pent-up demand to travel in general and to non-CMEA destinations in particular. This trend appears to have quickly abated, probably because of economic problems and insecurity related to the region's political-economic transition. Tourist expenditures in Hungary and Czechoslovakia doubled from about 1986 to 1992, providing hundreds of millions of dollars in net tourist income, much of it in convertible Western currencies (Fig. 12-14). On the other hand, between 1990 and 1991 alone, the former Yugoslavia experienced a more than 80 percent decline in revenues. Even peaceful and picturesque Slovenia experienced a more than 50 percent decline in visitors between 1990 and 1992. Priceless architectural treasures, like the ancient bridge at Mostar (see Fig. 12-5) and the Sarajevo bazaar, lie in ruins across Bosnia and along the Dalmatian coast. Once flourishing tourist destinations have been turned

FIGURE 12-14 View across the Danube to Buda from Pest. Budapest, like many other European capitals, is a major tourist center with a variety of attractions, including its castle district perched above the river in Buda and its stately Parliament building along the Danube in Pest. (Hungarian Press Agency)

into refugee centers. A resurrection of the former Yugoslavia's tourist industry does not appear to be near at hand. On the other hand, Albania, with its largely unspoiled Adriatic coast, stands to gain considerable revenue from expansion in tourism. Similarly, Black Sea resort towns in Romania (Constanța) and Bulgaria (Varna) experienced a rapid influx of foreign tourists in recent decades. These sites offer affordable, sunny beaches to Northern Europeans.

International Cooperation and Trade

An historical overview of trade within the ECSEE region must separately cover the Soviet-dominated CMEA on the one hand and Albania and the former Yugoslavia on the other. Neither Albania nor Yugoslavia played a long or active role in CMEA affairs. In fact, until recently Albania had a small and unnotable set of trade relationships. It should be noted, however, that the country's self-chosen policy of relatively strict economic autonomy resulted in little international commerce between it and other countries, other than politically motivated orientations first toward the USSR and then toward China. Ultimately it disengaged from both and chose to become a rather isolated, nonaligned state.

The former Yugoslavia's trade ties, in contrast to Albania's, were important and diverse. Yugoslav trade with the Soviets and other CMEA countries in ECSEE was at first important, but declined in relative importance after Tito's political break with the USSR. In the meantime, close trade ties were established with many Western countries, including the United States, which also assisted with massive economic aid to promote and support Yugoslavia's independent political course from Moscow. International aid, including that from the World Bank, during the postwar period made another important contribution to the rehabilitation and expansion of the Yugoslav economy. From a low of zero, Yugoslavia's trade with Western Europe and the United States expanded greatly until it reached about 65 percent of its total trade in 1991. Difficulties in trade with the EC and better relations with Moscow also led Yugoslavia to reexpand trade with the Soviet Union, which

was anxious to buy Yugoslavia's relatively high-quality goods. In the future, most of the former Yugoslav republics will no doubt have greater trade ties with Western Europe than with the former USSR, as is evident in Slovenia's and Croatia's emerging trade patterns. Serbia/Montenegro is more likely than the other republics to maintain long-held, closer ties with Russia.

The other countries in the ECSEE region were members of the CMEA and experienced several distinctive eras of trade development during the postwar era. A period of reduced foreign trade between 1947 and 1953 was characterized by overwhelming Soviet domination of the intrabloc market and a moderately well-enforced Western embargo on exportation of strategic goods to the East. Although trade with the USSR remained dominant for CMEA countries, intrabloc trade with countries other than the USSR then expanded for most countries from a low level in 1956 to reach approximately one-quarter of total trade flows throughout the 1970s. Trade with the West, though relatively small, also began to grow from the mid-1950s onward. After the late 1970s, East-West trade relations were punctuated by the East's need for technology and increased trade; East-West trade in 1987 accounted for 20 percent of the CMEA's exports and 15 percent of its imports.

The ECSEE's Soviet-dominated trade patterns in the postwar era represented an almost complete reorientation of pre-World War II trade relationships. In 1938 the ECSEE countries exported 68 percent of their products to Western Europe (14 % to other ECSEE countries), from which they also received 53 percent of their imports (15 % from ECSEE). Trade with the Soviet Union was negligible. Since the late 1980s, the former CMEA countries have again become much more closely tied to Western economies. By 1991 all of the former CMEA countries had more trade with Western Europe than with the former CMEA bloc, and in most cases Germany was replacing the former USSR as the region's major trade partner (Table 5-7).

Although the CMEA ultimately dissolved, the evolution of its trade and cooperation plays an important role in the economic history of ECSEE countries and will be briefly reviewed. International operation and trade within the organization made little headway during its first 10 years of existence until the early 1960s, when Khrushchev decided to use it as an important integrative instrument in the region. Bilateral agreements between individual ECSEE countries and the Soviet Union, and barter agreements between member states, were originally the basis for trade. A Soviet-dictated policy for each CMEA country to have priorities for development of selected sectors of its economy and pressure exerted by the USSR for closer integration among members based on these specializations generated resistance from some countries in the region, notably Romania. However, excepting Romania, the policies did impact member economies, and the raw material needs of ECSEE countries forced them into a variety of cooperative agreements with the Soviet Union. Cooperative undertakings included building of the Friendship pipeline from the Urals to refineries in East Germany, the construction of pipeline extensions into Hungary and Czechoslovakia, as well as completion of a parallel Brotherhood gas line into Czechoslovakia. Development of Soviet natural resources was also pursued with CMEA members' participation (often with labor), such as construction of a pulp mill (Ust-Ilim), an asbestos combine (Urals), the Orenburg gas pipeline from the southern part of the Urals to Eastern Europe, and expansion of facilities for the production of alloy metals for the iron and steel industry.

The increase in postwar intra-CMEA trade can also be ascribed to the Soviet Union's and member states' large but not very demanding market for consumer goods and industrial products, which enabled the pursuit of economies of scale by CMEA producers. CMEA goods sold poorly in Western markets, and in the absence of a convertible currency and balance of payment problems, barter arrangements between individual CMEA countries contributed to the growth of their economies. Increased trade also resulted in part from imports of machinery and technology used to build modern industries, paid for by exports to and loans from the West. The loans resulted in sizable foreign debts by most CMEA countries by the 1980s.

The poorer CMEA states and those that were hoping to implement extensive modernization programs discovered that the burden imposed by joint investments with the USSR, combined with their international debts, restricted domestic economic options. The impact of the deteriorating economic situation in the CMEA economic realm beginning in the 1970s increased their economic dependence on the Soviet Union. This made resistance to Soviet demands more difficult and at the same time reduced ECSEE's ability to contribute their full share (as seen by the Soviets) to joint economic efforts. All these conditions created a real dilemma for the ECSEE countries as well as for the Soviet Union. With sizable Western debts and a growing desire to improve economic relations with the West, the Soviet Union's desire to bind the socialist countries closer to them by ever larger investments in their own raw material industries was countered by their CMEA allies' increasing demands for technology and capital available from the West.

When the CMEA dissolved, its members still had international debts totaling approximately $100 billion. Problems with these debts still haunt the ECSEE countries. At one time Romania had completely wiped out its debt by draconian economic measures (e.g., greatly reduced consumption of domestic electricity and sharply curtailed food sales), but it has been reamassing a debt since the overthrow of Ceausescu (see Inset 12-1). In recent years, direct and indirect aid from the West has lessened the debt problem somewhat for Poland but debts have grown rapidly for Hungary, Romania, and the Czech and Slovak Republics.

Although economic integration within the CMEA bloc did not progress very far, especially in comparison to its Western counterpart (the EU), it did achieve modest success in interregional cooperation and in coordination of individual development plans. Much more is hoped from expected future ties between at least some ECSEE countries and the EU. Many countries have expressed interest in membership, which would bring access to a huge market and to hefty development subsidies. Membership would also assure investors and trade partners of a country's political and economic stability. However, a number of factors will probably complicate EU expansion into ECSEE. Expansion would result not only in a larger mar-

INSET 12-1

LIFE IN ROMANIA UNDER CEAUSESCU

Conditions for average Romanians during the time of Ceausescu were exceedingly difficult. During the 1980s, the "Great Conductor," as he was known officially, exported up to 50 percent of total agricultural output, so food shortages were common. Meat, vegetables, cooking oil, and "luxuries" such as coffee were often not available. Lighting was limited to one 40 watt bulb per room, hot water was usually available for only a few hours per day, and heating was limited. In typical East European fashion, people made jokes about the situation. One joke ran as follows: Why do people in Bucharest keep their apartment windows closed in winter? So that pedestrians walking below them on the street won't catch cold!

Romania was also one of the most repressive and intimidating countries in Europe. Estimates place the number of Securitate (secret police) at one for every three citizens. Romanians were forbidden from speaking with foreigners. A professor of geography who spoke unofficially to a visiting professor read his own obituary, published in a newspaper as a not so gentle warning. Another individual who allowed a foreign student to spend the night at his apartment was hauled into jail, given a stiff fine, and branded a traitor. Virtually everyone in the country suffered at the hands of the government, which Ceausescu ran in dictatorial fashion.

---

ket, but also in increased competition and increased net operating costs, especially without substantial reduction of EU agricultural subsidies. There is also fear of introducing political and economic instability into the EU that could follow from too hasty inclusion of new members. Binational disputes between member and nonmember states further complicate things (e.g., between Italy and Slovenia over expulsion of the Italians after World War II from the Istrian Peninsula, and between Greece and Macedonia over an appropriate official name for Macedonia). Nonetheless, it is widely speculated that Hungary, the Czech Republic, and probably Poland will be serious candidates for membership fairly soon and could join within a decade. Small, relatively stable, prosperous Slovenia could also be a serious candidate before long—if it can resolve its problems with Italy, which will likely block entry until agreements are hammered out.

Of course, EU membership is only one possible avenue for countries of the region. The Czech Republic became the first Eastern bloc country to join the OECD, and other East European countries are expected to join soon. Other, smaller alignments and trading blocs are emerging to fill the vacuum left by the collapse of the CMEA and the former simple division of Europe into West and East. These regional "clubs" aim to promote cooperation in such areas as trade, transportation,

tourism, energy use, and environmental protection. Alpen-Adria is such an organization, founded in 1978, and includes Slovenia, Croatia, five *Länder* of Austria, three counties of western Hungary, four regions of northern Italy, and Bavaria of southern Germany. The association obviously reflects the sphere of influence of the former Hapsburg Empire. The Pentagonale, launched in 1989 by Italy, Austria, Czechoslovakia, Hungary, and Yugoslavia, was intended to form a barrier to unbridled German expansion into former Eastern Europe. The Visegrad Group, formed in 1991 by Hungary, Poland, and Czechoslovakia (now including the Czech and Slovak Republics), was initiated to coordinate efforts to join the EU, as well as to cooperate in trade, economic reforms, and security. The Group, now called the Central European Free Trade Agreement (CEFTA), has admitted Slovenia and intends to eliminate internal trade tariffs by 1998. The *Donauländer*, begun by Austria in 1990, includes lands along the Danube from Bavaria to Moldova and seeks to coordinate transportation, tourism, and conservation. Finally, the Black Sea Economic Co-operation, begun in 1991, includes Turkey, Bulgaria, Romania, and areas of the former USSR surrounding the Black Sea.

In the 1990s Germany has become a dominant trading partner for most of this region—as it is for most of the rest of Europe. Austria, however, has also carved out a portion of the trade flows, reestablishing some of its historic economic ties with the former Austro-Hungarian lands. Potentially increased intraregional trade flows associated with the regional trade blocs such as CEFTA have yet to be very evident.

ENVIRONMENTAL PROBLEMS

It is hoped that, one of the positive, postsocialist changes in ECSEE will be amelioration, if not complete resolution, of the catastrophic environmental problems in some parts of the region. Economic development in ECSEE under socialism was achieved at an exceedingly high cost to the environment and human health. The air was heavily polluted, especially in industrial areas (Fig. 12-15); water was fouled both above and below ground; agricultural soils were heavily polluted with toxins and compacted by heavy tractors; forests were stricken by the effects of acid rain; cavernous pits stretched across the countryside in lignite production regions like the southern GDR and northern Bohemia; buildings were corroded and blackened

by acid rain and fallout from air pollution (see Fig. 11-16); and everyone and everything lived under a threat of catastrophic nuclear accidents. Around Copsa Mica, Romania, the entire landscape has been blackened by sooty fallout. In many places darkened snow has fallen from smoke-laden skies. The human health costs of problems like these and the Chernobyl accident are practically incalculable. Life expectancies in many ECSEE countries have fallen in recent years, while they have been steadily lengthening in Western Europe.

Many of the industrial activities that caused these problems continue to pollute today, owing to the need for output and for the many jobs associated with them. Where pollutant-generating activities have ended, such as lignite and potash mines in eastern Germany, high levels of regional unemployment have developed along with the cleaner air. Where polluting firms have remained open, high levels of pollution continue. In eastern Germany alone, it is estimated that it will cost up to $150 billion to resolve major environmental problems, and to refit factories and other facilities to meet German pollution standards. However, even this huge investment (over $10,000 per east German inhabitant) will not soon restore satisfactory conditions to the area's soils, water bodies, and

FIGURE 12-15 One of many air pollution sources at Nowa Huta, Poland. Socialist efforts to increase industrialization in the Cracow region after World War II, in part to inject a larger number of blue collar workers into a region considered to be otherwise bourgeois-oriented and politically suspect, led to both economic failings and environmental calamity. (W. H. Berentsen)

forests. Cleanup may take decades. Retrofitting factories also cannot eradicate the long-term, adverse health impacts of past pollution.

The countries of East Central Europe, owing in large part to their high level of industrialization, dependence on coal, and inefficient use of energy, produced the ECSEE's highest levels of sulfur dioxide and nitrogen oxide emissions. In 1988 East German per capita sulfur dioxide emissions were four times higher and Czechoslovakia's twice as high as those of the United States, itself a relatively great polluter by international or European standards. On a per capita basis, sulfur dioxide emissions in Hungary and Southeastern Europe were also very high by international standards. The situation in the ECSEE countries is all the more serious when we consider the very high levels of pollution per square mile or pollution output per unit of production. The air pollution and associated forest problems in a large "dirty triangle" including Silesia (e.g., as far east as Ostrava and Katowice), northern Moravia and western Bohemia, and Saxony (north to Leipzig and Hoyerswerda) are among the worst in the world over a large area. Especially poor conditions and serious problems exist in Polish and Czech Silesia. Lignite mining creates what often appears to be a "lunar landscape" from strip mining. A similarly scarred landscape, as well as air pollution visible from Helsinki across the wide Gulf of Finland, results from oil shale mining in northeastern Estonia. Whatever standard is applied, the record of socialist environmental degradation is virtually criminal, given the extent of the damage and government's efforts to hide the problems and silence critics.

In addition to these problems are the real but rather poorly documented, negative impacts of improper use and disposal of nuclear materials, as well as the impacts of known (and possibly undisclosed) nuclear accidents. Given the myriad potential causes of ill-health in ECSEE (e.g., poor eating habits, excessive drinking and smoking, air and water pollution), the geographic mobility of the population, and the temporal lag between exposure to nuclear materials and the onset of associated illness, it is difficult to assess the extent of health problems associated with one-time exposure of humans to hazardous nuclear materials,

including those improperly discarded into air, soil, and water. Serious health problems in uranium mining areas of the former southern GDR and Czechoslovakia, not to mention the emerging problems in East Central Europe linked to the Chernobyl nuclear accident, indicate the ultimate potential impact of poor nuclear safety practices of the Soviet/CMEA nuclear power and military products' industries. Many of the Soviet-style reactors in the region, especially those at Kosloduy in Bulgaria, are outdated and in imminent danger of a Chernobyl-type mishap.

In regional terms, it can be argued that the Czech Republic is Europe's most heavily polluted country, in part because of the prevailing westerly and southwesterly winds by which it receives polluted air from both western and eastern Germany, adding to problems created by its own domestic emissions. The Czech Republic, surrounded by wooded mountain ranges, also has been especially hard hit by acid rain. Conifers, seriously weakened by the intake of harmful chemicals, easily topple during strong winds or heavy snow, and from attacks by various pests.

Central Europe's largest forest regions are in danger of denudation by acid rain from industrial pollution. The worst affected area is the Krusne Horty Mountains (Ore Mountains or in German, Erzgebirge) of northwestern Bohemia and southeastern Germany. Large parts of the mountains northwest of Prague resemble a wasteland when seen from the air.

Grave environmental problems also emanate from Romania, where chlorine and sodium products have produced an ecological catastrophe in the Giurigiu-Ruse area, two Danube ports on the Romanian-Bulgarian border. A plant built in 1984 is polluting the air of southern Romania as well as the Bulgarian city of Ruse. Romania's inability and unwillingness to cope with this problem has become so serious that it has at times threatened relations between Romania and its neighbor. Similarly, the negative environmental impact of the Gabcikovo-Nagymaros hydroelectric project on the Danube River along the Austrian, Hungarian and Slovak borders has strained relations between Austria, Hungary (both have backed out of the project), and Slovakia. Feeling that it had few viable alternatives to replace electricity that will be

SOCIALIST PHILOSOPHY AND THE ENVIRONMENT

The severity of environmental issues in East Central and Southeast Europe in part stems from socialist philosophy. One of the basic tenets of socialism, as espoused by Marx, is that development occurs in harmony with nature. Environmental degradation is seen as a result of an exploitative development regime, which is a characteristic of capitalism but is not possible under socialism. This rationalization essentially gave governments a free hand to pursue development paths with little regard to their environmental consequences. Since acknowledgment of pollution would, in a sense, be an admission of the failure of socialism, an official blind eye was turned to environmental issues. The consequences of this inaction were failure to recognize mounting prob-

lems and to form appropriate institutions to combat the problems, and reluctance to publish any incriminating data.

Another aspect of Marxism that impacted the environment concerns its notions of materialism. According to Marxism, pristine nature has value only insofar as it can be used by people. As such, setting aside large tracts of land for habitat or wilderness preservation could not be justified. Accordingly, parks and heritage areas were given rather low priority. Furthermore, natural resources were seen as things to be used as needed; socialist governments therefore showed little restraint in mining and other forms of resource extraction.

---

generated from it, Slovakia has unilaterally completed its portion of the project.

A number of socialist policies led to the long-term and widespread environmental problems of this area (see Inset: 12-2). First, the emphasis on industrialization and increased agricultural production resulted in greater needs for fuel and power, preferably from domestic sources and often resulting in use of highly polluting resources like lignite. Second, the large industrial and other priority investments throughout the postwar period resulted in investment constraints in protecting the environment and thus in the ability of governments to provide enough efficient technical equipment to combat emissions. Third, lack of adequate data, political commitment, and oversight made it virtually impossible to identify problems and implement effective policies and ameliorative actions—had any been earnestly desired.

Today there is better information about environmental problems and how to deal with them. Opportunities for the public to exert political influence on economic and environmental policies have improved, and better technology has been implemented to reduce pollution and rehabilitate devastated regions. Still, governments and citizens of the ECSEE countries often have decided that too little money is available to adopt cleaner environmental practices and that it is too painful to elimi-

nate the jobs embedded within old, polluting industrial plants and practices. Thus, for example, the Czech and Slovak Republics face difficult choices between (1) using polluting lignite-fired or Soviet-style nuclear power plants for domestically produced energy, or (2) importing expensive oil, natural gas, or electricity. In short, for a number of reasons the environmental problems in ECSEE will probably remain visible, harmful, and controversial into the twenty-first century.

A POSTSOCIALIST, POSTSOVIET ECSEE

In what history seems likely to designate as the Revolution of 1989, the former socialist countries of Eastern Europe are experiencing radical changes in their political, economic, and social structures. Even if politically stable democracies and Western-style market economies do not emerge from this revolutionary era, the countries of the region will no doubt be remarkably different in the future than they were prior to the collapse of the Soviet Empire.

Many, if not most, citizens in the region view this period as a "time of troubles" rather than as a liberating revolution, however. The region now faces both a daunting set of problems and a wrenching set of perilous decisions. Following is an overview of these problems, as well as the difficult circumstances and choices facing the region and its people. The somewhat bewildering array of problems, opinions of how to solve them, and inherent tradeoffs and contradictions with many policy options (e.g., cleaning the air by eliminating jobs in polluting plants) indicate why the course of the "Revolution of 1989" will almost certainly be long, tortuous, and less than completely successful. Many of these problems plague Western countries as well, but the West has a longer established tradition of facing up to and living with them. And too, the West simply has more money available to cushion people when difficult trade-offs must be made between, for example, closing a dangerous nuclear facility, reducing power output, raising energy prices, and putting people out of work.

Political Transition

Although the political life in most countries in the region is now marked by greater levels of openness, information, and public input (albeit probably more, for example, in Hungary and less in Romania), unequal resources and dissimilar motivations and commitments to democracy among political contenders provide opportunity for democrat, demagogue, and dictator alike. Although people rejoice in their rights to more or less free speech and the reduced threat from secret police forces, they fret over political fragmentation, lack of forceful and beneficial action by government (at least as they perceive it), and the dearth of strong leadership.

Decisions must be made and traditions developed to divide responsibilities among local and regional versus national governments; government ministries, planners, and authorities versus private enterprises; national interests versus international realities and responsibilities; and personal freedom versus public responsibility. For example, decisions must be made on the appropriate level of government intervention in the economy and on how various segments and levels of government institutions should carry out their roles. How far should current efforts to support

local government be pushed? How can publicly based interest groups be developed and brought into the political process without creating even further political fragmentation and economic profiteering?

Decisions must be made about the level of services the state is to provide and the services people must purchase with their own resources. Funds to pay for public services must be collected and the political will to cut back on subsidies for other services must be achieved. Somehow citizens must recognize that the huge debts incurred by socialist governments to underwrite its overspending either will not be funded by domestic or international investors or will simply result in bankruptcy. Funding from the West to solve problems in the East has been less than many in the West would like, but will never approach the unrealistic expectations of many people in Eastern Europe, who have yet to understand the link between levels of production and real purchasing power. It is not entirely an exaggeration that many people in the East think that the West has so much money that there are no real budget limitations. Such is the legacy of the paternalistic socialist state and the mirage of Western opulence. These problems may be at their worst in Russia, where economic restructuring has been retarded by an entrenched, apparently socialist-minded bureaucracy, while constant, credible charges of rampant corruption undermine the public's faith in both government and private enterprise.

Choices must be made between maintaining national economic independence and the political importance of national "face-saving" in determining conditions for foreign ownership and investment. Somehow, for example, fairly commonplace hopes of salvation through German investment must be balanced with the fears of renewed German domination. Isolated earlier from choice, citizens must decide how the benefits of international investment and trade balance with their threat to local control, domestic employment, and national pride. Simplistic, unrealistic expectations of "send money, not responsibilities" must be combated.

A difficult balance must be achieved between protecting emerging and strategic industries and promoting long-term survival of efficient and internationally competitive firms. Difficult political-economic choices must be made, probably on a case by case basis, between supporting investments in more prosperous regions which have better infrastructure and in disadvantaged regions which have lower wage rates, more poorly skilled labor forces, and poor infrastructure. Differences of opinion on these choices played a prominent role in the dissolution of Czechoslovakia and will almost surely lead to years of support for "protest" political parties in eastern Germany and elsewhere.

How far can and should private initiative and personal freedom be encouraged before public security and stability are threatened? The new political systems in the East must develop a workable political consensus so that private enterprise can generate jobs, income, investment, innovation, and tax revenues without creating democracies rife with social and political strife and instability. Reelection of socialist governments in countries such as Poland, Hungary, and Lithuania underscore the East Europeans' yearning for benefits they valued under the earlier political-economic system.

New and reformed institutions are needed to guide and undertake aspects of transition in ECSEE. Respected and efficient public, quasi-public, and private institutions like those in the West will need to evolve to help societies govern themselves and avoid the concentration of power in the hands of the ruthless and incompetent dictators (e.g., Ceausescu) and isolated political elites (e.g., in East Germany and Bulgaria) who for so long have dominated in the region. The authority of and trust in entities such as courts, tax authorities, and specialized interest groups needs to be established. Each society must reach an acceptable and stable, yet malleable, politically tenable consensus on what the future can and cannot look like.

Finally, at the international level countries in East Central and Southeastern Europe need to forge new political and economic relationships with Russia, the EU, and NATO. Domestic economic and international political successes must be achieved to open the huge, protected EU market to its eastern neighbors. The perceived economic opportunity and political security that EU membership would bring to, for example, the earliest likely candidates in East Central Europe (Czech Republic, Hungary, and Poland) must be balanced with reassurances of friendly relations with Russia, in which nationalist demagogues are attempting to rally support for reestablishing the perceived glories of Soviet rule. Possible NATO membership for East Central European countries also presents a similar diplomatic tightrope walk for both the West and countries within the region. East European countries are anxious to join NATO before a feared renewal of Russian imperialism comes to pass, such as was threatened by both Russian presidential candidates and some of President Yeltsin's ministers during the 1996 Russian election campaign. The acrimonious debate about NATO expansion eastward involves the West, the East Central European countries that are likely to join first, the Baltic states that will probably be left out of NATO until at least the next century, and Russia. The debate is likely to remain a major international political issue for many years to come.

Social Implications of Transition

These difficult political tasks suggest a number of related social problems facing the East European countries. Incomes are now low, social services have been cut, and economic security has been eroded. How long will people be willing and able to accept these conditions while some citizens as well as foreign interlopers prosper? Economic inequalities are widening in ECSEE, while poverty and conspicuous consumption commingle on the streets of major cities. Organized and street-level crime, indigent and homeless beggars, social segregation, and more obvious political corruption are new and menacing phenomena for East Europeans. Job availability and security for women, dramatic changes in the organization of child care, and escalating housing and transportation costs in the face of job insecurity are among several pressing social, and ultimately political, issues. The psychological impacts of these issues are apparent at the sociobiological level; birth rates have plunged in many parts of the former socialist world. For example, in 1993 they were at about one-third their 1986 level in eastern Germany, and 50 percent declines are rather common elsewhere.

Socioeconomic and political insecurities in the

East compared to real and imagined opportunities in the West have generated increased streams of interregional migration which are exacerbating ethnic prejudices and socioeconomic jealousies across Europe. Restrictions on immigration and citizenship in Germany, Switzerland, and Austria are justified in these countries as protection of national interests, but in the East they can be interpreted as racist and selfish actions inconsistent with both Cold War protestations of unity and promises of help at the beginning of the "Revolution of 1989."

Demagogues in Eastern Europe could exaggerate and exploit these problems to take power—with unknown consequences. The rhetoric of populist, nationalistic demagogues has found a considerable following from Vienna and Bratislava to Moscow.

The Economic Transition

The issues noted above are interrelated with economic problems, although economic issues themselves often generate more headlines. Especially prominent in the transition in East Central and Southeastern Europe is a belated restructuring of the region's productive activities and labor forces. The socialists' overemphasis on industry, especially heavy industry, now haunts the economies of ECSEE, which, with greater exposure to the international economy, must become much more efficient and innovative in all sectors. Most economies of the region are rapidly shifting employment out of unproductive, overstaffed manufacturing and agricultural activities, while long-neglected service sectors are starting to grow. In fact, in selected service sectors and places, things are booming (e.g., construction in eastern Germany and tourist-oriented services in Prague). Change is most difficult for large, state-owned factories and for many huge, formerly state-owned or -dominated farms. Hundreds of thousands of workers have lost their jobs as their former employers dissolved. More job losses are still pending in countries where the breakup of big firms has been slow, such as in Poland, or where economic restructuring has been delayed, as in much of Southeastern Europe and the former Soviet Union.

Especially vexing problems are involved in making the devilish choice between a healthier, cleaner, safer environment or cheaper energy and continuation of employment in the region's coal mines and nuclear power plants. For countries that suffer some of the world's worst pollution but that have little money for investment to refit polluting plants or pay for alternative (often imported) energy sources, the available choices often seem equally awful.

Similarly, in order to get their economies off the ground again, many countries will undoubtedly be forced to do an about-face in their policies concerning regional economic inequalities. Under socialism there was much rhetoric and some action (e.g., by way of establishing of new industrial complexes in lagging regions) in order to reduce regional inequalities, particularly those between rural and urban areas. These efforts were never completely successful owing to a number of enduring advantages of cities, including centralized political and economic administration in urban areas as well as the advantages of cities as the base for the large economic enterprises favored by the socialist system. Now, with many former socialist countries' economies facing ongoing employment cuts in agriculture and industry, cities, especially larger cities and capitals, stand to gain most from an expansion of service sector employment. This results from the traditional and rational concentration of more highly specialized service activities such as finance and professional consulting activities in cities, as well as a concentration of foreign investment and expanded tourist activity in them. Prague provides a classic example of the geographic concentration of foreign investment and tourism. Rapid expansion of economic activity, especially in tourism, has transformed a dour socialist city into a vibrant market and tourist center.

A tendency toward greater economic growth in those parts of ECSEE closest to Western Europe also threatens to further widen social and regional inequalities within the socialist countries. Because of the lower time and transport costs of moving goods and people, as well as the greater probability of exchange of ideas by way of face-to-face contacts between West and East Europeans, the western parts of many formerly socialist countries are experiencing greater economic dynamism than eastern regions, often further entrenching already existing patterns of regional development and socioeconomic well-being. Thus, for example, western Hungary, Poland, and Estonia are developing more rapidly than eastern areas—as is the Czech Republic as opposed to Slovakia, and Slovenia and Croatia as opposed to the other former Yugoslav republics. These western areas have, in general, more rapid rates of integration and transformation into the West European economic structure (e.g., with more entrepreneurial activity and more foreign direct investment activities). For example, a recent World Bank report rating countries by generalized levels of economic liberalization and growth ranks Slovenia, Poland, Hungary, and Croatia highly, while Albania, Romania, Russia, and Belarus lag. (Despite its location and poor economic performance, Macedonia is an exception to the generalized pattern—it received a favorable rating.) An indication of economic change is provided by plunging levels of subsidies, which, for example, fell from 11—17 percent of GDP in 1989 to 3—5 percent in 1993 in Bulgaria, Hungary, Poland, Slovakia, and Slovenia. Unfortunately, another indication of change has been the surge of "gray" (questionably legal but tolerated) and "black" (illegal) markets, which are estimated to comprise as much as 20 percent of all economic activity (probably higher in Yugoslavia).

The Landscape and Land Use

The "Revolution of 1989" has also brought dramatic changes to ECSEE landscapes. Increased competition for central city space between expanding retail and administrative functions and reestablishment of a market for urban land are transforming cities in ECSEE. The urban landscape has become dramatically more commercially oriented; there are both more retail and consumer-oriented activities, including shops, restaurants, bars, and hotels, as well as a profusion of advertising to alert consumers to their products and services. Political placards, once common in many socialist countries, have been replaced by the colorful commercial signs so common in the West (Fig. 12-16). The "Marlboro man" now often stands

where party leader photos once dominated. Graffiti scrawled on building walls, often politically motivated, has replaced the once common exhortations to workers to fill their quotas and beware of the evils of the West and capitalism. Collapsing facades have in many places been repaired to provide some evidence of gentrification in urban centers, although city dwellers in places like Prague will hasten to note that, thus far, building facades are often as far as change has gone. This results from shortages of funds, uncertainty about the potential return for investments, and desire of investors to gain the quickest, surest profit by improving the appearance of potential shop and office quarters on busy streets. Nonetheless,

FIGURE 12-16 A commercial street in Poznan. (W. H. Berentsen)

cityscapes across the region are displaying more economic dynamism and greater opportunity for shoppers, as well as presenting cities' architectural treasures in a more colorful way than during the dull and dreary days of socialism.

At the same time that central cities are changing, pressures for suburbanization are increasing. Greater demand for central city space by retailers, business offices, and tourist services, together with the likely associated decline in the availability and increased cost of central city residences, will probably reinforce other suburbanizing tendencies and conditions. Among the suburbanizing factors are the already existing, massive housing estates built on the fringes of ECSEE cities, as well as the increased ownership of private automobiles. In eastern Germany these forces, as well as a further constrained inner-city land market, owing to uncertainty about title to land and buildings and uncharacteristically lax land use controls, are leading to particularly strong suburban development, but suburbanization is occurring in other parts of ECSEE as well. Suburbanization is still constrained, however, by relatively low levels of private auto ownership, extensive public transport networks focused on city centers, cultural preference for strong and vibrant central cities, and long traditions of government ownership of urban land, housing, transport, and retail facilities. Hence American levels of suburban development and central city decay are as yet unknown and unlikely to evolve anytime soon in Eastern Europe.

Although capital cities are and probably will hold great advantages over smaller provincial cities early in the transition era, eventually a more complex and balanced urban system is expected to develop than the politically dominated urban system under socialism. The socialist political and economic administrative system allocated the location of all manner of activities (e.g., enterprise offices and factories, warehouses, retail outlets, and social service centers) to cities based on political criteria. Under a more market-oriented system, one could expect to see, at least in some countries, both a greater balance in the urban hierarchy and the development of specializations among the countries' cities. For example, although Budapest and East Berlin were unquestioned centers for providing virtually all major, specialized urban func-

tions under socialism, the distribution of functions was far wider among West Germany cities. Though also based on long historical traditions, the dominance of Budapest and Berlin was enhanced during the socialist era, and the future evolution of the region's urban systems could begin diverging from twentieth-century patterns by the early part of the twenty-first century. The first impacts of transition on urban systems have often favored capital cities like Prague and Tallinn owing to high concentrations of the countries' foreign investment and tourism in these places. Ultimate patterns of development are still unclear.

Future Prospects for Transition in ECSEE

The problems, potentials, and prospects for transition in the ECSEE reflect the revolutionary, but also rather uncertain, nature of change in the region. Undoubtedly, individual countries' successful socioeconomic and political transitions will require some common approaches and display some common paths and lessons. However, all the countries have at least somewhat different political and economic conditions at the outset that will affect policies and development patterns in them during the transition. For example, Slovenia, Slovakia, Ukraine, Belarus, and Moldova are either truly independent countries for the first time in their history or for the first time in centuries. The former Soviet and Yugoslav republics as well as the Czech and Slovak Republics have emerged from the dissolution of larger entities. A host of small countries with even smaller relative market sizes must somehow integrate into a world economy with dominant national economies, such as Germany in Europe, and with hugely resourceful multinational corporations. The Baltic states; Slovak Republic and former Yugoslav republics; and Moldova probably face the stiffest challenges in this regard. A small number of countries have somewhat advantageous early leads in implementing political and economic change (e.g., Czech Republic, Hungary, and Poland) and in acquiring foreign investment (most notably Hungary), whereas other countries such as Bosnia-Herzegovina, Moldova, Yugoslavia, and Romania are off to inauspicious beginnings during the transition era—most for somewhat different reasons. A couple of countries face particularly severe levels of poverty and isolation from the rest of Europe—Albania and Macedonia. Only one former ECSEE country has a more or less assured long-term source of capital to rebuild its infrastructure and economy, while assuring a modicum of consumer well-being—the former GDR. During the first five years of the "postsocialist" era all of the former Eastern bloc countries experienced negative economic growth, but the economies of ECSEE countries, including the Baltic states, are now beginning to expand (Fig. 12-17).

In short, for the countries of ECSEE, problems are many, resources and guidelines for transition are few, and time may be short. Patterns of future political, economic, and social development in

ECSEE will be among Europe's most important, interesting, and imponderable issues of the late twentieth and early twenty-first centuries.

Regional Economic Patterns in the Mid-1990s

The dramatic political and economic developments in the ECSEE from 1989 to the present are generating changes in a wide array of socioeconomic-geographic patterns at the international, national, and regional scales across the region. Although it is now difficult to predict the geographic impacts of the revolutionary era, some trends appear to be developing and others can be reasonably expected to become evident before

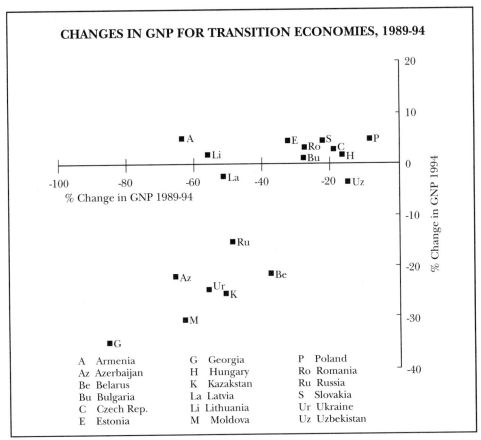

FIGURE 12-17 Status (1994) and changes in GNP in the former "Eastern bloc."

long. First, at the international level, the countries of Southeastern Europe not only are Europe's poorest, but also have its greatest current economic problems. They are likely to become even poorer in comparison to the rest of Europe. Despite dramatic transformations in the post–World War II era, these countries remain the ones most dependent on agriculture and with the least well-developed service sectors. Available data indicate that manufacturing and related economic activities such as mining sustained serious production cuts in the early 1990s, tourist income fell (drastically in the former Yugoslavia), international investment remained low (Bulgaria had less than 5% of what Hungary received in the early 1990s), economic activity continued to be constrained by the international embargo on Serbia, unemployment was high, and trade balances were negative. Continued delay in actions to overcome the region's historic economic-geographic disadvantages, as well as destruction associated with armed conflict, bode poorly for the short- to mid-term future of this part of ECSEE. Early results from more vigorous reform efforts and relatively peaceful conditions in East Central Europe offer much more hope for economic progress in Slovenia, Poland, the Czech and Slovak Republics, and Hungary. Still, economic conditions in these countries remain worse than in most parts of Western Europe, although, as noted earlier, some of the East Central European countries are the most likely next set of candidates for inclusion in the EU, perhaps as early as the turn of the century.

Recent economic conditions in ECSEE vary considerably by country and region, and dramatic changes in, for example, output, employment, inflation, and economic policy have been common. Briefly, the situation as it existed by about 1995 is as follows.

By 1994 in ECSEE, only Poland's industrial economy had recovered to a large extent from the sharp downturn of the late 1980s and early 1990s, and in most other countries (especially Hungary), the steep slide in industrial and overall production had at least been halted. During 1994 and 1995 Slovakia and Slovenia also demonstrated the kind of rapid growth in manufacturing that occurred a bit earlier in Hungary and Poland. Rapid declines in industrial output were continuing into 1995 in the

European successor states of the FSU; only in Estonia and Lithuania did output data during 1995 offer some hope for a turnaround in manufacturing.

During the early postsocialist era, Poland undertook a controversial policy course favoring radical, swift economic restructuring; the result was an estimated 25 percent of total economic production in the private sector as early as 1992 and over 50 percent by 1995. (Private sector production had been an estimated 5 percent or less in most CMEA countries during the socialist period.) Employment in privately owned manufacturing plants was at about 5 percent of the total in 1985 but 60 percent by 1995. Between 1990 and mid-1995 the country received sizable levels of foreign investment, though far lower on a per capita basis ($51) than those in Hungary ($717) and the Czech Republic ($365). Much more important in absolute terms was Poland's attainment of a high level of Western financial assistance—about 40 percent of all aid given to ECSEE countries during 1990–1992. Despite indications of economic success and recovery, Poland also suffered official unemployment levels (over 15% in 1995) that were among the region's highest. The Czech Republic and Hungary also displayed some early, positive indications of success in the transition process. The employment structures of these countries are far closer to those of Western countries than the other ECSEE states. The Czech Republic and the GDR were the most prosperous countries in the CMEA. Despite the fact that per capita income estimates from ECSEE countries do not now provide consistent figures, both continue to have relatively high income levels by ECSEE standards, though rather low by Western standards. The Czech Republic also has one of Europe's lowest official unemployment rates (below 3% in mid-1995) and a balanced trade account. The Czech Republic's efforts to modernize its economy and draw closer to Western European lifestyles and institutions have been assisted by billions of dollars worth of foreign investment (second to Hungary in per capita terms) and Western financial assistance, much from Germany and Austria.

Hungary began economic reform many years before other CMEA countries and appears to have benefited from this head start. Its average income per capita may now be at least as high as that in

INSET 12-3

FOREIGN INVESTMENT IN HUNGARY: THE MORNING AFTER

The fall of communism in Europe was a time of great joy for people both east and west of the Iron Curtain. Many U.S. and other companies quickly took advantage of the new opportunities to invest in firms, to form joint ventures, and to gain market access. Manufacturers were attracted to the region by the relatively skilled, but quite low wage labor (usually only 10% of Western rates) and what seemed like unlimited demand for Western products.

After four years, however, these initial hopes have not been met by reality. For example, General Electric (GE) made a spectacular entrance onto the scene when it entered into a joint venture with the Hungarian light bulb producer Tungsram. GE publicized the deal with a high-profile ad campaign featuring upbeat television commercials, and backed the arrangement with $50 million investment over the first three years. By 1993 GE had soured on the

deal, stopped the flow of investment, and moved operations to China. In another case, Schwinn Bicycle Company opened a factory in an old munitions plant on Csepel Island in Budapest. At first, labor costs were low, and the venture seemed profitable. However, poor worker habits, unacceptable levels of rejected articles, and numerous problems with suppliers forced the company out. Schwinn found that far from being cost effective, the production costs of a bicycle made in Hungary were some seven to eight times higher than elsewhere. Other such disappointing experiences on the part of both Western investors, Hungary, and other ECSEE countries have led to reassessment of the net costs and benefits of foreign investment. At this point in the economic transition of the region, this is probably a necessary and prudent step.

---

the Czech Republic. It received about one-half of all foreign investment and a large share (especially in per capita terms) of Western financial assistance in the ECSEE region during the early 1990s (see Inset 12-3). In early 1994 it had a reasonable balance of imports and exports and growing private and service sectors of the economy. Manufacturing output grew rapidly during 1994–1995 after several years of decline. However, certain social and political costs and strains are associated with Hungary's postsocialist transition. Unemployment is relatively high; many Hungarians continue to work long hours at more than one job, with notable apparent negative side effects on health; and income inequalities within the society have become a serious social and political issue. An indication of the severity of these problems were the surprising results of the national elections in 1994 when socialists (avowedly reformed) were returned to leadership. No doubt, more surprises like this one, as well as problems, lie ahead for Hungary and the other rapidly restructuring economies and societies in ECSEE (eastern Germany, Czech Republic, and Poland).

Other ECSEE countries began to show indications of economic improvement and stabilization

by 1994. Slovenia, the most economically prosperous of the former Yugoslav republics, began experiencing recoveries in manufacturing and total output during 1993, although unemployment levels remain high. Albania, probably Europe's poorest country and still experiencing high unemployment rates, had one of Europe's highest economic growth rates in 1993–1994 after about a 33-percent drop in output during 1990–1992. Proud Albanian leaders were pointing at vigorous reform and privatization policies as the basis for the turnaround. Slovakia exhibited poorer economic conditions in virtually all categories than its more prosperous former partner, the Czech Republic, until 1995 when it drew closer in performance. Especially troubling, however, was a steep decline in Slovak manufacturing, which once was overly oriented toward military production. The country had some good news by the mid-1990's: the slide in manufacturing production abated, and declines in total economic output appeared to have been checked in 1993–1994. During 1995 signs of economic growth appeared. In addition, a high percentage of service sector activity has now been privatized, and a good start has been made in expanding the private sector share in total output (25% in 1994).

Some countries in the region—Macedonia, Bosnia-Herzegovina and Latvia—continued to have serious economic problems into the mid-1990s following similarly serious slides in the early 1990s. Unemployment levels were high and economic growth rates low or negative. Macedonia and Bosnia-Herzegovina have poorly developed infrastructures and economies that are overly dependent on agriculture. Bosnia, of course, also was still battered by war in the mid-1990s, and Macedonia's economy suffered from Greece's embargo on most trade with it until 1995. A radical reform program to bring greater self-sufficiency and economic stability to Serbia was showing some success. However, economic conditions in Yugoslavia and Bosnia-Herzegovina remained poor, and reliable information was difficult to obtain. As an example of the volatile nature of the Serb economy, in the mid-1990s inflation rates reached levels exceeding 500 percent per week.

Resurgent Nationalism, Increased Inequalities

Sadly, expressions of nationalism and associated boundary disputes, ethnically based discrimination, and economic problems are likely to continue, particularly in Southeastern Europe. At the worst a Balkan war could erupt; at the best, perhaps, these problems can be contained so that a (likely generations-long) process of improved relations can be initiated.

At the national level, both ethnically and socially based economic inequalities and inequities in political power will probably bring problems for most ECSEE countries. These problems are in most cases centuries old and, although a lot of rhetoric about resolving them was voiced under socialism, most remain. Although most inhabitants of the region have been relieved by the end of autocratic rule under the old socialists, no clear-cut political consensus has appeared favoring either a small number of strong parties or West European-style capitalism. The region has deep concerns about security for jobs, retirement, women's rights, and health care; about crime and corruption; and about income inequalities. These factors played a critical role in the election of reformed socialist parties as

noted earlier. Numerous political parties based on different philosophies of governance and ethnic appeal could so complicate governing ECSEE countries, as has often been the case in the past, that governments' socioeconomic development plans will be difficult to draft and implement.

At the regional and local levels, new geographic patterns of socioeconomic conditions could evolve. Regional economic inequalities could easily increase, as cities, with better infrastructure and skilled workers, could attract new economic activities, while some rural areas with labor-intensive agriculture and overspecialized industrial regions may languish. Residential segregation in cities might increase by way of economic forces. That is, the despised workers' slums so common in European cities during the early stages of capitalism may again become more conspicuous. Greater emphasis on consumption and personal choice is already bringing more private automobiles onto the roads and more commercial placards onto the landscape, and may generate land use structures and landscapes similar to those in Western Europe. Whatever their nature, changes emanating from this revolutionary era in the ECSEE are bound to include a wide variety of new patterns within its economic, social, and political geography.

The Former Yugoslavia

The most dramatic and tragic contemporary issue in ECSEE is armed conflict in the former Yugoslavia and the potential for its spread to other parts of the region. The complex and ancient roots of the conflict there that must be understood in order to assess the contemporary situation. Even a relatively cursory overview of the bases of the conflicts quickly establishes the region's bewildering array of ethnic, religious, economic, and related political problems that has generated hostilities between population groups within the former Yugoslavia and between its successor states and neighboring countries.

The former Yugoslavia's complex ethnic composition and geography (see Table 12-1 and Fig. 12-6) was the result of migratory movements of people and related territorial struggles between empires and states for millennia, including the approximately 2700 years for which we have some written records. Archaeological records indicate that humans have lived in the area of the former Yugoslavia for at least 200,000 years. By about 600 B.C. the Greeks began to establish trading posts and, later, colonies on the Adriatic coast. They were displaced by the Romans, who also ultimately ruled most of the future Yugoslavia for about 400 years. In A.D. 395 the Roman Empire split between the west, dominated from Rome, and the east ruled from Constantinople (now Istanbul). The Eastern or Byzantine Empire maintained control over or had influence in parts of the former Yugoslavia for over a thousand years.

By the 4th century A.D., Slavic peoples began moving south into the region, displacing Illyrians, Greeks, and other inhabitants. The successful seventh century A.D. alliance of Avar and Slavic peoples resulted in the spread of the Slavs over an even greater area in Southeastern Europe. The land that is now Slovenia soon thereafter fell under the domination of Germanic peoples and was ultimately held for 640 years within the Habsburg Empire. Indications are that in the seventh century the Byzantine Empire used the Croats to secure and occupy what has become Croatia, which established its own independence in the tenth century. By 1102 ties between Croatia and Hungary developed that lasted until 1918. First Croatia and then Hungary contested Venice for control of the Dalmatian coast. Serbia and Bosnia-Herzegovina also played less important roles in the Dalmatian territorial conflict at various times.

Serbia achieved independence from Byzantium in the twelfth century and developed a flourishing state and culture until its subjugation by the Ottoman Turks for over 500 years. Some areas, notably Dubrovnik (earlier Ragusa), were able to remain relatively free of Turkish domination through payment of tribute. Serbs in what became Montenegro, however, resisted Turkish domination throughout the period through their near single-minded devotion to defense and independence. Over the centuries these Serbs defending Montenegro developed a sense of separate self-identity and became today's Montenegrins, who remain close political allies of the Serbs and Serbia. During the time of struggle with the Turks,

Serb and Montenegrin cultures were apparently imprinted by an heroic struggle for independence and, especially among the Serbs, for the sanctity of Kosovo as a legendary homeland. These factors have echoed across the centuries to impact contemporary Serbian and Montenegrin politics. Today's self-proclaimed "Yugoslavia" is comprised of Serb- and Montenegrin-controlled territories. The historical attachment to Kosovo also helps explain the Serbs' reticence to allow independence for this formerly autonomous province, in which up to the early 1990s over 90 percent of the population were ethnic Albanians (though reports of immigration of Serb refugees from Bosnia could be changing this situation).

In 1453 Byzantium also fell to the Turks, and before 1500 virtually all of Southeastern Europe was under their control. This initiated a period of over 400 years of armed struggle for territorial dominance in the region between Austria, Hungary, and the Ottoman Empire. This period began to produce the population movements that led to the twentieth century's geographically complex ethnic population distribution in the Balkans. At times, thousands of people fled from battle fronts; one such occasion brought, for example, thousands of Serbs to the Vojvodina region in what is now northern Serbia and even into settlements in what is now Hungary. The Austrians established a military frontier area (originally depopulated) in Croatia and Vojvodina; subsequently, they greatly complicated its ethnic geography by settling guards and farmers in it from among the Empire's highly diverse ethnic groups.

By the end of the nineteenth century, the Ottoman Empire's economic problems, its related political decadence and military weakness, the emergence of Slav nationalism, and Austro-Hungary's and Russia's political and territorial aspirations resulted in the establishment of many of today's Southeast European states. Bitter disputes, usually involving conflicting territorial claims, erupted among the numerous small states, the region's empires (Austro-Hungarian, Ottoman, and Russian), as well as other European powers. This competition is the basis for many of the territorial disputes now swirling around Bosnia-Herzegovina, Macedonia, and Transylvania in particular. Disputes over the former two regions led to the two Balkan Wars of 1912–1913, conflicts that portended World War I.

These historical events in the former Yugoslavia created complex ethnic patterns throughout Southeastern Europe, particularly in Bosnia-Herzegovina, Croatia (notably Slavonia in the east, Dalmatia in the west), and Macedonia, where geopolitical boundaries between empires were ever shifting. Ethnic and geopolitical conflicts ensued.

Related geographic patterns of cultural and economic development have further complicated this already chaotic picture. After A.D. 1054, the close ethnic and linguistic relationship between Croats and Serbs was splintered by the second schism between Roman Catholicism and Eastern Orthodoxy. This precipitated a greater cultural divide among the southern Slavs, especially the Serbs and Croats, not only in religious affairs, but also in the development of alphabets from spoken languages. Written languages were Cyrillic-based in the south and Latin-based in the north. Turkish occupation led to the political-economic ascendancy of the Greek clergy and the establishment of a large local Muslim population. The power of the Greek clergy led especially to antipathy between Slavic Macedonians and Greeks. Evolution of a large Muslim population, which many people attribute to the conversion of (perceived unscrupulous) Slavs to Islam for their personal political and economic gain, generated further ethnic and political problems. There are two other theories for the unclear origin of Muslim Yugoslavs who once inhabited much of Bosnia and Herzegovina. One is that today's Muslims descend from the Bogomiles, ethnic Slavs who followed a heretic religious sect that evolved in medieval times and spread from Bulgaria. The other suggests that Muslims descend from immigrant Anatolian Turks.

The almost complete lack of supportive economic development efforts (e.g., policies favoring the building of transport facilities, educational and financial institutions, and manufacturing plants) during the critical era of nineteenth-century industrialization, as well as autocratic rule in Ottoman Europe, greatly retarded economic development, especially in the southern parts of the former Yugoslavia. In Hungarian-held lands (Croatia and northern Serbia), these problems were somewhat less severe, whereas in Austrian-held Slovenia industrialization, education, and integration with life in more advanced Central and Western Europe was proceeding.

Some citizens of the former Yugoslavia have ascribed the great differences in postindependence standards of living within the former Yugoslavia, related to these developments, to the unfair/unscrupulous advantages attained by some people, such as Slovenes and Muslims, at the cost of others, such as Serbs, Montenegrins, Macedonians, and Albanians. In 1918 the vast majority of landowners in Bosnia were, in fact, Muslims. Whatever the actual cause of this pattern, local Croats and Serbs often choose to interpret this as evidence of unfair advantage and ethnic discrimination. Conversely, other Yugoslav citizens perceived Slovenes and Croats to be hard-working people who subsidized a leisurely, unproductive lifestyle of southern "Yugoslavs." Despite a variety of efforts to blunt these perceptions, a relatively poor economic performance gave the communist Yugoslav regime too few resources to provide its ethnically conscious and diverse population with enough improvement in their lives to reduce inequalities—which, in fact, increased alarmingly in the post–World War II era. By the late 1980s, Slovenia's per capita income levels were about eight times higher than Kosovo's, where per capita growth was held back by Europe's highest rate of natural population growth.

Given the high level of outside domination, "Yugoslavs" have long viewed their neighbors with suspicion. For example, as an early geography lesson, school children learned the names of the countries bordering Yugoslavia in this order: Bulgaria, Romania, Italy, Greece, Albania, Magyarorszag (Hungary), and Austria. The first letters of each country spell out the word "BRIGAMA," which in Serbo-Croatian means "troubles."

Thus, there are many bases—historical, religious-cultural, economic, and political—for the development of ethnic antipathy in the former Yugoslavia. In retrospect, then, it is astounding that the diverse peoples of the former Yugoslavia achieved political triumphs by establishing a state after World War I, surviving a worldwide recession, and reestablishing a unified Yugoslavia under Tito after World War II. During that war hundreds of thousands of Yugoslavs died in combat and as the result of "ethnic cleansing"—especially Serbs, who died by the thousands under a Nazi-supported Croatian government.

In the early postwar years, Yugoslavia followed the Soviet model of economic and political development, but Stalin's break with Tito in 1948 forced it to establish closer relations with the West. With a complete trade embargo by all CMEA countries and Albania, Yugoslavia's economy had to rely on its own resources, and in the 1950s it slowly developed closer economic and political ties with West European countries, Greece, and the United States, which extended important military and economic aid. Politically, Yugoslavia remained part of the nonaligned countries.

Economic development in Yugoslavia during the 1960s and 1970s was erratic, with its multinational character affecting the complicated decision-making processes between the Yugoslav Federation and the individual republics. Foreign borrowing played an important role in the Yugoslav economic development in the 1970s. Combating high inflation, streamlining a cumbersome administrative machinery, emphasizing at the same time economic growth, and reducing differences in development levels between the most developed northern republics and the poor southern republics, especially Kosovo, were important goals. In spite of the raw material wealth of the southern, less developed regions (with 75 % of the lignite coal, 96% of the iron ore reserves, and 86 % of the nonferrous metal resources), regional inequalities in per capita income increased after 1947.

The death of the Federation's president Tito in 1980 brought long-submerged differences between the advanced and underdeveloped republics to the forefront, especially the problems between Slovenia, Croatia, and Serbia. Tito's unifying influence certainly had complicated the country's cumbersome decision-making processes, especially in times of economic and political stress. Tito strongly believed that power in Yugoslavia should not be concentrated in any one of the six republics and that the age-old rivalry between Serbs and Croats could be controlled only through a decentralized decision-making system. With his death, the government and the party, which was deeply divided along regional-ethnic lines, found it more and

more difficult to control these conflicts. These differences affected political and economic policies throughout the 1980s. As a result, uncontrolled inflation, a drastically lower standard of living, and constant delays in implementing obviously needed economic reforms created many problems.

By 1989 a number of circumstances began to build upon the centuries-old legacies of ethnic, cultural, and political conflicts and upon the ever heightening desires for national independence by the country's ethnic groups, bringing about a tragedy of horrific proportions. The unwieldy post-Tito political system did not survive a number of tests and challenges; most of Yugoslavia's republics declared independence; and warfare broke out.

Yugoslavia's fragile internal political stability was perhaps first threatened by ever growing economic problems in the ECSEE states, which the autocratic, socialist/communist regimes were unable to resolve. In a related development, Gorbachev's critical posture with respect to long-held political and economic policies and his criticism of several ECSEE governments emboldened reformers and dissidents within the region. At the same time, the Soviets' economic problems grew, and their ability and willingness to maintain their ECSEE empire first wavered and then evaporated. Truly revolutionary events in, for example, Hungary, Czechoslovakia, Bulgaria, and the GDR began to raise questions about Yugoslavia's own future. Unfortunately, at the same time Yugoslav domestic politics were becoming ever more complex and strident. Highly nationalistic leaders held power in Croatia and Bosnia-Herzegovina, in part in response to the growing power and ever bolder policies of Slobodan Milosevic, the nationalistic leader of Serbia. In what many people view as a key factor in Yugoslavia's demise as a unified state and descent into war, the Serbian central government revoked local political autonomy in Kosovo and Vojvodina. The other republics interpreted these actions as an explicit threat. The citizens of these republics had long suspected and feared a (perceived or real) desire by Serbs to dominate all of Yugoslavia, if not simply to create a "greater Serbia."

Slovenia and Croatia, in particular, also pressed for both economic reform and greater economic autonomy (including reduced flows of north-to-south subsidies), positions that favored them but ran counter to Serb desires for greater centralized control and a slower pace of reforms. Many people argue that European and U.S. diplomatic efforts were also far too few during this critical period, in part because of these governments' preoccupation with the Iraqi occupation of Kuwait and the subsequent Gulf War. In a late 1990 referendum, Slovenians voted for separation from Yugoslavia, followed by the same action in Croatia during the spring of 1991; both actions were supported by the German government and, through its leadership, the EC as well.

Skirmishes within Slovenia broke out between Slovenian and the largely Serb-controlled Federal forces, but Slovenia was able to establish independent rule. However, armed conflict between Croatia and both Federal and Croatian Serb forces became intense and brutal, with Croatia fighting to establish independence and defend the territory it comprised within Federal Yugoslavia, and Serbs and Federal forces fighting to maintain central authority and prevent Serbs living in Croatia from once again falling under the power of a potentially threatening, nationalistic Croatian government. The Croatian capital of Zagreb was bombed by air; Serb-dominated forces seized and held territory in eastern Croatia (Slavonia) and central Dalmatia; and both charges and evidence of "ethnic cleansing" and widespread atrocities became common.

A similar, though more politically and territorially complex, conflict erupted in 1992 following Bosnia-Herzegovina's announcement of independence. Here combat, intrigue, terror, and unimaginable atrocities prevailed into the mid-1990s as the result of conflict between ethnic, religious, and political groups largely identifiable with the Serb, Croatian, and Muslim population groups. UN, European, and U.S. diplomacy achieved a reduction in hostilities but no clear resolutions to underlying problems until late 1995. A tenuous peace settlement was in place in 1996 (Fig. 12-18), but fear of renewed war still hangs over Croatia, Bosnia, and Serbia-Montenegro. Serbia-Montenegro continues to refer to itself as "Yugoslavia," though without official recognition from other countries.

Prophetically, the late George Hoffman, editor of the last edition of this textbook (1990), wrote that "Serbian nationalism has been counterpro-

ductive inasmuch as it aroused the strong opposition of Yugoslavia's non-Serbian population; this could easily become a serious strain on the viability of the state in the future." Perceived threats from Serbia as well as additional potential sources of conflict continue to undermine peace in still other parts of the former Yugoslavia. There is concern that political and territorial agreements between Serbia, Croatia, and Bosnia could lead to greater Serb pressure on Kosovo and possibly on Macedonia as well. Outbreak of war in Kosovo could well result in some kind of military action by Albania, as well as other countries with geopolitical interests and Muslim populations (e.g., Turkey). Such actions could then result in responses by Bulgaria and Greece, each with its own political-territorial problems with the former Yugoslavia, Albania, and Turkey. One scenario is another Balkan War that could draw in military forces from outside the region in hopes of ending such a conflict, but in the short term surely complicating and intensifying it.

The Macedonian situation provides a classic example of the tangled problems of ethnicity, nationalism, and geopolitics in the Balkans. Dominantly Slavic people in this former Yugoslav republic self-identify as Macedonians, an identification that is disputed or denied by members of other ethnic groups and governments in the region. For example, many Serbs and Bulgarians argue that self-proclaimed Macedonians are actually Serbs or Bulgarians, respectively. Many Greeks, and their government, argue that use of the name *Macedonia* by a Slavic people is unjustified, given that modern-day Slavs have no ethnic ties to the ancient Macedonians, who included Alexander the Great, and are viewed as Greek by many modern Greeks. Greeks also believe that the use of the term *Macedonia* for the state that has emerged from the Yugoslav Republic of Macedonia could be used at some time in the future to justify its attempts to incorporate within "Macedonia" the Macedonian region within modern Greece. The dispute became so serious that in 1994 Greece unilaterally closed most commerce between the new state of Macedonia and the seaport that serves it—Thessaloniki, Greece. This action created serious political tensions between Greece and its EU partners, and by 1996 the trade embargo had been lifted.

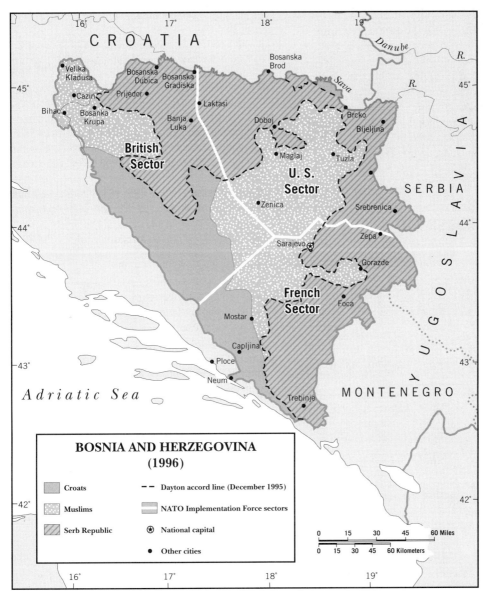

FIGURE 12-18 Delimitation of territorial agreements in Bosnia-Herzegovina associated with the Dayton Peace Plan.

In short, given the aspirations of some Serbs and Bulgarians for territory in Macedonia; the Macedonian-Greek dispute; tensions between the Macedonian government, ethnic Albanians (now 23% of the country's population), and other minorities; and Macedonia's relative poverty, it is a country that at best could face continued problems in international relations or at worst could spark a Balkan war. Such a war could be ignited by an invasion of Macedonia by Serbia or by some other event associated with conflicts within the former Yugoslavia.

In order to acquire a balanced understanding of the unfolding events in the former Yugoslavia, a broad background, including an understanding of the perspectives of the combatants and potential combatants in the overlapping conflicts, is needed. The preceding sketch of the situation provides a beginning toward such an understanding, as well as a geographical perspective on the issues. Note, however, that a textbook cannot present information on the most recent events and trends in the former Yugoslavia; referral to current sources of information is therefore recommended (e.g., the *New York Times* and other leading U.S. and international newspapers, or journals such as *Current History*).

BIBLIOGRAPHY

Berentsen, W. H. (1981). "Regional Change in the German Democratic Republic." *Annals Association of American Geographers* 71: 56–66.

———. (1989). "Regional Development and Regional Policy in Central Europe, 1950–1980." In *Regional Development Processes and Policies*, W. H. Berentsen, D. R. Danta, and E. Daroczi, eds. Budapest: Centre for Regional Studies, Hungarian Academy of Sciences pp. 156–177.

———. (1987). "Settlement Structure and Urban Development in the GDR, 1950–1985." *Urban Geography* 8: 405–419.

Büschenfeld, H. (1995). "Makedonien—jüngstereuropäischer Staat." *Geographische Rundschau* 47(3): 162–167.

Burghardt, A. F. (1962). *Borderland: A Historical and Geographical Study of Burgenland, Austria*. Madison: University of Wisconsin Press.

Carter, F. W. (1985). "Pollution Problems in Post-war Czechoslovakia." *Institute of British Geographers, Transaction New Series* 10: 17–44.

Central Intelligence Agency. (1990). *Atlas of Eastern Europe*. Washington, D.C.: CIA.

Comisso, E., and L. D'A. Tyson, eds. (1986). *Power, Purpose and Collective Choice, Economic Strategy in the Socialist States*. Ithaca, N.Y.: Comen.

Croan, M. (1989). "Lands In-between: The Politics of Cultural Identity in Contemporary Eastern Europe." *Eastern European Politics and Society* 3: 176–197.

Curtis, G. E., ed. (1992). *Yugoslavia: A Country Study*. Washington D.C.: U.S.G.P.O.

Danta, D. R. (1987). "Hungarian Urbanization and Socialist Ideology." *Urban Geography* 8: 391–404.

Dawson, A. H. (1987). *Planning in Eastern Europe*. New York: St. Martin's Press.

De Bardelleben, J., ed. (1989). *Environmental Problems and Policies in Eastern Europe*. Washington, D.C.: Wilson Center Press.

Domański, B., and R. Matykowski. (1996). "Regional Industrial Change in an Economy in Transition: The Case of Poland." Unpublished paper, Institute of Geography, Jagiellonian University, Cracow.

French, R. A., and F.E.I.Hamilton, eds. (1979). *The Socialist City. Spatial Structure and Urban Policy*. Chichester, Eng.: Wiley.

Georgescu, V. (1987). "Romania in the 1980s: The Legacy of Dynastic Socialism." *Eastern European Politics and Societies* 2: 69–93.

Gross, M. (1981). "On the Integration of the Croatian Nation—A Case Study in Nation Building." *East European Quarterly* 15: 209–225.

Grzegorz, G. (1986). "The Spatial Aspects of the Polish Crisis." *GeoJournal* 12: 81–88.

Hare, P. G. (1987). "Industrial Development in Hungary Since World War II." *Eastern European Politics and Societies* 2:115–151.

Hoffman, G.W. (1977). "The Evolution of the Ethnographic Map of Yugoslavia. An Historical Geographic Interpretation." In *Historical Geography of the Balkans*, F.W. Carter, ed. London: Seminar Press, pp. 437–491.

———. (1974). *Regional Development Strategy in Southeast Europe. A Comparative Analysis of Albania, Bulgaria, Greece, Romania and Yugoslavia*. 2nd ed. New York: Praeger.

———. (1952). "The Shatter Belt in Relation to the East-West Conflict." *Journal of Geography* 51: 266–275.

———. (1981). "Rural Transformation in Eastern Europe since World War II." In *The Process of Rural Transformation*, I. Volgyes et al., eds. New York: Pergamon Press, pp. 21–41.

———. (1986). "The Transformation of the Urban Landscape in Southeastern Europe." In *World Pattern of Modern Urban Change*, M. P. Conzens, ed. Chicago: University of Chicago, Department of Geography, Research Paper No. 217218, pp. 129–150.

Jancar, B. (1987). *Environmental Management in the Soviet Union and Yugoslavia*. Durham, N.C.: Duke University Press.

Jelavich, B. (1983). *History of the Balkans*. Cambridge: Cambridge University Press.

Jordan, P. (1995). "Rumänien–permanente Peripherie Europas?" *Erdkundeunterricht* 1995(2): 42–51.

Kaser, M., and M. C. Radice (1987). *The Economic History of Eastern Europe, 1919–1975*. London: Oxford.

Korcelli, P. (1995). "Regional Patterns in Poland's Transformation: The First Five Years." Institute of Geography and Spatial Organization, Polish Academy of Sciences, Working Paper no. 34 (Warsaw).

Krekic, B. (1987). *The Urban Society of Eastern Europe in Premodern Times*. Berkeley: University California Press.

Kuklinski, A. (1986). *Regional Studies in Poland: Experience and Prospects*. Warsaw: Panstwowe Wydnawnictwo Naukowe.

Lampe, J. R. (1986). *The Bulgarian Economy in the Twentieth Century*. New York: St. Martin's Press.

Lampe, J. R., and M. R. Jackson. (1982). *Balkan Economic History, 1550–1950. From Imperial Borderland to Developing Nation*. Bloomington: Indiana University Press.

Leff, C. S. (1988). *National Conflict in Czechoslovakia. The Making and Remaking of State*. Princeton, N.J.: Princeton University Press.

Magocsi, P. R. (1993). *Historical Atlas of East Central Europe*. Toronto: University of Toronto Press.

Misztal, S. (1996). "Regional Aspects of Ownership Transformation in Polish Industry." Unpublished paper, Institute of Geography and Spatial Organization, Polish Academy of Sciences, Warsaw.

Nelson, D. N., and W. Welsh (1989). *East European Politics*. Boulder, Colo: Westview.

Pearson, R. (1983). *National Minorities in Eastern Europe 1848–1945*. London: Macmillan.

Pecsi, M., and B. Sarfalvi. (1984). *The Geography of Hungary*. Budapest: Corvina.

Popescu, C. (1993). "Romanian Industry in Transition." *GeoJournal* 29(1): 41–48.

Pounds, N.J.G. (1969). *Eastern Europe*. London: Longman.

———. (1985). *An Historical Geography of Europe: 1800-1914*. Cambridge: Cambridge University Press.

Raagmaa, G. (1996). "Hidden Economy Growth as a General Phenomenon of Postsocialist Transition Economies." Unpublished paper, Estonian Institute for Future Studies and Institute of Geography, Tartu University.

Ramet, P. (1984). *Nationalism and Federalism in Yugoslavia 1963–1983*. Bloomington: Indiana University Press.

Rothschild, J. (1989). *Return to Diversity. A Political History of East Central Europe Since World War II*. New York: Oxford University Press.

Rugg, D. S. (1985). *Eastern Europe*. London and New York: Longman.

Rusinow, D., ed. (1988). *Yugoslavia. A Fractured Federalism*. Washington, D.C.: Wilson Center Press.

Seton-Watson, H. (1975). *The "Sick Heart" of Modern Europe: The Problem of the Danubian Lands*. Seattle, Wash.: University of Washington Press.

Stoianovich, T. A. (1967). *A Study in Balkan Civilization*. New York: Alfred A. Knopf.

Stokes, G. (1987). "The Social Origins of East European Politics." *Eastern European Politics and Societies* 1: 30–74.

Stryjakiewicz, T. (1996). "The Changing Industrial Enterprise in an 'Economy in Transition': Structural and Spatial Dimensions in Poland." Unpublished manuscript, Institute of Socio-Economic Geography and Spatial Planning, Adam Mickiewicz University, Poznan.

Sugar, P. F., and I. Cederer. (1969). *Nationalism in Eastern Europe*. Seattle, Wash.: University of Washington Press.

Terry, Meiklejohn S., ed. (1984). *Soviet Policy in Eastern Europe*. New Haven, Conn.: Yale University Press.

Turnock, D. (1988). *The Making of Eastern Europe. From the Earliest Times to 1815*. New York: Routledge.

United Nations (1995). *Economic Bulletin for Europe*. New York and Geneva: UN.

World Bank. (1995). *Transition* (various issues).

Zaniewski, K. (1992). "Regional Inequalities in Social Well-being in Central and Eastern Europe." *Tijdschrift voor economische en sociale geografie* 83 (5): 342–352.

13

RUSSIA AND
THE EUROPEAN NIS

No systematic geographical understanding of Europe would be complete without a discussion of the former Soviet Union, especially the Russian Federation (the USSR's Russian Republic) and some of its European newly independent states (NIS). Dramatic political and economic changes in Eastern Europe are closely related to changes within the Soviet Union—which now also no longer exists. In addition, no clear physical, linguistic, cultural, or historical barriers separate the newly independent states of the former Soviet Union (FSU) west of the Urals from the rest of Europe. Recent discoveries based on plate tectonic theory provide a geological basis for the traditional use of the Urals and Caucasus Mountain Ranges as borders between Europe and Asia, though most of the new national political borders within the geographical confines of the FSU have no such easily visible physiographic demarcations. In fact, the current configurations of these boundaries often represent the results of historical accidents, battle-field victories, early Stalinist gerrymandering, and 70-odd years of Soviet demographic, economic, linguistic, cultural, and political blurring. The Urals are useless as a defining border for Russia—the most economically, demographically and politically significant of the successor states. Even south of the Caucasus, Georgia and Armenia are more European historically, culturally, and linguistically than Asian. Nonetheless, Europe proper does contain the core area of Russia and all of the newly independent states of Estonia, Latvia, Lithuania, Belarus, Ukraine, and Moldova.

The aim here is not to present a comprehensive portrait of the geography of the former USSR, but rather to highlight some of the key issues, problems, and developments of the Soviet and post-Soviet era and to relate Russia and the other European successor states to the rest of Europe. The political, economic, and social developments of post–World War II Europe cannot be evaluated adequately without reference to the former Soviet

Union, and the contemporary problems and dynamism of Europe as a whole is inextricably linked to the fate of the European Soviet successor states. At this writing much uncertainty remains over the economic and political fates of several of these NIS, especially Ukraine, Moldova, and Belarus.

Nonetheless, as background for the post-Soviet era, a description of the physical environment and some cultural and historical highlights are warranted. Unlike Europe to the west, which may be characterized as maritime and peninsular, with mostly agreeable climates, the physical geography of Russia and the European NIS is much more aptly described by such terms as *continuity, massiveness,* and *continentality.* Although these countries contain much of the best and most easily inhabited regions of the former Soviet Union, continentality still poses a series of challenges to human habitation, especially in the Russian north and in regions east of the Urals.

SIZE AND RELATIVE LOCATION

To a significant extent, the economic, military, and political *superpower* status that the former Soviet Union achieved after the end of World War II was based on its *supersize.* Even after the breakup of the USSR, Russia with a total area of 6,592,692 sq miles (17,075,000 sq km) remains nearly twice the size of Canada, China, or the United States. Even without the resources of the other 14 former Soviet republics, Russia alone still has within its borders ample varieties and quantities of minerals and fossil fuels to make it the most nearly resource self-sufficient industrial country in the world. Ukraine's 233,206 sq miles (604,000 sq km) make it the second largest country in Europe, surpassing France's area by about 10 percent. In all European Russia and the European NIS occupy nearly one-half of the total area of Europe. The tremendous resource base of this extensive area has long been plagued by expensive transportation problems and, hence, problems of territorial-economic integration. At least in the short run, many of these problems will be intensified by the geographical

legacy of the Soviet-built infrastructure focused on serving the needs of Russia's core areas in Europe.

Focusing on Russia for the moment, we observe that both its east-west and its north-south spans are spectacular. The distance from the westernmost point of the country (20° E) near noncontiguous Kaliningrad on the Baltic Sea to Cape Dezhnev opposite Alaska on the Bering Strait (170° W), is over 6200 miles (9920 km) and over 170° longitude—nearly half the circumference of the earth and a span of 11 time zones. Within European Russia the maximum north-south extent is roughly 1860 miles (3000 km) from the southernmost Russian-Azerbaijan border to the Barents Sea coastline in the north. Notably, Russia lays claim to the entire polar region between the meridians of Murmansk (32° E) and the Bering Strait (168° 45' W) as far north as the North Pole itself.

Equally striking is Russia's location relative to other landmasses, oceans, and population centers. Perhaps the most critical feature of Russia's relative location is its northerly latitudinal position. Except for relatively small southern portions of the Far East and North Caucasus region, all of Russia is located at latitudes north of the coterminus 48 U.S. states. While about half of Ukraine's territory lies south of the U.S.-Canadian border, all of the other European NIS states lie to the north of it. St. Petersburg, Russia's second largest city, is only a bit farther south than Anchorage, Alaska; Moscow, the capital city, is slightly farther north than Ketichan in the Alaskan panhandle. Great circle distances from Moscow to Washington, D.C., and to Seattle are the same, and St. Petersburg and Vladivostok are nearly as far from each other as they are from Seattle.

Russia has replaced the former Soviet Union as having the longest coastline by far of any country. This is true despite the fact that more than half of the former Soviet Union's Black Sea coastline and most of the Baltic Sea coastline lies outside Russia. More than half of Russia's coastline is at extremely high latitudes along the Arctic Ocean. Most of these littoral regions are frozen much of the year, or are marshy and sparsely settled, or totally uninhabited. From the perspective of transportation significance, the seas bordering Russia and the European NIS can be classified into four groups:

(1) seas having direct access to the world's oceans; (2) the seasonally icebound Arctic and sub-Arctic seas; (3) the land-locked Caspian Sea; and (4) seas having access through straits controlled by other countries.

The first group includes the Barents Sea, White Sea, and Sea of Japan (see Fig. 13-1). Murmansk's harbor on the Barents Sea, kept open by the warm North Atlantic Drift (the eastern extension of the Gulf Stream), is Russia's only truly year-round port. The White Sea lumber port of Arkhangelsk, on the other hand, is useless between November and May because of ice. Although the Sea of Japan provides access to the Pacific Ocean, icebreakers are necessary to keep Vladivostok, Nakhodka, Vostochny, and Vanino open the year round.

The second group, the much-touted Arctic Sea Route, is of minor importance for shipping, and serves only a few scattered coastal settlements in northern and eastern Siberia during its short season, which is extended with the aid of icebreakers to 120 days from July through October. The few minor ports on the Bering and Okhotsk seas are also icebound much of the year. With the collapse of the centrally controlled Soviet economy, the survival of settlements dependent on the Arctic Sea Route is now very much in question.

The third group includes only the large, land-locked, saline lake called the Caspian Sea. Of the five major ports located along the shores of the Caspian Sea, only two, Astrakhan' and Makhachkala, remain Russian. Shipping on the Caspian Sea is likely to continue to decline as a result of the Soviet breakup, the building of new oil and natural gas pipelines, and the likely reorientation of much Central Asian trade southward.

The fourth group includes the Baltic Sea and Black Sea – Sea of Azov international bodies of water. Historically, the Soviets and before them the Russians shed much blood in efforts to acquire and maintain a foothold on the Baltic Sea, because it afforded Russia and the USSR the shortest and easiest route to the Atlantic Ocean and Western Europe. The independence of the three Baltic states has left Russia with only two major ports on the Baltic Sea—St. Petersburg and Kaliningrad. St. Petersburg can be kept open only by the use of ice-breakers through most of the winter season. Russian foreign maritime trade through Kaliningrad now requires transit through Lithuania and either Latvia or Belarus. Lithuania and Russia have been engaged in protracted negotiations because of the now geographically noncontiguous nature of Kaliningrad Oblast and its strategic naval and military facilities. Russia holds a number of bargaining chips in these deliberations, including financially important transit traffic through Baltic ports, energy supplies for the energy-scarce Baltic states and Belarus, and timetables for the complete withdrawal of Russian troops in some of these former Soviet republics. The non-Russian political players, in turn, wield power over surface-transit access privileges for Russian imports and exports to Kaliningrad and other Baltic ports, such as Tallinn in Estonia, Riga and Liepaja in Latvia, and Klaipeda in Lithuania. Ironically, some of the Russian exports leaving through these ports are illegal or smuggled goods. For example, Estonia has recently become the world's largest exporter of some nonferrous metals, such as copper, whereas in fact, it has no indigenous supplies of these metals or any refining or processing plants.

Like the Baltic Sea, access to the Black Sea was long a Russian objective and was finally achieved during the reign of Catherine the Great in the late eighteenth century. Winter ice is only a minor problem for the northern Black Sea ports, but Turkey's control of the Dardanelles and the Bosporus has long been a political and military problem for Russia and the Soviet Union. Since the breakup of the Soviet Union, however, a more acute problem has been the intramural contest between Ukraine and Russia over the division of ownership of the large Black Sea naval fleet and the large naval port facilities at Sevastopol' in Crimea. Ukraine possesses the biggest and most modern of the Black Sea commercial ports, namely, those at Odesa, Mykolayiv (formerly Nikolayev), and Kherson and the Sea of Azov ports at Berdyans'k and Mariupol' (formerly Zhdanov). Ukraine also retains control over the mouth of the Danube River, which would be of greater political significance in Ukraine's political and economic conflicts with Russia had not CMEA trade declined precipitously with both Russia and Ukraine since the USSR's breakup.

Russia still has two significant commercial Black Sea ports at Tuapse and Novorossiysk along the eastern margins of the Black Sea and in the North Caucasus region. The port of Sochi near the Russian-Georgian border is more important as a tourist port-of-call than as a commercial port. Along the northern shore of the Sea of Azov and a short distance upstream from the mouth of the Don River, Russia still has the ports of Taganrog and Rostov-na-Donu, respectively.

Thus, since the breakup of the Soviet Union, Russia has on all coasts become more restricted in terms of its direct maritime access. Today Russia may be aptly described as being a gigantic northerly landmass circumscribed along the north and east by cold, icy, uninviting seas and along the south and west by either rugged mountainous terrain or less than enthusiastic former political and economic partners.

PHYSICAL GEOGRAPHY

Topographic Regions and Resources

Tectonic forces, glaciation, and water erosion are the primary geomorphic processes responsible for the topographic configuration of Russia and the European NIS, which in general can be likened to a great pool table, bounded by a high mountainous rim along the southern margins and dissected plateaus and mountains in the east. Averaging only 300 to 600 ft. (90 to 180 m) in elevation, this enormous continuation of the North European Lowlands stretches from Poland to the Yenisey Valley in Siberia (see Fig. 13-1). The Appalachian-like north-south trending Ural Mountains form the only major relief barrier in this extensive lowland region. The highest peak, Gora Narodnaya (People's Pak), reaches only 6184 ft (1874 m), and much of the Urals range is below 3000 ft (900 m). The low-lying, heavily industrialized, middle Urals region through which the Trans-Siberian Railroad runs has extremely rich mineral deposits,

but some have been mined to exhaustion. Long famous for their iron-ore deposits, the Urals also have commercial-grade deposits of bauxite, chrome, asbestos, nickel, platinum, gold, copper, zinc, and various mineral salts. Very large oilfields and modest coalfields exist on both flanks of the range.

Including the three southern mountain ranges—the Carpathians, the Crimean Mountains, and the northern flank of the high, rugged Caucasus—the Great Russian Lowland is coterminous with the population and productive heartland of the former Soviet Union. Underlain by ancient Pre-Cambrian crystalline rocks with younger marine and continental sediments deposited on top, most of this rolling lowland topography is well below 600 ft (180 m) in elevation. The three areas of greater elevation, up to 1820 ft (560 m)—the Ukrainian Upland, the Central Russian Upland, and the Volga Uplands—are all the result of minor tectonic upthrusting. The high right banks along many of the southward-flowing rivers, including the Dnieper (Dnipro), Don, and Volga, formed strategic and easily defensible locations for early settlements such as Kiev (Kyyiv).

Much of the detailed relief of the Great Russian Lowland is the result of recent continental glaciation (see Fig. 2-5). Similar to the ice-scraped Pre-Cambrian shield areas of Ontario and Minnesota in North America, Karelia and the Kola Peninsula in the northwest are dotted with thousands of lakes and are rich in mineral deposits, especially nephelite (a low-grade aluminum ore), apatite (phosphate rock), iron, and nickel ores. The northern part of European Russia exhibits strong geomorphic evidence of recent glaciation, including extensive marshes, lakes, and a deranged drainage network, with festooned terminal moraines forming common and conspicuous features of the landscape. Even in the southern part of the plain, glaciation has left its mark. At its maximum extent, two glacial lobes of ice extended down the Don and Dnieper valleys. Thick layers of finely ground (loess) silt from the outwash plains of the melting ice sheet were deposited south of the morainic features. Subsequent water erosion of these wind-blown deposits has created the gullies and ravines

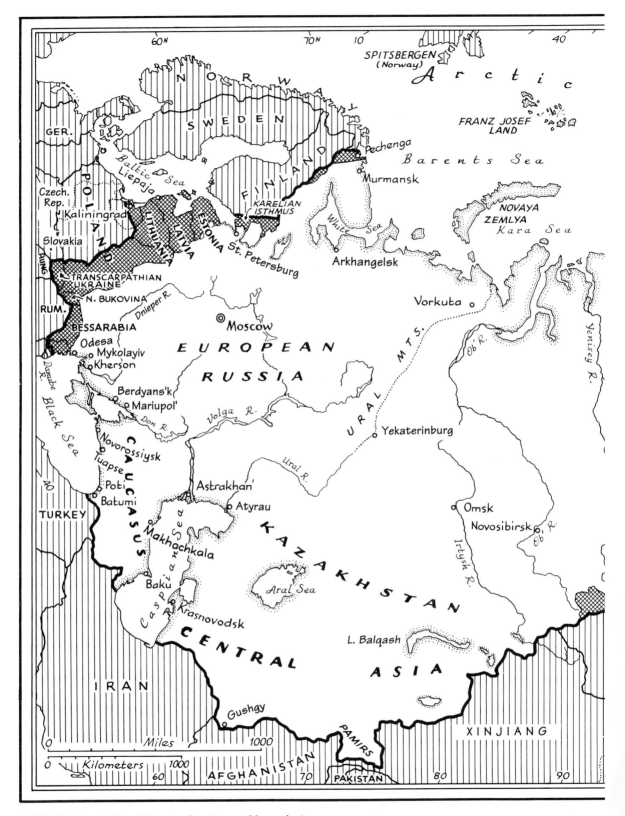

FIGURE 13-1 The NIS and Russia—location and boundaries.

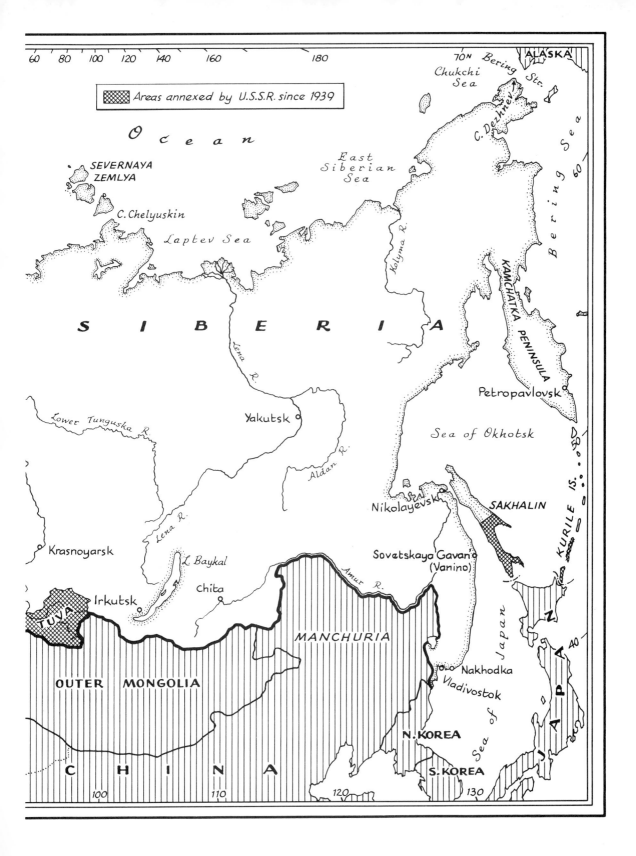

Areas annexed by U.S.S.R. since 1939

O c e a n

SEVERNAYA
ZEMLYA

C. Chelyuskin

Laptev Sea

Chukchi
Sea

70N Bering Str.

ALASKA

East
Siberian
Sea

C. Dezhnev

Bering Sea

60

S I B E R I A

KAMCHATKA PENINSULA

Lena R.

Yakutsk

Lower Tunguska R.

Aldan R.

Lena R.

Kolyma R.

Petropavlovsk

Sea of Okhotsk

Nikolayevsk

SAKHALIN

KURILE IS.

Krasnoyarsk

L. Baykal

Amur R.

Sovetskaya Gavan'
(Vanino)

Irkutsk

Chita

TUVA

MANCHURIA

JAPAN

40

Sea of Japan

OUTER   MONGOLIA

Nakhodka

Vladivostok

N. KOREA

C H I N A

S. KOREA

100

110

120

130

characteristic of the many parts of the Ukrainian landscape (Fig. 13-2).

In addition to the metallic mineral deposits in the northwest and the iron ore at Kryvyy Rih (also called Krivoi Rog) in Ukraine, the Great Russian Lowland contains other rich fuel and nonmetallic resources. The metamorphic rocks of the Kursk Magnetic Anomaly (KMA) just north of Ukraine are reputed to contain the world's largest mass of iron ore reserves. Coal and peat are abundant in the sedimentary mantle of the lowland, including the bituminous deposits of the Moscow Basin, and the hard coal of the Donets Basin in south-eastern Ukraine and the Pechora Basin in the northern Urals region. After World War II the Volga-Urals region became the most important Soviet oil- and natural gas-producing area. The North Caucasus foreland is also important for oil and gas deposits. Other resources such as potash, rock salt, phosphates, manganese, oil shale, and polymetallic ores are also mined in the Great Russian Lowland.

Beyond the Urals, the West Siberian Lowland stretches for hundreds of monotonous miles to the Yenisey Valley. Lower in elevation and with far less relative relief than its European counterpart, the West Siberian Lowland displays morainic features above 60° N and extensive outwash plains and swamp in areas between rivers (interfluves) below the 60th parallel. Although far from having a hospitable environment, Western Siberia has been the focus of much international interest since the mid-1960's because of its huge proven and predicted reserves of both natural gas and oil. Currently, this region produces about 90 percent and 70 percent of total Russian Federation gas and oil, respectively.

Much of the region near the Caspian Sea is below sea level, by as much as 90 ft (27 m). Except for oil- and gas-bearing strata underlying Kazakhstan along the northeastern Caspian depression and various mineral salts, this lowland is devoid of commercially important mineral and fuel resources.

Between the Yenisey and Lena rivers lies a dissected upland called the Central Siberian Plateau. Nearly the size of the West Siberian Lowland, most of the plateau is less than 3000 ft (900 m) above sea level. Although inaccessible and sparse-

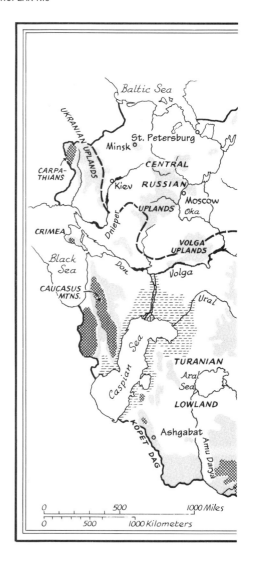

ly inhabited, the region is potentially rich in natural resources, especially coal, gas, and diamonds in the Sakha region (formerly Yakutiya).

Eastern Siberia consists of a complex series of mountain ranges with peaks cresting between 6000 and 10,000 ft (1800 and 3000 m). The Kamchatka Peninsula is composed of a series of coalesced volcanoes. In this still active geothermal area, some of this energy has been harnessed to generate local power supplies and to provide for local space-heating. The peninsula and the Kuril

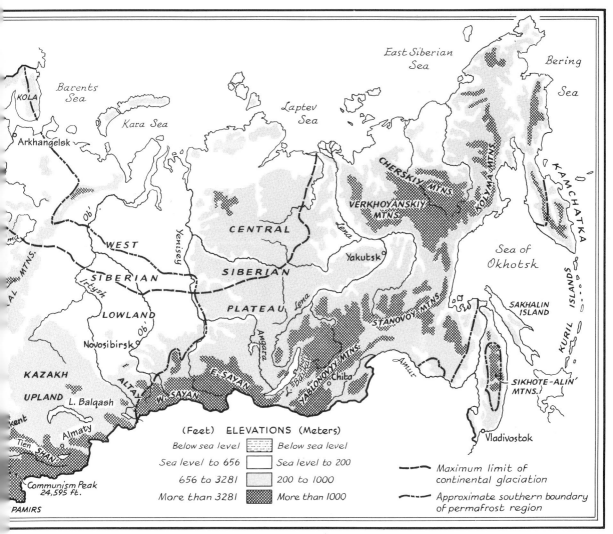

FIGURE 13-2 Topographic regions of the NIS and Russia.

Islands to the southwest are geologically part of an oceanic island-arc created by the northwestern Pacific oceanic crust being forced beneath the marine extension of the less dense Asian continental rock.

The Verkhoyanskiy and Cherskiy Ranges were also created by tectonic forces associated with continental drift and seafloor spreading. As the ancestral European and North American landmasses drifted apart, the drift velocity was faster in the southern part of the North Atlantic Ocean than in the north; thus, the region of the New Siberian Islands served as a fulcrum point, and the region south of these islands is subjected to an east-west-oriented compressional stress field creating the rugged terrain of northeastern Siberia. Much of eastern Siberia lies within an active seismic area, especially along the southern Russian border. Faulting has produced many rift valleys (areas between parallel faults), including the deep depression filled by the world-famous Lake Baykal (nearly 4900 ft deep [1500 m]).

The crystalline rocks of northeastern Siberia have yielded a rich supply of diamonds and gold. In addition, several tin and coal deposits exist in the region, and oil is extracted on Sakhalin Island. Of questionable economic viability under the Soviet planned economy, development of many of these resources may be even more doubtful under world market conditions. Although no ice sheet covered eastern Siberia, ancient and recent alpine glaciation has sculptured much of the landscape within the northeastern highlands. Approximately half of the entire Russian Federation—including nearly all the region east of the Yenisey River—is plagued by permafrost (permanently frozen ground) ranging in frigid thickness from a few to a thousand feet (300 m). Permafrost, of course, creates difficult transportation, construction, and agricultural conditions.

Only the mountain portions of the southern perimeter of Russia and the NIS remain to be mentioned. The low Ukrainian Carpathians, the Crimean Mountains (3900–5850 ft high/1200–1800 m), and the Caucasus are eastern extensions of the Alpine system of Europe. The Caucasus Ranges, in particular, has long constituted a significant barrier to easy overland transit. Along the southern margins of Siberia lie the taller Sayan and Altay Mountains (8800–13,650 ft high/2700–4200 m) which form a series of high and wide plateaus. The headwaters of three mighty Siberian rivers—the Yenisey, the Ob', and the Irtysh—have deeply scarred these plateaus through erosion. Glaciers are common in the Altay Range. This region has the chief Russian supplies of lead and zinc, while the famous Kuznetsk coal basin is situated along its northern slopes.

When Kazakhstan and the other four Central Asian republics were part of the Soviet Union, the high mountainous rim that formed the southern border of the Central Asian republics constituted an effective political as well as a physical border for the Soviet Union. This southern mountain system, from the Carpathians in the west to the trans-Baykal Ranges in the east, is the result of compressional forces associated with continental drift—the folded mountains in the west from the collision of the African with the Eurasian tectonic plate, and the plateau-like ranges in the east by the ramming of the Indian subcontinent or tectonic plate into it as well. Now, however, the southern border of Russia and the northern border of Kazakhstan pass through thousands of miles of undifferentiated rolling steppe landscape.

Climates: Continentality *par excellence*

The mere sound of the words *troyka* or *Siberia* seems able to set listeners shivering with cold, and well it should. With the minor exceptions of the Mediterranean-like climate along the southern Crimean coast, the humid subtropical coastal margins around the southeastern Black Sea near Sochi, and the monsoonal section of the southern Russian Far East (which does, however, have cold winters), the climate of the entire Russian Federation and nearly all of the NIS can be aptly characterized by one word: *continentality*. Simply stated, this means long, cold winters; short, cool-to-hot summers; and relatively dry conditions.

Because of the vastness of this landmass area, the cold Arctic Ocean, the distance from the Atlantic Ocean, and the southern and eastern mountain barriers, little of the combined Russian and NIS territory enjoys moderating marine influences on its climate. Hence, this Eurasian landmass cools rapidly during the winters and heats rapidly during the summers. These heating and cooling characteristics are primarily responsible for the creation of a persistent, frigid but sunny, high-pressure air mass over northeastern Siberia in the winter season. Conversely, a large, less well-defined, low-pressure system occurs over eastern Asia in the summer. Everywhere the average annual temperature range is great. For example, Verkhoyansk in eastern Siberia has a range of 118°F (65.5°C)—from a low of -58°F (-50°C) average for January to a high of 60°F (15.5°C) average for July—the greatest annual range in the world. Temperatures as low as -94°F (-70°C) have been recorded at Oymyakon in Sakha in northeastern Siberia. In such low temperatures, hypothermia develops rapidly, and even steel becomes brittle and fractures easily. Moscow has a 52°F (29°C) annual temperature range, and the Baltic and Pacific coastal region experiences 30° and 60°F (17° and 33°C) ranges, respectively.

The moderating influence of the Atlantic's westerly winds and the cold Siberian high-pressure system in combination produces a roughly northwest-southeast alignment of equivalent January average temperatures or isotherms (see Fig. 13-3). Latitudinal effects together with narrowly confined coastal maritime influences account for the alignment of the July isotherms (see Fig. 13-4). Only a few areas along the Crimean coast and the southeastern Black Sea littoral zone have average January temperatures above freezing. The snow cover lasts from 260 days in the Siberian north to 40 days in the southern Ukrainian steppe.

The human significance of these climatological facts is mixed. On the one hand, snow cover serves as a protective blanket and moisture reserve for the following growing season for winter grains. On the other hand, in spite of its vastness, much of the territory of Russia and the European NIS has a harsh climate, a relatively limited growing season, and conditions that are difficult for developing infrastructure such as railroads.

An investigation of precipitation patterns reveals additional environmental constraints (see fig. 13-5). Although Northern Europe normally receives abundant moisture from the Atlantic westerlies, by the time these modified maritime air masses reach the Great Russian Lowland, they have already lost much of their moisture content. Nonetheless, these Atlantic air masses are the predominant source of precipitation for the entire Russian landscape, except for the summer monsoonal zone in the Far East. Since the storm tracks generally traverse the landmass astride the 60th parallel, precipitation totals tend to decrease to the north and south of this line. The reliability of rainfall follows a similar pattern, while also decreasing from west to east across Siberia.

Orographic precipitation accounts for the relatively high rainfall in the Urals, Crimea, and western Caucasia. Except for these southern highlands, the entire territory of Russia and the European NIS experiences summer rainfall maxima. Low-pressure systems produce the Mediter-

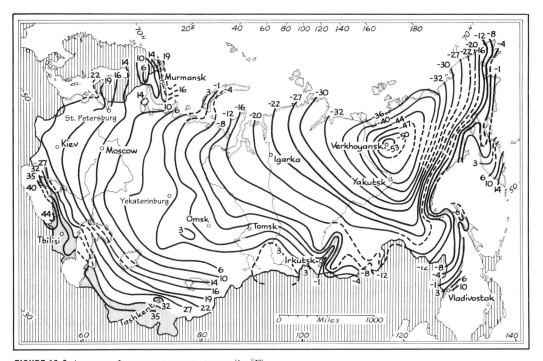

FIGURE 13-3 Average January temperatures (in °F).

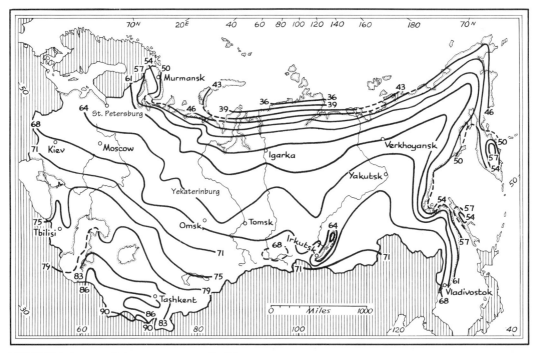

FIGURE 13-4 Average July temperatures (in °F).

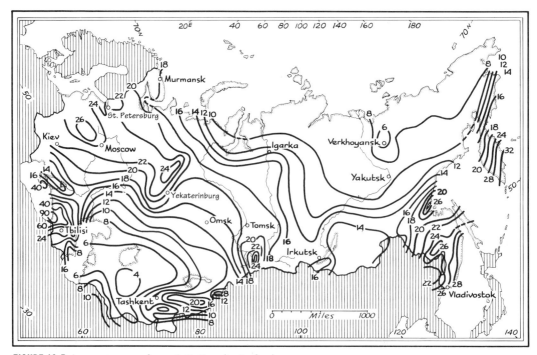

FIGURE 13-5 Average annual precipitation (in inches).

ranean-like winter precipitation maxima along the Black Sea.

The geographic generalization to be drawn from considerations of Russian and European NIS temperature and rainfall patterns is that there is little overlap of regions receiving sufficient or abundant precipitation with regions receiving abundant solar insulation. Thus, from human settlement and agricultural perspectives, essentially all of the territory lying south of a imaginary line drawn from Odesa on the Black Sea to Irkutsk near Lake Baykal (excluding the southern Black Sea coastal areas) suffers to varying degrees from chronic water shortages. Territory lying north of an imaginary line from St. Petersburg to Irkutsk has a chronic deficit of solar radiation. The roughly cone-shaped territory in between, often referred to as the "fertile triangle," is in fact not well suited for agriculture in many areas and offers nothing approaching the natural advantages of the United States' "cornbelt."

Natural Regions: The Latitudinal Brush Strokes

Close interdependencies exist among climate, soils, and vegetation. Vegetation mirrors climate, while climate, together with vegetation, exerts a major influence on soil formation. Precipitation and evaporation affect the rates of soil generation and the movement of soluble plant nutrients within the soil. Nowhere else in the world has nature's climatic and geologic phenomena interacted so decisively to create clearly defined natural soil and vegetation regions as on the Eurasian landmass (Fig. 13-6). The continentality of much of the landmass has allowed nature to use a simple nine- to ten-color palette and a wide brush to make broad latitudinal biogeographic bands across the landscape. Partly for this reason, Russian natural scientists and physical geographers were the scientific parents of modern soil science and ecological biogeography.

Aside from the rich mineral and fossil-fuel deposits previously discussed, only parts of these zones are of major agroeconomic importance. Although the tundra is useless agriculturally except for reindeer herding and modest berry

gathering, the vast coniferous forest or taiga—especially in the European north and across southern Siberia—supplies the raw material for the large Russian timber industry. Although not underlain by particularly fertile soils, the mixed-forest zone to the south has agricultural production that has long supported a relatively dense population. The forest steppe or wooded steppe is a transitional zone between the forests to the north and the true steppe to the south. A prime region of former Soviet and current Russian and Ukrainian agriculture, it reflects both a southward increase in temperature and a decrease in moisture. The vegetation alternates between deciduous forests and grasslands. As the climate gets still warmer and drier, true chernozem ("black earth") soils and grasslands appear. Although these soils are highly fertile and the steppe zone is crucial for Russian and Ukrainian grain production, much of the steppe zone—especially toward the east—suffers chronic drought problems. The Virgin Lands of southern West Siberia (mainly these lands are in northern Kazakhstan) are within this biotic zone, as are much of the Ukrainian and Russian North Caucasus *breadbasket* areas. The truly arid desert regions lie in the former Soviet Central Asian republics and Kazakhstan. The exotic biotic zone is limited, yet symbolically very significant. The mild, wet winters and the hot, damp summer along the Russian southeastern Black Sea coast allow for a modest amount of Russian tea cultivation.

ENVIRONMENTAL PROBLEMS

Water Resources: Quantity and Quality

Although many of the major rivers in European Russia are frozen over from two to seven months of the year and tend to flow either northward or southward against the general east-west direction of both historical and present human movement and commerce, Baltic, Russian, and Ukrainian rivers have long served as important transportation and trade routes. As a result of nineteenth- and twentieth-century canal digging, channel

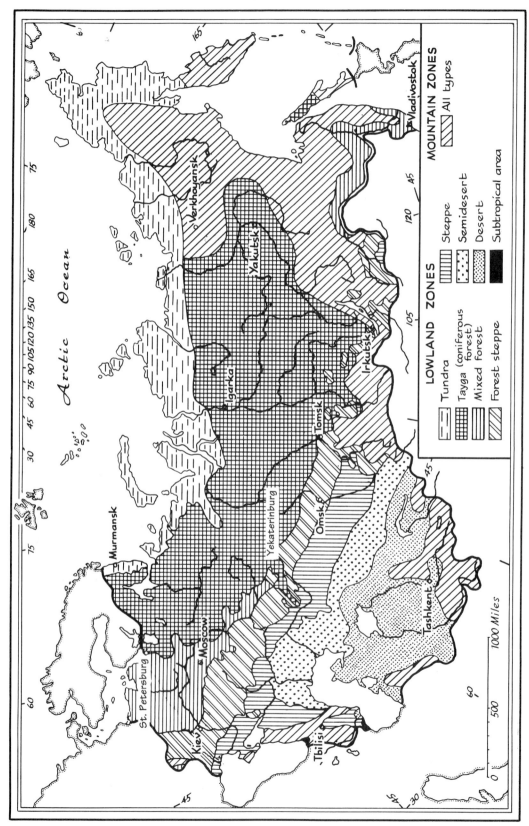

FIGURE 13-6 Natural regions.

dredging, and lock-and-dam construction, European Russia and the NIS now possess important and highly integrated, navigable waterway systems (Fig. 13-7). The Azov, Black, Caspian, Baltic, and White seas are all connected for navigation.

Because of the difficulty and expense of building and maintaining highways and railroads in much of Siberia, rivers are used during the short navigation season (three to four months) to transport durable, bulky supplies to settlements and cities

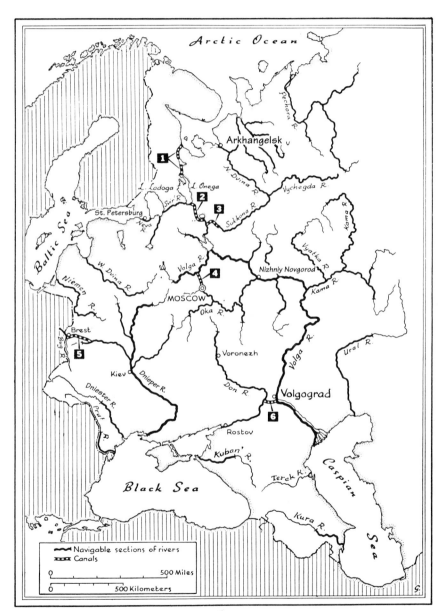

FIGURE 13-7 Major navigable waterways of the NIS and Russia. 1: Baltic-White Sea Canal 2: Volga-Baltic Canal 3: Sukhona River Canal (The Volga-Baltic and Sukona River Canals have been part of the "Northwestern Project" to divert otherwise north-flowing water toward the south into the Rybinsk Reservoir and the Volga River.) 4: Moscow-Volga Canal 5: Bug-Pripyat Canal 6: Volga-Don Canal

located on the Ob'-Irtysh, Yenisey-Angara, Lena-Aldan, and Amur-Zeya river systems.

Even though river transit is still important in Russia and the European NIS, agricultural, municipal, and industrial uses of water have been for some time of far more critical concern. Unfortunately, a severe geographical disparity exists between the locations of major water supply and demand areas. Essentially, the demand for water is concentrated in the west and south, whereas the greatest natural surface water supplies are located in the north and east. Low evapotranspiration rates and high surface runoff caused by permafrost more than compensate for the low average annual precipitation in the north and east.

The high demand for water in the southern half of European Russia and the European NIS, combined with the skewed seasonal rainfall distribution and highly irregular annual precipitation, contributed to a convincing rationale for the Soviet construction of a series of hydroelectric cascades on the Dnieper and Volga rivers. In addition, grandiose schemes were planned to divert from the Vychegda and Pechora rivers of the European north copious volumes of river water southward into the Kama-Volga-Caspian system and from the Ob'-Itrysh into the Aral-Caspian Basin of Kazakhstan and Central Asia. Increased agricultural, municipal, and industrial extraction of water from the Volga, increased evapotranspiration from the surfaces of the chain of Soviet-built Volga reservoirs, and a period of increased aridity in the Caspian region all combined to produce a significant decline in the level of the Caspian Sea between 1930 and the mid-1970s. Because of the shallowness of the northern end of the sea, the former seacoast city and port of Astrakhan' became situated as far as 30 miles (48 km) upstream on the Volga. Also during this interim, officially planned, but inappropriate, construction occurred along the newly exposed, nearly flat coastal shoreline. However, owing in part to improved water management practices and increased precipitation patterns, the situation reversed itself. Since 1978 the Caspian Sea has been rising an average of 6 in. (15 cm) per year. As a result, at least portions of four cities and 109 villages, with a total population of 197,000 and with 2650 acres (1072 ha) of land, are under immediate threat of being inundated by the rising Caspian waters. Over 7950 acres (3220 ha) of valuable lands have already been "recovered" from the sea at great cost.

Over the past few decades, the Soviet and post-Soviet press and technical journals have published a large number of accounts dealing with specific water pollution problems. These articles acknowledge that serious chronic water problems exist in many lakes and rivers in the Baltic republics and Karelia; along the Baltic, the Black, the Caspian, and the Azov Sea coasts; within many lakes and rivers in Northern and Central European Russia; within the Southern Bug (Buh), Dniester (Dnestr), Dnieper, Don, and Sivers'kyy Donets drainage basins in Southern European Russia and Ukraine; along various waterways in the North Caucasus including the Kuban Basin; in many locations within the Ural-Volga-Caspian Basin; along various rivers draining the heavily industrialized Ural Mountains; along the Ob'-Irtysh-Tom', Yenisey-Angara river systems and the shores of Lake Baykal in Siberia; and in various freshwater lakes, including Lake Khanka, and rivers in Primorskoye Kray and coastal waters of the Sea of Japan near Vladivostok, especially in Amur Bay and Peter the Great Bay in the Russian Far East.

Volumes have been written about this appalling Soviet environmental legacy. Nonetheless, some of these problems merit slightly more detail here. After more than 30 years of argument and debate, the pollution problems at Lake Baykal still remain unsolved. From a medical standpoint, some of the most problematic contamination comes from river water in the Urals, the Northern Dvina, the Ob' and several of its tributaries, the Don, and several others. The waters from these rivers have become documented sources of outbreaks of dysentery, cholera, viral hepatitis, typhoid fever, and toxic and chemical poisonings. Effluents from the chemical and pulp and paper industries are still contaminating Lake Imandra in the Kola Peninsula and Lakes Ladoga and Onega in Karelia.

A huge flood control project, including nearly 16 miles (25.4 km) of complex dam structures, was started in 1979 on the Neva estuary near St. Petersburg, linking the Kronstadt island naval base with both sides of the mainland. From a hydrological perspective, this was a sound flood control project designed to protect St. Petersburg from severe flooding that has repeatedly occurred over the centuries. What has resulted, however, is a virtual cesspool at the mouth of the Neva River in St. Petersburg, because the dam traps the high volume of wastes discharged into the Neva both by St. Petersburg and by upstream cities and industries. Unfortunately, instead of attacking the pollution sources, officials and well-meaning, but misguided, environmental groups have attacked the dam itself as the problem. Thus, the severe pollution of the Neva has continued. Ironically, the concentrated pollution near St. Petersburg has lessened water pollution problems in the Gulf of Finland.

Both the Caspian Sea and the Sea of Azov have experienced phenomenal increases in the average concentration of pesticides, including pesticides such as DDT, though long ago it was officially outlawed in the former Soviet Union. This is especially true of the Caspian Sea where the long-term average equals 44 milligrams per liter (mg/l), and the current annual levels range from 7 mg/l up to 143 mg/l. Even the northern section of the Caspian is seriously contaminated with phenols and oil products. Presumably, these contaminants originate from polluted Volga River waters, as well as from the petroleum industries in Kazakhstan around the northeastern perimeter of the sea. Contamination in the Black Sea continues, especially the serious and widespread buildup of hydrogen sulfide which is making the sea into a "watery" biological desert. Even the top layers of much of the Black Sea coastal regions are depleted of oxygen owing to large-scale industrial pollution. The primary sources seem to be the massive amounts of pollutants being discharged into the Black Sea by the Danube, Don, Dnieper, and Southern Bug rivers. The major pollutants are nitrogen and phosphorus fertilizer runoff, oil products, iron and iron oxides, and heavy metals such as mercury, arsenic, and cadmium. The Crimean resort district seems to be especially troubled. An indicator of the increased recent severity of this pollution is that the Black Sea fish catch declined by fully two-thirds between 1985 and 1992. Elevated levels of pesticides and heavy metals, in some cases at toxic levels, are observed around the margins of the Arctic Sea, on the adjacent landmasses, and in the floral and faunal food chains in the region. In addi-

tion, large amounts of toxic and radioactive materials from the mammoth Soviet military-industrial complex have been dumped into northern seas, with what many people believe pose ominous future problems.

Long a major problem, multiple pipeline ruptures, transshipment spillage, and surface oil seepage have greatly increased in recent years. Environmentalists estimate that Russia may lose from 1 to 3 percent of its oil output annually through pipeline leaks. The most recent large oil spill occurred near the city of Usinsk in the northern part of the Komi Republic where the U.S. Energy Department's claim of 270,000 tons of spilled oil greatly exceeds that of the official local government's and Komineft's (Komi Oil Company) claim of 14,000 tons. Internal documents from Komineft alone admit to over 1900 such oil leaks between 1986 and 1991. Several miles of the Kolva and Usa rivers and their tributaries' river banks have been covered in crude oil, and the Pechora River is threatened as well. The scale of the oil spill problems is undoubtedly worse in the West Siberian oilfields where multiple leaks have severely contaminated extensive areas of the Ob'-Irtysh watershed.

In Russia, approximately 17.4 cubic miles (28 cu km) of polluted water are discharged into reservoirs each year. Of the waste-water effluent that passes through the woefully inadequate and inefficient municipal treatment plants, some 52 percent of the volume is composed of industrial waste streams, over 34 percent from agricultural waste water, and 13 percent from domestic sewage. About 50 percent of Russia's population drinks water that does not meet safety standards. One of the major obstacles compounding the problems of potable water quality is that both the sewer pipes and water supply pipes are in poor condition in most Russian and NIS cities. Accordingly, low water pressure is a chronic problem, and contaminated sewage water enters the groundwater and, thus, in turn enters into the water supply network. In summary, in 1991 the USSR Ministry of Ecology acknowledged that the following percentages of surface waters in the former Soviet Union exceeded the MPC (maximal permitted concentration) safety limits for various contaminants depending on location: ammonia, 30–39; copper compounds,

72–75; nitric acid, 28–43; oil and petroleum products, 40–49; organic substances, 30–37; phenols, 46–60; surface-active detergents, 6–8; and zinc, 34–36 percent.

On the positive side, over the past two decades recirculating industrial water supply systems and sewage treatment plant capacities have expanded significantly. Ironically, perhaps the most positive improvements in water quality are associated indirectly with the precipitous downturn in the industrial production of Russia and the European NIS following the collapse of the USSR and the related, severe economic recession in the region.

Air Pollution Problems and Prevention

The relative contributions of various sources to air pollution in Russia and the European NIS differ dramatically from those in the United States. This is true simply because motorized vehicles rule the streets and their noxious gases fill the air over major U.S. cities, whereas industrial smokestacks have been performing the same "fouling" job over the skies of the former Soviet Union. Nonetheless, vehicle emissions are also becoming a major source of air contamination in some large Russian cities.

More than 60 million people in the Russian Federation live in urban environments where the concentration of hazardous substances in the air exceeds the MPCs by a factor of at least five. Of these citizens, 50 million live in cities with extreme air pollution—where the concentration of hazardous substances exceeds the MPCs by a factor of ten or more. Only 15 percent of Russia's citizens reside in areas where the ambient air quality meets health standards. The recent reduction in emission of air pollutants is associated almost exclusively with the "nonproduction" of industrial plants as a result of many strikes, fuel and raw material supply shortages, industrial plant closures caused by the breakup of the USSR, and disarray in air monitoring agencies.

One of the worst and most widespread pollutants is benzo(a)pyrene (BP), a known carcinogen. By 1991 BP was detected in 160 of the 350 Russian Federation cities monitored by the Ministries of Health and Environment. In 92 of these cities the detected BP levels were at hazardous levels. Unlike the emissions of many other air contaminants that have declined since 1989 because of the economic downturn, the emissions of BP and dioxin actually increased owing to the low combustion temperatures being allowed in industrial and municipal thermal power plants. There appears to be a strong statistical link between urban air concentration levels of BP and dioxin and malignant tumors (cancers), particularly among the young, in Russian cities. In addition to thermal power plant emissions, the other main sectors responsible for air pollution include the chemical industry, ferrous and nonferrous metallurgy, the fuel and energy sector, machine building, household heating, and transport.

In 1990 the Russian Republic government issued Resolution No. N93, which identified 43 Russian cities where priority pollution abatement measures were desperately needed. The contamination levels of the two primary greenhouse gases, methane and carbon dioxide, were not even considered in this listing. Fully 28 of the 29 cities that have significant chemical industry production related to the defense sector are listed as having significant human health problems. Dioxin contamination is strongly suggested as being one of the chief causes of these medical problems. Finally, Russia's atmospheric releases of nine major industrial heavy metals and hydrogen fluoride (from aluminum refining) as recently as 1992 ranged from over 750 percent to nearly 12,000 percent greater than combined EU releases of these substances, respectively.

Not all of the air pollution problems of Russia and the NIS are of their own making. For example, more than 80 percent of the atmospheric pollution afflicting Belarus originates from upwind foreign sources, especially as a result of the burning of poor-quality, high-sulfur coals in Central and East European industrial plants. The three Baltic countries and Russia also suffer to varying degrees from similar downwind pollution, including St. Petersburg from the noxious exhausts of oil shale burning in northeastern Estonia.

In summary, the most positive improvement in urban air quality in the former Soviet Union was associated with the shift away from oil and coal toward natural gas for electricity generation and space-heating within major urban areas. Hard currency and domestic fuel shortages in some of the NIS, such as Ukraine, now threaten to create a significant backsliding in this regard. Finally, although recent foreign technological assistance has created the potential for modest improvements in ambient air quality, the biggest recent improvements represent only short-run pollutant reductions associated with the disruption of industrial production.

The Chernobyl' (Chornobyl') Accident

The most spectacular lingering environmental disaster of the FSU is associated with the nuclear reactor accident at the Chernobyl' nuclear power plant on April 26, 1986. Located about 75 miles (120 km) north of Kiev, Ukraine's capital city, the explosions that shattered the Unit Number 4 reactor released about 50 times more radioactive material into the atmosphere than the combined atomic bombs detonated over Hiroshima and Nagasaki. Changing weather patterns and upper air winds in the days following the accident dispersed a large plume of radioactive gas and particles containing about 30 million curies initially (50 million curies total, compared to only 50 curies discharged at the accident at Three Mile Island) to the northwest as far as Sweden and Finland, to the west into Poland, Austria, Germany, and Switzerland, and as far south as Yugoslavia and Greece. Another 20 million curies were deposited onto some 50,000 sq miles (130,000 sq km) of western Russia, Belarus, and Ukraine. The fallout consisted mainly of cesium 137 with a half-life of 30 years, strontium 90 with a half-life of 28 years, and radioactive iodine with a seven-day half-life. The first two radio nuclides will remain dangerous sources of irradiation to the soil, water, and food chain of the affected areas at least until the year 2135. Both the Dnieper and Pripet (Pripyat) rivers were threatened initially with radioactive wastes, and in the long term as well because of the slow hydrologic release of radioactive particles from the highly contaminated Pripyat marsh lands and radioactive runoff from Chernobyl's cooling ponds. Construction of a

totally new water supply system for the city of Kiev was begun shortly after the accident.

Although a huge concrete and steel sarcophagus tomb was hastily built around the reactor, it has been impossible to seal off the still hot reactor; more than 10,750 sq ft (1000 sq m) of leaks have formed. Of the 100,000 workers who built the sarcophagus, several thousand are reputed to have died from radiation poisoning. In 1991 a fire also raged through the Number 2 Chernobyl' reactor, and reactors 1 and 3 are still operating.

Despite Premier Gorbachev's policy of *glasnost* (openness), much secrecy and concealment surrounded this disaster. For example, radiation fallout maps for contamination zones in Belarus and Ukraine were not published until March 1989 and those of the four most contaminated oblasts in the Russian SFSR not until February 1990. Recent reports indicate that cesium 137 contaminates 16 oblasts in the Russian Federation (including Mordovia), all six oblasts of Belarus, and eight in Ukraine, whereas originally only one oblast in the Russian Federation and two oblasts in Belarus and Ukraine, respectively, were reported. Despite the high levels of soil and water contamination, agricultural production continued on much of the contaminated lands. Produce was mixed with production from other nonaffected areas, and "diluted" products were widely distributed throughout the former USSR.

The initial Chernobyl' cleanup costs were vastly understated at a fraction of their actual cost. Calculation of costs must also include long-term medical costs of the affected populations and the costs of bringing alternative (nonnuclear) energy supplies on line. Only time will reveal the full extent of the long-term environmental and human health effects of this disastrous event. With the passage of time, one thing has become clear: the seriousness of the accident and its human health impacts far exceed the initial reports. Several other nuclear power station accidents and incidents of less seriousness have occurred, including a partial core meltdown at the Shevchenko power and desalinization reactor on the Mangyshlak Peninsula along the Caspian Sea in southwest Kazakhstan and a number of reported electrical fires at the Ignalina nuclear power station in eastern Lithuania.

The Military: Radioactive and Chemical Wastes

It is extremely important to note the linkage between military issues and environmental concerns. International attention has focused primarily on the potential post-Soviet nuclear brain drain, nuclear accidents, and nuclear terrorism; but similar concerns are warranted with regard to chemical and bacteriological warfare experts. The recently created Ecology and Special Protection Systems Directorate of the Russian Ministry of Defense reflects the seriousness of the environmental contamination legacy of the Soviet military, both in the former territory of the USSR and at former Soviet military bases on foreign soil. The "green" helmets of the new ministry are charged with an active role in cleanup operations, as opposed to monitoring activities at test ranges, firing ranges, airfields, tank training areas, warehouses, and arsenals. In addition, disaster relief operations, such as the post-Chernobyl' accident, earthquake relief, and ecological disaster relief operations are under this new Directorate's jurisdiction.

The Soviet nuclear industry, run primarily by the military, had a long-secret history of serious accidents before Chernobyl'. Safety had a low priority compared with weapons development and with bringing nuclear power stations on line. For example, nuclear power plants were built without radiation containment vessels. New information indicates that many accidental atmospheric releases of radiation have resulted from the so-called Atomic Cities Network (*atomgrad*)—an estimated 16 to 87 secret cities that Stalin initially established to develop the atom bomb.

The first large-scale accident in the USSR occurred in September 1957 at Kyshtym (now renamed Mayak) in the Urals, about 56 miles (90 km) northwest of Chelyabinsk. A failure in the cooling mechanism of a nuclear waste storage tank produced a massive steam explosion, which ejected some 70 to 80 tons of radioactive material containing about 20 million curies into the atmosphere. There had also been more than a decade of dumping of cesium- and strontium-laden nuclear wastes from the nearby top-secret Mayak (alternatively called Chelyabinsk-40 and later Chelyabinsk-65) bomb-making factory into

the bottom of Lake Karachay, a small, 642-acre (260-ha) lake. As a result, this reservoir received (and leaked into the surrounding groundwater) 120 million curies worth of hazardous nuclear waste, an amount equal to about 2.4 times the radioactive content of the debris released by the Chernobyl' accident. During the hot, dry summer of 1967, Lake Karachay evaporated, and winds dispersed the exposed radioactive dust as far as 50 miles (80 km) downwind, directly contaminating an estimated 41,000 people. As recently as 1990, radiation levels measured on the downwind lake shore, 600 roentgens per hour, were still sufficiently high to produce a lethal human dose within 60 minutes of exposure! Similar dosages can result from exposures along the nearby Techa River which drained Lake Karachay and into which radioactive wastes were directly discharged. Smaller scale accidents releasing plutonium into the atmosphere have occurred as recently as April 1993 at Tomsk-7 in East Siberia and in July 1993 again at Chelyabinsk-65. Serious problems have resulted from nuclear waste dumping into the waters of the Arctic north and the Pacific coastal seas, including the sea burial of spent naval reactors, combined with several nuclear submarine accidents and the current storage of nuclear waste aboard ships anchored along coastal inlets in the northern and eastern seas.

In addition to atmospheric testing of nuclear weapons, especially in the Semey (formerly, Semipalatinsk) region of Kazakhstan and on Novaya Zemlya in the north from 1949 to 1962, the Soviet Union set off 116 nuclear explosions for "technical purposes," such as for dam construction projects, coal, gas and oil exploration, and mining projects between 1965 and 1988. For example, underground blasts were used to shatter rock formations in the oilfields of the Kazakhstan Republic and the diamond mines of Sakha. These blasts ranged from the equivalent of 1000 tons of TNT (size of the bomb dropped on Hiroshima) up to 165,000 tons of TNT. Forty-three of these detonations were in the range of 5500 to 11,000 tons of TNT. Despite being underground, several blasts heaved contaminated dirt into the atmosphere. Unfortunately, significantly elevated rates of cancer, especially leukemia, stillbirths, and birth defects, appear to be strongly associated with populations living in or near these nuclear-impacted regions and cities.

By far the most distressing example of massive Soviet and now Russian nuclear roulette is the recent disclosure of the secret injection of billions of gallons of atomic waste, up to 3 billion curies or about half of total Soviet accumulated nuclear wastes, directly into the earth at three sites—Dimitrovgrad near the middle Volga, at Tomsk near the Ob' River, and at Krasnoyarsk on the Yenisey River. The current radioactivity of these injected wastes is still estimated to be 1.45 billion curies. In the worst case scenario, the wastes could leak to the surface and create large regional calamities downstream, contaminate large aquifers, or spread to the Caspian Sea in the case of the Dimitrovgrad site and to the Arctic Ocean in the last two cases. In the most benign and hopeful scenario, these wastes may stay deep underground for a sufficiently long time to render them more or less harmless by the long natural process of radioactive decay.

Activities associated with chemical weapons are probably an even greater human health threat than radioactivity, especially throughout Russia, Ukraine, and the Baltic states. Such weapons were designed, tested, produced, and stored in over 300 cities and towns of the former Soviet Union. Until at least the mid-1980s, chemical weapons were dumped into seas bordering the USSR. Soils, groundwater, and surface waters are widely contaminated by military weapons production. These contamination problems appear to be linked to high rates of congenital abnormalities among people in many cities with chemical-military activities. Unfortunately, similar to other environmental problems, governmental funds available for the required cleanup and ameliorative tasks are highly insufficient.

Other Environmental Problems

This brief overview of Soviet environmental problems must of course omit much detail. Problems associated with faunal and floral nature preservation and poaching, overfishing, the destruction of spawning beds, land reclamation and irrigation,

soil erosion, chemical contamination of soils, soil salinization, timber harvesting and replanting rates, solid waste disposal and landfills, and a host of other resource management conflicts are all major environmental issues that have actually worsened since the dissolution of the Soviet Union.

Four interwoven factors have aggravated these environmental problems. First, even before the breakup of the Soviet Union, the financial resources necessary to solve or at least ameliorate these problems were lacking, and the political will to do so was at best questionable. The worsening economic downturn in some NIS such as Ukraine, problems in the tax collection systems nearly everywhere, and the practically unprecedented demands on governmental coffers from the social-political safety net mean that the priority on redressing environmental problems has been diminished. Second, the centrifugal political forces unleashed since the breakup of the USSR continue and have threatened the legitimacy of any and all central governmental functions, agencies, and policies. Hence, enforcement of environmental laws and regulations has suffered nearly everywhere. Third, the transformation to a market economy has created "free rider" problems—private economic incentives to pollute the environment by casting off private production costs on society. Similarly, natural, biological, and environmental resources that were once officially protected have become marketable commodities that can be and are being converted into hard currency. Examples include poaching and effectively unregulated hunting, fishing, mining, timber harvesting, and all sorts of resource smuggling induced by hard currency. Fourth, interjurisdictional environmental pollution control and abatement problems have increased, as formerly "regional" environmental problems have been recast into "international" environmental problems. Several projects funded by the United States Agency for International Development (USAID) and the EU are underway to try to come to grips with both the environmental problems that are a tragic legacy of the Soviet era and with the new environmental management problems and issues engendered by the ongoing economic changes in Russia and the NIS.

HISTORICAL AND ADMINISTRATIVE BACKGROUND

Historical Geography

Countries the size and influence of the UK, France, the United States, the former Soviet Union, or the current Russian Federation are not created overnight; rather, they evolve through time from spatially localized centers of power. This evolution can be conceived of as a series of spatial diffusion processes. The things being diffused might be referred to collectively as geopolitical glue; that is, they effectively bind a state together. Examples include military-political influence or control, people, political and economic institutions, transportation networks, language, and culture. At this historical juncture, it is equally important to ask the converse question; namely, what processes can result in the disintegration and fragmentation of a country?

In these two opposing contexts, a number of geographic questions need to be raised. First, for example, what were the source or sources of the *binding* agents; why did the diffusion or geographic spread take certain directions at certain times and not others; how and why were political controls established with such diffusions; and what modifications in indigenous cultures and sociopolitical institutions resulted from the successful dissemination of new geopolitical control agents? Second, what were the internal and external geographic, historical, economic, social, political, ethnic, religious, linguistic, and cultural factors and processes, which to varying degrees helped to dissolve the original geopolitical glue that kept the Soviet Union together for more than seven decades? These and many other subsidiary questions constitute a systematic framework within which much of the historical, political, and economic data of any country can be examined in a realistic and geographical manner. Let us take a glimpse at a thousand years of Russian-Soviet experience and try to piece together the important sets of spatial diffusion processes leading first to the "cohesive" Soviet state of this century and then, in turn to its recent breakup.

Long before the name *Russia* appeared on the historical landscape, there had already been three areas of advanced civilization within what makes up the former Soviet territory—in Central Asia, in Transcaucasia, and around the northern Black Sea littoral regions (where there were Hellenic settlements). The first Russian state, however, was situated around the present city of Kiev. By the eighth century A.D., Slavic-speaking peoples had migrated into the Dnieper, Volkhov, and upper Volga basins, possibly eastward and northward from the Carpathian region. Starting early in the ninth century, invading Norse traders, or Varangians, began settling among the Slavs along the same Volkhov-Dnieper axis. Both Slavs and Varangians were interested in trade and needed protection from marauding steppe nomads. As a result, the Scandinavian intruders were gradually able to consolidate jointly settled lands under their leadership into a political entity called *Rus* (or Russia); and the original capital of Novgorod was replaced by Kiev in 882.

Environmental factors helped make Kiev a strategic location. First, it was on the high right bank of the Dnieper and easily defensible. The Dnieper location was vital in allowing the Kievan influence to spread along the main water route between the Baltic region to the north and Constantinople to the south. This medieval mercantile state exported furs, amber, honey, salt, and slaves to Byzantium, in return for textiles, fruit, wine, and gold. Second, Kiev was situated near the forest-steppe boundary. Shifting agriculture coexisted with fixed settlement among the eastern Slavs around Kiev. Cereal growing on the potentially rich agricultural lands of the steppes thus allowed Kievan Russia both to diversify and to expand its trading commodities. Hence, using the Volkhov-Dnieper river system network to good advantage for both trade and military conquest, the Kievan royal house was able to assemble a loose confederation of essentially city-state principalities.

The penetration of Eastern Orthodox Christianity from Constantinople was an additional nation-binding force for the Kievan core. After Saint Vladimir's conversion to Christianity in A.D. 988 Kievan Russia ruled in relative comfort, however for only a short period, until the death of

Vladimir's successor Yaroslav in 1054. The partition of Kievan Russia among Yaroslav's sons in that year led to the gradual fragmentation of this once powerful eastern Slav kingdom. In addition to the domestic feud within the royal family, many of the city-states began flexing their independent muscle, especially Vladimir, Suzdal, Tver' (Kalinin in Soviet times), and Moscovy (Moscow) within the upper Volga principality of Vladimir-Suzdal. The Republic of Novgorod, having already obtained self-government from Kievan Russia in 997, achieved complete independence in 1136. A few decades later, in 1169, a raiding party from Suzdal actually sacked Kiev. The Volga Bulgars to the east, marauding Polovtsi people to the south, and Khazars and Pechenegs to the southeast became increasingly troublesome.

The invasion by the Mongols or Tatars in the thirteenth century marked the final eclipse of Kievan Russia. After the Mongol conquest, the indigenous population scattered basically along two exodus routes. One of the major pathways led west and northwest to Poland and Lithuania, whereas the other led north and northeast to the headwaters of the Volga. Successfully escaping the subjugation of the Tatars, the first group fell easy victims to Lithuanian and Polish expansion after 1240. The latter migration route proved more fortuitous. In addition to being safe from regular incursions by nomads, the upper Volga region had an extremely well-linked natural transportation network. The Valday Hills northwest of Moscow are the headwaters region for the rivers that drain into the White, Baltic, Black, and Caspian seas. This radial drainage pattern played no small part in Moscow's rise to prominence (see Figs. 13-7 and 13-8).

Moscow was first mentioned in 1147 and was part of the principality of Vladimir-Suzdal. The area was less congenial than Kiev, with poorer soils, heavy forests requiring clearing, swampy land, and a much more severe climate, but the inhospitable environment ironically increased the security of the area. Although it is a moot question why Moscow rather than one of the other settlements arose as the strongest, three plausible factors may be cited. First, Moscow's location near the hub of the radial drainage network meant that it

was well located. Second, it seems that the early Moscow princes were strong and clever politicians. Because they collected Tatar tribute from the other Russian cities and principalities, the Tatar yoke rested lightly on them. Having thus gained the Mongol's favor, the Moscow princes were made the sovereign princes of all Russia. Third, the Metropolitan of the Orthodox church moved from Vladimir to Moscow in 1310, signaling the decline of one of Moscow's strongest rivals. In 1453 another important event occurred: after the fall of Constantinople to the Turks, Moscow became the third Rome. Although Russia considered itself part of Europe, later events set Russia off along a quite different historical path. Various theological, philosophical, and intellectual currents—for example, scholasticism, the Renaissance, the Reformation, the Counter-Reformation, and Reason and Enlightenment—which greatly affected the European countries drawing their Christianity from Rome, only touched the ruling elite of Russia. Orthodoxy and autocracy prevented these moderating influences in Russia until the Bolshevik Revolution (see Fig. 13-9). Indirectly, then, the fall of Constantinople may perhaps be the origin of many east-west dichotomies.

Regardless of the causes, Moscow, or Moscovy, became the new core of the eastern Slavs. Beginning by way of local territorial expansion along the river systems, Moscow gradually acquired more power and wealth, until in 1478 Ivan III (1462–1505), the Grand Prince of Moscovy, successfully invaded and subdued Novgorod—the only Russian principality to have avoided Mongol control. Two years later Moscovy stopped paying tribute to the Tatars. Ivan III and his successor Vasili II (1505–1533) successfully pursued a policy of "gathering in the Russian lands." As a result of this conscious strategy of aggrandizement, the Grand Principality of Tver was annexed in 1485, Vyatka in 1489, Pskov in 1510, and Ryazan' in 1521. The reconquest of Smolensk from the Lithuanians took place in 1514.

During this consolidation of Russian lands, a return migration, or recolonization, was taking place by descendants of the earlier Russian peoples who had fled to the west instead of the northeast. Hence, by the sixteenth century the middle

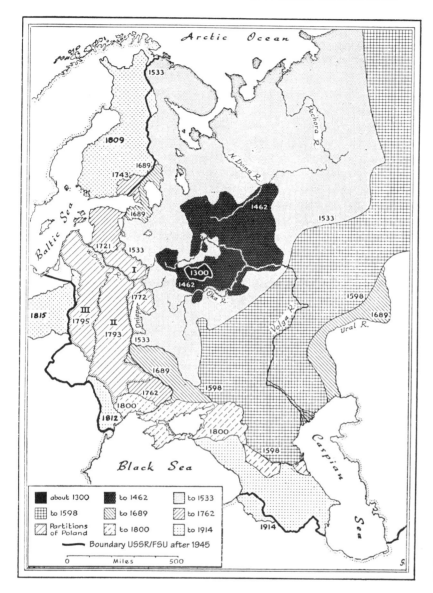

FIGURE 13-8 Growth of the Russian Empire in Europe.

and upper Dnieper regions were populated by two new ethnic nations, with variant forms of the Russian language, the Little Rus (Ukrainians) and Belarussians (White Russians), respectively.

Ivan IV (1533–1584) or "Ivan the Terrible," was crowned the "Tsar of All the Russias" in 1547 and soon embarked on the first conquest of non-Russian lands. At the time, Russia was virtually surrounded by hostile powers—by the powerful Swedes to the northwest, a united Poland-Lithuania to the west and southwest, Black Sea Tatars to the south, and Tatars to the east. Ivan IV's foreign adventures were marked with dismal failure in the west and spectacular successes in the east. His invasion of Livonia (roughly comprising modern Estonia and Latvia) in 1558 developed into a protracted war with Sweden, Poland, and Lithuania which lasted until 1583 and cost him all of the Russian possessions on the Gulf of Finland, as well as those on the western shore of Lake Ladoga. Along the eastern frontier, however, the disintegrated Tatar khanates (kingdoms) proved relative-

FIGURE 13-9 A snowy night in Red Square. GUM, Russia's and the former Soviet Union's largest department store, is on the left and St. Basil's Cathedral is in the center. (C. ZumBrunnen)

ly easy prey, with Kazan' on the central Volga being captured in 1552 and Astrakhan' at the river's mouth in 1556. In order to protect and exploit these newly acquired lands, numerous fortress towns—such as Samara (Kuybyshev in Soviet times), Saratov, Voronezh, and Tsaritsyn (later Stalingrad and now Volgograd)—were established by the advancing Russians between 1586 and 1590. With these victories, Russia had possession of much valuable steppe land as well as access to the Caspian Sea.

The march of the Russian Empire across Siberia was rapid. Beginning in 1581, the wave of Slavic eastward expansion reached the Pacific shores in 1640. The Baykal area was annexed in 1652, and in 1689 the Treaty of Nerchinsk between Russia and China granted to Russia all the territory north of the watershed of the Stanovoy Mountains, but thus granted China land on both sides of the Amur and all its tributaries east of the Argun River. This treaty may be one of the long-term sources of the Sino-Soviet conflict of the past few decades, because it was violated in the mid-nineteenth century by Russian expansion south of the Amur.

Thus, over the three centuries of 1550–1858, the Russian Empire expanded eastward—most rapid-

ly between 1550 and 1650. This diffusion process was politically organized, with military and semi-military Cossacks leading the way, extracting fur tribute from the small indigenous populations and constructing small forts along the way. These military outposts subsequently served as nucleation points for development of surrounding areas. All of this activity resulted in the diffusion of Russian people, political (tsarist) control, bureaucracy, religion, and customs over a vast, formerly non-Russian area. Partly from this experience, the former USSR claimed to be, and the current Russian Federation claims to be, an Asian country.

Having reached the Pacific, Russia turned westward. Although the reign of Peter I ("the Great," 1689–1725) symbolizes this period, his father, Alexis, can be credited with several important military successes, especially the recapture of Smolensk, Kiev, and the left bank of the Dnieper from the Poles between 1656 and 1667. Peter revolutionized Russia politically, economically, and culturally. Despite his often stringent, even despotic, methods of implementing his various reforms, he was the one tsar lionized by the former Soviet regime. Peter began the industrialization of the Urals. From nearby iron, copper, and lead deposits, the Ural smelters supplied arms factories. Having obtained a relatively secure foothold on the Baltic in 1703, Peter began carving St. Petersburg (renamed Leningrad during the Soviet era) out of the swampy terrain along the Baltic shore near the mouth of the Neva River. In 1713 the capital of the empire was transferred from Moscow to St. Petersburg, where it remained until 1918. The signing of the Treaty of Nystad in 1721, which marked the end of the Northern Wars with Sweden, gave Estonia, Livonia, and Karelia to Russia. Russian foreign trade gradually became dominated by St. Petersburg, from which furs, timber, grain, flax, and iron were exported to Europe in return for coffee, sugar, dyes, and wine. Peter's northern triumphs were not matched by his southern probes. Nonetheless, by creating a navy, modernizing the army, and remolding the administrative organization of the empire, Peter reoriented the entire country from St. Petersburg—his *window on Europe.*

Internal dissension and revolt have characterized Russia from the early days of Kievan Russia until today. It took all the efforts of the lackluster rulers between Peter I and Catherine II ("the Great") to preserve the previous Russian territorial gains. During Catherine's reign (1762–1796), Russia won back the *western lands* from Poland-Lithuania. With the successive partitions of Poland (1772, 1793, 1795) the Russian Empire's western boundary approximated the most recent Soviet one, minus East Prussia, Galicia, and Bessarabia. More important, however, were Russia's conquests in the south. Catherine's wars against Turkey culminated in Russia's capture of all the southern steppe lands from the Dniester to the Kuban' River. These acquisitions, of course, contained superior agricultural land.

Catherine's successors became entangled in the French Revolutionary and Napoleonic wars, and chiefly as a result of its involvement in these and other conflicts, Russia annexed a large portion of the Caucasus (1801–1819), Finland (1809), Bessarabia (1812), and the Grand Duchy of Warsaw (1815). After this time and except for minor changes, the European border of the Russian Empire remained unaltered until World War I. During the rest of the nineteenth century, Russian control and influence spread primarily to the remainder of the Caucasus,

throughout the territory that today comprises the five former Soviet Central Asian republics, and into the Far East.

During the nineteenth century, the Russian Empire underwent a significant economic transformation. Acquisition of the rich black earth zone in the southern steppe and construction of nearby Black Sea ports made the Russian Ukraine the breadbasket of Europe. The Moscow-Ivanovo textile belt flourished. The old manufacturing complexes in St. Petersburg grew and diversified somewhat. The charcoal-based metallurgy of the Urals was rapidly eclipsed in importance by the coking coal of the Donets Basin (Donbas) and the nearby high-grade iron ore deposits of Kryvyy Rih in central Ukraine. Expanding foreign markets for lumber invigorated the European north and the port of Arkhangelsk. The emancipation of the serfs in 1861 symbolized Russia's attempt to cast off its medieval image and enter the era of Western industrial capitalism. In very general terms, these were the conditions that existed on the eve of World War I and the Bolshevik Revolution of 1917.

In short, thanks to the spatial integrators mentioned earlier—political control, bureaucracy, people, language, customs, and transportation networks—it is evident that the Russian Empire bequeathed a relatively cohesive empire to the Soviets. In terms of strategic geographic connectivity, the tsarist rail network (see Fig. 13-12), including the famous Trans-Siberian line begun in 1891 and completed in 1917, was an especially vital asset to the triumphant Red Army of the Bolsheviks during and after the period of foreign intervention and civil war between 1918 and 1921. In many ways, Soviet efforts were directed toward further increasing the geographic, economic, and political integration of what was already the world's largest state.

Boundary Changes Since World War I

During World War I and the internal turmoil that followed, the position of the Russian-Soviet western border changed frequently. After the situation stabilized, however, with the Bolsheviks in firm control, the infant Soviet state was forced to concede significant territorial losses along its European perimeter. As part of the terms of the 1920 Treaty of Riga, Finland, Estonia, Latvia, and Lithuania were granted independence. Parts of what are now western Belarus and Ukraine were also lost to Poland. Bessarabia (now largely in Moldova) was annexed by Romania in 1918. Finally, the Kars region south of Batumi was ceded to Turkey in March of 1921.

The territorial losses were more than recouped by Soviet annexations between 1939 and 1945. The Russo-German Pact of August 23, 1939, led to the military partition of Poland. In spite of the Finns' tenacious defense during the Russo-Finnish Winter War of 1939–1940, the USSR gained three small, but strategic, pieces of territory from Finland (see Fig. 13-10). Also during the autumn of 1939, Soviet troops invaded and occupied the three Baltic states as well as Eastern Galicia, Bukovina, and Bessarabia in the west and southwest.

In 1940 the three Baltic republics and Bessarabia were formerly reincorporated into the Soviet Union. The annexation of Bessarabia brought the Soviet Union to the Danube Delta. Territorial readjustments along ethnic settlement lines resulted in the cession to the Soviet Union of northern Bukovina and Transcarpathian Ukraine, formerly part of Czechoslovakia. The USSR lost a small section of Poland it had occupied in 1939, since the post–World War II Polish-Soviet border was also drawn along ethnic-language lines, but it still acquired a large swath of what had been eastern Poland prior to 1939. Former East Prussia was partitioned between Poland and the Soviet Union. The Soviet section was resettled with Russians after the relocation of its German population. This area formed a noncontiguous unit within the former Russian Republic, called Kaliningrad Oblast, and is still part of the Russian Federation. As a result of the western border changes, the Soviet Union gained strategic, direct access to Czechoslovakia, Hungary, and Norway. Of these, only the common border with Norway remains for Russia. Along the Asian frontier, Tuva was formally incorporated into the USSR in 1944. In the Far East, the Soviets took advantage of their tardy entry into the Pacific theater of the war by reclaiming the southern half of Sakhalin Island and the southern Kuril Islands from Japan. The Soviet territorial war reparations, especially the Kuril Islands, are still a major source of friction between Japan and the former Soviet Union.

Evolution of the Soviet Political— Administrative Structure

After the success of the 1917 Bolshevik Revolution, the Soviets made changes in the political-administrative territorial structure based on two criteria. First, territorial units were created based on ethnic population distribution and boundaries. Second, attempts were made to delineate territorial-administrative units, using the concept of functional economic regions.

Considering the vast areas of non-Russian territory incorporated into the Russian Empire, the ethnic complexity of Russia and the former Soviet Union comes as no surprise. At present slightly over 100 distinct ethnic groups live within the boundary of the territory of the former Soviet Union, speaking over 40 different languages. Even at the time of the 1897 Census, Great Russians constituted only 43 percent of the total population. During the early days of the Russian Revolution of 1917, the ethnic diversity of the country was given explicit recognition in the Declaration of Rights of the Peoples of Russia. Officially, certain legal guarantees were offered: (1) the equality and sovereignty of the various ethnic groups of Russia, (2) the free development of national minorities and ethnic groups, (3) their right to self-determination, including the right of secession and independence, and (4) the abolition of all national and national-religious privileges and restrictions. The Declaration also formed the legal basis for the Soviet political-administrative structure that subsequently evolved.

Although the spirit of this piece of human rights legislation was abrogated, circumvented, deliberately violated, or simply ignored in a number of instances, the principle of national autonomy was nonetheless responsible for the organization of the former USSR into the country's primary political-administrative units—the former 15 Union Republics, or Soviet Socialist Republics (Fig. 13-10)—that now constitute the 15 newly independent states (NIS) carved out of the former Soviet Union. These 15 units represented most of the

FIGURE 13-10 The NIS and administrative regions within Russia.

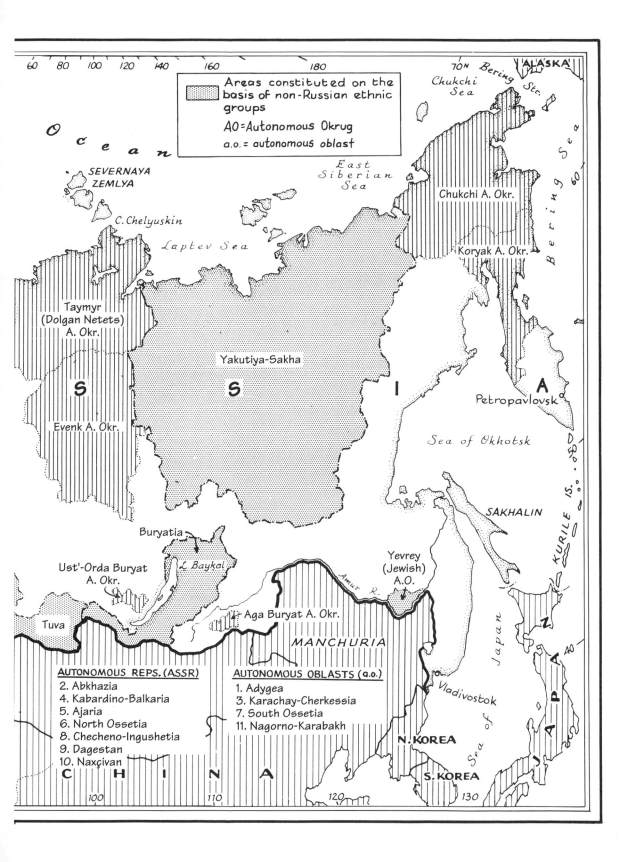

Areas constituted on the basis of non-Russian ethnic groups

AO=Autonomous Okrug
a.o. = autonomous oblast

O c e a n

SEVERNAYA ZEMLYA

C. Chelyuskin

Laptev Sea

East Siberian Sea

Chukchi Sea

70N Bering Str.

ALASKA

Bering Sea

60

Chukchi A. Okr.

Koryak A. Okr.

Taymyr (Dolgan Netets) A. Okr.

Yakutiya-Sakha

S

S

S

I

A

Petropavlovsk

Sea of Okhotsk

Evenk A. Okr.

KURILE IS.

SAKHALIN

Buryatia

L. Baykal

Ust'-Orda Buryat A. Okr.

Yevrey (Jewish) A.O.

Amur R.

Tuva

Aga Buryat A. Okr.

MANCHURIA

Z

Japan I.

40

JAPA

Vladivostok

AUTONOMOUS REPS. (ASSR)
2. Abkhazia
4. Kabardino-Balkaria
5. Ajaria
6. North Ossetia
8. Checheno-Ingushetia
9. Dagestan
10. Naxçivan

AUTONOMOUS OBLASTS (a.o.)
1. Adygea
3. Karachay-Cherkessia
7. South Ossetia
11. Nagorno-Karabakh

N. KOREA

Sea of Japan

S. KOREA

C H I N A

100

110

120

130

large ethnic groups within the former Soviet Union. Technically speaking, the largest and most important of the former Union Republics, Russia, was a federation of a number of major nationalities associated with the Russian state and hence was known as the Russian Soviet Federated Socialist Republic (RSFSR). This multiethnic nature is still implied by the name of the new country formed out of the RSFSR—the Russian Federation. Prior to the breakup of the Soviet Union, the former 15 Union Republics were administratively similar to the 50 states of the United States.

The second tier of the Soviet territorial administrative hierarchy consisted of three different units: Autonomous Soviet Socialist Republics (ASSRs), *oblasts* (regions), and *krays* (territories). All three units were on the same jurisdictional level, directly subservient to their respective Union Republics. The differences were as follows. The ASSR boundaries were laid out to give important ethnic minorities political recognition and representation in the former Soviet of Nationalities, one of the USSR's two legislative bodies. An oblast contains no significant minority group other than the titular group of its given republic. Thus, oblasts are purely administrative units created by using the principle of functional economic regions. The final unit, the kray, has more arbitrarily drawn boundaries, which reflect economic-administrative considerations; at the same time, it contains one or more minor political subdivisions that are predicated on ethnic or national groups. These subdivisions are either autonomous oblasts (A.O.— autonomous regions) or autonomous okrugs (A.Okr.— autonomous districts), or both. An oblast may also have contained one or more national okrugs. The oblasts and krays are somewhat analogous to counties in the United States, though generally far larger. The lowest level units of the political-economic administrative scheme are called *rayons*. Rayons are either rural or urban and are similar to American townships and city wards. Several large cities have special status that places them directly subordinate to their respective republics. With a few exceptions, the political-economic organization of the former USSR followed the above-outlined three-tier hierarchy.

Thus far since the breakup of the Soviet Union on December 25, 1991, few, if any, boundary changes have occurred along any of these Soviet-era political-administrative boundaries either between Russia and the other NIS or within Russia itself. On the other hand, innumerable place name changes and spellings have occurred, and the terms for the various political-administrative units have changed. For example, the term *oblast* is now used only in Russia and Ukraine (*voblast* in Belarus). Within the Russian Federation former ASSRs have become republics and the designation *national okrugs* (N.Okr.), which constituted a separate jurisdictional level greater than a rayon, but less than a kray or an oblast, is no longer used. In Ukraine the ethnically Russian-dominated former Krym Oblast (Crimea) (with tens of thousands of once expelled but now newly returned Crimean Tatars) has been designated a republic.

As previously mentioned, the administrative structure evolved over time. In a number of situations, Stalin used a "divide and conquer" form of boundary drawing, such as the splitting of Ossetian peoples into a North Ossetia administrative unit in Russia and a South Ossetia unit within Georgia, or the splitting of the Abkhazian people between Russia and Georgia. Nonetheless, it could reasonably be argued that during the Soviet era the nationality principle functioned as a stabilizing force by maintaining Soviet power. Much of this has now changed since the breakup of the Soviet Union. The misapplication of the Declaration of Rights of the Peoples of Russia in the past in terms of the actual drawing of various political-administrative boundaries has now become one of the many sources of centrifugal forces, both between various successor states and within some of them, especially within Russia and Georgia. Although control over resources is now often the source of conflict (such as for oil and gas revenues in Tatarstan, Bashkortostan, Yamal Nenets A. O., and Khanty-Mansi A. O., and various resources such as gas, coal, timber, and diamonds in Sakha), ethnicity/national identity "wrongs" of the past are being used as an excuse for greater regional and local autonomy.

Although few Kremlin watchers would have disagreed with the assertion that the real legislative power of the country was concentrated in the hands of the Central Committee of the Communist party, the USSR did have a bicameral legislature composed of a House of the Union and a House of Nationalities that rubber-stamped party initiatives. The House of the Union was analogous to the U.S. House of Representatives in that representation was based on population—specifically, one deputy for every 300,000 inhabitants—and the House of Nationalities was composed of representatives chosen from the various nationality-based political units. The bicameral Supreme Soviet was the source of both the formal executive and legislative branches of the Soviet government. The real political-executive force, however, resided in a Council of Ministers, arising from its central administrative direction of the entire national economy. Because many high-echelon Communist party officials were also members of the Council of Ministers, the party had effective control over all branches of government.

Even though many representatives were not directly elected and some positions were allocated to various organizations such as the Soviet Academy of Sciences, the spring 1989 Soviet elections for the short-lived Congress of People's Deputies represented the closest thing to a democratic election since the triumph of the Bolshevik Revolution. Although the coup d'état against Gorbachev in August 1991 failed, his rescue by Boris Yeltsin (Yel'tsin) signaled the final demise of Gorbachev's real political power and the ascendancy of an independent Russia under Yeltsin's leadership. Yeltsin's recognition of the independence of the three Baltic republics in autumn 1991 and the formation of the Commonwealth of Independent States (CIS) were the final centrifugal acts that fractured the remaining power of the "center" of the Soviet Union. Since the Soviet Union was officially dissolved on December 25, 1991, Russia and all of the other European NIS, but not all of the other former Soviet republics, have conducted free and democratic presidential elections and have created truly democratically elected parliaments (or Dumas), some of them bicameral. In October 1993 Yeltsin successfully waged his own short-lived military battle against anti-reformers, conservative members of the Russian Parliament, after he chose to end the political stalemate between the presidency and Parliament by issuing a decree dissolving the Parliament and ordering new elections for December 1993. Yeltsin won re-election in 1996 against right- and left-wing opponents.

Having now sketched in the cultural and historical background, it is time to return to a discussion of some of the major accomplishments and unresolved problems of the Soviet era which helped precipitate its final disintegration. Theories and hypotheses about the breakup of the former Soviet Union will also be presented.

THE NATURE OF SOVIET ECONOMIC DEVELOPMENT

Overview of Soviet Economic History

From the Russian Revolution of 1917 to the 1950s, a predominantly agrarian society was transformed into a military, industrialized superpower. With the exception of the full 1940s decade which encompassed the World War II destruction and reconstruction period, a high rate of economic development characterized much of the Soviet era from about 1930 until perhaps the mid-1960s. Moreover, the unique Soviet system and approach to development had no close historical analogs except, perhaps ironically, in the tsarist industrial development strategy of the late nineteenth century.

Marx's criticisms of capitalism, though voluminous, fell painfully short of presenting a blueprint for the supposed future communist utopia; the Soviet regime was therefore forced both to build on the past and to innovate. The peculiarly Soviet result may be called the Soviet development model. This model constituted the only serious challenge and alternative to Western market or mixed-market models of development for the underdeveloped countries of Asia, Africa, and Latin America. It is also relevant here that the countries of Eastern Europe that fell under Soviet influence after World War II were coerced into adopting the Soviet model. Until Stalin's death in 1953, the economic policies and institutions of Eastern Europe closely paralleled those of the Soviet Union.

We focus here on the theme of Soviet economic development for two reasons. First, the centrally planned economic development was largely a Russian-Soviet innovation and a pervasive Soviet policy goal after 1928. Second, and more importantly, this preoccupation had profound geographic impacts on the former Soviet Union's economic structure and population, placing major constraints on the current political and economic transformation of the former Soviet republics. The current behaviors of the newly emerging rich elite of Russia (the *novo riche*) have an unfortunate, powerful resonance with pre-Revolutionary patterns of the wealthy, as noted in the following section. Although entrepreneurial skills now appear to be developing rapidly in the Baltics and Russia, this does not appear to be the case uniformly across all the former Soviet republics. Unlike pre-Revolutionary times, Russia and the European NIS have educated and skilled labor forces, which are often lacking in Asian republics. Nonetheless, as we will see, decades of distorted economic development policies are forcing Russia to survive primarily by exporting its mineral, energy, and other natural resources rather than value-added, manufactured commodities. Before investigating former Soviet institutions and strategies of development and their geographic impacts, however, an overview of early Soviet economic history is in order, especially focusing on the Revolution and War Communism, New Economic Policy (NEP), and Industrialization Debate eras.

At the time of the 1917 Russian Revolution, Russia was socially and economically backward, despite tsarist Russia's high rates of economic growth in the 1890s. The rural population consisted predominantly of poor and illiterate agricultural peasants. Essentially, there were two socioeconomic classes, (1) the wealthy landed gentry and aristocracy, and (2) the peasantry—with no significant middle class. Also, the urban-industrial proletariat was small. In general, the upper-class lifestyle was characterized by lavish consumption, commonly of expensive imported goods, and the wealthy exhibited little propensity to save or invest. Because of the weak domestic entrepreneurial tradition, much of Russia's industry was foreign owned and its profits were expatriated. The country's potential wealth rested in its vast, virtually untapped mineral and other natural resources, and its enormous but unskilled, under-

employed, agricultural labor force. Russia's citizens were also ravaged and exhausted by World War I, from which the newly created USSR extricated itself by making great territorial and human sacrifices. Control over much of its best land and the newer industrial regions of Ukraine was being contested between the Bolsheviks on the one side and interventionists and counterrevolutionary forces on the other. In civil war conditions of military urgency and extreme economic scarcity, Lenin and the Bolshevik leadership resorted to stern economic policies between 1917 and 1921 that have come to be known as War Communism.

The key policies of the austere War Communism period included the nationalization of all businesses with five or more employees and the elimination of markets in agriculture and retail trade. Agriculture, however, remained under private ownership and control, following the spontaneous peasant land seizures and massive land redistribution of 1917. Industrial labor was conscripted and received payments-in-kind from the state stores of requisitioned agricultural produce. In the demonetized economic environment, the leadership imposed a tax-in-kind on the peasants and rationed practically all foodstuffs.

These policies initially brought the results required of them, but problems developed rapidly after the end of the civil war in 1920. The peasants resisted passively by reducing production, which helped precipitate the devastating famine of 1921. The continued policy of labor conscription created more vociferous dissent among the urban proletariat, culminating in the 1921 Kronstadt Naval Revolt. Realizing the disastrous political consequences of continuing these policies, Lenin proposed a tactical retreat—the New Economic Policy (NEP), which came into effect in 1922.

The New Economic Policy ushered in a revival of private ownership and a market economy in the consumer sector. At the same time, it did not truly herald a complete return to capitalism, for all medium- and large-scale industries and transportation facilities remained nationalized. These measures were taken to provide incentives for the peasants to produce food for distribution to the increasingly hungry cities. In the industrial sector, the NEP seemed to produce spectacularly rapid increases in output. These large increases were primarily the result of restoring to production the country's grossly underutilized pre-Revolutionary industrial capacity. In essence, the NEP was introduced to restore the collaboration or alliance (*smychka*) between the proletariat and the peasant, strained by War Communism. By 1926 private market agriculture under the NEP had already resulted in significant economic differentiation between the *kulaks*, or "rich" peasants. and the mass of the peasantry, once again fraying the fragile alliance between workers and farmers. With time, the potential conflict between Soviet power and the peasants increased. NEP, similarly to War Communism, was only an interim program, geared to buy time for resolving the difficult questions of industrialization, agricultural organization, and capital accumulation.

Some Bolsheviks believed that neither domestic nor international conditions would be found conducive to a measured pace of development. The famous industrialization debate between 1924 and 1928 focused on questions of the sources of investment, sectoral allocation of investment, and tempo of industrialization. With hindsight we now also know that the debate served as a backdrop for Stalin's political maneuvering to consolidate his position of absolute political power following the death of Lenin in 1924. Unlike the years between 1928 and the late 1980s (Gorbachev's *glasnost* era), the years before 1928 were characterized by political pluralism within the Communist party, the participation of nonparty members in high-level discussions, and the flourishing of theory in a number of fields, especially economics. In essence, the industrialization debate was conducted by the two major factions of the party. The gradualist group, or right, stressed agricultural development, while the intensive industrialization group, or left, argued for the rapid and radical restructuring of the economic system.

Pervading the industrialization debate was the irony that according to Marxism, *primitive capitalist accumulation*, with its concomitant increasing misery of the working class, was to provide the material basis for socialism. In general, the rightists' strategies would have followed this "natural" socioeconomic development. The leftist position in essence amounted to a violation of Marxist doctrine by attempting to achieve socialism and com-

munism without having experienced the full capitalist phase of the Marxist historical materialism. The debate was resolved by Stalin's successful struggle to consolidate his position of power—with the leaders of both factions losing, some losing their lives as well as their political positions.

After 1928 Stalin had a free hand and embarked on a series of decisive, radically new policies. The deteriorating economic conditions of 1927 and 1928 had been rapidly eroding the feasibility of the gradualist proposition. Having already embraced the leftist policies on industrialization with the inception of the First Five-Year Plan for 1928 to 1932, Stalin took drastic measures in the agricultural sector to solve the acute marketing problem and at the same time destroy the political clout of the *kulaks*, the country's successful small farmers. In December 1929, he issued orders to collectivize agriculture, and less than three months later over half of the agricultural labor force was in the collectives. Collectivization was predicated on its theoretical efficacy to (1) increase the marketed share of agricultural production, (2) shift resources from consumption into industrial investments, (3) eliminate private ownership of land, and (4) vanquish the *kulak* opposition to the regime.

Many Soviet leaders probably judged collectivization as successful in achieving these four objectives. In the short run, however, the policy yielded phenomenal losses in capital, livestock, and human lives. To a significant degree, the Soviet agricultural capital and labor base had not yet fully recovered from the direct and indirect or echo effects of the collectivization era before the demise of the Soviet Union. In fact, the legacy of Soviet agricultural organizational, capital investment, infrastructural, and incentive problems still severely plagues post-Soviet agriculture directly and hence the entire economic transition process.

The Soviet Development Model

The Soviet development model, thus, evolved from a mixture of ideological and, more pragmatically based, political and economic motives. At least three major **preconditions** of the model can be cited. The first precondition, involving the elimination of economic domination by foreign capitalists, was satisfied by nationalizing foreign-owned and -controlled enterprises during the Revolution and the Bolshevik victory in the civil war. (Ironically, nearly six decades later, Russia and the NIS are now trying, with limited to mixed success, to encourage foreign economic investment.) The second precondition was economic self-sufficiency; although Soviet development did not preclude foreign trade, the country's vast resource base allowed the USSR to avoid the economic vicissitudes of capitalist countries—especially the economic depression of the 1930s that engulfed Europe as well as the United States. The third precondition was a redistribution of economic and political power. Accordingly, the expropriation of industrial enterprises by the state and the landed estates by the peasants in 1917 unequivocally heralded a radical social revolution. Political power, however, instead of being decentralized, rapidly became centralized within the Communist party.

From the Revolution to 1928 many social and economic institutions were destroyed, leaving a socioeconomic vacuum that had to be filled if the whole country and its economy were not to descend rapidly into chaos and collapse. Four **new institutional forms** were substituted. Just as peasant proprietorship had earlier replaced the landed estates, *collectivized* and *state agriculture* supplanted private landownership. *State ownership* and *control of industry* displaced private and foreign ownership and operation. These latter two institutions did not represent novel ideas conceived by the Bolshevik regime, for they were fundamental socialist institutions described by Marx. But the other two institutions had no, or at best only very nebulous, Marxist antecedents.

The deliberate demise of the market mechanism and the profit motive in the fledgling Soviet economy necessitated the creation of alternative institutions to perform the functions of resource allocation and economic coordination. The evolving Soviet command economy introduced *central planning* and a concomitant *centralized "materials-balance"* approach to resource allocation in place of the functions that the market mechanism normally performed in Western economies. Finally, a *system of administrative control and pressure*, and a *worker and managerial incentive system*, involving both monetary and nonmonetary rewards, were introduced to supersede many of the economic functions normally attributed to the private profit motive. Thus, various auditors, Communist party overseers, the Plan, production quotas, and bonuses became part of the day-to-day milieu of both workers and managers in order to prod them to perform in compliance with the leadership's economic goals. Although these various measures worked adequately during the earlier decades of "extensive" growth, by the later years of Khrushchev's leadership (1960–1964) Soviet market substitute institutions were becoming increasingly ineffectual and inappropriate for an environment that was calling for ever-increasing emphasis on quality control and efficient resource management to achieve growth.

A half-dozen or so key Soviet **development strategies** were implemented. First, industry was given development priority. The consumer sector was slighted, as was agriculture. Investment in agriculture was deliberately limited to the minimum required to permit agriculture to supply the industrial sector with a growing marketed surplus of technical crops and foodstuffs for the rapidly burgeoning urban labor force. Investment in mechanized agriculture was designed to produce rapid increases in labor productivity, thus enabling hundreds of thousands of rural workers to migrate to the cities to seek employment in industry.

Second, a skewed or unbalanced growth pattern within industry was pursued by allocating the lion's share of industrial investment to heavy industries such as coal, steel, electric power, machine building, and petroleum, while slighting light industries, consumer goods, housing, and transportation.

Third, by effectively suppressing personal consumption and using an exceedingly low discount rate, a high rate of savings or investment was generated and maintained. In other words, by foregoing consumption initially, the planners hoped rapidly to develop an industrial capacity capable of yielding high per capita consumption rates at some indefinite future time. This structural disequilibrium between producer and consumer goods persisted throughout the entire Soviet period, but less flagrantly so in recent decades than in the first few decades of Soviet power. Even today there is considerable scarcity of domestically produced consumer goods.

Fourth, an import-substitution policy was adopted in foreign trade. This autarkic policy was designed to maintain the Soviet Union's independence from foreign political and economic entanglements, and at the same time reserve the country's meager foreign exchange for the purchase of high-priority capital goods, primarily machine tools.

Fifth, the central planner's selection of productive techniques was guided by the rational need to conserve the country's two scarcest resources—capital and skilled labor. Accordingly, planners often opted for dual technologies. For example, in many basic industrial processes, advanced Western technologies were adopted, while low technology, labor intensive techniques were favored in auxiliary and subsidiary processes. Hence, modern blast furnaces were often loaded by manual laborers using wheel barrows. Economies of scale were attempted by constructing large integrated capital intensive factories. (This "gigantomania" legacy is a serious, current impediment to market competition in post-Soviet industries.) Intensive multiple-shift operations for capital goods were also applied to economize on scarce capital. For instance, in the transport sector Soviet rolling stock was used much more intensively than in the West. In rural areas low-skilled, underemployed, and seasonally unemployed labor was used for the construction of roads, schools, irrigation canals, and farm buildings as well as in cultivating the land and tending livestock.

Sixth, Soviet planners invested heavily in human capital. One of the most impressive achievements of the Soviet regime was their swift reduction of widespread illiteracy. The teaching of at least rudimentary language skills was often combined with vocational and on-the-job technical training. The emphasis on investment in human capital also extended to areas of public health, hospitals, and medical care.

Finally, until the post-Khrushchev era the Soviet leadership used a strategy that might be referred to as *input infusion*. In other words, the planners'

ability to rapidly augment input supplies—especially of labor and raw materials—was primarily responsible for the rapid increase in output. Only in the last decade or so did Soviet leaders and their plans stress factory productivity or efficient resource use as a stimulus to economic growth. This change in relative emphasis evolved naturally as Soviet labor reserves began to dwindle and as the stocks of many accessible, high-quality raw materials began to decline.

As a result of this development model, Soviet industrial development was impressive by any standard, in contrast to the stagnation in the agricultural and consumer sectors (Table 13-1). Only during the 1960s did the high overall GNP growth rate, averaging about 7 percent per year after World War II, begin to slacken. Growth still remained above an internationally respectable 5 percent, with industrial growth rates somewhat higher.

By the end of the 1970s and into the early Gorbachev period, however, overall economic growth had stagnated, ranging from nearly zero to at best 2 percent annually. Most of this deceleration in growth could be accounted for by an aging capital stock overdue for replacement, bureaucratic and planning bottlenecks and shortcomings, inclement weather for agriculture, the gradual depletion of readily accessible high-quality natural resources, and a taxing level of military expenditures. Although Gorbachev through his early economic reform efforts tried to reinvigorate the economy, his efforts to modernize heavy industry with the importation of foreign technology were probably misguided and met with limited success.

The Geographic Components of Soviet Industrial Location Policy

Although in the aggregate the former Soviet Union had (and Russia still has) the largest and most complete inventories of mineral ores and fossil-fuel deposits of any country, this was blurred by the relatively low-quality and increasing remoteness of most of these resource reserves. Similar to water resources, a sizable fraction of the deposits are located in distant Siberia, especially energy

TABLE 13-1

DYNAMICS OF SOVIET PRODUCTION OF SELECTED INDUSTRIAL PRODUCTS

Item	1913	1928	1940	1960	1985	1990	1991
Electric power—billion kwh	2.0	5.0	48.3	292.3	1544.1	1726.0	1675.9
Oil—million metric tons	10.3	11.6	31.1	147.9	595.3	570.8	515.0
Gas—billion m³	0.02	0.3	3.2	45.3	642.9	814.8	810.5
Coal—million metric tons	29.2	35.5	166.0	509.6	726.4	703.3	629.5
Steel—million metric tons	4.3	4.3	18.3	65.3	154.5	154.4	133.1
Mineral fertilizers[a]—million metric tons	0.09	0.1	3.2	13.9	33.2	34.3[b]	NA
Turbine generators—million kW	—	0.04	1.2	9.2	21.6	16.4[b]	NA
Autos, trucks, and buses—thousand	—	0.8	145.4	523.6	2197[c]	NA	NA
Tractors—thousand	—	1.3	31.6	238.5	585	532[b]	NA
Pulp—million metric tons	0.3	0.2	0.5	2.3	8.4	8.5[b]	NA
Fabrics—million m²	2194	2198	3320	6636	12052	13137[b]	NA
Cement—million metric tons	1.8	1.9	5.8	45.5	130.8	140.4[b]	NA
TV sets—thousand	—	—	0.3	1726.0	9371	9938[b]	NA
Household refrigerators—thousand	—	—	3.5	529	5860	6465[b]	NA
Meat and meat byproducts —thousand metric tons	—	—	1544	4406	10808	131164[b]	NA

[a]Conventional units; in terms of conventional content: nitrogenous fertilizer (N)—20.5 percent; potassium fertilizer (K$_2$O)—41.6 percent; phosphate fertilizer (P$_2$O$_5$)—18 7 percent; and phosphate meal (P$_2$O$_5$)—19 percent.

[b]Data for 1989.

[c]Data for 1980.

Sources: Daily Review 22, No. 11 (March 2, 1976); *Handbook of Economic Statistics 1976* (Washington, D.C.: Office of Economic Research, CIA, September 1976), various pages; *Narodnoye khozyaystvo SSSR v 1974 godu* (Moscow: Statistika, 1975), various pages; *Narodnoye khozyaystvo SSSR v 1987 godu* (Moscow: Finansy i statistika, 1988), various pages; *Narodnoye khozyaystvo SSSR v 1989 godu* (Moscow: Finansy i statistika, 1990), various pages; *Narodnoye khozyaystvo za 70 let* (Moscow: Finansy i statistika, 1987), *Pravda* (January 21, 1989); *Post-Soviet Geography* (April 1992): 237–268; *Post-Soviet Geography* (February 1994): 114; *SSSR v tsifrakh v 1973 godu* (Moscow: Statistika, 1974), various pages.

supplies, while the domestic markets for energy and raw materials were and are still heavily concentrated from the Urals westward. For a few decades the European part of the country, and now the European successor states, have had a rapidly growing energy deficit. A combination of the size, quality, and location of resource deposits had long been the chief geographical constraint on Soviet industrial location policy, and will undoubtedly continue to be in the post-Soviet era. The enormous physical size, generally harsh climate, and locational mismatch between people and resources, and the attendant transportation and development problems, have become even more problematic in the post-Soviet era because of the new international (formerly internal) boundaries, foreign trade issues, and regional resource disputes that have arisen since the dissolution.

Greater possibilities of success existed for consciously influencing the location of industrial rather than agricultural activities. Because of various ideological constraints, however, a theoretical basis for the location of industry had long been a sensitive problem for Soviet economists. Industrial location problems can nonetheless be put within the general context of investment decisions; accordingly, three questions had to be answered with respect to investment. Fundamental, of course, was the allocation of the former Soviet Union's income between consumption and investment. Marx answered this question for Soviet leaders by indicating that investment should be maximized. Strict political control and central economic planning provided the means for accomplishing such a program. The second question involved division of investment funds among the various sectors of the economy. Again, Marx provided the answer by stressing industrial producer goods as opposed to consumer goods. The logical final question pertained to the spatial allocation of investment funds within each sector. Although Marx stated some general criteria, he produced nothing comparable to modern Western location theory.

Location Policy Under Stalin Soviet industrial location or resource-use policy can be divided into two periods—the Stalin era of the 1920s to mid-1950s, and the post–Stalin era with its various reform programs. For many years during Stalin's reign, economic calculations were not employed in locational decisions. As a consequence, during the first few decades of Soviet rule, economic decision making became the realm of the politician, with a resulting disregard for economic efficiency in locational decisions. Location doctrine was thus filled with inconsistencies, ambiguities, and even contradictions.

During the Stalin era the general trend was to move labor eastward to resource locations, which thus became new industrial centers. This eastward movement was motivated by at least four major factors. First, locating industries at raw material sites reduced the transportation burden and at the same time facilitated the economic goal of regional self-sufficiency. Second, the pre-Revolutionary location of industry was presupposed to be exploitative, because resources were claimed to be transported to more developed regions for processing in a mercantilist or colonialist fashion. The Soviets believed that on-site or near-site resource use was ideologically purer. Third, the political argument was that by industrializing the once-

backward minority areas, the indigenous ethnic groups would gain a sense of achievement and thus become willing to give their loyalty to the Soviet regime. Finally, because most known and untapped resources were located in and beyond the Urals, the buildup of heavy industry would be located in the relatively safe and inaccessible interior of the country. Simultaneously, the buildup of strategic industries in the east would create a more dispersed pattern of industry, making the defense posture of the country more secure.

The first significant consequence of Stalin's push eastward was the creation of the Ural-Kuznets Combine. As initially set up, Urals' iron ore was transported 1200 miles (1900 km) by rail to the Kuznetsk Basin (Kuzbas) of western Siberia. On the return trip, Kuznetsk coking coal was hauled to the Urals. As a result of this exchange, two new major steel centers were created—Novokuznetsk in the Kuzbas and Magnitogorsk in the Urals (see Fig. 13-11). In recent decades, the western Siberian steel complex relied more on local iron ore deposits, while Magnitogorsk began being switched to closer coking coal from Qaraghandy (formerly Karaganda).

The German invasion of June 1941 provided a strong *ex post facto* rationalization for Stalin's eastward push. Despite the Axis armies' capture of the principal economic regions of the USSR in 1941 and 1942, the eastward expansion of industrial production during the First and Second Five-Year Plans, as well as the dismantling, transporting, and relocating of some 1300 factories in the Urals, Middle Asia, and Siberia to avoid the advancing Germans, played a critical role in ultimately halting the German advance at Stalingrad (now Volgograd). Primarily as a result of these factory relocations, industrial output in Siberia, the Urals, and the Volga Valley increased three- to fourfold. (Lend-lease shipments of supplies by the Allies were also instrumental in turning the tide along the eastern front in favor of the Soviet armed forces.)

Although Soviet industrial progress was rapid during the first two Five-Year Plans (1928–1932 and 1933–1937), a conflict in location policy became evident by the end of the period. Based on Marxist doctrine, the Soviets began to favor extremely large-scale industrial facilities to take

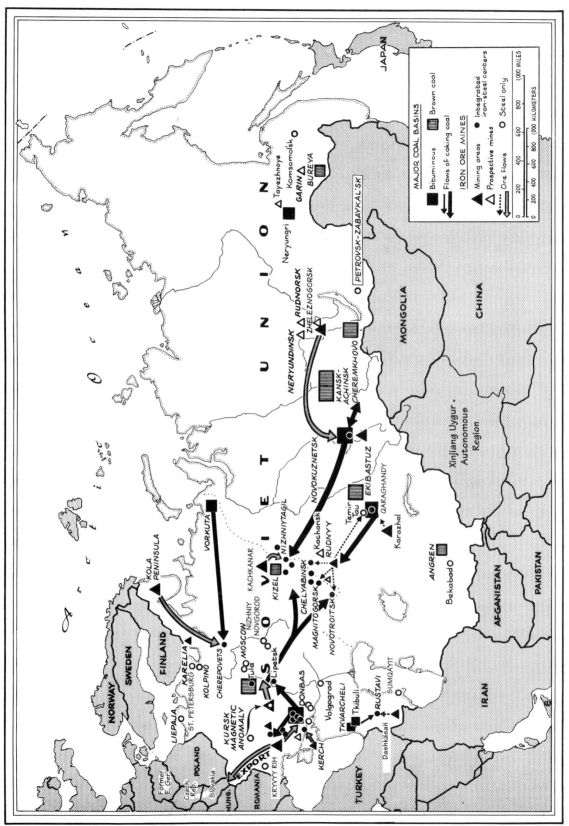

FIGURE 13-11 FSU coal and steel resources and flows to major production centers.

advantage of gains from economies of scale. In fact, Soviet industry became by far the most highly concentrated in the world in the sense of the number of workers per enterprise or factory. This *gigantomania* of the 1930s, in which a few huge plants were constructed to serve excessively large market areas, placed a considerable strain on the railroad sector and led to a general trend toward regional specialization. Accordingly, Stalin and the central planners were faced with a dilemma. Continuation of regional specialization plans would have required massive investment funds for the transportation sector. At the same time, Hitler's menacing actions in the rest of Europe meant that resources were needed for the defense industry. The war-interrupted Third Five-Year Plan (1938–1942) attempted to resolve the dilemma by giving greater official support to a regional approach for the development of the economy—a new emphasis away from sectoral planning. More importantly, however, the new regional approach represented a change from the *gigantomania* of the earlier regional specialization era toward achievement of regional self-sufficiency. This stress on regional autarky was predicated on minimizing of both transportation burdens and the threat of military defeat.

The Fourth Five-Year Plan (1946–1950) represented a rapid and successful national war reconstruction program. Approximately 60 percent of total Soviet industrial plant had been destroyed during the war. The reconstruction was aided by the movement of industries from East Germany, Poland, and Manchuria to the USSR. Although the Soviet Union officially considered these relocations of industrial plants and equipment to be German and Japanese war reparations, the losses were actually suffered by East Germany, Poland and China.

Explicit or implicit in Stalinist, and more generally Soviet, location principles were three major contradictions: the goals of regional autarky and regional specialization were in opposition; the Soviet proclivity for large-scale enterprises conflicted with the goal of minimizing the use of transportation facilities; and the general geographic distribution of raw materials and energy on the one hand, and laborers and consumers on the other, often produced a conflict between raw material

sites and market-oriented locations for manufacturing industries. Military considerations always received high priority, often subordinating other locational objectives.

Attempts at Spatial Profitability (Khozraschyot) Over time the Soviets did indeed become more aware of opportunity costs (costs of foregone investment opportunities) and comparative advantage (focusing production on commodities with the greatest international competitive advantage). Beginning with the revival of cost consciousness in the 1950s, post-Stalin era policies minimized total production costs, while the goal of spatially uniform development received less emphasis. Because of labor supply problems and high infrastructural costs in the east, planners tried for nearly two decades to concentrate labor-intensive activities in the European part of the country and energy- and resource-intensive developments in the east. Operationally, such a dichotomization of economic activities is rarely easy. Nonetheless, the Soviet economic planners consciously tried to create growth poles or territorial production complexes (TPCs) to take advantage of potential industrial linkages. For example, ferrous-metallurgy/machine-building complexes and the newer petrochemical complexes represent successful attempts to reap positive external benefits of spatial agglomeration. Thus, despite the clear ideological doctrine of uniform spatial development, the post-Stalinist Soviet planners opted for a more pragmatic economic development strategy. By the late 1950s, the Soviet leadership and planners had discovered the paradoxical, but probably inevitable, fact that in order to expedite the future development of underdeveloped regions, the growth of industrially advanced regions had to be encouraged.

Still, despite higher development costs in much of Siberia and the Far East, the pro-Eastern development lobby again had influence: 5 of the 11 territorial production complexes singled out for priority development during the eleventh Five-Year Plan (1981–1985) and beyond were located in Siberia. Four complexes were in Central Asia and only two in the European core. Conscious efforts were being made to create TPCs that took advantage of industrial linkages, thereby yielding agglomeration economies that at least partially offset higher development costs in these mostly (from a Soviet perspective) peripheral regions. Excluding the Baykal-Amur-Mainline rail project (BAM) and the Kursk Magnetic Anomaly (KMA) ferrous metallurgy and Karatau-Dzhambul industrial chemicals projects, the other eight complexes were all heavily energy development schemes predicated on the growing energy shortages in the European USSR. At the same time, after the death of Stalin, in 1953, a number of labor-intensive industries, such as auto, truck, and tractor manufacturing, electronics, and precision instrument manufacturing, were located in the European heartland.

Soviet industrial development policy and history did *not* closely parallel those of Europe and North America. Fundamental differences obtained with regard to (1) tempo of development, (2) sectoral priorities, (3) human sacrifice, and (4) degree of political control over development. Finally, although the Soviets rationally retreated from the spatially uniform development doctrine, they did manipulate wages, consumer prices, and infrastructural investment so as to reduce significantly the inherited pre-Revolutionary inequity among regions in terms of real per capita income, education, and health care. Within regions, however, as we will see, the sharp urban-rural disparities persisted, owing primarily to the long-term chronic low priority on tertiary or service sector investment.

Gorbachev: The Promises and Failures of *Perestroika*, and *Glasnost*

After a series of lackluster leaders following Khrushchev's fall, the arrival of the charismatic Mikhail Gorbachev on the Soviet political center stage in 1985 was marked by promises of dynamic changes in the structure of the Soviet economy and in the everyday life of its people. This dynamic "new" reform climate was ushered in on the supposedly synergistic winds of *perestroika* and *glasnost*. A great many hoped-for positive changes were encapsulated in these two Russian terms. *Perestroika*, or "restructuring," became the catch-all term for Soviet economic reform, whereas, *glas-*

nost, or more "openness" in public discussion and debate, referred to greater freedom of expression in the arts and to steps toward achieving political democratization. *Glasnost* brought the March 26, 1989, more or less free election of 1500 candidates to the new Congress of USSR People's Deputies. The word "new" is used advisedly here because we can look back into Russian and Soviet history and easily find at least weak analogues for many of Gorbachev's policies and reforms, which collectively fell under the twin rubrics of *perestroika* and *glasnost*. For example, Gorbachev's economic reformers, to a certain degree, could glance over their shoulders to the previously discussed NEP period. Then, too, *glasnost* had precedents in the wave of de-Stalinization of the Khrushchev era, when even the politically critical early writings of Aleksandr Solzhenitsyn were officially published.

More specifically, then, what were some of the key aspects of Gorbachev's economic reform package, and why did it fail in terms of reforming as opposed to disintegrating the former Soviet Union? The goal of Gorbachev's *perestroika* was to make significantly greater use of normally understood economic methods to operate the Soviet economy, and hence, to shift away from its overly centralized command system of management. During the summer of 1987, the Party Central Committee approved a four-year reform blueprint and accordingly, introduced more reliance on market methods and profit incentives. For the first time since the 1920s, the Soviets began allowing direct foreign investment and joint ventures. The mandate of *Gosplan*, the State Planning Committee, was curtailed in terms of strategic and day-to-day operational planning. Individual plant managers began to be required, and were given the freedom to make, more of their own decisions, and workers' compensation was supposed to be much more closely tied to their productive performance. In theory, firms were to be "allowed" to go bankrupt, and worker layoffs were to be permitted. In the Russian Federation fears of massive social unrest associated with such bankruptcies and layoffs have continued to result in the central government "cranking up the money presses" and maintaining "soft-budget constraints" (flexible budgets with the possibility of continued subsidies, rather than fixed budgets) to bail out scores of the large state and newly "privatized" industrial enterprises, even into the mid-1990s.

In effect, the government's actions represented a greater fear of massive social unrest associated with potential bankruptcies and massive layoffs than the hyperinflation which their money printing helped engender. Profit-motivated "contract brigades" proliferated among both agricultural and industrial workers. In May 1987 a law went into effect that allowed individual and (cooperative) family businesses to be created. Within a matter of months, over 200,000 Soviet citizens started up small service sector businesses, and by early 1989 over 2 million people were already employed in co-ops and private businesses. Moscow bore witness to a proliferation of private restaurants, employing up to 25 workers, almost overnight.

Prior to the breakup of the Soviet Union, the economic reform plans called for most industrial products to be purchased and sold in wholesale trade by 1992, free from state central control. Such a revolutionary change had little chance of being successful without a dramatic shift to rational market pricing. For decades *Gosnab*, the state supply agency, had constructed fixed price lists for about 200,000 Soviet products. From a theoretical basis, the freeing up of such prices seemed essential before enterprises could realize the benefits of the new managerial autonomy. Yet such a rapid return to market prices had significant political risks for Gorbachev. Two key consumer sectors, food and housing, had for a long time been *highly* subsidized. Strong fears were voiced that the presumably large, required price increases could set off a torrent of widespread passive and active resistance to economic reforms.

Also, an entrenched cadre of approximately 18 million bureaucrats posed a formidable obstacle to Gorbachev's reform plans. The record reveals that Gorbachev's reform package attempted to use old Soviet fist (punitive) approaches too often. For example, labor discipline campaigns in terms of massive crackdowns on drunkenness, absenteeism, waste, and corruption were conspicuous parts of Gorbachev's policy. They all ended up being counterproductive and failed miserably.

Informed opinion varies as to why the reform processes Gorbachev initiated failed to bring about their intended results, assuming the demise of the Soviet Union was not one of their intended goals. It appears that at least at some level Gorbachev was trying to create a civil society in the Soviet Union. His political weaving and dodging while trying to maintain his position of power may detract from this interpretation. Nonetheless, as the first Soviet leader since Lenin who was a lawyer, he seemed to have embarked on a course leading to a society that would be ruled more by law than by political fiat. One thing seems certain: *glasnost* quickly took on a life of its own. It seems to have functioned literally like a breath of fresh air or oxygen, helping to flame the denied, suppressed, and long-smoldering embers and feelings of ethnic nationalism and regionalism.

Fundamental to economic reform are the codification and enforcement of clear property rights and governmental taxation schemes. With the possible exception of the Baltic republics, where efforts to restore pre-annexation property rights are actively underway, none of the former Soviet republics has comprehensively resolved the complex property rights issues. Nonetheless, aside from the Baltics, Russia seems to have attempted to initiate the most radical property rights reforms thus far, but has made no pretense of restoring pre-Revolutionary property ownership. Even so, many of the property rights issues in Russia remain far from resolved, especially land ownership questions. Yet to be resolved are major practical and political questions surrounding which of the myriad of old all-Union legislation remains in effect versus new Russian Federation legislation. Certainly, political stability and clearly delineated property rights are crucial if the regions and republics of the former USSR are to develop private market relationships and induce domestic private entrepreneurial investment, let alone to attract significant foreign capital investment.

Another major controversy about economic reform in Russia has centered on the pace of reform. Those favoring rapid reform could be considered proponents of so-called "shock-therapy", and those favoring a slower pace of reform could be considered proponents of "evolutionary reform." Shock therapy is commonly associated with a young Soviet economist, Yegor Gaidar, whose team was composed of both Russian and foreign economic advisers, including Jeffrey Sachs of Harvard University. Shock therapy was used in Poland, and essentially calls for freeing commodity prices, eliminating "soft-budget constraints," imposing strong restraints on the printing of money in order to prevent hyperinflation, rapidly privatizating economic enterprises including agriculture, granting freedom for foreign economic competition, and allowing inefficient firms to go bankrupt. This economic medicine will necessarily heighten the pain in the short run, but will result in faster, more rational, efficient market transformation. The evolutionary perspective calls for the more gradual reform, including continued subsidization of state and formerly state enterprises in order to prevent massive unemployment and social upheaval.

A debate still rages as to whether or not "shock therapy" failed in Russia or, for that matter, whether it was even tried. For example, most prices were freed in January 1992 (exceptions were food and some other consumer goods), prior to major privatization efforts. Foreign competition was still severely limited; thus the Soviet legacy of *gigantomania* allowed many enterprises to respond as monopolists by simultaneously raising prices and cutting back on production. The dismantling of *Gosplan* and the system of central planning and state orders led to a vacuum in coordination of the economy. In the short run, hundreds of private and mixed private-state enterprise-owned commodity exchanges proliferated to perform this coordinating role, functioning as auction houses for everything from socks to jet aircraft.

In essence, reform efforts may still be characterized as consisting of bold steps, half-steps, contradictory steps, and retreats in the face of strong political opposition. All of the economic medicines that a "shock therapy" regime prescribes were probably not administered, let alone in a rationally coordinated way. At the same time, a number of strong arguments could be made suggesting that the Soviet economic-geographic legacy and patterns of spatial and sectoral development, as well as ethnic and political factors, did not and do not lend themselves easily to "shock

therapy" approaches. Unfolding has been a series of events and reform processes that are neither representative of "shock therapy" nor well thought out, coordinated "evolutionary reform;" rather, they could be referred to as attempts to "muddle through."

Nonetheless, important pieces of enterprise property reform legislation were enacted before and after the dissolution of the Soviet Union between 1990 and 1992. Unfortunately, and not surprisingly, before laws were in place, and even afterward, much privatization of formerly state assets took place and continue to occur by a variety of other means. Collectively these can be labeled de facto spontaneous privatization processes on the part of the bureaucracy, enterprise directors and other insiders, and former party officials, rather than the more orderly, open and democratic processes specified by various legislative acts. Accordingly, we may ask whether or not the market transition/privatization processes that have taken place to date can be better characterized as yielding economically desirable efficiency gains or as *personalizing* (frankly speaking "stealing") state property, with monopolistic inefficiencies remaining intact.

During the 1992–1993 active phase of privatization, enterprises were officially and legally privatized by a variety of means. Yeltsin signed a revised privatization program on December 24, 1993, and it went into effect on January 1, 1994. This program retains most of the main features of the earlier program but includes important changes. These current post-Soviet reforms are too recent, too uncertain, too weakly entrenched, and too fluid for anyone to speculate with any degree of confidence about how they may alter the post-Soviet economic landscape in the long term. One thing seems certain: economic prosperity and an autonomous, efficient, integrated market economy will not manifest themselves any time soon.

DEMOGRAPHY AND URBANIZATION

Imperial Russian, Soviet, and post-Soviet governments' policies and actions have, of course, had profound impacts on their countries' large and diverse populations. Before turning to a geographically based analysis of the Soviet and Russian economies, the following section provides an overview of the policies, trends, and characteristics of the Soviet and Russian populations.

Distinguishing Soviet and Post-Soviet Demographic Characteristics

As previously noted, the Soviet Union was highly multinational. The supposed ethnic *melting pot* of the United States does not come close to the former

Soviet Union in cultural, linguistic, and ethnic pluralism (Table 13-2). Besides its multinational composition, the USSR experienced three other demographic developments in this century—calamitous population losses, rapid urbanization, and massive internal migrations, which, at least in scale, distinguished it from the rest of Europe and the United States.

The tumultuous events of World War I, the civil war from 1919 to 1921 (2 million deaths), the epidemics from 1917 to 1923 (3 million deaths), the famines during the 1920s (5.5 million deaths), the forced collectivization in the 1930s (10 million

---

TABLE 13-2

LANGUAGES OF THE FORMER USSR

(Number of People in Ethnic Group, in Thousands)

Language Family	Language Subgroup	Major Languages	1970 Census	1979 Census	1989 Census
Indo-European	Slavic	Russian	129,015	137,397	145,155
		Ukrainian	40,753	42,347	44,186
		Belarussian	9,052	9,463	10,036
		Polish	1,167	1,151	1,126
		Bulgarian	351	361	373
	Baltic	Latvian	1,430	1,439	1,459
		Lithuanian	2,665	2,851	3,067
	Iranian	Tadzhik	2,136	2,898	4,215
		Ossetian	488	542	598
		Tat	17	24	31
		Kurdish	89	116	153
	Armenian	Armenian	3,559	4,151	4,623
	Germanic	German	1,846	1,936	2,039
		Yiddish	2,151	1,811	1,449
	Romance	Moldovian	2,698	2,968	3,352
	Greek	Greek	337	344	358
	Indic	Gypsy	175	209	262

continued

continued

TABLE 13-2

(Number of People in Ethnic Group, in Thousands)

Language Family	Language Subgroup	Major Languages	1970 Census	1979 Census	1989 Census
Turkic		Tatar	5,931	6,317	6,649
		Bashkir	1,240	1,371	1,449
		Azerbaijani	4,380	5,477	6,770
		Uzbek	9,195	12,456	16,698
		Kazakh	5,299	6,556	8,136
		Kyrgyz	1,452	1,906	2,529
		Turkmen	1,525	2,028	2,729
		Yakut	296	328	382
		Karakalpak	236	303	424
		Tuvinian	139	166	207
Finnic	Eastern Branch	Komi	475	478	497
		Mordvinian	1,263	1,192	1,154
		Chuvash	1,694	1,751	1,842
		Mari	599	622	671
		Udmurt	704	714	747
		Nentsy (Samoyedes)	29	30	35
	Western Branch	Estonian	1,007	1,020	1,027
		Karelian (Finnish)	230	215	131
		Lappish	2	2	2
Caucasian	Southern	Georgian	3,245	3,571	3,981
	Northern	Abkhaz	83	91	105
		Cherkess (Circassian)	40	46	52
		Kabardian	280	322	391
		Chechen-Ingush	771	942	1,194
		Dagestan group	1,365	1,657	2,064
Mongolian		Buryat	315	353	421
		Kalmyk	137	147	174
Manchurian		Evenki (Tungus)	25	28	30
Paleoasiatic		Minor Siberian	97	98	117

Sources: *Narodnoye khozyaystvo SSSR v 1970 g.* (Moscow: Statistika, 1971), pp. 15–17; *Narodnoye khozyaystvo SSSR v 1979 g.* (Moscow: Statistika, 1980) p. 30; *Narodnoye khozyaystvo SSSR v 1989 g.* (Moscow: Finansy I Statistika, 1990), pp. 30–33; *Naseleniye SSSR* (Moscow: Politizdat, 1980); *Vestnik Statistiki*, No. 2, 1980.

kulaks died or were murdered), the famines and purges in the 1930s (15 million deaths), World War II (25 to 30 million deaths, with another 15 million in indirect losses as birth deficits), and continuing emigration have been responsible directly or indirectly, through birth deficits and other subsequent population *echo effects*, for population deficits totaling an estimated 150 million people by 1991. These staggering figures are essentially equal to the entire current population of Russia, 148 million, or more than 50 percent of the current combined population of the 15 former republics, now over 293 million. The direct and indirect population losses suffered during World War II, of course, were the Soviet Union's major demographic disaster. For comparison it may be noted that the United States' war losses amounted to about 300,000 people. Falsification of the 1939 Census and subsequent secrecy mean, however, that the World War II deaths are only now being distinguished from the 1930s purges, collectivization, and prison camp deaths.

The western part of the country suffered the most from the German occupation. As a measure of this hardship, Belarus did not recover its prewar population level until the early 1970s. For the country as a whole, the prewar population was not attained until 1955. The strong gender bias resulting from World War II deaths is also still evident in Russia and the European NIS.

Life expectancies reached post–1960 lows in the USSR in 1984 and then began to improve somewhat before dramatic declines following the breakup, especially for men. Infant mortality rates (IMR—deaths before the age of one year) rose throughout the 1970s. While on the decline during most of the 1980s, they never returned to an all-time national low of 22.9 deaths per 1000 live births reached in 1971. In the late 1980s, IMR again started to increase, rapidly following the breakup, and now averages overall about 30/per 1000 for all 15 of the former republics (highest in Tajikistan, 47, lowest in Belarus—12.5). Russia and the six European NIS countries all experienced increases in the IMR after the breakup. Presumably in the case of life expectancy, these erratic, deteriorating health statistics are associated with the increased use of tobacco, alcohol, and their often associated increased incidents of industrial accidents. The infant mortality figures may be associated with pervasive high levels of prenatal alcohol consump-

tion by Soviet women. Since the breakup, health-related economic dislocations such as the deterioration of medical care and shortages of medicines and vaccines, and even murder, have become major factors in the dramatic retrogression of life expectancy and infant mortality figures.

Concomitant with the forced industrialization program, the Soviet Union experienced a spectacular rate of urbanization after the 1930s, the second of the aforementioned distinguishing demographic characteristics of the Soviet and post-Soviet eras. Before World War I, the Russian Empire was predominantly rural, with only 18 percent of the population classified as urban. The civil war and famines of the early 1920s reduced this figure to 16 percent by the end of 1922. However, by 1940 as compared with 1922, the urban population had nearly tripled, from 22 million to 63 million, making the country's population one-third urban. The 50 percent urban level was achieved in 1961. According to official census data of January 12, 1989, the Soviet Union's population was nearly 66 percent urban. The urban population increased from 28.5 million before World War I to 189 million in 1989. During the same time period, the rural population experienced an absolute decline from 131 million to 98 million. Currently, Moldova remains by far the least urban (47%) of the seven European NIS states and Russia (73%) the most urban. The others range from a low of 68 percent urban in Ukraine to 70 in Estonia. Although there has been some urban depopulation and return to the countryside since the breakup, this process is undoubtedly transitory.

The USSR's and FSU's third distinguishing demographic feature have been the extremes of state-sponsored internal migration of large segments of the population. The forced exile of *kulaks* and other peasants to Siberia during the 1930s was the first of these massive population movements. Stalin's political purges in the middle and late 1930s added to this phenomenon and supplied forced labor for many Soviet projects in the European north and Siberia. Another sort of compulsory migration took place during World War II, when several ethnic groups accused of collaboration with the Germans and other subversive activities were forcibly evicted from their historic homelands and exiled to Central Asia and Siberia. Among these groups were the Karachai, Kalkar, Chechen, and

Ingush peoples of the northern Caucasus, as well as the Kalmyks, the Volga Germans, and the Crimean Tatars. Smaller numbers of people were exiled after World War II, including tens of thousands of people from the Baltic republics. In the early years of Khrushchev's power, these exiled peoples regained their civil rights, and most were returned to their homelands, the Volga Germans and the Crimean Tatars being notable exceptions. Beginning in the late 1980s under *glasnost* and *perestroika*, tens of thousands of Germans emigrated to West Germany. Crimean Tatars under the supposed democratic umbrella of *glasnost* mounted several protests in Moscow and elsewhere, and tens of thousands simply demonstrated with their feet and returned to the Crimea, building large squatter settlements. Long suppressed as an ethnic category in the official census, Crimean Tatars numbered 272,000 in the official 1989 Soviet Census.

Two mass migrations occurred after the war. First, large numbers of Russians from the densely inhabited regions of Central European Russia were moved to the annexed areas of northern East Prussia, to the Baltic republics, to southern Sakhalin Island, and to other annexed territories along the Soviet western frontier. These inmigrations, especially in the Baltics, were not welcomed by the local ethnic populations and have resulted in numerous problems in the post-Soviet era, usually focused on citizenship rights and definitions. Second, in the 1950s, hundreds of thousands of young people, predominantly Russians and Ukrainians, were induced, and in part conscripted, to work in the Virgin Lands of Kazakhstan.

In more recent times, three other types of large-scale migrations have been occurring. First, beginning in earnest in the 1970s, cycles of essentially Jewish emigration have taken place, primarily to Israel and the United States, and since the breakup hundreds of thousands of people have emigrated out of the former Soviet Union to Western countries. For example, from 1989 through 1994 a total of 559,900 people emigrated from Russia, including 224,200 to Germany, 164,000 to Israel, and 42,000 to the United States.

Second, also since the breakup, large-scale migration between the former republics has been continuing, mainly in what might be characterized as "returning to the motherland(s)." For example, large numbers of Russians have been leaving the Central Asian republics in particular and returning to "mother Russia," even though many or perhaps most had spent their entire lives in these other republics. From 1989 through 1994 there was a net positive migration of 2.4 million people into Russia from the other republics. Except for inter-republic flows between Belarus-Russia and Ukraine-Russia, all of these flows have been net positive flows into Russia in all years since 1989. The largest inmigration streams have been from Central Asia (in thousands): Kazakhstan (656), Uzbekistan (436), Tadjikistan (236), Kyrgyzstan (237), and Turkmenistan (51); from Transcaucasia: Armenia (249), Georgia (228), and Azerbaijan (97); and from the combined Baltics (183). In the case of the Baltics, many Russians probably felt that their freedom and standard of living would remain higher if they remained than if they emigrated to an uncertain future in Russia. These flows have been growing dramatically since 1991, when 104,900 net migrants came into Russia from the other former republics, compared to 1994 with 914,600 (304,500 from Kazakhstan alone). The sums for this six-year period include net outflows from Russia into Belarus (3000) and Ukraine (21,800). In both cases, however, these trends may be rapidly reversing themselves as there were net flows into Russia from Belarus in 1994 (15,600) and from Ukraine (135,400 in 1994). The adoption of national language laws and rising local nationalism in the former republics may yet lead to accelerated Russian outmigration.

The third migration pattern involves the return of large numbers of military personnel and their families from Eastern Europe, especially from the former East Germany. The provision of housing and jobs for these inmigrants has been very problematic. The West German government provided significant funds to the Russian government for military personnel relocations as part of the agreement for the Soviet/Russian troop withdrawals from East Germany in 1994.

Population Size and Distribution— People in Space

According to official Soviet estimates, the population of the USSR passed the 250 million mark in the early 1970s. Increasing at a modest annual rate of about 2 million, the Soviet Union ranked third behind China and India in population among the world's countries. Considering the catastrophic demographic losses after 1913, Soviet population growth was rapid (Table 13-3). The rate of natural increase was high throughout the 1950s, reaching a high of 17.8 per 1000 (or 1.78% per year) in 1960. During the 1960s, there was a steady decline in both urban and rural fertility rates (average number of children per woman) and a slight increase in the death rate. Hence, the population growth rate decreased to a nadir of 8.9 per 1000 (or 0.89% per year) in 1969. After 1970, the growth rate again increased slightly. Currently, however, the growth rate for the entire former Soviet Union has plum-

TABLE 13-3

POPULATION OF THE FORMER SOVIET REPUBLICS

Republic	1926	1940	1959	1979	1989	1994	1970–1994	1993-1994
			In Thousands				Pop. Growth In Pct.	Pop. Growth In Pct.
Russia	93,395	110,098	117,534	137,551	147,386	148,366	0.4	0.2
European NIS								
Ukraine	29,018[a]	41,340	41,869	49,755	51,704	52,114	0.4	0.2
Belarus	4,983	9,046	8,056	9,560	10,200	10,367	0.6	0.2
Moldova	572[b]	2,468	2,885	3,947	4,341	4,353	0.8	0.1
Lithuania	—	2,925	2,711	3,398	3,690	3,739	0.6	0.3
Latvia	—	1,886	2,093	2,521	2,681	2,566	0.3	1.5
Estonia	—	1,054	1,197	1,466	1,573	1,507	0.4	1.3
Transcaucasia								
Azerbaijan	2,315	3,274	3,698	6,028	7,029	7,431	1.6	0.9
Georgia	2,666	3,612	4,044	5,015	5,449	5,426	0.6	0.4
Armenia	880	1,320	1,763	3,031	3,283	3,742	1.7	0.5
Central Asia								
Uzbekistan	4,446	6,551	8,119	15,391	19,906	22,200	2.6	2.2
Kazakhstan	6,503	6,148	9,295	14,684	16,538	16,942	1.1	0.3
Tajikistan	827	1,525	1,981	3,801	5,112	5,704	2.8	2.3
Kyrgyzstan	993	1,528	2,066	3,529	4,291	4,463	1.7	0.9
Turkmenistan	1,001	1,302	1,516	2,759	3,534	4,361	2.9	2.5
FSU[c] Total	147,028	194,077	208,827	262,436	286,717	293,274	0.8	0.1

[a]1926 boundaries.

[b]Moldovian ASSR of 1926.

[c]FSU = former Soviet Union.

Sources: Narodnoye khozyaystvo SSSR za 70 let (Moscow: Finansy i statistika, 1987, p. 374; *Izvestiya* (April 28, 1989), p. 1; Carl Haub, "Population Change in the Former Soviet Republics," *Population Bulletin*, 49, No. 4 (December 1994): 7 & 48.

meted to 0.1 percent per year. The European NIS countries currently have negative growth rates, except Belarus (0.2%/year) and Moldova (0.1%/year). In the three Baltic countries the negative rate averages -0.9 percent per year.

Until the late 1980s, the general aging of the population was principally responsible for the mild increase in the death rate. In the 1980s and since the breakup, degenerative diseases, infectious diseases, alcohol abuse, accidents, and murder/suicide have become the major causes of increased deaths. The myriad problems associated with the economic dislocations, such as the increased numbers of divorces and decreased number of marriages, since the breakup have resulted in sharp declines in fertility rates in all 15 former republics. On the other hand, after a string of eight straight years of declines, 1994 was the first year when a increase rather than total decrease in births was recorded.

Between 1950 and 1970, the median age of the population increased by over 5 years, to an average of 30 years. More economically and politically problematic was the slow rise in the dependency ratio—the number of nonworking young and old persons per 1000 persons of working age—which added aggregate labor supply problems to the chronic problems of the regional distribution of labor and low labor productivity. In the short run, the dearth of births since the breakup will moderate this figure, but in the long run it could well intensify labor supply problems.

Not surprisingly, climatic and physical factors have had a profound impact on the geographic distribution of both rural and urban population. Essentially, the European NIS population is concentrated in a population wedge that has apexes at St. Petersburg, Odesa, and the middle Urals, with a relatively high-density population ribbon about 400 miles (640 km) wide astride the Trans-Siberian Railway from the Urals to the Kuzbas (Figs. 13-12 and 13-13). A number of widely spaced cities and settlements exist along the Trans-Siberian Railway east of the Kuzbas, much like beads on a necklace.

By 1989 about 196 million Soviet citizens resided in the European part of the country, including Transcaucasia and the European Urals, and 91 million in the Asiatic portions. In 1940 the respective figures were 160 million and 34 million. Thus,

the eastward trend in economic development has been reflected in a similar long-term eastward population shift from 17.7 percent living east of the Urals in 1940 to 31.7 percent by 1989. This Soviet eastward population movement will likely emerge as a major economic and political problem for post-Soviet Russia. Much of the population movement was based on the development of remote natural resources, many of which are losing whatever artificial advantages they might have had under the irrational pricing structure of the former command economy. In effect, despite decades of complaints about the inadequate urban and transportation infrastructure in Siberian settlements, the Soviet forced-industrialization machine probably overinvested in settlements in many of these regions. Now many of these cities and settlements are finding themselves without viable economic rationales.

Recent Trends in Urban and Rural Population Growth

The remarkably rapid Soviet urbanization after the First Five-Year Plan can be attributed to several factors. Of first importance was the rural-to-urban migration needed to satisfy the burgeoning labor demands of Soviet industry, a process that continued unabated for decades. A natural expansion in the urban population itself also contributed a large share of the increase. The industrialization drive concurrently resulted in the rapid creation of a number of new or essentially new industrial cities, particularly in the Urals and eastern regions of the country, such as Magnitogorsk, Chelyabinsk, Omsk, Novosibirsk, Novokuznetsk, and Kemerovo. The final factor was simply one of redefinition. In other words, the total Soviet urban population was increased by merely redefining some rural settlements and centers as urban settlements once they reached a certain size.

During the long census interim of 1939–1959, the core population growth area of the USSR was in the region between Moscow and Lake Baykal, which had rapidly growing cities. The highest proportion of these growth centers was associated with resource extraction—primarily coal, oil, and iron ore. The five main growth subregions were:

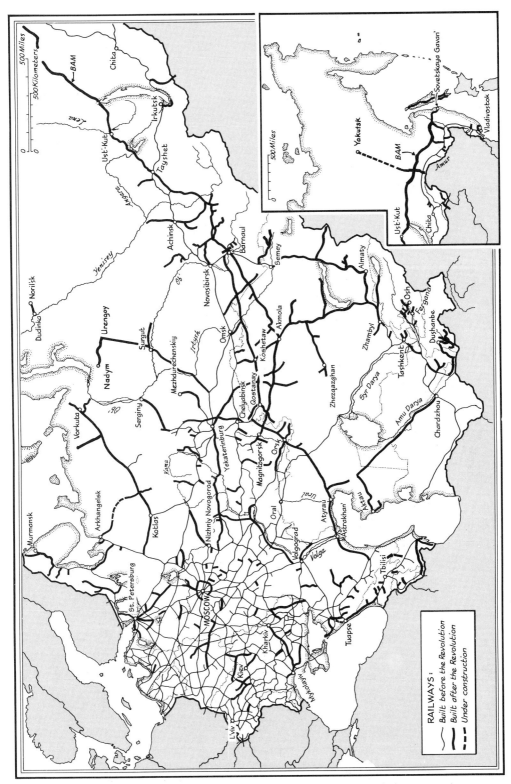

FIGURE 13-12 FSU railroad network.

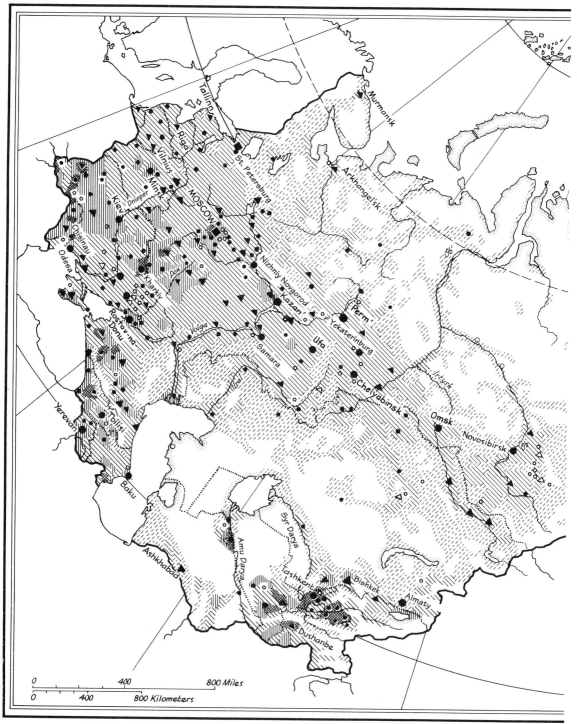

FIGURE 13-13 FSU population density.

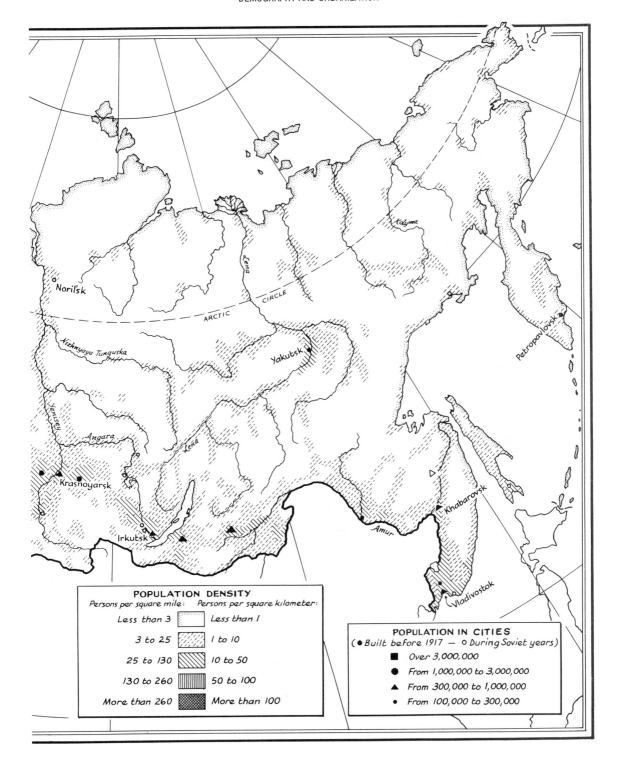

POPULATION DENSITY

Persons per square mile:	Persons per square kilometer:
Less than 3	Less than 1
3 to 25	1 to 10
25 to 130	10 to 50
130 to 260	50 to 100
More than 260	More than 100

POPULATION IN CITIES
(● Built before 1917 — ○ During Soviet years)

- ■ Over 3,000,000
- ● From 1,000,000 to 3,000,000
- ▲ From 300,000 to 1,000,000
- • From 100,000 to 300,000

(1) the Komi coal- and oilfields in the European north, (2) the Tula coal basin south of Moscow, (3) the Volga-Urals oilfield, (4) the Kuzbas coal basin in southern West Siberia, and (5) the Qaraghandy (Karaganda) coal and iron ore deposits in Kazakhstan. Logically, the only agricultural region with high rates of urbanization was the Virgin Lands area of northern Kazakhstan and southern West Siberia, which was rapidly developed in the 1950s (and is discussed later in this chapter).

After 1959 the distribution of rapidly growing cities was more widely spread, extending throughout the European part of the Soviet Union all the way to Lake Baykal. The only regional concentration of rapidly growing cities was in Kazakhstan and parts of Central Asia, which was plagued with rural overpopulation. The greater dispersion of the urban growth pattern after 1959 was associated with renewed emphasis on labor-intensive industrial development in the neglected and smaller cities of the western parts of the country.

The rapid pace of urbanization can be summarized by way of time-series data sets. For example, at the time of the Revolution and even as late as l939, Moscow and St. Petersburg (then Leningrad) were the only Soviet cities exceeding one million in population (Table 13-4). Although Kiev, the Ukrainian capital, was the only additional city to join the million-plus category in 1959, 21 more cities attained the million or more mark by 1990. In fact, urban growth was so rapid, particularly for the medium- and large-sized cities, that the Soviets long attempted to curb it (a topic we will return to later). Then, too, spatial expansion of cities resulted in the gradual coalescence of three regional conurbations in Russia: (1) the greater Moscow region, (2) the middle and southern Urals, and (3) the Kuzbas, as well as two conurbations in Ukraine, the Donbas and the Dnieper bend region. Despite the bias against large cities, during the past few decades the Soviets experienced a significant problem with declining towns and their associated economic and social woes.

The rural population as a proportion of the total population within Russia and the European NIS is highest today in Moldova (53%) and the southwest Ukraine (44%). In the years following 1970, the rural population increased rapidly in practically all of West Siberia and Crimea. The other dramatic

demographic development was the net rural exodus from European Russia, Ukraine, the Urals, and most of southern Siberia. Between 1980 and 1990, the absolute rural population totals in 23 of the 25 Ukrainian oblasts decreased. In European Russia most administrative divisions suffered similar absolute declines in rural population.

Some major trend reversals in the patterns of rural population decline in Russia have been occurring since the breakup. For example, between 1992 and 1993, the total Russian Federation population declined 707,000, urban population declined by 1,634,000, and rural population grew by 927,000. The reversals in general rural population growth rates most likely reflect short-term adjustments to the post-Soviet economic travail, whereby people returned to the countryside where at least a reliable food supply could be grown for personal consumption. On the other hand, the long-term general trend of rural outmigration to industrialized cities probably plays a significant negative role in terms of the agricultural transformation/reform of the countryside, for there has long been a marked tendency for outmigrants to be higher skilled and younger workers.

Two final trends in rural and urban population dynamics should be mentioned, because if they continue in the long run they will have profound impacts on the human and economic landscapes of Russia and the other former Soviet republics. Compared with the pre-World War II era, the Soviet Union experienced a sharp decline in fertility rates during the 1950s and 1960s. The decline had two major spatial-temporal dimensions: (1) a rural-urban dimension, and (2) an ethnic dimension. In essence, the downward trend in crude birth rates and age-specific birth rates began in the urban areas of the Baltic republics and spread eastward and southward like a series of radiating waves. Thus, at present, the lowest fertility rates are in the urban areas of European Russia (less than 1.4 children/woman) and the Baltic republics (ranging from 1.4 in "Protestant" Estonia to 1.7 in "Catholic" Lithuania). The highest rates are in the four Central Asian republics, ranging from a low of 3.3 in Kyrgyzstan to a high of 4.3 in Tajikistan.

The fertility decline has been associated with urbanization and industrialization factors similar to those to which fertility declines in the West have

TABLE 13-4

POPULATION OF THE LARGEST RUSSIAN AND EUROPEAN NIS CITIES

Year	In Thousands						
	1926	1939	1959	1970	1989[a]	1990	1992
Russian Federation							
Moscow	2026	4542	6044	7077	8972	9080	8957
St. Petersburg (Leningrad)	1614	3401	3340	3897	5024	5035	5004
Nizhni Novgorod (Gorki)	185	644	941	1170	1438	1443	1441
Novosibirsk	120	404	885	1161	1437	1443	1442
Yekaterinburg (Sverdlovsk)	136	423	779	1025	1365	1372	1371
Samara (Kuybyshev)	176	390	806	1045	1241	1258	1239
Omsk	162	289	581	821	1148	1159	1169
Chelyabinsk	59	273	689	875	1142	1148	1143
Kazan	176	406	667	869	1094	1103	1104
Perm	85	306	629	850	1091	1094	1099
Ufa	99	258	547	771	1078	1094	1097
Rostov-on-Don	308	510	600	789	1019	1025	1027
Volgagrad	148	445	591	818	999	1005	1006
Ukraine							
Kiev (Kyyiv)	514	851	1110	1632	2587	2616	
Kharkiv	417	840	953	1223	1611	1618	
Dnipropetrovs'k	233	528	661	862	1179	1187	
Odesa	421	599	664	892	1115	1106	
Donets'k	106	474	708	879	1110	1117	
Belarus							
Minsk	132	237	509	917	1589	1613	

[a]Census as of January 12, 1989.

Sources: *Narodnoye khozyaystvo SSSR v 1974 g.* (Moscow: Statistika, 1975); Chauncy Harris, *Cities of Soviet Union* (Chicago: Rand McNally, 1970); Theodore Shabad, *Soviet Geography* (October 1979), pp. 481–488; *Narodnoye khozyaystvo SSSR v 1980 g.* (Moscow: Statistika, 1981), pp. 18–23; *Narodnoye khozyaystvo za 70 let* (Moscow: Finansy i statistika, 1987), pp. 395–400.; and Izvestiya (April 28, 1989), pp. 2–3; *Narodnoye khozyaysta-vo rossiiskoy federatsii 1992* (Moscow: Gosudarstvennyy komitet Rossiyskiy Federatsii po statistike, 1992), pp. 87–90; *Demograficheskiy yezhegod-nik SSSR 1990* (Moscow: Finansy i statistika, 1990), pp. 14–26.

been attributed. Female employment, relatively easy availability of abortion (a high of 216 abortions/100 live births in Russia to a low of 18 abortions/100 life births in Azerbaijan during 1990–1993), and a shortage of housing, however, have been more important factors in the former USSR than in Western Europe or other areas where the demographic transition began earlier.

Nonetheless, at least two major resistances to the fertility decline are evident. The first, of course, might be labeled *relative degree of ruralism*. The second has a strong ethnic dimension, for which the non-Western percentage of the population is important, with *Western* defined as including the three Baltic nationalities plus Russians, Ukrainians, Belarusians, Germans, Poles, Jews, Finns, and Karelians. The changes in the total population by administrative area (Table 13-3) between 1959 and 1994 can be explained to a considerable extent by ethnic variations in fertility, with the rates for Kazakh, Azerbaijani, and Central Asian nationalities still being roughly three times higher than the former Soviet national average, whereas the rates of the three major Slavic nationalities—Ukrainians, Belarusians, and Russians—are all less than the national average, and Russian, Estonian, and Latvian rates are especially low. Migration for reasons of employment and climatic amenity were second-order factors in regional population growth patterns over the previous couple of decades. However, since the breakup, inter-republic migration, which has often been ethnic or nationality based, has become a significant factor in regional population growth patterns, as noted previously.

Problems of Soviet and Post-Soviet Urbanization

The Soviets acknowledged urban problems associated with housing and urban amenities, excessive urban growth, and underdevelopment of rural settlements and small cities. The Soviet housing shortage was neither a new nor a particularly Soviet problem; urban crowding and poor-quality structures were associated with the labor influx of the tsarist period of industrialization from the 1860s until the Revolution. Because of the urban influx in the 1930s and the devastating housing losses of World War II, average living space per urban resident was about 65 sq ft (6 sq m) after the war, approximately 10 sq ft (1 sq m) less than during the late pre-Revolutionary period. By 1980 the average rose to 147 sq ft (13.6 sq m) and, as a result of the massive housing campaigns of the 1980s, the figure rose to 168 sq ft per capita (15.5 sq m) at the end of the decade. Regionally there were and are great differences. For example, citizens of the former Central Asian republics live in less than one-third the space per resident and in significantly

poorer quality housing than citizens in the Baltic republics. Overall, in spite of improvements, both in terms of per capita living space and its quality, all parts of the former Soviet Union still lag far behind Europe and the United States in living space per capita.

The former USSR has significantly different degrees of urban crowding, with the European part of the country being much better supplied with housing than the Asian part, especially Central Asia. The relatively low level of Soviet urban housing space is the combined result of small apartment sizes and a high number of occupants per apartment. Even at the time of the Soviet breakup, the housing shortage was reflected in average waiting periods for obtaining apartments of 1.5 to 3 years in the European parts of the country—up to 4 to 5 years in Siberia, and even longer in Central Asia. Because the highly subsidized rental charges for state-owned apartments were a nominal 5 percent of wages, nearly everyone could have afforded more housing. Hence, problems of establishing criteria for rationing presented themselves, including legal criteria for waiting lists and the payment of various kinds of bribes. In contrast to the urban areas, there was and is a surplus of rural housing, associated principally with rural outmigration and to a lesser extent with second homes or *dachas* owned or assigned to certain privileged elite of the society (the *nomenklatura*). Rural collective (*kolkhoz*) and state farm (*sovkhoz*) workers seem to prefer their private cottages adjacent to their private plots over the state-owned collective apartment buildings.

Paralleling space constraints is the low quality of Soviet urban housing, as compared with that of other industrialized countries. Besides its bland and unimaginative architecture, quality of construction is shoddy, and utilities and services are poor—with approximately 10 percent of the urban dwelling new units still without water and sewerage. Beginning with Gorbachev's reforms and accelerating since the breakup, at least in Russia and the Baltics, a great deal of both private and cooperative housing construction has been underway, especially of new detached houses around the urban periphery of most cities, as well as the major renovation activity of existing dwellings within major cities.

A second urban problem emanating from the Soviet period are problems associated with large cities. The Soviets long had a bias against large cities and tried to control their growth (see Fig. 13-14). Part of this old bias stemmed from the lingering vestiges of Russia's pervasive rural village past. Among the supposed disadvantages of large cities are the negative externalities of pollution, lower health and hygienic conditions, traffic congestion, long journeys to work, and strains on and rising per capita costs for public service facilities. Automobile congestion and exhaust pollution have now become additional major urban problems in major Russian and Baltic cities.

On the other hand, large cities have many advantages that could not be suppressed even during the Soviet era of irrational prices. Such advantages include agglomeration economies and the many more opportunities and amenities that large cities afford their populations. Thus, the real question should always have been not just the costs per urban resident, which admittedly increased with cities above 50,000 in the former Soviet Union, but rather the net productivity per capita after subtracting for the negative externalities (Fig. 13-14).

Part of the efforts to control urban growth were predicated on the ideological goal of equalizing rural and urban living conditions. Accordingly, many Soviet specialists perceived small cities as having distinct investment advantages over large cities. First, of course, they do not usually have the same scale of congestion, transportation, and pollution problems. More importantly, however, it was argued that small cities contain pools of underutilized labor. But in reality smaller cities have lower-skilled workers and poorly developed infrastructures. Hence, ratios of capital investment compared to total production (capital output ratios) in small cities were likely to have been significantly higher than in large cities. On the whole, the Soviet concern with excessive city size seems to have been economically unwarranted. Thus, because of the myriad difficulties associated with taking account of the various negative externalities, it can be assumed that emerging market forces will continue to result in ever more people individually "voting with their feet" and trying to move into, or close to, the already large Russian and NIS cities once disruptive effects of economic change subside.

Incredible disparities in the distribution of urban amenities and consumer products existed in the former Soviet Union, with urban areas being favored over rural areas and larger cities over smaller cities. Beginning with Gorbachev's reforms, decrees allowing for the creation of private restaurants and service-oriented businesses began to help improve the urban consumer's overall amenities and began reducing the marked dichotomies within the urban hierarchy and between the cities and the countryside. While prices are very high, today stores in even small Russian settlements are much better stocked with food and consumer items, many imported, than they ever were during the Soviet era.

FIGURE 13-14 Moscow apartment complex (C. ZumBrunnen)

National Ethnic Composition and Nagging Population Problems

Although a number of issues could be considered under the general topic of population problems and policy, we will restrict ourselves here to a brief discussion of three interrelated general issues—Russification and nationalism, labor supply, and social and demographic problems.

Over the years, the general multinational character of the former Soviet Union posed a number of problems for the Bolshevik leadership. Essentially, the regime simultaneously pursued two seemingly contradictory policies. On the one hand, it was ideologically committed to allowing the various national groups and ethnic minorities to maintain, practice, and develop their own native language, customs, ethnic transitions, and, to a lesser extent, religions. On the other hand, the Soviet leaders consistently promoted, though with varying zeal, a policy of Russification—the promotion of Russian language and culture across all regions and cultures within the USSR.

Such tangible physical manifestations of ethnic pluralism as native-language schools, massive multilanguage book and newspaper publication, performances of ethnic music and other art forms, native-language radio and television programs, and native dress were allowed and encouraged. Nonetheless, the Russian language, customs, institutions, and nationality were always *first among equals*. With few exceptions, a fluent command of Russian was a prerequisite for professional-occupational success and mobility. The degree of Russian cultural assimilation is indicated by the following statistics. There were only 145 million Russians according to the 1989 Census, yet an estimated 165 million Soviet citizens considered Russian their first language and an additional 69 million considered it their second language. Thus, of a total 1989 population of 286 million, Russian was either the first or second language for approximately 234 million Soviet citizens. In terms of language assimilation, Jews, Poles, and Germans seem to be the most Russified of the larger national minorities.

The most blatant and resented forms of Russification involved strong preferential treatment of Russians in employment and advancement or the actual moving of Russians into national minority areas, such as took place in the Baltic republics and in annexed western borderlands after World War II and in the Kazakh Republic somewhat later. Since the breakup of the Soviet Union, disputes over national language knowledge, use, or language requirements for citizenship have erupted in the Baltics and several other NIS locations. Essentially, all these disputes involve a "reverse Russification," with local Russian speakers now claiming it is they who are being unfairly discriminated against. There is more than a little irony in this turn of events. For example, there are about 7 million Ukrainians in the Russian Federation without a single Ukrainian-language elementary school, yet the 11 million Russians in Ukraine receive their educational instruction overwhelmingly in Russian.

To be sure, the negative aspects of ethnic consciousness in the former USSR did not lead to social separation, such as that of the Indian caste system, the former South African apartheid system, or the formerly institutionalized racial segregation of the United States. At the same time, ethnic *pecking orders* and feelings of nationalism were still pronounced among certain groups. Nationalism and anti-Russian feelings tended to be highest among the Baltic nationalities and some Transcaucasian groups, notably the Georgians. The Baltic peoples, Georgians, Armenians, and to a lesser extent Ukrainians, looked down on the Russians and at the same time resented what they considered to be Russian chauvinism. In turn, the Russians tended to feel superior to many of the Asian and Muslim minorities. Several religious sects—notably Jews, Catholics, Uniates, and Baptists—and such independent minorities as Gypsies were discriminated against and sometimes officially scorned and ridiculed.

One should not be left with the impression that all nationalist feelings were and are polarized between Russians on the one hand and other nationalities on the other. Under Gorbachev's *glasnost* policy, a number of other fairly serious ethnic rivalries and conflicts openly manifested themselves. For example, violent rioting was reported in various Central Asian cities in the late 1980s, some of which was reportedly related to corruption by party officials. Crimean Tatars openly demonstrated in Moscow for the right to return to their ancestral homelands. The unrest between Armenia and Azerbaijan, beginning in the winter of 1988, involved Armenian demands that the predominantly Armenian Nagorno-Karabakh Autonomous Oblast (see Fig. 13-10, Autonomous Oblast no. 11) become a noncontiguous part of the Armenian Republic. These demands escalated into what has become a protracted, debilitating inter-republic war. Another bloody clash based on ethnic nationalism occurred in April 1989 in Tbilisi, the capital of the Georgian Republic, between Soviet army troops and demonstrators. This confrontation, in which at least 19 people were officially reported as killed, was precipitated by the nationalistic demands for fully independent republic-level status (and hence, political succession and independence from the Georgian Republic) by ethnic Abkhazians of the Abkhaz ASSR along the Black Sea coast of the Georgian Republic (see Fig. 13-10). The confrontation ultimately developed into a civil war between Abkhazians and Georgians involving Russian army troops. The desire of the Ossetian people, divided by the Caucasus Mountains into South Ossetia within Georgia and North Ossetia with the Russian Federation, to be politically united led to another civil war within Georgia. In hindsight, it appears that these and other sorts of heated political and nationality conflicts, including bloody events in the Lithuanian capital of Vilnius involving Russian troops, posed fatal problems of governance for Gorbachev, leading to the initial breakaway of the Baltic republics and then the failed *coup d'état* in August 1991.

The long-espoused goal and claim of the Soviet leadership had been the elimination rather than the fostering of national and ethnic friction, notwithstanding the regime's official promotion of *scientific atheism* and, beginning with Stalin, the deliberate manipulation of such friction to maintain and consolidate Soviet power. Nonetheless, the persistence of smoldering and recently violent flames of nationalist feelings and ethnic antagonisms attest to the regime's failure ever to create the *ideal Soviet* man and woman. Unfortunately, these problems have taken an even bloodier trajectory in the post-Soviet era, especially in Chechnya and Dagestan in the North Caucasus, and in all three states of Transcaucasia, in Tadjikistan, and in the Trans-Dniester region of Moldova. The potential implications of Yeltsin's and the Russian Army's bungled and indiscriminately bloody attempts to crush independence-seeking Chechnya are ominous indeed. Even in the nineteenth century it took decades and 400,000 tsarist troops to subdue the region.

Another thorny, ethnically based Soviet population issue was the changing ethnic composition of the country. As previously discussed, the Kazakh and Central Asian nationalities have much higher rates of natural increase than the three principal Slavic groups—the Russians, Ukrainians, and Belarusians. During the intercensal period 1959 to 1970, all three Slavic groups grew less rapidly than the national average. Although Russians still constituted a distinct majority (about 51.3% in the 1989 Census), their numerical superiority declined slightly from 1959 (54.3%). The three Slavic groups' combined share of the total Soviet population declined from 76.3 percent in 1959 to 72.0 percent in 1979 to 69.8 percent in 1989. Because of their high rates of natural increase, the titular ethnic groups in the Central Asian republics, Kazakhstan, and Transcaucasia all increased as a fraction of the population in each republic. Had the Soviet Union not split apart, the ethnic Russian population share was projected to decline to 48.2 percent by 2000. These divergent trends in ethnic and nationality population growth patterns underlie, to a significant degree, some of the major centrifugal forces that led to the dismemberment of the Soviet Empire. For example, the increased Asian component ("yellowing") of military forces was an increasing Soviet concern, especially following the Soviet military intervention into Afghanistan. The Soviet press openly admitted the existence of interethnic conflicts and fights among Soviet recruits. With Russian or at least Slavic officers leading increasingly Asian troops, troop loyalty in the long run became a real concern to the Kremlin.

Ethnic and age-structure issues were also important aspects of a second important Soviet population problem—assuring a labor supply. Even without all of the rather abrupt changes in fertility, life expectancy, and migration flows associated with the social and economic turmoil of the breakup, the former Soviet Union was facing only a modest growth of the working-age population through the 1990s. Aggregate Soviet labor force shortages began in the 1960s. In fact, the total size of the labor force in 1970 fell some 1.7 million below the official projection of Soviet planners. In response to this serious long-term problem, in 1967 the regime began to create administrative organizations to discover and mobilize unused and underutilized reserves of labor.

Quite aside from aggregate labor shortages, the regional-ethnic differences in population growth presented a number of labor force distribution problems. The new locational cost consciousness of the Gorbachev regime called for priority investment of scarce capital in the older European core of the country, while the existing reserve labor pools were (and will be) situated in its economically and culturally remote southern regions. The prospect of transferring substantial numbers of Central Asian populations to the labor-deficit regions appeared dim. Even under the forced labor policies of Stalin, the Central Asian groups proved quite resistant to such relocations. The notorious Siberian labor turnover problems, in which policymakers also quickly faced diminishing returns to wage inducements and fringe benefits reinforced the planners' dilemma over the location of investment. In Siberia, higher wages had even helped accelerate the rate of labor turnover. In other words, the higher the wages the Siberian workers received, the sooner they could *retire* to their private *dachas* on the Black Sea.

The multifarious ethnic and labor force problems of the former Soviet Union made the articulation of an official population policy very difficult. On the one hand, Soviet planners might have wanted to pursue a regionally differentiated population policy that in essence would have been a pronatalist policy in the European USSR and Siberia, and an antinatalist one in the Transcaucasus and Central Asia. Adoption of such a racially ominous approach, however, could easily have precipitated profound negative political consequences for the Slavic majority, both internally and externally. The Soviet Union's world image would have been tarnished severely, especially in the eyes of Third World countries.

Regulations on abortion, contraception, and family payments and allowances suggest that the Soviet Union had neither a strong nor a consistent official population policy (refer to Table 13-5). For example, abortion was legalized in 1920 under Lenin's direction. Subsequently, the number of abortions grew rapidly, exceeding births by 271 percent in 1934. After 1936, the government limited legal abortions to cases in which either the mother's health was in danger or the fetus was possibly suffering from a hereditary defect. The declining birth rate and the possible need for military and industrial personnel were probably the chief considerations behind the more restrictive policy. Ostensibly to eliminate the serious health problems created by the performance of illegal abortions, the prohibition on abortion was repealed in 1955. At present, the Russian abortion policy as expressed through its health officials is to discourage abortion in principle, but to accept it as a lesser evil than illegal abortion. Although the pill, IUDs, and other devices are available, condoms appear to be the only contraceptive method widely used. As Table 13-5 suggests, contraception is not widely practiced. Abortion rates are correlated with nationality and religion, with the rates being highest among Estonian, Latvian, and Slavic nationality groups (in terms of both total abortions per woman and abortions per 100 live births. The rates were lowest among Transcausasians and Central Asians, with the abortion rates in Westernized and Catholic Lithuania being intermediate. The high percentage of Russians in Kazakhstan and Kyrgyzstan strongly affects the rates for those republics.

Divorce, suicide, and children born outside of marriage also are strongly correlated with nationality and religion. The highest rates are in the Baltics (excepting Catholic Lithuania for the case of children born outside of marriage), intermediate but still high rates in Slavic regions, and the lowest rates among the Muslim populations of Central Asia. All regions have experienced dramatic increases in the percentage of children born outside of marriage except the Muslim countries of the Caucasus and Central Asia, which have low percentages of Russians and high percentages of titular nationalities.

As mentioned previously, alcoholism and its attendant antisocial ramifications, such as crimes against individuals and property, have now become a full-blown national tragedy within Russia and most of the other former republics, even including most of the Muslim NIS. Although the roots of the alcohol problem clearly predated the Bolshevik Revolution, the day-to-day drabness of Soviet life exacerbated rather than diminished this social problem which, to be fair, seems to varying degrees to afflict all industrial societies. High rates of worker absenteeism, alcohol-related health problems, industrial accidents, shoddy workmanship, and poor worker morale may all be linked to heavy alcohol consumption by all segments of

TABLE 13-5

ETHNICITY AND SELECTED SOCIAL CHARACTERISTICS OF RUSSIA AND THE NIS

Region/ Country	Ethnicity		Divorce As pct. of Marriages 1990–1993	Pct. Women Using Contraception 1990	Abortions		Suicides per 100,000 1990	Pct. Births Outside Marriage	
	Percent Titular Nationality	Percent Russian			Total per Women 1989	per 100 Birth 1990–1993		1980	1990–1993
Slavic & Moldova									
Belarus	77.9	13.2	50	13	3.1	78	20	6	9
Moldova	64.5	13.0	37	15	2.4	65	15	7	11
Russia	81.5	81.5	68	22	3.5	216	26	11	17
Ukraine	72.7	22.1	57	15	2.7	156	21	9	12
Baltic									
Estonia	63.2	29.4	74	26	2.2	169	27	18	38
Latvia	54.2	33.1	71	19	2.2	117	26	13	23
Lithuania	81.1	8.5	59	12	1.7	90	26	5	9
Caucasus									
Armenia	93.3	1.6	14	12	0.8	40	3	—	12
Azerbaijan	82.7	5.6	14	7	0.6	18	2	0	4
Georgia	70.1	6.3	20	8	1.5	45	4	5	19
Central Asia									
Kazakhstan	39.7	37.8	30	22	2.5	98	19	10	13
Kyrgyzstan	52.4	21.5	20	25	2.4	61	12	11	12
Tajikistan	62.3	7.6	10	15	1.2	26	5	7	8
Turkmenistan	72.0	9.5	13	12	1.2	28	8	3	4
Uzbekistan	71.4	8.3	14	19	1.2	31	7	4	4

Source: Adapted from Table A-6 & Table A-7 in Carl Haub, "Population Change in the Former Soviet Republics," *Population Bulletin* 49, No. 4 (December 1994): 50.

Soviet and post-Soviet society. Ironically, the Soviets long used high turnover taxes on alcohol to fill government coffers and at the same time to "mop up" surplus consumer income created by chronic shortages of consumer goods.

The series of anti-alcoholism resolutions enacted in 1985 presumably signaled recognition of the seriousness of Soviet alcoholism. These measures limited the production, distribution, and consumption of alcohol and imposed penalties on public drunkenness. Prohibition on private production of *samogon* (home distilling) was also in effect. The short-term positive results of the anti-alcohol campaign were impressive. Rates for crime and various types of accidents were reportedly down 20 to 25 percent. Industrial absenteeism rates had declined 33 percent, with absenteeism rates among construction workers down 40 percent. Though most impressive, similar to the American experience with prohibition, lots of unanticipated social, economic, and political obstacles sabotaged Gorbachev's good intentions and the campaign was relaxed. In the post-Soviet era it appears that the import of foreign alcoholic beverages, combined with the expansion of alcoholic beverage production by newly privatized firms, has resulted in the alcoholism problems becoming significantly worse than at any time in the Soviet era.

Finally, violent crime and theft have mushroomed in post-Soviet Russia. Mafia contract murders and armed robbery and break-ins are now commonplace in Russian cities. For the first time in decades, large numbers of Russian citizens are fearful to walk the streets alone, take taxi rides, and use subways in major cities late at night. These fears helped to generate votes for politicians calling for "a return to order" in Russia's December 1995 parliamentary and 1996 presidential elections.

INTRODUCTION TO GEOGRAPHIC ECONOMIC HIGHLIGHTS

Geographic manifestations of Soviet development policies and their economic development model, as well as current economic trends and patterns remain to be explored. In this section we present selected highlights of Soviet and post-Soviet achievements and problems in four areas: (1) transportation, (2) agriculture, (3) energy resources, and (4) key industries. Subsequent major sections touch on international relations and foreign trade.

Transportation and Infrastructural Problems

Transport is intimately intertwined with the efficient operation of any modern, urban, industrial state. The topography and climate of the territory of the former Soviet Union favored railroad transit as opposed to river, coastal, or highway movement. The immense size of the country predetermined that the laudatory, long-espoused Soviet goal of uniform spatial development would be preposterously expensive.

As Figure 13-12 illustrates, the Bolsheviks inherited an extensive, but European-focused, rail network. This network was doubled during the Soviet era in the pursuit of two objectives. The most overriding objective was to lay new rail lines in order to gain access to raw materials and potential industrial sites in the underdeveloped regions of the country. Examples of this Soviet *rails to resources* policy include the Turkestan-Siberian Railroad, the Magnitogorsk to Ust'-Kut lines, and the construction by forced labor of the Pechora line to the Vorkuta coal basin. Even the more recent, and increasingly economically nonviable, Baykal-Amur-Mainline (BAM) from Ust-Kut to Komsomol'sk on the Amur and the West Siberian line from Surgut to Yamburg can be characterized to a considerable degree as outgrowths of this policy.

The second objective was to eliminate bottlenecks and increase the capacity of intensively used lines by double-tracking and electrifying the lines. The rail network and rolling stock were used intensively as a capital savings measure. Despite economic stagnation in the 1980s, Soviet freight traffic density (ton-miles per mile of roadbed) was approximately six times that of the United States and significantly higher than that of Western Europe as well. As a means of stretching capital, the Soviets utilized steam locomotives much longer than did North America or the rest of Europe.

In the early 1990s, railroads in the Russian Federation accounted for a dominant but declining 43 percent of all freight ton-miles and 34 percent of passenger miles, essentially the same as for buses (33 percent). Prior to the disruptions in transport associated with the economic upheavals of the breakup, all modes of transport had been expanding, but the fastest growing modes in terms of tonnage annually had been oil and natural gas pipelines, especially within the Russian Federation. In the early 1990s, gas and oil pipelines combined accounted for nearly one-half of total estimated Russian freight movement. At the same time, there are tremendous problems with pipeline breaks and leaks from poor-quality pipes, poor engineering, shoddy construction, and inadequately inspected welds.

Despite a rapid increase in the Soviet mileage of hard-surfaced roads over the past few decades, still less than half of the surface road network has asphalt or concrete paving. Most of the road improvements have taken place in the European part of Russia and the NIS on intercity links, whereas the conditions of most of the rural road network have continued to fluctuate with the weather between mud and dust. Since the breakup of the USSR, intercity truck travel in the European core has increased dramatically, much of it hauling imported food and consumer goods from port cities or overland across Northern Europe. The number of cars on the streets of the larger cities has increased dramatically, much of the increase being the result of the import of new and used foreign automobiles. Whereas in the Soviet period rush-hour took place on the sidewalks and enormously overcrowded city buses, tramways, trolley buses, and subway trains, now the streets are congested with automobiles as well.

The Soviet Union had a dense airline network linking remote places in Siberia, in the north, and in the Far East, but *heavily* focused on one major hub—Moscow. In terms of ton-miles, freight traffic was trivial, but in terms of passenger miles it accounted for nearly 20 percent of all traffic. Until the breakup, the Soviet Union also had the world's largest airline fleet by far in the form of the state-owned Aeroflot. After the breakup, Aeroflot's planes were initially divided up among the 15 republics into new national airlines. More recently,

privatization processes have led to the formation of many private airline companies and the cannibalization of planes, because shortages of spare parts have led to a reduction of the overall fleet size. Also, fuel shortages have resulted in chaotic flight schedules and poor maintenance; and safety problems have resulted in a record number of (now reported) air crashes. Aeroflot continues to fly and has purchased some Boeing and Airbus planes to operate on some of their international routes that earn hard currency. Communication technology, safety standards, and airport infrastructures are in dire need of modernizing and improvement.

Agriculture

A number of questions may be asked about the contribution of the agricultural sector to Soviet and post-Soviet economic development and about the geographic and human impacts of Soviet and post-Soviet agricultural strategies. Agriculture may contribute to economic development by creating capital in the form of food and raw materials; by producing exports to increase foreign exchange; by supplying a significant fraction of an expanding industrial labor demand; by meeting the increasing demand for food that is normally concomitant with economic development, failing which further development may be impeded; and by generating demand for industrial and consumer goods as agricultural incomes rise. The USSR called upon agriculture only to satisfy the first three functions. Governmental controls kept food demands from rising concurrently with economic growth. Because the Five-Year Plan determined the size and composition of demand through its wage and price controls, and agricultural wages were held artificially low for a long time, rural incomes were a relatively unimportant source of demand.

Collectivization and Agricultural Organization To fulfill the three roles assigned by Stalin and his planners, agriculture had to create a growing marketed surplus and release redundant labor, through a structural reorganization and through increases in labor productivity. The collectivization campaign was designed to provide these two solutions. However, the initial impact of collectivization was disastrous in terms of human, livestock, and capital losses. Although the campaign was ordained to be voluntary and slow, Stalin began a forced consolidation of individual landholdings, equipment, and farm animals. At the end of 1929, on the eve of the campaign, only 1.7 percent of the farms were collective types, and two months later, on March 1, 1930, fully 55 percent of households were in collective farms. Taking Stalin at his word—in his "dizzy with success" speech, in which he blamed local functionaries for extremism and reiterated that collectivization should be voluntary—the peasants responded by rapidly dissolving collectives until only 23.6 percent of households remained collectivized. Swiftly, Stalin again resorted to forced collectivization and with harsh treatment for peasants who resisted, especially the richer *kulaks*. For example, by July 1, 1930, over 1.5 million peasants had been exiled to Siberia. The new wave of collectivization was permanent, with 90–95 percent of the peasant households in collectives by 1937. Between 1931 and 1933, the loss of human life attributed to the excesses of the collectivization process and the attendant famines has been estimated at over 8 million people. Many peasants slaughtered their livestock rather than surrender them to the collectives. The livestock losses of this tempestuous period of Soviet history, combined with those resulting from World War II, were not made up until the late 1950s.

Despite heavy social and capital deprivations, collectivization produced a profound structural reorganization of agriculture. The consolidation of small land parcels into large collective farm fields facilitated mechanization, and hence improved labor productivity. The state monopoly of trade allowed the regime to extract forced savings from agriculture by (1) keeping agricultural procurement prices low relative to those of manufactured goods, (2) reselling agricultural commodities to the urban population at relatively high prices, and (3) retaining the resulting profit as a source of investment. With the effective demand for consumer goods throttled by low wages, Soviet planners were able to concentrate most investment in capital goods industries, which increased the growth rate of the strategic sectors of the economy.

The collective farm system also enabled the marketed share of output to be determined relatively independently of the size of the total agricultural output. For example, socialized agriculture delivered 25 million tons of grain to the state in 1937, and in 1939, 24 million tons, despite a total crop reduction of 20 million tons, with the peasants absorbing the loss. At the same time, acreages of such industrial crops as cotton and sugar beets were rapidly expanded in order to replace imports and hence free foreign exchange for capital goods imports.

The collective farm system provided surplus labor in two ways. First, the seasonally unemployed were mobilized for other work. More importantly, surplus agricultural labor was released for permanent relocation in urban areas. Agricultural mechanization provided the *push*, and higher urban wages and amenities provided the *pull* for this massive labor migration stream.

There were three major organizational forms of Soviet agriculture: (1) collective farms (*kolkhozy*), (2) state farms (*sovkhozy*), and (3) private holdings. The *kolkhoz* was (and is) a cooperative enterprise whose members shared profits among themselves in accord with their labor contribution to the collective. Besides the normal agricultural pursuits of crop and livestock raising, many kolkhozy engaged in such subsidiary activities as the manufacture of building materials and food processing. Wages were based on the arduousness and required skills of the work as well as actually recorded individual labor-time effort. Also, state bonuses were paid for production exceeding the individual kolkhoz plan.

Initially the most common organizational forms of socialized agriculture, kolkhozy were created in the older, better, and more densely settled agricultural regions. At the close of collectivization in the late 1930s, there were nearly 250,000 small kolkhozy averaging fewer than 100 families each. Until 1958 central planners and party officials kept a tight rein on kolkhoz operations through the use of the Machine Tractor Stations (MTSs) that supplied, maintained. and operated much of the equipment used in mechanized fieldwork. Just prior to the breakup of the Soviet Union, the individual kolkhoz averaged 480 persons but ranged up to several thousands. Between 1958 and 1972, the policy of kolkhoz consolidation, as well as a policy of converting kolkhozy to sovkhozy, reduced the number of kolkhozy from 67,700 to 32,300. By 1986 the number of kolkhozy had fallen to 26,300, averaging nearly 16,000 acres (6456 ha) each, of which over one-half was actually planted. After passage of the Law on Cooperatives in 1988, the number of cooperatives again grew to 29,000 by 1990. In the Russian Federation the total number of collective farm workers decreased monotonically during the 1980s from 4.8 million in 1980 to 3.9 million in 1991. A dramatic decline down to 2.2 million Russian collective workers in 1992 is highly misleading, for it primarily reflects how kolkhozy are registered and membership is reported.

Implicit in the post-1958 emphasis on sovkhozy at the expense of kolkhozy was that the regime considered the sovkhozy to be ideologically purer. Accordingly, all sovkhoz means of production was state property, and sovkhozy workers were salaried state employees. Wages were at piece rates, differentiated according to difficulty and importance. Similarly to the *kolkhozniki*, sovkhoz workers received annual bonuses for production exceeding the farm's plan or goal. Initially created from nationalized landlords' estates, sovkhozy were few in number and were intended to demonstrate to kolkhozy and private farmers the advantages of capital-intensive, scientific agriculture. In 1990 there were 23,500 sovkhozy, of which 13,000 were in the Russian Federation. Between 1980 and 1991 the number of *sovkhozniki* in the Russian Federation declined from 6.1 million to 4.5 million.

Although sovkhozy generally have cultivated their land less intensively, they have tended to be larger and better equipped than kolkhozy—in the late 1980s the average sovkhoz employed 390 workers on about 39,300 acres (15,900 ha) of land, with on average 30 percent sown in crops. Sovkhozy have predominated over kolkhozy in the European northwest, the Urals, Kazakhstan, and Siberia. Many of the massive state farms in the last three regions (averaging about 49,500 acres in grain [20,000 ha]) were created as part of Khrushchev's Virgin and Idle Lands Program of the 1950s. In other regions of the USSR, the state farms have tended to be smaller. Sovkhozy have also tended to be more specialized than kolkhozy —for example, approximately 40 percent of all sovkhozy have specialized in dairy farming, or

dairy farming combined with beef raising. Also, sovkhozy located in the urban periphery concentrate on truck gardens, milk, egg, and poultry production for distribution to neighboring cities.

Besides the kolkhozy and sovkhozy, private plots have always been an important part of Soviet and Russian agriculture. Seventy years after the famous industrialization debates, the post-Soviet leadership is still plagued with the problem of transferring state production into private hands. As suggested previously, ever since the War Communism era, peasant allegiance has been a nagging problem for the regime. Repeated coercive attempts to enlist peasant cooperation to increase production were met with passive or active resistance. Hence, after collectivization Stalin reluctantly, but pragmatically, yielded to a *carrot* approach —the private plots. It was pragmatic in the sense of providing a steady flow of human foodstuffs, appeasing the peasants politically, and alleviating somewhat, but by no means solving, the problem of worker motivation on collective and state farms. In fact, the side-by-side coexistence of private and socialized agriculture was contradictory, as we will see shortly.

The small (not over 1 acre [0.4 ha]) private plots (Fig. 13-15) of kolkhoz and sovkhoz farmers constituted the bulk of the private holdings. In addition, many urban workers have long tilled small patches of land assigned to their factories or offices. Kitchen gardens are also ubiquitously

FIGURE 13-15 Shelekov, East Siberia, small *dachas* and private plots or kitchen gardens in foreground; air pollution plumes from Shelekov aluminum refinery in background. (C. ZumBrunnen)

interspersed among urban apartment buildings. Then, too, for decades large tracts of land composed of tiny gardens, each with a diminutive tool shed-*dacha* (summer cottage), have constituted a common landscape feature of the urban environs of all Soviet cities of all sizes. Food production from these "kitchen gardens" became even more important in the early post-Soviet period.

Prior to the fragmentation of the Soviet Union, private holdings produced about 30 percent of the total value of Soviet agricultural output, while directly utilizing only 2 to 3 percent of the sown acreage. Private agriculture's share of high-value, labor-intensive crops was even higher, especially for vegetables, potatoes, fruit, meat, and even milk and eggs.

While they are very important, it would be very misleading to attribute this apparent high level of private plot productivity to the wonders of private initiative and profit motivations alone. The other important factors include the nature of commodities produced on the private plots, subsidies, and a contradictory incentive system. Tillers of their private plots have rationally chosen to use their scarce land resources to grow or raise the most valuable crops, such as those that are commonly foods for direct human consumption. Second, there has always been a high level of hidden state farm or collective farm subsidization in these products through legal and quasilegal payments-in-kind and peasant purchases from state and collective granaries, as well as pervasive pilfering of state and collective resources that directly and indirectly have long been channeled to and through these private plots.

Even at the end of the Soviet era, private plots accounted for only a fraction of 1 to 2 percent of Soviet forage crop acreage, an amount totally inadequate to feed private sector livestock. Accordingly, the output of up to 20 percent of the total arable land—hay land, pasture, and sown land—is used to support, or rather subsidize, the livestock production of the private sector. During the 1950s and 1960s as much as 90 percent of kolkhoznik wages consisted of payments-in-kind—50 percent in fodder. In more recent times, kolkhoz and sovkhoz workers were also purchasing feed from the collective and state farms. As already noted, since the early 1930s peasants have also been pilfering vast

quantities of state and collective resources, a process that became ever more open and flagrant after the country's breakup.

Why such a subsidization pattern evolved can basically be explained in terms of the incentive structure of Soviet agriculture. Since the output from private plots could be used personally or sold in the various collective farm markets at free market prices, the tillers of the private plots and tenders of private livestock captured the entire benefit stream of their *private* work efforts, whereas they were forced to share the benefits of their *social* work efforts on both collective and state farms. In other words, the marginal rate of return to private effort vastly exceeded that to the social-collective effort. Besides being an ideological contradiction—one that has persisted with vacillating tolerance for over 65 years and into the post-Soviet era—the dual, but unequal, reward structure undercut socialized agriculture and explained many of the shortcomings of Soviet agriculture. Hence, it should be no surprise that worker motivation had long been a serious chronic problem of both forms of Soviet agriculture.

The Geography of Agricultural Production The agricultural zone of the NIS corresponds to that of the wheat-growing areas (Figs. 13-16 and 13-17). The physical constraints of soil and climate discussed in the beginning of this chapter confine most crop production to the so-called *Fertile Triangle*, which has its apexes at Odesa in Ukraine, St. Petersburg in the northeast and Irkutsk in East Siberia, as well as outlying regions in the Far East. Areas of barley, oats, rye, and corn production essentially mirror the spring wheat acreage indicated in Figure 13-17. Cereal grains are still the predominant crops, with wheat of first importance. Corn is much less important in the NIS than in the United States. Because of the shorter growing season, ear corn ripens only in Moldova and parts of Ukraine, and elsewhere it is harvested green for silage. The Soviet Union produced over one-half of the world's sunflower crop and about one-third of the world's sugar beets. Both were grown in a broad latitudinal band corresponding roughly to the black earth, steppe, and wooded steppe natural regions.

The Soviet Union led the world in cotton production, producing 15 percent more than the Unit-

FIGURE 13-16 Wheat fields north of Belgorod in the chernozem soil region of southern European Russia. (C. ZumBrunnen)

pre-Revolutionary "colonial times" has been concentrated in a number of cities in the Central European region northeast of Moscow. This supply problem developed early in the post-Soviet era when cotton still being sent to Russia from Central Asia was sold by Russia for hard currency. This angered the Central Asian producing countries. Since then, they have sought successfully to market their cotton on the world market themselves, leaving the Russian textile industry in dire condition. Another major Soviet fiber crop, flax, is grown principally in the temperature zone of Northwestern European NIS.

Potatoes, the Soviets' second staple besides bread, are grown nearly everywhere, but the Baltic republics plant the greatest acreage and produce the highest yields. Vegetable production has long lagged behind that of the United States, reaching at most only one-third of U.S. levels even in the Soviet era, and consisting of a much less varied type of product. The as yet negligible soybean cultivation has been confined to the Far East in Amur Oblast. Fruit production is concentrated around the Black Sea. Hardy products, such as pears and apples, extend into the temperate northern areas,

ed States. But since it was concentrated on the irrigated lands of Central Asia and Azerbaijan, especially in Uzbekistan, European NIS cotton production is now zero. Recently, the Central Asian republics have been selling their cotton on hard currency markets and elsewhere in the world. This has created major raw material supply problems for Russia's textile industry, which since

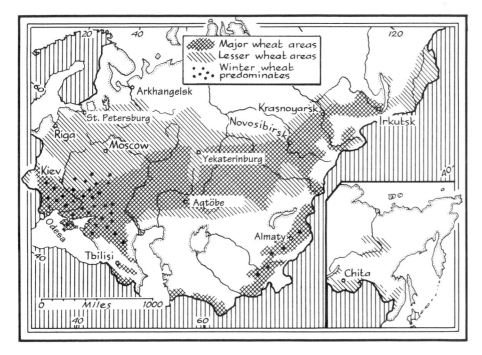

FIGURE 13-17
Agricultural zones.

where plantings commonly serve as windbreaks, whereas plums, apricots, and both wine and table grapes are restricted to the warmer southern areas. Tea is still grown along the Black Sea coasts in Krasnodar Kray of the Russian Federation, but the best tea plantations were located to the south in newly independent Georgia.

Although undertaken nearly everywhere except in the tayga and tundra zones, cattle and swine production is still highest in Ukraine and European Russia. Since the breakup, production of both has declined significantly. Although sheep raising and goat herding were practiced chiefly in the mountainous regions of Crimea, Transcaucasia, and Central Asia during the Soviet era, the production of both sheep and goats has declined in the European NIS even more sharply than that of cattle and swine. Beginning with the Khrushchev era, there was a quantum increase in Soviet land allocated to forage crops, which supported the sizable increase in kolkhoz and sovkhoz output of livestock products after the early 1950s. However, the economic hardships of the transition period resulted in higher than normal rural direct consumption of meat products, which has cut down the size of the herds.

Soviet Agricultural Performance The Soviet agricultural sector was immense. It employed nearly 23 percent of the labor force and received approximately one-third of all capital investment (including housing and services). Long neglected, agriculture did not begin to receive substantial investment, except for the Virgin and Idle Lands program, until the mid-1960s. For comparison, agriculture in the United States employs less than 3 percent of the workforce and claims less than 5 percent of investment. The USSR had about one-third again as much land under cultivation as the United States, but on a per acre basis it produced on average only about 56 percent of the value of that of American farmland. Not surprisingly then, Soviet state agricultural subsidies still accounted for 15 percent of the state budget in 1991.

Throughout the vast majority of the Soviet period, the large overall increase in Soviet agricultural output came primarily through expansion of the sown acreage. For instance, after 1950 the USSR increased its total sown acreage by 106 million acres (43 million ha), an area equivalent in size to the state of California. Not surprisingly, this expansion meant an ever-continuing push to use marginal farmland. The Virgin and Idle Lands scheme proposed under Khrushchev is an example. In an attempt to improve the animal protein content in the average Soviet diet, Khrushchev decided to shift a significant portion of Soviet wheat production into western Siberia and northern Kazakhstan, thus freeing the better European *chernozem* (black earth) lands for corn and other livestock forage crops. Between 1953 and 1958, over 71 million acres (29 million ha) of previously untilled lands were plowed up and sown to spring wheat—equivalent to about one-fifth of the total U.S. land currently under cultivation. Much of this land is marginal, being susceptible to drought and wind erosion. Luckily for the Soviets, droughts tend not to occur simultaneously in the European and Asian wheat-growing zones, but the scheme has been less than a stunning success.

Overall grain production reached 205 million tons annually during the 1976–1980 Plan period and fluctuated thereafter. For comparison purposes, the 1940 figure for Soviet grain production was 105 million tons. From 1980 through 1992, grain imports averaged 40 million tons per year, ranging from a low of 30 million tons between June 1986 and July 1987 to a high of 61 million tons between June 1991 and July 1992. Throughout the period 1980–1992, approximately 20 percent of the total produced and imported grain was used for direct human food consumption, whereas around 55 percent was used for animal fodder, 10 to 12 percent was saved for seed, and on average 15 percent or more was lost after harvest.

From the time of Leonid Brezhnev's rule (1964–1982), the Soviet Union demonstrated an increasing willingness to rely on agricultural imports, which implicitly admitted the seeming intractability of Soviet agricultural production problems, while recognizing the realities of comparative advantage in economic production and the mutual benefits of trade. Furthermore, such purchases dipped into increasingly scarce Soviet reserves of foreign currency. The Soviet leadership needed to, but fundamentally failed to solve a number of nagging agricultural production problems in order to be able to use this hard currency to modernize the country's industrial plant.

In summary, the Soviet agricultural performance was reasonably adequate, but far from remarkable, especially as compared to Soviet industrial growth. Soviet planning and organizational problems, in addition to the heavy losses resulting from collectivization and World War II, go far to explain the relatively poor performance of agriculture vis-à-vis industry. However, aforementioned environmental constraints and vicissitudes of weather phenomena also proved serious impediments to Soviet agricultural progress. Nonetheless, substantial increases in overall production of vegetables, fruits, meat, eggs, and dairy products did benefit the Soviet consumer. Although the average Soviet caloric diet still contained over twice as much grain and potatoes as the U.S. diet, a significant decline in the consumption of these starchy foodstuffs was achieved after 1950. Unfortunately for the average Soviet citizen's heart, the increases in sugar, fats, and oil exceeded those in meat, dairy products, vegetables, fruits, and eggs.

Agricultural Reform in the Gorbachev and Yeltsin Eras

Gorbachev had a long-standing interest in agriculture. Beginning in 1978, he was the supervisor of the Central Committee's national policy for agriculture and a key player in Brezhnev's 1982 Food Program. Gorbachev's agricultural policies and reforms responded to many nagging problems in the agricultural sector. The myth of unlimited agricultural resources, Soviet faith in the human efficacy to transform nature, various central planning mistakes, the irrational Soviet price structure, and weak worker incentives coalesced to produce some economically and environmentally inefficient agricultural land use patterns. Long-standing problems plagued Soviet, and still plague post-Soviet agriculture, including: (1) stemming the exodus of young rural workers, (2) increasing capital investment, (3) satisfying rural consumer pressures for improved living conditions, (4) improving labor productivity (at best only about one-sixth that of the United States), (5) improving farm worker incentives, (6) reducing chronic organiza-

tional and planning inefficiencies, (7) intensifying land use through the diffusion of new and better technology, (8) reducing waste and spoilage, (9) improving the transportation infrastructure, (10) increasing on-farm crop storage facilities, and (11) improving the performance of industries that are linked to agriculture.

Given these problems and Gorbachev's background in agriculture, it is not surprising that he assigned a high priority to the task of improving agricultural efficiency in order to be able to cut back on government spending on this highly subsidized sector. Essentially, his approach was threefold: (1) shifting around rather than increasing investment, (2) streamlining and improving the bureaucracy to better synchronize production in the food chain, and (3) strengthening economic market incentives to improve efficiency.

Reasoning that methods to reduce on-farm waste would be far more cost effective in improving agricultural efficiency than additional direct investments, the first approach involved shifting some investment away from agriculture and directly toward secondary industries linked to farming. Nonetheless, investments in the transport infrastructure, such as better roads, more trucks, and more and better crop storage facilities would have been needed and still are needed to reduce the recognized large-scale losses and spoilage of harvested crops. A major step in the direction of his second approach occurred in 1985 with the creation of the USSR State Agroindustrial Committee (*Gosagroprom*). The staffs and functions of five ministries and one state committee were amalgamated to form this superministry, yielding a 47 percent reduction in administrative staff. The objectives of Gosagroprom were: (1) to eliminate bureaucratic vested interests that chronically kept the agriculture "input-production-processing food chain" out of sync, and (2) to shift decision making closer to the local level. The report card on Gosagroprom, however, was very mixed. The third part of Gorbachev's agricultural reform was the most problematic. A March 1986 decree gave farms the freedom to dispose of above-plan production at market-influenced prices, to sell perishable produce locally at market prices, and to exchange food between localities.

Gorbachev did not remain in power long enough to see these reforms bear significant fruit. Unproductive farms and heavy agriculture subsidies continued into the post-Soviet era.

Although Gorbachev's chief concern was the revitalization of agriculture's socialist sectors, at the same time, he was arguably one of the staunchest supporters of the private sector. In effect, Gorbachev tried but did not succeed in achieving a closer economic and social integration between socialized and private farming. In fairness to him, one could persuasively state that the internal contradictions between the two were perhaps too great and the resistance to fundamental change too unwieldy.

Agricultural reform during the Yeltsin, post-Soviet era thus far has comprised the formation of private peasant farms, and the reorganization of kolkhozy and sovkhozy. As mentioned earlier, private peasant farms began in a limited way under Gorbachev's series of laws and reforms. However, the first significant impetus for private peasant farms began in December 1990 and was furthered by a Yeltsin decree in November 1993.

Land for private peasant farms has come from two sources: (1) the share that a given peasant was entitled to, based on membership in a state or collective farm and (2) a Special Land Fund established by each rayon or city council. There have been many obstacles to such farms. Even if they were allocated land from a state or collective farm, the land parcels that individual peasants received were often undesirable, with poorer soils, difficult access, or poor location in sites remote from the peasant's base of operation. In addition, the land parcels have commonly been small, noncontiguous fields, and hence, uneconomic to farm. Access to credit, equipment, seeds, fertilizer, transportation, and markets—often controlled by local or regional mafias—have provided other strong impediments to private farming. Despite these major obstacles and a modest beginning of 4433 farms in January 1991, the number increased rapidly to 284,000 by November 1995. At the same time, failure rates have been high, increasing from 4 per 100 new farms in 1992 to 14 in 1993, and up to 36 in the first quarter of 1994.

The second route of reform, kolkhoz and sovkhoz reorganization, dates from Yeltsin's decree of December 1991 that required all collective and state farms to reorganize by January 1, 1993.

However, this entire process appears to have been much more of a reform on paper than a reform in the fields. Most enterprises chose some collective form of agriculture, and most have continued to operate with few or no real changes, except for increasing ambiguity and uncertainty about real ownership rights and responsibilities. The best documented examples of genuine agricultural land reform and farm creation have occurred in Nizhniy Novgorod Oblast (formerly Gor'kiy Oblast) located about 250 miles (400 km) east-northeast of Moscow. These demonstration projects had heavy involvement of foreign consultants and significant financial resources to carry them out. Although they are good models for market reform, they do not represent a viable economic agricultural reform option for the entire country because of the large number of trained personnel and large amount of financial resources that would be required to conduct such a process on the national scale—and neither the personnel nor the money is available.

As of early November 1995, the Russian government retained 3.7 billion acres (1.5 billion ha) of land; re-registered and reorganized cooperatives and state farms held 420 million acres (170 million ha); and private owners held 74 million acres (30 million ha). A total of 45 million Russian citizens own landplots. Apparently, then, approximately 494 million acres (200 million ha) out of the Russian Federation's 549 million acres (222.1 million ha) of agricultural land had been transferred.

Lacking a Land Code that clearly defines landownership rights, post-Soviet agriculture appears to be operating in a vast sea of slippery, unstable mud. At this vantage point, it appears that agriculture and its reform will continue to be problematic in post-Soviet Russia, with meaningful reform in other former republics such as Belarus and Ukraine lagging behind Russia's uncertain agricultural reforms. Even within Russia, the reform picture has no clear focus as a result of its great complexity and uncertainty, political conflicts, and regional diversity.

Energy in the Soviet and the NIS Economies

The key to any type of modern economic development is energy. The following section discusses the tremendous reserves of energy resources, especially in the Russian Federation, as well as their general geographical distribution, and the past, current, and future energy problems that faced Soviet planners and are facing post-Soviet leaders.

The previous discussion of industrial location policies and decision making indicated a significant shift toward the east during the Soviet era. Nowhere was this eastward geographical shift more evident than within the Soviet energy and fuels sectors. Not surprisingly, the control over and supply of energy resources have become the foci of innumerable core-periphery disputes among Russia and the other former republics,

between the Russian "center" and the Russian Federation regions that possess the developed supplies and reserves, and between the old *nomenklatura* who have manipulated the energy privatization processes to become the extremely wealthy *novo riche* (newly rich) and the hordes of the newly dispossessed individual citizens.

Coal NIS coal production peaked in 1988 at 848 million tons, or 725 percent above the 1940 figure (see Fig. 13-11 and Table 13-6). Economic dislocations, including labor strife, since the Soviet Union's breakup have led to an overall decline in coal production greater than 22 percent. Before World War II, the Donets'k Basin in Ukraine produced about 57 percent of the USSR's total coal, while at present it produces less than 20 percent of total NIS coal. It is still the second largest coal pro-

---

TABLE 13-6

REGIONAL OUTPUT OF NIS FUEL AND POWER

	1980	1985	1990	1992
Coal Production	**Millions of Metric Tons**			
Former USSR	716.4	726.4	703.3	605.8
Russia	391.4	395.2	395.3	337.2
European USSR	86.3	80.2	71.5	54.0
Donbas (east)	32.3	31.1	28.9	20.4
Urals	38.8	28.0	23.9	22.6
Siberia	266.3	287.0	299.9	260.6
Kuznetsk Basin	145.0	146.2	150.4	109.4
Kansk-Achinsk	34.8	41.4	52.3	46.0
So. Yakutia	2.1	11.9	16.9	12.4
Ukraine	197.1	189.0	164.8	134.0
Donets Basin	173.3	167.5	145.0	119.0
Kazakhstan	115.4	130.8	131.6	127.0
Qaraghandy	48.6	49.8	48.7	45.0
Ekibastuz	66.8	80.5	81.9	81.0
Central Asia	11.0	10.0	10.7	7.1
Georgia	1.9	1.7	2.0	0.5

continued

continued

TABLE 13-6

	1980	1985	1990	1992
Petroleum Production	**Millions of Metric Tons**			
Former USSR	603.2	595.3	570.8	449.5
Russia	546.7	542.3	516.2	395.8
European USSR	153.9	105.5	79.6	66.0
Volga	113.4	73.8	54.3	46.2
Urals	77.6	66.0	59.2	52.4
Siberia	315.2	370.7	377.4	277.4
West Siberia	312.7	368.1	375.2	275.7
Sakhalin	2.5	2.6	2.2	1.7
Ukraine	7.5	5.8	5.3	4.4
Belarus	2.6	2.0	2.1	2.0
Kazakhstan	18.7	22.8	25.8	27.5
Other Central Asia	9.9	8.6	8.7	8.5
Transcaucasia	17.9	13.6	12.7	11.1
Natural Gas Production	**Billions of Cubic Meters**			
Former USSR	435.2	642.9	814.8	781.2
Russia	254.0	462.0	640.6	640.4
European USSR	41.3	30.3	19.7	15.9
Urals	51.0	48.9	43.3	41.7
Siberia	161.7	382.8	577.6	582.8
West Siberia	156.4	375.8	569.3	574.6
Ukraine	56.7	42.9	28.1	20.9
Belarus	0.3	0.2	0.3	0.2
Kazakhstan	4.3	5.5	7.1	8.8
Uzbekistan	34.8	34.6	40.8	42.8
Turkmenistan	70.5	83.2	87.8	60.1
Transcaucasia	14.3	14.2	9.9	7.8
Electric Power Output	**Billions of Kilowatt hours**			
Former USSR	1293.9	1544.1	1726.0	1574.1
Thermal	1037.1	11622.2	1281.0	1126.2
Hydro	183.9	214.5	233.0	240.0
Nuclear	72.9	167.4	212.0	207.9
Russia	804.9	962.0	1082.2	1014.6
Ukraine	236.0	272.0	298.5	252.6

continued

TABLE 13-6

Electric Power Output	1980	1985	1990	1992
		Billions of Kilowatt hours		
Belarus	34.1	33.2	39.5	37.6
Moldova	15.6	16.8	15.7	11.1
Baltic states	35.3	43.8	52.2	48.0
Kazakhstan	61.5	81.3	87.4	81.3
Central Asia	63.4	85.1	102.4	92.6
Transcaucasia	43.2	50.0	47.8	36.2

Sources: Matthew Sagers, "The Energy Industries of the Former U.S.S.R.: A Mid-Year Survey," *Post-Soviet Geography* 34, No. 6 (June 1993): 344, 378, 392, 404; PlanEcon 10, Nos. 37–38 (1994): 6; and *Statistical Handbook 1995: States of the Former USSR* (Washington, D.C.: World Bank, 1995), p. 445.

ducer among the former republics, but not much above that of Kazakhstan. Ukraine's economy has been seriously impacted by its lack of oil and natural gas resources and its dependence on coal from antiquated, dangerous, underground mines with thin coal seams. Despite large increases in the controlled price of Ukrainian coal in the early 1990s, the gap between Donbas coal production costs and prices has widened significantly. Mine worker strikes have been widespread and chronic, and the Ukrainian government is extremely hard pressed to find the financial resources to continue its large budget subsidy for the coal industry.

The eastward energy shift in Soviet exploitation of energy resources was first reflected in coal mining. Between World War II and the breakup of the USSR, the big coal production increases, in both relative and absolute terms, came from the Kuznetsk Basin or Kuzbas in western Siberia and the Qaraghandy Basin of Kazakhstan. Because of the thick seams and shallow depths, much of the Kuzbas coal was suitable for open-pit mining. Because of its low cost and the fuel deficit of European Russia, much of the Kuzbas coal was shipped west as coke for iron and steel production. Mine worker strikes and other problems in the Kuzbas resulted in its 1992 production being less than 69 percent of the basin's peak production of 175 million tons in 1988. The third and fourth leading coalfields in the former USSR, Ekibastuz and

Qaraghandy in Kazakhstan, have large reserves of open-pit accessible sub-bituminous coals and underground shaft-mine coking coals, respectively. Although its output was shipped chiefly to the Urals, in recent years Qaraghandy coal was also moved to Central Asia and European Russia. Production at both of these basins has held up surprisingly well, considering that much of their production was based on what are now foreign markets—directly in the case of Qaraghandy's output and indirectly in terms of Ekibastuz's minehead thermal power stations. Much of their electricity is carried by wire to markets across the border into Russia. The Pechora Basin (Vorkuta) in the Russian European north was developed during World War II with forced labor and produces a modest 7 percent of the Russian Federation's total coal production.

By far the largest coal *reserves* are in eastern Siberia in the Tunguska, Lena, Kansk-Achinsk, Taymyr, and Kuznetsk basins. The future use of the low-quality lignite coals of the Kansk-Achinsk Basin for synthetic fuel production and in thermal power plants at the minehead, which had long encountered serious delays in the Soviet era, are now even more questionable owing to the high costs of thermal electricity produced from these low-quality coals compared to the abundant and the significantly cheaper hydropower available in eastern Siberia.

Oil Baku on the Caspian Sea, Maykop in the North Caucasus region , and Groznyy, the capital of troubled Chechnya in the Caucasus area, extracted about 88 percent of the USSR's total output of crude oil in 1940 (Fig. 13-18). Between 1940 and the peak oil production year, 1988, Soviet crude production increased over 22-fold (1988 total production was 686 million tons). However, instead of reaching its planned output target of 698 million tons in 1990, crude oil production dropped to 627 million tons, and in 1992 to 494 million tons for the former republics combined. Of this decline of 192 million tons, all but 2 million tons occurred within the largest producing former republic, the Russian Federation.

Baku's modest oil production leveled off long ago and now represents slightly over 2 percent of the total output of the former union. The relative production of the Russian North Caucasus fields dropped from about 45 percent in 1940 to about 1.6 percent in the early 1990s. From 1940 until the 1970s, the major growth region was in the Russian Volga-Urals fields of Bashkortostan (formerly Bashkir ASSR), Samara, Perm', Orenburg, the Udmurt Republic, and Tatarstan (formerly Tatar ASSR). However, their relative share of the total output has decreased from above 70 percent in the mid-1960s to about 22 percent today. During the late 1970s and 1980s, the rate of absolute decline in the Volga-Urals fields was significant and was precipitated by excessively high rates of extraction that damaged many of the wells and oil pools.

The phenomenal growth in Soviet crude oil production oil between 1960 (163 million tons) and 1988 (686 million tons) was based overwhelmingly on the discovery and development of the large West Siberian oilfields surrounding Nizhnevartovsk, especially the super giant Samotlar field (see Fig. 13-18). Yielding its first crude in 1964, this field alone in 1980 produced 213 million tons, equivalent to more than 130 percent of total Soviet oil production in 1960! West Siberia's crude oil production was about 10 percent of the Soviet total in 1970, yet reached 67 percent in 1988 as well as having about 60 percent of the known reserves. Many of these large fields are now facing depletion. For example, even before some of the economic factors behind the post-Soviet decline in oil production came into play in the early 1990s, out-

put from the Nizhnevartovsk fields had declined in 1992 to less than one-quarter of its 1980 output.

The only other significant growth province within the territory of the former Soviet Union in recent years has been in the North Caspian Sea fields in the second largest oil-producing former republic, Kazakhstan. Chevron has become a major player in the post-independence Kazakh oil industry. Full development of the highly viscous and high-sulfur oil from the large Tengiz field will require upwards of $40 billion in investment over the expected 40-year life of the project. Chevron is to receive half of the oil output in exchange for its hard currency investment in the project. Because of incentives, taxes, and bonuses, this joint Chevron-Kazakh agreement leaves Kazakhstan with over 80 percent of the profit and Chevron with slightly less than 20 percent. Development of Caspian Sea offshore deposits in Turkmenistan and Azerbaijan has also attracted the interest of foreign petroleum firms.

Thus, depletion of the reserve base of large Russian fields has forced a switch to the exploitation of smaller, widely scattered fields that have lower rates of flow and higher infrastructure requirements such as collection field piping. An increasingly large fraction of the flow from new wells has been necessary merely to replace the diminished flow from wells that are nearing the end of their productive life.

In spite of the dramatic decline in Russian oil extraction in the early 1990s, crude oil production in the Russian Federation still accounts for nearly 90 percent of the combined oil output of the former republics. This economic reality combined with the geography of the oil- and gas-producing fields, reserves, and the pipeline network system provides the Russian Federation with a large economic control lever over many of the former republics and their efforts independently to develop and export their indigenous energy resources. Getting oil out of land-locked Kazakhstan is a clear example. With the large Russian fields in western Siberia reaching maturity, known and yet to be discovered large reserves are located mainly in remote, inhospitable, and fragile environments in the north, the east, and offshore in the Arctic and Pacific basins. Hence, these new potential supply sources are difficult and expensive to bring into

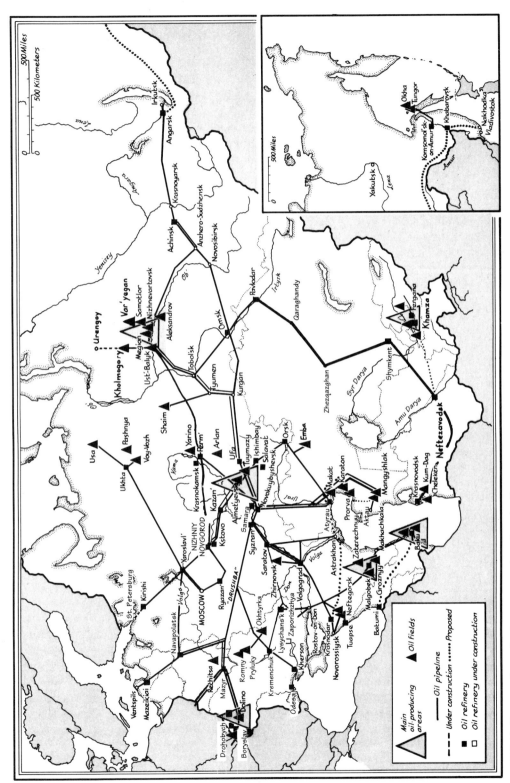

FIGURE 13-18 FSU oil-producing areas and major pipelines.

production. Even under the best of circumstances, including the infusion of much needed foreign equipment, technology, personnel, and investment, Russian oil output will not likely be returned to physically sustainable levels (495 million tons) until after the turn of the century—if ever.

Natural Gas Natural gas output was negligible in the USSR until the late 1950s. During the 1950s as part of Khrushchev's campaign for developing the petrochemical branches of industry, gas discoveries and output grew geometrically, registering nearly an 18-fold increase in output between 1960 and the peak output year of 1990 (28.8 trillion cu ft/814.8 billion cu m). Widespread use of gas had to await the pipeline construction of the 1960s (Fig. 13-19). The major producing fields are in West Siberia, the Central Asian republics, the North Caucasus, and Ukraine. Similar to the case with oil, the Russian Federation's gas output (82% of the former republics' total 1992 output) has long dominated the gas industry. Although Russia's gas production declined slightly in 1992 for the first time ever, compared with other economic sectors this performance must be considered exemplary given the severity of the economic crisis within Russia.

The gas industry's problems are different, and its prospects are brighter than those of the Russian oil industry. First, the Russian reserves of gas are huge, and though concentrated in the north, they most often exist in shallow and geologically simple formations that are easy to develop. Second, the necessary infrastructural developments are much less elaborate and costly than those for oil, which requires refineries and separate production pipelines. Third, as a result of the two above factors, the need for foreign investment is much less in the gas than the oil industry. Fourth, the continuing monopolistic nature of the gas industry has allowed it to respond proactively to maintain its dominance, whereas the more decentralized oil industry has had many more organizational problems.

On the other hand, the gas industry appears to have more of a "soft demand" problem, whereas the oil industry has a problem with developing new supplies. In order to capture new sources of unserved and underserved demands, such as the dispersed housing and municipal sectors (only 13% of total gas demand in 1990), the gas industry needs to invest vast sums in the construction of pipeline distribution networks to serve these dispersed potential consumers. At the same time, there is no apparent economic incentive for such investments. For example, gas prices for these consumer uses have remained highly subsidized and controlled, with 1993 prices being only equivalent to 6.5 percent of the gas prices paid by Russian industrial customers.

The gas industry has also been plagued by serious financial problems, such as delinquent payments to it, which have created difficulties for the huge *Gazprom* monopoly to pay its employees. Zealously protecting its privileged position and its domestic market from foreign competition, Gazprom has successfully maneuvered the government into removing offshore Barents Sea energy development rights from a Western consortium and giving them to *Rosshelf* organized by Gazprom. The huge reserves in Sakha also promise to be important for Gazprom in the more distant future, and a South Korean consortium of companies has been negotiating with Russia and Sakha for gas deliveries and a direct 3725-mile (6000-km) pipeline to South Korea. Offshore Sakhalin gas deposits have attracted considerable foreign interest. As for oil, the northern part of western Siberia looms into the future as the major natural gas-producing region. Nearly 70 percent of the reserves are located in the permafrost wilderness of northwest Siberia, and roughly 15 percent are in the deserts of the former Central Asian republics.

Uzbekistan gas has been exported primarily to the energy-deficit Urals, and Turkmenistan gas to Ukraine and recently to the Volga region. In the post-Soviet era, all of these flow patterns have become problematic for two major reasons: (1) disputes over gas prices on the one hand and nonpayment for gas deliveries on the other, and (2) disputes because of Russian control of the current gas transmission lines out of Central Asia. Similar to the case with proposed oil transmission pipelines from Central Asian and Kazakhstan oilfields, several controversial gas pipeline proposals are being discussed. Some would exit Central Asia through Iran, a route that concerns the West. Another proposed pipeline would cross Azerbai-

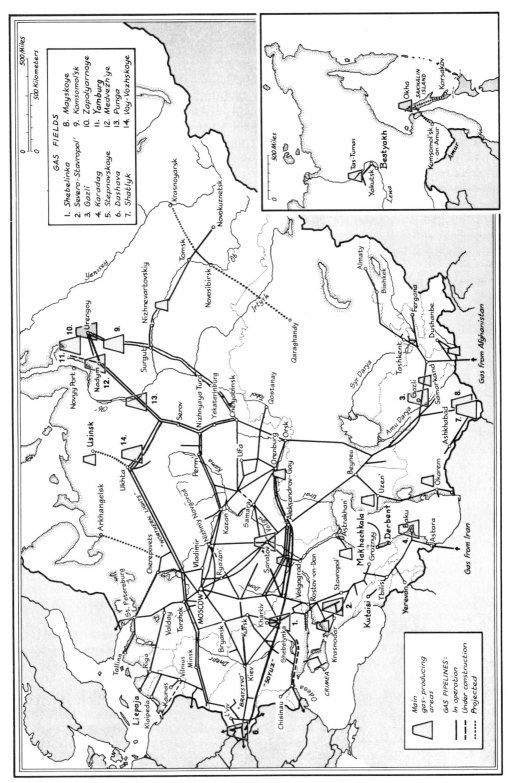

FIGURE 13-19 FSU gas-producing areas and major pipelines.

jan and Georgia. Others would skirt the southern Caspian Sea coast of Iran and exit through Turkey.

Although Ukraine has sizable gas reserves, financial constraints make major Ukrainian gas developments unlikely for a considerable time period. Ukraine has long been dependent on huge gas deliveries from Russia. Disputes over new prices and chronic nonpayment by Ukraine have led to significant disruptions of its economy. Both sides have economic levers here, although Russia needs to use gas pipelines that cross Ukraine for its gas exports to parts of Eastern, Southern and Western Europe. Then, too, no two former republics' economies were as interconnected and dependent on each other as those of Russia and Ukraine. Thus, without gas deliveries from Russia, Ukrainian factories cannot produce industrial goods needed by Russian industries. As the post-Soviet economies convert away from military production, many of these industrial linkages between Ukraine and Russia should weaken. Ukraine is trying to negotiate with Iran for alternative gas supplies. Because of Russian policies and the geography of the new states and the old energy distribution networks, all of the other republics with export potential for oil and gas have major unsolved transportation problems remaining before they are able to control their own energy export developments.

Other Energy Sources Peat has long been used locally for fuel in power stations and for space-heating in Belarus, the Baltic republics, Ukraine, and northern European Russia, including the Urals. Oil shale is mined and burned in power stations in Estonia, near St. Petersburg, and near Samara on the middle Volga. Even under the old Soviet system of administrative prices, these two fuels were competitive only for nearby markets in fuel-deficit areas, and their use is destined to disappear. The oil shale mining industry in Estonia is highly charged politically. This environmentally dirty industry was predicated on the introduction of large numbers of Russian miners into the country and partially fueled large thermal plants (in which oil shale is mixed with fuel oil), which once supplied electricity for the greater St. Petersburg region of northwest Russia. Owing to both currently severe political tensions between Russia and Estonia and to the high cost of the oil shale energy,

its use has dropped and most generated electricity is now sold within Estonia itself.

In the early 1990s, the share of electricity production from thermal, hydro, and nuclear plants amounted to 72, 15, and 13 percent, respectively. Strikes in the coalfields and mines and interrupted coal deliveries throughout the former Soviet Union have resulted in brownouts, power disruptions, and chronic shortages of electricity in some regions, such as the Trans-Baykal region and the Far East.

Although most of the former USSR's hydroelectric power potential lies in Siberia, the European potential was first developed as part of Lenin's original electrification goal for the country (Fig. 13-20). The first large-scale hydro-installation went into production in 1932 at Zaporizhzhya on the Dnieper River. This dam was destroyed during World War II and later rebuilt. Before the war, several hydrostations on the Volga were opened. The large energy demands of European Russia after the war led to the construction of many more large hydroelectric dams on the Volga and Dnieper in the 1950s and early 1960s and more recently in Siberia on the Yenisey and Angara rivers, in the Far East, and in Central Asia. A number of large-capacity thermal plants have been constructed since the 1950s.

Nuclear energy was severely sidetracked by the Chernobyl' accident in the spring of 1986, and no new reactors have been put into production since 1990. Nonetheless, two of the original four Chernobyl' units went back on line as early as the autumn of 1986. Despite the Chernobyl' nuclear plant accident, the shortage of fossil fuel energy reserves in the European NIS, and the lack of major domestic alternatives in the case of the Ignalina nuclear plant in Lithuania, seems to be keeping the nuclear power industry limping along. Russia has again announced major nuclear power initiatives. The International Atomic Energy Agency (IAEA) and other energy organizations have recommended the permanent closing of the 15 RBMK Chernobyl'-type reactors still operating in Russia. Russia has firmly resisted such a move, stating that to do so would result in a loss of about $60 billion.

Although safety issues have received much more attention since 1986, nuclear power plants within the former Soviet Union continue to be

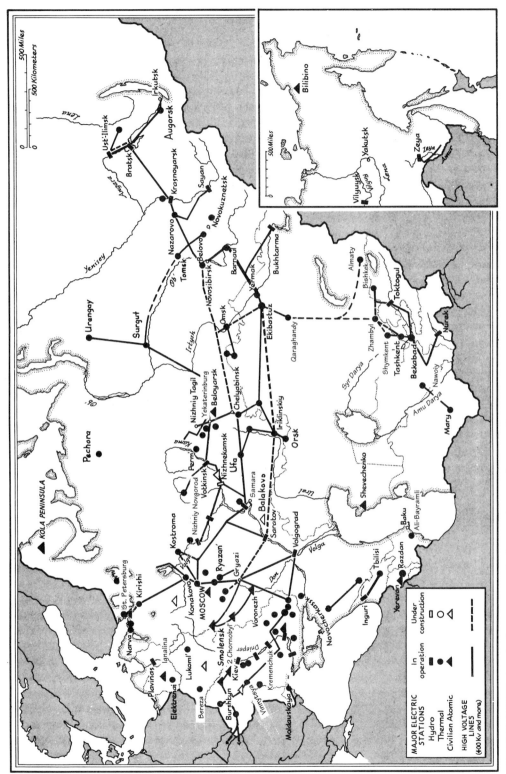

FIGURE 13-20 FSU electrical power-producing stations and power lines.

plagued by a number of "unscheduled stoppages" and minor accidents and fires. In general, most power plant facilities under construction at the time of the breakup of the Soviet Union have experienced major completion delays. Work on several plants appears to have been halted owing to lack of financial resources.

Energy Problems and Trends We have only skimmed the surface of the myriad post-Soviet energy problems. Nevertheless, we can safely conclude that Russia and the NIS will be confronted by serious energy-related issues for decades to come. The European part of the NIS, including the Urals, is faced with increasing net energy deficits. During the Soviet era, these long-standing regional supply problems stimulated Soviet pioneering research in high-voltage direct-current transmission of electricity for transferring the energy of Siberian hydropower and energy from Siberian and Kazakhstan coals to the energy-starved western parts of the country. More importantly, the vast proven and predicted reserves of oil and gas remaining in western Siberia have engendered a number of complex interrelated issues. For example, should Russia continue to export oil and gas to the West in exchange for much coveted Western technology and consumer goods? Or should it augment supplies only to meet its own growing needs, fulfilling a Russia first policy? To what extent will energy be used as a diplomatic tool or ploy? Will reserves prove adequate to honor long-term commitments to former republics, to satisfy other current and potential purchasers, and to meet the changing domestic demand for lighter distillates like gasoline? How should, can, or must the Russian and NIS energy balances evolve in the future? For example, beyond the year 2000 will coal, or will nuclear energy predominate over gas and oil? Many other economic, political, and technical aspects of energy issues, such as the tempo and order of development and the end use of newly developing energy sources, also still remain unsettled.

Manufacturing: An Overview

The Production Giant—The Iron and Steel Industry Although resource extraction is tied to resource sites, resource use and processing are not. The most fun-

damental of the heavy, resource-based industries is iron and steel production. The first Russian ironworks were situated between Moscow and Tula in the seventeenth century. Ferrous metallurgy was launched in the Urals under Peter I and in the nineteenth century in Ukraine. Despite the Soviet rehabilitation of the Urals' metal industry and the new iron and steel centers built by the Soviets in Siberia and Kazakhstan, the Ukraine has maintained its dominance (see Fig. 13-11 and Table 13-7). This republic has four clusters of iron and steel plants. The most important one is in the heart of the Donets'k coking-coal district of Ukraine and adjacent Russia. The iron ore capital of Kryvyy Rih has a very large capacity plant. The Dnieper River cluster is situated midway between Kryvyy Rih iron ore and Donbas coal. The final cluster consists of two seaboard iron and steel plants at Mariupol' and a steel-smelting plant located at Taganrog, both on the Sea of Azov. The Mariupol' plants receive their iron ore from Kerch. Since Kerch ore is phosphoric, the Mariupol' plants also produce phosphate fertilizer as a byproduct. These southern European locations received continued emphasis from the early years of Soviet power simply because of their advantageous geographical proximity to both raw materials and large markets. After the war, new plants were built and old ones expanded in accordance with the new resource-use policies.

The second largest regional concentration of ferrous metal industry is in the Urals. Expanded during the 1930s and World War II, the dwindling supplies of local iron ore caused the relative share of Urals' pig-iron production to peak out in 1956 at 36 percent of total Soviet output. Because of the local availability of scrap metal, however, the Urals' fraction of steel production has been somewhat greater. There are 11 integrated iron and steel plants in the Urals, the largest ones being at Magnitogorsk, Novotroitsk, Nizhniy Tagil, and Chelyabinsk. The region also has 11 steel-smelting plants.

East of the Urals, the Soviets built ferrous metal centers in the Russian Kuzbas and in the Qaraghandy region of Kazakhstan. In the Kuzbas, the previously mentioned Novokuznetsk plant, opened in 1932, was supplemented in the mid-1960s by the so-called West Siberian plant at Gur'yevsk.

TABLE 13-7

REGIONAL DISTRIBUTION OF THE SOVIET IRON ORE AND STEEL INDUSTRIES
(MILLIONS OF METRIC TONS)

Iron Ore	1940	1960	1970	1980	1985	1990	1992
Total former USSR	29.9	105.9	197.3	244.7	247.6	236.0	175.4
Russian Federation	(10.3)	(39.0)	66.5	92.4	103.8	106.8	80.9
European Russia	(2.2)	(2.0)	25.4	50.0	64.2	68.6	(54.4)
Kola	—	(1.7)	7.6	10.7	12.0	11.7	(9.0)
Karelia	—	—	—	—	8.6	9.3	(8.0)
Kursk (KMA)	—	(0.3)	17.8	39.3	43.6	47.6	(37.3)
Urals	8.1	27.3	26.5	25.0	23.0	20.7	(12.8)
Siberia	0.5	9.7	12.9	17.0	16.7	17.5	(15.0)
Ukraine	19.1	(63.7)	111.2	125.5	120.0	105.0	75.7
Kazakhstan	—	2.0	18.2	25.8	23.0	23.8	17.3
Steel							
Total former USSR	18.3	65.3	115.91	147.9	154.7	154.4	118.1
Russian Federation	9.3	36.6	63.9	84.4	88.7	89.5	67.0
European Russia	3.4	9.3	18.5	(26)	29.5	32.3	(27)
Urals	4.0	21.8	36.0	(42)	44.5	42.7	(30)
Siberia	1.89	5.5	9.4	(16)	14.7	14.6	(10)
Ukraine	8.9	26.2	46.6	53.7	55.0	52.6	41.7

Quantities in parentheses are estimates. NA means regional data not obtained.

Sources: Strana sovetov za 50 let (Moscow: Statistika, 1967; Theodore Shabad, "News Notes," *Soviet Geography : Review & Translation* (April 1977): 277–281; *Narodnoye khozyaystvo SSSR v 1970 g.* (Moscow: Statistika, 1971), p. 191; Matthew J. Sagers, "Review of the Iron and Steel Industry in the Former USSR in 1992 and Thereafter," *Post-Soviet Geography* (September 1993): 454–460; Paul Lydolph, *Geography of the U.S.S.R.*, 2nd ed. (New York: John Wiley & Sons, 1970), p. 509.

In the European heartland of Russia, three integrated iron and steel centers—Tula, Lipetsk. and Cherepovets—are important because of their proximity to high-consumption areas. As high-grade Kryvyy Rih ores became scarcer, the enriched ores of the Kursk Magnetic Anomaly (KMA) supplied increasing quantities of ore for the Donbas, Central Industrial Region, Cherepovets, Urals, and East European plants, as well as a new plant in the southern KMA region itself. Other ferrous metallurgical installations shown on Figure 13-11 serve only local markets. Nonetheless, their construction during the Soviet era was consistent with the political goal of industrializing the regions inhabited by national minorities.

Significantly, all aspects of Soviet ferrous metallurgy—iron ore mining, coking coal production, and steel production—became stagnant in the late 1970s for a variety of reasons related to raw materials, energy, technology, labor, demand, and management. Nonetheless, Soviet crude steel production reached its highest output of 179 million tons in 1988, more than double the U.S. production total of 82 million metric tons. As Table 13-7 indicates, production of iron ore, pig iron, and steel within the former Soviet republics has declined dramatically since the breakup. A variety of reasons can be cited, including all of those previously noted, which accounted for the decline in the late 1970s, amplified by all the labor strikes, supply disruptions, delinquent inter-firm and inter-republic payments problems, and a softening of demand in the military machine building sectors. In addition, the freeing of prices allowed newly privatized firms to raise prices and cut back production in classic monopolistic types of firm behavior.

For the most part, the ferrous metallurgical plants of the former USSR were not nearly as modern and appealing for private investment as the oil and gas enterprises. Accordingly, these old, dirty hallmark industries of the Soviet development system might well be expected to continue to decline and languish for a long time. In general, nonferrous metal industries have fared even worse than ferrous metals since the breakup of the Soviet Union. Exceptions tend to be accessible, high-grade, or high-value precious metals with foreign markets such as gold and the platinum groups.

Machine Building In the early years, Soviet machine building was concentrated in the regions of St. Petersburg, Moscow, Nizhniy Novgorod in the Russian SFSR, Kharkiv in Ukraine, and Riga in Latvia. Although these European centers retained their dominance, manufacturing became distributed, albeit unevenly, across the entire country. For example, the European NIS region still manufactures about 75 percent of the total machinery output of the former 15 republics, with the Urals in the Russian Federation and the rest of the former republics sharing equally in the remaining 25 percent. Heavy machinery, such as mining and metallurgical equipment, railroad equipment, locomotives, and railroad rolling stock, gravitated toward the centers of steel production in the southeast Ukraine, the old industrial core around Moscow, the Urals, the Kuzbas, and the Angara River Valley downstream from Irkutsk in East Siberia. On the other hand, textile machinery and bulky farm implements are more market oriented in location of production. Accordingly, textile machinery production is concentrated in the Moscow-Ivanovo textile belt. Farm equipment manufacturing plants are located in Ukraine and in several Russian Federation locations (Moscow region, Sea of Azov region, Volga Valley, Urals, and West Siberia). Automobile production, which was still modest by European and U.S. standards

at the time of the breakup, is concentrated in the central industrial regions of Moscow, Nizhniy Novgorod, and Yaroslavl'. Auto and truck plants in the Urals, the Volga Valley, Belarus, and Ukraine were completed during and after World War II. The Zhiguli or Lada/Fiat auto plant at Togliatti near Samara, and Kamaz, the world's largest truck plant, situated in the new city of Naberezhnyye Chelny along the Kama River in Tatarstan symbolized the Soviets' late, yet substantial, commitment to the automobile age. Furthermore, both projects were and are still heavily dependent on Western technology.

Chemicals—The Last of the Soviet-Era Growth Industries Although Soviet industrial investment since Khrushchev's "Chemicalization Drive" (1958–1965) resulted in some eastward drift of chemical industries to the Asian parts of the country, the predominant trend was one of dispersion within European economic core areas. For example, mineral fertilizer factories are located near either raw material sites or market areas, namely, European Russia, the Baltic republics, Ukraine, and the Urals. The major recent geographical shift was in the production of nitrogen fertilizer. Originally, nitrogen fertilizer was manufactured by utilizing byproduct hydrogen from coking coal (from the Donbas and Urals) and low-grade lignite (from the Moscow region) to produce ammonia. After the Soviet natural gas revolution that began in the 1950s, Central Asia and the Volga Valley became significant sites of nitrogen fertilizer production. The older locations also switched to piped-in natural gas.

The petroleum industry also revolutionized the Soviet synthetic rubber industry, beginning in 1957 in Azerbaijan near Baku. Since then, three new plants were opened in the Volga Valley and one at Omsk in western Siberia, all near oil refining complexes. Agglomeration or industrial linkage factors accounted for the siting of new petrochemical industries adjacent to petroleum refineries or natural gas pipelines. Examples of such industries include plastics, synthetic fibers, synthetic resins, and detergents. Market factors as well as agglomeration effects resulted in the siting of most of these new industrial facilities in the old European heartland.

Under Brezhnev, the Soviets made enormous increases in the purchases of imported technology for their chemical industries, including the purchase of entire plants. This policy appears to have been predicated on three factors. First, the Soviets lacked the design and engineering capability to mass produce the needed modern equipment. Second, the relaxed Western trade constraints during détente enabled the Soviet Union to sign favorable trade and technology agreements with Western countries. Third, because nearly all such purchases were paid for at least in part by guaranteed export markets for the resulting chemical products, the Soviets were able to pay for the foreign equipment and plant purchases with smaller up-front outlays of scarce foreign-currency reserves. Priorities changed after the Brezhnev era, and the chilling of East-West relations in the early 1980s helps to explain why the chemical industry languished in the 1980s. Although the official Russian figure of a 45 percent economic decline in the chemical and petroleum processing industries between 1990 and 1994 probably overstates the case, nonetheless, in the post-Soviet years, the problems in the chemical industries have resulted in shortages of numerous types of chemical products and renewed efforts to obtain modern imported Western equipment and plants within the context of a variety of problematic, joint-venture type agreements.

Timber Market and raw material accessibility also explain why the NIS timber industries remain centered in the European NIS. Paper mills use coniferous softwoods and hence are concentrated in the European North. Because the plywood industry uses deciduous birch and alder, it is focused farther south and west in the mixed-forest belt of the European NIS. Sawmills are commonly situated near the mouths of rivers in the European North. The timber industry has been languishing since 1960, and Soviet efforts to improve productivity by utilizing imported Western technology were not successful. Since the breakup of the USSR, the timber industry in Russia has developed three strong regional trends. Declines in the European NIS core areas have been moderated by strong recent increases in the exports of hewn timber, plywood, cellulose pulp, and especially newsprint. Ironically, the strong export market has resulted in domes-

tic supply shortages of newsprint in Russia. Strong export markets in East Asia, especially in Japan, North and South Korea—partially resulting from timber-cutting restrictions in the western United States and Canada—have resulted in significant foreign timber harvesting and export activities in the Far East. Extensive clear-cutting near railroad and river transportation avenues associated with these export-based activities have become controversial because of accelerated soil erosion and other environmental problems.

The timber enterprises in the vast Siberian taygal forests between the Urals and the Trans-Baykal region have been the most negatively impacted by the breakup. Their local demand has declined, their traditional domestic market areas in the Central Asian republics have been disrupted; and their remoteness and high transport costs have made their outputs, except for higher value-added commodities such as pulp and paper, noncompetitive even in western Russia.

In both the near and long term, Russia's vast forests are in dire need of much better silviculture management. The desperate lure of immediate export earnings does not augur well for the Russian forests.

The Food Industry Russian and European NIS food processing centers, though widely distributed, tend to gravitate toward large urban consumption centers, especially dairy and meat-processing plants. The location of food-canning facilities, on the other hand, mirrors that of the production areas, chiefly Ukraine and Moldova for fruits and vegetables. Fish-canning plants quite naturally are distributed along the coastal margins, especially in the Far East.

The entire food industry in Russia and the European NIS is in a state of flux. On the one hand, since the breakup, tremendous quantities of food are being imported—primarily from Western Europe into European Russia and from Japan and the western United States into the Far East. A steady stream of tractor-trailers filled with foodstuffs travel the major roads from port cities on the Black Sea and Baltic and across Northern Europe to urban markets throughout the European NIS. On the other hand, new private restaurants and catering enterprises are flourishing, and joint ventures in new food-processing facilities seem to be taking hold rapidly.

INTERRELATIONSHIPS BETWEEN THE FORMER SOVIET UNION AND EUROPE

Political-Military Interaction

We can derive a great deal of insight into the political, military, and economic relationships between the former Soviet Union and the rest of Europe by drawing on the historical relationship between Russia and Europe. Many of the fundamental aspects of their twentieth-century interactions have strong historical parallels and antecedents. The former Soviet regime's actions were often predicated on an inherited Russian legacy of suspicion, xenophobia, and aggressive inferiority. Learning from the historical repetition of military invasion by European powers—including the poignant example of the foreign military interventions in the tumultuous period following the October Revolution—it is not at all surprising that the Soviet regime pursued an isolationist-autarkic political posture from the mid-1920s until just before World War II. Even without the stimulus of the German invasion, the goal of rapidly building a strong defense capacity would have been highly consistent with this combined foreign and domestic political policy. The chief, early Soviet tasks of holding onto the territorial conquests of the tsarist era and keeping a firm lid on internal dissension parallel long-standing imperial Russian goals.

On more than one occasion, the Soviets pragmatically forsook Marxist ideology to ensure these two overriding objectives. Certainly, the excesses of collectivization, the political purges of the 1930s, and the forced labor camps of the Stalinist period had more in common with tsarist practices and with Marx's criticisms of the worst features of labor exploitation under capitalism than they did with the expected policies in a Marxist worker's state. On the international front, the 1939 German-Soviet nonaggression pact brought together two ideologically estranged bedfellows. Stalin's pragmatic attempt to purchase vital time for military preparedness can also be linked to the nagging

Soviet suspicion that the UK, France, and the United States were, if not outright aiding, at least doing pitifully little to forestall, the creation of a large and sophisticated German war machine designed to accomplish the goal that their own interventionist forces had earlier failed to achieve—the destruction of Bolshevism.

Thus, when Soviet leaders found themselves in a strategic military position at the culmination of World War II hostilities, they embarked on a swift and thorough campaign to create a territorial buffer along the Soviet Union's western perimeter. In many ways, the successful prosecution of an unprovoked and unwanted war left the Soviet regime within easy grasp of Russia's long-sought hope of a secure western frontier. The disastrous capital and human losses inflicted on the Soviet peoples by the Axis powers served as both a convenient and a convincing rationale for the heavy Soviet extraction of war reparations in equipment, factories, and raw materials from East European countries. Only a tortured logic, however, could justify the compulsory deliveries of artificially cheap Polish coal to the Soviet Union after the war. Poland was not an Axis ally and proportionally suffered more from the war than any European country, including the USSR.

The Soviet response to the U.S.-inspired Marshall Plan, the Council for Mutual Economic Assistance (CMEA), also has its logical roots in the historically justified Soviet fear of an economically and militarily resurrected Germany. Similarly, the Warsaw Military Pact was a Soviet counterstroke to NATO. It is sufficient here to note that until the Hungarian and Polish revolts of 1956, the CMEA functioned somewhat like a reverse mercantilist trading bloc. In simple terms, the controlling partner, the Soviet Union, exported raw materials and food to Eastern European workshops and in return imported finished goods, such as machinery, consumer goods, and railroad equipment and rolling stock. With the terms of trade artificially set in favor of the Soviets, the Eastern European countries in effect subsidized the Soviet war reconstruction program.

Despite Soviet domination of Eastern Europe from 1945 through 1989, at first the economic relationship between them was at least in part mutually beneficial, for much of the Eastern bloc countries' economies had been geared for export to Germany. Thus, the rebuilding of the postwar Soviet economy provided a captive market for Eastern European industries and fostered the recovery of their own structurally unbalanced economies.

In response to the East Berlin revolt of 1953, the Soviet Union canceled the delivery of war reparations, turned over control of Soviet-owned and mixed Soviet-East European-owned companies to their respective host countries, and extended development aid and credits to Eastern Europe for economic reconstruction. But the Soviets' lingering reluctance to permit the Eastern European countries to oversee the development of their own economies, and Stalinist suppression of internal political freedoms, were nonetheless primary causes of additional social unrest in Eastern Europe in the mid-1950s.

The period from the late 1950s to August 1968 showed an apparently gradual Soviet relaxation of its tight military, economic, and political grip on the fortunes of Eastern Europe. For example, after 1963 the Eastern bloc states exercised a freer hand in foreign trade and over their own paths of economic development. The Soviet and Warsaw Pact military invasion of Czechoslovakia in 1968, however, again demonstrated to Europe and the rest of the world the degree of decisive action that the Soviets were still willing and able to execute in defense of their perceived vital interests. Notwithstanding the long Sino-Soviet rift, the Soviet leadership still believed Germany to be its major foreign military threat.

Casual inspection of a map of Europe reveals the geopolitical logic behind the Soviet intolerance of a *renegade* Czechoslovakia. Even a truly independent Czechoslovakia would have strategically split the Warsaw Pact and the CMEA countries. More alarming for the USSR, a future alliance between West Germany and Czechoslovakia could have transformed Czechoslovakia into an unsheathed dagger menacingly pointed directly at the Soviet motherland. Whether any of these Soviet military fears were justified is a moot point, because of the post-Revolutionary Soviet-European historical experience. In comparison to Soviet military actions in Eastern Europe from 1945 through the Czechoslovak invasion in 1968, the Soviet involvement in the Polish crisis of the late

1970s and early 1980s was far more restrained. With hindsight, one could interpret this as but a highly subtle precursor of the unprecedented Soviet acquiescent response to the astonishing events that swept Eastern Europe in the late 1980s and early 1990s, especially the tearing down of the Berlin Wall and the reunification of Germany.

Then, too, although the original Soviet military intervention in Afghanistan revealed a continuing Soviet determination to forcibly invoke the Brezhnev Doctrine, which asserted that the Soviet Union had the right to intervene on behalf of "fraternal" socialist governments threatened by "counterrevolutionary" forces, Gorbachev found a graceful method of disengagement. Americans may not like the analogy, but the Brezhnev Doctrine was quite similar to the American Monroe Doctrine.

In terms of international public relations savvy and personal charisma, Gorbachev represented a distinct departure from his predecessors. To a significant degree throughout much of Western Europe, Gorbachev seized on the antinuclear war movement and peace initiative, while the United States and its "Star Wars" missile interception program appeared to be aggressive in nature. To many knowledgeable people, Gorbachev, albeit possibly only for pragmatic economic reasons—the arms race was bankrupting the Soviet Union—came across as a strong proponent of international peace. It also appears that Gorbachev was given American assurances that if the Soviet Union "let go" of Eastern Europe, NATO would not attempt to incorporate this region into the Western Alliance. In the mid-1990s NATO's intentions to do just that are generating strong words of objection and threats of military action from a spectrum of Russian government leaders and politicians.

The foregoing discussion is in no way to be taken as an apology for the numerous heavy-handed Soviet policies and actions in the world political arena, but rather as a cursory attempt to understand the motivation, logic, and rationale behind Soviet behavior in European foreign affairs.

Foreign Trade

Before the mid-1950s the Bolshevik regime's desire for self-sufficiency limited Soviet imports of critical prototype Western machinery and equipment. Accordingly, it held exports—primarily timber and grain—to the level necessary to pay for the foreign technology. Thus, the commodity profile of trade was similar to that of the pre-Revolutionary era; so, too, were the trading partners, dominantly the industrialized Western European countries and the United States. The depression in the West and the industrialization drive in the Soviet Union made the trading arrangements mutually beneficial. Except for lend-lease imports, World War II greatly curtailed Soviet foreign trade. Although this trade recovered during the 1950s, its growth with the West was hamstrung by a series of U.S.-inspired export controls enacted at the height of the Cold War. The creation of CMEA, of course, was one of the Soviet responses to the various Western trade deterrent measures. As a result, the Soviet Union substituted East European countries for its long-term Western trading partners.

After 1955, the Soviet Union employed trade as a political and propaganda instrument, especially through use of long-term bilateral agreements with individual developing countries. For example, although the total value of Soviet foreign trade increased 16-fold between 1950 and 1988, its trade with developing states increased 53-fold. During the same period, trade between the USSR and developed capitalist countries increased 27-fold, and trade with all socialist countries increased only 12-fold. In order not to be misled by these figures, it must be noted that the absolute volumes of Soviet foreign trade with both developing countries and developed capitalist countries combined only represented one-fourth the value of Soviet trade with socialist countries in 1950. A sizable fraction of the trade with developing countries was with India, African and Middle Eastern Arab countries, and Turkey. Obviously, trade with all of these states was based at least as much on political as on economic factors.

Given the nature of the USSR's economy, state agencies conducted foreign trade. Primarily as a result of the Soviet Union's defaults on tsarist foreign debts and its World War II lend-lease obligations, as well as its low trade volume, the Soviet ruble had no recognized value in foreign exchange. Thus, the Soviet Union was commonly forced to arrange bilateral barter agreements or

else use gold or precious foreign reserves to purchase foreign goods, especially from countries outside CMEA. In fact, even most CMEA trade was based on long-term barter agreements. Simple two-country complementarity of trading commodities is not always easy to achieve, especially in the politically motivated trade with developing states. Thus, lack of a convertible currency, problematic international credit, and until near the very end of the Soviet Union, rigid central resource allocation, reduced the Soviet Union's flexibility in foreign trade. As Table 13-8 enumerates, at their maximum value Soviet exports totaled $110 billion in 1988, whereas imports reached their maximum in 1990 at $118 billion. The table also indicates the traumatic, disruptive impact that the breakup of the Soviet Union has had on foreign trade throughout all 15 of the former republics. By the end of 1994 only Estonia, Latvia and Turkmenistan (the last-named a natural gas exporter) had export trading volumes above those of 1990, and only Estonia had import levels above 1990 values. However, even the Baltic republic data are suspect, for some of their exports are really transshipped commodities, such as nonferrous precious metals, mainly from Russia. These were being exported to the world market through the Baltic states to circumvent export quotas and taxes, and they made a few Baltic traders instantly wealthy.

The commodity structure of Soviet trade evolved considerably compared to pre-Revolutionary and even pre-World War II times (see Tables 13-9 and 13-10 for current commodity trade structures). After 1940, machinery equipment and transport rolling stock grew slowly from about one-third of the total value of imports to over 40 percent by the time of the breakup, but this figure has since fallen back to about one-third. Other significant changes between 1940 and the breakup of the USSR were the large drop in ores and metals as a share of imports and the substantial rise in the relative position of consumer goods. In terms of total imports, the annual relative share of foodstuffs increased, but vacillated with the Soviet weather and hence with agricultural conditions. Thus, the Soviet Union of the late 1960s through the mid-1980s could no longer uphold its image as Europe's breadbasket.

Furs, diamonds, and precious metals had long been major foreign exchange earners for both the

TABLE 13-8

FOREIGN TRADE OF THE USSR AND NIS, 1988–1994 (MILLION U.S)

Year	EXPORTS			
	1988	**1990**	**1992**	**1994**
Total	110,219	103,296	52,334	58,434
Russia	87,254	79,473	41,600	46,974
Ukraine	12,535	13,389	3,774	4,648
Kazakhstan	1,610	1,777	1,451	1,327
Belarus	3,162	3,438	1,061	1,053
Uzbekistan	1,414	1,390	869	912
Lithuania	821	679	557	855
Estonia	251	198	242	730
Latvia	497	305	429	524
Turkmenistan	179	195	1,145	371
Azerbaijan	937	724	737	360
Tajikistan	457	610	111	319
Moldova	378	406	157	121
Kyrgyz Republic	72	88	71	112
Georgia	580	514	90	86
Armenia	72	110	40	42

Year	IMPORTS			
	1988	**1990**	**1992**	**1994**
Total	106,958	117,663	44,198	47,232
Russia	75,815	79,539	37,196	35,100
Ukraine	14,697	15,908	2,219	4,347
Kazakhstan	2,670	3,250	565	1,694
Estonia	638	592	254	1,251
Uzbekistan	1,271	2,217	924	1,106
Lithuania	1,414	1,543	342	1,063
Belarus	3,921	5,256	755	690
Latvia	1,022	1,641	423	581
Tajikistan	332	655	132	306
Turkmenistan	281	523	543	298
Azerbaijan	1,280	1,413	329	275
Georgia	1,065	1,542	180	189
Moldova	1,061	1,431	170	134
Armenia	575	855	95	110
Kyrgyz Republic	917	1,299	71	88

Source: Misha V. Belkindas, and Olga V. Ivanova, eds., *Foreign Trade Statistics in the USSR and Successor States: Studies of Economies in Transformation* (Washington, D.C.: World Bank, 1995), pp. 163 & 168.

TABLE 13-9

RUSSIAN, BELARUSSIAN AND UKRAINIAN FOREIGN EXPORT COMMODITY TRADE, 1994 (IN PCT.)

Commodity Group	Belarus	Estonia	Russia	Ukraine	Latvia	Commodity Group	Lithuania*	Moldova†
Total U.S.$	975.8	1,306.7	63,243.0	9,708.2	524.0	Total U.S.$	557.0	360.0
Total %	100.0	100.0	100.0	100.0	100.0	Total %	100.0	100.0
Animal & animal products	1.5	7.7	0.6	3.5	n.a.	Industry total	92.3	93.3
Foodstuffs, beverages, tobacco	0.8	12.3	0.9	5.8	n.a.	Power	6.3	13.1
Mineral products	5.1	8.2	44.1	10.5	n.a.	Ferrous metallurgy	1.3	4.0
Chemicals	34.4	6.8	7.0	10.5	n.a.	Chemical & petroleum	9.2	1.2
Plastics	3.6	1.8	1.7	3.1	n.a.	Machinery & metal works	23.4	19.6
Wood & wood products	1.9	10.2	2.6	0.2	n.a.	Sawmill & lumber industry	4.6	3.0
Textiles	18.8	13.7	1.9	1.6	n.a.	Building materials	3.3	1.2
Precious stones & metals	2.8	0.4	10.2	0.0	n.a.	Light industry	18.0	8.5
Base metals	7.6	8.0	17.8	36.2	n.a.	Food industry	18.3	41.8
Machinery	5.2	9.3	4.8	14.1	n.a.	Other industries	4.4	0.2
Transport equipment	11.5	7.6	3.8	7.3	n.a.	Agriculture	1.3	6.3
						Other material production	6.4	0.4

Source: Statistical Handbook 1995: States of the Former USSR (Washington, D.C., World Bank, 1995), pp. 120–121, 163–164, 355, 394, 434–435, 536–537; Misha V. Belkindas, and Olga V. Ivanova, eds., Foreign Trade Statistics in the USSR and Successor States: Studies of Economies in Transformation (Washington, D.C.: World Bank, 1995), p. 168.

*1992
†1993

TABLE 13-10

RUSSIAN AND EUROPEAN NIS FOREIGN IMPORT COMMODITY TRADE, (IN PCT.)

Commodity Group	1994 Belarus	1994 Estonia	1994 Russia	1994 Ukraine	Commodity Groups	1992 Lithuania	1993 Moldova
Total U.S.$	535.8	1658.4	38,649.6	9,989.2	Total U.S.$	342	210
Total %	100.0	100.0	100.0	100.0	Total %	100.0	100.0
Animal & animal products	0.4	2.1	4.8	0.6	Industry total	94.6	86.0
Vegetable products	12.3	2.7	6.5	1.0	Power	0.6	3.1
Foodstuffs, beverages, tobacco	3.8	9.9	15.8	1.6	Oil & gas	40.3	38.2
Mineral products	2.7	14.1	6.5	55.0	Coal	3.8	10.6
Chemicals	25.8	7.6	7.7	5.6	Ferrous metallurgy	3.7	3.7
Plastics	6.2	3.9	2.2	3.9	Chemicals and petroleum	10.5	7.8
Wood & wood products	0.2	1.4	0.2	2.7	Machinery & metal works	15.3	8.4
Pulp & paper	0.3	2.6	1.2	0.8	Sawmill & lumber industry	1.5	3.7
Textiles	6.2	10.3	6.0	2.7	Building materials	1.8	1.5
Footwear, etc.	1.2	1.6	1.9	0.4	Light industry	6.2	3.9
Base metals	3.2	5.9	6.5	4.1	Food industry	2.3	3.4
Machinery	30.9	19.7	24.6	14.2	Other industries	4.8	1.3
Transport equipment	2.3	8.6	6.6	4.1	Agriculture	5.3	13.8
Instruments	1.9	2.4	4.1	1.2			

Source: Statistical Handbook 1995: States of the Former USSR (Washington, D.C.: World Bank, 1995), pp. 122–123, 165–166, 356, 395, 436–437, 538–539; Misha V. Belkindas, and Olga V. Ivanova, eds., *Foreign Trade Statistics the USSR and Successor States: Studies of Economies in Transformation* (Washington, D.C.: World Bank, 1995), p. 168.

Russians and Soviets. In the case of furs, although the ruble value of fur exports is several times greater today than it was in 1940, the large overall expansion of Soviet exports resulted in the fractional share of furs plummeting from 9.4 percent to less than 0.2 percent of current FSU (overwhelmingly Russian) exports.

The economic transformation of the USSR by the mid-1960s was reflected in the extraordinary rise of machinery and manufactured equipment in the Soviet export commodity mix from 2 percent in 1940 to around 16 percent at the end of the Soviet era. At the same time, closer inspection reveals that these manufactured goods exports were destined primarily for the CMEA or Third World countries. Of far greater international importance was the spectacular increase in the export of Soviet fuels and electricity. While the physical quantities of coal exported grew about 2.4-fold between 1960 and 1991, those for crude oil, petroleum products, natural gas, and electricity (none exported in 1960) grew more rapidly. Oil and oil product exports reached a maximum in terms of natural units in 1988. Since then, there has been a dramatic drop in petroleum exports although they continue, along with gas exports, to generate billions of dollars of export earnings and remain significant within the international energy market.

The legacy of Russia's dominance of the former Soviet economy and its domestic trade linkages are still evident in terms of the current inter-republic trade of Russia and the six European NIS states (see Table 13-11). As a result of the need for energy imports and the continuing transshipment of Russian exports through the Baltics, these three non-CIS members (though less so Estonia) still conduct much of their foreign trade dealings with the Russian Federation. In contrast, their extra-FSU trade has dramatically shifted away from Eastern Europe toward the industrialized Western countries (see Table 13-12).

Although the USSR produced nearly 20 percent of the world's industrial output, it accounted for less than 3 percent of world trade. In summary, the changes in the commodity profile of Soviet foreign trade overstated the success of forced industrialization. At the same time, trade data hint at the structural imbalances created—that is,

the relative neglect or poor performance of the agricultural and consumer goods sector vis-à-vis heavy industry.

Europe, Trade, and Development of Siberia and the Far East

The course of current and future Siberian development appears to be closely intertwined with international trade in energy and raw materials. The general geographical disparity between Soviet natural resource supplies and industrial demands has been noted on a number of previous occasions. Coal, oil, gas, water power, and many valuable ores, minerals, and timber are concentrated in Siberia, often in environmentally inaccessible regions. The problems and costs of labor turnover, transportation infrastructure, long transport distances, housing and factory construction, and lack of urban amenities in Siberia have also been mentioned.

In an energy-dependent world, the military-strategic importance of oil and natural gas cannot be understated. From the late 1970s until the Soviet breakup at the end of 1991, the Soviet Union's energy resources were problematic for the Western alliance. On the one hand, energy-poor Europe understandably was far more willing to import Soviet oil and natural gas than the more energy-independent United States would have liked. Yet such a trading policy was mutually advantageous by diversifying Europe's energy supplies away from the increasingly politically unstable Middle East and by creating jobs and markets for European products needed by the former Soviet Union. This allowed the country to develop its energy deposits quickly as well as providing the Soviets with the hard currency needed to purchase Western technology and foodstuffs.

Differences between West European and U.S. policies were most clearly evident in the clash over West European participation in the West Siberian gas pipeline project. West Europeans justifiably interpreted America's attempts to place sanctions on Western companies participating in this Soviet energy project, while at the same time lifting America's grain embargo on the USSR, as blatantly hypocritical interference in their domestic

TABLE 13-11

MAJOR INTER-REPUBLIC FLOWS IN RUSSIAN AND EUROPEAN NIS FOREIGN TRADE, 1994 (IN PCT.)

Republic	Major Trade Partners (% of all intra-FSU exports /% of all intra-FSU imports)				
Russia	Ukraine (39/38)	Belarus (12/15)	Kazakhstan (12/6)	Uzbekistan (8/7)	Lithuania (5/4)
Belarus	Russia (81/87)	Ukraine (14/9)			
Ukraine	Russia (75/70)	Turkmenistan (4/19)	Belarus (7/4)		
Moldova	Russia (70/65)	Ukraine (17/25)	Belarus (6/4)		
Estonia	Russia (53/63)	Latvia (20/8)	Lithuania (9/12)	Ukraine (8/6)	Belarus (3/5)
Latvia	Russia (55/50)	Lithuania (11/13)	Ukraine (12/6)	Belarus (9/6)	Estonia (5/7)
Lithuania	Russia (50/77)	Ukraine (17/9)	Belarus (11/5)	Latvia (11/2)	

Sources: Statistical Handbook 1995: States of the Former USSR (Washington, D.C.: World Bank, 1995), p. 12; Misha V. Belkindas, and Olga V. Ivanova, eds., Foreign Trade Statistics in the USSR and Successor States: Studies of Economies in Transformation (Washington, D.C.: World Bank, 1995), pp. 175–176, 185–186, 187–188.

TABLE 13-12

FOREIGN TRADE OF RUSSIA ACCORDING TO CUSTOMS STATISTICS BY FOREIGN COUNTRY, 1994 (MILLIONS U.S.$).[a]

Exports			Imports		
Country		U.S.$	Country		U.S.$
Total Exports	Rank	63,243	Total Imports	Rank	38,650
Ukraine	1	6,700	Germany	1	5,640
Germany	2	5,355	*Ukraine*	2	4,402
United Kingdom	3	3,688	*Belarus*	3	2,092
Switzerland	4	3,686	United States	4	2,069
United States	5	3,372	*Kazakhstan*	5	1,996
Belarus	6	3,103	Finland	6	1,627
China	7	2,834	Netherlands	7	1,611
Italy	8	2,770	Italy	8	1,596
Netherlands	9	2,348	Japan	9	1,114
Japan	10	2,245	France	10	1,002

[a]NIS countries are in italics.

Source: Misha V. Belkindas and Olga V. Ivanova, eds., Foreign Trade Statistics in the USSR and Successor States: Studies of Economies in Transformation (Washington, D.C.: World Bank, 1995), pp. 208–209.

affairs. These policy differences among the Western allies, combined with the groundswell of anti-nuclear popular opinion that was sweeping Europe in the 1980s, weakened rather than strengthened the NATO alliance. In any event, recent data and research on the Russian oil industry's performance and the adequacy of Russian oil reserves cast a long shadow over Russia's physical ability to sustain even the recently curtailed crude oil export levels. On the other hand, Siberian natural gas reserves seem more than sufficient to maintain high levels of exports.

THE END OF DÉTENTE, THE NEAR-ABROAD, AND GEOPOLITICS IN THE POST-SOVIET ERA

From the vantage point of the mid-1970s and the era of so-called détente, the prospects of peaceful coexistence of the USSR and the West seemed good. Détente was always a somewhat nebulous and precarious international arrangement and was seriously questioned in many Western circles, especially the United States. Essentially, the criticism was that the benefits of détente accrued disproportionately to the Soviet Union. In many ways, the 1975 European Security Conference in Helsinki and the signing of the European security agreement represented the crowning culmination of centuries of Russian, and then decades of Soviet, foreign policy—an international guarantee affirming the country's western borders. While the geographic and prestige value of the security treaty for the Soviet Union was quite evident, the benefits to the West lacked a similar clarity. It appeared at the time that the West had yielded a significant diplomatic bargaining point to the USSR—the issue of the international legitimacy of post–World War II European frontiers. Nonetheless, from a broader world perspective, détente was generally perceived as a positive step toward continued peaceful international rapprochement.

Domestically, the Soviet Union was still confronted by some centuries-old Russian problems, chiefly a population demanding an ever more consumer-oriented economy. The Brezhnev era never came to terms with the changing domestic economic conditions that required greater emphasis on factor productivity. Brezhnev, while achieving many foreign policy and military-strategic objectives, failed to muster the wherewithal to carry out the requisite economic reforms necessary to make the Soviet economy dynamic once again. Much like America's leadership during the Vietnam era, Brezhnev's consensus rule led him to defer continually from making radical changes in domestic economic policy. After more than a half-century of Bolshevik rule, the Soviet system had developed a self-serving bureaucracy that was more interested in preserving its privileged position than in making rational economic changes that would have better served a broader socioeconomic spectrum of the population. The centralized institutions and policies that had stimulated the rapid growth of a backward agrarian society in the 1930s had become increasingly inappropriate and inefficient for a complex, myriad goods-producing economy exhibiting increasing resource scarcities and conflicting resource uses. With rational market price allocation mechanisms forced out the door, a huge "second economy" or black market mushroomed and came through the windows, cracks, and crannies of all Soviet socioeconomic structures.

At the same time, this reticence to enact reform was not politically irrational for the Brezhnev leadership, especially in the short run. The situation presented a classic "Catch-22." In essence, the overriding economic problems cried out for much greater decentralized decision making and rational markets to get the sluggish economy moving again. While tolerated by the Soviets in such CMEA countries as Hungary, such domestic approaches had traditionally been anathema for the leadership for fear that the untethered economy might veer off in an undesirable or even uncontrollable trajectory. Then, too, Khrushchev had rocked the ship of state with his party reforms and *sovnarkhozy* scheme (organized on regional rather than national sectoral planning) and had found himself cast adrift, no longer at the helm. Having been in effect one of the anti-Khrushchev usurpers, Brezhnev remained cautious about making anything more than minor "adjustments" in the command economy's planning, coordination, and compliance apparatus. Thus, it was that he bequeathed an increasingly corrupt, inefficient, noninnovative, technologically backward, and stagnating economy to his successors.

Whereas Yuri Andropov (1982–1984) and Konstantin Chernenko (1984–1985) served as short-term caretakers of the stagnating economy they inherited from Brezhnev, Gorbachev quickly made important changes in both the domestic and international arenas. Yet many old questions remained. For example, would the Soviet Union continue to try to overcome its relative technological and productivity gaps by continued importation of Western capital and high-technology goods, or would a reassessment reveal that such efforts had not been cost effective owing to systemic problems incorporating the foreign plants and equipment with domestic capital and the indigenous labor force? Strong efforts to invigorate the lagging agricultural sector were initiated, but their success was far from certain and distant at best. It remained an open question whether Gorbachev's crackdown on pervasive economic corruption would be successful, let alone whether his reforms and twin policies of *perestroika* and *glasnost* could enlist the masses' aid in overcoming the entrenched bureaucratic inertia and vested interests. Instead of serving as a controllable societal pressure release valve, *glasnost* appears to have intensified many social pressures until the lid was blown off long-pent-up nationality issues, ethnic problems, and regional rivalries. Once released, these forces rapidly developed their own dynamic, vigorous, centrifugal trajectories. Apparently having underestimated or incorrectly understood these geographically expressed forces, Gorbachev could no longer choreograph them.

From the vantage point of the late 1980s and the signed IMF treaty, it seemed more plausible than ever that Soviet military spending would be curtailed. Furthermore, anyone with an appreciation of the human and economic suffering inflicted on the European Soviet Union during World War II would have had to invoke a tortuous logic to argue that the Soviet people and their leadership wanted war. On the other hand, few foresaw that *glasnost* combined with the failure to meet pent-up consumer demands would finally constitute a fatal challenge to the regime's legitimacy. Gorbachev

did not appear to be militarily adventurous; in fact, he seemed realistically and pragmatically willing to rein in and curb the Soviet Union's heavy economic and military commitments in the international arena. The Soviet economy seemed to be merely stagnating rather than disintegrating; and the Soviet society's capacity to endure inhuman hardships was legendary.

Because of the pace of events following Gorbachev's ascendance and his subsequent fall from power, any speculation on future events would be hazardous, for too much weight may have to be placed on what may turn out to be merely transient events. One thing is certain: the reform road has been rocky and muddy, with many unforeseen, perilous detours, and many more detours lie ahead. The ensuing years and decades will present difficult choices for the citizens of Russia and the NIS. Accordingly, many pitfalls as well as opportunities exist for Europe, the United States, China, Japan, and the rest of the world in terms of their diplomatic, military, and economic relationships with the Soviet successor states.

In its euphoria over having "won" the Cold War, the West risks several fundamental confusions, namely: democracy cannot be equated with elections; privatization of state monopolies does not create profit-seeking, free market enterprises, but, rather private rent-seeking monopolies and oligopolies; and quiescence does not equate to political stability. Except for the Baltics, democracy does not have a legacy in the former Soviet Union in the form of social and political institutions that transcend their leaders. *Demokratizatsiya* is not the equivalent of "democracy" and *privatizatsiya* does not mean "private free market enterprise." The privatization process in Russia thus far can be more accurately characterized as a "golden parachute" safely landing a cornucopia of treasures (oil, gas, timber, metal ores, and minerals) for the former *nomenklatura, apparatchiks* (bureaucrats), and Communist party bosses than as democratic, free market, private enterprise reform for the benefit of the masses.

The breakup of the Soviet Union is probably the most momentous event of the twentieth century in a century of momentous events, and in 1991–1992 the West through its failure to extend aid to the region may well have missed the opportunity of the century to give global peace and stability a lasting positive chance. When a program on the scale of a Marshall Plan was required, perhaps some $25 billion per year for five to ten years, collectively the West responded with meager promises of stingy levels of aid and assistance. To comprehend the potential gravity of this situation, we need to understand the profound losses that the Russians as a people and a state have experienced. They are engulfed in a deep indentity crisis and collective grief process, including denial, anger, negotiation, and depression, with no clear vision of acceptance yet on the horizon.

These processes are fraught with potentially violent consequences. First and foremost, though greatly weakened, the nuclear-equipped Russian military is still enormous compared to the defense forces of any of the other former republics. Russia still has military bases in all 11 of the other republics in the Commonwealth of Independent States (CIS). The CIS has generated over 600 paper agreements, but only 25 have been signed and ratified. Fundamentally, the CIS is an effort to reimpose Russian power. The Russian Federation is not a federation, for federal-state (or region) relations are a zero-sum game. Fifty-three percent of the territory of the Russian Federation is composed of various "autonomous," non-Russian units created by the former Soviet center, and 18.5 percent of the population is non-Russian. Hence, the original RSFSR's boundaries were, in effect, drawn by negation, and Russians were given "extraterritorial" status. Today 25.4 million of these Russians live in the "near-abroad" republics, ammunition for Russian nationalists and jingoistic politicians seeking to resurrect the former Soviet Union's superpower status.

In October 1993 President Yeltsin used military force to dissolve the duly elected Parliament. In December 1993 a new Russian constitution, with strong presidential powers, was forced on the Russian Federation with a 51.2 percent positive vote, only after the total number of eligible voters was "revised" downward three times. President Yeltsin has enacted thousands of decrees, yet with each decree more and more citizens become alienated and drop out of the political process. For the first time ever, feelings of anti-Americanism are developing and are being expressed by ordinary Russian citizens. As the center gets weaker, will the leadership turn to "near-abroad adventurism" in an effort to deflect and rationalize domestic shortcomings and to retake what was lost? What could be more beneficial to the reestablishment of Russian control over Central Asia than the United States' dual containment policy of Iraq and Iran, which prevents land-locked Central Asian countries from exporting their resources, especially oil and gas, except through Russia? With hindsight, will the Gulf War be seen as a diversion contributing to the missed Western opportunity to change the course of history in Eastern Europe and the former Soviet Union? This is not meant to discount the justifiable Western concerns about nuclear proliferation posed by the military aspirations of Saddam Hussein.

Certainly, the results of the December 1995 Russian parliamentary elections—in which the Russian Federation's Communist party garnered 22.2 percent of the vote, the ultranationalist Liberal Democratic party of Russia 11.8 percent, and the reform-identified party, Russia Is Our Home, only 10.13 percent—suggest that Russia may be headed towards a late twentieth-century new "time of troubles." An imminent political challenge appears to be the likely requirement for Russia to choose a leader to succeed Yeltsin; whose ill-health casts doubt on his ability to complete his second term of office. In any event, Russia, like the USSR, despite all of its problems and weaknesses—and because of them—remains a crucial actor in European and world affairs.

BIBLIOGRAPHY

Aganbegyan, A. (1987). "The Economics of Perestroika." *International Affairs* 64,(2): 177–185.

_____. (1989). *Inside Perestroika: The Future of the Soviet Economy*. New York: Harper & Row.

Aslund, A, ed. (1994). *Economic Transformation in Russia*. New York: St. Martin's Press.

_____. (1989). *Gorbachev's Struggle for Economic Reform: The Soviet Reform Process, 1985–88*. Ithaca, NY: Cornell University Press.

_____. (1995) *How Russia Became a Market*. Washington, D.C.: Brookings Institution.

Barr, B. M., and K. E. Braden (1988). *The Disappearing Russian Forest: A Dilemma in Soviet Resource Management*. Totowa, N.J.: Rowman & Littlefield.

Braden, K. (1988). "Environmental Issues in Soviet Forest Management." *Soviet Geography* 29: 599–607.

Bradshaw, M. J., ed. (1993). *The Soviet Union: A New Regional Geography*. New York: John Wiley & Sons.

Craumer, P. R. (1994). "Regional Patterns of Agricultural Reform in Russia." *Post-Soviet Geography* 35: 329–351.

Crew, A. F. (1967). *An Atlas of Russian History: Eleven Centuries of Changing Borders*. New Haven, Conn.: Yale University Press.

DeBardeleben, J. (1985). *The Environment and Marxism-Leninism: The Soviet and East German Experience*. Boulder, Colo.: Westview Press.

Dienes, L. (1987). "Regional Planning and the Development of Soviet Asia." *Soviet Geography* 28: 287–314.

_____. (1987). *Soviet Asia: Economic Development and National Policy Choices*. Boulder, Colo. and London: Westview Press.

_____. (1987). "The Soviet Oil Industry in the Twelfth Five-Year Plan." *Soviet Geography* 28: 617–655.

Dienes, L., I. Dobozi, and M. Radetzki (1994). *Energy and Economic Reform in the Former Soviet Union: Implications for Production, Consumption and Exports, and for the International Energy Markets*. New York : St. Martin's Press.

Dienes, L., and T. Shabad (1979). *The Soviet Energy System*. New York: V. H. Winston.

Feshbach, M. (1995). *Ecological Disaster: Cleaning Up the Hidden Legacy of the Soviet Regime*. New York: Twentieth Century Fund Press.

_____, ed. (1995). *Environmental and Health Atlas of Russia*. Moscow: Paims Publishing House.

Feshbach, M., and A. Friendly, Jr. (1992). *Ecocide in the USSR: Health and Nature under Siege*. New York: Basic Books.

Filatotchev, I. V., and R. P. Bradshaw. (1995). "The Geographical Impact of the Russian Privatization Program." *Post-Soviet Geography* 36: 371–384.

Friedberg, M., and H. Isham, eds. (1987). *Soviet Society Under Gorbachev: Current Trends and the Prospects for Reform*. New York: M. E. Sharpe.

Fuchs, R., and G. Demko, eds. (1984). *Geographical Studies on the Soviet Union: Essays in Honor of Chauncy D. Harris*. Chicago: University of Chicago, Department of Geography. Research Paper No. 211.

Gorbachev, M. (1987). *Perestroika: New Thinking for Our Country and the World*. New York: Harper & Row.

Gorbachev's Economic Plans. Vols. 1 & 2. (1987). Study Papers, Joint Economic Committee, Congress of the United States. Washington, D.C.: U.S. Government Printing Office.

Hanson, P. (1990). "Property Rights in the New Phase of Reforms." *Soviet Economy* 6,(2):

Harris, C. D. (1970). *Cities of the Soviet Union*. Chicago: Rand McNally.

_____(1993). "The Russian Minorities: A Statistical Overview." *Post-Soviet Geography* 34:1–27.

_____(1993). "A Geographic Analysis of Non-Russian Minorities in Russia and Its Ethnic Homelands." *Post-Soviet Geography* 34: 543–597.

Haub, C. (1994). "Population Change in the Former Soviet Republics." *Population Bulletin* 49,(4): 50.

Holzner, L., and J. M., Knapp, eds. (1987). *Soviet Geographic Studies In Our Time: A Festschrift for Paul E. Lydolph*. Milwaukee: University of Wisconsin Press.

Hooson, D.J.M. (1966). *The Soviet Union: People and Regions*. Belmont. Calif.: Wadsworth.

Jensen, R., T., Shabad, and A., Wright, eds. (1983). *Soviet Natural Resources in the World Economy*. Chicago: University of Chicago Press.

Johnson, S., and H. Kroll. (1992). "Managerial Strategies for Spontaneous Privatization." *Soviet Economy* 7,(4): 281–316..

Kaiser, R. J. (1994). *The Geography of Nationalism in Russia and the USSR*. Princeton, NJ: Princeton Univervary Press.

Kingkade, W. W. (1988). "Recent and Prospective Population Growth in the U.S.S.R.: 1979–2025." *Soviet Geography* 29: 394–412.

Kotlyakov, V. M. (1988). "The Role and Place of Geography in the Solution of Ecological Problems: Results of a Conference at the Institute of Geography." *Soviet Geography* 29: 569–576.

Kroll, H. (1991). "Monopoly and Transition to the Market." *Soviet Economy* 7,(2): 143–174.

Liebowitz, R., ed. (1988). *Gorbachev's New Thinking: Prospects for Joint Ventures*. Cambridge, Mass.: Ballinger Publishing Co.

Lydolph, P. E. (1979). *Geography of the USSR: Topical Analysis*. Elkhart Lake, Wis.: Misty Valley Publishing.

Marples, D. R. (1995). "Belarus' Ten Years After Chernobyl'." *Post-Soviet Geography* 36: 323–350.

Matlock, J. F., Jr. (1995). *Autopsy on an Empire: The American Ambassador's Account of the Collapse of the Soviet Union*. New York: Random House.

Medvedkov, O. (1990). *Soviet Urbanization*. New York: Routledge.

Nove, A. (1989). *Glasnost in Action: Cultural Renaissance in Russia*. Boston: Unwin Hyman.

Pallot, J., and D. Shaw (1981). *Planning in the Soviet Union*. Athens: University of Georgia Press.

Pryde, P. R. (1991). *Environmental Management in the Soviet Union*. New York: Cambridge University Press.

_____,ed. (1995). *Environmental Resources and Constraints in the Former Soviet Republics*. Boulder, Colo.: Westview Press.

Rodgers, A., ed. (1990). *The Soviet Far East: Geographical Perspectives on Development*. London and New York: Routledge.

Rowland, R. H. (1995). "Rapidly Growing Towns in the Former USSR and Russia, 1970–1993." *Post-Soviet Geography* 36: 133–156.

Sacks, M. P. (1995). "Ethnic and Gender Divisions in the Work Force of Russia." *Post-Soviet Geography* 36: 1–12.

Sagers, M. (1993). "The Energy Industries of the Former U.S.S.R.: A Mid-Year Survey." *Post-Soviet Geography* 34: 341–418.

Sagers, M. J., and M. G. Green. (1986). *The Transportation of Soviet Energy Resources*. Totowa, N.J.: Rowman & Littlefield.

Sagers, M. J., and T. Shabad. (1990). *The Chemical Industry in the USSR: An Economic Geography*. Boulder, Colo.: Westview Press.

Sallnow, J. (1989). *Reform in the Soviet Union: Glasnost & the Future*. New York: St. Martin's Press.

Schroeder, G. E. (1994). "Observations on Economic Reform in the Successor States." *Post-Soviet Geography* 35: 1–13.

Shabad, T. (1969). *Basic Industrial Resources of the USSR*. New York: Columbia University Press.

Shabad, T. and V. Mote. (1977). *Gateway to Siberian Resources*. New York: Scripta Publishing Co.

Shaw, D. J., R. A., French, R. R., North, J., Pallot, G. E., Smith, and M.J. Bradshaw. (1995). *The Post-Soviet Republics: A Systematic Geography*. New York: Halsted Press.

Tabata, S. (1994). "The Anatomy of Russian Foreign Trade Statistics." *Soviet Geography* 35: 433–454.

USSR Energy Atlas. (1985). Washington, D.C.: U.S. Government Printing Office.

Van Atta, D. (1993). "The Human Dimension of Agrarian Reform in Russia." *Post-Soviet Geography* 34: 258–267.

Wegren, S. K. (1994). "New Perspectives on Spatial Patterns of Agrarian Reform: A Comparison of Two Russian Oblasts." *Post-Soviet Geography* 35: 455–481.

Weiner, D. R. (1988). *Models of Nature: Ecology, Conservation and Cultural Revolution in Soviet Russia*. Bloomington: Indiana University Press.

Wilber, C. K. (1969). *The Soviet Model and Underdeveloped Countries*. Chapel Hill: University of North Carolina Press.

Wood, A., ed. (1987). *Siberia: Problems and Prospects for Regional Development*. London: Croom Helm.

Ziegler, C. E. (1987). *Environmental Policy in the USSR*. Amherst: University of Massachusetts Press.

ZumBrunnen, C. (1973). "The Geography of Water Pollution in the Soviet Union." Ph.D. thesis, University of California at Berkeley.

_____(1993). "Problems and Prospects for the Development of New Commercial Structures in Russia and the Russian Far East." *Annals of the Japan Association of Economic Geographers* 39: 50–67.

_____,ed. (1992). *Urban Geography in the Soviet Union and the United States*. Totowa, N.J.: Rowman & Littlefield.

_____(1987). "Soviet Ferro-Ores Policies and Trends." In *Mineral Resource Development: Geopolitics, Economics, and Policy*, H. E. Johansen, O. P. Matthews, and G. Rudzitis, eds. Boulder Colo.: Westview Press, pp. 121–165.

_____(1984). "A Review of Soviet Water Quality Management: Theory and Practice." In *Geographical Studies on the Soviet Union: Essays in Honor of Chauncy D. Harris*, R. Fuchs and G. Demko, eds. Chicago: The University of Chicago, Department of Geography, Research Paper 211, pp. 257–294.

ZumBrunnen, C., and J. Osleeb. (1986). *The Soviet Iron and Steel Industry*. Totowa, N.J.: Rowman & Allanheld.

CHAPTER

14

CONCLUSION

Europe has changed—is changing—dramatically from day to day. The Soviet Union, Czechoslovakia, and Yugoslavia no longer exist. By 1992 Poland's neighbors were entirely different states than they had been in 1990. Eastern Europe has more than a dozen new states, which, rather than being adversaries of their West European neighbors, are now being integrated into pan-European institutions. During 1996 Russia became the Council of Europe's thirty-ninth member, punctuating the extent of Europe's changed post–Cold War geopolitical configuration and providing just one of several indications that Russia and many of its successor states are, indeed, part of Europe.

Contemporary Europe, nearing the start of the twenty-first century, is a very different place than it was only a few years ago—although one could have made this same statement about the region at virtually any time during the past two centuries, the period that historians call Europe's "modern" era. The ever-unfolding changes in Europe reflect at least one important characteristic of the region—its great internal diversity—as well as

indicating a characteristic of the contemporary era, which is experiencing rapid technological change. The significance and combined impacts of these factors are reflected in many of this book's major themes, including: human impacts on Europe's complex physical environment; pressure for economic restructuring in order for Western and Northern Europe to maintain and for Southern and Eastern Europe to achieve economic competitiveness and prosperity; political and social challenges to manage ethnic diversity, which continues to evolve owing to the movements of peoples within Europe and into it; related challenges to keep socioeconomic differences between regions and social groups from becoming politically untenable; and political and economic forces that are simultaneously resulting in the integration and disintegration of European states.

On the one hand, unfettered economic development threatens Europe's natural environment; on the other, "green movements" based on heightened awareness of the threat reflect a countervailing tendency for humans to preserve both the natural and human environments. Although air and water remain fouled, especially in parts of Eastern Europe and the FSU, many efforts are being made to remedy the situation—including dismantling dangerous nuclear plants in Eastern Europe, developing water treatment services on the Elbe River in Central Europe, and building tunnels under the Alps to try to protect mountain landscapes and air quality. Many countries are expanding their nature preserves and are developing national park systems like the one in the United States. Improved standards of living and greater interest in historic architecture have also been leading to greater efforts to preserve human landscapes. These are responses both to pressures for preserving national heritages and to opportunities for developing tourist industries—two goals that can at times be complementary and at other times contradictory.

Concern for environmental protection is tempered, and often overwhelmed, by greater concern for economic growth. Expectations for higher standards of living everywhere in Europe as well as intensifying competition for Europe's national economies and private firms, both within the region and from without, are driving economic change and generating political confrontation. In sectors such as shipbuilding and textile production, West European firms, in particular, are in trouble. During 1996, for example, Germany's biggest shipbuilding firm went bankrupt. Jobs in coal mining and steel production continued a long-term decline. High-technology sectors offer more hope. For example, multinational Airbus, the producer of aircraft, has become a serious competitor to the world's leading producer, Boeing of the United States.

Individual firms in all sectors are scrambling to meet changing technology and competition. Many European firms are joining with related firms in other countries in order to be better prepared for competition within Europe and the global economy. An increasing number of alliances are being forged among Europe's formerly small, nationally based auto producers and passenger airline companies. In a related trend, efforts to improve service quality and reduce costs have led to a wave of privatizations of formerly government controlled economic ventures. In the mid-1990s the telecommunication industry is being particularly impacted by this trend. In this sector, as in passenger air travel, there are an increasing number of alliances between European and American firms.

Privatization and increased competition are also bringing layoffs and pressure for reduced benefits to workers and lower subsidies to producers, generating political confrontations across the region. In 1995 France was rocked by public worker strikes, and disagreements among German political parties have sharpened—parties on the right pushing for lower taxes to bolster German competitiveness and left of center parties battling to maintain the "welfare state." In the UK this struggle seems already to have been won by the conservatives. Similar political struggles are evolving in Eastern Europe and are probably looming in Northern Europe.

Compounding the politically volatile agendas of Europe's states, as well as the EU, are issues of nationalism and ethnic conflict. Such problems have subsided somewhat in places like Belgium and the UK, but they continue to fester on Corsica, in the Basque lands of Spain, and in Estonia and Latvia; in 1996 they remained barely under control in Bosnia. Also affecting all of Europe are related problems of xenophobia associated with the inmigration of ethnic minorities. This issue of minorities has long been a social and political problem in Germany and France, an underlying cause of a troublesome regeneration of the far right political movement in Austria, and a prominent problem in countries such as the UK, Switzerland, and Italy.

Ethnic conflict and discrimination against immigrant minority groups are among the factors generating conflict among Europe's states, resulting in forces of political disintegration that stand in stark contrast to forces of integration, sponsored by EU leadership. Besides the disintegration of larger states into smaller, ethnically based ones, there remain serious conflicts between states resulting from the historically based territorial mixing of ethnic groups and related international boundary disputes. Such problems are especially prominent between Greece and Turkey over Cyprus and the Aegean Sea islands, between the UK and Ireland over Ulster, between Hungary and Romania over Transylvania, and between most Yugoslav successor states and their neighbors. At the same time, strong forces of integration emanate from a relatively dynamic European Union that accepted three new members in the 1990s, is considering and encouraging membership for several other countries, has forged a close economic relationship with EFTA, is developing improved economic ties to all of the East European states, and appears to be on the verge of establishing a unified currency—the "euro"—among its financially strongest members. In short, at the turn of the twenty-first century, Europe displays strong tendencies toward integration, especially in the West, while paradoxically suffering disintegrative pressures, most notably in the historic East European "shatterbelt."

In broad terms, it could be argued that contemporary Europe has entered an EU era after successfully weathering a threatening, bipolar Cold War era. The Cold War was characterized by confrontational politics, heated rhetorical propaganda, and the huge military might of NATO and the Warsaw Pact poised for war on either side of an Iron Curtain that divided Germany. Now Germany is united, the Warsaw Pact no longer exists, the Soviet army has dissolved, Russian forces have withdrawn eastward, the American military presence in Europe has lessened, and Russia is being invited into the "European house," as Gorbachev had insisted it should be several years ago. "Post-Soviet" issues have replaced Cold War issues in Europe.

Instead of preparing for the possibility of a military confrontation, EU states are girding themselves for intensifying global economic competition. More competitive firms are being formed by way of the processes noted earlier—privatization of cumbersome, subsidized state-owned entities and collaboration among or consolidation of formerly small, nationally based firms.

Governance in the post-Soviet era could also be changing. The role of supranational and subnational governments could increase at the expense of the state level, while nonstate actors such as multinational firms and citizen action groups like Greenpeace have unquestionably gained greater opportunity for influence. For example, state-controlled militaries no longer have the level of priority and urgency they commanded during the Cold War. France announced the formation of volunteer armed forces in 1996, while in Germany and elsewhere armed forces are being reduced.

The preeminent supranational government in Europe is without doubt the EU, but other entities, such as NATO, are also important, or at least show indications of becoming more important, such as

in the case of the Council of Europe. Subnational-level entities such as Germany's *Länder* and the Spanish autonomous regions like Catalonia, as well as individual city governments, are increasing contacts between people and institutions across national boundaries. These contacts are specifically fostered by the EU Interegio program and are logical outcomes during an era of proliferating telecommunications options and increasing imperatives for coordinating cross-boundary economic, environmental, and civil security issues. Pan-European contacts between political parties have also evolved with the slowly increasing responsibilities of the European Parliament.

The trend toward the increasing importance of subnational political associations and the growing importance of supra- and multinational commercial firms in Europe is undeniable, although state-level actions remain quite dominant, especially in the political arena. It is unclear how great the absolute importance of substate and nonstate actors may become in the future, but the tendency poses opportunities and problems. As nonstate entities like multinational firms grow in importance, people in local areas are feeling more removed from centers of decision making and more at the mercy of unseen forces. Similarly, state and substate governments have less and less power to control social and economic conditions in states where, by American standards, government has usually played a huge role in developing existing "welfare state" conditions. On the other hand, substate and nonstate organizational contacts across borders could lessen political problems in countries like Belgium and Spain by giving regions such as Wallonia and Catalonia a sense of political autonomy and importance on the European political stage, and reducing the importance of their political conflicts with their respective central governments.

In addition to coverage of these broad themes, this textbook has also used classic approaches within the field of geography to provide an overview of Europe in the mid-1990s. Much of the text reflects one of the discipline's oldest, now sometimes maligned, fields of descriptive regional geography. This factually based approach to presenting information remains an efficient method of providing basic background information on regions to people who are beginning to study them. The next steps in gaining more in-depth understanding of topics in the geography of Europe include both study of material in books similar to this one focusing on specialized topics and exposure to more analytically and theoretically oriented research presented in specialized journals. Portions of this book that, for example, evaluate the locational advantages and disadvantages of regions for attracting economic activities, offer a glimpse at the way specialists use a less descriptive and more analytical approach to understanding what is happening and why within the European space economy. In short, advanced study of the geography of Europe only begins where this introductory, descriptive text ends.

No matter the approach that is used or the depth that one seeks in understanding Europe, all "students" of the region seem uniformly fascinated by its historical, cultural, and geographic diversity. Despite obvious social, economic, environmental, and political problems, there is quite evident beauty in many things "European." The region's diversity offers an entire palette of opportunities for studying the successes and failures of human societies, and the region is hardly as monocultural as simple, ideologically loaded references to "Eurocentrism" might suggest. In fact, owing to Europe's diversity, what is actually "Europe" and who is a "European" are themselves not entirely clear. It is perhaps both heart-

FIGURE 14-1 "Citizen democracy instead of party dictatorship"—sloganeering in East Berlin, then still within the GDR. (W. H. Berentsen)

ening and troubling that upon arrival in Berlin in 1995 this author's taxi driver complained about the flood of "foreigners" into the city—this from an ethnic Turk, who came as a "guest worker" 27 years earlier, but now apparently feels, appropriately, like a "local" resident.

Studying Europe is a challenging, fulfilling, entertaining, yet frustrating undertaking. Through time, the object of study changes rapidly, and any

FIGURE 14-2 A play on words: literally "cabbage to the compost heap," but actually intended to be read as the political statement, "[Chancellor] Kohl to the compost heap," reflecting growing east German dissatisfaction with the realities of German unification. (eastern Berlin, W. H. Berentsen)

FIGURE 14-3 Europe: past...present ...future. A rural dweller plods homeward, away from once beautiful Sarajevo, Yugoslavia. (W. H. Berentsen)

given perspective taken in interpreting events and trends in the region can and will be both supported and criticized. While one person will argue that Europe is the font of all that is good in Western civilization, another will argue that Europe bears much responsibility for all that is wrong within the regions and societies it colonized and subsequently dominated. In like manner, Europe's "welfare states" can be held up as a model, or derided as inappropriate intrusions into the lives of individuals. Pan-European economic and political integration can be applauded, or it can be questioned in the face of the chaos and inhumanity in Yugoslavia that Europe itself has been unable to resolve. European traditions offer hope (Fig. 14-1) at the same time that dreams and illusions are crushed (Fig. 14-2). Europe is an ever-changing, always fascinating place, for which even a lifetime of study is too short. A study of the contemporary geography of Europe provides a good entree to further study of the region's history, economy, politics, culture, or society—not to mention its value in preparing one to experience life in Europe through study abroad and travel. The authors of this text all embarked decades ago on the adventurous undertaking of learning about Europe—an endeavor as long, as challenging, and as rewarding as the *Odyssey* undertaken at the dawn of European civilization's written record (Fig. 14.3).

BIBLIOGRAPHY

Andric, I. (1977). *The Bridge on the Drina.* Chicago: U. of Chicago Press.

Delouche, Frederic ed. (1992). *Illustrated History of Europe.* New York: Henry Holt and Co.

Dinan, Desmond (1994). *Ever Closer Union? An Introduction to the European Community.* Houndsmills, UK: Lynne Rienner Publishers, Inc. and MacMillan Press Ltd.

European Union, *Europe Magazine.* Brussels: EU, various dates.

German Information Center (New York), *The Week in Germany,* various dates.

Jordan, T.G. (1996). *The European Culture: A Systematic Geography,* 3rd ed. New York: HarperCollins.

Magocsi, P.R. (1993) *Historical Atlas of East Central Europe.* Toronto: University of Toronto Press.

Palmer, A. (1970). *The Lands Between: A History of East-Central Europe since the Congress of Vienna.* New York, N.Y.: Macmillan.

Pond, E. (1993). *Beyond the Wall: Germany's Road to Unification.* Washington, D.C.: Brookings Institution.

Poulsen, T.M. (1995). *Nations and States: A Geographic Background to World Affairs.* Englewood Cliffs, New Jersey: Prentice-Hall.

Pounds, N.J.G. (1990). *An Historical Geography of Europe.* Cambridge, UK: Cambridge University Press.

GLOSSARY

Agricultural Revolution   A term sometimes used to refer to two different eras in the development of agriculture. The earliest "revolution" dates back 10,000 years to the time of the domestication of plants and animals. A second "revolution" occurred at the beginning of the "Industrial Revolution", when during the 18th to early 20th centuries improved crop rotation and other land management techniques, improved animal breeding, and mechanization resulted in rapidly increasing levels of agricultural output.

Anticyclones   These are high pressure systems in the atmosphere characterized by clear skies, relatively dry air, and still conditions. In summer the resulting weather is clear and hot, in winter it will be clear and cold.

Arête   The sharp, rocky edge of a mountain peak formed by the location of cirques on opposite sides of the peak.

Autarky   A policy seeking economic self-sufficiency and independence by a country or region, as practiced, for example, by Albania's communist regime.

Balance of payments   The net balance of receipts and payments between a given country and the rest of the world. A negative balance of payments means that a country may, for example, be spending more for imports than it is earning in exports, though other types of exchanges such as tourist earnings/expenditures and interest earnings/disbursements also play roles in determining balance of payments.

Balkanization   The fragmentation of territory into small political states, often resulting from extreme levels of nationalism and hostility between neighboring ethnic groups and states. The term derives from this process in the "Balkans", a Turkish term used to refer to Southeastern Europe, where a large number of small states emerged as the result of break-up of such political entities as Austro-Hungary, the Ottoman Empire, and the former Yugoslavia.

Bastide   A planned, walled town built during the Middle Ages, especially common in southern France.

Boreal forest   The coniferous forest common in latitudes between 45° and 75° latitude. These forests cover much of Alaska, Canada, and Russia.

Calcareous   An adjective used to describe rocks or soils with calcium carbonate content, such as limestone and chalk rocks and rendzina soils.

Centrally planned economy   An economy that relies predominantly on the planned decisions of a government's planning apparatus rather than on the innumerable, uncoordinated actions of large numbers of independent economic decision-makers as is common in a market economy. The Soviet Union and other CMEA countries were classic examples of centrally planned economies.

Chernozem   A Russian word meaning "black earth". Chernozem soils are highly fertile, forming from the decay of grasses on mid-latitude grasslands. These have been heavily exploited by humans for agriculture, notably in Ukraine.

Cirque   Small circular depressions with steep rock backwalls high in glaciated terrain and often below mountain peaks. They resulted from erosion caused by small glaciers and are common in the Alps.

Classical era   The era of Greek and Roman cultural ascendancy in Southern Europe, from approximately 1000 B.C. to 400 A.D.

Comparative advantage   A technical, economic term that in effect means that a region has an advantage in the production of a good or service compared to another region. An absolute advantage exists when a place can produce something cheaper than another place. In reality, the lowest cost production site for one good may also be the lowest cost production site for many goods, but given resource limitations the site can only make use of some of these absolute advantages. Other, less favored sites, then may actually produce the product under a comparative advantage. A classic example is provided by the U.S. "corn belt" which has an absolute advantage within the USA for production of an array of agricultural products, including corn and wheat. However, the "corn belt" grows more corn than wheat, because the former is a more valuable crop, allowing the less well naturally endowed Great Plains region to specialize in wheat production. Compared to the "corn belt" (which must sacrifice much valuable corn to allow space for the less valuable wheat), the Great Plains has an advantage, a comparative advantage, in wheat production.

Convectional precipitation   Precipitation caused by the formation of convection cells in the atmosphere formed by rapid heating of land surfaces, usually during summer months, owing to intense solar radiation. Air masses at the ground are heated, rise, cool, and reach their dew point; water vapor then condenses and precipitation begins.

Crystalline rock   Generally quite hard rock that contains crystals resulting first from application of great pressure and related high temperatures, and then a slow cooling process that allows crystals to form. Both igneous rock (associated with vulcanism) and metamorphic rock (sedimentary rock exposed to great pressure and heat, usually resulting from tectonic movements in the earth's crust) may be crystalline.

Current account   That portion of the balance of payments resulting from trade in goods and services, as well as financial movements resulting from interest payments (but excluding money transferred in response to new or old debts, which defines the "capital account").

Cyclonic storm   A large, swirling low pressure system up to hundreds of miles across, identifiable by clouds and precipitation formed by the clash of unlike air masses along contact zones (fronts). The storm draws winds into it in a counter-clockwise fashion. Tropical cyclones, called hurricanes or typhoons, have much less impact on Europe than mid-latitude cyclones that drift east under the influence of westerly winds and bring Europe much of its precipitation.

Economic restructuring   Changes in the sectoral structure of an economy, usually resulting from competitive forces associated with the international (or "global") economy and/or domestic political changes (e.g., such as the recent demise of central economic planning and expansion of market mechanisms in Eastern Europe).

Deranged drainage   A drainage system with many short streams that often focus on internal drainage systems (i.e., with no direct outlet to the sea). This type of drainage is common in heavily glaciated areas such as Northern Europe and northern parts of Russia.

Distributary   A stream channel that diverges from a larger channel such as occurs in a delta or a braided stream. At its mouth the Rhine, for example, has several distributaries.

Economies of scale   Per unit production cost reductions (economies) that result from increasing the number of units (scale) of production. Economies of scale are realized by spreading fixed production costs (such as for buildings and machinery) over a larger number of units produced. Thus, for example, a farmer with large holdings or a factory with a large output of a particular product can more easily pay the fixed cost of machinery than smaller scale producers.

Esker   A sinuous deposit of partially sorted waterborne rock and coarse soil that builds up at the bottom of a stream of water flowing within a glacier. High levels of water pressure under a glacier means that esker deposits may snake both up and down modest slopes. The deposits can be huge in size but are usually a few feet high and wide, and frequently crudely resemble abandoned railroad beds.

Feudalism   A form of political and economic organization common during Europe's Medieval era in which peasants gave labor and agricultural produce to a lord in exchange for protection and the right to use land. There were a number of varieties of feudalism through time and space, some which resulted in sharply limiting peasants' civil rights and personal mobility.

Fodder crop   A coarse agricultural product that is used to feed animals, such as hay.

Fordist   A term referring to the type of organization of manufacturing plant closely associated with Henry Ford—large, assembly-line plants producing a limited range of closely related products such as automobile models.

GDP   Gross domestic product, the value of all goods and services produced and traded within an economy by commercial means (exchanged with the use of money) at market prices. This frequently used measure excludes, for example, the value of goods and services produced by subsistence activities and resulting from international trade in goods and transfer of funds.

Geopolitics   A general term used to refer to geographic factors associated with relationships between territorial political units (e.g., countries), but the term also has another quite specific meaning derived from *Geopolitik*, a perspective on international relations that was much abused by Nazi theorists and propagandists during the era of Germany's Third Reich.

Growth center   A city or town that provides an epicenter for the spread of economic growth and change across adjacent territory. The term is usually used to denote a consciously government-planned center. The related term "growth pole" is sometimes used virtually synonymously, although the latter, in fact, originally described relations between a variety of economic sectors impacted by a rapidly growing sector (the "pole").

Hercynian   One of the major mountain-building eras of European history (along with the Caledonian and Alpine eras). Many of Central Europe's mountain and hill regions date from this era, including the Harz of Germany from which the era derives its name.

Horn   A sharp, steep mountain peak formed by the coalescence of three or more cirques, as on the Matterhorn.

Horst   A raised block of rock covering a large area resulting from faulting and uplifting. The Black Forest and Vosges hill regions are horsts that lie on either side of a related feature, the Rhine Graben, which was formed at the same time but was affected by faulting and subsidence rather than uplift.

Humus   Organic material in soil that enhances its fertility.

Industrial Revolution   A general term used to describe the application of dramatically improved technology in manufacturing and transportation beginning in the UK about 1750 and extending to about the year 1900. Some people would argue that the Industrial Revolution was, in fact, simply the earliest part of an on-going period of scientific revolution.

Infrastructure   Facilities and institutions that are fundamental bases for economic activities but do not themselves directly produce a consumable product. A narrow definition of infrastructure includes transportation and communication, water and sewage, and power production facilities; a broader definition includes facilities and institutions such as those in education, health care, and finance. Many infrastructural facilities are often developed and related services provided at public expense or with public subsidies.

Invisibles or invisible payments   That part of the balance of payments of a country that derive from trade in services between countries (e.g., banking, insurance, tourism) as opposed to trade in "visible" commodities.

Irredentism   A movement in late 19th century Italy to acquire territory that was considered by its adherents to be "rightfully" Italian. The term is now used more generally to refer to any political effort that uses nationalistic propaganda to justify addition of territory to a country, by military means if necessary.

Leeward   The side of something, like a mountain range, facing away (sheltered) from the wind.

Loess   A German-derived word for highly fertile soils formed by the deposition of fine, wind-blown sediments eroded by the wind from unvegetated areas covered by glacial deposits, often following the retreat of ice masses. Large areas of loess deposits were formed during the ice ages at the contact zone of the North European Plain and the Central Uplands.

Low Countries   A term used to designate the three countries of Belgium, the Netherlands, and Luxembourg. The term derives from the low elevation plain in the northern portions of Belgium and the Netherlands.

Mercantilism   An economic philosophy especially dominant in the 17th and 18th centuries that argued that countries' economies would prosper from a good deal of state control, especially control over international trade, which, it was believed, most benefitted countries when exports regularly exceeded imports.

Monadnock An isolated hill, usually comprised of parent material relatively resistant to erosion. The landform gets its name from Mt. Monadnock in southern New Hampshire, USA.

Moraine A landform feature created by a poorly sorted mixture of varying sizes of rock and soil particles deposited by glacial action. A terminal moraine is an example—deposits that build up where a glacier may be stationary for some time owing to the fact that it is melting at a place at the same rate it is advancing, resulting in accumulation of material that is deposited as if at the end of a conveyer belt.

Orographic precipitation Precipitation caused by moist air masses being forced aloft by landforms, usually mountain ranges.

Paleolithic The early human cultural era corresponding to the Pleistocene geologic era.

Paleozoic The geologic era ranging from about 640 to 230 million years ago—the early era of complex lifeforms on earth.

Pleistocene The geologic era spanning most of the Quaternary era (the past two million years), excepting the most recent 10,000 years (the Holocene or Recent era). The Pleistocene is noted for eras of continental glaciation and the appearance of humans on the planet.

Podzolic soils Typical soils of moist mid-latitude forests with distinctive layers (horizons) and, at best moderate fertility.

Polder A Dutch term for land that is "reclaimed" for economic use by using dikes and pumps to remove water from it.

PPP A measure used in EU income reports to assess purchasing power parity—the average income level of people in a given territory taking into account costs of goods and services in the region. Thus, high cost regions' PPP levels will be lower than low cost regions which have identical income levels.

Quaternary era See "Pleistocene".

Regional specialization The relative specialization of a portion of a region's labor force within a particular sector of economic activity, usually resulting from a combination of advantages related to its human and natural resources.

Restructuring See "economic restructuring".

Rift valley A landform caused by the drop of a large, relatively narrow strip of terrain between parallel faults.

Siltation The deposition of very fine-grained material, silt, into a water body so that the mass of the water body and depth of the water course lessens, a common occurrence and problem behind dams and in canals.

Solstice A date when the direct rays of the sun at noon strike 23 1/2° north latitude at the Tropic of Cancer (on about June 21) and 23 1/2° south latitude at the Tropic of Capricorn (on about December 22).

Space economy A term used by economic geographers to refer to the spatial structure of an economy, including the geographic distribution of economic activities and the pattern of flows of goods, information, and people between regions (i.e. across space).

Taiga A Russian term for the boreal forest that covers much of its territory.

Windward The side of something, like a mountain range, facing the wind.

AREA AND DEMOGRAPHIC DATA FOR SELECTED STATES

(Smallest Microstates Omitted)

	Area (1000 sq mi)	Population (Millions) 1997	Population (Millions) 2004	Population (Millions) 2010	1997 Population Density (per sq mi)	Annual Rate of Natural Incr (Percent)	Doubling Time (years)	Life Expectancy at Birth (years)	Percent Urban Population	1993 Gross Nat'l Product Per Capita ($US)
World	51,510.8	5,878.5	6,425.6	7,023.6	114	1.5	45	66	43	4,500
Europe	2,261.0	581.9	587.3	592.8	257	0.2	332	73	72	11,870
Albania	11.1	3.6	3.8	4.1	322	1.8	39	72	37	340
Austria	32.4	8.1	8.2	8.3	250	0.1	533	77	54	23,120
Belarus	80.2	10.3	10.6	10.9	128	-0.2		69	68	2,840
Belgium	11.8	10.2	10.3	10.4	862	0.1	578	77	97	21,210
Bosnia	19.7	3.5	3.9	4.4	178	0.7	95	72	34	
Bulgaria	42.8	8.4	8.2	7.9	196	-0.3		71	67	1,160
Croatia	21.8	4.5	4.4	4.4	206	-0.1		70	54	
Cyprus	3.6	0.8	0.8	0.8	210	0.9	76	77	68	10,380
Czech Republic	30.6	10.4	10.4	10.5	339	0.0		73	75	2,730
Denmark	16.6	5.2	5.3	5.3	314	0.1	770	75	85	26,510
Estonia	17.4	1.5	1.4	1.4	84	-0.5		70	71	3,040
Finland	130.1	5.1	5.2	5.2	40	0.3	227	76	64	18,970
France	211.2	58.5	60.1	61.7	277	0.3	217	78	74	22,360
Germany	137.8	81.5	81.3	81.2	591	-0.1		76	85	23,560
Greece	50.9	10.5	10.3	10.2	206	0.0		77	63	7,390
Hungary	35.9	10.2	10.0	9.9	284	-0.3		69	63	3,330
Iceland	39.8	0.3	0.3	0.3	7	1.1	64	79	91	23,620
Ireland	27.1	3.6	3.6	3.5	134	0.5	139	75	57	12,580
Italy	116.3	57.7	57.1	56.5	496	0.0		77	68	19,620
Latvia	24.9	2.5	2.5	2.4	100	-0.5		68	69	2,030
Liechtenstein	0.1	0.1	0.1	0.1	523	0.6	108			
Lithuania	25.2	3.7	3.7	3.8	147	0.0		71	68	1,310
Luxembourg	1.0	0.4	0.4	0.4	411	0.4	193	76	86	35,850
Macedonia	9.9	2.2	2.2	2.3	218	0.8	85	72	58	780

	Area (1000 sq mi)	Population (Millions)			1997 Population Density (per sq mi)	Annual Rate of Natural Incr (Percent)	Doubling Time (years)	Life Expectancy at Birth (years)	Percent Urban Population	1993 Gross Nat'l Product Per Capita ($US)
		1997	2004	2010						
Malta	0.3	0.4	0.4	0.4	1,257	0.7	102	75	85	
Moldova	13.0	4.4	4.6	4.8	337	0.4	193	68	47	1,180
Netherlands	15.9	15.6	16.2	16.9	980	0.4	182	77	89	20,710
Norway	125.2	4.4	4.5	4.7	35	0.3	224	77	73	26,340
Poland	120.7	38.8	39.5	40.2	321	0.2	301	72	62	2,270
Portugal	34.3	9.9	9.9	9.9	290	0.1	866	75	34	7,890
Romania	91.7	22.7	22.4	22.2	247	-0.1		70	55	1,120
Serbia	26.9	10.9	11.0	11.1	406	0.3	204	72	47	
Slovakia	18.8	5.4	5.6	5.7	288	0.4	178	71	57	1,900
Slovenia	7.8	2.0	2.0	2.0	254	0.1	1,386	73	50	6,310
Spain	194.9	39.2	39.1	39.0	201	0.1	578	77	64	13,650
Sweden	173.7	8.9	9.0	9.2	51	0.1	990	78	83	24,830
Switzerland	15.9	7.1	7.3	7.6	446	0.3	224	78	68	36,410
Ukraine	233.1	51.6	52.3	53.0	222	-0.4		69	68	1,910
United Kingdom	94.2	59.0	60.0	61.0	626	0.2	385	76	92	17,970
Russia	6,592.8	145.7	147.6	149.5	22	-0.6		65	73	2,350
Armenia	11.5	3.8	4.0	4.2	331	0.8	83	71	68	660
Azerbaijan	33.4	7.5	8.2	9.0	225	1.6	43	71	54	730
Georgia	26.9	5.4	5.6	5.7	202	0.2	462	73	56	560
Turkey	301.4	63.3	70.8	79.2	210	1.6	44	67	51	2,120
North America	7,509.9	296.8	314.9	334.2	40	0.7	105	76	75	24,340
Canada	3,831.0	30.0	31.7	33.6	8	0.7	102	78	77	20,670
United States	3,678.9	266.7	283.0	300.4	72	0.7	105	76	75	24,750

INDEX